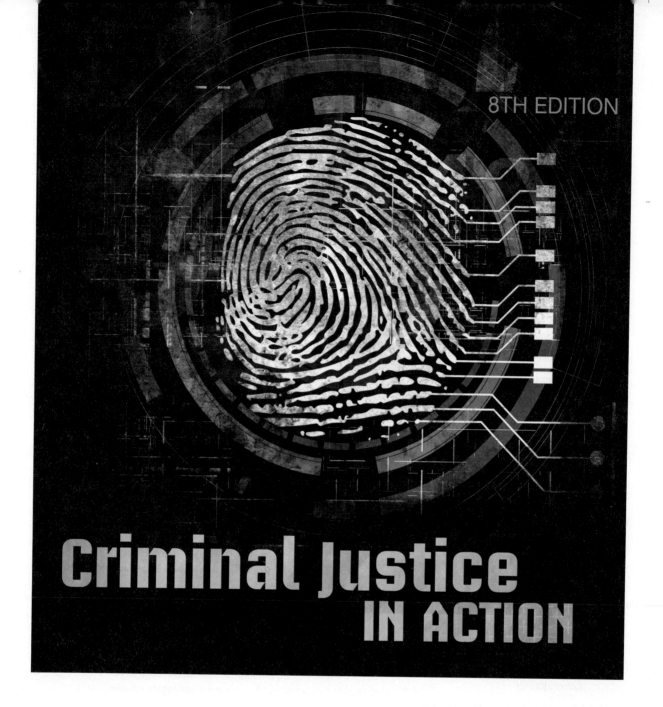

8TH EDITION

Criminal Justice
IN ACTION

LARRY K. GAINES

California State University
San Bernardino

ROGER LeROY MILLER

Institute for University Studies
Arlington, Texas

CENGAGE
Learning

Australia • Brazil • Japan • Mexico • Singapore • United Kingdom • United States

CENGAGE
Learning

Criminal Justice in Action, 8th Edition
Larry K. Gaines and **Roger LeRoy Miller**

Senior Vice President, Global Product Management Higher Education: Jack W. Calhoun

Vice President and General Manager, Social Sciences & Qualitative Business: Erin Joyner

Product Director: Jaime Perkins

Senior Product Manager: Carolyn Henderson Meier

Product Assistant: Audrey Espey

Senior Content Developer: Bob Jucha

Content Coordinator: Casey Lozier

Media Developer: Andy Yap

Sr. Content Digitization Project Manager: Lezlie Light

Executive Brand Manager: Melissa Larmon

Market Development Manager: Molly Felz

Production Manager: Brenda Ginty

Manufacturing Planner: Judy Inouye

Sr. Content Project Manager: Ann Borman

Rights Acquisition Specialist: Don Schlotman

Sr. Rights Acquisition Director: Robert Kauser

Art Director, Interior and Cover Design: Brenda Carmichael, PreMedia Global

Cover Image: agsandrew/Shutterstock

Copyeditor: Sue Bradley

Proofreader: Pat Lewis

Index: Terry Casey

Compositor: Parkwood Composition Service

Library of Congress Control Number: 2013947999

ISBN-13: 978-1-285-45898-4

Cengage Learning
200 First Stamford Place, 4th Floor
Stamford, CT 06902
USA

Cengage Learning is a leading provider of customized learning solutions with office locations around the globe, including Singapore, the United Kingdom, Australia, Mexico, Brazil, and Japan. Locate your local office at: **www.cengage.com/global**.

Cengage Learning products are represented in Canada by Nelson Education, Ltd.

To learn more about Cengage Learning, visit **www.cengage.com**.

Purchase any of our products at your local college store or at our preferred online store **www.cengagebrain.com**.

Printed in the United States of America
1 2 3 4 5 6 7 17 16 15 14 13

Contents in Brief

Contents

Robert Nickelsberg/Getty Images

Wilfred Y. Wong/Getty Images

PART TWO: The Police and Law Enforcement

Spencer Platt/Getty Images

PART THREE: Criminal Courts

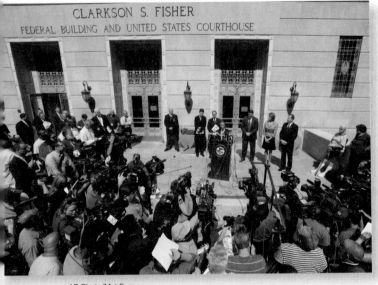

CLARKSON S. FISHER
FEDERAL BUILDING AND UNITED STATES COURTHOUSE

AP Photo/Mel Evans

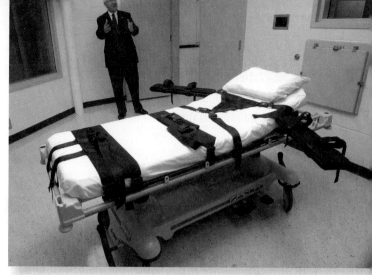

AP Photo/Dave Martin

10 THE CRIMINAL TRIAL 312

11 PUNISHMENT AND SENTENCING 346

PART FOUR: Corrections

AP Photo/*Rapid City Journal*, Benjamin Brayfield

AP Photo/Rich Pedroncelli

PART FIVE: Special Issues

Reuters/Jim Urquhart

16 TODAY'S CHALLENGES: THE TERROR THREAT, CYBER CRIME, AND WHITE-COLLAR CRIME 524

FEATURES OF SPECIAL INTEREST

COMPARATIVE CRIMINAL JUSTICE

YOU BE THE _____

In Chapter 14 of this Eighth Edition of *Criminal Justice in Action,* Julie Howe, a halfway house program manager, tells students that her favorite part of her job is that she "has an impact on people's lives." In Chapter 5, FBI Agent Arnold Bell describes a "particularly interesting time" that he spent in Los Angeles solving bank robberies. In Chapter 12, Peggy McCarthy, a probation officer, says that, although her duties can be demanding, when she helps a client make a "positive change" in his or her life, she realizes that "what I'm doing day in and day out is 100 percent worthwhile."

Impactful. Interesting. Worthwhile. In their own words, Howe, Bell, and McCarthy capture the essence of a career in the American criminal justice system. As in previous editions, each chapter of *Criminal Justice in Action, Eighth Edition,* includes a **Careers in CJ feature** in which a criminal justice practitioner presents a personal account of his or her profession. Combining this first-person insight with a solid pedagogical foundation and numerous real-world examples, *Criminal Justice in Action* offers students unmatched insight into the world of crime and justice that goes well beyond the clichés of Hollywood or the rhetoric of politicians. With the help and advice of the many criminal justice professors who have adopted this best-selling textbook over the years, we believe we have created an invaluable introduction to the field.

Social Media, Careers, and Criminal Justice

We are well aware that many students using this text are interested in a criminal justice career. Furthermore, it is evident that social media are crucial to the twenty-first-century job search. Accordingly, each Career in CJ feature, mentioned above, now includes a **new Social Media Career Tip** to help students succeed in today's difficult labor market. These tips will help students use Web sites such as Facebook and LinkedIn to find potential employers, network, and present themselves as viable candidates for employment.

Criminal Justice in Action, Eighth Edition, also acknowledges that criminal justice–related organizations, from police departments to special interest groups to university departments, rely on social media to interact with their target audiences. We take advantage of this wealth of information by offering a **new social media margin feature** in each chapter. These features direct students to a specific Web site—the FBI's Twitter account, for example, or the Electronic Privacy Information Center's Facebook page—where they can access a ready stream of information concerning various aspects of American criminal justice.

Further Changes to the Eighth Edition

As in previous editions of *Criminal Justice in Action,* each chapter in the Eighth Edition begins with a new "ripped from the headlines" vignette that introduces the themes to be covered in the pages that follow. Furthermore, the text continues to reflect the ever-changing nature of our topic with approximately **170 new references to recent research involving crime and criminal behavior** and **140 new real-life examples of actual crimes.** The Eighth Edition also includes about **thirty new features and twenty new figures, as well as discussions of twenty new United States Supreme Court cases and more than one hundred new photos.** Additionally, we allow both expert and lay witnesses to give their opinions of criminal justice matters, with **more than eighty new quotes from professionals and thirty new quotes from "ordinary" citizens in the text.**

Two other extensive changes to the Eighth Edition involve topics crucial to the American criminal justice system:

- **Terrorism.** The bombing of the Boston Marathon on April 15, 2013, only underscores the threat that domestic terrorism poses to the population and infrastructure of the United States. Recognizing this, a **new feature entitled Countering Domestic Terrorism** highlights the ever-shifting perils of this phenomenon and the various strategies taken by American law enforcement, courts, and corrections in response.

- **Victims.** For much of the history of American criminal justice, the role of the crime victim was limited to taking the witness stand in court. This is no longer the case, and we have **greatly expended our coverage of victims' rights and responsibilities** in today's crime picture. Seven of the chapters of *Criminal Justice in Action* now include in-depth discussions of victims, covering a variety of issues relating to the legal and ethical aspects of victim participation in the criminal justice system.

Concentrated Critical Thinking

In addition to the changes already covered, we have added three critical analysis questions to the introductory page of each chapter. These questions, which relate back to the chapter-opening vignette and introduce themes important to the upcoming chapter, continue our commitment to developing students' abilities to think critically about criminal justice. Indeed, each feature and most photograph captions in the textbook end with a question that requires an innovative, inquisitive response. Other critical-thinking tools in *Criminal Justice in Action, Eighth Edition,* include:

- **Learning Objectives.** At the beginning of each chapter, students are introduced to up to ten learning objectives (LOs) for that chapter. For example, in Chapter 4, "Inside Criminal Law," Learning Objective 5 (LO5) asks students to "Explain how the doctrine of strict liability applies to criminal law." The area of text that furnishes the information is marked with a square LO5 graphic, and, finally, the correct answer is found in the chapter-ending materials. This constant active learning will greatly expand students' understanding of dozens of crucial criminal justice topics.

- **Self Assessment Boxes.** Students are not, however, required to wait until they have finished reading a chapter to engage in self-assessment. We have placed a self assessment box at the end of each major section of each chapter. Three to five sentences long, these items require students to fill in the blanks, thereby reinforcing the most important points in the section they have just read. (All answers are found at the end of each chapter.)

- **CJ in Action Features.** Each of the chapter-ending CJ in Action features introduces students to a controversial topic from the chapter and provides them with "for" and "against" arguments related to that topic. Then, using information and knowledge gained from the chapter, the student is asked to write a short essay giving her or his opinion on the controversy. These features not only help students improve their writing and critical-thinking skills, but they also act as a review for the material in the chapter. The Eighth Edition of *Criminal Justice in Action* includes many new such chapter-ending features, covering topics such as domestic violence and police officers in schools.

CHAPTER-BY-CHAPTER ORGANIZATION OF THE TEXT

This edition's sixteen chapters blend the principles of criminal justice with current research and high-interest examples of what is happening in the world of crime and crime prevention right now. What follows is a summary of each chapter, along with a description of some of the revisions to the Eighth Edition.

Part 1: The Criminal Justice System

Chapter 1 provides an introduction to the criminal justice system's three major institutions: law enforcement, the courts, and corrections. The chapter also answers conceptual questions such as "what is crime?" and "what are the values of the American criminal justice system?"

- The chapter has been expanded with a **new section** entitled **"Discretion and Ethics,"** which focuses on the importance of informal decision making in the criminal justice system and the role that ethics plays in shaping the choices made by criminal justice professionals.

- The chapter closes with a **new discussion of the growing role of social media** in American criminal justice. Students are introduced to the use of these Internet-based technologies as means both to enforce the law and to break it.

Chapter 2 focuses on criminology, giving students insight into why crime occurs before shifting their attention toward how society goes about fighting it. The chapter addresses the most widely accepted and influential criminological hypotheses, including choice theories, trait theories, sociological theories, social process theories, and social conflict theories.

- To give students a better understanding of the major strains of criminology, this chapter has been **reorganized** with **new sections** entitled "The Brain and the Body" (focusing on choice and trait theories), "Bad Neighborhoods" (focusing on economic and environmental influences on crime), and "Life Lessons" (focusing on the social processes of crime).

- A **new** chapter-ending CJ in Action feature ("Legalizing Marijuana") explores the ramifications of legalizing the possession of small amounts of marijuana in Colorado and Washington.

Chapter 3 furnishes students with an understanding of two areas fundamental to criminal justice: (1) the practical definitions of crime, such as the difference between felonies and misdemeanors and different degrees of criminal conduct, and (2) the various modes of measuring crime, including the FBI's Uniform Crime Reports and the U.S. Department of Justice's National Crime Victimization Survey.

- Providing the starting point for our increased coverage of the topic throughout the textbook, a **new section entitled "Victims of Crime"** outlines the legal rights of crime victims and explores the context of victimization in the larger crime picture.

- A **new** chapter-ending CJ in Action feature ("Victims of Domestic Violence") asks students to determine whether victims of domestic violence should have a voice in determining the sentencing and punishment of their abusers.

Chapter 4 lays the foundation of criminal law. It addresses constitutional law, statutory law, and other sources of American criminal law before shifting its focus to the legal framework that allows the criminal justice system to determine and punish criminal guilt.

- A **new** Countering Domestic Terrorism feature ("Homegrown Support") describes how the federal government uses the legal concept of material support to detain terrorist suspects who use words as weapons.

- A **new** CJ and Technology feature ("Due Process and Predator Drones") explains the debate surrounding the federal government's decision to kill a U.S. citizen in Yemen without following the procedure of criminal law.

Part 2: The Police and Law Enforcement

Chapter 5 acts as an introduction to law enforcement in the United States today. This chapter offers a detailed description of the country's numerous local, state, and federal law enforcement agencies and examines the responsibilities and duties that come with a career in law enforcement.

- A **new** chapter-opening vignette ("What's Going On?") provides insight into the Seattle Police Department's attempts to better inform locals about crime through its "Tweets-by-beat" initiative.

- As part of a **new** consideration of intelligence-led policing and the need for law enforcement agencies to do "more with less," students will learn about police strategies such as using Predpol, which is software that

attempts to predict when and where crimes are most likely to occur.

Chapter 6 puts students on the streets and gives them a gritty look at the many challenges of being a law enforcement officer. It starts with a discussion of the importance of discretion in law enforcement and then moves on to policing strategies and issues in modern policing, such as use of force, corruption, and the "thin blue line."

- Students' understanding of split-second decision making with life-or-death ramifications is underscored by a **new** You Be the Police Officer feature ("High-Speed Discretion") that puts them behind the wheel during a high-speed pursuit.

- A **new** discussion of how aggressive investigative strategies such as **informants and undercover agents** are used to combat **domestic terrorism** includes an in-depth examination of the **pros and cons of preventive policing.**

Chapter 7 examines the sometimes uneasy relationship between law enforcement and the U.S. Constitution by explaining the rules of being a police officer. Particular emphasis is placed on the Fourth, Fifth, and Sixth Amendments, giving students an understanding of crucial concepts such as probable cause, reasonableness, and custodial interrogation.

- An **updated** section entitled "Electronic Surveillance" illuminates the constitutional issues surrounding law enforcement use of closed-circuit television (CCTV) cameras as crime-fighting tools. The section includes **new** discussions of the United States Supreme Court's recent ruling on technological tracking of citizens and the future of unmanned drones in law enforcement.

- In the context of racial profiling, we have added a **new** discussion of the Supreme Court's decision regarding Arizona's "papers, please" law that requires local police officers, "when practicable," to check the legal status of potential undocumented immigrants.

Part 3: Criminal Courts

Chapter 8 takes a big-picture approach in describing the American court system, giving students an overview of the basic principles of our judicial system, the state and federal court systems, and the role of judges in the criminal justice system.

- The court system's ability to live up to societal expectations of truth and justice, a running theme of the third part of this textbook, is explored in the chapter's **new** opening vignette ("Dark Honeymoon") concerning the nontrial of Gabe Watson for the alleged murder of his wife. Despite the fact that Watson pleaded guilty to manslaughter in Australia, an Alabama judge threw the case out of an American criminal court for lack of evidence.

- A **new** CJ and Technology feature ("Lie Detection in Court") investigates the use—or lack thereof—of polygraph exams in American criminal courts.

Chapter 9 provides students with a rundown of pretrial procedures and highlights the role that these procedures play in America's adversary system. Thus, pretrial procedures such as establishing bail and plea bargaining are presented as part of the larger "battle" between the prosecution and the defense.

- A **new** discussion is designed to give students an appreciation of the often difficult **relationship between prosecutors and crime victims,** who often expect these officers of the court to strive for conviction at any cost.
- The section on plea bargaining now includes a **new** analysis of the United States Supreme Court's potentially "game-changing" recent decision providing defendants with a constitutional right to effective representation during plea negotiations.

Chapter 10 puts the student in the courtroom and gives her or him a strong understanding of the steps of the criminal trial. The chapter also attempts to answer the fascinating but ultimately frustrating question, "Are criminal trials in this country fair?"

- Three **new** figures use excerpts from actual court records to give students a first-hand understanding of three crucial aspects of the criminal trial: jury selection, the opening statement, and the closing argument.
- The student's understanding of constitutional protections against double jeopardy will be enhanced by a **new** Comparative Criminal Justice feature ("Double Trouble") describing the plight of Amanda Knox, a former American exchange student in danger of being charged a second time for murder by Italian judicial officials.

Chapter 11 links the many different punishment options for those who have been convicted of a crime with the theoretical justifications for those punishments. The chapter also examines punishment in the policy context, weighing the public's desire for ever-harsher criminal sanctions against the consequences of such governmental strategies.

- As part of our continuing exploration of the underlying concepts of **restorative justice,** this chapter offers a **new** discussion of the **practical aspects of restitution** and of **victim-offender dialogue programs** that provide convicts with the opportunity to apologize in person to the victims of their crimes.
- A **new** You Be the Juror feature ("Life or Death?") asks students to decide whether a man who has been found guilty of hiring another person to kill his fourteen-year-old, pregnant girlfriend should be sentenced to death or given a life prison term without parole.

Part 4: Corrections

Chapter 12 makes an important point, and one that is often overlooked in the larger discussion of the American corrections system: not all of those who are punished need to be placed behind bars. This chapter explores the community corrections options, from probation to parole to intermediate sanctions such as intensive supervision and home confinement.

- A **new** section **comparing probation and parole** is designed to help the student distinguish between these two forms of community corrections, whose similarities can tend to obscure very important conceptual differences.
- Continuing our focus on crime victims, we have added a **new** discussion of the sometime murky **role of the victim** in determining an offender's chances of being **granted parole.**

Chapter 13 focuses on prisons and jails. Record-high rates of incarceration have pushed these institutions to the forefront of the criminal justice system, and this chapter explores the various issues—such as overcrowding and the emergence of private prisons—that have resulted from the prison population boom.

- A **new** section entitled **"Inmate Population Trends"** describes a surprising recent decrease in the American prison population as well as efforts by certain states to reduce their inmate numbers in order to lower the unfeasible costs of expensive corrections systems.
- A **new** Question of Ethics feature ("The Strip Search") introduces students to the ethical issues raised by the practice of strip searching jail inmates who have not been charged with committing any crime.

Chapter 14 is another example of our efforts to get students "into the action" of the criminal justice system, this time putting them in the uncomfortable position of being behind bars. It also answers the question, "What happens when the inmate is released back into society?"

- The repercussions of prison overcrowding are discussed in the **new** chapter-opening vignette ("Business as Usual") concerning recurrent prison violence at the Lee Correctional Institution in Bishopville, South Carolina.
- An **updated** discussion of America's sex offender laws is highlighted by a **new** CJ and Technology feature ("Crime Registries") that asks the question, "What if the government created registry lists of other criminals, as is commonly done for sex offenders?"

Part 5: Special Issues

Chapter 15 examines the juvenile justice system, giving students a comprehensive description of the path taken by delinquents from first contact with police to trial and punishment. The chapter contains a strong criminological component as well, scrutinizing the various theories of why certain juveniles turn to delinquency and what steps society can take to stop them from doing so before it is "too late."

- A **new** discussion examines the United States Supreme Court's 2012 ruling that juveniles who are convicted of murder may not be automatically sentenced to life in prison without the possibility of parole.
- A **new** chapter-ending CJ in Action feature ("Police in Schools") requires students to grapple with the thorny question of whether schools are better or worse off when being policed by law enforcement officers.

Chapter 16 concludes the text by taking an expanded look at three crucial criminal justice topics: (1) law enforcement and anti-terrorism, (2) cyber crime, and (3) white-collar crime.

- Concluding the focus on domestic terrorism found throughout the text, the **new** chapter-opening vignette ("Do-It-Yourself Terror") describes the ramifications of the homemade-bomb attack on the Boston Marathon on April 15, 2013.
- Combining the chapter's themes of terrorism and cyber crime, a **new** section explores the **growing danger** to the nation's population and infrastructure **posed by cyberattacks.**

SPECIAL FEATURES

Supplementing the main text of *Criminal Justice in Action, Eighth Edition,* are some ninety eye-catching, instructive, and penetrating special features. These features, described

below with examples, have been designed to enhance the student's understanding of a particular criminal justice issue.

CAREERS IN CJ: As stated before, many students reading this book are planning a career in criminal justice. We have provided them with an insight into some of these careers by offering first-person accounts of what it is like to work as a criminal justice professional.

- In Chapter 15, Carl McCullough, a former professional football player, provides an inside look at his duties as a resident youth worker at a juvenile detention center in Hennepin County, Minnesota.

COUNTERING DOMESTIC TERRORISM: This **new** feature, as noted earlier in the Preface, focuses on the challenges posed by homegrown terrorism to law enforcement, the courts, and the corrections system.

- "Diversity of Hate" (Chapter 1) introduces students to the federal government's definition of terrorism and makes the point that homegrown terrorists are, despite media portrayals, a diverse criminal class not limited to any single race, ethnicity, or religion.

MASTERING CONCEPTS: Some criminal justice topics require additional explanation before they become crystal clear in the minds of students. This feature helps students to master many of the essential concepts in the textbook.

- In Chapter 7, this feature helps students understand the legal differences between a police stop and a police arrest.

YOU BE THE ____: This feature puts students into the position of a criminal justice actor in a hypothetical case or situation that is based on a real-life event. The facts of the case or situation are presented with alternative possible outcomes, and the student is asked to "be the _____" and make a decision. Students can then consult Appendix B at the end of the text to learn what actually happened in the offered scenario.

- You Be the Legislator, "Banning Distracted Walking" (Chapter 1), a **new** feature, asks students to consider the extent to which government should enact criminal laws to protect citizens from their own risky behavior.

CJ AND TECHNOLOGY: Advances in technology are constantly transforming the face of criminal justice. In these features, which appear in nearly every chapter, students learn of one such emergent technology and are asked to critically evaluate its effects.

- This **new** feature in Chapter 9 describes how defense attorneys are challenging the use of DNA fingerprinting evidence—seemingly infallible—against their clients in criminal court.

COMPARATIVE CRIMINAL JUSTICE: The world offers a dizzying array of different criminal customs and codes, many of which are in stark contrast to those accepted in the United States. This feature provides dramatic and sometimes perplexing examples of foreign criminal justice practices in order to give students a better understanding of our domestic ways.

- "The Great Firewall of China" (Chapter 16), an **updated** feature, describes China's recent efforts to limit and control the use of the Internet through criminal laws to an extent that is unimaginable to most Americans.

A QUESTION OF ETHICS: Ethical dilemmas occur in every profession, but the challenges facing criminal justice professionals often have repercussions beyond their own lives and careers. In this feature, students are asked to place themselves in the shoes of police officers, prosecutors, defense attorneys, and other criminal justice actors facing ethical dilemmas: Will they do the right thing?

- In a **new** feature entitled "Fake Friends" (Chapter 7), students examine the issue of privacy on social media. Specifically, are law enforcement agents acting ethically when they use fake identities on Facebook to further criminal investigations?

LANDMARK CASES: Rulings by the United States Supreme Court have shaped every area of the criminal justice system. In this feature, students learn about and analyze the most influential of these cases.

- Chapter 14 presents a **new** feature on *Brown v. Plata* (2011) in which the Supreme Court ordered California corrections officials to reduce the state's prison population after deciding that overcrowding was denying inmates satisfactory levels of health care.

MYTH VERSUS REALITY: Nothing endures like a good myth. In this feature, we try to dispel some of the more enduring myths in the criminal justice system while at the same time asking students to think critically about their consequences.

- "Are Too Many Criminals Found Not Guilty by Reason of Insanity?" (Chapter 4) dispels the notion that the criminal justice is "soft" because it lets scores of "crazy" defendants go free due to insanity.

Extensive Study Aids

Criminal Justice in Action, Eighth Edition, includes a number of pedagogical devices designed to complete the student's active learning experience. These devices include:

- Concise **chapter outlines** appear at the beginning of each chapter. The outlines give students an idea of what to expect in the pages ahead, as well as a quick source of review when needed.

- Dozens of **key terms and a running glossary** focus students' attention on major concepts and help them master the vocabulary of criminal justice. The chosen terms are boldfaced in the text, allowing students to notice their importance without breaking the flow of reading. On the same page that a key term is highlighted, a margin note provides a succinct definition of the term. For further reference, a glossary at the end of the text provides a full list of all the key terms and their definitions. This edition includes over forty new key terms.

- Each chapter has at least six **figures,** which include graphs, charts, and other forms of colorful art that reinforce a point made in the text. This edition includes twenty new figures.

- Hundreds of **photographs** add to the overall readability and design of the text. Each photo has a caption, and most of these captions include a critical-thinking question dealing with the topic at hand. This edition includes more than one hundred new photos.

- At the end of each chapter, students will find five **Questions for Critical Analysis.** These questions will help the student assess his or her understanding of the just-completed chapter, as well as develop critical-thinking skills.

- Our teaching/learning package offers numerous opportunities for using **online technology** in the classroom. As noted earlier, students will find new Social Media & CJ features in the margins of each chapter, directing them to areas of criminal justice interest on the Internet.

ACKNOWLEDGMENTS

Throughout the creation of the eight editions of this text, we have been aided by hundreds of experts in various criminal justice fields and by professors throughout the country, as well as by numerous students who have used the text. We list below the reviewers for this Eighth Edition, followed by the class-test participants and reviewers for the first seven editions. We sincerely thank all who participated on the revision of *Criminal Justice in Action*. We believe that the Eighth Edition is even more responsive to the needs of today's criminal justice instructors and students alike because we have taken into account the constructive comments and criticisms of our reviewers and the helpful suggestions of our survey respondents.

Reviewers for the Eighth Edition

We are grateful for the participation of the reviewers who read and reviewed portions of our manuscript throughout its development, and for those who gave us valuable insights through their responses to our survey.

Diana R. Grant
Sonoma State University

Michele Grillo
Monmouth University

Lisa A. Houston
Allegheny College of Maryland

Paul Klenowski
Clarion University

Janine Kremling
California State University at San Bernardino

Tom Lawrence
Tri-County Technical College

David F. Owens
Onondaga Community College

Jason B Waller
Tyler Junior College

CLASS-TEST PARTICIPANTS

We also want to acknowledge the participation of the professors and their students who agreed to class-test portions of the text. Our thanks go to:

Tom Arnold
College of Lake County

Paula M. Broussard
University of Southwestern Louisiana

Mike Higginson
Suffolk Community College

Andrew Karmen
John Jay College of Criminal Justice

Fred Kramer
John Jay College of Criminal Justice

Anthony P. LaRose
Western Oregon University

Anne Lawrence
Kean University

Jerry E. Loar
Walters State Community College

Phil Reichel
University of Northern Colorado

Albert Sproule
Allentown College

Gregory B. Talley
Broome Community College

Karen Terry
John Jay College of Criminal Justice

Angelo Tritini
Passaic County Community College

Gary Uhrin
Westmoreland County Community College

Robert Vodde
Fairleigh Dickinson University

REVIEWERS OF THE FIRST, SECOND, THIRD, FOURTH, FIFTH, SIXTH, AND SEVENTH EDITIONS

We appreciate the assistance of the following reviewers whose guidance helped create the foundation for this best seller. We are grateful to all.

Lorna Alvarez-Rivera
Ohio University

Angela Ambers-Henderson
Montgomery County Community College

Gaylene Armstrong
Southern Illnois University

Judge James Bachman
Bowling Green State University

Tom Barclay
University of South Alabama

Julia Beeman
University of North Carolina at Charlotte

Lee Roy Black
California University of Pennsylvania

Anita Blowers
University of North Carolina at Charlotte

Stefan Bosworth
Hostos Community College

Michael E. Boyko
Cuyahoga Community College

John Bower
Bethel College

Steven Brandl
University of Wisconsin–Milwaukee

Scott Brantley
Chancellor University

Charles Brawner III
Heartland Community College

Timothy M. Bray
University of Texas–Dallas

Susan Brinkley
University of Tampa

Paula Broussard
University of Southwestern Louisiana

Michael Brown
Ball State College

Theodore Byrne
California State University, Dominguez Hills

Patrick Buckley
San Bernardino Valley College

Joseph Bunce
Montgomery College–Rockville

James T. Burnett
SUNY, Rockland Community College

Ronald Burns
Texas Christian University

Paul Campbell
Wayne State College

Dae Chang
Wichita State University

Sheri Chapel
Ridley-Lowell Business and Technical Institute and Keystone College

Steven Chermak
Indiana University

Charlie Chukwudolue
Northern Kentucky University

Monte Clampett
Asheville-Buncombe Community College

John Cochran
University of South Florida

Ellen G. Cohn
Florida International University

Corey Colyer
West Virginia University

Mark Correia
University of Nevada–Reno

Theodore Darden
College of Du Page

John del Nero
Lane Community College

Richard H. De Lung
Wayland Baptist University

John Dempsey
Suffolk County Community College

Tom Dempsey
Christopher Newport University

Joyce Dozier
Wilmington College

Frank J. Drummond
Modesto Junior College

M. G. Eichenberg
Wayne State College

Frank L. Fischer
Kankakee Community College

Linda L. Fleischer
The Community College of Baltimore County

Aric Steven Frazier
Vincennes University

Frederick Galt
Dutchess Community College

Phyllis Gerstenfeld
California State University Stanislaus

James Gilbert
University of Nebraska–Kearney

Dean Golding
West Chester University of Pennsylvania

Debbie Goodman
Miami-Dade Community College

Cecil Greek
Florida State University

Donald Grubb
Northern Virginia Community College

Sharon Halford
Community College of Aurora

Michael Hallett
Middle Tennessee State University

Mark Hansel
Moorhead State University

Pati Hendrickson
Tarleton State University

Michelle Heward
Weber State University

Gerald Hildebrand
Austin Community College

Dennis Hoffman
University of Nebraska–Omaha

Richard Holden
Central Missouri State University

Ronald Holmes
University of Louisville

Marilyn Horace-Moore
Eastern Michigan University

Matrice Hurrah
Shelby State Community College

Nicholas Irons
County College of Morris

Michael Israel
Kean University

J. D. Jamieson
Southwest Texas State University

James Jengeleski
Shippensburg University

Robert Jerin
Endicott College

Paul Johnson
Weber State University

Jason R. Jolicoeur
Cincinnati State Technical and Community College

Casey Jordan
Western Connecticut State University

Matthew Kanjirathinkal
Texas A & M University–Commerce

Bill Kelly
University of Texas–Austin

Paul Klenowski
Clarion University

David Kotajarvi
Lakeshore Technical College

John H. Kramer
Pennsylvania State University

Janine Kremling
California State University at San Bernardino

Kristen Kuehnle
Salem State University

Karl Kunkel
Southwest Missouri State

James G. Larson
National University

Barry Latzer
John Jay College of Criminal Justice

Deborah Laufersweiler-Dwyer
University of Arkansas at Little Rock

Paul Lawson
Montana State University

Nella Lee
Portland State University

Walter Lewis
St. Louis Community College–Meramec

Larry Linville
Northern Virginia Community College

Faith Lutze
Washington State University

Richard Martin
Elgin Community College

Richard H. Martin
University of Findlay

William J. Mathias
University of South Carolina

Janet McClellan
Southwestern Oregon Community College

Pat Murphy
State University of New York–Geneseo

Rebecca Nathanson
Housatonic Community Technical College

Ellyn Ness
Mesa Community College

Kenneth O'Keefe
Prairie State College

Michael Palmiotto
Wichita State University

Rebecca D. Petersen
University of Texas, San Antonio

Gary Prawel
Monroe Community College

Mark Robarge
Mansfield University

Matt Robinson
Appalachian State University

Debra Ross
Buffalo State College

William Ruefle
University of South Carolina

Gregory Russell
Washington State University

John Scheb II
University of Tennessee–Knoxville

Melinda Schlager
University of Texas at Arlington

Ed Selby
Southwestern College

Larry Snyder
Herkimer County Community College

Ronald Sopenoff
Brookdale Community College

Domenick Stampone
Raritan Valley Community College

Katherine Steinbeck
Lakeland Community College

Hallie Stephens
Southeastern Oklahoma State University

Kathleen M. Sweet
St. Cloud State University

Gregory Talley
Broome Community College

Karen Terry
John Jay College of Criminal Justice

Amy B. Thistlethwaite
Northern Kentucky University

Rebecca Titus
New Mexico Junior College

Lawrence F. Travis III
University of Cincinnati

Kimberly Vogt
University of Wisconsin–La Crosse

Robert Wadman
Weber State University

Ron Walker
Trinity Valley Community College

John Wyant
Illinois Central College

Others were instrumental in bringing this Eighth Edition to fruition. We continue to appreciate the extensive research efforts of Shawn G. Miller and the additional legal assistance of William Eric Hollowell. Robert Jucha, our Content Developer, provided equal parts elbow grease and creative energy; it was a pleasure to work with him. Product Manager Carolyn Hendersen Meier supplied crucial guidance to the project through her suggestions and recommendations. At the production end, we once again feel fortunate to have enjoyed the services of our tireless content project manager, Ann Borman, who oversaw virtually all aspects of this book. Additionally, we wish to thank the designer of this new edition, PreMedia Global, who has created what we believe to be the most dazzling and student-friendly design of any text in the field. We are also thankful for the services of all those at Parkwood Composition who worked on the Eighth Edition, particularly Lee Branjord. The eagle eyes of Sue Bradley and Pat Lewis, who shared the duties of copy editing and proofreading, were invaluable. A special word of thanks must also go to the team responsible for the extensive multimedia package included in this project, including Media Developer for Criminal Justice, Andy Yap, and writer Robert C. De Lucia of John Jay College of Criminal Justice. In addition, we appreciate the work of Julia Campbell of the University of Nebraska–Kearney, who revised the Instructor's Resource Manual, and Nathan Moran of Midwestern State University who created the Lesson Plans and PowerPoints. We also appreciate the work of Janine Kremling of California State University, San Bernardino for revising the Study Guide and Pamela Donovan of Bloomsburg University for revising the web quizzing. We are also grateful for the aid of Product Assistant Audrey Espey, Andy Yap, Media Developer, and Content Coordinator Casey Lozier who ensured the timely publication of supplements. A final thanks to all of the great people in marketing and advertising who helped to get the word out about the book, including marketing manager Michelle Williams, who has been tireless in her attention to this project.

Any criminal justice text has to be considered a work in progress. We know that there are improvements that we can make. Therefore, write us with any suggestions that you may have.

L. K. G.
R. L. M.

Dedication

This book is dedicated to my good friend and colleague, Lawrence Walsh, of the Lexington, Kentucky Police Department. When I was a rookie, he taught me about policing. When I became a researcher, he taught me about the practical applications of knowledge. He is truly an inspiring professional in our field.

L.K.G.

To Mac,

from whom I learned
so much.

R.L.M.

CHAPTER

1 Criminal Justice Today

CHAPTER OUTLINE		CORRESPONDING LEARNING OBJECTIVES
What Is Crime?		Describe the two most common models of how society determines which acts are criminal.
		Define *crime*.
The Purpose of the Criminal Justice System		
The Structure of the Criminal Justice System		Outline the three levels of law enforcement.
		List the essential elements of the corrections system.
Discretion and Ethics		Explain the difference between the formal and informal criminal justice processes.
		Define ethics, and describe the role that it plays in discretionary decision making.
Criminal Justice Today		Contrast the crime control and due process models.
		Explain the defining aspects of a terrorist act, and identify one common misperception concerning terrorism.
		List the major issues in criminal justice today.

To target your study and review, look for these numbered Learning Objective icons throughout the chapter.

Photo by Joshua Lott/Getty Images

GANGLAND STORIES

THE TWO MURDERS took place within five miles and five days of each other during the winter of 2013. First, on the afternoon of January 28, high school student Hadiya Pendleton was fatally shot in the back while talking with friends at a park on Chicago's South Side. Then, early on the morning of February 1, thirty-two-year-old Michelle Smith died when an assailant sprayed the van she was driving on the Stevenson Expressway with a torrent of bullets.

The homicides, in themselves, were not particularly unusual. Over the past several years, Chicago has surpassed New York and Los Angeles as the nation's center of attention for deadly crime. The Chicago police reported forty-two murders in the first month of 2013, after the city experienced 506 during the previous year. Much of the violence can be attributed to gangs and guns, as was the case in the deaths of both Pendleton and Smith. Pendleton was the innocent victim of a gang member who mistook her and her friends for rivals on the wrong turf. Similarly, police investigators said that the incident involving Smith stemmed from "drug and gang activity."

The community's reaction to the two murders, however, was markedly different. Smith was a convicted felon and a documented gang member, and her death barely registered. In contrast, Pendleton was an honors student and a member of her school's majorette team, which had just returned from performing at President Barack Obama's inauguration in Washington, D.C. City officials offered a $40,000 award for information leading to the capture of her killer. A week after Pendleton's death, 150 people marched through Chicago streets in her name to raise awareness of gun violence. "Every single day, people are shot out here, and it's us kids," said one of her classmates. "We're supposed to be burying our mothers. Not our mothers burying us."

1. Following Hadiya Pendleton's murder, the mayor of Chicago deployed two hundred additional police officers to the parts of the city plagued by gang violence. What are some of the ways that extra officers could prevent shootings such as Pendleton's and Michelle Smith's?
2. According to government statistics, about 40 percent of criminals obtain their guns from family and friends. What can law enforcement officials do to reduce this source of illegal guns? How could social media such as Facebook and Twitter be used to help?
3. Should gangs themselves be illegal? Why or why not?

Scott Olson/Getty Images

At the entrance of a Chicago funeral home, a police officer walks past a painting of fifteen-year-old Hadiya Pendleton, killed by gang violence in February 2013.

WHAT IS CRIME?

Two decades ago, Chicago did, in essence, make gangs illegal. The city passed an ordinance that allowed police to tell young men "loitering with no apparent purpose" to disperse. If these orders were not followed, police could—and did—detain the loiterers. Over the course of three years, Chicago police made 42,000 arrests under this law.[1]

Eventually, the United States Supreme Court overturned Chicago's anti-loitering ordinance. The problem, according to the Court, was that law enforcement could not arrest people who were merely standing together in a group without any further evidence of criminal behavior.[2] For a short time, however, doing just that constituted a **crime** within Chicago city limits. As this rather extreme example shows, a crime is not simply an act that seems dishonest or dangerous or taboo. It is a wrong against society that is *proclaimed by law* and that, if committed under specific circumstances, is punishable by the criminal justice system.

Determining Criminal Behavior

One problem with the definition of crime just provided is that it obscures the complex nature of societies. A society is not static—it evolves and changes, and its concept of criminality evolves and changes as well. As Chicago's short-lived anti-loitering law shows, different communities can have vastly different ideas of what constitutes a crime. To give an international example, in 2012, police in West Sumatra, Indonesia, arrested Alexander Aan for writing "God is not great" on Facebook. An Indonesian court sentenced Aan to two and a half years in prison for violating a criminal prohibition against "inciting religious hatred." Such legislation would not be allowed in the United States because of our country's long traditions of freedom of speech and religion. (See the feature *Comparative Criminal Justice—Speech Crime* on the following page to learn about another foreign criminal law that runs counter to America's legal traditions.)

To more fully understand the concept of crime, it will help to examine the two most common models of how society "decides" which acts are criminal: the consensus model and the conflict model.

THE CONSENSUS MODEL The term *consensus* refers to general agreement among the majority of any particular group. Thus, the **consensus model** rests on the assumption that as people gather together to form a society, its members will naturally come to a basic agreement with regard to shared norms and values. Those individuals whose actions deviate from the established norms and values are considered to pose a threat to the well-being of society as a whole and must be sanctioned (punished). The society passes laws to control and prevent unacceptable behavior, thereby setting the boundaries for acceptable behavior within the group.[3]

The consensus model, to a certain extent, assumes that a diverse group of people can have similar **morals.** In other words, they share an ideal of what is "right" and "wrong." Consequently, as public attitudes toward morality change, so do laws. In seventeenth-century America, a person found guilty of *adultery* (having sexual relations with someone other than one's spouse) could expect to be publicly whipped, branded, or even executed. Furthermore, a century ago, one could walk into a pharmacy and purchase heroin. Today, social attitudes have shifted to consider adultery a personal issue, beyond the reach of the state, and to consider the sale of heroin a criminal act.

Crime An act that violates criminal law and is punishable by criminal sanctions.

Consensus Model A criminal justice model in which the majority of citizens in a society share the same values and beliefs. Criminal acts are acts that conflict with these values and beliefs and that are deemed harmful to society.

Morals Principles of right and wrong behavior, as practiced by individuals or by society.

 LEARNING 1 OBJECTIVE Describe the two most common models of how society determines which acts are criminal.

SPEECH CRIME

Travel on the cramped, overcrowded London subway system is often unpleasant. For those riders stuck in the same car as Jacqueline Williams on the afternoon of October 30, 2012, however, the trip was nearly unbearable. At that time, Williams, who is white, unleashed a verbal rant against black commuters on the train, saying "Go home where you belong . . . . You might have been born here, but I bet your grandparents weren't." "You make me sick," Williams continued, adding, "If you belonged here, you'd be pink-skinned, blonde-haired, blue eyes, green eyes." She also told one black passenger that she walked "like a monkey."

Williams's actions were ugly and offensive, but were they criminal? In the United States, no. As interpreted by American courts, the First Amendment to the U.S. Constitution does not allow laws punishing speech unless that speech is likely to provoke immediate violence. England's Crime and Disorder Act, in contrast, prohibits "threatening, abusive, or insulting words"

within the "hearing or sight" of someone "likely to be caused harassment, alarm, or distress which was racially aggravated." Consequently, British Transport Police identified Williams using a YouTube video of the incident and arrested her for committing a racially aggravated public order offense.

If convicted, Williams faced a significant punishment. Six months earlier, another Londoner, Jacqueline Woodhouse, was found guilty of similarly insulting black passengers on a subway car. In sentencing Woodhouse to twenty-one weeks behind bars, a British judge lamented that "our citizens could be subject to such behavior."

FOR CRITICAL ANALYSIS

Do you think that the United States should criminalize "threatening, abusive, or insulting words" aimed at members of a minority group? What would be the consequences—both intended and unintended—of such a law?

Conflict Model A criminal justice model in which the content of criminal law is determined by the groups that hold economic, political, and social power in a community.

THE CONFLICT MODEL Some people reject the consensus model on the ground that moral attitudes are not constant or even consistent. In large, democratic societies such as the United States, different groups of citizens have widely varying opinions on controversial issues of morality and criminality such as abortion, the war on drugs, immigration, and assisted suicide. These groups and their elected representatives are constantly coming into conflict with one another. According to the **conflict model,** then, the most politically powerful segments of society—based on class, income, age, and race—have the most influence on criminal laws and are therefore able to impose their values on the rest of the community.

Consequently, what is deemed criminal activity is determined by whichever group happens to be holding power at any given time. Because certain groups do not have access to political power, their interests are not served by the criminal justice system. To give one example, with the exception of Oregon and Washington State, physician-assisted suicide for the terminally ill is illegal in the United States. Although opinion polls show that the general public is evenly divided on the issue,[4] several highly motivated interest groups have been able to convince lawmakers that the practice goes against America's shared moral and religious values.

An Integrated Definition of Crime

Define *crime.* **2** LEARNING OBJECTIVE

Considering both the consensus and conflict models, we can construct a definition of crime that will be useful throughout this textbook. For our purposes, crime is an action or activity that is:

1. Punishable under criminal law, as determined by the majority or, in some instances, by a powerful minority.
2. Considered an *offense against society as a whole* and prosecuted by public officials, not by victims and their relatives or friends.
3. Punishable by sanctions based on laws that bring about the loss of personal freedom or life.

At this point, it is important to understand the difference between crime and **deviance,** or behavior that does not conform to the norms of a given community or society. Deviance is a subjective concept. For example, some segments of society may think that smoking marijuana or killing animals for clothing and food is deviant behavior. Deviant acts become crimes only when society as a whole, through its legislatures, determines that those acts should be punished—as is the situation today in the United States with using illegal drugs but not with eating meat. Furthermore, not all crimes are considered particularly deviant—little social disapproval is attached to those who fail to follow the letter of parking laws. In essence, criminal law reflects those acts that we, as a society, agree are so unacceptable that steps must be taken to prevent them from occurring.

Several years ago, the federal government and several state governments banned the sale of Four Loko, here being enjoyed by college students in Fort Collins, Colorado. The drink, known as "blackout in a can," combines the alcohol content of nearly six beers with a strong dose of caffeine. Why might society demand that the sale of this product be made a criminal offense?
Matthew Staer/Landov

Types of Crime

The manner in which crimes are classified depends on their seriousness. Federal, state, and local legislation has provided for the classification and punishment of hundreds of thousands of different criminal acts, ranging from jaywalking to first degree murder. For general purposes, we can group criminal behavior into six categories: violent crime, property crime, public order crime, white-collar crime, organized crime, and high-tech crime.

VIOLENT CRIME Crimes against persons, or *violent crimes,* have come to dominate our perspectives on crime. There are four major categories of violent crime:

- **Murder,** or the unlawful killing of a human being.
- **Sexual assault,** or *rape,* which refers to coerced actions of a sexual nature against an unwilling participant.
- **Assault** and **battery,** two separate acts that cover situations in which one person physically attacks another (battery) or, through threats, intentionally leads another to believe that he or she will be physically harmed (assault).
- **Robbery,** or the taking of funds, personal property, or any other article of value from a person by means of force or fear.

As you will see in Chapter 4, these violent crimes are further classified by *degree,* depending on the circumstances surrounding the criminal act. These circumstances include the intent of the person committing the crime, whether a weapon was used,

Deviance Behavior that is considered to go against the norms established by society.

Murder The unlawful killing of one human being by another.

Sexual Assault Forced or coerced sexual intercourse (or other sexual acts).

Assault A threat or an attempt to do violence to another person that causes that person to fear immediate physical harm.

Battery The act of physically contacting another person with the intent to do harm, even if the resulting injury is insubstantial.

Robbery The act of taking property from another person through force, threat of force, or intimidation.

Courtesy F. W. Gill

CAREERS IN CJ

F. W. GILL

GANG INVESTIGATOR

The problem, for most of these kids, is that nobody cares. Their parents don't, or can't, get involved in their children's lives. (How many times have I heard parents deny that their son or daughter is a gang banger, even though it's obvious?) Teachers are in the business of teaching and don't, or can't, take the time to get to know their most troubled students. So, when I'm dealing with gang members, the first thing I do is listen. I don't lecture them, I don't tell them that they are throwing away their lives. I just listen. You'd be amazed how effective this can be—these kids, who look so tough on the outside, just want an adult to care.

Not that there is any magic formula for convincing a gang member to go straight. It is very difficult to get someone to change his or her lifestyle. If they don't want to change— really want to change—then nothing I can say or do is going to make much of a difference. Unfortunately, there are many lost causes. I've even had a couple of cases in which a juvenile was afraid to leave the gang because his father was a gang member, and he insisted that the boy stay in the gang. I have had some success in convincing gang members to turn their lives around by joining the military. The military provides discipline and a new outlook on life, things that these kids badly need. The way I look at it, in some cases, war is the best shot these kids have at saving their own lives.

SOCIAL MEDIA CAREER TIP When you are posting on Facebook, assume that your post will be published in your local newspaper and read by a potential employer. So, if you think the post might reflect poorly on you as a potential employee, keep it offline.

and (in cases other than murder) the level of pain and suffering experienced by the victim.

PROPERTY CRIME The most common form of criminal activity is *property crime,* or those crimes in which the goal of the offender is some form of economic gain or the damaging of property. Pocket picking, shoplifting, and the stealing of any property that is not accomplished by force are covered by laws against **larceny,** also known as *theft.* **Burglary** refers to the unlawful entry of a structure with the intention of committing a serious crime such as theft. *Motor vehicle theft* describes the theft or attempted theft of a motor vehicle, including all cases in which automobiles are taken by persons not having lawful access to them. *Arson* is also a property crime. It involves the willful and malicious burning of a home, automobile, commercial building, or any other construction.

PUBLIC ORDER CRIME The concept of **public order crimes** is linked to the consensus model discussed earlier. Historically, societies have always outlawed activities that are considered contrary to public values and morals. Today, the most common public order crimes include public drunkenness, prostitution, gambling, and illicit drug use. These crimes are sometimes referred to as *victimless crimes* because they often harm only the offender. As you will see throughout this textbook, however, that term is rather misleading. Public order crimes may create an environment that gives rise to property and violent crimes.

Larceny The act of taking property from another person without the use of force with the intent of keeping that property.

Burglary The act of breaking into or entering a structure (such as a home or office) without permission for the purpose of committing a felony.

Public Order Crime Behavior that has been labeled criminal because it is contrary to shared social values, customs, and norms.

FAST FACTS

YOUTH INTERVENTION SPECIALIST/GANG INVESTIGATOR JOB DESCRIPTION:

- Conducts assessments and refers at-risk youth to appropriate activities, programs, or agencies.
- Serves as a liaison between the police department, schools, other agencies, and the community regarding gang and other youth-related matters.

WHAT KIND OF TRAINING IS REQUIRED?

- A bachelor's degree in counseling, criminal justice, or other social science-related field. Bilingual (English/Spanish) skills are desired.

ANNUAL SALARY RANGE?

- $40,000–$49,000

WHITE-COLLAR CRIME Business-related crimes are popularly referred to as **white-collar crimes.** The term *white-collar crime* is broadly used to describe an illegal act or series of acts committed by an individual or business entity using some nonviolent means to obtain a personal or business advantage. As you will see in Chapter 16, when we consider the topic in much greater detail, certain property crimes fall into this category when committed in a business context. Although the extent of this criminal activity is difficult to determine with any certainty, the Association of Certified Fraud Examiners estimates that white-collar crime costs businesses worldwide as much as $3.5 trillion a year.[5]

ORGANIZED CRIME White-collar crime involves the use of legal business facilities and employees to commit illegal acts. For example, a bank teller can't embezzle unless he or she is first hired as a legal employee of the bank. In contrast, **organized crime** describes illegal acts by illegal organizations, usually geared toward satisfying the public's demand for unlawful goods and services. Organized crime broadly implies a conspiratorial and illegal relationship among any number of persons engaged in unlawful acts. More specifically, groups engaged in organized crime employ criminal tactics such as violence, corruption, and intimidation for economic gain. The hierarchical structure of organized crime operations often mirrors that of legitimate businesses, and, like any corporation, these groups attempt to capture a sufficient percentage of any given market to make a profit. For organized crime, the traditional preferred markets are gambling, prostitution, illegal narcotics, and loan sharking (lending funds at higher-than-legal interest rates), along with more recent ventures into counterfeiting and credit-card scams.

HIGH-TECH CRIME The newest variation on crime is directly related to the increased presence of computers in everyday life. The Internet, with approximately 2.5 billion users worldwide, is the site of numerous *cyber crimes,* such as selling pornographic materials, soliciting minors, and defrauding consumers through bogus financial investments. The dependence of businesses on computer operations has left corporations vulnerable to sabotage, fraud, embezzlement, and theft of proprietary data. Figure 1.1 below describes

White-Collar Crime Nonviolent crimes committed by business entities or individuals to gain a personal or business advantage.

Organized Crime Illegal acts carried out by illegal organizations engaged in the market for illegal goods or services, such as illicit drugs or firearms.

FIGURE 1.1 Types of Cyber Crime

Cyber Crimes against Persons and Property

- *Cyber Fraud:* Any misrepresentation knowingly made over the Internet with the intention of deceiving another person.
- *Identity Theft:* The appropriation of identity information, such as a person's name, driver's license, or Social Security number, to illegally access the victim's financial resources.
- *Cyberstalking:* Use of the Internet, e-mail, or any other form of electronic communication to attempt to contact and/or intimidate another person.

Cyber Crimes in the Business World

- *Hacking/Cracking:* The act of employing one computer to gain illegal access to the information stored on another computer.
- *Malware Production:* The creation of programs harmful to computers, such as worms, Trojan horses, and viruses.
- *Intellectual Property Theft:* The illegal appropriation of property that results from intellectual creative processes, such as films, video games, and software, without compensating its owners.

Cyber Crimes against the Community

- *Online Child Pornography:* The illegal selling, posting, and distributing of material depicting children engaged in sexually explicit conduct.
- *Online Gambling:* The use of the Internet to conduct gambling operations that would be illegal if carried out in the "real" world.

several of the most common cyber crimes, and we will address this particular criminal activity in much greater detail in Chapter 16.

SELF ASSESSMENT

Fill in the blanks and check your answers on page 31.

A criminal act is a wrong against _____ and therefore is "avenged," or prosecuted, by _____ _____, not by the individual victims of a crime. A crime is not the same as an act of _____, the term for behavior that is nonconformist but not necessarily criminal. Murder, assault, and robbery are labeled _____ crimes because they are committed against persons. The category of crime that includes larceny, motor vehicle theft, and arson is called _____ crime. When a criminal acts to gain an illegal business advantage, he or she has committed what is commonly known as a _____-_____ crime.

THE PURPOSE OF THE CRIMINAL JUSTICE SYSTEM

Defining which actions are to be labeled "crimes" is only the first step in safeguarding society from criminal behavior. Institutions must be created to apprehend alleged wrongdoers, to determine whether these persons have indeed committed crimes, and to punish those who are found guilty according to society's wishes. These institutions combine to form the **criminal justice system.** As we begin our examination of the American criminal justice system in this introductory chapter, it is important to have an idea of its purpose.

Maintaining Justice

As its name implies, the explicit goal of the criminal justice system is to provide *justice* to all members of society. Because **justice** is a difficult concept to define, this goal can be challenging, if not impossible, to meet. Broadly stated, justice means that all individuals are equal before the law and that they are free from arbitrary arrest or seizure as defined by the law. In other words, the idea of justice is linked with the idea of fairness. Above all, we want our laws and the means by which they are carried out to be fair.

Justice and fairness are subjective terms, which is to say that people may have different concepts of what is just and fair. If a woman who has been beaten by her husband retaliates by killing him, what is her just punishment? Reasonable persons could disagree, with some thinking that the homicide was justified and that she should be treated leniently. Others might insist that she should not have taken the law into her own hands. Police officers, judges, prosecutors, prison administrators, and other employees of the criminal justice system must decide what is "fair." Sometimes, their course of action is obvious, but often, as we shall see, it is not.

Protecting Society

Within the broad mandate of "maintaining justice," Megan Kurlychek of the University at Albany, New York, has identified four specific goals of our criminal justice system:

1. To protect society from potential future crimes of the most dangerous or "risky" offenders.
2. To determine when an offense has been committed and provide the appropriate punishment for that offense.
3. To rehabilitate those offenders who have been punished so that it is safe to return them to the community.

Criminal Justice System The interlocking network of law enforcement agencies, courts, and corrections institutions designed to enforce criminal laws and protect society from criminal behavior.

Justice The quality of fairness that must exist in the processes designed to determine whether individuals are guilty of criminal wrongdoing.

4. To support crime victims and, to the extent possible, return them to their pre-crime status.[6]

Again, though these goals may seem straightforward, they are fraught with difficulty. Take the example of James Holmes, who was charged with twenty-four counts of murder and 116 counts of attempted murder by law enforcement officials on July 30, 2012. Ten days earlier, Holmes—armed with an assault rifle and three other guns—had apparently opened fire on the audience at a late-night screening of a Batman movie in Aurora, Colorado. Following the incident, authorities at the University of Colorado, where Holmes had been a graduate student, came under heavy criticism for not reacting more forcefully to staff concerns about his behavior. Next chapter, we will revisit Holmes's behavior as part of a discussion on the challenges of predicting criminality.

A month after the attack, Holmes's defense attorneys told a district judge that their client was mentally ill, causing many in Aurora and throughout the country to worry that he would never receive an appropriate punishment for his actions (see the photo alongside). In Chapter 4, you will learn how insanity can be used as a defense to criminal wrongdoing. Furthermore, regardless of his mental state, should Holmes ever be set free? In Chapters 11 and 14, we will discuss the concept of rehabilitation and the role that victims play in the eventual return of offenders to the community. Throughout this textbook, you will come to better understand the criminal justice system by exposure to differing opinions on these topics and many others. (The feature *You Be the Legislator—Banning Distracted Walking* on the following page examines just how far criminal law should stretch to protect citizens from harm.)

Review the four goals of the criminal justice system listed on this and the facing page. Which of the goals would be met by rehabilitating James Holmes, shown here in a Colorado court, and returning him to society? Which would be met by putting him in prison for life?
RJ Sangosti-Pool/Getty Images

SELF ASSESSMENT

Fill in the blanks and check your answers on page 31.

The concept of _____ is closely linked with ideas of fairness and equal treatment for all, and it is a primary goal of American police officers, judges, and prison administrators. Other goals include _____ society from criminal behavior, _____ those who are guilty of criminal wrongdoing, and supporting the _____ of crime.

THE STRUCTURE OF THE CRIMINAL JUSTICE SYSTEM

Society places the burden of maintaining justice and protecting our communities on those who work for the three main institutions of the criminal justice system: law enforcement, the courts, and corrections. In this section, we take an introductory look at these institutions and their role in the criminal justice system as a whole.

The Importance of Federalism

To understand the structure of the criminal justice system, you must understand the concept of **federalism,** which means that government powers are shared by the national (federal) government and the states. The framers of the U.S. Constitution, fearful of tyranny and a too-powerful central government, chose the system of federalism as a compromise.

The appeal of federalism was that it established a strong national government capable of handling large-scale problems while allowing for state powers and local

Federalism A form of government in which a written constitution provides for a division of powers between a central government and several regional governments.

traditions. For example, earlier in the chapter we noted that physician-assisted suicide, though banned in most of the country, is legal in Oregon and Washington State. Several years ago, the federal government challenged the decision made by voters in these two states to allow the practice. The United States Supreme Court sided with the states, ruling that the principle of federalism supported their freedom to differ from the majority viewpoint in this instance.[7]

The Constitution gave the national government certain express powers, such as the power to coin money, raise an army, and regulate interstate commerce. All other powers were left to the states, including police power, which allows the states to enact whatever laws are necessary to protect the health, morals, safety, and welfare of their citizens. As the American criminal justice system has evolved, the ideals of federalism have ebbed somewhat. Specifically, the powers of the national government have expanded significantly. In Chapter 2, we will see how these powers have been challenged by the efforts of several states to legalize the possession and sale of marijuana for recreational use, thereby directly violating federal drug laws.

LAW ENFORCEMENT The ideals of federalism can be clearly seen in the local, state, and federal levels of law enforcement. Though agencies from the different levels cooperate if the need arises, they have their own organizational structures and tend to operate independently of one another. We briefly introduce each level of law enforcement here and cover them in more detail in Chapters 5, 6, and 7.

YOU BE THE Legislator

BANNING DISTRACTED WALKING

THE SITUATION A twenty-four-year-old woman walks into a telephone pole while texting. A twelve-year-old boy, his attention focused on a handheld video game, is struck by a pickup truck as he crosses the street. Over a period of six years, according to a University of Maryland study, 116 pedestrians have been killed or seriously injured while wearing headphones. These are examples of the dangers of "distracted walking," which—by some measures—has become a national safety concern. Although driver traffic fatalities in the United States are dropping, pedestrian traffic fatalities and injuries are increasing. Young people seem particularly vulnerable. One special interest group found that the number of teens injured in pedestrian accidents rose 25 percent from 2006 to 2010. Many observers explain these figures by pointing to an epidemic of distracted walking.

THE LAW At present, no state has passed a criminal law banning any form of distracted walking. (By contrast, thirty-nine states ban texting while driving, and ten states prohibit all drivers from using handheld cell phones.)

YOUR DECISION Suppose that you are a member of your state legislature. One of your colleagues puts forth a bill prohibiting the act of walking while using an electronic device such as a smartphone. In supporting this potential legislation, your colleague cites a University of Washington study showing that distracted walking is as risky for a pedestrian as drunk driving is for a driver. Would you favor such legislation? Why or why not? Under what circumstances do you believe the criminal justice system has a responsibility to protect citizens from their own risky behavior?

To see how several state legislatures have responded to the idea of banning distracted walking, go to Example 1.1 in Appendix B.

Somchai Rakin/Shutterstock.com

Local Law Enforcement On the local level, the duties of law enforcement agencies are split between counties and municipalities. The chief law enforcement officer of most counties is the county sheriff. The sheriff is usually an elected post, with a two- or four-year term. In some areas, where city and county governments have merged, there is a county police force, headed by a chief of police. As Figure 1.2 below shows, the bulk of all police officers in the United States are employed on a local level. The majority of these work in departments that consist of fewer than 10 officers, though a large city such as New York may have a police force of about 36,000.

Local police are responsible for the "nuts and bolts" of law enforcement work. They investigate most crimes and attempt to deter crime through patrol activities. They apprehend criminals and participate in trial proceedings, if necessary. Local police are also charged with "keeping the peace," a broad set of duties that includes crowd and traffic control and the resolution of minor conflicts between citizens. In many areas, local police have the added obligation of providing social services such as dealing with domestic violence and child abuse.

3 LEARNING OBJECTIVE Outline the three levels of law enforcement.

State Law Enforcement Hawaii is the only state that does not have a state law enforcement agency. Generally, there are two types of state law enforcement agencies, those designated simply as "state police" and those designated as "highway patrols." State highway patrols concern themselves mainly with infractions on public highways and freeways. Other state law enforcers include fire marshals, who investigate suspicious fires and educate the public on fire prevention; and fish, game, and watercraft wardens, who police a state's natural resources and often oversee its firearms laws. Some states also have alcoholic beverage control officers, as well as agents who investigate welfare and food stamp fraud.

Federal Law Enforcement The enactment of new national anti-terrorism, gun, drug, and violent crime laws over the past forty years has led to an expansion in the size and scope of the federal government's participation in the criminal justice system. The Department of Homeland Security, which we will examine in detail in Chapters 5 and 16, combines the police powers of twenty-four federal agencies to protect the United States from terrorist attacks. Other federal agencies with police powers include the Federal Bureau of Investigation (FBI), the Drug Enforcement Administration (DEA), the U.S. Secret Service, and the Bureau of Alcohol, Tobacco, Firearms and Explosives (ATF). In fact, almost every federal agency, including the postal and forest services, has some kind of police power.

FIGURE 1.2 Local, State, and Federal Employees in Our Criminal Justice System

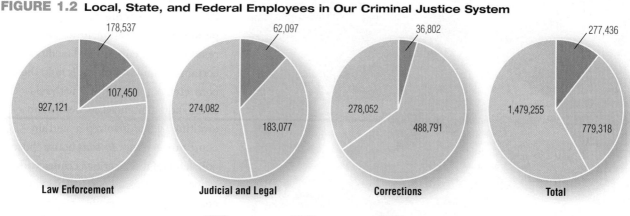

Source: Bureau of Justice Statistics, *Justice Expenditure and Employment in the United States, 2009* (Washington, D.C.: U.S. Department of Justice, May 2012), Table 2.

Unlike their local and state counterparts, federal law enforcement agencies operate throughout the United States. In May 2012, for example, the FBI conducted a nationwide sweep targeting health-care fraud, arresting more than one hundred doctors, nurses, and other medical professionals in seven cities ranging from Los Angeles to Chicago to Miami. Federal agencies are also able to provide support for local police departments, as happened several years ago when agents from the ATF joined forces with the Tulsa (Oklahoma) Police Department to combat a string of armed robberies that had plagued the city for nearly six months.

THE COURTS The United States has a *dual court system,* which means that we have two independent judicial systems, one at the federal level and one at the state level. In practice, this translates into fifty-two different court systems: one federal court system and fifty different state court systems, plus that of the District of Columbia. As allowed under the rules of federalism, the U.S. (federal) criminal code lists about 4,500 crimes, and each state has its own criminal statutes that determine illegal acts under state law. In general, those defendants charged with violating federal criminal law will face trial in federal court, while those defendants charged with violating state law will appear in state court.

The *criminal court* and its work group—the judge, prosecutors, and defense attorneys—are charged with the weighty responsibility of determining the innocence or guilt of criminal suspects. We will cover these important participants, their roles in the criminal trial, and the court system as a whole in Chapters 8, 9, 10, and 11.

LEARNING
List the essential elements of
the corrections system. **4**
OBJECTIVE

■ At midyear 2012, America's jails held approximately 744,000 inmates, including these residents of the Orange County jail in Santa Ana, California. What are the basic differences between jails and prisons?
Lucy Nicholson/Reuters/Landov

CORRECTIONS Once the court system convicts and sentences an offender, she or he is delegated to the corrections system. (Those convicted in a state court will be under the control of that state's corrections system, and those convicted of a federal crime will find themselves under the control of the federal corrections system.) Depending on the seriousness of the crime and their individual needs, offenders are placed on probation, incarcerated, or transferred to community-based correctional facilities.

- *Probation,* the most common correctional treatment, allows the offender to return to the community and remain under the supervision of an agent of the court known as a probation officer. While on probation, the offender must follow certain rules of conduct. When probationers fail to follow these rules, they may be incarcerated.
- If the offender's sentence includes a period of incarceration, he or she will be remanded to a correctional facility for a certain amount of time. *Jails* hold those convicted of minor crimes with relatively short sentences, as well as those awaiting trial or involved in certain court proceedings. *Prisons* house those convicted of more serious crimes with longer sentences. Generally speaking, counties and municipalities administer jails, while prisons are the domain of federal and state governments.

- *Community-based corrections* have increased in popularity as jails and prisons have been plagued with problems of funding and overcrowding. Community-based correctional facilities include halfway houses, residential centers, and work-release centers. They operate on the assumption that all convicts do not need, and are not benefited by, incarceration in jail or prison.

The majority of those inmates released from incarceration are not finished with the corrections system. The most frequent type of release from a jail or prison is *parole*, in which an inmate, after serving part of his or her sentence in a correctional facility, is allowed to serve the rest of the term in the community. Like someone on probation, a parolee must conform to certain conditions of freedom, with the same consequences if these conditions are not followed. Issues of probation, incarceration, community-based corrections, and parole will be covered in Chapters 12, 13, and 14.

The Criminal Justice Process

In its 1967 report, the President's Commission on Law Enforcement and Administration of Justice asserted that the criminal justice system

> is not a hodgepodge of random actions. It is rather a continuum—an orderly progression of events—some of which, like arrest and trial, are highly visible and some of which, though of great importance, occur out of public view.[8]

The commission's assertion that the criminal justice system is a "continuum" is one that many observers would challenge.[9] Some liken the criminal justice system to a sports team, which is the sum of an indeterminable number of decisions, relationships, conflicts, and adjustments.[10] Such a volatile mix is not what we generally associate with a "system." For most, the word **system** indicates a certain degree of order and discipline. That we refer to our law enforcement agencies, courts, and correctional facilities as part of a "system" may reflect our hopes rather than reality. Still, it will be helpful to familiarize yourself with the basic steps of the *criminal justice process,* or the procedures through which the criminal justice system meets the expectations of society. These basic steps are provided in Figure 1.3 on the following page.

In his classic study of the criminal justice system, Herbert Packer, a professor at Stanford University, compared the ideal criminal justice process to an assembly line "down which moves an endless stream of cases, never stopping."[11] In Packer's image of assembly-line justice, each step of the **formal criminal justice process** involves a series of "routinized operations" with the end goal of getting the criminal defendant from point A (his or her arrest by law enforcement) to point B (the criminal trial) to point C (if guilty, her or his punishment).[12] As Packer himself was wont to point out, the daily operations of criminal justice rarely operate so smoothly. In this textbook, the criminal justice process will be examined as the end product of many different decisions made by many different criminal justice professionals in law enforcement, the courts, and corrections.

SELF ASSESSMENT

Fill in the blanks and check your answers on page 31.

To protect against a too-powerful central government, the framers of the U.S. Constitution relied on the principle of _____ to balance power between the national government and the states. Consequently, the United States has a _____ court system—one at the federal level and one at the _____ level. One expert has compared the _____ criminal justice process to an assembly line involving a series of routine operations.

FIGURE 1.3 The Criminal Justice Process

This diagram provides a simplified overview of the basic steps of the criminal justice process, from criminal act to release from incarceration. Next to each step, you will find the chapter of this textbook in which the event is covered.

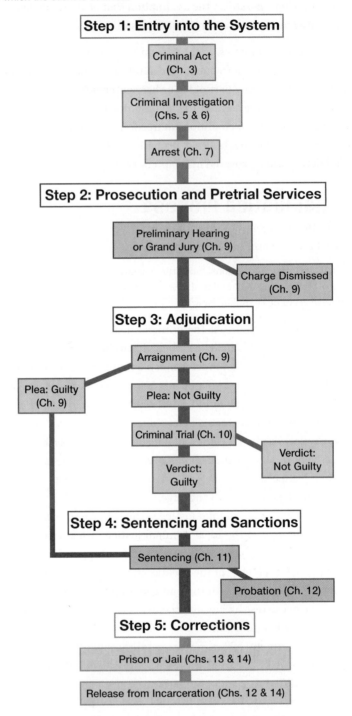

DISCRETION AND ETHICS

Practically, the formal criminal justice process suffers from a serious drawback: it is unrealistic. Law enforcement agencies do not have the staff or funds to investigate *every* crime, so they must decide where to direct their limited resources. Increasing caseloads and a limited amount of time in which to dispose of them constrict many of our nation's courts. Overcrowding in prisons and jails affects both law enforcement agencies and the courts—there is simply not enough room for all convicts.

The criminal justice system relies on *discretion* to alleviate these pressures. By **discretion,** we mean the authority to choose between and among alternative courses of action, based on individual judgment and conscience. Collectively, the discretionary decisions made by criminal justice professionals are said to produce an **informal criminal justice process** that does not operate within the rigid confines of formal rules and laws.

LEARNING **5** OBJECTIVE Explain the difference between the formal and informal criminal justice processes.

Informal Decision Making

By its nature, the informal criminal justice system relies on the discretion of individuals to offset the rigidity of criminal statutes and procedural rules. For example, even if a prosecutor believes that a suspect is guilty, she or he may decide not to bring charges against the suspect if the case is weak or the police erred during the investigative process. In many instances, prosecutors will not squander the scarce resource of court time on a case they might not win. Some argue that the informal process has made our system more just. Given the immense pressure of limited resources, the argument goes, only rarely will an innocent person end up before a judge and jury.[13]

DISCRETION IN ACTION Law enforcement also uses discretion to best allocate its scarce resources. For example, in the *You Be the Legislator* feature earlier in the chapter, we mentioned the proliferation of state laws banning texting while driving. Georgia's ban took effect in July 2010, yet over the next two years fewer than fifty people a month in the entire state were convicted of that offense.[14] Apparently, police officers in Georgia are using their discretion to loosely enforce the texting-while-driving law, given what we know to be the prevalence of such behavior.

There are several reasons for this use of discretion. First, it is difficult for police officers to prove that a person has been texting and driving. In court, the suspect will often claim that he or she was simply accessing a GPS navigation system or using his or her hands for some other legal activity. If a judge believes this argument, as is often the case, the police officer has wasted his or her time.[15] Second, police officers may not consider enforcement of texting-while-driving laws to be the best use of their limited time. From July 2010 to September 2012, Georgia law enforcement officers were able to secure about 22,500 convictions for drunk driving compared to 1,281 convictions for texting while driving.[16] Despite evidence that the two behaviors are comparably dangerous, Georgia police obviously give higher priority to getting drunk drivers off state roadways.

In Chapters 5, 6, and 7, we will examine many other circumstances that call for discretionary decision making by law enforcement officers. (See Figure 1.4 below for a

Discretion The ability of individuals in the criminal justice system to make operational decisions based on personal judgment instead of formal rules or official information.

Informal Criminal Justice Process A model of the criminal justice system that recognizes the informal authority exercised by individuals at each step of the criminal justice process.

FIGURE 1.4 Discretion in the Criminal Justice System

Criminal justice officials must make decisions every day concerning their duties. The officials listed below, whether they operate on a local, state, or federal level, rely heavily on discretion when meeting the following responsibilities.

Police	Judges
• Enforce laws • Investigate specific crimes • Search people or buildings • Arrest or detain people	• Set conditions for pretrial release • Accept pleas • Dismiss charges • Impose sentences
Prosecutors	**Correctional Officials**
• File charges against suspects brought to them by the police • Drop cases • Reduce charges	• Assign convicts to prison or jail • Punish prisoners who misbehave • Reward prisoners who behave well

description of some of the important discretionary decisions that make up the informal criminal justice process.)

THE PITFALLS OF DISCRETION Unfortunately, the informal criminal justice system does not always benefit from measured, rational decision making. Individual judgment can be tainted by personal bias, erroneous or irrational thinking, and plain ill will. When this occurs, discretion becomes "the power to *get away* with alternative decisions (emphasis added)."[17] Indeed, many of the rules of the formal criminal justice process are designed to keep its employees from substituting their own judgment for that of the general public, as expressed by the law.

Regarding the texting-while-driving bans discussed above, many observers worry that such laws will exacerbate the incidence of racial profiling in the United States.[18] As you will learn in Chapter 7, racial profiling is the police practice of improperly targeting members of minority groups based on personal characteristics such as race or ethnicity. Furthermore, associate Supreme Court justice Antonin Scalia has criticized discretion in the courts for its tendency to cause discriminatory and disparate criminal sentences, a subject we will discuss in Chapter 11. According to Scalia, the need for fairness and certainty in the criminal justice system outweighs the practical benefits of widespread and unpredictable discretionary decision making.[19]

Ethics and Justice

Define ethics, and describe the role that it plays in discretionary decision making. LEARNING OBJECTIVE 6

How can we reconcile the need for some sort of discretion in criminal justice with the ever-present potential for abuse? Part of the answer lies in our initial definition of discretion, which mentions not only individual judgment but also *conscience*. Ideally, actors in the criminal justice system will make moral choices about what is right and wrong based on the norms that have been established by society. In other words, they will behave *ethically*.

Ethics in criminal justice is closely related to the concept of justice. Because criminal justice professionals are representatives of the state, they have the power to determine whether the state is treating its citizens fairly. If some law enforcement officers in fact make the decision to pull over a texting driver based on that driver's race, then they are not only acting unethically but also unjustly.

ETHICS AND THE LAW The line between ethics and justice is often difficult to discern, as ethical standards are usually not written into criminal statutes. Consequently, individuals must often "fill in" the ethical blanks. To make this point, ethics expert John Kleinig uses the real-life example of a police officer who refused to arrest a homeless person for sleeping in a private parking garage. A local ordinance clearly prohibited such behavior. The officer, however, felt it would be unethical to arrest a homeless person under those circumstances unless he or she was acting in a disorderly manner. The officer's supervisors were unsympathetic to this ethical stance, and he was suspended from duty without pay.[20]

ETHICS AND CRITICAL THINKING Did the police officer in the above example behave ethically by inserting his own beliefs into the letter of the criminal law? Would an officer who arrested peaceful homeless trespassers be acting unethically? In some cases, the ethical decision will be *intuitive*, reflecting an automatic response determined by a person's background and experiences. In other cases, however, intuition is not enough. *Critical thinking* is needed for an ethical response.[21] Throughout this textbook, we will use the

Ethics The moral principles that govern a person's perception of right and wrong.

principle of critical thinking—which involves developing analytical skills and reasoning—to address the many ethical challenges inherent in the criminal justice system.

SELF ASSESSMENT

Fill in the blanks and check your answers on page 31.

At every level, the criminal justice system relies on the ＿＿＿ of its employees to keep it from being bogged down by formal rules. Some critics think that this freedom to make decisions leads to the dominance of an ＿＿＿ criminal justice system, which can, in some cases, result in unequal treatment and even discrimination. Ideally, to avoid this kind of injustice, criminal justice professionals will incorporate proper ＿＿＿ in their decision-making process.

Crime Control Model A criminal justice model that places primary emphasis on the right of society to be protected from crime and violent criminals.

Due Process Model A criminal justice model that places primacy on the right of the individual to be protected from the power of the government.

CRIMINAL JUSTICE TODAY

In describing the general direction of the criminal justice system as a whole, many observers point to two models introduced by Professor Herbert Packer: the *crime control model* and the *due process model*.[22] The underlying value of the **crime control model** is that the most important function of the criminal justice process is to punish and repress criminal conduct. The system must be quick and efficient, placing as few restrictions as possible on the ability of law enforcement officers to make discretionary decisions in apprehending criminals.

Although not in direct conflict with crime control, the underlying values of the **due process model** focus more on protecting the rights of the accused through formal, legal restraints on the police, courts, and corrections. That is, the due process model relies on the courts to make it more difficult to prove guilt. It rests on the belief that it is more desirable for society that ninety-nine guilty suspects go free than that a single innocent person be condemned.[23] (The *Mastering Concepts* feature on the following page provides a further comparison of the two models.)

LEARNING **7** OBJECTIVE Contrast the crime control and due process models.

Crime and Law Enforcement: The Bottom Line

It is difficult to say which of Packer's two models has the upper hand today. As we will see later in this section, homeland security concerns have brought much of the criminal justice system in line with crime control values. At the same time, decreasing arrest and imprisonment rates suggest that due process values are strong, as well. Indeed, despite that fact that most Americans believe our crime problem to be worsening,[24] the number of violent crimes in the United States is presently at its lowest level in four decades. Furthermore, property crimes have been declining every year for the past decade.[25]

As we will discuss in Chapter 3, such trends contradict conventional wisdom, which holds that when people are out of work and need money, they turn to crime as a last resort. Despite the economic downturn that has gripped the county for the past several years, the expected higher levels of criminality have not occurred. Juvenile crime rates are also declining, a subject we will address in Chapter 15. Alfred Blumstein of Carnegie Mellon University in Pittsburgh has called all this good news "striking," because it comes "at a time when everyone anticipated [crime rates] could be going up because of the recession."[26]

SMARTER POLICING Just as law enforcement inevitably gets a great deal of the blame when crime rates are high, American police forces have received much credit for the apparent decline in criminality. The consensus is that the police have become smarter and more disciplined over the past two decades, putting into practice strategies that allow

MASTERING CONCEPTS
CRIME CONTROL MODEL VERSUS DUE PROCESS MODEL

Crime Control Model	Due Process Model
GOAL	**GOAL**
• Deter crime by arresting and incarcerating criminals as quickly and efficiently as possible.	• Protect the individual charged with a crime against the immense and sometimes possibly unjust power of the state.
METHODS	**METHODS**
• Allow the police to "do their jobs" by limiting the amount of judicial oversight of law enforcement tactics.	• Assure the constitutional rights of those accused of crimes, at the hands of both the law enforcement officers who make the arrest and the prosecutors who prosecute the defendant in criminal court.
• Limit the number of rights and protections enjoyed by defendants in court.	• Whenever possible, allow nonviolent convicts to serve their sentences in the community rather than behind bars.
• Incarcerate criminals for lengthy periods of time by imposing harsh sentences, including the death penalty.	• Protect the civil rights of all inmates, and focus on rehabilitation rather than punishment in prisons and jails.

them to more effectively prevent crime. For example, the widespread use of *proactive policing* promotes more rigorous enforcement of minor offenses—such as drunkenness and public disorder—with an eye toward preventing more serious wrongdoing.[27] In addition, *hot-spot policing* has law enforcement officers focusing on high-crime areas rather than spreading their resources evenly throughout metropolitan areas.[28] These and other innovative policing strategies will be explored more fully in Chapter 6.

IDENTIFYING CRIMINALS Technology has also played a significant role in improving law enforcement efficiency. Police investigators are enjoying the benefits of perhaps the most effective new crime-fighting tool since fingerprint identification: DNA profiling. This technology allows law enforcement agents to identify a suspect from body fluid evidence (such as blood, saliva, or semen) or biological evidence (such as hair strands or fingernail clippings). As we will also see in Chapter 6, by collecting DNA from convicts and storing the information in databases, investigators have been able to reach across hundreds of miles and back in time to catch wrongdoers.

Law enforcement's ability to identify criminal suspects is set to receive another boost with the increased use of **biometrics.** The term refers to the various technological devices that read a person's unique physical characteristics and report his or her identity to authorities. The most common biometric devices record a suspect's fingerprints, but hand geometry, facial features, and the minute details of the human eye can also provide

Biometrics Methods to identify a person based on his or her unique physical characteristics, such as fingerprints or facial configuration.

biometric identification.[29] Public cameras equipped with facial recognition software can now scan crowds and pick out criminal suspects by matching their features against those stored in a database. We will address the privacy concerns brought about by such technology in Chapter 7.

CJ & TECHNOLOGY — MORIS (MOBILE OFFENDER RECOGNITION AND IDENTIFICATION SYSTEM)

Barry Chin/*Boston Globe* via Getty Image

It seems as though there is an app for everything these days—even biometrics. Several years ago, law enforcement agents in about forty counties began using the Mobile Offender Recognition and Identification System (MORIS). With the device, which weighs about twelve ounces and attaches to a smartphone, the police officer takes a photograph of a suspect's face from five feet away, or of the suspect's eyes from a distance of six inches. The app is then engaged to search for a facial or iris match from a national database to determine if the suspect has a previous record.

Without MORIS, a police officer must take the suspect back to the station house, take her or his fingerprints, and then wait up to a week to hear if the FBI was able to produce a match. With MORIS, the digital search is completed within seconds. "This is a game changer for law enforcement," says Pinal County (Arizona) sheriff Paul Babeu, who was happy to pay the $3,000 cost of each MORIS unit. "It's worth its weight in gold."

Thinking about MORIS
Why is MORIS a "game changer" for law enforcement? Should this technology be made available to ordinary citizens? Why or why not?

CONTINUING CHALLENGES FOR LAW ENFORCEMENT Not every policing trend is positive. Due to the worsening economic conditions discussed above, according to one recent survey, about half of the nation's local law enforcement agencies have been subject to budget cuts in recent years.[30] The impact of these cuts, which include officer layoffs and resource reductions, could seriously hamper efforts to combat three of the major challenges facing today's police: gangs, guns, and illegal drugs.

The Scourge of Street Gangs For many local law enforcement agencies, particularly those in large metropolitan areas, success is measured by their ability to control **street gangs.** These gangs are often identified as groups of offenders who band together to engage in violent, unlawful, or criminal activity. According to the most recent data, more than 33,000 gangs, with approximately 1.4 million members, are criminally active in the United States. The same study estimates that gangs are responsible for an average of 48 percent of violent crime in most cities, and for up to 90 percent in the worst-hit areas.[31] As we saw in the opening to this chapter, in 2012, Chicago—bucking the national trend—experienced its highest homicide levels in five years, with city officials attributing more than a quarter of the killings to a single gang, the Gangster Disciples.[32]

The FBI's "Safe Streets" initiative—in which the federal agency teams up with local police forces—has resulted in the arrest of more than 23,000 gang members over the past decade, but such efforts are threatened by budget cuts on the municipal and county levels. The topic of youth gangs and efforts to combat their criminal activity will be covered more extensively in Chapter 15.

Street Gang A group of people, usually three or more, who share a common identity and engage in illegal activities.

Gun Control Efforts by a government to regulate or control the sale of guns.

Drug Any substance that modifies biological, psychological, or social behavior. In particular, an illegal substance with those properties.

Psychoactive Drugs Chemicals that affect the brain, causing changes in emotions, perceptions, and behavior.

Gun Use and Crime Even though gangs are heavily involved in criminal activity, most gang-related homicides are not crime related. That is, the killings do not occur during drug deals or robberies "gone bad." Rather, according to data collected by the federal government, the great majority of gang deaths involve the deadly mix of inter-gang conflict (such as territorial or personal disputes) and firearms.[33] Taking this kind of data into consideration, Alfred Blumstein suggests that the most serious threat to America's positive crime outlook is not the economy but an increase in the number of guns in high-crime neighborhoods.[34] Overall, about 31,000 people are killed by gunfire in the United States each year, and illegally obtained firearms are a constant concern for law enforcement officials.

At the same time, legal ownership of guns is widespread, with almost one-third of American households possessing at least one gun.[35] In 2008, the United States Supreme Court further solidified the legal basis for this practice by ruling that the U.S. Constitution protects an individual's right to "bear arms."[36] The Court's decision has done little to lessen the debate over **gun control,** or the policies that the government implements to keep firearms out of the hands of the wrong people. The clamor surrounding this debate reached a fever pitch in 2012. That year, a series of high-profile, multiple-victim shootings culminated on December 14 with the death of twenty-six people—twenty of them children—following an attack at the Sandy Hook Elementary School in Newtown, Connecticut. We will take a closer look at the divisive topic of gun control in the *CJ in Action* feature at the end of this chapter.

FIGURE 1.5 Drug Use in the United States

According to the National Survey on Drug Use and Health, about 22.5 million Americans, or 9.7 percent of those over twelve years old, can be considered "illicit drug users." As you can see, most of these people used marijuana exclusively. Furthermore, eighteen- to twenty-five-year-olds were more likely to have used illegal drugs than any other segment of the population.

Habits of Illegal Drug Users

Used marijuana and some other drug
Used a drug other than marijuana
Used marijuana only

Percentage Using in Past Month

Category of Users

Age
12–17
18–25
26 and older

Gender
Male
Female

Race and Ethnicity
White
African American
American Indian
Asian American
Hispanic

Percentage Using in Past Month

Source: National Survey on Drug Use and Health, 2012.

The Illegal Drugs Problem One area in which the nation's crime outlook has not been particularly encouraging involves illegal drugs. Over the past two decades, while arrests for most criminal behavior declined, the arrest rate for illegal drug possession and use increased by 122 percent.[37] Today, more than six of every ten arrestees tests positive for at least one drug in their systems at the time of arrest.[38]

The broadest possible definition of a **drug,** which includes alcohol, is any substance that modifies biological, psychological, or social behavior. In popular terminology, however, the word *drug* has a more specific connotation. When people speak of the "drug" problem, or the war on "drugs," or "drug" abuse, they are referring specifically to illegal **psychoactive drugs,** which affect the brain and alter consciousness or perception. Almost all of the drugs that we will be discussing in this textbook, such as marijuana, cocaine, heroin, and amphetamines, are illegal and psychoactive.

Drug Use in the United States The main source of drug use data is the National Survey on Drug Use and Health, conducted annually by the National Institute on Drug Abuse (see Figure 1.5 alongside). According to the survey, only 8.7 percent of those questioned had used an illegal drug in the past month. Even so, this means that a significant number of Americans—about 22.5 million—are regularly using illegal drugs, and the figure mushrooms when users of legal substances such as alcohol (133 million users) and tobacco (68 million users) are included.[39] Furthermore, illegal drug use appears to be increasing in this country, particularly among young people. Drug abuse often leads to further criminal behavior in adolescents, as we will see when we look at the juvenile justice system in Chapter 15. In general, the massive market for illegal drugs causes significant damage both in the United States and in countries such as Mexico that supply America with its "fix."

Homeland Security and Domestic Terrorism

Without question, the attacks of September 11, 2001—when terrorists hijacked four commercial airlines and used them to kill nearly three thousand people in New York City, northern Virginia, and rural Pennsylvania—were the most significant events of the first decade of the 2000s as far as crime fighting is concerned. As we will see throughout this textbook, the resulting **homeland security** movement has touched nearly every aspect of criminal justice. This movement has the ultimate goal of protecting America from **terrorism**, which can be broadly defined as the random use of staged violence to achieve political goals.

COUNTERTERRORISM AND CIVIL LIBERTIES "September 11 is the day that never ends," wrote journalist Richard Cohen on the occasion of its tenth anniversary in 2011.[40] Certainly, the memory of that day's events has lingered in the public consciousness. In March 2012, nearly two-thirds of Americans still worried a "great deal" or a "fair amount" about the possibility of future terrorist attacks in the United States.[41] Mobilized by such fears, federal, state, and local governments spent about $600 billion from 2002 to 2011 to bolster the nation's homeland security apparatus.[42]

The Patriot Act The need to respond to the terrorist threat led American politicians and police officials to turn sharply toward crime control principles, as discussed on page 19. In particular, the Patriot Act,[43] passed six weeks after the 9/11 attacks, strengthened the ability of federal law enforcement agents to investigate and incarcerate suspects. The 342-page piece of legislation is difficult to summarize, but some of its key provisions include the following:

- An expansion of the definition of what it means to "engage in terrorist activity" to include providing "material support" through such activities as fund-raising or operating Web sites for suspected terrorist organizations.
- Greater leeway for law enforcement agents to track Internet use, access private financial records, and wiretap those suspected of terrorist activity.
- A reduction in the amount of evidence law enforcement agents need to gather before taking a terrorist suspect into custody.

Homeland Security and Civil Liberties In a recent poll, 34 percent of those questioned about the Patriot Act felt that the law "goes too far and poses a threat to *civil liberties.*" Another 42 percent considered the legislation "a necessary tool that helps the government find terrorists."[44] The term **civil liberties** refers to the personal freedoms guaranteed to all Americans by the U.S. Constitution, particularly the first ten amendments, known as the Bill of Rights.

Concerns about balancing personal freedoms and personal safety permeate our criminal justice system. In fact, an entire chapter of this textbook—Chapter 7—is needed to discuss the rules that law enforcement must follow to protect the civil liberties of

Homeland Security A concerted national effort to prevent terrorist attacks within the United States and reduce the country's vulnerability to terrorism.

Terrorism The use or threat of violence to achieve political objectives.

Civil Liberties The basic rights and freedoms for American citizens guaranteed by the U.S. Constitution, particularly in the Bill of Rights.

crime suspects. Many of the issues that we will address in that chapter are particularly relevant to counterterrorism efforts. For example:

1. The First Amendment to the U.S. Constitution states that the government shall not interfere with citizens' "freedom of speech." Does this mean that individuals should be allowed to support terrorist causes on the Internet?

2. The Fourth Amendment protects against "unreasonable searches and seizures." Does this mean that law enforcement agents should be able to seize the computer of a terrorist subject without any actual proof of wrongdoing?

3. The Sixth Amendment guarantees a trial by jury to a person accused of a crime. Does this mean that the U.S. military can find a suspect guilty of terrorist actions without providing a jury trial?

Critics of counterterrorism measures, including intercepting suspected terrorists' e-mails and increasing security at airports, believe that the government has overstepped its bounds. Supporters of these and other tactics point out that such efforts succeeded in protecting Americans from another large-scale terrorist attack until the bombings at the Boston Marathon on April 15, 2013.

DOMESTIC TERRORISM For most of the past decade, America's counterterrorism strategies have focused on international terrorism, represented by foreign terrorist organizations that possess the resources to carry out large-scale, coordinated attacks. There is a sense that the ability of such organizations to produce another September 11-style attack has diminished in recent years,[45] for reasons we will explore in Chapter 16. At the same time, concerns have grown surrounding **domestic terrorism,** which involves acts of terror that are carried out within one's own country, against one's own people, and with little or no direct foreign involvement.

Domestic terrorists are often alienated individuals who become emboldened after meeting others who share their extreme views. In many instances, these views involve outrage over American military excursions against Muslims in the Middle East, as well as contempt for Western cultural norms at home. For example, Dzhokhar Tsarnaev told investigators that he and his brother Tamerlan planted pressure-cooker bombs near the finish of the 2013 Boston Marathon as a protest against U.S.-led wars in Iraq and Afghanistan.[46] However, many domestic terrorists have no connection whatsoever to Islamic fundamentalism. According to one study, 25 percent of all known terrorist incidents in this country since 2001 have involved anti-government extremists or white supremacists,[47] a situation we examine in the feature *Countering Domestic Terror—Diversity of Hate* on the following page.

The Emergence of Victims' Rights

Just before Cook County (Illinois) Circuit Judge Charles Burns sentenced William Balfour to three life terms in prison for committing triple murder on July 24, 2012, the judge gave Greg King an opportunity to address the court. "It was like a chunk of my heart was ripped out," said King, whose seven-year-old son Julian was one of Balfour's victims. "I felt hopeless. I was filled with rage for . . . the man who murdered my son." Legally, King's statement had no impact, as Balfour's sentenced was mandated by state law. Emotionally, however, King's words resonated. "I would like to thank Judge Burns for the opportunity to express my emotions," he said at the end of his statement. "I have had this bottled up inside me for a long time."[48]

ADVOCATING FOR CRIME VICTIMS "There has been a huge movement in criminal law toward giving victims a voice in what happens—which provides both some solace and

Piotr Krzeslak/
Shutterstock.com

DIVERSITY OF HATE

LEARNING
8
OBJECTIVE
Explain the defining aspects of a terrorist act, and identify one common misperception concerning terrorism.

For many Americans, the term "terrorist" brings to mind a specific sort of person: a young male of Middle Eastern ancestry with strong anti-American views rooted in Islamic fundamentalism. As with many stereotypes, this one is flawed. Several years ago, for example, Colleen LaRose, a blonde Pennsylvania woman who called herself "JihadJane" pleaded guilty to plotting the death of a Swedish cartoonist whose work had offended some Muslims.

In one sense, LaRose does conform to popular perception—she is a convert to Islam. As a matter of fact, however, no working legal definition of terrorism includes any reference to race, religion, or ethnicity. According to the Federal Bureau of Investigation (FBI), terrorism "is the unlawful use of force or violence against persons or property to intimidate or coerce a government, the civilian population, or any segment thereof, in furtherance of political or social objectives."

Particularly when it comes to domestic terrorism, the wide variety of terrorists and terrorist behavior is evident. In May 2012, the FBI foiled a plot to blow up a bridge near Cleveland, Ohio, by five middle-class anarchists wanting to express their hatred of "Corporate America." That August, a white supremacist named Wade Michael Page shot and killed six people inside a Sikh temple in Wisconsin, apparently driven by the mistaken belief that he was murdering Muslims. Then, in February 2013, Floyd Lee Corkins II pleaded guilty to an armed act of terrorism for shooting an unarmed security guard in the Washington, D.C., headquarters of a think tank that opposes same-sex marriage. According to the FBI, Corkins said, "I don't like your politics" as he opened fire.

FOR CRITICAL ANALYSIS Using the FBI's definition of terrorism, explain why all three incidents described above are considered terrorist acts. Then, refer back to James Holmes's alleged crimes described earlier in the chapter. Why is Holmes's wrongdoing *not* considered terrorist behavior?

closure," notes Chicago Kent College of Law professor Doug Godfrey.[49] For our purposes, a **victim** is any person against whom a crime has been committed or who is directly or indirectly harmed by a criminal act.

Widespread recognition of crime victims is a relatively recent phenomenon. It was not until the 1970s that victims' rights advocates began addressing what they perceived to be an imbalance in favor of criminal defendants in the criminal justice system. These activists pointed out that crime victims had virtually no rights under state or federal law. Therefore, they were forced to deal with the physical, emotional, and financial consequences of victimization on their own. As a presidential task force concluded in 1982, "The victims of crime have been transformed into a group oppressively burdened by a system designed to protect them. This oppression must be redressed."[50]

LEGISLATIVE EFFORTS Over the past twenty years, all fifty states have redressed the situation by providing legal rights to victims in their statutory codes or state constitutions. Furthermore, in 2004, the U.S. Congress passed the Crime Victims' Rights Act.[51] These legislative actions have given victims a much greater presence in criminal proceedings, including, as was the case with Greg King, the right to be heard in criminal court.[52] Various government agencies also provide a broad range of services to crime victims, from crisis intervention to emotional support to financial compensation.

Not all observers believe that the emergence of victims' rights has had a positive impact. In many instances, these critics point out, the various legislative efforts have

Victim Any person who suffers physical, emotional, or financial harm as the result of a criminal act.

failed to protect victims' rights as promised. Furthermore, some feel that that the presence of victims in the courtroom adds an element of bias to criminal proceedings.[53] Throughout this textbook, we will examine the growing role of the victim in the criminal justice system to determine whether such criticisms are justified.

Inmate Population Trends

The proposition seems logical: if more criminals spend more time behind bars, crime rates will decline. Rising incarceration rates cannot be conclusively linked to the recent crime decline, however. For the first time in four decades, incarceration rates are not rising. After increasing by 500 percent from 1980 to 2008, the inmate population in the United States has leveled off and, as you can see in Figure 1.6 below, has even decreased slightly over the past several years. Certainly, these decreases have been small, and the American corrections system remains immense. More than 2.2 million offenders are in prison or jail in this country, and another 4.8 million are under community supervision.[54] Still, the new trend reflects a series of crucial changes in the American criminal justice system.

THE ECONOMICS OF INCARCERATION For many years, the growing prison population was fed by a number of "get tough on crime" laws passed by politicians in response to the crime wave of the late 1980s and early 1990s. These sentencing laws—discussed in Chapter 11—made it more likely that a person arrested for a crime would wind up behind bars and that, once there, he or she would not be back in the community for a long while. The recent reversal of this pattern does not mean that the due process model, which favors rehabilitation over incarceration, is beginning to dominate the American criminal justice system. Rather, as Ram Cnaan, a professor at the University of Pennsylvania, notes, it reflects a painful truth about prison and jail inmates: "They simply cost too much."[55] Each year, federal and state governments spend more than $57 billion on corrections.

Not surprisingly, a recent survey of state corrections officials found "budget cuts" to be the most pressing issue in the field.[56] One method of bringing corrections spending under control is to grant early release to nonviolent offenders. Another is to divert offenders from jail and prison through special courts that promote rehabilitation rather than punishment for certain offenders. Also, corrections officials are implementing a

FIGURE 1.6 Prison and Jail Populations in the United States, 1985–2011

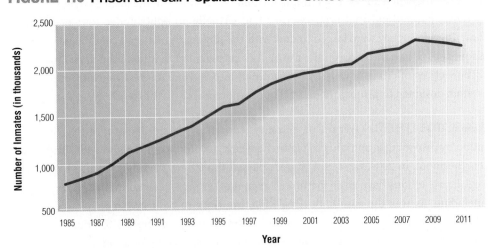

Sources: Bureau of Justice Statistics, *Correctional Populations in the United States, 1995* (Washington, D.C.: U.S. Department of Justice, June 1997), Table 1.1, page 12; and Bureau of Justice Statistics, *Correctional Populations in the United States, 2011* (Washington, D.C.: U.S. Department of Justice, November 2012), Table 2, page 3.

number of programs to reduce the *recidivism rate* of ex-convicts, which stands at about 45 percent.[57] **Recidivism** refers to the act of committing another crime (and possibly returning to incarceration) after a person has already been punished for previous criminal behavior. We will examine these policies and their ramifications for the nation's prisons and jails in Chapters 12, 13, and 14.

DECLINING USE OF THE DEATH PENALTY Another interesting corrections trend involves death row inmates, who are in prison awaiting execution after having been found guilty of committing a **capital crime.** At the beginning of 2013, the death row population in American prisons stood at 3,146, down from 3,653 in 2000.[58] During that same time period, the number of annual executions in this country dropped from 85 to 43.

Judges and juries, it seems, have become less willing to sentence the "worst of the worst" criminals to death. In 2011, the number of death sentences fell below one hundred for the first time since the early 1970s. In 2012, only seventy-seven convicts were sentenced to be executed, and Connecticut became the fifth state in five years to abolish the death penalty.[59] We will further explore *capital punishment,* one of the most controversial areas of the criminal justice system, in Chapter 11.

INCARCERATION AND RACE One troublesome aspect of capital punishment is that a black defendant is much more likely to be sentenced to death for killing a white victim than a white defendant is for killing a black victim.[60] Indeed, looking at the general statistics, a bleak picture of minority incarceration emerges. Even though African Americans make up only 13 percent of the general population in the United States, the number of black men in state and federal prisons (555,300) is significantly larger than the number of white men (465,100).[61] In federal prisons, one in every three inmates is Hispanic,[62] a ratio that has increased dramatically over the past decade as law enforcement and homeland security agencies have focused on immigration law violations, a subject we will consider in Chapter 16. The question of whether these figures reflect purposeful bias on the part of certain members of the criminal justice community will be addressed at various points in this textbook.

The Social Media Revolution

Not long after Trayvon Martin was shot and killed by George Zimmerman on February 26, 2012, in Sanford, Florida, angry protests erupted throughout the country. The demonstrations were spurred by the perception among many that Zimmerman, a Hispanic neighborhood watch volunteer, would escape punishment for the death of Martin, an unarmed African American teenager. (Zimmerman, eventually charged with second degree murder, claimed he was acting in self-defense, a subject we will cover in Chapter 4.)

Levels of national anger were certainly fueled by the wide availability and use of *social media,* the popular tem for Internet-based technologies that allow users to interact with each other and with the larger community of users. The most popular outlets are social networking sites such as Facebook and Google+, through which users can create and share personal profiles, and microblogs such as Twitter, where they can post short comments for public consumption. The protests following Martin's death were an outgrowth of countless Facebook postings on the subject, and opinions on Twitter captured the mood of the national debate.

TECHNOLOGICAL STRATEGIES Social media's impact on the criminal justice system goes well beyond increasing public interest in high-profile murder cases. Criminal justice

Recidivism The act of committing a new crime after a person has already been punished for a previous crime by being convicted and sent to jail or prison.

Capital Crime A criminal act that makes the offender eligible to receive the death penalty.

SOCIAL MEDIA & CJ

Many cities and counties in the United States offer **"crime stopper" Facebook pages** to keep the local community informed on relevant criminal justice topics. Go to Facebook and search for "Crimestoppers" plus the name of your city, county, or state.

LEARNING

9

OBJECTIVE

List the major issues in criminal justice today.

Local police patrol the grounds of the Ladue Middle School in Ladue, Missouri, on January 17, 2013. That day, school officials received a threatening post on Instagram that included a photo of Newton, Connecticut, shooter Adam Lanza. What particular challenges do threats delivered on social media pose to law enforcement agencies?
UPI/Bill Greenblatt /LANDOV

professionals are increasingly adapting the technology to their specific endeavors. Leading up to George Zimmerman's 2013 trial, his defense attorney Mark O'Meara set up a Twitter page and a Facebook account on behalf of his client. O'Meara consistently used these social media sites to deliver updates to the public about his strategy, avoiding journalists and other representatives of traditional news outlets. Prosecutors have also begun to mine social media, scouring sites for relevant information on defendants and witnesses.

As we will discuss in Chapter 5, law enforcement agents are benefiting from social media as an investigative tool. Departmental Facebook pages have proved to be a popular thoroughfare for anonymous crime tips, and police officers can develop important leads on suspects without leaving their desks. Several years ago, Houston police solved a bank robbery thanks to an incriminating trail of Facebook posts—including "Got $$$" and "Wipe my teeth with hundreds"—left by the perpetrators.[63] Law enforcement agencies are also using social media to provide information. The Hillsborough (New Jersey) Police Department, for example, has created a Twitter feed that allows residents to receive instant alerts about dangerous weather conditions, road closures, and "hot spots" of criminal activity.

TECHNOLOGICAL OFFENSES As a rule, technology that helps law enforcement provides new outlets for criminals as well. Social media are no exception. Groups of shoplifters employ Twitter and Facebook to organize "flash-robs," in which a certain establishment is targeted and raided within minutes. Street gangs go to the Internet to recruit new members and organize criminal enterprises, as do homegrown terrorists. After the FBI arrested four Southern California men in November 2012 for planning to kill U.S. soldiers overseas, the federal agents revealed that the aspiring terrorists had "liked" each others' anti-American sentiments on Facebook.[64]

Because of the anonymity they provide, social media are also natural outlets for stalking, bullying, and harassment, topics we address in Chapter 16's section on cyber crime. "The fascinating thing about technology is that once we open the door, it's going to move in ways that we can't always predict and are slow to control," says Scott Decker, a criminal justice professor at Arizona State University.[65]

SELF ASSESSMENT

Fill in the blanks and check your answers on page 31.

The _____ _____ model of criminal justice places great importance on high rates of apprehension and conviction of criminal suspects. In contrast, the _____ _____ model emphasizes the rights of the _____ over the powers of the government. Despite predictions to the contrary, crime rates in the United States have steadily _____ over the past several years. At the same time, _____ populations are also decreasing for the first time since the early 1970s.

CJ IN ACTION

GUN CONTROL VERSUS GUN RIGHTS

After Adam Lanza shot and killed twenty first-graders and six adults at an elementary school in Newtown, Connecticut, on December 14, 2012, the debate over gun violence revived along predictable lines. Advocates of gun control argued that fewer guns available to fewer people would reduce the likelihood of such massacres. Advocates of gun rights argued the opposite, claiming that more guns were needed to defend citizens against deranged criminals such as Lanza. Evidently, the vast majority of Americans who own guns are law-abiding citizens who keep their firearms at home for self-protection. This chapter's *CJ in Action* feature deals with the thorny issue of how best to protect the rights of this group while at the same time limiting the harm done by the illegal or improper use of firearms in the United States.

AS AMERICAN AS . . .

The Second Amendment to the U.S. Constitution states, "A well regulated Militia, being necessary to the security of a free State, the right of the people to keep and bear Arms, shall not be infringed." Recently, the United States Supreme Court has tried to clarify this somewhat unclear language. Over the course of two separate rulings, the Court has stated that the Second Amendment provides individuals with a constitutional right to bear arms, and that this right must be recognized at all levels of government—federal, state, and local.[66]

Although the Supreme Court emphasized in both cases that states could continue to prohibit certain individuals—such as criminals and the mentally ill—from legally purchasing firearms, critics of our nation's relatively lax gun laws were disappointed with the results. Pointing out that Adam Lanza—who possibly suffered from personality disorders—was able to steal his weapons from his mother (whom he also killed), they continue to argue for greater restrictions on gun ownership. Opponents of stricter gun control laws reject the notion that firearms themselves are to blame for violent crime. Said one gun seller, "That's like pointing a finger at Ford and blaming them for car deaths."[67]

THE CASE FOR MORE RESTRICTIVE GUN LAWS

- Each year, about 31,000 people in the United States die from gun violence, including about 20,000 suicides and 10,000 homicides.[68] About 70 percent of murders in the nation involve firearms.[69]

- The importance of guns for self-protection is overstated. Less than 1 percent of all gun deaths involve self-defense, with the rest being accidents, suicides, and homicides.[70]

- Considered too dangerous for public use, fully automatic weapons such as machine guns are already banned in the United States. For the same reason, the federal government should outlaw semiautomatic weapons, which can rapidly fire multiple rounds, and the high-capacity ammunition clips that allow them to do so. According to one editorial, the .223 Bushmaster semiautomatic rifle used by Adam Lanza is designed only for mass slaughter and "does not belong in private hands."[71]

THE CASE AGAINST MORE RESTRICTIVE GUN LAWS

- Gun control laws do not decrease crime, for the simple reason that someone who is going to commit a crime with a gun is probably going to obtain that firearm illegally. Consequently, stricter gun control would "prevent only law-abiding citizens from owning handguns."[72] Furthermore, as we saw earlier in the chapter, violent crime is at historically low levels in the United States, belying the argument that the country needs to change its gun laws.[73]

- Firearms offer protection from criminal attacks beyond that provided by public law enforcement.

- Nearly one in five American adults possesses a firearm, accounting for about 300 million total privately and legally guns owned in this country. Putting restrictions on that ownership would create a huge new criminal class in this country, not to mention the anger toward the government that such measures would provoke.

YOUR OPINION—WRITING ASSIGNMENT

When it comes to allowing concealed weapons on college campuses, the United States is a nation divided. Twenty-one states ban the practice outright. Twenty-four states permit the schools to decide for themselves. Five states—Colorado, Mississippi, Oregon, Utah, and Wisconsin—have passed bills expressly permitting the carrying of concealed weapons on campus grounds.[74] Should this practice be allowed? Does it make campuses safer or more dangerous? Would it be more desirable to have a single law that covered the entire nation? Before responding, you can review our discussions in this chapter concerning:

- Consensus and conflict models of crime (pages 5–6).

- Federalism and the structure of the criminal justice system (pages 11–12).

- Gun sales and gun control (page 22).

Your answer should include at least three full paragraphs.

CHAPTER SUMMARY

For more information on these concepts, look back to the Learning Objective icons throughout the chapter.

 Describe the two most common models of how society determines which acts are criminal. The consensus model argues that the majority of citizens will agree on which activities should be outlawed and punished as crimes. It rests on the assumption that a diverse group of people can have similar morals. In contrast, the conflict model argues that in a diverse society, the dominant groups exercise power by codifying their value systems into criminal laws.

 Define *crime.* Crime is any action punishable under criminal statutes and is considered an offense against society. Therefore, alleged criminals are prosecuted by the state rather than by victims. Crimes are punishable by sanctions that bring about a loss of personal freedom or, in some cases, fines.

 Outline the three levels of law enforcement. Because we have a federal system of government, law enforcement occurs at the (a) national, or federal, level and the (b) state level and within the states at (c) local levels. Because crime is mostly a local concern, most employees in the criminal justice system work for local governments. Agencies at the federal level include the FBI, the DEA, and the U.S. Secret Service, among others.

 List the essential elements of the corrections system. Criminal offenders are placed on probation, incarcerated in a jail or prison, transferred to community-based corrections facilities, or released on parole.

 Explain the difference between the formal and informal criminal justice processes. The formal criminal justice process involves the somewhat mechanical steps that are designed to guide criminal defendants from arrest to possible punishment. For every step in the formal process, though, someone has discretion, and such discretion leads to an informal process. Even when prosecutors believe that a suspect is guilty, they have the discretion not to prosecute, for example.

 Define ethics, and describe the role that it plays in discretionary decision making. Ethics consist of the moral principles that guide a person's perception of right and wrong. Most criminal justice professionals have a great deal of discretionary leeway in their day-to-day decision making, and their ethical beliefs can help ensure that they make such decisions in keeping with society's established values.

 Contrast the crime control and due process models. The crime control model assumes that the criminal justice system is designed to protect the public from criminals. Thus, its most important function is to punish and repress criminal conduct. The due process model presumes that the accused are innocent and provides them with the most complete safeguards, usually within the court system.

 Explain the defining aspects of a terrorist act, and identify one common misperception concerning terrorism. According to the federal government, the defining aspects of terrorism are (a) violence in the service of (b) intimidation or coercion, with the goal of furthering (c) political or social objectives. Terrorists need not represent a certain religion or support fundamentalist religious causes.

 List the major issues in criminal justice today. (a) Falling violent and property crime rates; (b) the impact of an extended recession on crime rates; (c) improved policing strategies; (d) street gangs; (e) gun sales and gun control; (f) use of illegal drugs; (g) homeland security; (h) the Patriot Act and civil liberties; (i) America's shrinking, though still massive, inmate population; (j) cost-cutting measures in the corrections system; (k) possible bias against minorities in the criminal justice system; and (l) social media in the criminal justice system.

QUESTIONS FOR CRITICAL ANALYSIS

1. How is it possible to have a consensus about what should or should not be illegal in a country with several hundred million adults from all races, religions, and walks of life?

2. What would be some of the drawbacks of having the victims of a crime, rather than the state (through its public officials), prosecute criminals?

3. Do you agree that public order crimes such as prostitution and illegal gambling are "victimless" crimes? Why or why not?

4. Refer back to the discussion of the police officer who refused to arrest the nonviolent homeless person in this chapter's discussion of ethics. Did the officer act properly in this situation, or should he have carried out the law regardless of his personal ethical beliefs? Explain your answer.

5. As noted earlier in the chapter, corrections officials are reducing prison budgets by releasing nonviolent offenders before their sentences are finished. What is your opinion of this strategy? What might be some of the consequences of large-scale early release programs for drug dealers and those convicted of property crimes?

KEY TERMS

assault   7
battery   7
biometrics   20
burglary   8
capital crime   27
civil liberties   23
conflict model   6
consensus model   5
crime   5
crime control model   19
criminal justice system   10
deviance   7
discretion   17

domestic terrorism   24
drug   22
due process model   19
ethics   18
federalism   11
formal criminal justice process   15
gun control   22
homeland security   23
informal criminal justice process   17
justice   10
larceny   8
morals   5
murder   7

organized crime   9
psychoactive drugs   22
public order crime   8
recidivism   27
robbery   7
sexual assault   7
street gang   21
system   15
terrorism   23
victim   25
white-collar crime   9

SELF ASSESSMENT ANSWER KEY

Page 10: i. society; **ii.** public officials/the government; **iii.** deviance; **iv.** violent; **v.** property; **vi.** white-collar

Page 11: i. justice; **ii.** protecting; **iii.** punishing; **iv.** victims

Page 15: i. federalism; **ii.** dual; **iii.** state; **iv.** formal

Page 19: i. discretion; **ii.** informal; **iii.** ethics

Page 28: i. crime control; **ii.** due process; **iii.** individual; **iv.** decreased; **v.** prison

NOTES

1. *City of Chicago v. Morales,* 527 U.S. 41 (1999). Many United States Supreme Court cases will be cited in this book, and it is important to understand these citations. *City of Chicago v. Morales* refers to the parties in the case that the Court is reviewing. "U.S." is the abbreviation for *United States Reports,* the official publication of United States Supreme Court decisions. "527" refers to the volume of the *United States Reports* in which the case appears, and "41" is the page number. The citation ends with the year the case was decided, in parentheses. Most, though not all, Supreme Court case citations in this book will follow this formula.

2. *Ibid.,* 49.

3. Herman Bianchi, *Justice as Sanctuary: Toward a New System of Crime Control* (Bloomington: Indiana University Press, 1994), 72.

4. *Health Poll: Physician Assisted Suicide* (Ann Arbor, MI: Truven Health Analytics, December 2012), at **healthcare.thomsonreuters.com/npr /assets/NPR_reports_PhysicianAssisted Suicide_1212.pdf**.

5. *2012 Report to the Nations: Occupational Fraud and Abuse* (Austin, TX: Association of Certified Fraud Examiners, 2012), 2.

6. Megan Kurlychek, "What Is My Left Hand Doing? The Need for Unifying Purpose and Policy in the Criminal Justice System," *Criminology & Public Policy* (November 2011), 909.

7. *Gonzales v. Oregon,* 546 U.S. 243 (2006).

8. President's Commission on Law Enforcement and Administration of Justice, *The Challenge of Crime in a Free Society* (Washington, D.C.: Government Printing Office, 1967), 7.

9. John Heinz and Peter Manikas, "Networks among Elites in a Local Criminal Justice System," *Law and Society Review* 26 (1992), 831–861.

10. James Q. Wilson, "What to Do about Crime: Blaming Crime on Root Causes," *Vital Speeches* (April 1, 1995), 373.

11 Herbert Packer, *The Limits of the Criminal Sanction* (Stanford, CA: Stanford University Press, 1968), 154–173.

12. *Ibid.*

13. Daniel Givelber, "Meaningless Acquittals, Meaningful Convictions: Do We Reliably Acquit the Innocent?" *Rutgers Law Review* 49 (Summer 1997), 1317.

14. Andrea Simmons, "Texting While Driving Laws Rarely Enforced," *Atlanta-Journal-Constitution* (October 30, 2012), A1.

15. "Texting While Driving Ban Is Hard to Enforce, Police Officers Say," *Associated Press* (November 12, 2012).

16. Simmons.

17. George P. Fletcher, "Some Unwise Reflections about Discretion," *Law & Contemporary Problems* (Autumn 1984), 279.

18. David Royce, "Texting and Driving Ban Bill Filed—Again—in Tallahassee," *Miami Herald* (November 22, 2012), at **www.miamiherald.com/2012/11/22/3109627/texting-and-driving-ban-bill-filed.html**.

19. Antonin Scalia, "The Rule of Law as a Law of Rules," *University of Chicago Law Review* 56 (1989), 1178–1180.

20. John Kleinig, *Ethics and Criminal Justice: An Introduction* (New York: Cambridge University Press, 2008), 33–35.

21. Elizabeth Banks, *Criminal Justice Ethics: Theory and Practice* (Los Angeles: Sage Publications, 2008), 13.

22. Packer, 154–173.

23. Givelber, 1317.

24. "Most Americans Believe Crime is U.S. is Worsening," *Gallup.com* (October 31, 2011), at **www.gallup.com/poll/150464/americans-believe-crime-worsening.aspx**.

25. Matt Pearce, "Crime Declines, Fear Remains," *Sun Sentinel* (Ft. Lauderdale, FL) (June 19, 2012), 9A.

26. Quoted in Richard Oppel, Jr., "Steady Decline in Major Crime Baffles Experts," *New York Times* (May 24, 2011), A1.

27. Charis E. Kubrin et al., "Proactive Policing and Robbery Rates across U.S. Cities," *Criminology* (February 2010), 57–91.

28. James Q. Wilson, "Hard Times, Fewer Crimes," *Wall Street Journal* (May 31, 2011), 9.

29. Thomas J. Baker, "Biometrics for Intelligence-Led Policing: The Coming Trends," *The Police Chief* (April 2011), 38–45.

30. Police Executive Research Forum, "Is the Economic Downturn Fundamentally Changing How We Police?" *Critical Issues in Policing*, vol. 16 (Washington, D.C.: Police Executive Research Forum, 2010).

31. Federal Bureau of Investigation, "2011 National Gang Threat Assessment Issued," *FBI National Press Office* (October 21, 2011).

32. Jeremy Gorner, "Gang Factions Fuel Violent Year," *Chicago Tribune* (October 3, 2012), 1.

33. Centers for Disease Control and Prevention, "Gang Homicides—Five Cities, 2003 to 2008," *Morbidity and Mortality Weekly Report* (January 27, 2012), at **www.cdc.gov/mmwr/preview/mmwrhtml/mm6103a2.htm**.

34. Alfred Blumstein, "The Crime Drop in America: An Exploration of Some Recent Crime Trends," *Journal of Scandinavian Studies in Criminology and Crime Prevention* (December 2006), 17–35.

35. James Lindgren, "Fall from Grace: Arming America and the Bellesiles Scandal," *Yale Law Journal* 111 (2002), 2203.

36. *District of Columbia v. Heller*, 554 U.S. 570 (2008).

37. Howard Snyder, *Arrests in the United States, 1980–2009* (Washington, D.C.: Bureau of Justice Statistics, September 2011), 12.

38. Office of National Drug Control Policy, *ADAM II: 2011 Annual Report* (Washington, D.C.: Executive Office of the President, May 2012), vii.

39. Substance Abuse and Mental Health Services Administration, *Results from the 2011 National Survey on Drug Use and Health: Summary of National Findings* (Washington, D.C.: National Institute on Drug Abuse, 2012), at 13, 31, 43.

40. Quoted in "9/11: Ten Years Later, How America Has Changed," *The Week* (September 16, 2011), 18.

41. "Terrorism in the United States," *Gallup.com*, at **www.gallup.com/poll/4909/terrorism-united-states.aspx#1**.

42. Scott Shane, "Shifting Mood May End Blank Check for U.S. Security Efforts," *New York Times* (October 25, 2012), A1.

43. Uniting and Strengthening America by Providing Appropriate Tools Required to Intercept and Obstruct Terrorism (USA PATRIOT) Act of 2001, Pub. L. No. 107-56, 115 Stat. 272 (2001).

44. Pew Research Center for the People and the Press, "Public Remains Divided over the Patriot Act" (February 15, 2011), at **pewresearch.org/pubs/1893/poll-patriot-actrenewal**.

45. Siohban Gorman, "Terror Risk Falls, U.S. Officials Say," *Wall Street Journal* (April 28-29, 2012), A4.

46. Greg Miller and Sari Horwitz, "Blasts Point to Gaps in U.S. Counterterror System," *Chicago Tribune* (May 6, 2013), 12.

47. "Terrorism: Are We Ignoring the Biggest Threat?" *The Week* (August 24-31, 2012), 19.

48. Gregory King, "Victim Impact Statement from Father of Murdered Julian King, 7," *Chicago Sun-Times* (July 25, 2012), at **www.suntimes.com/13971775-418/victim-impact-statement-from-father-of-murdered-julian-king-7.html**.

49. Quoted in Daniel B. Wood, "James Holmes Hearing: At Last, A Chance for Victims to Testify," *Christian Science Monitor* (January 7, 2013), at **www.csmonitor.com/USA/Justice/2013/0107/James-Holmes-hearing-At-last-a-chance-for-victims-to-testify**.

50. Lois Haight Herrington et al., *President's Task Force on Victims of Crime: Final Report* (1982), at **www.ojp.usdoj.gov/ovc/publications/presdntstskforcrprt/87299.pdf**.

51. 18 U.S.C. Section 3771 (2006).

52. Susan Herman, *Parallel Justice for Victims of Crime* (Washington, D.C.: The National Center for Victims of Crime), 46–47.

53. Danielle Levine, "Public Wrongs and Private Rights: Limiting the Victim's Role in a System of Public Prosecution," 104 *Northwestern University Law Review* (2010), 335-362.

54. Bureau of Justice Statistics, *Correctional Populations in the United States, 2011* (Washington, D.C.: U.S. Department of Justice, November 2012), Table 2, page 3.

55. Quoted in "U.S. Prison Population Rises despite a Drop in 20 States," *Associated Press* (December 9, 2009).

56. Association of State Correctional Administrators, "ASCA June 2011 Current Issues in Corrections," at **www.asca.net/system/assets/attachments/3505/ASCA%20June%202011%20Current%20Issues%20in%20Corrections%20Survey.pdf?1316119987**.

57. Pew Center on the States, *State of Recidivism: The Revolving Door of America's Prisons* (Washington, D.C.: The Pew Charitable Trusts, April 2011), 2.

58. Death Penalty Information Center, "Size of Death Row by Year—1968 to Present," at **www.deathpenaltyinfo.org/death-row-inmates-state-and-size-death-row-year#year**.

59. *The Death Penalty in 2012: Year End Report* (Washington, D.C.: Death Penalty Information Center, December 2012), 1.

60. Death Penalty Information Center, "National Statistics on Death Penalty and Race," at **www.deathpenaltyinfo.org/race-death-rowinmates-executed-1976**.

61. Bureau of Justice Statistics, *Prisoners in 2011* (Washington, D.C.: U.S. Department of Justice, December 2012), Appendix Table 7, page 7.

62. Federal Bureau of Prisons, "Inmate Breakdown," at **www.bop.gov/news/ quick.jsp#2**.

63. Zain Shauk, "Will They Post on Facebook Their Guilt in Heist?" *Houston Chronicle* (August 19, 2011), B2.

64. Joe Mozingo, "'They Saw This as Jihad,'" *Los Angeles Times* (November 21, 2012), 1.

65. Quoted in Patrik Jonsson, " 'Flash Robs': How Twitter Is Being Twisted for Criminal Gain," *Christian Science Monitor* (August 3, 2011), at **www.csmonitor.com/USA/2011/0803/Flash-robs-How-Twitter-is-being-twisted-for-criminal-gain-VIDEO**.

66. *District of Columbia v. Heller* (2008); and *McDonald v. Chicago*, 561 U.S. ____ (2010).

67. Quoted in Adam Magourney, "In an Ocean of Firearms, Tucson Is Far Away," *New York Times* (January 20, 2011), A15.

68. Donna L. Hoyert and Jiaquan Xu, "Deaths: Preliminary Data for 2011" in *National Vital Reports* (Washington, D.C.: National Center for Health Statistics, October 2012), 42, 60.

69. Federal Bureau of Investigation, *Crime in the United States, 2011* (Washington, D.C.: U.S. Department of Justice, 2012), at **www.fbi.gov /about-us/cjis/ucr/crime-in-the-u.s/2011/crime-in-the-u.s.-2011 /tables/expanded-homicide-data-table-7**.

70. Michael Grunwald, "The Tucson Tragedy: Fire Away," *Time* (January 24, 2011), 38.

71. "We Can Do Better," *Washington Post* (December 18, 2012), A20.

72. Quoted in David Nakamura and Robert Barnes, "Appeals Court Rules D.C. Handgun Ban Unconstitutional," *Washington Post* (March 10, 2007), A1.

73. Harry Wilson, quoted in David Espo and Nancy Benac, "Gun Control Agenda Seems Futile Despite Tragedies," *Arizona Daily Star* (July 22, 2012), A10.

74. Dan Frosch, "University Is Uneasy as Court Ruling Allows Guns on Campus," *New York Times* (September 23, 2012), 19.

CHAPTER ONE APPENDIX

How to Read Case Citations and Find Court Decisions

Many important court cases are discussed throughout this book. Every time a court case is mentioned, you will be able to check its citation using the endnotes on the final pages of the chapter. Court decisions are recorded and published on paper and on the Internet. When a court case is mentioned, the notation that is used to refer to, or to *cite*, the case denotes where the published decision can be found.

Decisions of state courts of appeals are usually published in two places, the state reports of that particular state and the more widely used *National Reporter System* published by West Group. Some states no longer publish their own reports. The *National Reporter System* divides the states into the following geographic areas: Atlantic (A. or A.2d), North Eastern (N.E. or N.E.2d), North Western (N.W. or N.W.2d), Pacific (P., P.2d, or P.3d), Southern (So., So.2d, or So.3d), and South Western (S.W., S.W.2d, or S.W.3d). The 2d and 3d in these abbreviations refer to the *Second Series* and *Third Series*, respectively.

Federal trial court decisions are published unofficially in West's *Federal Supplement* (F.Supp. or F.Supp.2d), and opinions from the circuit courts of appeals are reported unofficially in West's *Federal Reporter* (F., F.2d, or F.3d). Opinions from the United States Supreme Court are reported in the *United States Reports* (U.S.), the *Lawyers' Edition of the Supreme Court Reports* (L.Ed.), West's *Supreme Court Reporter* (S.Ct.), and other publications. The *United States Reports* is the official publication of United States Supreme Court decisions. It is published by the federal government. Many early decisions are missing from these volumes. The citations of the early volumes of the United States Reports include the names of the actual reporters, such as Dallas, Cranch, or Wheaton. *McCulloch v. Maryland,* for example, is cited as 17 U.S. (4 Wheat.) 316. Only after 1874 did the present citation system, in which cases are cited based solely on their volume and page numbers in the *United States Reports,* come into being. The *Lawyers' Edition of the Supreme Court Reports* is an unofficial and more complete edition of Supreme Court decisions. West's *Supreme Court Reporter* is an unofficial edition of decisions dating from October 1882. These volumes contain headnotes and numerous brief editorial statements of the law involved in a given case.

Citations to decisions of state courts of appeals give the name of the case; the volume, name, and page number of the state's official report (if the state publishes its own reports); and the volume, unit, and page number of the *National Reporter.* Federal court citations also give the name of the case and the volume, name, and page number of the reports. In addition to the citation, this textbook lists the year of the decision in parentheses. Consider, for example, the case *Miranda v. Arizona,* 384 U.S. 436 (1966). The Supreme Court's decision in this case may be found in volume 384 of the *United States Reports* on page 436. The case was decided in 1966.

2 Causes of Crime

To target your study and review, look for these numbered Learning Objective icons throughout the chapter.

Robert Nickelsberg/Getty Images

LONER GUNMAN

IN THEIR continuing efforts to make college campuses safer places, crime experts have tried to come up with a method to identify potential sources of violence. These efforts have led to the development of a "profile" of school shooters. According to this profile, such offenders are almost always male and often are older graduate students. They also tend to be socially awkward and isolated, and in many instances have experienced a "significant disruption" in their lives just prior to an eruption of violent behavior.

James Holmes did not open fire on a college campus. Instead, his attack occurred in a movie theater in Aurora, Colorado, on July 20, 2012. In a number of other ways, however, Holmes does fit the profile of a school shooter. He was a twenty-four-year-old graduate student, having spent a year at the University of Colorado's Center for Neuroscience. About a month before his shooting spree, in which he killed twelve moviegoers and wounded fifty-eight others, Holmes abruptly quit the program after performing poorly on an oral exam. Following the incident, one fellow graduate student remarked that Holmes was a silent loner who "always seemed to be off in his own world, which did not involve other people."

In retrospect, there were other hints that Holmes might pose a danger to the community. Six weeks before the shootings, a University of Colorado psychiatrist who had been treating Holmes expressed concerns about his mental well-being to the school's threat assessment team. Furthermore, Holmes himself planned the attack with "calculation and deliberation," stockpiling an arsenal of guns and ammunition over the course of several months. He also booby trapped his apartment with explosives on the day of the shootings and purchased his movie ticket twelve days in advance. For many, this showed that Holmes's behavior could only be explained one way. "He's not crazy," said Tom Teves, whose son had been killed during Holmes's rampage. "He's evil."

1. Does the criminal profile of the school shooter described above strike you as realistic? Why or why not? Of what use might such a profile be to university officials and campus law enforcement?

2. What was the "significant interruption" in James Holmes's life leading up to the attacks? Do you think this event lessened the University of Colorado's responsibility to protect the community from potential danger?

3. Why is it reassuring to label violent criminals "evil"? Why might this sort of labeling be irrelevant in the context of the criminal justice system?

AP Photo/*The Denver Post*, Hyoung Chang

With this memorial, community members show their support for the victims of James Holmes's July 2012 shooting spree in Aurora, Colorado.

Gray wall studio/Shutterstock.com

THE ROLE OF THEORY

The study of crime, or **criminology,** is rich with different reasons as to why people commit crimes. However, *criminologists,* or those who study the causes of crime, warn against using models or profiles to predict violent behavior. After all, not every socially awkward, male graduate student who suddenly drops out of school should be treated as a future mass murderer. To make such a judgment, researchers Michael L. Sulkowski and Philip J. Lazarus point out, would lead to a "gross overidentification of potential threats."[1]

Still, in the case of James Holmes, there did seem to be some connection between his characteristics and his violent outburst, particularly when one considers that he may have been suffering from mental illness. That is, there may have been a *correlation* between his behavior and his crimes, a concept that is crucial to criminology.

Correlation and Cause

Correlation between two variables means that they tend to vary together. **Causation,** in contrast, means that one variable is responsible for the change in the other. As we will see later in the chapter, there is a correlation between drug abuse and criminal behavior: statistically, many criminals are also drug abusers. But drug abuse does not cause crime: not everyone who abuses drugs is a criminal.

To give another example, the states with the strictest gun laws, such as Hawaii and Massachusetts, generally have low gun death rates. The states with the most lenient gun laws, such as Alabama and Alaska, generally have high gun death rates.[2] Nevertheless, few criminologists would assert that gun laws *cause* gun deaths, though many might argue that such laws are a contributing factor. Many more elements must be taken into account to get a full picture of the root causes of firearm homicides in any particular geographical area.

So, correlation does not equal cause. Such is the quandary for criminologists. We can say that there is a correlation between many factors and criminal behavior, but it is quite difficult to prove that the factors directly cause criminal behavior. Consequently, the question that is the underpinning of criminology—What causes crime?—has yet to be definitively answered.

Criminological Theories

Criminologists have, however, uncovered a wealth of information concerning a different, and more practically applicable, inquiry: Given a certain set of circumstances, why do individuals commit criminal acts? This information has allowed criminologists to develop a number of *theories* concerning the causes of crime.

LEARNING **1** OBJECTIVE Discuss the difference between a hypothesis and a theory in the context of criminology.

THE SCIENTIFIC METHOD Most of us tend to think of a *theory* as some sort of guess or a statement that is lacking in credibility. In the academic world, and therefore for our purposes, a **theory** is an explanation of a happening or circumstance that is based on observation, experimentation, and reasoning. Scientific and academic researchers observe facts and their consequences to develop *hypotheses* about what will occur when a similar fact pattern is present in the future. A **hypothesis** is a proposition that can be tested by researchers or observers to determine if it is valid. If enough authorities do find the hypothesis valid, it will be accepted as a theory. See Figure 2.1 on the next page for an example of this process, known as the *scientific method,* in action.

THEORY IN ACTION Criminological theories are primarily concerned with attempting to determine the reasons for criminal behavior. For example, two criminologists from

FIGURE 2.1 The Scientific Method

The scientific method is a process through which researchers test the accuracy of a hypothesis. This simple example should provide an idea of how the scientific method works.

 Observation: I left my home at 7:00 this morning, and I was on time for class.

 Hypothesis: If I leave home at 7:00 every morning, then I will never be late for class.
(Hypotheses are often presented in this "If . . . , then . . ." format.)

 Test: For three straight weeks, I left home at 7:00 every morning. Not one time was I late for class.

 Verification: Four of my neighbors have the same morning class. They agree that they are never late if they leave by 7:00 A.M.

 Theory: As long as I leave home at 7:00 A.M., I don't have to worry about being late for class.

 Prediction: Tomorrow morning I'll leave at 7:00, and I will be on time for my class.

Note that even a sound theory supported by the scientific method such as this one does not *prove* that the prediction will be correct. Other factors not accounted for in the test and verification stages, such as an unexpected traffic accident, may disprove the theory. Predictions based on complex theories such as the criminological ones we will be discussing in this chapter are often challenged in such a manner.

Arizona State University, Matthew Larson and Gary Sweeten, recently wanted to test their hypothesis that young people involved in romantic breakups are at high risk for destructive behavior. Relying on a survey of high school and college students who were asked about issues in their personal lives, Larson and Sweeten found some support for their hypothesis. According to the data, breakups do indeed correlate with higher rates of criminal offending and substance abuse among young men and higher rates of substance abuse among young women.[3]

SELF ASSESSMENT

Fill in the blanks and check your answers on page 62.

Researchers who study the causes of crime are called _____. These researchers test hypotheses, or educated guesses, using the _____ method. If a hypothesis proves valid, it can be used to support a _____, or explanation based on observation and reasoning, that explains a possible cause of crime.

THE BRAIN AND THE BODY

As you read this chapter, keep in mind that theories are not the same as facts, and most, if not all, of the criminological theories described in these pages have their detractors. Over the past century, however, a number of theories of crime have gained wide, if not total, acceptance. We now turn our attention to these theories, starting with those that focus on the psychological and physical aspects of criminal behavior.

Crime and Free Will: Choice Theories of Crime

For the purposes of the American criminal justice system, the answer to why a person commits a crime is rather straightforward: because that person chooses to do so. This application of **choice theory** to criminal law is not absolute. If a defendant can prove that she or he lacked the ability to make a rational choice, in certain circumstances the defendant will not be punished as harshly for a crime as would normally be the case. But such allowances are relatively recent. From the early days of this country, the general presumption in criminal law has been that behavior is a consequence of free will.

THEORIES OF CLASSICAL CRIMINOLOGY An emphasis on free will and human rationality in the realm of criminal behavior has its roots in **classical criminology.** Classical theorists believed that crime was an expression of a person's rational decision-making process: before committing a crime, a person would weigh the benefits of the crime against the costs of being apprehended. Therefore, if punishments were stringent enough to outweigh the benefits of crime, they would dissuade people from committing the crime in the first place.

The earliest popular expression of classical theory came in 1764 when the Italian Cesare Beccaria (1738–1794) published his *Essays on Crime and Punishments*. Beccaria

Choice Theory A school of criminology that holds that wrongdoers act as if they weigh the possible benefits of criminal or delinquent activity against the expected costs of being apprehended.

Classical Criminology A school of criminology based on the belief that individuals have free will to engage in any behavior, including criminal behavior.

criticized existing systems of criminal law as irrational and argued that criminal procedures should be more consistent with human behavior. He believed that, to be just, criminal law should reflect three truths:

1. All decisions, including the decision to commit a crime, are the result of rational choice.
2. Fear of punishment can have a deterrent effect on the choice to commit crime.
3. The more swift and certain punishment is, the more effective it will be in controlling crime.[4]

Beccaria believed that any punishment that purported to do anything other than deter crime was cruel and arbitrary.

POSITIVISM AND MODERN RATIONAL THEORY By the end of the 1800s, the positivist school of criminologists had superseded classical criminology. According to **positivism,** criminal behavior is determined by biological, psychological, and social forces and is beyond the control of the individual. The Italian physician Cesare Lombroso (1835–1909), an early adherent of positivism who is known as the "Father of Criminology," believed that criminals were throwbacks to the savagery of early humankind and could therefore be identified by certain physical characteristics such as sharp teeth and large jaws. He also theorized that criminality was similar to mental illness and could be genetically passed down from generation to generation in families that had cases of insanity, syphilis, epilepsy, and even deafness. Such individuals, according to Lombroso and his followers, had no free choice when it came to wrongdoing—their criminality had been predetermined at birth.[5]

LEARNING OBJECTIVE **2** Contrast positivism with classical criminology.

Positivist theory lost credibility as crime rates began to climb in the 1970s. If crime was caused by external factors, critics asked, why had the proactive social programs of the 1960s not brought about a decrease in criminal activity? An updated version of classical criminology, known as *rational choice theory,* found renewed acceptance. James Q. Wilson (1931–2012), one of the most prominent critics of the positivist school, summed up rational choice theory as follows:

> At any given moment, a person can choose between committing a crime and not committing it. The consequences of committing a crime consist of rewards (what psychologists call "reinforcers") and punishments; the consequences of not committing the crime also entail gains and losses. The larger the ratio of the net rewards of crime to the net rewards of [not committing a crime], the greater the tendency to commit a crime.[6]

In other words, a person, before committing a crime, acts as if she or he is weighing the benefits (which may be money, in the case of a robbery) against the costs (the possibility of being caught and going to prison or jail). If the perceived benefits are greater than the potential costs, the person is more likely to commit the crime.

"THRILL OFFENDERS" Expanding on rational choice theory, sociologist Jack Katz has stated that the "rewards" of crime may be sensual as well as financial. The inherent danger of criminal activity, according to Katz, increases the "rush" a criminal experiences on successfully committing a crime. Katz labels the rewards of this "rush" the *seduction of crime.*[7] For example, the National Coalition for the Homeless documented nearly 900 unprovoked attacks against the homeless in the decade that ended in 2010, including 244 fatalities.[8] In most of these incidents, the assailants were "thrill offenders" who kicked, punched, or set on fire homeless persons for the sport of it. Katz believes that such seemingly "senseless" crimes can be explained by rational choice theory only if the intrinsic (inner) reward of the crime itself is considered.

CHOICE THEORY AND PUBLIC POLICY The theory that wrongdoers choose to commit crimes is a cornerstone of the American criminal justice system. Because crime is seen as the end result of a series of rational choices, policymakers have reasoned that severe punishment can deter criminal activity by adding another variable to the decision-making process. Supporters of the death penalty—now used by thirty-two states and the federal government—emphasize its deterrent effects, and legislators have used harsh mandatory sentences to control illegal drug use and trafficking.

"Born Criminal": Biological and Psychological Theories of Crime

As we have seen, Cesare Lombroso believed in the "criminal born" man and woman and was confident that he could distinguish criminals by their apelike physical features. Such far-fetched notions have long been relegated to scientific oblivion. Nevertheless, many criminologists do believe that *trait theories* have validity. These theories suggest that certain *biological* or *psychological* traits in individuals could incline them toward criminal behavior given a certain set of circumstances. **Biology** is a very broad term that refers to the scientific study of living organisms, while **psychology** pertains more specifically to the study of the mind and its processes. "All behavior is biological," pointed out geneticist David C. Rowe. "All behavior is represented in the brain, in its biochemistry, electrical activity, structure, and growth and decline."[9]

GENETICS AND CRIME Criminologists who study biological theories of crime often focus on the effect that *genes* have on human behavior. Genes are coded sequences of DNA that control every aspect of our biology, from the color of our eyes and hair to the type of emotions we have. Every person's genetic makeup is determined by genes inherited from his or her parents. Consequently, when scientists study ancestral or evolutionary developments, they are engaging in **genetics,** a branch of biology that deals with traits that are passed from one generation to another through genes.

Twin and Adoption Studies Genetics is at the heart of criminology's "nurture versus nature" debate. In other words, are traits such as aggressiveness and antisocial behavior, both of which often lead to criminality, a result of a person's environment (nurture) or her or his genes (nature)? To tip the balance toward "nature," a criminologist must be able to prove that, all other things being equal, the offspring of aggressive or antisocial parents are at risk to exhibit those same traits.

Many criminologists have turned to *twin studies* to determine the relationship between genetics and criminal behavior. If the "nature" argument is correct, then twins should exhibit similar antisocial tendencies. The problem with twin studies is that most twins grow up in the same environment, so it is difficult, if not impossible, to determine whether their behavior is influenced by their genes or by their surroundings.[10] Because of the inconsistencies of twin studies, some criminologists have turned to *adoption studies,* which eliminate the problem of family members sharing the same environment. A number of well-received adoption studies have shown a correlation between rates of criminality among adopted children and antisocial or criminal behavior by their biological parents.[11]

The "Crime Gene" About twenty years ago, Dutch scientists claimed to have determined that males who possessed a mutant copy of the MAOA gene were abnormally aggressive.[12] Dubbed the "warrior gene," MAOA suddenly became the center of a great deal of criminological attention. Additional research, however, proved that this genetic mutation does not, by itself, lead to criminal behavior. Rather, a person with low levels of MAOA, which regulates emotion, exhibits an increased risk for violent behavior only when that person was also abused as a child.[13]

Further studies have shown a genetic basis for such traits as attention deficit hyperactivity disorder (ADHD) and low self-control, both of which have been linked to antisocial behavior and crime.[14] Keep in mind, however, that no single gene or trait has been proved to *cause* criminality. Even for those with mutated MAOA, the "warrior gene" mentioned above, the risk of criminal activity is minimal.[15] As a result, the best that genetics can do is raise the possibility for a predisposition toward aggression or violence in an individual based on her or his family background.

■ In 2012, Wayne Treacy, right, was convicted of attempted first degree murder for nearly beating fifteen-year-old Josie Lou Ratley to death. Treacy's attorneys claimed that, at the time of the crime, Treacy was suffering from a form of temporary insanity. If true, should this fact have had any bearing on Treacy's guilt or innocence?
Taimy Alvarez/*Sun Sentinel*/MCT via Getty Images)

HORMONES AND AGGRESSION Chemical messengers known as **hormones** have also been the subject of much criminological study. Criminal activity in males has been linked to elevated levels of hormones—specifically, **testosterone,** which controls secondary sex characteristics and has been associated with traits of aggression. Testing of inmate populations shows that those incarcerated for violent crimes exhibit higher testosterone levels than other prisoners.[16] Elevated testosterone levels have also been used to explain the age-crime relationship, as the average testosterone level of men under the age of twenty-eight is double that of men between thirty-one and sixty-six years old.[17]

A very specific form of female violent behavior is believed to stem from hormones. In 2012, Rasesh Patel of Lakeland, Florida, told investigators that his wife Neha was suffering from *postpartum psychosis* when she drowned their one-year-old son in a bathtub. This temporary illness, believed to be caused partly by the hormonal changes that women experience after childbirth, triggers abnormal behavior in a small percentage of new mothers.[18]

THE BRAIN AND CRIME The study of brain activity, or *neurophysiology,* has also found a place in criminology. Cells in the brain known as *neurons* communicate with each other by releasing chemicals called **neurotransmitters.** Criminologists have isolated three neurotransmitters that seem to be particularly related to aggressive behavior:

1. Serotonin, which regulates moods, appetite, and memory.
2. Norepinephrine, which regulates sleep-wake cycles and controls how we respond to anxiety, fear, and stress.
3. Dopamine, which regulates perceptions of pleasure and reward.[19]

Researchers have established that, under certain circumstances, low levels of serotonin and high levels of norepinephrine are correlated with aggressive behavior.[20] Dopamine plays a crucial role in drug addiction, as we shall see later in the chapter.

According to the federal government, more than half of all prison and jail inmates have mental health problems, with smaller percentages suffering from severe brain disorders.[21] After fatally shooting six people and wounding fourteen others on January 8, 2011, in Tucson, Arizona, Jared Loughner was diagnosed with *schizophrenia,* a chronic brain disorder that can lead to erratic, uncontrollable behavior. Persons suffering from

Hormone A chemical substance, produced in tissue and conveyed in the bloodstream, that controls certain cellular and body functions such as growth and reproduction.

Testosterone The hormone primarily responsible for the production of sperm and the development of male secondary sex characteristics such as the growth of facial and pubic hair and the change of voice pitch.

Neurotransmitter A chemical that transmits nerve impulses between nerve cells and from nerve cells to the brain.

this disease are at an unusually high risk for committing suicide or harming others. Psychiatrist E. Fuller Torrey estimates that schizophrenics commit about a thousand homicides each year.[22]

Further research shows that even moderate use of alcohol or drugs increases the chances that a schizophrenic will behave violently.[23] Still, it is important to note that about 2.4 million Americans—1 percent of the adult population—have been diagnosed with schizophrenia, and the vast majority of them will never become criminal offenders. That is, there may be a correlation between schizophrenia and violence, but the brain disorder cannot be said to cause violence.

CJ & TECHNOLOGY — MAPPING THE BRAIN

Johan Swanepoel/Shutterstock.com

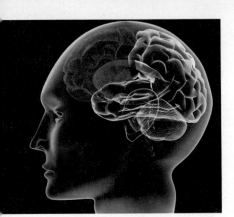

Yakobchuk Vasyl/Shutterstock.com

LEARNING OBJECTIVE 3 Explain how brain-scanning technology is able to help scientists determine if an individual is at risk for criminal offending.

Today, technology has made it relatively easy (if not always inexpensive) for scientists (and defense attorneys) to show brain irregularities such as schizophrenia. Computer axial tomography (CAT) scans combine X-ray technology with computer technology to provide an exact three-dimensional image of the brain. Magnetic resonance imaging (MRI) technology uses a very powerful magnet to create a magnetic field, which is then bombarded with radio waves. These waves can provide a very detailed image of brain tissue, allowing doctors to determine whether the tissue is damaged or diseased. Functional magnetic resonance imaging (MRI) permits researchers to study the function of the brain as well as its structure. This technique determines which areas of the brain are in use by measuring blood flow patterns. When a brain area is active, it consumes more oxygen and therefore requires increased amounts of blood.

Thinking about Brain-Scanning Devices
The technologies discussed above allow scientists to discover and measure brain malfunctions that are associated with various neurological disorders such as schizophrenia. Given the correlation between schizophrenia and violent behavior, how could brain scanners be used to prevent crime? What would be some of the problems with using these devices to identify potential criminals before they had in fact committed any crimes?

PSYCHOLOGY AND CRIME Like biological theories of crime, psychological theories of crime operate under the assumption that individuals have traits that make them more or less predisposed to criminal activity. To a certain extent, however, psychology rests more heavily on abstract ideas than does biology. Even Sigmund Freud (1856–1939), perhaps the most influential of all psychologists, considered the operations of the mind to be, like an iceberg, mostly hidden.

Freud's Psychoanalytic Theory For all his accomplishments, Freud rarely turned his attention directly toward the causes of crime. His **psychoanalytic theory,** however, has provided a useful approach for thinking about criminal behavior. According to Freud, most of our thoughts, wishes, and urges originate in the *unconscious* region of the mind, and we have no control—or even awareness of—these processes. Freud believed that, on an unconscious level, all humans have criminal tendencies and that each of us is continually struggling against these tendencies.

To explain this struggle, Freud devised three abstract systems that interact in the brain: the *id,* the *ego,* and the *superego.* The id is driven by a constant desire for pleasure and self-gratification through sexual and aggressive urges. The ego, in contrast, stands for reason and common sense, while the superego "learns" the expectations of family and society and acts as the conscience. When the three systems fall into disorder, the id can take control, causing the individual to act on his or her antisocial urges and, possibly, commit crimes.[24]

Social Psychology and "Evil" Behavior Another crucial branch of psychology—*social psychology*—focuses on human behavior in the context of how human beings relate to and influence one another. Social psychology rests on the assumption that the way we view ourselves is shaped to a large degree by how we think others view us. Generally, we act in the same manner as those we like or admire because we want them to like or admire us. Thus, to a certain extent, social psychology tries to explain the influence of crowds on individual behavior.

About three decades ago, psychologist Philip Zimbardo highlighted the power of group behavior in dramatic fashion. Zimbardo randomly selected some Stanford University undergraduate students to act as "guards" and other students to act as "inmates" in an artificial prison environment. Before long, the students began to act as if these designations were real, with the "guards" physically mistreating the "inmates," who rebelled with equal violence. Within six days, Zimbardo was forced to discontinue the experiment out of fear for its participants' safety.[25] One of the basic assumptions of social psychology is that people are able to justify improper or even criminal behavior by convincing themselves that it is actually acceptable behavior. This delusion, researchers have found, is much easier to accomplish with the support of others behaving in the same manner.[26]

■ On May 1, 2012, police struggle to control anticapitalism protesters in Seattle, Washington. How does social psychology help explain acts of violence or disorder by large groups of people?
Stuart Isett/Bloomberg via Getty Images

TRAIT THEORY AND PUBLIC POLICY Whereas choice theory justifies punishing wrongdoers, biological and psychological views of criminality suggest that antisocial behavior should be identified and treated before it manifests itself in first-time or further criminal activity. Though the focus on treatment diminished somewhat in the 1990s, rehabilitation practices in corrections have made somewhat of a comeback over the past few years. The primary motivation for this new outlook, as we will see in Chapters 11 through 14, is the pressing need to divert nonviolent offenders from the nation's overburdened prison and jail system.

SELF ASSESSMENT

Fill in the blanks and check your answers on page 62.

_____ theory holds that criminals make a deliberate decision to commit a crime after weighing the possible rewards or punishments involved. Twin studies are used to determine the role of _____ in possibly passing an inherited proclivity for criminal behavior from one generation to the next. Social _____ focuses on how individuals justify their own antisocial or criminal behavior by comparing it to similar behavior by others.

BAD NEIGHBORHOODS AND OTHER ECONOMIC DISADVANTAGES

While America's current economic problems have not, as yet, resulted in national crime increases, the same cannot be said for local trouble spots. The city of Chicago, for example, experienced 506 homicides in 2012, a 16 percent increase over the previous year. The vast majority of these murders (more than 80 percent) took place in neighborhoods on the south and west sides of the city.[27] These areas are marked by long-term financial hardship, unemployment, abandoned buildings, and high levels of gang activity. Indeed, for decades, criminologists focusing on **sociology** have argued that neighborhood conditions are perhaps the most important variable in predicting criminal behavior.

Sociological Theories of Crime

The problem with trait theory, many criminologists contend, is that it falters when confronted with certain crime patterns. Why is the crime rate in Detroit, Michigan, many times that of Sioux Falls, South Dakota? Do high levels of air pollution cause an increase in abnormal brain activity or higher levels of testosterone? As no evidence has been found that would suggest that such biological factors can be so easily influenced, several generations of criminologists have instead focused on social and physical environmental factors in their study of criminal behavior.

THE CHICAGO SCHOOL The importance of sociology in the study of criminal behavior was established by a group of scholars who were associated with the Sociology Department at the University of Chicago in the early 1900s. These sociologists, known collectively as the Chicago School, gathered empirical evidence from the slums of the city that showed a correlation between conditions of poverty, such as inadequate housing and poor sanitation, and high rates of crime. Chicago School members Ernest Burgess (1886–1966) and Robert Ezra Park (1864–1944) argued that neighborhood conditions, be they of wealth or poverty, had a much greater determinant effect on criminal behavior than ethnicity, race, or religion.[28] The methods and theories of the Chicago School, which stressed that humans are social creatures whose behavior reflects their environment, have had a profound effect on criminology over the past century.

The study of crime as correlated with social structure revolves around three specific theories: (1) social disorganization theory, (2) strain theory, and (3) cultural deviance theory.

SOCIAL DISORGANIZATION THEORY Studies have shown that neighborhoods with high concentrations of liquor stores and payday lenders tend to have abnormally high levels of crime.[29] Again, to revisit a theme of this chapter, these studies do not suggest that such businesses cause crime. Rather, the availability of "take-away" alcohol and cash reflect other problems in the neighborhoods that have a more direct relationship to criminality.

The theory that crime is largely a product of unfavorable conditions in certain communities was popularized by Clifford Shaw and Henry McKay, contemporaries of the Chicago School mentioned above.[30] Shaw and McKay's influence is shown in the widespread acceptance of **social disorganization theory** in contemporary criminology.

Disorganized Zones Studying juvenile delinquency in Chicago, Shaw and McKay discovered certain "zones" that exhibited high rates of crime. These zones were characterized by "disorganization," or a breakdown of the traditional institutions of social control such

Learning **4** Objective
List and describe the three theories of social structure that help explain crime.

as family, school systems, and local businesses. In contrast, in the city's "organized" communities, residents had developed certain agreements about fundamental values and norms. Shaw and McKay found that residents in high-crime neighborhoods had to a large degree abandoned these fundamental values and norms. Also, a lack of social controls had led to increased levels of antisocial, or criminal, behavior.[31] According to social disorganization theory, factors that lead to crime in these neighborhoods are perpetuated by continued elevated levels of high school dropouts, unemployment, deteriorating infrastructures, and single-parent families. (See Figure 2.2 below to better understand social disorganization theory.)

The Value of Role Models In the late 1990s, sociologist Elijah Anderson of the University of Pennsylvania took Shaw and McKay's theories one step further. According to Anderson, residents in high-crime, African American "disorganized" zones separate themselves into two types of families: "street" and "decent." "Street" families are characterized by a lack of consideration for others and poorly disciplined children. In contrast, "decent" families are community minded, instill values of hard work and education in their children, and generally have "hope for the future."[32]

Spending time in these disadvantaged areas, Anderson discovered that most "decent" families included an older man who held a steady job, performed his duties as husband and father, and was interested in the community's well-being. When external factors such as racial discrimination and lack of employment opportunities reduce the presence of these traditional role models, Anderson theorizes, "street" codes fill the void and youth violence escalates.[33] In a study released several years ago, criminologists Eric A. Stewart and Ronald L. Simons tested Anderson's theories. They studied the behavior of more than seven hundred African American adolescents and found that, indeed, in disorganized neighborhoods where a violent street culture dominates, juveniles are much more likely to commit acts of violent delinquency.[34]

FIGURE 2.2 **The Stages of Social Disorganization Theory**

Social disorganization theory holds that crime is related to the environmental pressures that exist in certain communities or neighborhoods. These areas are marked by the desire of many of their inhabitants to "get out" at the first possible opportunity. Consequently, residents tend to ignore the important institutions in the community, such as businesses and education, causing further erosion and an increase in the conditions that lead to crime.

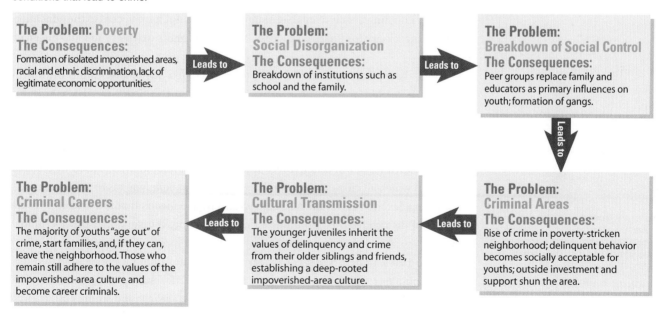

Source: Adapted from Larry J. Siegel, *Criminology*, 10th ed. (Belmont, CA: Thomson/Wadsworth, 2009), 180.

ROBERT AGNEW
CRIMINOLOGIST

Courtesy Robert Agnew

FAST FACTS

CRIMINOLOGIST, JOB DESCRIPTION:

- Work for local, state, and federal governments, on policy advisory boards, or for legislative committees. In some cases, he or she may work for privately funded think tanks or for a criminal justice or law enforcement agency. Most often, employment as a criminologist will be through a college or university, where both teaching and research will be conducted.

WHAT KIND OF TRAINING IS REQUIRED?

- An advanced degree is required. Specifically, some combination of degrees in criminology, criminal justice, sociology, or psychology is preferable. Graduate level education is a must for any research position.

ANNUAL SALARY RANGE?

- $40,000–$122,000

When I first became interested in criminology, my research led me to "strain" or *anomie* theories that said when a person stumbles in achieving financial success or middle-class status due to social factors beyond his or her control, he or she may turn to crime. While strain theory made a lot of sense to me, I felt that the theory was incomplete. When I looked around me, it was easy to spot other sources of frustration and anger, such as harassment by peers, conflict with parents or romantic partners, poor grades in school, or poor working conditions.

I outlined sources of strain as the loss of "positively valued stimuli" such as romantic relationships, or the threat of "negatively valued stimuli" such as an insult or physical assault. I also pointed out that monetary success was just one among many "positively valued goals" that might cause strain when not achieved. Furthermore, I noted that people who experience strain may turn to crime for several reasons—crime might allow them to achieve their monetary and status goals, protect positively valued stimuli, escape negative stimuli, achieve revenge against wrongs, or simply deal with the strain (such as taking drugs to forget problems). I drew on these observations and my own experiences to develop a new "general strain theory."

SOCIAL MEDIA CAREER TIP Find groups on Facebook and LinkedIn in which people are discussing the criminal justice career or careers that interest you. Participate in the discussions to get information and build contacts.

STRAIN THEORY Another self-perpetuating aspect of disorganized neighborhoods is that once residents gain the financial means to leave a high-crime community, they usually do so. This desire to escape the inner city is related to the second branch of social structure theory: **strain theory.** Most Americans have similar life goals, which include gaining a certain measure of wealth and financial freedom. The means of attaining these goals, however, are not universally available. Many citizens do not have access to the education or training necessary for financial success. This often results in frustration and anger, or *strain.*

Strain theory has its roots in the works of French sociologist Emile Durkheim (1858–1917) and his concept of **anomie** (derived from the Greek word for "without norms"). Durkheim believed that *anomie* resulted when social change threw behavioral norms into a flux, leading to a weakening of social controls and an increase in deviant behavior.[35] Another sociologist, American Robert K. Merton, expanded on Durkheim's ideas in his own theory of strain. Merton believed that *anomie* was caused by a social structure in which all citizens have similar goals without equal means to achieve them.[36] One way to alleviate this strain is to gain wealth by the means that are available to the residents of disorganized communities: drug trafficking, burglary, and other criminal activities.

In the 1990s, Robert Agnew of Emory University in Atlanta, Georgia, updated this line of criminology with his *general strain theory,* or GST.[37] Agnew reasoned that of all "strained" individuals, very few actually turn to crime to relieve the strain. GST tries to determine what factors, when combined with strain, actually lead to criminal activity. By

Strain Theory The assumption that crime is the result of frustration felt by individuals who cannot reach their financial and personal goals through legitimate means.

Anomie A condition in which the individual feels a disconnect from society due to the breakdown or absence of social norms.

the early 2000s, Agnew and other criminologists settled on the factor of negative emotionality, a term used to cover personality traits of those who are easily frustrated, quick to lose their tempers, and disposed to blame others for their own problems.[38] Thus, GST mixes strain theory with aspects of psychological theories of crime.

CULTURAL DEVIANCE THEORY Combining elements of social disorganization and strain theories, **cultural deviance theory** asserts that people adapt to the values of the subculture to which they belong. A **subculture** (a subdivision that exists within the dominant culture) has its own standards of behavior, or norms. By definition, a disorganized neighborhood is isolated from society at large, and the strain of this isolation encourages the formation of subcultures within the slum. According to cultural deviance theory, members of low-income subcultures are more likely to conform to value systems that celebrate behavior, such as violence, that directly confronts the value system of society at large and therefore draws criminal sanctions.

SOCIAL STRUCTURE THEORY AND PUBLIC POLICY If criminal behavior can be explained by the conditions in which certain groups of people live, then it stands to reason that changing those conditions can prevent crime. Indeed, government programs to decrease unemployment, reduce poverty, and improve educational facilities in low-income neighborhoods have been justified as part of large-scale attempts at crime prevention.

Social Conflict Theories

Strain theory and the concept of *anomie* seem to suggest that the unequal structure of our society is, in part, to blame for criminal behavior. This argument forms the bedrock of **social conflict theories** of crime. These theories, which entered mainstream criminology in the 1960s, hold capitalism responsible for high levels of violence and crime because of the disparity of income that it encourages.

MARXISM VERSUS CAPITALISM The genesis of social conflict theory can be found in the political philosophy of a German named Karl Marx (1818–1883). Marx believed that capitalist economic systems necessarily produce income inequality and lead to the exploitation of the working classes.[39] Consequently, social conflict theory is often associated with a critique of our capitalist economic system.

Capitalism is seen as leading to high levels of violence and crime because of the disparity of income that results. The poor commit property crimes for reasons of need and because, as members of a capitalist society, they desire the same financial rewards as everybody else. They commit violent crimes because of the frustration and rage they feel when these rewards seem unattainable. Laws, instead of reflecting the values of society as a whole, reflect only the values of the segment of society that has achieved power and is willing to use the criminal justice system as a tool to keep that power.[40] Thus, the harsh penalties for "lower-class" crimes such as burglary can be seen as a means of protecting the privileges of the "haves" from the aspirations of the "have-nots."

It is important to note that, according to social conflict theory, power is not synonymous with wealth. Women and members of minority groups can be wealthy and yet still be disassociated from the benefits of power in our society. Richard Quinney, one of the most influential social conflict theorists of the past forty years, encompasses issues of race, gender, power, and crime in a theory known as the **social reality of crime.**[41] For Quinney, along with many of his peers, criminal law does not reflect a universal moral code, but instead is a set of "rules" through which those who hold power can control and subdue

Cultural Deviance Theory
A branch of social structure theory based on the assumption that members of certain subcultures reject the values of the dominant culture by exhibiting deviant behavior patterns.

Subculture A group exhibiting certain values and behavior patterns that distinguish it from the dominant culture.

Social Conflict Theories
A school of criminology that views criminal behavior as the result of class conflict.

Social Reality of Crime The theory that criminal laws are designed by those in power to help them keep power at the expense of those who do not have power.

those who do not. Any conflict between the "haves" and the "have-nots," therefore, is bound to be decided in favor of the "haves," who make the law and control the criminal justice system. Following this reasoning, Quinney sees violations of the law not as inherently criminal acts, but rather as political ones—as revolutionary acts against the power of the state.

ISSUES OF RACE AND GENDER Those who perceive the criminal justice system as an instrument of social control point to a number of historical studies and statistics to support their argument. In the nineteenth century, nearly three-quarters of female inmates had been incarcerated for sexual misconduct. They were sent to institutions such as New York's Western House of Refuge at Albion to be taught the virtues of "true" womanhood.[42] Today, about 69 percent of the approximately 44,000 Americans arrested for prostitution each year are women.[43] After the Civil War (1861–1865), many African Americans were driven from the South by "Jim Crow laws" designed to keep them from attaining power in the postwar period. Today, the criminal justice system performs a similar function. One out of every ten black men in their thirties is in prison or jail on any given day,[44] and African American males are incarcerated at about 6.3 times the rate of white males.[45]

Apparent injustices only add to the sense of oppression in minority communities. In September 2012, for example, evidence came to light suggesting that Milwaukee (Wisconsin) police had misled the public concerning the death—ten months earlier—of robbery suspect Derek Williams. Authorities initially claimed that Williams, who was African American, had died from natural causes in the back of a police car. The new evidence showed, however, that Williams's death might have been caused by injuries he suffered in a fight with the arresting officers. "[The police] need to stop identifying black folks aged eighteen to thirty as criminals to be eliminated," said one angry resident after learning of the possible cover-up.[46]

RACIAL THREAT THEORY Over the past few decades, disproportionate arrest and incarceration rates of African Americans have sparked interest in *racial threat theory*. First developed to describe the reaction of many whites to the growing social, economic, and political power of African Americans in the 1960s,[47] today the theory focuses on the amount of control the criminal justice system exerts on the African American community. Racial threat theory is based on the hypothesis that as the size of a minority group increases, members of the majority group take steps to repress that group.[48]

This hypothesis has found support in a number of studies that link increases in the proportion of black residents to increases in the size and funding of local police departments in the same area.[49] Similarly, as we shall see in Chapter 7, those states with the largest numbers of undocumented Hispanic immigrants have been most active in passing anti-immigrant legislation over the past few years. Proponents of this legislation often cite the criminal threat posed by undocumented immigrants, though the data do not support such assertions.[50]

■ Two law enforcement officers investigate a murder in the Desire neighborhood of New Orleans. How would a criminologist who advocates social conflict theories of criminal behavior explain high crime rates in low-income neighborhoods such as Desire? Michael DeMocker/*The Times-Picayune/* Landov

SOCIAL CONFLICT THEORY AND PUBLIC POLICY Given its radical nature, social conflict theory has had a limited impact on public policy. Even in the aftermath of situations in which class conflict has had serious and obvious repercussions, such as the Los Angeles riots of 1991, few observers feel that enough has been accomplished to improve the conditions that led to the violence. Indeed, many believe that the best hope for a shift in the power structure is the employment of more women and minorities in the criminal justice system itself.

SELF ASSESSMENT

Fill in the blanks and check your answers on page 62.

Social _____ theory examines living conditions to explain the crime rate in any given neighborhood or community. _____ theory focuses on the frustrations experienced by individuals who may lack the means to achieve upward mobility. Social _____ theories are rooted in the concept of power, and contend that the American criminal justice system is designed to repress members of _____ groups through arrest and incarceration.

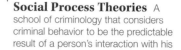
LIFE LESSONS AND CRIMINAL BEHAVIOR

Some criminologists find class theories of crime overly narrow. Surveys that ask people directly about their criminal behavior have shown that the criminal instinct is pervasive in middle- and upper-class communities, even if it is expressed differently. Anybody, these criminologists argue, has the potential to act out criminal behavior, regardless of class, race, or gender.

Family, Friends, and the Media: Social Processes of Crime

Philip Zimbardo conducted a well-known, if rather unscientific, experiment to show the broad potential for misbehavior. The psychologist placed an abandoned automobile with its hood up on the campus of Stanford University. The car remained in place, untouched, for a week. Then, Zimbardo smashed the car's window with a sledgehammer. Within minutes, passersby had joined in the destruction of the automobile, eventually stripping its valuable parts.[51] **Social process theories** function on the same basis as Zimbardo's "interdependence of decisions experiment": the potential for criminal behavior exists in everyone and will be realized depending on an individual's interaction with various institutions and processes of society. Social process theory has three main branches: (1) learning theory, (2) control theory, and (3) labeling theory.

LEARNING THEORY Popularized by Edwin Sutherland in the 1940s, **learning theory** contends that criminal activity is a learned behavior. In other words, a criminal is taught both the practical methods of crime (such as how to pick a lock) and the psychological aspects of crime (how to deal with the guilt of wrongdoing). Sutherland's *theory of differential association* held that individuals are exposed to the values of family and peers such as school friends or co-workers. If the dominant values one is exposed to favor criminal behavior, then that person is more likely to mimic such behavior.[52] Sutherland concentrated particularly on familial relations, believing that a child was more likely to commit crimes if she or he saw an older sibling or a parent doing so.

LEARNING **5** OBJECTIVE List and briefly explain the three branches of social process theory.

More recently, learning theory has been expanded to include the growing influence of the media. In the latest in a long series of studies, psychologists at the University of Michigan's Institute for Social Research released data in 2003 showing that exposure to high levels of televised violence increases aggressive behavior among young children.[53] Such findings have spurred a number of legislative attempts to curb violence on television.[54] James Holmes, whose crimes were described at the beginning of this chapter, was a devoted player of "hack and slash" video games such as Diablo III and World of Warcraft. Two years prior to Holmes's attacks, the issue of whether such games can be blamed for violent behavior was addressed by the United States Supreme Court, as shown in the feature *Landmark Cases—Brown v. EMA* below.

LANDMARK CASES:
Brown v. Entertainment Merchants Association (EMA)

Reacting to studies linking violent video games to violent behavior in children, in 2006 then California governor Arnold Schwarzenegger signed a bill prohibiting the sale or rental of games that portray "killing, maiming, dismembering or sexually assaulting an image of a human being" to people younger than eighteen years old. The law imposed a $1,000 fine on violators. Immediately, video game sellers sued the state, saying it had violated their constitutional right to freedom of speech. After two lower courts accepted this argument and invalidated California's law, the issue finally arrived before the United States Supreme Court.

Brown v. EMA
United States Supreme Court
559 S.Ct. 1448 (2010)

IN THE WORDS OF THE COURT . . .
JUSTICE SCALIA, MAJORITY OPINION

* * * *

Like the protected books, plays, and movies that preceded them, video games communicate ideas—and even social messages—through many familiar literary devices (such as characters, dialogue, plot, and music) and through features distinctive to the medium (such as the player's interaction with the virtual world). That suffices to confer First Amendment protection. Under our Constitution, "esthetic and moral judgments about art and literature * * * are for the individual to make, not for the Government to decree, even with the mandate or approval of a majority."

* * * *

No doubt a State possesses legitimate power to protect children from harm, but that does not include a free-floating power to restrict the ideas to which children may be exposed.

* * * *

California relies primarily on * * * research psychologists whose studies purport to show a connection between exposure to violent video games and harmful effects on children. These studies have been rejected by every court to consider them, and with good reason: They do not prove that violent video games *cause* minors to act aggressively (which would at least be a beginning). Instead, "[n]early all of the research is based on correlation, not evidence of causation * * * ." They show at best some correlation between exposure to violent entertainment and minuscule real-world effects, such as children's feeling more aggressive or making louder noises in the few minutes after playing a violent game than after playing a nonviolent game.

DECISION
In the absence of any provable negative effects on minors from violent video games, the Court ruled that California's ban was unconstitutional and therefore could not be enforced.

FOR CRITICAL ANALYSIS
If states have the "legitimate power" to "protect children from harm," why did the Court invalidate California's violent video game law? How did Justice Scalia use the concepts of *cause* and *correlation* to support the Court's decision? (You can review those terms from our discussion earlier in the chapter.)

Kentoh/Shutterstock.com

CONTROL THEORY Criminologist Travis Hirschi focuses on the reasons why individuals do not engage in criminal acts, rather than why they do. According to Hirschi, social bonds promote conformity to social norms. The stronger these social bonds—which include attachment to, commitment to, involvement with, and belief in societal values—the less likely that any individual will commit a crime.[55] **Control theory** holds that although we all have the potential to commit crimes, most of us are dissuaded from doing so because we care about the opinions of our family and peers. James Q. Wilson and George Kelling described control theory in terms of the "broken windows" effect. Neighborhoods in poor condition are filled with cues of lack of social control (for example, broken windows) that invite further vandalism and other deviant behavior.[56] If these cues are removed, according to Wilson and Kelling, so is the implied acceptance of crime within a community.

Janet Lauritsen, a criminologist at the University of Missouri–St. Louis, contends that familial control is more important than run-down surroundings in predicting whether crime will occur. Lauritsen found that adolescents residing in two-parent households were victims of crime at similar rates, regardless of the levels of disadvantage in the neighborhoods in which they lived. By contrast, adolescents from single-parent homes who lived in highly disorganized neighborhoods were victimized at much higher rates than their counterparts in more stable locales. In Lauritsen's opinion, the support of a two-parent household offers crucial protection for children, whatever the condition of their neighborhood.[57]

LABELING THEORY James Caston was a big fan of the James Gang, a group of outlaws famous for robbing trains, banks, and stagecoaches in southern and midwestern states near the end of the nineteenth century. Consequently, Caston decided to name his first two sons after gang members "Jesse" and "Frank." Today, both brothers are serving life sentences in a Louisiana state prison for murder. "We never had a chance," said Jesse James Caston when asked about the influence of his name.[58]

The Caston brothers serve as a rather literal example of a third social process theory. **Labeling theory** focuses on perceptions of criminal behavior rather than the behavior itself. Labeling theorists study how being labeled a criminal—a "whore" or a "junkie" or a "thief"—affects that person's future behavior. Sociologist Howard Becker contends that deviance is

> a consequence of the application by others of rules and sanctions to an offender. The deviant is one to whom that label has successfully been applied; deviant behavior is behavior that people so label.[59]

Such labeling, some criminologists believe, becomes a self-fulfilling prophecy. Someone labeled a "junkie" will begin to consider himself or herself a deviant and continue the criminal behavior for which he or she has been labeled. Following this line of reasoning, the criminal justice system is engaged in artificially creating a class of criminals by labeling victimless crimes such as drug use, prostitution, and gambling as "criminal."

SOCIAL PROCESS THEORY AND PUBLIC POLICY Because adult criminals are seen as too "hardened" to unlearn their criminal behavior, crime prevention policies associated with social process theory focus on juvenile offenders. Many youths, for example, are diverted from the formal juvenile justice process to keep them from being labeled "delinquent." Furthermore, many schools have implemented programs that attempt to steer children away from crime by encouraging them to "just say no" to drugs and stay in school. As we shall see in Chapter 6, implementation of Wilson and Kelling's "broken windows"

Control Theory A series of theories that assume that all individuals have the potential for criminal behavior, but are restrained by the damage that such actions would do to their relationships with family, friends, and members of the community.

Labeling Theory The hypothesis that society creates crime and criminals by labeling certain behavior and certain people as deviant.

principles has been credited with lowering the violent crime rate in New York and in a number of other major cities.

Looking Back to Childhood: Life Course Theories of Crime

If crime is indeed learned behavior, some criminologists are asking, shouldn't we be focusing on early childhood—the time when humans do the most learning? Many of the other theories we have studied in this chapter tend to attribute criminal behavior to factors—such as unemployment or poor educational performance—that take place long after an individual's personality has been established. Practitioners of **life course criminology** believe that lying, stealing, bullying, and other conduct problems that occur in childhood are the strongest predictors of future criminal behavior and have been seriously undervalued in the examination of why crime occurs.[60]

SELF-CONTROL THEORY Focusing on childhood behavior raises the question of whether conduct problems established at a young age can be changed over time. Michael Gottfredson and Travis Hirschi, whose 1990 publication *A General Theory of Crime* is one of the foundations of life course criminology, think not.[61] Gottfredson and Hirschi believe that criminal behavior is linked to "low self-control," a personality trait that is formed before a child reaches the age of ten and can usually be attributed to poor parenting.[62]

Someone with low self-control is generally impulsive, thrill seeking, and likely to solve problems with violence rather than his or her intellect. Gottfredson and Hirschi think that once low self-control has been established, it will persist. In other words, childhood behavioral problems are not "solved" by positive developments later in life, such as healthy personal relationships or a good job.[63] Thus, these two criminologists ascribe to what has been called the *continuity theory of crime*, which essentially says that once negative behavior patterns have been established, they cannot be changed.

THE POSSIBILITY OF CHANGE Not all of those who practice life course criminology follow the continuity theory. Terrie Moffitt, for example, notes that youthful offenders can be divided into two groups. The first group are life-course-persistent offenders: they are biting playmates at age five, skipping school at ten, stealing cars at sixteen, committing violent crimes at twenty, and perpetrating fraud and child abuse at thirty.[64] The second group are adolescent-limited offenders: as the name suggests, their "life of crime" is limited to the teenage years.[65] So, according to Moffitt, change is possible, if not for the life-course-persistent offenders (who are saddled with psychological problems that lead to continued social failure and misconduct), then for the adolescent-limited offenders.

Robert Sampson and John Laub take this line of thinking one step further. While acknowledging that "antisocial behavior is relatively stable" from childhood to old age, Sampson and Laub have gathered a great deal of data showing, in their opinion, that offenders may experience "turning points" when they are able to veer off the road from a life of crime.[66] A good deal of research in this area has concentrated on the positive impact of getting married, having children, and finding a job,[67] but other turning points are also being explored. John F. Frana of Indiana State University and Ryan D. Schroeder of the University of Louisville argue that military service can act as a "rehabilitative agent."[68] Several researchers have studied the role that religion and spirituality can play as "hooks for change."[69] Furthermore, particularly for drug abusers, the death of a loved one or friend from shared criminal behavior can provide a powerful incentive to discontinue that behavior.

Describe the importance of early childhood behavior for those who subscribe to self-control theory. **LEARNING 6 OBJECTIVE**

SOCIAL MEDIA & CJ

The American Society of Criminology operates **Critical Criminology** as a forum for ideas and information relating to the causes of crime. Look up "Critical Criminology" on Facebook to browse the wide variety of links and posts on its Facebook page.

Ankomando/Shutterstock.com

MASTERING CONCEPTS
THE CAUSES OF CRIME

CHOICE THEORIES

Key Concept: Crime is the result of rational choices made by those who decide to engage in criminal activity for the rewards—financial and otherwise—that it offers.

Example: A Texas judge sentenced Jimmy Billingsley to fifteen years in prison for knowingly infecting a woman with the HIV virus. The victim testified that Billingley "insisted on having unprotected sex."

BIOLOGICAL AND PSYCHOLOGICAL TRAIT THEORIES

Key Concept: Criminal behavior is explained by the biological and psychological attributes of an individual.

Example: A Polk County, Tennessee, jury acquitted Bradley Waldroup of first degree murder after hearing testimony that he suffered from a genetic mutation that predisposed him to violence. This finding allowed Waldroup to avoid a life sentence in prison.

SOCIOLOGICAL THEORIES

Key Concept: Crime is not something one is "born to do." Rather, crime is the result of the social conditions such as poverty, poor schools, unemployment, and discrimination with which a person lives.

Example: Researchers at Boston's Northeastern University estimate that, on any given day, about one in ten young male high school dropouts is in prison or jail, whereas only one in thirty-five young male high school graduates are incarcerated.

SOCIAL CONFLICT THEORIES

Key Concept: Through criminal laws, the dominant members of society control the minority members, using institutions such as the police, courts, and prisons as tools of oppression.

Example: In 2011, of the 684,330 people stopped and searched by New York City police officers, 87 percent were African American or Hispanic. As those groups comprise only about 25 percent and 28 percent of the city's population, respectively, the police force opened itself to charges of racial profiling, covered in Chapter 7.

SOCIAL PROCESS THEORIES

Key Concept: Family, friends, and peers have the greatest impact on an individual's behavior, and it is the interactions with these groups that ultimately determine whether a person will become involved in criminal behavior.

Example: According to the U.S. Department of Justice, nearly 50 percent of inmates in state prisons have relatives who have also been incarcerated.

LIFE COURSE THEORIES

Key Concept: Criminal and antisocial behavior is evident at each stage of a person's life. By focusing on such behavior in early childhood, criminologists may be able to better understand and predict offending patterns that emerge as a person grows older.

Example: After interviewing 261 inmates serving time for violent crimes in state prison, criminologists found that more than half had behaved with cruelty toward animals when they were children.

LIFE COURSE THEORIES AND PUBLIC POLICY Life course theories intersect with public policy mainly with regard to two crucial institutions that influence early childhood: parenting and school. In many jurisdictions, parenting-skills classes are available (or mandatory) for mothers and fathers of children with behavioral problems. Often, such problems are first identified by preschool teachers, and public school systems generally offer in-house intervention and counseling services. (See *Mastering Concepts* above for a review of theories discussed so far in this chapter.)

SELF ASSESSMENT

Fill in the blanks and check your answers on page 62.

Among social process theories, _____ theory could be used to explain why the younger sibling of a gang member would be more likely to join a gang. Similarly, _____ theory could be used to explain why someone who lives in a heavily vandalized neighborhood would be more likely to commit acts of vandalism. Supporters of _____ _____ theories of crime believe that stealing, bullying, and other conduct problems that occur during _____ can, in some instances, predict adult offending.

THE LINK BETWEEN DRUGS AND CRIME

Earlier in this chapter, we discussed the difference between correlations and causes. As you may recall, criminologists are generally reluctant to declare that any one factor causes a certain result. Richard B. Felson of Penn State University and Keri B. Burchfield of Northern Illinois University, however, believe that alcohol consumption has a causal effect on crime victimization under certain circumstances.[70] Felson and Burchfield found that "frequent and heavy" drinkers are at a great risk of assault when they are drinking, but do not show abnormal rates of victimization when sober. They hypothesize that consuming alcohol leads to aggressive and offensive behavior, particularly in men, which in turn triggers violent reactions from others.

In Chapter 1, we learned that about 22.5 million Americans regularly use illegal drugs such as marijuana and cocaine, with another 200 million using legal drugs such as alcohol and nicotine. Here, we will discuss two questions concerning these habits. First, why do people use drugs? Second, what are the consequences for the criminal justice system?

The Criminology of Drug Use

At first glance, the reason people use drugs, including legal drugs such as alcohol, is obvious: such drugs give the user pleasure and provide a temporary escape for those who may feel tension or anxiety. Ultimately, though, such explanations are unsatisfactory because they fail to explain why some people use drugs while others do not.

THEORIES OF DRUG USE Several of the theories we discussed earlier in the chapter have been used by experts to explain drug use. *Social disorganization theory* holds that rapid social change can cause people to become disaffiliated from mainstream society, causing them to turn to drugs. *Control theory* suggests that a lack of social control, as provided by entities such as the family or school, can lead to antisocial behavior.

DRUGS AND THE "LEARNING PROCESS" Focusing on the question of why first-time drug users become habitual users, sociologist Howard Becker sees three factors in the "learning process." He believes first-time users:

1. Learn the techniques of drug use.
2. Learn to perceive the pleasurable effects of drug use.
3. Learn to enjoy the social experience of drug use.[71]

Becker's assumptions are evident in the widespread belief that positive images of drug use in popular culture "teach" adolescents that such behavior is not only acceptable but desirable. The entertainment industry, in particular, has been criticized for glamorizing various forms of drug use.

■ Do you think that drug abusers, such as this man injecting heroin into his arm, should be treated as criminals to be punished or as ill people in need of treatment? Explain your answer.
Bob Combs/Photo Researchers via Getty Images

Drug Addiction and Dependency

Another theory rests on the assumption that some people possess overly sensitive drug receptors in their brains and are therefore biologically disposed toward drug use.[72] Though there is little conclusive evidence that biological factors can explain initial drug experimentation, scientific research has provided a great deal of insight into patterns of long-term drug use.

DRUG USE AND DRUG ABUSE In particular, science has aided in understanding the difference between drug *use* and drug *abuse*. **Drug abuse** can be defined as the use of any drug—licit or illicit—that causes either psychological or bodily harm to the abuser or to third parties. Just as most people who drink beer or wine avoid abusing alcohol, most users of illegal substances are not abusers. For most drugs except nicotine, only between 7 and 20 percent of all users suffer from compulsive abuse.[73]

Despite their relatively small numbers, drug abusers have a disparate impact on the drug market. The 20 percent of Americans, for example, who drink the most consume more than 80 percent of all alcoholic beverages sold in the United States. The data are similar for illicit substance abusers, leading to the conclusion that, to a large extent, abusers and addicts sustain the market for illegal drugs. As Figure 2.3 below shows, alcohol is, by a large margin, the most frequently abused drug in the United States.

ADDICTION BASICS The most extreme abusers are addicted to, or physically dependent on a drug. To understand the basics of addiction and physical dependence, you must understand the role of *dopamine* in the brain. Dopamine, mentioned earlier in the chapter, is the neurotransmitter responsible for delivering pleasure signals to brain nerve endings in response to behavior—such as eating good food or engaging in sex—that makes us feel good. The bloodstream delivers drugs to the area of the brain that produces dopamine, thereby triggering the production of a large amount of the substance in the brain. Over time, the continued use of drugs physically changes the nerve endings, called *receptors*. To continue operating in the presence of large amounts of dopamine, the receptors become less sensitive, meaning that greater amounts of any particular drug are required to create the amount of dopamine needed for the same

> **Drug Abuse** The use of drugs that results in physical or psychological problems for the user, as well as disruption of personal relationships and employment.

FIGURE 2.3 Drug Abuse and Dependency in the United States

In 2011, about 20.6 million Americans were classified as being addicted to or abusing drugs. As this figure shows, the majority of this substance abuse involves alcohol, with marijuana being the most abused illicit drug.

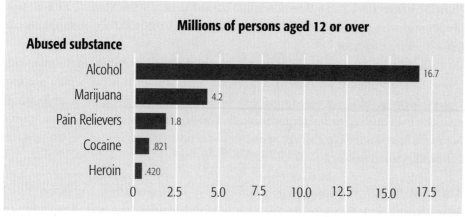

Source: Substance Abuse and Mental Health Services Administration, *Results from the 2011 National Survey on Drug Use and Health: Summary of National Findings* (Washington, D.C.: National Institute on Drug Abuse, 2012), 74–75.

Prescription Drugs Medical
drugs that require a physician's
permission for purchase.

Methamphetamine (meth)
An easily produced, relatively
inexpensive stimulant that creates a
strong feeling of euphoria in the user
and is highly addictive.

levels of pleasure. When the supply of the drug is cut off, the brain strongly feels the lack of dopamine stimulation, and the abuser will suffer symptoms of withdrawal until the receptors readjust.[74]

Addiction and physical dependence are interrelated, though not exactly the same. Those who are physically dependent on a drug suffer withdrawal symptoms when they stop using it, but after a certain time period, they are generally able to emerge without further craving. Addicts, in contrast, continue to feel a need for the drug long after withdrawal symptoms have passed. For many years, researchers have been striving to determine if some people are more likely than others to become addicts for biological reasons. In 2008, a group of researchers from Peking University in China made significant headway toward doing so by showing that many addicts share a particular set of *enzymes,* or proteins that trigger chemical reactions in the body.[75]

The Drug-Crime Relationship

Of course, because many drugs are illegal, anybody who sells, uses, or in any way promotes the use of these drugs is, under most circumstances, breaking the law. The drug-crime relationship goes beyond the language of criminal drug statutes, however. About 37 percent of state prisoners and 33 percent of jail inmates incarcerated for a violent crime were under the influence of alcohol at the time of their arrest.[76] Similarly, according to one recent study, about two-thirds of all arrestees in ten major American cities tested positive for illicit drugs when apprehended.[77] As we will see throughout this textbook, the prosecution of illegal drug users and suppliers has been one of the primary factors in the enormous growth of the American correctional industry.

PRESCRIPTION DRUG ABUSE According to both law enforcement officials and public-policy experts, the last few years have seen a dramatic shift in America's drug problem. Although marijuana continues to be the most widely abused drug in the United States, **prescription drugs** are next on the list.[78] These powerful drugs—which include types of pain relievers, tranquilizers, stimulants, and sedatives—are not available for sale "over the counter." Rather, they can be obtained only with the permission of a licensed health-care professional.

According to the National Survey on Drug Use and Health, 2.3 million people over the age of twelve used prescription drugs for nonmedical purposes for the first time in 2011.[79] In total, the number of people addicted to painkillers increased from 936,000 in 2002 to 1.8 million in 2011.[80] From 2007 to 2010, more than 1,800 pharmacy robberies occurred in the United States, with the offenders targeting prescription drugs such as the painkillers oxycodone and hydrocodone and the antianxiety agent Xanax.[81] Prescription drugs are also implicated in more than half of the nearly 40,000 fatal overdoses that occur in the country each year.[82]

Finally, legal, over-the-counter substances are the main ingredient in the manufacture of **methamphetamine (meth),** a highly addictive stimulant to the central nervous system. Meth is relatively easy to make in home laboratories using the ingredients of common cold medicines and farm chemicals. Consequently, the drug provides a "cheap high" and has become the scourge of many poor rural areas, particularly in the western half of the United States.

SYNTHETIC DRUGS Numerous drug manufacturers—at least one thousand in the United States alone—have found an innovative way to circumvent drug laws. They produce *synthetic drugs* that simulate the effects of illicit substances but are created using legal chemical compounds. Synthetic cannabinoids, for example, mimic the active ingredient in marijuana, and methadrone crystals, packaged as "bath salts," can be snorted to produce the same "rush" as cocaine or meth. Ingesting bath salts causes elevated blood pressure and heart rates and can lead to extreme, violent behavior. For example, Ryan Foley of Scranton, Pennsylvania, recently admitted that he was under the influence of bath salts when he broke into a monastery and stabbed a priest.

Even though every state has passed some form of legislation banning these substances, it is fairly easy for manufacturers to create new variations. Spurred by Internet orders, the use of synthetic drugs has spread rapidly. By one estimate, synthetic cannabinoid sales are now approaching $5 billion annually.[83] In 2010, the nation's poison control centers handled 303 calls linked to bath salt use. In the first half of 2011, that number spiked to 3,470.[84]

MODELS OF ADDICTION Is criminal conviction and incarceration the best way for society to deal with addicts? Those who follow the **medical model of addiction** believe that addicts are not criminals, but mentally or physically ill individuals who are forced into acts of petty crime to "feed their habit." Those who believe in the *enslavement theory of addiction* advocate treating addiction as a disease and hold that society should not punish addicts but rather attempt to rehabilitate them, as would be done for any other unhealthy person.[85]

Although a number of organizations, including the American Medical Association, recognize alcoholism and other forms of drug dependence as diseases, the criminal justice system tends to favor the **criminal model of addiction** over the medical model. The criminal model holds that illegal drug abusers and addicts endanger society with their behavior and should be punished the same as persons who commit non-drug-related crimes.[86]

LEGALIZATION BASICS A third model has recently begun to challenge the two well-established approaches to illegal drug use described above. This model is based on the concept of *legalization*. By "legalizing" drugs, we mean treating them in the same manner as alcohol or tobacco. That is, heavily regulated but legally available to persons over the age of twenty-one.

Today, thanks to the crime that goes along with the illegal drug trade in Latin America and the Caribbean, eight of the world's ten most violent-crime-ridden countries are in that part of the world.[87] This led the president of Mexico, whose struggles with drug-related violence are detailed in the feature *Comparative Criminal Justice—A Real War on Drugs* on the next page, to call for a "national debate on legalization."[88] In 2012, the South American country of Uruguay took steps to legalize marijuana. That same year, so did Colorado and Washington, creating a controversy in the United States that we will address in the *Criminal Justice in Action* feature at the end of the chapter.

SELF ASSESSMENT

Fill in the blanks and check your answers on page 62.

Drug _____ is defined as the use of any drug that causes harm to the user or a third party. People who are _____, meaning that they desire the drug long after use has stopped, need greater amounts of the drug to stimulate a neurotransmitter in the brain called _____. Harms associated with the abuse of _____ drugs, which require a physician's permission, and _____ drugs, which mimic the effects of substances such as marijuana and cocaine, have increased in recent years.

> **Medical Model of Addiction**
> An approach to drug addiction that treats drug abuse as a mental illness and focuses on treating and rehabilitating offenders rather than punishing them.
>
> **Criminal Model of Addiction**
> An approach to drug abuse that holds that drug offenders harm society by their actions to the same extent as other criminals and should face the same punitive sanctions.

LEARNING

7
OBJECTIVE

Contrast the medical model of addiction with the criminal model of addiction.

A REAL WAR ON DRUGS

For most of the past decade, Mexico and its citizens have suffered through a bloody and seemingly endless "war on drugs." Each year, illegal drugs worth from $25 to $40 billion are smuggled over the border from Mexico into the United

■ A soldier stands guard over fifty tons of burning marijuana seized from drug dealers by the Mexican army.
Keith Dannermiller/Corbis

States, and various cartels are willing to fight—and kill—for their cut. From 2007 to 2012, nearly 58,000 Mexicans were murdered in drug-related slayings. "I really characterize this as a civil war," says Howard Campbell of the University of Texas at El Paso. "We're seeing all the casualties of a war, people murdered, people wounded, people fleeing their homes, disintegration and chaos."

Mexico's leaders have not stood idly by in the face of this carnage. Mistrustful of corrupt local police, the Mexican government has sent tens of thousands of federal troops to the areas where the drug trade is most active, primarily along the U.S.–Mexican border. Although numerous drug kingpins have been captured, these efforts have apparently only exacerbated the problem.

FOR CRITICAL ANALYSIS

According to Tony Garza, who spent six years (2002–2008) as the U.S. ambassador to Mexico, the country would not "be experiencing this level of violence were the United States not the largest consumer of illicit drugs and the main supplier of weapons to the cartels." The U.S. government has provided Mexico with $1.9 billion in aid to use in its war on drugs, and numerous American federal, state, and local law enforcement agencies are working with their Mexican counterparts to stem the violence. Is the United States morally obligated to provide this financial and tactical aid? What other steps could our government take to weaken the link between illegal drugs and crime in Mexico?

CRIMINOLOGY FROM THEORY TO PRACTICE

You have almost completed the only chapter in this textbook that deals primarily with theory. The chapters that follow will concentrate on the more practical and legal aspects of the criminal justice system: how law enforcement agencies fight crime, how our court systems determine guilt or innocence, and how we punish those who are found guilty. Criminology can, however, play a crucial role in the criminal justice system. "A lot of my colleagues just want to write scholarly articles for scholarly journals," notes Professor James Alan Fox of Northeastern University in Boston. "But I think if you're in a field with specialized knowledge that can be useful to the community, you should engage the public and policymakers."[89]

Criminology and the Chronic Offender

Perhaps the most useful criminological contribution to crime fighting in the past half century was *Delinquency in a Birth Cohort*, published by the pioneering trio of Marvin Wolfgang, Robert Figlio, and Thorsten Sellin in 1972. This research established the idea of the **chronic offender,** or career criminal, by showing that a small group of juvenile offenders—6 percent—was responsible for a disproportionate amount of the violent crime attributed to a group of nearly 10,000 young males: 71 percent of the murders, 82 percent of the robberies, 69 percent of the aggravated assaults, and 73 percent of the rapes.[90]

Further research has supported the idea of a "chronic 6 percent,"[91] and law enforcement agencies and district attorneys' offices have devised specific strategies to apprehend and prosecute repeat offenders, with dozens of local police agencies forming career criminal units to deal with the problem. Legislators have also reacted to this research: habitual offender laws that provide harsher sentences for repeat offenders have become quite popular. We will discuss these statutes, including the controversial "three-strikes-and-you're-out" laws, in Chapter 11.

Chronic Offender A delinquent or criminal who commits multiple offenses and is considered part of a small group of wrongdoers who are responsible for a majority of the antisocial activity in any given community.

LEARNING **8** OBJECTIVE

Explain the theory of the chronic offender and its importance for the criminal justice system.

Criminology and the Criminal Justice System

There is a sense, however, that criminology has not done enough to make our country a safer place. Eminent criminologist James Q. Wilson, for one, criticized his peers for trying to understand crime rather than reduce it.[92] Many criminal justice practitioners also argue that too much of the research done by criminologists is inaccessible to them. As Sarah J. Hart, director of the National Institute of Justice, has noted, an overwhelmed police chief simply does not have the time or patience to wade through the many scientific journals in which crime research appears.[93]

This criticism may be too harsh. As we discuss further in Chapter 6, Wilson himself (in collaboration with George Kelling) developed the "broken windows" theory, which reshaped police strategy in the 1990s. Furthermore, as we will also see in Chapter 6, criminological theories about the "hot spots" in which crime takes place, also known as *applied geography,* have led dozens of police departments to adopt computer-based crime mapping prevention strategies.[94]

David Kennedy, a criminologist at John Jay College in New York, has partnered with law enforcement agencies in a number of American cities to implement his drug-market intervention (DMI) initiative. As part of DMI, known drug dealers are approached by police and given a choice: stop dealing and we will help you turn your life around, or keep dealing and we will arrest you. Those who choose to participate in the program are offered educational classes, drug treatment, and job training and placement. Four years after DMI came to Cincinnati, Ohio, gang homicides dropped by 41 percent.[95] Indeed, in the opinion of many observers, researchers know more today about "what works" in criminology than at any other time in our nation's history.[96]

SELF ASSESSMENT

Fill in the blanks and check your answers on page 62.

In 1972, Marvin Wolfgang and his colleagues established the idea of the _____ offender, by showing that a _____ percentage of offenders is often responsible for a disproportionately _____ amount of crime. Research on this subject has led law enforcement agencies to focus resources on _____ offenders.

CJ IN ACTION

LEGALIZING MARIJUANA

The popularity of marijuana, the most commonly used illegal drug in the United States, is growing. Over the past five years, the number of regular users has swollen from about 15 million to 18 million.[97] If, as some observers believe, the reason for this increase is pot's cultural acceptance in our society,[98] then, as of November 6, 2012, we can expect the trend to continue. On that day, Colorado and Washington became the first two states to legalize the possession and sale of marijuana for personal use. These steps reflect a growing "get soft" movement regarding the nation's marijuana laws that we now address in this chapter's *CJ in Action* feature.

FEDERALISM IN ACTION

Over the past two decades, many jurisdictions have decided to reject the absolute prohibition of marijuana use. Nineteen states and the District of Columbia allow for the medical use of the drug to alleviate pain. Eight states have *decriminalized* marijuana, meaning that possession of small amounts of pot is treated as an infraction, like a traffic ticket, rather than a crime. Six states treat marijuana possession as a fine-only misdemeanor, with no prison or jail time.[99] Marijuana legalization in Colorado and Washington takes things further. In both states, possession of up to an ounce is no longer against the law for those twenty-one years of age and older. The substance is now sold and taxed in state-licensed stores, much as is the case with alcohol and tobacco.

In the immediate future, two questions remain to be answered regarding these new guidelines. First, will federal law enforcement enforce federal laws prohibiting marijuana possession and sale in Colorado and Washington? As we learned in Chapter 1, the federal government certainly has the power to do so. Second, what will be the health consequences of legal marijuana in the affected communities?

THE CASE FOR LEGALIZATION

- The "peace dividend" of legalization would be substantial. On the one hand, 850,000 Americans are arrested each year on marijuana-related charges. Removing these offenders from the criminal justice system would save U.S. taxpayers billions of dollars annually.[100] On the other hand, the country would reap a windfall in taxes on the controlled sale of a previously illegal drug. One Harvard University economist has estimated that the net economic gain to the United States for legalizing marijuana would be between $10.1 billion and $13.9 billion a year.[101]

- Legalization would put the black market for marijuana—estimated at $15 to $30 billion a year[102]—out of business,

ending violent crime associated with the pot trade and depriving thousands of criminals of their livelihood.

- Legalization would result in a more efficient criminal justice system, as scarce law enforcement resources would be diverted away from marijuana offenses, and the pressure on both overloaded courts and overcrowded prisons would be alleviated.[103]

THE CASE AGAINST LEGALIZATION

- As one health professional puts it, "Marijuana is not good for you."[104] Frequent marijuana use has been linked to mental disorders such as depression and anxiety. It is also associated with respiratory problems, IQ reduction, and immune system weakness.[105]

- Legalization would greatly decrease the price of marijuana (perhaps by as much as 80 percent), thus increasing the number of users and societal impact of the drug's negative consequences.[106]

- Minors can often easily obtain legal but controlled drug products such as cigarettes and alcohol. If marijuana is legalized, we can expect that minors would have greater access to it as well.

YOUR OPINION—WRITING ASSIGNMENT

What is your opinion of marijuana legalization? Drug policy expert Kevin Sabet opposes the practice. "People tend to think that if you are against legalization, you're in favor of increasing the jail population," he says. "The reality is, we can reduce marijuana use as well as incarceration rates."[107] Do you agree with Sabet that there is a realistic strategy that lies between widespread legalization and widespread prohibition? If so, what would be the most important aspects of this "third way"? Or, are you in favor of continued strict measures to punish marijuana users and sellers? Before responding, you can review our discussions in this chapter concerning:

- Social psychology (page 43).

- The criminology of drug use (page 54).

- The drug-crime relationship (pages 56–57).

Your answer should include at least three full paragraphs.

CHAPTER SUMMARY

For more information on these concepts, look back to the Learning Objective icons throughout the chapter.

 Discuss the difference between a hypothesis and a theory in the context of criminology. A hypothesis is a proposition, usually presented in an "If . . . , then . . ." format, that can be tested by researchers. If enough different authorities are able to test and verify a hypothesis, it will usually be accepted as a theory. Because theories can offer explanations for behavior, criminologists often rely on them when trying to determine the causes of criminal behavior.

 Contrast positivism with classical criminology. Whereas classical theorists believe criminals make rational choices, those of the positivist school believe that criminal behavior is determined by psychological, biological, and social forces that the individual cannot control.

 Explain how brain-scanning technology is able to help scientists determine if an individual is at risk for criminal offending. Brain scanning technologies such as CAT scans, MRIs, and fMRIs provide scientists with detailed depictions of brain structure and brain activity. When these depictions show disease or dysfunction such as schizophrenia that is correlated with violent behavior, the subject is at greater risk of criminal offending.

 List and describe the three theories of social structure that help explain crime. Social disorganization theory states that crime is largely a product of unfavorable conditions in certain communities, or zones of disorganization. The strain theory argues that most people seek increased wealth and financial security and that the strain of not being able to achieve these goals through legal means leads to criminal behavior. Finally, cultural deviance theory asserts that people adapt to the values of the subculture—which has its own standards of behavior—to which they belong.

 List and briefly explain the three branches of social process theory. (a) Learning theory, which contends that people learn to be criminals from their family and peers. (b) Control theory, which holds that most of us are dissuaded from a life of crime because we place importance on the opinions of family and peers. (c) Labeling theory, which holds that a person labeled a "junkie" or a "thief" will respond by becoming or remaining whatever she or he is labeled.

 Describe the importance of early childhood behavior for those who subscribe to self-control theory. Advocates of self-control theory believe that violent and antisocial behavior in adulthood can be predicted, to a large extent, by low levels of self-control in early childhood. Therefore, a child who is impulsive and tends to solve problems with violence is at risk for adult offending.

 Contrast the medical model of addiction with the criminal model of addiction. Those who support the former believe that addicts are not criminals, but mentally or physically ill individuals who are forced into acts of petty crime to "feed their habit." Those in favor of the criminal model of addiction believe that abusers and addicts endanger society with their behavior and should be treated like any other criminals.

 Explain the theory of the chronic offender and its importance for the criminal justice system. A chronic offender is a juvenile or adult who commits multiple offenses. According to research conducted by Marvin Wolfgang and others in the 1970s, chronic offenders are responsible for a disproportionately large percentage of all crime. In the decades since, law enforcement agencies and public prosecutors have developed strategies to identify and convict chronic offenders with the goal of lessening overall crime rates. In addition, legislators have passed laws that provide longer sentences for chronic offenders in an attempt to keep them off the streets.

QUESTIONS FOR CRITICAL ANALYSIS

1. Research shows that when levels of single-family mortgage foreclosures rise in a neighborhood, so do levels of violent crime. Explain the correlation between these two sets of statistics. Why is it false to say that single-family mortgage foreclosures *cause* violent crimes to occur?

2. Why would someone who subscribes to choice theory believe that increasing the harshness of a penalty for a particular crime would necessarily lead to fewer such crimes being committed?

3. Consider the following statement: "The government should protect the public from mentally ill persons who are potentially dangerous, even if that means hospitalizing those persons against their will." Do you agree or disagree? Why?

4. Review the theory of differential association in this chapter. Then, review the definition of white-collar crime in Chapter 1. How could the theory of differential association be used to describe high levels of white-collar crime in any particular business or industry?

5. Naloxone is a drug that counteracts the effects of heroin and is routinely used by ambulance crews and hospital emergency room staffers to save heroin abusers from fatal overdoses. Recently, public health officials have been distributing naloxone for free to heroin addicts in some parts of the country. What are the positives and negatives of this policy?

KEY TERMS

anomie   46
biology   40
causation   37
choice theory   38
chronic offender   59
classical criminology   38
control theory   51
correlation   37
criminal model of addiction   57
criminology   37
cultural deviance theory   47
drug abuse   55

genetics   40
hormone   41
hypothesis   37
labeling theory   51
learning theory   49
life course criminology   52
medical model of addiction   57
methamphetamine (meth)   56
neurotransmitter   41
positivism   39
prescription drugs   56

psychoanalytic theory   42
psychology   40
social conflict theories   47
social disorganization theory   44
social process theories   49
social reality of crime   47
sociology   44
strain theory   46
subculture   47
testosterone   41
theory   37

SELF ASSESSMENT ANSWER KEY

Page 38: i. criminologists; **ii.** scientific; **iii.** theory

Page 43: i. Choice (or Rational Choice); **ii.** genetics (or genes); **iii.** psychology

Page 49: i. disorganization; **ii.** Strain; **iii.** conflict; **iv.** minority

Page 53: i. learning; **ii.** control; **iii.** life course; **iv.** childhood

Page 57: i. abuse; **ii.** addicted; **iii.** dopamine; **iv.** prescription; **v.** synthetic

Page 59: i. chronic; **ii.** small; **iii.** large; **iv.** repeat or habitual

NOTES

1. Michael L. Sulkowski and Philip J. Lazarus, "Contemporary Responses to Violent Attacks on College Campuses," *Journal of School Violence* (October 2011), 343.

2. Ethan Bronner, "Other States, and Other Times, Would Have Posed Obstacles for Gunman," *New York Times* (July 25, 2012), A12.

3. Matthew Larson and Gary Sweeten, "Breaking Up Is Hard to Do: Romantic Dissolution, Offending, and Substance Abuse During the Transition to Adulthood," *Criminology* (August 2012), 605–635.

4. James Q. Wilson and Richard J. Hernstein, *Crime and Human Nature: The Definitive Study of the Causes of Crime* (New York: Simon & Schuster, 1985), 515.

5. Cesare Lombroso, *Criminal Man*, eds. Mary Gibson and Nicole Hahn Rafter (Durham, NC: Duke University Press, 2006).

6. Wilson and Hernstein, 44.

7. Jack Katz, *Seductions of Crime: Moral and Sensual Attractions of Doing Evil* (New York: Basic Books, 1988).

8. National Coalition for the Homeless, "Hate Crimes and Violence against People Experiencing Homelessness," at **www.nationalhomeless.org/factsheets/hatecrimes.html**.

9. David C. Rowe, *Biology and Crime* (Los Angeles: Roxbury, 2002), 2.

10. David C. Rowe, "Genetic and Environmental Components of Antisocial Behavior: A Study of 265 Twin Pairs," *Criminology* 24 (1986), 513–532.

11. Raymond R. Crowe, "An Adoption Study of Antisocial Personality," *Archives of General Psychiatry* (1974), 785–791; Sarnoff A. Mednick, William F. Gabrielli, and Barry Hutchings, "Genetic Influences on

Criminal Convictions: Evidence from an Adoption Cohort," *Science* (1994), 891–894; and Remi J. Cadoret, "Adoption Studies," *Alcohol Health & Research World* (Summer 1995), 195–201.

12. Hans G. Brunner et al., "Abnormal Behavior Associated with a Point Mutation in the Structural Gene for Monoamine Oxidase A," *Science* (October 22, 1993), 578–580.

13. Avshalom Caspi et al., "Role of Genotype in the Cycle of Violence in Maltreated Children," *Science* (August 2, 2002), 851–854.

14. Gail S. Anderson, *Biological Influences on Criminal Behavior* (Boca Raton, FL: CRC Press, 2007), 105–118.

15. Judith G. Edersheim, Bruce H. Price, and Jordan W. Smoller, "'Your Honor, My Genes Made Me Do It,'" *Wall Street Journal* (October 23, 2012), A21.

16. L. E. Kreuz and R. M. Rose, "Assessment of Aggressive Behavior and Plasma Testosterone in Young Criminal Population," *Psychosomatic Medicine* 34 (1972), 321–332.

17. H. Persky, K. Smith, and G. Basu, "Relation of Psychological Measures of Aggression and Hostility to Testosterone Production in Men," *Psychosomatic Medicine* 33 (1971), 265, 276.

18. Benjamin J. Sadock, Harold I. Kaplan, and Virginia A. Sadock, *Kaplan & Sadock's Synopsis of Psychiatry* (Philadelphia: Lippincott Williams & Wilkins, 2007), 865.

19. Robert J. Meadows and Julie Kuehnel, *Evil Minds: Understanding and Responding to Violent Predators* (Upper Saddle River, NJ: Pearson Prentice Hall, 2005), 156–157.

20. *Ibid.,* 157, 169.

21. Bureau of Justice Statistics, *Health Problems of Prison and Jail Inmates* (Washington, D.C.: U.S. Department of Justice, September 2006), 1.

22. Quoted in Eileen Sullivan, "Loners Like Tucson Gunman 'Fly below the Radar,'" *Associated Press* (January 17, 2011).

23. Herman Bianchi, *Justice as Sanctuary: Toward a New System of Crime Control* (Bloomington: Indiana University Press, 1994), 72.

24. David G. Myers, *Psychology,* 7th ed. (New York: Worth Publishers, 2004), 576–577.

25. Philip Zimbardo, "Pathology of Imprisonment," *Society* (April 1972), 4–8.

26. David Canter and Laurence Alison, "The Social Psychology of Crime: Groups, Teams, and Networks," in *The Social Psychology of Crime: Groups, Teams, and Networks,* ed. David Canter and Laurence Alison (Hanover, NH: Dartmouth, 2000), 3–4.

27. Monica Davey, "In a Soaring Homicide Rate, a Divide in Chicago," *New York Times* (January 3, 2013), A1.

28. Robert Park, Ernest Burgess, and Roderic McKenzie, *The City* (Chicago: University of Chicago Press, 1929).

29. Caterina Gouvis Roman et al., *Alcohol Outlets as Attractors of Violence and Disorder: A Closer Look at the Neighborhood Environment* (Washington, D.C.: Urban Institute, 2008), 5–15; and Charis E. Kubrin et al., "Does Fringe Banking Exacerbate Neighborhood Crime Rates?" *Criminology and Public Policy* (May 2011), 437–463.

30. Clifford R. Shaw, Henry D. McKay, and Leonard S. Cottrell, *Delinquency Areas* (Chicago: University of Chicago Press, 1929).

31. Clifford R. Shaw and Henry D. McKay, *Report on the Causes of Crime,* vol. 2: *Social Factors in Juvenile Delinquency* (Washington, D.C.: National Commission on Law Observance and Enforcement, 1931).

32. Elijah Anderson, *Code of the Street: Decency, Violence and the Moral Life of the Inner City* (New York: W. W. Norton, 2000), 35–65.

33. *Ibid.,* 180.

34. Eric A. Stewart and Ronald L. Simons, "Race, Code of the Street, and Violent Delinquency: A Multilevel Investigation of Neighborhood Street Culture and Individual Norms of Violence," *Criminology* (May 2010), 569–603.

35. Emile Durkheim, *The Rules of Sociological Method,* trans. Sarah A. Solovay and John H. Mueller (New York: Free Press, 1964).

36. Robert K. Merton, *Social Theory and Social Structure* (New York: Free Press, 1957). See the chapter on "Social Structure and Anomie."

37. Robert Agnew, "Foundation for a General Strain Theory of Crime and Delinquency," *Criminology* 30 (1992), 47–87.

38. Robert Agnew, Timothy Brezina, John Paul Wright, and Francis T. Cullen, "Strain, Personality Traits, and Delinquency: Extending General Strain Theory," *Criminology* (February 2002), 43–71.

39. Lawrence L. Shornack, "Conflict Theory and the Family," *International Social Science Review* 62 (1987), 154–157.

40. Robert Meier, "The New Criminology: Continuity in Criminology Theory," *Journal of Criminal Law and Criminology* 67 (1977), 461–469.

41. Richard Quinney, *The Social Reality of Crime* (Boston: Little, Brown, 1970).

42. Nicole Hahn Rafter, *Partial Justice: Women, Prisons, and Social Control* (New Brunswick, NJ: Transaction Publishers, 1990).

43. Federal Bureau of Investigation, *Crime in the United States, 2011* (Washington D.C.: U.S. Department of Justice, 2012), at **www.fbi.gov/about-us/cjis/ucr/crime-in-the-u.s/2011/crime-in-the-u.s.-2011/tables/table=42**.

44. The Sentencing Project, at **www.sentencingproject.org/template/page.cfm?id=122**.

45. Bureau of Justice Statistics, *Bulletin: Prisoners in 2011* (Washington, D.C.: U.S. Department of Justice, December 2012), Table 8, page 8.

46. Quoted in Gina Barton, "Rally Demands Police Change," *Milwaukee Journal Sentinel* (October 4, 2012), 1.

47. Hubert M. Blalock, *Toward a Theory of Minority-Group Relations* (New York: Capricorn Books, 1967).

48. *Ibid.*

49. These studies are discussed in Ted Chiricos, Kelly Welch, and Marc Gertz, "Racial Typification of Crime and Support for Punitive Measures," *Criminology* (May 1, 2004), 359–390.

50. Xia Wang, "Undocumented Immigrants as Perceived Criminal Threat: A Test of the Minority Threat Perspective," *Criminology* (August 2012), 744–745.

51. Philip G. Zimbardo, "The Human Choice: Individuation, Reason, and Order versus Deindividuation, Impulse, and Chaos," in *Nebraska Symposium on Motivation,* ed. William J. Arnold and David Levie (Lincoln, NE: University of Nebraska Press, 1969), 287–293.

52. Edwin H. Sutherland, *Criminology,* 4th ed. (Philadelphia: Lippincott, 1947).

53. L. Rowell Huesmann, Jessica Moise-Titus, Cheryl-Lynn Podolski, and Leonard D. Eron, "Longitudinal Relations between Children's Exposure to TV Violence and Their Aggressive and Violent Behavior in Young Adulthood: 1977–1992," *Developmental Psychology* (March 2003), 201.

54. Telecommunications Act of 1996, 47 U.S.C. Section 303 (1999).

55. Travis Hirschi, *Causes of Delinquency* (Berkeley: University of California Press, 1969).

56. James Q. Wilson and George L. Kelling, "Broken Windows," *Atlantic Monthly* (March 1982), 29.

57. Janet L. Lauritsen, *How Families and Communities Influence Youth Victimization* (Washington, D.C.: Office of Juvenile Justice and Delinquency Prevention, 2003).

58. Quoted in Kevin Johnson, "For Many of USA's Inmates, Crime Runs in the Family," *USA Today* (January 29, 2008), 1A.

59. Howard S. Becker, *Outsiders: Studies in the Sociology of Deviance* (New York: Free Press, 1963).

60. Francis T. Cullen and Robert Agnew, *Criminological Theory, Past to Present: Essential Readings,* 2d ed. (Los Angeles: Roxbury Publishing Co., 2003), 443.

61. Michael R. Gottfredson and Travis Hirschi, *A General Theory of Crime* (Stanford, CA: Stanford University Press, 1990).

62. *Ibid.,* 90.

63. *Ibid.*

64. Terrie Moffitt, "Adolescent-Limited and Life-Course-Persistent Antisocial Behavior: A Developmental Taxonomy," *Psychological Review* 100 (1993), 679–680.

65. *Ibid.*, 674.

66. Robert J. Sampson and John H. Laub, *Crime in the Making: Pathways and Turning Points through Life* (Cambridge, MA: Harvard University Press, 1993), 11.

67. *Ibid.*; John H. Laub and Robert J. Sampson, *Shared Beginnings, Divergent Lives: Delinquent Boys to Age 70* (Cambridge, MA: Harvard University Press, 2003); and Derek A. Kreager, Ross L. Matsueda, and Elena A. Erosheva, "Motherhood and Criminal Desistance in Disadvantaged Neighborhoods," *Criminology* (February 2010), 221–257.

68. John F. Frana and Ryan D. Schroeder, "Alternatives to Incarceration," *Justice Policy Journal* (Fall 2008), available at **www.cjcj.org/files/alternatives_to.pdf**.

69. Peggy C. Giordano, Monica A. Longmore, Ryan D. Schroeder, and Patrick M. Seffrin, "A Life-Course Perspective on Spirituality and Desistance from Crime," *Criminology* (February 2008), 99–132.

70. Richard B. Felson and Keri B. Burchfield, "Alcohol and the Risk of Physical and Sexual Assault Victimization," *Criminology* (November 1, 2004), 837.

71. Becker.

72. Myers, 75–76.

73. Peter B. Kraska, "The Unmentionable Alternative: The Need for and Argument against the Decriminalization of Drug Laws," in *Drugs, Crime, and the Criminal Justice System,* ed. Ralph Weisheit (Cincinnati, OH: Anderson Publishing, 1990).

74. Anthony A. Grace, "The Tonic/Phasal Model of Dopamine System Regulation," *Drugs and Alcohol* 37 (1995), 111.

75. Li Chuan-Yun, Mao Xizeng, and Wei Liping, "Genes and (Common) Pathways Underlying Drug Addiction," *Public Library of Science*, at **www.ploscompbiol.org/articleinfo%3Adoi%2F10.1371%2F journal.pcbi.0040002**.

76. Bureau of Justice Statistics, "Alcohol and Crime: Data from 2002 to 2008," at **bjs.ojp.usdoj.gov/content/acf/29_prisoners_and _alcoholuse.cfm and bjs.ojp.usdoj.gov/content/acf/30_jails _and_alcoholuse .cfm**.

77. *ADAM II: 2011 Annual Report* (Washington, D.C.: Office of National Drug Policy, May 2012), vii.

78. *Epidemic: Responding to America's Prescription Drug Crisis* (Washington, D.C.: Executive Office of the President of the United States, 2011), 1.

79. Substance Abuse and Mental Health Services Administration, *Results from the 2011 National Survey on Drug Use and Health: Summary of National Findings* (Washington, D.C.: National Institute on Drug Abuse, September 2012), 58.

80. Donna L. Leger, "Painkiller Abuse Declines in 2011," *USA Today* (September 25, 2012), 1A.

81. Abby Goodnough, "Pharmacies Besieged by Addicted Thieves," *New York Times* (February 7, 2011), A1.

82. Damien Cave and Michael S. Schmidt, "Rise in Pill Abuse Forces New Look at U.S. Drug Fight," *New York Times* (July 17, 2012), A1.

83. Ben Paynter, "The Money Is Huge: The Unlicensed, Ingenious, and Increasingly Scary World of Synthetic Drugs," *Bloomberg Businessweek* (June 20–26, 2011).

84. Abby Goodnough and Katie Zezima, "An Alarming New Stimulant, Legal in Many States," *New York Times* (July 17, 2011), A1.

85. James A. Inciardi, *The War on Drugs: Heroin, Cocaine, and Public Policy* (Palo Alto, CA: Mayfield, 1986), 148.

86. *Ibid.*, 106.

87. "Burn-Out and Battle Fatigue," *The Economist* (March 17, 2012), 43.

88. Quoted in *ibid.*

89. Quoted in Timothy Egan, "After Seven Deaths, Digging for an Explanation," *New York Times* (June 25, 2006), 12.

90. Marvin Wolfgang, Robert Figlio, and Thorsten Sellin, *Delinquency in a Birth Cohort* (Chicago: University of Chicago Press, 1972).

91. Lawrence W. Sherman, "Attacking Crime: Police and Crime Control," in *Modern Policing,* ed. Michael Tonry and Norval Morris (Chicago: University of Chicago Press, 1992), 159.

92. James Q. Wilson, "What to Do about Crime," *Commentary* (September 1994), 25–34.

93. Sarah J. Hart, "A New Way of Doing Business at the NIJ," *Law Enforcement News* (January 15/31, 2002), 9.

94. David Weisburg, "Shifting Crime and Justice Resources from Prisons to Police: Shifting Police from People to Place," *Criminology & Public Policy* (February 2011), 153–163.

95. David Kennedy, "'God, It's Got to Stop,'" *Newsweek* (October 3, 2011), 25–27.

96. Richard Rosenfeld, "Book Review: *The Limits of Crime Control,*" *Journal of Criminal Law and Criminology* (Fall 2002).

97. *Results from the 2011 Annual Survey on Drug Use and Health: A Summary of National Findings,* 1, 55; and Tony Dokoupil, "High Times in America," *Newsweek* (October 29, 2012), 28.

98. David Frum, "Weed Whacked," *Newsweek* (December 17, 2012), 22.

99. "Briefing: How America's Views of Marijuana Are Changing," *The Christian Science Monitor Weekly* (June 18, 2012), 13.

100. Walter Simpson, "A Joint Venture," *Buffalo News* (February 27, 2011), G1.

101. Jeffrey A. Miron, "The Budgetary Implications of Marijuana Prohibition" (June 2005), at **www.prohibitioncosts.org/mironreport.html**.

102. Beau Kilmer, "The Marijuana Exception," *Wall Street Journal* (April 21–22, 2012), C2.

103. James A. Inciardi and Duane C. McBride, "Debating the Legalization of Drugs," in *Handbook of Drug Control in the United States,* ed. James A. Inciardi (New York: Greenwood Press, 1990), 285–289.

104. Susan Weiss, policy chief for the National Institute on Drug Abuse, quoted in "Is Marijuana Bad for You?" *The Week* (November 30, 2012), 11.

105. *Fact Sheet: Office of National Drug Control Policy* (Washington, D.C.: Executive Office of the President, October 2010), 2.

106. Beau Kilmer et al., *Altered State? Assessing How Marijuana Legalization in California Could Influence Marijuana Consumption and Public Budgets* (Santa Monica, CA: RAND Corporation 2010).

107. Quoted in Frum.

DO NOT CROSS · TEXT A T... OR CALL

CHAPTER

3

The Crime Picture:
Offenders and Victims

CHAPTER OUTLINE	CORRESPONDING LEARNING OBJECTIVES	
Classifications of Crime		Discuss the primary goals of civil law and criminal law and explain how these goals are realized.
		Explain the differences between crimes *mala in se* and *mala prohibita*.
Measuring Crime in the United States		Identify the publication in which the FBI reports crime data and list the two main ways in which the data are reported.
		Distinguish between the National Crime Victimization Survey (NCVS) and self-reported surveys.
Victims of Crime		Describe the three ways that victims' rights legislation increases the ability of crime victims to participate in the criminal justice system.
		Discuss one major concern regarding victim participation in the criminal justice process.
Crime Trends in the United States		Identify the three factors most often used by criminologists to explain changes in the nation's crime rate.
		Explain why income level appears to be more important than race or ethnicity when it comes to crime trends.
		Discuss the prevailing explanation for the rising number of women incarcerated in the United States.

To target your study and review, look for these numbered Learning Objective icons throughout the chapter.

Scott Olson/Getty Images

A HISTORY OF VIOLENCE

LATE AT NIGHT, Juan Morales enters a sleeping woman's dark bedroom after watching her boyfriend leave. Pretending to be the boyfriend, he proceeds to have sexual intercourse with the woman, who does not realize what is happening until too late. Has Morales committed a crime? "The answer is no," ruled a Los Angeles court on January 2, 2013, somewhat reluctantly. The problem was a "historic anomaly" in California's legal definition of rape. According to a state law passed in the 1870s, such trickery is rape only if the perpetrator pretends to be the victim's *husband.* Because Morales's victim was not married, his actions were not—technically—criminal.

Understandably, the court's decision caused a fair amount of controversy. One Long Beach assemblywoman compared the ruling to "applying horse-and-buggy standards to our freeways." Indeed, the term *rape* has a difficult legal history in the United States. For many years, both federal and state and criminal law required that "force" be used to raise a sexual assault to the level of a crime. That is, the offender (by definition, male) had to use violence against the victim (by definition, female), who was similarly required to strenuously resist the attack. Most rapes, however, occur through coercion and threats and feature physical contact such as pinning the victim to the ground that does not leave obvious traces of harm. The Centers for Disease Control estimates that only 14 percent of rape cases involve armed rapists and victims with outwardly obvious injuries like bruises or broken bones.

Today, only six states require evidence of overt physical force for a rape to have occurred, and most criminal codes in the United States recognize male victims. Additionally, the U.S. Department of Justice recently expanded the way that it measures the national occurrence of criminal sexual assault. Now, for the purposes of federal statistics, almost any sexual act committed against a person—female or male—without her or his consent meets the standard for rape.

1. In the Morales case described above, the victim had no way to directly contest the court's decision. Even if California politicians do amend the law, any change will come too late to impact her case. Should victims of crime be given an outlet to challenge court outcomes that they believe to be incorrect or unfair? Why or why not?

2. What is your opinion of rape laws that focus on lack of victim consent rather than the use of physical force by the alleged rapist?

3. Until recent decades, many states defined rape as the forcible sexual intercourse with a person other than the wife of the accused. What do you think was the purpose of this "marital exemption"? How has American society changed so that this exemption is now unacceptable?

AP Photo/*The News & Observer,* Travis Long

On the Chapel Hill campus of the University of North Carolina, students protest the school's policy on sexual assault, a contentious subject for many crime victims.

CLASSIFICATION OF CRIMES

The federal government's decision regarding its official definition of rape was met with widespread approval. The new definition "comes much closer to reflecting the reality of the crime," said Scott Berkowitz, head of the Rape, Abuse, and Incest National Network.[1] As you will see later in this chapter, definitions and measurements of crime are specific tools that both criminal justice professionals and community leaders can use for crime prevention and victim assistance.

We start, however, with a broad overview of three classifications that are crucial to understanding the crime picture of the United States: the differences between (1) civil law and criminal law, (2) felonies and misdemeanors, and (3) crimes *mala in se* and *mala prohibita*.

Civil Law and Criminal Law

All law can be divided into two categories: civil law and criminal law. As U.S. criminal law has evolved, it has diverged from U.S. civil law. These two categories of law are distinguished by their primary goals. The criminal justice system is concerned with protecting society from harm by preventing and prosecuting crimes. A crime is an act so reprehensible that it is considered a wrong against society as a whole, as well as against the individual victim. Therefore, the state prosecutes a person who commits a criminal act. If the state is able to prove that a person is guilty of a crime, the government will punish her or him with imprisonment or fines, or both.

Civil law, which includes all types of law other than criminal law, is concerned with disputes between private individuals and between entities. Proceedings in civil lawsuits are normally initiated by an individual or a corporation (in contrast to criminal proceedings, which are initiated by public prosecutors). Such disputes may involve, for example, the terms of a contract, the ownership of property, or an automobile accident. Under civil law, the government provides a forum for the resolution of *torts*—or private wrongs—in which the injured party, called the **plaintiff,** tries to prove that a wrong has been committed by the accused party, or the **defendant.** (Note that the accused party in both criminal and civil cases is known as the *defendant.*)

GUILT AND RESPONSIBILITY A criminal court is convened to determine whether the defendant is *guilty*—that is, whether the defendant has, in fact, committed the offense charged. In contrast, civil law is concerned with responsibility, a much more flexible concept. For example, when baby Sofia Blunt developed cerebral palsy soon after her birth, a civil court in San Louis Obispo, California, blamed Kurt Haupt, the presiding doctor. Apparently, Haupt failed to take proper steps to increase blood flow to Sofia's brain during delivery. Even though Haupt was never charged with any crime, the civil court decided that he was **liable,** or legally responsible, for Sofia's condition because of his carelessness.

Most civil cases involve a request for monetary damages to compensate for the wrong that has been committed. Thus, in 2012, the civil court had Kurt Haupt's insurance company pay $74 million to Sofia Blunt's parents to cover the medical costs they will incur over their daughter's lifetime.

THE BURDEN OF PROOF Although criminal law proceedings are completely separate from civil law proceedings in the modern legal system, the two systems do have some similarities. Both attempt to control behavior by imposing sanctions on those who violate

Civil Law The branch of law dealing with the definition and enforcement of all private or public rights, as opposed to criminal matters.

Plaintiff The person or institution that initiates a lawsuit in civil court proceedings by filing a complaint.

Defendant In a civil court, the person or institution against whom an action is brought. In a criminal court, the person or entity who has been formally accused of violating a criminal law.

Liability In a civil court, legal responsibility for one's own or another's actions.

 LEARNING OBJECTIVE 1 Discuss the primary goals of civil law and criminal law and explain how these goals are realized.

Beyond a Reasonable Doubt
The degree of proof required to find the defendant in a criminal trial guilty of committing the crime. The defendant's guilt must be the only reasonable explanation for the criminal act before the court.

Preponderance of the Evidence The degree of proof required to decide in favor of one side or the other in a civil case. In general, this requirement is met when a plaintiff proves that a fact more likely than not is true.

Felony A serious crime, usually punishable by death or imprisonment for a year or longer.

Misdemeanor A criminal offense that is not a felony; usually punishable by a fine and/or a jail term of less than one year.

society's definition of acceptable behavior. Furthermore, criminal and civil law often supplement each other. In certain instances, a victim may file a civil suit against an individual who is also the target of a criminal prosecution by the government.

Because the burden of proof is much greater in criminal trials than civil ones, it is almost always easier to win monetary damages than a criminal conviction. Several years ago, for example, store manager Richard Moore was found not guilty of sexually abusing an employee in O'Fallon, Illinois, because investigators could not match his DNA to physical evidence found near the alleged incident. A separate civil court, however, ruled that Moore had sexually abused the woman and ordered his employer, the furniture chain Aaron's, to pay her $41 million in damages. During the criminal trial, the court did not find enough evidence to prove **beyond a reasonable doubt** (the burden of proof in criminal cases) that Moore was guilty of any crime. Nevertheless, the civil trial established by a **preponderance of the evidence** (the burden of proof in civil cases) that Moore had thrown the employee to the floor and sexually abused her. (See the *Mastering Concepts feature* below for a comparison of civil and criminal law.)

Felonies and Misdemeanors

Depending on their degree of seriousness, crimes are classified as *felonies* or *misdemeanors*. **Felonies** are crimes punishable by death or by imprisonment in a federal or state penitentiary for one year or longer (though some states, such as North Carolina, consider felonies to be punishable by at least two years' incarceration). The Model Penal Code, a general guide for criminal law that you will learn more about in the next chapter, provides for four degrees of felony:

1. Capital offenses, for which the maximum penalty is death.
2. First degree felonies, punishable by a maximum penalty of life imprisonment.
3. Second degree felonies, punishable by a maximum of ten years' imprisonment.
4. Third degree felonies, punishable by a maximum of five years' imprisonment.[2]

For the most part, felonies involve crimes of violence such as armed robbery or sexual assault, or other "serious" crimes such as stealing a large amount of money or selling illegal drugs.

TYPES OF MISDEMEANORS Under federal law and in most states, any crime that is not a felony is considered a **misdemeanor.** Misdemeanors are crimes punishable by a fine or by confinement for up to a year. If imprisoned, the guilty party goes to a local jail instead

MASTERING CONCEPTS
CIVIL LAW VERSUS CRIMINAL LAW

ISSUE	CIVIL LAW	CRIMINAL LAW
Area of concern	Rights and duties between individuals	Offenses against society as a whole
Wrongful act	Harm to a person or business entity	Violation of a statute that prohibits some type of activity
Party who brings suit	Person who suffered harm (plaintiff)	The state (prosecutor)
Party who responds	Person who supposedly caused harm (defendant)	Person who allegedly committed a crime (defendant)
Standard of proof	Preponderance of the evidence	Beyond a reasonable doubt
Remedy	Damages to compensate for the harm	Punishment (fine or incarceration)

of a penitentiary. Disorderly conduct and trespassing are common misdemeanors. Most states distinguish between *gross misdemeanors,* which are offenses punishable by thirty days to a year in jail, and *petty misdemeanors,* or offenses punishable by fewer than thirty days in jail. Probation and community service are often imposed on those who commit misdemeanors, especially juveniles. As you will see in Chapter 8, whether a crime is a felony or misdemeanor can also determine in which criminal court the case will be tried.

INFRACTIONS The least serious form of wrongdoing is often called an **infraction** and is punishable only by a small fine. Even though infractions such as parking tickets or traffic violations technically represent illegal activity, they generally are not considered "crimes." Therefore, infractions rarely lead to jury trials and are deemed to be so minor that they do not appear on the offender's criminal record. In some jurisdictions, the terms *infraction* and *petty offense* are interchangeable. In others, however, they are different. Under federal guidelines, for example, an infraction can be punished by up to five days of prison time, while a petty offender is only liable for a fine.[2] Finally, those who string together a series of infractions (or fail to pay the fines that come with such offenses) are in danger of being criminally charged. In Illinois, having three or more speeding violations in one year is considered criminal behavior.[3]

■ A police officer writes a citation after making a traffic stop in Mount Pocono, Pennsylvania. What is the difference between an infraction, such as a speeding violation, and a crime? Why does it make sense that infractions do not appear on a person's criminal record?
AP Photo/*Pocono Record,* Keith R. Stevenson

Mala in Se and *Mala Prohibita*

Criminologists often express the social function of criminal law in terms of *mala in se* or *mala prohibita* crimes. A criminal act is referred to as **mala in se** if it would be considered wrong even if there were no law prohibiting it. *Mala in se* crimes are said to go against "natural laws"—that is, against the "natural, moral, and public" principles of a society. Murder, rape, and theft are examples of *mala in se* crimes. These crimes are generally the same from country to country or culture to culture.

In contrast, the term **mala prohibita** refers to acts that are considered crimes only because they have been codified as such through statute—"human-made" laws. A *mala prohibita* crime is considered wrong only because it has been prohibited. It is not inherently wrong, though it may reflect the moral standards of a society at a given time. Thus, the definition of a *mala prohibita* crime can vary from country to country and even from state to state. Bigamy, or the offense of having two legal spouses, could be considered a *mala prohibita* crime.

LEARNING OBJECTIVE **2** Explain the differences between crimes *mala in se* and *mala prohibita.*

MAKING THE DISTINCTION Some observers question the distinction between *mala in se* and *mala prohibita.* In many instances, it is difficult to define a "pure" *mala in se* crime. That is, it is difficult to separate a crime from the culture that has deemed it a crime.[4] Even murder, under certain cultural circumstances, is not considered a criminal act. In a number of poor, traditional areas of the Middle East and Asia, the law excuses "honor killings" in which men kill female family members suspected of sexual indiscretion. Our own legal system excuses homicide in extreme situations, such as self-defense or when a law enforcement agent kills in the course of upholding the law. Therefore, "natural" laws

Infraction In most jurisdictions, a noncriminal offense for which the penalty is a fine rather than incarceration.

Mala in Se A descriptive term for acts that are inherently wrong, regardless of whether they are prohibited by law.

Mala Prohibita A descriptive term for acts that are made illegal by criminal statute and are not necessarily wrong in and of themselves.

can be seen as culturally specific. Similar difficulties occur in trying to define a "pure" *mala prohibita* crime. More than 150 countries, including most members of the European Union, have legalized prostitution. With the exception of seven rural counties of Nevada, prostitution is illegal in the United States.

ELECTRONIC EAVESDROPPING

1000 Words/Shutterstock.com

"Our society is going through a technological transformation," notes Adam Schwartz, a civil liberties lawyer. "We are at a time where tens of millions of Americans carry around a telephone or other device in their pocket that has an audio-video capacity. Ten years ago, [we] weren't walking around with all these devices." This widespread ability to record interactions with others has increased the possibility that Americans are breaking the law, often without their knowledge. The criminal codes of twelve states require the consent of all parties involved before any conversation can be recorded.

In some cases, the penalties for breaking these laws can be quite harsh. Under the Illinois Eavesdropping Act, audio-recording a civilian without consent is a Class 4 felony, punishable by up to three years in prison. Audio-recording an Illinois law enforcement official who is performing her or his duties without consent is a Class 1 felony, punishable by up to fifteen years in prison.

Thinking about Electronic Eavesdropping

Are these eavesdropping statutes *mala in se* laws or *mala prohibita* laws? While explaining your answer, remember that smartphones and other easily portable devices with one-touch recording capabilities did not exist when most eavesdropping statutes were passed.

THE DRUG DILEMMA In spite of these difficulties, the *mala in se/mala prohibita* split can help explain seeming contradictions in criminal law. Take the law's treatment of *stimulants,* which are drugs that act on the nervous system to produce feelings of well-being and euphoria. *Nicotine,* a naturally occurring substance in the tobacco plant, and *caffeine,* found in coffee, tea, and soft drinks, are both stimulants. So are *cocaine,* an active ingredient in the South American coca plant, and *amphetamine,* developed in the 1920s to treat asthma sufferers. Nicotine and caffeine are considered **licit drugs,** or socially acceptable substances, if used by adults. In contrast, cocaine and many amphetamines are considered **illicit drugs,** or drugs whose sale and use have been made illegal. The most widely used drug in the United States is *alcohol,* consumed, at least occasionally, by approximately two-thirds of adult Americans.[5]

Distinguishing between Licit and Illicit Drugs Why has society prohibited the use of certain drugs, while allowing the use of others? The answer cannot be found in the risk of harm caused by the substances. Just as with illicit drugs, many licit drugs, if abused, can have serious consequences for the health of the user or of others. Improper consumption of the nonprescription pain reliever Tylenol (acetaminophen) is a leading cause of liver failure in the United States today,[6] and about 10,000 Americans are killed in alcohol-related car crashes each year.[7] Nor is illegality linked to the addictive quality of the drug. According to the American Medical Association, nicotine is the most habit-forming substance, with over two-thirds of people who smoke cigarettes becoming "hooked."[8] The next most addictive drug is heroin, followed by cocaine, alcohol, amphetamines, and marijuana, in that order.

Licit Drugs Legal drugs or substances, such as alcohol, caffeine, and nicotine.

Illicit Drugs Certain drugs or substances whose use or sale has been declared illegal.

The drug most widely associated with violent behavior, especially domestic violence, is alcohol.[9] One professor of preventive medicine has concluded that "there are no scientific . . . or medical bases on which the legal distinctions between various drugs are made."[10]

Society and the Law If drug laws are not based on science or medicine, on what are they based? The answers lies in the concept of *mala prohibita:* certain drugs are characterized as illicit while others are not because of presiding social norms and values. The general attitude of American society toward drugs has changed dramatically over the past century and a half. With the notable exception of alcohol, many drugs were considered useful, medicinal substances in the 1800s. Cocaine was promoted as a remedy for dozens of ailments. Coca-Cola, introduced in 1886, was marketed as providing the benefits of cocaine without the dangers of alcohol.[11]

As these attitudes have changed, the law has changed as well. Today, licit and illicit drugs are regulated under the Controlled Substances Act (CSA), which is part of the Comprehensive Drug Abuse Prevention and Control Act of 1970.[12] The CSA specifies five hierarchical categories for drugs and the penalties for the manufacture, sale, distribution, possession, or consumption of these drugs, based on the substances' medical use, potential for abuse, and addictive qualities (see Figure 3.1 below). The CSA explicitly excludes "distilled spirits, wine, malt beverages, and tobacco" from the legal definition of a "controlled substance."[13] Therefore, alcohol and tobacco are legal not because they have pharmacological effects that are considerably different or safer than those of illicit drugs, but rather because the law, as supported by society, says so.[14] Furthermore, as we saw in last chapter's discussion of the legalization of marijuana, sometimes certain segments of society challenge the status quo, placing pressure on criminal law to adjust accordingly.

SELF ASSESSMENT

Fill in the blanks and check your answers on page 93.

_____ law is concerned with disputes between private individuals and other entities, whereas criminal law involves the _____'s duty to protect society by preventing and prosecuting crimes. A _____ is a serious crime punishable by more than a year in prison or the death penalty, while a person found guilty of a _____ will usually spend less than a year in jail or pay a fine.

FIGURE 3.1 Schedules of Narcotics as Defined by the Federal Controlled Substances Act

The Comprehensive Drug Abuse Prevention and Control Act of 1970 continues to be the basis for the regulation of drugs in the United States. Substances named by the act were placed under direct regulation of the Drug Enforcement Administration (DEA). The act "ranks" drugs from I to V, with Schedule I drugs being the most heavily controlled and carrying the most severe penalties for abuse.

	CRITERIA	EXAMPLES
SCHEDULE 1	Drugs with high abuse potential that are lacking therapeutic utility or adequate safety for use under medical supervision.	Marijuana, heroin, LSD, peyote, PCP, mescaline
SCHEDULE II	Drugs with high abuse potential that are accepted in current medical practice despite high physical and psychological dependence potential.	Opium, cocaine, morphine, Benzedrine, methadone, methamphetamine
SCHEDULE III	Drugs with moderate abuse potential that are utilized in current medical practice despite dependence potential.	Barbiturates, amphetamine
SCHEDULE IV	Drugs with low abuse potential that are accepted in current medical practice despite limited dependence potential.	Valium, Darvon, phenobarbital
SCHEDULE V	Drugs with minimal abuse potential that are used in current medical practice despite limited dependence potential.	Cough medicine with small amounts of narcotic

Source: The Comprehensive Drug Abuse Prevention and Control Act of 1970.

MEASURING CRIME IN THE UNITED STATES

So far in this textbook, you have been exposed to numerous studies relating to the criminal justice system. For the most part, these analyses have dealt with narrow topics such as the police response to texting-while-driving, the relationship between states' gun laws and their gun death rates, and the nationwide prevalence of prescription drug abuse. The best-known annual survey of criminal behavior, however, tries to answer the broadest of questions: How much crime is there in the United States?

The Uniform Crime Report

Suppose that a firefighter dies while fighting a fire at an office building. Later, police discover that the building manager intentionally set the fire. All of the elements of the crime of arson have certainly been met, but can the manager be charged with murder? In some jurisdictions, the act might be considered a form of murder, but according to the U.S. Department of Justice, arson-related deaths and injuries of police officers and firefighters due to the "hazardous natures of their professions" are not murders.[15]

Identify the publication in which the FBI reports crime data and list the two main ways in which the data are reported.

LEARNING 3 OBJECTIVE

The distinction is important because the Department of Justice provides us with the most far-reaching and oft-cited set of national crime statistics. Each year, the department releases the **Uniform Crime Report (UCR).** Since its inception in 1930, the UCR has attempted to measure the overall rate of crime in the United States by organizing "offenses known to law enforcement."[16] To produce the UCR, the Federal Bureau of Investigation (FBI) relies on the voluntary participation of local law enforcement agencies. These agencies—approximately 18,200 in total, covering 95 percent of the population—base their information on three measurements:

1. The number of persons arrested.
2. The number of crimes reported by victims, witnesses, or the police themselves.
3. Police employee data.[17]

Once this information has been sent to the FBI, the agency presents the crime data in two important ways:

1. As a *rate* per 100,000 people. So, for example, suppose the crime rate in a given year is 3,500. This means that, for every 100,000 inhabitants of the United States, 3,500 *Part I offenses* (explained on the facing page) were reported to the FBI by local police departments. The crime rate is often cited by media sources when discussing the level of crime in the United States.
2. As a *percentage* change from the previous year or other time periods. From 2000 to 2010, there was a 20.2 percent decrease in violent crime and an 18.7 percent decrease in property crime. Thus, according to the UCR, the first decade of the twenty-first century saw a significant reduction in criminal behavior in the United States.[18]

The Department of Justice publishes its data annually in *Crime in the United States.* Along with the basic statistics, this publication offers an exhaustive array of crime information, including breakdowns of crimes committed by city, county, and other geographic designations and by the demographics (gender, race, age) of the individuals who have been arrested for crimes.

Uniform Crime Report (UCR)
An annual report compiled by the FBI to give an indication of criminal activity in the United States.

Part I Offenses

The UCR divides the criminal offenses it measures into two major categories: Part I and Part II offenses. **Part I offenses** are those crimes that, due to their seriousness and frequency, are recorded by the FBI to give a general idea of the "crime picture" in the United States in any given year. For a description of the seven Part I offenses, see Figure 3.2 below.

Part I violent offenses are those most likely to be covered by the media and, consequently, inspire the most fear of crime in the population. These crimes have come to dominate crime coverage to such an extent that, for most Americans, the first image that comes to mind at the mention of "crime" is one person physically attacking another person or a robbery taking place with the use or threat of force.[19] Furthermore, in the stereotypical crime, the offender and the victim usually do not know each other.

Given the trauma of violent crimes, this perception is understandable, but it is not accurate. According to UCR statistics, a relative or other acquaintance of the victim commits at least 44 percent of the homicides in the United States.[20] Furthermore, as is evident from Figure 3.2, the majority of Part I offenses committed are property crimes. Notice that 60 percent of all reported Part I offenses are larceny/thefts, and another 21 percent are burglaries.[21]

Part II Offenses

Not only do violent crimes represent the minority of Part I offenses, but Part I offenses are far outweighed by **Part II offenses,** which include all crimes recorded by the FBI that do not fall into the category of Part I offenses. While Part I offenses are almost always felonies, Part II offenses include criminal behavior that is often classified as a misdemeanor.

Part I Offenses Crimes reported annually by the FBI in its Uniform Crime Report. Part I offenses include murder, rape, robbery, aggravated assault, burglary, larceny, and motor vehicle theft.

Part II Offenses All crimes recorded by the FBI that do not fall into the category of Part I offenses. These crimes include both misdemeanors and felonies.

FIGURE 3.2 **Part I Offenses**

Every month local law enforcement agencies voluntarily provide information on serious offenses in their jurisdiction to the FBI. These serious offenses, known as Part I offenses, are defined here. (Arson is not included in the national crime report data, but it is sometimes considered a Part I offense nonetheless, so its definition is included here.) As the graph shows, most Part I offenses reported by local police departments in any given year are property crimes.

Murder. The willful (nonnegligent) killing of one human being by another.

Forcible rape. The carnal knowledge of a female forcibly and against her will.*

Robbery. The taking or attempting to take of anything of value from the care, custody, or control of a person or persons by force or threat of force or violence and/or by putting the victim in fear.

Aggravated assault. An unlawful attack by one person on another for the purpose of inflicting severe or aggravated bodily injury. This type of assault is usually accompanied by the use of a weapon or by means likely to produce death or great bodily harm.

Burglary—breaking or entering. The unlawful entry of a structure to commit a felony or a theft. Attempted forcible entry is included.

Larceny/theft (except motor vehicle theft). The unlawful taking, carrying, leading, or riding away of property from the possession or constructive possession of another.

Motor vehicle theft. The theft or attempted theft of a motor vehicle.

Arson. Any willful or malicious burning or attempt to burn, with or without intent to defraud, a dwelling house, public building, motor vehicle or aircraft, personal property of another, and the like.

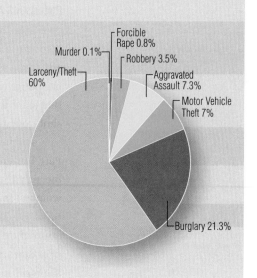

*The new definition of rape, as indicated in the opening to this chapter, had not yet gone into effect for these data.

Sources: Federal Bureau of Investigation, *Crime in the United States, 2011* (Washington, D.C.: U.S. Department of Justice, 2012), at **www.fbi.gov/about-us/cjis/ucr/crime-in-the-u.s/2011/crime-in-the-u.s.-2011/offense-definitions** and **www.fbi.gov/about-us/cjis/ucr/crime-in-the-u.s/2011/crime-in-the-u.s.-2011/tables/table-1**.

Of the nineteen categories that make up Part II offenses, the most common are drug abuse violations, simple assaults (in which no weapons are used and no serious harm is done to the victim), driving under the influence, and disorderly conduct.[22]

Information gathered on Part I offenses reflects those offenses "known," or reported to the FBI by local agencies. Part II offenses, in contrast, are measured only by arrest data. In 2011, the FBI recorded about 2.1 million arrests for Part I offenses in the United States. That same year, about 10.2 million arrests for Part II offenses took place.[23] In other words, a Part II offense was five times more common than a Part I offense. Such statistics have prompted Marcus Felson, a professor at Rutgers University School of Criminal Justice, to comment that "most crime is very ordinary."[24]

The UCR: A Flawed Method?

Even though the UCR is the predominant source of crime data in the country, there are numerous questions about the accuracy of its findings. For one, there is scattered evidence that some local police departments manipulate their crime reports. In a recent anonymous survey of nearly two thousand retired New York City police officers, more than 80 percent reported instances in which the severity of offenses was downgraded for statistical purposes.[25] Furthermore, the UCR most likely suffers from the twin problems of underreporting and inconsistency.

POLICE NOTIFICATION For the UCR to be accurate, citizens must report criminal activity to the police, and the police must then pass this information on to the FBI. Criminologists have long been aware that neither citizens nor police can be expected to perform these roles with consistency.[26] Citizens may not report a crime for any number of reasons, including fear of reprisal, embarrassment, or a personal bias in favor of the offender. Many also feel that police cannot do anything to help them in the aftermath of a crime, so they do not see the point of involving law enforcement agents in their lives. Surveys of crime victims reveal that only 49 percent of violent crimes and 37 percent of property crimes are reported to the police.[27] In general, people seem more willing to notify police about robberies and aggravated assaults by strangers than about rapes or violence that occurs within the family context.[28]

PROBLEMS WITH DISCRETION AND DEFINITIONS Local police departments have a great deal of discretion in interpreting what constitutes a Part I offense, which can lead to inconsistencies. In Illinois, for example, if one person strikes another person but does not cause any harm, the offender is usually charged with a misdemeanor. If the victim is a police officer or a teacher, however, the misdemeanor becomes felony assault. So, in that state, an incident in which a teacher's finger is scratched and one where a victim is shot nonfatally could both be reported to the FBI as "aggravated assaults."[29]

Furthermore, the FBI and local law enforcement agencies do not always interpret Part I offenses in the same manner. As we saw in the opening of this chapter, until recently the FBI employed a very narrow definition of rape: "carnal knowledge" of a woman "forcibly and against her will." Many local agencies would define the crime more loosely, including any nonconsensual act of a sexual nature as a rape. This situation often forced employees at local police departments to sift through yearly reports of sexual assaults and discard those that did not match the FBI's definition. Sometimes, the resulting discrepancies could be dramatic. In 2010, for example, the Chicago Police Department investigated nearly 1,400 sexual assaults, yet did not report a single one to the FBI for inclusion in the UCR because of differences in agency definitions.[30]

The National Incident-Based Reporting System

In the 1980s, well aware of the various criticisms of the UCR, the Department of Justice began seeking ways to revise its data-collecting system. The result was the National Incident-Based Reporting System (NIBRS). In the NIBRS, local agencies collect data on each single crime occurrence within twenty-two offense categories made up of forty-six specific crimes called Group A offenses. These data are recorded on computerized record systems provided—though not completely financed—by the federal government.

The NIBRS became available to local agencies in 1989. Twenty-four years later, thirty-six states have been NIBRS certified, with about 40 percent of the agencies in those states using the updated system.[31] Even in its limited form, however, criminologists have responded enthusiastically to the NIBRS because the system provides information about four "data sets"—offenses, victims, offenders, and arrestees—unavailable through the UCR. The NIBRS also presents a more complete picture of crime by monitoring all criminal "incidents" reported to the police, not just those that lead to an arrest.[32] Furthermore, because jurisdictions involved with the NIBRS must identify bias motivations of offenders, the procedure is very useful in studying hate crimes, a topic we will address in the next chapter. (See Figure 3.3 below to get a clearer sense of the differences between the UCR and the NIBRS.)

Victim Surveys

One alternative method of data collecting attempts to avoid the distorting influence of the "intermediary," or the local police agencies. In **victim surveys,** criminologists or other researchers ask the victims of crime directly about their experiences, using techniques such as interviews or e-mail and phone surveys. The first large-scale victim survey took place in 1966, when members of 10,000 households answered questionnaires as part of the President's Commission on Law Enforcement and the Administration of Justice. The results indicated a much higher victimization rate than had been previously expected, and researchers felt the process gave them a better understanding of the **dark figure of crime,** or the actual amount of crime that occurs in the country.

Victim Surveys A method of gathering crime data that directly surveys participants to determine their experiences as victims of crime.

Dark Figure of Crime A term used to describe the actual amount of crime that takes place. The "figure" is "dark," or impossible to detect, because a great number of crimes are never reported to the police.

FIGURE 3.3 Comparing the UCR and the NIBRS

As the following scenario shows, the process of crime data collection under the NIBRS is much more comprehensive that the reporting system of the UCR.

At approximately 9:30 p.m. on March 22, 2013, two young males approach a thirty-two-year-old African American woman in the parking garage of a movie theater. The first man, who is white, puts a knife to the woman's throat and grabs her purse, which contains $150. The second man, who is Hispanic, then puts a gun to the woman's temple and rapes her. When he is finished, he shoots her in the chest, a wound that does not prove to be fatal. The two men flee the scene and are not apprehended by law enforcement.

	UCR	NIBRS
Crime reported to FBI	One rape. Under the UCR, when more than one crime is involved in a single incident, only the most serious is reported. Also, attempts are not recorded.	One rape, one robbery, and one attempted murder.
Age, sex, and race of the victim	Not recorded.	Recorded.
Age, sex, and race of the offenders	Not recorded.	Recorded.
Location and time of the attack	Not recorded.	Recorded.
Type and value of lost property	Not recorded.	Recorded.

Source: U.S. Department of Justice.

THE NATIONAL CRIME VICTIMIZATION SURVEY Criminologists were so encouraged by the results of the 1966 experiment that the federal government decided to institute an ongoing victim survey. The result was the National Crime Victimization Survey (NCVS), which started in 1972. Conducted by the U.S. Bureau of the Census in cooperation with the Bureau of Justice Statistics of the Justice Department, the NCVS conducts an annual survey of nearly 80,000 households with about 143,000 occupants over twelve years of age. Participants are interviewed twice a year concerning their experiences with crimes in the prior six months. As you can see in Figure 3.4 below, questions are quite detailed in determining the experiences of crime victims.

ADVANTAGES AND DISADVANTAGES Proponents of the NCVS highlight a number of aspects in which the victim survey is superior to the UCR:

1. It measures both reported and unreported crime.
2. It is unaffected by police bias and distortions in reporting crime to the FBI.
3. It does not rely on victims directly reporting crime to the police.[33]

As we shall discuss further in the next section, one of the most celebrated aspects of victim surveys is that they give the victim a voice in the criminal justice system. This "voice" was certainly heard in the debate over rape definitions and statistics that we have mentioned several times in this chapter. In 2011, the NCVS reported about 243,000 sexual assaults, compared with the nearly 83,500 incidents of "forcible rape" indicated by the UCR.[34] Authors of another recent victim survey—defining the crime as "forced penetration" or "attempted forced penetration"—estimate that as many as 1.3 million American women are raped each year.[35] These comparisons provided a measure of proof that the FBI was underreporting rape in its annual publication.

In the past, the NCVS has been criticized for the use of confusing, technical jargon in its questions. As is clear from Figure 3.4 below, efforts have been made to simplify the survey's language so that it is more easily understood. Another problem with any victim

FIGURE 3.4 Sample Questions from the NCVS (National Crime Victimization Survey)

31a. What were the injuries you suffered, if any?
a. None
b. Raped
c. Attempted rape
d. Sexual assault other than rape or attempted rape
e. Knife or stab wounds
f. Gun shot, bullet wounds
g. Broken bones or teeth knocked out
h. Internal injuries
i. Knocked unconscious
j. Bruises, black eye, cuts, scratches, swelling, chipped teeth

37. Still thinking about your distress associated with being a victim of this crime, did you feel any of the following ways for A MONTH OR MORE?
a. Worried or anxious?
b. Angry?
c. Sad or depressed?
d. Vulnerable?
e. Violated?
f. Like you couldn't trust people?
g. Unsafe?

63. How old would you say the offender was?
a. Under 12
b. 12–14
c. 15–17
d. 18–20
e. 21–29
f. 30 or older
g. Don't know

78a. Were any of the offenders a member of a street gang?
a. Yes.
b. No.
c. Don't know.

78b. Were any of the offenders drinking or on drugs?
a. Yes
b. No.
c. Don't know.

104b. What was the value of the PROPERTY that was taken?
a. $ _____.

Source: Adapted from U.S. Department of Justice, *National Crime Victimization Survey 2009* (Washington, D.C.: Bureau of Justice Statistics, 2011).

survey is that the responses cannot be verified. If a participant, for whatever reason, fails to answer truthfully, the faulty response is recorded as fact.[36]

Self-Reported Surveys

Based on many of the same principles as victim surveys, but focusing instead on offenders, **self-reported surveys** are a third source of data for criminologists. In this form of data collection, persons are asked directly—through personal interviews or questionnaires, or over the telephone—about specific criminal activity to which they may have been a party. Self-reported surveys are most useful in situations in which the group to be studied is already gathered in an institutional setting, such as a juvenile facility or a prison. One of the most widespread self-reported surveys in the United States, the Drug Use Forecasting Program, collects information on narcotics use from arrestees who have been brought into booking facilities.

Because there is no penalty for admitting to criminal activity in a self-reported survey, subjects tend to be more forthcoming in discussing their behavior. Researchers interviewing a group of male students at a state university, for example, found that a significant number of them admitted to committing minor crimes for which they had never been arrested.[37] This fact points to the most striking finding of self-reported surveys: the dark figure of crime, referred to earlier as the *actual* amount of crime that takes place, appears to be much larger than the UCR or NCVS would suggest.

SELF ASSESSMENT

Fill in the blanks and check your answers on page 93.

To produce its annual _____ _____ _____ , the FBI relies on the cooperation of local law enforcement agencies. _____ surveys rely on those who have been the subject of criminal activity to discuss the incidents with researchers, while _____- _____ surveys ask participants to detail their own criminal behavior. These two methods show that the _____ _____ of crime, or the actual amount of crime that takes place in this country, is much _____ than official crime data would suggest.

VICTIMS OF CRIME

It is no coincidence that the U.S. Department of Justice launched the first version of the National Crime Victimization Survey in the 1970s. The previous decade had seen a dramatic increase in the rights afforded to criminal defendants. To offset what they saw as a growing imbalance in the American criminal justice system, advocates began to argue that crime victims also needed greater protection under the law. Initially, the victims' rights movement focused on specific areas of crime, such as domestic violence, sexual assault, and, through the efforts of Mothers Against Drunk Driving, vehicular homicide.[38] Today, an emphasis on the rights of all crime victims has a profound impact on the workings of law enforcement, courts, and corrections in the United States.

Self-Reported Survey A method of gathering crime data that relies on participants to reveal and detail their own criminal or delinquent behavior.

LEARNING
4
OBJECTIVE
Distinguish between the National Crime Victimization Survey (NCVS) and self-reported surveys.

In May 2012, family members of murder victim Martin Caballero address a criminal court in Mays Landing, New Jersey. Should crime victims and their families have the "right" to participate in the criminal justice system? Why or why not?
AP Photo/*Press of Atlantic City*, Danny Drake

Legal Rights of Crime Victims

Thirty years ago, a presidential task force invited federal and state legislatures to "address the needs of the millions of Americans and their families who are victimized by crime every year and who often carry its scars into the years to come."[39] This call to action was, in large part, a consequence of the rather peculiar position of victims in our criminal justice system. That is, once a crime has occurred, the victim is relegated to a single role: being a witness against the suspect in court. Legally, he or she has no say in the prosecution of the offender, or even whether such a prosecution is to take place. Such powerlessness can be extremely frustrating, particularly in the wake of a traumatic, life-changing event.

Describe the three ways that victims' rights legislation increases the ability of crime victims to participate in the criminal justice system.

LEARNING

5

OBJECTIVE

LEGISLATIVE ACTION To remedy this situation, all states have passed legislation creating certain rights for victims. On a federal level, such protections are encoded in the Crime Victims' Rights Act of 2004 (CVRA), which gives victims "the right to participate in the system."[40] This participation primarily focuses on three categories of rights:

1. The right to be *informed*. This includes receiving information about victims' rights in general, as well as specific information such as the dates and time of court proceedings relating to the relevant crime.
2. The right to be *present*. This includes the right to be present at those court hearings involving the case at hand, as long as the victim's presence does not interfere with the rights of the accused.
3. The right to be *heard*. This includes the ability to consult with prosecutorial officials before the criminal trial (addressed in Chapter 9), to speak during the sentencing phase of the trial (Chapter 11), and to offer an opinion when the offender is scheduled to be released from incarceration (Chapter 12).[41]

Some jurisdictions also provide victims with the right of law enforcement protection from the offender during the time period before a criminal trial. In addition, most states require *restitution,* or monetary payment, from offenders to help victims repay any costs associated with the crime and rebuild their lives. One victim of child pornography has collected restitution totaling $1.6 million from more than 150 men who viewed or sold her image illegally.[42] (To learn about one potential downside of the victims' rights movement, see the feature *A Question of Ethics—With a Vengeance* on the facing page.)

ENFORCEABILITY Although many victims have benefited from the legislation described above, advocates still find fault with the manner in which the legislation is applied. The main problem, they say, is that the federal and state laws do not contain sufficient enforcement mechanisms. That is, if a victim's rights are violated in some way, the victim has little recourse.

For example, in 2005 a dangerous gas leak led to an explosion that killed fifteen people and injured dozens of others in Texas City, Texas. Without conferring with the victims, federal prosecutors decided not to press any criminal charges against the oil company responsible for the accident. A federal judge dismissed the victims' claim that their rights had been breached by the government, because, under the CVRA, prosecutors have discretionary powers in this area of the law.[43] Indeed, almost all victims' rights legislation gives criminal justice officials the discretion to deny such rights. Consequently, according to one observer, victims' rights are often more illusion than reality.[44]

Victim Services

The consequences for crime victims go well beyond frustrations with the criminal justice system. Many feel some degree of anger, guilt, shame, and grief. In particular, victims of violent crimes are at a high risk of post-traumatic stress disorder (PTSD), a condition that burdens sufferers with extreme anxiety and flashbacks relating to the traumatic event. Crime victims also experience higher-than-normal levels of depression, drug abuse, and suicidal tendencies.[45]

In addition to the emotional support of family and friends, a number of victim services exist to help with these symptoms of victimization. Hundreds of *crisis intervention* centers operate around the country, providing a wide range of aid. For example, the Donald W. Reynolds Crisis Intervention Center in Fort Smith, Arkansas, offers counseling, shelter, and relocation guidance to victims of domestic violence and sexual assault. These centers also allow for contact with *victim advocates,* or individuals that help victims gain access to public benefits, health care, employment and educational assistance, and numerous other services. The impact of such programs is, however, somewhat limited. Only about 9 percent of victims of violent crimes avail themselves of victim service agencies.[46]

SOCIAL MEDIA & CJ

The National Center for Victims of Crime supports victims' rights and provides training for victim advocates. To learn more, go to their Web page and click on the Facebook icon.

Ankomando/Shutterstock.com

The Risks of Victimization

Anybody can be a victim of crime. This does not mean, however, that everybody is at an equal risk of being victimized. In the previous chapter, for instance, we noted that residents of neighborhoods with heavy concentrations of payday lending businesses

---

A QUESTION OF ETHICS: With a Vengeance

LEARNING **6** OBJECTIVE Discuss one major concern regarding victim participation in the criminal justice process.

THE SITUATION During the recent trial of her son's murderer in San Mateo, California, Adriana Frias looked in the eyes of the defendant and said, "I hope that you die of sadness." Her husband Moises then told the judge, "These type of people should never be allowed to get out of jail. Let them rot there."

THE ETHICAL DILEMMA Such feelings are understandable, but they cause a certain amount of distrust regarding the victims' rights movement's impact on our criminal justice system. In most cases, victims cannot be expected to be objective or impartial. A victim would never, for example, be allowed to sit on a jury. Indeed, some worry that increasing the legal rights of victims creates an imbalance in our criminal justice system. According to one expert, this trends forces "prosecutors and judges [to] elevate victims over the defendant and the public" and "may threaten the fair and just adjudication of a crime case."

WHAT IS THE SOLUTION? Does the concept of revenge have a place in the American criminal justice system? Most observers would assert strongly that it does not. Ideally, criminal justice professionals have an ethical obligation to be fair, objective, and impartial, and to avoid the desire to inflict harm on a criminal for reasons of vengeance, no matter how heinous the crime. What about victims of crime?

During the colonial period of the 1600s, crime victims played a dominant role in the American criminal justice system. A victim would hire a sheriff to pursue and arrest the defendant, and pay court officials to run the trial. What are the disadvantages of such as system for society? Are there any advantages?

Manfredxy/Shutterstock.com

Repeat Victimization
The theory that certain people and places are more likely to be subject to repeated criminal activity and that past victimization is a strong indicator of future victimization.

are targeted by criminals at unusually high rates.[47] To better explain the circumstances surrounding this type of victimization, criminologists Larry Cohen and Marcus Felson devised the *routine activities theory*. According to Cohen and Felson, most criminal acts require the following:

1. A likely offender.
2. A suitable target (a person or an object).
3. The absence of a capable guardian—that is, any person (not necessarily a law enforcement agent) whose presence or proximity prevents a crime from happening.[48]

When these three factors are present, the likelihood of crime rises. Cohen and Felson cite routine activities theory in explaining the link between payday lenders and crime. People who use payday lenders often leave those establishments with large sums of cash, late at night or during weekends when there is less street traffic. Consequently, they act as suitable targets, attracting likely offenders to neighborhoods where the payday lenders are located.[49]

REPEAT VICTIMIZATION Cohen and Felson also hypothesize that offenders attach "values" to suitable targets. The higher the value, the more likely that target is going to be the subject of a crime.[50] A gold watch, for example, would obviously have a higher value for a thief than a plastic watch and therefore is more likely to be stolen. Similarly, people who are perceived to be weak or unprotected can have high value for criminals. Law enforcement officials in southern Florida, for example, believe that undocumented immigrants in the area have high victimization rates because criminals know they are afraid to report crimes to authorities for fear of being removed from the country.

Resources such as the National Crime Victimization Survey provide criminologists with an important tool for determining which types of people are most valued as potential victims. Statistics clearly show that a relatively small number of victims are involved in a disproportionate number of crimes. These findings support an approach to crime analysis known as **repeat victimization.** This theory is based on the premise that certain populations—mostly low-income resident of urban areas—are more likely to be victims of crimes than others and, therefore, past victimization is a strong predictor of future victimization.[51]

THE VICTIM-OFFENDER CONNECTION Not only does past victimization seem to increase the risk of future victimization, but so does past criminal behavior. In New Orleans, for example, 64 percent of homicide victims have previously been arrested for a felony. In Milwaukee, the number is even higher, at 75 percent.[52] "The notion that [violent crimes] are random bolts of lightning, which is the commonly held image, is not the reality at all," says David Kennedy, a professor at New York's John Jay College of Criminal Justice.[53]

Kennedy's point is further made by Figure 3.5 on the left, which identifies young African American males from urban neighborhoods as the most common victims of crimes. This demographic, as will become clear later in the chapter, is also at the highest risk for criminal

FIGURE 3.5 Crime Victims in the United States

According to the U.S. Department of Justice, African Americans, residents of urban areas, and people between the ages of eighteen and twenty-four are most likely to be victims of violent crime in this country.

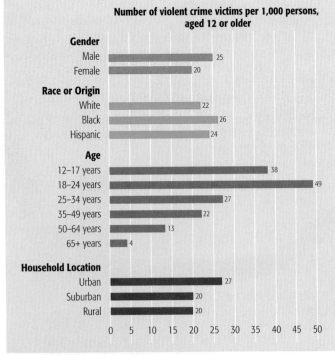

Source: Bureau of Justice Statistics, *Criminal Victimization, 2011* (Washington, D.C.: U.S. Department of Justice, October 2012), 5, 6.

behavior. Increasingly, law enforcement agencies are applying the lessons of repeat victimization and other victim studies to concentrate their attention on "hot spots" of crime, a strategy we address in Chapter 6.

SELF ASSESSMENT

Fill in the blanks and check your answers on page 93.

Historically, crime victims have been relegated to the role of being a _____ to the crime. Victims' rights legislation attempts to increase victim participation in the criminal justice system by giving victims the right to be _____, _____, and _____. The _____ _____ theory predicts that a combination of factors concerning a victim's environment make that victim more susceptible to crime. The theory of _____ victimization holds that past victimization is a strong predictor of future victimization.

CRIME TRENDS IN THE UNITED STATES

The UCR, NCVS, and other statistical measures we have discussed so far in this chapter, though important, represent only the tip of the iceberg of crime data. Thanks to the efforts of government law enforcement agencies, educational institutions, and private individuals, more information on crime is available today than at any time in the nation's history. When interpreting and predicting general crime trends, experts tend to rely on what University of California at Berkeley law professor Franklin Zimring calls the three "usual suspects" of crime fluctuation:

LEARNING **7** OBJECTIVE

Identify the three factors most often used by criminologists to explain changes in the nation's crime rate.

1. *Imprisonment,* based on the principle that (a) an offender in prison or jail is unable to commit a crime on the street, and (b) a potential offender on the street will not commit a crime because he or she does not want to wind up behind bars.
2. *Youth populations,* because offenders commit fewer crimes as they grow older.
3. The *economy,* because when legitimate opportunities to earn income become scarce, some people will turn to illegitimate methods such as crime.[54]

Pure statistics do not always tell the whole story, however, and crime rates often fail to behave in the ways that the experts predict.

Looking Good: Crime in the 1990s and 2000s

In 1995, eminent crime expert James Q. Wilson, noting that the number of young males was set to increase dramatically over the next decade, predicted that "30,000 more young muggers, killers, and thieves" would be on the streets by 2000. "Get ready," he warned.[55] Other criminologists offered their own dire projections. John DiIulio foresaw a swarm of "juvenile super-predators" on the streets,[56] and James A. Fox prophesied a "blood bath" by 2005.[57] Given previous data, these experts could be fairly confident in their predictions. Fortunately for the country, they were wrong. As is evident from Figure 3.6 on the following page, starting in 1994 the United States experienced a steep crime decline that we are still enjoying today.

THE GREAT CRIME DECLINE The crime statistics of the 1990s are startling. Even with the upswing at the beginning of the decade, from 1990 to 2000 the homicide rate dropped 39 percent, the robbery rate 44 percent, the burglary rate 41 percent, and the auto theft rate 37 percent. By most measures, this decline was the longest and deepest of the twentieth century.[58] In retrospect, the 1990s seem to have encompassed a "golden era" for the

FIGURE 3.6 Violent Crime in the United States, 1990–2011

According to statistics gathered each year by the FBI, American violent crime rates dropped steadily in the second half of the 1990s, leveled off for several years, and now have begun to decrease anew.

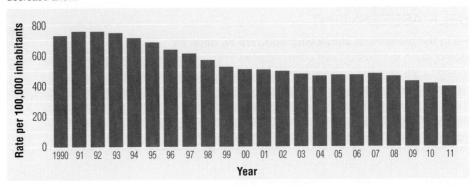

Source: Federal Bureau of Investigation.

leading indicators of low crime rates. The economy was robust. The incarceration rate was skyrocketing. Plus, despite the misgivings of James Q. Wilson and many of his colleagues, the percentage of the population in the high-risk age bracket in 1995 was actually lower than it had been in 1980.[59]

Several other factors also seemed to favor lower crime rates. Police tactics, many of which we will discuss in Chapter 6, became more effective—thanks in no small part to "zero-tolerance" policies inspired by Wilson's writings. Furthermore, many of those most heavily involved in a crack cocaine boom that shook the nation in the late 1980s had been killed or imprisoned, or were no longer offending. Without their criminal activity, the United States became a much safer place.[60]

CONTINUING DECREASES In the early years of the 2000s, the nation's crime rate flattened for a time before resuming its downward trend. By 2011, property crime rates had dropped for the eighth straight year, and violent crime rates had shrunk to their lowest levels since the early 1970s. Given that, in recent years, the economy has been mired in a recession, with unemployment running at unusually high levels, the positive crime figures have come as something of a surprise.

Gary LaFree, a criminology professor at the University of Maryland, calls this trend "fascinating," because "we'd normally expect crime to go up when we are in an economic downturn."[61] Again, as in the 1990s, law enforcement is receiving much of the credit for the good news, particularly information-based policing techniques that use computer programs to focus crime prevention tactics on "hot spots" of criminal activity. In addition, LaFree points out, the median age in the United States is around thirty-seven years, the highest of any time in the nation's history.[62] As noted earlier, older people tend to commit fewer crimes than younger ones.

THE IMMEDIATE FUTURE Not all of the experts are confident that crime rates will continue to decline. To alleviate financial pressures on strained budgets, local governments are reducing their police forces, and, as we will see in Chapter 13, states are releasing prisoners. Both strategies could have negative consequences for crime in the United States.[63] In 2012, certain cities such as Chicago, Detroit, and Los Angeles saw murder rates increase. Furthermore, in a relatively rare divergence from the UCR, the 2011 NCVS reported a rise in violent crime of 17 percent and a rise in property crime of 11 percent. Although many criminologists labeled this disparity either a "one-year fluctuation" or statistically insignificant, others—aware of the advantages of victim surveys we discussed earlier in the chapter—worry that it could signal the beginning of an upward shift in crime rates.[64]

Crime, Race, and Poverty

One group has noticeably failed to benefit from the positive crime trends of the past fifteen years: young African American males. According to data compiled by Alexia Cooper and Erica L. Smith of the Bureau of Justice Statistics, black males between the ages of fourteen and twenty-four, who represent 1 percent of the country's total population, make up a quarter of its homicide offenders and 16 percent of its homicide victims.[65] Overall, since 2000, while the total number of murders in the United States has dropped by 5 percent, the number of male black victims has increased by more than 10 percent.[66] In the cities with rising murder rates mentioned above, a large part of the violence is taking place within the African American community—nationwide, most murder victims are killed by someone of the same race (93 percent for blacks, 85 percent for whites).[67]

By some measures, black citizens are twice as likely as whites to live in poverty and hold low-wage jobs. What is your opinion of the theory that economic disadvantage, rather than skin color, accounts for the disproportionate number of African Americans in U.S. prisons, such as these inmates at Florida's Dade County Correctional Facility? Joe Sohm/Visions of America/Newscom

RACE AND CRIME Homicide rates are not the only area in which there is a divergence in crime trends between the races. Official crime data seem to indicate a strong correlation between minority status and crime: African Americans—who make up 13 percent of the population—constitute 38 percent of those arrested for violent crimes and 30 percent of those arrested for property crimes.[68] A black man is almost twelve times more likely than a white man to be sent to prison for a drug-related conviction, while black women are about five times more likely than white women to be incarcerated for a drug offense.[69] (See the feature *Myth versus Reality—Race Stereotyping and Drug Crime* on the following page.) Furthermore, a black juvenile in the United States is nearly three times more likely than a white juvenile to wind up in delinquency court.[70]

CLASS AND CRIME The racial differences in the crime rate are one of the most controversial areas of the criminal justice system. At first glance, crime statistics seem to support the idea that the subculture of African Americans in the United States is disposed toward criminal behavior. Not all of the data, however, support that assertion. A recent research project led by sociologist Ruth D. Peterson of Ohio State University gathered information on nearly 150 neighborhoods in Columbus, Ohio. Peterson and her colleagues separated the neighborhoods based on race and on levels of disadvantage such as poverty, joblessness, lack of college graduates, and high levels of female-headed families. She found that whether the neighborhoods were predominantly white or predominantly black had little impact on violent crime rates. Those neighborhoods with higher levels of disadvantage, however, had uniformly higher violent crime rates.[71]

LEARNING **8** OBJECTIVE Explain why income level appears to be more important than race or ethnicity when it comes to crime trends.

Income Level and Crime Peterson's research suggests that, regardless of race, a person is at a much higher risk of violent offending or being a victim of violence if he or she lives in

Race Stereotyping and Drug Crime

Crack cocaine–related violence spread like wildfire through the nation's inner cities in the 1980s. In response, then president Ronald Reagan vowed to escalate the "war on drugs." As a consequence, law enforcement efforts focused on arresting and incarcerating the wrongdoers in those communities, most of whom were African American. Even though this urban violence has largely subsided, the tactics continue: every year between 1980 and 2010, blacks were arrested on drug charges at rates between 2.8 and 5.5 times higher than whites. Today, even though African Americans make up about 13 percent of the U.S. population, they represent more than 50 percent of sentenced drug offenders.

THE MYTH African Americans are sent to prison for drug crimes in greater numbers than whites because more of them buy, sell, and use drugs.

THE REALITY The use of illegal drugs by blacks and whites in the United States is roughly equal. According to data gathered by the federal government, about 10.7 percent of African Americans and about 9.1 percent of whites admit to using drugs within the previous month. A recently released study conducted by Duke University researchers showed that black adolescents are only about half as likely as their white counterparts to become dependent on illegal drugs and alcohol.

These figures are not reflected in criminal justice trends. African Americans who use drugs are arrested at about three times the rate of whites who use drugs. Furthermore, although blacks account for only 28 percent of all drug arrests, they represent 49 percent of those convicted of drug crimes and 44 percent of all Americans sentenced for drug crimes. Finally, more than four out of every five drug arrests are for possession of the banned substance, not for its sale or manufacture. Thus, the racial disparity in arrests cannot be due to a large class of African American drug dealers.

Although these statistics leave the criminal justice system open to charges of institutionalized racism, the disparities are possibly the result of practical considerations. Several years ago, criminologists Robin Engel, Michael Smith, and Francis Cullen compared police deployment patterns and drug arrests in Seattle. They found that, as police presence is necessarily greater in crime-prone areas, the numbers of drug arrests in those areas were higher than normal. Because crime-prone areas have large concentrations of minority residents, that population is subject to greater law enforcement scrutiny. The authors concluded, therefore, that citizens' demand for protection played a much more significant role than possible police bias in the disproportionate drug arrest rates for African Americans in the city.

FOR CRITICAL ANALYSIS

Heather Mac Donald, a crime expert at the Manhattan Institute in New York, suggests that the racial disparities in the "war on drugs" make sense because the urban street trade often leads to violence and other crimes that harm inner-city communities. Drug use by whites, in contrast, generally takes place in suburban homes, hidden from view, without the same level of negative side effects. What is your opinion of Mac Donald's theory?

---

a disadvantaged neighborhood. Given that African Americans are two times more likely than whites to live in poverty and hold low-wage-earning jobs, they are, as a group, more susceptible to the factors that contribute to criminality.[72]

Indeed, a wealth of information suggests that income level is more important than skin color when it comes to crime trends. A 2002 study of nearly 900 African American children (400 boys and 467 girls) from neighborhoods with varying income levels showed that family earning power had the only significant correlation with violent behavior.[73] More recent research conducted by William A. Pridemore of Indiana University found a "positive and significant association" between poverty and homicide.[74] Lack of education, another handicap most often faced by low-income citizens, also seems to correlate with criminal behavior. Forty-one percent of all inmates in state and federal prisons failed to obtain a high school education, compared with 18 percent of the population at large.[75]

The Class-Crime Relationship The sociological theories of crime you studied in Chapter 2 predict that those without the financial means to acquire the consumer goods and services that dominate our society will turn to illegal methods to "steal" purchasing power. But, logic aside, many criminologists are skeptical of such an obvious class-crime relationship. After all, poverty does not *cause* crime. The majority of residents in low-income neighborhoods are law-abiding. Furthermore, self-reported surveys indicate that high-income citizens are involved in all sorts of criminal activities[76] and are far more likely to commit white-collar crimes, which are not included in national crime statistics. These facts tend to support the theory that high crime rates in low-income communities are at least partly the result of a greater willingness of police to arrest poor citizens and of the court system to convict them.

ETHNICITY AND CRIME Another point to remember when reviewing statistical studies of minority offenders and victims is that they tend to focus on race, which distinguishes groups based on physical characteristics such as skin color, rather than *ethnicity,* which denotes national or cultural background. Thus, the bulk of criminological research in this area has focused on the differences between European Americans and African Americans, both because the latter have been the largest minority group in the United States for most of its history and because the racial differences between the two groups are easily identifiable.

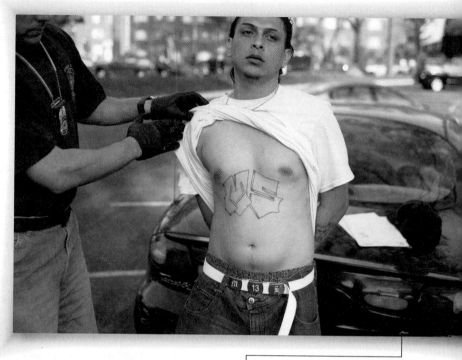

A member of Prince George's County's Anti-Gang Unit makes an arrest during a crackdown on Hispanic gangs in Langley Park, Maryland. Why is it likely that crime experts will increase their focus on issues of Hispanic offenders and victims in the United States over the next few decades?
Photo by Robert Nickelsberg/Getty Images

Americans of Hispanic descent have either been excluded from many crime studies or been linked with whites or blacks based on racial characteristics. Other minority groups, such as Asian Americans, Native Americans, and immigrants from the South Pacific or Eastern Europe, have been similarly underreported in crime studies.

This state of affairs will more than likely change in the near future. At present rates of growth, the Hispanic population will triple by 2050, when it will account for approximately one-third of the total U.S. population. Hispanics are also the fastest-growing minority group in the U.S. prison population.[77] Because of an increased emphasis on immigration law enforcement, more than half of the inmates in federal prisons in this country today are Hispanic.[78]

In fact, crime experts have already begun to focus on issues of Hispanic criminality. For example, Robert J. Sampson of Harvard University, examining the criminal behavior of more than 11,000 residents of 180 Chicago neighborhoods, found lower rates of violence among Mexican Americans than among either whites or blacks. Sampson and his colleagues theorize that strong social ties in immigrant populations create an environment that is incompatible with crime.[79]

Women and Crime

To put it bluntly, crime is an overwhelmingly male activity. More than 68 percent of all murders involve a male victim and a male perpetrator, and in only 2.2 percent of homicides are both the offender and the victim female.[80] Only 13 percent of the national jail population and 7 percent of the national prison population are female, and in 2011 only 26 percent of all arrests involved women.[81]

A GROWING PRESENCE The statistics cited above fail to convey the startling rate at which the female presence in the criminal justice system has been increasing. Between

1991 and 2011, the number of men arrested each year declined by approximately 90,000. Over that time period, annual arrests for women increased by almost 700,000.[82] In 1970, there were about 6,000 women in federal and state prisons, but today, there are more than 111,000.[83] There are two possible explanations for these increases. Either (1) the life circumstances and behavior of women have changed dramatically in the past forty years, or (2) the criminal justice system's attitude toward women has changed over that time period.[84]

In the 1970s, when female crime rates started surging upward, many observers accepted the former explanation. "You can't get involved in a bar fight if you're not allowed in the bar," said feminist theorist Freda Adler in 1975.[85] It has become clear, however, that a significant percentage of women arrested are involved in a narrow band of wrongdoing, mostly drug- and alcohol-related offenses or property crimes.[86] Research shows that as recently as the 1980s, many of the women now in prison would not have been arrested or would have received lighter sentences for their crimes.[87] Consequently, more scholars are convinced that rising female criminality is the result of a criminal justice system that is "more willing to incarcerate women."[88]

Discuss the prevailing explanation for the rising number of women incarcerated in the United States. LEARNING OBJECTIVE 9

WOMEN AS CRIME VICTIMS The most striking aspect of women as victims of crime is the extent to which such victimization involves a prior relationship. According to the National Crime Victimization Survey, a male is twice as likely as a female to experience violence at the hands of a stranger.[89] With regard to intimate partner violence—involving a spouse, ex-spouse, boyfriend, girlfriend, ex-boyfriend, or ex-girlfriend—the gender difference is even more pronounced. Women are about five times more likely then men to be victims of intimate partner violence.[90]

Common Crimes against Women In general, about six of every ten crimes in the United States are committed by someone known to the victim. Those crimes that usually involve strangers, such as robbery and assault, most often target male victims. In contrast, women have a greater chance of being victimized in nonstranger crimes, such as sexual assault.[91] Indeed, women are the victims in 86 percent of all intimate partner violence prosecutions.[92] The highest rate of victimization occurs among women between the ages of twelve and thirty-four, and one study estimates that between one-fifth and one-quarter of female college students have experienced a rape or attempted rape.[93]

Statistically, women are also at a greater risk of being victims of **domestic violence.** This umbrella term covers a wide variety of maltreatment, including physical violence and psychological abuse, inflicted among family members and others in close relationships. Though government data show that women are significantly more likely to be victims of domestic violence than men, these findings are not unquestioned. Men, many observers assume, are less likely to report abuse because of the social stigma surrounding female-on-male violence.[94] As you will see in the *Criminal Justice in Action* feature at the end of the chapter, domestic violence presents a number challenges for the criminal justice system.

A third crime that appears to mainly involve female victims is **stalking,** or a course of conduct directed at a person that would reasonably cause that person to feel fear. Such behavior includes unwanted phone calls, following or spying, and a wide range of online activity that we will address in Chapter 16. Stalkers target women at about three times the rate they target men, and seven out of ten stalking victims have had some prior relationship with their stalkers.[95]

Domestic Violence The act of willful neglect or physical violence that occurs within a familial or other intimate relationship.

Stalking The criminal act of causing fear in a person by repeatedly subjecting that person to unwanted or threatening attention.

Increased Exposure Previously, we noted that women's changing place in American society over the past four decades is believed to have contributed to climbing female arrest and incarceration numbers. Some criminologists contend that these changing circumstances are similarly responsible for a shift in female victimization characteristics. Since 1970, the number of women in the workplace has increased significantly, as has the participation of women in the political arena. As a result, women more commonly find themselves at work or other activities away from home that expose them to stranger violence.[96] And, indeed, although women are still at much less risk for stranger violence than men, the gap between the sexes has been steadily shrinking since at least the early 1990s.[97]

Mental Illness and Crime

After Eddie Ray Routh fatally shot two men at a gun range in Glen Rose, Texas, on February 2, 2013, his sister told police that Routh was "psychotic." She added that Routh said he "could smell the pigs" and "was going to get their souls before they took his."[98] Given that one of Routh's victims was Chris Kyle, a well-known Navy SEAL sniper, the incident received a great deal of attention, thus contributing to the public perception that "psychotics" pose a particular danger to society. The reality concerning mental illness and crime is much more nuanced and complex.

RISK FACTORS FOR VIOLENT CRIME In the context of the criminal justice system, the term *mental illness* covers a wide variety of symptoms, ranging from reoccurring depression and anger to hallucinations and schizophrenia (described in Chapter 2). It also indicates recent treatment from a mental health care practitioner. Government research indicates that, using this description, about 11 percent of Americans over the age of eighteen suffer from some form of mental illness.[99] Does this mean that 26 million adults in this country are at a high risk for violent behavior? Not necessarily.

Gun Control After Adam Lanza killed twenty children and six adults at an elementary school in Newtown, Connecticut, on December 14, 2012, many observers called for stricter laws to keep guns out of the hands of the mentally ill. Although Lanza had never been diagnosed with any specific mental illness, at least half a dozen states moved to revise their mental health laws to that effect. In New York, for example, the legislature passed a bill requiring mental health practitioners to report potentially dangerous clients to government gun control authorities.[100] Today, forty-four states regulate the sale of firearms to the mentally ill, and the federal government bars such sales to any person who is a "mental defective."[101]

Drug Abuse Critics say that the emphasis on the mentally ill in the gun control debate is unfair and inaccurate. Of the tens of thousand of gun deaths that occur in this country, few are caused by people with mental illness.[102] Furthermore, a 2006 study published in the *American Journal of Psychiatry* claimed that only 4 percent of violent crime in the United States can be attributed to people with a mental illness.[103] Although the possibility of violent behavior increases for those with serious conditions such as schizophrenia or bipolar disorder,[104] the most significant risk factor for the mentally ill is substance abuse. Between 80 and 90 percent of all mentally ill inmates in American prisons and jails are abusers of alcohol or other drugs.[105]

RISK FACTORS FOR VICTIMIZATION Those who suffer from mental illness are much more likely to be victims of crime than perpetrators. Such maladies often interfere with a person's ability to find and keep employment and therefore lead to poverty, which, we have seen, correlates with victimization. The mentally ill are also more likely to be homeless, a circumstance that leaves them particularly susceptible to crime.[106] In addition, mental illness can interfere with a person's ability to make prudent decisions in potentially dangerous situations, increasing her or his chances of being assaulted.[107]

A recent review of the subject found that rates of victimization among people with mental illnesses are up to 140 times higher than in the general population.[108] Mental health advocates insist that increasing services for America's mentally ill will reduce the harm they cause themselves and others, a subject we will explore more fully in Chapter 12.

SELF ASSESSMENT

Fill in the blanks and check your answers on page 93.

According to many experts, the three factors that most strongly affect national crime figures are the rate at which offenders are _____, the percentage of the population that is _____ the age of twenty-four, and the economy. Despite continued declining crime rates in the 2000s, young _____ _____ males continue to experience high levels of offending and victimization. Men are more likely than women to be victims of crimes committed by a _____. Despite public perception to the contrary, the _____ _____ are more likely to be victims of crime than offenders.

CJ IN ACTION

VICTIMS OF DOMESTIC VIOLENCE

First, Dale Jones slapped Shenera Norris, his girlfriend, and threatened her with a butcher knife. Then, he punched her in the face, leading to his arrest. Norris, however, pleaded with Baltimore officials not to press criminal charges against Jones. "Please let a loving father and a caring man free," she wrote. "He's all I have."[109] Without Norris's cooperation, prosecutors felt compelled to release Jones. Several months later, he stabbed her to death. Norris's murder underscores the often contradictory relationship between victims of domestic violence and the criminal justice system. In this chapter's *Criminal Justice in Action,* we address the debate surrounding one widespread method of dealing with a crime where the defendant and victim frequently live together.

NO-DROP POLICIES

Legally, crime victims are not the clients of public prosecutors. That is, as you will see in Chapter 9, prosecutors have the ultimate authority to decide when to bring a case to court, regardless of the victim's wishes. In practice, domestic violence cases unfold somewhat differently. Because the victim is usually the only witness to the violence, if she or he refuses to participate, such cases can be very difficult to prosecute successfully.[110] For a number of reasons, domestic violence victims such as Shenera Norris frequently choose not to side with law enforcement against their abusers. These reasons include fear of retaliation, financial dependence on the offender, issues of custody and child support, and complex emotional ties.[111]

Faced with uncooperative victims, prosecutors will consistently "drop" domestic violence cases. To remedy this situation, many jurisdictions in the United States have implemented "no-drop" policies. Such policies require prosecutors to carry through with a domestic violence case once an arrest has been made, even if this goes against the wishes of the victim. There is little question that no-drop policies increase the prosecution and conviction rates of domestic violence offenders.[112] The question is, do such policies actually benefit domestic violence victims?

THE CASE FOR NO-DROP POLICIES

- If a domestic violence victim decides to cooperate with law enforcement officials, she or he becomes more vulnerable to retaliatory attacks by the abuser. By taking this decision out of the victim's hands, no-drop policies promote victim safety.[113]

- Without no-drop policies, prosecutors dismiss 50 to 80 percent of all domestic violence charges. With such policies, dismissal rates fall to 10 to 35 percent. Therefore, no-drop policies show a commitment to treat domestic violence as a serious crime.[114]

- No-drop policies deter domestic violence by increasing the likelihood that offenders will be prosecuted and punished.

THE CASE AGAINST NO-DROP POLICIES

- No-drop policies send the paternalistic message that victims of domestic violence cannot make rational choices about themselves and their futures.[115]

- Domestic violence victims are in a better position than public officials to determine the risk of continued abuse. If a victim feels that prosecuting the abuser will only increase the likelihood of further violence, prosecutors should respect her or his decision to forgo such action.[116]

- Several studies show that no-drop policies increase the risk of victimization. This can be attributed to "separation assault," which is violence that occurs as retaliation after a victim is separated from her or his abuser. Such separation is a common result of no-drop policies.[117]

YOUR OPINION—WRITING ASSIGNMENT

No-drop policies certainly increase the chances that an offender will be convicted and punished. The policies do not, however, make the punishment more severe. Most domestic violence charges are misdemeanors, not felonies, and therefore offenders are usually sentenced to little or no jail time.[118] Does this leniency change your opinion of no-drop policies? Why or why not? Do you feel such policies properly balance the needs of society and the needs of domestic violence victims? Before responding, you can review our discussions in this chapter concerning:

- Felonies and misdemeanors (pages 70–71).

- Legal rights of victims (page 80).

- Women as crime victims (pages 88–89).

Your answer should include at least three full paragraphs.

CHAPTER SUMMARY

For more information on these concepts, look back to the Learning Objective icons throughout the chapter.

 Discuss the primary goals of civil law and criminal law and explain how these goals are realized. Civil law is designed to resolve disputes between private individuals and other entities such as corporations. In these disputes, one party, called the plaintiff, tries to gain monetary damages by proving that the accused party, or defendant, is to blame for a tort, or wrongful act. In contrast, criminal law exists to protect society from criminal behavior. To that end, the government prosecutes defendants, or persons who have been charged with committing a crime.

 Explain the differences between crimes *mala in se* and *mala prohibita*. A criminal act is *mala in se* if it is inherently wrong, while a criminal act *mala prohibita* is illegal only because it is prohibited by the laws of a particular society. It is sometimes difficult to distinguish between these two sorts of crimes because it is difficult to define a "pure" *mala in se* crime—that is, it is difficult to separate a crime from the culture that has deemed it a crime.

 Identify the publication in which the FBI reports crime data and list the two main ways in which the data are reported. Every year the FBI releases the Uniform Crime Report (UCR), in which it presents different crimes as (a) a rate per 100,000 people and (b) a percentage change from the previous year.

 Distinguish between the National Crime Victimization Survey (NCVS) and self-reported surveys. The NCVS involves an annual survey of more than 40,000 households conducted by the Bureau of the Census along with the Bureau of Justice Statistics. The survey queries citizens on crimes that have been committed against them. As such, the NCVS includes crimes not necessarily reported to police. Self-reported surveys, in contrast, involve asking individuals about criminal activity to which they may have been a party.

 Describe the three ways that victims' rights legislation increases the ability of crime victims to participate in the criminal justice system. (a) The right to be informed of victims' rights in general and of specific information relating to the relevant criminal case; (b) the right to be present at court proceedings involving the victim; and (c) the right to be heard on matters involving the prosecution, punishment, and release of the offender.

 Discuss one major concern regarding victim participation in the criminal justice process. Criminal justice professionals have an ethical obligation to be fair, objective, and impartial in their duties. Understandably, crime victims are usually not impartial toward an offender who has allegedly wronged them. Therefore, by allowing crime victims to participate, public officials allow a measure of partiality into criminal justice proceedings.

 Identify the three factors most often used by criminologists to explain changes in the nation's crime rate. (a) Levels of incarceration, because an offender behind bars cannot commit any additional crimes and the threat of imprisonment acts as a deterrent to criminal behavior; (b) the size of the youth population, because those under the age of twenty-four commit the majority of crimes in the United States; and (c) the health of the economy, because when income and employment levels fall, those most directly affected may turn to crime for financial gain.

 Explain why income level appears to be more important than race or ethnicity when it comes to crime trends. Criminologists have found that the most consistent indicators of criminal behavior are circumstances such as low family earning power and the absence of a parent. In addition, failure to obtain a high school diploma appears to have a positive correlation with criminal activity, regardless of the race or ethnicity of the individual. Finally, some believe that high arrest rates in low-income minority neighborhoods can be attributed to a willingness of police to arrest residents of these communities and of the court system to convict them.

 Discuss the prevailing explanation for the rising number of women incarcerated in the United States. Experts believe that many women are arrested and given harsh punishment for activity that would not have put them behind bars several decades ago. For the most part, this activity is nonviolent: the majority of female arrestees are involved in drug- and alcohol-related offenses and property crimes.

QUESTIONS FOR CRITICAL ANALYSIS

1. Give an example of how one person could be involved in a civil lawsuit and a criminal lawsuit for the same action.

2. Why is murder considered a *mala in se* crime? What argument can be made that murder is not a *mala in se* crime?

3. Assume that you are a criminologist who wants to determine the extent to which high school students engage in risky behavior such as abusing alcohol and illegal drugs, carrying weapons, and contemplating suicide. How would you go about gathering these data?

4. Research shows that female college students who have been the victim of rape or attempted rape are at an unusually high risk of repeat victimization if they engage in binge alcohol drinking. What victim services should colleges provide to reduce the chances that this group of victims will be revictimized?

5. Critics of laws that limit ownership of firearms for people with mental illness claim that these laws discourage such people from seeking treatment. Why would this be the case?

KEY TERMS

beyond a reasonable doubt   70
civil law   69
dark figure of crime   77
defendant   69
domestic violence   88
felony   70
illicit drugs   72
infraction   71

liability   69
licit drugs   72
mala in se   71
mala prohibita   71
misdemeanor   70
Part I offenses   75
Part II offenses   75

plaintiff   69
preponderance of the evidence   70
repeat victimization   82
self-reported survey   79
stalking   88
Uniform Crime Report (UCR)   74
victim surveys   77

SELF ASSESSMENT ANSWER KEY

Page 73: i. Civil; **ii.** state/government; **iii.** felony; **iv.** misdemeanor

Page 79: i. Uniform Crime Report; **ii.** Victim; **iii.** self-report; **iv.** dark figure; **v.** greater/larger

Page 83: i. witness; **ii.** informed; **iii.** present; **iv.** heard; **v.** routine activities; **vi.** repeat

Page 90: i. imprisoned/incarcerated; **ii.** under; **iii.** African American; **iv.** stranger; **v.** mentally ill

NOTES

1. Quoted in "Justice Department Redefines Rape," National Public Radio, January 6, 2012, transcript at **www.npr.org/2012/01/06/144801667 /justicedepartment-redefines-rape**.

2. *Federal Criminal Rules Handbook*, Section 2.1 (West 2008).

3. 625 Illinois Compiled Statutes Annotated Section 5/16-104 (West 2002).

4. Johannes Andenaes, "The Moral or Educative Influence of Criminal Law," *Journal of Social Issues* 27 (Spring 1971), 17, 26.

5. *Summary Health Statistics for U.S. Adults: National Health Interview Survey, 2011* (Hyattsville, MD: National Center for Health Statistics, December 2012), 36.

6. "Tylenol Top Dose Cut to Prevent Overdoses," *Chicago Sun Times* (July 30, 2011), 3.

7. National Highway Traffic Safety Administration, *2011 Motor Vehicle Crashes: Overview* (Washington, D.C.: U.S. Department of Transportation, December 2012), Table 3, page 2.

8. John Slade, "Health Consequences of Smoking: Nicotine Addiction," *Hearings before the Subcommittee on Health and the Environment of the House Committee on Energy and Commerce* (Washington, D.C.: U.S. Government Printing Office, 1988), 163–164.

9. Ethan Nadelmann, "Should We Legalize Drugs? History Answers: Yes," *Hofstra Law Review* 18 (1990), 41.

10. Steven Jonas, "Solving the Drug Problem: A Public Health Approach to the Reduction of the Use and Abuse of Both Legal and Recreational Drugs," *Hofstra Law Review* 18 (1990), 753.

11. David F. Musto, *The American Disease: Origins of Narcotic Control* (New York: Oxford University Press, 1987), 1.

12. Codified as amended at 21 U.S.C. Sections 801–966 (1994).

13. Uniform Controlled Substances Act (1994), Section 201(h).

14. Douglas N. Husak, *Drugs and Rights* (New York: Cambridge University Press, 2002), 21.

15. Federal Bureau of Investigation, *Uniform Crime Reporting Handbook* (Washington, D.C.: U.S. Department of Justice, 2004), 74.

16. Federal Bureau of Investigation, *Crime in the United States, 2011* (Washington, D.C.: U.S. Department of Justice, 2012), at **www.fbi.gov /about-us/cjis/ucr/crime-in-the-u.s/2011/crime-in-the-u.s. -2011/about-cius**.

17. *Ibid.*

18. Federal Bureau of Investigation, *Crime in the United States, 2010* (Washington, D.C.: U.S. Department of Justice, 2011), at **www.fbi.gov /about-us/cjis/ucr/crime-in-the-u.s/2010/crime-in-the-u.s. -2010/tables/10tbl01.xls.**

19. Jeffrey Reiman, *The Rich Get Richer and the Poor Get Prison,* 4th ed. (Boston: Allyn & Bacon, 1995), 59–60.

20. *Crime in the United States, 2011,* at **www.fbi.gov/about-us/cjis/ucr /crime-in-the-u.s/2011/crime-in-the-u.s.-2011/tables/expanded -homicide-data-table-10.**

21. *Ibid.,* at **www.fbi.gov/about-us/cjis/ucr/crime-in-the-u.s/2011 /crime-in-the-u.s.-2011/tables/table-1.**

22. *Ibid.,* at **www.fbi.gov/about-us/cjis/ucr/crime-in-the-u.s/2011 /crime-in-the-u.s.-2011/tables/table-29 and www.fbi.gov/about -us/cjis/ucr/crime-in-the-u.s/2011/crime-in-the-u.s.-2011 /offense-definitions.**

23. *Ibid.,* at **www.fbi.gov/about-us/cjis/ucr/crime-in-the-u.s/2011 /crime-in-the-u.s.-2011/tables/table-29.**

24. Marcus Felson, *Crime in Everyday Life* (Thousand Oaks, CA: Pine Forge Press, 1994), 3.

25. Wendy Ruderman, "Crime Report Manipulation Is Common among New York Police, Study Finds," *New York Times* (June 29, 2012), A17.

26. Eric P. Baumer and Janet L. Lauritsen, "Reporting Crime to the Police, 1973-2005: A Multivariate Analysis of Long-Term Trends in the National Crime Survey (NCS) and National Crime Victimization Survey (NCVS)," *Criminology* (February 2010), 132–133.

27. Bureau of Justice Statistics, *Crime Victimization, 2011* (Washington, D.C.: U.S. Department of Justice, October 2012), Table 8, page 8.

28. Lynn Langton et al., *Victimizations Not Reported to the Police, 2006– 2010* (U.S. Department of Justice, August 2012), 4.

29. Dave Gathman, "Counting Crime in the Smaller Towns," *Courier News (Elgin, Ill.)* (November 14, 2012), 8.

30. Charlie Savage, "U.S. to Expand Its Definition of Rape in Statistics," *New York Times* (January 7, 2012), A10.

31. *Crime in the United States, 2011,* at **wwwfbi.gov/about-us/cjis/ucr /crime-in-the-u.s/2011/crime-in-the-u.s.-2011/about-cius.**

32. David Hirschel, "Expanding Police Ability to Report Crime: The National Incident-Based Reporting System," *In Short: Toward Criminal Justice Solutions* (Washington, D.C.: National Institute of Justice, July 2009), 1–2.

33. Victor E. Kappeler, Mark Blumberg, and Gary W. Potter, *The Mythology of Crime and Criminal Justice,* 2d ed. (Prospect Heights, IL: Waveland Press, 1993), 31.

34. *Criminal Victimization, 2011,* Table 1, page 2; and *Crime in the United States, 2011,* at **www.fbi.gov/about-us/cjis/ucr/crime-in -the-u.s/2011/crime-in-the-u.s.-2011/tables/table-1.**

35. M. C. Black et al., *The National Intimate Partner and Sexual Violence Survey: 2010 Summary Report* (Atlanta, GA: National Center for Injury Prevention and Control, 2011), 3.

36. Frank A. Hagan, *Introduction to Criminology: Theories, Methods, and Criminal Behavior* 7th ed. (Thousand Oaks, CA: Sage Publications, 2011), 41.

37. Peter B. Wood, Walter R. Grove, James A. Wilson, and John K. Cochran, "Nonsocial Reinforcement and Criminal Conduct: An Extension of Learning Theory," 35 *Criminology* (May 1997), 335–366.

38. Lynne N. Henderson, "The Wrongs of Victims' Rights," 37 *Stanford Law Review* (1985), 947–948.

39. Lois H. Harrington et al., *President's Task Force on Victims of Crime: Final Report* (Washington, D.C.: U.S. Department of Justice, December 1982), viii.

40. 18 U.S.C. Section 3771 (2006).

41. Susan Herman, *Parallel Justice for Victims of Crime* (Washington, D.C.: The National Center for Victims of Crime, 2010), 45–48.

42. Emily Bazelon, "Money Is No Cure," *New York Times Magazine* (January 27, 2013), 28.

43. *In re Dean,* 527 F. 3d, 391, 394 (5th Cir. 2008).

44. Douglas E. Beloof, "The Third Wave of Crime Victims' Rights: Standing, Remedy, and Review," *Brigham Young University Law Review* 2 (2005), 258.

45. Herman, 17–21.

46. Lynn Langton, *Use of Victim Service Agencies by Victims of Serious Violent Crime, 1993–2009* (Washington, D.C.: U.S. Department of Justice, August 2011), 1.

47. Chris E. Kubrin, et al., "Does Fringe Banking Exacerbate Neighborhood Crime Rates?" *Criminology and Public Policy* (May 2011), 437–464.

48. Larry Cohen and Marcus Felson, "Social Change and Crime Rate Trends: A Routine Activity Approach," *American Sociological Review* (1979), 588–608.

49. Kubrin, et al., 441.

50. Cohen and Felson.

51. Herman, 13–16.

52. Katy Reckdahl, "NOPD Release of Murder Victims Criminal Records Is Challenged," *New Orleans Times–Picayune* (January 1, 2012), 1.

53. Quoted in Kevin Johnson, "Criminals Target Each Other, Trend Shows," *USA Today* (August 31, 2007), 1A.

54. Franklin E. Zimring, *The Great American Crime Decline* (New York: Oxford University Press, 2007), 45–72.

55. James Q. Wilson, "Concluding Essay in Crime," in James Q. Wilson and Joan Petersilia, eds., *Crime* (San Francisco: Institute for Contemporary Studies Press, 1995), 507.

56. John DiIulio, *How to Stop the Coming Crime Wave* (New York: Manhattan Institute, 1996), 4.

57. James Fox, *Trends in Juvenile Violence* (Boston: Northeastern University Press, 1996), 1.

58. Zimring, 6.

59. *Ibid.,* 197–198.

60. *Ibid.,* 82.

61. Quoted in Andrew Mach, "Violent Crime Rates in the U.S. Drop, Approach Historical Lows," *msnbc.com* (June 11, 2012), at **usnews .nbcnews.com/_news/2012/06/11/12170947-fbi-violent-crime -rates-in-the-us-drop-approach-historic-lows?lite.**

62. *Ibid.*

63. Heather Mac Donald, "A Crime Theory Demolished," *Wall Street Journal* (January 4, 2010), at **online.wsj.com/article/SB10001424052748703 5809045746380240557355900.html.**

64. Danielle Ryan, "2011 Saw 17 Percent Jump in Violent Crimes," *Los Angeles Times* (October 18, 2012), 12; and Kevin Johnson, "Violent Crime Rises Sharply," *USA Today* (October 18, 2012), 3A.

65. Alexia Cooper and Erica L. Smith, *Homicide Trends in the United States, 1980–2008* (Washington, D.C.: Bureau of Justice Statistics, November 2011), 16.

66. Cameron McWhirter and Gary Fields, "Communities Struggle to Break a Grim Cycle of Killing," *Wall Street Journal* (August 18–19, 2012), A1.

67. Cooper and Smith, 13.

68. *Crime in the United States, 2011,* at **www.fbi.gov/about-us/cjis/ucr /crime-in-the-u.s/2011/crime-in-the-u.s.-2011/tables/table-43.**

69. *Targeting Blacks: Drug Law Enforcement and Race in the United States* (New York: Human Rights Watch, May 2008), 3.

70. Charles Puzzanchera, Benjamin Adams, and Melissa Sickmund, *Juvenile Court Statistics, 2008* (Washington, D.C.: National Center for Juvenile Justice, July 2011), 20.

71. Ruth D. Peterson, "The Central Place of Race in Crime and Justice— The American Society of Criminology's 2011 Sutherland Address," *Criminology* (May 2012), 303–327.

72. Patricia Y. Warren, "Inequality by Design: The Connection between Race, Crime, Victimization, and Social Policy," *Criminology & Public Policy* (November 2010), 715.

73. Eric A. Stewart, Ronald L. Simons, and Rand D. Donger, "Assessing Neighborhood and Social Psychological Influence on Childhood

Violence in an African American Sample," *Criminology* (November 2002), 801–829.

74. William Alex Pridemore, "A Methodological Addition to the Cross-National Empirical Literature on Social Structure and Homicide: A First Test of the Poverty-Homicide Thesis," *Criminology* (February 2008), 133.

75. Caroline Wolf Harlow, *Education and Correctional Populations* (Washington, D.C.: Bureau of Justice Statistics, January 2003), 1.

76. Charles Tittle and Robert Meier, "Specifying the SES/Delinquency Relationship," *Criminology* 28 (1990), 270–301.

77. Marguerite Moeller, *America's Tomorrow: A Profile of Latino Youth* (New York: National Council of La Raza, 2010).

78. *Preliminary Fiscal Year 2011 Data* (Washington, D.C.: U.S. Sentencing Commission, September 2011), Table 23, page 44.

79. Robert J. Sampson, Jeffrey Morenoff, and Stephen W. Raudenbush, "Social Anatomy of Racial and Ethnic Disparities in Violence," *American Journal of Public Health* 95 (2005), 231.

80. Cooper and Smith, Table 4, page 9.

81. Bureau of Justice Statistics, *Jail Inmates at Midyear 2011—Statistical Tables* (Washington, D.C.: U.S. Department of Justice, April 2012), Table 6, page 6; Bureau of Justice Statistics, *Prisoners in 2011* (Washington, D.C.: U.S. Department of Justice, December 2012), Table 1, page 2; and *Crime in the United States, 2011* at **www.fbi.gov/about-us/cjis/ucr/crime-in-the-u.s/crime-in-the-u.s.-2011/persons-arrested/persons-arrested**.

82. Federal Bureau of Justice, *Crime in the United States, 2000* (Washington, D.C.: U.S. Department of Justice, 2001), Table 33, page 221; and *Crime in the United States, 2011* at **www.fbi.gov/about-us/cjis/ucr/crime-in-the-u.s/2011/crime-in-the-u.s.-2011/tables/table-33**.

83. *Prisoners in 2011*, Table 1, page 2.

84. Jennifer Schwartz and Bryan D. Rookey, "The Narrowing Gender Gap in Arrests: Assessing Competing Explanations Using Self-Report, Traffic Fatality, and Official Data on Drunk Driving, 1980–2004," *Criminology* (August 2008), 637–638.

85. Quoted in Barry Yeoman, "Violent Tendencies: Crime by Women Has Skyrocketed in Recent Years," *Chicago Tribune* (March 15, 2000), 3.

86. *Crime in the United States, 2011*, at **www.fbi.gov/about-us/cjis/ucr/crime-in-the-u.s/2011/crime-in-the-u.s.-2011/tables/table-42**.

87. Schwarz and Rookey, 637–671.

88. Meda Chesney-Lind, "Patriarchy, Prisons, and Jails: A Critical Look at Trends in Women's Incarceration," *Prison Journal* (Spring/Summer 1991), 57.

89. Erika Harrell, *Violent Victimization Committed by Strangers, 1993–2010* (Washington, D.C.: U.S. Department of Justice, December 2012), 2.

90. Shannan Catalano, *Intimate Partner Violence, 1993–2010* (Washington, D.C.: U. S. Department of Justice, November 2012), Table 1, page 2.

91. Harrell, Table 1, page 2.

92. Bureau of Justice Statistics, *Female Victims of Violence* (Washington, D.C.: U.S. Department of Justice, September 2009), Table 2, page 5.

93. Bonnie S. Fisher, Francis T. Cullen, and Michael G. Turner, *The Sexual Victimization of College Women* (Washington, D.C.: U.S. Department of Justice, December 2000), 10.

94. Eve S. Buzawa, "Victims of Domestic Violence," in Robert C. Davis, Arthur Lurigio, and Susan Herman, eds., *Victims of Crime*, 4th ed. (Los Angeles: Sage, 2013), 36–37.

95. Shannan Catalano, *Stalking Victims in the United States—Revised* (Washington, D.C.: U.S. Department of Justice, September 2012), 1, 5.

96. Min Xie, Karen Heimer, and Janet L. Lauritsen, "Violence against Women in U.S. Metropolitan Areas: Changes in Women's Status and Risk, 1980–2004," *Criminology* (February 2012), 106–107, 131.

97. Harrell, Figure 2, page 2.

98. Quoted in Tanya Eiserer and Melissa Repko, "Sister of Suspect in Slaying of Navy SEAL Sniper Chris Kyle Told 911 She Was Terrified When Brother Showed Up," *Dallas Morning News* (February 6, 2013), A1.

99. Doris J. James and Lauren E. Glaze, *Mental Heath Problems of Prison and Jail Inmates* (Washington, D.C.: U.S. Department of Justice, September 2006), 3.

100. Erica Goode and Jack Healy, "Focus on Mental Health Laws to Curb Violence Is Unfair, Some Say," *New York Times* (February 1, 2013), A13.

101. The Gun Control Act of 1968, 18 U.S.C. Section 922(g).

102. Richard A. Friedman, "In Gun Debate, a Misguided Focus on Mental Illness," *New York Times* (December 18, 2012), D5.

103. Seena Fazel and Martin Grann, "The Population Impact of Severe Mental Illness on Violent Crime," *American Journal of Psychiatry* (August 2006), 1397–1403.

104. Jeffrey W. Swanson et al., "Violence and Psychiatric Disorder in the Community: Evidence from the Epidemiologic Catchment Area Surveys," *Hospital & Community Psychiatry* (July 1990), 761–770.

105. James and Glaze, 6.

106. Arthur J. Lurigio, Kelli E. Canada, and Matthew W. Epperson, "Crime Victimization and Mental Illness" in *Victims of Crime*, 216–217.

107. *Ibid.*, 217–218.

108. Roberto Maniglio, "Severe Mental Illness and Criminal Victimization: A Systematic Review," *Acta Psychiactra Scandinavica* 119 (2009), 180–191.

109. Quoted in Julie Bykowicz, "City Targets Domestic Violence," *Baltimore Sun* (February 25, 2008), 1A.

110. Naomi R. Cahn, "Innovative Approaches to the Prosecution of Domestic Violence Crimes: An Overview," in Eve S. Buzawa and Carl G. Buzawa, eds., *Domestic Violence: The Changing Criminal Justice Response* (Santa Barbara, CA: Praeger, 1992), 163.

111. Erin L. Han, "Mandatory Arrest and No-Drop Policies: Victim Empowerment in Domestic Violence Cases," 23 *Boston College Third World Law Journal* (2003), 159–192.

112. Andrew R. Klein, *Practical Implications of Current Domestic Violence Research: For Law Enforcement, Prosecutors, and Judges* (Washington, D.C.: National Institute of Justice, June 2009), 44, 45.

113. Malinda L. Seymore, "Isn't It a Crime?: Feminist Perspectives on Spousal Immunity and Spousal Violence," 90 *Northwestern University Law Review* (1996), 1079–1080.

114. Kalyani Robbins, "No-Drop Prosecution of Domestic Violence: Just Good Policy, or Equal Protection Mandate?" 52 *Stanford Law Review* (1999), 205–233.

115. Jessica Dayton, "The Silencing of a Woman's Choice: Mandatory Arrest and No Drop Prosecution Policies in Domestic Violence Cases," 9 *Cardozo Women's Law Journal* (2003), 281.

116. Tamara L. Kuennen, "Private Relationships and Public Problems: Applying Principles of Relational Contract Theory to Domestic Violence," *Brigham Young University Law Review* (2010), 528–530.

117. *Ibid.*, 529–530.

118. *Ibid.*, 574–575.

CHAPTER

4 Inside Criminal Law

CHAPTER OUTLINE		CORRESPONDING LEARNING OBJECTIVES
The Development of American Criminal Law		List the four written sources of American criminal law.
		Explain precedent and the importance of the doctrine of *stare decisis*.
The Purposes of Criminal Law		Explain the two basic functions of criminal law.
The Elements of a Crime		Delineate the elements required to establish *mens rea* (a guilty mental state).
		Explain how the doctrine of strict liability applies to criminal law.
Defenses under Criminal Law		List and briefly define the most important excuse defenses for crimes.
		Discuss a common misperception concerning the insanity defense in the United States.
		Describe the four most important justification criminal defenses.
Procedural Safeguards		Distinguish between substantive and procedural criminal law.
		Explain the importance of the due process clause in the criminal justice system.

To target your study and review, look for these numbered Learning Objective icons throughout the chapter.

MURDER OR A HEART ATTACK?

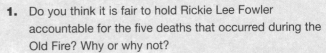

ACCORDING TO police investigators, Rickie Lee Fowler was angry about being thrown out of a family member's house in California's San Bernardino Mountains. As retaliation, Fowler started one of the largest wildfires in state history. Known as the Old Fire, the 91,000-acre blaze lasted nine days, destroyed 1,003 homes, and caused the deaths of five men. Fowler was eventually convicted on two counts of arson and five counts of murder. In January 2013, a jury sentenced him to be executed. "You're not going to find a better case than this for the death penalty," said San Bernardino County deputy district attorney Robert Bullock.

Not everybody in the legal community agreed. "I've never heard of a case like this," said Loyola (Los Angeles) Law School professor Stan Goldman. The legal definition of murder requires the offender to have some prior intent to harm the victim. Though Fowler intentionally started the Old Fire, there was no indication that he intended to hurt any people. Furthermore, the five victims did not die of smoke inhalation or burn injuries. Rather, they all died of heart attacks brought about by stress experienced due to the fire. One of the victims, who lost his house and his business to the flames, did not suffer his fatal heart attack until a week after the event.

Fowler's attorneys claimed that their client obviously never intended to kill anyone, and that it was ludicrous to blame him for the heart attacks. Professor Goldman believes that the "real question is whether we should be executing people when the [murders] were not an easily foreseeable consequence of the criminal act." Local law enforcement officials, however, insist that criminal law must be flexible enough to punish behavior that is not marked by obvious intent yet still poses a threat to society. "The fact of the matter is that these lives were directly lost as a result of Rickie Fowler's actions," observed deputy district attorney Bullock.

1. Do you think it is fair to hold Rickie Lee Fowler accountable for the five deaths that occurred during the Old Fire? Why or why not?

2. A few months after the Old Fire was finally extinguished, a huge mudslide occurred in the burn area, flooding a church camp and killing fourteen people. The mudslide would not have taken place without the fire. Using the reasoning of Robert Bullock described above, make the argument that Fowler was responsible for those deaths as well. (He was never charged with any crime in connection with the mudslide.)

3. Why is the issue of intent so crucial to criminal law? That is, why do we sometimes feel uncomfortable charging people with crimes they did not intend to commit?

AP Photo/*The Sun*, LaFonzo Carter

Rickie Lee Fowler, right, was convicted of two counts of arson and five counts of murder for the damage he caused by starting the Old Fire in California's San Bernardino Mountains.

THE DEVELOPMENT OF AMERICAN CRIMINAL LAW

Given the various functions of *law,* a single definition of this term is difficult to establish. To the Greek philosopher Aristotle (384–322 B.C.E.), law was a "pledge that citizens of a state will do justice to one another." Aristotle's mentor, Plato (427–347 B.C.E.), saw the law as primarily a form of social control. The British jurist Sir William Blackstone (1723–1780) described law as "a rule of civil conduct prescribed by the supreme power in a state, commanding what is right, and prohibiting what is wrong." In the United States, jurist Oliver Wendell Holmes, Jr. (1841–1935), contended that law was a set of rules that allowed one to predict how a court would resolve a particular dispute.

The Conception of Law

Although these definitions vary in their particulars, they are all based on the following general observation: law consists of enforceable rules governing relationships among individuals and between individuals and their society.[1] Searching back into history, several sources for modern American law can be found in the rules laid out by ancient societies. One of the first known examples of written law was created during the reign of Hammurabi (1792–1750 B.C.E.), the sixth king of the ancient empire of Babylon. The Code of Hammurabi set out crimes and their punishments based on *lex Talionis,* or "an eye for an eye." This concept of retribution is still important and will be discussed in Chapter 11.

Another ancient source of law can be found in the Mosaic Code of the Israelites (1200 B.C.E.). According to tradition, Moses—acting as an intermediary for God—presented the code to the tribes of Israel. The two sides entered into a covenant, or contract, in which the Israelites agreed to follow the code and God agreed to protect them as the chosen people. Besides providing the basis for Judeo-Christian teachings, the Mosaic Code is also reflected in modern American law, as evident in similar prohibitions against murder, theft, adultery, and perjury.

Modern law also owes a debt to the Code of Justinian, promulgated throughout the Roman Empire in the sixth century. This code collected many of the laws that Western society had produced. It was influential in the development of the legal systems of the European continent. To some extent, it also influenced the common law of England.

English Common Law

The English system of law as it stands today was solidified during the reign of Henry II (1154–1189). Henry sent judges on a specific route throughout the country, known as a circuit. These circuit judges established a **common law** in England. In other words, they solidified a national law in which legal principles applied to all citizens equally, no matter where they lived or what the local customs had dictated in the past. When confusion about any particular law arose, the circuit judges could draw on English traditions, or they could borrow from legal decisions made in other European countries. Once a circuit judge made a ruling, other circuit judges faced with similar cases generally followed that ruling. Each interpretation became part of the law on the subject and served as a legal **precedent**—a decision that furnished an example or authority for deciding subsequent cases involving similar legal principles or facts. Over time, a body of general rules that prescribed social conduct and that was applied throughout the entire English realm was established, and subsequently it was passed on to British colonies, including those in the New World that would eventually become the thirteen original United States.

Common Law The body of law developed from custom or judicial decisions in English and U.S. courts and not attributable to a legislature.

Precedent A court decision that furnishes an example of authority for deciding subsequent cases involving similar facts.

LEARNING **1** OBJECTIVE

List the four written sources of American criminal law.

What is important about the formation of the common law is that it developed from the customs of the populace rather than simply the will of a ruler. As such, the common law came to reflect the social, religious, economic, and cultural values of the people. In any society that is, like our own, governed by the **rule of law,** all persons and institutions, including the government itself, must abide by the law. Furthermore, the law must be applied equally and enforced fairly, and must not be altered arbitrarily by any individual or group, no matter how powerful.

Written Sources of American Criminal Law

Originally, common law was *uncodified.* That is, it relied primarily on judges following precedents, and the body of the law was not written down in any single place. Uncodified law, however, presents a number of drawbacks. For one, if the law is not recorded in a manner or a place in which the citizenry has access to it, then it is difficult, if not impossible, for people to know exactly which acts are legal and which acts are illegal. Furthermore, citizens have no way of determining or understanding the procedures that must be followed to establish innocence or guilt. Consequently, U.S. history has seen the development of several written sources of American criminal law, also known as "substantive" criminal law. These sources include:

1. The U.S. Constitution and the constitutions of the various states.
2. Statutes, or laws, passed by Congress and by state legislatures, plus local ordinances.
3. Regulations, created by regulatory agencies, such as the federal Food and Drug Administration.
4. Case law (court decisions).

We describe each of these important written sources of law in the following pages. (For a preview, see Figure 4.1 on the facing page.)

CONSTITUTIONAL LAW The federal government and the states have separate written constitutions that set forth the general organization and powers of, and the limits on, their respective governments. **Constitutional law** is the law as expressed in these constitutions.

The U.S. Constitution is the supreme law of the land. As such, it is the basis of all law in the United States. Any law that violates the Constitution, as ultimately determined by the United States Supreme Court, will be declared unconstitutional and will not be enforced. The Tenth Amendment, which defines the powers and limitations of the federal government, reserves to the states all powers not granted to the federal government. Under our system of federalism (see Chapter 1), each state also has its own constitution. Unless they conflict with the U.S. Constitution or a federal law, state constitutions are supreme within their respective borders. (You will learn more about how constitutional law applies to our criminal justice system throughout this textbook.)

STATUTORY LAW Statutes enacted by legislative bodies at any level of government make up another

George Washington, standing at right, presided over the constitutional convention of 1787. The convention resulted in the U.S. Constitution, the source of a number of laws that continue to form the basis of our criminal justice system today.
Bettmann/Corbis

FIGURE 4.1 Sources of American Law

Constitutional law	**Definition:** The law as expressed in the U.S. Constitution and the various state constitutions.	**Example:** The Fifth Amendment to the U.S. Constitution states that no person shall "be compelled in any criminal case to be a witness" against himself or herself.
Statutory law	**Definition:** Laws or *ordinances* created by federal, state, and local legislatures and governing bodies.	**Example:** Texas state law considers the theft of cattle, horses, or exotic livestock or fowl a felony.
Administrative law	**Definition:** The rules, orders, and decisions of federal or state government administrative agencies.	**Example:** The federal Environmental Protection Agency's rules criminalize the use of lead-based paint in a manner that causes health risks to the community.
Case law	**Definition:** Judge-made law, including judicial interpretations of the other three sources of law.	**Example:** A federal judge overturns a Nebraska state law making it a crime for sex offenders to use social networking sites on the ground that the statute violated the constitutional right of freedom of speech.

source of law, which is generally referred to as **statutory law.** *Federal statutes* are laws that are enacted by the U.S. Congress. *State statutes* are laws enacted by state legislatures, and statutory law also includes the ordinances passed by cities and counties. A federal statute, of course, applies to all states. A state statute, in contrast, applies only within that state's borders. City or county ordinances (statutes) apply only to those jurisdictions where they are enacted.

The Model Penal Code Until the mid-twentieth century, state criminal statutes were disorganized, inconsistent, and generally inadequate for modern society. In 1952, the American Law Institute began to draft a uniform penal code in the hopes of solving this problem. The first **Model Penal Code** was released ten years later and has had a broad effect on state statutes.[2] Though not a law itself, the Code defines the general principles of criminal responsibility. The majority of states have adopted parts of the Model Penal Code into their criminal statutes, and some states, such as New York, have adopted a large portion of the Code.

Legal Supremacy It is important to keep in mind that there are essentially fifty-two different criminal codes in this country—one for each state, the District of Columbia, and the federal government. Originally, the federal criminal code was quite small. The U.S. Constitution mentions only three federal crimes: treason, piracy, and counterfeiting. Today, according to a recent study, federal law includes about 4,500 offenses that carry criminal penalties.[3] Inevitably, these federal criminal statutes are bound to overlap or even contradict state statutes. In such cases, thanks to the **supremacy clause** of the Constitution, federal law will almost always prevail. Simply put, the supremacy clause holds that federal law is the "supreme law of the land."

So, in 2012, U.S. district judge Donald Molloy ruled that federal law enforcement agents were justified in arresting Montana residents for possessing medical marijuana, even though use of the drug for medicinal purposes is legal under the law of that state. As we discussed in Chapter 2, federal drug law does not allow for medical marijuana use, and, as Judge Molloy stated, "we are all bound by federal law, like it or not."[4] Along the same lines, any statutory law—federal or state—that violates the Constitution will be overturned. In the late 1980s, for example, the United States Supreme Court ruled that any state laws banning the burning of the American flag were unconstitutional because they impinged on the individual's right to freedom of expression.[5]

Statutory Law The body of law enacted by legislative bodies.

Model Penal Code A statutory text created by the American Law Institute that sets forth general principles of criminal responsibility and defines specific offenses.

Supremacy Clause A clause in the U.S. Constitution establishing that federal law is the "supreme law of the land" and shall prevail when in conflict with state constitutions or statutes.

■ Smoking marijuana in this Denver park no longer carries a high risk of arrest by state and local police. What method did Colorado voters use to legalize the possession of small amounts of marijuana in 2012? What are some of the pros and cons of this method of creating new criminal laws?
AP Photo/Brennan Linsley

Ballot Initiatives On a state and local level, voters can write or rewrite criminal statutes through a form of direct democracy known as the **ballot initiative.** In this process, a group of citizens draft a proposed law and then gather a certain number of signatures to get the proposal on that year's ballot. If a majority of the voters approve the measure, it is enacted into law. Currently, twenty-four states and the District of Columbia accept ballot initiatives, and these special elections have played a crucial role in shaping criminal law in those jurisdictions.

In the mid-1990s, for example, California voters approved a "three-strikes" measure (discussed in Chapter 11) that increased penalties for third-time felons, transforming the state's criminal justice system in the process. In 2012, when Colorado and Washington decided to legalize the sale and possession of small amounts of marijuana, voters in those states approved this dramatic legal change through ballot initiatives. As we just noted, however, ballot initiatives do not supplant federal law, and marijuana sellers and users in these states are still subject to arrest under federal drug laws.

ADMINISTRATIVE LAW A third source of American criminal law consists of **administrative law**—the rules, orders, and decisions of *regulatory agencies.* A regulatory agency is a federal, state, or local government agency established to perform a specific function. The Occupational Safety and Health Administration (OSHA), for example, oversees the safety and health of American workers. The Environmental Protection Agency (EPA) is concerned with protecting the natural environment, and the Food and Drug Administration (FDA) regulates food and drugs produced in the United States.

Disregarding certain laws created by regulatory agencies can be a criminal violation. Federal statutes, such as the Clean Water Act, authorize a specific regulatory agency, such as the EPA, to enforce regulations to which criminal sanctions are attached.[6] So, in 2012, following a criminal investigation led by the EPA, a North Carolina hog farm was found guilty of discharging waste into the Waccamaw River watershed. As punishment, a federal judge sentenced the company to pay $1.5 million in fines and sent its president to prison for six months.

CASE LAW As is evident from the earlier discussion of the common law tradition, another basic source of American law consists of the rules of law announced in court decisions, or precedents. These rules of law include interpretations of constitutional provisions, of statutes enacted by legislatures, and of regulations created by administrative agencies. Today, this body of law is referred to variously as the common law, judge-made law, or **case law.**

Case law is the basis for a doctrine called *stare decisis* ("to stand on decided cases"). Under this doctrine, judges are obligated to follow the precedents established within their jurisdiction. For example, any decision of a particular state's highest court will control the outcome of future cases on that issue brought before all the lower courts within that same state. Per the supremacy clause, discussed earlier, all U.S. Supreme

LEARNING **2** OBJECTIVE
Explain precedent and the importance of the doctrine of *stare decisis.*

Ballot Initiative A procedure in which the citizens of a state, by collecting enough signatures, can force a public vote on a proposed change to state law.

Administrative Law The body of law created by administrative agencies (in the form of rules, regulations, orders, and decisions) in order to carry out their duties and responsibilities.

Case Law The rules of law announced in court decisions.

Stare Decisis (pronounced *ster-ay dih-si-ses*). A legal doctrine under which judges are obligated to follow the precedents established under prior decisions.

Court decisions involving the U.S. Constitution are binding on *all* courts, because the U.S. Constitution is the supreme law of the land.

The doctrine of *stare decisis* does not require the U.S. Supreme Court *always* to follow its own precedent, though the Court often does so. At times, a change in society's values will make an older ruling seem obsolete, at least in the eyes of the Supreme Court justices. In 1986, for example, the Court upheld a state law that banned certain homosexual acts that were lawful when performed by a man and a woman.[7] Seventeen years later, the Court overturned that decision, ruling that the government does not have the ability to treat one class of citizens differently from the rest of society when it comes to sexual practices between consenting adults. The original case "was not correct when it was decided, and it is not correct today," wrote Justice Anthony Kennedy.[8]

SELF ASSESSMENT

Fill in the blanks and check your answers on page 128.

The U.S. _____ is the supreme law of this country. Any law that violates this document will be declared _____ by the United States Supreme Court. Laws enacted by legislative bodies are known as _____, while the body of law created by judicial decisions is known as _____ law. The doctrine of _____ _____ reflects the tradition of relying on the _____ of decided cases to settle new ones.

THE PURPOSES OF CRIMINAL LAW

Why do societies need laws? Many criminologists believe that criminal law has two basic functions: one relates to the legal requirements of a society, and the other pertains to the society's need to maintain and promote social values.

LEARNING
3
OBJECTIVE

Explain the two basic functions of criminal law.

Protect and Punish: The Legal Function of the Law

The primary legal function of the law is to maintain social order by protecting citizens from *criminal harm*. This term refers to a variety of harms that can be generalized to fit into two categories:

1. Harms to individual citizens' physical safety and property, such as the harm caused by murder, theft, or arson.
2. Harms to society's interests collectively, such as the harm caused by unsafe foods or consumer products, a polluted environment, or poorly constructed buildings.[9]

Because criminal law has the primary goal of protecting people from harm, new criminal laws are often passed in response to specific acts. So, following the fatal shooting of twenty children and six adults at an elementary school in Newtown, Connecticut, on December 14, 2012, many states moved to tighten their gun laws.

One of the country's most important counterterrorism laws was passed in response to the 1995 truck bombing of the Alfred P. Murrah Federal Building in Oklahoma City, Oklahoma, which killed 168 people. The primary goal of the Antiterrorism and Effective Death Penalty Act (AEDPA) is to hamper terrorist organizations by cutting off their funding. The law prohibits persons from "knowingly providing material support or resources" to any group that the United States has designated a "foreign terrorist organization."[10] "Material support" is defined very broadly in the legislation, covering funding, financial services, lodging, training, expert advice or assistance, communications equipment, transportation, and other physical assets.[11] For an example of how the AEDPA has been used in the wake of the September 11, 2001, terrorist attacks against the United States, see the feature *Countering Domestic Terrorism—Homegrown Support* below.

Maintain and Teach:
The Social Function of the Law

If criminal laws against acts that cause harm or injury to others are almost universally accepted, the same cannot be said for laws that criminalize "morally" wrongful activities that may do no obvious, physical harm outside the families of those involved. Why criminalize gambling or prostitution if the participants are consenting?

EXPRESSING PUBLIC MORALITY The answer lies in the social function of criminal law. Many observers believe that the main purpose of criminal law is to reflect the values and norms of society, or at least of those segments of society that hold power. Legal scholar Henry Hart has stated that the only justification for criminal law and punishment is "the judgment of community condemnation."[12]

Take, for example, the misdemeanor of bigamy, which occurs when someone knowingly marries a second person without terminating her or his marriage to an original husband or wife. Apart from moral considerations, there would appear to be no victims in a bigamous relationship, and indeed many societies have allowed and continue to allow bigamy to exist. In the American social tradition, however, as John L. Diamond of the University of California's Hastings College of the Law points out:

COUNTERING Domestic Terrorism

Piotr Krzeslak/Shutterstock.com

HOMEGROWN SUPPORT

About a decade ago, Tarek Mehanna traveled to the Middle Eastern country of Yemen wanting to train with the international terrorist group al Qaeda. Failing in this endeavor, Mehanna, an American citizen born in Pittsburgh, returned home and began to spread his extremist ideology via the Internet. He posted videos and documents that glorified suicide bombings and translated propaganda documents such as "39 Ways to Make and Participate in *Jihad*" into English. He supported radical Islam on various Web sites and IM chat rooms. In one instance, he referred to the remains of mutilated American soldiers in Iraq as "Texas BBQ."

After following his online trail for several years, federal agents arrested Mehanna and charged him with conspiracy to provide material support for al Qaeda and other terrorist groups. The government offered no proof that Mehanna planned or attempted to execute a terrorist act. Nor did it provide any evidence that he had been in contact with any terrorist groups, including al Qaeda. Rather, in this case, Mehanna's material support consisted of his efforts to motivate others to take up arms against the United States and its

citizens. Mehanna was eventually convicted and, in April 2012, sentenced to spend 210 months in prison.

Andrew F. March of Yale University calls the Mehanna conviction "a frightening and unnecessary attempt to expand the kinds of religious and political speech that the government can criminalize." Proponents of this use of the material support law counter that Mehanna clearly intended to cause violence, and that his punishment would deter others from following his example. According to a government statement, "Mehanna's actions are the kind that most individuals who are radicalized in the United States are likely to contemplate replicating—traveling overseas to get terrorism experience, and using the Internet to connect with and support other terrorists."

FOR CRITICAL ANALYSIS One commentator compared Tarek Mehanna to a mob boss who says, "I think it's a good idea if Johnny Boots gets whacked," and then claims, "I was only expressing my opinion," after the murder is carried out. Do you agree with this comparison? Why or why not?

Marriage is an institution encouraged and supported by society. The structural importance of the integrity of the family and a monogamous marriage requires unflinching enforcement of the criminal laws against bigamy. The immorality is not in choosing to do wrong, but in transgressing, even innocently, a fundamental social boundary that lies at the core of social order.[13]

Of course, public morals are not uniform across the entire nation, and a state's criminal code often reflects the values of its residents. Illinois and the District of Columbia, for example, are the only parts of the United States where people cannot, under any circumstances, carry a concealed weapon in public. Sometimes, local values and federal law will conflict with one another. In South Carolina, operating a cockfighting operation is a misdemeanor, and violators are often let off with a fine. Under federal animal welfare laws, however, the same activity carries a potential five-year prison term.[14] In 2012, five South Carolinians arrested by federal agents for cockfighting claimed—unsuccessfully—in court that their convictions were illegitimate because the federal government has no authority to regulate the "sport" within state borders.[15]

■ Why does the supremacy clause make it unlikely that residents of states with lenient cockfighting laws will be able to escape the harsher punishments of federal animal welfare laws that prohibit the practice?
Al Bello/Getty Images

TEACHING SOCIETAL BOUNDARIES Some scholars believe that criminal laws not only express the expectations of society, but "teach" them as well. Professor Lawrence M. Friedman of Stanford University thinks that just as parents teach children behavioral norms through punishment, criminal justice "'teaches a lesson' to the people it punishes, and to society at large." Making burglary a crime, arresting burglars, putting them in jail—each step in the criminal justice process reinforces the idea that burglary is unacceptable and is deserving of punishment.[16]

This teaching function can also be seen in traffic laws. There is nothing "natural" about most traffic laws: Americans drive on the right side of the street, the British on the left side, with no obvious difference in the results. These laws, such as stopping at intersections, using headlights at night, and following speed limits, do lead to a more orderly flow of traffic and fewer accidents—certainly socially desirable goals. The laws can also be updated when needed. Over the past few years, several states have banned the use of handheld cell phones while driving because of the safety hazards associated with that behavior. Various forms of punishment for breaking traffic laws teach drivers the social order of the road.

SELF ASSESSMENT

Fill in the blanks and check your answers on page 128.

The _____ function of the law is to protect citizens from _____ harm by assuring their physical safety. The _____ function of the law is to teach citizens proper behavior and express public _____ by codifying the norms and values of the community.

Corpus Delicti The body of circumstances that must exist for a criminal act to have occurred.

Actus Reus (pronounced *ak*-tus ⌊*ray*-uhs). A guilty (prohibited) act.

THE ELEMENTS OF A CRIME

In fictional accounts of police work, the admission of guilt is often portrayed as the crucial element of a criminal investigation. Although an admission is certainly useful to police and prosecutors, it alone cannot establish the innocence or guilt of a suspect. Criminal law normally requires that the **corpus delicti,** a Latin phrase for "the body of the crime," be proved before a person can be convicted of wrongdoing.[17] *Corpus delicti* can be defined as "proof that a specific crime has actually been committed by someone."[18] It consists of the basic elements of any crime, which include (1) *actus reus,* or a guilty act; (2) *mens rea,* or a guilty intent; (3) concurrence, or the coming together of the criminal act and the guilty mind; (4) a link between the act and the legal definition of the crime; (5) any attendant circumstances; and (6) the harm done, or result of the criminal act. (See *Mastering Concepts* below for an example showing some of the various elements of a crime.)

Criminal Act: *Actus Reus*

Suppose Mr. Smith walks into a police department and announces that he just killed his wife. In and of itself, the confession is insufficient for conviction unless the police find Mrs. Smith's corpse, for example, with a bullet in her brain and establish through evidence that Mr. Smith fired the gun. (This does not mean that an actual dead body has to be found in every homicide case. Rather, it is the fact of the death that must be established in such cases.)

Most crimes require an act of *commission,* meaning that a person must *do* something in order to be accused of a crime. The prohibited act is referred to as the **actus reus,** or guilty act. Furthermore, the act of commission must be voluntary. For example, if Mr. Smith had an epileptic seizure while holding a hunting rifle and accidentally shot his wife, he normally would not be held criminally liable for her death. (To better understand this principle, see the feature *You Be the Judge—A Voluntary Act?* on the facing page.)

MASTERING CONCEPTS
THE ELEMENTS OF A CRIME

Camilo Torres/Shutterstock.com

Carl Robert Winchell walked into the SunTrust Bank in Volusia County, Florida, and placed a bag containing a box on a counter. Announcing that the box held a bomb, he demanded to be given an unspecified amount of cash. After receiving several thousand dollars in cash, Winchell fled, leaving the box behind. A Volusia County Sheriff's Office bomb squad subsequently determined that the box did not in fact contain any explosive device. Winchell was eventually arrested and charged with robbery.

Winchell's actions were criminal because they satisfy the three elements of a crime:

1. *Actus Reus:* Winchell **physically** committed the crime of bank robbery.
2. *Mens Rea:* Winchell **intended** to commit the crime of bank robbery.
3. *Concurrence:* Winchell's intent to rob the bank and his use of the false bomb threat* **came together** to create a criminal act.

*Note that the fact that there was no bomb in the box has no direct bearing on the three elements of the crime. It could, however, lead to Winchell's receiving a lighter punishment than if he had used a real bomb.

A LEGAL DUTY In some cases, an act of *omission* can be a crime, but only when a person has a legal duty to perform the omitted act. One such legal duty is assumed to exist based on a "special relationship" between two parties, such as a parent and child, adult children and their aged parents, and spouses.[19] Those persons involved in contractual relationships with others, such as physicians and lifeguards, must also perform legal duties to avoid criminal penalty. Hawaii, Minnesota, Rhode Island, Vermont, and Wisconsin have even passed "duty to aid" statutes requiring their citizens to report criminal conduct and help victims of such conduct if possible.[20] Another example of a criminal act of omission is failure to file a federal income tax return when required by law to do so.

A PLAN OR ATTEMPT The guilty act requirement is based on one of the premises of criminal law—that a person is punished for harm done to society. Planning to kill someone or to steal a car may be wrong, but the thoughts do no harm and are therefore not criminal until they are translated into action. Of course, a person can be punished for *attempting* murder or robbery, but normally only if he or she took substantial steps toward the criminal objective and the prosecution can prove that the desire to commit the crime was present. Furthermore, the punishment for an **attempt** normally is less severe than if the act had succeeded.

Mental State: *Mens Rea*

A wrongful mental state—**mens rea**—is usually as necessary as a wrongful act in determining guilt. The mental state, or requisite *intent,* required to establish guilt of a crime is indicated in the applicable statute or law. For theft, the wrongful act is the taking of another person's property, and the required mental state involves both the awareness that the property belongs to another and the desire to deprive the owner of it.

Attempt The act of taking substantial steps toward committing a crime while having the ability and the intent to commit the crime, even if the crime never takes place.

Mens Rea (pronounced mehns ray-uh). Mental state, or intent. A wrongful mental state is usually as necessary as a wrongful act to establish criminal liability.

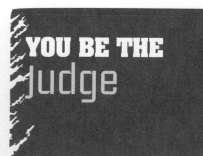

YOU BE THE Judge

A VOLUNTARY ACT?

THE FACTS On a bright, sunny afternoon, Emil was driving on Delaware Avenue in Buffalo, New York. As he was making a turn, Emil suffered an epileptic seizure and lost control of his automobile. The car careened onto the sidewalk and struck a group of six schoolgirls, killing four of them. Emil knew that he was subject to epileptic attacks that rendered him likely to lose consciousness.

THE LAW An "act" committed while one is unconscious is in reality not an act at all. It is merely a physical event or occurrence over which the defendant has no control—that is, such an act is involuntary. If the defendant voluntarily causes the loss of consciousness by, for example, using drugs or alcohol, however, then he or she will usually be held criminally responsible for any consequences.

YOUR DECISION Emil was charged in the deaths of the four girls. He asked the court to dismiss the charges, as he was unconscious at the time of the accident and therefore had not committed a voluntary act. In your opinion, is there an *actus reus* in this situation, or should the charges against Emil be dismissed?

To see how the appellate court in New York ruled in this case, go to Example 4.1 in Appendix B.

THE CATEGORIES OF *MENS REA* A guilty mental state includes elements of purpose, knowledge, negligence, and recklessness.[21] A defendant is said to have *purposefully* committed a criminal act when he or she desires to engage in certain criminal conduct or to cause a certain criminal result. For a defendant to have *knowingly* committed an illegal act, he or she must be aware of the illegality, must believe that the illegality exists, or must correctly suspect that the illegality exists but fail to do anything to dispel (or confirm) his or her belief.

Negligence Criminal **negligence** involves the mental state in which the defendant grossly deviates from the standard of care that a reasonable person would use under the same circumstances. The defendant is accused of taking an unjustified, substantial, and foreseeable risk that resulted in harm. In 2012, for example, a San Diego County, California, man named Richard Fox killed his girlfriend by accidentally shooting her with a homemade cannon. The fireworks enthusiast obviously did not intend for his girlfriend to die. At the same time, there is certainly a foreseeable risk inherent in operating homemade cannons around other people. Eventually, Fox was arrested for negligently discharging an explosive instead of murder.

Recklessness A defendant who commits an act recklessly is more blameworthy than one who is criminally negligent. The Model Penal Code defines criminal **recklessness** as "consciously disregard[ing] a substantial and unjustifiable risk."[22] So, in 2012, a Waldo County, Maine, jury found Luke Bryant guilty of criminal recklessness in the death of his friend Tyler Seaney. Bryant killed Seaney while the two were playing a game that involved pointing unloaded shotguns at each other and pulling the trigger. Even though Bryant was unaware that the gun was actually loaded in this instance, the risk of harm associated with this game was so great that the jury felt he should have taken greater safety measures. (As you can see, the difference between negligence and recklessness is not always clear. One could certainly argue that Richard Fox's behavior in causing the death of his girlfriend, described above, rose to the level of recklessness.)

DEGREES OF CRIME In the previous chapter, you learned that crimes are graded by degree. Generally speaking, the degree of a crime is a reflection of the seriousness of that crime, and is used to determine the severity of any subsequent punishment.

With many crimes, degree is a function of the criminal act itself, as determined by statute. For example, most criminal codes consider a burglary that involves a nighttime forced entry into a home to be a burglary in the first degree. If the same act takes place during the day and involves a nonresidential building, then it is burglary in the second degree. As you might expect, burglary in the first degree carries a harsher penalty than burglary in the second degree.

Willful Murder With murder, the degree of the crime is, to a large extent, determined by the mental state of the offender. Murder is generally defined as the willful killing of a human being. It is important to emphasize the word *willful*, as it precludes homicides caused by accident or negligence. A death that results from negligence or accident generally is considered a private wrong and therefore a matter for civil law.

In addition, criminal law punishes those who plan and intend to do harm more harshly than it does those who act wrongfully because of strong emotions or other extreme circumstances. First degree murder—usually punishable by life in prison or the death penalty—occurs under two circumstances:

Negligence A failure to exercise the standard of care that a reasonable person would exercise in similar circumstances.

Recklessness The state of being aware that a risk does or will exist and nevertheless acting in a way that consciously disregards this risk.

1. When the crime is premeditated, or contemplated beforehand by the offender, instead of being a spontaneous act of violence.
2. When the crime is deliberate, meaning that it was planned and decided on after a process of decision making. Deliberation does not require a lengthy planning process. A person can be found guilty of first degree murder even if she or he made the decision to kill only seconds before committing the crime.

Second degree murder, usually punishable by a minimum of fifteen to twenty-five years in prison, occurs when no premeditation or deliberation was present, but the offender did have *malice aforethought* toward the victim. In other words, the offender acted with wanton disregard for the consequences of his or her actions. (*Malice* means "wrongful intention" or "the desire to do evil.")

The difference between first and second degree murder is illustrated in a case involving a California man who beat a neighbor to death with a partially full brandy bottle. The crime took place after Ricky McDonald, the victim, complained to Kazi Cooksey, the offender, about the noise coming from a late-night barbecue Cooksey and his friends were holding. The jury could not find sufficient evidence that Cooksey's actions were premeditated, but he certainly acted with wanton disregard for his victim's safety. Therefore, the jury convicted Cooksey of second degree murder rather than first degree murder.

Types of Manslaughter A homicide committed without malice toward the victim is known as *manslaughter* and is commonly punishable by up to fifteen years in prison. **Voluntary manslaughter** occurs when the intent to kill may be present, but malice is lacking. Voluntary manslaughter covers crimes of passion, in which the emotion of an argument between two friends may lead to a homicide. Voluntary manslaughter can also occur when the victim provoked the offender to act violently.

Involuntary manslaughter covers incidents in which the offender's acts may have been careless, but he or she had no intent to kill. Several years ago, for example, Dr. Conrad Murray was convicted of involuntary manslaughter for his role in the death of pop star Michael Jackson. Murray had provided Jackson with a powerful anesthetic to help Jackson sleep, and the dosage proved fatal. Although Murray had certainly not intended for Jackson to die, he was held criminally responsible for the singer's death and sentenced to four years in prison. As Figure 4.2 on the next page shows, the distinction between manslaughter and murder is not always clear, and rests on intent.

STRICT LIABILITY For certain crimes, criminal law holds the defendant to be guilty even if intent to commit the offense is lacking. These acts are known as **strict liability crimes** and generally involve endangering the public welfare in some way.[23] Drug-control statutes, health and safety regulations, and traffic laws are all strict liability laws.

Protecting the Public To a certain extent, the concept of strict liability is inconsistent with the traditional principles of criminal law, which hold that *mens rea* is required for an act to be criminal. The goal of strict liability laws is to protect the public by eliminating the possibility that wrongdoers could claim ignorance or mistake to absolve themselves of criminal responsibility.[24] Thus, a person caught dumping waste in a protected pond or driving 70 miles per hour in a 55 miles-per-hour zone cannot plead a lack of intent in his or her defense.

The principle is often applied in more serious situations as well. In December 2012, Cody Trailes was charged with first degree murder in connection with the heroin

Voluntary Manslaughter A homicide in which the intent to kill was present in the mind of the offender, but malice was lacking.

Involuntary Manslaughter A homicide in which the offender had no intent to kill her or his victim.

Strict Liability Crimes Certain crimes, such as traffic violations, in which the defendant is guilty regardless of her or his state of mind at the time of the act.

LEARNING **5** OBJECTIVE Explain how the doctrine of strict liability applies to criminal law.

FIGURE 4.2 Murder or Manslaughter?

As this case shows, different degrees of murder are determined by the *mens rea* of the offender.

The Crime: University of Virginia senior George Huguely, drunk, decides to pay a visit to his ex-girlfriend Yeardley Love's off-campus apartment after midnight. When she refuses to answer the door, he kicks it down, grabs Love by the neck, and wrestles her to the floor. Several hours later, Love's roommate finds her lying face down on a pillow, in a pool of blood, dead.

The Prosecution: Prosecutors charge Huguely with **first degree murder,** punishable by life in prison. They argue that Huguely was enraged because Love was dating someone else, and the murder was **premeditated and deliberate.**

The Defense: Huguely's defense lawyers claim that the crime was **manslaughter,** punishable by one to ten years in prison. They argue that their drunken client **did not intend** to harm Love, much less kill her, and point out that Love **died from suffocation** well after Huguely left her apartment.

The Jury: The jurors found Huguely guilty of **second degree murder,** punishable by twenty-six years in prison. They found that although Huguely **did not intend** to kill Love, he did act with **malice aforethought** and caused her death.

■ On February 22, 2012, George Huguely V is led to court for jury deliberations in Charlottesville, Virginia.
AP Photo/Steve Helber

overdose death of John Simmons, Jr. There was no evidence that Trailes intended for Simmons to die, or even knew him. He did, however, supply Simmons with the heroin that led to the overdose. In most jurisdictions, Trailes would only be charged with a drug offense under these circumstances. Under New Jersey law, however, strict liability murder is imposed on anybody who helps another person obtain drugs that lead to a fatal overdose.[25] As a result, Trailes's *mens rea* concerning Simmons's death was irrelevant.

Protecting Minors One of the most controversial strict liability crimes is **statutory rape,** in which an adult engages in a sexual relationship with a minor. In most states, even if the minor consents to the sexual act, the crime still exists because, being underage, he or she is considered incapable of making a rational decision on the matter.[26] Therefore, statutory rape has been committed even if the adult was unaware of the minor's age or was misled to believe that the minor was older.

ACCOMPLICE LIABILITY Under certain circumstances, a person can be charged with and convicted of a crime that he or she did not actually commit. This occurs when the suspect has acted as an *accomplice,* helping another person commit the crime. Generally, to be found guilty as an accomplice, a person must have the "dual intent" (1) to aid the person who committed the crime and (2) that such aid would lead to the commission of the crime.[27] As for the *actus reus,* the accomplice must have helped the primary actor in either a physical sense (for example, by providing the getaway car) or a psychological sense (for example, by encouraging her or him to commit the crime).[28]

In some states, a person can be convicted as an accomplice even without intent if the crime was a "natural and probable consequence" of his or her actions.[29] This principle has led to a proliferation of **felony-murder** legislation. Felony-murder is a form of first degree murder that applies when a person participates in any of a list of serious felonies that results in the death of a human being. Under felony-murder law, if two men

Statutory Rape A strict liability crime in which an adult engages in a sexual act with a minor.

Felony-Murder An unlawful homicide that occurs during the attempted commission of a felony.

rob a bank, and the first man intentionally kills a security guard, the second man can be convicted of first degree murder as an accomplice to the bank robbery, even if he had no intent to hurt anyone. Along these same lines, if a security guard accidentally shoots and kills a customer during a bank robbery, the bank robbers can be charged with first degree murder because they committed the underlying felony.

In the case that opened this chapter, authorities were able to charge Rickie Lee Fowler under California's felony-murder law. Even though Fowler, at worst, intended to commit arson, that particular crime is a felony and the wildfire was found to have caused the five fatal heart attacks. These kinds of laws have come under criticism because they punish individuals for unintended act or acts committed by others. Nevertheless, the criminal codes of more than thirty states include some form of the felony-murder rule.[30]

Concurrence

According to criminal law, there must be *concurrence* between the guilty act and the guilty intent. In other words, the guilty act and the guilty intent must occur together.[31] Suppose, for example, that a woman intends to murder her husband with poison in order to collect his life insurance. Every evening, this woman drives her husband home from work. On the night she plans to poison him, however, she swerves to avoid a cat crossing the road and runs into a tree. She survives the accident, but her husband is killed. Even though her intent was realized, the incident would be considered an accidental death because she had not planned to kill him by driving the car into a tree.

Attendant Circumstances
The facts surrounding a criminal event that must be proved to convict the defendant of the underlying crime.

Hate Crime Law A statute that provides for greater sanctions against those who commit crimes motivated by bias against an individual or a group based on race, ethnicity, religion, gender, sexual orientation, disability, or age.

Causation

Criminal law also requires that the criminal act cause the harm suffered. In 1989, for example, nineteen-year-old Mike Wells shook his two-year-old daughter, Christina, so violently that she suffered brain damage. Soon after the incident, Wells served prison time for aggravated child abuse. Seventeen years later, in 2006, Christina died. When a coroner ruled that the cause of death was the earlier brain injury, Pasco County (Florida) authorities decided that, despite the passage of time, Wells was criminally responsible for his daughter's death. In 2010, Wells pleaded guilty to second degree murder and received a fifteen-year prison sentence.

Attendant Circumstances

In certain crimes, **attendant circumstances**—also known as accompanying circumstances—are relevant to the *corpus delicti*. Most states, for example, differentiate between simple assault and the more serious offense of aggravated assault depending on the attendant circumstance of whether the defendant used a weapon such as a gun or a knife while committing the crime. Criminal law also classifies degrees of property crimes based on the attendant circumstance of the amount stolen. According to federal statutes, the theft of less than $1,000 from a bank is a misdemeanor, while the theft of any amount over $1,000 is a felony.[32] (To get a better understanding of the role of attendant circumstances in criminal statutes, see Figure 4.3 below.)

REQUIREMENTS OF PROOF AND INTENT Attendant circumstances must be proved beyond a reasonable doubt, just like any other element of a crime.[33] Furthermore, the *mens rea* of the defendant regarding each attendant circumstance must be proved as well. Consider the case of Christopher Jones, who was recently convicted of third degree rape in a South Dakota criminal court. Under state law, third degree rape occurs when the victim is incapable of giving consent to the sex act due to severe intoxication.

A South Dakota appeals court overturned Jones's conviction, ruling that prosecutors did not prove beyond a reasonable doubt that the defendant knew of his victim's drunken state and, thus, her inability to give consent. The court added that if the state legislature wanted to remove such knowledge from the definition of the crime, it must say so in the statute, thus making awareness of the victim's intoxication a *strict liability* (see the previous discussion) attendant circumstance.[34]

HATE CRIME LAWS In most cases, a person's motive for committing a crime is irrelevant—a court will not try to read the accused's mind. Over the past few decades, however, nearly every state and the federal government have passed *hate crime laws* that make the suspect's motive an important attendant circumstance to his or her criminal act. In general, **hate crime laws** provide for greater sanctions against those who com-

FIGURE 4.3 Attendant Circumstances in Criminal Law

Most criminal statutes incorporate three of the elements we have discussed in this section: the act (*actus reus*), the intent (*mens rea*), and attendant circumstances. This diagram of the federal false imprisonment statute should give you an idea of how these elements combine to create the totality of a crime.

| Intent | Act | Attendant Circumstances |

Whoever intentionally confines, restrains, or detains another against that person's will is guilty of felony false imprisonment.

mit crimes motivated by bias against a person based on race, ethnicity, religion, gender, sexual orientation, disability, or age. The concept of a hate crime as measurable, definable criminal behavior is a relatively new one and, as we will see in the *Criminal Justice in Action* feature at the end of this chapter, has its detractors.

Harm

For most crimes to occur, some harm must have been done to a person or to property. A certain number of crimes are actually categorized depending on the harm done to the victim, regardless of the intent behind the criminal act. Take two offenses, both of which involve one person hitting another in the back of the head with a tire iron. In the first instance, the victim dies, and the offender is charged with murder. In the second, the victim is only knocked unconscious, and the offender is charged with battery. Because the harm in the second instance was less severe, so was the crime with which the offender was charged, even though the act was exactly the same. Furthermore, most states have different degrees of battery depending on the extent of the injuries suffered by the victim.

Many acts are deemed criminal if they could do harm that the laws try to prevent. Such acts are called **inchoate offenses.** They exist when only an attempt at a criminal act was made. If Jenkins solicits Peterson to murder Jenkins's business partner, this is an inchoate offense on the part of Jenkins, even though Peterson fails to carry out the act. Threats and *conspiracies* also fall into the category of inchoate offenses. In 2012, a Cedar Lake, Indiana, man was arrested on charges of felony intimidation for threatening to set his wife on fire and "kill as many people as possible" at the school where she worked. The United States Supreme Court has ruled that a person could be convicted of criminal **conspiracy** even though police intervention made the completion of the illegal plan impossible.[35]

SELF ASSESSMENT

Fill in the blanks and check your answers on page 128.

Proof that a crime has been committed is established through the elements of the crime, which include the _____ _____, or the physical act of the crime; the _____ _____, or the intent to commit the crime; and the _____ of the guilty act and the guilty intent. With _____ _____ crimes, the law determines that a defendant is guilty even if he or she lacked the _____ to perform a criminal act. _____ circumstances are those circumstances that accompany the main criminal act in a criminal code, and they must be proved _____ _____ _____ _____, just like any other elements of a crime.

DEFENSES UNDER CRIMINAL LAW

According to prosecutors, Derrick Francois fatally shot Chandrick Harris in the head as part of a family feud that had gotten out of control in Gretna, Louisiana. On January 7, 2013, however, the day before Francois's murder trial was to begin, his defense attorneys presented pay stubs backing Francois's claim that he was working in Pascagoula, Mississippi, at the time of Harris's killing in Gretna. That is, they raised an **alibi** defense, saying that their client could not possibly have committed this murder because he was somewhere else when it occurred. Along with presenting an alibi, defendants can raise a number of other defenses for wrongdoing in our criminal courts. These defenses generally rely on one of two arguments: (1) the defendant is not responsible for the crime, or (2) the defendant was justified in committing the crime.

Criminal Responsibility and the Law

The idea of responsibility plays a significant role in criminal law. In certain circumstances, the law recognizes that even though an act is inherently criminal, society will not punish the actor because he or she does not have the requisite mental condition. In other words, the law "excuses" the person for his or her behavior. Insanity, intoxication, and mistake are the most important excuse defenses today, but we start our discussion of the subject with one of the first such defenses recognized by American law: infancy.

INFANCY Under the earliest state criminal codes of the United States, children younger than seven years of age could never be held legally accountable for crimes. Those between seven and fourteen years old were presumed to lack the capacity for criminal behavior, while anyone over the age of fourteen was tried as an adult. Thus, early American criminal law recognized **infancy** as a defense in which the accused's wrongdoing is excused because he or she is too young to fully understand the consequences of his or her actions.

With the creation of the juvenile justice system in the early 1900s, the infancy defense became redundant, as youthful delinquents were automatically treated differently from adult offenders. Today, most states either designate an age (eighteen or under) under which wrongdoers are sent to juvenile court or allow prosecutors to decide whether a minor will be charged as an adult on a case-by-case basis. We will explore the concept of infancy as it applies to the modern American juvenile justice system in much greater detail in Chapter 15.

INSANITY After Leo Kwaska killed and decapitated Shirley Meeks, his downstairs neighbor, he told psychiatrists that Meeks was a demon and that he needed to kill her to avert the end of the world. In 2012, a Jackson County, Mississippi, judge found that Kwaska's severe mental illness kept him from knowing that his actions were wrong. As a result, Kwaska was sent to a psychiatric hospital rather than prison. Thus, **insanity** may be a defense to a criminal charge when the defendant's state of mind is such that she or he cannot claim legal responsibility for her or his actions.

Measuring Sanity The general principle of the insanity defense is that a person is excused for his or her criminal wrongdoing if, as a result of a mental disease or defect, he or she

- Does not perceive the physical nature or consequences of his or her conduct;
- Does not know that his or her conduct is wrong or criminal; or
- Is not sufficiently able to control his or her conduct so as to be held accountable for it.[36]

Although criminal law has traditionally accepted the idea that an insane person cannot be held responsible for criminal acts, society has long debated what standards should be used to measure sanity for the purposes of a criminal trial. This lack of consensus is reflected in the diverse tests employed by different American jurisdictions to determine insanity. The tests include the following:

1. *The* M'Naghten *rule.* Derived from an 1843 British murder case, the **M'Naghten rule** states that a person is legally insane and therefore not criminally responsible if, at the time of the offense, he or she was not able to distinguish between right and wrong.[37] As Figure 4.4 on the facing page shows, half of the states still use a version of the *M'Naghten* rule. One state, New Hampshire, uses a slightly different version of this rule called the "product test." Under this standard, a defendant is not guilty if the unlawful act was the product of a mental disease or defect.

Infancy A condition that, under early American law, excused young wrongdoers of criminal behavior because presumably they could not understand the consequences of their actions.

Insanity A defense for criminal liability that asserts a lack of criminal responsibility due to mental instability

M'Naghten Rule A common law test of criminal responsibility, derived from *M'Naghten's* Case in 1843, that relies on the defendant's inability to distinguish right from wrong.

2. *The ALI/MPC test.* In the early 1960s, the American Law Institute (ALI) included an insanity standard in its Model Penal Code (MPC), discussed earlier in the chapter. Also known as the **substantial-capacity test,** the **ALI/MPC test** requires that the defendant lack "substantial capacity" to either "appreciate the wrongfulness" of his or her conduct or to conform that conduct "to the requirements of the law."[38]

3. *The irresistible-impulse test.* Under the **irresistible-impulse test,** a person may be found insane even if he or she was aware that a criminal act was "wrong," provided that some "irresistible impulse" resulting from a mental deficiency drove him or her to commit the crime.[39]

The ALI/MPC test is considered the easiest standard of the three for a defendant to meet because the defendant needs only to show a lack of "substantial capacity" to be released from criminal responsibility. Defense attorneys generally consider it more difficult to prove that the defendant could not distinguish "right" from "wrong" or that he or she was driven by an irresistible impulse.

Determining Competency Whatever the standard, the insanity defense is rarely entered and is even less likely to result in an acquittal, as it is difficult to prove.[40] (See the feature *Myth versus Reality—Are Too Many Criminals Found Not Guilty by Reason of Insanity?* on the following page.) Psychiatry is far more commonly used in the courtroom to determine the "competency" of a defendant to stand trial. If a judge believes that the defendant is unable to understand the nature of the proceedings or to assist in his or her own defense, the trial will not take place.

Substantial-Capacity Test (ALI/MPC Test) A test for the insanity defense that states that a person is not responsible for criminal behavior when he or she "lacks substantial capacity" to understand that the behavior is wrong or to know how to behave properly.

Irresistible-Impulse Test A test for the insanity defense under which a defendant who knew his or her action was wrong may still be found insane if he or she was unable, as a result of a mental deficiency, to control the urge to complete the act.

FIGURE 4.4 Insanity Defenses

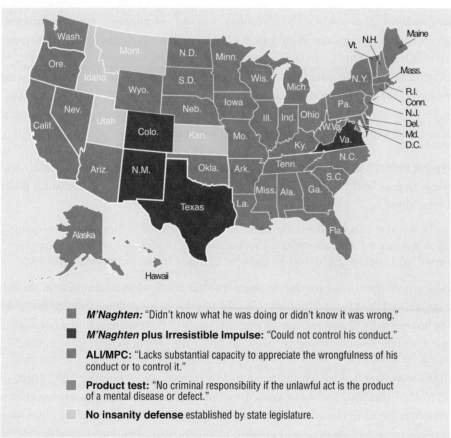

- ■ *M'Naghten:* "Didn't know what he was doing or didn't know it was wrong."
- ■ *M'Naghten* plus **Irresistible Impulse:** "Could not control his conduct."
- ■ **ALI/MPC:** "Lacks substantial capacity to appreciate the wrongfulness of his conduct or to control it."
- ■ **Product test:** "No criminal responsibility if the unlawful act is the product of a mental disease or defect."
- ■ **No insanity defense** established by state legislature.

Are Too Many Criminals Found Not Guilty by Reason of Insanity?

Saicle/
Shutterstock.com

LEARNING OBJECTIVE 7 Discuss a common misperception concerning the insaniy defense in the United States.

To many Americans, it seems likely that any person who commits a gruesome murder or any other sort of violent crime has psychological problems. The question, then, is, how do we balance the need to punish such a person with the possibility that he or she may be seriously ill?

THE MYTH The American system of criminal justice answers this question by stating that a person may not be tried for an offense if that person cannot be held legally responsible for her or his actions. Because of the publicity surrounding the insanity defense, many people are under the impression that it is a major loophole in our system, allowing criminals to be "let off" no matter how heinous their crimes.

THE REALITY In fact, the insanity defense is raised in only about 1 percent of felony trials, and it is successful only one out of every four times it is raised. The reason: it is extremely difficult to prove insanity under the law. For example, Andre

Thomas cut out the hearts of his wife, their young son, and her thirteen-month-old daughter. Before his murder trial, Thomas pulled his right eye out of its socket. (Several years later, while on death row, he ripped out the other eye and apparently ate it.) Nonetheless, prosecutors were able to convince a Texas jury that Brown understood the difference between right and wrong at the time of the murders, and an appeals court upheld the conviction. Thomas is "clearly 'crazy,'" said one of the appellate judges who heard his case, "but he is also 'sane' under Texas law."

Even if Thomas had succeeded with the insanity defense, he would not have been "let off" in the sense that he would have been set free. Many defendants found not guilty by reason of insanity spend more time in mental hospitals than criminals who are convicted of similar acts spend in prison.

FOR CRITICAL ANALYSIS
What do the relatively limited use and success rate of the insanity defense indicate about the impact of public opinion on criminal law?

When **competency hearings** (which may also take place after the initial arrest and before sentencing) reveal that the defendant is in fact incompetent, criminal proceedings come to a halt. For example, in January 2013, an Alameda County (California) judge ruled that because One L. Goh suffered from paranoid schizophrenia, he was not fit to stand trial. Goh had been charged with seven counts of murder resulting from a shooting rampage on the campus of Oikos University in Oakland. As a result of the judge's decision, Goh would receive psychiatric treatment to restore his competency. When this goal was achieved, the criminal proceedings would continue.

Guilty but Mentally Ill Public backlash against the insanity defense caused six state legislatures to pass "guilty but mentally ill" statutes. Under these laws, a defendant is guilty but mentally ill if

> at the time of the commission of the act constituting the offense, he [or she] had the capacity to distinguish right from wrong . . . but because of mental disease or defect he [or she] lacked sufficient capacity to conform his [or her] conduct to the requirements of the law.[41]

Competency Hearing A court proceeding to determine whether the defendant is mentally well enough to understand the charges filed against him or her and cooperate with a lawyer in presenting a defense.

Intoxication A defense for criminal liability in which the defendant claims that the taking of intoxicants rendered him or her unable to form the requisite intent to commit a criminal act.

In other words, the laws allow a jury to determine that a defendant is "mentally ill," though not insane, and therefore criminally responsible for her or his actions. Defendants found guilty but mentally ill generally spend the early years of their sentences in a psychiatric hospital and the rest of the time in prison, or they receive treatment while in prison.

INTOXICATION The law recognizes two types of **intoxication,** whether from drugs or from alcohol: *voluntary* and *involuntary.* Involuntary intoxication occurs when a person is physically forced to ingest or is injected with an intoxicating substance, or is unaware that a substance contains drugs or alcohol. Involuntary intoxication is a viable defense to a crime if the substance leaves the person unable to form the mental state necessary to understand that the act committed while under the influence was wrong.[42] In Colorado, for example, the murder conviction of a man who shot a neighbor was overturned on the basis that the jury in the initial trial was not informed of the possibility of involuntary intoxication. At the time of the crime, the man had been taking a prescription decongestant that contained phenylpropanolamine, which has been known to cause psychotic episodes.

Voluntary drug or alcohol intoxication is also used to excuse a defendant's actions, though it is not a defense in itself. Rather, it is used when the defense attorney wants to show that the defendant was so intoxicated that *mens rea* was negated. In other words, the defendant could not possibly have had the state of mind that a crime requires. Many courts are reluctant to allow voluntary intoxication arguments to be presented to juries, however. After all, the defendant, by definition, voluntarily chose to enter an intoxicated state.

Twelve states have eliminated voluntary intoxication as a possible defense, a step that has been criticized by many legal scholars but was upheld by the United States Supreme Court in *Montana v. Egelhoff* (1996).[43] The case concerned a double murder committed by James Allen Egelhoff, who was extremely drunk at the time of the crime. Egelhoff was convicted on two counts of deliberate homicide, which is defined by Montana law as "knowingly" or "purposefully" causing the death of another human being.[44] Egelhoff appealed his conviction, arguing that the state statute prohibiting evidence of voluntary intoxication kept his attorneys from showing the jury that he was too inebriated to "knowingly" or "purposefully" commit the murders.[45] The Court allowed Egelhoff's conviction, ruling that states were constitutionally within their rights to abolish the voluntary intoxication defense.

■ According to prosecutors, seventeen-year-old Tyler Hadley beat his parents to death with a hammer in Port St. Lucie, Florida. Hadley claims that he took three pills of the psychoactive drug ecstasy before the homicides. How could Hadley's defense attorneys use this information in defending their client against first degree murder charges?
(AP Photo/St. Lucie County Sheriff's office)

MISTAKE Everyone has heard the saying, "Ignorance of the law is no excuse." Ordinarily, ignorance of the law or a *mistaken idea* about what the law requires is not a valid defense.[46] For example, several years ago retired science teacher Eddie Leroy Anderson and his son dug for arrowheads near their favorite campground site in Idaho, unaware that the land was a federally protected archaeological site. Facing two years in prison for this mistake, they pleaded guilty and were given a year's probation and a $1,500 fine each. "Folks need to pay attention to where they are," said U.S. attorney Wendy Olson.[47]

Mistake of Law As the above example suggests, strict liability crimes specifically preclude the *mistake of law* defense, because the offender's intent is irrelevant. For practical reasons, the mistake of law defense is rarely allowed under any circumstances. If "I didn't know" was a valid defense, the courts would be clogged with defendants claiming ignorance of all aspects of criminal law. In some rare instances, however, people who claim that they honestly did not know that they were breaking a law may have a valid defense if (1) the law was not published or reasonably known to the public or (2) the person relied on an official statement of the law that was erroneous.[48]

Mistake of Fact A *mistake of fact*, as opposed to a *mistake of law,* operates as a defense if it negates the mental state necessary to commit a crime. If, for example, Oliver mistakenly walks off with Julie's briefcase because he thinks it is his, there is no theft. Theft requires knowledge that the property belongs to another. The mistake-of-fact defense has proved very controversial in rape and sexual assault cases, in which the accused claims a mistaken belief that the sex was consensual, while the victim insists that he or she was coerced.

Justification Criminal Defenses and the Law

Describe the four most important justification criminal defenses.

LEARNING
8
OBJECTIVE

In certain instances, a defendant will accept responsibility for committing an illegal act, but contend that—given the circumstances—the act was justified. In other words, even though the guilty act and the guilty intent are present, the particulars of the case relieve the defendant of criminal liability. In 2011, for example, there were 653 "justified" killings of those who were in the process of committing a felony: 393 were killed by law enforcement officers and 260 by private citizens.[49] Four of the most important justification defenses are duress, self-defense, necessity, and entrapment.

DURESS **Duress** exists when the *wrongful* threat of one person induces another person to perform an act that she or he would otherwise not perform. In such a situation, duress is said to negate the *mens rea* necessary to commit a crime. For duress to qualify as a defense, the following requirements must be met:

1. The threat must be of serious bodily harm or death.
2. The harm threatened must be greater than the harm caused by the crime.
3. The threat must be immediate and inescapable.
4. The defendant must have become involved in the situation through no fault of his or her own.[50]

Note that some scholars consider duress to be an excuse defense, because the threat of bodily harm negates any guilty intent on the part of the defendant.[51]

When ruling on the duress defense, courts often examine whether the defendant had the opportunity to avoid the threat in question. Two narcotics cases illustrate this point. In the first, the defendant claimed that an associate threatened to kill him and his wife unless he participated in a marijuana deal. Although this contention was proved true during the course of the trial, the court rejected the duress defense because the defendant made no apparent effort to escape, nor did he report his dilemma to the police. In sum, the drug deal was avoidable—the defendant could have made an effort to extricate himself, but he did not, thereby surrendering the protection of the duress defense.[52]

In the second case, a taxi driver in Bogotá, Colombia, was ordered by a passenger to swallow cocaine-filled balloons and take them to the United States. The taxi driver was warned that if he refused, his wife and three-year-old daughter would be killed. After a series of similar threats, the taxi driver agreed to transport the drugs. On arriving at customs at the Los Angeles airport, the defendant consented to have his stomach X-rayed, which led to discovery of the contraband and his arrest. During his trial, the defendant told the court that he was afraid to notify the police in Colombia because he believed them to be corrupt. The court accepted his duress defense, on the grounds that it met the four requirements listed above and the defendant had notified American authorities when given the opportunity to do so.[53]

JUSTIFIABLE USE OF FORCE—SELF-DEFENSE A person who believes he or she is in danger of being harmed by another is justified in defending himself or herself with the use of force, and any criminal act committed in such circumstances can be justified as **self-defense.** Other situations that also justify the use of force include the defense of another person, the defense of one's dwelling or other property, and the prevention of

Duress Unlawful pressure brought to bear on a person, causing the person to perform an act that he or she would not otherwise perform.

Self-Defense The legally recognized privilege to protect one's self or property from injury by another.

a crime. In all these situations, it is important to distinguish between deadly and non-deadly force. Deadly force is likely to result in death or serious bodily harm.

The Amount of Force Generally speaking, people can use the amount of nondeadly force that seems necessary to protect themselves, their dwellings, or other property or to prevent the commission of a crime. Deadly force can be used in self-defense if there is a *reasonable belief* that imminent death or bodily harm will otherwise result, if the attacker is using unlawful force (an example of lawful force is that exerted by a police officer), if the defender has not initiated or provoked the attack, and if there is no other possible response or alternative way out of the life-threatening situation.[54]

Deadly force normally can be used to defend a dwelling only if the unlawful entry is violent and the person believes deadly force is necessary to prevent imminent death or great bodily harm. In some jurisdictions, it is also a viable defense if the person believes deadly force is necessary to prevent the commission of a felony (such as arson) in the dwelling. Authorities will often take an expansive view of lawful deadly force when it is used to protect another person, particularly a loved one. So, in 2012, a Shiner, Texas, man was not charged with any crime after he beat to death a man who was in the process of sexually molesting the assailant's five-year-old daughter.

The Duty to Retreat When a person is outside the home or in a public space, the rules for self-defense change somewhat. Until relatively recently, almost all jurisdictions required someone who is attacked under these circumstances to "retreat to the wall" before fighting back. In other words, under this **duty to retreat** one who is being assaulted may not resort to deadly force if she or he has a reasonable opportunity to "run away" and thus avoid the conflict. Only when this person has run into a "wall," literally or otherwise, may deadly force be used in self-defense.

Recently, however, several states have changed their laws to eliminate this duty to retreat. For example, a Florida law did away with the duty to retreat outside the home, stating that citizens have "the right to stand [their] ground and meet force with force, including deadly force," if they "reasonably" fear for their safety.[55] The Florida law also allows a person to use deadly force against someone who unlawfully intrudes into her or his house (or vehicle), even if that person does not fear for her or his safety.[56]

The George Zimmerman Case At least twenty-five states have broadened their self-defense laws to include a version of Florida's "stand your ground" statute. These laws became a topic of much debate when George Zimmerman shot and killed unarmed seventeen-year-old Trayvon Martin in Sanford, Florida, on February 26, 2012. Zimmerman told police that he had encountered Martin during his rounds as a neighborhood watchman, and that he had pulled the trigger only after being attacked by the younger man. Initially, Florida authorities accepted this version of events and did not arrest Zimmerman, who appeared to have acted within the limits of the state's "stand your ground" law.

Duty to Retreat The requirement that a person claiming self-defense prove that she or he first took reasonable steps to avoid the conflict that resulted in the use of deadly force.

George Zimmerman, shown here in a Seminole County (Florida) courthouse, insisted that his voice could be heard screaming for help on a 911 recording of his deadly encounter with Trayvon Martin. How might this piece of evidence have helped Zimmerman's self-defense claims?
Stephen M. Dowell-Pool/Getty Images

Necessity A defense against criminal liability in which the defendant asserts that circumstances required her or him to commit an illegal act.

Entrapment A defense in which the defendant claims that he or she was induced by a public official—usually an undercover agent or police officer—to commit a crime that he or she would otherwise not have committed.

This decision was met with a national outcry. Much of the anger focused on aspects of the incident that seemed to indicate racial bias. (Zimmerman is Hispanic, while Martin was African American.) Furthermore, critics worry that the proliferation of "stand your ground" laws has created a "nation where disputes are settled by guns instead of gavels, and where suspects are shot by civilians instead of arrested by police."[57] A special prosecutor eventually charged Zimmerman with second degree murder. In July 2013, a jury acquitted Zimmerman. The jurors, apparently influenced by photos of the defendant's bloodied head taken by police after the incident, agreed that he could have acted reasonably in defending himself against great bodily harm or death.[58]

NECESSITY The **necessity** defense requires courts to weigh the harm caused by the crime actually committed against the harm that would have been caused by the criminal act avoided. If the avoided harm is greater than the committed harm, then the defense has a chance of succeeding. Several years ago, for example, a San Francisco jury acquitted a defendant of illegally carrying a concealed weapon because he was avoiding the "greater evil" of getting shot himself. The defendant had testified that he needed the gun for protection while entering a high-crime neighborhood to buy baby food and diapers for his crying niece.[59] Murder is the one crime for which the necessity defense is not applicable under any circumstances.[60]

ENTRAPMENT **Entrapment** is a justification defense that criminal law allows when a police officer or government agent deceives a defendant into wrongdoing. Although law enforcement agents can legitimately use various forms of subterfuge—such as informants or undercover agents—to gain information or apprehend a suspect in a criminal act, the law places limits on these strategies. Police cannot persuade an innocent person to commit a crime, nor can they coerce a suspect into doing so, even if they are certain she or he is a criminal.

The guidelines for determining entrapment were established in the 1932 case of *Sorrells v. United States*.[61] The case, which took place during Prohibition, when the sale of alcoholic beverages was illegal, involved a federal law enforcement agent who repeatedly urged the defendant to sell him bootleg whiskey. The defendant initially rejected the agent's overtures, stating that he "did not fool with whiskey." Eventually, however, he sold the agent a half-gallon of the substance and was summarily convicted of violating the law. The United States Supreme Court held that the agent had improperly induced the defendant to break the law and reversed his conviction.

This case set the precedent for focusing on the defendant's outlook in entrapment cases. In other words, the Court decided that entrapment occurs if a defendant who is not predisposed to commit the crime is convinced to do so by an agent of the government.[62] (For an overview of justification and excuse defenses, see Figure 4.5 on the facing page.)

SELF ASSESSMENT

Fill in the blanks and check your answers on page 128.

Criminal law recognizes that a defendant may not be _____ for a criminal act if her or his mental state was impaired, by either _____—the psychological inability to separate right from wrong—or _____ due to drugs or alcohol. Defendants may also claim that they were _____ in committing an act either because they were under _____ to perform an act that they would not otherwise have performed or because they were acting in _____-_____ to protect themselves from serious bodily harm. _____ occurs when a government agent deceives a defendant into committing a crime.

FIGURE 4.5 Justification and Excuse Defenses

Justification Defenses: Based on a defendant admitting that he or she committed the particular criminal act, but asserting that, under the circumstances, the criminal act was justified.

	The defendant must prove that:	Example
DURESS	She or he performed the criminal act under the use or threat of use of unlawful force against her or his person that a reasonable person would have been unable to resist.	A mother assists her boyfriend in committing a burglary after he threatens to kill her children if she refuses to do so.
SELF-DEFENSE	He or she acted in a manner to defend himself or herself, others, or property, or to prevent the commission of a crime.	A husband awakes to find his wife standing over him, pointing a shotgun at his chest. In the ensuing struggle, the firearm goes off, killing the wife.
NECESSITY	The criminal act he or she committed was necessary in order to avoid a harm to himself or herself or another that was greater than the harm caused by the act itself.	Four people physically remove a friend from her residence on the property of a religious cult, arguing that the crime of kidnapping was justified in order to remove the victim from the damaging influence of cult leaders.
ENTRAPMENT	She or he was encouraged by agents of the state to engage in a criminal act she or he would not have engaged in otherwise.	The owner of a boat marina agrees to allow three federal drug enforcement agents, posing as drug dealers, to use his dock to unload shipments of marijuana from Colombia.

Excuse Defenses: Based on a defendant admitting that she or he committed the criminal act, but asserting that she or he cannot be held criminally responsible for the act due to lack of criminal intent.

	The defendant must prove that:	Example
INFANCY	Because he or she was under a statutorily determined age, he or she did not have the maturity to make the decisions necessary to commit a criminal act.	A thirteen-year-old takes a handgun from his backpack at school and begins shooting at fellow students, killing three. (In such cases, the offender is often processed by the juvenile justice system rather than the criminal justice system.)
INSANITY	At the time of the criminal act, he or she did not have the necessary mental capacity to be held responsible for his or her actions.	A man with a history of mental illness pushes a woman in front of an oncoming subway train, which kills her instantly.
INTOXICATION	She or he had diminished control over her or his actions due to the influence of alcohol or drugs.	A woman who had been drinking malt liquor and vodka stabs her boyfriend to death after a domestic argument. She claims to have been so drunk as to not remember the incident.
MISTAKE	He or she did not know that his or her actions violated a law (this defense is very rarely even attempted), or that he or she violated the law believing a relevant fact to be true when, in fact, it was not.	A woman, thinking that her divorce in another state has been finalized when it has not, marries for a second time, thereby committing bigamy.

PROCEDURAL SAFEGUARDS

To this point, we have focused on **substantive criminal law,** which defines the acts that the government will punish. We will now turn our attention to **procedural criminal law.** (The section that follows will provide only a short overview of criminal procedure. In later chapters, many other constitutional issues will be examined in more detail.) Criminal law brings the force of the state, with all its resources, to bear against the individual.

Criminal procedures, drawn from the ideals stated in the Bill of Rights, are designed to protect the constitutional rights of individuals and to prevent the arbitrary use of power by the government.

The Bill of Rights

For various reasons, proposals related to the rights of individuals were rejected during the framing of the U.S. Constitution in 1787. In fact, the original constitution contained only three provisions that referred to criminal procedure. Article I, Section 9, Clause 2, states that the "Privilege of the Writ of Habeas Corpus shall not be suspended." As will be

LEARNING **9** OBJECTIVE
Distinguish between substantive and procedural criminal law.

Substantive Criminal Law
Law that defines the rights and duties of individuals with respect to one another.

Procedural Criminal Law
Rules that define the manner in which the rights and duties of individuals may be enforced.

discussed in Chapter 10, a writ of *habeas corpus* is an order that requires jailers to bring a person before a court or judge and explain why the person is being held in prison. Article I, Section 9, Clause 3, holds that no "Bill of Attainder or ex post facto Law shall be passed." A bill of attainder is a legislative act that targets a particular person or group for punishment without a trial, while an *ex post facto* law operates retroactively, making an event or action illegal though it took place before the law was passed. Finally, Article III, Section 2, Clause 3, maintains that the "Trial of all Crimes" will be by jury and "such Trial shall be held in the State where the said crimes shall have been committed."

AMENDING THE CONSTITUTION The need for a written declaration of rights of individuals eventually caused the first Congress to draft twelve amendments to the Constitution and submit them for approval by the states. Ten of these amendments, commonly known as the **Bill of Rights,** were adopted in 1791. Since then, seventeen more amendments have been added.

The Bill of Rights, as interpreted by the United States Supreme Court, has served as the basis for procedural safeguards of the accused in this country. These safeguards include the following:

1. The Fourth Amendment protection from unreasonable searches and seizures.
2. The Fourth Amendment requirement that no warrants for a search or an arrest can be issued without probable cause.
3. The Fifth Amendment requirement that no one can be deprived of life, liberty, or property without "due process" of law.
4. The Fifth Amendment prohibition against *double jeopardy* (trying someone twice for the same criminal offense).
5. The Fifth Amendment guarantee that no person can be required to be a witness against (incriminate) himself or herself.
6. The Sixth Amendment guarantees of a speedy trial, a trial by jury, a public trial, the right to confront witnesses, and the right to a lawyer at various stages of criminal proceedings.
7. The Eighth Amendment prohibitions against excessive bails and fines and cruel and unusual punishments. (For the full text of the Bill of Rights, see Appendix A.)

EXPANDING THE CONSTITUTION The Bill of Rights initially offered citizens protection only against the federal government. Over the years, however, the procedural safeguards of most of the provisions of the Bill of Rights have been applied to the actions of state governments through the Fourteenth Amendment.[63] Furthermore, the states, under certain circumstances, have the option to grant even more protections than are required by the federal Constitution. As these protections are crucial to criminal justice procedures in the United States, they will be afforded much more attention in Chapter 7, with regard to police action, and in Chapter 10, with regard to the criminal trial.

In 2012, several members of Congress introduced a proposed Victims' Rights Amendment to the U.S. Constitution.[64] This proposed amendment would contain many of the same rights that are present in state victims' rights laws and the federal Victims' Rights Act, as discussed in Chapter 3. The difference, claim its supporters, is that such an amendment would give some "teeth" to protections that are now, as

Why do most Americans accept certain precautions taken by the federal government—such as full body scans at airports—that restrict our individual freedom or compromise our privacy?
John Moore/Getty Images

you also learned in Chapter 3, mostly discretionary.[65] Victims' rights supporters have been trying, without success, to amend the Constitution in favor of victims since 1996, showing just how important constitutional protections are in the criminal justice system.

Due Process

Both the Fifth and Fourteenth Amendments provide that no person should be deprived of "life, liberty, or property without due process of law." This **due process clause** basically requires that the government not act unfairly or arbitrarily. In other words, the government cannot rely on individual judgment and impulse when making decisions, but must stay within the boundaries of reason and the law. Of course, disagreements as to the meaning of these provisions have plagued courts, politicians, and citizens since this nation was founded, and will undoubtedly continue to do so.

To understand due process, it is important to consider its two types: procedural due process and substantive due process.

PROCEDURAL DUE PROCESS According to **procedural due process,** the law must be carried out by a *method* that is fair and orderly. It requires that certain procedures be followed in administering and executing a law so that an individual's basic freedoms are not violated.

The American criminal justice system's adherence to due process principles is evident in its treatment of the death penalty. To ensure that the process is fair, as we will see in Chapter 11, a number of procedural safeguards have been built into capital punishment. Much to the dismay of many victims' groups, these procedures make the process expensive and lengthy. In California, for example, the average time between conviction for a capital crime and execution is twenty-five years.[66]

LEARNING **10** OBJECTIVE Explain the importance of the due process clause in the criminal justice system.

CJ & TECHNOLOGY — DUE PROCESS AND PREDATOR DRONES

Johan Swanepoel/Shutterstock.com

Between 2008 and 2013, American Predator drones—remote controlled, unmanned aircraft armed with missiles—killed upwards of 3,000 suspected terrorists in Afghanistan, Pakistan, and Yemen. Although that tally includes an unknown number of innocent civilians, the most controversial target has been Islamist cleric Anwar al-Awlaki, who failed to survive a drone strike in Yemen on September 30, 2011.

Through his online sermons in English, Awlaki had been linked to more than a dozen terrorist operations, including a plot to blow up cargo airplanes bound for the United States. He was also a United States citizen. Because of Awlaki's citizenship, critics argued that his death by drone attack was illegal, given that the U.S. Constitution forbids the execution of American citizens without due process of law. Legal expert Glenn Greenwald noted that there had been no effort to charge Awlaki with committing any crime, and he had not been afforded a trial to prove his innocence. "[Awlaki] was simply ordered killed by the president: his judge, jury and executioner," Greenwald said.

Oleg Yarko/Shutterstock

Thinking about Due Process and Predator Drones

In 2013, President Barack Obama's administration justified targeted assassinations of suspected terrorists—including U.S. citizens—as "lawful acts of self-defense." After reviewing our discussion of self-defense earlier in the chapter, what is your opinion of this argument?

SUBSTANTIVE DUE PROCESS Fair procedures would obviously be of little use if they were used to administer unfair laws. For example, suppose a law requires everyone to wear a red shirt on Mondays. You wear a blue shirt on Monday, and you are arrested, convicted, and sentenced to one year in prison. The fact that all proper procedures were followed and your rights were given their proper protections would mean very little because the law that you broke was unfair and arbitrary.

Thus, **substantive due process** requires that the laws themselves be reasonable. The idea is that if a law is unfair or arbitrary, even if properly passed by a legislature, it must be declared unconstitutional. In the 1930s, for example, Oklahoma instituted the Habitual Criminal Sterilization Act. Under this statute, a person who had been convicted of three felonies could be "rendered sexually sterile" by the state (that is, the person would no longer be able to produce children). The United States Supreme Court held that the law was unconstitutional, as there are "limits to the extent which a legislatively represented majority may conduct biological experiments at the expense of the dignity and personality and natural powers of a minority."[67]

THE JUDICIAL SYSTEM'S ROLE IN DUE PROCESS As the last example suggests, the United States Supreme Court often plays the important role of ultimately deciding when due process has been violated and when it has not. (See Figure 4.6 below for a list of important Supreme Court due process cases.)

The Court is also called on from time to time to determine whether a due process right exists in the first place. For example, in Figure 4.4 on page 115, you will notice that four states—Idaho, Kansas, Montana, and Utah—do not provide defendants with access to the insanity defense. In 2007, John Delling killed two men in Idaho whom he believed had conspired to steal his soul. Because Idaho does not allow the insanity defense, Delling pleaded guilty to the murders and was sentenced to life in prison. In 2012, his lawyers asked the Supreme Court to rule that the insanity defense was a constitutional right that should be available to all defendants in the United States. The Court refused to so, allowing individual states to prohibit the insanity defense if they so wish.[68]

FIGURE 4.6 Important United States Supreme Court Due Process Decisions

YEAR	ISSUE	AMENDMENT INVOLVED	COURT CASE
1948	Right to a public trial	VI	*In re Oliver*, 333 U.S. 257
1952	Police searches cannot be so invasive as to "shock the conscience"	IV	*Rochin v. California*, 342 U.S. 165
1961	Exclusionary rule	IV	*Mapp v. Ohio*, 367 U.S. 643
1963	Right to a lawyer in all criminal felony cases	VI	*Gideon v. Wainwright*, 372 U.S. 335
1964	No compulsory self-incrimination	V	*Malloy v. Hogan*, 378 U.S. 1
1964	Right to have counsel when taken into police custody and subjected to questioning	VI	*Escobedo v. Illinois*, 378 U.S. 478
1965	Right to confront and cross-examine witnesses	VI	*Pointer v. Texas*, 380 U.S. 400
1966	Right to an impartial jury	VI	*Parker v. Gladden*, 385 U.S. 363
1966	Confessions of suspects not notified of due process rights ruled invalid	V	*Miranda v. Arizona*, 384 U.S. 436
1967	Right to a speedy trial	VI	*Klopfer v. North Carolina*, 386 U.S. 21
1967	Juveniles have due process rights, too	V	*In re Gault*, 387 U.S. 1
1968	Right to a jury trial ruled a fundamental right	VI	*Duncan v. Louisiana*, 391 U.S. 145
1969	No double jeopardy	V	*Benton v. Maryland*, 395 U.S. 784

SOCIETY'S BEST INTERESTS The due process clause does not automatically doom laws that may infringe on procedural or substantive rights. In certain circumstances, the lawmaking body may be able to prove that its interests are greater than the due process rights of the individual, and in those cases the statute may be upheld. Several years ago, for example, a U.S. appellate court upheld the immediate suspension of a kindergarten student who said "I'm going to shoot you" to classmates during recess. Although a school generally must follow certain steps before suspending a student, the court felt that in this instance the kindergarten's interest in limiting this kind of violent speech was more important than the student's due process rights.[69]

Spectators line up to enter the U.S. Supreme Court building in Washington, D.C. The Court recently upheld a federal law broadening the government's power to eavesdrop on international e-mails and phone calls. Why might the Court tend to defer to the federal government where questions of national security are concerned? Mark Wilson/Getty Images

DUE PROCESS AND NATIONAL SECURITY The U.S. court system, including the Supreme Court, is put under particular pressure when national security is threatened. Certainly, as was clear in the earlier *CJ and Technology* feature concerning Predator drones, many of the controversies concerning antiterrorism strategies that we will discuss in this textbook have their basis in due process concerns. Despite several important rulings to the contrary, which will be covered in Chapter 16, some observers feel that the judiciary has favored the government over terrorism suspects when it comes to due process rights.

In 2003, for example, U.S. citizen Abdullah al-Kidd was arrested and spent two weeks in federal prison without being charged of having committed a crime. Usually, the due process clause does not allow persons to be locked up in this manner. Under the federal *material witness* law, however, the government can detain individuals who have witnessed crimes so that they can testify at trial.

Al-Kidd was never called to testify at any time before being released. In retrospect, it seemed obvious that al-Kidd was held as a material witness because, though they suspected him of terrorism-related activities, federal law enforcement officers had no evidence of any actual wrongdoing. In 2011, the Supreme Court upheld al-Kidd's detention, essentially saying that that the federal officials had followed the correct procedure in holding him as a material witness, and thus the fact that he had not committed any crime was irrelevant.[70]

SELF ASSESSMENT

Fill in the blanks and check your answers on page 128.

The basis for procedural safeguards for the accused is found in the ____ ____ ____ of the U.S. Constitution. According to these safeguards, no person shall be deprived of life or liberty without ____ ____ of law. This means that the ____ by which the law is carried out must be fair and orderly and the laws themselves must be ____. The ____ ____ ____ ____ ultimately decides whether these rights have been violated.

HATE CRIME LAWS

It was every commuter's worst nightmare. On December 29, 2012, Erika Mendez pushed Sunando Sen onto the tracks of an elevated subway station in Queens, New York. Sen, born in India, was immediately killed by an oncoming train. Mendez told the police that she chose Sen, whom she believed to be a Muslim, "because I hate Hindus and Muslims ever since 2001 when they put down the twin towers I've been beating them up [sic]."[71] New York officials charged Mendez with second degree murder as a *hate crime,* meaning that, if convicted, she faces a minimum prison sentence of twenty years instead of fifteen years. The philosophy behind hate crime legislation, which punishes the defendant not only for acts but also for motives, is the subject of this chapter's *CJ in Action* feature.

PUNISHING BIAS

Nearly every state and the federal government have hate crime laws that, as noted earlier in the text, apply when the underlying crime is committed because of the victim's race, color, religion, ancestry, national origin, political affiliation, gender, sexual orientation, age, or disability. These laws are based on a model created by the Anti-Defamation League (ADL) in 1981. The ADL model was centered on the concept of "penalty enhancement": just as someone who robs a convenience store using a gun will face a greater penalty than if he or she had been unarmed, so will someone who commits a crime because of prejudice against her or his victim or victims.[72]

Critics of hate crime laws feel that such "penalty enhancements" rest on shaky legal grounds. It is one thing to prove that a robber used a gun, but it is another thing to prove what was in a defendant's mind. Even when an offender's bias is obvious, as is the case with Erika Mendez, should it affect how many years she spends behind bars? Despite these misgivings, the United States Supreme Court has upheld the constitutionality of hate crime laws as long as the prohibited motive (1) is specifically listed as an attendant circumstance (see page 112) in the legislation and (2) is proved beyond a reasonable doubt during the trial.[73]

THE CASE FOR HATE CRIME LAWS

- Hate crimes target groups, not just an individual—if one Muslim or Hindu in New York is attacked, for example, then all Muslims or Hindus in New York suffer intimidation and fear. Thus, such acts need to be punished more harshly.

- Historically, the groups listed in hate crime legislation have received inadequate protection from the American criminal justice system. Hate crime laws redress these shortcomings.

- Hate crime laws do not punish a defendant's speech or beliefs, which are protected by the U.S. Constitution. Rather, they allow jurors to learn whether the defendant's speech or beliefs were the reason for the choice of victim.

THE CASE AGAINST HATE CRIME LAWS

- Hate crime laws punish political views that, though unpopular and even appalling, are protected by the First Amendment, which states that the government shall make no law "abridging the freedom of speech."

- For the most part, motive is irrelevant in criminal law. Defendants are punished for what they did, not for why they did it.

- Hate crime laws indicate that some victims are worthy of more protection than others. It is unjust that Erika Mendez would receive a lesser sentence if her victim were not a member of a minority group.[74]

YOUR OPINION —WRITING ASSIGNMENT

Harold, who is white, is at a party, and he is drunk. He sees Mary, his ex-girlfriend, talking with James, who is African American. Harold knows that Mary and James have been dating for several weeks. Harold shouts racial epithets at James and is thrown out of the party. Later that night, Harold stalks James and attacks him with a baseball bat.

Did Harold commit a hate crime deserving of a harsher penalty? How does this case influence your opinion of hate crime laws in general? Before responding, you can review our discussion in this chapter concerning:

- The purposes of criminal law (pages 103–105).

- *Mens rea* and criminal acts (pages 107–111).

- Attendant circumstances (pages 112–113).

Your answer should include at least three full paragraphs.

CHAPTER SUMMARY

For more information on these concepts, look back to the Learning Objective icons throughout the chapter.

 List the four written sources of American criminal law. (a) The U.S. Constitution and state constitutions; (b) statutes passed by Congress and state legislatures (plus local ordinances); (c) administrative agency regulations; and (d) case law.

 Explain precedent and the importance of the doctrine of *stare decisis*. Precedent is a common law concept in which one decision becomes the example or authority for deciding future cases with similar facts. Under the doctrine of *stare decisis,* judges in a particular jurisdiction are bound to follow precedents of that same jurisdiction. The doctrine of *stare decisis* leads to efficiency in the judicial system.

 Explain the two basic functions of criminal law. The primary function is to protect citizens from harms to their safety and property and from harms to society's interest collectively. The second function is to maintain and teach social values as well as social boundaries—for example, speed limits and laws against bigamy.

 Delineate the elements required to establish *mens rea* (a guilty mental state). (a) Purpose, (b) knowledge, (c) negligence, or (d) recklessness.

 Explain how the doctrine of strict liability applies to criminal law. Strict liability crimes do not allow the alleged wrongdoer to claim ignorance or mistake to avoid criminal responsibility—for example, exceeding the speed limit and statutory rape.

 List and briefly define the most important excuse defenses for crimes. Insanity—different tests of insanity can be used, including (a) the *M'Naghten* rule (right-wrong test); (b) the ALI/MPC test, also known as the substantial-capacity test; and (c) the irresistible-impulse test. **Intoxication**—voluntary and involuntary, the latter being a possible criminal defense. **Mistake**—sometimes valid if the law was not published or reasonably known or if the alleged offender relied on an official statement of the law that was erroneous. Also, a mistake of fact may negate the mental state necessary to commit a crime.

 Discuss a common misperception concerning the use of the insanity defense in the United States. Contrary to popular opinion, the insanity defense is not an oft-used loophole that allows criminals to avoid responsibility for committing heinous crimes. Insanity defenses are difficult to mount and very rarely succeed. Even when a defendant is found not guilty by reason of insanity, she or he does not "go free." Instead, such defendants are sent to mental health care institutions.

 Describe the four most important justification criminal defenses. Duress—requires that (a) the threat is of serious bodily harm or death, (b) the harm is greater than that caused by the crime; (c) the threat is immediate and inescapable; and (d) the defendant became involved in the situation through no fault of his or her own. **Justifiable use of force**—the defense of one's person, dwelling, or property, or the prevention of a crime. **Necessity**—justifiable if the harm sought to be avoided is greater than that sought to be prevented by the law defining the offense charged. **Entrapment**—that the criminal action was induced by certain governmental persuasion or trickery.

 Distinguish between substantive and procedural criminal law. The former concerns questions about what acts are actually criminal. The latter concerns procedures designed to protect the constitutional rights of individuals and to prevent the arbitrary use of power by the government.

 Explain the importance of the due process clause in the criminal justice system. The due process clause acts to limit the power of government. In the criminal justice system, the due process clause requires that certain procedures be followed to ensure the fairness of criminal proceedings and that all criminal laws be reasonable and in the interest of the public good.

QUESTIONS FOR CRITICAL ANALYSIS

1. Give an example of a criminal law whose main purpose seems to be teaching societal boundaries rather than protecting citizens from harm. By searching the Internet, can you find examples of other countries where this behavior is *not* considered criminal? How is the behavior perceived in those countries?

2. Nine-year-old Savannah lies to her grandmother Jessica about eating candy bars. As punishment, Jessica forces Savannah to run for three hours without a rest. Severely dehydrated, the girl has a seizure and dies. What should be the criminal charge against Jessica, and why?

3. Keith lends his car to Jermaine, who drives with two other friends to the home of a marijuana dealer. The three men break into the home, intending to steal a safe full of cash. The drug dealer is unexpectedly at home, however, and in a struggle Jermaine winds up murdering him. What rule allows local prosecutors to charge Keith with first degree murder? Why?

4. Critics have derogatorily labeled the "stand your ground laws" passed by Florida and many other states (see page 119) "license to kill" laws. Why would they do so? What is your opinion of these laws?

5. Suppose that Louisiana's legislature passes a law allowing law enforcement officers to forcibly remove residents from their homes in the face of an imminent hurricane. Why might a court uphold this law even though, in most circumstances, such forcible removal would violate the residents' due process rights? If you were a judge, would you uphold Louisiana's new law?

KEY TERMS

SELF ASSESSMENT ANSWER KEY

Page 103: i. Constitution; **ii.** unconstitutional; **iii.** statutes; **iv.** case/judge-made/common; **v.** *stare decisis;* **vi.** precedents

Page 105: i. legal; **ii.** criminal; **iii.** social; **iv.** morality

Page 113: i. *actus reus;* **ii.** *mens rea;* **iii.** concurrence; **iv.** strict liability; **v.** intent/*mens rea*/mental state; **vi.** Attendant; **vii.** beyond a reasonable doubt

Page 120: i. responsible; **ii.** insanity; **iii.** intoxication; **iv.** justified; **v.** duress; **vi.** self-defense; **vii.** Entrapment

Page 125: i. Bill of Rights; **ii.** due process; **iii.** procedures; **iv.** reasonable/fair; **v.** United States Supreme Court

NOTES

1. Roger LeRoy Miller and Gaylord A. Jentz, *Business Law Today, Comprehensive Edition,* 7th ed. (Cincinnati, OH: South-Western, 2007), 2–3.

2. Joshua Dressler, *Understanding Criminal Law,* 2d ed. (New York: Richard D. Irwin, 1995), 22–23.

3. John S. Baker, Jr., *Measuring the Explosive Growth of Federal Crime Legislation* (Washington, D.C.: The Federalist Society for Law and Public Policy Studies, 2008), 1.

4. Quoted in "Judge: Federal Law Trumps Montana's Medical Pot Law," *Associated Press* (January 23, 2012).

5. *Texas v. Johnson,* 491 U.S. 397 (1989).

6. Clean Water Act Section 309, 33 U.S.C.A. Section 1319 (1987).

7. *Bowers v. Hardwick,* 478 U.S. 186 (1986)

8. *Lawrence v. Texas,* 539 U.S., 558, 578 (2003).

9. Joel Feinberg, *The Moral Limits of the Criminal Law: Harm to Others* (New York: Oxford University Press, 1984), 221–232.

10. 18 U.S.C. Section 2339B(a)(1) (1996).

11. 18 U.S.C. Section 2339A(b) (Supp. I 2001).

12. Henry M. Hart, Jr., "The Aims of the Criminal Law," *Law & Contemporary Problems* 23 (1958), 405–406.

13. John L. Diamond, "The Myth of Morality and Fault in Criminal Law Doctrine," *American Criminal Law Review* 34 (Fall 1996), 111.

14. The Humane Society of the United States, "Ranking of State Cockfighting Laws," June 2010, at **www.humanesociety.org/assets/pdfs/animal _fighting/cockfighting_statelaws.pdf**; and Animal Welfare Act Amendments of 2007, Pub. L. No. 110-246, 122 Statute 223 (2007).

15. John Monk, "Cockfighters Take Fight to Federal Appeals Court,") *The State (Columbia, SC)* (December 4, 2011), A1.

16. Lawrence M. Friedman, *Crime and Punishments in American History* (New York: Basic Books, 1993), 10.

17. Thomas A. Mullen, "Rule without Reason: Requiring Independent Proof of the *Corpus Delicti* as a Condition of Admitting Extrajudicial Confession," *University of San Francisco Law Review* 27 (1993), 385.

18. *Hawkins v. State,* 219 Ind. 116, 129, 37 N.E.2d 79 (1941).

19. David C. Biggs, "'The Good Samaritan Is Packing': An Overview of the Broadened Duty to Aid Your Fellowman, with the Modern Desire to Possess Concealed Weapons," *University of Dayton Law Review* 22 (Winter 1997), 225.

20. Terry Halbert and Elaine Ingulli, *Law and Ethics in the Business Environment,* 6th ed. (Mason, OH: South-Western Cengage Learning, 2009), 8.

21. Model Penal Code Section 2.02.

22. Model Penal Code Section 2.02(c).

23. *Black's Law Dictionary,* 1423.

24. *United States v. Dotterweich,* 320 U.S. 277 (1943).

25. New Jersey Statutes Annotated Section 2C:35-9 (West 2004).

26. *State v. Stiffler,* 763 P.2d 308, 311 (Idaho Ct.App. 1988).

27. *State v. Harrison,* 425 A.2d 111 (1979).

28. Richard G. Singer and John Q. LaFond, *Criminal Law: Examples and Explanations* (New York: Aspen Law & Business, 1997), 322.

29. *State v. Linscott,* 520 A.2d 1067 (1987).

30. Adam Liptak, "Serving Life for Providing Car to Killers," *New York Times* (December 4, 2007), A1.

31. *Morissette v. United States,* 342 U.S. 246, 251–252 (1952).

32. Federal Bank Robbery Act, 18 U.S.C.A. Section 2113.

33. *In re Winship,* 397 U.S. 358, 364, 368–369 (1970).

34. *State v. Jones,* 2011 S.D. 60 (2011).

35. *United States v. Jiminez Recio,* 537 U.S. 270 (2003).

36. Paul H. Robinson, *Criminal Law Defenses* (St. Paul, MN: West, 2008), Section 173, Ch. 5Bl

37. *M'Naghten's* Case, 10 Cl.&F. 200, Eng.Rep. 718 (1843). Note that the name is also spelled M'Naughten and McNaughten.

38. Model Penal Code Section 401 (1952).

39. Joshua Dressler, *Cases and Materials on Criminal Law,* 2d ed. (St. Paul, MN: West Group, 1999), 599.

40. Stephen Lally, "Making Sense of the Insanity Plea," *Washington Post Weekly Edition* (December 1, 1997), 23.

41. South Carolina Code Annotated Section 17-24-20(A) (Law. Co-op. Supp. 1997).

42. Lawrence P. Tiffany and Mary Tiffany, "Nosologic Objections to the Criminal Defense of Pathological Intoxication: What Do the Doubters Doubt?" *International Journal of Law and Psychiatry* 13 (1990), 49.

43. 518 U.S. 37 (1996).

44. Montana Code Annotated Section 45-5-102 (1997).

45. Montana Code Annotated Section 45-2-203 (1997).

46. Kenneth W. Simons, "Mistake and Impossibility, Law and Fact, and Culpability: A Speculative Essay," *Journal of Criminal Law and Criminology* 81 (1990), 447.

47. Quoted in Gary Fields and John R. Emshwiller, "As Criminal Laws Proliferate, More Are Ensnared," *Wall Street Journal* (July 23, 2011), at **online.wsj.com/article/SB10001424052748703749504576172714184601654.html**.

48. *Lambert v. California,* 335 U.S. 225 (1957).

49. Federal Bureau of Investigation, *Crime in the United States, 2011* (Washington, D.C.: U.S. Department of Justice, 2012), at **www.fbi.gov /about-us/cjis/ucr/crime-in-the-u.s/2011/crime-in-the-u.s.-2011 /tables/expanded-homicide-data-table-14**; and **www.fbi.gov/about -us/cjis/ucr/ucr/crime-in-the-u.s/2011/crime-in-the-u.s.-2011 /tables/expanded-homicide-data-table-15**.

50. Craig L. Carr, "Duress and Criminal Responsibility," *Law and Philosophy* 10 (1990), 161.

51. Arnold N. Enker, "In Supporting the Distinction between Justification and Excuse," *Texas Tech Law Review* 42 (2009), 277.

52. *United States v. May,* 727 F.2d 764 (1984).

53. *United States v. Contento-Pachon,* 723 F.2d 691 (1984).

54. *People v. Murillo,* 587 N.E.2d 1199, 1204 (Ill.App.Ct. 1992).

55. Florida Statutes Section 776.03 (2005).

56. *Ibid.*

57. Michael Bloomberg, quoted in "A Lethal Right to Self-Defense," *The Week* (May 4, 2012), 13.

58. Molly Hennessy-Fiske and Michael Muskal, "Jury Finds George Zimmerman Not Guilty," *Los Angeles Times* (July 13, 2013), A1.

59. "Man Acquitted of Concealed Weapon Charge on 'Necessity' Defense," *San Francisco Examiner* (July 10, 2011), at **www.sfexaminer.com/local /crime/2011/07/man-acquitted-concealed-weapon-charge -necessity-defense**.

60. *People v. Petro,* 56 P.2d 984 (Cal.Ct.App. 1936); and *Regina v. Dudley and Stephens,* 14 Q.B.D. 173 (1884).

61. 287 U.S. 435 (1932).

62. Kenneth M. Lord, "Entrapment and Due Process: Moving toward a Dual System of Defenses," *Florida State University Law Review* 25 (Spring 1998), 463.

63. Henry J. Abraham, *Freedom and the Court: Civil Liberties in the United States,* 7th ed. (New York: Oxford University Press, 1998), 38–41.

64. House Joint Resolution 106, 112th Congress (2012).

65. Paul G. Cassell, "The Victims' Rights Amendment: A Sympathetic, Clause-by-Clause Analysis," *Phoenix Law Review* (Spring 2012), 301.

66. Arthur L. Alarcon and Paula M. Mitchell, "Executing the Will of the Voters? A Legislature's Multi-Billion Dollar Death Penalty Debacle," *Loyola of Los Angeles Law Review* 44 (2011), S109.

67. *Skinner v. Oklahoma,* 316 U.S. 535, 546–547 (1942).

68. Jonathan Stempel, "Supreme Court Declines to Review Insanity Defense Appeal," *Reuters* (November 26, 2012).

69. "*S.G.V. Sayreville Board of Education et al.,* No. 02-2384," *New Jersey Law Journal* (July 14, 2003), 139.

70. *Ashcroft v. Al-Kidd,* 563 U.S. _____ (2011).

71. Quoted in Marc Santora, "Woman Is Charged with Murder as a Hate Crime in a Fatal Subway Push," *New York Times* (December 30, 2012), A15.

72. Steve M. Freeman, "Hate Crime Laws: Punishment Which Fits the Crime," *Annual Survey of American Law* 4 (1992/1993), 581–585.

73. *Wisconsin v. Mitchell,* 508 U.S. 476 (1993); and *Apprendi v. New Jersey,* 530 U.S. 466 (2000).

74. Richard Cohen, "When Thought Becomes a Crime," *Washington Post* (October 19, 2010), at **www.realclearpolitics.com/articles/2010/10 /19/punish_crime_not_thought_107629.html**.

CHAPTER

5 Law Enforcement Today

Jared Wickerham/Getty Images

To target your study and review, look for these numbered Learning Objective icons throughout the chapter.

WHAT'S GOING ON?

LIKE THE REST of American society, law enforcement has been swept up by the tide of social media. Over the past few years, most local police departments have taken advantage of Facebook and Twitter to improve their ability to communicate with the public. None have gone as far as the Seattle Police Department (SPD), however, and its new "Tweets-by-beat" initiative. Residents in fifty-one Seattle neighborhoods can now receive constant updates of nearby criminal activity directly from the police. Over the course of a single Sunday, for example, people living on Olive Way near downtown Seattle would have been notified of an "intoxicated person" on their street, along with two burglaries and several reports of "suspicious vehicles," accident investigations, and noise complaints.

"More and more people want to know what's going on on their piece of the rock," says Seattle police chief John Diaz. "This is just a different way we could put out as much information as possible as quickly as possible."

Are the Seattle police providing the public with *too much* information? Eugene O'Donnell, a professor at John Jay College of Criminal Justice in New York City, worries that a greater awareness of local crime could lead to a greater, and unwarranted, fear of becoming a victim. Such awareness might also give residents the impression that the police are not doing their jobs effectively.

Furthermore, as highlighted by an incident in New Jersey, social media can be notoriously difficult to control. In January 2013, two West Orange police officers apparently joined a Facebook discussion concerning the shooting death of Raymar Lecky outside a Newark nightclub. One of the officers claimed that Lecky was a gang member and posted his criminal record. The other then wrote, "Live by the gun die by the gun BOOM" and added, referring to Lecky and his killer, "two birds with one stone. One dead and one will eventually go to jail." Amid the resulting outcry, Lecky's mother demanded that the two officers be "terminated—no less."

1. The Seattle Police Department will not send tweets regarding sex crimes or domestic violence. Also, all other tweets are delayed for one hour after the initial report to law enforcement. What might be the purpose of these safeguards?

2. The West Orange Police Department has a social media policy that prohibits officers from discussing any information relating to their duties online. What is your opinion of this policy?

3. Several years ago, an Albuquerque, New Mexico, detective lost his job for tweeting an insensitive joke about Muslims. He also used his Twitter account to provide a link to a Web site that compared the administration of President Barack Obama to the Nazis. Do you think that law enforcement officers should be prohibited from using social media to make controversial statements that do not directly concern their duties? Why or why not?

Michael Hanson/*New York Times*

Neighborhood Twitter accounts allow the Seattle Police Department to keep community members up to date on local crime information, such as the status of this suspicious white van investigated by a patrol officer.

THE RESPONSIBILITIES OF THE POLICE

Police officers are the most visible representatives of our criminal justice system. Indeed, they symbolize the system for many Americans who may never see the inside of a court-room or a prison cell. Still, the general perception of a "cop's life" is often shaped by television dramas such as the *CSI* series and *Hawaii Five-O*. Another stated goal of the Seattle Police Department's "Tweets-by-beat" project is to counteract this perception by giving the public a better understanding of the day-to-day work of law enforcement.[1] In reality, police spend a great deal of time on such mundane tasks as responding to noise complaints, confiscating firecrackers, and poring over paperwork.

Sociologist Egon Bittner warned against the tendency to see the police primarily as agents of law enforcement and crime control. A more inclusive accounting of "what the police do," Bittner believed, would recognize that they provide "situationally justified force in society."[2] In other words, the function of the police is to solve any problem that may *possibly,* though not *necessarily,* require the use of force.

Within Bittner's rather broad definition of "what the police do," we can pinpoint four basic responsibilities of the police:

1. To enforce laws.
2. To provide services.
3. To prevent crime.
4. To preserve the peace.

LEARNING OBJECTIVE 1 List the four basic responsibilities of the police.

As will become evident over the next two chapters, there is a great deal of debate among legal and other scholars and law enforcement officers over which responsibilities deserve the most police attention and what methods should be employed by the police in meeting those responsibilities.

Enforcing Laws

In the public mind, the primary role of the police is to enforce society's laws—hence, the term *law enforcement officer.* In their role as "crime fighters," police officers have a clear mandate to seek out and apprehend those who have violated the law. The crime-fighting responsibility is so dominant that all police activity—from the purchase of new automobiles to a plan to hire more minority officers—must often be justified in terms of its law enforcement value.[3]

Police officers also see themselves primarily as crime fighters, or "crook catchers," a perception that often leads people into what they believe will be an exciting career in law enforcement. Although the job certainly offers challenges unlike any other, police officers normally do not spend the majority of their time in law enforcement duties. After surveying a year's worth of dispatch data from the Wilmington (Delaware) Police Department, researchers Jack Greene and Carl Klockars found that officers spent only about half of their time enforcing the law or dealing with crimes. The rest of their time was spent on order maintenance, service provision, traffic patrol, and medical assistance.[4]

Furthermore, information provided by the Uniform Crime Report shows that most arrests are made for "crimes of disorder" or public annoyances rather than violent or property crimes.[5] In 2011, for example, police made about 10.2 million arrests for drunkenness, liquor law violations, disorderly conduct, vagrancy, loitering, and other minor offenses, but only about 535,000 arrests for violent crimes.[6] (For Iranian law enforcement, preventing "crimes of disorder" includes enforcing laws that may strike many Americans as overly intrusive, as described in the feature *Comparative Criminal Justice—Morality Police* below.)

Providing Services

The popular emphasis on crime fighting and law enforcement tends to overshadow the fact that a great deal of a police officer's time is spent providing services for the community. The motto "To Serve and Protect" has been adopted by thousands of local police departments, and the *Law Enforcement Code of Ethics* recognizes the duty "to serve the community" in its first sentence.[7] The services that police provide are numerous—a partial list would include directing traffic, performing emergency medical procedures, counseling those involved in domestic disputes, providing directions to tourists, and finding lost children.

Along with firefighters, police officers are among the first public servants called to conduct search and rescue operations. This particular duty adds considerably to the dangers faced by law enforcement agents (discussed in more detail in Chapter 6). As we will see in the next section, a majority of police departments have adopted a strategy called community policing that requires officers to provide assistance in areas that are not, at first glance, directly related to law enforcement. In many ways, law enforcement agents are on the front lines when it comes to national health issues such as mental illness and substance abuse. Of all contacts that police officers have with members of the public, an estimated 20 percent involve those who are mentally ill or intoxicated.[8]

COMPARATIVE CRIMINAL JUSTICE

Saicle/Shutterstock.com

THE MORALITY POLICY

A decade ago, Tehran—the capital of Iran, with a population of about 12 million people—had almost no coffee shops. Today, however, the city is filled with hundreds of cafés. "The coffee shops are our hideaways," explains twenty-four-year-old Nima Manzouri while sitting in one of the establishments with his girlfriend. "If we hold hands on the streets, we can be arrested."

In Iran, criminal law dictates public behavior. Showing affection in public is illegal, particularly if one happens to be unmarried. So is showing too much skin, particularly if one is a woman. A mandatory dress code, known as *hijab*, requires that Iranian women cover their head, arms, and legs when appearing in public. *Hijab* is enforced by the *Gashte Ershad*, Iran's morality police force. Those who violate the dress code face fines, imprisonment, and, in extreme cases, a lashing. In the summer of 2012, the *Gashte Ershad* closed down 140 coffee shops and restaurants in Tehran for *hijab* violations and other gender-related offenses such as permitting women to smoke.

Iran's morality police take other steps to "promote virtue and prevent vice." In recent years, they have arrested young boys and girls for taking part in a squirt-gun war (considered too intimate) and banned women and girls from skiing unless accompanied by a male relative. The *Gashte Ershad* also recently banned the sale of Barbie dolls for having "destructive cultural and social consequences."

FOR CRITICAL ANALYSIS

Under what circumstances do American law enforcement officers act as "morality police"? Can you make the argument that enforcing public values is the responsibility of any nation's police force?

Preventing Crime

Perhaps the most controversial responsibility of the police is to *prevent* crime, terrorist related or otherwise. According to Jerome Skolnick, co-director of the Center for Research in Crime and Justice at the New York University School of Law, there are two predictable public responses when crime rates begin to rise in a community. The first is to punish convicted criminals with stricter laws and more severe penalties. The second is to demand that the police "do something" to prevent crimes from occurring in the first place. Is it, in fact, possible for the police to "prevent" crimes? The strongest response that Professor Skolnick is willing to give to this question is "maybe."[9]

A Los Angeles police officer oversees community efforts to clean up trash and graffiti. What are the benefits and drawbacks of having law enforcement agents provide services that do not directly involve preventing and solving crimes?
Monica Almeida/*New York Times*/Redux Pictures

On a limited basis, police can certainly prevent some crimes. If a rapist is dissuaded from attacking a solitary woman because a patrol car is cruising the area, then the police officer behind the wheel has prevented a crime. Furthermore, exemplary police work can have a measurable effect. "Quite simply, cops count," says William Bratton, who has directed police departments in Boston, Los Angeles, and New York. "[T]he quickest way to impact crime is with a well-led, managed, and appropriately resourced police force."[10] In Chapter 6, we will study a number of policing strategies that have been credited, by some, for decreasing crime rates in the United States.

In general, however, the deterrent effects of police presence are unclear. Carl Klockars has written that the "war on crime" is a war that the police cannot win because they cannot control the factors—such as unemployment, poverty, immorality, inequality, political change, and lack of educational opportunities—that contribute to criminal behavior in the first place.[11]

Preserving the Peace

To a certain extent, the fourth responsibility of the police, that of preserving the peace, is related to preventing crime. Police have the legal authority to use the power of arrest, or even force, in situations in which no crime has yet occurred, but might occur in the immediate future.

In the words of James Q. Wilson, the police's peacekeeping role (which Wilson believed to be the most important role of law enforcement officers) often takes on a pattern of simply "handling the situation."[12] For example, when police officers arrive on the scene of a loud late-night house party, they may feel the need to disperse the party and even arrest some of the partygoers for disorderly conduct. By their actions, the officers have lessened the chances of serious and violent crimes taking place later in the evening. The same principle is often used when dealing with domestic disputes, which, if escalated, can lead to homicide. Such situations are in need of, to use Wilson's terminology again, "fixing up," and police can use the power of arrest, or threat, or coercion, or sympathy, to do just that.

The basis of Wilson and George Kelling's zero-tolerance theory is similar: street disorder—such as public drunkenness, urination, and loitering—signals to both law-abiding citizens and criminals that the law is not being enforced and therefore leads to

Night Watch System An early
form of American law enforcement
in which volunteers patrolled their
community from dusk to dawn to keep
the peace.

more violent crime. Hence, if police preserve the peace and "crack down" on the minor crimes that make up street disorder, they will in fact be preventing serious crimes that would otherwise occur in the future.[13]

SELF ASSESSMENT

Fill in the blanks and check your answers on page 163.

Both the public and law enforcement officers themselves believe that the police's primary job is to _____ laws. A large and crucial part of policing, however, involves providing _____ such as directing traffic. The ability of the police to actually _____ crime is a matter of great debate, and some experts believe that the most important role of a police officer is to _____ the peace.

A SHORT HISTORY OF THE AMERICAN POLICE

Although modern society relies on law enforcement officers to control and prevent crime, in the early days of this country police services had little to do with crime control. The policing efforts in the first American cities were directed toward controlling certain groups of people (mostly slaves and Native Americans), delivering goods, regulating activities such as buying and selling in the town market, maintaining health and sanitation, controlling gambling and vice, and managing livestock and other animals.[14] Furthermore, these police services were for the most part performed by volunteers, as a police force was an expensive proposition. Often, the volunteers were organized using the **night watch system,** brought over from England by colonists in the seventeenth century. Under this system, all physically fit males were required to offer their services to protect the community on a rotating nightly basis.[15]

The Evolution of American Law Enforcement

The night watch system did not ask much of its volunteers, who were often required to do little more than loudly announce the time and the state of the weather. Furthermore, many citizens avoided their duties by hiring others to "go on watch" in their place, and those who did serve frequently spent their time on watch sleeping and drinking.[16] Eventually, as the populations of American cities grew in the late eighteenth and early nineteenth centuries, so did the need for public order and the willingness to devote public resources to the establishment of formal police forces. The night watch system was insufficient to meet these new demands, and its demise was inevitable.

EARLY POLICE DEPARTMENTS In 1829, the British home secretary Sir Robert "Bobbie" Peel took a dramatic step to organize law enforcement in London—then as now one of the largest cities in the Western world. He pushed the Metropolitan Police Act through Parliament, forming the London Metropolitan Police. One thousand strong at first, the members of this police force were easily recognizable in their uniforms that featured blue coats and top hats. Under Peel's direction, the "bobbies," as the police were called in honor of their founder, did not carry any firearms and were assigned to specific areas, or "beats," to prevent crime. Peel also believed that the police should be organized along military lines under the control of local, elected officials.[17]

London's police operation was so successful that it was soon imitated in smaller towns throughout England and, eventually, in the United States. In 1833, Philadelphia became the first city to employ both day and night watchmen. Five years later, working from Peel's model, Boston formed the first organized police department, consisting of six full-time officers. In 1844, New York City laid the foundation for the modern police department by combining its day and night watches under the control of a single police chief. By the onset of the Civil War in 1861, a number of American cities, including Baltimore, Boston, Chicago, Cincinnati, New Orleans, and Philadelphia, had similarly consolidated police departments, modeled on the Metropolitan Police of London.[18]

THE POLITICAL ERA Like their modern counterparts, many early police officers were hard working, honest, and devoted to serving and protecting the public. On the whole, however, in the words of historian Samuel Walker, "The quality of American police service in the nineteenth century could hardly have been worse."[19] This poor quality can be attributed to the fact that the recruitment and promotion of police officers were intricately tied to the politics of the day. Police officers received their jobs as a result of political connections, not because of any particular skills or knowledge. Whichever political party was in power in a given city would hire its own cronies to run the police department. Consequently, the police were often more concerned with serving the interests of the political powers than with protecting the citizens.[20]

Corruption was rampant during this *political era* of policing, which lasted roughly from 1840 to 1930. Police salaries were relatively low, and many police officers saw their positions as opportunities to make extra income through any number of illegal activities. Bribery was common, as police would use their close proximity to the people to request "favors," which went into the police officers' own pockets or into the coffers of the local political party as "contributions."[21] This was known as the **patronage system,** or the "spoils system," because to the political victors went the spoils.

The political era also saw police officers take an active role in providing social services for their bosses' constituents. In many instances, this role even took precedence over law enforcement duties. Politicians realized that they could attract more votes by offering social services to citizens than by arresting them, and they required the police departments under their control to act accordingly.

THE REFORM ERA The abuses of the political era of policing did not go unnoticed. Nevertheless, it was not until 1929 that President Herbert Hoover appointed the national Commission on Law Observance and Enforcement to assess the American criminal justice system. The Wickersham Commission, named after its chairman, George Wickersham, focused on two areas of American policing that were in need of reform: (1) police brutality and (2) "the corrupting influence of politics." According to the commission, this reform should come about through higher personnel standards, centralized police administrations, and the increased use of technology.[22] Reformers of the time took the commission's findings as a call for the professionalization of American police and initiated the progressive (or *reform*) era in American policing.

■ A horse-drawn police wagon used by the New York City Police Department, circa 1886. Why might this new form of transportation have represented a "revolution" for early American police forces?
Corbis/Bettmann

LEARNING
2
OBJECTIVE

Tell how the patronage system affected policing.

Patronage System A form of corruption in which the political party in power hires and promotes police officers, receiving job-related "favors" in return.

Professionalism and Administrative Reforms Many of the Wickersham Commission's recommendations echoed the opinions of one of its contributors—August Vollmer, the police chief of Berkeley, California, from 1905 to 1932.[23] Along with his protégé O. W. Wilson, Vollmer promoted a style of policing known as the **professional model.** Under the professional model, police chiefs, who had been little more than figureheads during the political era, took more control over their departments. A key to these efforts was the reorganization of police departments in many major cities. To improve their control over operations, police chiefs began to add midlevel positions to the force. These new officers, known as majors or assistant chiefs, could develop and implement crime-fighting strategies and more closely supervise individual officers. Police chiefs also tried to consolidate their power by bringing large areas of a city under their control so that no local ward, neighborhood, or politician could easily influence a single police department.

The professionalism trend benefited law enforcement agents in a number of ways. Salaries and working conditions improved, and for the first time, women and members of minority groups were given opportunities—albeit limited—to serve.[24] At the same time, police administrators controlled officers to a much greater extent than in the past, expecting them to meet targets for arrests and other numerical indicators that were seen as barometers of effectiveness. Any contact with citizens that did not explicitly relate to law enforcement was considered "social work" and discouraged.[25] As police expert Chris Braiden puts it, American police officers were expected to "park their brains at the door of the stationhouse" and simply "follow orders like a robot."[26] The isolation of officers from the public was made complete by an overreliance on the patrol car, a relatively new technological innovation at the time. In the political era, officers walked their beats, interacting with citizens. In the reform era, they were expected to stay inside their "rolling fortresses," driving from one call to the next without wasting time or resources on public relations.[27]

CJ & TECHNOLOGY — HIGH-TECH COP CARS

Michael Hanson/*New York Times*

When patrol cars came into common use by police departments in the 1930s, they changed the face of American policing. Nine decades later, the technology associated with patrol cars continues to evolve. Today, approximately 80 percent of all police cars in the United States are equipped with on-board computers. Specialized software for these computers allows law enforcement agents to turn cars into mobile offices. So, for example, if a patrol officer receives a call concerning an incident involving a known suspect, he or she can use the in-car computer to immediately access the suspect's criminal files. In Tampa, Florida, patrol officers have access to NC4 Safecop software, which allows them to analyze neighborhood crime data from the driver's seat.

Other recent innovations include Automatic License Plate Recognition, a three-camera computer-operated system that performs a "20-millisecond" background check on every license plate it sees, and the StarChase launcher, a small, laser-guided cannon that shoots a small, sticky radio transmitter at a fleeing vehicle. Once the offending car has been "tagged" with this device, police can track the fugitive at a safe distance without the need for a dangerous, high-speed pursuit.

Thinking about Police Automobile Technology

One criminal justice expert has suggested that all police car computers be equipped with voice-to-text software, which would allow an officer's spoken words to be digitized immediately onto department databases. What would be some of the benefits of this technological upgrade?

Turmoil in the 1960s and 1970s By the 1950s, America prided itself on having the most modern and professional police force in the world. As efficiency became the goal of the reform-era police chief, however, relations with the community suffered. Instead of being members of the community, police officers were now seen almost as intruders, patrolling the streets in the anonymity of their automobiles. The drawbacks of this perception—and of the professional model in general—became evident in the 1960s, one of the most turbulent decades in American history. The civil rights movement, though not inherently violent, intensified feelings of helplessness and impoverishment in African American communities. These frustrations resulted in civil unrest, and many major American cities experienced race riots in the middle years of the decade. Concurrently, America was experiencing rising crime rates and often violent protests against U.S. involvement in the war in Vietnam (1964-1975).

By the early 1970s, many observers believed that poor policing was contributing to the national turmoil. The National Advisory Commission on Civil Disorders stated bluntly that poor relations between the police and African American communities were partly to blame for the violence that plagued many of those communities.[28] In striving for professionalism, the police appeared to have lost touch with the citizens they were supposed to be serving. To repair their damaged relations with a large segment of the population, police would have to rediscover their community roots.

THE COMMUNITY ERA The beginning of the *community era* may be traced to several government initiatives that took place in 1968. Of primary importance was the Omnibus Crime Control and Safe Streets Act, which was passed that year.[29] Under this act, the federal government provided state and local police departments with funds to create a wide variety of police-community programs. Most large-city police departments established entire units devoted to community relations, implementing programs that ranged from summer recreation activities for inner-city youths to "officer-friendly" referral operations that encouraged citizens to come to the police with their crime concerns.

In the 1970s, as this vital rethinking of the role of the police was taking place, the country was hit by a crime wave. Thus, police administrators were forced to combine efforts to improve community relations with aggressive and innovative crime-fighting strategies. As we will see in Chapter 6 when we discuss these strategies in more depth, the police began to focus on stopping crimes before they occur, rather than concentrating only on solving crimes that have already been committed. A dedication to such proactive strategies led to widespread acceptance of *community policing* in the 1980s and 1990s.

Community policing is based on the notion that meaningful interaction between officers and citizens will lead to a partnership in preventing and fighting crime.[30] Though the idea of involving members of the community in this manner is hardly new—a similar principle was set forth by Sir Robert Peel in the 1820s—community policing has had a major impact on the culture of American law enforcement by asking the average police officer to be a problem solver as well as a crime fighter.[31] (See Figure 5.1 on the following page for an overview of the three eras of policing described in this section.)

Policing Today: Intelligence, Terrorism, and Technology

Many law enforcement experts believe that the events of September 11, 2001, effectively ended the community era of policing.[32] Though police departments have not, in general, abandoned the idea of partnering with the community, their emphasis has shifted

FIGURE 5.1 The Three Eras of American Policing

George L. Kelling and Mark H. Moore have separated the history of policing in the United States from 1840 to 2000 into three distinct periods. Below is a brief summarization of these three eras.

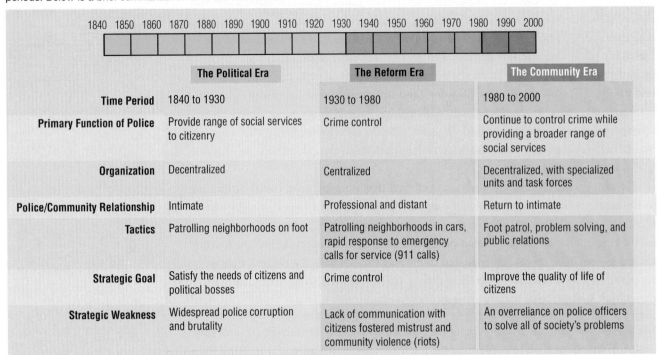

	The Political Era	The Reform Era	The Community Era
Time Period	1840 to 1930	1930 to 1980	1980 to 2000
Primary Function of Police	Provide range of social services to citizenry	Crime control	Continue to control crime while providing a broader range of social services
Organization	Decentralized	Centralized	Decentralized, with specialized units and task forces
Police/Community Relationship	Intimate	Professional and distant	Return to intimate
Tactics	Patrolling neighborhoods on foot	Patrolling neighborhoods in cars, rapid response to emergency calls for service (911 calls)	Foot patrol, problem solving, and public relations
Strategic Goal	Satisfy the needs of citizens and political bosses	Crime control	Improve the quality of life of citizens
Strategic Weakness	Widespread police corruption and brutality	Lack of communication with citizens fostered mistrust and community violence (riots)	An overreliance on police officers to solve all of society's problems

Sources: Adapted from George L. Kelling and Mark H. Moore, "From Political to Reform to Community: The Evolving Strategy of Police," in *Community Policing: Rhetoric or Reality,* ed. Jack R. Greene and Stephen D. Mastrofski (New York: Praeger Publishers, 1991), 14–15, 22–23; plus authors' updates. Reproduced with permission of Greenwood Publishing Group, Inc., Westport, Connecticut.

toward developing new areas of expertise, including counterterrorism and surveillance through technology. In particular, the process of collecting, analyzing, and mapping crime data has become a hallmark of law enforcement in the twenty-first century.

INTELLIGENCE-LED POLICING "Humans are not nearly as random as we think," says Jeff Brantingham, an anthropologist at the University of California, Los Angeles. "Crime is a physical process, and if you can explain how offenders move and how they mix with victims, you can understand an incredible amount."[33] Relying on this basic principle, Brantingham and several colleagues developed Predpol, a software program that strives to predict when and where crimes are most likely to occur. The software relies on a basic truism of criminal behavior: most crime is local. That is, offenders tend to commit crimes close to home, and they tend to victimize the same people and neighborhoods repeatedly.[34] (Remember, from Chapter 3, the concept of repeat victimization.)

The Predpol approach is known as predictive policing, or **intelligence-led policing** (IPL), because it relies on data—or intelligence—concerning past crime patterns to predict future crime patterns. In theory, IPL is relatively simple. Just as commercial fishers are most successful when they concentrate on the areas of the ocean where the fish are, law enforcement does well to focus its scarce resources on the areas where the most crime occurs. With programs such as Predpol and other "hot spot" technologies that we will discuss in the next chapter, police administrators are able to deploy small forces to specific locations, rather than blanketing an entire city with random patrols. Doing "more with less" in this manner is a particularly important consideration as police budgets shrink around the country.[35]

Explain how intelligence-led policing works and how it benefits modern police departments.
LEARNING
3
OBJECTIVE

Intelligence-Led Policing
An approach that measures the risk of criminal behavior associated with certain individuals or locations so as to predict when and where such criminal behavior is most likely to occur in the future.

THE CHALLENGES OF COUNTERTERRORISM If the importance of intelligence-based policing was not evident before September 11, 2001, the tragic events of that day made it clear that the nation's law enforcement agencies could not simply react to the crime of terrorism. With such a high toll in human lives, such attacks needed to be prevented. "Intelligence used to be a dirty word" for local police departments, according to David Carter, a professor of criminal justice at Michigan State University.[36] Today, however, financial support from the federal government has helped create more than one hundred local and state police intelligence units, with at least one in each state.[37] The New York Police Department, in a class by itself, has more than one thousand personnel assigned to homeland security and has stationed agents in six foreign countries. Furthermore, that city's 2,500 subway police conduct tens of thousands of random bag checks each year and watch for commuters walking in a stiff manner and talking to themselves—potential signs of a suicide bomber.[38]

Indeed, all police officers in the country are now expected to prepare for a terrorist attack in their communities, and counterterrorism has become part of the day-to-day law enforcement routine. (See the feature *Countering Domestic Terrorism—Under Suspicion* below to learn about a particular aspect of these daily responsibilities.) This transition has not always been smooth. Many local police departments have had to shift personnel from traditional crime units, such as antigang or white-collar crime, to counterterrorism. Limited funds are also an issue. Raymond Kelly, police commissioner of New York, has testified to the "huge expenses" of counterterrorism and intelligence strategies.[39] Although the federal government provided $31 billion in grants to state and local governments for homeland security between 2003 and 2010, many law enforcement

COUNTERING Domestic Terrorism

UNDER SUSPICION

LEARNING OBJECTIVE 4 Describe the usefulness of Suspicious Activity Reports in countering domestic terrorism.

First, the unidentified male walking around the harbor in Newport Beach, California, took several photographs of the Orange County Sheriff's Department's fireboat and the Balboa Ferry with his cell phone camera. Then he made a phone call, walked to his car, and returned five minutes later to take more pictures. Next, he met another person, with whom he watched boat traffic. Finally, another adult with two children joined the pair, and the group boarded the ferry.

Was this behavior suspicious? Apparently, it was suspicious enough to be noted by a local law enforcement officer and filed as Suspicious Activity Report (SAR) NO3821, to be passed along to the federal government. The goal of the SAR program is to have officers from every local police and sheriff's department provide tips about potential terrorism

activity to one of seventy-two *fusion centers* across the United States. At these fusion centers, federal terrorism experts examine the reports to determine if any actual threat exists. An SAR rarely leads to further legal action. The first 161,000 such reports resulted in only five arrests, none of which had to do with terrorism. "Ninety-nine percent don't pan out or lead to anything," said one Federal Bureau of Investigation special agent of the information from local police officers. "But we're happy to wade through these things."

FOR CRITICAL ANALYSIS The federal government's definition of *suspicious activity* is "observed behavior reasonably indicative of pre-operational planning related to terrorism or other criminal activity." What is your opinion of this definition? Is it too broad? Why do you think the actions of the Newport Beach suspect described above resulted in an SAR? What potential for abuse, if any, do you see in the SAR program?

agencies continue to rely on already–stretched-thin city budgets to cover the extra costs of anti-terrorism responsibilities.[40]

LAW ENFORCEMENT 2.0 Fortunately, just as more intelligence has become crucial to police work, the means available to gather such intelligence have also increased greatly. Nearly every successful anti-terrorism investigation has relied on information gathered from the Internet. More and more often, traditional criminals are also getting caught on the Web. Police in South Charleston, West Virginia, arrested six young men who photographed themselves destroying a local hotel room and then posted the incriminating pictures on various Twitter accounts. Utah police discovered material on a convicted sex offender's MySpace account that proved forbidden contact with two youths. Memphis detectives were able to apprehend two burglars who had stolen alcohol from a restaurant when one of them wrote on Facebook, "I'd like to collect some of the booty we liberated Sunday, if there's any left." According to a recent poll, more than 80 percent of local police departments also use social media as a form of outreach to the public, as we saw at the beginning of this chapter.[41]

As the leaders of the reform movement envisioned, technology also continues to improve the capabilities of officers in the field. Using special applications on smartphones or tablet computers, police can instantly access the addresses of wanted persons, registered sex offenders, gang members, and recent crime locations. As we saw earlier in this section, the modern police car is quickly evolving into a command center on wheels, and police officers also enjoy the use of mobile fingerprint readers, less lethal weapons such as laser beams (discussed in Chapter 6), and dozens of other technological innovations.

Some law enforcement veterans are concerned that the "art" of policing is being lost in an era of intelligence-led policing and increased reliance on technology. "If it becomes all about the science," says Los Angeles Police Department Deputy Chief Michael Downing, "I worry we'll lose the important nuances."[42] As the remainder of this chapter and the two that follow show, however, the human element continues to dominate all aspects of policing in America.

SELF ASSESSMENT

Fill in the blanks and check your answers on page 163.

During the _____ era of American policing, which lasted roughly from 1840 to 1930, police officers used the _____ system to enrich themselves. The _____ era, which followed, saw the modernization of our nation's law enforcement system through innovations like Vollmer and Wilson's _____ model of policing. Following the national turmoil of the 1960s and early 1970s, _____ era strategies encouraged a partnership between citizens and the police. Today, _____-led policing efforts attempt to make law enforcement agencies more efficient and better able to prevent future _____ attacks.

RECRUITMENT AND TRAINING: BECOMING A POLICE OFFICER

In 1961, police expert James H. Chenoweth commented that the methods used to hire police officers had changed little since 1829 when the Metropolitan Police of London was created.[43] The past half-century, however, has seen a number of improvements in the way that police administrators handle the task of **recruitment,** or the development of a pool of qualified applicants from which to select new officers. Efforts have been made

Recruitment The process by which law enforcement agencies develop a pool of qualified applicants from which to select new members.

to diversify police rolls, and recruits in most police departments undergo a substantial array of tests and screens—discussed below—to determine their aptitude. Furthermore, annual starting salaries that can exceed $70,000, along with the opportunities offered by an interesting profession in the public service field, have attracted a wide variety of applicants to police work. (To learn what a police officer can expect to earn in his or her first year on the job, see Figure 5.2 below.)

Basic Requirements

The selection process involves a number of steps, and each police department has a different method of choosing candidates. Most agencies, however, require at a minimum that a police officer:

- Be a U.S. citizen.
- Not have been convicted of a felony.
- Have or be eligible to have a driver's license in the state where the department is located.
- Be at least twenty-one years of age.
- Meet weight and eyesight requirements.

In addition, few departments will accept candidates older than forty-five years of age.

BACKGROUND CHECKS AND TESTS Beyond these minimum requirements, police departments usually engage in extensive background checks, including drug tests; a review of the applicant's educational, military, and driving records; credit checks; interviews with spouses, acquaintances, and previous employers; and a background search to determine whether the applicant has been convicted of any criminal acts. Police agencies generally require certain physical attributes in applicants: normally, they must be able to pass a physical agility or fitness test. (For an example of one such test, see Figure 5.3 on the following page.)

FIGURE 5.2 Average Annual Salary for Entry-Level Officers by Size of Population Served

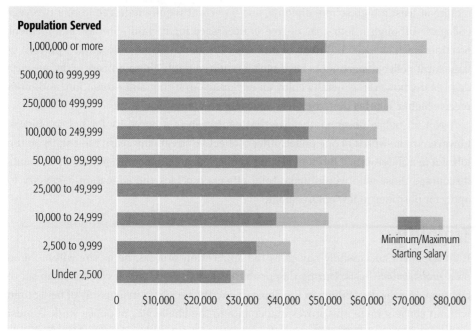

Source: Bureau of Justice Statistics, *Local Police Departments, 2007* (Washington, D.C.: U.S. Department of Justice, December 2010), Table 7, page 12.

FIGURE 5.3 Physical Agility Exam for the Henrico County (Virginia) Division of Police

Those applying for the position of police officer must finish this physical agility exam within 3 minutes, 30 seconds. During the test, applicants are required to wear the equipment (with a total weight of between 9 and 13 pounds) worn by patrol officers, which includes the police uniform, leather gun belt, firearm, baton, portable radio, and ballistics vest.

Getty Images

1. Applicant begins test seated in a police vehicle, door closed, seat belt fastened.
2. Applicant must exit vehicle and jump or climb a six-foot barrier.
3. Applicant then completes a one-quarter mile run or walk, making various turns along the way, to simulate a pursuit run.
4. Applicant must jump a simulated five-foot culvert/ditch.
5. Applicant must drag a "human simulator" (dummy) weighing 175 pounds a distance of 50 feet (to simulate a situation in which an officer is required to pull or carry an injured person to safety).
6. Applicant must draw his or her weapon and fire five rounds with the strong hand and five rounds with the weak hand.

Getty Images

In some departments, particularly those that serve large metropolitan areas, the applicant must take a psychological screening test to determine if he or she is suited to law enforcement work. Generally, such suitability tests measure the applicant's ability to handle stress, follow rules, use good judgment, and avoid off-duty behavior that would reflect negatively on the department.[44] Along these same lines, according to the International Association of Chiefs of Police, more than one-third of American police agencies now review an applicant's social media activity on sources such as Facebook, MySpace, and Twitter.[45] In one instance, the Middletown (New Jersey) Police Department rejected an applicant because he had posted photos of himself with "scantily clad women" online.

EDUCATIONAL REQUIREMENTS One of the most dramatic differences between today's police recruits and those of several generations ago is their level of education. In the 1920s, when August Vollmer began promoting the need for higher education in police officers, few had attended college. Today, 82 percent of all local police departments require at least a high school diploma, and 9 percent require a degree from a two-year college.[46] Although a four-year degree is necessary for certain elite law enforcement positions such as Federal Bureau of Investigation special agent, only about 5 percent of large local police departments have such a requirement.[47] Those officers with four-year degrees do, however, generally enjoy an advantage in hiring and promotion, and often receive higher salaries than their less educated co-employees.

Not all police observers believe that education is a necessity for police officers, however. In the words of one police officer, "effective street cops learn their skills on the job, not in a classroom."[48] By emphasizing a college degree, say some, police departments discourage those who would make solid officers but lack the education necessary to apply for positions in law enforcement.

Identify the differences between the police academy and field training as learning tools for recruits. LEARNING OBJECTIVE **5**

Training

If an applicant successfully navigates the application process, he or she will be hired on a *probationary* basis. During this **probationary period,** which can last from six to eighteen months depending on the department, the recruit is in jeopardy of being fired without cause if he or she proves inadequate to the challenges of police work. Almost every state requires that police recruits pass through a training period while on probation. During this time, they are taught the basics of police work and are under constant

Probationary Period A period of time at the beginning of a police officer's career during which she or he may be fired without cause.

supervision by superiors. The training period usually has two components: the police academy and field training. On average, local police departments serving populations of 250,000 or more require 1,648 hours of training—972 hours in the classroom and 676 hours in the field.[49]

ACADEMY TRAINING The *police academy,* run by either the state or a police agency, provides recruits with a controlled, militarized environment in which they receive their introduction to the world of the police officer. They are taught the laws of search, seizure, arrest, and interrogation; how and when to use weapons; the procedures of securing a crime scene and interviewing witnesses; first aid; self-defense; and other essentials of police work. Nine in ten police academies also provide terrorism-related training to teach recruits how to respond to terrorist incidents, including those involving weapons of mass destruction.[50] Academy instructors evaluate the recruits' performance and send intermittent progress reports to police administrators.

A recruit performs pushups under duress at the Cleveland Police Academy. Why are police academies an important part of the learning process for a potential police officer?
Marvin Fong/*Cleveland Plain Dealer*/Landov

IN THE FIELD **Field training** takes place outside the confines of the police academy. A recruit is paired with an experienced police officer known as a field training officer (FTO). The goal of field training is to help rookies apply the concepts they have learned in the academy "to the streets," with the FTO playing a supervisory role to make sure that nothing goes awry. According to many, the academy introduces recruits to the formal rules of police work, but field training gives the rookies their first taste of the informal rules. In fact, the initial advice to recruits from some FTOs is often along the lines of "O.K., kid. Forget everything you learned in the classroom. You're in the real world now." Nonetheless, the academy is a critical component in the learning process, as it provides rookies with a road map to the job.

SELF ASSESSMENT

Fill in the blanks and check your answers on page 163.
Most police agencies require that recruits be at least _____-_____ years of age and have no prior _____ convictions. During the _____ period, which can last as long as eighteen months, a recruit will attend a _____ _____ to learn the rules of police work in an institutional setting. Then, she or he will leave the classroom and partner with an experienced officer for _____ _____.

WOMEN AND MINORITIES IN POLICING TODAY

For many years, the typical American police officer was white and male. As recently as 1968, African Americans represented only 5 percent of all sworn officers in the United States, and the percentage of "women in blue" was even lower.[51] Only within the past thirty years has this situation been addressed, and only within the past twenty years have

Field Training The segment of a police recruit's training in which he or she is removed from the classroom and placed on the beat, under the supervision of a senior officer.

Discrimination The illegal use of characteristics such as gender or race by employers when making hiring or promotion decisions.

Affirmative Action A hiring or promotion policy favoring those groups, such as women, African Americans, or Hispanics, who have suffered from discrimination in the past or continue to suffer from discrimination.

many police departments actively tried to recruit women, African Americans, Hispanics, Asian Americans, and members of other minority groups. The result, as you will see, has been a steady though not spectacular increase in the diversity of the nation's police forces. When it comes to issues of gender, race, and ethnicity, however, mere statistics rarely tell the entire story.

Antidiscrimination Law and Affirmative Action

To a certain extent, external forces have driven law enforcement agencies to increase the number of female and minority recruits. The 1964 Civil Rights Act and its 1972 amendments guaranteed members of minority groups and women equal access to jobs in law enforcement, partly by establishing the Equal Employment Opportunity Commission (EEOC) to ensure fairness in hiring practices. The United States Supreme Court has also ruled on several occasions that **discrimination** by law enforcement agencies violates federal law.[52] In legal terms, discrimination occurs when hiring and promotion decisions are based on individual characteristics such as gender or race, and not on job-related factors.

CONSENT DECREES Since the early 1970s, numerous law enforcement agencies have instituted **affirmative action** programs to increase the diversity of their employees. These programs are designed to give women and members of minority groups certain advantages in hiring and promotion to remedy the effects of past discrimination and prevent future discrimination. Often, affirmative action programs are established voluntarily. Sometimes, however, they are the result of lawsuits brought by employees or potential employees who believe that the employer has discriminated against them. In such instances, if the court finds that discrimination did occur, it will implement a *consent decree* to remedy the situation. Under a consent decree, the law enforcement agency often agrees to meet certain numerical goals in hiring women and members of minority groups. If it fails to meet these goals, it is punished with a fine or some other sanction.[53]

RECRUITING CHALLENGES Over the past two decades, the EEOC has brought about two dozen discrimination lawsuits against local and state law enforcement agencies on behalf of wronged individuals. In almost every case, the agency agreed to resolve the problem through a consent decree.[54] As the Rochester (New York) Police Department (RPD) has learned, however, simply being willing to increase diversity in recruiting may not be enough. The RPD is operating under a voluntary consent decree that requires at least one in four new hires to come from a minority group. Despite an affirmative action program and a population of potential recruits that is 52 percent nonwhite, from 2005 to 2010 the RPD added only 21 members of minority groups to its force, out of a total of 186 new hires.[55]

In some instances, creative recruiting methods can bolster diversity. For example, Vermont's Step Up to Law Enforcement program provides women interested in law enforcement with a series of courses designed to make the application process less intimidating. The curriculum includes preparation for the physical and written exams, along with lectures on the challenges facing women police officers. In its first four years, twenty of the program's graduates were hired by local police departments or state correctional facilities.[56] Nonetheless, too often the "multiple hurdles" of the police recruiting process discourage or disqualify women and minorities despite efforts to attract them. In the *CJ in Action* feature at the end of this chapter, we will examine the controversial practice of lowering these hurdles to help diversify American police departments.

Working Women: Gender and Law Enforcement

In 1987, about 7.6 percent of all local police officers were women. Twenty years later, that percentage had risen to almost 12 percent.[57] That increase seems less impressive, however, when one considers that women make up more than half of the population of the United States, meaning that they are severely underrepresented in law enforcement.

ADDED SCRUTINY There are several reasons for the low levels of women serving as police officers. First, relatively few women hold leadership positions in American policing. More than half of this country's large police departments have no women in their highest ranks,[58] and fewer than 1 percent of the police chiefs in the United States are women.[59] Consequently, female police officers have few superiors who might be able to mentor them in what can be a hostile work environment. In addition to the dangers and pressures facing all law enforcement agents, which we will discuss in the next chapter, women must deal with an added layer of scrutiny. Many male police officers feel that their female counterparts are mentally soft, physically weak, and generally unsuited for the rigors of the job. At the same time, male officers often try to protect female officers by keeping them out of hazardous situations, thereby denying the women the opportunity to prove themselves.[60]

LEARNING
6
OBJECTIVE

Describe the challenges facing women who choose law enforcement as a career.

Women in law enforcement also face the problem of *tokenism,* or the belief that they have been hired or promoted to fulfill diversity requirements and have not earned their positions. Tokenism creates pressure to prove the stereotypes wrong. As one female officer told researcher Teresa Lynn Wertsch:

> The guys can view you as a sex object instead of a professional. It makes me try harder to put up more fronts and play more of the macho, boy role rather than accept that I am a female. . . . You can't be meek or mild, too quiet. You can't be too loud or boisterous because then you would be a dike, too masculine. I wish it didn't have to be this way, but you're either a bitch, a dike, or a slut.[61]

In fact, most of the negative attitudes toward women police officers are based on prejudice rather than actual experience. A number of studies have shown that there is very little difference between the performances of men and women in uniform.[62] (For more on this topic, see the feature *Myth versus Reality—Women Make Bad Cops* on the following page.)

SEXUAL HARASSMENT The female officer quoted above observed that male officers see her as a "sex object." Anecdotal evidence suggests that this attitude is commonplace in police departments and often leads to **sexual harassment** of female police officers. Sexual harassment refers to a pattern of behavior that is sexual in nature, such as inappropriate touching or lewd jokes, and is unwelcome by its target.[63] Over a nine-month period in 2010, the National Police Misconduct Statistics and Reporting Project confirmed eighty-six incidents of sexual harassment in police departments nationwide.[64] Self-reported surveys, however, suggest that the actual incidence is much higher, with most incidents going unreported.[65]

Despite having to deal with problems such as sexual harassment, outdated stereotypes, and tokenism, female police officers have generally shown that they are capable law enforcement officers, willing to take great risks if necessary to do their job. The names of nearly three hundred women are included on the National Law Enforcement Memorial in Washington, D.C.

Sexual Harassment A repeated pattern of unwelcome sexual advances and/or obscene remarks in the workplace. Under certain circumstances, sexual harassment is illegal and can be the basis for a civil lawsuit.

Since the formation of the earliest police departments in the nineteenth century, policing has been seen as "man's work." Only men were considered to have the physical strength necessary to deal with the dangers of the street.

THE MYTH The perception that women are not physically strong enough to be effective law enforcement officers prevails both in the public mind and within police forces themselves. Criminologist Susan Martin has found that policewomen are under "constant pressure to demonstrate their competence and effectiveness vis-à-vis their male counterparts." One female police officer describes her experience:

> I got a call. They send another male officer and then another male officer. The attitude is—get a guy. I'm there with the one male officer and when the other guy shows up, the first male officer says to the second, this is right in front of me—"I'm glad you came."

THE REALITY Female police officers are certainly capable of acts of bravery and physical prowess. In fact, a number of studies have shown that policewomen can be as effective as men in most situations, and often more so. Citizens appear to prefer dealing with a female police officer rather than a male during service calls—especially those that involve domestic violence. In general, policewomen are less aggressive and more likely to reduce the potential for a violent situation by relying on verbal skills rather than their authority as law enforcement agents. According to a study conducted by the National Center

for Women and Policing, payouts in lawsuits for claims of brutality and misconduct involving male officers exceed those involving females by a ratio of 43 to 1.

FOR CRITICAL ANALYSIS

Do you believe that female police officers can be just as effective as men in protecting citizens from criminal behavior? Why or why not?

A female member of the Miami (Florida) Police Department provides security during a public event.
Joe Raedle/Getty Images

Minority Report: Race and Ethnicity in Law Enforcement

As Figure 5.4 on the facing page shows, like women, members of minority groups have been slowly increasing their presence in local police departments since the late 1980s. Specifically, in 2007, African American officers comprised about 12 percent of the nation's police officers; Hispanic officers, about 10 percent; and other minority groups such as Asians, American Indians, and Pacific Islanders, about 3 percent.[66] By some measures, members of minority groups are better represented than women in policing. Cities such as Detroit and Washington have local police departments that closely match their civilian populations in terms of diversity, and in recent years, a majority of police recruits in New York City have been members of minority groups. On other measures, such as promotion, minorities in law enforcement continue to seek parity.[67]

DOUBLE MARGINALITY According to Peter C. Moskos, a professor at the John Jay College of Criminal Justice in New York, "black and white police officers remain two distinct shades of blue, with distinct attitudes toward each other and the communities they

FIGURE 5.4 Members of Minority Groups in Local Law Enforcement, 1987–2007

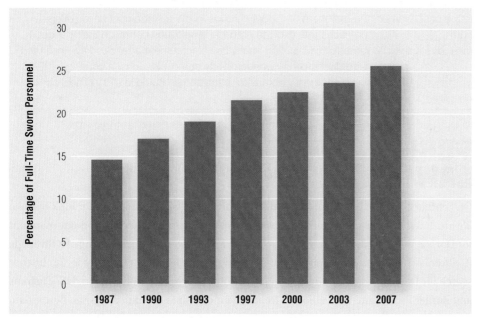

Note: Includes blacks or African Americans, Hispanics or Latinos, Asians, Native Hawaiians or other Pacific Islanders, American Indians, Alaska Natives, and persons identifying two or more races.

Source: Bureau of Justice Statistics, *Local Police Departments, 2007* (Washington, D.C.: U.S. Department of Justice, December 2010), Figure 9, page 14.

serve."[68] While that may be true, minority officers generally report that they have good relationships with their white fellow officers.[69] Often, though, members of minority groups in law enforcement—particularly African Americans and Hispanics—do face the problem of **double marginality.** This term refers to a situation in which minority officers are viewed with suspicion by both sides:

1. White police officers believe that minority officers will give members of their own race or ethnicity better treatment on the streets.
2. Those same minority officers face hostility from members of their own community who are under the impression that black and Hispanic officers are traitors to their race or ethnicity.

In response, minority officers may feel the need to act more harshly toward minority offenders to prove that they are not biased in favor of their own racial or ethnic group.[70]

THE BENEFITS OF A DIVERSE POLICE FORCE In 1986, Supreme Court justice John Paul Stevens spoke for many in the criminal justice system when he observed that "an integrated police force could develop a better relationship [with a racially diverse citizenry] and therefore do a more effective job of maintaining law and order than a force composed of white officers."[71] Indeed, despite the effects of double marginality, African American officers may have more credibility in a predominantly black neighborhood than white police officers, leading to better community-police relations and a greater ability to solve and prevent crimes. Certainly, in the Mexican American communities typical of border states such as Arizona, Texas, and California, many Hispanic officers are able to gather information that would be very difficult for non-Spanish-speaking officers to collect. Finally, however, the best argument for a diverse police force is that members of minority groups represent a broad source of talent in this country, and such talent can only enhance the overall effectiveness of American law enforcement.

Double Marginality The double suspicion that minority law enforcement officers face from their white colleagues and from members of the minority community to which they belong.

In the past, women and members of minority groups in law enforcement have suffered from _____, or hiring practices that exclude potential employees based on their gender, race, or ethnicity. To remedy this situation, many law enforcement agencies have instituted _____ _____ programs to diversify their workforces. In some instances, a court will issue a _____ _____, under which an agency agrees to reach certain numerical hiring goals or be penalized.

PUBLIC AND PRIVATE LAW ENFORCEMENT

On February 12, 2013, during a shootout with the police, Christopher Dorner took his own life inside a mountain cabin near Big Bear, California. The suicide ended a ten-day manhunt for Dorner, who was a suspect in three murders, including the ambush killing of a Riverside (California) police officer. Thousands of law enforcement agents took part in the intense search for Dorner, including members of the Federal Bureau of Investigation, U.S. Customs and Border Protection, the California Department of Fish and Wildlife, the San Bernardino County Sheriff's Department, and the Las Vegas and Los Angeles Police Departments.

As the effort to capture Dorner, which stretched across the southwest United States and into Mexico, shows, Americans are served by a multitude of police organizations. Overall, there are about 18,000 law enforcement agencies in the United States, employing about 880,000 officers.[72] For the most part, these agencies operate on three different levels: local, state, and federal. Each level has its own set of responsibilities, which we shall discuss starting with local police departments.

Municipal Law Enforcement Agencies

According to federal statistics, there is one local or state police officer for every 400 residents of the United States.[73] About two-thirds of all *sworn officers,* or those officers with arrest powers, work in small- and medium-sized police departments serving cities with populations from 10,000 to one million.[74] While the New York City Police Department employs about 38,000 police personnel, 50 percent of all local police departments have ten or fewer law enforcement officers.[75]

Of the three levels of law enforcement, municipal agencies have the broadest authority to apprehend criminal suspects, maintain order, and provide services to the community. Whether the local officer is part of a large force or the only law enforcement officer in the community, he or she is usually responsible for a wide spectrum of duties, from responding to noise complaints to investigating homicides. Larger police departments will often assign officers to specialized task forces or units that deal with a particular crime or area of concern. For example, in Washington, D.C., the police department features a Gay and Lesbian Liaison Unit that deals with anti-homosexual crimes in the city. The Knoxville (Tennessee) Police Department has a squad devoted to combating Internet crimes against children, while the three hundred officers assigned to the New York Police Department's Emergency Services Unit are trained in suicide rescue, hostage negotiation, and SCUBA operations.

Sheriffs and County Law Enforcement

The **sheriff** is a very important figure in American law enforcement. Almost every one of the more than three thousand counties in the United States (except those in Alaska) has a sheriff. In every state except Rhode Island and Hawaii, sheriffs are elected by members

Sheriff The primary law enforcement officer in a county, usually elected to the post by a popular vote.

of the community for two- or four-year terms and are paid a salary set by the state legislature or county board.

As elected officials who do not necessarily need a background in law enforcement, modern sheriffs resemble their counterparts from the political era of policing in many ways. Simply stated, the sheriff is also a politician. When a new sheriff is elected, she or he will sometimes repay political debts by appointing new deputies or promoting those who have given her or him support.

SIZE AND RESPONSIBILITY OF SHERIFFS' DEPARTMENTS Like municipal police forces, sheriffs' departments vary in size. The largest is the Los Angeles County Sheriff's Department, with more than 9,400 deputies. Of the 3,063 sheriffs' departments in the country, thirteen employ more than 1,000 officers, while forty-five have only one.[76]

■ Lane County (Oregon) sheriff's deputies take part in an "active shooter" training exercise to protect local grade schools students. Why do sheriffs' departments and municipal police agencies often find themselves policing the same geographical areas?
AP Photo/*The Register-Guard*, Brian Davies

Keep in mind that cities, which are served by municipal police departments, often exist within counties, which are served by sheriffs' departments. Therefore, police officers and sheriffs' deputies often find themselves policing the same geographical areas. Police departments, however, are generally governed by a local political entity such as a mayor's office, while most sheriffs' departments are assigned their duties by state law. About 80 percent of all sheriffs' departments have the primary responsibility for investigating violent crimes in their jurisdictions. Other common responsibilities of a sheriff's department include:

- Investigating drug crimes.
- Maintaining the county jail.
- Carrying out civil and criminal processes within county lines, such as serving eviction notices and court summonses.
- Keeping order in the county courthouse.
- Collecting taxes.
- Enforcing orders of the court, such as overseeing the isolation of a jury during a trial.[77]

It is easy to confuse sheriffs' departments and local police departments. Both law enforcement agencies are responsible for many of the same tasks, including crime investigation and routine patrol. There are differences, however. Sheriffs' departments are more likely to be involved in county court and jail operations and to perform certain services such as search and rescue. Local police departments, for their part, are more likely to perform traffic-related functions than are sheriffs' departments.[78]

THE COUNTY CORONER Another elected official on the county level is the **coroner,** or medical examiner. Duties vary from county to county, but the coroner has a general mandate to investigate "all sudden, unexplained, unnatural, or suspicious deaths" reported to the office. The coroner is ultimately responsible for determining the cause of death in these cases. Coroners also perform autopsies and assist other law enforcement

Coroner The medical examiner of a county, usually elected by popular vote.

A Connecticut State Police officer provides advice for a motorist stuck in a snowstorm on Interstate 84 in East Hartford. In what ways do state law enforcement officers supplement the efforts of local police officers?
AP Photo/Jessica Hill

agencies in homicide investigations. For example, after singer Whitney Houston died in February 2012, the Los Angeles County coroner needed to determine the cause of death. After a two-month investigation, the coroner confirmed that Houston drowned in her bathtub, with heart disease and cocaine use listed as contributing factors.

State Police and Highway Patrols

The most visible state law enforcement agency is the state police or highway patrol agency. Historically, state police agencies were created for three reasons:

1. To assist local police agencies, which often did not have adequate resources or training to handle their law enforcement tasks.
2. To investigate criminal activities that crossed jurisdictional boundaries (such as when bank robbers committed a crime in one county and then fled to another part of the state).
3. To provide law enforcement in rural and other areas that did not have local or county police agencies.

THE DIFFERENCE BETWEEN STATE POLICE AND HIGHWAY PATROLS Today, there are twenty-three state police agencies and twenty-six highway patrols in the United States. State police agencies have statewide jurisdiction and are authorized to perform a wide variety of law enforcement tasks. Thus, they provide the same services as city or county police departments and are restricted only by the boundaries of the state. In contrast, highway patrols have limited authority. Their duties are generally defined either by their jurisdiction or by the specific types of offenses they have the authority to control. As their name suggests, most highway patrols concentrate primarily on regulating traffic. Specifically, they enforce traffic laws and investigate traffic accidents. Furthermore, they usually limit their activity to patrolling state and federal highways.

Trying to determine what state agency has which duties can be confusing. The Washington State Highway Patrol, despite its name, also has state police powers. In addition, thirty-five states have investigative agencies that are independent of the state police or highway patrol. Such agencies are usually found in states with highway patrols, and they have the primary responsibility of investigating criminal activities. For example, in addition to its highway patrol, Oklahoma runs a State Bureau of Investigation and a State Bureau of Narcotics and Dangerous Drugs. Each state has its own methods of determining the jurisdictions of these various organizations.

LIMITED-PURPOSE LAW ENFORCEMENT AGENCIES Even with the agencies just discussed, a number of states have found that certain law enforcement areas need more specific attention. As a result, a wide variety of limited-purpose law enforcement agencies have sprung up in the fifty states. For example, most states have an alcoholic beverage control commission (ABC), or a similarly named organization, which monitors the sale and distribution of alcoholic beverages. The ABC monitors alcohol distributors to ensure that all taxes are paid on the beverages and is responsible for revoking or suspending the liquor licenses of establishments that have broken relevant laws.

Many states have fish and game warden organizations that enforce all laws relating to hunting and fishing. Motor vehicle compliance (MVC) agencies monitor interstate carriers or trucks to make sure that they are in compliance with state and federal laws. MVC officers generally operate the weigh stations that are commonly found on interstate highways. Other limited-purpose law enforcement agencies deal with white-collar and computer crime, regulate nursing homes, and provide training to local police departments.

Federal Law Enforcement Agencies

Statistically, employees of federal agencies do not make up a large part of the nation's law enforcement force. In fact, the New York City Police Department has about one-third as many employees as all of the federal law enforcement agencies combined. Nevertheless, the influence of these federal agencies is substantial.

Unlike local police departments, which must deal with all forms of crime, federal agencies have been authorized, usually by Congress, to enforce specific laws or attend to specific situations. The U.S. Coast Guard, for example, patrols the nation's waterways, while U.S. Postal Inspectors investigate and prosecute crimes perpetrated through the use of the U.S. mails. In this section, you will learn the elements and duties of the most important federal law enforcement agencies, which are grouped according to the federal department or bureau to which they report. (See Figure 5.5 on the following page for the current federal law enforcement "lineup.")

THE DEPARTMENT OF HOMELAND SECURITY Comprising twenty-two federal agencies, the Department of Homeland Security (DHS) coordinates national efforts to protect the United States against international and domestic terrorism. While most of the agencies under DHS control are not specifically linked with the criminal justice system, the department does oversee three agencies that play an important role in counterterrorism and fighting crime: U.S. Customs and Border Protection, U.S. Immigration and Customs Enforcement, and the U.S. Secret Service.

LEARNING **7** OBJECTIVE Indicate some of the most important law enforcement agencies under the control of the Department of Homeland Security.

U.S. Customs and Border Protection (CBP) In 2012, the federal government spent nearly $18 billion on enforcing immigration law.[79] A large chunk of these funds went to **U.S. Customs and Border Protection (CBP),** which polices the flow of goods and people across the United States' international borders. In general terms, this means that the agency has two primary goals: (1) to keep undocumented immigrants, illegal drugs, and drug traffickers from crossing our borders, and (2) to facilitate the smooth flow of legal trade and travel. Consequently, CBP officers are stationed at every port of entry and exit to the United States. The officers have widespread authority to investigate and search all international passengers, whether they arrive on airplanes, ships, or other forms of transportation.

The U.S. Border Patrol, a branch of the CBP, has the burden of policing both the Mexican and Canadian borders between official ports of entry. Its primary focus has been on the Mexican border, which is patrolled by nearly 21,500 agents, more than double the number of a decade ago. This increase in personnel seems to have had a deterrent effect. In 2011, about 325,000 illegal crossers were apprehended on that border. A decade earlier, that number was close to 1.6 million.[80] (The recent economic downturn in the United States, which has removed some of the economic incentives for illegal crossing,

U.S. Customs and Border Protection (CBP) The federal agency responsible for protecting U.S. borders and facilitating legal trade and travel across those borders.

FIGURE 5.5 Federal Law Enforcement Agencies

A number of federal agencies employ law enforcement officers who are authorized to carry firearms and make arrests. The most prominent ones are under the control of the U.S. Department of Homeland Security, the U.S. Department of Justice, or the U.S. Department of the Treasury.

Department of Homeland Security

DEPARTMENT NAME	APPROXIMATE NUMBER OF OFFICERS	MAIN RESPONSIBILITIES
U.S. Customs and Border Protection (CBP)	37,000	• (1) Prevent the illegal flow of people and goods across America's international borders; (2) facilitate legal trade and travel
U.S. Immigration and Customs Enforcement (ICE)	12,500	• Uphold public safety and homeland security by enforcing the nation's immigration and customs laws
U.S. Secret Service	5,000	• (1) Protect the president, the president's family, former presidents and their families, and other high-ranking politicians; (2) combat currency counterfeiters

Department of Justice

DEPARTMENT NAME	APPROXIMATE NUMBER OF OFFICERS	MAIN RESPONSIBILITIES
Federal Bureau of Investigation (FBI)	13,000	• (1) Protect national security by fighting international and domestic terrorism; (2) enforce federal criminal laws such as those dealing with cyber crime, public corruption, and civil rights violations
Drug Enforcement Administration (DEA)	4,500	• Enforce the nation's laws regulating the sale and use of drugs
Bureau of Alcohol, Tobacco, Firearms and Explosives (ATF)	2,500	• (1) Combat the illegal use and trafficking of firearms and explosives; (2) investigate the illegal diversion of alcohol and tobacco products
U.S. Marshals Service	3,500	• (1) Provide security at federal courts; (2) protect government witnesses; (3) apprehend fugitives from the federal court or corrections system

Department of the Treasury

DEPARTMENT NAME	APPROXIMATE NUMBER OF OFFICERS	MAIN RESPONSIBILITIES
Internal Revenue Service (IRS)	2,500	• Investigate potential criminal violations of the nation's tax code

Source: Bureau of Justice Statistics, *Federal Law Enforcement Officers, 2008* (Washington, D.C.: U.S. Department of Justice, June 2012), Table 1, page 2.

has probably also affected these figures.) Border Patrol agents also keep a significant amount of illegal drugs from entering the country—5 million pounds in 2011.[81]

U.S. Immigration and Customs Enforcement (ICE) The CBP shares responsibility for locating and apprehending those persons illegally in the United States with special agents from **U.S. Immigration and Customs Enforcement (ICE).** While the CBP focuses almost exclusively on the nation's borders, ICE has a broader mandate to investigate and to enforce our country's immigration and customs laws. Simply stated, the CBP covers the borders, and ICE covers everything else. The latter agency's duties include detaining undocumented aliens and deporting (removing) them from the United States, ensuring that those without permission do not work or gain other benefits in this country, and disrupting human trafficking operations.

U.S. Immigration and Customs Enforcement (ICE) The federal agency that enforces the nation's immigration and customs laws.

ICE and Local Cooperation Recently, ICE has become more aggressive in its efforts to apprehend and remove undocumented immigrants with criminal records. In 2012, it removed about 410,000 undocumented immigrants from the United States. Approximately 55 percent of these immigrants had been convicted of felonies or misdemeanors.[82] These numbers were the highest in the agency's history, and reflect, in part, the success of its Secure Communities initiative. Under this program, started in 2008, information on every suspect arrested by state and local police officers is transmitted electronically to ICE during the booking process. If this instant background check shows that the suspect is in the country illegally and has a history of criminal or immigration law violations that makes him or her eligible for removal, ICE will issue a *detainer*.

In Douglas, Arizona, Border Patrol agents detain a man suspected of smuggling marijuana across the U.S. border from Mexico. What is the difference between U.S. Customs and Border Protection, which oversees the Border Patrol, and U.S. Immigration and Customs Enforcement?
Joshua Lott/*New York Times*/Redux Pictures

This document allows ICE to take custody of the suspect at the conclusion of his or her contact with the criminal justice system, usually after the suspect has been released by police or has completed a jail or prison sentence. According to the DHS, the priority of Secure Communities is to identify and remove those undocumented immigrants who have been charged with or convicted of serious crimes.[83] The program has come under considerable criticism, however, for ensnaring those guilty of misdemeanors or even traffic tickets.[84] Furthermore, as we will see in Chapter 7, Arizona and several other states have passed controversial laws concerning local law enforcement's ability to influence immigration law.

The U.S. Secret Service When it was created in 1865, the **U.S. Secret Service** was primarily responsible for combating currency counterfeiters. In 1901, the agency was given the added responsibility of protecting the president of the United States, the president's family, the vice president, the president-elect, and former presidents. These duties have remained the cornerstone of the agency, with several expansions. After a number of threats against presidential candidates in the 1960s and early 1970s, including the shootings of Robert Kennedy of New York and Governor George Wallace of Alabama, in 1976 Secret Service agents became responsible for protecting those political figures as well.

In addition to its special plainclothes agents, the agency also directs two uniformed groups of law enforcement officers. The Secret Service Uniformed Division protects the grounds of the White House and its inhabitants, and the Treasury Police Force polices the Treasury Building in Washington, D.C. This responsibility includes investigating threats against presidents and those running for presidential office. To aid its battle against counterfeiters and forgers of government bonds, the agency has the use of a laboratory at the Bureau of Engraving and Printing in the nation's capital.

Additional DHS Agencies Besides the three already discussed—CBP, ICE, and the U.S. Secret Service—three other DHS agencies play a central role in preventing and responding to crime and terrorist-related activity:

- The *U.S. Coast Guard* defends the nation's coasts, ports, and inland waterways. It also combats illegal drug shipping and enforces immigration law at sea.

U.S. Secret Service A federal law enforcement organization with the primary responsibility of protecting the president, the president's family, the vice president, and other important political figures.

- The *Transportation Security Administration* is responsible for the safe operation of our airline, rail, bus, and ferry services. It also operates the Federal Air Marshals program that places undercover federal agents on commercial flights.
- The *Federal Emergency Management Agency* holds a position as the lead federal agency in preparing for and responding to disasters such as hurricanes, floods, terrorist attacks, and *infrastructure* concerns. Our national **infrastructure** includes all of the facilities and systems that provide the daily necessities of modern life, such as electric power, food, water, transportation, and telecommunications.

THE DEPARTMENT OF JUSTICE The U.S. Department of Justice, created in 1870, is still the primary federal law enforcement agency in the country. With the responsibility of enforcing criminal law and supervising the federal prisons, the Justice Department plays a leading role in the American criminal justice system. To carry out its responsibilities to prevent and control crime, the department has a number of law enforcement agencies, including the Federal Bureau of Investigation, the federal Drug Enforcement Administration, the Bureau of Alcohol, Tobacco, Firearms and Explosives, and the U.S. Marshals Service.

The Federal Bureau of Investigation (FBI) Initially created in 1908 as the Bureau of Investigation, this agency was renamed the **Federal Bureau of Investigation (FBI)** in 1935. One of the primary investigative agencies of the federal government, the FBI has jurisdiction over nearly two hundred federal crimes, including white-collar crimes, espionage (spying), kidnapping, extortion, interstate transportation of stolen property, bank robbery, interstate gambling, and civil rights violations. With its network of agents across the country and the globe, the FBI is also uniquely positioned to combat worldwide criminal activity such as terrorism and drug trafficking. In fact, since 2001, the agency has shifted its focus from traditional crime to national security. Over a recent two-year period, more than half of all FBI investigations have focused on groups or individuals suspected of terrorist activity as opposed to "ordinary" crimes.[85]

The FBI and Local Cooperation The FBI is also committed to providing valuable support for local and state law enforcement agencies. Its Identification Division maintains a large database of fingerprint information and offers assistance in finding missing persons and identifying the victims of fires, airplane crashes, and other disfiguring disasters. The services of the FBI Laboratory, the largest crime laboratory in the world, are available at no cost to other agencies. Finally, the FBI's National Crime Information Center (NCIC) provides lists of stolen vehicles and firearms, missing license plates, vehicles used to commit crimes, and other information to local and state law enforcement officers.

The FBI's latest information-sharing program, the Law Enforcement National Data Exchange (N-DEx), acts as an electronic search engine for suspected criminals. So, for example, several years ago, Philadelphia police identified a suspect in a home invasion/murder investigation. Unable to locate the suspect locally, they turned to N-DEx for help. The N-DEx search indicated that the suspect had been involved in a domestic violence incident in Wilmington, Delaware. With the aid of Wilmington law enforcement, Philadelphia police were subsequently able to learn the suspect's home address and arrest him.[86]

The Drug Enforcement Administration (DEA) The mission of the **Drug Enforcement Administration (DEA)** is to enforce domestic drug laws and regulations and to assist

Identify the duties of the FBI. — **8** LEARNING OBJECTIVE

Photo Courtesy of FBI.gov

ARNOLD E. BELL

FEDERAL BUREAU OF INVESTIGATION (FBI) AGENT

I came to the FBI from the U.S. Army, where I worked as a crewman on a UH-1 helicopter and subsequently as a special agent with the U.S. Army Criminal Investigation Command. My work experience in the U.S. Army and degree from St. Leo College (now University) provided the educational foundation that allowed entry into the FBI. After graduating from the FBI Academy in Quantico, Virginia, I was assigned to our Los Angeles division, where I spent the next twelve years. It was a particularly interesting time to be working in Los Angeles, which was experiencing a boom in bank robberies. During the most intense stretches, we were averaging between five and seven bank robberies a day! When I wasn't chasing down a bank robber, I had my hands full with hunting down fugitives, working against organized crime, and dealing with public corruption.

I am currently assigned to the FBI's cyber division as an assistant section chief. The primary mission of my division is to combat cyber-based terrorism and hostile-intelligence operations conducted via the Internet, and to address general cyber crime. Since September 11, 2001, our primary focus has shifted from criminal work to counterterrorism. This has been a difficult transformation for many of us "old-timers" because we grew up in the Bureau doing criminal work. We all recognize, however, the importance of this new challenge, and, despite the difficulties, I believe we have been successful in fulfilling both missions.

fbi.gov

SOCIAL MEDIA CAREER TIP Be aware of your e-mail address/screen name/login name and what it represents. Stay away from nicknames. Use a professional and unique name to represent yourself consistently across social media platforms.

---

other federal and foreign agencies in combating illegal drug manufacture and trade on an international level. The agency also enforces the provisions of the Controlled Substances Act (see Chapter 3), which governs the manufacture, distribution, and dispensing of legal drugs, such as prescription drugs.

DEA agents often work in conjunction with local and state authorities to prevent illicit drugs from reaching communities. The agency also conducts extensive operations with law enforcement entities in other drug-producing countries. For example, the DEA consistently works with the Mexican military to combat Mexico's powerful drug cartels. Furthermore, on January 6, 2013, DEA agents informed Honduras's government of a suspicious boat operating off the coast of that Central American republic. The Honduran coast guard chased down the vessel and discovered that it was carrying nearly 800 pounds of cocaine.

Like the FBI, the DEA operates a network of six regional laboratories used to test and categorize seized drugs. Local law enforcement agencies have access to the DEA labs and often use them to ensure that information about particular drugs that will be presented in court is accurate and up to date. In recent years, Congress has given the FBI more authority to enforce drug laws, and the two agencies now share a number of administrative controls.

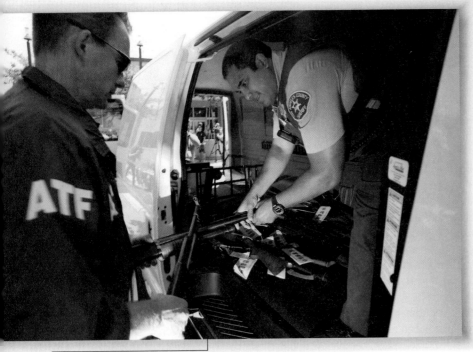

A sheriff's deputy transfers confiscated firearms to an ATF agent in Los Angeles. Some law enforcement experts have suggested that the ATF could do its job more effectively if handguns sold in the United States were listed in a national database. What would be the benefits and drawbacks of such a database?
David McNew/Getty Images

SOCIAL & CJ
MEDIA

The **ATF Press Office** operates a Twitter page that doubles as a newsroom for the federal crime-fighting agency. To find this page, enter "ATF" and "Twitter" in your search engine.

Ankomando/Shutterstock.com

The Bureau of Alcohol, Tobacco, Firearms and Explosives (ATF) As its name suggests, the Bureau of Alcohol, Tobacco, Firearms and Explosives (ATF) is primarily concerned with the illegal sale, possession, and use of firearms and the control of untaxed tobacco and liquor products. The Firearms Division of the agency has the responsibility of enforcing the Gun Control Act of 1968, which sets the circumstances under which firearms may be sold and used in this country. The bureau also regulates all gun trade between the United States and foreign nations and collects taxes on all firearm importers, manufacturers, and dealers. In keeping with these duties, the ATF is also responsible for policing the illegal use and possession of explosives. Furthermore, the ATF is charged with enforcing federal gambling laws.

Because it has jurisdiction over such a wide variety of crimes, especially those involving firearms and explosives, the ATF is a constant presence in federal criminal investigations. So, following Adam Lanza's December 2012 shooting rampage in Newtown, Connecticut, ATF agents raided a Hartford gun shop where Lanza's mother had purchased one of the guns used by her son in the attack. Furthermore, the ATF is engaged in an ongoing and crucial operation to keep American firearms out of the hands of Mexican drug cartels. The ATF has also formed multijurisdictional antigang task forces with other federal and local law enforcement agencies to investigate gang-related crimes involving firearms.

The U.S. Marshals Service The oldest federal law enforcement agency is the U.S. Marshals Service. In 1789, President George Washington assigned thirteen U.S. Marshals to protect his attorney general. That same year, Congress created the office of the U.S. Marshals and Deputy Marshals. Originally, the U.S. Marshals acted as the main law enforcement officers in the western territories. Following the Civil War (1861–1865), when most of these territories had become states, these agents were assigned to work for the U.S. district courts, where federal crimes are tried. The relationship between the U.S. Marshals Service and the federal courts continues today and forms the basis for the officers' main duties, which include:

1. Providing security at federal courts for judges, jurors, and other courtroom participants.
2. Controlling property that has been ordered seized by federal courts.
3. Protecting government witnesses who put themselves in danger by testifying against the targets of federal criminal investigations. This protection is sometimes accomplished by relocating the witnesses and providing them with different identities.
4. Transporting federal prisoners to detention institutions.
5. Investigating violations of federal fugitive laws.[87]

THE DEPARTMENT OF THE TREASURY The Department of the Treasury, formed in 1789, is mainly responsible for all financial matters of the federal government. It pays all the federal government's bills, borrows funds, collects taxes, mints coins, and prints paper currency. The largest bureau of the Treasury Department, the Internal Revenue Service (IRS), is concerned with violations of tax laws and regulations. The bureau has three divisions, only one of which is involved in criminal investigations. The examination branch of the IRS audits the tax returns of corporations and individuals. The collection division attempts to collect taxes from corporations or citizens who have failed to pay the taxes they owe. Finally, the criminal investigation division investigates cases of tax evasion and tax fraud. Criminal investigation agents can make arrests.

The IRS has long played a role in policing criminal activities such as gambling and selling drugs for one simple reason: those who engage in such activities almost never report any illegally gained income on their tax returns. Therefore, the IRS is able to apprehend them for tax evasion. The most famous example took place in the early 1930s, when the IRS finally arrested famed crime boss Al Capone—responsible for numerous violent crimes—for not paying his taxes.

Private Security The practice of private corporations or individuals offering services traditionally performed by police officers.

Private Security

Even with increasing numbers of local, state, and federal law enforcement officers, the police do not have the ability to prevent every crime. Recognizing this, many businesses and citizens have decided to hire private guards for their properties and homes. In fact, according to the Freedonia Group, an industry-research firm, demand for **private security** generates revenues of nearly $50 billion a year.[88] More than 10,000 firms employing around 1.1 million people provide private security services in this country, compared with about 880,000 public law enforcement agents.

LEARNING **9** OBJECTIVE
Analyze the importance of private security today.

A private security guard makes the rounds near the Food Court at Landmark Mall in Alexandria, Virginia. Why is being visible such an important aspect of many private security jobs?
Newhouse News Service/Landov

PRIVATIZING LAW ENFORCEMENT As there are no federal regulations regarding private security, each state has its own rules for this form of employment. In several states, including California and Florida, prospective security guards must have at least forty hours of training. Ideally, a security guard—lacking the extensive training of a law enforcement agent—should only observe and report criminal activity unless use of force is needed to prevent a felony.[89]

As a rule, private security is not designed to replace law enforcement. It is intended to deter crime rather than stop it.[90] A uniformed security guard patrolling a shopping mall parking lot or a bank lobby has one primary function—to convince a potential criminal to search out a shopping mall or bank that does not have private security. For the same reason, many citizens hire security personnel to drive marked cars through their neighborhoods, making them a less attractive target for burglaries, robberies, vandalism, and other crimes.

CONTINUED HEALTH OF THE INDUSTRY Indicators point to continued growth for the private security industry. The *Hallcrest Report II,* a far-reaching overview of private security trends funded by the National Institute of Justice, identifies four factors driving this growth:

1. An increase in fear on the part of the public triggered by media coverage of crime.
2. The problem of crime in the workplace. According to the University of Florida's National Retail Security Survey, American retailers lose about $34 billion a year because of shoplifting and employee theft.
3. Budget cuts in states and municipalities that have forced reductions in the number of public police, thereby raising the demand for private ones.
4. A rising awareness of private security products (such as home burglar alarms) and service as cost-effective protective measures.[91]

Another reason for the industry's continued health is terrorism. Private security is responsible for protecting more than three-fourths of the nation's likely terrorist targets such as power plants, financial centers, dams, malls, oil refineries, and transportation hubs.

SELF ASSESSMENT

Fill in the blanks and check your answers on page 163.

Municipal police departments and _____ departments are both considered "local" organizations and have many of the same responsibilities. On the state level, the authority of the _____ _____ is usually limited to enforcing traffic laws. Nationally, the _____ has jurisdiction over all federal crimes, while the _____ focuses on federal drug laws and the _____ regulates the sale and possession of guns. Private security is designed to _____ crime rather than prevent it.

CJ IN ACTION

AFFIRMATIVE ACTION IN LAW ENFORCEMENT

In 2008, racial tensions in Lima, Ohio, reached a boiling point when white police officers accidentally shot and killed an African American woman during a botched drug raid. At the time, the eighty-person police force of Lima, a town that is one-quarter black, had only two African American officers. Community leaders vowed to increase minority police hires. Five years later, however, nothing had changed. "We're struggling to get minorities to want to participate in the hiring process even," admitted Lima police chief Kevin Martin in 2013.[92] Should the Lima city government *force* diversity through an affirmative action program? In this *CJ in Action* feature, we will attempt to answer two questions concerning such programs. First, do they work? Second, and just as important, are they fair?

STRATEGIES FOR DIVERSITY

For potential female police officers, the physical fitness test often poses the greatest barrier to hiring. In California, for example, all applicants must scale a six-foot wall to be considered for a police job. Officials estimate that this requirement eliminates half of the women who apply.[93] Some police departments, however, adjust their physical fitness tests to level the playing field. The Champaign (Illinois) Police Department, for example, requires male applicants to run 1.5 miles in thirteen minutes and female applicants to complete the course in sixteen minutes.[94] Thus, affirmative action programs represent an "active effort" to support the employment of women and members of minority groups in law enforcement.[95]

THE CASE FOR AFFIRMATIVE ACTION IN LAW ENFORCEMENT

- For most of the nation's history, women and minorities suffered from widespread discrimination in policing. Affirmative action remedies these past wrongs.

- The existence of a diverse police force improves community-police relations and makes it easier for all officers to do their jobs because it assures the community that the police will not act in a discriminatory manner.

- Affirmative action works. In Pittsburgh, the percentage of female police officers rose from 1 percent to 27 percent after an affirmative action program went into effect, but it began to decline as soon as the program ended.[96] In

Chicago, the African American share of new police hires rose from 10 percent to 40 percent in just two years after the implementation of a consent decree.[97]

THE CASE AGAINST AFFIRMATIVE ACTION IN LAW ENFORCEMENT

- A stigma is attached to persons perceived to have benefited from affirmative action. "I don't want to be in a department where I was hired because of my skin color," said one African American applicant in Dayton, Ohio. "I want it because I earned it."[98]

- Public safety requires that all police officers be the most competent and skilled, regardless of their gender, race, or ethnicity.

- There are no "special skills" unique to women or minority law enforcement agents. Studies show that, for the most part, "cops act like cops."[99]

YOUR OPINION—WRITING ASSIGNMENT

The city of Springfield wants to test seventy-seven of its police officers for possible promotion to lieutenant. The exam—part written multiple choice and part oral—is specifically designed to avoid bias against minority candidates. Of the seventy-seven candidates, forty-three are white, nineteen are black, and fifteen are Hispanic. All of the top ten performers on the exam, immediately eligible for promotion, are white.

A city official argues that these results should be disregarded because black and Hispanic candidates have been unfairly excluded from the opportunity for promotion. What do you think of this argument? Would it be fair to the successful white candidates to invalidate the results? What would be in the best interests of the citizens of Springfield? Before responding, you can review our discussions in this chapter concerning:

- The reform era of policing (pages 137–139).

- Antidiscrimination law and affirmative action (page146).

- Gender, race, and ethnicity in law enforcement (pages 147–149).

Your answer should include at least three full paragraphs.

CHAPTER **SUMMARY**

For more information on these concepts, look back to the Learning Objective icons throughout the chapter.

 List the four basic responsibilities of the police. (a) To enforce laws, (b) to provide services, (c) to prevent crime, and (d) to preserve the peace.

 Tell how the patronage system affected policing. During the political era of policing (1840–1930), bribes paid by citizens and business owners often went into the coffers of the local political party. This became known as the patronage system.

 Explain how intelligence-led policing works and how it benefits modern police departments. Intelligence-led policing uses past crime patterns to predict when and where crime will occur in the future. In theory, intelligence-led policing allows police administrators to use fewer resources because it removes costly and time-consuming "guesswork" from the law enforcement equation.

 Describe the usefulness of Suspicious Activity Reports in countering domestic terrorism. A Suspicious Activity Report is filed with the federal government when a local or state law enforcement agent witnesses behavior that may be connected with domestic terrorist activities. Even though thousands of such reports have been provided to fusion centers across the United States, the program has yet to yield significant benefits for homeland security.

 Identify the differences between the police academy and field training as learning tools for recruits. The police academy is a controlled environment where police recruits learn the basics of policing from instructors in classrooms. In contrast, field training takes place in the "real world": the recruit goes on patrol with an experienced police officer.

 Describe the challenges facing women who choose law enforcement as a career. Many male officers believe that their female counterparts are not physically or mentally strong enough for police work, which puts pressure on women officers to continually prove themselves. Female officers must also deal with tokenism, or the stigma that they were hired only to fulfill diversity requirements, and sexual harassment in the form of unwanted advances or obscene remarks.

 Indicate some of the most important law enforcement agencies under the control of the Department of Homeland Security. (a) U.S. Customs and Border Protection, which polices the flow of goods and people across the United States' international borders and oversees the U.S. Border Patrol; (b) U.S. Immigration and Customs Enforcement, which investigates and enforces our nation's immigration and customs laws; and (c) the U.S. Secret Service, which protects high-ranking federal government officials and federal property.

 Identify the duties of the FBI. The FBI has jurisdiction to investigate hundreds of federal crimes, including white-collar crime, kidnapping, bank robbery, and civil rights violations. The FBI is also heavily involved in combating terrorism and drug-trafficking operations in the United States and around the world. Finally, the agency provides support to state and local law enforcement agencies through its crime laboratories and databases.

 Analyze the importance of private security today. In the United States, businesses and citizens spend billions of dollars each year on private security. Heightened fear of crime and increased crime in the workplace have fueled the growth in spending on private security.

QUESTIONS FOR **CRITICAL ANALYSIS**

1. Which of the four basic responsibilities of the police do you think is most important? Why?

2. Increased professionalism in police forces has been made possible by two-way radios, telephones, and automobiles. In what way has society not benefited from this increased professionalism? Explain your answer.

3. Review the discussion of double marginality in this chapter. Why would members of a minority community think that police officers of the same race or ethnicity were "traitors"? What can police departments do to dispel this misperception?

4. One of the major differences between a local police chief and a sheriff is that the sheriff is elected, while the police

chief is appointed. What are some of the possible problems with having a law enforcement official who, like any other politician, is responsible to voters? What are some of the possible benefits of this situation?

5. Critics of programs such as Secure Communities, described in this chapter, that link local police to immigration law contend that such programs make it less likely that undocumented immigrants will cooperate with law enforcement, either as witnesses or victims. Why might this be the case?

KEY **TERMS**

affirmative action   146

coroner   151

discrimination   146

double marginality   149

Drug Enforcement Administration (DEA)   156

Federal Bureau of Investigation (FBI)   156

field training   145

infrastructure   156

intelligence-led policing   140

night watch system   136

patronage system   137

private security   159

probationary period   144

professional model   138

recruitment   142

sexual harassment   147

sheriff   150

U.S. Customs and Border Protection (CBP)   153

U.S. Immigration and Customs Enforcement (ICE)   154

U.S. Secret Service   155

SELF ASSESSMENT **ANSWER KEY**

Page 136: i. enforce; **ii.** services; **iii.** prevent; **iv.** preserve

Page 142: i. political; **ii.** patronage; **iii.** reform; **iv.** professional; **v.** community; **vi.** intelligence; **vii.** terrorist

Page 145: i. twenty-one; **ii.** felony; **iii.** probationary; **iv.** police academy; **v.** field training

Page 150: i. discrimination; **ii.** affirmative action; **iii.** consent decree

Page 160: i. sheriffs'; **ii.** highway patrol; **iii.** FBI (Federal Bureau of Investigation); **iv.** DEA (Drug Enforcement Administration); **v.** ATF (Bureau of Alcohol, Tobacco, Firearms and Explosives); **vi.** deter

NOTES

1. Kirk Johnson, "Hey, @SeattlePD: What's the Latest?" *New York Times* (October 2, 2012), A16.

2. Egon Bittner, *The Functions of Police in a Modern Society,* Public Health Service Publication No. 2059 (Chevy Chase, MD: National Institute of Mental Health, 1970), 38–44.

3. Carl Klockars, "The Rhetoric of Community Policing," in *Community Policing: Rhetoric or Reality,* ed. Jack Greene and Stephen Mastrofski (New York: Praeger Publishers, 1991), 244.

4. Jack R. Greene and Carl B. Klockars, "What Do Police Do?" in *Thinking about Police,* 2d ed., ed. Carl B. Klockars and Stephen D. Mastrofski (New York: McGraw-Hill, 1991), 273–284.

5. John S. Dempsey and Linda S. Forst, *An Introduction to Policing,* 6th ed. (Clifton Park, NY: Delmar Cengage Learning, 2012), 380–381.

6. Federal Bureau of Investigation, *Crime in the United States, 2011* (Washington, D.C.: U.S. Department of Justice, 2011), at **www.fbi.gov /about-us/cjis/ucr/crime-in-the-u.s/2011/crime-in-the-u.s.-2011 /tables/table-29**.

7. Reprinted in *The Police Chief* (January 1990), 18.

8. Robert J. Kaminski, Clete DiGiovanni, and Raymond Downs, "The Use of Force between the Police and Persons with Impaired Judgment," *Police Quarterly* (September 2004), 311–338.

9. Jerome H. Skolnick, "Police: The New Professionals," *New Society* (September 5, 1986), 9–11.

10. Quoted in Nancy Ritter, ed., "LAPD Chief Bratton Speaks Out: What's Wrong with Criminal Justice Research—and How to Make It Right," *National Institute of Justice Journal* 257 (2007), 29.

11. Klockars, 250.

12. James Q. Wilson, *Varieties of Police Behavior: The Management of Law and Order in Eight Communities* (Cambridge, MA: Harvard University Press, 1968).

13. James Q. Wilson and George L. Kelling, "Broken Windows," *Atlantic Monthly* (March 1982), 29.

14. M. K. Nalla and G. R. Newman, "Is White-Collar Crime Policing, Policing?" *Policing and Society* 3 (1994), 304.

15. Mitchell P. Roth, *Crime and Punishment: A History of the Criminal Justice System,* 2d ed. (Belmont, CA: Wadsworth Cengage Learning, 2011), 65.

16. *Ibid.*

17. Peter K. Manning, *Police Work* (Cambridge, MA: MIT Press, 1977), 82.

18. Mark H. Moore and George L. Kelling, "'To Serve and Protect': Learning from Police History," *Public Interest* 70 (1983), 53.

19. Samuel Walker, *The Police in America: An Introduction* (New York: McGraw-Hill, 1983), 7.

20. Moore and Kelling, 54.

21. Mark H. Haller, "Chicago Cops, 1890–1925," in *Thinking about Police,* ed. Carl Klockars and Stephen Mastrofski (New York: McGraw-Hill, 1990), 90.

22. William J. Bopp and Donald O. Shultz, *A Short History of American Law Enforcement* (Springfield, IL: Charles C Thomas, 1977), 109–110.

23. Roger G. Dunham and Geoffrey P. Alpert, *Critical Issues in Policing: Contemporary Issues* (Prospect Heights, IL: Waveland Press, 1989).

24. Ken Peak and Emmanuel P. Barthe, "Community Policing and CompStat: Merged, or Mutually Exclusive?" *The Police Chief* (December 2009), 73.

25. *Ibid.,* 74.

26. Quoted in *ibid.*

27. Peter K. Manning, "The Police: Mandate, Strategies, and Appearances," in *Crime and Justice in American Society,* ed. Jack D. Douglas (Indianapolis, IN: Bobbs-Merrill, 1971), 149–163.

28. National Advisory Commission on Civil Disorder, *Report* (Washington, D.C.: U.S. Government Printing Office, 1968), 157–160.

29. 18 U.S.C.A. Sections 2510–2521.

30. Jayne Seagrave, "Defining Community Policing," *American Journal of Police* 1 (1996), 1–22.

31. Peak and Barthe, 78.

32. Jason Vaughn Lee, "Policing after 9/11: Community Policing in an Age of Homeland Security," *Police Quarterly* (November 2010), 351–353.

33. Quoted in Ronnie Garrett, "Predict and Serve," *Law Enforcement Technology* (January 2013), 19.

34. *Ibid.*

35. Charlie Beck and Colleen McCue, "Predictive Policing: What Can We Learn from Wal-Mart and Amazon about Fighting Crime in a Recession?" *The Police Chief* (November 2009), 19.

36. Quoted in "Spies among Us," *U.S. News & World Report* (May 8, 2006), 43.

37. *Ibid.,* 41–43.

38. Tom Hays, "Post-9/11, Biggest Terror Threat Is Underground," *Associated Press* (July 18, 2011).

39. Raymond W. Kelly, "Homeland Security Preparedness in New York City," prepared statement before the U.S. House of Representatives, 2005.

40. Dana Priest and William M. Arkin, "Monitoring America," *Washington Post* (December 20, 2010), A1; and Lois M. Davis et al., *Law Enforcement's Post-9/11 Focus on Counterterrorism and Homeland Security* (Santa Monica, CA: RAND Corporation, 2010), 8.

41. Sara Schreiber, "Social Media and the Mob," *Law Enforcement Technology* (September 2012), 38–39.

42. Quoted in Joel Rubin, "Stopping Crime before It Starts," *Los Angeles Times* (August 21, 2010), A17.

43. James H. Chenoweth, "Situational Tests: A New Attempt at Assessing Police Candidates," *Journal of Criminal Law, Criminology and Police Science* 52 (1961), 232.

44. Yossef S. Ben-Porath et al., "Assessing the Psychological Suitability of Candidates for Law Enforcement Positions," *The Police Chief* (August 2011), 64-70.

45. D. P. Hinkle, "College Degree: An Impractical Prerequisite for Police Work," *Law and Order* (July 1991), 105.

46. Bureau of Justice Statistics, *Local Police Departments, 2007* (Washington, D.C.: U.S. Department of Justice, December 2010), Table 5, page 11.

47. Kevin Johnson, "Police Agencies Find It Hard to Require Degrees," *USA Today* (September 18, 2006), 3A.

48. D. P. Hinkle, "College Degree: An Impractical Prerequisite for Police Work," *Law and Order* (July 1991), 105.

49. *Local Police Departments, 2007,* 12.

50. Bureau of Justice Statistics, *State and Local Law Enforcement Training Academies, 2006* (Washington, D.C.: U.S. Department of Justice, February 2009), 7.

51. National Advisory Commission on Civil Disorder, *Report* (Washington, D.C.: U.S. Government Printing Office, 1968), Chapter 11.

52. *Griggs v. Duke Power Co.,* 401 U.S. 424 (1971); and *Abermarle Paper Co. v. Moody,* 422 U.S. 405 (1975).

53. Gene L. Scaramella, Steven M. Cox, and William P. McCamey, *Introduction to Policing* (Thousand Oaks, CA: Sage Publications, 2011), 30–31.

54. Lucas Sullivan, "Black Applicants Protest Lowering Scores," *Dayton (OH) Daily News* (March 6, 2011), A13.

55. Brian Sharp, "Minority Recruiting Poses Test for Police," *Democrat and Chronicle (Rochester, NY)* (March 29, 2010), 1.

56. Lianne M. Tuomey and Rachel Jolly, "Step Up to Law Enforcement: A Successful Strategy for Recruiting Women into the Law Enforcement Profession," *The Police Chief* (June 2009), 70, 73.

57. *Local Police Departments, 2007,* 14.

58. National Center for Women and Policing, *Equality Denied: The Status of Women in Policing: 2001* (Washington, D.C.: U.S. Government Printing Office, 2002), 4.

59. Jacqueline Mroz, "Female Police Chiefs: A Novelty No More," *New York Times* (April 6, 2008), 3.

60. Scaramella, Cox, and McCamey, 318.

61. Quoted in Teresa Lynn Wertsch, "Walking the Thin Blue Line: Policewomen and Tokenism Today," *Women and Criminal Justice* (1998), 35–36.

62. Katherine Stuart van Wormer and Clemens Bartollas, *Women and the Criminal Justice System,* 3d ed. (Upper Saddle River, NJ: Pearson Education, 2011), 318–319.

63. Susan L. Webb, *The Global Impact of Sexual Harassment* (New York: Master Media Limited, 1994), 26.

64. The Cato Institute, "National Police Misconduct Statistics and Reporting Project: 2010 Quarterly Q3 Report," at **www.policemisconduct.net /statistics/2010-quarterly-q3-report**.

65. Joseph L. Gustafson, "Tokenism in Policing: An Empirical Test of Kanter's Hypothesis," *Journal of Criminal Justice* 36 (2008), 5–7.

66. *Local Police Departments, 2007,* 14.

67. David Alan Sklansky, "Not Your Father's Police Department: Making Sense of the New Demographics of Law Enforcement," *Journal of Criminal Law and Criminology* (Spring 2006), 1209–1243.

68. Peter C. Moskos, "Two Shades of Blue: Black and White in the Blue Brotherhood," *Law Enforcement Executive Forum* (2008), 57.

69. Scaramella, Cox, and McCamey, 324.

70. Dempsey and Forst, 183.

71. *Wygant v. Jackson Board of Education,* 476 U.S. 314 (1986).

72. Bureau of Justice Statistics, *Census of State and Local Law Enforcement Agencies, 2008* (Washington, D.C.: U.S. Department of Justice, July 2011), 1; and Bureau of Justice Statistics, *Federal Law Enforcement Officers, 2008* (Washington, D.C.: U.S. Department of Justice, June 2012), 1.

73. *Census of State and Local Law Enforcement Agencies, 2008,* 3.

74. *Local Police Departments, 2007,* Table 3, page 9.

75. *Census of State and Local Law Enforcement Agencies, 2008,* 4.

76. *Ibid.,* Table 4, page 5.

77. Bureau of Justice Statistics, *Sheriffs' Offices, 2003* (Washington, D.C.: U.S. Department of Justice, May 2006), 15–18.

78. Bureau of Justice Statistics, *Sheriffs' Departments, 1997* (Washington, D.C.: U.S. Department of Justice, February 2000), 14.

79. Doris Meissner et al., *Immigration Enforcement in the United States: The Rise of a Formidable Machinery* (Washington, D.C.: Migration Policy Institute, January 2013), 2.

80. Marc Lacey, "At the Border, on the Night Watch," *New York Times* (October 13, 2011), A17.

81. "CBP's 2011 Fiscal Year in Review," at **www.cbp.gov/xp/cgov/newsroom /news_releases/national/2011_news_archive/12122011.xml**.

82. U.S. Immigration and Customs Enforcement, "FY 2012: ICE Announces Year-End Removal Numbers" (December 21, 2012), at **www.ice.gov /news/releases/1212/121221washingtondc2.htm**.

83. Martin J. Mayer, "Secure Communities Program: Mandatory or Optional?" *The Police Chief* (February 2013), 10.

84. Fernanda Santos, "After Immigration Arrests, Online Outcry, and Release," *New York Times* (January 12, 2013), A9.

85. Charlie Savage, "F.B.I. Focusing on Security Over Ordinary Crime," *New York Times* (August 24, 2011), A15.

86. Charlie Bush, "Enhancing Criminal Justice and Homeland Security Capabilities: N-DEx Fulfilling Its Vision to Support Law Enforcement," *The Police Chief* (February 2013), 34–37.

87. United States Marshals Service, "Fact Sheet," at **www.justice.gov /marshals/duties/factsheets/general-1209.html**.

88. *Private Security Services to 2014* (Cleveland, OH: Freedonia Group, November 2010), 15.

89. John B. Owens, "Westec Story: Gated Communities and the Fourth Amendment," *American Criminal Law Review* (Spring 1997), 1138.

90. National Retail Federation, "Retail Fraud, Shoplifting Rates Decrease, According to National Retail Security Survey," at **www.nrf.com /modules.php?name=News&op=viewlive&sp_id=945**.

91. William C. Cunningham, John J. Strauchs, and Clifford W. Van Meter, *The Hallcrest Report II: Private Security Trends, 1970 to 2000* (Boston: Butterworth-Heinemann, 1990), 236.

92. Quoted in Bob Blake, "Lima Struggling with Minority Hiring," *The Lima News (Ohio)* (January 21, 2013), 1A.

93. Liz Tascio, "Women Recruits Meet High Standard," *Contra Coast Times* (March 16, 2003), 4.

94. "DOJ Decides Suit Is a Bad Fit," *Law Enforcement News* (October 31, 2001), 1.

95. Dempsey and Forst, 188.

96. Kim Lonsway *et al.,* "Under Scrutiny: The Effect of Consent Decrees on the Representation of Women in Sworn Law Enforcement," National Center for Women and Policing (2003), at **www.womenandpolicing. org/pdf/Fullconsentdecreestudy.pdf**.

97. Justin McCrary, "The Effect of Court-Ordered Hiring Quotas on the Composition and Quality of Police," National Bureau of Economic Research (2006), at **www.nber.org/papers/w12368**.

98. Quoted in Sullivan.

99. Sklansky, 1224–1228.

6 Problems and Solutions in Modern Policing

To target your study and review, look for these numbered Learning Objective icons throughout the chapter.

AP Photo/Jae C. Hong

JUSTIFIED?

ONE MORNING in January 2012, thirteen-year-old Jaime Gonzalez walked into a first-period class at Cummings Middle School in Brownsville, Texas, and, for no apparent reason, punched another student in the face. As school administrators tried to calm an agitated Gonzalez in the hallway, their puzzlement turned to alarm—the eighth grader had a gun tucked into his pants. Within minutes, the school was in lockdown and two local police officers had arrived on the scene. They shouted at Gonzalez to "Put the gun down! Put it on the floor!" Disregarding these orders, Gonzalez raised his weapon. The officers fired three times and hit the teenager twice, once in the chest and once in the abdomen. "Subject shot," one of the officers said as he called for emergency medical aid.

After Gonzalez died from his wounds in a local hospital, an already-shaken community learned one more piece of disturbing news. Although the weapon Gonzalez had been brandishing looked like a black Glock semiautomatic pistol, it was actually a relatively harmless .177-caliber BB gun, available on the Internet for $60. As might be expected, this development opened the Brownsville police to a great deal of criticism. "Why was so much excess force used on a minor?" asked Gonzalez's father, Jaime Sr. "What happened was an injustice," insisted Noralva, the boy's mother.

Brownsville interim police chief Orlando Rodriguez defended his officers' decision making. He stressed that, as far as the two men knew, they were dealing with an armed suspect who posed a serious threat to more than seven hundred students and about seventy-five staff members. "When I looked at that gun, there is no doubt [that] from a distance it's absolutely real," agreed school official Carl A. Montoya. "I think the officers responded, obviously, from their training. From that perspective, it was a real gun."

1. Do you think the two Brownsville police officers acted reasonably under the circumstances? Why or why not?
2. It is not uncommon for law enforcement agents to shoot children or adults armed with BB guns or other types of air pistols that appear to be deadly weapons. Should society expect police officers to wait to determine the full extent of the threat posed by an apparent shooter before using deadly force as a protective measure? Explain your answer.
3. After thirty-year police veteran Michael A. Black retired, he said, "Although my gun left its holster on [many] occasions, I am grateful that I never had to shoot anyone." Does this statement surprise you? What might be some of the psychological consequences for a law enforcement agent who fatally shoots a suspect, even if the shooting is justified?

AP Photo/*Brownsville Herald*, Yvette Vela

Noralva and Jaime Gonzalez embrace at the funeral of their son, who was fatally shot by Brownsville, Texas, police after brandishing what appeared to be a handgun at his school.

Gray wall studio/Shutterstock.com

THE ROLE OF DISCRETION IN POLICING

One of the ironies of law enforcement is that patrol officers—often the lowest-paid members of an agency with the least amount of authority—have the greatest amount of discretionary power. Part of the explanation for this is practical. Patrol officers spend most of the day on the streets, beyond the control of their supervisors. Usually, only two people are present when a patrol officer must make a decision: the officer and the possible wrongdoer. In most cases, the law enforcement officer has a great deal of freedom to take the action that he or she feels the situation requires.

Without this freedom, many police officers might find their duties unrewarding. Indeed, numerous studies have shown that higher levels of officer autonomy are reflected in higher levels of officer job satisfaction.[1] At the same time, discretion can lead to second guessing on the part of the public, an officer's superiors, and the officer him- or herself. Certainly, the Brownsville police officers just discussed would have preferred not to have shot and killed Jaime Gonzalez, whether the boy was wielding a real gun or not. Their decisions were made in a split second, under stressful circumstances, and without the benefit of the evidence that came to light following the shooting.

Justification for Police Discretion

Despite the possibility of mistakes, courts generally have upheld the patrol officer's freedom to decide "what law to enforce, how much to enforce it, against whom, and on what occasions."[2] This judicial support of police discretion is based on the following factors:

- Police officers are considered trustworthy and are therefore assumed to make honest decisions, regardless of contradictory testimony by a suspect.
- Experience and training give officers the ability to determine whether certain activity poses a threat to society, and to take any reasonable action necessary to investigate or prevent such activity.
- Due to the nature of their jobs, police officers are extremely knowledgeable in human, and by extension criminal, behavior.
- Police officers may find themselves in danger of personal, physical harm and must be allowed to take reasonable and necessary steps to protect themselves.[3]

LEARNING OBJECTIVE 1 — Explain why police officers are allowed discretionary powers.

Dr. Anthony J. Pinizzotto, a psychologist with the Federal Bureau of Investigation (FBI), and Charles E. Miller, an instructor in the bureau's Criminal Justice Information Services Division, take the justification for discretion one step further. These two experts argue that many police officers have a "sixth sense" that helps them handle on-the-job challenges. Pinizzotto and Miller believe that although "intuitive policing" is often difficult to explain to those outside law enforcement, it is a crucial part of policing and should not be discouraged by civilian administrators.[4]

Factors of Police Discretion

There is no doubt that subjective factors influence police discretion. The officer's beliefs, values, personality, and background all enter into his or her decisions. To a large extent, however, a law enforcement agent's actions are determined by the rules of policing set down in the U.S. Constitution and enforced by the courts. These rules are of paramount importance and will be discussed in great detail in Chapter 7.

■ Regarding high-speed auto pursuits, one police administrator says, "Every chase is like a no-win situation for us. We can be criticized if we do chase but also if we don't." Explain why the administrator might feel this way. SVLumagraphica/Shutterstock

ELEMENTS OF DISCRETION Assuming that most police officers stay on the right side of the Constitution in most instances, four other factors generally enter the discretion equation in any particular situation. First, and most important, is the nature of the criminal act. The less serious a crime, the more likely a police officer is to ignore it. A person driving 60 miles per hour in a 55-miles-per-hour zone, for example, is much less likely to be ticketed than someone doing 80 miles per hour. A second element often considered is the attitude of the wrongdoer toward the officer. A motorist who is belligerent toward a highway patrol officer is much more likely to be ticketed than one who is contrite and apologetic. Third, the relationship between the victim and the offender can influence the outcome. If the parties are in a familial or other close relationship, police officers may see the incident as a personal matter and be hesitant to make an arrest.

LIMITING POLICE DISCRETION The fourth factor of the discretion equation is departmental policy.[5] A **policy** is a set of guiding principles that law enforcement agents must adhere to in stated situations. If a police administrator decides that all motorists who exceed the speed limit by 10 miles per hour will be ticketed, that policy will certainly influence the patrol officer's decisions. Policies must be flexible enough to allow for officer discretion, but at the same time be specific enough to provide the officer with a clear sense of her or his duties and obligations.

Discretion and High-Speed Pursuits At about 12:30 A.M. on December 14, 2012, a Cayce (South Carolina) police officer spotted a blue Hyundai heading down the street with its headlights off. When the officer signaled for the Hyundai to pull over, its driver sped away, leading to a two-minute chase at ninety miles per hour. Although such police action is often necessary, in this case it ended in tragedy when the Hyundai struck a mini-van. The accident killed not only the driver of the Hyundai, who was legally drunk, but also Chamberlain Branch, a forty-eight-year-old father of three who was in the minivan.

In fact, about 35 percent of all such police pursuits end in car crashes, causing around 350 fatalities each year. One-third of the victims are third parties—drivers or passengers in other cars or pedestrian bystanders.[6] Following the chase that led to Branch's death, many wondered whether the police officer was justified in taking such risks in response to a minor traffic violation. The Cayce Police Department's own guidelines for high-speed chases require that officers weigh "the seriousness of the original offense" against the "dangers created by the pursuit."[7]

To limit the discretion that can result in these kinds of tragedies, 94 percent of the nation's local police departments have implemented police pursuit policies, with 61 percent restricting the discretion of officers to engage in a high-speed chase.[8] The success of such policies can be seen in the results from Los Angeles, which features more high-speed chases than any other city in the country by a wide margin. In 2003, Los Angeles

Policy A set of guiding principles designed to influence the behavior and decision making of police officers.

police officers were ordered to conduct dangerous pursuits only if the fleeing driver was suspected of a serious crime. Within a year, the number of high-speed pursuits decreased by 62 percent, and injuries to third parties dropped by 58 percent.[9] (To learn how one police officer's split-second decision on the road led to a ruling by the U.S. Supreme Court, see the feature *You Be the Police Officer—High-Speed Discretion* below.)

Discretion and Domestic Violence In Chapter 3, we saw that many prosecutors are reluctant to charge domestic abusers with a crime. Similarly, police officers often hesitate to make an arrest in a domestic violence situation, even when the officer has strong evidence of an assault.[10] In light of this apparent reluctance, in the 1970s jurisdictions began passing legislation that severely limits police discretion in domestic violence cases. Today, twenty-one states have **mandatory arrest laws** that require a police officer to arrest a person who has abused someone related by blood or marriage.[11] The theory behind mandatory arrest policies is relatively straightforward: they act as a deterrent to criminal behavior. Costs are imposed on the person who is arrested. He or she must go to court and face the possibility of time in jail. Statistically, these laws appear to have met their goals. Researchers have found significantly higher arrest rates for domestic violence offenders in states with mandatory arrest laws than in states without them.[12]

Even so, mandatory arrest laws do not always trump police discretion. In a 2005 case, the United States Supreme Court refused to allow a civil lawsuit against Castle Rock

HIGH-SPEED DISCRETION

YOU BE THE
Police
Officer

THE SITUATION You are a police officer who, late at night, clocks a car traveling 73 miles per hour on a road with a 55-mile-per-hour speed limit. You follow the car, activating your blue flashing lights to indicate that the driver, a young man named Victor, should pull over. Instead, Victor speeds up to 85 miles per hour and proceeds to lead you on a chase that seems right out of a Hollywood movie. Going down a narrow, two-lane street, Victor swerves through traffic, forcing numerous other cars off the road, and runs several red lights. You mimic these dangerous maneuvers, and, about six minutes after the chase began, you find yourself directly behind Victor's bumper, both of you speeding at 90 miles per hour. For a short period, there are no other cars nearby.

THE LAW Your department has no specific policy regarding high-speed pursuits. According to case law, law enforcement agents must act "reasonably" in such situations, weighing the risks to themselves, the suspects, and any innocent bystanders before taking any action.

YOUR DECISION Use your discretion to consider your various options. You can abandon the chase as too dangerous and allow Victor to escape. You can continue the pursuit. Or, you can attempt to force Victor off the road, thereby exposing both of you to possible injury or even death. What will you do?

[To see how a police officer in rural Georgia reacted in a similar situation, go to Example 6.1 in Appendix B.]

Bureaucracy A hierarchically structured administrative organization that carries out specific functions.

(Colorado) police officers who failed to enforce a court order mandating that Jessica Gonzales's estranged husband keep at least one hundred yards away from her house at all times. (He eventually kidnapped and killed their three daughters.) In the decision, Justice Antonin Scalia pointed out that there is a "well established tradition of police discretion [that] has long coexisted with apparently mandatory arrest statutes."[13]

SELF ASSESSMENT

Fill in the blanks and check your answers on page 205.

In general, a law enforcement officer has a great deal of _____ when it comes to his or her duties. When a police administration wants to curtail this freedom of action, it can institute a departmental _____ to guide the officer's decision making in certain situations, such as high-speed chases. With regard to domestic violence, many states have passed _____ _____ legislation to further restrict police discretion in this area.

POLICE ORGANIZATION AND FIELD OPERATIONS

Brownsville police administrators placed the two officers involved in Jaime Gonzalez's death, discussed at the beginning of this chapter, on *administrative leave* pending an investigation into the incident. In other words, the officers were temporarily relieved of their duties, with pay. This step does not imply that they were suspected of any wrongdoing. Most law enforcement agencies react similarly when a firearm is fired in the line of duty, both to allow for a full investigation of the event and to give the officer a chance to recover from what can be a traumatic experience.

Administrative leave is a *bureaucratic* response to an officer-involved shooting. In a **bureaucracy,** formal rules govern an individual's actions and relationships with co-employees. The ultimate goal of any bureaucracy is to reach its maximum efficiency—in the case of a police department, to provide the best service for the community within the confines of its limited resources such as staff and budget. Although some police departments are experimenting with alternative structures based on a partnership between management and the officers in the field, most continue to rely on the hierarchical structure described below.

■ A lieutenant (in the white shirt) gives instructions to two sergeants. On his left, a patrol officer appears to be awaiting instructions. How do the delegation of authority and the chain of command contribute to police efficiency?
Elyse Rieder/Photo Researchers

The Structure of the Police Department

Each police department is organized according to its environment: the size of its jurisdiction, the type of crimes it must deal with, and the demographics of the population it must police. A police department in a racially diverse city often faces different challenges than a department in a homogeneous one. Geographic location also influences police organization. The makeup of the police department in Miami, Florida, for example, is partially determined by the fact that the city is a gateway for illegal drugs smuggled from Central and South America. Consequently, the department directs a high percentage of its resources to special drug-fighting units. It has also formed cooperative partnerships with federal agencies such as the FBI and U.S. Customs and Border Protection in an effort to stop the flow of narcotics and weapons into the South Florida area.

CHAIN OF COMMAND Whatever the size or location of a police department, it needs a clear rank structure and strict accountability to function properly.[14] One of the goals of the police reformers, especially beginning in the 1950s, was to lessen the corrupting influence of politicians. The result was a move toward a militaristic organization of police.[15] As you can see in Figure 6.1 on the right, a typical police department is based on a "top-down" chain of command that leads from the police chief down to detectives and patrol officers. In this formalized structure, all persons are aware of their place in the chain and of their duties and responsibilities within the organization.

Delegation of authority is a critical component of the chain of command, especially in larger departments. The chief of police delegates authority to division chiefs, who delegate authority to commanders, and on down through the organization. This structure creates a situation in which nearly every member of a police department is directly accountable to a superior. As was the original goal of police reformers, these links encourage discipline and control and lessen the possibility that any individual police employee will have the unsupervised freedom to abuse her or his position.[16] Furthermore, experts suggest that no single supervisor should be responsible for too many employees. The ideal number of subordinates for a police sergeant, for example, is eight to ten patrol officers. This number is often referred to as the *span of control.* If the span of control rises above fifteen, then it is assumed that the superior officer will not be able to effectively manage his or her team.[17]

ORGANIZING BY AREA AND TIME In most metropolitan areas, police responsibilities are divided according to zones known as *beats* and *precincts*. A beat is the smallest stretch that a police officer or a group of police officers regularly patrol. A precinct—also known as a *district* or a *station*—is a collection of beats. A precinct commander, or captain, is held responsible by his or her superiors at police headquarters for the performance of the officers in that particular precinct.[18]

Police administrators must also organize their personnel by time. Most departments separate each twenty-four-hour day into three eight-hour *shifts*, also called *tours* or *platoons*. The night shift generally lasts from midnight to 8 A.M., the day shift from 8 A.M. to 4 P.M., and the evening shift from 4 P.M. to midnight. Officers either vary their hours by, say, working days one month and nights the next, or they have fixed tours in which they consistently take day, night, or evening shifts.[19] A number of police departments have implemented compressed workweeks, in which officers work longer shifts (ten or twelve hours) and fewer days. Such schedules are believed to improve the officers' quality of life by providing more substantial blocks of time off the job to recover from the stresses of police work.[20]

LAW ENFORCEMENT IN THE FIELD To a large extent, the main goal of any police department is the most efficient organization of its *field services.* Also known as "operations" or "line services," field services include patrol activities, investigations, and special operations. According to Henry M. Wrobleski and Karen M. Hess, most police departments are "generalists." Thus, police officers are assigned to general areas and perform all field service functions within the boundaries of their beats. Larger departments may be more specialized, with personnel assigned to specific types of crime, such as illegal drugs or white-collar crime, rather than geographic locations. Smaller departments, which make up the bulk of local law enforcement agencies, rely almost exclusively on general patrol.[21]

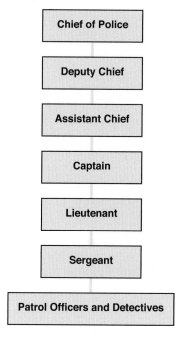

FIGURE 6.1 A Typical Police Department Chain of Command

Most American police departments follow this model of the chain of command, though smaller departments with fewer employees often eliminate several of these categories.

Chief of Police

Deputy Chief

Assistant Chief

Captain

Lieutenant

Sergeant

Patrol Officers and Detectives

Delegation of Authority The principles of command on which most police departments are based, in which personnel take orders from and are responsible to those in positions of power directly above them.

Police on Patrol:
The Backbone of the Department

Every police department has a patrol unit, and patrol is usually the largest division in the department. More than two-thirds of the sworn officers, or those officers authorized to make arrests and use force, in local police departments in the United States have patrol duties.[22]

"Life on the street" is not easy. Patrol officers must be able to handle any number of difficult situations, and experience is often the best and, despite training programs, the only teacher. As one patrol officer commented:

> You never stop learning. You never get your street degree. The person who says . . . they've learned it all is the person that's going to wind up dead or in a very compromising position. They've closed their minds.[23]

It may take a patrol officer years to learn when a gang is "false flagging" (trying to trick rival gang members into the open) or what to look for in a suspect's eyes to sense if he or she is concealing a weapon. This learning process is the backdrop to a number of different general functions that a patrol officer must perform on a daily basis.

THE PURPOSE OF PATROL In general, patrol officers do not spend most of their shifts chasing, catching, and handcuffing suspected criminals. The vast majority of patrol shifts are completed without a single arrest.[24] Officers spend a great deal of time meeting with other officers, completing paperwork, and patrolling with the goal of preventing crime in general rather than focusing on any specific crime or criminal activity.

LEARNING
List the three primary purposes of police patrol. **2** OBJECTIVE

As police accountability expert Samuel Walker has noted, the basic purposes of the police patrol have changed very little since 1829, when Sir Robert Peel founded the modern police department. These purposes include:

1. The deterrence of crime by maintaining a visible police presence.
2. The maintenance of public order and a sense of security in the community.
3. The twenty-four-hour provision of services that are not crime related.[25]

Given that most patrol shifts end without an officer making a single arrest, what activities take up most of a patrol officer's time?
Rod Lamkey Jr/AFP/Getty Images

The first two goals—deterring crime and keeping order—are generally accepted as legitimate police functions. The third, however, has been more controversial.

COMMUNITY CONCERNS As noted in Chapter 5, the community era saw a resurgence of the patrol officer as a provider of community services, many of which have little to do with crime. The extent to which noncrime incidents dominate patrol officers' time is evident in the Police Services Study, a survey of 26,000 calls to police in sixty different neighborhoods. The study found that only one out of every five calls involved the report of criminal activity.[26] (See Figure 6.2 on the facing page for the results of another survey of crime calls.)

There is some debate over whether community services should be allowed to dominate patrol officers' duties. The question, however, remains: If the

FIGURE 6.2 Calls for Service

Over a period of two years, the Project on Policing Neighborhoods gathered information on calls for service in Indianapolis, Indiana, and St. Petersburg, Florida. As you can see, the largest portion of these calls involved disputes where no violence or threat of violence existed. Be aware also that nearly two-thirds of the nonviolent dispute calls and nearly half of the assault calls answered by police dealt with domestic confrontations.

Description of Violation	Percentage of Total Calls
NONSERIOUS CRIME CALLS	
Nonviolent disputes	42
Public disorder (examples: drunk, disorderly, begging, prostitution)	22
Assistance (examples: missing persons, traffic accident, damaged property)	10
Minor violations (examples: shoplifting, trespassing, traffic/parking offense, refusal to pay)	4
SERIOUS CRIME CALLS	
Assaults (examples: using violence against a person, kidnapping, child abuse)	26
Serious theft (examples: motor vehicle theft, burglary, purse snatching)	5
General disorder (examples: illicit drugs, fleeing police, leaving the scene of an accident)	2

Source adapted from: Stephen D. Mastrofski, Jeffrey B. Snipes, Roger B. Parks, and Christopher D. Maxwell, "The Helping Hand of the Law: Police Control of Citizens on Request," *Criminology* 38 (May 2000), Table 5, page 328.

Eldad Carin/iStockphoto

police do not handle these problems, who will? Few cities have the financial resources to hire public servants to deal specifically with, for example, finding shelter for homeless persons. Furthermore, the police are the only public servants on call twenty-four hours a day, seven days a week, making them uniquely accessible to citizen needs.

PATROL ACTIVITIES To recap, the purposes of police patrols are to prevent and deter crime and also to provide social services. How can the police best accomplish these goals? Of course, each department has its own methods and strategies, but William Gay, Theodore Schell, and Stephen Schack are able to divide routine patrol activity into four general categories:

1. *Preventive patrol.* By maintaining a presence in a community, either in a car or on foot, patrol officers attempt to prevent crime from occurring. This strategy, which O. W. Wilson called "omnipresence," was a cornerstone of early policing philosophy and still takes up roughly 40 percent of patrol time.
2. *Calls for service.* Patrol officers spend nearly a quarter of their time responding to 911 calls for emergency service or other citizen problems and complaints.
3. *Administrative duties.* Paperwork takes up nearly 20 percent of patrol time.
4. *Officer-initiated activities.* Incidents in which the patrol officer initiates contact with citizens, such as stopping motorists and pedestrians and questioning them, account for 15 percent of patrol time.[27]

The category estimates made by Gay, Schell, and Schack are not universally accepted. Professor of law enforcement Gary W. Cordner argues that administrative duties account for the largest percentage of patrol officers' time. According to Cordner, when officers are not consumed with paperwork and meetings, they are either answering calls for service (which takes up 67 percent of the officers' time on the street) or initiating activities themselves (the remaining 33 percent).[28]

Detective The primary police investigator of crimes.

"NOISE, BOOZE, AND VIOLENCE" Indeed, there are dozens of academic studies that purport to answer the question of how patrol officers spend their days and nights. Perhaps it is only fair, then, to give a police officer the chance to describe the duties patrol officers perform. In the words of Anthony Bouza, a former police chief:

> [Patrol officers] hurry from call to call, bound to their crackling radios, which offer no relief—especially on summer weekend nights.... The cops jump from crisis to crisis, rarely having time to do more than tamp one down sufficiently and leave for the next. Gaps of boredom and inactivity fill the interims, although there aren't many of these in the hot months. Periods of boredom get increasingly longer as the nights wear on and the weather gets colder.[29]

Bouza paints a picture of a routine beat as filled with "noise, booze, violence, drugs, illness, blaring TVs, and human misery." This may describe the situation in high-crime neighborhoods, but it certainly does not represent the reality for the majority of patrol officers in the United States. Duties that all patrol officers have in common, whether they work in Bouza's rather nightmarish city streets or in the quieter environment of rural America, include controlling traffic, conducting preliminary investigations, making arrests, and patrolling public events.

Detective Investigations

Investigation is the second main function of police, along with patrol. Whereas patrol is primarily preventive, investigation is reactive. After a crime has been committed and the patrol officer has gathered the preliminary information from the crime scene, the responsibility of finding "who dunnit" is delegated to the investigator, generally known as the **detective.** The most common way for someone to become a detective is to be promoted from patrol officer. Detectives have not been the focus of nearly as much reform attention as their patrol counterparts, mainly because the scope of the detective's job is limited to law enforcement, with less emphasis given to social services or order maintenance.

The detective's job is not quite as glamorous as it is sometimes portrayed by the media. Detectives spend much of their time investigating common crimes such as burglaries and are more likely to be tracking down stolen property than a murderer. They must also prepare cases for trial, which involves a great deal of time-consuming paperwork. Furthermore, a landmark RAND Corporation study estimated that more than 97 percent of cases that are "solved" can be attributed to a patrol officer making an arrest at the scene, witnesses or victims identifying the perpetrator, or detectives undertaking routine investigative procedures that could easily be performed by clerical personnel.[30] For example, even though a task force of up to thirty-five Los Angeles detectives worked around the clock for a week on the January 2012 murder of seventeen-year-old Francisco Rodriguez, it was an informant's tip that finally directed police to two suspects in the killing. "There is no Sherlock Holmes," said one investigator. "The good detective on the street is the one who knows all the weasels and one of the weasels will tell him who did it."[31]

Aggressive Investigation Strategies

LEARNING OBJECTIVE 3 Indicate some investigation strategies that are considered aggressive.

Detective bureaus also have the option of implementing aggressive strategies. For example, if detectives suspect that a person was involved in the robbery of a Mercedes-Benz parts warehouse, one of them might pose as a "fence"—or purchaser of stolen goods. In what is known as a "sting" operation, the suspect is deceived into thinking that the detective (fence) wants to buy stolen car parts. After the transaction takes place, the suspect can be arrested.

UNDERCOVER OPERATIONS Perhaps the most dangerous and controversial operation a law enforcement agent can undertake is to go *undercover,* or to assume a false identity in order to obtain information concerning illegal activities. Though each department has its own guidelines on when undercover operations are necessary, all that is generally required is the suspicion that illegal activity is taking place. Today, undercover officers are commonly used to infiltrate large-scale narcotics operations or those run by organized crime.

■ New York City Detective Debra Lawson has worked undercover as part of an elite unit devoted to seizing illegal firearms. Recently, a New York state legislator proposed a bill that would limit the amount of time that a law enforcement officer would be allowed to go undercover. What might be the reasoning behind this legislation?
Beatrice de Gea/*The New York Times*

In some situations, a detective bureau may not want to take the risk of exposing an officer to undercover work or may believe that an outsider cannot infiltrate an organized crime network. When the police need access and information, they have the option of turning to a **confidential informant (CI).** A CI is a person who is involved in criminal activity and gives information about that activity and those who engage in it to the police. As many as 80 percent of all illegal drug cases in the United States involve confidential informants. "They can get us into places we can't go," says one police administrator. "Without them, narcotics cases would practically cease to function."[32]

PREVENTIVE POLICING AND DOMESTIC TERRORISM Aggressive investigative strategies also play a crucial role in the federal government's efforts to combat domestic terrorism. Because would-be terrorists often need help to procure the weaponry necessary for their schemes, they are natural targets for well-placed informants and undercover agents. According to the Center on Law and Security at New York University, about two-thirds of the federal government's major terrorism prosecutions have relied on evidence provided by informants.[33]

Preventive Strikes On February 17, 2012, a Moroccan immigrant named Amine El Khalifi was arrested near the U.S. Capitol Building in Washington, D.C. El Khalifi, who had bragged that he "would be happy killing thirty people," was carrying an automatic weapon and wearing a suicide vest packed with what he thought were explosives.[34]

In Chapter 4, we saw that criminal law generally requires intent and action. A person must have both intended to commit a crime and taken some steps toward doing so. In most cases, criminal law also requires that a harm has been done and that the criminal act caused that harm. According to federal officials, however, El Khalifi never managed to contact an established terrorist group. His gun was inoperable, and his explosives were inert. Both had been provided by an FBI undercover agent acting as an al Qaeda operative. Indeed, El Khalifi had been under FBI surveillance for more than a year.

Confidential Informant (CI)
A human source for police who provides information concerning illegal activity in which he or she is involved.

The case of Amine El Khalifi provides a clear example of *preventive policing*. With preventive policing, the goal is not to solve the crime after it has occurred, but rather to prevent it from happening in the first place. Even though El Khalifi posed no immediate threat to the public, federal authorities were not willing to take the risk that he might eventually develop into a dangerous terrorist. Although some observers claim that law enforcement officials are exaggerating the threat posed by many of these accused plotters, the government points to a record of successes to justify this new approach. From the beginning of 2009 to 2012, preventive policing tactics aided in the arrests of nearly forty domestic terrorism suspects similar to El Khalifi.[35] (See Figure 6.3 below for more examples of preventive policing.)

Entrapment Issues The aggressive tactics employed by federal agents in preventing terrorist attacks have drawn criticism from some quarters. In February 2013, for example, American citizen Mohamed Osman Mohamud was convicted of attempting to use a weapon of mass destruction. Several years earlier, Mohamud had pushed a cell phone button in the belief that he was detonating a car bomb that would kill thousands of people in downtown Portland, Oregon. In reality, the bomb was a fake, built by FBI technicians. FBI undercover agents also provided Mohamud with $3,000 to purchase the fake bomb components, took him to a remote location to test the bomb, and helped him load the vehicle with six 55-gallon drums of explosives and diesel fuel.

During Mohamud's trial, his defense attorney Stephen R. Sady asked, "Did the government create the crime? Did the FBI foil its own plot?"[36] As you learned in Chapter 4, entrapment is a possible defense for criminal behavior when a government agent plants the idea of committing a crime in a defendant's mind. Although the entrapment defense has often been raised in domestic terrorism cases such as Mohamud's involving informants or undercover agents, it has yet to succeed. The law requires that the suspect

FIGURE 6.3 Preventive Policing: The Age of the Foiled Plot

When it comes to potential domestic terrorists, the federal government has decided to "Prevent first, prosecute second." This blueprint has led to dozens of "quick strikes" against domestic terrorism suspects, including the three examples listed here.

Facebook Farce December 2010	Family Affair March 2011	Bridge Party May 2012
The Plot: Antonio Martinez, a recent American convert to Islam, tried to blow up a U.S. military recruitment center in Catonsville, Maryland. On his Facebook page, Martinez wrote that all he "thinks about is *jihad*."	**The Plot:** Lonnie and Karen Vernon, members of an Alaskan militia group, planned to kill federal judge Ralph Beistline and several of the judge's family members. The deaths were to be retaliation for an unfavorable tax ruling that cost the couple their home.	**The Plot:** Five disgruntled members of the Occupy Cleveland movement decided to destroy a bridge in Cuyahoga Valley National Park. Their goal was to strike a violent blow against corporate America.
How Far It Got: Martinez loaded an SUV with barrels of explosives and parked the vehicle next to the recruitment center. He then dialed a cell phone number that he believed would detonate the bombs, but they were actually fakes provided by an FBI undercover agent.	**How Far It Got:** The Vernons purchased a silencer-equipped pistol and grenades, telling the seller about their criminal intentions. As it turned out, the seller was a confidential informant, and the Vernons were arrested on the spot.	**How Far It Got:** The five self-described "anarchists" spent months discussing potential targets and purchased several devices that they believed to be filled with the powerful explosive C-4. In reality, the fake C-4 was provided by an FBI informant who also recorded a number of the group's "secret" conversations.
The Result: Martinez pleaded guilty to attempted use of a weapon of mass destruction, and in April 2012, a federal judge sentenced him to twenty-five years in prison.	**The Result:** The Vernons pleaded guilty to charges of conspiring to kill a federal judge. In January 2013, Lonnie was sentenced to twenty-six years in prison and Karen to twelve years in prison.	**The Result:** In late 2012, four of the plotters were convicted of various attempted terrorist acts and received sentences ranging from 6½ to 11½ years in prison. Sentencing for the fifth participant was delayed pending a psychiatric evaluation.

show no predisposition to commit the crime, and in most cases domestic terrorism suspects are given numerous opportunities to "back out" by the undercover government agents.[37]

Clearance Rates and Cold Cases

The ultimate goal of all law enforcement activity is to *clear* a crime, or secure the arrest and prosecution of the offender. Even a cursory glance at **clearance rates,** which show the percentage of reported crimes that have been cleared, reveals that investigations succeed only part of the time. In 2011, just 65 percent of homicides and 48 percent of total violent crimes were solved, while police cleared only 19 percent of property crimes.[38] For the most part, the different clearance rates for different crimes reflect the resources that a law enforcement agency expends on each type of crime. The police generally investigate a murder or a rape more vigorously than the theft of an automobile or a computer.

As a result of low clearance rates, police departments are saddled with an increasing number of **cold cases,** or criminal investigations that are not cleared after a certain amount of time. (The length of time before a case becomes "cold" varies from department to department. In general, a cold case must be "somewhat old" but not "so old that there can be no hope of ever solving it".[39]) Even using various technologies we will explore in the next section, cold case investigations rarely succeed. A recent RAND study found that only about one in twenty cold cases results in an arrest, and only about one in a hundred results in a conviction.[40]

Forensic Investigations and DNA

Although the crime scene typically offers a wealth of evidence, some of it is incomprehensible to a patrol officer or detective without assistance. For that aid, law enforcement officers rely on experts in **forensics,** or the practice of using science and technology to investigate crimes. Forensic experts apply their knowledge to items found at the crime scene to determine crucial facts such as:

- The cause of death or injury.
- The time of death or injury.
- The type of weapon or weapons used.
- The identity of the crime victim, if that information is unavailable.
- The identity of the offender (in the best-case scenario).[41]

To assist forensic experts, many police departments operate or are affiliated with approximately 400 publicly funded crime laboratories in the United States. As we noted in the previous chapter, the FBI also offers the services of its crime lab to agencies with limited resources. The FBI's aid in this area is crucial, given that the nation's crime labs are burdened with a backlog of nearly one million requests for forensic services.[42]

CRIME SCENE FORENSICS The first law enforcement agent to reach a crime scene has the important task of protecting any **trace evidence** from contamination. Trace evidence is generally very small—often invisible to the naked human eye—and often requires technological aid for detection. Hairs, fibers, blood, fingerprints, broken glass, and footprints are all examples of trace evidence. A study released by the National Institute of Justice in 2010 confirmed that when police are able to link such evidence to a suspect, the likelihood of a conviction rises dramatically.[43]

Police will also search a crime scene for bullets and spent cartridge casings. These items can provide clues as to how far the shooter was from the target. They can also be

Clearance Rate A comparison of the number of crimes cleared by arrest and prosecution with the number of crimes reported during any given time period.

Cold Case A criminal investigation that has not been solved after a certain amount of time.

Forensics The application of science to establish facts and evidence during the investigation of crimes.

Trace Evidence Evidence such as a fingerprint, blood, or hair found in small amounts at a crime scene.

Photo Courtesy of Martha Blake

CAREERS IN CJ

MARTHA BLAKE
FORENSIC SCIENTIST

In high school, I was interested in science, but didn't want to end up being a technician doing the same thing every day. I was looking in college catalogues and came across criminalistics at U.C. Berkeley. The coursework included such courses as microscopy, instrumental analysis, trace evidence, criminal law, and statistics, and it sounded fascinating. I decided in my senior year of high school to become a forensic scientist.

As quality assurance manager at the San Francisco Police Department's crime lab, I am often called to criminal court to testify about evidence that has passed through our lab. I am always nervous when I testify, and I think it is healthy to be a little nervous. As an expert witness, the most challenging part of my testimony is describing my findings to a jury of primarily nonscientists in a way that will make my testimony understandable and credible. I've found that juries tend to understand evidence that is part of their lives. Everyone can identify the writing of a family member or spouse, so describing how handwriting is identified is not too hard. Explaining how DNA analysis works is more difficult.

SOCIAL MEDIA CAREER TIP When people search for you online, they won't click past the first page. Check to see where your material appears on a regular basis.

Ballistics The study of firearms, including the firing of the weapon and the flight of the bullet.

DNA Fingerprinting The identification of a person based on a sample of her or his DNA, the genetic material found in the cells of all living things.

compared with information stored in national firearms databases to determine, under some circumstances, the gun used and its most recent owner. The study of firearms and its application to solving crimes goes under the general term **ballistics.** Comparing shell casings found at three different crime scenes, New York City police ballistics experts were able to determine that the same .22-caliber pistol was used to kill three Brooklyn-area merchants over a five-month period in 2012.

For more than a century, the most important piece of trace evidence has been the human fingerprint. Because no two fingerprints are alike, they are considered reliable sources of identification. Forensic scientists compare a fingerprint lifted from a crime scene with that of a suspect and declare a match if there are between eight and sixteen "points of similarity." This method of identification is not infallible, however. It is often difficult to lift a suitable print from a crime scene, and researchers have uncovered numerous cases in which innocent persons were convicted based on evidence obtained through faulty fingerprinting procedures.[44]

THE DNA REVOLUTION The technique of **DNA fingerprinting,** or using a suspect's DNA to match the suspect to a crime, emerged in the mid-1990s and has now all but replaced fingerprint evidence in many types of criminal investigations. The shift has been a boon to crime fighters: one law enforcement agent likened DNA fingerprinting to "the finger of God pointing down" at a guilty suspect.[45]

DNA, which is the same in each cell of a person's body, provides a "genetic blueprint" or "code" for every living organism. DNA fingerprinting is useful in criminal investigations because no two people, save for identical twins, have the same genetic code. Therefore, lab technicians, using the process described in Figure 6.4 on the facing page, can compare the DNA sample of a suspect to the evidence found at the crime scene. If the

Describe how forensic experts use DNA fingerprinting to solve crimes.

LEARNING 4 OBJECTIVE

FIGURE 6.4 Unlocking Evidence in DNA

Deoxyribonucleic acid, or DNA, is the genetic material that carries the code for all living cells. Through DNA profiling, a process explained here, forensic scientists test DNA samples to see if they match the DNA profile of a known criminal or other test subject.

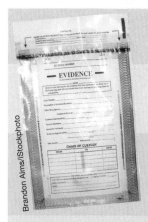

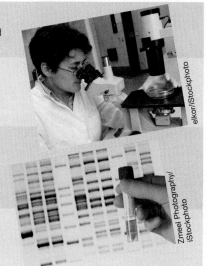

1. DNA samples can be taken from a number of sources, including saliva, blood, hair, or skin. These samples are labeled and shipped to a forensic lab.

2. The DNA is extracted from the cells of the sample using complex proteins known as enzymes. An electrical charge is then sent through the resulting DNA fragments to separate them according to size.

3. Another set of enzymes is added to the now separate DNA fragments. These enzymes attach themselves to different categories of genetic material within the DNA fragments and become distinct when exposed to photographic film. The "photograph" of this visible pattern is the DNA fingerprint.

4. Crime lab technicians will look for thirteen points on the DNA fingerprint called "markers." These thirteen markers are then compared with a suspect's DNA or with DNA found at a crime scene. If a match is found for each of the thirteen markers, there is almost no chance that the two DNA samples came from different persons.

match is negative, it is certain that the two samples did not come from the same source. If the match is positive, the lab will determine the odds that the DNA sample could have come from someone other than the suspect. Those odds are so high—sometimes reaching 30 billion to one—that a match is practically conclusive.[46]

The initial use of DNA to establish criminal guilt took place in Britain in 1986. The FBI used it for the first time in the United States two years later. The process begins when forensic technicians gather blood, semen, skin, saliva, or hair from the scene of a crime. Blood cells and sperm are rich in DNA, making them particularly useful in murder and rape cases, but DNA has also been extracted from sweat on dirty laundry, skin cells on eyeglasses, and saliva on used envelope seals. Once a suspect is identified, her or his DNA can be used to determine whether she or he can be placed at the crime scene. Several years ago, for example, investigators connected Aaron Thomas, the "East Coast Rapist," to a series of sexual assaults that took place from Rhode Island to Virginia by obtaining Thomas's DNA sample from a discarded cigarette.

DNA IN ACTION The ability to "dust" for genetic information on such a wide variety of evidence, as well as that evidence's longevity and accuracy, greatly increases the chances that a crime will be solved. Indeed, police no longer need a witness or even a suspect in custody to solve crimes. What they do need is a piece of evidence and a database.

In 1985, for example, Saba Girmai was found strangled to death in a dumpster in Mountain View, California. For nearly three decades, police were unable to establish any useful leads concerning Girmai's murderer. This changed when technicians at the Santa Clara County District Attorney's Crime Laboratory developed a DNA profile of the suspect using evidence found underneath Girmai's fingerprints. Checking these results against the state's crime database, the technicians found a match with Daniel Garcia, who had been previously convicted of a different crime. Twenty-eight years after the fact, in 2013, Garcia finally was arrested in connection with Girmai's death.

Databases and Cold Hits The identification of Daniel Garcia is an example of what police call a **cold hit,** which occurs when law enforcement finds a suspect "out of nowhere" by

Cold Hit The establishment of a connection between a suspect and a crime, often through the use of DNA evidence, in the absence of an ongoing criminal investigation.

■ How did "familial DNA" lead investigators to Lonnie Franklin, Jr., left, shown here in a Los Angeles courtroom? Why might privacy advocates criticize this method of using DNA to identify criminal suspects?
AP Photo/Irfan Khan, Pool

comparing DNA evidence from a crime scene against the contents of a database. The largest and most important database is the National Combined DNA Index System (CODIS). Operated by the FBI since 1998, CODIS gives local and state law enforcement agencies access to the DNA profiles of those who have been convicted of various crimes. CODIS contains DNA records of over 10 million people, and as of January 2013, the database had produced 200,300 cold hits nationwide.[47]

New Developments The investigative uses of DNA fingerprinting are expanding rapidly. Taking advantage of a new technique known as "touch DNA," investigators can collect evidence from surfaces that are not marked by obvious clues such as bloodstains or well-preserved fingerprints. With this technique, forensic scientists can gather enough microscopic cells to test for the presence of DNA by scraping a piece of food or an article of clothing. In addition, although CODIS was designed to help police solve murders and rapes, it is becoming increasingly useful in identifying suspects in burglaries and other property crimes. A recent study funded by the National Institute of Justice found that twice as many suspects were arrested when DNA fingerprinting was added to property crime investigations.[48]

Because relatives have similar DNA, law enforcement agents are now conducting "familial searches" of parents, siblings, and other relatives to gain more information about suspects. One such search led to the 2010 arrest of Los Angeles's "Grim Sleeper"—so called because there was a fourteen-year gap between the murders he committed in the 1980s and those in the 2000s. Investigators were able to narrow their focus to Lonnie Franklin, Jr., after DNA evidence from various Grim Sleeper crime scenes exhibited similarities to the DNA of Lonnie's son Christopher, who had recently been convicted on a weapons charge (see the photo above). Forensic experts are also raising the possibility that DNA will be able to act as a "genetic witness." That is, a DNA sample taken from a crime scene soon may be able to provide law enforcement with a physical description of a suspect, including her or his eye, skin, and hair color and age.[49]

Privacy and civil rights advocates protest that DNA collection has gone too far. Specifically, authorities in many states now collect samples from those who have been convicted of nonviolent crimes and, in some instances, from those who have merely been arrested for a crime but not convicted. We will examine the controversy surrounding that practice, which was the subject of a recent decision by the United States Supreme Court, in the *CJ in Action* feature at the end of the chapter.

SELF ASSESSMENT

Fill in the blanks and check your answers on page 205.

_____ officers make up the backbone of a police department. One of their primary functions is to _____ crime by maintaining a visible _____ in the community. _____, in contrast, investigate crimes that have already occurred. In the past two decades, _____, or the science of crime investigation, has been revolutionized by the technique of _____ _____, in which crime labs use samples of a person's genetic material to match suspects to crimes.

POLICE STRATEGIES: WHAT WORKS

In October 2012, the Detroit Police Officers Association surprised and angered that city's politicians by warning visitors to stay away. Because of $75 million in law enforcement budget cuts, the union declared that Detroit's police force was "grossly understaffed" and thus unable to protect the public from violent crime.[50] Bargaining tactics aside, Detroit's plight is not uncommon. Nearly two-thirds of local American law enforcement agencies have faced budget cuts over the past five years.[51]

Anecdotal evidence suggests that reducing the size of a police force, for whatever reason, leads to higher crime rates. In San Bernardino, California, for example, the homicide rate recently increased by 50 percent the first year after a large portion of the city's police were laid off for financial reasons.[52] Similarly, in Sacramento, California, a reduction in the police force coincided with a 48 percent increase in gun violence. "You've got to figure out within the new rules of the game how to [be] better," admitted Sacramento Police Chief Rick Braziel.[53] In this section, we will examine the most important law enforcement strategies being implemented to ensure that the outcome of this "game" is an increase in police efficiency rather than an increase in crime.

Calls for Service

Even as his department was being depleted by budget cuts, Sacramento Police Chief Braziel remained steadfast in his commitment to respond to 911 calls in a timely manner. While law enforcement officers do not like to think of themselves as being at the "beck and call" of citizens, that is the operational basis of much police work. All police departments practice **incident-driven policing,** in which calls for service are the primary instigators of action. Between 40 and 60 percent of police activity is the result of 911 calls or other citizen requests, which means that police officers in the field initiate only about half of such activity.[54]

RESPONSE TIME AND EFFICIENCY The speed with which the police respond to calls for service has traditionally been seen as a crucial aspect of crime fighting and crime prevention. In incident-driven policing, the ideal scenario is as follows: a citizen sees a person committing a crime and calls 911, and the police arrive quickly and catch the perpetrator in the act. Alternatively, a citizen who is the victim of a crime, such as a mugging, calls 911 as soon as possible, and the police arrive to catch the mugger before she or he can flee the immediate area of the crime.

Although such scenarios are quite rare in real life, **response time,** or the time elapsed between the instant a call for service is received and the instant the police arrive on the scene, has become a benchmark for police efficiency. If these times lag, as was the case in December 2012 when the Tucson, Arizona, police took nearly three hours to respond to a fight in a public library, local law enforcement comes under criticism. Tucson Police Chief Robert Villanseñor explained his department's sluggish reaction to the fight by pointing out that he had recently lost 150 officers due to city budget cuts.[55] Indeed, many police administrators believe that maintaining acceptable response times is primarily a function of the number of police officers available to respond.

IMPROVING RESPONSE TIME EFFICIENCY Many police departments have come to realize that overall response time is not as critical as response time for the most important calls. For this reason, a number of metropolitan areas have introduced 311 nonemergency call

Incident-Driven Policing A reactive approach to policing that emphasizes a speedy response to calls for service.

Response Time The rapidity with which calls for service are answered.

Differential Response
A strategy for answering calls for service in which response time is adapted to the seriousness of the call.

Random Patrol A patrol strategy that relies on police officers monitoring a certain area with the goal of detecting crimes in progress or preventing crime due to their presence. Also known as *general* or *preventive patrol.*

Explain why differential response strategies enable police departments to respond more efficiently to 911 calls.
LEARNING **5** **OBJECTIVE**

systems to reduce the strain on 911 operations.[56] Another popular method of improving performance in this area is a **differential response** strategy, in which the police distinguish among different calls for service so that they can respond more quickly to the most serious incidents.

Suppose, for example, that a police department receives two calls for service at the same time. The first caller reports that a burglar is in her house, and the second says that he has returned home from work to find his automobile missing. If the department employs differential response, the burglary in progress—a "hot" crime—will receive immediate attention. The missing automobile—a "cold" crime that could have been committed several hours earlier—will receive attention "as time permits," and the caller may even be asked to make an appointment to come to the police station to formally report the theft. (See Figure 6.5 on the facing page for possible responses to calls to a 911 operator.)

NEXT GENERATION 911 The most pressing shortcomings of America's 911 systems are not organizational, but rather technological. These systems were developed more than forty years ago, when copper-wire landlines ran between telephones and a central switch. Today, more than 70 percent of emergency calls for service come from mobile phones, and increasing numbers of consumers are taking advantage of VoIP (voice-over-Internet protocol) technology to turn their computers into telephones. Furthermore, by 2012, 35 percent of American households were wireless only—a percentage that is certain to increase in the near future.[57]

This situation presents a problem for law enforcement. Standard 911 systems cannot pinpoint the exact location of a mobile phone or a computer. If a caller is unable to provide that information, then it can prove very difficult for police officers to determine the site of the emergency. To resolve this issue, law enforcement is making the slow transition to Next Generation 911. This new system will rely on the Internet and will make it possible for officers to receive text messages, videos, photos, and location data about crime incidents. For example, a store clerk who has just been robbed at gunpoint will be able to take a photo of the offender's getaway car and send that photo to police along with the emergency call for service.[58]

■ A communications supervisor monitors 911 calls and police dispatches for the Boynton Beach, Florida, police department. What are some reasons that a 911 caller might not be able to relate her or his exact location and the nature of the emergency?
Mark Randall/MCT/Landov

Patrol Strategies

Although rapid response strategies are popular with the public, police experts have found little evidence that they lead to the apprehension of suspects or decrease crime.[59] Similarly, another traditional police strategy, *random patrol,* is increasingly felt to be an inefficient use of law enforcement resources.[60] **Random patrol** refers to police officers making the rounds of a specific area with the general goal of detecting and preventing crime. Every police department in the United States randomly patrols its jurisdiction using automobiles. In addition, 53 percent utilize foot patrols, 32 percent bicycle patrols, 16 percent motorcycle patrols, 4 percent boat patrols, and 1 percent horse patrols.[61]

FIGURE 6.5 Putting the Theory of Differential Response into Action

Differential response strategies are based on a simple concept: treat emergencies like emergencies and nonemergencies like nonemergencies. As you see, calls for service that involve "hot crimes" will be dealt with immediately, while those that report "cold crimes" will be dealt with at some point in the future.

"HOT" CALLS FOR SERVICE—IMMEDIATE RESPONSE	
Complaint to 911 Officer	**Rationale**
"I just got home from work and I can see someone in my bedroom through the window."	Possibility that the intruder is committing a crime.
"My husband has a baseball bat, and he says he's going to kill me."	Crime in progress.
"A woman in a green jacket just grabbed my purse and ran away."	Chances of catching the suspect are increased with immediate action.
"COLD" CALLS FOR SERVICE—ALTERNATIVE RESPONSE	
"I got to my office about two hours ago, but I just noticed that the fax machine was stolen during the night."	The crime occurred at least two hours earlier.
"The guy in the apartment above me has been selling pot for years, and I'm sick and tired of it."	Not an emergency situation.
"My husband came home late two nights ago with a black eye, and I finally got him to admit that he didn't run into a doorknob. Larry Smith smacked him."	Past crime with a known suspect who is unlikely to flee.

Source: Adapted from John S. Dempsey and Linda S. Forst, *An Introduction to Policing,* 6th ed. (Clifton Park, NY: Delmar Cengage Learning, 2011), 260–261.

TESTING RANDOM PATROL Police researchers have been questioning the effectiveness of random patrols since the influential Kansas City Preventive Patrol Experiment of the early 1970s. As part of this experiment, different neighborhoods in the city were subjected to three different levels of patrol: random patrol by a single police car, random patrol by multiple police cars, and no random patrol whatsoever. The results of the Kansas City experiment were somewhat shocking. Researchers found that increasing or decreasing preventive patrol had little or no impact on crimes, public opinion, the effectiveness of the police, police response time, traffic accidents, or reports of crime to police.[62]

For some, the Kansas City experiment and other similar data prove that patrol officers, after a certain threshold, are not effective in preventing crime and that scarce law enforcement resources should therefore be diverted to other areas. "It makes about as much sense to have police patrol routinely in cars to fight crime as it does to have firemen patrol routinely in fire trucks to fight fire," said University of Delaware professor Carl Klockars.[63] Still, random patrols are important for maintaining community relations, and they have been shown to reduce fear of crime in areas where police have an obvious presence.[64]

DIRECTED PATROLS In contrast to random patrols, **directed patrols** target specific areas of a city and often attempt to prevent a specific type of crime. Directed patrols have found favor among law enforcement experts as being a more efficient use of police resources than random patrols, as indicated by the recent Philadelphia Foot Patrol Experiment. During this experiment, extra foot patrols were utilized in sixty Philadelphia locations plagued by high levels of violent crime. During three months of directed patrols, arrests increased by 13 percent in the targeted areas, and violent crime decreased by 23 percent. In addition, an estimated fifty-three violent crimes were prevented over the three-month period.[65]

Predictive Policing and Crime Mapping

In the previous chapter, we discussed how predictive, or intelligence-led, policing strategies help law enforcement agencies anticipate patterns of criminal activity, allowing them to respond to, or even prevent, crime more effectively. Predictive policing is

Directed Patrol A patrol strategy that is designed to focus on a specific type of criminal activity at a specific time.

Hot Spots Concentrated areas of high criminal activity that draw a directed police response.

Crime Mapping Technology that allows crime analysts to identify trends and patterns of criminal behavior within a given area.

Reactive Arrests Arrests that come about as part of the ordinary routine of police patrol and responses to calls for service.

increasingly attractive to police administrators because, in theory, it requires fewer resources than traditional policing. "We're facing a situation where we have thirty percent more calls for service but twenty percent less staff than in the year 2000," says Zach Friend, a crime analyst for the Santa Cruz (California) Police Department. "So, we have to deploy our resources in a more effective way."[66] Friend and his colleagues are doing so by using computer models for predicting aftershocks from earthquakes to generate projections about where property crimes are most likely to take place.

FINDING "HOT SPOTS" Predictive policing strategies are strongly linked with directed patrols, which seek to improve on random patrols by targeting specific high-crime areas already known to law enforcement.[67] The target areas for directed patrols are often called **hot spots** because they contain greater numbers of criminals and have higher-than-average levels of victimization. Needless to say, police administrators are no longer sticking pins in maps to determine where hot spots exist. Rather, police departments are using **crime mapping** technology to locate and identify hot spots and "cool" them down. Crime mapping uses geographic information systems (GIS) to track criminal acts as they occur in time and space. Once sufficient information has been gathered, it is analyzed to predict future crime patterns.

Why does hot spot policing work? Criminologists Lawrence Sherman and David Weisburd provided a clue more than twenty years ago by observing the anti-crime impact of patrol officers. Sherman and Weisburd observed that after a police officer left a certain high-crime area, about fifteen minutes elapsed before criminal activity occurred at that spot.[68] Therefore, a police officer on patrol is most efficient when she or he spends a certain amount of time at a hot spot and then returns after fifteen minutes.

A recent experiment involving the Sacramento Police Department supports this hypothesis. Over a three-month period, twenty-one crime hot spots in the city received fifteen-minute randomized patrols, while another twenty-one crime hot spots received normal random patrols. Using calls for service as a measuring stick, the hot spots subject to fifteen-minute patrols were found to experience much less criminal activity.[69]

THE RISE OF COMPSTAT Computerized crime mapping was popularized when the New York Police Department launched CompStat in the mid-1990s. Still in use, CompStat starts with police officers reporting the exact location of crime and other crime-related information to department officials. These reports are then fed into a computer, which prepares grids of a particular city or neighborhood and highlights areas with a high incidence of serious offenses. (See Figure 6.6 on the facing page for an example of a GIS crime map.)

In New York and many other cities, the police department holds "Crime Control Strategy Meetings" during which precinct commanders are held accountable for CompStat's data-based reports in their districts. In theory, this system provides the police with accurate information about patterns of crime and gives them the ability to "flood" hot spots with officers at short notice. About two-thirds of large departments now employ some form of computerized crime mapping,[70] and Wesley Skogan, a criminologist at Northwestern University, believes that CompStat and similar technologies are the most likely cause of recent declines in big-city crime.[71]

Arrest Strategies

Like patrol strategies, arrest strategies can be broken into two categories that reflect the intent of police administrators. **Reactive arrests** are those arrests made by police officers, usually on general patrol, who observe a criminal act or respond to a call for

FIGURE 6.6 A GIS Crime Map for a Neighborhood in New Orleans

This crime map shows the incidence of various crimes during a two-week period in a neighborhood near downtown New Orleans.

The Omega Group/crimemapping.com

service. **Proactive arrests** occur when the police take the initiative to target a particular type of criminal or behavior. Proactive arrests are often associated with directed patrols of hot spots, and thus are believed by many experts to have a greater influence on an area's crime rates.[72]

THE BROKEN WINDOWS EFFECT To a certain extent, the popularity of proactive theories was solidified by a magazine article that James Q. Wilson and George L. Kelling wrote in 1982.[73] In their piece, entitled "Broken Windows," Wilson and Kelling argued that reform-era policing strategies focused on violent crime to the detriment of the vital police role of promoting the quality of life in neighborhoods. As a result, many communities, particularly in large cities, had fallen into a state of disorder and disrepute, with two very important consequences. First, these neighborhoods—with their broken windows, dilapidated buildings, and lawless behavior by residents—send out "signals" that criminal activity is tolerated. Second, this disorder spreads fear among law-abiding citizens, dissuading them from leaving their homes or attempting to improve their surroundings.

Thus, the **broken windows theory** is based on "order maintenance" of neighborhoods by cracking down on "quality-of-life" crimes such as panhandling, public drinking and urinating, loitering, and graffiti painting. Only by encouraging directed arrest strategies with regard to these quality-of-life crimes, the two professors argued, could American cities be rescued from rising crime rates.

SUPPORTERS AND CRITICS Like CompStat, the implementation of Wilson and Kelling's theory as a police strategy has been given a great deal of credit for crime decreases in American cities (particularly New York) over the past three decades.[74] It has remained in

Proactive Arrests Arrests that occur because of concerted efforts by law enforcement agencies to respond to a particular type of criminal or criminal behavior.

Broken Windows Theory Wilson and Kelling's theory that a neighborhood in disrepair signals that criminal activity is tolerated in the area. By cracking down on quality-of-life crimes, police can reclaim the neighborhood and encourage law-abiding citizens to live and work there.

Two Washington, D.C., police officers offer suggestions to a six-year-old during the annual "Shop with a Cop" event in the nation's capital. How can establishing friendly relations with citizens help law enforcement agencies reduce crime?
Andrew Harnik/*Washington Times*/Landov

Explain community policing and its contribution to the concept of problem-oriented policing. **LEARNING** **6** **OBJECTIVE**

Community Policing
A policing philosophy that emphasizes community support for and cooperation with the police in preventing crime.

favor among police administrators, despite debate in the academic community over whether the tactics have any measurable impact on violent crime in blighted neighborhoods.[75] Critics insist that instituting "zero-tolerance" arrest policies for lesser crimes in low-income neighborhoods not only discriminates against the poor and minority groups but also fosters a strong mistrust of police.[76]

Community Policing and Problem Solving

In "Broken Windows," Wilson and Kelling insisted that, to reduce fear and crime in high-risk neighborhoods, police had to rely on the cooperation of citizens. For all its drawbacks, the political era of policing (see Chapter 5) did have characteristics that observers such as Wilson and Kelling have come to see as advantageous. During the nineteenth century, the police were much more involved in the community than they were after the reforms. Officers performed many duties that today are associated with social services, such as operating soup kitchens and providing lodging for homeless people. They also played a more direct role in keeping public order by "running in" drunks and intervening in minor disturbances.[77] To a certain extent, **community policing** advocates a return to this understanding of the police mission.

RETURN TO THE COMMUNITY Community policing can be defined as an approach that promotes community-police partnerships, proactive problem solving, and community engagement to address issues such as fear of crime and the causes of such fear in a particular area. Neighborhood watch programs, in which police officers and citizens work together to prevent local crime and disorder, are a popular version of a community policing initiative. Under community policing, patrol officers have the freedom to improvise. They are expected to develop personal relationships with residents and to encourage those residents to become involved in making the community a safer place. As part of Operation Heat Wave, for instance, Dallas detectives go door-to-door in neighborhoods plagued by burglary and auto theft. During these face-to-face meetings, the detectives are able to gather information concerning recent victimizations and encourage attendance at community crime-watch meetings.[78]

The Quiet Revolution The strategy of increasing police presence in the community has been part of, in the words of George Kelling, a "quiet revolution" in American law enforcement.[79] Today, nearly two-thirds of police departments mention community policing in their mission statements, and a majority of the departments in large cities offer community police training for employees.[80] Furthermore, the idea seems to be popular among law enforcement agents. A 2011 survey of more than 1,200 officers in eleven police departments found that between 60 and 95 percent agreed with the idea that "police officers should try to solve non-crime problems on their beat."[81] A majority of the officers also reported having positive relations with members of the public, who they felt generally appreciated community policing efforts.[82]

Criticisms of Community Policing Nevertheless, despite, or maybe because of, its "feel good" associations, community policing has been the target of several criticisms. First, more than half of the police chiefs and sheriffs in a survey conducted by the National Institute of Justice were unclear about the actual meaning of "community policing,"[83] leading one observer to joke that Professor Kelling's revolution is even quieter than expected.[84] Second, since its inception, community policing has been criticized—not the least by police officials—as having more to do with public relations than with actual crime fighting.[85]

PROBLEM-ORIENTED POLICING A drawback inherent in most police strategies can be summed up with the truism, "Catch a thief, there will always be another one to take his [or her] place." In other words, common street criminals such as burglars, auto thieves, and shoplifters are so numerous that arresting one seems to have little or no impact.[86] By itself, community policing may not offer much hope for solving this dilemma. But having law enforcement establish a cooperative presence in the community is a crucial part of a strategy that focuses on long-term crime prevention. Introduced by Herman Goldstein of the Police Executive Research Forum in the 1970s, **problem-oriented policing** is based on the premise that police departments devote too many of their resources to reacting to calls for service and too few to "acting on their own initiative to prevent or reduce community problems."[87] To rectify this situation, problem-oriented policing moves beyond simply responding to incidents and attempts instead to control or even solve the root causes of criminal behavior.

Goldstein's theory encourages police officers to stop looking at their work as a day-to-day proposition. Rather, they should try to shift the patterns of criminal behavior in a positive direction. For example, instead of responding to a 911 call concerning illegal drug use by simply arresting the offender—a short-term response—the patrol officers should also look at the long-term implications of the situation. They should analyze the pattern of similar arrests in the area and interview the arrestee to determine the reasons, if any, that the site was selected for drug activity.[88] Then additional police action should be taken to prevent further drug sales at the identified location. (For an example of problem-oriented policing in action, see Figure 6.7 on the next page.)

> **Problem-Oriented Policing**
> A policing philosophy that requires police to identify potential criminal activity and develop strategies to prevent or respond to that activity.

SELF ASSESSMENT

Fill in the blanks and check your answers on page 205.

Without exception, modern police departments practice _____-driven policing, in which officers respond to calls for _____ such as 911 phone calls after a crime has occurred. Along the same lines, most patrol officers work _____ patrols, in which they cover designated areas and react to the incidents they encounter. _____ patrols, which often focus on "hot spots" of crime, and _____ arrest policies, which target a particular type of criminal behavior, have both been shown to be very effective. _____ policing is a popular strategy in which officers are encouraged to develop partnerships with citizens to prevent and combat crime.

"US VERSUS THEM": ISSUES IN MODERN POLICING

The night after two police officers shot and killed Jaime Gonzalez, described in the opening to this chapter, the Brownsville police received several death threats. Apparently, some members of the community were unconvinced by the argument that

FIGURE 6.7 "Pulling Levers" in Nashville

A form of problem-oriented policing known as "pulling levers" has gained a place in departmental strategies over the past decade. This approach administers a variety of sanctions, or levers, to deter groups of chronic offenders from continuing their criminal behavior.

In Nashville, Tennessee, a "pulling levers" strategy was applied to the problem of street-level drug dealing. For years, law enforcement's response to this problem was to perpetuate a cycle in which drug dealers were arrested and prosecuted only to be replaced by another group of drug dealers. The Nashville Drug Market Initiative (NDMI) attempts to break this cycle with a four-stage process of problem-oriented policing:

Stage 1: Identification	Analyze crime data to determine which areas of the city have the highest levels of drug crime.
Stage 2: Preparation	Coordinate with local law enforcement, politicians, social service providers, and residents to ensure that the initiative will receive community support.
Stage 3: Notification	Following a large-scale crackdown on known drug dealers, those criminals are given the options of "turning their lives around" with the help of social services or being convicted and imprisoned.
Stage 4: Resource Delivery	Those drug dealers who so choose are provided with assistance such as drug treatment, education and skills training, and job-interview skills.

According to city officials, NDMI brought about a significant to moderate reduction in violent crime, property crime, drug offenses, and calls for service in the affected areas. As we noted in Chapter 2, DMI initiatives have found success in other cities as well.

---

the officers' actions were justified because Gonzalez appeared to be in possession of an actual handgun. Indeed, there seems to be a public perception, fueled by heavy coverage of police shootings, that American law enforcement agents are "trigger happy" when it comes to using their weaponry. The reality is that such fatal shootings are quite rare.[89] According to one estimate, the average New York City police officer would have to work 694 years to shoot and kill someone, and the likelihood is more remote in most other cities.[90]

The question of when to use lethal force is one of many on-the-job issues that make law enforcement such a challenging and often dangerous career. When faced with a scenario such as the one in the halls of Brownsville's Cummings Middle School, sometimes police officers make the right decisions, and sometimes they make the wrong ones. Often, it is difficult to tell the two apart.

Police Subculture

As a rule, police officers do not appreciate being second-guessed when it comes to their split-second shooting decisions. To officers, it often seems that civilians believe that suspects with weapons should be given a "free shot" before being fired at by law enforcement.[91] Feelings of frustration and mistrust toward civilians are hallmarks of **police subculture,** a broad term used to describe the basic assumptions and values that permeate law enforcement agencies and are taught to new members of a law enforcement agency as the proper way to think, perceive, and act. Every organization has a subculture, with values shaped by the particular aspects and pressures of that organization. In the police subculture, those values are formed in an environment characterized by danger, stress, boredom, and violence.

THE CORE VALUES OF POLICE SUBCULTURE From the first day on the job, rookies begin the process of **socialization,** in which they are taught the values and rules of police work. This process is aided by a number of rituals that are common to the law enforcement

Police Subculture The values and perceptions that are shared by members of a police department and, to a certain extent, by all law enforcement agents.

Socialization The process through which a police officer is taught the values and expected behavior of the police subculture.

experience. Police theorist Harry J. Mullins believes that the following rituals are critical to the police officer's acceptance, and even embrace, of police subculture:

- Attending a police academy.
- Working with a senior officer, who passes on the "lessons" of police work and life to the younger officer.
- Making the initial felony arrest.
- Using force to make an arrest for the first time.
- Using or witnessing deadly force for the first time.
- Witnessing major traumatic incidents for the first time.[92]

Each of these rituals makes it clear to the police officer that this is not a "normal" job. The only other people who can understand the stresses of police work are fellow officers, and consequently law enforcement officers tend to insulate themselves from civilians. Eventually, the insulation breeds mistrust, and the police officer develops an "us versus them" outlook toward those outside the force. In turn, this outlook creates what sociologist William Westly called the **blue curtain,** also known as the "blue wall of silence" or simply "the code."[93] This curtain separates the police from the civilians they are meant to protect.

POLICE CYNICISM A cynic is someone who universally distrusts human motives and expects nothing but the worst from human behavior. *Police cynicism* is characterized by a rejection of the ideals of truth and justice—the very values that an officer is sworn to uphold.[94] As cynical police officers lose respect for the law, they replace legal rules with those learned in the police subculture, which are believed to be more reflective of "reality." The implications for society can be an increase in police misconduct, corruption, and brutality.[95]

Police cynicism is exacerbated by a feeling of helplessness—to report another officer's wrongdoing is a severe breach of the blue wall of silence. As one officer said:

> As one officer told a columnist for the *New York Times,* the prevailing attitude among law enforcement officers is that, as long as one's supervisors accept a certain form of questionable behavior without comment, there is no reason to curtail that behavior. Indeed, according to the officer, any hint of disapproval can lead to accusations of being a "rat." "You've gotta work with a lot of these guys," the officer explained. "You go on a gun job, the next thing you know, you got nobody following you up the stairs."[96]

The officer's statement highlights one of the reasons why the police subculture resonates beyond department walls—he has basically admitted that he will not report wrongdoing by his peers. In this manner, the police subculture influences the actions of police officers, sometimes to the detriment of society. In the next sections, we will examine two areas of the law enforcement work environment that help create the police subculture and must be fully understood if the cynical nature of the police subculture is ever to be changed: (1) the dangers of police work and (2) the need for police officers to establish and maintain authority.

The Physical Dangers of Police Work

At 9:28 A.M. on February 28, 2013, Sergeant Gary Morales of the St. Lucie County (Florida) Sheriff's Office pulled over a driver for a traffic violation. At some point during the stop, the suspect grabbed a gun that was hidden in the car and opened fire on Morales, killing him. As this incident shows, there is no such thing as a "routine" traffic stop. For that matter, police officers learn early in their careers that nothing about their job is "routine"—they face the threat of physical harm every day.

OFFICERS KILLED AND ASSAULTED According to the Officer Down Memorial Page, Gary Morales was one of 147 law enforcement agents who died in the line of duty from January

Body Armor Protective covering that is worn under a police officer's clothing and designed to minimize injury from being hit by a fired bullet.

2012 to February 2013, and one of fifty-seven who were killed by hostile gunfire.[97] In addition, about 55,000 assaults were committed against police officers in 2011, with 27 percent of these assaults resulting in an injury.[98] These numbers are hardly surprising. As police experts John S. Dempsey and Linda S. Forst point out, police "deal constantly with what may be the most dangerous species on this planet—the human being."[99]

At the same time, Dempsey and Forst note that according to data compiled by the federal government, citizens and the police come into contact about 40 million times a year.[100] Given this figure, the police have relatively low death and injury rates. The statistical safety of police officers can be attributed to two factors. First, police academies emphasize officer safety, focusing on areas such as self-defense, firearm proficiency, arrest tactics, and nonlethal weapons (which will be addressed later in the chapter).[101] Second, police officers take extraordinary precautions to protect their physical safety, including wearing protective **body armor** underneath their clothing.[102] The body armor most widely used by American police officers is made of Kevlar, a high-strength fiber discovered in 1964 by a chemist named Stephanie Kwolek. Low-level Kevlar can stop .357 and .9mm shots, while high-level "tactical armor" can deflect rifle and machine gun bullets. Ninety-two percent of all police departments require their officers to wear body armor, which has saved at least 3,000 law enforcement lives since 1987.[103]

ACCIDENTAL DEATHS Despite perceptions to the contrary, a high percentage of deaths and injuries suffered by police officers are not the result of assaults by criminal suspects. Generally speaking, half of all law enforcement officer injuries are due to accidents, and about two-thirds of those injuries occur when officers are doing something other than making an arrest.[104] In particular, traffic accidents cause as many line-of-duty deaths as do firearms.[105] One reason for the fatalities is that a number of law enforcement officers do not take simple precautions when behind the wheel. A recent study conducted by the National Highway Traffic Safety Administration found that 42 percent of police officers killed in vehicle crashes were not wearing seat belts.[106]

Also, as Craig Floyd of the National Law Enforcement Officers Memorial Fund points out, nearly every police officer will be involved in a high-speed automobile response or chase during her or his career, but only 10 percent will be involved in a gunfight. Yet firearms training is common, while driver training is not. Furthermore, although great strides have been made in protective body armor for police officers, the same cannot be said for safety measures in patrol cars.[107]

A fellow officer pays his respects during the funeral of Chattahoochee Hills, Georgia, police officer Mike Vogt, who was shot and killed while on patrol. Besides physical violence, what are some of the other occupational threats that police officers face on a daily basis?
AP Photo/Brant Sanderlin

Stress and the Mental Dangers of Police Work

In addition to physical dangers, police work entails considerable mental pressure and stress. Professor John Violanti and his colleagues at the University at Buffalo have determined that police officers experience unusually high levels of *cortisol,* otherwise known as the "stress hormone," which is associated with serious health problems such as diabetes and heart disease.[108] "Intervention is necessary to help officers deal with this difficult and stressful occupation," says Violanti. "[Police officers] need to learn how to relax, how to think differently about things they experience as a cop."[109]

POLICE STRESSORS The conditions that cause stress—such as worries over finances or relationships—are known as **stressors.** Each profession has its own set of stressors, but police are particularly vulnerable to occupational pressures and stress factors such as the following:

- The constant fear of being a victim of violent crime.
- Exposure to violent crime and its victims.
- The need to comply with the law in nearly every job action.
- Lack of community support.
- Negative media coverage.

Police face a number of internal pressures as well, including limited opportunities for career advancement, excessive paperwork, and low wages and benefits.[110] The unconventional hours of shift work can also interfere with an officer's private life and contribute to lack of sleep. Each of these is a primary stressor associated with police work.[111]

THE CONSEQUENCES OF POLICE STRESS Police stress can manifest itself in different ways. The University at Buffalo study cited above found that the stresses of law enforcement often lead to high blood pressure and heart problems.[112] Other research shows that police officers are three times more likely to suffer from alcoholism than the average American.[113] If stress becomes overwhelming, an officer may suffer from **burnout,** becoming listless and ineffective as a result of mental and physical exhaustion. Another problem related to stress is *post-traumatic stress disorder (PTSD).* Often recognized in war veterans and rape victims, PTSD is a reaction to a stressor that evokes significant stress. For police officers, such stressors might include the death of a fellow agent or the shooting of a civilian. An officer suffering from PTSD will:

1. Re-experience the traumatic event through nightmares and flashbacks.
2. Become less and less involved in the outside world by withdrawing from others and refusing to participate in normal social interactions.
3. Experience "survival guilt," which may lead to loss of sleep and memory impairment.[114]

To put it bluntly, law enforcement officers are exposed to more disturbing images—of violent death, bloody crime scenes, horrible accidents, and human cruelty—in their first few years on the job than most people will see in a lifetime. Though some studies suggest that police officers have higher rates of suicide than the general population, it appears that most develop an extraordinary ability to handle the difficulties of the profession and persevere.[115]

Authority and the Use of Force

If the police subculture is shaped by the dangers of the job, it often finds expression through authority. The various symbols of authority that decorate a police officer—including the uniform, badge, nightstick, and firearm—establish the power she or he holds over civilians. For better or for worse, both police officers and civilians tend to equate terms such as *authority* and *respect* with the ability to use force.

Stressors The aspects of police work and life that lead to feelings of stress.

Burnout A mental state that occurs when a person suffers from exhaustion and has difficulty functioning normally as a result of overwork and stress.

Near the beginning of the twentieth century, a police officer stated that his job was to "protect the good people and treat the crooks rough."[116] Implicit in the officer's statement is the idea that to do the protecting, he had to do some roughing up as well. This attitude toward the use of force is still with us today. Indeed, it is generally accepted that not only is police use of force inevitable, but that police officers who are unwilling to use force in certain circumstances cannot do their jobs effectively.

USE OF FORCE IN LAW ENFORCEMENT In general, the use of physical force by law enforcement personnel is very rare, occurring in only about 1.4 percent of the 40 million annual police-public encounters mentioned earlier. Still, the Department of Justice estimates that law enforcement officers threaten to use force or use force in encounters with 770,000 civilians a year, and nearly 14 percent of those incidents result in an injury.[117] Federal authorities also report that about 690 deaths occur in the process of an arrest on an annual basis.[118] Of course, police officers are often justified in using force to protect themselves and other citizens. As we noted earlier, they are the targets of tens of thousands of assaults each year. Law enforcement agents are also usually justified in using force to make an arrest, to prevent suspects from escaping, to restrain suspects or other individuals for their own safety, or to protect property.[119]

At the same time, few observers would be naïve enough to believe that the police are *always* justified in the use of force. A 2009 survey of emergency room physicians found that 98 percent believed that they had treated patients who were victims of excessive police force.[120] How, then, is "misuse" of force to be defined? To provide guidance for officers in this tricky area, nearly every law enforcement agency designs a *use of force matrix.* As the example in Figure 6.8 on the left shows, such a matrix presents officers with the proper force options for different levels of contact with a civilian.

TYPES OF FORCE To comply with the various, and not always consistent, laws concerning the use of force, a police officer must understand that there are two kinds of force: *nondeadly force* and *deadly force.* Most force used by law enforcement is nondeadly force. In most states, the use of nondeadly force is regulated by the concept of **reasonable force,** which allows the use of nondeadly force when a reasonable person would assume that such force was necessary. In contrast, **deadly force** is force that an objective police officer realizes will place the subject in direct threat of serious injury or death.

THE UNITED STATES SUPREME COURT AND USE OF FORCE The United States Supreme Court set the limits for the use of deadly force by law enforcement officers in *Tennessee v. Garner*

FIGURE 6.8 The Orlando (Florida) Police Department's Use of Force Matrix

Like most local law enforcement agencies, the Orlando Police Department has a policy to guide its officers' use of force. These policies instruct an officer on how to react to an escalating series of confrontations with a civilian and are often expressed visually, as shown here.

Source: Michael E. Miller, "Taser Use and the Use-of-Force Continuum," *Police Chief* (September 2010), 72.

(1985).[121] The case involved an incident in which Memphis police officer Elton Hymon shot and killed a suspect who was trying to climb over a fence after stealing ten dollars from a residence. Hymon testified that he had been trained to shoot to keep a suspect from escaping, and indeed Tennessee law at the time allowed police officers to apprehend fleeing suspects in this manner.

In reviewing the case, the Supreme Court focused not on Hymon's action but on the Tennessee statute itself, ultimately finding it unconstitutional:

> When the suspect poses no immediate threat to the officer and no threat to others, the use of deadly force is unjustified. . . . It is not better that all felony suspects die than that they escape.[122]

The Court's decision forced twenty-three states to change their fleeing felon rules, but it did not completely eliminate police discretion in such situations. Police officers still may use deadly force if they have probable cause to believe that the fleeing suspect poses a threat of serious injury or death to the officers or others. (We will discuss the concept of probable cause in the next chapter.)

In essence, the Court recognized that police officers must be able to make split-second decisions without worrying about the legal ramifications. Four years after the *Garner* case, the Court tried to clarify this concept in *Graham v. Connor* (1989), stating that the use of any force should be judged by the "reasonableness of the moment."[123] In 2004, the Court modified this rule by suggesting that an officer's use of force could be "reasonable" even if, by objective measures, the force was not needed to protect the officer or others in the area.[124] (See the feature *You Be the Sheriff's Deputy—Threat Level* below.)

THREAT LEVEL

LEARNING **7** OBJECTIVE — Determine when police officers are justified in using deadly force.

THE SITUATION You receive a call from dispatch telling you that Lee Dylan, a mentally unstable man, has just escaped from a local jail where he was being held on suspicion of committing a nonviolent felony. Driving toward the jail, you see a man matching Dylan's description running down a back alley. Jumping out of your car, you and your partner follow on foot. Eventually, you and your partner corner the man, who is indeed Dylan, in a construction site. Dylan, who is of average height and build, grabs a loose brick and makes threatening motions with it. You pull your gun and, along with your partner, move toward Dylan. You yell, "Drop the brick!" He screams, "You're going to have to kill me!" and rushes at you.

THE LAW The use of force by a law enforcement agent—even deadly force—is based on the concept of reasonableness. In other words, would a reasonable police officer in this officer's shoes have been justified in using force?

YOUR DECISION Does Dylan pose a threat of serious bodily harm to you or your partner? How you answer this question will determine the type of force you use against him. Keep in mind that almost all police officers experience an adrenaline rush in stressful situations, and this may influence your reaction.

[To see how a law enforcement officer in Cincinnati reacted in similar circumstances, go to Example 6.2 in Appendix B.]

Somchai Rakin/Shutterstock.com

Conducted Energy Device (CED) A less lethal weapon designed to disrupt a target's central nervous system by means of a charge of electrical energy.

Professionalism Adherence to a set of values that show a police officer to be of the highest moral character.

LESS LETHAL WEAPONS Regardless of any legal restrictions, violent confrontations between officers and suspects are inevitable. To decrease the likelihood that such confrontations will result in death or serious injury, many police departments use *less lethal weapons,* which are designed to subdue but not seriously harm suspects. The most common less lethal weapon is Oleoresin Capsicum, or OC pepper spray, which is used by 97 percent of all local police departments.[125] An organic substance that combines ingredients such as resin and cayenne pepper, OC causes a sensation similar to having sand or needles in the eyes when sprayed into a suspect's face. Other common less lethal weapons include tear gas, water cannons, and **conducted energy devices (CEDs),** which rely on an electrical shock to incapacitate uncooperative suspects.

The best-known, and most controversial, CED is the Taser—a handheld electrical stun gun that fires blunt darts up to 21 feet at speeds of 200 to 220 feet per second. The darts deliver 50,000 volts into the target for a span of about five seconds. Nationally, more than 15,000 law enforcement agencies deploy Tasers, and, when properly used, the devices increase the safety of both officers and suspects.[126] According to a study conducted by researchers at Wake Forest University, 99.7 percent of people shocked by Tasers had minor or no injuries.[127] Nevertheless, according to the human rights organization Amnesty International, as of 2012 more than 500 people have died after being Tasered by police.[128] Often, these deaths occurred because the target had a weakened heart or was in ill health because of drug use.[129]

SELF ASSESSMENT

Fill in the blanks and check your answers on page 205.

Like any organization, a police department has a _____ that determines the values of its employees. In law enforcement, these values are shaped by the _____ dangers, such as assault, and mental dangers, such as high levels of _____, that officers face every day. Laws regulating police use of force rely on two concepts: _____ force, which is the amount of force that a rational person would consider necessary in a given situation, and _____ force, which is a level of force that will place the subject in grave bodily danger.

POLICE MISCONDUCT AND ETHICS

If police culture is, as we noted earlier, marked by a certain mistrust of the public, it is only fair to note that the reverse is often true as well. Police are held to a high standard of behavior that can be summarized by the umbrella term **professionalism.** A professional law enforcement agent is expected to be honest, committed to ideals of justice, respectful of the law, and intolerant of misconduct by his or her fellow officers. When police act unprofessionally, or are perceived to have done so, then their relationship with the community will inevitably suffer.

Indeed, Yale University professor Tom Tyler believes that the public's perception of police *legitimacy* is the basis of law enforcement–community relations. That is, if citizens fail to see their moral and social norms reflected in police behavior, then they will be less likely to respect criminal law themselves or aid the police in fighting crime.[130]

Racial and Ethnic Biases in Policing

According to research conducted by sociologists Matthew S. Crow and Brittany Adrion of the University of West Florida, police officers are more likely to use Tasers against members of minority groups than against whites.[131] Such statistics contribute to the perception among minorities that they do not receive equal treatment from the criminal justice system. When polled, African Americans consistently express less confidence in the police than do whites (see Figure 6.9 on the right). Consequently, the legitimacy of the police for many minorities is compromised by the specter of bias.

PERCEIVED BIAS In the next chapter's discussion of racial profiling, we will see that many African Americans believe that they are often targeted for a particular "offense"—DWB, or "driving while black." To a certain extent, statistics bear out these suspicions. A recent Justice Department study reports that although police pull over black, white, and Hispanic drivers at similar rates, blacks and Hispanics are almost three times more likely to be searched following the stop.[132]

The same study found that police officers are more than three times more likely to use force when coming into contact with African Americans than with whites and slightly more likely with Hispanics than with whites.[133] Furthermore, criminologists Tammy Rinehart Kochel, David B. Wilson, and Stephen Mastrofski recently published a study concluding that, "consistent with what most of the American public perceives," racial minority suspects are more likely to be arrested than whites for similar wrongdoing.[134] These data reinforce the notion that police bias is responsible for the disproportionate numbers of minorities in American prisons and jails discussed throughout this textbook.

POLICE ATTITUDES AND DISCRETION Although everyone would agree that some individual officers may be influenced by prejudice, the greater police presence and arrest rates in minority neighborhoods should not be accepted as automatic evidence of law enforcement discrimination. As we learned earlier in the chapter, the primary operational tactic of all metropolitan police forces is responding to calls for service. According to research by law enforcement expert Richard J. Ludman, the greater police presence in these communities is mainly the result of calls for service from residents, which, in turn, are caused by higher local crime rates. Indeed, Randall Kennedy believes that such "selective law enforcement" should be, and for the most part is, welcomed by those who live in high-crime areas and appreciate the added protection.[135]

Furthermore, as several experts point out, cultural differences often exist between police officers and the residents of the neighborhoods they patrol. One survey found that police working in minority areas perceived higher levels of abuse and less respect from those citizens than from those in nonminority areas.[136] In looking at police abuse in Inglewood, California, the *Los Angeles Times* found that most of the victims claimed they were assaulted after "contempt of cop" incidents, such as not immediately following orders or verbally challenging the officer.[137] Judging someone's demeanor is often a subjective task and can be influenced by a lack of communication between two people

FIGURE 6.9 Racial Attitudes toward the Police

As these polls conducted by the federal government show, members of minority groups are more likely than whites to have negative views of the police.

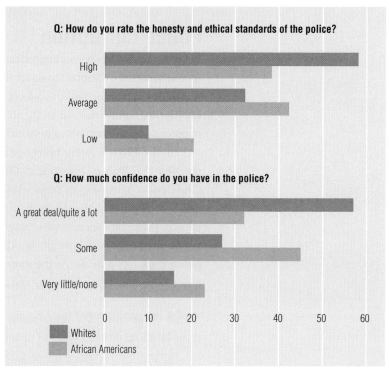

Source: U.S. Department of Justice.

of different backgrounds—another reason why it is so important for police departments to attract members of minority groups, as noted in our discussion of recruiting strategies in the previous chapter.

Police Corruption

Police *corruption* has been a concern since the first organized American police departments. As you recall from Chapter 5, a desire to eradicate, or at least limit, corruption was one of the motivating factors behind the reform movement of policing. For general purposes, **police corruption** can be defined as the misuse of authority by a law enforcement officer "in a manner designed to produce personal gain."

In the 1970s, a police officer named Frank Serpico went public about corruption in the New York Police Department. City authorities responded by establishing the Knapp Commission to investigate Serpico's claims. The inquiry uncovered widespread institutionalized corruption in the department. In general, the Knapp Commission report divided corrupt police officers into two categories: "grass eaters" and "meat eaters." "Grass eaters" are involved in passive corruption—they simply accept the payoffs and opportunities that police work can provide. As the name implies, "meat eaters" are more aggressive in their quest for personal gain, initiating and going to great lengths to carry out corrupt schemes.[138]

TYPES OF CORRUPTION Specifically, the Knapp Commission's investigation identified three basic, traditional types of police corruption:

Identify the three traditional forms of police corruption.
LEARNING
8
OBJECTIVE

1. *Bribery,* in which the police officer accepts money or other forms of payment in exchange for "favors," which may include allowing a certain criminal activity to continue or misplacing a key piece of evidence before a trial. Related to bribery are *payoffs,* in which an officer demands payment from an individual or a business in return for certain services.
2. *Shakedowns,* in which an officer attempts to coerce money or goods from a citizen or criminal.
3. *Mooching,* in which the police officer accepts free "gifts" such as cigarettes, liquor, or services in return for favorable treatment of the gift giver.[139]

Additionally, corrupt police officers have many opportunities to engage in theft or burglary by taking money or property in the course of their duties. Vice investigations, for example, often uncover temptingly large amounts of illegal drugs and cash. Several years ago, a Wake County (North Carolina) sheriff 's deputy was arrested after she improperly "confiscated" a package of marijuana and $6,435 in cash seized during an arrest.

Another scenario involves police misconduct that becomes pervasive, infecting a group of officers. In 2012, dozens of Baltimore police officers were implicated in a $1 million kickback scheme. For years, the officers had been diverting autos damaged in traffic accidents to the Majestic Body Shop in return for a payoff of several hundred dollars per car (see photo alongside). Sometimes, the

■ In the wake of the Majestic Body Shop scandal, then Police Commissioner Frederick H. Bealefeld III, left, hired former federal counternarcotics chief Grayling G. Williams, right, to run the Baltimore City Police Department's anticorruption division. What steps can police administrators take to lessen the likelihood of such scandals?
Matt Roth/*The New York Times*

officers themselves would cause further damage to the cars to increase the portion of the insurance payout that went into their own pockets.

CORRUPTION IN POLICE SUBCULTURE   There is no single reason why police misconduct occurs. Certain types of officers do, however, seem more likely to engage in corruption—the young, the relatively uneducated (lacking a college degree), those with records of prior criminality and citizens' complaints, and those unlikely to be promoted.[140] Lawrence Sherman has identified several stages in the moral decline of these "bad cops."[141]

In the first stage, the officers accept minor gratuities, such as the occasional free meal from a restaurant on their beats. These gratuities gradually evolve into outright bribes, in which the officers receive the gratuity for overlooking some violation. For example, a law officer may accept pay from a bar owner to ensure that the establishment is not investigated for serving alcohol to minors. In the final stage, officers no longer passively accept bribes but actively seek them out. The officers may even force the other party to pay for unwanted police services. This stage often involves large amounts of money and may entail protection of or involvement in illegal drug, gambling, or prostitution organizations.

Police Accountability

Even in a police department with excellent recruiting methods, state-of-the-art ethics and discretionary training programs, and a culturally diverse workforce that nearly matches the makeup of the community, the problems discussed earlier in this chapter are bound to occur. The question then becomes—given the inevitability of excessive force, corruption, and other misconduct—*who shall police the police?*

INTERNAL INVESTIGATIONS   "The minute the public feels that the police department is not investigating its own alleged wrongdoing well, the police department will not be able to function credibly in even the most routine of matters," says Sheldon Greenberg, a professor of police management at Johns Hopkins University.[142] The mechanism for these investigations within a police department is the **internal affairs unit (IAU).** In many smaller police departments, the police chief conducts internal affairs investigations, while midsized and large departments have a team of internal affairs officers. The New York Police Department's IAU has an annual budget of nearly $62 million and consists of 650 officers.

As much as police officers may resent internal affairs units, most realize that it is preferable to settle disciplinary matters in house. The alternatives may be worse. In 2012, after conducting a ten-month investigation that uncovered widespread corruption, excessive use of force, and discrimination against minority civilians, the U.S. Department of Justice ordered a reorganization of the New Orleans Police Department (NOPD). As part of this reorganization, federal officials required the NOPD to implement hundreds of new policies in areas ranging from the treatment of women victims to the identification of crime suspects. These changes are expected to cost the city nearly $60 million.[143]

CITIZEN OVERSIGHT   Many communities also rely on an external procedure for handling citizen complaints against the police, known as **citizen oversight.** In this process, citizens—people who are not sworn officers and, by inference, not biased in favor of law enforcement officers—review allegations of police misconduct or brutality. According to data gathered by police accountability expert Samuel Walker, nearly one hundred cities now operate some kind of review procedure by an independent body.[144] For the

Internal Affairs Unit (IAU)
A division within a police department that receives and investigates complaints of wrongdoing by police officers.

Citizen Oversight   The process by which citizens review complaints brought against individual police officers or police departments.

most part, citizen review boards can only recommend action to the police chief or other executive. They do not have the power to discipline officers directly. Police officers generally resent this intrusion by civilians, and most studies have shown that civilian review boards are not widely successful in their efforts to convince police chiefs to take action against their subordinate officers.[145]

One form of citizen oversight that has been highly successful in curbing police misconduct is cheap digital video. Every week, it seems, recordings taken by citizens using a handheld camera, smartphone, or some other device go "viral" online, flooding the Internet with examples of police brutality or some other form of misbehavior. In 2012, a Philadelphia police lieutenant lost his job after a cell phone video captured him punching a woman in the face during the city's annual Puerto Rican Day parade. Four days after the incident, 1.3 million people had viewed the video online. "All of our people should be conducting themselves like they are being recorded all the time," says Robin Larson of the Broward County (Florida) Sheriff's Department.[146]

CJ & TECHNOLOGY — SELF-SURVEILLANCE

AP Photo/*The Topeka Capital Journal*, Thad Allton

Law enforcement agents may soon be under constant surveillance—by their own superiors. At least 1,100 police agencies in the United States are using body-mounted video cameras to document traffic stops, arrests, and other encounters with suspects. These small, self-contained units clip to the officer's uniform, and include tiny radio microphones to record sound.

Some departments are also using head-worn video systems that "look" wherever an officer moves his or her head. Law enforcement agents hope that these devices will help protect them against unfounded charges of misconduct. "In this job we're frequently accused of things we haven't done, or things that [were] kind of embellished," says Bainbridge Island (Washington) police officer Ben Sias. "And the cameras show a pretty unbiased opinion of what actually did happen."

Thinking about Self-Surveillance
Dennis Kenney, a professor at New York's John Jay College of Criminal Justice, warns that this technology "raises tremendous privacy concerns." What are some of those concerns?

Ethics in Law Enforcement

Police corruption is intricately connected with the ethics of law enforcement officers. As you saw in Chapter 1, ethics has to do with fundamental questions of the fairness, justice, rightness, or wrongness of any action. Given the significant power that police officers hold, society expects very high standards of ethical behavior from them. These expectations are summed up in the *Police Code of Conduct,* which was developed by the International Association of Chiefs of Police in 1989.

To some extent, the *Police Code of Conduct* is self-evident: "A police officer will not engage in acts of corruption or bribery." In other aspects, it is idealistic, perhaps unreasonably so: "Officers will never allow personal feelings, animosities, or friendships to influence official conduct." The police working environment—rife with lying, cheating, lawbreaking, and violence—often does not allow for such ethical absolutes.

ETHICAL DILEMMAS Some police actions are obviously unethical, such as the behavior of the police officers who received kickbacks from the Baltimore auto body shop, described in a previous section. The majority of ethical dilemmas that a police officer will face are not so clear cut. Criminologists Joycelyn M. Pollock and Ronald F. Becker define an ethical dilemma as a situation in which law enforcement officers:

- Do not know the right course of action;
- Have difficulty doing what they consider to be right; and/or
- Find the wrong choice very tempting.[147]

Because of the many rules that govern policing—the subject of the next chapter—police officers often find themselves tempted by a phenomenon called **noble cause corruption.** This type of corruption occurs when, in the words of John P. Crank and Michael A. Caldero, "officers do bad things because they believe the outcomes will be good."[148] Examples include planting evidence or lying in court to help convict someone the officer knows to be guilty and the situation discussed in the feature *A Question of Ethics—The "Dirty Harry" Problem* below.

ELEMENTS OF ETHICS Pollock and Becker, both of whom have extensive experience as ethics instructors for police departments, further identify four categories of ethical dilemmas, involving discretion, duty, honesty, and loyalty.[149]

- *Discretion.* The law provides rigid guidelines for how police officers must act and how they cannot act, but it does not offer guidelines for how officers *should act* in many circumstances. As mentioned at the beginning of this chapter, police officers often use discretion to determine how they should act, and ethics plays an important role in guiding discretionary actions.

> **Noble Cause Corruption**
> Knowing misconduct by a police officer with the goal of attaining what the officer believes is a "just" result.

LEARNING **9** OBJECTIVE Explain what an ethical dilemma is and name four categories of ethical dilemmas that a police officer typically may face.

A QUESTION OF ETHICS   The "Dirty Harry" Problem

THE SITUATION A young girl has been kidnapped by a psychotic killer named Scorpio. Demanding a $200,000 ransom, Scorpio has buried the girl alive, leaving her with just enough oxygen to survive for a few hours. Detective Harry Callahan manages to find Scorpio, but the kidnapper stubbornly refuses to reveal the location of the girl. Callahan comes to the conclusion that the only way he can get this information from Scorpio in time is to beat it out of him.

THE ETHICAL DILEMMA The U.S. Constitution, as interpreted by the United States Supreme Court, forbids the torture of criminal suspects. Following proper procedure, Callahan should arrest Scorpio and advise him of his constitutional rights. If Scorpio requests an attorney, Callahan must comply. If the attorney then advises Scorpio to remain silent, there is nothing Callahan can do. Of course, after all this time, the girl will certainly be dead.*

WHAT IS THE SOLUTION? What should Detective Callahan do? According to the late Carl B. Klockars of the University of Delaware,

"Each time a police officer considers deceiving a suspect into confessing by telling him that his [or her] fingerprints were found at the scene or that a conspirator has already confessed, each time a police officer considers adding some untrue details to his [or her] account of a probable cause to legitimate a crucial stop or search [that police officer] faces" the same problem as Detective Callahan. Are police ever justified in using unlawful methods, no matter what good may ultimately be achieved?

* This scenario is taken from *Dirty Harry* (1971), one of the most popular police dramas of all time. In the film, Detective Callahan, played by Clint Eastwood, shoots Scorpio and then tortures him. Although Callahan eventually gets the information he needs, it is too late to save the girl.

Manfredxy/Shutterstock.com

On February 20, 2013, Vice President Joseph Biden presented Kitsap County (Washington) Deputy Sheriff Krista McDonald with the Public Safety Officer Medal of Valor. McDonald earned the honor for placing herself in the line of fire to rescue two fellow deputies who had been wounded in a shootout with a suspected sex offender. What role does the concept of duty play in a law enforcement agent's decision, regardless of her or his own safety, to protect the life of another person?
Mandel Ngan/AFP/Getty Images

- *Duty.* The concept of discretion is linked with **duty,** or the obligation to act in a certain manner. Society, by passing laws, can make a police officer's duty clearer and, in the process, help eliminate discretion from the decision-making process. But an officer's duty will not always be obvious, and ethical considerations can often supplement "the rules" of being a law enforcement agent.
- *Honesty.* Of course, honesty is a critical attribute for an ethical police officer. A law enforcement agent must make hundreds of decisions in a day, and most of them require him or her to be honest in order to properly do the job.
- *Loyalty.* What should a police officer do if he or she witnesses a partner using excessive force on a suspect? The choice often sets loyalty against ethics, especially if the officer does not condone the violence.

Although an individual's ethical makeup is determined by a multitude of personal factors, police departments can create an atmosphere that is conducive to professionalism. Brandon V. Zuidema and H. Wayne Duff, both captains with the Lynchburg (Virginia) Police Department, believe that law enforcement administrators can encourage ethical policing by:

1. Incorporating ethics into the department's mission statement.
2. Conducting internal training sessions in ethics.
3. Accepting "honest mistakes" and helping the officer learn from those mistakes.
4. Adopting a zero-tolerance policy toward unethical decisions when the mistakes are not so honest.[150]

SELF ASSESSMENT

Fill in the blanks and check your answers on page 205.

Police officers are held to high standards of _____, meaning that they are expected to be honest and respectful of the law. Misconduct such as accepting bribes or shaking down citizens is known as _____, and such behavior is investigated by _____ _____ units within police departments. In matters of ethics, a police officer is often guided by his or her sense of _____, or the obligation to act in a certain manner, and a feeling of _____ toward fellow officers.

Duty The moral sense of a police officer that she or he should behave in a certain manner.

CJ IN ACTION

THE DNA JUGGERNAUT

In August 2003, Katie Sepich, a graduate student at the University of New Mexico, was raped and strangled to death. Using a tiny amount of skin tissue from under Sepich's fingernails, the police were able to recover the DNA of her attacker. Authorities did not find a match until four years later, when Gabriel Avila was found guilty of burglary and was forced to provide a DNA sample. As it turned out, Avila had been arrested for other crimes just weeks after killing Sepich, and if his DNA had been taken at that point, he would quickly have been identified as her murderer. Collecting DNA from a person who has been arrested but not convicted of a crime is controversial, however, as we discuss in this chapter's *CJ in Action*.

EXPANDING DNA SAMPLING
Today, nearly every state collects DNA from all persons convicted of a felony. In addition, sixteen states gather DNA from those found guilty of a misdemeanor, and thirty-five do the same for juvenile felony offenders.[151] Twenty-eight states—including New Mexico, in the wake of the Katie Sepich situation—and the federal government are taking the process one step further. They have passed legislation that allows for DNA fingerprinting of those who have not been convicted of a felony but have merely been arrested.[152] Supporters of this strategy see it as similar, if not identical, to the common practice of recording the actual fingerprints of all arrestees.

THE CASE FOR
COLLECTING DNA FROM ARRESTEES
- The more comprehensive our DNA data banks, the higher the number of cold hits and other matches by law enforcement agencies. As a Virginia prosecutor puts it, "enhanced databases increase the chances of solving crimes."[153]

- Such measures are preventive, as they increase the odds that individuals who have committed violent crimes and are subsequently arrested on separate, less serious charges will wind up behind bars. One study conducted in Chicago identified fifty-three murders and rapes that could have been prevented by DNA fingerprinting of arrestees.[154]

- The public interest in law enforcement is more important than the privacy interests of individuals who have been arrested for criminal behavior.

THE CASE AGAINST
COLLECTING DNA FROM ARRESTEES
- Our criminal justice system is based on the premise that someone is innocent until proven guilty. An arrest does not equal guilt, and a person should not suffer the consequences of guilt until it has been proved in court. In California alone, approximately 420,000 people are arrested each year and never found guilty of wrongdoing.[155]

- Unlike fingerprints, DNA samples provide a wealth of personal information about a person, including genetic conditions and predisposition to disease. The government should not have access to this information following an arrest that does not lead to conviction.

- Forty percent of DNA profiles in the federal database belong to African Americans, and, given a greater law enforcement emphasis on immigration offenses, Hispanics could dominate such databases in the future.[156] Consequently, the system will exacerbate the perception by many that our criminal justice system is inherently biased.

YOUR OPINION—WRITING ASSIGNMENT
During a 2013 case involving the issue of DNA and arrestees, Supreme Court Justice Elena Kagan asked, "Why don't we [take DNA samples from] everybody who comes in for a driver's license?"[157] Taking into account that Kagan was being sarcastic, what point is she trying to make? What is your opinion of collecting DNA from arrestees, in general? Given what you learned about family DNA searching in this chapter, how might taking DNA from arrestees give police officers an incentive to act unethically? Before responding, you can review our discussions in this chapter concerning:

- Proactive arrest strategies (pages 180–182).

- DNA fingerprinting (pages 186–188).

- Police ethics and noble cause corruption (pages 200–202).

Your answer should include at least three full paragraphs.

CHAPTER **SUMMARY**

For more information on these concepts, look back to the Learning Objective icons throughout the chapter.

 Explain why police officers are allowed discretionary powers. Police officers are considered trustworthy and able to make honest decisions. They have experience and training. They are knowledgeable in criminal behavior. Finally, they must have the discretion to take reasonable steps to protect themselves.

 List the three primary purposes of police patrol. (a) The deterrence of crime, (b) the maintenance of public order, and (c) the provision of services that are not related to crime.

 Indicate some investigation strategies that are considered aggressive. Using undercover officers is considered an aggressive (and often dangerous) investigative technique. The use of informants is also aggressive, but involves danger for those who inform.

 Describe how forensic experts use DNA fingerprinting to solve crimes. Law enforcement agents gather trace evidence such as blood, semen, skin, or hair from the crime scene. Because these items are rich in DNA, which provides a unique genetic blueprint for every living organism, crime labs can create a DNA profile of the suspect and test it against other such profiles stored in databases. If the profiles match, then law enforcement agents have found a strong suspect for the crime.

 Explain why differential response strategies enable police departments to respond more efficiently to 911 calls. A differential response strategy allows a police department to distinguish among calls for service so that officers may respond to important calls more quickly. Therefore, a "hot" crime, such as a burglary in progress, will receive more immediate attention than a "cold" crime, such as a missing automobile that disappeared several days earlier.

 Explain community policing and its contribution to the concept of problem-oriented policing. Community policing involves proactive problem solving and a community-police partnership in which the community engages itself along with the police to address crime and the fear of crime in a particular geographic area. By establishing a cooperative presence in a community, police officers are better able to recognize the root causes of criminal behavior there and apply problem-oriented policing methods when necessary.

 Determine when police officers are justified in using deadly force. Police officers must make a reasonable judgment in determining when to use force that will place the suspect in threat of injury or death. That is, given the circumstances, the officer must reasonably assume that the use of such force is necessary to avoid serious injury or death to the officer or someone else.

 Identify the three traditional forms of police corruption. The three traditional forms are bribery, shakedowns, and mooching.

 Explain what an ethical dilemma is and name four categories of ethical dilemmas that a police officer typically may face. An ethical dilemma is a situation in which police officers (a) do not know the right course of action, (b) have difficulty doing what they consider to be right, and/or (c) find the wrong choice very tempting. The four types of ethical dilemmas involve (a) discretion, (b) duty, (c) honesty, and (d) loyalty.

QUESTIONS FOR **CRITICAL ANALYSIS**

1. Mandatory arrest laws regarding domestic violence have had two unintended consequences. First, more women are being arrested for assault. Second, more dual arrests are occurring, in which police officers arrest both parties in a domestic violence incident. Why are these trends a natural consequence of limiting police discretion in this area?

2. In speaking with a domestic terrorism suspect, a paid FBI informant said, "Allah has more work for you to do," adding, "Revelation is going to come in your dreams that you have to do this thing." The "thing" was to shoot down American military airplanes with handheld missiles. If you were defending the terrorism suspect in court, how would you use this evidence? Why would your efforts be likely to fail?

3. Criminologists John and Emily Beck suggest that crime reduction strategies should treat crime as if it were a form of pollution. How does this comparison make sense in the context of predictive policing and crime mapping?

4. Relate the concept of "broken windows" to high-crime neighborhoods and potential ways to combat crime in such neighborhoods.

5. How might cultural differences between police officers and residents of the neighborhoods they patrol contribute to increased use of officer force in those neighborhoods?

KEY **TERMS**

ballistics   180
blue curtain   191
body armor   192
broken windows theory   187
bureaucracy   172
burnout   193
citizen oversight   199
clearance rate   179
cold case   179
cold hit   181
community policing   188
conducted energy device (CED)   196
confidential informant (CI)   177
crime mapping   186

deadly force   194
delegation of authority   173
detective   176
differential response   184
directed patrol   185
DNA fingerprinting   180
duty   202
forensics   179
hot spots   186
incident-driven policing   183
internal affairs unit (IAU)   199
mandatory arrest law   171
noble cause corruption   201
police corruption   198

police subculture   190
policy   170
proactive arrests   187
problem-oriented policing   189
professionalism   196
random patrol   184
reactive arrests   186
reasonable force   194
response time   183
socialization   190
stressors   193
trace evidence   179

SELF ASSESSMENT **ANSWER KEY**

Page 172: i. discretion; **ii.** policy; **iii.** mandatory arrest

Page 182: i. Patrol; **ii.** deter; **iii.** presence; **iv.** Detectives; **v.** forensics; **vi.** DNA fingerprinting

Page 189: i. incident; **ii.** service; **iii.** random; **iv.** Directed; **v.** proactive; **vi.** Community

Page 196: i. subculture; **ii.** physical; **iii.** stress; **iv.** reasonable; **v.** deadly

Page 202: i. professionalism; **ii.** corruption; **iii.** internal affairs; **iv.** duty; **v.** loyalty

NOTES

1. Richard R. Johnson, "Police Officer Job Satisfaction: A Multidimensional Analysis," *Police Quarterly* (June 2012), 158–160.

2. Kenneth Culp David, *Police Discretion* (St. Paul, MN: West Publishing Co., 1975).

3. C. E. Pratt, "Police Discretion," *Law and Order* (March 1992), 99–100.

4. "More than a Hunch," *Law Enforcement News* (September 2004), 1.

5. Herbert Jacob, *Urban Justice* (Boston: Little, Brown, 1973), 27.

6. Larry Copeland, "Chases by Police Yield High Fatalities," *USA Today* (April 23, 2010), 3A.

7. John Monk, "Deadly December Car Chase into Columbia Raises Questions," *The Slate (Columbia, SC)* (December 23, 2012), at **www.thestate.com/2013/01/19/2595602/deadly-december-car-chase-into.html**.

8. Bureau of Justice Statistics, *Local Police Departments, 2003* (Washington, D.C.: U.S. Department of Justice, May 2006), 24.

9. Jack Richter, "Number of Police Pursuits Drop Dramatically in Los Angeles," *Los Angeles Police Department Press Release* (August 20, 2003).

10. L. Craig Parker, Robert D. Meier, and Lynn Hunt Monahan, *Interpersonal Psychology for Criminal Justice* (St. Paul, MN: West Publishing Co., 1989), 113.

11. National Institute of Justice, "Table 1. States with Mandatory Arrest Provisions," at **www.nij.gov/publications/dv-dual-arrest-222679/exhibits/table1.htm**.

12. David Hirschel, Eve Buzawa, April Pattavina, and Don Faggiani, "Domestic Violence and Mandatory Arrest Laws: To What Extent Do They Influence Police Arrest Decisions?" *Journal of Criminal Law and Criminology* (Fall 2007), 255–298.

13. *Town of Castle Rock v. Gonzales,* 545 U.S. 748, 760 (2005).

14. Peter K. Manning, *Police Work: The Social Organization of Policing,* 2d ed. (Prospect Heights, IL: Waveland Press, 1997), 96.

15 Samuel Walker, *The Police in America: An Introduction,* 2d ed. (New York: McGraw-Hill, 1992), 16.

16. George L. Kelling and Mark H. Moore, "From Political to Reform to Community: The Evolving Strategy of Police," in *Community Policing:*

Rhetoric or Reality, ed. Jack Greene and Stephen Mastrofski (New York: Praeger Publishers, 1988), 13.

17. Michael White, *Controlling Officer Behavior in the Field* (New York: John Jay College of Criminal Justice, 2011), 19.

18. John S. Dempsey and Linda S. Forst, *An Introduction to Policing,* 6th ed. (Clifton Park, NY: Delmar Cengage Learning, 2011), 84.

19. *Ibid.,* 86–87.

20. Karen L. Amendola, "Schedule Matters: The Movement to Compressed Work Weeks," *The Police Chief* (May 2012), 30–35.

21. Henry M. Wrobleski and Karen M. Hess, *Introduction to Law Enforcement and Criminal Justice,* 7th ed. (Belmont, CA: Wadsworth/ Thomson Learning, 2003), 119.

22. Bureau of Justice Statistics, *Local Police Departments, 2007* (Washington, D.C.: U.S. Department of Justice, December 2010), 6.

23. Connie Fletcher, "What Cops Know," *On Patrol* (Summer 1996), 44–45.

24. David H. Bayley, *Police for the Future* (New York: Oxford University Press, 1994), 20.

25. Walker, 103.

26. Eric J. Scott, *Calls for Service: Citizens Demand an Initial Police Response* (Washington, D.C.: National Institute of Justice, 1981), 28–30.

27. William G. Gay, Theodore H. Schell, and Stephen Schack, *Routine Patrol: Improving Patrol Productivity,* vol. 1 (Washington, D.C.: National Institute of Justice, 1977), 3–6.

28. Gary W. Cordner, "The Police on Patrol," in *Police and Policing: Contemporary Issues,* ed. Dennis Jay Kenney (New York: Praeger Publishers, 1989), 60–71.

29. Anthony V. Bouza, *The Police Mystique: An Insider's Look at Cops, Crime, and the Criminal Justice System* (New York: Plenum Press, 1990), 27.

30. Peter W. Greenwood and Joan Petersilia, *The Criminal Investigation Process: Summary and Policy Implications* (Santa Monica, CA: RAND Corporation, 1975).

31. Fletcher, 46.

32. Quoted in Sarah Stillman, "The Throwaways," *New Yorker* (September 3, 2012), 38–39.

33. Center on Law and Security, *Terrorist Trial Report Card: September 11, 2001–September 11, 2009* (New York: New York University School of Law, January 2010), 42–44.

34. Richard A. Serrano, "D.C. Bomb Plot Foiled," *Baltimore Sun* (February 18, 2012), 10A.

35. Debbie Siegelbaum, "Authorities Foil Planned Suicide Bombing Attack on Capitol Building," *The Hill* (February 17, 2012), at **thehill.com /homenews/news/211447-authoritiesfoil-planned-suicide -bombing-attack-on-capitol-building**.

36. Quoted in Kirk Johnson, "In 2010 Portland Bomb Plot, a Question of Manipulation or Violent Extremism," *New York Times* (January 12, 2013), A12.

37. David Shipler, "Terrorist Plots, Hatched by the FBI," *New York Times* (April 29, 2012), SR4.

38. Federal Bureau of Investigation, *Crime in the United States, 2011* (Washington, D.C.: U.S. Department of Justice, 2012), at **www.fbi.gov /about-us/cjis/ucr/crime-in-the-u.s/2011/crime-in-the-u.s. -2011/tables/table_25**.

39. James M. Cronin, Gerard R. Murphy, Lisa L. Spahr, Jessica I. Toliver, and Richard E. Weger, *Promoting Effective Homicide Investigations* (Washington, D.C.: Police Executive Research Forum, August 2007), 102–103.

40. Robert C. Davis, Carl Jenses, and Karin E. Kitchens, *Cold Case Investigations: An Analysis of Current Practices and Factors Associated with Successful Outcomes* (Santa Monica, CA: RAND Corporation, 2011), xii.

41. Ronald F. Becker, *Criminal Investigations,* 2d ed. (Sudbury, MA: Jones & Bartlett, 2004), 7.

42. Bureau of Justice Statistics, *Census of Publicly Funded Forensic Crime Laboratories, 2009* (Washington, D.C.: U.S. Department of Justice, August 2012), 1.

43. Joseph Peterson, Ira Sommers, Deborah Baskin, and Donald Johnson, *The Role and Impact of Forensic Evidence in the Criminal Justice Process* (Washington, D.C.: National Institute of Justice, September 2010), 8–9.

44. Simon A. Cole, "More Than Zero: Accounting for Error in Latent Fingerprinting Identification," *Journal of Criminal Law and Criminology* (Spring 2005), 985–1078.

45. Quoted in "New DNA Database Helps Crack 1979 N.Y. Murder Case," *Miami Herald* (March 14, 2000), 18A.

46. Judith E. Lewter, "The Use of Forensic DNA in Criminal Cases in Kentucky as Compared with Other Selected States," *Kentucky Law Journal* (1997–1998), 223.

47. "CODIS—NDIS Statistics," at **www.fbi.gov/about-us/lab/biometric -analysis/codis/ndis-statistics**.

48. Nancy Ritter, "DNA Solves Property Crimes (But Are We Ready for That?)," *NIJ Journal* (October 2008), 2–12.

49. Evan Pellegrino, "UA Team Adds Precision to DNA Forensics," *Arizona Daily Star* (March 3, 2009), A1; and Gautam Naik, "To Sketch a Thief: Genes Draw Likeness of Suspects," *Wall Street Journal* (March 29, 2009), A9.

50. NBC News Staff, "Visit Detroit at Your Own Risk" (October 8, 2012), at **usnews.nbcnews.com/_news/2012/10/08/14294269-visit-detroit -at-your-own-risk-police-union-warns?lite**.

51. "63 Percent of Local Police Departments Are Facing Cuts in Their Total Funding, Survey Shows." Police Executive Research Forum, January 2009, at **www.policeforum.org/library/press-releases/PERF %20Survey%20on%20Policing%20&%20Economy.pdf**.

52. Ian Lovett, "A Poorer San Bernardino, and a More Dangerous One, Too," *New York Times* (January 15, 2013), A12.

53. Quoted in Erica Goode, "Crime Increases in Sacramento after Deep Cuts to Police Force," *New York Times* (November 4, 2012), A26.

54. Wrobleski and Hess, 173.

55. Quoted in Darren DaRonco, "Cash Cuts Faulted for Cops' Slow Response," *Arizona Daily Star* (December 9, 2012), C1.

56. National Institute of Justice, *Managing Calls to the Police with 911/311 Systems* (Washington, D.C.: U.S. Department of Justice, February 5, 2005).

57. Stephen J. Blumberg and Julian V. Luke, *Wireless Substitution: Early Release of Estimates From the National Health Interview Survey, January– June 2012* (Washington, D.C.: Centers for Disease Control, December 2012), 1.

58. Eddie Reyes, "Next Generation 9-1-1: What It Is—and Why Police Chiefs Should Care," *The Police Chief* (December 2012), 86–87.

59. Cody W. Telep and David Weisburd, "What Is Known about the Effectiveness of Police Practices in Reducing Crime and Disorder?" *Police Quarterly* (December 2012), 344.

60. *Ibid.*

61. *Local Police Departments, 2007,* Table 12, page 15.

62. George L. Kelling, Tony Pate, Duane Dieckman, and Charles Brown, *The Kansas City Preventive Patrol Experiment: A Summary Report* (Washington, D.C.: The Police Foundation, 1974), 3–4.

63. Carl B. Klockars and Stephen D. Mastrofski, "The Police and Serious Crime," in *Thinking about Police,* ed. Carl B. Klockars and Stephen Mastrofski (New York: McGraw-Hill, 1990), 130.

64. Anthony M. Pate, "Experimenting with Foot Patrol: The Newark Experience," in Dennis P. Rosenbaum, ed., *Community Crime Prevention: Does It Work?* (Newbury Park, CA: Sage, 1986).

65. Jerry H. Ratcliffe, et al., "The Philadelphia Foot Patrol Experiment: A Randomized Controlled Trial of Police Patrol Effectiveness in Violent Crime Hotspots," *Criminology* (August 2011), 795–830.

66. Quoted in Erica Goode, "Sending the Police before There's a Crime," *New York Times* (August 16, 2011), A11.

67. Lawrence W. Sherman, "Policing for Crime Prevention," in *Contemporary Policing: Controversies, Challenges, and Solutions,* ed. Quint C. Thurman and Jihong Zhao (Los Angeles: Roxbury Publishing Co., 2004), 62.

68. Lawrence W. Sherman and David Weisburd, "General Deterrent Effects of Police Patrol in Crime 'Hot Spots': A Randomized Controlled Trial," *Justice Quarterly* (December 1995), 625–648.

69. Renée J. Mitchell, "Hot-Spot Randomized Control Works for Sacramento," *The Police Chief* (February 2013), 12.

70. David Weisburd and Cynthia Lum, "The Diffusion of Computerized Crime Mapping in Policing: Linking Research and Practice," *Police Practice and Research* 6 (2005), 419–434.

71. Quoted in "New Model Police," *Economist* (June 9, 2007), 29.

72. Sherman, 63–66.

73. *Ibid.*, 65.

74. William Sousa and George L. Kelling, "Of 'Broken Windows,' Criminology, and Criminal Justice," in *Police Innovation: Contrasting Perspectives*, ed. David L. Weisburd and Anthony A. Braga (New York: Cambridge University Press, 2006), 77–97.

75. Anthony A. Braga and Brenda J. Bond, "Policing Crime and Disorder Hot Spots: A Randomized Controlled Trial," *Criminology* (August 2008), 579.

76. Ralph B. Taylor, "Incivilities Reduction Policing, Zero Tolerance, and the Retreat from Coproduction: Weak Foundations and Strong Pressures," in *Police Innovation: Contrasting Perspectives*, ed. David L. Weisburd and Anthony A. Braga (New York: Cambridge University Press, 2006), 133–153.

77. Mark H. Moore and George L. Kelling, "'To Serve and Protect': Learning from Police History," *Public Interest* (Winter 1983), 54–57.

78. Brigitte Gassaway, Steven Armon, and Dana Perez, "Engaging the Community: Operation Heat Wave," *Geography and Public Safety* (October 2011), 8–9.

79. George Kelling, "Police and Community: The Quiet Revolution," in *Perspectives in Policing* (Washington, D.C.: National Institute of Justice, 1988).

80. *Local Police Departments, 2003*, 19.

81. Wesley K. Skogan and Megan Alderden, *Police and the Community* (Washington, D.C.: National Police Research Platform, February 2011), 4.

82. *Ibid.*, 5–6.

83. National Institute of Justice Preview, *Community Policing Strategies* (Washington, D.C.: Office of Justice Programs, November 1995), 1.

84. Jihong Zhao and Quint C. Thurman, "Community Policing: Where Are We Now?" *Crime and Delinquency* (July 1997), 345–357.

85. Robert C. Trojanowicz and David Carter, "The Philosophy and Role of Community Policing," at **www.cj.msu.edu/~people/cp/cpphil.html**.

86. Tom Casady, "Beyond Arrest: Using Crime Analysis to Prevent Crime," *The Police Chief* (September 2008), 24.

87. Herman Goldstein, "Improving Policing: A Problem-Oriented Approach," *Crime and Delinquency* 25 (1979), 236–258.

88. Bureau of Justice Assistance, *Problem-Oriented Drug Enforcement: A Community-Based Approach for Effective Policing* (Washington, D.C.: Office of Justice Programs, 1993), 5.

89. J. Pete Blair, et al., "Reasonableness and Reaction Time," *Police Quarterly* (December 2011), 324.

90. William A. Geller and Michael S. Scott, *Deadly Force: What We Know* (Washington, D.C.: Police Executive Research Forum, 1992).

91. Blair, et al., 327.

92. Harry J. Mullins, "Myth, Tradition, and Ritual," *Law and Order* (September 1995), 197.

93. William Westly, *Violence and the Police: A Sociological Study of Law, Custom, and Morality* (Cambridge, MA: MIT Press, 1970).

94. Wallace Graves, "Police Cynicism: Causes and Cures," *FBI Law Enforcement Bulletin* (June 1996), 16–21.

95. Robert Regoli, *Police in America* (Washington, D.C.: R. F. Publishing, 1977).

96. Bob Herbert, "A Cop's View," *New York Times* (March 15, 1998), 17.

97. Officer Down Memorial Page, at **www.odmp.org/search/year/2013?ref=sidebar and www.odmp.org/search/year?year=2012**.

98. Federal Bureau of Investigation, *Law Enforcement Officers Killed and Assaulted, 2011* (Washington, D.C.: U.S. Department of Justice, 2012), at **www.fbi.gov/about-us/cjis/ucr/leoka/2011/officers-assaulted-1/officers-assaulted**.

99. John S. Dempsey and Linda S. Forst, *An Introduction to Policing*, 6th ed. (Clifton Park, NY: Delmar Cengage Learning, 2011), 170.

100. Bureau of Justice Statistics, *Contacts between Police and the Public, 2008* (Washington, D.C.: U.S. Department of Justice, October 2011), 1.

101. Joseph A. Schafer, *Policing 2020: Exploring the Future of Crime, Communities, and Policing* (Washington, D.C.: Federal Bureau of Investigation, 2007), 381–387.

102. Dempsey and Forst, 170.

103. Heath Grant, et al., *Body Armor Use, Care, and Performance in Real World Conditions: Findings from a National Survey* (Washington, D.C.: Police Executive Research Forum, November 2012), 2, 49.

104. Steven G. Brandl and Meghan S. Stroshine, "The Physical Hazards of Police Work Revisited," *Police Quarterly* (September 2012), 263.

105. The Officer Down Memorial Page; and Craig W. Floyd and Kevin P. Morrison, "Officer Safety on Our Roadways: What the Numbers Say about Saving Lives," *The Police Chief* (July 2010), 28.

106. National Highway Traffic Safety Administration, *Characteristics of Law Enforcement Officers' Fatalities in Motor Vehicle Crashes* (Washington, D.C.: U.S. Department of Transportation, January 2011), Figure 15, page 25.

107. Rebecca Kanable, "Going Home at Night," *Law Enforcement Technology* (January 2009), 23–24.

108. University at Buffalo, "Impact of Stress on Police Officers' Physical and Mental Health," *Science Daily* (September 29, 2008), at **www.sciencedaily.com/releases/2008/09/080926105029.htm**.

109. Quoted in *ibid.*

110. Gail A. Goolsakian, et al., *Coping with Police Stress* (Washington, D.C.: National Institute of Justice, 1985).

111. J. L. O'Neil and M. A. Cushing, *The Impact of Shift Work on Police Officers* (Washington, D.C.: Police Executive Research Forum, 1991), 1.

112. "Impact of Stress on Police Officers' Physical and Mental Health."

113. James Hibberd, "Police Psychology," *On Patrol* (Fall 1996), 26.

114. M. J. Horowitz, N. Wilner, N. B. Kaltreider, and W. Alvarez, "Signs and Symptoms of Post Traumatic Stress Disorder," *Archives of General Psychiatry* 37 (1980), 85–92.

115. Daniel W. Clark, Elizabeth K. White, and John M. Violanti, "Law Enforcement Suicide: Current Knowledge and Future Directions," *The Police Chief* (May 2012), 48.

116. Lawrence M. Friedman, *Crime and Punishment in American History* (New York: Basic Books, 1993), 362.

117. Bureau of Justice Statistics, *Contacts between Police and the Public, 2008*, 14.

118. Bureau of Justice Statistics, *Arrest-Related Deaths, 2003–2009, Statistical Tables* (Washington, D.C.: U.S. Department of Justice, November 2011), 1.

119. David J. Spotts, "Reviewing Use-of-Force Practices," *The Police Chief* (August 2012), 12.

120. H. Range Hutson, Deirdre Anglin, Phillip Rice, Demetrious N. Kyriacou, Michael Guirguis, and Jared Strote, "Excessive Use of Force by Police: A Survey of Academic Emergency Physicians," *Emergency Medicine Journal* (January 2009), 20–22.

121. 471 U.S. 1 (1985).

122. 471 U.S. 1, 11 (1985).

123. 490 U.S. 386 (1989).

124. *Brosseau v. Haugen*, 543 U.S. 194 (2004).

125. *Local Police Departments, 2007*, Table 14, page 17.

126. Geoffrey P. Alpert, et al., *Police Use of Force, Tasers, and other Less-than-Lethal Weapons* (Washington, D.C.: National Institute of Justice, 2011), 1–3.

127. William P. Bozeman, et al., "Safety and Injury Profile of Conducted Electrical Weapons Used by Law Enforcement Officers against Criminal Suspects," *Annals of Emergency Medicine* 53 (2009), 480–489.

128. Amnesty International, Press Release, "Amnesty International Urges Stricter Limits on Police Taser Use as U.S. Death Toll Reaches 500" (February 15, 2012), at **www.amnestyusa.org/news/press-releases /amnesty-international-urges-stricter-limits-on-police-taser -use-as-us-death-toll-reaches-500**.

129. Michael D. White, et al., "An Incident-Level Profile of TASER Device Deployments in Arrest-Related Deaths," *Police Quarterly* (March 2013), 97–98.

130. Tom Tyler, "Legitimacy and Cooperation: Why Do People Help the Police Fight Crime in Their Communities?" *Yale Law School Legal Scholarship Repository* (January 2008), 234–236.

131. Matthew S. Crow and Brittany Adrion, "Focal Concerns and Police Use of Force: Examining the Factors Associated with Taser Use," *Police Quarterly* (December 2011), 381.

132. *Contacts between Police and the Public, 2008,* 1.

133. *Ibid.,* Table 8, page 12.

134. Tammy Rinehart Kochel, David B. Wilson, and Stephen Mastrofski, "Effect of Suspect Race on Officers' Arrest Decisions," *Criminology* (August 2011), 498.

135. Randall L. Kennedy, "*McClesky v. Kemp,* Race, Capital Punishment, and the Supreme Court," *Harvard Law Review* 101 (1988), 1436–1438.

136. Douglas A. Smith, "Minorities and the Police: Attitudinal and Behavioral Questions," in *Race and Criminal Justice,* ed. Michael J. Lynch and E. Britt Patterson (New York: Harrow & Heston, 1991), 28–30.

137. Matt Lait and Scott Glover, "Inglewood Police Accused of Abuse in Other Cases," *Los Angeles Times* (July 15, 2002), A1.

138. Bouza, 72.

139. Knapp Commission, *Report on Police Corruption* (New York: Brazilier, 1973).

140. Robert J. Kane and Michael D. White, "Bad Cops: A Study of Career-Ending Misconduct among New York City Police Officers," *Criminology & Public Policy* (November 2009), 764.

141. Lawrence W. Sherman, "Becoming Bent: Moral Careers of Corrupt Policemen," in *Police Corruption: A Sociological Perspective,* ed. Lawrence W. Sherman (Garden City, NY: Doubleday, 1974), 191–208.

142. Quoted in Jennifer Dukes and Loren Keller, "Can Police Be Police to Selves?" *Omaha World-Herald* (February 22, 1998), 1A.

143. John Schwartz, "New Orleans Police, Mired in Scandal, Accept Plan for Overhaul," *New York Times* (July 25, 2012), A1.

144. "Roster of Civilian Oversight Agencies in the U.S.," National Association for Civilian Oversight of Law Enforcement, at **www.nacole.org**.

145. Hazel Glenn Beh, "Municipal Liability for Failure to Investigate Citizen Complaints against Police," *Fordham Urban Law Journal* 23 (Winter 1998), 209.

146. Quoted in Kevin Johnson, "For Cops, Citizen Videos Bring Increased Scrutiny," *USA Today* (October 15, 2010), 1A.

147. Jocelyn M. Pollock and Ronald F. Becker, "Ethics Training Using Officers' Dilemmas," *FBI Law Enforcement Bulletin* (November 1996), 20–28.

148. Quoted in Thomas J. Martinelli, "Dodging the Pitfalls of Noble Cause Corruption and the Intelligence Unit," *The Police Chief* (October 2009), 124.

149. Pollock and Becker, 20–28.

150. Brandon V. Zuidema and H. Wayne Duff, "Organizational Ethics through Effective Leadership," *Law Enforcement Bulletin* (March 2009), 8–9.

151. Solomon Moore, "FBI and States Vastly Expanding Databases of DNA," *New York Times* (April 19, 2009), 1.

152. Julie Samuels, Elizabeth Davies, Dwight Pope and Ashleigh Holand, "Collecting DNA From Arrestees: Implementation Lessons," *NIJ Journal* (June 2012), 19–21.

153. Quoted in Ellen Sorokin, "Attorney General Hopefuls Favor More DNA Collection," *Washington Times* (August 7, 2001), C1.

154. Referenced in Eileen Sullivan, "Feds to Collect DNA from Every Person They Arrest," *Associated Press* (April 16, 2008).

155. Kamala D. Harris, *Crime in California, 2011* (Sacramento, CA: California Department of Justice, 2012), 2, 18.

156. Moore, 19.

157. Quoted in Adam Liptak, "Justices Wrestle Over Allowing DNA Sampling at Time of Arrest," *New York Times* (February 27, 2013), A18.

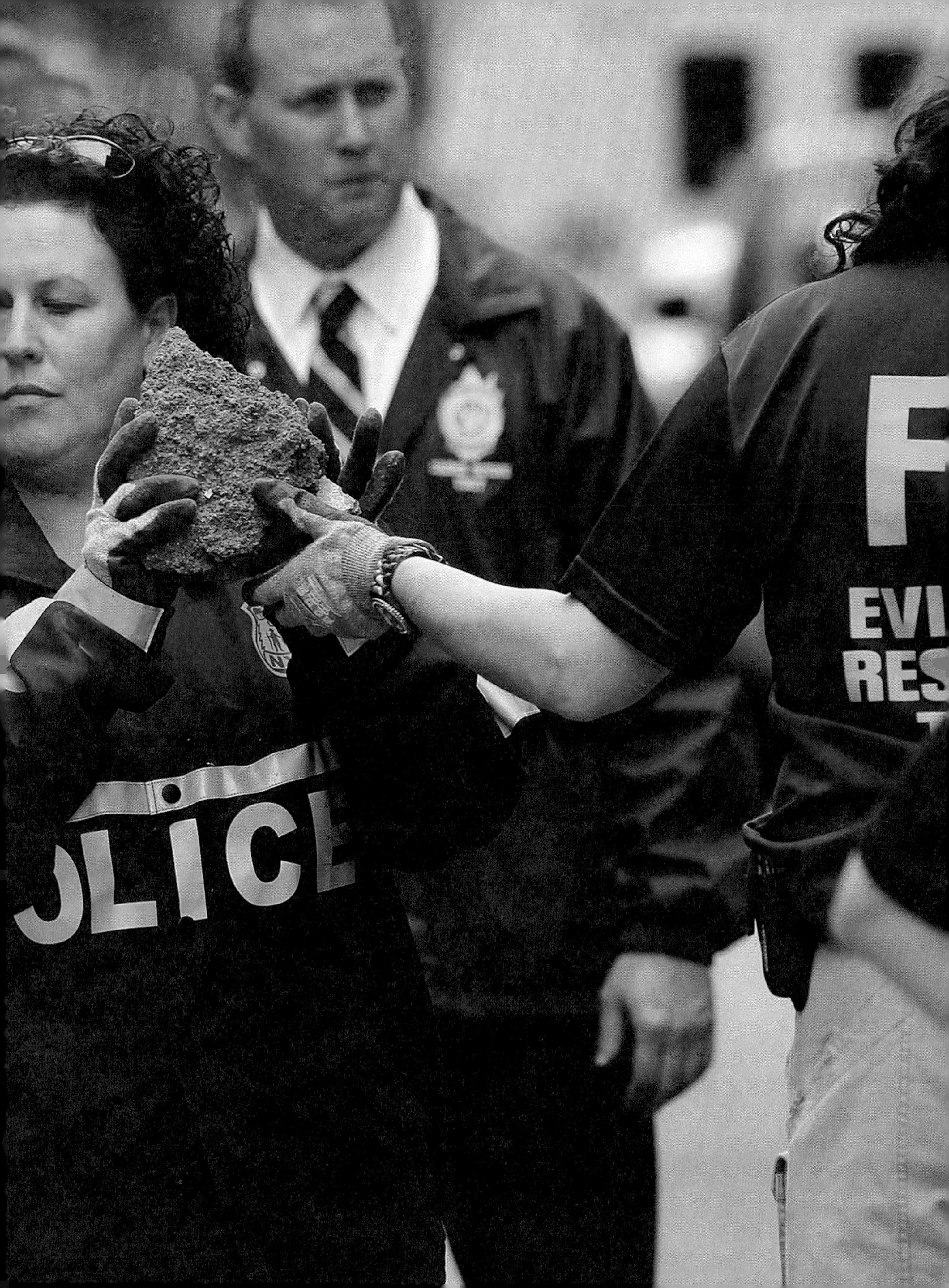
OLICE
EVI
RES

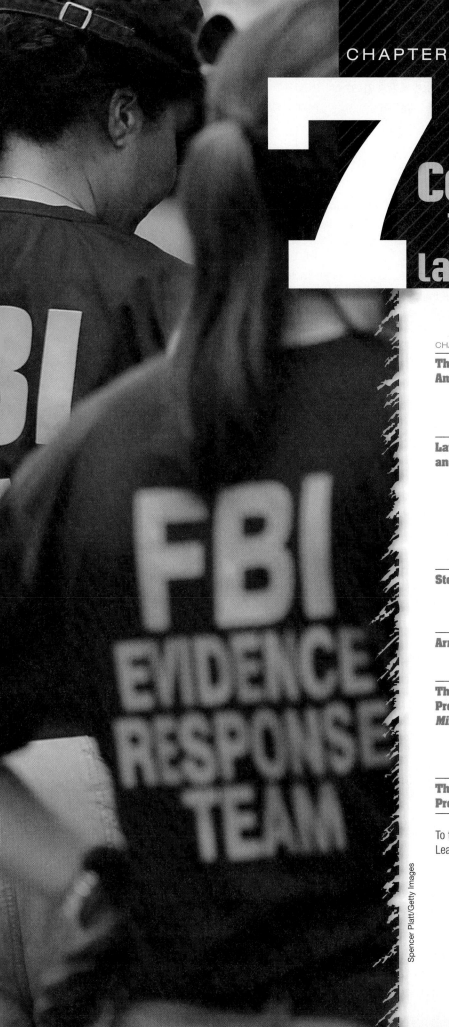

CHAPTER

7 Police and the Constitution: The Rules of Law Enforcement

To target your study and review, look for these numbered Learning Objective icons throughout the chapter.

Spencer Platt/Getty Images

WHAT'S THAT SMELL?

FOR THE THREE Lexington-Fayette (Kentucky) narcotics officers, the odds of making the correct decision seemed fifty-fifty. They had just followed a suspected drug dealer into the breezeway of an apartment complex and saw two doors, one on the left and one on the right. They knew the suspect had entered one of the apartments, but they had no way of determining which one. Then the officers smelled marijuana smoke coming from the apartment on the left. They immediately started banging on that door, yelling, "This is the police!" After hearing suspicious movements inside, the officers forced themselves into the apartment.

They did not find their suspect. Instead, the officers discovered Hollis King and two friends sitting on his sofa, smoking marijuana. A quick search of the apartment uncovered a stash of marijuana, powder and crack cocaine, and cash. King was arrested, convicted of several drug-related offenses, and sentenced to eleven years in prison. He appealed the conviction, claiming that the narcotics officers had improperly burst into and searched his apartment.

Generally, law enforcement agents cannot enter any sort of dwelling without consent from an inhabitant or written permission from a judge, called a *warrant*. As you will learn later in the chapter, however, the warrant requirement does not apply under certain "exigent," or urgent, circumstances. In this case, the narcotics officers believed that the suspicious noises they heard were made by someone destroying evidence, thus creating an exigent circumstance. Several years ago, the United States Supreme Court ruled in favor of the Lexington-Lafayette officers, holding that their actions were justified even though, as it turned out, the original suspect was not in King's apartment. According to Justice Samuel Alito, the officers' "warrantless entry to prevent the destruction of evidence is reasonable and thus allowed."

1. Hollis King's lawyers argued that if the police officers had not erroneously knocked on their client's door, they would not have heard the mysterious noises that allowed them to enter his apartment. Should law enforcement agents be able to benefit from their own mistakes in this manner? Why or why not?

2. In this case, the "exigent" circumstance that allowed the police to enter King's apartment was the possible destruction of evidence. Can you think of some other urgent circumstances that might allow law enforcement agents to enter a house without consent or a warrant?

3. In Chapter 3, we learned that possession of small amounts of marijuana is now legal in the states of Colorado and Washington. In a scenario with the same facts as the King arrest, how would the legalization of marijuana affect the "reasonableness" of the police officers' actions?

Robert Nickelsberg/Getty Images

Through its decisions, the United States Supreme Court determines the guidelines that law enforcement officers must follow when entering and searching apartments and other dwellings.

THE FOURTH AMENDMENT

In *Kentucky v. King*, the Supreme Court did not address whether Hollis King was guilty or innocent of the charges against him. That was for the trial court to decide. Rather, the Court ruled that the Lexington-Fayette narcotics officers had not overstepped the boundaries of their authority in entering and searching King's apartment.[1] In the previous chapter, we discussed the importance of discretion for police officers. This discretion, as we noted, is not absolute. A law enforcement agent's actions are greatly determined by the rules for policing set down in the U.S. Constitution and enforced by the courts.

To understand these rules, law enforcement officers must understand the Fourth Amendment, which reads as follows:

> The right of the people to be secure in their persons, houses, papers, and effects, against unreasonable searches and seizures, shall not be violated, and no Warrants shall issue, but upon probable cause, supported by Oath or affirmation, and particularly describing the place to be searched, and the persons or things to be seized.

This amendment contains two critical legal concepts: a prohibition against *unreasonable* **searches and seizures** and the requirement of **probable cause** to issue a warrant.

Searches and Seizures The legal term, as found in the Fourth Amendment to the U.S. Constitution, that generally refers to the searching for and the confiscating of evidence by law enforcement agents.

Probable Cause Reasonable grounds to believe the existence of facts warranting certain actions, such as the search or arrest of a person.

Reasonableness

Law enforcement personnel use searches and seizures to look for and collect the evidence prosecutors need to convict individuals suspected of crimes. As you have just read, when police are conducting a search or seizure, they must be *reasonable*. Though courts have spent innumerable hours scrutinizing the word, no specific meaning for *reasonable* exists. A thesaurus can provide useful synonyms—logical, practical, sensible, intelligent, plausible—but because each case is different, those terms are relative.

In the *King* case, the Supreme Court rejected the argument that the search had been so unreasonable as to violate the Fourth Amendment's prohibition against unreasonable searches and seizures. That does not mean that the police officers' actions would have been reasonable under any circumstances. What if the narcotics officers, after having lost the trail of their suspected drug dealer, had begun randomly kicking down doors in the apartment complex, eventually discovering Hollis King and his illegal drug stash? Under those circumstances, their conduct would almost certainly have been considered unreasonable.

Indeed, one Supreme Court justice, Ruth Bader Ginsburg, did believe that the officers in the *King* case had acted unreasonably. The Court's decision, she warned, "arms the police with a way routinely to dishonor the Fourth Amendment's warrant requirement."[2] For example, she noted, law enforcement agents can now simply roam the hallways of apartment buildings, knock whenever they smell marijuana, and make a forced entry if they think they hear something suspicious.[3]

Probable Cause

The concept of reasonableness is linked to probable cause. The Supreme Court has ruled, for example, that any arrest or seizure is unreasonable unless it is supported by probable cause.[4] The burden of probable cause requires more than mere suspicion on a police officer's part. The officer must know of facts and circumstances that would reasonably lead to "the belief that an offense has been or is being committed."[5]

SOURCES OF PROBABLE CAUSE If no probable cause existed when a police officer took a certain action, it cannot be retroactively applied. If, for example, a police officer stops a

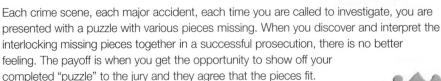

WILLIAM HOWE
POLICE DETECTIVE

FAST FACTS

POLICE DETECTIVE, JOB DESCRIPTION:

- Collect evidence and obtain facts pertaining to criminal cases.
- Conduct interviews, observe suspects, examine records, and help with raids and busts.

WHAT KIND OF TRAINING IS REQUIRED?

- 2–5 years' experience as a police patrol officer is required before testing to become a detective.
- Larger departments require 60 units of college credit or an associate's degree.

ANNUAL SALARY RANGE?

- $43,920–$76,350

Each crime scene, each major accident, each time you are called to investigate, you are presented with a puzzle with various pieces missing. When you discover and interpret the interlocking missing pieces together in a successful prosecution, there is no better feeling. The payoff is when you get the opportunity to show off your completed "puzzle" to the jury and they agree that the pieces fit. When I once thrilled at the chase of the bad guy through the alleys and neighborhoods, I now enjoy even more pursuing them with the mental skills I have developed—accident reconstruction, fingerprint identification, and the interpretation of crime scenes. This can be every bit as rewarding as the foot pursuit, not to mention ever so much easier on the body.

Having been in police work for thirty-five years, I have been assaulted only four times on the job (two of which were at gunpoint). This confirmed for me, once and for all, the importance of being able to use your mind rather than your size to, first, talk your way out of trouble and, second, talk the bad guys into going along with your plans for them.

SOCIAL MEDIA CAREER TIP For your profile photo, stick with a close-up, business-appropriate photo in which you are smiling and wearing something you would wear as a potential employee. Avoid symbols, party photos, long-distance shots, or baby pictures.

---

person for jaywalking and then finds several ounces of marijuana in that person's pocket, the arrest for marijuana possession would probably be disallowed. Remember, suspicion does not equal probable cause. If, however, an informant had tipped the officer off that the person was a drug dealer, probable cause might exist and the arrest could be valid. Informants are one of several sources that may provide probable cause. Others include:

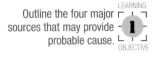

Outline the four major sources that may provide probable cause. **LEARNING OBJECTIVE 1**

1. *Personal observation.* Police officers may use their personal training, experience, and expertise to infer probable cause from situations that may not be obviously criminal. If, for example, a police officer observes several people in a car slowly circling a certain building in a high-crime area, that officer may infer that the people are "casing" the building in preparation for a burglary. Probable cause could be established for detaining the suspects.

2. *Information.* Law enforcement officers receive information from victims, eyewitnesses, informants, and official sources such as police bulletins or broadcasts. Such information, as long as it is believed to be reliable, is a basis for probable cause.

3. *Evidence.* In certain circumstances, which will be examined later in this chapter, police have probable cause for a search or seizure based on evidence—such as a shotgun—in plain view.

4. *Association.* In some circumstances, if the police see a person with a known criminal background in a place where criminal activity is openly taking place, they have probable cause to stop that person. Generally, however, association is not adequate to establish probable cause.[6]

In 2013, the Supreme Court confirmed that drug-sniffing dogs are important sources of probable cause. The case involved a "free air sniff" by a German shepherd named Aldo at a traffic stop. The dog's efforts led to the discovery of methamphetamine ingredients in the back of a truck. The defendant claimed that Aldo, who did not have an extensive record of finding illegal drugs, was an unreliable source of probable cause. The Court disagreed, ruling that the possibility of a dog making a mistake is not enough to overcome probable cause when the animal correctly leads its handler to hidden contraband.[7]

THE PROBABLE CAUSE FRAMEWORK In a sense, the concept of probable cause allows police officers to do their job effectively. Most arrests are made without a warrant because most arrests are the result of quick police reaction to the commission of a crime. Indeed, it would not be practical to expect a police officer to obtain a warrant before making an arrest on the street. Thus, probable cause provides a framework that limits the situations in which police officers can make arrests, but also gives officers the freedom to act within that framework. In 2003, the Supreme Court reaffirmed this freedom by ruling that Baltimore (Maryland) police officers acted properly when they arrested all three passengers of a car in which cocaine had been hidden in the back seat. "A reasonable officer," wrote Chief Justice William H. Rehnquist, "could conclude that there was probable cause to believe" that the defendant, who had been sitting in the front seat, was in "possession" of the illicit drug despite his protestations to the contrary.[8]

Once an arrest is made, the arresting officer must prove to a judge that probable cause existed. In *County of Riverside v. McLaughlin* (1991),[9] the Supreme Court ruled that this judicial determination of probable cause must be made within forty-eight hours after the arrest, even if this two-day period includes a weekend or holiday.

■ The U.S. Supreme Court has ruled that a dog's sniff is an acceptable source of probable cause in certain *public places,* such as the Los Angeles International Airport, shown here. In 2013, the Court held that a dog's sniff is not an acceptable source of probable cause if it alone leads police to search *private property.* Why do you think the Court looks at the two situations differently?
AP Photo/Reed Saxon

The Exclusionary Rule

Historically, the courts have looked to the Fourth Amendment for guidance in regulating the activity of law enforcement officers, as the language of the Constitution does not expressly do so. The courts' most potent legal tool in this endeavor is the **exclusionary rule,** which prohibits the use of illegally seized evidence. According to this rule, any evidence obtained by an unreasonable search or seizure is inadmissible (may not be used) against a defendant in a criminal trial.[10] Even highly incriminating evidence, such as a knife stained with the victim's blood, usually cannot be introduced at a trial if illegally obtained. Furthermore, any physical or verbal evidence police are able to acquire by using illegally obtained evidence is known as the **fruit of the poisoned tree** and is also inadmissible. For example, if the police use the existence of the bloodstained knife to get a confession out of a suspect, that confession will be excluded as well.

One of the implications of the exclusionary rule is that it forces police to gather evidence properly. If they follow appropriate procedures, they are more likely to be

LEARNING OBJECTIVE **2** Explain the exclusionary rule and the exceptions to it.

Exclusionary Rule A rule under which any evidence that is obtained in violation of the accused's rights, as well as any evidence derived from illegally obtained evidence, will not be admissible in criminal court.

Fruit of the Poisoned Tree Evidence that is acquired through the use of illegally obtained evidence and is therefore inadmissible in court.

"Inevitable Discovery" Exception The legal principle that illegally obtained evidence can be admissible in court if police using lawful means would have "inevitably" discovered it.

"Good Faith" Exception The legal principle that evidence obtained with the use of a technically invalid search warrant is admissible during trial if the police acted in good faith when they sought the warrant from a judge.

rewarded with a conviction. If they are careless or abuse the rights of the suspect, they are unlikely to get a conviction. A strict application of the exclusionary rule, therefore, will permit guilty people to go free because of police carelessness or innocent errors. In practice, relatively few apparently guilty suspects benefit from the exclusionary rule. Research shows that about 3 percent of felony arrestees avoid incarceration because of improper police searches and seizures.[11]

THE "INEVITABLE DISCOVERY" EXCEPTION Critics of the exclusionary rule maintain that, regardless of statistics, the rule hampers the police's ability to gather evidence and causes prosecutors to release numerous suspects before their cases make it to court. Several Supreme Court decisions have mirrored this view and provided exceptions to the exclusionary rule.

The **"inevitable discovery" exception** was established in the wake of the disappearance of ten-year-old Pamela Powers of Des Moines, Iowa, on Christmas Eve, 1968. The primary suspect in the case, a religious fanatic named Robert Williams, was tricked by a detective into leading police to the site where he had buried Powers. The detective convinced Williams that if he did not lead police to the body, he would soon forget where it was buried. This would deny his victim a "Christian burial." Initially, in *Brewer v. Williams* (1977),[12] the Court ruled that the evidence (Powers's body) had been obtained illegally because Williams's attorney had not been present during the interrogation that led to his admission. Several years later, in *Nix v. Williams* (1984),[13] the Court reversed itself, ruling that the evidence was admissible because the body would have eventually ("inevitably") been found by lawful means.

THE "GOOD FAITH" EXCEPTION The scope of the exclusionary rule has been further diminished by two cases involving faulty warrants. In the first, *United States v. Leon* (1984),[14] the police seized evidence on authority of a search warrant that had been improperly issued by a judge. In the second, *Arizona v. Evans* (1995),[15] due to a computer error, a police officer detained Isaac Evans on the mistaken belief that he was subject to an arrest warrant. As a result, the officer found a marijuana cigarette on Evans's person and, after a search of his car, discovered a bag of marijuana.

In both cases, the Court allowed the evidence to stand under a **"good faith" exception** to the exclusionary rule. Under this exception, evidence acquired by a police officer using a technically invalid warrant is admissible if the officer was unaware of the error. In these two cases, the Court said that the officers acted in "good faith." By the same token, if police officers use a search warrant that they know to be technically incorrect, the good faith exception does not apply, and the evidence can be suppressed.

SELF ASSESSMENT

Fill in the blanks and check your answers on page 244.

The Fourth Amendment contains two critically important restrictions on police authority: a prohibition against _____ searches and seizures and a requirement of _____ _____ that a crime has been committed before a warrant for a search or seizure can be issued. Judges rely on the _____ rule to keep _____ that has been improperly obtained by the police out of criminal courts.

LAWFUL SEARCHES AND SEIZURES

How far can law enforcement agents go in searching and seizing private property? Consider the steps taken by Jenny Stracner, an investigator with the Laguna Beach (California) Police Department. After receiving information that a suspect, Greenwood, was engaged in drug trafficking, Stracner enlisted the aid of the local trash collector in procuring evidence. Instead of taking Greenwood's trash bags to be incinerated, the collector agreed to give them to Stracner. The officer found enough drug paraphernalia in the garbage to obtain a warrant to search the suspect's home. Subsequently, Greenwood was arrested and convicted on narcotics charges.[16]

Remember, the Fourth Amendment is quite specific in forbidding unreasonable searches and seizures. Were Stracner's search of Greenwood's garbage and her seizure of its contents "reasonable"? The Supreme Court thought so, holding that Greenwood's garbage was not protected by the Fourth Amendment.[17]

The Role of Privacy in Searches

A crucial concept in understanding search and seizure law is *privacy*. By definition, a **search** is a governmental intrusion on a citizen's reasonable expectation of privacy. The recognized standard for a "reasonable expectation of privacy" was established in *Katz v. United States* (1967).[18] The case dealt with the question of whether the defendant was justified in his expectation of privacy in the calls he made from a public phone booth. The Supreme Court held that "the Fourth Amendment protects people, not places," and Katz prevailed.

In his concurring opinion, Justice John Harlan, Jr., set a two-pronged test for a person's expectation of privacy:

1. The individual must prove that she or he expected privacy, and
2. Society must recognize that expectation as reasonable.[19]

Accordingly, the Court agreed with Katz's claim that he had a reasonable right to privacy in a public phone booth. Even though the phone booth was a public place, accessible to anyone, Katz had taken clear steps to protect his privacy.

A LEGITIMATE PRIVACY INTEREST Despite the *Katz* ruling, simply taking steps to protect one's privacy is not enough to protect against law enforcement intrusion. The steps must be reasonably certain to ensure privacy. If a person is unreasonable or mistaken in expecting privacy, he or she may forfeit that expectation. For instance, in *California v. Greenwood* (1988),[20] described above, the Court did not believe that the suspect had a reasonable expectation of privacy when it came to his garbage bags. The Court noted that when we place our trash on a curb, we expose it to any number of intrusions by "animals, children, scavengers, snoops, and other members of the public."[21] In other words, if Greenwood had truly intended for the contents of his garbage bags to remain private, he would not have left them on the side of the road.

To give another example, the Court also upheld the search in a case in which a drug-sniffing dog was used to detect marijuana in the trunk of a car after the driver was stopped for speeding. The Court ruled that no one has a legitimate privacy interest in possessing illegal drugs or other contraband such as explosives in the trunk of his or her car.[22]

PRIVACY AND SATELLITE MONITORING As you can see, a number of factors go into determining whether a reasonable expectation of privacy exists. In *United States v. Jones* (2012),[23] the U.S. Supreme Court emphasized the important roles that time and technology play in this equation. The Court's ruling invalidated the efforts of federal agents who had placed a GPS tracking device on the car of Antoine Jones, a Washington, D.C., nightclub owner suspected of drug trafficking. Using the device, which relies on satellite

Search The process by which police examine a person or property to find evidence that will be used to prove guilt in a criminal trial.

transmissions to determine location, the agents were able to follow Jones's movements for a month. This evidence helped bring about Jones's conviction for conspiring to distribute cocaine.

The Court found that the government had "physically occupied" private property—Jones's car—for an unreasonably long amount of time. As a result, all evidence gathered by the GPS device was ruled inadmissible. Several Supreme Court justices also pointed out that most citizens do not expect the police to be monitoring every drive they make over the course of twenty-eight days.[24] As one commentator stated, the ruling seemed to acknowledge that just because technology now permits greater levels of surveillance, this "does not mean that society has decided there's no such thing as privacy anymore."[25] (See the feature *A Question of Ethics—Fake Friends* below to learn more about expectation of privacy issues on the Internet.)

Search and Seizure Warrants

The Supreme Court's ruling in the case of Antoine Jones discussed above does not mean that law enforcement officers can *never* track someone for a month using a GPS device or any other technology. Rather, it means that, to do so, they need to obtain a **search warrant**, a step that the federal agents failed to take before beginning their surveillance of Jones. A search warrant is a court order that authorizes police to search a certain area. Before a judge or magistrate will issue a search warrant, law enforcement officers must provide:

A QUESTION OF ETHICS

Fake Friends

THE SITUATION Adam, a college student in Wisconsin, accepts an offer from a "good looking girl" to be Facebook friends. Several days later, the local police call Adam to the station, show him photos that he has posted on his Facebook page of him with a beer, and ticket him for underage drinking. As it turned out, the "good looking girl" was an "undercover" police officer using a fake profile to get access to Adam's private photos. Even though Facebook policy bans users from providing false information, many law enforcement agencies have no reservations about using fake identities as part of online criminal investigations.

THE ETHICAL DILEMMA Clearly, Facebook users have no reasonable expectation of privacy regarding information they post in the social networking site's public spaces. Facebook does, however, provide users with a number of controls to restrict certain information to "friends." It seems logical that users do have an expectation of privacy with this content, and that it should be unethical, if not illegal, for police officers using fake identities to operate on Facebook.

Actually, police investigators have legal access to *all* information on Facebook, no matter what the status of that information. In its privacy policy, Facebook states that it will disclose user material to the government if required to do so by law. Furthermore, Facebook

employees routinely monitor "private" user content. As far as the courts are concerned, if a person exposes information to any potential third party, there is no reasonable expectation of privacy (as with the garbage bags in the text). Consequently, though its one billion users may not be aware of the fact, everything on Facebook is fair game for law enforcement.

WHAT IS THE SOLUTION? What is your opinion of the ethics of police officers using fake identities to go undercover on Facebook? Should users have an expectation of privacy when they take active steps to protect certain personal information as "private"? Why or why not? Keep in mind that, as we saw in the previous chapter, undercover agents and informants routinely use fake identities in the "real world" to fool criminal suspects.

Manfredxy/Shutterstock.com

- Information showing probable cause that a crime has been or will be committed.
- Specific information on the premises to be searched, the suspects to be found and the illegal activities taking place at those premises, and the items to be seized.

The purpose of a search warrant is to establish, before the search takes place, that a *probable cause to search* justifies infringing on the suspect's reasonable expectation of privacy.

PARTICULARITY OF SEARCH WARRANTS The members of the First Congress specifically did not want law enforcement officers to have the freedom to make "general, exploratory" searches through a person's belongings.[26] Consequently, the Fourth Amendment requires that a warrant describe with "particularity" the place to be searched and the things—either people or objects—to be seized.

This "particularity" requirement places a heavy burden on law enforcement officers. Before going to a judge to ask for a search warrant, they must prepare an **affidavit** in which they provide specific, written information on the property that they wish to search and seize. They must know the specific address of any place they wish to search. General addresses of apartment buildings or office complexes are not sufficient. Furthermore, courts generally frown on vague descriptions of goods to be seized. For example, several years ago, a federal court ruled that a warrant permitting police to search a home for "all handguns, shotguns and rifles" and "evidence showing street gang membership" was too broad. As a result, the seizure of a shotgun was disallowed for lack of a valid search warrant.[27]

A **seizure** is the act of taking possession of a person or property by the government because of a (suspected) violation of the law. In general, four categories of items can be seized by use of a search warrant:

1. Items resulting from the crime, such as stolen goods.
2. Items that are inherently illegal for anybody to possess (with certain exceptions), such as narcotics and counterfeit currency.
3. Items that can be called "evidence" of the crime, such as a bloodstained sneaker or a ski mask.
4. Items used in committing the crime, such as an ice pick or a printing press used to make counterfeit bills.[28]

See Figure 7.1 on the right for an example of a search warrant.

REASONABLENESS DURING A SEARCH AND SEIZURE No matter how "particular" a warrant is, it cannot provide for all the conditions that are bound to come up during its service. Consequently, the law gives law enforcement officers the ability to act "reasonably" during a search and seizure in the event of unforeseeable circumstances. For example, if a police officer is searching an apartment for a stolen MacBook Pro laptop computer and notices a vial of crack cocaine sitting on the suspect's bed, that contraband is considered to be in "plain view" and can be seized.

Note that if law enforcement officers have a search warrant that authorizes them to search for a stolen laptop computer, they would not be justified in opening small drawers.

Affidavit A written statement of facts, confirmed by the oath or affirmation of the party making it and made before a person having the authority to administer the oath or affirmation.

Seizure The forcible taking of a person or property in response to a violation of the law.

LEARNING **3** OBJECTIVE

List the four categories of items that can be seized by use of a search warrant.

FIGURE 7.1 Example of a Search Warrant

United States District Court

DISTRICT OF

In the Matter of the Search of

(Name, address or brief description of person or property to be searched)

SEARCH WARRANT

CASE NUMBER:

TO:_____ and any Authorized Officer of the United States

Affidavit(s) having been made before me by_____ who has reason to

believe that ☐ on the person of or ☐ on the premises known as (name, description and/or location)

in the_____ District of_____ there is now concealed a certain person or property, namely (describe the person or property)

I am satisfied that the affidavit(s) and any recorded testimony establish probable cause to believe that the person or property so described is now concealed on the person or premises above-described and establish grounds for the issuance of this warrant.

YOU ARE HEREBY COMMANDED to search on or before_____
Date

(not to exceed 10 days) the person or place named above for the person or property specified, serving this warrant and making the search (in the daytime — 6:00 A.M. to 10:00 P.M.) (at any time in the day or night as I find reasonable cause has been established) and if the person or property be found there to seize same, leaving a copy of this warrant and receipt for the person or property taken, and prepare a written inventory of the person or property seized and promptly return this warrant to_____
as required by law.

U.S. Judge or Magistrate

Date and Time Issued_____ at_____
City and State

Name and Title of Judicial Officer_____ Signature of Judicial Officer_____

Because a computer could not fit in a small drawer, an officer would not have a basis for reasonably searching one. Hence, officers are restricted in terms of where they can look by the items they are searching for.

Searches and Seizures without a Warrant

Although the Supreme Court has established the principle that searches conducted without warrants are *per se* (by definition) unreasonable, it has set "specifically established" exceptions to the rule.[29] In fact, most searches take place in the absence of a judicial order. Warrantless searches and seizures can be lawful when police are in "hot pursuit" of a subject or when they search bags of trash left at the curb for regular collection. Because of the magnitude of smuggling activities in "border areas" such as airports, seaports, and international boundaries, a warrant normally is not needed to search property in those places. Furthermore, in 2006 the Court held unanimously that police officers do not need a warrant to enter a private home in an emergency, such as when they reasonably fear for the safety of the inhabitants.[30] The two most important circumstances in which a warrant is not needed, though, are (1) searches incidental to an arrest and (2) consent searches.

LEARNING OBJECTIVE 4 Explain when searches can be made without a warrant.

SEARCHES INCIDENTAL TO AN ARREST The most frequent exception to the warrant requirement involves **searches incidental to arrests,** so called because nearly every time police officers make an arrest (a procedure discussed in detail later in the chapter), they also search the suspect. As long as the original arrest was based on probable cause, these searches are valid for two reasons, established by the Supreme Court in *United States v. Robinson* (1973):

1. The need for a police officer to find and confiscate any weapons a suspect may be carrying.
2. The need to protect any evidence on the suspect's person from being destroyed.[31]

Law enforcement officers are, however, limited in the searches they may make during an arrest. These limits were established by the Supreme Court in *Chimel v. California* (1969).[32] In that case, police arrived at Chimel's home with an arrest warrant but not a search warrant. Even though Chimel refused their request to "look around," the officers searched the entire three-bedroom house for nearly an hour, finding stolen coins in the process. Chimel was convicted of burglary and appealed, arguing that the evidence of the coins should have been suppressed.

The Supreme Court held that the search was unreasonable. In doing so, the Court established guidelines as to the acceptable extent of searches incidental to an arrest. Primarily, the Court ruled that police may search any area within the suspect's "immediate control" to confiscate any weapons or evidence that the suspect could destroy. The Court found, however, that there was no justification

> for routinely searching rooms other than that in which the arrest occurs—or, for that matter, for searching through all desk drawers or other closed or concealed areas in that room itself. Such searches, in the absence of well-recognized exceptions, may be made only under the authority of a search warrant.[33]

The exact interpretation of the "area within immediate control" has been left to individual courts, but in general it has been taken to mean the area within the reach of the arrested person. Thus, the Court is said to have established the "arm's reach doctrine" in its *Chimel* decision.

SEARCHES WITH CONSENT **Consent searches,** the second most common type of warrantless searches, take place when individuals voluntarily give law enforcement officers permission to search their persons, homes, or belongings. The most relevant factors in determining whether consent is voluntary are

1. The age, intelligence, and physical condition of the consenting suspect;
2. Any coercive behavior by the police, such as the language used to request consent; and
3. The length of the questioning and its location.[34]

If a court finds that a person has been physically threatened or otherwise coerced into giving consent, the search is invalid.[35] Furthermore, the search consented to must be reasonable. Several years ago, the North Carolina Supreme Court invalidated a consent search that turned up a packet of cocaine. As part of this search, the police had pulled down the suspect's underwear and shone a flashlight on his groin. The court ruled that a reasonable person in the defendant's position would not consent to such an intrusive examination.[36]

Two deputy sheriffs walk past open lockers at the Wyoming Area High School in Exeter, Pennsylvania, during a search for weapons on campus. Under what circumstances do you think that law enforcement should be able to search school lockers without consent from students or their parents?
AP Photo/*The Citizens' Voice*, Kristen Mullen

The Citizen's Decision The standard for consent searches was set in *Schneckcloth v. Bustamonte* (1973),[37] in which, after being asked, the defendant told police officers to "go ahead" and search his car. A packet of stolen checks found in the trunk was ruled valid evidence because the driver consented to the search. Numerous court decisions have also supported the "knock and talk" strategy, in which the law enforcement agent simply walks up to the door of a residence, knocks, and asks to come in and talk to the resident.[38] The officer does not need reasonable suspicion or probable cause that a crime has taken place in this situation because the decision to cooperate rests with the civilian.

The Intimidation Factor Critics of consent searches hold that such searches are rarely voluntary because most people are intimidated by police and will react to a request for permission to make a search as if it were an order.[39] Furthermore, most people are unaware that they have the option *not* to comply with a request for a search. Thus, if a police officer asks to search an individual's car after issuing a speeding ticket, the individual is well within her or his rights to refuse. According to the United States Supreme Court in *Florida v. Bostick* (1991),[40] so long as police officers do not improperly coerce a suspect to cooperate, they are not *required* to inform the person that he or she has a choice in the matter.

Consequently, in *Ohio v. Robinette* (1996),[41] the Court held that police officers do *not* need to notify people that they are "free to go" after an initial stop when no arrest is involved. Similarly, in 2002, the Court ruled that the inside of a bus is not an inherently coercive environment and thus officers do not need to advise passengers that they can refuse to be searched.[42] The significance of this line of cases is underscored by data presented in connection with the *Robinette* ruling: in the two years leading up to that case,

Consent Searches Searches by police that are made after the subject of the search has agreed to the action. In these situations, consent, if given of free will, validates a warrantless search.

four hundred Ohio drivers were convicted of narcotics offenses that resulted directly from search requests that could have been denied but were not.[43] (For an overview of the circumstances under which warrantless searches are allowed, see Figure 7.2 below.)

Searches of Automobiles

In *Carroll v. United States* (1925),[44] the Supreme Court ruled that the law could distinguish among automobiles, homes, and persons in questions involving police searches. In the years since its *Carroll* decision, the Court has established that the Fourth Amendment does not require police to obtain a warrant to search automobiles or other movable vehicles when they have probable cause to believe that a vehicle contains contraband or evidence of criminal activity.[45] The reasoning behind such leniency is straightforward: requiring a warrant to search an automobile places too heavy a burden on police officers. By the time the officers could communicate with a judge and obtain the warrant, the suspects could have driven away and destroyed any evidence. Consequently, the Court has consistently held that someone in a vehicle does not have the same reasonable expectation of privacy as someone at home or even in a phone booth.

WARRANTLESS SEARCHES OF AUTOMOBILES For nearly three decades, police officers believed that if they lawfully arrested the driver of a car, they could legally make a warrantless search of the car's entire front and back compartments. This understanding was based on the Supreme Court's ruling in *New York v. Benton* (1981),[46] which seemed to allow this expansive interpretation of the "area within immediate control" with regard to automobiles.

In *Arizona v. Gant* (2009), however, the Court announced that its *Benton* decision had been misinterpreted. Such warrantless searches are allowed only if (1) the person being arrested is close enough to the car to grab or destroy evidence or a weapon inside the car or (2) the arresting officer reasonably believes that the car contains evidence pertinent to the same crime for which the arrest took place.[47] So, for example, police will no longer be able to search an automobile for contraband if the driver has been arrested for failing to pay previous speeding tickets—unless the officer reasonably believes the suspect has the ability to reach and destroy any such contraband.

FIGURE 7.2 Exceptions to the Requirement That Officers Have a Search Warrant

In many instances, it would be impractical for police officers to leave a crime scene, go to a judge, and obtain a search warrant before conducting a search. Therefore, under the following circumstances, a search warrant is not required.

INCIDENT TO LAWFUL ARREST
Police officers may search the area within immediate control of a person after they have arrested him or her.

CONSENT
Police officers may search a person without a warrant if that person voluntarily agrees to be searched and has the legal authority to authorize the search.

STOP AND FRISK
Police officers may frisk, or "pat down," a person if they suspect that the person may be involved in criminal activity or pose a danger to those in the immediate area.

HOT PURSUIT
If police officers are in "hot pursuit" or chasing a person they have probable cause to believe committed a crime, and that person enters a building, the officers may search the building without a warrant.

AUTOMOBILE EXCEPTION
If police officers have probable cause to believe that an automobile contains evidence of a crime, they may, in most instances, search the vehicle without a warrant.

PLAIN VIEW
If police officers are legally engaged in police work and happen to see evidence of a crime in "plain view," they may seize it without a warrant.

ABANDONED PROPERTY
Any property, such as a hotel room that has been vacated or contraband that has been discarded, may be searched and seized by police officers without a warrant.

BORDER SEARCHES
Law enforcement officers on border patrol do not need a warrant to search vehicles crossing the border.

Significant Powers As you can imagine, the law enforcement community reacted negatively to the new restrictions outlined in the *Gant* decision.[48] Police officers, however, still can conduct a warrantless search of an automobile based on circumstances other than the incidental-to-an-arrest doctrine. These circumstances include probable cause of criminal activity, consent of the driver, and "protective searches" to search for weapons if police officers have a reasonable suspicion that such weapons exist.[49] In addition, an officer may order passengers as well as the driver out of a car during a traffic stop. The Court has reasoned that the danger to an officer is increased when there is a passenger in the automobile.[50]

Pretextual Stops Law enforcement agents also have a great deal of leeway regarding automobile stops. Crucially, as long as an officer has probable cause to believe that a traffic law has been broken, her or his "true" motivation for making a stop is irrelevant.[51] So, even if the police officer does not have a legally sufficient reason to search for evidence of a crime such as drug trafficking, the officer can use a minor traffic violation to pull over the car and investigate his or her "hunch." (To learn more about such "pretextual stops," see the feature *You Be the Judge—A Valid Pretext?* below.)

CONTAINER SEARCHES In keeping with the principles of the "movable vehicle" exception, the Supreme Court has also provided law enforcement agents with a great deal of leeway

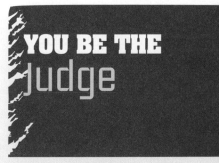

A VALID PRETEXT?

Somchai Rakin/Shutterstock.com

THE SITUATION Officers Soto and Littlejohn are patrolling a "high drug area" of Washington, D.C., in an unmarked car. They become suspicious of a truck with temporary plates being driven slowly by Michael, a young African American. The officers follow the truck, and when Michael fails to signal while making a right turn, they pull him over for a traffic violation. During the traffic stop, the officers legally notice two large bags of crack cocaine in Michael's possession and arrest him on drug charges. Michael's lawyers claim that the police officers had no probable cause that Michael was carrying drugs, and that the evidence against their client should be suppressed under the exclusionary rule (discussed earlier in the chapter).

THE LAW As far as Fourth Amendment law is concerned, any subjective reasons that a police officer might have for stopping a suspect, including any motives based on racial stereotyping or bias, are irrelevant. As long as the officer has objective probable cause to believe a traffic violation or other wrongdoing has occurred, the stop is valid.

YOUR DECISION During Michael's trial, Soto is asked whether the "real" reasons for stopping the truck were that it had temporary plates, its driver was African American, and it was moving slowly in an area known for drug dealing. His answer convinces you that, in fact, the traffic violation was a pretext for the police officers' decision to stop Michael's car in the hope that he was carrying illegal drugs. There is no question, however, that Michael did fail to signal while making a right turn. Do you think the evidence against Michael should be allowed in court?

[To see how the United States Supreme Court ruled in a similar situation, go to Example 7.1 in Appendix B.]

for warrantless searches of containers within a vehicle. In one case, Washington, D.C., detectives received a reliable tip that a man known as the "Bandit" was selling drugs from his car. Without first getting a warrant, the detectives searched the Bandit's trunk and found heroin in a closed paper bag. The Court refused to suppress the evidence, ruling that in such situations police officers can search every part of the vehicle that might contain the items they are seeking, as long as they have probable cause to believe that the items are somewhere in the car.[52]

Nevertheless, there are limits to what can be searched. As Justice John Paul Stevens stated in his opinion, "probable cause to believe that undocumented aliens are being transported in a van will not justify a warrantless search of a suitcase" in that van.[53] By the same token, if the tipster had told the police specifically that "Bandit has a bag of heroin in his trunk," they would not have been justified in searching the front area of the car without a warrant or probable cause.[54]

The Plain View Doctrine

LEARNING OBJECTIVE **5** Describe the plain view doctrine and indicate one of its limitations.

As we have already seen several times in this chapter, the Constitution, as interpreted by our courts, provides very little protection to evidence *in plain view*. For example, suppose a traffic officer pulls over a person for speeding, looks in the driver's side window, and clearly sees what appears to be a bag of heroin resting on the passenger seat. In this instance, under the **plain view doctrine,** the officer would be justified in seizing the drugs without a warrant.

The plain view doctrine was first enunciated by the Supreme Court in *Coolidge v. New Hampshire* (1971).[55] The Court ruled that law enforcement officers may make a warrantless seizure of an item if four criteria are met:

1. The item is positioned so as to be detected easily by an officer's sight or some other sense.
2. The officer is legally in a position to notice the item in question.
3. The discovery of the item is inadvertent. That is, the officer had not intended to find the item.
4. The officer immediately recognizes the illegal nature of the item. No interrogation or further investigation is allowed under the plain view doctrine.

New York City police officers search a limousine for explosives at a checkpoint set up in response to a credible terrorist threat. If the officers found a stack of counterfeit one hundred dollar bills during this search, would the plain view doctrine allow the seizure of the fake cash? Why or why not?
Justin Sullivan/Getty Images

Advances in technology that allow law enforcement agents to "see" beyond normal human capabilities have raised new issues in regard to plain view principles. *Thermal imagers,* for example, measure otherwise invisible levels of infrared radiation. These devices are particularly effective in detecting marijuana plants grown indoors because of the heat thrown off by the "grow lights" that the plants need to survive. The question for the courts has been whether a warrantless search of a dwelling through its walls by means of a thermal imager violates Fourth Amendment protections of privacy. According to the Supreme Court, an item is not in plain view if law enforcement agents need the aid of this technology to "see" it.[56] Thus, information from a thermal imager is not by itself justification for a warrantless search.

Electronic Surveillance

Electronic Surveillance The use of electronic equipment by law enforcement agents to record private conversations or observe conduct that is meant to be private.

During the course of a criminal investigation, law enforcement officers may decide to use **electronic surveillance,** or electronic devices such as wiretaps or hidden microphones ("bugs"), to monitor and record conversations, observe movements, and trace or record telephone calls.

BASIC RULES: CONSENT AND PROBABLE CAUSE Given the invasiveness of electronic surveillance, the Supreme Court has generally held that the practice is prohibited by the Fourth Amendment. In *Burger v. New York* (1967),[57] however, the Court ruled that it was permissible under certain circumstances. That same year, *Katz v. United States* (discussed at the beginning of this section) established that recorded conversations are inadmissible as evidence unless certain procedures are followed.

In general, law enforcement officers can use electronic surveillance only if consent is given by one of the parties to be monitored, or, in the absence of such consent, with a warrant.[58] For the warrant to be valid, it must:

1. Detail with "particularity" the conversations that are to be overheard.
2. Name the suspects and the places that will be under surveillance.
3. Show probable cause to believe that a specific crime has been or will be committed.[59]

Once the specific information has been gathered, the law enforcement officers must end the electronic surveillance immediately.[60] In any case, the surveillance cannot last more than thirty days without a judicial extension.

FORCE MULTIPLYING Pervasive forms of electronic surveillance are allowed under the theory that people who are in public places have no reasonable expectation of privacy.[61] For example, many Americans would be surprised to learn how often they are under the watchful eye of law enforcement via closed-circuit television (CCTV) cameras. CCTV surveillance relies on strategically placed video cameras to record and transmit all activity in a targeted area, such as on a public street or in a government building. The images are monitored in real time so that law enforcement personnel can investigate any suspicious or criminal activity captured by the cameras.

CCTV is an example of a *force multiplier,* so called because this form of electronic surveillance allows laws enforcement agencies to expand their capabilities without a significant increase in personnel. Speaking of CCTV, Brian Harvey, a deputy chief with the Dallas Police Department, says, "One camera operator can cover a lot more area than field officers can."[62]

Covering large areas is the attraction of another force multiplier: the unmanned drone, which we saw in the military context in Chapter 4. In a law enforcement context, such drones would carry cameras rather than weapons and could be used for a host of policing duties, such as patrolling high-crime neighborhoods or tracking fleeing felons. Although only a few police departments are presently experimenting with unmanned police drones, federal regulations for their widespread use should be in effect by 2015.[63]

AUTOMATIC LICENSE PLATE RECOGNITION

Suzanne Kreiter/*The Boston Globe* via Getty Images

An increasingly popular force multiplier involves computerized infrared cameras that take digital photos of license plates. Usually mounted on police cars, these automatic license-plate recognition (ALPR) devices convert the images to text. Then the numbers are instantly checked against databases that contain records of the license plates of stolen cars and automobiles driven by a wide variety of targets, from wanted felons to citizens with unpaid parking tickets. In heavy-traffic areas, ALPR units can check thousands of license plates each hour. After adding ALPR technology to cameras mounted on just two patrol cars, police in Columbia, Missouri, used the system to make fifty arrests in three months. "It allows us to do our job better and more efficiently," says Columbia police lieutenant Brian Richenberger.

Thinking about Automatic License Plate Recognition

How might law enforcement use ALPR not only to identify "hot" license plates but also as part of ongoing criminal investigations? For example, how might narcotics officers on a stakeout of a suspected drug dealer's house take advantage of ALPR technology?

CONSTITUTIONAL CONCERNS Critics of CCTV cameras, ALPR, and other forms of high-tech surveillance contend that these technologies infringe on individual privacy, allowing law enforcement to create "digital dossiers" on people without probable cause.[64] Police in Charlottesville, Virginia, are prohibited by local ordinance from using evidence gathered by an unmanned drone in criminal court, even though that city's police department does not yet own any drones. Numerous other state and local laws preemptively restrict the use of drones, as politicians and citizens worry about the ramifications of technology that can, in the words of one expert, "detect a milk carton from sixty thousand feet."[65]

The Supreme Court's ruling in *United States v. Jones,* the GPS monitoring case discussed earlier in the chapter, did little to clarify this area of the law, as it applies only to lengthy periods of surveillance. Generally speaking, law enforcement agents do not need a search warrant when using CCTV, ALPR, or other surveillance technologies that record short periods of time in public places. As noted earlier, no reasonable expectation of privacy exists in such situations. American courts have been less consistent in determining the constitutionality of other increasingly common forms of police surveillance, such as downloading the contents of a suspect's smartphone or tracking a suspect's movements by his or her use of that device.

Homeland Security and the Fourth Amendment

Passed in the wake of the September 11, 2001, terrorist attacks, the Patriot Act (discussed in Chapter 1) has generally made it easier for law enforcement agents to conduct searches. For example, to search a suspect's apartment and examine the contents of his or her computer, agents previously needed a warrant based on probable cause that a crime had taken place or was about to take place. The Patriot Act amends the law to allow the Federal Bureau of Investigation (FBI) or other federal agencies to obtain warrants for "terrorism" investigations, "chemical weapons" investigations, or "computer fraud and abuse" investigations as long as agents can prove that such actions have a "significant purpose."[66] In other words, no proof of criminal activity need be provided.

THE PATRIOT ACT AND SURVEILLANCE The Patriot Act also gives law enforcement agents more leeway when conducting surveillance. The Foreign Intelligence Surveillance Act of 1978 (FISA) allowed for surveillance of a suspect without a warrant as long as the "primary purpose" of the surveillance was to investigate foreign spying and not to engage in criminal law enforcement.[67] The Patriot Act amends FISA to allow for searches and surveillance if a "significant purpose" of the investigation is intelligence gathering or any other type of antiterrorist strategy.[68] The statute also provides federal agents with "roving surveillance authority," allowing them to continue monitoring a terrorist suspect on the strength of the original warrant even if the suspect moves to an area outside the control of the court that issued the warrant.[69]

CONGRESS AND WIRETAPPING Following a series of controversies concerning the ability of the National Security Agency (NSA) to wiretap telephone and e-mail communications of terrorism suspects, in 2008 Congress passed an amended version of FISA.[70] The revised law allows the NSA to wiretap for seven days, without a court order, any person "reasonably believed" to be outside the United States, if the surveillance is necessary to protect national security. It also permits the wiretapping of Americans for seven days without a court order, if federal officials have probable cause to believe that the target is linked to terrorism. Supporters of the amendments claim that the average American has nothing to fear from the law "unless you have al Qaeda on your speed dial." Critics, however, see it as a further erosion of Fourth Amendment protections in the name of homeland security.[71]

SOCIAL MEDIA & CJ

To learn more about online privacy issues, go to the home page of the **Electronic Privacy Information Center (EPIC)** and click on the Facebook icon. You'll see posts by EPIC staff members and other parties interested in the subject.

Ankomando/Shutterstock.com

SELF ASSESSMENT

Fill in the blanks and check your answers on page 244.

A search is a governmental intrusion on the _____ of an individual. To protect these rights, law enforcement agents must procure a _____ _____ before examining a suspect's home or personal possessions. During a properly executed search, officers may _____ any items that may be used as evidence or that are inherently illegal to possess. Law enforcement agents do not need a judge's prior approval to conduct a search incidental to an _____ or when the subject of the search gives his or her _____. Under the Patriot Act, government agents no longer have to show _____ cause to obtain warrants for terrorist investigations. Rather, they only need to show that their actions have a "_____ purpose."

STOPS AND FRISKS

Several years ago, an Indianapolis (Indiana) police officer was patrolling a high-crime neighborhood when he saw a bicycle sitting next to a car in a gas station parking lot. The officer watched as Michael Woodson got out of the car, put on a backpack, and began to cycle away. After stopping Woodson, the officer searched the backpack, finding more than thirty contraband DVDs. Woodson challenged his eventual conviction on two charges of fraud, claiming that the police officer had no good reason to stop him in the first place.

A three-judge Indiana appeals panel agreed and overturned Woodson's conviction. The panel rejected the argument that, given the setting and Woodson's behavior, the police officer was justified in thinking that a drug deal was taking place. That is, no *reasonable suspicion* existed that a crime had been committed in the gas station parking lot.[72] When such reasonable suspicion does exist, police officers are well within their rights to *stop and frisk* a suspect. In a stop and frisk, law enforcement officers (1) briefly detain a person they reasonably believe to be suspicious, and (2) if they believe the person to be armed, proceed to pat down, or "frisk," that person's outer clothing.[73]

The Elusive Definition of Reasonable Suspicion

Like so many elements of police work, the decision of whether to stop a suspect is based on the balancing of conflicting priorities. On the one hand, a police officer feels a sense of urgency to act when he or she believes that criminal activity is occurring or is about to occur. On the other hand, law enforcement agents do not want to harass innocent individuals, especially if doing so runs afoul of the U.S. Constitution. In stop-and-frisk law, this balancing act rests on the fulcrum of reasonable suspicion.

Distinguish between a stop and a frisk, and indicate the importance of the case *Terry v. Ohio.* LEARNING OBJECTIVE 6

TERRY V. OHIO The precedent for the ever-elusive definition of a "reasonable" suspicion in stop-and-frisk situations was established in *Terry v. Ohio* (1968).[74] In that case, a detective named McFadden observed two men (one of whom was Terry) acting strangely in downtown Cleveland. The men would walk past a certain store, peer into the window, and then stop at a street corner and confer. While they were talking, another man joined the conversation and then left quickly. Several minutes later the three men met again at another corner a few blocks away. Detective McFadden believed the trio was planning to break into the store. He approached them, told them who he was, and asked for identification. After receiving a mumbled response, the detective frisked the three men and found handguns on two of them, who were tried and convicted of carrying concealed weapons.

The Supreme Court upheld the conviction, ruling that Detective McFadden had reasonable cause to believe that the men were armed and dangerous and that swift action was necessary to protect himself and other citizens in the area.[75] The Court accepted McFadden's interpretation of the unfolding scene as based on objective facts and practical conclusions. It therefore concluded that his suspicion was reasonable. In contrast, in the case described on the previous page, the Indianapolis police officer's grounds for stopping Michael Woodson—activity that looked like an illegal drug deal in a part of town where such activity is common—were not seen by the Indiana appeals court as reasonable.

THE "TOTALITY OF THE CIRCUMSTANCES" TEST For the most part, the judicial system has refrained from placing restrictions on police officers' ability to make stops. In the *Terry* case, the Supreme Court did say that an officer must have "specific and articulable facts" to support the decision to make a stop, but added that the facts may be "taken together with rational inferences."[76] The Court has consistently ruled that because of their practical experience, law enforcement agents are in a unique position to make such inferences and should be given a good deal of freedom in doing so.

In the years since the *Terry* case was decided, the Court has settled on a "totality of the circumstances" test to determine whether a stop is based on reasonable suspicion.[77] In 2002, for example, the Court ruled that a U.S. Border Patrol agent's stop of a minivan in Arizona was reasonable.[78] On being approached by the Border Patrol car, the driver had stiffened, slowed down his van, and avoided making eye contact with the agent. Furthermore, the children in the van waved at the officer in a mechanical manner, as if ordered to do so. The agent pulled over the van and found 128 pounds of marijuana.

In his opinion, Chief Justice William Rehnquist pointed out that such conduct might have been unremarkable on a busy city highway, but on an unpaved road thirty miles from the Mexican border it was enough to reasonably arouse the agent's suspicion.[79] The justices also made clear that the need to prevent terrorist attacks is part of the "totality of the circumstances" and, therefore, law enforcement agents will have more leeway to make stops near U.S. borders.

A Stop

The terms *stop* and *frisk* are often used in concert, but they describe two separate acts. A **stop** takes place when a law enforcement officer has reasonable suspicion that a criminal activity is about to take place. Because an investigatory stop is not an arrest, there are limits to the extent police can detain someone who has been stopped. For example, in one situation an airline traveler and his luggage were detained for ninety minutes while the police waited for a drug-sniffing dog to arrive. The Supreme Court ruled that the initial stop of the passenger was constitutional, but that the ninety-minute wait was excessive.[80]

In 2004, the Court held that police officers could require suspects to identify themselves during a stop that is otherwise valid under the *Terry* ruling.[81] The case involved a Nevada rancher who was fined $250 for refusing to give his name to a police officer investigating a possible assault. The defendant argued that such requests force citizens to incriminate themselves against their will, which is prohibited, as we shall see later in the chapter, by the Fifth Amendment. Justice Anthony Kennedy wrote, however, that "asking questions is an essential part of police investigations" that would be made much more difficult if officers could not determine the identity of a suspect.[82] The ruling validated "stop-and-identify" laws in twenty states and numerous cities and towns.

A Frisk

The Supreme Court has stated that a **frisk** should be a protective measure. Police officers cannot conduct a frisk as a "fishing expedition" simply to try to find items besides weapons, such as illegal narcotics, on a suspect.[83] A frisk does not necessarily follow a stop and in fact may occur only when the officer is justified in thinking that the safety of police officers or other citizens may be endangered.

Again, the question of reasonable suspicion is at the heart of determining the legality of frisks. In the *Terry* case, the Court accepted that Detective McFadden reasonably believed that the three suspects posed a threat. The suspects' refusal to answer McFadden's questions, though within their rights because they had not been arrested, provided him with sufficient motive for the frisk. In 2009, the Court extended the "stop and frisk" authority by ruling that a police officer could order a passenger in a car that had been pulled over for a traffic violation to submit to a pat-down.[84] To do so, the officer must have a reasonable suspicion that the suspect may be armed and dangerous.

Race and Reasonable Suspicion

By the letter of the law, a person's race or ethnicity alone cannot provide reasonable suspicion for stops and frisks.[85] Some statistical measures, however, seem to show that these factors do, at times, play a troubling role in this area of policing. Over a twelve-month period in Los Angeles, African Americans were 127 percent more likely to be stopped than whites, and Hispanics

Stop A brief detention of a person by law enforcement agents for questioning.

Frisk A pat-down or minimal search by police to discover weapons.

A police officer frisks a suspect in San Francisco, California. What is the main purpose behind a frisk? When are police justified in frisking someone?
Mark Richards/PhotoEdit

Racial Profiling The practice of targeting people for police action based solely on their race, ethnicity, or national origin.

were 43 percent more likely than whites to be frisked.[86] These two minority groups represented 87 percent of the nearly 700,000 stops made by New York City police officers in 2011, even though they constitute a relatively small percentage of the city's population.[87]

RACIAL PROFILING Referring to the situation in New York City, law professor Randolph McClaughlin of Pace University said, "People are starting to wonder: 'What's really going on here?'"[88] The suspicion among many is that police are using **racial profiling** in deciding which suspects to stop. Racial profiling occurs when a police action is based on the race, ethnicity, or national origin of the suspect rather than any reasonable suspicion that he or she has broken the law.

As you may recall from our discussion of pretextual stops earlier in the chapter, as long as a police officer can provide a valid reason for a stop, any racial motivation on his or her part is often legally irrelevant. When statistics show that a law enforcement agency is inexplicably focusing its attention on members of minority groups, public officials may, however, take policy measures to stop the practice. Several years ago, for example, the Philadelphia Police Department confronted racial profiling within its ranks by limiting officer discretion to make stops based on reasonable suspicion.[89] Furthermore, racial profiling can leave law enforcement agencies open to lawsuits for violating provisions of the U.S. Constitution that require all citizens to be treated fairly and equally by the government. We will take a closer look at racial profiling in the *CJ in Action* feature at the end of the chapter.

IMMIGRATION LAW AND PROFILING During a recent lawsuit alleging racial profiling, evidence was provided that Sheriff Joe Arpaio of Maricopa County, Arizona, ordered his deputies to check the immigration status of those who "look like they come from another country."[90] The issue of immigration and racial profiling in Arizona has garnered national attention since 2010, when Arizona passed a law aimed at policing its large number of undocumented immigrants. The legislation, known as S.B. 1070, *requires* state and local police officers, "when practicable," to check the immigration status of someone they have a reasonable suspicion is in the country illegally.[91]

The language of Arizona's law does prohibit officers from using a suspect's race or ethnicity as the sole consideration in determining reasonable suspicion. Furthermore, officers can inquire about immigration status only after a suspect has been stopped for another reason, such as a traffic violation. The law's critics, however, believe that police will have no choice but to focus on Arizona's Hispanic population, as determined primarily by skin color.

Much to the disappointment of these critics, in 2012 the U.S. Supreme Court upheld the so-called "papers, please" provision of the Arizona law.[92] The Court based its ruling on the fact that state and local police officers are not actually enforcing immigration law, which is the domain of the federal government. Rather, they are notifying federal immigration officials about the presence

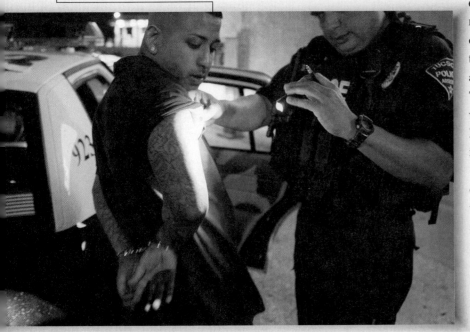

■ Under a new state law, Arizona law enforcement agents such as this Tucson police officer would be required to detain anyone they suspected of being an "unauthorized alien." Why do critics of this law believe that it requires racial profiling on the part of police officers? Do you agree with this criticism? Why or why not? Photo by Scott Olson/Getty Images

of undocumented immigrants who have been detained for other forms of misconduct. If, however, the implementation of S.B 1070 and similar laws in five other states does lead to blatant levels of racial profiling, experts believe that the Court will revisit the constitutionality of these laws.[93]

SELF ASSESSMENT

Fill in the blanks and check your answers on page 244.

A police officer can make a _____ , which is not the same as an arrest, if she or he has a _____ suspicion that a criminal act is taking place or is about to take place. Then, the officer has the ability to _____ the suspect for weapons as a protective measure.

ARRESTS

As happened in the *Terry* case discussed earlier, a stop and frisk may lead to an **arrest.** An arrest is the taking into custody of a citizen for the purpose of detaining him or her on a criminal charge. It is important to understand the difference between a stop and an arrest. In the eyes of the law, a stop is a relatively brief intrusion on a citizen's rights, whereas an arrest—which involves a deprivation of liberty—is deserving of a full range of constitutional protections (see *Mastering Concepts—The Difference between a Stop and an Arrest* below). Consequently, while a stop can be made based on reasonable suspicion, a law enforcement officer needs probable cause, as defined earlier, to make an arrest.[94]

Elements of an Arrest

When is somebody under arrest? The easy—and incorrect—answer would be whenever the police officer says so. In fact, the state of being under arrest is dependent not only on the actions of the law enforcement officers but also on the perception of the suspect. Suppose Mr. Smith is stopped by plainclothes detectives, driven to the police station, and detained for three hours for questioning. During this time, the police never tell Mr. Smith he is under arrest, and in fact, he is free to leave at any time. But if Mr. Smith or any other reasonable person *believes* he is not free to leave, then, according to the Supreme Court, that person is in fact under arrest and should receive the necessary constitutional protections.[95]

MASTERING CONCEPTS
THE DIFFERENCE BETWEEN A STOP AND AN ARREST

Both stops and arrests are considered seizures because both police actions involve the restriction of an individual's freedom to "walk away." Both must be justified by a showing of reasonableness as well. You should be aware, however, of the differences between a stop and an arrest. **During a stop,** police can interrogate the person and make a limited search of his or her outer clothing. If anything occurs during the stop, such as the discovery of an illegal weapon, then officers may arrest the person. **If an arrest is made,** the suspect is now in police custody and is protected by the U.S. Constitution in a number of ways that will be discussed later in the chapter.

PhotoDisc

	STOP	ARREST
Justification	Reasonable suspicion only	Probable cause
Warrant	None	Required in some, but not all, situations
Intent of Officer	To investigate suspicious activity	To make a formal charge against the suspect
Search	May frisk, or "pat down," for weapons	May conduct a full search for weapons or evidence
Scope of Search	Outer clothing only	Area within the suspect's immediate control or "reach"

Arrest Warrant A written order, based on probable cause and issued by a judge or magistrate, commanding that the person named on the warrant be arrested by the police.

Exigent Circumstances Situations that require extralegal or exceptional actions by the police.

LEARNING OBJECTIVE 7: List the four elements that must be present for an arrest to take place.

Criminal justice professor Rolando V. del Carmen of Sam Houston State University has identified four elements that must be present for an arrest to take place:

1. The *intent* to arrest. In a stop, though it may entail slight inconvenience and a short detention period, there is no intent on the part of the law enforcement officer to take the person into custody. Therefore, there is no arrest. As intent is a subjective term, it is sometimes difficult to determine whether the police officer intended to arrest. In situations when the intent is unclear, courts often rely—as in our hypothetical case of Mr. Smith—on the perception of the arrestee.[96]
2. The *authority* to arrest. State laws give police officers the authority to place citizens under custodial arrest, or take them into custody. Like other state laws, the authorization to arrest varies among the fifty states. Some states, for example, allow off-duty police officers to make arrests, while others do not.
3. *Seizure or detention.* A necessary part of an arrest is the detention of the subject. Detention is considered to have occurred as soon as the arrested individual submits to the control of the officer, whether peacefully or under the threat or use of force.
4. The *understanding* of the person that she or he has been arrested. Through either words—such as "you are now under arrest"—or actions, the person taken into custody must understand that an arrest has taken place. When a suspect has been forcibly subdued by the police, handcuffed, and placed in a patrol car, he or she is believed to understand that an arrest has been made. This understanding may be lacking if the person is intoxicated, insane, or unconscious.[97]

FIGURE 7.3 Example of an Arrest Warrant

United States District Court

DISTRICT OF

UNITED STATES OF AMERICA
V.

WARRANT FOR ARREST

CASE NUMBER:

To: The United States Marshal
and any Authorized United States Officer

YOU ARE HEREBY COMMANDED to arrest ____________
Name

and bring him or her forthwith to the nearest magistrate to answer a(n)

☐ Indictment ☐ Information ☐ Complaint ☐ Order of Court ☐ Violation Notice ☐ Probation Violation Petition

charging him or her with (brief description of offense)

in violation of Title ______ United States Code, Section(s) ______

Name of Issuing Officer — Title of Issuing Officer

Signature of Issuing Officer — Date and Location

Bail fixed at $ ______ by ______
Name of Judicial Officer

RETURN

This warrant was received and executed with the arrest of the above-named defendant at ______

DATE RECEIVED	NAME AND TITLE OF ARRESTING OFFICER	SIGNATURE OF ARRESTING OFFICER
DATE OF ARREST		

Arrests with a Warrant

When law enforcement officers have established probable cause to arrest an individual who is not in police custody, they obtain an **arrest warrant** for that person. An arrest warrant, similar to a search warrant, contains information such as the name of the person suspected and the crime he or she is suspected of having committed. (See Figure 7.3 on the left for an example of an arrest warrant.) Judges or magistrates issue arrest warrants after first determining that the law enforcement officers have indeed established probable cause.

ENTERING A DWELLING There is a perception that an arrest warrant gives law enforcement officers the authority to enter a dwelling without first announcing themselves. This is not accurate. In *Wilson v. Arkansas* (1995),[98] the Supreme Court reiterated the common law requirement that police officers must knock and announce their identity and purpose before entering a dwelling. Under certain conditions, known as **exigent circumstances,** law enforcement officers need not announce themselves. As you saw at the beginning of the chapter, these circumstances include situations in which the officers have a reasonable belief of any of the following:

- The suspect is armed and poses a strong threat of violence to the officers or others inside the dwelling.

- Persons inside the dwelling are in the process of destroying evidence or escaping because of the presence of the police.
- A felony is being committed at the time the officers enter.[99]

Warrantless Arrest An arrest made without first seeking a warrant for the action.

According to Peter Kraska, a professor at Eastern Kentucky University, the number of no-knock police raids based on exigent circumstances has increased from 2,000 to 3,000 per year in the mid-1980s to 70,000 to 80,000 per year today.[100] Critics worry that with these tactics police are increasingly endangering citizens, some of whom may be innocent.[101] Infamously, in 2006 Atlanta undercover police officers fatally shot a ninety-two-year-old woman during a botched no-knock drug raid.

THE WAITING PERIOD The Supreme Court severely weakened the practical impact of the "knock and announce" rule with its decision in *Hudson v. Michigan* (2006).[102] In that case, Detroit police did not knock before entering the defendant's home with a warrant. Instead, they announced themselves and then waited only three to five seconds before making their entrance, not the fifteen to twenty seconds suggested by a prior Court ruling.[103] Hudson argued that the drugs found during the subsequent search were inadmissible because the law enforcement agents did not follow proper procedure.

By a 5–4 margin, the Court disagreed. In his majority opinion, Justice Antonin Scalia stated that an improper "knock and announce" is not unreasonable enough to provide defendants with a "get-out-of-jail-free card" by disqualifying evidence uncovered on the basis of a valid search warrant.[104] Thus, the exclusionary rule, discussed earlier in this chapter, would no longer apply under such circumstances. Legal experts still advise, however, that police observe a reasonable waiting period after knocking and announcing to be certain that any evidence found during the subsequent search will stand up in court.[105]

Arrests without a Warrant

Arrest warrants are not always required, and in fact, most arrests are made on the scene without a warrant. A law enforcement officer may make a **warrantless arrest** if:

1. The offense is committed in the presence of the officer; or
2. The officer has probable cause to believe that the suspect has committed a particular crime; or
3. The time lost in obtaining a warrant would allow the suspect to escape or destroy evidence, and the officer has probable cause to make an arrest.[106]

The type of crime also comes to bear in questions of arrests without a warrant. As a general rule, officers can make a warrantless arrest for a crime they did not see if they have probable cause to believe that a felony has been committed. For misdemeanors, the crime must have been committed in the presence of the officer for a warrantless arrest to be valid. According to a 2001 Supreme Court ruling, even an arrest for a misdemeanor that involves "gratuitous humiliations" imposed by a police officer "exercising extremely poor judgment" is valid as long as the officer can satisfy probable cause requirements.[107] That case involved a Texas mother who was handcuffed, taken away from her two young children, and placed in jail for failing to wear her seat belt.

In certain situations, warrantless arrests are unlawful even though a police officer can establish probable cause. In *Payton v. New York* (1980),[108] for example, the Supreme Court held that when exigent circumstances do not exist and the suspect does not give consent to enter a dwelling, law enforcement officers cannot force themselves in for the purpose of making a warrantless arrest. (In contrast, in the situation discussed at the

Interrogation The direct questioning of a suspect to gather evidence of criminal activity and to try to gain a confession.

Coercion The use of physical force or mental intimidation to compel a person to do something—such as confess to committing a crime—against her or his will.

opening of this chapter, exigent circumstances—the need to prevent the destruction of evidence relating to criminal activity—provided the police officers with a compelling reason to enter Hollis King's apartment and arrest him without a warrant.) A year after the *Payton* ruling, the Court expanded its holding to cover the homes of third parties.[109] So, if police wish to arrest a criminal suspect in another person's home, they cannot enter that home to arrest the suspect without first obtaining a search warrant, a process we discussed earlier in the chapter.

SELF ASSESSMENT

Fill in the blanks and check your answers on page 244.

An arrest occurs when a law enforcement agent takes a suspect into _____ on a criminal charge. If the officer has prior knowledge of the suspect's criminal activity, she or he must obtain a _____ from a judge or magistrate before making the arrest. Officers can, however, make _____ arrests if an offense is committed in their presence or they have _____ _____ to believe that a crime was committed by the particular subject.

THE INTERROGATION PROCESS AND *MIRANDA*

After the Pledge of Allegiance, there is perhaps no recitation that comes more readily to the American mind than the *Miranda* warning:

> You have the right to remain silent. If you give up that right, anything you say can and will be used against you in a court of law. You have the right to speak with an attorney and to have the attorney present during questioning. If you so desire and cannot afford one, an attorney will be appointed for you without charge before questioning.

The *Miranda* warning is not a mere prop. It strongly affects one of the most important aspects of any criminal investigation—the **interrogation,** or questioning of a suspect from whom the police want to get information concerning a crime and perhaps a confession.

The Legal Basis for *Miranda*

The Fifth Amendment guarantees protection against self-incrimination. In other words, as we shall see again in Chapter 10, a defendant cannot be required to provide information about his or her own criminal activity. A defendant's choice *not* to incriminate himself or herself cannot be interpreted as a sign of guilt by a jury in a criminal trial. A confession, or admission of guilt, is by definition a statement of self-incrimination. How, then, to reconcile the Fifth Amendment with the critical need of law enforcement officers to gain confessions? The answer lies in the concept of **coercion,** or the use of physical or psychological duress to obtain a confession.

SETTING THE STAGE FOR *MIRANDA* The Supreme Court first recognized that a confession could not be physically coerced in a 1936 case concerning a defendant who was beaten and whipped until he confessed to a murder.[110] It was not until 1964, however, that the Court specifically recognized that the accused's due process rights should be protected during interrogation.

That year, the Court heard the case of *Escobedo v. Illinois*,[111] which involved a convicted murderer who had incriminated himself during a four-hour questioning session at a police station. Police officers ignored the defendant's requests to speak with his lawyer, who was actually present at the station while his client was being interrogated.

The Court overturned the conviction, setting forth a five-pronged test in the process. This test established that if police are interrogating a suspect in custody, they cannot deny the suspect's request to speak with an attorney and must warn the suspect of his or her constitutional right to remain silent under the Fifth Amendment. If any one of the five prongs was not satisfied, the suspect had effectively been denied his or her right to counsel under the Sixth Amendment.[112]

THE *MIRANDA* CASE The limitations of the *Escobedo* decision quickly became apparent. All five of the prongs had to be satisfied for the defendant to enjoy the Sixth Amendment protections it offered. In fact, the accused rarely requested counsel, rendering the *Escobedo* test irrelevant no matter what questionable interrogation methods the police used to elicit confessions. Consequently, two years later, the Supreme Court handed down its *Miranda* decision,[113] establishing the **Miranda rights** and introducing the concept of what University of Columbia law professor H. Richard Uviller called *inherent coercion.* This terms refers to the assumption that even if a police officer does not lay a hand on a suspect, the general atmosphere of an interrogation is in and of itself coercive.[114]

Though the *Miranda* case is best remembered for the procedural requirement it spurred, at the time the Supreme Court was more concerned about the treatment of suspects during interrogation. (See the feature *Landmark Cases*—Miranda v. Arizona on the following page.) The Court found that routine police interrogation strategies, such as leaving suspects alone in a room for several hours before questioning them, were inherently coercive. Therefore, the Court reasoned, every suspect needed protection from coercion, not just those who had been physically abused. The *Miranda* warning is a result of this need. In theory, if the warning is not given to a suspect before an interrogation, the fruits of that interrogation, including a confession, are invalid.

When a *Miranda* Warning Is Required

As we shall see, a *Miranda* warning is not necessary under several conditions, such as when no questions are asked of the suspect. Generally, *Miranda* requirements apply only when a suspect is in **custody.** In a series of rulings since *Miranda,* the Supreme Court has defined custody as an arrest or a situation in which a reasonable person would not feel free to leave.[115] Consequently, a **custodial interrogation** occurs when a suspect is under arrest or is deprived of her or his freedom in a significant manner. Remember, a *Miranda* warning is only required before a custodial interrogation takes place. For example, if four police officers enter a suspect's bedroom at 4:00 A.M., wake him, and form a circle around him, then they must give him a *Miranda* warning before questioning. Even though the suspect has not been arrested, he will "not feel free to go where he please[s]."[116]

The concept of custody is a fluid one, as the Court demonstrated with a 2012 ruling involving an imprisoned convict suspected of committing additional sex crimes. The inmate was taken from his prison cell to a conference room on a different floor, where he was questioned for five to seven hours without being read his *Miranda* rights. Even though the inmate was under armed guard and still in prison, the Court ruled that he was not in "custody" because the door to the room was open and he was told several times during the session that he was free to leave.[117]

When a *Miranda* Warning Is Not Required

A *Miranda* warning is not necessary in a number of situations:

1. When the police do not ask the suspect any questions that are *testimonial* in nature. Such questions are designed to elicit information that may be used against

Miranda Rights The constitutional rights of accused persons taken into custody by law enforcement officials, such as the right to remain silent and the right to counsel.

Custody The forceful detention of a person, or the perception that a person is not free to leave the immediate vicinity.

Custodial Interrogation The questioning of a suspect after that person has been taken into custody. In this situation, the suspect must be read his or her *Miranda* rights before interrogation can begin.

the suspect in court. Note that "routine booking questions," such as the suspect's name, address, height, and eye color, do not require a *Miranda* warning. Even though answering these questions may provide incriminating evidence (especially if the person answering is a prime suspect), the Supreme Court has held that they are absolutely necessary if the police are to do their jobs.[118] (Imagine the officer not being able to ask a suspect her or his name.)

2. When the police have not focused on a suspect and are questioning witnesses at the scene of a crime.

3. When a person volunteers information before the police have asked a question.

4. When the suspect has given a private statement to a friend or some other acquaintance. *Miranda* does not apply to these statements so long as the government did not orchestrate the situation.

LANDMARK CASES:
Miranda v. Arizona

LEARNING OBJECTIVE 8
Explain why the U.S. Supreme Court established the *Miranda* warnings.

In 1963, a rape and kidnapping victim identified produce worker Ernesto Miranda as her assailant in a lineup. Phoenix detectives questioned Miranda for two hours concerning the crimes, at no time informing him that he had a right to have an attorney present. When the police emerged from the session, they had a signed statement by Miranda confessing to the crimes. He was subsequently convicted and sentenced to twenty to thirty years in prison. After the conviction was confirmed by the Arizona Supreme Court, Miranda appealed to the United States Supreme Court, claiming that he had not been warned that any statement he made could be used against him, and that he had a right to counsel during the interrogation.

Miranda v. Arizona
United States Supreme Court
384 U.S. 436 (1966)

IN THE WORDS OF THE COURT . . .
CHIEF JUSTICE WARREN, MAJORITY OPINION

* * * *

The cases before us raise questions which go to the roots of our concepts of American criminal jurisprudence: the restraints society must observe consistent with the Federal Constitution in prosecuting individuals for crime. More specifically, we deal with the admissibility of statements obtained from an individual who is subjected to custodial police interrogation and the necessity for procedures which assure that the individual is accorded his privilege under the Fifth Amendment to the Constitution not to be compelled to incriminate himself.

* * * *

It is obvious that such an interrogation environment is created for no purpose other than to subjugate the individual to the will of his examiner. This atmosphere carries its own badge of intimidation. To be sure, this is not physical intimidation, but it is equally destructive of human dignity. The current practice of incommunicado interrogation is at odds with one of our Nation's most cherished principles—that the individual may not be compelled to incriminate himself. Unless adequate protective devices are employed to dispel the compulsion inherent in custodial surroundings, no statement obtained from the defendant can truly be the product of his free choice.

DECISION
The Court overturned Miranda's conviction, stating that police interrogations are, by their very nature, coercive and therefore deny suspects their constitutional right against self-incrimination by "forcing" them to confess. Consequently, any person who has been arrested and placed in custody must be informed of his or her right to be free from self-incrimination and to be represented by counsel during any interrogation. In other words, suspects must be told that they *do not have* to answer police questions. To accomplish this, the Court established the *Miranda* warning, which must be read prior to questioning a suspect in custody.

FOR CRITICAL ANALYSIS
What is meant by the phrase "coercion can be mental as well as physical"? What role does the concept of "mental coercion" play in Chief Justice Warren's opinion?

5. During a stop and frisk, when no arrest has been made.
6. During a traffic stop.[119]

LEARNING
9
OBJECTIVE

Indicate situations in which a *Miranda* warning is unnecessary.

In 1984, the Supreme Court also created a "public-safety exception" to the *Miranda* rule. The case involved a police officer who, after feeling an empty shoulder holster on a man he had just arrested, asked the suspect the location of the gun without informing him of his *Miranda* rights. The Court ruled that the gun was admissible as evidence because the police's duty to protect the public is more important than a suspect's *Miranda* rights.[120] In April 2013, federal law enforcement agents relied on this exception to question Boston Marathon bomber Dzhokhar Tsarnaev from a hospital bed without first "Mirandizing" him. Once the agents were satisfied that Tsarnaev knew of no other active plots or threats to public safety, they read the suspect his *Miranda* rights in the presence of a lawyer.[121]

WAIVING *MIRANDA* Suspects can *waive* their Fifth Amendment rights and speak to a police officer, but only if the waiver is made voluntarily. Silence on the part of a suspect does not mean that his or her *Miranda* protections have been relinquished. To waive their rights, suspects must state—either in writing or orally—that they understand those rights and that they will voluntarily answer questions without the presence of counsel.

To ensure that the suspect's rights are upheld, prosecutors are required to prove by a preponderance of the evidence that the suspect "knowing and intelligently" waived his or her *Miranda* rights.[122] To make the waiver perfectly clear, police will ask suspects two questions in addition to giving the *Miranda* warning:

1. Do you understand your rights as I have read them to you?
2. Knowing your rights, are you willing to talk to another law enforcement officer or me?

If the suspect indicates that she or he does not want to speak to the officer, thereby invoking her or his right to silence, the officer must *immediately* stop any questioning.[123] Similarly, if the suspect requests a lawyer, the police can ask no further questions until an attorney is present.[124]

CLEAR INTENT The suspect must be absolutely clear about her or his intention to stop the questioning or have a lawyer present. In *Davis v. United States* (1994),[125] the Supreme Court upheld the interrogation of a suspect after he said, "Maybe I should talk to a lawyer." The Court found that this statement was too ambiguous, saying that it did not want to force police officers to "read the minds" of suspects who make vague declarations. Along these same lines, in *Berghuis v. Thompkins* (2010),[126] the Court upheld the conviction of a suspect who implicated himself in a murder after remaining mostly silent during nearly three hours of police questioning. The defendant claimed that he had invoked his *Miranda* rights by being

■ What aspects of the situation shown in this photo indicate that the Aspen (Colorado) police officer is required to "Mirandize" the suspect before asking him any questions, even if he never formally places the suspect under arrest?
Photo by Chris Hondros/Getty Images

uncommunicative with the interrogating officers. The Court disagreed, saying that silence is not enough—a suspect must actually state that he or she wishes to cut off questioning for the *Miranda* protections to apply.

The Law Enforcement Response to *Miranda*

When the *Miranda* decision was first handed down, many people, particularly police officials, complained that it distorted the Constitution by placing the rights of criminal suspects above the rights of society as a whole.[127] In the four and a half decades since the ruling, however, law enforcement agents have adapted to the *Miranda* restrictions, and strategies to work within their boundaries have become a standard part of police training.

After an extensive on-site study of police interrogation tactics, Richard A. Leo, a criminologist at the University of San Francisco law school, noted a pattern of maneuvers that officers use to convince suspects to voluntarily waive their *Miranda* rights. Leo identifies three such strategies:

- The *conditioning* strategy is geared toward creating an environment in which the suspect is encouraged to think positively of the interrogator and thus is conditioned to cooperate. The interrogator will offer the suspect coffee or a cigarette and make pleasant small talk. These steps are intended to lower the suspect's anxiety level and generate a sense of trust that is conducive to a *Miranda* waiver and confession.
- The *de-emphasizing strategy* tries to downplay the importance of *Miranda* protections, giving the impression that the rights are unimportant and can be easily waived. For example, one officer told a suspect, "I need to advise you of your rights. It's a formality. I'm sure you've watched television with the cop shows and you hear them say their rights so you can probably recite this better than I can, but it's something I need to do and we can get this out of the way before we talk about what happened."
- When using the *persuasion* strategy, an officer will explicitly try to convince the suspect to waive her or his rights. Commonly, the detective will tell suspects that waiving the rights is the only way they will be able to get their side of the story out. Otherwise, the detective continues, only the victim's side of the story will be considered during the trial.[128]

Sometimes, officers go too far with their interrogation strategies and infringe on a suspect's rights. About twenty years ago, for example, police officers questioned seventeen-year-old Jonathan Doody overnight for more than twelve straight hours concerning the killing of nine people outside a Buddhist temple in Phoenix, Arizona. Although the officers told Doody at the outset that he had the right to remain silent, they reacted to his silence aggressively. At one point, when Doody refused to answer the same questions for the fourteenth time, a frustrated detective responded:

> Say something. Say something, Jonathan. Come on, man, this is ridiculous. Say something. What's your name? What's your name, Jonathan? Jonathan, what's your name? What's your last name?[129]

Finally, at 4 A.M., Doody confessed to his involvement in the killings and was eventually convicted on nine counts of murder. In 2010, however, a federal appeals court overturned the conviction, holding that the officers had effectively "de-Mirandized" Doody during the long and stressful interrogation session and therefore his confession was inadmissible in court.[130]

The Future of *Miranda*

"*Miranda* has become embedded in routine police practice to the point where the warnings have become part of our national culture," wrote Chief Justice William Rehnquist over a decade ago.[131] This may be true, but, at the same time, many legal scholars believe that a series of Supreme Court rulings have eroded *Miranda*'s protections. "It's death by a thousand cuts," says Jeffrey L. Fisher of the National Association of Criminal Defense Lawyers, who believes the Court is "doing everything it can to ease the admissibility of confessions that police wriggle out of suspects."[132]

VOLUNTARY STATEMENTS One such exception, created by the Supreme Court in 2004, is crucial to understanding the status of *Miranda* rights in current criminal law. The case involved a Colorado defendant who voluntarily told the police the location of his gun (which, being an ex-felon, he was not allowed to possess) without being read his rights.[133] The Court upheld the conviction, finding that the *Miranda* warning is merely *prophylactic*. In other words, it is only intended to prevent violations of the Fifth Amendment. Because only the gun, and not the defendant's testimony, was presented at trial, the police had not violated the defendant's constitutional rights. In essence, the Court was ruling that the "fruit of the poisoned tree" doctrine, discussed earlier in this chapter, does not bar the admission of physical evidence that is discovered based on voluntary statements by a suspect who has not been "Mirandized." (See Figure 7.4 below for a rundown of several other significant Court rulings that have weakened the *Miranda* requirements over the past decades.)

RECORDING CONFESSIONS *Miranda* may eventually find itself obsolete regardless of any decisions made in the courts. A relatively new trend in law enforcement has been for agencies to record interrogations and confessions digitally. Video recording technology has progressed to the point where it is reasonable to ask law enforcement agents to carry a personal video camera with them at all times.[134] Indeed, as we saw in the previous chapter, many police agencies in the United States now use body-mounted video cameras that record all contacts with suspects.

One of the benefits of recording confessions in this manner would be to lessen suspicions that police officers use verbal techniques like accusation and confrontation to elicit *false confessions*. Such videos contain clear evidence of how an interview is carried out,

FIGURE 7.4 Supreme Court Decisions Eroding *Miranda* Rights

Moran v. Burbine (475 U.S. 412 [1986]). **This case established that police officers are not required to tell suspects undergoing custodial interrogation that their attorney is trying to reach them.** The Court ruled that events that the suspect could have no way of knowing about have no bearing on his ability to waive his *Miranda* rights.

Arizona v. Fulminante (499 U.S. 279 [1991]). **In this very important ruling, the Court held that a conviction is not automatically overturned if the suspect was coerced into making a confession.** If the other evidence introduced at the trial is strong enough to justify a conviction without the confession, then the fact that the confession was illegally gained can be, for all intents and purposes, ignored.

Texas v. Cobb (532 U.S. 162 [2001]). When a suspect refuses to waive his or her *Miranda* rights, a police officer cannot lawfully continue the interrogation until the suspect's attorney arrives on the scene. In this case, however, **the Court held that a suspect may be questioned without having a lawyer present if the interrogation does not focus on the crime for which he or she was arrested,** even though it does touch on another, closely related, offense.

Florida v. Powell (559 U.S. ___ [2010]). Florida's version of the *Miranda* warning informs suspects that they have a right "to talk with an attorney," but does not clearly inform them of the right to a lawyer during any police interrogation. The Court upheld Florida's warning, **ruling that different jurisdictions may use whatever version of the *Miranda* warning they please, as long as it reasonably conveys the essential information about a suspect's rights.**

and whether law enforcement agents have used improper means to gain the confession. In Texas, where false confessions have led at least seven innocent suspects to be wrongfully convicted in recent years, legislators are considering requiring video interrogations in all cases involving violent felonies.[135] Three states—Alaska, Illinois, and Minnesota—and hundreds of municipalities already regularly engage in this practice. Some scholars have suggested that recording all custodial interrogations would satisfy the Fifth Amendment's prohibition against coercion and thus render the *Miranda* warning unnecessary.

SELF ASSESSMENT

Fill in the blanks and check your answers on page 244.

Miranda requirements apply only when law enforcement agents have the suspect in _____. The *Miranda* warning is only required _____ a custodial interrogation takes place. A suspect can _____ his or her *Miranda* rights, but this must be done "knowingly and intentionally." If the suspect indicates that he or she does not wish to speak, the police officer must _____ stop any questioning. The suspect can also end questioning any time by requesting the presence of an _____.

THE IDENTIFICATION PROCESS

LEARNING
10
OBJECTIVE

List the three basic types of police identification.

A confession is a form of self-identification; the suspect has identified herself or himself as the guilty party. If police officers are unable to gain a confession, they must use other methods to link the suspect with the crime. In fact, to protect against false admissions, police must use these other methods even if the suspect confesses.

Essential Procedures

Unless police officers witness the commission of the crime themselves, they must establish the identity of the suspect using three basic types of identification procedures:

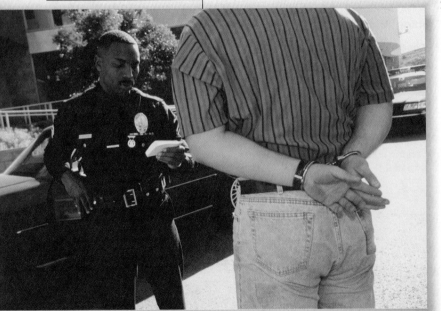

■ A Los Angeles police officer reads a handcuffed "suspect" his *Miranda* rights during a training exercise. Does a police officer need to take this action every time he or she arrests a suspect? If not, under what circumstances must an officer administer the *Miranda* warning?
Kim Kulish/Corbis

1. *Showups,* which occur when a suspect who matches the description given by witnesses is apprehended near the scene of the crime within a reasonable amount of time after the crime has been committed. The suspect is usually returned to the crime scene for possible identification by witnesses.

2. *Photo arrays,* which occur when no suspect is in custody but the police have a general description of the person. Witnesses and victims are shown "mug shots" of people with police records that match the description. Police will also present witnesses and victims with pictures of people they believe might have committed the crime.

3. *Lineups,* which entail lining up several physically similar people, one of whom is the suspect, in front of a witness or victim. The police may have each member of the lineup wear clothing similar to that worn by the criminal and say a phrase that was used during the crime. These visual and oral cues are designed to help the witness identify the suspect.

As with the other procedures discussed in this chapter, constitutional law governs the identification process, though some aspects are more tightly restricted than others. The Sixth Amendment right to counsel, for example, does not apply during showups or photo arrays. In showups, the police often need to establish a suspect quickly, and it would be unreasonable to expect them to wait for an attorney to arrive. According to the Supreme Court in *United States v. Ash* (1973),[136] however, the police must be able to prove this need for immediate identification, perhaps by showing that it was necessary to keep the suspect from fleeing the state.

As for photo arrays, courts have found that any procedure that does not require the suspect's presence does not require the presence of his or her attorney.[137] The lack of an attorney does not mean that police can "steer" a witness toward a positive identification with statements such as "Are you sure this isn't the person you saw robbing the grocery store?" Such actions would violate the suspect's due process rights.

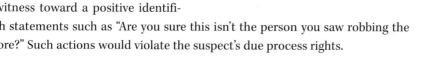

■ David Lee Wiggins, center, spent more than two decades in a Texas prison for the 1989 rape of a fourteen-year-old girl before DNA evidence proved his innocence. The victim, whose face was covered during most of the attack, picked Wiggins out of a photo array and then a live lineup. How does Wiggins's case expose some of the drawbacks of using these methods to identify suspects?
AP Photo/*The Fort Worth Star-Telegram*, Rodger Mallison

Nontestimonial Evidence

Some observers feel that the standard **booking** procedure—the process of recording information about the suspect immediately after arrest—infringes on a suspect's Fifth Amendment rights. During booking, the suspect is photographed and fingerprinted, and blood samples may be taken. If these samples lead to the suspect's eventual identification, according to some, they amount to self-incrimination. In *Schmerber v. California* (1966),[138] however, the Supreme Court held that such tests are not the equivalent of *testimonial* self-incrimination (where the suspect testifies verbally against himself or herself) and therefore do not violate the Fifth Amendment.

Using similar legal reasoning, the Court has also determined that voice and handwriting samples gathered by police may be used to identify a suspect.[139] Because alcohol dissipates quickly in the bloodstream, courts consistently allow the police to draw blood from suspected drunk drivers without consent or a search warrant.[140]

SELF ASSESSMENT

Fill in the blanks and check your answers on page 244.

Police employ several methods to _____ a suspect, or link that suspect to the crime. They will show witnesses a _____ _____ of suspect "mug shots" or present a number of physically similar persons, one of whom is the suspect, in a _____. The United States Supreme Court has determined that standard _____ procedures, during which police record information on the suspect, do not violate the Fifth Amendment.

Booking The process of entering a suspect's name, offense, and arrival time into the police log following her or his arrest.

CJ IN ACTION

RACIAL PROFILING AND THE CONSTITUTION

The plainclothes New York police officer overheard two Middle Eastern men speaking Urdu, a language common in Pakistan. They were complaining about airport security measures that they believed focused unfairly on Muslims. On the basis of this conversation alone, the two men became targets of the New York Police Department's Demographics Unit, a secret team dedicated to preventing terrorist attacks.[141] Particularly in the age of terrorism, when community suspicion rests heavily on Arab and Muslim Americans, the practice of racial profiling remains a controversial subject. In this *CJ in Action* feature, we will explore the difficult question of whether this police tactic can be justified.

A VALID STRATEGY?

The Fourth Amendment protects persons against "unreasonable searches and seizures." Intuitively, it would seem that when the police search or detain a person because of his or her race, an unreasonable search or seizure has taken place. Nevertheless, such profiling does seem to occur, as with the New York anti-terrorism unit mentioned above. Furthermore, the federal government recently opened an investigation into security officials at Boston's Logan International Airport for racially profiling passengers who fit certain stereotypes, such as Hispanics traveling to Miami or African Americans wearing baseball caps backward.[142]

In New York City, an overwhelming percentage of stops and frisks conducted by the police involve members of minority groups. Earlier in the chapter, you learned that, in these cases, as long as a police officer has probable cause that actual wrongdoing has occurred, any "racist intent" on his or her part is often irrelevant. Does this mean that racial profiling is a valid law enforcement strategy?

THE CASE FOR RACIAL PROFILING

- Crime rates are racially disproportionate. Young African American males are often more likely than other age and racial groups to commit drug-related crimes. Hispanics are more likely than other ethnic groups to have violated immigration laws. To ignore such evidence in the name of cultural sensitivity does a disservice to law-abiding citizens of all races.[143]

- Racial profiling sometimes can seem to work. Since the New York Police Department implemented its Stop, Question, and Frisk policy over a decade ago, the city has experienced a "historic" crime decline, and officers have confiscated 6,000 firearms.[144] At the same time, the murder rate in Philadelphia jumped by 10 percent in the first year after the city reined in its own aggressive stop-and-frisk policy.[145]

- Racial profiling is necessary to protect against terrorist acts, which, at present, have mostly been committed by men of Middle Eastern background. "We're at war with a terrorist network," says one commentator. "Are we really supposed to ignore the one identifiable fact that we know about them?"[146]

THE CASE AGAINST RACIAL PROFILING

- Racial profiling is indistinguishable from racism and humiliates thousands of innocent people.

- If members of minority groups are more likely to be carrying illegal drugs than are whites, then police should find drugs more often on them than on whites after a stop and search. In fact, such "hit rates" are remarkably similar among the races.[147]

- If terrorist groups know in advance that law enforcement agencies are focusing on certain races or ethnic groups, they will simply select individuals of different races or ethnic groups for future attacks.

YOUR OPINION—WRITING ASSIGNMENT

Over the course of six years, New York's Demographics Unit, mentioned above, infiltrated Muslim communities in New York, New Jersey, and Connecticut, without proof of any wrongdoing.[148] The law enforcement agents assembled databases on where Muslims lived, worked, and prayed, and placed informants in hundreds of Muslim student groups and mosques. Do you think there are any circumstances, such as providing an "early warning system" for terrorism, under which a suspect's race or ethnicity can be used to establish reasonable suspicion or probable cause? Or, do you think that law enforcement should always be "color blind"? Before responding, you can review our discussions in this chapter concerning:

- Probable cause (pages 213–215).

- The definition of reasonable suspicion (page 228).

- Arrests (pages 231–234).

Your answer should include at least three full paragraphs.

CHAPTER SUMMARY

For more information on these concepts, look back to the Learning Objective icons throughout the chapter.

 Outline the four major sources that may provide probable cause. (a) Personal observation, usually due to an officer's personal training, experience, and expertise; (b) information, gathered from informants, eyewitnesses, victims, police bulletins, and other sources; (c) evidence, which often has to be in plain view; and (d) association, which generally must involve a person with a known criminal background who is seen in a place where criminal activity is openly taking place.

 Explain the exclusionary rule and the exceptions to it. This rule prohibits illegally seized evidence, or evidence obtained by an unreasonable search and seizure in an inadmissible way, from being used against the accused in criminal court. Exceptions to the exclusionary rule are the "inevitable discovery" exception established in *Nix v. Williams* and the "good faith" exception established in *United States v. Leon* and *Arizona v. Evans.*

 List the four categories of items that can be seized by use of a search warrant. (a) Items resulting from a crime, such as stolen goods; (b) inherently illegal items; (c) evidence of the crime; and (d) items used in committing the crime.

 Explain when searches can be made without a warrant. Searches and seizures can be made without a warrant if they are incidental to an arrest (but they must be reasonable); when they are made with voluntary consent; when they involve the "movable vehicle" exception; when property has been abandoned; and when items are in plain view, under certain restricted circumstances (see *Coolidge v. New Hampshire*).

 Describe the plain view doctrine and indicate one of its limitations. Under the plain view doctrine, police officers are justified in seizing an item if (a) the item is easily seen by an officer who is legally in a position to notice it; (b) the discovery of the item is unintended; and (c) the officer, without further investigation, immediately recognizes the illegal nature of the item.

An item is not in plain view if the law enforcement agent needs to use technology such as a thermal imager to "see" it.

 Distinguish between a stop and a frisk, and indicate the importance of the case *Terry v. Ohio.* Though the terms *stop* and *frisk* are often used in concert, a stop is the separate act of detaining a suspect when an officer reasonably believes that a criminal activity is about to take place. A frisk is the physical "pat-down" of a suspect. In *Terry v. Ohio,* the Supreme Court ruled that an officer must have "specific and articulable facts" before making a stop, but those facts may be "taken together with rational inferences."

 List the four elements that must be present for an arrest to take place. (a) Intent, (b) authority, (c) seizure or detention, and (d) the understanding of the person that he or she has been arrested.

 Explain why the U.S. Supreme Court established the *Miranda* warnings. The Supreme Court recognized that police interrogations are, by their nature, coercive. Consequently, to protect a suspect's constitutional rights during interrogation, the Court ruled that the suspect must be informed of those rights before being questioned.

 Indicate situations in which a *Miranda* warning is unnecessary. (a) When no questions that are testimonial in nature are asked of the suspect; (b) when there is no suspect and witnesses in general are being questioned at the scene of a crime; (c) when a person volunteers information before the police ask anything; (d) when a suspect has given a private statement to a friend without the government orchestrating it; (e) during a stop and frisk when no arrests have been made; (f) during a traffic stop; and (g) when a threat to public safety exists.

 List the three basic types of police identification. (a) Showups, (b) photo arrays, and (c) lineups.

QUESTIONS FOR CRITICAL ANALYSIS

1. What are the two most significant legal concepts contained in the Fourth Amendment, and why are they important?

2. Should law enforcement agents be required to get a search warrant before accessing records that reveal a cell phone user's location? Those who think a warrant

is unnecessary in this situation argue that once users turn their phones on, they have decided to waive their expectations of privacy by "voluntarily" transmitting their locations. What is your opinion of this argument?

3. A suspect discards his half-smoked cigarette on the sidewalk. The cigarette is picked up by a police officer, and the saliva on it allows law enforcement to obtain a sample of the suspect's DNA. Without a search warrant, should this evidence be allowed in court? Why or why not?

4. Suppose that a police officer stops a person who "looks funny." The person acts strangely, so the police officer decides to frisk him. The officer feels a bulge in the suspect's coat pocket, which turns out to be a bag of cocaine. Would the arrest for cocaine possession hold up in court? Why or why not?

5. What if, in the case that opens this chapter, the Kentucky narcotics officers had not smelled marijuana and had simply knocked on Hollis King's door and asked to talk with him? What would King's options have been in that situation?

KEY **TERMS**

affidavit   219

arrest   231

arrest warrant   232

booking   241

coercion   234

consent searches   221

custodial interrogation   235

custody   235

electronic surveillance   225

exclusionary rule   215

exigent circumstances   232

frisk   229

fruit of the poisoned tree   215

"good faith" exception   216

"inevitable discovery" exception   216

interrogation   234

Miranda rights   235

plain view doctrine   224

probable cause   213

racial profiling   230

search   217

search warrant   218

searches and seizures   213

searches incidental to arrests   220

seizure   219

stop   229

warrantless arrest   233

SELF ASSESSMENT **ANSWER KEY**

Page 216: i. unreasonable; **ii.** probable cause; **iii.** exclusionary; **iv.** evidence

Page 227: i. privacy; **ii.** search warrant; **iii.** seize; **iv.** arrest; **v.** consent; **vi.** probable; **vii.** significant

Page 231: i. stop; **ii.** reasonable; **iii.** frisk

Page 234: i. custody; **ii.** warrant; **iii.** warrantless; **iv.** probable cause

Page 240: i. custody; **ii.** before; **iii.** waive; **iv.** immediately; **v.** attorney

Page 241: i. identify; **ii.** photo array; **iii.** lineup; **iv.** booking

NOTES

1. *Kentucky v. King*, 131 S.Ct. 1849 (2011).

2. *Ibid.*, 1858.

3. *Ibid.*, 1869.

4. *Michigan v. Summers*, 452 U.S. 692 (1981).

5. *Brinegar v. United States*, 338 U.S. 160 (1949).

6. Rolando V. del Carmen, *Criminal Procedure for Law Enforcement Personnel* (Monterey, CA: Brooks/Cole Publishing Co., 1987), 63–64.

7. *Florida v. Harris*, ____ U.S. ____ (2013).

8. *Maryland v. Pringle*, 540 U.S. 366 (2003).

9. 500 U.S. 44 (1991).

10. *United States v. Leon*, 468 U.S. 897 (1984).

11. Thomas Y. Davis, "A Hard Look at What We Know (and Still Need to Learn) about the 'Costs' of the Exclusionary Rule: The NIJ Study and Other Studies of 'Lost' Arrests," *A.B.F. Research Journal* (1983), 680.

12. 430 U.S. 387 (1977).

13. 467 U.S. 431 (1984).

14. 468 U.S. 897 (1984).

15. 514 U.S. 1 (1995).

16. *California v. Greenwood*, 486 U.S. 35 (1988).

17. *Ibid.*

18. 389 U.S. 347 (1967).

19. *Ibid.*, 361.

20. 486 U.S. 35 (1988).

21. *Ibid.*

22. *Illinois v. Caballes,* 543 U.S. 405 (2005).

23. 565 U.S. _____ (2012).

24. *Ibid.*

25. Quoted in James Vicini, "Supreme Court Limits Police Use of GPS to Track Suspects," *Reuters* (January 23, 2012).

26. *Coolidge v. New Hampshire,* 403 U.S. 443, 467 (1971).

27. *Millender v. Messerschmidt,* 620 F.3d 1016 (9th Cir. 2010).

28. del Carmen, 158.

29. *Katz v. United States,* 389 U.S. 347, 357 (1967).

30. *Brigham City v. Stuart,* 547 U.S. 398 (2006).

31. 414 U.S. 234–235 (1973).

32. 395 U.S. 752 (1969).

33. *Ibid.,* 763.

34. Carl A. Benoit, "Questioning 'Authority': Fourth Amendment Consent Searches," *FBI Law Enforcement Bulletin* (July 2008), 24.

35. *Bumper v. North Carolina,* 391 U.S. 543 (1968).

36. *State v. Stone,* 362 N.C. 50, 653 S.E.2d 414 (2007).

37. 412 U.S. 218 (1973).

38. Jayme W. Holcomb, "Knock and Talks," *FBI Law Enforcement Bulletin* (August 2006), 22–32.

39. Ian D. Midgley, "Just One Question before We Get to *Ohio v. Robinette:* 'Are You Carrying Any Contraband . . . Weapons, Drugs, Constitutional Protections . . . Anything Like That?'" *Case Western Reserve Law Review* 48 (Fall 1997), 173.

40. 501 U.S. 429 (1991).

41. 519 U.S. 33 (1996).

42. *United States v. Drayton,* 536 U.S. 194 (2002).

43. Linda Greenhouse, "Supreme Court Upholds Police Methods in Vehicle Drug Searches," *New York Times* (November 19, 1996), A23.

44. 267 U.S. 132 (1925).

45. *United States v. Ross,* 456 U.S. 798, 804–809 (1982); and *Chambers v. Maroney,* 399 U.S. 42, 44, 52 (1970).

46. 453 U.S. 454 (1981).

47. *Arizona v. Gant,* 556 U.S. 332 (2009).

48. Adam Liptak, "Justices Significantly Cut Back Officers' Searches of Cars of People They Arrest," *New York Times* (April 22, 2009), A12.

49. Dale Anderson and Dave Cole, "Search and Seizure after *Arizona v. Gant,*" *Arizona Attorney* (October 2009), 15.

50. *Maryland v. Wilson,* 519 U.S. 408 (1997).

51. *Whren v. United States,* 517 U.S. 806 (1996).

52. *United States v. Ross,* 456 U.S. 798 (1982).

53. *Ibid.,* 824.

54. *California v. Acevedo,* 500 U.S. 565 (1991).

55. 403 U.S. 443 (1971).

56. *Kyollo v. United States,* 533 U.S. 27 (2001).

57. 388 U.S. 42 (1967).

58. 18 U.S.C. Sections 2510(7), 2518(1)(a), 2516 (1994).

59. Christopher K. Murphy, "Electronic Surveillance," in "Twenty-Sixth Annual Review of Criminal Procedure," *Georgetown Law Journal* (April 1997), 920.

60. *United States v. Nguyen,* 46 F.3d 781, 783 (8th Cir. 1995).

61. Joseph Siprut, "Privacy through Anonymity: An Economic Argument for Expanding the Right of Privacy in Public Places," *Pepperdine Law Review* 33 (2006), 311, 320.

62. Quoted in Rebecca Kanable, "Dallas' First Year with CCTV," *Law Enforcement Technology* (February 2008), 35.

63. Nick Paumgarten, "Here's Looking at You," *New Yorker* (May 14, 2012), 48.

64. Sharon B. Franklin, "Watching the Watchers: Establishing Limits on Public Video Surveillance," *Champion* (April 2008), 40.

65. Quoted in Paumgarten, 48.

66. Pub. L. No. 107-56, Section 201-2-2, 115 Stat. 272, 278 (2001).

67. 50 U.S.C. Section 1803 (2000).

68. Patriot Act, Section 203(d)(1), 115 Stat. 272, 280 (2001).

69. Patriot Act, Section 206, amending Section 105(c)(2)(B) of the Foreign Intelligence Surveillance Act.

70. FISA Amendments Act of 2008, Pub. L. No. 110-261, 122 Stat. 2436 (2008).

71. Eric Lichtblau, "Senate Approves Bill to Broaden Wiretap Powers," *New York Times* (July 10, 2008), A1.

72. *Woodson v. Indiana,* No. 49A05-1106-CR-306 (2011).

73. Karen M. Hess and Henry M. Wrobleski, *Police Operation: Theory and Practice* (St. Paul, MN: West Publishing Co., 1997), 122.

74. 392 U.S. 1 (1968).

75. *Ibid.,* 20.

76. *Ibid.,* 21.

77. See *United States v. Cortez,* 449 U.S. 411 (1981); and *United States v. Sokolow,* 490 U.S. 1 (1989).

78. *United States v. Arvizu,* 534 U.S. 266 (2002).

79. *Ibid.,* 270.

80. *United States v. Place,* 462 U.S. 696 (1983).

81. *Hibel v. Sixth Judicial District Court,* 542 U.S. 177 (2004).

82. *Ibid.,* 182.

83. *Minnesota v. Dickerson,* 508 U.S. 366 (1993).

84. *Arizona v. Johnson,* 555 U.S. 328 (2009).

85. *United States v. Avery,* 137 F.3d 343, 353 (6th Cir. 1997).

86. Ian Ayres and Jonathan Borowsky, *A Study of Racially Disparate Outcomes in the Los Angeles Police Department* (Los Angeles: ACLU of Southern California, October 2008), i.

87. Raymond W. Kelly, *2011 Reasonable Suspicion Stops* (New York: City of New York Police Department, 2012), 4.

88. Quoted in Russ Buettner and William Glaberson, "Courts Putting Stop-and-Frisk Policy on Trial," *New York Times* (July 11, 2012), A1.

89. Reuben Kramer, "Philly Police Settle Suit over 'Stops and Frisks,'" *Courthouse News Service* (June 24, 2011), at **www.courthousenews .com/2011/06/24/37675.htm.**

90. Quoted in Fernando Santos, "Arizona Sheriff's Trial begins with Focus on Complaints about Illegal Immigrants," *New York Times* (July 20, 2012), A11.

91. Arizona Revised Statutes Sections 11-1051(B), 13-1509, 13-2929(C).

92. *Arizona v. United States,* 567 U.S. ___ (2012).

93. Julia Preston, "Immigration Ruling Leaves Issues Unresolved," *New York Times* (June 27, 2012), A14.

94. Rolando V. del Carmen and Jeffrey T. Walker, *Briefs of Leading Cases in Law Enforcement,* 2d ed. (Cincinnati, OH: Anderson, 1995), 38–40.

95. *Florida v. Royer,* 460 U.S. 491 (1983).

96. See also *United States v. Mendenhall,* 446 U.S. 544 (1980).

97. del Carmen, 97–98.

98. 514 U.S. 927 (1995).

99. Linda J. Collier and Deborah D. Rosenbloom, *American Jurisprudence,* 2d ed. (Rochester, NY: Lawyers Cooperative Publishing, 1995), 122.

100. Quoted in Ron Barnett and Paul Alongi, "Critics Knock No-Knock Police Raids," *USA Today* (February 14, 2011), 3A.

101. Radley Balko, *Overkill: The Rise of Paramilitary Police Raids in America* (Washington, D.C.: Cato Institute, 2006), 2–15.

102. 547 U.S. 586 (2006).

103. *United States v. Banks,* 540 U.S. 31, 41 (2003).

104. *Hudson v. Michigan,* 547 U.S. 586, 593 (2006).

105. Tom Van Dorn, "Violation of Knock-and-Announce Rule Does Not Require Suppression of All Evidence Found in Search," *The Police Chief* (October 2006), 10.

106. "Warrantless Searches and Seizures" in *Georgetown Law Journal Annual Review of Criminal Procedure, 2011* (Washington, D.C.: Georgetown Law Journal, 2011), 955.

107. *Atwater v. City of Lago Vista,* 532 U.S. 318, 346–347 (2001).

108. 445 U.S. 573 (1980).

109. *Steagald v. United States,* 451 U.S. 204 (1981).

110. *Brown v. Mississippi,* 297 U.S. 278 (1936).

111. 378 U.S. 478 (1964).

112. *Ibid.,* 490–491.

113. *Miranda v. Arizona,* 384 U.S. 436 (1966).

114. H. Richard Uviller, *Tempered Zeal* (Chicago: Contemporary Books, 1988), 188–198.

115. *Orozco v. Texas,* 394 U.S. 324 (1969); *Oregon v. Mathiason,* 429 U.S. 492 (1977); and *California v. Beheler,* 463 U.S. 1121 (1983).

116. *Orozco,* 325.

117. *Howes v. Fields,* 132 S.Ct. 1181 (2012).

118. *Pennsylvania v. Muniz,* 496 U.S. 582 (1990).

119. del Carmen, 267–268.

120. *New York v. Quarles,* 467 U.S. 649 (1984).

121. Ethan Bonner and Michael S. Schmidt, "In Questions at First, No *Miranda* for Suspect," *New York Times* (April 23, 2013), A13.

122. *Moran v. Burbine,* 475 U.S. 412 (1986).

123. *Michigan v. Mosley,* 423 U.S. 96 (1975).

124. *Fare v. Michael C.,* 442 U.S. 707, 723–724 (1979).

125. 512 U.S. 452 (1994).

126. 560 U.S. ___ (2010).

127. Patrick Malone, "You Have the Right to Remain Silent: *Miranda* after Twenty Years," *American Scholar* 55 (1986), 367.

128. Richard A. Leo, "The Impact of *Miranda* Revisited," *Journal of Criminal Law and Criminology* 86 (Spring 1996), 621–692.

129. *Doody v. Schriro,* 596 F.3d 620, 624 (9th Cir. 2010).

130. *Ibid.,* 620.

131. *Dickerson v. United States,* 530 U.S. 428 (2000).

132. Quoted in Jesse J. Holland, "High Court Trims *Miranda* Warning Rights Bit by Bit," *Associated Press* (August 2, 2010).

133. *United States v. Patane,* 542 U.S. 630 (2004).

134. James Schnabl, "Are Video Police Reports the Answer?" *The Police Chief* (September 2012), 32.

135. Maurice Chammah, "'80 Murder Confession Raises Calls to Require Police to Record Interrogations," *New York Times* (December 28, 2012), A19.

136. 413 U.S. 300 (1973).

137. *United States v. Barker,* 988 F.2d 77, 78 (9th Cir. 1993).

138. 384 U.S. 757 (1966).

139. *United States v. Dionisio,* 410 U.S. 1 (1973); and *United States v. Mara,* 410 U.S. 19 (1973).

140. *State v. Johnson,* 774 N.W.2d 340 (Iowa 2008).

141. Adam Goldman and Matt Apuzzo, "NYPD: Muslim Spying Led to No Leads, Terror Cases," *Associated Press* (August 21, 2012).

142. Michael S. Schmidt and Eric Lichtblau, "Racial Profiling Rife at Airport, U.S. Officials Say," *New York Times* (August 12, 2012), A1.

143. Dinesh D'Souza, *The End of Racism: Principles for a Multicultural Society* (New York: Free Press, 1995), 260–261.

144. "Spread 'Em!" *The Economist* (June 2, 2012), 36–37.

145. *Ibid.,* 37.

146. Michael Kinsley, "When Is Racial Profiling Okay?" *Washington Post* (September 30, 2001), A1.

147. Bureau of Justice Statistics, *Contacts between Police and the Public, 2005* (Washington, D.C.: U.S. Department of Justice, April 2007).

148. Adam Goldman and Matt Puzo, "Inside the Spy Unit That NYPD Says Doesn't Exist," *Associated Press* (August 31, 2011).

8 Courts and the Quest for Justice

To target your study and review, look for these numbered Learning Objective icons throughout the chapter.

AP Photo/Mel Evans

DARK HONEYMOON

ACCORDING TO Gabe Watson, his wife Tina's drowning death was a tragic accident. According to Alabama prosecutors, he committed murder. The incident occurred when, eleven days after being married in October 2003, the couple decided to go scuba diving on Australia's Barrier Reef during their honeymoon. In Gabe's version of events, Tina, a novice diver, started to panic underwater. When he tried to save her, she accidentally dislodged his mask and regulator, forcing him to the surface without her. Prosecutors in Alabama countered that Gabe killed Tina to collect on a life insurance policy. He did so, they claimed, by turning off her air supply and holding her in a bear hug until she lost consciousness.

Originally charged with murder by Australian officials, Gabe pleaded guilty to manslaughter for not doing enough to save Tina from drowning. After spending eighteen months in an Australian prison, in 2010 he was sent back to Alabama to face similar charges in his and Tina's home state. If found guilty in an Alabama court, he could have been sentenced to a lifetime in prison. Jefferson County Circuit Judge Tommy Nail, however, was suspicious of the prosecution's arguments from the beginning of trial proceedings. The judge scoffed at Gabe's alleged financial motives, pointing out that the life insurance policy in question was remarkably modest. Furthermore, the only witness who saw Gabe and Tina together underwater testified that he thought Gabe was trying to save her life.

Although a jury had been selected to hear Gabe's murder trial, it never got the chance to find him guilty or innocent. On February 23, 2012, Nail, as was his judicial prerogative, ruled that there was no evidence that Gabe had committed the crime and dismissed the charges against him. "The only way to convict him of intentional murder is to speculate," Nail said. "'Nobody knows exactly what happened in the water." The judge's ruling shocked Tommy Thomas, Tina's father. "It should have gone to the jury for them to decide," he insisted.

1. Following Judge Tommy Nail's decision, law professor Robert Jarvis of Nova Southeastern University said, "Most judges prefer to let even the weakest of cases go to the jury and let them decide if there was sufficient evidence." Why do you think judges usually defer to juries in this manner? Do you agree with the judge's ruling in Gabe Watson's case?

2. The alleged murder took place in Australia, and Gabe had already served a prison term there. Should Alabama officials even have been given the chance to prosecute him? Why or why not?

3. Trying to show that Gabe had "murder on his mind" before Tina's death, prosecutors claimed that Gabe took back his wife's engagement ring before she was buried. If you were a judge in this case, would you accept this as evidence that Gabe was greedy enough to commit murder? Explain your answer.

AP Photo/Dave Martin

Gabe Watson, left, confers with his lawyer in a Birmingham, Alabama, courtroom before Jefferson County Circuit Judge Tommy Nail dismissed charges that Watson had murdered his wife.

Gray wall studio/Shutterstock.com

FUNCTIONS OF THE COURTS

Following the dismissal of murder charges against Gabe Watson, his attorney said, "It has been a nightmare for Gabe and his family and a nightmare for Tina and her family. We all wanted justice."[1] Did each side get *justice* from the court system? Famed jurist Roscoe Pound once characterized "justice" as society's demand "that serious offenders be convicted and punished," while at the same time "the innocent and unfortunate are not oppressed."[2]

This somewhat idealistic definition obscures the fact that there are two sides to each court proceeding, and Gabe's and Tina's families certainly had different ideas of what would have been a just outcome to the Alabama case. On a more practical level, then, a court is a place where arguments are settled. At best, the court provides a just environment in which the basis of the argument can be decided through the application of the law.

Courts have extensive powers in our criminal justice system: they can bring the authority of the state to seize property and to restrict individual liberty. Given that the rights to own property and to enjoy personal freedom are enshrined in the U.S. Constitution, a court's *legitimacy* in taking such measures must be unquestioned by society. This legitimacy is based on two factors: impartiality and independence.[3] In theory, each party involved in a courtroom dispute must have an equal chance to present its case and must be secure in the belief that no outside factors are going to influence the decision rendered by the court. In reality, as we shall see over the next four chapters, it does not always work that way.

Due Process and Crime Control in the Courts

As mentioned in Chapter 1, the criminal justice system has two sets of underlying values: due process and crime control. Due process values focus on protecting the rights of the individual, whereas crime control values stress the punishment and repression of criminal conduct. The competing nature of these two value systems is often evident in the nation's courts.

LEARNING **1** OBJECTIVE

Define and contrast the four functions of the courts.

THE DUE PROCESS FUNCTION The primary concern of early American courts was to protect the rights of the individual against the power of the state. Memories of injustices suffered at the hands of the British monarchy were still strong, and most of the procedural rules that we have discussed in this textbook were created with the express purpose of giving the individual a "fair chance" against the government in any courtroom proceedings. Therefore, the due process function of the courts is to protect individuals from the unfair advantages that the government—with its immense resources—automatically enjoys in legal battles.

■ Why is it important that American criminal courtrooms, such as this one in Cape May, New Jersey, are places of impartiality and independence?
AP Photo/*The Press of Atlantic City*, Dale Gerhard

Seen in this light, constitutional guarantees such as the right to counsel, the right to a jury trial, and protection from self-incrimination are equalizers in the "contest" between the state and the individual. The idea that the two sides in a courtroom dispute are adversaries is, as we shall discuss in the next chapter, fundamental in American courts.

THE CRIME CONTROL FUNCTION Advocates of crime control distinguish between the court's obligation to be fair to the accused and its obligation to be fair to society. The crime control function of the courts emphasizes punishment and retribution—criminals must suffer for the harm done to society, and it is the courts' responsibility to see that they do so. Given this responsibility to protect the public, deter criminal behavior, and "get criminals off the streets," the courts should not be concerned solely with giving the accused a fair chance. Rather than using due process rules as "equalizers," the courts should use them as protection against blatantly unconstitutional acts. For example, a detective who beats a suspect with a tire iron to get a confession has obviously infringed on the suspect's constitutional rights. If, however, the detective uses trickery to gain a confession, the court should allow the confession to stand because it is not in society's interest that law enforcement agents be deterred from outwitting criminals.

The Rehabilitation Function

A third view of the court's responsibility is based on the "medical model" of the criminal justice system. In this model, criminals are analogous to patients, and the courts perform the role of physicians who dispense "treatment."[4] The criminal is seen as sick, not evil, and therefore treatment is morally justified. Of course, treatment varies from case to case, and some criminals require harsh penalties such as incarceration. In other cases, however, it may not be in society's best interest for the criminal to be punished according to the formal rules of the justice system. Perhaps the criminal can be rehabilitated to become a productive member of society and thus save taxpayers the costs of incarceration or other punishment.

The Bureaucratic Function

To a certain extent, the crime control, due process, and rehabilitation functions of a court are secondary to its bureaucratic function. In general, a court may have the goal of protecting society or protecting the rights of the individual, but on a day-to-day basis that court has the more pressing task of dealing with the cases brought before it. Like any bureaucracy, a court is concerned with speed and efficiency, and loftier concepts such as justice can be secondary to a judge's need to wrap up a particular case before six o'clock so that administrative deadlines can be met. Indeed, many observers feel that the primary adversarial relationship in the courts is not between the two parties involved but between the ideal of justice and the reality of bureaucratic limitations.[5]

SELF ASSESSMENT

Fill in the blanks and check your answers on page 276.

The _____ _____ function of American courts is to protect _____ from the unfair advantages that the government enjoys during legal proceedings. In contrast, the _____ _____ function of the courts emphasizes punishment—criminals must suffer for the harm they do to _____. A third view of the court system focuses on the need to _____ a criminal, in much the same way as a doctor would treat a patient.

THE BASIC PRINCIPLES OF THE AMERICAN JUDICIAL SYSTEM

One of the most often cited limitations of the American judicial system is its complex nature. In truth, the United States does not have a single judicial system, but fifty-two different systems—one for each state, the District of Columbia, and the federal government. As each state has its own unique judiciary with its own set of rules, some of which may be in conflict with the federal judiciary, it is helpful at this point to discuss some basics—jurisdiction, trial and appellate courts, and the dual court system.

Jurisdiction

In Latin, *juris* means "law," and *diction* means "to speak." Thus, **jurisdiction** literally refers to the power "to speak the law." Before any court can hear a case, it must have jurisdiction over the persons involved in the case or its subject matter. The jurisdiction of every court, even the United States Supreme Court, is limited in some way.

GEOGRAPHIC JURISDICTION One limitation is geographic. Generally, a court can exercise its authority over residents of a certain area. A state trial court, for example, normally has jurisdictional authority over crimes committed in a particular area of the state, such as a county or a district. A state's highest court (often called the state supreme court) has jurisdictional authority over the entire state, and the United States Supreme Court has jurisdiction over the entire country.

In the case that opened this chapter, Gabe Watson's attorneys contended that the state of Alabama did not have the power to try their client, as his alleged crime took place in Australia. Prosecutors, however, successfully argued that, since Watson would have planned the alleged murder of his wife in Alabama, that state had geographic jurisdiction over the crime. For the most part, criminal jurisdiction is determined by legislation. The U.S. Congress or a state legislature can determine what acts are illegal within the geographic boundaries it controls, thus giving federal or state courts jurisdiction over those crimes. What happens, however, when more than one court system has jurisdiction over the same criminal act?

Federal versus State Jurisdiction Most criminal laws are state laws, so the majority of all criminal trials are heard in state courts. Many acts that are illegal under state law, however, are also illegal under federal law. As a general rule, when Congress "criminalizes" behavior that is already prohibited under a state criminal code, the federal and state courts both have jurisdiction over that crime unless Congress states otherwise in the initial legislation. Thus, **concurrent jurisdiction,** which occurs when two different court systems have simultaneous jurisdiction over the same case, is quite common.

Less common is the situation in which federal law and state law contradict each other. As we saw in Chapter 3, Colorado and Washington legalized possession of small amounts of marijuana in 2012. Furthermore, nineteen states and the District of Columbia allow the use of marijuana for medical purposes. Federal law, however, continues to treat the possession, sale, or distribution of marijuana as a crime. Consequently, federal law enforcement officials will have to rely on their discretion in deciding whether to prosecute users of the drug in states where such use is "legal."

State versus State Jurisdiction Multiple states can also claim jurisdiction over the same defendant or criminal act, depending on state legislation and the circumstances

Jurisdiction The authority of a court to hear and decide cases within an area of the law or a geographic territory.

Concurrent Jurisdiction The situation that occurs when two or more courts have the authority to preside over the same criminal case.

LEARNING
2
OBJECTIVE

Define *jurisdiction* and contrast geographic and subject-matter jurisdiction.

At the MedMar Healing Center in San Jose, California, an employee examines young marijuana plants that will eventually be sold for medicinal purposes. How does medical marijuana present a situation of concurrent jurisdiction in which federal law and state law are contradictory?
David Paul Morris/Bloomberg via Getty Images

of the crime. For example, if Billy is standing in State A and shoots Frances, who is standing in State B, the two states could have concurrent jurisdiction to try Billy for murder. Similarly, if a property theft takes places in State A but police recover the stolen goods in State B, concurrent jurisdiction could exist. Some states have also passed laws stating that they have jurisdiction over their own citizens who commit crimes in other states, even if there is no other connection between the home state and the criminal act.[6]

The concept of jurisdiction encourages states to cooperate with each other regarding fugitives from the law. In 2013, for example, Michael Boysen was suspected of killing his grandparents in Renton, Washington. Boysen fled south to Oregon, where local police apprehended him in a Lincoln City hotel room. Oregon officials subsequently *extradited* Boysen back to Washington to stand trial for the double murder. **Extradition** is the formal process by which one legal authority, such as a state or a nation, transfers a fugitive or a suspect to another legal authority that has a valid claim on that person.

Multiple Trials When different courts share jurisdiction over the same defendant, multiple trials can result. From 2007 to 2010, for example, religious sect leader Warren Jeffs appeared in the courts of three different states—Arizona, Texas, and Utah—to face charges related to sex with underage girls. Because officials in each state had probable cause that he had committed crimes within state limits, each state had jurisdiction over him and the right to conduct a criminal trial.

Although some believe that such multiple trials are a waste of taxpayer money, state and county prosecutors often argue that local victims of crimes deserve the "sense of closure" that comes with criminal proceedings.[7] In addition, as we will see in Chapter 10, guilty verdicts can be appealed and reversed, and extra convictions serve as "insurance" against that possibility. In most situations, however, convictions in one jurisdiction end the prosecution of the same case in another jurisdiction.

INTERNATIONAL JURISDICTION Under international law, each country has the right to create and enact criminal law for its territory. Therefore, the notion that a nation has jurisdiction over any crimes committed within its borders is well established. The situation becomes more delicate when one nation feels the need to go outside its own territory to enforce its criminal law. International precedent does, however, provide several bases for expanding jurisdiction across international borders.

For example, anti-terrorism efforts have been aided by the principle that the United States has jurisdiction over persons who commit crimes against Americans even when the former are citizens of foreign countries and live outside the United States. In October 2012, British authorities extradited Egyptian-born preacher Abu Hamza al-Masri to the United States to face multiple terrorism charges, including conspiring to set up a terrorist training camp in Oregon. Similarly, that same year Thailand

Extradition The process by which one jurisdiction surrenders a person accused or convicted of violating another jurisdiction's criminal law to the second jurisdiction.

extradited Ukrainian citizen Maksym Shynkarenko to New Jersey, where he was to face trial for operating several child pornography Web sites. Even though Shynkarenko had never been to New Jersey before, the fact that at least thirty men in that state accessed his Web sites provided a basis for jurisdiction.

To facilitate the process of international jurisdiction, the United States has entered into extradition treaties with a number of countries. In these treaties, the nations agree to extradite fugitives to each other following a formal request. For example, operating under an extradition treaty, from 2007 to 2011 the Mexican government sent 478 criminal suspects—mostly alleged murderers and drug traffickers—to the United States.[8] Furthermore, some behavior, such as piracy and genocide, is considered a crime against all nations collectively and, according to the principles of *universal jurisdiction,* can be prosecuted by any nation having custody of the wrongdoer.

In August 2013, the United States formally requested the extradition of Eric Marques, alleging that the Irish citizen, shown here after being arrested in Dublin, had disseminated "countless" child pornography images to the U.S. via the Internet. Do you think that the American government should have jurisdiction over suspects such as Marques who commit their crimes on foreign soil? Press Association via AP Images

SUBJECT-MATTER JURISDICTION Jurisdiction over subject matter also acts as a limitation on the types of cases a court can hear. State court systems include courts of *general* (unlimited) *jurisdiction* and courts of *limited jurisdiction.* Courts of general jurisdiction have no restrictions on the subject matter they may address, and therefore deal with the most serious felonies and civil cases. Courts of limited jurisdiction, also known as lower courts, handle misdemeanors and civil matters under a certain amount, usually $1,000.

As we will discuss later in the chapter, many states have created special subject-matter courts that only dispose of cases involving a specific crime. For example, a number of jurisdictions have established drug courts to handle an overload of illicit narcotics arrests. Furthermore, under the Uniform Code of Military Justice, the U.S. military has jurisdiction over active personnel who commit crimes, even if those crimes occur outside the course of duty.[9] In such cases, military officials can either attempt to *court-martial* the suspect in military court or allow civilian prosecutors to handle the case in state or federal court. (As the feature *Myth versus Reality—Reservation Rules* on the next page shows, a jurisdictional "void" on tribal land in the United States has had dire consequences for the Native American population.)

Trial and Appellate Courts

Another distinction is between courts of original jurisdiction and courts of appellate, or review, jurisdiction. Courts having *original jurisdiction* are courts of the first instance, or **trial courts.** Almost every case begins in a trial court. It is in this court that a trial (or a guilty plea) takes place, and the judge imposes a sentence if the defendant is found guilty. Trial courts are primarily concerned with *questions of fact.* They are designed to determine exactly what events occurred that are relevant to questions of the defendant's guilt or innocence.

Courts having *appellate jurisdiction* act as reviewing courts, or **appellate courts.** In general, cases can be brought before appellate courts only on appeal by one of the parties in the trial court. (Note that because of constitutional protections against being tried twice for the same crime, prosecutors who lose in criminal trial court *cannot* appeal the verdict.) An appellate court does not use juries or witnesses to reach its decision. Instead, its judges make a decision on whether the case should be *reversed* and *remanded,* or sent back to the court of original jurisdiction for a new trial. Appellate judges present written

LEARNING
3
OBJECTIVE
Explain the difference between trial and appellate courts.

Trial Courts Courts in which most cases usually begin and in which questions of fact are examined.

Appellate Courts Courts that review decisions made by lower courts, such as trial courts; also known as *courts of appeals.*

Opinions Written statements by the judges expressing the reasons for the court's decision in a case.

Dual Court System The separate but interrelated court system of the United States, made up of the courts on the national level and the courts on the state level.

explanations for their decisions, and these **opinions** of the court are the basis for a great deal of the precedent in the criminal justice system.

It is important to understand that appellate courts do not determine the defendant's guilt or innocence—they only make judgments on questions of procedure. In other words, they are concerned with *questions of law* and normally accept the facts as established by the trial court. Only rarely will an appeals court question a jury's decision. Instead, the appellate judges will review the manner in which the facts and evidence were provided to the jury and rule on whether errors were made in the process.

The Dual Court System

As we saw in Chapter 1, America's system of federalism allows the federal government and the governments of the fifty states to hold authority in many areas. As a result, the federal government and each of the fifty states, as well as the District of Columbia, have their own separate court systems. Because of the split between the federal courts and the state courts, this is known as the **dual court system.** (See Figure 8.1 on the facing page to get a better idea of how federal and state courts operate as distinct yet parallel entities.)

MYTH vs REALITY   Reservation Rules

Saicle/Shutterstock.com

Thanks to freedom from state antigambling laws and "sin" taxes on alcohol and cigarettes, Native American reservations are often considered somewhat outside the law. Indeed, Vernon Roanhorse, a Navajo tribal official, calls his reservation a "lawless land." The problems, however, go much deeper than casinos and cheap cigarettes.

THE MYTH In its earliest days, the U.S. government treated the various Native American tribes as individual sovereign nations. Ever since, the American government has allowed American Indians a considerable amount of self-rule. Consequently, many non-Native Americans believe that tribal leaders enjoy complete jurisdiction over all events that occur on tribal lands, including crimes.

THE REALITY There is no single justice system for the 310 Native American reservations that exist in the United States. Some have their own police departments, while others rely on federal or state law enforcement agents. Tribes do run their own court systems, but federal law denies tribal courts criminal jurisdiction over defendants who are not American Indians or who are from a different tribe. Furthermore, serious felonies including violent crimes such as rape and murder are generally

under federal jurisdiction. For these crimes, tribal authorities often must rely on federal agents to investigate and U.S. attorneys to prosecute.

The federal government's record in this area has been dismal, particularly when it comes to crimes against women. Native American women suffer incidents of domestic violence and rape at rates more than double the national average. About 75 percent of such crimes on reservations are committed by non-Native Americans, meaning that tribal courts lack jurisdiction over most potential defendants. Yet, in two-thirds of these cases, federal prosecutors fail to take action. As a result, reservations have become a form of "safe haven" for sexual criminals. In 2013, a federal law was passed to remedy this situation. The new legislation extends tribal jurisdiction to cover non-Native Americans who commit crimes of domestic violence or rape against a Native American spouse or partner.

FOR CRITICAL ANALYSIS
What is the jurisdictional loophole in the new federal law just mentioned? (Hint: What happens when a *stranger* from outside the reservation sexually assaults a Native American on reservation land?) How does this loophole limit the new law's effectiveness?

FIGURE 8.1 The Dual Court System

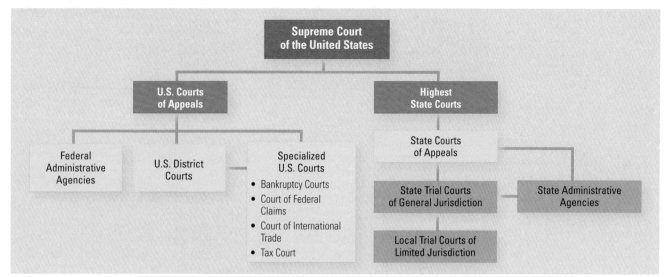

Federal and state courts both have limited jurisdiction. Generally, federal courts preside over cases involving violations of federal law, and state courts preside over cases involving violations of state law. The distinction is not always clear, however. Federal courts have jurisdiction over more than four thousand crimes, many of which also exist in state criminal codes. In 2012, for instance, local and federal law enforcement agents cooperated in apprehending Damon Quick, who had committed a string of armed robberies of stores and restaurants in the Durham, North Carolina, area. Broadly interpreting a federal law outlawing robbery that obstructs commerce between states,[10] the federal government claimed jurisdiction over Quick, as did North Carolina. Following an agreement between the two sides, Quick was prosecuted—and found guilty—in federal court.

SELF ASSESSMENT

Fill in the blanks and check your answers on page 276.

Before any court can hear a case, it must have _____ over the persons involved or the _____ _____ of the dispute. Almost every case begins in a _____ court, which is primarily concerned with determining the facts of the dispute. After this first trial, the participants can, under some circumstances, ask an _____ court to review the proceedings for errors in applying the law. The American court system is called a _____ court system because _____ courts address violations of federal law and _____ courts address violations of state law.

STATE COURT SYSTEMS

Typically, a state court system includes several levels, or tiers, of courts. State courts may include (1) lower courts, or courts of limited jurisdiction; (2) trial courts of general jurisdiction; (3) appellate courts; and (4) the state's highest court. As previously mentioned, each state has a different judicial structure, in which different courts have different jurisdictions, but there are enough similarities to allow for a general discussion. Figure 8.2 on the following page shows a typical state court system.

LEARNING OBJECTIVE **4** Outline the several levels of a typical state court system.

Courts of Limited Jurisdiction

Most states have local trial courts that are limited to trying cases involving minor criminal matters, such as traffic violations, prostitution, and drunk and disorderly conduct. Although these minor courts usually keep no written record of the trial proceedings and

FIGURE 8.2 A Typical State Court System

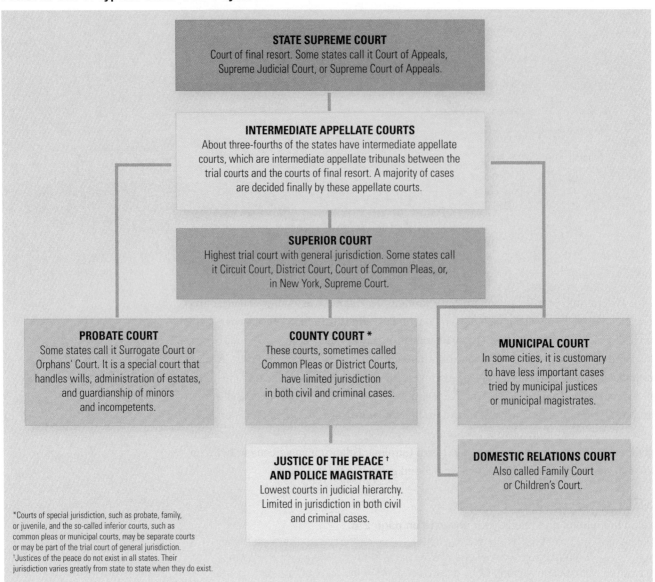

STATE SUPREME COURT
Court of final resort. Some states call it Court of Appeals, Supreme Judicial Court, or Supreme Court of Appeals.

INTERMEDIATE APPELLATE COURTS
About three-fourths of the states have intermediate appellate courts, which are intermediate appellate tribunals between the trial courts and the courts of final resort. A majority of cases are decided finally by these appellate courts.

SUPERIOR COURT
Highest trial court with general jurisdiction. Some states call it Circuit Court, District Court, Court of Common Pleas, or, in New York, Supreme Court.

PROBATE COURT
Some states call it Surrogate Court or Orphans' Court. It is a special court that handles wills, administration of estates, and guardianship of minors and incompetents.

COUNTY COURT *
These courts, sometimes called Common Pleas or District Courts, have limited jurisdiction in both civil and criminal cases.

MUNICIPAL COURT
In some cities, it is customary to have less important cases tried by municipal justices or municipal magistrates.

**JUSTICE OF THE PEACE †
AND POLICE MAGISTRATE**
Lowest courts in judicial hierarchy. Limited in jurisdiction in both civil and criminal cases.

DOMESTIC RELATIONS COURT
Also called Family Court or Children's Court.

*Courts of special jurisdiction, such as probate, family, or juvenile, and the so-called inferior courts, such as common pleas or municipal courts, may be separate courts or may be part of the trial court of general jurisdiction.
†Justices of the peace do not exist in all states. Their jurisdiction varies greatly from state to state when they do exist.

cases are decided by a judge rather than a jury, defendants have the same rights as those in other trial courts. The majority of all minor criminal cases are decided in these lower courts. Courts of limited jurisdiction can also be responsible for the preliminary stages of felony cases. Arraignments, bail hearings, and preliminary hearings often take place in these lower courts.

MAGISTRATE COURTS One of the earliest courts of limited jurisdiction was the justice court, presided over by a *justice of the peace,* or JP. In the early days of this nation, JPs were found everywhere in the country. One of the most famous JPs was Judge Roy Bean, the "hanging judge" of Langtry, Texas, who presided over his court at the turn of the twentieth century. Today, more than half the states have abolished justice courts, though JPs still serve a useful function in some cities and rural areas, notably in Texas. The jurisdiction of justice courts is limited to minor disputes between private individuals and to crimes punishable by small fines or short jail terms. The equivalent of a county JP in a city is known as a **magistrate** or, in some states, a municipal court judge. Magistrate

Magistrate A public civil officer or official with limited judicial authority within a particular geographic area, such as the authority to issue an arrest warrant.

courts have the same limited jurisdiction as do justice courts in rural settings. In most jurisdictions, magistrates are responsible for providing law enforcement agents with search and seizure warrants, discussed in Chapter 7.

SPECIALTY COURTS As mentioned earlier, many states have created **problem-solving courts** that have jurisdiction over very narrowly defined areas of criminal justice. Not only do these courts remove many cases from the existing court systems, but they also allow court personnel to become experts in a particular subject. Problem-solving courts include:

Judge Sarah Smith, left, talks with an offender at her drug court in downtown Tulsa, Oklahoma. What are some of the benefits of drug courts and other problem-solving courts?
Photo by Adam Wisneski/*Tulsa World*

1. Drug courts, which deal only with illegal substance crimes.
2. Gun courts, which have jurisdiction over crimes that involve the illegal use of firearms.
3. Juvenile courts, which specialize in crimes committed by minors. (We will discuss juvenile courts in more detail in Chapter 15.)
4. Domestic courts, which deal with crimes of domestic violence, such as child and spousal abuse.
5. Mental health courts, which focus primarily on the treatment and rehabilitation of offenders with mental health problems.

As we will see in Chapter 12, many state and local governments are searching for cheaper alternatives to locking up nonviolent offenders in prison or jail. Because problem-solving courts offer a range of treatment options for wrongdoers, these courts are becoming increasingly popular in today's more budget-conscious criminal justice system. For example, at least 2,500 drug courts are now operating in the United States, a number that is expected to increase as the financial benefits of diverting drug law violators from correctional facilities become more attractive to politicians.

Trial Courts of General Jurisdiction

State trial courts that have general jurisdiction may be called county courts, district courts, superior courts, or circuit courts. In Ohio, the name is the court of common pleas and in Massachusetts, the trial court. (The name sometimes does not correspond with the court's functions. For example, in New York the trial court is called the supreme court, whereas in most states the supreme court is the state's highest court.) Courts of general jurisdiction have the authority to hear and decide cases involving many types of subject matter, and they are the setting for criminal trials (discussed in Chapter 10).

State Courts of Appeals

Every state has at least one court of appeals (known as an appellate, or reviewing, court), which may be an intermediate appellate court or the state's highest court. About three-fourths have intermediate appellate courts. The highest appellate court in a state is usually called the supreme court, but in both New York and Maryland, the highest state court is called the court of appeals. The decisions of each state's highest court on all

Problem-Solving Courts
Lower courts that have jurisdiction over one specific area of criminal activity, such as illegal drugs or domestic violence.

questions of state law are final. Only when issues of federal law or constitutional procedure are involved can the United States Supreme Court overrule a decision made by a state's highest court.

SELF ASSESSMENT

Fill in the blanks and check your answers on page 276.

State court systems include several levels of courts. Lower courts, or courts of _____ jurisdiction, hear only cases involving minor criminal matters or narrowly defined areas of crime such as domestic violence. Trial courts of _____ jurisdiction hear cases involving many different subject matters. The state courts of _____ make the final decisions on all questions of state law.

THE FEDERAL COURT SYSTEM

Outline the federal court system.

LEARNING
5
OBJECTIVE

The federal court system is basically a three-tiered model consisting of (1) U.S. district courts (trial courts of general jurisdiction) and various courts of limited jurisdiction, (2) U.S. courts of appeals (intermediate courts of appeals), and (3) the United States Supreme Court.

Unlike state court judges, who are usually elected, federal court judges—including the justices of the Supreme Court—are appointed by the president of the United States, subject to the approval of the Senate. All federal judges receive lifetime appointments (because under Article III of the Constitution they "hold their offices during Good Behavior").

U.S. District Courts

On the lowest tier of the federal court system are the U.S. district courts, or federal trial courts. These are the courts in which cases involving federal laws begin, and a judge or jury decides the case (if it is a jury trial). Every state has at least one federal district court, and there is one in the District of Columbia. The number of judicial districts varies over time, primarily owing to population changes and corresponding caseloads. At the present time, there are ninety-four judicial districts. The federal system also includes other trial courts of limited jurisdiction, such as the Tax Court and the Court of International Trade.

U.S. Courts of Appeals

In the federal court system, there are thirteen U.S. courts of appeals—also referred to as U.S. circuit courts of appeals. The federal courts of appeals for twelve of the circuits hear appeals from the district courts located within their respective judicial circuits (see Figure 8.3 on the facing page). The Court of Appeals for the Thirteenth Circuit, called the Federal Circuit, has national appellate jurisdiction over certain types of cases, such as cases in which the U.S. government is a defendant. The decisions of the circuit courts of appeals are final unless a further appeal is pursued and granted. In that case, the matter is brought before the Supreme Court.

The United States Supreme Court

Alexander Hamilton, writing in *Federalist Paper* No. 78 (1788), predicted that the United States Supreme Court would be the "least dangerous branch" of the federal government because it had neither the power of the purse nor the power of the sword (that is, it could not raise any revenue, and it lacked an enforcement agency).[11] Unless the other two branches of the government—the president and Congress—would accept its decisions, the Court would be superfluous.

FIGURE 8.3 Geographic Boundaries of the Federal Circuit Courts of Appeals

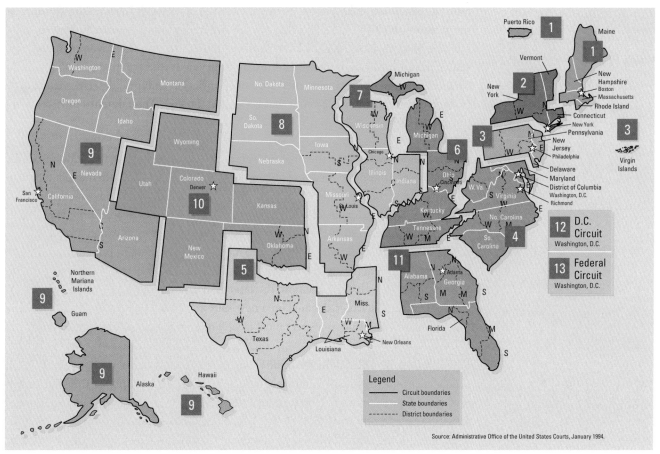

Source: Administrative Office of the United States Courts, January 1994.

In the Supreme Court's earliest years, it appeared that Hamilton's prediction would come true. The first chief justice of the Supreme Court, John Jay, resigned to become governor of New York because he thought the Court would never play an important role in American society. The next chief justice, Oliver Ellsworth, quit to become an envoy to France. In 1801, when the federal capital was moved to Washington, D.C., no one remembered to include the Supreme Court in the plans. It did not have its own meeting space until 1835.[12]

INTERPRETING AND APPLYING THE LAW Despite these early bouts of inconsequence, the Supreme Court has come to dominate the country's legal culture. Although the Court reviews a minuscule percentage of the cases decided in the United States each year, its decisions profoundly affect our lives. The impact of Court decisions on the criminal justice system is equally far reaching: *Gideon v. Wainwright* (1963)[13] established every American's right to be represented by counsel in a criminal trial; *Miranda v. Arizona* (1966)[14] transformed pretrial interrogations; *Furman v. Georgia* (1972)[15] ruled that the death penalty was unconstitutional; and *Gregg v. Georgia* (1976)[16] spelled out the conditions under which it could be allowed. As you have no doubt noticed from references in this textbook, the Court has addressed nearly every important facet of criminal law.

Judicial Review The Supreme Court "makes" criminal justice policy in two important ways: through *judicial review* and through its authority to interpret the law. **Judicial review** refers to the power of the Court to determine whether a law or action by the other branches of the government is constitutional. For example, in the late 1990s

Judicial Review The power of a court—particularly the United States Supreme Court—to review the actions of the executive and legislative branches and, if necessary, declare those actions unconstitutional.

Congress passed a law restricting Internet sales of "crush" videos, which showed women crushing small animals to death with their bare feet or high heels.[17] The wording of the statute prohibited the sale of videos showing any form of graphic violence against animals. Several years after the law's passage, Robert Stevens of Pittsville, Virginia, was sentenced to three years in prison for distributing videos that featured pit bull fights. In 2010, the Supreme Court overturned Stevens's conviction and invalidated the federal law as unconstitutional on the ground that it violated the First Amendment's protections of freedom of expression.[18]

Statutory Interpretation As the final interpreter of the Constitution, the Supreme Court must also determine the meaning of certain statutory provisions when applied to specific situations. In the previous chapter, you learned that a law enforcement officer must immediately stop questioning a suspect who invokes her or his *Miranda* rights. In *Maryland v. Shatzer* (2010),[19] the Court considered a situation in which a sexual abuse suspect invoked his *Miranda* rights, spent more than two years in prison (for an unrelated crime), and then waived his *Miranda* rights. The Court rejected the suspect's claim that due to his much earlier action, the later waiver, although made willingly, "did not count." Instead, the Court decided on a new rule: a *Miranda* invocation is good for only fourteen days. After that, a suspect must clearly reestablish her or his right to silence.

JURISDICTION OF THE SUPREME COURT The United States Supreme Court consists of nine justices—a chief justice and eight associate justices. The Supreme Court has original, or trial, jurisdiction only in rare instances (set forth in Article III, Section 2, of the Constitution). In other words, only rarely does a case originate at the Supreme Court level. Most of the Court's work is as an appellate court. It has appellate authority over cases decided by the U.S. courts of appeals, as well as over some cases decided in the state courts when federal questions are at issue.

Explain briefly how a case is brought to the Supreme Court. LEARNING **6** OBJECTIVE

John G. Roberts, Jr., pictured here, is the seventeenth chief justice of the United States Supreme Court. What does it mean to say that Roberts and the eight associate members of the Court "make criminal justice policy"?
AP Photo/Lawrence Jackson, File

WHICH CASES REACH THE SUPREME COURT? There is no absolute right to appeal to the United States Supreme Court. Although thousands of cases are filed with the Supreme Court each year, in 2011–2012 the Court heard only seventy-seven. With a **writ of *certiorari*** (pronounced sur-shee-uh-*rah*-ree), the Supreme Court orders a lower court to send it the record of a case for review. A party can petition the Supreme Court to issue a writ of *certiorari,* but whether the Court will do so is entirely within its discretion. More than 90 percent of the petitions for writs of *certiorari* (or "certs," as they are popularly called) are denied. A denial is not a decision on the merits of a case, nor does it indicate agreement with the lower court's opinion. Therefore, the denial of the writ has no value as a precedent.

The Court will not issue a writ unless at least four justices approve of it. This is called the **rule of four.** Although the justices are not required to give their reasons for refusing to hear a case, most often the discretionary decision is based on whether the legal issue involves a "substantial federal question." Often, such questions arise when lower courts split on a particular issue. For example, in recent years different federal and state courts have produced varying opinions on the question of whether police officers can search the contents of cell phones without a search warrant.[20] To clear up confusion on this increasingly important matter, the Court will likely hear a case involving cell phone searches in the near future. Practical considerations aside, if the justices feel that a case does not address an important federal law or constitutional issue, they will vote to deny the writ of *certiorari*.

SUPREME COURT DECISIONS   Like all appellate courts, the Supreme Court normally does not hear any evidence. The Court's decision in a particular case is based on the written record of the case and the written arguments (briefs) that the attorneys submit. The attorneys also present **oral arguments**—arguments presented in person rather than on paper—to the Court, after which the justices discuss the case in *conference*. The conference is strictly private—only the justices are allowed in the room.

Majorities and Pluralities   When the Court has reached a decision, the chief justice, if in the majority, assigns the task of writing the Court's opinion to one of the justices. When the chief justice is not in the majority, the most senior justice voting with the majority assigns the writing of the Court's opinion. The opinion outlines the reasons for the Court's decision, the rules of law that apply, and the decision.

From time to time, the justices agree on the outcome of a case, but no single reason for that outcome gains five votes. When this occurs, the rationale that gains the most votes is called the *plurality* opinion. Plurality opinions are problematic, because they do not provide a strong precedent for lower courts to follow. Although still relatively rare, the incidence of plurality opinions has increased over the past fifty years as the Court has become more ideologically fractured.[21]

Concurrence and Dissent   Often, one or more justices who agree with the Court's decision may do so for different reasons than those outlined in the majority opinion. These justices may write **concurring opinions** setting forth their own legal reasoning on the issue. Frequently, one or more justices disagree with the Court's conclusion. These justices may write **dissenting opinions** outlining the reasons why they feel the majority erred. Although a dissenting opinion does not affect the outcome of the case before the Court, it may be important later. In a subsequent case concerning the same issue, a justice or attorney may use the legal reasoning in the dissenting opinion as the basis for an argument to reverse the previous decision and establish a new precedent.

Oral Arguments   The verbal arguments presented in person by attorneys to an appellate court. Each attorney presents reasons why the court should rule in his or her client's favor.

Concurring Opinions   Separate opinions prepared by judges who support the decision of the majority of the court but who want to make or clarify a particular point or to voice disapproval of the grounds on which the decision was made.

Dissenting Opinions   Separate opinions in which judges disagree with the conclusion reached by the majority of the court and expand on their own views about the case.

SELF ASSESSMENT

Fill in the blanks and check your answers on page 276.
The lowest tier of the federal court system contains U.S. _____ courts, also known as federal trial courts. Appeals from this lower tier are heard in the thirteen U.S. _____ courts of appeals. A decision handed down by a court in this second tier is final unless the United States _____ Court issues a writ of _____, indicating that it has agreed to review the case.

JUDGES IN THE COURT SYSTEM

Supreme Court justices are the most visible and best-known American jurists, but in many ways they are unrepresentative of the profession as a whole. Few judges enjoy three-room office suites fitted with a fireplace and a private bath, as do the Supreme

Court justices. Few judges have four clerks to assist them. Few judges get a yearly vacation that stretches from July through September. Most judges, in fact, work at the lowest level of the system, in criminal trial courts, where they are burdened with overflowing caseloads and must deal daily with the pettiest of criminals.

One attribute a Supreme Court justice and a criminal trial judge in any small American city do have in common is the expectation that they will be just. Of all the participants in the criminal justice system, no single person is held to the same high standards as the judge. From her or his lofty perch in the courtroom, the judge is counted on to be "above the fray" of the bickering defense attorneys and prosecutors. When the other courtroom contestants rise at the entrance of the judge, they are placing the burden of justice squarely on the judge's shoulders.

The Roles and Responsibilities of Trial Judges

One of the reasons that judicial integrity is considered so important is the amount of discretionary power a judge has over the court proceedings. In the opening of this chapter, you saw an example of a judge who ruled that the prosecution's evidence against defendant Gabe Watson was so weak that no trial was necessary. Figure 8.4 below shows that nearly every stage of the trial process includes a decision or action to be taken by the presiding judge.

BEFORE THE TRIAL A great deal of the work done by a judge takes place before the trial even starts, free from public scrutiny. These duties, some of which you have seen from a different point of view in the section on law enforcement agents, include determining the following:

FIGURE 8.4 The Role of the Judge in the Criminal Trial Process
In the various stages of a felony case, judges must undertake the actions described here.

1. **Pre-Arrest**
   - Decide whether law enforcement officers have provided sufficient probable cause to justify a search or arrest warrant.

2. **Initial Appearance**
   - Inform the suspect of the charges against him or her and of his or her rights.
   - Review the charges to see if probable cause exists that the suspect committed the crime. If not, the judge will dismiss the case.
   - Set the amount of bail (or deny bail) and determine any other conditions of pretrial release.

3. **Preliminary Hearing**
   - Based on evidence provided by the prosecution and defense, decide whether there is probable cause that the suspect committed the crime.
   - Continue to make sure that the defendant's constitutional rights are not being violated.

4. **Arraignment**
   - Ensure that the defendant has been informed of the charges against him or her.
   - Ensure that the defendant understands the plea choices before him or her (to plead guilty, not guilty, or *nolo contendere*).

5. **Plea Bargain**
   - Assist with the plea bargaining process, if both sides are willing to "make a deal."
   - If the defendant decides to plead guilty in return for charges being lessened, ensure that the defendant understands the nature of the plea bargain and has not been pressured into pleading guilty by his or her attorney.

6. **Pretrial Motions**
   - Rule on pretrial motions presented by the defense.
   - Decide whether to grant continuances (the postponement of the trial to allow more time for gathering evidence).

7. **Trial**
   - Ensure that proper procedure is followed in jury selection.
   - "Officiate" at the trial, making sure that both the prosecutor and the defense follow procedural rules in presenting evidence and questioning witnesses.
   - Explain to the jury points of law that affect the case.
   - Provide jury instructions, or instruction to jurors on the meaning of the laws applicable to the case.
   - Receive the jury's final verdict of guilty or not guilty.

8. **Sentencing**
   - If the verdict is "guilty," impose the sentence on the convict.

1. Whether there is sufficient probable cause to issue a search or arrest warrant.
2. Whether there is sufficient probable cause to authorize electronic surveillance of a suspect.
3. Whether enough evidence exists to justify the temporary incarceration of a suspect.
4. Whether a defendant should be released on bail, and if so, the amount of the bail.
5. Whether to accept pretrial motions by prosecutors and defense attorneys.
6. Whether to accept a plea bargain.

Docket The list of cases entered on a court's calendar and thus scheduled to be heard by the court.

During these pretrial activities, the judge takes on the role of the *negotiator*.[22] As most cases are decided through plea bargains rather than through trial proceedings, the judge often offers his or her services as a negotiator to help the prosecution and the defense "make a deal." The amount at which bail is set is often negotiated as well. Throughout the trial process, the judge usually spends a great deal of time in his or her *chambers*, or office, negotiating with the prosecutors and defense attorneys.

DURING THE TRIAL When the trial starts, the judge takes on the role of *referee*. In this role, she or he is responsible for seeing that the trial unfolds according to the dictates of the law and that the participants in the trial do not overstep any legal or ethical bounds. Furthermore, the judge is expected to be neutral, determining the admissibility of testimony and evidence on a completely objective basis. The judge also acts as a *teacher* during the trial, explaining points of law to the jury. If the trial is not a jury trial, then the judge must also make decisions concerning the guilt or innocence of the defendant.

At the close of the trial, if the defendant is found guilty, the judge must decide on the length of the sentence and the type of sentence. (Different types of sentences, such as incarceration, probation, and other forms of community-based corrections, will be discussed in Chapters 11 and 12.) The sentencing phase also gives the judge a chance to make personal comments about the proceedings, if he or she wishes. While sentencing Dr. Conrad Murray to the maximum four years behind bars for the involuntary manslaughter of pop singer Michael Jackson in 2011, Los Angeles County Superior Court Judge Michael Pastor delivered a thirty-minute scolding. Pastor chastised the defendant for being motivated by a desire for "money, fame, and prestige" and criticized Murray for suggesting, in a documentary film, that Jackson was responsible for his own death. "Yikes," said Pastor at the hearing. "Talk about blaming the victim!"[23]

THE ADMINISTRATIVE ROLE Judges are also *administrators* and are responsible for the day-to-day functioning of their courts. A primary administrative task of a judge is scheduling. Each courtroom has a **docket,** or calendar of cases, and it is the judge's responsibility to keep the docket current. This entails not only scheduling the trial, but also setting pretrial motion dates and deciding whether to grant attorneys' requests for *continuances,* or additional time to prepare for the trial. Judges must also keep track of the immense paperwork generated by each case and manage the various employees of the court. In some instances, judges are even responsible for the budgets of their courtrooms.[24] In 1939, Congress, recognizing the burden of such tasks, created the Administrative Office of the United States Courts to provide administrative assistance for federal court judges.[25] Most state court judges, however, do not have the luxury of similar aid, though they are supported by a court staff.

LIE DETECTION IN COURT

AP Photo/Cecil Whig, Matthew Given

During a polygraph test, rubber tubes are placed on a person's chest and abdominal area to record his or her breathing patterns. In addition, two small metal plates are attached to the subject's fingers to measure sweat levels, and a blood pressure cuff indicates her or his heart rate. The examiner asks a series of questions, keeping track of changes in the body's responses to determine if the subject is telling the truth. Law enforcement agents routinely employ polygraphs in the course of criminal investigations, and the technology is widely used by the government to test job applicants and those seeking a security clearance.

In criminal courtrooms, however, polygraph exams are surprisingly absent. The decision to allow evidence of such exams rests primarily with the judge, particularly in federal court. In exercising this discretion, the judge must decide whether the results of the exam are reliable. Even though properly administered polygraphs are, by some measures, accurate about 75 percent of the time, many judges are suspicious of what they believe to be "junk science" and therefore are reluctant to allow it in their courtrooms.

Thinking about Polygraph Exams

In particular, polygraph exams are popular with defendants who want to use the tests to prove their innocence. Assuming that such exams do have 75 percent accuracy rates, are judges justified in keeping the results out of court? Explain your answer.

Selection of Judges

Explain the difference between the selection of judges at the state level and at the federal level. LEARNING OBJECTIVE 7

In the federal court system, all judges are appointed by the president and confirmed by the Senate. It is difficult to make a general statement about how judges are selected in state court systems, however, because the procedure varies widely from state to state. In some states, such as New Jersey, all judges are appointed by the governor and confirmed by the upper chamber of the state legislature. In other states, such as Alabama, **partisan elections** are used to choose judges. In these elections, a judicial candidate declares allegiance to a political party, usually the Democrats or the Republicans, before the election. States such as Kentucky that conduct **nonpartisan elections** do not require a candidate to affiliate herself or himself with a political party in this manner. Finally, some states, such as Missouri, select judges based on a subjective definition of merit.

The two key concepts in discussing methods of selecting judges are *independence* and *accountability*.[26] Those who feel that judicial fairness is dependent on the judges' belief that they will not be removed from office as the result of an unpopular ruling support methods of selection that include appointment.[27] In contrast, some observers feel that judges are "politicians in robes" who make policy decisions every time they step to the bench. Following this line of thought, judges should be held accountable to those who are affected by their decisions and therefore should be chosen through elections, as legislators are.[28] The most independent, and therefore least accountable, judges are those who hold lifetime appointments. They are influenced neither by the temptation to make popular decisions to impress voters nor by the need to follow the ideological or party line of the politicians who provided them with their posts.

APPOINTMENT OF JUDGES Article II, Section 2, of the Constitution authorizes the president to appoint the justices of the Supreme Court with the advice and consent of the

Partisan Elections Elections in which candidates are affiliated with and receive support from political parties.

Nonpartisan Elections Elections in which candidates are presented on the ballot without any party affiliation.

Senate. Subsequent laws enacted by Congress provide that the same procedure is used for appointing judges to the lower federal courts as well.

Federal Appointments On paper, the appointment process is relatively simple. After selecting a nominee, the president submits the name to the Senate for approval. The Senate Judiciary Committee then holds hearings and makes its recommendation to the Senate, where a majority vote is needed to confirm the nomination. In practice, the process does not always proceed smoothly.

Given the importance of the Supreme Court in shaping the nation's laws and values, the appointment process for its justices is highly politicized. Presidents choose candidates who reflect the political beliefs of their party, and members of the opposing party in the Senate do their best to discredit these individuals. In recent years, heated debate over controversial issues such as abortion and gay rights has characterized the proceedings to the point that one commentator likens them to elections rather than the appointments envisioned by the nation's founders.[29]

Patronage Issues Five states, as well as Puerto Rico, employ similar selection methods, with the governor offering nominees for the approval of the state legislature. Judges in these states, as would be expected, serve longer terms than their counterparts in nonappointment judicial systems.[30] They are also regarded as products of *patronage*, as are judges appointed to federal positions by the president. In other words, appointed judges often obtain their positions because they belong to the same political party as the president (or governor, at the state level) and also have been active in supporting the candidates and ideology of the party in power. One of the most prevalent criticisms of appointing judges is that the system is based on "having friends in high places" rather than on merit.[31]

ELECTION OF JUDGES Most states moved from an appointive to an elective system for judges in the mid-nineteenth century. The reasoning behind the move was to make judges more representative of the communities in which they served. Today, all but eleven states choose at least some of their judges through elections.[32] Nearly 90 percent of all state judges face elections at some point in their judicial careers.[33] Even though the practice is widespread, as we will see in the *CJ in Action* feature at the end of the chapter, many observers feel that judicial elections raise unavoidable questions about the impartiality that lies at the heart of the profession.

MERIT SELECTION In 1940, Missouri became the first state to combine appointment and election in a single merit selection. When all jurisdiction levels are counted, nineteen states and the District of Columbia now utilize the **Missouri Plan,** as merit selection has been labeled. The Missouri Plan consists of three basic steps:

- When a vacancy on the bench arises, candidates are nominated by a nonpartisan committee of citizens.
- The names of the three most qualified candidates are sent to the governor or executive of the state judicial system, and that person chooses who will be the judge.
- A year after the new judge has been installed, a "retention election" is held so that voters can decide whether the judge deserves to keep the post.[34]

The goal of the Missouri Plan is to eliminate partisan politics from the selection procedure, while at the same time giving the citizens a voice in the process. (For a review of the selection processes, see *Mastering Concepts—The Selection of State and Federal Judges* on the next page.)

Missouri Plan A method of selecting judges that combines appointment and election.

MASTERING CONCEPTS
THE SELECTION OF STATE AND FEDERAL JUDGES

FEDERAL JUDGES	STATE JUDGES	
1. The president nominates a candidate and presents the nominee to the U.S. Senate. 2. The Senate Judiciary Committee holds hearings concerning the qualifications of the candidate and makes its recommendation to the full Senate. 3. The full Senate votes to confirm or reject the president's nominee.	**Partisan Elections** • Judicial candidates, supported by and affiliated with political parties, place their names before the voters for consideration for a particular judicial seat. • The electorate votes to decide who will retain or gain the seat. **Executive Apointment** • The governor nominates a candidate to the state legislature. • The legislature votes to confirm or reject the governor's nominee.	**Nonpartisan Elections** • Judicial candidates, not supported by or affiliated with political parties, place their names before the voters for consideration for a particular judicial seat. • The electorate votes to decide who will retain or gain the seat. **Missouri Plan** • A nominating commission provides a list of worthy candidates. • An elected official (usually the governor) chooses from the list submitted by the commission. • A year later, a "retention election" is held to allow voters to decide whether the judge will stay on the bench.

THE REMOVAL OF JUDGES Besides losing an election, sitting judges can be removed from office for **judicial misconduct**, or behavior that diminishes public confidence in the judiciary. Nearly every state has a *judicial conduct commission,* which consists of lawyers, judges, and other prominent citizens and is often a branch of the state's highest court. This commission investigates charges of judicial misconduct and may recommend removal if warranted. The final decision to discipline a judge generally is made by the state supreme court.[35]

Several state judges are removed from office each year. Recent examples include Michigan District Judge Sylvia James, who lost her seat for a wide variety of misconduct that included misappropriating more than $100,000 that was supposed to be restitution for crime victims. James used some of the funds to buy personal items and redirected the rest to community charities of her choice.

THE IMPEACHMENT PROCESS Such transgressions as those committed by Sylvia James, however deplorable, would be unlikely to result in a similar outcome if committed by a federal judge. Appointed under Article II of the U.S. Constitution, federal judges can be removed from office only if found guilty of "Treason, Bribery, or other high Crimes and Misdemeanors." Before a federal judge can be **impeached,** the U.S. House of Representatives must be presented with specific charges of misconduct and vote on whether these charges merit further action. If the House votes to impeach by a simple majority (more than 50 percent), the U.S. Senate—presided over by the chief justice of the United States Supreme Court—holds a trial on the judge's conduct. At the conclusion of this trial, a two-thirds majority vote is required in the Senate to remove the judge.

This disciplinary action is extremely rare: only eight federal judges have been impeached and convicted in the nation's history. Most recently, in 2010 U.S. District Court Judge G. Thomas Porteous was removed from office for accepting tens of thousands of dollars in cash from lawyers to pay gambling debts and then lying about his misbehavior to federal investigators. (See the feature *Comparative Criminal Justice—Back to School* on the facing page to learn about France's preferred method for producing ethical judges.)

Judicial Misconduct A general term describing behavior—such as accepting bribes or consorting with known felons—that diminishes public confidence in the judiciary.

Impeachment The formal process by which a public official is charged with misconduct that could lead to his or her removal from office.

COMPARATIVE CRIMINAL JUSTICE

BACK TO SCHOOL

Elections for judges are extremely rare outside the United States. Indeed, only two nations—Japan and Switzerland—engage in the practice, and then only in very limited situations. To the rest of the world, according to one expert, "American adherence to judicial elections is as incomprehensible as our rejection of the metric system." Much more common, for example, is the French system, crafted to provide extensive training for potential judges.

French judicial candidates must pass two exams. The first, open to law school graduates only, combines oral and written sections and lasts at least four days. In some years, only 5 percent of the applicants overcome this hurdle. Not surprisingly, the pressure is intense. "It gives you nightmares for years afterwards," says Jean-Marc Baissus, a judge in Toulouse. "You come out of [the exam] completely shattered." Those who do survive the first test enter a two-year program at the École Nationale de la Magistrature,

> **LEARNING OBJECTIVE 8**
> Describe one alternative, practiced in other countries, to the American method of choosing judges.

a judicial training academy. This school is similar to a police training academy in the United States, in that candidates spend half of their time in the classroom and the other half in the courtroom.

At the end of this program, judicial candidates are subject to a second examination. Only those who pass the exam may become judges. The result, in the words of Mitchell Lasser, a law professor at Cornell University, is that French judges "actually know what the hell they are doing. They've spent years in school taking practical and theoretical courses on how to be a judge." The French also pride themselves on creating judges who are free from the kind of political pressures faced by American judges who must go before the voters.

FOR CRITICAL ANALYSIS

Do you think that the French system of training judges is superior to the American system of electing them? Before explaining your answer, consider that French judges lack the practical courtroom experience of American judges, many of whom served as lawyers earlier in their careers.

Diversity on the Bench

According to a recent report by the Brennan Center for Justice in New York City, "Americans who enter the courtroom often face a predictable presence on the bench: a white male."[36] Overall, about two-thirds of all state appellate judges are white males, and women in particular are notably absent from the highest courts of most states.[37] On both a national and state level, members of minority groups are underrepresented. Arizona's population, for example, is 40 percent nonwhite, but the state has no minority supreme court justices and minorities hold less than 20 percent of other state judgeships.[38]

The federal judiciary shows a similar pattern. Of the nearly 1,800 federal judges in this country, about 10 percent are African American, 6 percent are Hispanic, and less than 2 percent are Asian American. Furthermore, only 19 percent are women.[39] Of the 111 justices who have served on the United States Supreme Court, two have been African American: Thurgood Marshall (1970–1991) and Clarence Thomas (1991–present). In 2009, Sonia Sotomayor became the first Hispanic appointed to the Court and the third woman, following Sandra Day O'Connor (1981–2006) and Ruth Bader Ginsburg (1993–present). A year later, Elena Kagan became the fourth woman appointed to the Court.

The Impact of Past Discrimination

Edward Chen, a federal judge for the Northern District of California, identifies a number of reasons for the low minority representation on the bench. Past discrimination in law schools has limited the pool of experienced minority attorneys who have the political

Before his appointment, New Jersey Superior Court Judge Sohail Mohammed, a native of India, represented nearly three dozen suspects detained following the 9/11 terrorist attacks. He has also trained more than 7,000 law enforcement agents to better understand the Muslim American community. What are the benefits of having judges with a wide range of cultural experiences on the bench?
New Jersey Governor's Office/Tim Larsen

ties, access to "old boy" networks, and career opportunities that lead to judgeships.[40] Only recently, as increased numbers of minorities have graduated from law schools, have rates of minority judges begun to creep slowly upward. Traditionally, efforts to diversify American judges by race, ethnicity, and gender have been met with resistance from those who argue that because judges must be impartial, it makes no difference whether a judge is black, Asian, Hispanic, or white.[41]

Sherrilyn A. Ifill of the University of Maryland School of Law rejects this argument. She believes that "diversity on the bench" can only enrich our judiciary by introducing a variety of voices and perspectives into what are perhaps the most powerful positions in the criminal justice system. By the same token, Ifill credits the lack of diversity in many trial and appeals courts with a number of harmful consequences, such as more severe sentences for minority youths than for white youths who have committed similar crimes, disproportionate denial of bail to minority defendants, and the disproportionate imposition of the death penalty on minority defendants accused of killing white victims.[42]

SELF ASSESSMENT

Fill in the blanks and check your answers on page 276.

In the federal court system, judges are appointed by the _____ and confirmed by the _____. In state court systems, however, the selection process varies. Some states mirror the federal system, with the _____ making judicial appointments with the approval of the legislature. Others conduct either _____ elections, in which political parties openly support judicial candidates, or _____ elections, in which the candidate is not affiliated with any political group. Finally, a number of states rely on _____ selection, which combines appointment and election. Federal judges can be removed only through the process of _____, while state judges face removal if they engage in serious _____.

THE COURTROOM WORK GROUP

Television dramas often depict the courtroom as a battlefield, with prosecutors and defense attorneys spitting fire at each other over the loud and insistent protestations of a frustrated judge. Consequently, many people are somewhat disappointed when they witness a real courtroom at work. Rarely does anyone raise his or her voice, and the courtroom professionals appear—to a great extent—to be cooperating with each other. In Chapter 6, we discussed the existence of a police subculture, based on the shared values of law enforcement agents. A courtroom subculture exists as well, centered on the **courtroom work group.**

The most important feature of any work group is that it is a *cooperative* unit, whose members establish shared values and methods that help the group efficiently reach its goals. Though cooperation is not a concept usually associated with criminal courts, it is in fact crucial to the adjudication process.

Courtroom Work Group The social organization consisting of the judge, prosecutor, defense attorney, and other court workers.

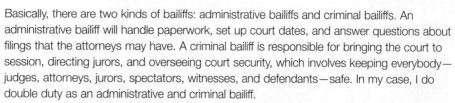

CAREERS IN CJ

Photo Courtesy of Shawn Davis

SHAWN DAVIS

BAILIFF

FASTFACTS

**BAILIFF
JOB DESCRIPTION:**

- Maintain order and provide security in the courtroom during trials.
- Open and close court, call cases, call witnesses, and the like.
- Escort and guard juries, prevent juries from having contact with the public.

**WHAT KIND OF
TRAINING IS REQUIRED?**

- At a minimum, a high school diploma or GED.

ANNUAL SALARY RANGE?

- $30,000–$38,000

Basically, there are two kinds of bailiffs: administrative bailiffs and criminal bailiffs. An administrative bailiff will handle paperwork, set up court dates, and answer questions about filings that the attorneys may have. A criminal bailiff is responsible for bringing the court to session, directing jurors, and overseeing court security, which involves keeping everybody—judges, attorneys, jurors, spectators, witnesses, and defendants—safe. In my case, I do double duty as an administrative and criminal bailiff.

Violence in the courtroom is rare. Most inmates are on their best behavior in front of the judge. It can flare up in an instant, however, and you have to be constantly on guard. One time, an inmate under my control made a run for it as we were transporting him back to the jail from his court appearance. His leg shackles broke, giving him a short-lived sense of freedom. We were able to tackle him in front of the courthouse just before he could jump into a waiting convertible. We later learned that the accomplice—the inmate's brother—was supposed to bring a handgun and shoot us as part of the escape plan. Another time, a defendant started taking off his shirt and tried to attack the victim, who had just given testimony. He was quickly tackled, cuffed, and carted off to jail.

SOCIAL MEDIA CAREER TIP Networking is crucial. Develop as many useful social media contacts as possible, and cultivate those contacts. Also, reciprocate. If you help others establish online contacts, they are likely to remember you and return the favor.

Members of the Courtroom Work Group

The courtroom work group is made up of those individuals who are involved with the defendant from the time she or he is arrested until sentencing. The most prominent members are the judge, the prosecutor, and the defense attorney (the latter two will be discussed in detail in the next chapter). Three other court participants complete the work group:

LEARNING
9
OBJECTIVE

List and describe the members of the courtroom work group.

1. The *bailiff of the court* is responsible for maintaining security and order in the judge's chambers and the courtroom. Bailiffs lead the defendant in and out of the courtroom and attend to the needs of the jurors during the trial. A bailiff, often a member of the local sheriff's department but sometimes an employee of the court, also delivers summonses in some jurisdictions.

2. The *clerk of the court* has an exhausting list of responsibilities. Any plea, motion, or other matter to be acted on by the judge must go through the clerk. The large amount of paperwork generated during a trial, including transcripts, photographs, evidence, and any other records, is maintained by the clerk. The clerk also issues subpoenas for jury duty and coordinates the jury selection process. In the federal court system, judges select clerks, while state clerks are either appointed or, in nearly a third of the states, elected.

3. *Court reporters* record every word that is said during the course of the trial. They also record any *depositions,* or pretrial question-and-answer sessions in which a party or a witness answers an attorney's questions under oath.

Three trial lawyers confer as the judge waits at the Sedgwick County Courthouse in Wichita, Kansas. How is working in a courtroom similar to working in a corporate office? How is it different?
Jaime Oppenheimer/MCT/Landov

Formation of the Courtroom Work Group

The premise of the work group is based on constant interaction that fosters relationships among the members. As legal scholar David W. Neubauer describes:

> Every day, the same group of courthouse regulars assembles in the same courtroom, sits or stands in the same places, and performs the same tasks as the day before. The types of defendants and the nature of the crimes they are accused of committing also remain constant. Only the names of the victim, witnesses, and defendants are different.[43]

After a period of time, the members of a courtroom work group learn how the others operate. The work group establishes patterns of behavior and norms, and cooperation allows the adjudication process to function informally and smoothly.[44] In some cases, the members of the work group may even form personal relationships, which only strengthen the courtroom culture.

One way in which the courtroom work group differs from a traditional work group at a company such as Facebook, Inc., is that each member answers to a different sponsoring organization. Although the judge has ultimate authority over a courtroom, he or she is not the "boss" of the attorneys. The prosecutor is hired by the district attorney's office, the defense attorney by a private individual or the public defender's office, and the judge by the court system itself.

The Judge in the Courtroom Work Group

The judge is the dominant figure in the courtroom and therefore exerts the most influence over the values and norms of the work group. A judge who runs a "tight ship" follows procedure and restricts the freedom of attorneys to deviate from regulations, while a *"laissez-faire"* judge allows more leeway to members of the work group. A judge's personal philosophy also affects the court proceedings. If a judge has a reputation for being "tough on crime," both prosecutors and defense attorneys will alter their strategies accordingly. In fact, a lawyer may be able to manipulate the system to "shop" for a judge whose philosophy best fits the attorney's goals in a particular case.[45] If a lawyer is caught trying to influence the assignment of judges, however, she or he is said to be "corrupting judicial independence" and may face legal proceedings.

Although preeminent in the work group, a judge must still rely on other members of the group. To a certain extent, the judge is the least informed member of the trio. Like a juror, the judge learns the facts of the case as they are presented by the attorneys. If the attorneys do not properly present the facts, then the judge is hampered in making rulings. Furthermore, if a judge deviates from the norms of the work group—by, for example, refusing to grant continuances—the other members of the work group can "discipline" the judge. Defense attorneys and prosecutors can request further continuances, fail to produce witnesses in a timely manner, and slow down the proceeding through a general lack of preparedness. The delays caused by such acts can ruin a judge's calendar—especially in large courts—and bring pressure from the judge's superiors.

Assembly-Line Justice

In discussing the goals of the courtroom work group, several general concepts figure prominently—efficiency, cooperation, rapidity, and socialization. One aim of the work group, however, is glaring in its absence: justice. One of the main criticisms of the American court system is that it has sacrificed the goal of justice for efficiency. Some observers claim that only the wealthiest can afford to receive justice as promised by the Constitution, while the rest of society is left with a watered-down version of *assembly-line justice.*

THE IMPACT OF EXCESSIVE CASELOADS Given the caseloads that most courts face, some degree of assembly-line justice seems inevitable. A quick survey of the nation's court system provides clear examples of the extent of the problem and its consequences. Many, if not most, state courts are consistently behind on their dockets.[46] After watching a judge in Lynwood (Washington) Municipal Court handle more than one hundred misdemeanor cases in four hours, a researcher noted that each defendant got less time before the judge "than it takes to get a hamburger from a McDonald's drive-through."[47]

Several years ago, about 300 criminal cases in Riverside County, California, were dismissed because of a shortage of available judges.[48] Although the situation is less extreme in the federal court system, some of those courts also struggle to meet their obligations. In 2012, the district court in Connecticut needed to import nine out-of-state volunteer federal judges to relieve its caseload.[49]

THE COURTROOM WORK GROUP AND OVERLOADED COURTS A judge's worth is increasingly measured by her or his ability to keep the "assembly line" of cases moving, rather than by the quality of her or his judicial work. Consequently, the judicial process is accused of being "careless and haphazard" and of routinely supporting decisions made on the basis of incomplete information. Though definitive statistics on the subject have never been adequately gathered, many observers feel that assembly-line justice affects the actions of others in the criminal justice system as well:

- Beyond filling out a crime report, police officers often do not investigate misdemeanors and less serious felonies unless the offender was caught in the act.
- Police officers often are encouraged to obtain confessions—using whatever means necessary—from defendants, rather than find incriminating evidence, because a confession is more likely to lead to conviction.
- Prosecutors often press charges for misdemeanors and nonviolent felonies only when the case is a "slam dunk"—that is, when conviction is certain.
- To wrap up cases quickly, prosecutors generally bargain reduced sentences for guilty verdicts. As a result, criminals spend less time in prison than is in society's best interests.[50]

If the public is under the impression that police, judges, and lawyers are more interested in speed than in justice, the pressure of caseloads may also lead to loss of respect for the criminal justice system as a whole.

SELF ASSESSMENT

Fill in the blanks and check your answers on page 276.

The three most prominent members of the courtroom work group are the _____, the _____, and the _____ _____. As a rule, these professionals must _____ with each other to ensure the smooth functioning of the court system. A condition known as _____-_____ _____ exists when courtroom work groups sacrifice justice for the sake of efficiency.

ELECTING JUDGES

The television advertisement voice-over started by rhetorically asking viewers if they would "give probation to a sex offender convicted of two counts of rape." Then, it continued: "Judge Phyllis McMillen did." The negative ad went on to claim that, after McMillen's leniency, the "career criminal and sex offender" went on to commit armed robbery.[51] As it turned out, the facts presented in the advertisement—paid for by supporters of McMillen's opponent in a 2012 Oakland, Michigan, judicial election—were false. McMillen had in fact sentenced the suspect to up to fifteen years in prison for breaking and entering, and had not been involved in his earlier sexual conduct convictions.[52] The airing of blatant misinformation is only one of the issues that contributes to the continuing controversy over judicial elections, the subject of this chapter's *CJ in Action* feature.

POPULARITY AND ACCOUNTABILITY

As was the case with Judge Phyllis McMillen—who won her reelection bid—attack ads in judicial campaigns often focus on crime. The subject is seen as a "hot button issue" that will anger voters and, at least theoretically, get them to the polls. Proponents of judicial elections insist that unless judges are regularly forced to submit themselves to the will of the electorate, there is no way to hold them accountable for their actions.

Critics, such as Hans A. Linde, a retired justice of the Oregon Supreme Court, counter "'Judicial accountability' has a virtuous ring to it until one asks, accountability for what?"[53] The answer to Linde's rhetorical question, at least in his mind, is that the public will hold a judge accountable for making unpopular rulings, but not necessarily for making "incorrect" ones. If Linde's assertion is true, the negative impact will fall most heavily on defendants in criminal trials, who are among the most unpopular participants in the judicial process.

THE CASE FOR JUDICIAL ELECTIONS

- In a democracy, voters have the right to select government officials such as judges who make important policy decisions.

- Elections ensure that the people have a measure of control over the judiciary. If a judge repeatedly makes unpopular decisions involving the punishment of criminals or other important issues, he or she deserves to be voted out of office.

- Campaigning requires judges to interact with the community, thereby broadening their perspective. One judicial candidate noted that he was forced to "leave his comfort zone of similarly minded lawyers" and talk to "nurses in Pearland [Texas], stay-at-home moms in Galveston, shrimpers in Chambers County, doctors in Houston's vast medical center, [and] farmers in Sealy."[54]

THE CASE AGAINST JUDICIAL ELECTIONS

- Judges are not like politicians. They must be neutral in applying the law to the facts, regardless of any political consequences. In other words, "courts are supposed to do what is right, not what is popular."[55]

- The need to raise funds for judges' election campaigns raises concerns of undue influence by major contributors such as lawyers and other special interests. In one poll, more than a quarter of 2,428 state judges felt that campaign contributions had some influence on judges' decisions.[56] In another, nearly 80 percent of citizens agreed with the statement: "Elected judges are influenced by having to raise campaign funds."[57]

- Voters not only lack knowledge of the issues of a judicial election, but do not even know who the candidates are. A poll in Michigan found that nine out of ten voters could not identify a single sitting state supreme court justice.[58]

YOUR OPINION—WRITING ASSIGNMENT

In the criminal justice context, under what circumstances, if any, should a judge be required to remove himself or herself from a trial because of statements made or contributions accepted during a campaign? Note that, according to the Model Code of Judicial Conduct, "A judge shall disqualify himself or herself in a proceeding in which the judge's impartiality might reasonably be questioned."[59] Before completing this assignment, you can review our discussions in this chapter concerning:

- The legitimacy of courts (page 251).

- The roles and responsibilities of trial judges (pages 264–265).

- Selection of judges (pages 266–268).

Your answer should include at least three full paragraphs.

CHAPTER SUMMARY

For more information on these concepts, look back to the Learning Objective icons throughout the chapter.

 Define and contrast the four functions of the courts. The four functions are (a) due process, (b) crime control, (c) rehabilitation, and (d) bureaucratic. The most obvious contrast is between the due process and crime control functions. The former is mainly concerned with the procedural rules that allow each accused individual to have a "fair chance" against the government in a criminal proceeding. For crime control, the courts are supposed to impose enough "pain" on convicted criminals to deter criminal behavior. For the rehabilitation function, the courts serve as "doctors" who dispense "treatment." In their bureaucratic function, courts are more concerned with speed and efficiency.

 Define *jurisdiction* and contrast geographic and subject-matter jurisdiction. Jurisdiction relates to the power of a court to hear a particular case. Courts are typically limited in geographic jurisdiction—for example, to a particular state. Some courts are restricted in subject matter, such as a small claims court, which can hear only cases involving civil matters under a certain monetary limit.

 Explain the difference between trial and appellate courts. Trial courts are courts of the first instance, where a case is first heard. Appellate courts review the proceedings of a lower court. Appellate courts do not have juries.

 Outline the several levels of a typical state court system. (a) At the lowest level are courts of limited jurisdiction, (b) next are trial courts of general jurisdiction, (c) then appellate courts, and (d) finally, the state's highest court.

 Outline the federal court system. (a) At the lowest level are the U.S. district courts in which trials are held, as well as various minor federal courts of limited jurisdiction; (b) next are the U.S. courts of appeals, otherwise known as circuit courts of appeals; and (c) finally, the United States Supreme Court.

 Explain briefly how a case is brought to the Supreme Court. Cases decided in U.S. courts of appeals, as well as cases decided in the highest state courts (when federal questions arise), can be appealed to the Supreme Court. If at least four justices approve of a case filed with the Supreme Court, the Court will issue a writ of *certiorari,* ordering the lower court to send the Supreme Court the record of the case for review.

 Explain the difference between the selection of judges at the state level and at the federal level. The president nominates all judges at the federal level, and the Senate must approve the nominations. A similar procedure is used in some states. In other states, all judges are elected on a partisan ballot or on a nonpartisan ballot. Some states use merit selection, or the Missouri Plan, in which a citizen committee nominates judicial candidates, the governor or executive of the state judicial system chooses among the top three nominees, and a year later a "retention election" is held.

 Describe one alternative, practiced in other countries, to the American method of choosing judges. The practice of electing judges is quite rare, with the United States being one of the few countries that allows it. Other nations, including France, require candidates for judicial positions (generally law school graduates) to complete an academic program that includes several difficult exams and has a low success rate.

 List and describe the members of the courtroom work group. (a) The judge; (b) the prosecutor, who brings charges in the name of the people (the state) against the accused; (c) the defense attorney; (d) the bailiff, who is responsible for maintaining security and order in the judge's chambers and the courtroom; (e) the clerk, who accepts all pleas, motions, and other matters to be acted on by the judge; and (f) court reporters, who record what is said during a trial as well as at depositions.

QUESTIONS FOR CRITICAL ANALYSIS

1. "The primary adversarial relationship in the courts is not between the plaintiff (prosecutor, or state) and defendant, but rather between the ideal of justice and the reality of bureaucratic limitations." Explain why you agree or disagree with this statement.

2. Several years ago, authorities in Thailand extradited Russian citizen and alleged international arms dealer Viktor Bout to the United States. The evidence against Bout included an audio recording of a conversation he had with American agents posing as Colombian rebels.

During this conversation, Bout agreed to furnish the "revolutionaries" with weapons for the purpose of killing American pilots. How does this evidence give the United States jurisdiction over Bout?

3. In 2012, the United States Supreme Court "denied cert" in the case of Joel Tenenbaum, who had been ordered to pay a recording company $675,000 in fines for illegally downloading thirty-one songs using a file-sharing Web site. Tenebaum claimed that the fine was excessive and unfair. What does it mean for the Court to "deny cert"?

In this instance, what might have been some reasons for the Court's refusal to consider Tenenbaum's case?

4. Why do federal judges have more job security than state judges? How does this give them more freedom to make unpopular decisions?

5. Which of the methods of selecting judges that you learned about in the chapter—elections, appointments, or the Missouri Plan—would be most likely to increase judicial diversity? Explain your answer.

KEY TERMS

appellate courts   255
concurrent jurisdiction   253
concurring opinions   263
courtroom work group   270
dissenting opinions   263
docket   265
dual court system   256
extradition   254

impeachment   268
judicial misconduct   268
judicial review   261
jurisdiction   253
magistrate   258
Missouri Plan   267
nonpartisan elections   266
opinions   256

oral arguments   263
partisan elections   266
problem-solving courts   259
rule of four   262
trial courts   255
writ of *certiorari*   262

SELF ASSESSMENT ANSWER KEY

Page 252: i. due process; **ii.** individuals; **iii.** crime control; **iv.** society; **v.** rehabilitate

Page 257: i. jurisdiction; **ii.** subject matter; **iii.** trial; **iv.** appellate; **v.** dual; **vi.** federal; **vii.** state

Page 260: i. limited; **ii.** general; **iii.** appeals

Page 263: i. district; **ii.** circuit; **iii.** Supreme; **iv.** *certiorari*

Page 270: i. president; **ii.** Senate; **iii.** governor; **iv.** partisan; **v.** nonpartisan; **vi.** merit; **vii.** impeachment; **viii.** misconduct

Page 273: i. judge; **ii.** prosecutor; **iii.** defense attorney; **iv.** cooperate; **v.** assembly-line justice.

NOTES

1. Quoted in Eric Velasco, "Watson Acquitted of Wife's Murder," *Birmingham News* (February 24, 2012), 1.

2. Roscoe Pound, "The Administration of Justice in American Cities," *Harvard Law Review* 12 (1912).

3. Russell Wheeler and Howard Whitcomb, *Judicial Administration: Text and Readings* (Englewood Cliffs, NJ: Prentice Hall, 1977), 3.

4. Larry J. Siegel, *Criminology: Instructor's Manual,* 6th ed. (Belmont, CA: West/Wadsworth Publishing Co., 1998), 440.

5. Gerald F. Velman, "Federal Sentencing Guidelines: A Cure Worse Than the Disease," *American Criminal Law Review* 29 (Spring 1992), 904.

6. Wayne R. LaFave, "Section 4.6. Multiple Jurisdiction and Multiple Prosecution," *Substantive Criminal Law,* 2d ed. (C.J.S. Criminal Section 254), 2007.

7. William Wan, "Snipers to Be Tried in Maryland," *Baltimore Sun* (May 11, 2005), 1A.

8. Elliot Spagat, "Mexican Extradited to U.S. under New President," *Associated Press* (March 8, 2013).

9. 18 U.S.C. Section 3231; and *Solorio v. United States,* 483 U.S. 435 (1987).

10. 18 U.S.C.A. Section 1951.

11. Alexander Hamilton, *Federalist Paper* No. 78, in *The Federalist Papers,* ed. Clinton Rossiter (New York: New American Library, 1961), 467–470.

12. G. Edward White, *History of the Supreme Court,* vols. 3–4: *The Marshall Court and Cultural Change* (New York: Oxford University Press, 1988), 157–200.

13. 372 U.S. 335 (1963).

14. 384 U.S. 436 (1966).

15. 408 U.S. 238 (1972).

16. 428 U.S. 153 (1976).

17. 18 U.S.C. Section 48 (1999).

18. *United States v. Stevens,* 559 U.S. ____ (2010).

19. 559 U.S. ____ (2010).

20. Somini Sengupta, "Courts Divided Over Searches of Cellphones," *New York Times* (November 26, 2012), A1.

21. David R. Stras and James F. Spriggs II, "Explaining Plurality Opinions," *Georgetown Law Journal* 99 (March 2010), 519.

22. Barry R. Schaller, *A Vision of American Law: Judging Law, Literature, and the Stories We Tell* (Westport, CT: Praeger, 1997).

23. Quoted in Linda Deutsch, "Murray Gets 4-Year Sentence, Tongue-Lashing from Judge," *Associated Press* (November 29, 2011).

24. Harlington Wood, Jr., "Judiciary Reform: Recent Improvements in Federal Judicial Administration," *American University Law Review* 44 (June 1995), 1557.

25. Pub. L. No. 76-299, 53 Stat. 1223, codified as amended at 28 U.S.C. Sections 601–610 (1988 & Supp. V 1993).

26. Patrick Emery Longan, "Judicial Professionalism in a New Era of Judicial Selection," *Mercer Law Review* (Spring 2005), 913.

27. Andrew F. Hanssen, "Learning about Judicial Independence: Institutional Change in the State Courts," *Journal of Legal Studies* (2004), 431–474.

28. Brian P. Anderson, "Judicial Elections in West Virginia," *West Virginia Law Review* (Fall 2004), 243.

29. Richard Davis, *Electing Justice: Fixing the Supreme Court Nomination Process* (New York: Oxford University Press, 2005), 6–9.

30. Daniel R. Deja, "How Judges Are Selected: A Survey of the Judicial Selection Process in the United States," *Michigan Bar Journal* 75 (September 1996), 904.

31. Edmund V. Ludwig, "Another Case against the Election of Trial Judges," *Pennsylvania Lawyer* 19 (May/June 1997), 33.

32. American Judicature Society, "Judicial Selection in the States," at **www.judicialselection.com**.

33. David K. Scott, "Zero-Sum Judicial Elections: Balancing Free Speech and Impartiality through Recusal Reform," *Brigham Young University Law Review* (2009), 481, 485.

34. James E. Lozier, "The Missouri Plan a.k.a. Merit Selection Is the Best Solution for Selecting Michigan's Judges," *Michigan Bar Journal* 75 (September 1996), 918.

35. John Gardiner, "Preventing Judicial Misconduct: Defining the Role of Conduct Organizations," *Judicature* 70 (1986), 113–121.

36. Ciara Torres-Spelliscy, Monique Chase, and Emma Greenman, *Improving Judicial Diversity,* 2d ed. (New York: Brennan Center for Justice, 2010), 1.

37. *Ibid.*

38. *Ibid.*

39. Federal Judicial Center, "Diversity on the Bench," at **www.fjc.gov/history/home.nsf/page/judges_diversity.html**.

40. Edward M. Chen, "The Judiciary, Diversity, and Justice for All," *California Law Review* (July 2003), 1109.

41. Theresa B. Beiner, "The Elusive (but Worthwhile) Quest for a Diverse Bench in the New Millennium," *University of California at Davis Law Review* (February 2003), 599.

42. Sherrilyn A. Ifill, "Racial Diversity on the Bench: Beyond Role Models and Public Confidence," *Washington and Lee Law Review* (Spring 2000), 405.

43. David W. Neubauer, *America's Courts and the Criminal Justice System,* 5th ed. (Belmont, CA: Wadsworth Publishing Co., 1996), 41.

44. Alissa P. Worden, "The Judge's Role in Plea Bargaining: An Analysis of Judges' Agreement with Prosecutors' Sentencing Recommendations," *Justice Quarterly* 10 (1995), 257–278.

45. Kimberly Jade Norwood, "Shopping for Venue: The Need for More Limits," *University of Miami Law Review* 50 (1996), 295–298.

46. Court Statistics Project, "Examining the Work of State Courts: An Analysis of 2010 State Court Caseloads," at **www.courtstatistics.org/Other-Pages/~/media/Microsites/Files/CSP/DATA%20PDF/CSP_DEC.ashx**.

47. Robert C. Boruchowitz, Malia N. Brink, and Maureen Dimino, *Minor Crimes, Massive Waste* (Washington, D.C.: National Association of Criminal Defense Lawyers, April 2009), 32.

48. Maura Dolan and Victoria Kim, "State Supreme Court Upholds Riverside County's Dismissal of Criminal Cases," *Los Angeles Times* (October 26, 2010), at **articles.latimes.com/2010/oct/26/local/la-me-dismiss-20101026**.

49. Martha Nell, "9 Out-of-State Colleagues Will Help Overwhelmed Federal Court in Conn. Get on Top of Caseload," *ABA Journal* (September 24, 2012), at **www.abajournal.com/news/article/9_out-of-state_colleagues_will_help_overwhelmed_federal_court_in_conn._get_/**.

50. Malcolm Feeley, *Felony Arrests: Their Prosecutions and Disposition in New York Courts* (New York: Vera Institute, 1981), xii.

51. "Money Talks? Out-of-State Cash Funding Circuit Court Hopefuls' Campaigns; Negative Ad Arrives," *Spinal Column: West Oakland's News Weekly* (September 19, 2012), at **spinalcolumnonline.com/2012/09/19/money-talks-out-of-state-cash-funding-circuit-court-hopefuls-campaigns-negative-ad-arrives/**.

52. *Ibid.*

53. Quoted in Daniel Burke, "Code of Judicial Conduct Canon 7B(1)(c): Toward the Proper Regulation of Speech in Judicial Campaigns," *Georgetown Journal of Legal Ethics* 81 (Summer 1993), 181.

54. Martin J. Siegel, "In Defense of Judicial Election (Sort Of)," *Litigation* (Summer 2010), 24–25.

55. Owen Fiss, "The Right Degree of Independence," in *The Law As It Could Be* (New York: New York University Press, 2003), 61.

56. Justice at Stake Campaign, "Justice at Stake—State Judges Frequency Questionnaire" (2002), at **www.justiceatstake.org/media/cms/JASJudgesSurveyResults_EA8838C0504A5.pdf**.

57. Referenced in Thomas J. Moyer, "Commission on the 21st Century Judiciary," *Akron Law Review* (2005), 556.

58. William Ballenger, "In Judicial Wilderness, Even Brickley's Not Safe," *Michigan Politics* 28 (1996), 1–3.

59. *Model Code of Judicial Conduct,* Canon 3(E)(1) (2007).

9 Pretrial Procedures: The Adversary System in Action

CHAPTER OUTLINE	CORRESPONDING LEARNING OBJECTIVES
The Prosecution	List the different names given to public prosecutors and indicate the general powers that they have.
	Contrast the prosecutor's roles as an elected official and as a crime fighter.
The Defense Attorney	Delineate the responsibilities of defense attorneys.
	Explain why defense attorneys must often defend clients they know to be guilty.
Truth, Victory, and the Adversary System	List the three basic features of an adversary system of justice.
Pretrial Detention	Identify the steps involved in the pretrial criminal process.
	Indicate the three influences on a judge's decision to set bail.
Establishing Probable Cause	Identify the main difference between an indictment and an information.
The Prosecutorial Screening Process	Explain how a prosecutor screens potential cases.
Pleading Guilty	Indicate the ways that both defense attorneys and prosecutors can induce plea bargaining.

To target your study and review, look for these numbered Learning Objective icons throughout the chapter.

AP Photo/Atlanta Journal-Constitution, Kent D. Johnson

DEATH BY HAZING

IT TOOK Orange County (Florida) prosecutor Lawson Lamar a long time to figure out what to do about the killing of Robert Champion. On November 19, 2011, Champion, a twenty-six-year-old drum major with Florida A&M University's renowned marching band, was beaten to death before a football game in Orlando. As part of a hazing ritual, he had been forced to walk from one end of a school bus to the other while fellow band members punched, kicked, and struck him with various objects, including drumsticks. Following the abuse, according to the local medical examiner, Champion died of hemorrhagic shock caused by blunt-force trauma.

Five months after the incident, Lamar finally announced that his office was charging eleven band members with third degree felony hazing for Champion's death. Many observers felt that the charge, which carries a maximum penalty of five years in prison, was too soft. Lamar defended his decision, saying that it would be nearly impossible to prove which of the defendants was primarily responsible for the homicide. "We do not have a blow or a shot or a knife thrust that killed Mr. Champion," the prosecutor explained. Other legal experts agreed. "Charging someone with murder certainly sounds sexier," said a former member of the Miami–Dade County State Attorney's Office. "But it's not the prosecutor's job to make headlines—it's to find justice."

As it turned out, Jeff Ashton had a different notion of justice in this case. After defeating Lamar in an election, Ashton moved quickly to toughen the prosecution's stance. Without explanation, in March 2013 he upgraded the charges against the defendants to manslaughter, which, in Florida, carries a maximum fifteen-year prison sentence. "We applaud and commend [Ashton's] actions," said the attorney for the Champion family. "Robert wasn't hurt by hazing. He was killed by hazing. We are fortunate that someone with the courage to act has been elected in Orange County."

1. One observer called the Champion case a "nightmare" for a prosecutor because there were twenty-five people on the bus when the crime took place. How would these circumstances make it difficult for investigators to determine who was responsible for what during the hazing incident?

2. Under Florida law, hazing is defined as any action—under the sanction of a college-sponsored organization—in which participants recklessly or intentionally endanger the mental or physical health of a student. Third degree felony hazing occurs when the act leads to the bodily injury or death of another person. State law defines manslaughter as acting without reasonable caution in a way that puts another person at risk of death. Which prosecutor, Lawson Lamar or Jeff Ashton, do you think chose the correct charges in the case of Robert Champion? Why?

3. After the initial charges against her son's hazers were announced, Champion's mother, Pam, expressed her disappointment that the potential penalties weren't more severe. Should government prosecutors take into account the views of crime victims when deciding how to punish an offender? Explain your answer.

AP Photo/*The Tampa Tribune*, Joseph Brown III

Twenty-six-year-old Robert Champion, a drum major in Florida A&M's marching band, died as the result of a hazing ritual conducted by bandmates on a school bus.

THE PROSECUTION

Public Prosecutors Individuals, acting as trial lawyers, who initiate and conduct cases in the government's name and on behalf of the people.

Attorney General The chief law officer of a state; also, the chief law officer of the nation.

Bill Sharpe, representing one of the defendants charged with manslaughter by Jeff Ashton, called the move a "scare tactic" to persuade his client to plead guilty (a strategy we discuss later in the chapter).[1] "Dueling lawyers" such as Sharpe and Ashton are the main combatants of the American adversary system. Contrary to public opinion, however, these struggles start well before the beginning of the criminal trial. Indeed, cases rarely make it as far as trial. Instead, the issue of guilt and innocence is usually negotiated beforehand, with the terms largely dictated by government lawyers called **public prosecutors.**

Prosecutorial Duties

The public prosecutor in federal criminal cases is called a U.S. attorney. In cases tried in state or local courts, the public prosecutor may be referred to as a *prosecuting attorney, state attorney, district attorney, county attorney,* or *city attorney.* Given their great autonomy, prosecutors are generally considered the most dominant figures in the American criminal justice system.

 LEARNING OBJECTIVE 1 List the different names given to public prosecutors and indicate the general powers that they have.

In some jurisdictions, the district attorney is the chief law enforcement officer, with broad powers over police operations. Prosecutors have the power to bring the resources of the state against the individual and hold the legal keys to meting out or withholding punishment. Ideally, this power is balanced by a duty of fairness and a recognition that the prosecutor's ultimate goal is not to win cases, but to see that justice is done. In *Berger v. United States* (1935), Justice George Sutherland called the prosecutor

> in a peculiar and very definite sense the servant of the law, the twofold aim of which is that guilt shall not escape or innocence suffer. He may prosecute with earnestness and vigor— indeed, he should do so. But, while he may strike hard blows, he is not at liberty to strike foul ones. It is as much his duty to refrain from improper methods calculated to produce a wrongful conviction as it is to use every legitimate means to bring about a just one.[2]

In part to lessen the opportunity for "foul" behavior by prosecutors, they are not permitted to keep evidence from the defendant that may be useful in showing his or her innocence.[3] For example, in 1995, Juan Smith was convicted of five murders at a party in New Orleans and eventually sentenced to death. The only eyewitness to the crime gave conflicting comments to police, including that he could not "ID anyone because [he] couldn't see faces."[4] Obviously, Smith's defense attorneys could have used such statements to create reasonable doubt about their client's guilt. Because prosecutors never provided them with this evidence, in 2012 the Supreme Court overturned Smith's conviction and ordered a new trial.[5]

The Office of the Prosecutor

When he or she is acting as an *officer of the law* during a criminal trial, there are limits on the prosecutor's conduct, as we shall see in the next chapter. During the pretrial process, however, prosecutors hold a great deal of discretion in deciding the following:

1. Whether an individual who has been arrested by the police will be charged with a crime.
2. The level of the charges to be brought against the suspect.
3. If and when to stop the prosecution.[6]

There are more than eight thousand prosecutor's offices around the country, serving state, county, and municipal jurisdictions. Even though the **attorney general** is the chief

FIGURE 9.1 The Baltimore City State's Attorney's Office

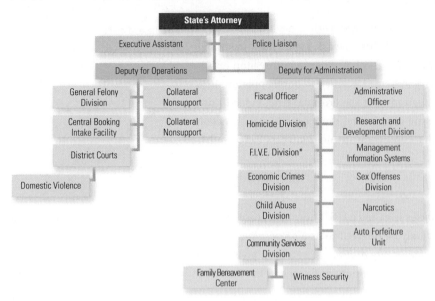

*F.I.V.E. is an acronym for "Firearms Investigation Violence Enforcement."

Source: Baltimore City State's Attorney's Office.

law enforcement officer in any state, she or he has limited (and in some states, no) control over prosecutors within the state's boundaries.

Each jurisdiction has a chief prosecutor, who is sometimes appointed but more often elected. As an elected official, he or she typically serves a four-year term, though in some states, such as Alabama, the term is six years. In smaller jurisdictions, the chief prosecutor has several assistants, and they work closely together. In larger ones, the chief prosecutor may have numerous *assistant prosecutors,* many of whom he or she rarely meets. Assistant prosecutors—for the most part, young attorneys recently graduated from law school—may be assigned to particular sections of the organization, such as criminal prosecutions in general or areas of *special prosecution,* such as narcotics or gang crimes. (See Figure 9.1 above for the structure of a typical prosecutor's office.)

The Prosecutor as Elected Official

The chief prosecutor's autonomy is not absolute. As an elected official, she or he must answer to the voters. (There are exceptions: U.S. attorneys are nominated by the president and approved by the Senate, and chief prosecutors in Alaska, Connecticut, New Jersey, Rhode Island, and the District of Columbia are either appointed or hired as members of the attorney general's office.) The prosecutor may be part of the political machine. In many jurisdictions, the prosecutor must declare a party affiliation and is expected to reward fellow party members with positions in the district attorney's office if elected.

PROSECUTORIAL POLITICS A prosecutor's electability is often enhanced by his or her involvement in high-profile cases. Several years ago, for example, Florida state attorney Lawson Lamar assigned Jeff Ashton as lead prosecutor in the trial of Casey Anthony, accused of murdering her two-year-old daughter. Even though Anthony was acquitted, Ashton took advantage of the national media attention garnered by the case to defeat his boss Lamar in a subsequent election, as we saw in the opening of this chapter.

The post of prosecutor is also considered a "stepping-stone" to higher political office, and many prosecutors have gone on to serve in legislatures or as judges. Sonia Sotomayor (see the photo on the facing page), the first Hispanic member of the United States Supreme Court, started her legal career in 1979 as an assistant district attorney in New York City. While at that job, she first came to public attention by helping to prosecute the "Tarzan Murderer," an athletic criminal responsible for at least twenty burglaries and four killings.

ELECTIONS AND IMPARTIALITY Just as judicial elections can raise concerns that judges' decisions may be influenced by politics, as we discussed in the previous chapter, the specter of an upcoming election can cast doubt on the impartiality of a prosecutor's decisions. For example, researchers recently found that during an election year, incum-

LEARNING
2
OBJECTIVE

Contrast the prosecutor's roles as an elected official and as a crime fighter.

bent prosecutors in North Carolina are more likely to take cases to trial and less likely to allow defendants to plead guilty. In contrast, when that state's prosecutors do not face an election, fewer cases are taken to trial and more are plea bargained.[7] Similar research in New York found that convictions won by prosecutors within six months of an election are 5 to 7 percent more likely to be later overturned by an appeals court. This is interpreted as evidence that prosecutors under electoral pressure are more apt to make mistakes while aggressively trying to win cases and attract positive publicity.[8]

The Prosecutor as Crime Fighter

One of the reasons the prosecutor's post is a useful first step in a political career is that it is linked to crime fighting. Thanks to savvy public relations efforts and television police dramas such as *Law & Order*—with its opening line, "In the criminal justice system, the people are represented by two separate yet equally important groups: the police who investigate crime and the district attorneys who prosecute the offenders"—prosecutors are generally seen as law enforcement agents. Indeed, the prosecutors and the police do have a symbiotic relationship. Prosecutors rely on police to arrest suspects and gather sufficient evidence, and police rely on prosecutors to convict those who have been apprehended.

■ Give several reasons why experience as a prosecutor would make someone such as United States Supreme Court justice Sonia Sotomayor a more effective judge.
AP Photo/Pablo Martinez Monsivais

Despite, or perhaps because of, this mutual dependency, the relationship between the two branches of law enforcement is often strained. Part of this can be attributed to different backgrounds. Most prosecutors come from middle- or upper-class families, while police are often recruited from the working class. Furthermore, prosecutors are required to have a level of education that is not attained by most police officers.

More important, however, is a basic divergence in the concept of guilt. For a police officer, a suspect is guilty if he or she has in fact committed a crime. For a prosecutor, a suspect is guilty if enough evidence can be legally gathered to prove such guilt in a court of law. In other words, police officers often focus on *factual guilt,* whereas prosecutors are ultimately concerned with *legal guilt.*[9] Thus, police officers will feel a great deal of frustration when a suspect they "know" to be guilty is set free. Similarly, a prosecutor may become annoyed when police officers do not follow the letter of the law in gathering evidence, thereby greatly reducing the chances of conviction.

Prosecutors and Victims

Because prosecutors have the responsibility of trying and convicting offenders, crime victims often see themselves as being on "the same side" as the prosecution. This perception is only strengthened when prosecutors publicly align themselves with victims. In 2012, for example, Florida special prosecutor Angela Corey met and prayed with the family of Trayvon Martin, who had been killed in controversial fashion by George Zimmerman (described in Chapter 4's discussion of self-defense).

CONFLICTS OF INTEREST In fact, prosecutors do not represent crime victims. Understandably, most victims are focused primarily on the fate of the defendant who caused them harm. Prosecutors, in contrast, must balance the rights of the victims with those of the accused and the best interests of the public at large.

Indeed, if a prosecutor becomes too involved in the personal tragedies of crime victims, he or she runs the risk of losing the neutrality that is the hallmark of the office.[10]

Furthermore, prosecutors who actively seek the support of crime victims sometimes create the impression of a conflict of interest, even if such a conflict does not actually exist.[11] After meeting with Martin's family, whom she called "lovely people," Florida prosecutor Corey charged Zimmerman with second degree murder. In many circles, Corey's decision was criticized for being politically motivated and her prayer session with the Martins derided as a publicity stunt.[12]

PROSECUTORS AND VICTIMS' RIGHTS A prosecutor's duty of neutrality does not mean that he or she should ignore crime victims or their wishes. Practically, prosecutors rely on victims as sources of information and valuable witnesses. Believable victims are also quite helpful if a case goes to trial, as they may be able to elicit a sympathetic response from the jury.[13] Furthermore, as we saw in Chapter 3, federal and state victims' rights legislation requires the prosecutor to confer with victims at various stages of the criminal justice process.

In keeping with the spirit of these laws, Brooklyn district attorney Charles Hynes sends a letter to victims of crimes that are being prosecuted by his office. The letter contains information regarding victims' rights under state law, possible victim compensation, and the victims' services unit operated by Hynes's office. It begins, "What happened to you was wrong, and I want you to know that my staff will do everything it can to assist you."[14]

SELF ASSESSMENT

Fill in the blanks and check your answers on page 309.

Public prosecutors initiate and conduct cases on behalf of the _____ against the defendant. During the pretrial process, prosecutors must decide whether to _____ an individual with a particular crime. Ideally, a prosecutor's ultimate goal is not to _____ cases, but rather to see _____ done.

THE DEFENSE ATTORNEY

The media provide most people's perception of defense counsel: the idealistic public defender who nobly serves the poor, the "ambulance chaser," or the celebrity attorney in the $3,000 suit. These stereotypes, though not entirely fictional, tend to obscure the crucial role that the **defense attorney** plays in the criminal justice system. Most persons charged with crimes have little or no knowledge of criminal procedure. Without assistance, they would be helpless in court. By acting as a staunch advocate for her or his client, the defense attorney (ideally) ensures that the government proves every point against that client beyond a reasonable doubt, even for cases that do not go to trial. In sum, the defense attorney provides a counterweight against the state in our adversary system.

The Responsibilities of the Defense Attorney

The Sixth Amendment right to counsel is not limited to the actual criminal trial. In a number of instances, the United States Supreme Court has held that defendants are entitled to representation as soon as their rights may be denied, which, as we have seen, includes the custodial interrogation and lineup identification procedures.[15] Therefore, an important responsibility of the defense attorney is to represent the defendant at the various stages of the custodial process, such as arrest, interrogation, lineup, and arraignment. Other responsibilities include:

- Investigating the incident for which the defendant has been charged.
- Communicating with the prosecutor, which includes negotiating plea bargains.

Delineate the responsibilities of defense attorneys. **3** LEARNING OBJECTIVE

- Preparing the case for trial.
- Submitting defense motions, including motions to suppress evidence.
- Representing the defendant at trial.
- Negotiating a sentence, if the client has been convicted.
- Determining whether to appeal a guilty verdict.[16]

Defending the Guilty

At one time or another in their careers, all defense attorneys will face a difficult question: Must I defend a client whom I know to be guilty? According to the American Bar Association's code of legal ethics, the answer is almost always, "yes."[17] The most important responsibility of the criminal defense attorney is to be an advocate for her or his client. As such, the attorney is obligated to use all ethical and legal means to achieve the client's desired goal, which is usually to avoid or lessen punishment for the charged crime.

As Supreme Court justice Byron White once noted, defense counsel has no "obligation to ascertain or present the truth." Rather, our adversarial system insists that the defense attorney "defend the client whether he is innocent or guilty."[18] Indeed, if defense attorneys refused to represent clients whom they believed to be guilty, the Sixth Amendment guarantee of a criminal trial for all accused persons would be rendered meaningless. (To learn more about the difficult situations that can arise with a guilty defendant, see the feature *A Question of Ethics—The Right Decision?* below.)

A QUESTION OF ETHICS   The Right Decision?

THE SITUATION Gerard Marrone is the defense attorney for Levi Aron, charged with kidnapping, murdering, and dismembering eight-year-old Leiby Kletzky in Brooklyn, New York. There is little question of Aron's guilt, as he provided the police with a signed confession and has no alibi for his whereabouts at the time of the crime. Marrone is uncertain about whether he wants to continue representing this "horrific" client. "You can't look at your kids and then look at yourself in the mirror, knowing that a little boy, who's close in age to my eldest son, was murdered so brutally," Marrone said about his conflicting feelings.

Explain why defense attorneys must often defend clients they know to be guilty. **LEARNING 4 OBJECTIVE**

THE ETHICAL DILEMMA The criminal justice system would not be able to function if lawyers refused to represent clients they knew to be guilty. At the same time, a lawyer must be guided by his or her own conscience. If a client is so repugnant to the lawyer as to impair the quality of representation, then perhaps the lawyer should drop the case.

WHAT IS THE SOLUTION? What would you do in Marrone's shoes? Several years ago, he decided that his conscience prevented him from representing Aron, and he withdrew from the case. His replacement, Jennifer McCann, criticized Marrone's actions. "To sit there and say, 'This is a hard case, I don't want to take it.'" McCann said. "That's for somebody else, that's not who I am." She added, "It's not about defending [Aron's] actions. It's about defending his rights."

■ Defense attorneys Pierre Bazile, right, and Jennifer McCann appear with their client Levi Aron at the State Supreme Court in Brooklyn in New York.
Jesse Ward via *New York Times*/Redux Pictures

The Public Defender

Generally speaking, there are two different types of defense attorneys: (1) private attorneys, who are hired by individuals, and (2) **public defenders,** who work for the government. The distinction is not absolute, as many private attorneys accept employment as public defenders, too. The modern role of the public defender was established by the Supreme Court's interpretation of the Sixth Amendment in *Gideon v. Wainwright* (1963).[19]

In that case, the Court ruled that no defendant can be "assured a fair trial unless counsel is provided for him," and therefore the state must provide a public defender to those who cannot afford to hire one for themselves. Subsequently, the Court extended this protection to juveniles in *In re Gault* (1967)[20] and those faced with imprisonment for committing misdemeanors in *Argersinger v. Hamlin* (1972).[21] The impact of these decisions has been substantial: about 90 percent of all criminal defendants in the United States are represented by public defenders or other appointed counsel.[22]

ELIGIBILITY ISSUES Although the Supreme Court's *Gideon* decision obligated the government to provide attorneys for poor defendants, it offered no guidance on just how poor the defendant needs to be to qualify for a public defender. In theory, counsel should be provided for those who are unable to hire an attorney themselves without "substantial hardship."[23] In reality, each jurisdiction has its own guidelines, and a defendant refused counsel in one area might be entitled to it in another. A judge in Kittitas County, Washington, to give an extreme example, frequently denies public counsel for college student defendants. This judge believes that any person who chooses to go to school rather than work automatically falls outside the *Gideon* case's definition of indigence.[24]

DEFENSE COUNSEL PROGRAMS In most areas, the county government is responsible for providing indigent defendants with attorneys. Three basic types of programs are used to allocate defense counsel:

1. *Assigned counsel programs,* in which local private attorneys are assigned clients on a case-by-case basis by the county.
2. *Contracting attorney programs,* in which a particular law firm or group of attorneys is hired to regularly assume the representative and administrative tasks of indigent defense.
3. *Public defender programs,* in which the county assembles a salaried staff of full-time or part-time attorneys and creates a public (taxpayer-funded) agency to provide services.[25]

Much to the surprise of many indigent defendants, these programs are not entirely without cost. Government agencies can charge fees for "free" legal counsel when the fees will not impose a "significant legal financial hardship" on the defendant. Today, more than 80 percent of all local public defender offices charge some form of so-called cost recoupment.[26] Florida, North Carolina, and Virginia have mandatory public defender fees, meaning that judges cannot waive such costs under any circumstances. In Virginia, indigent defendants may be charged up to $1,235 per count for certain felonies.[27]

EFFECTIVENESS OF PUBLIC DEFENDERS Under the U.S. Constitution, a defendant who is paying for her or his defense attorney has a right to choose that attorney without interference from the court. This right of choice does not extend to indigent defendants. According to the United States Supreme Court, "a defendant may not insist on an attorney he cannot afford."[28] In other words, an indigent defendant must accept the public

defender provided by the court system. (Note that, unless the presiding judge rules otherwise, a person can waive her or his Sixth Amendment rights and act as her or his own defense attorney.) This lack of control contributes to the widespread belief that public defenders do not provide an acceptable level of defense to indigents.

Statistics show, however, that conviction rates of defendants with private counsel and those represented by publicly funded attorneys are generally the same.[29] The main difference seems to be between private attorneys who are assigned indigent clients and full-time public defenders. A recent study of 3,412 Philadelphia indigent murder defendants found that, compared with private appointed counsel, public defenders reduce the conviction rate by 19 percent and the overall expected time served in prison by 24 percent.[30]

The main reason for this discrepancy, at least in Philadelphia, appears to be financial. Court-appointed defense attorneys in that city receive a flat fee for each client, which essentially works out to an average of $2 an hour. Furthermore, they are afforded limited public funds to investigate their client's innocence. Philadelphia's public defenders, by contrast, are paid an annual salary and supported by a staff of investigators and various experts.[31]

Unreasonable Caseloads The American Bar Association recommends that a public defender handle no more than 150 felony cases and 400 misdemeanor cases each year. Nationwide, about three-quarters of all county-based public defender programs exceed these limits.[32] In Florida, for example, each public defender averages about 500 felony cases and more than 2,000 misdemeanor cases annually.[33] Several years ago, New York City lawmakers passed a law that caps the number of criminal cases for court-appointed lawyers.[34] Supporters expressed hope that the legislation would serve as a model to alleviate oppressive client caseloads plaguing public defenders throughout the country.

The *Strickland* Standard In one Louisiana murder trial, not only did the court-appointed defense attorney spend only eleven minutes preparing for trial on a charge that carries a mandatory life sentence, but she also represented the victim's father and had been representing the victim at the time of his death. Not surprisingly, her defendant was found guilty. Such behavior raises a critical question: When a lawyer does such a poor job, has the client essentially been denied his or her Sixth Amendment right to assistance of counsel? In *Strickland v. Washington* (1984),[35] the Supreme Court set up a two-pronged test to determine whether constitutional requirements have been met. To prove that prior counsel was not sufficient, a defendant must show (1) that the attorney's performance was deficient *and* (2) that this deficiency *more likely than not* caused the defendant to lose the case.

In practice, it has been very difficult to prove the second prong of this test. A prosecutor can always argue that the defendant would have lost the case even if his or her lawyer had not been inept. Sometimes, however, such ineptness is so intolerable that it meets the *Strickland* standard and a new trial is required. In 2013, the Kansas Supreme Court overturned the capital conviction of Phillip Cheatham, Jr., for the shooting deaths of two Topeka women a decade earlier. Most crucially, Cheatham's defense attorney had failed to present evidence that his client was driving to Chicago at the time of the shootings. The lawyer also spent only sixty hours preparing for the trial (being busy running for governor at the time) and referred to Cheatham as a "professional drug dealer" and "shooter of people" in court.[36]

The Attorney-Client Relationship

The implied trust between an attorney and her or his client usually is not in question when the attorney has been hired directly by the defendant—as an "employee," the attorney well understands her or his duties. Relationships between public defenders and their clients, however, are often marred by suspicion on both sides. As Northwestern University professor Jonathan D. Casper discovered while interviewing indigent defendants, many of them feel a certain amount of respect for the prosecutor. Like police officers, prosecutors are just "doing their job" by trying to convict the defendant. In contrast, the defendants' view of their own attorneys can be summed up in the following exchange between Casper and a defendant:

> Did you have a lawyer when you went to court the next morning?
> No, I had a public defender.[37]

This attitude is somewhat understandable. Given the caseloads that most public defenders carry, they may have as little as five or ten minutes to spend with a client before appearing in front of a judge. How much, realistically, can a public defender learn about the defendant in that time? Furthermore, the defendant is well aware that the public defender is being paid by the same source as the prosecutor and the judge. "Because you're part of the system, your indigent client doesn't trust you," admitted one court-appointed attorney.[38]

The situation handcuffs the public defenders as well. With so little time to spend on each case, they cannot validate the information provided by their clients. If the defendant says he or she has no prior offenses, the public defender often has no choice but to believe the client. Consequently, many public defenders later find that their clients have deceived them. Along with the high pressures of the job, a client's lack of cooperation and disrespect can limit whatever satisfaction a public defender may find in the profession.

Attorney-Client Privilege

To defend a client effectively, a defense attorney must have access to all the facts concerning the case, even those that may be harmful to the defendant. To promote the unrestrained flow of information between the two parties, legislatures and lawyers themselves have constructed rules of **attorney-client privilege.** These rules require that communications between a client and his or her attorney be kept confidential, unless the client consents to the disclosure.

THE PRIVILEGE AND CONFESSIONS Attorney-client privilege does not stop short of confessions. Indeed, if, on hearing any statement that points toward guilt, the defense attorney could alert the prosecution or try to resign from the case, attorney-client privilege would be rendered meaningless. Even if the client says, "I have just killed seventeen women. I selected only pregnant women so I could torture them and kill two people at once. I did it. I liked it. I enjoyed it," the defense attorney must continue to do his or her utmost to serve that client.[39]

Without attorney-client privilege, observes legal expert John Kaplan, lawyers would be forced to give their clients the equivalent of the *Miranda* warning before representing them.[40] In other words, lawyers would have to make clear what clients could or could not say in the course of preparing for trial, because any incriminating statement might be used against the client in court. Such a development would have serious ramifications for the criminal justice system.

THE EXCEPTION TO THE PRIVILEGE The scope of attorney-client privilege is not all encompassing. In *United States v. Zolin* (1989),[41] the Supreme Court ruled that lawyers may disclose the contents of a conversation with a client if the client has provided information concerning a crime that has yet to be committed. This exception applies only to communications involving a crime that is ongoing or will occur in the future. If the client reveals a past crime, the privilege is still in effect, and the attorney may not reveal any details of that particular criminal act.

■ Defense attorney John Amabile makes a point on behalf of his client in a Woburn, Massachusetts, courtroom. Why are the rules of attorney-client privilege necessary for a defense attorney to properly do his or her job?
ZUMA Press/Newscom

SELF ASSESSMENT

Fill in the blanks and check your answers on page 309.

The _____ Amendment states that every person accused of a crime has a right to counsel. There are two types of defense attorneys: (1) _____ attorneys hired by individuals and (2) _____ defenders, provided to _____ defendants by the government. Because of attorney-client _____, any admissions of guilt for past crimes that a client makes to her or his defense attorney are _____, unless the client _____ to their disclosure.

LEARNING OBJECTIVE **5** List the three basic features of an adversary system of justice.

TRUTH, VICTORY, AND THE ADVERSARY SYSTEM

In strictly legal terms, three basic features characterize the **adversary system:**

1. A neutral and passive decision maker, either the judge or the jury.
2. The presentation of evidence from both parties.
3. A highly structured set of procedures (in the form of constitutional safeguards) that must be followed in the presentation of that evidence.[42]

Some critics of the American court system believe that it has been tainted by overzealous prosecutors and defense attorneys. Gordon Van Kessel, a professor at Hastings College

Attorney-Client Privilege A rule of evidence requiring that communications between a client and his or her attorney be kept confidential, unless the client consents to disclosure.

Adversary System A legal system in which the prosecution and defense are opponents, or adversaries, and present their cases in the light most favorable to themselves.

of Law in California, complains that American lawyers see themselves as "prize fighters, gladiators, or, more accurately, semantic warriors in a verbal battle," and bemoans the atmosphere of "ritualized aggression" that exists in the courts.[43]

Our discussion of the courtroom work group in the last chapter, however, seems to contradict this image of "ritualized aggression." As political scientists Herbert Jacob and James Eisenstein have written, "pervasive conflict is not only unpleasant; it also makes work more difficult."[44] The image of the courtroom work group as "negotiators" rather than "prize fighters" seems to be supported by the fact that more than nine out of every ten cases conclude with negotiated "deals" rather than trials. Jerome Skolnick of the University of California at Berkeley found that work group members grade each other according to "reasonableness"[45]—a concept criminal justice scholar Abraham S. Blumberg embellished by labeling the defense attorney a "double agent." Blumberg believed that a defense attorney is likely to cooperate with the prosecutor in convincing a client to accept a negotiated plea of guilty because the defense attorney's main object is to finish the case quickly so as to collect the fee and move on.[46]

Perhaps, then, the most useful definition of the adversary process tempers Professor Van Kessel's criticism with the realities of the courtroom work group. University of California at Berkeley law professor Malcolm Feeley observes:

> In the adversary system the goal of the advocate is not to determine truth but to win, to maximize the interests of his or her side within the confines of the norms governing the proceedings. This is not to imply that the theory of the adversary process has no concern for the truth. Rather, the underlying assumption of the adversary process is that truth is most likely to emerge as a by-product of vigorous conflict between intensely partisan advocates, each of whose goal is to win.[47]

Blumberg took a more cynical view when he called the court process a "confidence game" in which "victory" is achieved when a defense attorney—with the implicit aid of the prosecutor and judge—is able to persuade the defendant to plead guilty.[48] As you read the rest of the chapter, which deals with pretrial procedures, keep in mind Feeley's and Blumberg's contentions concerning "truth" and "victory" in the American courts.

CJ & TECHNOLOGY — CHALLENGING DNA EVIDENCE

Johan Swanepoel/Shutterstock.com

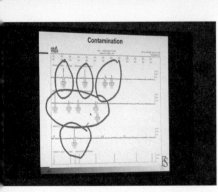

AP Photo/Red Huber, Pool

In Chapter 6, we described how DNA fingerprinting has become the "gold standard" of police investigations. Indeed, DNA evidence would seem to leave defense attorneys with little recourse once it has been used against their clients. This is not, however, the case. The pressures of the adversary system have forced these lawyers to devise a number of strategies to challenge DNA technology. Many of these strategies were evident in the recent trial of Richard Hirschfield for the abduction, rape, and murder of two University of California, Davis students more than thirty years ago.

Prosecutors linked Hirschfield to the crime through traces of his DNA on a blanket in the van where the two victims were killed. Facing odds of 240 trillion to one that the DNA did not belong to Hirschfield, his attorneys tried various methods to introduce doubt into the proceedings. They argued that their client might have had consensual sex with someone else in the van after the murders. They suggested that the blanket might have been stolen, come in contact with Hirschfield's DNA, and then placed back in the van. They asserted that the scientists who lifted the DNA from the blanket were biased because they worked for the prosecution, or that the DNA sample might have been contaminated through human error. Although each of these types of arguments has been successful in other criminal trials, Hirschfield's jury was unimpressed. They convicted him of the charges, and in January 2013 a Sacramento judge sentenced him to death.

Thinking about Challenging DNA Evidence
Several years ago, scientists in Israel demonstrated that, using information stored in a DNA database, it is possible to re-create a person's DNA without access to that person's biological material. In the future, how might defense attorneys use the existence of such "fabricated" DNA to challenge DNA evidence found at a crime scene?

PRETRIAL DETENTION

After an arrest has been made, the first step toward determining the suspect's guilt or innocence is the **initial appearance** (for an overview of the entire process, see Figure 9.2 on the next page). During this brief proceeding, a magistrate (see Chapter 8) informs the defendant of the charges that have been brought against him or her and explains his or her constitutional rights—particularly, the right to remain silent (under the Fifth Amendment) and the right to be represented by counsel (under the Sixth Amendment). At this point, if the defendant cannot afford to hire a private attorney, a public defender may be appointed, or private counsel may be hired by the state to represent the defendant. As the U.S. Constitution does not specify how soon a defendant must be brought before a magistrate after arrest, it has been left to the judicial branch to determine the timing of the initial appearance. The Supreme Court has held that the initial appearance must occur "promptly," which in most cases means within forty-eight hours of booking.[49]

LEARNING OBJECTIVE 6 Identify the steps involved in the pretrial criminal process.

In misdemeanor cases, a defendant may decide to plead guilty and be sentenced during the initial appearance. Otherwise, the magistrate will usually release those charged with misdemeanors on their promise to return at a later date for further proceedings. For felony cases, however, the defendant is not permitted to make a plea at the initial appearance because a magistrate's court does not have jurisdiction to decide felonies. Furthermore, in most cases the defendant will be released only if she or he posts **bail**—an amount paid by the defendant to the court and retained by the court until the defendant returns for further proceedings.

Defendants who cannot afford bail are generally kept in a local jail or lockup until the date of their trial, though many jurisdictions are searching for alternatives to this practice because of overcrowded incarceration facilities. Government statisticians estimate that 58 percent of felony defendants are released before their trials.[50]

Setting Bail

Bail is provided for under the Eighth Amendment. The amendment does not, however, guarantee the right to bail. Instead, it states that "excessive bail shall not be required." This has come to mean that in all cases except those involving a capital crime (where bail is prohibited), the amount of bail required must be reasonable compared with the seriousness of the wrongdoing. It does *not* mean that the amount of bail must be within the defendant's ability to pay.

BAIL GUIDELINES There is no uniform system for pretrial detention. Each jurisdiction has its own *bail tariffs,* or general guidelines concerning the proper amount of bail. For

Initial Appearance An accused's first appearance before a judge or magistrate following arrest.

Bail The dollar amount or conditions set by the court to ensure that an individual accused of a crime will appear for further criminal proceedings.

FIGURE 9.2 The Steps Leading to a Trial

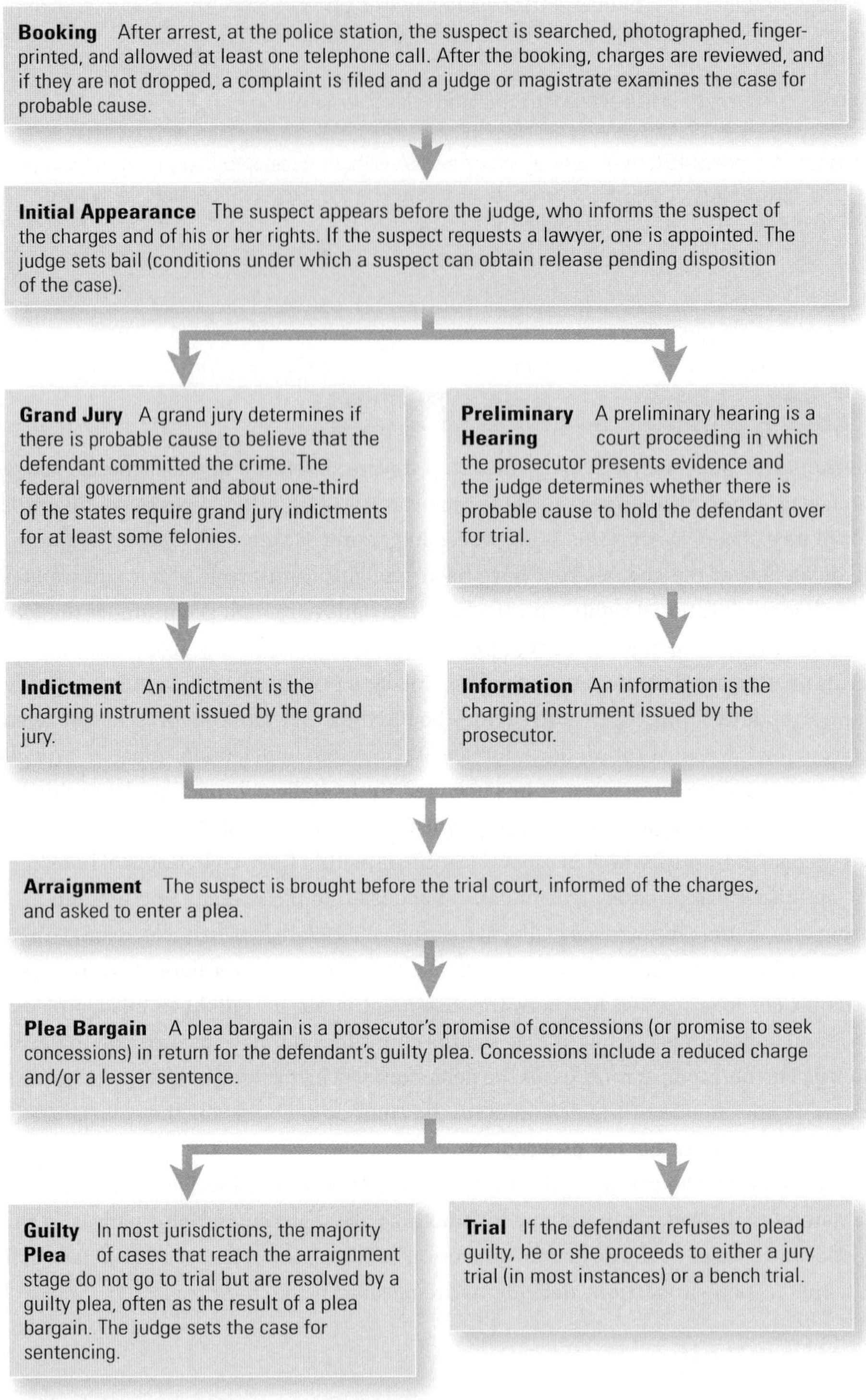

Booking After arrest, at the police station, the suspect is searched, photographed, finger-printed, and allowed at least one telephone call. After the booking, charges are reviewed, and if they are not dropped, a complaint is filed and a judge or magistrate examines the case for probable cause.

Initial Appearance The suspect appears before the judge, who informs the suspect of the charges and of his or her rights. If the suspect requests a lawyer, one is appointed. The judge sets bail (conditions under which a suspect can obtain release pending disposition of the case).

Grand Jury A grand jury determines if there is probable cause to believe that the defendant committed the crime. The federal government and about one-third of the states require grand jury indictments for at least some felonies.

Preliminary Hearing A preliminary hearing is a court proceeding in which the prosecutor presents evidence and the judge determines whether there is probable cause to hold the defendant over for trial.

Indictment An indictment is the charging instrument issued by the grand jury.

Information An information is the charging instrument issued by the prosecutor.

Arraignment The suspect is brought before the trial court, informed of the charges, and asked to enter a plea.

Plea Bargain A plea bargain is a prosecutor's promise of concessions (or promise to seek concessions) in return for the defendant's guilty plea. Concessions include a reduced charge and/or a lesser sentence.

Guilty Plea In most jurisdictions, the majority of cases that reach the arraignment stage do not go to trial but are resolved by a guilty plea, often as the result of a plea bargain. The judge sets the case for sentencing.

Trial If the defendant refuses to plead guilty, he or she proceeds to either a jury trial (in most instances) or a bench trial.

misdemeanors, the police usually follow a preapproved bail schedule created by local judicial authorities. In felony cases, the primary responsibility to set bail lies with the judge. Figure 9.3 on the facing page shows typical bail amounts for violent offenses.

Bail guidelines can be quite extensive. In Illinois, for example, a judge is required to take thirty-eight different factors into account when setting bail: fourteen involve the crime itself, two refer to the evidence gathered, four to the defendant's record, nine to the defendant's flight risk and immigration status, and nine to the defendant's general character.[51] For the most part, however, judges are free to use such tariffs as loose guidelines, and they have a great deal of discretion in setting bail according to the circumstances in each case.

JUDGES AND BAIL Extralegal factors may also play a part in bail setting. University of New Orleans political scientist David W. Neubauer has identified three contexts that may influence a judge's decision-making process:[52]

1. *Uncertainty.* To a certain extent, predetermined bail tariffs are unrealistic, given that judges are required to set bail within forty-eight hours of arrest. It is often difficult to get information on the defendant in that period of time, and even if a judge can obtain a "rap sheet," or list of prior arrests ("priors"), she or he will probably not have an opportunity to verify its accuracy. Due to this uncertainty, most judges have no choice but to focus primarily on the seriousness of the crime in setting bail.

2. *Risk.* There is no way of knowing for certain whether a defendant released on bail will return for his or her court date, or whether he or she will commit a crime while free. Judges are aware of the criticism they will come under from police groups, prosecutors, the press, and the public if a crime is committed during that time. Consequently, especially if she or he is up for reelection, a judge may prefer to "play it safe" and set a high bail to detain a suspect or refuse outright to offer bail when legally able to do so. In general, risk aversion also dictates why those who are charged with a violent crime such as murder are usually less likely to be released prior to trial than those who are charged with property crimes such as larceny or motor vehicle theft.

3. *Overcrowded jails.* As we will discuss in detail in Chapter 13, many of the nation's jails are overcrowded. This may force a judge to make a difficult distinction between those suspects she or he believes must be detained and those who might need to be detained. To save jail space, a judge might be more lenient in setting bail for members of the latter group.[53]

Judges can also administer multiple bail amounts for defendants charged with multiple crimes. For instance, in April 2012 Judge William Hiddle set bail at $9.16 million each for two defendants who allegedly killed three victims and wounded two others during a racially motivated shooting rampage in Tulsa, Oklahoma. The total reflected $3 million for three counts of first degree murder, $75,000 for two counts of shooting with intent to kill, and $10,000 for a single count of possession of a firearm in the commission of a felony.[54]

Gaining Pretrial Release

Earlier, we mentioned that many jurisdictions are looking for alternatives to the bail system. One of the most popular options is **release on recognizance (ROR)**. This is used when the judge, based on the advice of trained personnel, decides that the defendant is not at risk to "jump" bail and does not pose a threat to the community. The defendant is then released at no cost with the understanding that he or she will return at the time of the trial. The Vera Institute, a nonprofit organization in New York City, introduced

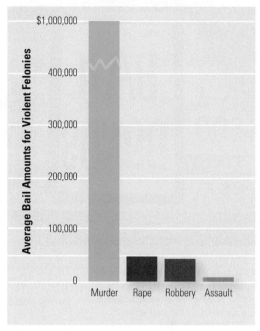

FIGURE 9.3 **Average Bail Amounts for Violent Felonies**

These figures represent the mean bail figures for the seventy-five largest counties in the nation.

Source: Adapted from Bureau of Justice Statistics, *Felony Defendants in Large Urban Counties, 2006* (Washington, D.C.: U.S. Department of Justice, May 2010), Table 7, page 7.

 LEARNING **7** **OBJECTIVE** Indicate the three influences on a judge's decision to set bail.

Release on Recognizance (ROR) A judge's order that releases an accused from jail with the understanding that he or she will return of his or her own will for further proceedings.

What is your opinion of legislation that abolishes bail bonding for profit? What other ethical issues are raised by the bail system? Christine Osborne/Corbis

the concept of ROR as part of the Manhattan Bail Project in the 1960s, and such programs are now found in nearly every jurisdiction. When properly administered, ROR programs seem to be successful, with less than 5 percent of the participants failing to show for trial.[55]

POSTING BAIL Those suspected of committing a felony, however, are rarely released on recognizance. These defendants may post, or pay, the full amount of the bail in cash to the court. The money will be returned when the suspect appears for trial. Given the large amount of funds required, and the relative lack of wealth of many criminal defendants, a defendant can rarely post bail in cash. Another option is to use real property, such as a house, instead of cash as collateral. These **property bonds** are also rare because most courts require property valued at double the bail amount. Thus, if bail is set at $5,000, the defendant (or the defendant's family and friends) will have to produce property valued at $10,000.

BAIL BOND AGENTS If unable to post bail with cash or property, a defendant may arrange for a **bail bond agent** to post a bail bond on the defendant's behalf. The bond agent, in effect, promises the court that he or she will turn over to the court the full amount of bail if the defendant fails to return for further proceedings. The defendant usually must give the bond agent a certain percentage of the bail (frequently 10 percent) in cash. This amount, which is often not returned to the defendant later, is considered payment for the bond agent's assistance and assumption of risk. Depending on the amount of the bail bond, the defendant may also be required to sign over to the bond agent rights to certain property (such as a car, a valuable watch, or other asset) as security for the bond.

Although bail bond agents obviously provide a service for which there is demand, the process is widely viewed with distaste. Indeed, the Philippines is the only other nation where bail bonding is an accepted part of the pretrial release process. Four states—Illinois, Kentucky, Oregon, and Wisconsin—have abolished bail bonding for profit. The rationale for such reform focuses on three perceived problems with the practice:

1. Bail bond agents provide opportunities for corruption, as they may improperly influence officials who are involved in setting bail to inflate the bail.
2. Because they can refuse to post a bail bond, bail bond agents are, in essence, making a business decision concerning a suspect's pretrial release. This is considered the responsibility of a judge, not a private individual with a profit motive.[56]
3. About 40 percent of defendants released on bail are eventually found not guilty of any crime. These people, although innocent, have had to pay what amounts to a bribe if they wanted to stay out of jail before their trial.[57]

The states that have banned bail bond agents have established an alternative known as *ten percent cash bail*. This process, pioneered in Chicago in the early 1960s, requires the court, in effect, to take the place of the bond agent. An officer of the court will accept a deposit of 10 percent of the bail amount, refundable when the defendant appears at the

Property Bond An alternative to posting bail in cash, in which the defendant gains pretrial release by providing the court with property valued at the bail amount as assurance that he or she will return for trial.

Bail Bond Agent A businessperson who agrees, for a fee, to pay the bail amount if the accused fails to appear in court as ordered.

assigned time. A number of jurisdictions allow for both bail bond agents and ten percent cash bail, with the judge deciding whether a defendant is eligible for the latter.

Preventive Detention

The vagueness of the Eighth Amendment's requirement that "excessive bail shall not be required" allows the practice to serve another purpose: the protection of the community. That is, if a judge feels that the defendant poses a threat should he or she be released before trial, the judge will set bail at a level the suspect cannot possibly afford. In January 2012, for example, a Los Angeles superior court judge set the bail for indigent defendant Harry Burkhart, accused of setting dozens of fires across the city during the New Year's weekend, at $2.85 million.

Alternatively, more than thirty states have passed **preventive detention** legislation to the same effect. These laws allow judges to act "in the best interests of the community" by denying bail to arrestees with prior records of violence, thus keeping them in custody prior to trial. The federal Bail Reform Act of 1984 similarly affirms that federal offenders can be held without bail to ensure "the safety of any other person and the community."[58]

Critics of the 1984 act believe that it violates the U.S. Constitution by allowing the freedom of a citizen to be restricted before he or she has been proved guilty in a court of law. For many, the act also brings up the troubling issue of *false positives*—erroneous predictions that defendants, if given pretrial release, would commit a crime, when in fact they would not. In *United States v. Salerno* (1987),[59] however, the Supreme Court upheld the act's premise. Then Chief Justice William Rehnquist wrote that preventive detention was not a "punishment for dangerous individuals" but a "potential solution to a pressing social problem." Therefore, "there is no doubt that preventing danger to the community is a legitimate . . . goal." In fact, about 18 percent of released defendants are rearrested before their trials begin, 11 percent for violent felonies.[60]

SELF ASSESSMENT

Fill in the blanks and check your answers on page 309.

During the _____ _____, a magistrate informs the defendant of the charges brought against her or him and explains her or his _____ rights. Following this proceeding, the defendant will be detained until trial unless he or she can post _____, the amount of which is determined by the _____. Even if the defendant can afford to pay this amount, he or she may be kept in jail until trial under a _____ detention statute if the court decides that he or she poses a risk to the community.

ESTABLISHING PROBABLE CAUSE

Once the initial appearance has been completed and bail has been set, the prosecutor must establish *probable cause*. In other words, the prosecutor must show that a crime was committed and link the defendant to that crime. There are two formal procedures for establishing probable cause at this stage of the pretrial process: preliminary hearings and grand juries.

The Preliminary Hearing

During the **preliminary hearing,** the defendant appears before a judge or magistrate who decides whether the evidence presented is sufficient for the case to proceed to trial. Normally, every person arrested has a right to this hearing within a reasonable amount of time after his or her initial arrest—usually, no later than ten days if the defendant is in custody or within thirty days if he or she has gained pretrial release.

Preventive Detention The retention of an accused person in custody due to fears that she or he will commit a crime if released before trial.

Preliminary Hearing An initial hearing in which a magistrate decides if there is probable cause to believe that the defendant committed the crime with which he or she is charged.

THE PRELIMINARY HEARING PROCESS The preliminary hearing is conducted in the manner of a mini-trial. Typically, a police report of the arrest is presented by a law enforcement officer, supplemented with evidence provided by the prosecutor. Because the burden of proving probable cause is relatively light (compared with proving guilt beyond a reasonable doubt), prosecutors rarely call witnesses during the preliminary hearing, saving them for the trial. During this hearing, the defendant has a right to be represented by counsel, who may cross-examine witnesses and challenge any evidence offered by the prosecutor. In most states, defense attorneys can take advantage of the preliminary hearing to begin the process of **discovery,** in which they are entitled to have access to any evidence in the possession of the prosecution relating to the case. Discovery is considered a keystone in the adversary process, as it allows the defense to see the evidence against the defendant prior to making a plea.

WAIVING THE HEARING The preliminary hearing often seems rather perfunctory, although in some jurisdictions it replaces grand jury proceedings. It usually lasts no longer than five minutes, and the judge or magistrate rarely finds that probable cause does not exist. For this reason, defense attorneys commonly advise their clients to waive their right to a preliminary hearing. Once a judge has ruled affirmatively, in many jurisdictions the defendant is bound over to the **grand jury,** a group of citizens called to decide whether probable cause exists. In other jurisdictions, the prosecutor issues an **information,** which replaces the police complaint as the formal charge against the defendant for the purposes of a trial.

The Grand Jury

The federal government and about one-third of the states require a grand jury to make the decision as to whether a case should go to trial. Grand juries are *impaneled,* or created, for a period of time usually not exceeding three months. During that time, the grand jury sits in closed (secret) session and hears only evidence presented by the prosecutor—the defendant cannot present evidence at this hearing. The prosecutor presents to the grand jury whatever evidence the state has against the defendant, including photographs, documents, tangible objects, the testimony of witnesses, and other items. If the grand jury finds that probable cause exists, it issues an **indictment** (pronounced in-*dyte*-ment) against the defendant.

Like an information in a preliminary hearing, the indictment becomes the formal charge against the defendant. As Figure 9.4 on the facing page shows, some states require a grand jury to indict for certain crimes, while in other states a grand jury indictment is optional.

THE "SHIELD" AND THE "SWORD" The grand jury has a long history in the United States, having been brought over from England by the colonists and codified in the Fifth Amendment to the U.S. Constitution. Historically, it has acted as both a "shield" and a "sword" in the criminal justice process. By giving citizens the chance to review government charges of wrongdoing, it "shields" the individual from the power of the state. At the same time, the grand jury offers the government a "sword"—the opportunity to provide evidence against the accused—in its efforts to fight crime and protect society.[61]

A "RUBBER STAMP" Today, the protective function of the grand jury is in doubt—critics say that the "sword" aspect works too well and the "shield" aspect not at all. Statistically, the grand jury is even more prosecutor friendly than the preliminary hearing. Defendants

FIGURE 9.4 State Grand Jury Requirements

As you can see, in some states a grand jury indictment is required to charge an individual with a crime, while in others it is either optional or prohibited. When a grand jury is not used, the discretion of whether to charge is left to the prosecutor, who must then present his or her argument at the preliminary hearing (discussed earlier in the chapter).

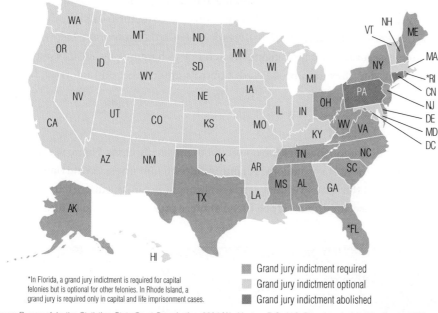

*In Florida, a grand jury indictment is required for capital felonies but is optional for other felonies. In Rhode Island, a grand jury is required only in capital and life imprisonment cases.

- Grand jury indictment required
- Grand jury indictment optional
- Grand jury indictment abolished

Source: Bureau of Justice Statistics, *State Court Organization, 2004* (Washington, D.C.: U.S. Department of Justice, August 2006), 215–217.

are indicted at a rate of more than 99 percent,[62] leading to the common characterization of the grand jury as little more than a "rubber stamp" for the prosecution.

Certainly, the procedural rules of the grand jury favor prosecutors. The exclusionary rule (see Chapter 7) does not apply in grand jury investigations, so prosecutors can present evidence that would be disallowed at any subsequent trial. Furthermore, because the grand jury is given only one version of the facts—the prosecution's—it is likely to find probable cause. In the words of one observer, a grand jury would indict a "ham sandwich" if the government asked it to do so.[63] As a result of these concerns, a number of jurisdictions have abolished grand juries.

SELF ASSESSMENT

Fill in the blanks and check your answers on page 309.

If a case is to proceed to trial, the prosecutor must establish _____ _____ that the defendant committed the crime in question. One way of doing this involves a _____ hearing, in which a judge or magistrate rules whether the prosecutor has met this burden. In the other method, the decision rests with a group of citizens called a _____ _____ who will hand down an _____ if they believe the evidence is sufficient to support the charges.

THE PROSECUTORIAL SCREENING PROCESS

Some see the high government success rates in pretrial proceedings as proof that prosecutors successfully screen out weak cases before they get to a grand jury or preliminary hearing. If, however, grand juries have indeed abandoned their traditional duties in favor of "rubber stamping" most cases set in front of them, and preliminary hearings are little better, what is to keep prosecutors from using their charging powers indiscriminately?

Nothing, say many observers. Once the police have initially charged a defendant with committing a crime, the prosecutor can prosecute the case as it stands, reduce or increase the initial charge, file additional charges, or dismiss the case. In a system of government and law that relies on checks and balances, asked legal expert Kenneth Culp Davis, why should the prosecutor be "immune to review by other officials and immune to review by the courts?"[64] (For information on another prosecutor-friendly system, see the feature *Comparative Criminal Justice—Japan's All-Powerful Prosecutors* below.) Though American prosecutors have far-ranging discretionary charging powers, it is not entirely correct to say that they are unrestricted. Controls are indirect and informal, but they do exist.

Case Attrition

Prosecutorial discretion includes the power *not* to prosecute cases. Figure 9.5 on the facing page depicts the average outcomes of one hundred felony arrests in the United States. As you can see, of the sixty-five adult arrestees brought before the district attorney, only thirty-five are prosecuted, and only eighteen of these prosecutions lead to incarceration.

Saicle/Shutterstock.com

COMPARATIVE
CRIMINAL JUSTICE

JAPAN'S ALL-POWERFUL PROSECUTORS

Prosecutors in the United States are generally believed to have a great deal of charging discretion. The discretionary power of American prosecutors, however, does not equal that of their Japanese counterparts. With the ability to "cherry pick" their cases, prosecutors in Japan routinely have annual conviction rates of about 99 percent.

THE "CONFESSION MILL"

One observer described the Japanese courts as a "confession mill." Unlike the American system, Japan has no arraignment procedure during which the accused can plead guilty or innocent. Instead, the focus of the Japanese criminal justice system is on extracting confessions of guilt: police can hold and question suspects for up to twenty-three days without pressing charges. Furthermore, the suspect has no absolute right to counsel during the interrogation, and police are often able to get confessions that make for open-and-shut convictions. The prosecutor also has the "benevolent" discretion to drop the case altogether if the suspect expresses remorse.

In addition, the extraordinarily high conviction rate is a product of Japanese culture. To fail in an attempt to convict results in a loss of face, not only for the individual prosecutor

but also for the court system as a whole. The Japanese Justice Ministry estimates that, to avoid the risk of losing, prosecutors decline to press charges against 35 percent of indictable suspects each year. Japanese judges—there are almost no juries—contribute to the high conviction rate by rarely questioning the manner in which prosecutors obtain confessions.

NO PLEA BARGAINING

Interestingly, given the amount of prosecutorial discretion, the Japanese criminal justice system does not allow for plea bargaining. The Japanese see the practice of "trading" a guilty plea for a lesser sentence as counterproductive, as a defendant may be tempted to confess to crimes she or he did not commit if the prosecution has a strong case. For the Japanese, a confession extracted after, say, twenty-three days of interrogation may be "voluntary," but a confession gained through a promise of leniency is "forced" and therefore in conflict with the system's goals of truth seeking and accuracy.

FOR CRITICAL ANALYSIS

Explain the fundamental differences between the American and Japanese criminal justice systems. Do you think the lack of a comparable adversarial system weakens or strengthens the Japanese system in comparison with the American one?

FIGURE 9.5 Following One Hundred Felony Arrests: The Criminal Justice Funnel

100 people arrested
35 juveniles go to juvenile court
65 adults considered for prosecution
30 put on probation or dismissed
35 cases accepted for prosecution
30 cases dropped
5 jump bail
30 cases go to trial
3 acquitted
23 plead guilty
4 found guilty
27 sentenced
9 placed on probation
Incarcerated: 18 adults 5 juveniles

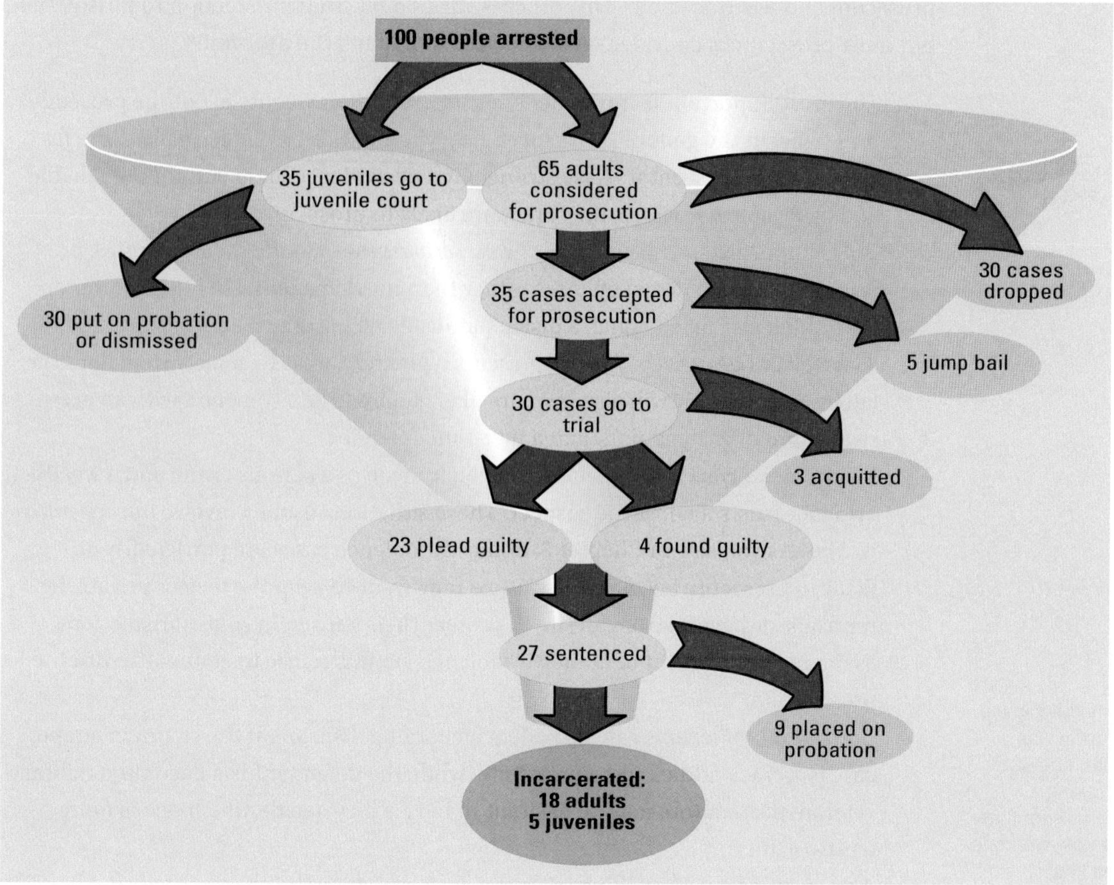

Source: Adapted from Todd R. Clear, George F. Cole, and Michael D. Reisig, *American Corrections*, 9th ed. (Belmont, CA: Wadsworth, 2011), 134.

Consequently, fewer than one in three adults arrested for a felony sees the inside of a prison or jail cell. This phenomenon is known as **case attrition,** and it is explained in part by prosecutorial discretion.

SCARCE RESOURCES About half of those adult felony cases brought to prosecutors by police are dismissed through a *nolle prosequi* (Latin for "unwilling to pursue"). Why are these cases "nolled," or not prosecuted by the district attorney? In the section on law enforcement, you learned that the police do not have the resources to arrest every lawbreaker in the nation. Similarly, district attorneys do not have the resources to prosecute every arrest. They must choose how to distribute their scarce resources. Several years ago, for example, Shawnee County (Kansas) district attorney Chad Taylor reacted to a 10 percent cut in his budget by announcing that his staff no longer had the funds to prosecute misdemeanors. As a result, eighteen domestic violence suspects were freed from the county jail, causing an immediate uproar among local and national victims' rights groups. After a month of criticism, Taylor agreed to resume prosecuting such cases "with less staff, less resources, and severe restraints on our ability to effectively seek justice."[65]

In some cases, the decision is made for prosecutors, such as when police break procedural law and negate important evidence. This happens rarely—less than 1 percent of felony arrests are dropped because of the exclusionary rule, and almost all of these are the result of illegal drug searches.[66]

Case Attrition The process through which prosecutors, by deciding whether to prosecute each person arrested, effect an overall reduction in the number of persons prosecuted.

SCREENING FACTORS Most prosecutors have a *screening* process for deciding when to prosecute and when to "noll." This process varies a bit from jurisdiction to jurisdiction, but most prosecutors consider several factors in making the decision:[67]

Explain how a prosecutor screens potential cases.

LEARNING
9
OBJECTIVE

- The most important factor in deciding whether to prosecute is not the prosecutor's belief in the guilt of the suspect, but whether there is *sufficient evidence for conviction.* If prosecutors have strong physical evidence and a number of reliable and believable witnesses, they are quite likely to prosecute.

- Prosecutors also rely heavily on *offense seriousness* to guide their priorities, preferring to take on felony offenses rather than misdemeanors. In other words, everything else being equal, a district attorney will prosecute a rapist instead of a jaywalker because the former presents a greater threat to society than does the latter. A prosecutor will also be more likely to prosecute someone with an extensive record of wrongdoing than a first-time offender.

- Sometimes a case is dropped even when it involves a serious crime and a wealth of evidence exists against the suspect. These situations usually involve *uncooperative victims.* As you saw in Chapter 3, domestic violence cases are particularly difficult to prosecute because the victims may want to keep the matter private, fear reprisals, or have a strong desire to protect their abuser. In some jurisdictions, as many as 80 percent of domestic violence victims refuse to cooperate with the prosecution.[68]

- *Unreliability of victims* can also affect a charging decision. If the victim in a rape case is a crack addict and a prostitute, while the defendant is a decorated military veteran, prosecutors may be hesitant to have a jury decide which one is more trustworthy.

- A prosecutor may be willing to drop a case or reduce the charges against *a defendant who is willing to testify against other offenders.* Federal law encourages this kind of behavior by offering sentencing reductions to defendants who provide "substantial assistance in the investigation or prosecution of another person who has committed an offense."[69]

Often, prosecutors are motivated by a sense of doing "the right thing" for their community. This can lead them to establish *case priorities* concerning certain types of crime. For example, following the heroin overdose death of a teenage cheerleader in Troy, Illinois, recently appointed Madison County state's attorney Tom Gibbons teamed with local law enforcement to address the issue of drug-related deaths. Now, police in southern Illinois hand out small cards to persons arrested for heroin possession. One side of each card has a phone number for drug treatment. The other side has a contact number for the police and encourages the arrestees to identify their dealers. In the five years before Gibbons took office, the county prosecuted just one case of drug-induced homicide. In the fifteen months after he took office, Gibbons filed six such cases.[70] (To get a better idea of the difficulty of some charging decisions, see the feature *You Be the Prosecutor—A Battered Woman* on the facing page.)

When Wayne County (Michigan) Prosecutor Kym Worthy was a first-year law student, she was sexually assaulted during a nighttime jog. Drawing from that experience, Worthy now works to have cold case rape kits, which contain swabs of saliva, semen, and other evidence, tested for DNA fingerprinting. How might the backlog of untested rape kits—more than 11,000 in Detroit alone—discourage sexual assault victims from reporting the crime to police? AP Photo/*Detroit News*, Steve Perez

A BATTERED WOMAN

THE SITUATION For more than twenty years, John regularly beat his wife, Judy. He even put out cigarettes on her skin and slashed her face with glass. John was often unemployed and forced Judy into prostitution to earn a living. He regularly denied her food and threatened to maim or kill her. Judy left home several times, but John always managed to find her, bring her home, and punish her. Finally, Judy took steps to get John put in a psychiatric hospital. He told her that if anybody came for him, he would "see them coming" and cut her throat before they arrived. That night, Judy shot John three times in the back of the head while he was asleep, killing him. You are the prosecutor with authority over Judy.

THE LAW In your jurisdiction, a person can use deadly force in self-defense if it is necessary to kill an unlawful aggressor to save himself or herself from imminent death. (See pages 118–119 for a review of self-defense.) Voluntary manslaughter is the intentional killing of another human being without malice. It covers crimes of passion. First degree murder is premeditated killing, with malice. (See pages 108–109 for a review of the different degrees of murder.)

YOUR DECISION Will you charge Judy with voluntary manslaughter or first degree murder? Alternatively, do you believe she was acting in self-defense, in which case you will not charge her with any crime? Explain your choice.

[To see how a Rutherford County, North Carolina, prosecutor decided a case with similar facts, go to Example 9.1 in Appendix B.]

Prosecutorial Charging and the Defense Attorney

For the most part, there is little the defense attorney can do when the prosecutor decides to charge a client. If a defense attorney feels strongly that the charge has been made in violation of the defendant's rights, he or she can, however, submit *pretrial motions* to the court requesting that a particular action be taken to protect his or her client. For example, a defense attorney has the option of filing a motion to dismiss the charges against her or his client completely because of lack of evidence. In the case that opened this chapter, Florida A&M band member Ryan Dean, one of the defendants, asked that the felony hazing charges against him be thrown out. Through his lawyer, Dean claimed that police investigators failed to produce "a single witness" who saw him beating Robert Champion on the school bus.[71] (A judge dismissed the motion.)

Other common pretrial motions include the following:

1. Motions to suppress evidence obtained illegally.
2. Motions for a change of venue because the defendant cannot receive a fair trial in the original jurisdiction.
3. Motions to invalidate a search warrant.
4. Motions to dismiss the case because of a delay in bringing it to trial.
5. Motions to obtain evidence that the prosecution may be withholding.

As we shall soon see, defense attorneys sometimes use these pretrial motions to pressure the prosecution into offering a favorable deal for their client.

Arraignment A court proceeding in which the suspect is formally charged with the criminal offense stated in the indictment.

Nolo Contendere Latin for "I will not contest it." A criminal defendant's plea, in which he or she chooses not to challenge, or contest, the charges brought by the government.

Plea Bargaining The process by which the accused and the prosecutor work out a mutually satisfactory conclusion to the case, subject to court approval.

SELF ASSESSMENT

Fill in the blanks and check your answers on page 309.

On average, of sixty-five adult arrestees, a district attorney will prosecute only thirty-five. This process, which is known as case _____, requires that the prosecutor _____ all potential cases and dismiss the ones where the likelihood of _____ is weakest. The most important factor in this decision is whether there is sufficient _____ to find the defendant guilty.

PLEADING GUILTY

Based on the information (delivered during the preliminary hearing) or indictment (handed down by the grand jury), the prosecutor submits a motion to the court to order the defendant to appear before the trial court for an **arraignment.** Due process of law, as guaranteed by the Fifth Amendment, requires that a criminal defendant be informed of the charges brought against her or him and be offered an opportunity to respond to those charges. The arraignment is one of the ways in which due process requirements are satisfied by criminal procedure law.

At the arraignment, the defendant is informed of the charges and must respond by pleading not guilty or guilty. In some but not all states, the defendant may also enter a plea of *nolo contendere,* which is Latin for "I will not contest it." The plea of *nolo contendere* is neither an admission nor a denial of guilt. (The consequences for someone who pleads guilty and for someone who pleads *nolo contendere* are the same in a criminal trial, but the latter plea cannot be used in a subsequent civil trial as an admission of guilt.) Most frequently, the defendant pleads guilty to the initial charge or to a lesser charge that has been agreed on through *plea bargaining* between the prosecutor and the defendant. If the defendant pleads guilty, no trial is necessary, and the defendant is sentenced based on the crime he or she has admitted committing.

Plea Bargaining in the Criminal Justice System

Plea bargaining most often takes place after the arraignment and before the beginning of the trial. In its simplest terms, it is a process by which the accused, represented by the defense counsel, and the prosecutor work out a mutually satisfactory disposition of the case, subject to court approval. Usually, plea bargaining involves the defendant's pleading guilty to the charges against her or him in return for a lighter sentence, but other variations are possible as well. The defendant can agree to plead guilty in exchange for having the charge against her or him reduced from, say, felony burglary to the lesser offense of breaking and entering. Or a person charged with multiple counts may agree to plead guilty if the prosecutor agrees to drop one or more of the counts. Whatever the particulars, the results of a plea bargain are generally the same: the prosecutor gets a conviction, and the defendant a lesser punishment.

In *Santobello v. New York* (1971),[72] the Supreme Court held that plea bargaining "is not only an essential part of the process but a highly desirable part for many reasons." Some observers would agree, but with ambivalence. They understand that plea bargaining offers the practical benefit of saving court resources, but question whether it is the best way to achieve justice.[73] We will address the question of whether plea bargaining is an acceptable means of determining the defendant's fate in the *CJ in Action* feature at the end of the chapter.

Motivations for Plea Bargaining

Given the high rate of plea bargaining—accounting for 97 percent of criminal convictions in state courts[74]—it follows that the prosecutor, defense attorney, and defendant each have strong reasons to engage in the practice.

PROSECUTORS AND PLEA BARGAINING In most cases, a prosecutor has a single goal after charging a defendant with a crime: conviction. If a case goes to trial, no matter how certain a prosecutor may be that the defendant is guilty, there is always a chance that a jury or judge will disagree. Plea bargaining removes this risk. Furthermore, the prosecutorial screening process described earlier in the chapter is not infallible. Sometimes, a prosecutor will find that the evidence against the accused is weaker than first thought or will uncover new information that changes the complexion of the case. In these situations, the prosecutor may decide to drop the charges or, if he or she still feels that the defendant is guilty, turn to plea bargaining to "save" a questionable case.

The prosecutor's role as an administrator also comes into play. She or he may be interested in the quickest, most efficient manner to dispose of caseloads, and plea bargains reduce the time and money spent on each case. Personal philosophy can affect the proceedings as well. A prosecutor who feels that a mandatory minimum sentence for a particular crime, such as marijuana possession, is too strict may plea bargain in order to lessen the penalty. Similarly, some prosecutors will consider plea bargaining only in certain instances—for burglary and theft, for example, but not for more serious felonies such as rape and murder.

DEFENSE ATTORNEYS AND PLEA BARGAINING Political scientist Milton Heumann has said that the most important lesson that a defense attorney learns is that "most of his [or her] clients are guilty."[75] Given this stark reality, favorable plea bargains are often the best a defense attorney can do for clients, aside from helping them to gain acquittals. Some have suggested that defense attorneys have other, less savory motives for convincing a client to plead guilty, such as a desire to increase profit margins by quickly disposing of cases[76] or a wish to ingratiate themselves with the other members of the courtroom work group by showing their "reasonableness."[77]

DEFENDANTS AND PLEA BARGAINING The plea bargain allows the defendant a measure of control over his or her fate. In August 2012, for example, Jared Loughner pleaded guilty to killing six people and wounding thirteen others, including Arizona congresswoman Gabrielle Giffords, in Tucson twenty months earlier (see photo alongside). Had his case gone to trial, Loughner risked being convicted and given the death penalty. Under the terms of the plea agreement, Loughner will spend the rest of his life in prison. As Figure 9.6 on the following page shows, defendants who plea bargain receive significantly lighter sentences on average than those who are found guilty at trial.

VICTIMS AND PLEA BARGAINING One of the major goals of the victims' rights movement has been to

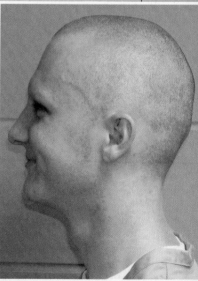

▪ Why did Jared Loughner agree to plead guilty to multiple charges stemming from his shooting rampage in Tucson, Arizona? What incentives might federal prosecutors have had for accepting Loughner's guilty plea and declining to seek his execution?
AP Photo/U.S. Marshal's Office, File

FIGURE 9.6 Sentencing Outcomes for Guilty Pleas

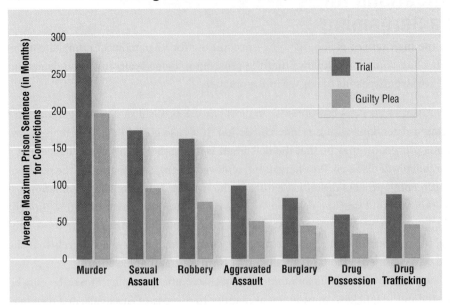

Source: Bureau of Justice Statistics, *Felony Sentences in State Courts, 2006—Statistical Tables* (Washington, D.C.: U.S. Department of Justice, December 2009), Table 4.3.

increase the role of victims in the plea bargaining process. In recent years, the movement has had some success in this area. About half of the states now allow for victim participation in plea bargaining. Many have laws similar to North Carolina's statute that requires the district attorney's office to offer victims "the opportunity to consult with the prosecuting attorney" and give their views on "plea possibilities."[78] On the federal level, the Crime Victims' Rights Act grants victims the right to be "reasonably heard" during the process.[79]

Crime victims often have mixed emotions regarding plea bargains. On the one hand, any form of "negotiated justice" that lessens the offender's penalty may add insult to the victim's emotional and physical injuries. "This is too little, too late," said Suzi Hillman, who had been shot multiple times by Jared Loughner in Tucson.[80] On the other hand, trials can bring up events and emotions that some victims would rather not have to re-experience. In the words of Mark Kelley, Gabrielle Giffords's husband, "Avoiding trial [for Loughner] will allow us, and we hope the whole Southern Arizona community, to continue with our recovery and move forward with our lives."[81]

Plea Bargaining and the Adversary System

One criticism of plea bargaining is that it subverts the adversary system, the goal of which is to determine innocence or guilt. Although plea bargaining does value negotiation over conflict, it is important to remember that it does so in a context in which legal guilt has already been established. Even within this context, plea bargaining is not completely divorced from the adversary process.

STRATEGIES TO INDUCE A PLEA BARGAIN Earlier, we pointed out that the most likely reason why a prosecutor does not bring charges is the lack of a strong case. This is also the most common reason why a prosecutor agrees to a plea bargain once charges have been brought. Defense attorneys are well aware of this fact and often file numerous pretrial motions in an effort to weaken the state's case. Even if the judge does not accept the motions, the defense may hope that the time required to process them will wear on the prosecutor's patience. As one district attorney has said, "the usual defense strategy today

Indicate the ways that both defense attorneys and prosecutors can induce plea bargaining. LEARNING **10** OBJECTIVE

is to bring in a stack of motions as thick as a Sunday newspaper; defense attorneys hope that we won't have the patience to ride them out."[82]

Prosecutors have their own methods of inducing a plea bargain. The most common is the ethically questionable practice of *overcharging*—that is, charging the defendant with more counts than may be appropriate. There are two types of overcharging:

1. In *horizontal overcharging,* the prosecutor brings a number of different counts for a single criminal incident.
2. In *vertical overcharging,* the prosecutor raises the level of a charge above its proper place. For example, as we saw in the opening of this chapter, the facts of a case may have warranted a charge of felony hazing, but the prosecutor charged the defendants with manslaughter.

After overcharging, prosecutors allow themselves to be "bargained down" to the correct charge, giving the defense attorney and the defendant the impression that they have achieved some sort of victory.

PROTECTING THE DEFENDANT Watching the defense attorney and the prosecutor maneuver in this manner, the defendant often comes to the conclusion that the plea bargaining process is a sort of game with sometimes incomprehensible rules. The Supreme Court is also aware of the potential for taking advantage of the defendant in plea bargaining and has taken steps to protect the accused. (For a summary of notable Supreme Court cases involving plea bargaining procedures, see Figure 9.7 below.) Until *Boykin v. Alabama* (1969),[83] judges would often accept the defense counsel's word that the defendant wanted to plead guilty. In that case, the Court held that the defendant must make a clear statement that he or she accepts the plea bargain. As a result, many jurisdictions now ask the accused to sign a **Boykin** form waiving his or her right to a trial.

In 2012, the Supreme Court dramatically affected this area of the law by ruling that defendants have a constitutional right to effective representation during plea negotiations.[84] That year, the Court considered the plight of Anthony Cooper, who had shot a

> **Boykin Form** A form that must be completed by a defendant who pleads guilty. The defendant states that she or he has done so voluntarily and with full comprehension of the consequences.

FIGURE 9.7 Notable United States Supreme Court Decisions on Plea Bargaining

The constitutional justification of the plea bargain as an accepted part of the criminal justice process has been fortified by these Supreme Court rulings.

Brady v. United States (397 U.S. 742 [1970]). In this case the defendant entered a guilty plea in order to avoid the death penalty. In allowing this action, the Court ruled that **plea bargains are a legitimate part of the adjudication process as long as they are entered into voluntarily and the defendant has full knowledge of the consequences of pleading guilty.**

North Carolina v. Alford (400 U.S. 25 [1970]). Although maintaining he was innocent of the first degree murder with which he was charged, Alford pleaded guilty to second degree murder in order to avoid the possibility of the death penalty that came with the original charges. After being sentenced to thirty years in prison, Alford argued that he was forced to plea bargain because of the threat of the death penalty.

The Court refused to invalidate Alford's guilty plea, stating that **plea bargains are valid even if the defendant claims innocence, as long as the plea was entered into voluntarily.**

Santobello v. New York (404 U.S. 257 [1971]). This case focused on the prosecutor's role in the plea bargain process. The Court ruled that **if a prosecutor promises a more lenient sentence in return for the defendant's guilty plea, the promise must be kept.**

Ricketts v. Adamson (483 U.S. 1 [1987]). In return for a reduction of charges, Ricketts agreed to plead guilty and to testify against a co-defendant in a murder case. When the co-defendant's conviction was reversed on appeal, Ricketts refused to testify a second

time. Therefore, the prosecutor rescinded the offer of leniency. The Court ruled that the prosecutor's action was justified, and that **defendants must uphold their side of the plea bargain in order to receive its benefits.**

United States v. Mezzanatto (513 U.S. 196 [1995]). The Court ruled that a prosecutor can refuse to plea bargain with a defendant unless the defendant agrees that any statements made by him or her during the bargaining process can be used against him or her in a possible trial. In other words, **if the defendant admits to committing the crime during plea bargain negotiations, and then decides to plead not guilty, the prosecution can use the admission as evidence during the trial.**

woman in Detroit. Based on faulty legal advice from his attorney, Cooper rejected a plea bargain that called for a sentence of four to seven years behind bars. Instead, he lost at trial and was sentenced to fifteen to thirty years. In essence, the Court found that the *Strickland* standard, discussed earlier in the chapter, applies to ineffective counsel during plea bargaining as well as ineffective counsel during the criminal trial.

Consequently, defendants like Cooper will be given the chance to argue that had they received proper legal advice, they would have accepted the plea bargain rather than risk a trial. If a defendant successfully proves ineffective counsel during plea bargaining, he or she will be given another chance to make a favorable plea.[85] The four members of the Court who dissented from this decision warned that it would give defendants who lose at trial an unfair opportunity to revisit a rejected plea bargain. "It's going to be tricky," agrees Stephanos Bibas, a law professor at the University of Pennsylvania. "There are going to be a lot of defendants who say after they're convicted that they really would have taken the plea."[86]

Pleading Not Guilty

Despite the large number of defendants who eventually plead guilty, the plea of not guilty is fairly common at the arraignment. This is true even when the facts of the case seem stacked against the defendant. Generally, a not guilty plea in the face of strong evidence is part of a strategy to (1) gain a more favorable plea bargain, (2) challenge a crucial part of the evidence on constitutional grounds, or (3) submit one of the affirmative defenses discussed in Chapter 4.

Of course, if either side is confident in the strength of its arguments and evidence, it will obviously be less likely to accept a plea bargain. Both prosecutors and defense attorneys may favor a trial to gain publicity, and sometimes public pressure after an extremely violent or high-profile crime will force a chief prosecutor (who is, remember, normally an elected official) to take a weak case to trial. Also, some defendants may insist on their right to a trial, regardless of their attorneys' advice. In the next chapter, we will examine what happens to the roughly 3 percent of indictments that do lead to the courtroom.

SELF ASSESSMENT

Fill in the blanks and check your answers on page 309.

A _____ _____ occurs when the prosecution and the defense work out an agreement that resolves the case. Generally, a defendant will plead guilty in exchange for a reduction of the _____ against him or her or a lighter _____, or both. To ensure that the defendant understands the terms of the plea, he or she must sign a _____ form waiving his or her right to a _____.

CJ IN ACTION

THE PLEA BARGAIN PUZZLE

In May 2012, William Cummins pleaded guilty to second degree unintentional murder for killing Patrick Jaworski during a fight over a cell phone in St. Paul, Minnesota. As part of the plea agreement, Cummins was sentenced to about twelve years in prison. This punishment enraged Jaworski's family. His sister, Samantha Latraille, said that Cummins "deserves more time for taking my little brother's life."[87] Prosecutor John Choi did not disagree, but defended his decision as a "tough call."[88] Because the prosecution had no evidence that the killing was premeditated, Cummins might have received an even lighter sentence had the case gone to trial. In this *CJ in Action* feature, we will examine the pros and cons of plea bargaining, a source of constant frustration for defendants, attorneys, and victims that the American court system apparently cannot live without.

ADVERSARIAL AND INEVITABLE

Those who support plea bargaining often do so because they cannot imagine life without it. In 1970, Supreme Court chief justice Warren Burger warned that "a reduction from 90 percent to 80 percent in guilty pleas requires the assignment of twice the judicial manpower and facilities—judges, court reporters, bailiffs, clerks, jurors, and courtrooms." Burger added, "A reduction to 70 percent trebles this demand."[89] This practicality bothers some observers. "Because of plea bargaining, I guess we can say, 'Gee, the trains run on time,'" notes criminologist Franklin Zimring. "But do we like where they're going?"[90]

THE CASE FOR PLEA BARGAINING

- Plea bargaining provides prosecutors and defense attorneys with the flexibility to quickly dispose of some cases while allocating scarce resources to the cases that require them.

- Because of mandatory minimum sentencing, which you will study in Chapter 11, criminal defendants who go to trial risk very harsh punishment if they lose. Plea bargaining allows them to mitigate that risk and accept a lesser sentence.

- The practice spares victims from reliving the horrors of their victimization as courtroom witnesses.

THE CASE AGAINST PLEA BARGAINING

- Plea bargaining gives innocent people an incentive to plead guilty if they feel that there is even a slight chance that a jury or judge might decide against them.

- Plea bargaining gives prosecutors too much power to coerce defendants, either by overcharging or by claiming to have evidence that the prosecutor knows would actually be inadmissible at trial, such as contraband gained by an illegal search. (Incidentally, the Supreme Court has ruled that prosecutors are within their rights to threaten defendants with harsher sentences to induce a guilty plea.)[91]

- The practice allows dangerous criminals to "beat the system" by negotiating for lighter sentences than they deserve. Consequently, it undermines the deterrent effects of punishment and the public's confidence in the criminal justice system.

YOUR OPINION—WRITING ASSIGNMENT

About fifteen years ago, Shelby County (Tennessee) district attorney General Bill Gibbons instituted a "no deals" policy for certain crimes prosecuted by his office. The policy covers many violent crimes, including first degree murder, second degree murder, aggravated robbery, aggravated rape, carjacking, and attempted first degree murder. The idea is simple: should a defendant in Shelby County be indicted for one of these, he or she will not get the "benefit" of a plea bargain for a lesser punishment or a lesser charge.

What is your opinion of "no deals" policies for specific crimes? What impact do such policies have on prosecutors, defense attorneys, and defendants? If you agree with this strategy, to which crimes would you apply it and why? Before responding, you can review our discussions in this chapter concerning:

- Defense attorneys (pages 284–289).

- Case attrition (pages 298–300).

- Plea bargaining (pages 302–306).

Your answer should include at least three full paragraphs.

CHAPTER SUMMARY

For more information on these concepts, look back to the Learning Objective icons throughout the chapter.

 List the different names given to public prosecutors and indicate the general powers that they have. At the federal level, the prosecutor is called the U.S. attorney. In state and local courts, the prosecutor may be referred to as the prosecuting attorney, state attorney, district attorney, county attorney, or city attorney. Prosecutors in general have the power to decide when and how the state will pursue an individual suspected of criminal wrongdoing. In some jurisdictions, the district attorney is also the chief law enforcement officer, holding broad powers over police operations.

 Contrast the prosecutor's roles as an elected official and as a crime fighter. In most instances, the prosecutor is elected and therefore may feel obliged to reward members of her or his party with jobs. To win reelection or higher political office, the prosecutor may feel a need to bow to community pressures. As a crime fighter, the prosecutor is dependent on the police, and indeed prosecutors are generally seen as law enforcement agents. Prosecutors, however, generally pursue cases only when they believe there is sufficient legal guilt to obtain a conviction.

 Delineate the responsibilities of defense attorneys. (a) Representation of the defendant during the custodial process; (b) investigation of the supposed criminal incident; (c) communication with the prosecutor (including plea bargaining); (d) preparation of the case for trial; (e) submission of defense motions; (f) representation of the defendant at trial; (g) negotiation of a sentence after conviction; and (h) appeal of a guilty verdict.

 Explain why defense attorneys must often defend clients they know to be guilty. In our adversary system, the most important responsibility of a defense attorney is to be an advocate for her or his client. This means ensuring that the client's constitutional rights are protected during criminal justice proceedings, regardless of whether the client is guilty or innocent.

 List the three basic features of an adversary system of justice. (a) A neutral decision maker (judge or jury); (b) presentation of evidence from both parties; and (c) a highly structured set of procedures that must be used when evidence is presented.

 Identify the steps involved in the pretrial criminal process. (a) Suspect taken into custody or arrested; (b) initial appearance before a magistrate, at which time the defendant is informed of his or her constitutional rights and a public defender may be appointed or private counsel may be hired by the state to represent the defendant; (c) the posting of bail or release on recognizance; (d) preventive detention, if deemed necessary to ensure the safety of other persons or the community, or regular detention, if the defendant is unable to post bail; (e) preliminary hearing (mini-trial), at which the judge rules on whether there is probable cause and the prosecutor issues an information; or in the alternative (f) grand jury hearings, after which an indictment is issued against the defendant if the grand jury finds probable cause; (g) arraignment, in which the defendant is informed of the charges and must respond by pleading not guilty or guilty (or in some cases *nolo contendere*); and (h) plea bargaining.

 Indicate the three influences on a judge's decision to set bail. (a) Uncertainty about the character and past criminal history of the defendant; (b) the risk that the defendant will commit another crime if out on bail; and (c) overcrowded jails, which may influence a judge to release a defendant on bail.

 Identify the main difference between an indictment and an information. An indictment is the grand jury's declaration that probable cause exists to charge a defendant with a specific crime. In jurisdictions that do not use grand juries, the prosecution issues an information as the formal charge of a crime.

 Explain how a prosecutor screens potential cases. (a) Is there sufficient evidence for conviction? (b) What is the priority of the case? The more serious the alleged crime, the higher the priority. The more extensive the defendant's criminal record, the higher the priority. (c) Are the victims cooperative? Violence against family members often yields uncooperative victims, so these cases are rarely prosecuted. (d) Are the victims reliable? (e) Might the defendant be willing to testify against other offenders?

 Indicate the ways that both defense attorneys and prosecutors can induce plea bargaining. Defense attorneys can file numerous pretrial motions in an effort to weaken the state's case. Prosecutors can engage in horizontal or vertical overcharging so that they can be "bargained down" in the process of plea bargaining.

QUESTIONS FOR **CRITICAL ANALYSIS**

1. According to the United States Supreme Court, prosecutors cannot face civil lawsuits for misconduct, even if they have deliberately sent an innocent person to prison. In practical terms, why do you think prosecutors are protected in this manner? Do you think the Supreme Court should lift this immunity for prosecutors? Why or why not?

2. Critics argue that charging low-income defendants fees for the services of public defenders is unconstitutional. Why might this practice go against the Supreme Court's ruling in *Gideon v. Wainwright?*

3. Preventive detention laws raise the troubling issue of *false positives,* or erroneous predictions that defendants, if released before trial, would commit a crime when in fact they would not. Why do you think that legislators, judges, and citizens are willing to accept the possibility of false positives when denying pretrial release to certain defendants?

4. In practice, the constitutional right to a lawyer does not cover initial bail hearings. What are the disadvantages for an indigent defendant who is not represented by a lawyer at this point in the pretrial process?

5. Do you think that a prosecutor should offer a favorable plea bargain to a defendant who provides helpful information concerning a different defendant? What are the pros and cons of this practice?

KEY **TERMS**

adversary system   289
arraignment   302
attorney general   281
attorney-client privilege   289
bail   291
bail bond agent   294
Boykin form   305
case attrition   299

defense attorney   284
discovery   296
grand jury   296
indictment   296
information   296
initial appearance   291
nolo contendere   302
plea bargaining   302

preliminary hearing   295
preventive detention   295
property bond   294
public defenders   286
public prosecutors   281
release on recognizance (ROR)   293

SELF ASSESSMENT **ANSWER KEY**

Page 284: i. government/state; **ii.** charge; **iii.** win; **iv.** justice

Page 289: i. Sixth; **ii.** private; **iii.** public; **iv.** poor/indigent; **v.** privilege; **vi.** confidential; **vii.** consents

Page 295: i. initial appearance; **ii.** constitutional; **iii.** bail; **iv.** judge; **v.** preventive

Page 297: i. probable cause; **ii.** preliminary; **iii.** grand jury; **iv.** indictment

Page 302: i. attrition; **ii.** screen; **iii.** conviction; **iv.** evidence

Page 306: i. plea bargain; **ii.** charges; **iii.** sentence; **iv.** *Boykin;* **v.** trial

NOTES

1. Quoted in Andrew Raffery, "Former Florida A&M Band Members Face Stiffer Charges for Hazing Death," *NBCNews.com* (March 4, 2013), at **usnews.nbcnews.com/_news/2013/03/04/17184496-former -florida-am-band-members-face-stiffer-charges-for-hazing-death?lite**.

2. 295 U.S. 78 (1935).

3. *Brady v. Maryland,* 373 U.S. 83 (1963).

4. *Smith v. Cain,* 132 S.Ct. 627 (2012).

5. *Ibid.*

6. Celesta Albonetti, "Prosecutorial Discretion: The Effects of Uncertainty," *Law and Society Review* 21 (1987), 291–313.

7. Siddhartha Bandyopadhyay and Bryan C. McCannon, "The Effect of the Election of Public Prosecutors on Criminal Trials," Working Paper (October 12, 2010), at **editorialexpress.com/cgi-bin/conference /download.cgi?db_name=res2011&paper_id=436**.

8. Bryan C. McCannon, "Prosecutor Elections, Mistakes, and Appeals," 7th Annual Conference on Empirical Legal Studies Paper (July 3, 2012), at **papers.ssrn.com/sol3/papers.cfm?abstract_id=2099730**.

9. Herbert Packer, *Limits of the Criminal Sanction* (Stanford, CA: Stanford University Press, 1968), 166–167.

10. Bennett L. Gershman, "Prosecutorial Ethics and Victims' Rights: The Prosecutor's Duty of Neutrality," *Lewis & Clark Law Review* 9 (2005), 561.

11. *Ibid.,* 569–572.

12. "And So to Court," *New York Post* (April 13, 2012), 30.

13. Gershman, 560–561.

14. Susan Herman, *Parallel Justice for Victims of Crime* (Washington, D.C.: National Center for Victims of Crime, 2010), 89.

15. *Gideon v. Wainwright,* 372 U.S. 335 (1963); *Massiah v. United States,* 377 U.S. 201 (1964); *United States v. Wade,* 388 U.S. 218 (1967); *Argersinger v. Hamlin,* 407 U.S. 25 (1972); and *Brewer v. Williams,* 430 U.S. 387 (1977).

16. Larry Siegel, *Criminology,* 6th ed. (Belmont, CA: West/Wadsworth Publishing Co., 1998), 487–488.

17. Center for Professional Responsibility, *Model Rules of Professional Conduct* (Washington, D.C.: American Bar Association, 2003), Rules 1.6 and 3.1.

18. *United States v. Wade,* 388 U.S. 218, 256–258 (1967).

19. 372 U.S. 335 (1963).

20. 387 U.S. 1 (1967).

21. 407 U.S. 25 (1972).

22. Laurence A. Benner, "Eliminating Excessive Public Defender Workloads," *Criminal Justice* (Summer 2011), 25.

23. American Bar Association, "Providing Defense Services," Standard 5-7.1, at **www.abanet.org/crimjust/standards/defsvcs_blk.html#7.1**.

24. Robert C. Boruchowitz, "The Right to Counsel: Every Accused Person's Right," *Washington State Bar Association Bar News* (January 2004), at **www.wsba.org/media/publications/barnews/2004/jan-04 -boruchowitz.htm**.

25. Bureau of Justice Statistics, *County-Based and Local Public Defender Offices, 2007* (Washington, D.C.: U.S. Department of Justice, September 2010), 3.

26. *Ibid.,* 6.

27. Alicia Bannon, Mitali Nagrecha, and Rebekah Diller, *Criminal Justice Debt: A Barrier to Reentry* (New York: Brennan Center for Justice, October 2010), 12.

28. *Wheat v. United States,* 486 U.S. 153, 159 (1988).

29. Bureau of Justice Statistics, *Defense Counsel in Criminal Cases* (Washington, D.C.: U.S. Department of Justice, 2000), 3.

30. James M. Anderson and Paul Heaton, *Measuring the Effect of Defense Counsel on Homicide Case Outcomes: Executive Summary* (Santa Monica, CA: RAND Corporation, December 2012), 1.

31. Peter A. Joy and Kevin C. McMunigal, "Does a Lawyer Make a Difference? Public Defender v. Appointed Counsel," *Criminal Justice* (Spring 2012), 46–47.

32. *County-Based and Local Public Defender Offices, 2007,* 1.

33. Brenner, 25.

34. John Eligon, "New Law to Limit Public Defenders' Caseloads in New York City," *New York Times* (April 6, 2009), A19.

35. 466 U.S. 668 (1984).

36. Sherman Smith, "Cheatham 'Elated' by Court's Decision to Give Him New Trial," *Topeka Capital Journal (Kansas)* (January 26, 2013), A1.

37. Jonathan D. Casper, *American Criminal Justice: The Defendant's Perspective* (Englewood Cliffs, NJ: Prentice Hall, 1972), 101.

38. Quoted in Mark Pogrebin, *Qualitative Approaches to Criminal Justice* (Thousand Oaks, CA: Sage Publications, 2002), 173.

39. Randolph Braccialarghe, "Why Were Perry Mason's Clients Always Innocent?" *Valparaiso University Law Review* (Fall 2004), 65.

40. John Kaplan, "Defending Guilty People," *University of Bridgeport Law Review* (1986), 223.

41. 491 U.S. 554 (1989).

42. Johannes F. Nijboer, "The American Adversary System in Criminal Cases: Between Ideology and Reality," *Cardozo Journal of International and Comparative Law* 5 (Spring 1997), 79.

43. Gordon Van Kessel, "Adversary Excesses in the American Criminal Trial," *Notre Dame Law Review* 67 (1992), 403.

44. James Eisenstein and Herbert Jacob, *Felony Justice* (Boston: Little, Brown, 1977), 24.

45. Jerome Skolnick, "Social Control in the Adversary System," *Journal of Conflict Resolution* 11 (1967), 52–70.

46. Abraham S. Blumberg, "The Practice of Law as Confidence Game: Organizational Cooption of a Profession," *Law and Society Review* 4 (June 1967), 115–139.

47. Malcolm Feeley, "The Adversary System," in *Encyclopedia of the American Judicial System,* ed. Robert J. Janosik (New York: Scribners, 1987), 753.

48. Blumberg, 115.

49. *Riverside County, California v. McLaughlin,* 500 U.S. 44 (1991).

50. Thomas H. Cohen, *Pretrial Release and Misconduct in Federal District Courts, 2008–2010* (Washington, D.C.: U.S. Department of Justice, November 2012), Table 2, page 4.

51. Illinois Annotated Statutes Chapter 725, Paragraph 5/110-5.

52. David W. Neubauer, *America's Courts and the Criminal Justice System,* 5th ed. (Belmont, CA: Wadsworth Publishing Co., 1996), 179–181.

53. Roy Flemming, C. Kohfeld, and Thomas Uhlman, "The Limits of Bail Reform: A Quasi Experimental Analysis," *Law and Society Review* 14 (1980), 947–976.

54. Manny Fernandez, "Two Suspects Confessed in Tulsa Shootings That Killed Three, Police Say," *New York Times* (April 10, 2012), A12.

55. Wayne H. Thomas, Jr., *Bail Reform in America* (Berkeley, CA: University of California Press, 1976), 4.

56. John S. Goldkamp and Michael R. Gottfredson, *Policy Guidelines for Bail: An Experiment in Court Reform* (Philadelphia: Temple University Press, 1985), 18.

57. Adam Liptak, "Illegal Globally, Bail Profit Remains Pillar of U.S. Justice," *New York Times* (January 28, 2008), A1.

58. 18 U.S.C. Sections 3141–3150 (Supp. III 1985).

59. 481 U.S. 739 (1987).

60. Bureau of Justice Statistics, *Felony Defendants in Large Urban Counties, 2006* (Washington, D.C.: U.S. Department of Justice, April 2008), Table 9, page 9.

61. Andrew D. Leipold, "Why Grand Juries Do Not (and Cannot) Protect the Accused," *Cornell Law Review* 80 (January 1995), 260.

62. Sam Skolnick, "Grand Juries: Power Shift?" *The Legal Times* (April 12, 1999), 1.

63. New York Court of Appeals Judge Sol Wachtler, quoted in David Margolik, "Law Professor to Administer Courts in State," *New York Times* (February 1, 1985), B2.

64. Kenneth C. Davis, *Discretionary Justice: A Preliminary Inquiry* (Baton Rouge, LA: Louisiana State University Press, 1969), 189.

65. Quoted in "DA Says He May File Some Topeka Domestic Violence Cases," *The Morning Sun (Pittsburg, KS)* (October 13, 2011), A2.

66. Milton Hirsh and David Oscar Markus, "Fourth Amendment Forum," *Champion* (December 2002), 42.

67. Bruce Frederick and Don Stemen, *The Anatomy of Discretion: An Analysis of Prosecutorial Decision Making—Summary Report* (New York: Vera Institute of Justice, December 2012), 4–16.

68. Tom Lininger, "Evidentiary Issues in Federal Prosecutions of Violence against Women," *Indiana Law Review* 36 (2003), 709.

69. 18 U.S.C. Section 3553(e) (2006).

70. Jim Salter and Jim Suhr, "Law Gets Tough against Cheaper, Deadlier Heroin," *Associated Press* (April 15, 2012).

71. Stephan Hudak, "Ex-FAMU Band Member Asks Judge to Throw Out Felony Hazing Charge," *Orlando Sentinel* (October 26, 2012), B3.

72. 404 U.S. 257 (1971).

73. Fred C. Zacharias, "Justice in Plea Bargaining," *William and Mary Law Review* 39 (March 1998), 1121.

74. Bureau of Justice Statistics, *Prosecutors in State Courts, 2007—Statistical Tables* (Washington, D.C.: U.S. Department of Justice, December 2011), 2.

75. Milton Heumann, *Plea Bargaining: The Experiences of Prosecutors, Judges, and Defense Attorneys* (Chicago: University of Chicago Press, 1978), 58.

76. Albert W. Alschuler, "The Defense Attorney's Role in Plea Bargaining," *Yale Law Journal* 84 (1975), 1200.

77. Stephen J. Schulhofer, "Plea Bargaining as Disaster," *Yale Law Journal* 101 (1992), 1987.

78. North Carolina General Statutes Section 15A-832(f) (2003).

79. 18 U.S.C. Section 3771 (2004).

80. Quoted in Fernanda Santos, "Life Term for Gunman after Guilty Plea in Tucson Killings," *New York Times* (August 8, 2012), A9.

81. Quoted in *ibid.*

82. Albert W. Alschuler, "The Prosecutor's Role in Plea Bargaining," *University of Chicago Law Review* 36 (1968), 53.

83. 395 U.S. 238 (1969).

84. *Lafler v. Cooper,* 132 S.Ct. 1376 (2012); and *Missouri v. Frye,* 132 S.Ct. 1399 (2012).

85. Laurence Benner, "Expanding the Right to Effective Counsel at Plea Bargaining," *Criminal Justice* (Fall 2012), 4-11.

86. Quoted in Adam Liptak, "Justices' Ruling Expands Rights of Accused in Plea Bargains," *New York Times* (March 22, 2012), A1.

87. Quoted in Emily Gurnon, "Man Sentenced in Fatal New Year's Stabbing: 11 Years Not Enough, Victim's Family Says," *St. Paul Pioneer Press* (May 17, 2012), B5.

88. Quoted in *ibid.*

89. Warren Burger, "Address to the American Bar Association Annual Convention," *New York Times* (August 11, 1970), 24.

90. Quoted in "Is Plea Bargaining a Cop-Out?" *Time* (August 28, 1978), at **www.time.com/time/magazine/article/0,9171,916340-3,00.html**.

91. *Bordenkircher v. Hayes,* 434 U.S. 357 (1978).

CHAPTER

10 The Criminal Trial

CHAPTER OUTLINE		CORRESPONDING LEARNING OBJECTIVES
Special Features of Criminal Trials	**1**	Identify the basic protections enjoyed by criminal defendants in the United States.
	2	Explain what "taking the Fifth" really means.
Jury Selection	**3**	List the requirements normally imposed on potential jurors.
	4	Contrast challenges for cause and peremptory challenges during *voir dire*.
The Trial	**5**	List the standard steps in a criminal jury trial.
	6	Explain the difference between testimony and real evidence, between lay witnesses and expert witnesses, and between direct and circumstantial evidence.
	7	Identify the primary method that defense attorneys use in most trials to weaken the prosecution's case against their client.
The Final Steps of the Trial and Postconviction Procedures	**8**	Delineate circumstances in which a criminal defendant may be tried a second time for the same act.
	9	List the five basic steps of an appeal.

To target your study and review, look for these numbered Learning Objective icons throughout the chapter.

AP Photo/Keith Srakocic, Pool

THE MISSING WITNESS

PROSECUTORS faced several obstacles in proving that Drew Peterson killed Kathleen Savio, his third wife. To start with, no physical evidence or witnesses linked Peterson to any crime. In addition, when Savio was found dead in her bathtub in 2004, the coroner ruled that she had slipped, hit her head, and accidentally drowned. It was not until Peterson's fourth wife, Stacy, disappeared in 2007 that local police reopened the investigation into Savio's death. In the process, they became convinced that Peterson "took out" Stacy because she knew that he had killed Savio. Though suspicions regarding Peterson's role in Stacy's disappearance were never confirmed, the renewed law enforcement interest did lead to his indictment for murdering Savio.

Peterson and Savio had divorced a year before her death. Prosecutors believed that Peterson killed Savio to avoid splitting his financial assets with her. To succeed in court, they needed to convince a Will County, Illinois, jury that (1) Savio's death was not an accident, and (2) despite lack of evidence, Peterson was the obvious culprit. The first objective was met with the help of experts who explained that Savio's exhumed body showed signs of fourteen separate injuries—too many to have been caused by a single fall in a relatively small bathtub. The second objective was trickier, because it relied on statements made by an unavailable witness: Stacy Peterson.

Despite protests by the defense, jurors did hear a number of these statements. For example, Stacy's pastor testified that she told him that Peterson got out of bed and left their house in the middle of the night around the time of Savio's death. Savio's divorce attorney also spoke in court, recounting a conversation with Stacy in which she "wanted to know if, in my opinion, the fact [that Peterson] killed Kathy could be used against him in the divorce proceeding." This evidence swayed the jury, and it convicted Peterson of murdering Savio. In February 2013, a judge sent him to prison for thirty-eight years.

1. Jurors in this case also heard testimony that Drew Peterson had tried to hire a hit man to kill Kathleen Savio and, from a friend of Savio's, that he had choked Savio and asked her, "Why don't you just die?" What is your opinion of prosecutor Chris Koch's assertion that, "When you use your common sense, it is obvious this man killed Kathleen Savio"?

2. According to Joe Lopez, Peterson's defense attorney, "It's a very dark day in America" when statements made by a person not available to be in court are used to gain a conviction. Why might Lopez feel this way?

3. The judge in this case refused to allow any mention in court of Stacy Peterson's disappearance or of suspicions that Drew Peterson was responsible for this disappearance. How would it have been unfair to Drew Peterson to allow a jury to hear these details?

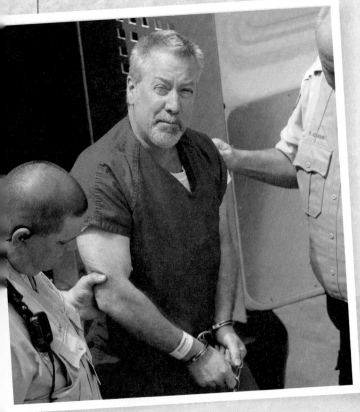

AP Photo/M. Spencer Green

Drew Peterson, shown here arriving at the Will County Courthouse in Joliet, Illinois, was convicted of murdering Kathleen Savio, his third wife.

SPECIAL FEATURES OF CRIMINAL TRIALS

Not surprisingly, given the sordid nature of Kathleen Savio's death and Stacy Peterson's mysterious disappearance, Drew Peterson's murder trial attracted national attention. Those who followed the proceedings might have gotten a skewed version of how the criminal justice system works. According to the *"wedding cake" model* of our court system, only the top, and smallest, "layer" of trials comes close to meeting constitutional standards of procedural justice.[1] In these celebrity trials, such as Peterson's, committed (and expensive) attorneys argue minute technicalities for days, with numerous (and expensive) expert witnesses taking the stand for both sides.

LEARNING OBJECTIVE 1 — Identify the basic protections enjoyed by criminal defendants in the United States.

On the bottom, largest layer of the wedding cake, the vast majority of defendants are dealt with informally, and the end goal seems to be speed rather than justice. Indeed, misdemeanor cases comprise about 80 percent of criminal court dockets, and for these defendants "convictions are largely a function of being selected for arrest."[2] Ideally, of course, criminal trial procedures are designed to protect *all* criminal defendants against the power of the state by providing them with a number of rights. Many of the significant rights of the accused are spelled out in the Sixth Amendment, which reads, in part, as follows:

> In all criminal prosecutions, the accused shall enjoy the right to a speedy and public trial, by an impartial jury of the State and the district wherein the crime shall have been committed, . . . and to be informed of the nature and cause of the accusation; to be confronted with the witnesses against him; to have compulsory process for obtaining witnesses in his favor; and to have the Assistance of Counsel for his defense.

In the last chapter, we discussed the Sixth Amendment's guarantee of the right to counsel. In this section, we will examine the other important aspects of the criminal trial, beginning with two protections explicitly stated in the Sixth Amendment: the right to a speedy trial by an impartial jury.

A "Speedy" Trial

As you have just read, the Sixth Amendment requires a speedy trial for those accused of a criminal act. The reason for this requirement is obvious: depending on various factors, the defendant may lose his or her right to move freely and may be incarcerated prior to trial. Also, the accusation that a person has committed a crime jeopardizes that person's reputation in the community. If the defendant is innocent, the sooner the trial is held, the sooner his or her innocence can be established in the eyes of the court and the public.

THE DEFINITION OF A SPEEDY TRIAL The Sixth Amendment does not specify what is meant by the term *speedy.* The United States Supreme Court has refused to quantify "speedy" as well, ruling instead in *Barker v. Wingo* (1972)[3] that only in situations in which the delay is unwarranted and proved to be prejudicial can the accused claim a violation of Sixth Amendment rights.

SPEEDY-TRIAL LAWS To meet constitutional requirements, all fifty states have their own speedy-trial statutes. For example, the Illinois Speedy Trial Act holds that a defendant must be tried within 120 days of arrest unless both the prosecution and the defense agree otherwise.[4] Keep in mind, however, that a defendant does not automatically go free if her or his trial is not "speedy" enough. There must be judicial action, which is rare but does occur from time to time. In 2012, for example, Ernest Burnett spent 106 days

Statute of Limitations A law limiting the amount of time prosecutors have to bring criminal charges against a suspect after the crime has occurred.

Jury Trial A trial before a judge and a jury.

Bench Trial A trial conducted without a jury, in which a judge makes the determination of the defendant's guilt or innocence.

in the Schenectady County (New York) jail—sixteen days more than allowed under state law—without prosecutors starting his trial process. As a result of this oversight, a county judge was forced to release Burnett, who had been arrested for kidnapping and trying to kill an ex-girlfriend.

Nearly half of all criminal trials in state courts are settled within three months of the defendant's arrest. About 12 percent take more than a year to adjudicate.[5] At the national level, the Speedy Trial Act of 1974[6] (amended in 1979) specifies the following time limits for those in the federal court system:

1. No more than thirty days between arrest and indictment.
2. No more than ten days between indictment and arraignment.
3. No more than sixty days between arraignment and trial.

Federal law allows extra time for hearings on pretrial motions, mental competency examinations, and other procedural actions.

Note that the Sixth Amendment's guarantee of a speedy trial does not apply until a person has been accused of a crime. Citizens are protected against unreasonable delays before accusation by **statutes of limitations,** which are legislative time limits that require prosecutors to charge a defendant with a crime within a certain amount of time after the illegal act took place. If the statute of limitations on a particular crime is ten years, and the police do not identify a suspect until ten years and one day after the criminal act occurred, then that suspect cannot be charged with that particular offense.

In general, prosecutions for murder and other offenses that carry the death penalty do not have a statute of limitations. This exception provides police with the ability to conduct cold case investigations that last for decades. In 2012, for example, New York City police received a tip that led them to arrest Pedro Hernandez for the abduction and murder of six-year-old Etan Patz in 1979. The problem with prosecuting such cases, of course, is that so much time has passed since the criminal act that witnesses may be missing or dead, memories may be unreliable, and other evidence may have been lost.

■ Several years ago, New York prosecutors gathered "credible" evidence that former Syracuse University assistant basketball coach Bernie Fine, right, had sexually abused a minor. Because the statute of limitations for the crime had expired, however, authorities could not charge Fine with any wrongdoing. What are the arguments for and against statutes of limitations in sexual abuse cases?
Jim McIsaac/Getty Images

The Role of the Jury

The Sixth Amendment also states that anyone accused of a crime shall be judged by "an impartial jury." In *Duncan v. Louisiana* (1968),[7] the Supreme Court solidified this right by ruling that in all felony cases, the defendant is entitled to a **jury trial.** The Court has, however, left it to the individual states to decide whether juries are required for misdemeanor cases.[8] If the defendant waives her or his right to trial by jury, a **bench trial** takes place in which a judge decides questions of legality and fact, and no jury is involved.

JURY SIZE The predominant American twelve-person jury is not the result of any one law—the Constitution does not require that the jury be a particular size. Historically, the number was inherited from the size of English juries, which was fixed at twelve during the fourteenth century.

In 1970, responding to a case that challenged Florida's practice of using a six-person jury in all but capital cases, the Supreme Court ruled that the accused did not have the right to be tried by a twelve-person jury. Indeed, the Court labeled the number twelve "a historical accident, wholly without significance except to mystics."[9] In *Ballew v. Georgia* (1978),[10] however, the Court did strike down attempts to use juries with fewer than six members, stating that a jury's effectiveness was severely hampered below that limit. About half the states allow fewer than twelve persons on criminal juries, though rarely for serious felony cases. In federal courts, defendants are entitled to have the case heard by a twelve-member jury unless both parties agree in writing to a smaller jury.

UNANIMITY In most jurisdictions, jury verdicts in criminal cases must be *unanimous* for **acquittal** or conviction. As will be explained in more detail later, if the jury cannot reach unanimous agreement on whether to acquit or convict the defendant, the result is a *hung jury,* and the judge may order a new trial. The Supreme Court has held that unanimity is not a rigid requirement. It declared that jury verdicts must be unanimous in federal criminal trials, but has given states leeway to set their own rules.[11] As a result, Louisiana and Oregon continue to require only ten votes for conviction in criminal cases.

The Privilege against Self-Incrimination

In addition to the Sixth Amendment, which specifies the protections we have just discussed, the Fifth Amendment to the Constitution also provides important safeguards for the defendant. The Fifth Amendment states that no person "shall be compelled in any criminal case to be a witness against himself." Therefore, a defendant has the right not to testify at a trial if to do so would implicate him or her in the crime.

Witnesses may also refuse to testify on this ground. For example, if a witness, while testifying, is asked a question and the answer would reveal her or his own criminal wrong-doing, the witness may "take the Fifth." In other words, she or he can refuse to testify on the ground that such testimony may be self-incriminating. Such a refusal rarely occurs, however, as witnesses are often granted *immunity* before testifying, meaning that no information they disclose can be used to bring criminal charges against them. Witnesses who have been granted immunity cannot refuse to answer questions on the basis of self-incrimination.

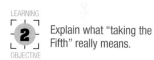

LEARNING
2 Explain what "taking the
OBJECTIVE Fifth" really means.

It is important to note that not only does the defendant have the right to "take the Fifth," but also that the decision to do so should not prejudice the jury in the prosecution's favor. The Supreme Court came to this controversial decision while reviewing *Adamson v. California* (1947),[12] a case involving the convictions of two defendants who had declined to testify in their own defense against charges of robbery, kidnapping, and murder. The prosecutor in the *Adamson* proceedings frequently and insistently brought this silence to the notice of the jury in his closing argument, insinuating that if the pair had been innocent, they would not have been afraid to testify. The Court ruled that such tactics effectively invalidated the Fifth Amendment by using the defendants' refusal to testify against them. Now judges are required to inform the jury that an accused's decision to remain silent cannot be held against him or her.

The Presumption of a Defendant's Innocence

The presumption in criminal law is that a defendant is innocent until proved guilty. The burden of proving guilt falls on the state (the public prosecutor). Even if a defendant did in fact commit the crime, she or he will be "innocent" in the eyes of the law unless the

During the 2013 trial of alleged mob boss Whitey Bulger, shown here being transported to a Boston courthouse, several criminal associates provided testimony regarding Bulger's illegal activity. Why is it necessary that such witnesses be granted immunity before testifying?
David L Ryan/*The Boston Globe* via Getty Images

prosecutor can substantiate the charge with sufficient evidence to convince a jury (or judge in a bench trial) of the defendant's guilt.[13]

Sometimes, especially when a case involves a high-profile violent crime, pretrial publicity may have convinced many members of the community—including potential jurors—that a defendant is guilty. In these instances, a judge has the authority to change the venue of the trial to increase the likelihood of an unbiased jury. In 2012, defense attorneys for Thayne Ormsby requested a change of venue for their client's trial for the brutal murders of two men and a ten-year-old boy in Houlton, Maine. Given the size of Houlton—population 6,123—and the case's local notoriety, Ormsby's lawyers successfully argued that the trial should be moved to Caribou, sixty miles to the north. (See the feature *Myth versus Reality—Spectator Demonstrations* on the facing page to see how a particular form of victim conduct tests the limits of presumed innocence.)

A Strict Standard of Proof

In a criminal trial, the defendant is not required to prove his or her innocence. As mentioned earlier, the burden of proving the defendant's guilt lies entirely with the state. Furthermore, the state must prove the defendant's guilt *beyond a reasonable doubt*. In other words, the prosecution must show that, based on all the evidence, the defendant's guilt is clear and unquestionable. In *In re Winship* (1970),[14] a case involving the due process rights of juveniles, the Supreme Court ruled that the Constitution requires the reasonable doubt standard because it reduces the risk of convicting innocent people and therefore reassures Americans of the law's moral force and legitimacy.

This high standard of proof in criminal cases reflects a fundamental social value—the belief that it is worse to convict an innocent individual than to let a guilty one go free. The consequences to the life, liberty, and reputation of an accused person from an erroneous conviction for a crime are substantial, and this has been factored into the process. Placing a high standard of proof on the prosecutor reduces the margin of error in criminal cases (at least in one direction).

SELF ASSESSMENT

Fill in the blanks and check your answers on page 343.

The defendant in any felony case is entitled to a trial by _____. If the defendant waives this right, a _____ trial takes place, in which the _____ decides questions of law and fact. Another benefit for the defendant is the privilege against _____-_____, which gives her or him the right to "take the Fifth." Perhaps the most important protection for the defendant, however, is the presumption in criminal law that she or he is _____ until proved _____. Thus, the burden is on the _____ to prove the defendant's culpability beyond a _____ _____.

JURY SELECTION

The initial step in a criminal trial involves choosing the jury. The framers of the Constitution ensured that the importance of the jury would not be easily overlooked. The right to a trial by jury is explicitly mentioned no fewer than three times

If pretrial publicity can improperly influence jurors' adherence to the presumption of innocence, what about publicity inside the courtroom during a trial? That is, should victims or other spectators be able to demonstrate their belief that a defendant is guilty in view of the jury?

THE MYTH Judges are resolute in maintaining an absolute air of impartiality within the courtroom. Therefore, they will take all necessary measures to ensure that the jury's opinion of the defendant's innocence or guilt is established only through the evidence presented during the trial. Any actions taken by spectators that might influence a jury's opinion, therefore, will not be allowed.

THE REALITY Historically, American courts have operated on the belief that juries are "likely to be impregnated by the environing atmosphere" and have strictly banned spectators from making their opinions known. Since the emergence of the victims' rights movement, however, many courts are now allowing spectators greater leeway in demonstrating during criminal trials. Victims' family members have been permitted to don remembrance ribbons, wear shirts with written messages, and carry an urn holding the victim's ashes in court. During one murder trial, members of the victim's family sat in the front row of the spectator gallery displaying his photo on large buttons. The U.S. Supreme Court ruled that the buttons did not create an atmosphere of intimidation within the courtroom, and upheld the defendant's conviction.

FOR CRITICAL ANALYSIS
Do you think that a defendant's presumption of innocence can be compromised by buttons with a picture of the victim displayed in court? Supreme Court justice Anthony Kennedy has suggested that "as a preventative matter" all such items should be prohibited from the spectator gallery of criminal trials. What is your opinion of this suggestion?

---

in the Constitution: in Section 2 of Article III, in the Sixth Amendment, and again in the Seventh Amendment. The use of a peer jury not only provided safeguards against the abuses of state power that the framers feared, but also gave Americans a chance—and a duty—to participate in the criminal justice system.

In the early years of the country, a jury "of one's peers" meant a jury limited to white, landowning males. Now, as the process has become fully democratized, there are still questions about what "a jury of one's peers" actually means and how effective the system has been in providing the necessary diversity in juries.

Initial Steps: The Master Jury List and *Venire*

The main goal of jury selection is to produce a cross section of the population in the jurisdiction where the crime was committed. As we saw earlier, sometimes a defense attorney may argue that his or her client's trial should be moved to another community to protect against undue prejudice. In practice, judges, mindful of the intent of the Constitution, are hesitant to grant such pretrial motions.

A JURY OF PEERS This belief that trials should take place in the community where the crime was committed is central to the purpose of selecting a jury of the defendant's "peers." The United States is a large, diverse nation, and the outlook of its citizens varies accordingly. Two very different cases, one tried in rural Maine and the other in San Francisco, illustrate this point.[15] In Maine, the defendant had accidentally shot and killed a woman standing in her backyard because he had mistaken her white mittens for a deer's tail. His attorney argued that it was the responsibility of the victim to wear bright-colored clothing in the vicinity of hunters during hunting season. The jury agreed, and the defendant was acquitted of manslaughter. In the San Francisco case, two people were charged with distributing sterile needles to intravenous drug users. Rather than

A Boston jury waits to be dismissed after finding Christian K. Gerhartsreiter guilty of kidnapping his seven-year-old daughter during a supervised visit. Why is it important for a defendant to be tried by a jury of her or his "peers"?
AP Photo/CJ Gunther, Pool

denying that the defendants had distributed the needles, the defense admitted the act but insisted that it was necessary to stem the transmission of AIDS and, thus, to save lives. The jury voted 11–1 to acquit, causing a mistrial.

These two outcomes may surprise or even anger people in other parts of the country, but they reflect the values of the regions where the alleged crimes were committed. Thus, a primary goal of the jury selection process is to ensure that the defendant is judged by members of her or his community—peers in the true sense of the word.

THE MASTER JURY LIST Besides having to live in the jurisdiction where the case is being tried, there are very few restrictions on eligibility to serve on a jury. State legislatures generally set the requirements, and they are similar in most states. For the most part, jurors must be

1. Citizens of the United States.
2. Eighteen years of age or over.
3. Free of felony convictions.
4. Healthy enough to function in a jury setting.
5. Sufficiently intelligent to understand the issues of a trial.
6. Able to read, write, and comprehend the English language (with one exception—New Mexico does not allow non-English-speaking citizens to be eliminated from jury lists simply because of their lack of English-language skills).

The **master jury list,** sometimes called the *jury pool,* is made up of all the eligible jurors in a community. This list is usually drawn from voter-registration lists or driver's license rolls, which have the benefit of being easily available and timely.

VENIRE The next step in gathering a jury is to draw together the **venire** (Latin for "to come"). The *venire* is composed of all those people who are notified by the clerk of the court that they have been selected for jury duty. Those selected to be part of the *venire* are ordered to report to the courthouse on the date specified by the notice.

Some people are excused from answering this summons. Persons who do not meet the qualifications listed above either need not appear in court or, in some states, must appear only in order to be officially dismissed by court officials. Also, people in some professions, including teachers, physicians, and judges, can receive exemptions due to the nature of their work. Each court sets its own guidelines for the circumstances under

LEARNING **3** OBJECTIVE
List the requirements normally imposed on potential jurors.

Master Jury List The list of citizens in a court's district from which a jury can be selected; compiled from voter-registration lists, driver's license lists, and other sources.

Venire The group of citizens from which the jury is selected.

which it will excuse jurors from service, and these guidelines can be as strict or as lenient as the court desires.

Voir Dire

Voir Dire The preliminary questions that the trial attorneys ask prospective jurors to determine whether they are biased or have any connection with the defendant or a witness.

At the courthouse, prospective jurors are gathered, and the process of selecting those who will actually hear the case begins. This selection process is not haphazard. The court ultimately seeks jurors who are free of any biases that may affect their willingness to listen to the facts of the case impartially. To this end, both the prosecutor and the defense attorney have some input into the ultimate makeup of the jury. Each attorney questions prospective jurors in a proceeding known as ***voir dire*** (French for "to speak the truth"). During *voir dire,* jurors are required to provide the court with a significant amount of personal information, including home address, marital status, employment status, arrest record, and life experiences.

QUESTIONING POTENTIAL JURORS The *voir dire* process involves both written and oral questioning of potential jurors. Attorneys fashion their inquiries in such a manner as to uncover any biases on the parts of prospective jurors and to find persons who might identify with the plights of their respective sides. As one attorney noted, though a lawyer will have many chances to talk to a jury as a whole, *voir dire* is his or her only chance to talk with the individual jurors. (To better understand the specific kinds of questions asked during this process, see Figure 10.1 below.)

To ensure that the jury is as sympathetic to their clients as possible, trial lawyers will hire a *jury selection consultant* to help with the *voir dire* process. These experts provide a number of services, from investigating the background of potential jurors to running mock trials that assist in determining what types of jurors will be most likely to provide the desired outcome.[16] As you might imagine, these services can be quite expensive, with fees reaching tens of thousands of dollars. A less costly alternative for attorneys is to conduct their own research by scouring Facebook and Twitter for valuable information on potential jurors' media habits, interests, hobbies, and religious affiliations.

CHALLENGING POTENTIAL JURORS During *voir dire,* the attorney for each side may exercise a certain number of challenges to prevent particular persons from serving on the jury. Both sides can exercise two types of challenges: challenges "for cause" and peremptory challenges.

FIGURE 10.1 **Sample Juror Questionnaire**

Drew Peterson, featured in the opening of this chapter, had gone through seemingly endless marital difficulties with Kathleen Savio, his third wife and alleged murder victim. As Peterson's relationship with Savio would play a significant role in the criminal proceedings, both the prosecution and the defense were interested in learning about the personal lives of potential jurors. The lawyers also wanted to determine whether prospective jurors had been exposed to media coverage of Peterson. The following excerpt from the juror questionnaire reflects both of these concerns.

7A. Has your marital status changed since 2010?

8A. Have you ever witnessed or been involved in a domestic dispute in which the police were called? If the answer is yes, did it result in an arrest?

9A. Do you now or have you ever paid or received child support or maintenance, sometimes called alimony?

12A. The *Lifetime* network commissioned and broadcast a made-for-television movie which purported to be about Drew Peterson. Have you seen this movie?

Challenge for Cause *A voir dire* challenge for which an attorney states the reason why a prospective juror should not be included on the jury.

Peremptory Challenges *Voir dire* challenges to exclude potential jurors from serving on the jury without any supporting reason or cause.

Challenges for Cause If a defense attorney or prosecutor concludes that a prospective juror is unfit to serve, the attorney may exercise a **challenge for cause** and request that that person not be included on the jury. Attorneys must provide the court with a sound, legally justifiable reason for why potential jurors are "unfit" to serve. For example, jurors can be challenged for cause if they are mentally incompetent, do not understand English, or are proved to have a prior link—be it personal or financial—with the defendant or victim.

Jurors can also be challenged if they express opinions that would prejudice them for or against the defendant. During jury selection for the 2013 trial of Gilberto Valle, a New York City police officer charged with conspiring to kidnap, rape, torture, and mutilate various women, one potential juror was dismissed for admitting that "Anything that relates to the subjugation of women is abhorrent to me." Another was kept off the jury for not being able to "stomach" the graphic nature of the evidence.[17]

The Supreme Court has ruled that individuals may also be legally excluded from a jury in a capital case if they would under no circumstances vote for a guilty verdict if it carried the death penalty.[18] At the same time, potential jurors cannot be challenged for cause if they have "general objections" or have "expressed conscientious or religious scruples" against capital punishment.[19] The final responsibility for deciding whether a potential juror should be excluded rests with the judge, who may choose not to act on an attorney's request.

Contrast challenges for cause and peremptory challenges during *voir dire.*

LEARNING **4** **OBJECTIVE**

Peremptory Challenges Each attorney may also exercise a limited number of **peremptory challenges.** These challenges are based solely on an attorney's subjective reasoning, and the attorney usually is not required to give any legally justifiable reason for wanting to exclude a particular person from the jury. Because of the rather random nature of peremptory challenges, each state limits the number that an attorney may utilize: between five and ten for felony trials (depending on the state) and between ten and twenty for trials that could possibly result in the death penalty (also depending on the state). Once an attorney's peremptory challenges are used up, he or she must accept forthcoming jurors, unless a challenge for cause can be used.

An attorney's decision to exclude a juror may sometimes seem whimsical. One state prosecutor who litigated drug cases was known to use a peremptory challenge whenever he saw a potential juror with a coffee mug or backpack bearing the insignia of the local public broadcasting station. The attorney presumed that this was evidence that the potential juror had donated funds to the public station, and that anybody who would do so would be too "liberal" to give the government's case against a drug offender a favorable hearing.[20] Lawyers have been known to similarly reject potential jurors for reasons of demeanor, dress, and posture.

Race and Gender Issues in Jury Selection

For many years, prosecutors used their peremptory challenges as an instrument of segregation in jury selection. Prosecutors were able to keep African Americans off juries in cases in which an African American was the defendant. The argument that African Americans—or members of any other minority group—would be partial toward one of their own was tacitly supported by the Supreme Court. Despite its own assertion, made in *Swain v. Alabama* (1965),[21] that blacks have the same right to appear on a jury as whites, the Court mirrored the apparent racism of society as a whole by protecting the questionable actions of many prosecutors.

THE *BATSON* REVERSAL The Supreme Court reversed this policy in 1986 with *Batson v. Kentucky.*[22] In that case, the Court declared that the Constitution prohibits prosecutors

CAREERS IN CJ

FASTFACTS

TRIAL COURT ADMINISTRATOR JOB DESCRIPTION:

- Oversees court operations, budget and accounting, technology, emergency management, and human resources.

WHAT KIND OF TRAINING IS REQUIRED?

- A B.A. in court administration, management, or a related area, and five years of professional experience in court administration or government administration, plus five years in a supervisory capacity.

ANNUAL SALARY RANGE?

- $66,000–$116,000

COLLINS E. IJOMA
TRIAL COURT ADMINISTRATOR

As the trial court administrator, I serve principally as the chief administrative officer for the largest trial and municipal court system in New Jersey. We provide technical and managerial support to the court (more than sixty superior court judges and thirty-six municipal court judges) on such matters as personnel, program development, case flow, resources, and facilities management. This description may sound "highfalutin" considering that most people can only describe a court in terms of a judge, one or two courtroom staff, and a few other employees associated with the visible activities in the courthouse. Obviously, there is a lot more going on behind the scenes of which the average citizen is not aware.

One thing that keeps me going and enthused about this profession is the resolve and dedication of our judges and staff. The family division embraces a host of issues, and in some cases those who seek help are hurting and desperate. The court may be their only hope.

SOCIAL MEDIA CAREER TIP Many businesses and organizations have their own career Web sites for potential employees. Some have even set up *talent communities* to interact with applicants. Explore these options if you have a specific job in mind.

---

from using peremptory challenges to strike possible jurors on the basis of race. Under the *Batson* ruling, the defendant must prove that the prosecution's use of a peremptory challenge was racially motivated. Doing so requires a number of legal steps:[23]

1. First, the defendant must make a *prima facie* case that there has been discrimination during *venire*. (*Prima facie* is Latin for "at first sight." Legally, it refers to a fact that is presumed to be true unless contradicted by evidence.)
2. To do so, the defendant must show that he or she is a member of a recognizable racial group and that the prosecutor has used peremptory challenges to remove members of this group from the jury pool.
3. Then, the defendant must show that these facts and other relevant circumstances raise the possibility that the prosecutor removed the prospective jurors solely because of their race.
4. If the court accepts the defendant's charges, the burden shifts to the prosecution to prove that its peremptory challenges were race neutral. If the court finds against the prosecution, it rules that a *Batson* violation has occurred.

The Court has revisited the issue of race a number of times in the years since its *Batson* decision. In *Powers v. Ohio* (1991),[24] it ruled that a defendant may contest race-based peremptory challenges even if the defendant is not of the same race as the excluded jurors. In *Georgia v. McCollum* (1992),[25] the Court placed defense attorneys under the same restrictions as prosecutors when making race-based peremptory challenges. Finally, in 2008, the Court, reaffirming its *Batson* decision of twenty-two years earlier, overturned the conviction of an African American death row inmate because a Louisiana prosecutor improperly picked an all-white jury for his murder trial.[26]

These rulings do not mean that a black defendant can never be judged by a jury made up entirely of whites. Rather, they indicate that attorneys cannot use peremptory challenges to reject a prospective juror because of her or his race. Indeed, there is evidence that African Americans are still being kept off juries, particularly in parts of the South.[27] A study conducted by researchers at Michigan State University found that, from 1990 to 2010, African Americans were more than twice as likely as whites to be struck from juries in trials with black defendants facing the death penalty.[28] "Anyone with any sense at all can think up a race-neutral reason [to exclude a potential minority juror] and get away with it," says Atlanta defense attorney Stephen B. Bright.[29]

WOMEN ON THE JURY In *J.E.B. v. Alabama ex rel. T.B.* (1994),[30] the Supreme Court extended the principles of the *Batson* ruling to cover gender bias in jury selection. The case was a civil suit for paternity and child support brought by the state of Alabama. Prosecutors used nine of their ten challenges to remove men from the jury, while the defense made similar efforts to remove women. When challenged, the state defended its actions by referring to what it called the rational belief that men and women might have different views on the issues of paternity and child support. The Court disagreed and held this approach to be unconstitutional.

Alternate Jurors

Because unforeseeable circumstances or illness may necessitate that one or more of the sitting jurors be dismissed, the court may also seat several *alternate jurors* who will hear the entire trial. Depending on the rules of the particular jurisdiction, two or three alternate jurors may be present throughout the trial. If a juror has to be excused in the middle of the trial, an alternate may take his or her place without disrupting the proceedings.

SELF ASSESSMENT

Fill in the blanks and check your answers on page 343.

The _____ is composed of all those people who have been identified as potential jurors for a particular trial. These people are then gathered for the process of _____ _____, in which the prosecution and defense choose the actual members of the jury. Both sides can remove jurors in two ways: (1) through unlimited challenges for _____, which require the attorney to give a reason for the removal, and (2) through a limited number of _____ challenges, for which no reason is necessary. According to the United States Supreme Court, potential jurors cannot be removed for reasons of _____ or _____.

THE TRIAL

Once the jury members have been selected, the judge swears them in and the trial itself can begin. (See Figure 10.2 on the facing page for a preview of the stages of a jury trial that will be detailed in this section.) A rather pessimistic truism among attorneys is that every case "has been won or lost when the jury is sworn." This reflects the belief that a juror's values are the major, if not dominant, factor in the decision of guilt or innocence.[31]

In actuality, it is difficult to predict how a jury will go about reaching a decision. Despite a number of studies on the question, researchers have not been able to identify any definitive consistent patterns of jury behavior. Sometimes, jurors in a criminal trial will follow instructions to find a defendant guilty unless there is a reasonable doubt, and sometimes they seem to follow instinct or prejudice and apply the law any way they choose.

List the standard steps in a criminal jury trial.
LEARNING 5 OBJECTIVE

Opening Statements

Attorneys may choose to open the trial with a statement to the jury, though they are not required to do so. In these **opening statements,** the attorneys give a brief version of the

FIGURE 10.2 The Steps of a Jury Trial

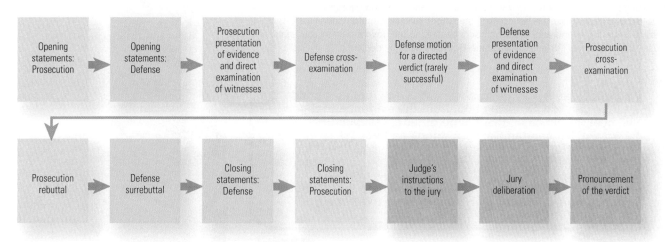

Opening statements: Prosecution → Opening statements: Defense → Prosecution presentation of evidence and direct examination of witnesses → Defense cross-examination → Defense motion for a directed verdict (rarely successful) → Defense presentation of evidence and direct examination of witnesses → Prosecution cross-examination →

Prosecution rebuttal → Defense surrebuttal → Closing statements: Defense → Closing statements: Prosecution → Judge's instructions to the jury → Jury deliberation → Pronouncement of the verdict

facts and the supporting evidence that they will present during the trial. Because some trials can drag on for weeks or even months, it is extremely helpful for jurors to hear a summary of what will unfold. In short, the opening statement is a kind of "road map" that describes the destination that each attorney hopes to reach and outlines how she or he plans to reach it.

The danger for attorneys is that they will offer evidence during the trial that might contradict an assertion made during the opening statement. This may cause jurors to disregard the evidence or shift their own thinking further away from the narrative being offered by the attorney.[32] (For an example of an opening statement, see Figure 10.3 on the following page.)

The Role of Evidence

Once the opening statements have been made, the prosecutor begins the trial proceedings by presenting the state's evidence against the defendant. Courts have complex rules about what types of evidence may be presented and how the evidence may be brought out during the trial. **Evidence** is anything that is used to prove the existence or nonexistence of a fact. For the most part, evidence can be broken down into two categories: testimony and real evidence. **Testimony** consists of statements by competent witnesses. **Real evidence,** presented to the court in the form of exhibits, includes any physical items—such as the murder weapon or a bloodstained piece of clothing—that affect the case.

Rules of evidence are designed to ensure that testimony and exhibits presented to the jury are relevant, reliable, and not unfairly prejudicial against the defendant. One of the tasks of the defense attorney is to challenge evidence presented by the prosecution by establishing that the evidence is not reliable. Of course, the prosecutor also tries to demonstrate the irrelevance or unreliability of evidence presented by the defense. The final decision on whether evidence is allowed before the jury rests with the judge, in keeping with his or her role as the "referee" of the adversary system.

TESTIMONIAL EVIDENCE A person who is called to testify on factual matters that would be understood by the average citizen is referred to as a **lay witness.** If asked about the condition of a victim of an assault, for example, a lay witness could relate certain facts, such as "she was bleeding from her forehead" or "she was unconscious on the ground

> **Evidence** Anything that is used to prove the existence or nonexistence of a fact.
>
> **Testimony** Verbal evidence given by witnesses under oath.
>
> **Real Evidence** Evidence that is brought into court and seen by the jury, as opposed to evidence that is described for a jury.
>
> **Lay Witness** A witness who can truthfully and accurately testify on a fact in question without having specialized training or knowledge.

LEARNING **6** OBJECTIVE

Explain the difference between testimony and real evidence, between lay witnesses and expert witnesses, and between direct and circumstantial evidence.

FIGURE 10.3 The Opening Statement

Several years ago, Casey Anthony went on trial in Orlando, Florida, for murdering her two-year-old daughter, Caylee. In her opening statement, lead prosecutor Linda Drane-Burdick (pictured at right) spent more than two hours describing the government's case against Casey in great detail. For emphasis, Drane-Burdick ended by declaring:

> As difficult as it may be to accept that any mother would intentionally kill her own child, from the evidence that you will hear in this case, there is no other conclusion that can be drawn. No one but Casey Anthony had access to all the pieces of evidence in this case. No one else lied to their friends, to the family, to investigators. No one else benefited from the death of Caylee Marie Anthony. At the end of this case, you will have no trouble concluding that Caylee Anthony was murdered by her mother, Casey Anthony.

AP Photo/Joe Burbank, Pool

During the thirty-three-day trial, the prosecution offered more than four hundred pieces of evidence in its effort to prove the defendant's guilt. At the trial's conclusion, however, the jury found Casey Anthony not guilty of murdering her daughter.

for several minutes." A lay witness could not, however, give information about the medical extent of the victim's injuries, such as whether she suffered from a fractured skull or internal bleeding. Coming from a lay witness, such testimony would be inadmissible.

Expert Witnesses When the matter in question requires scientific, medical, or technical skill beyond the scope of the average person, prosecutors and defense attorneys may call an **expert witness** to the stand. The expert witness is an individual who has professional training, advanced knowledge, or substantial experience in a specialized area, such as medicine, computer technology, or ballistics. The rules of evidence state that expert witnesses may base their opinions on three types of information:

1. Facts or data of which they have personal knowledge.
2. Material presented at trial.
3. Secondhand information given to the expert outside the courtroom.[33]

Expert witnesses are considered somewhat problematic for two reasons. First, they may be chosen for their "court presence"—whether they speak well or will appear sympathetic to the jury—rather than their expertise. Second, attorneys pay expert witnesses for their services. Given human nature, the attorneys expect a certain measure of cooperation from an expert they have hired, and an expert witness has an interest in satisfying the attorneys so that he or she will be hired again.[34] Under these circumstances, some have questioned whether the courts can rely on the professional nonpartisanship of expert witnesses.[35]

Challenging Expert Testimony If a trial lawyer wants to challenge an expert witness's validity or reliability, he or she must follow guidelines established by a Supreme Court decision from 1993. These guidelines call on the judge to determine whether the technique on which the expert witness is relying has been accepted by the scientific community at large.[36] Such challenges are fairly commonplace and have been used to question expert analysis of polygraph tests (see Chapter 8) and DNA evidence (see Chapter 9). This procedure has also been employed in efforts to undermine the legitimacy of fingerprint matches, described in Chapter 6.

Expert Witness A witness with professional training or substantial experience qualifying her or him to testify on a certain subject.

The predominant method of fingerprint identification, known as ACE-V (Analysis Comparison Evaluation Verification), relies on infrared or X-ray imaging of secretions from the body to produce fingerprint matches. If these samples are incomplete or in some way damaged, a faulty match between the print lifted from a crime scene and that of a suspect may result. Several scientific studies have shown that fingerprint matching is not infallible, though error rates are quite low at less than 1 percent.[37] Nevertheless, since 2000 defense attorneys have launched more than forty challenges to expert testimony regarding this process in American courts. None of these challenges has been successful, with judges finding that such small error rates should not keep fingerprint evidence from a jury.[38]

Direct Evidence Evidence that establishes the existence of a fact that is in question without relying on inference.

Circumstantial Evidence Indirect evidence that is offered to establish, by inference, the likelihood of a fact that is in question.

Relevant Evidence Evidence tending to make a fact in question more or less probable than it would be without the evidence. Only relevant evidence is admissible in court.

DIRECT VERSUS CIRCUMSTANTIAL EVIDENCE Two types of testimonial evidence may be brought into court: direct evidence and circumstantial evidence. **Direct evidence** is evidence that has been witnessed by the person giving testimony. "I saw Bill shoot Chris" is an example of direct evidence. **Circumstantial evidence** is indirect evidence that, even if believed, does not establish the fact in question but only the degree of likelihood of the fact. In other words, circumstantial evidence can create an inference that a fact exists.

Suppose, for example, that the defendant owns a gun that shoots bullets of the type found in the victim's body. This circumstantial evidence, by itself, does not establish that the defendant committed the crime. Combined with other circumstantial evidence, however, it may do just that. For instance, if other circumstantial evidence indicates that the defendant had a motive for harming the victim and was at the scene of the crime when the shooting occurred, the jury might conclude that the defendant committed the crime. The prosecutor's successful case against Drew Peterson for the murder of Kathleen Savio, described in the opening of the chapter, was based entirely on circumstantial evidence.

THE "CSI EFFECT" When possible, defense attorneys will almost always make the argument that the state has failed to present any evidence other than circumstantial evidence against their client. Recently, this tactic has been aided by a phenomenon known as the "CSI effect," taking its name from the popular television series *CSI: Crime Scene Investigation* and its spin-offs. According to many prosecutors, these shows have fostered unrealistic notions among jurors as to what high-tech forensic science can accomplish as part of a criminal investigation. In reality, the kind of physical evidence used to solve crimes on *CSI* is often not available to the prosecution, which must rely instead on witnesses and circumstantial evidence.

Several years ago, researchers surveyed more than one thousand jurors in Washtenaw County, Michigan, and found that nearly half "expected the prosecutor to present scientific evidence in every criminal case." This expectation was particularly strong in rape trials and trials lacking direct evidence of a crime.[39] Indeed, some observers believe the CSI effect was responsible for Casey Anthony's acquittal of charges that she murdered her two-year-old daughter (see Figure 10.3 earlier in the chapter). During that trial, prosecutors could provide only circumstantial evidence of Anthony's guilt, and even that evidence sometimes worked against them. For example, one of the prosecution's main contentions was that Anthony used duct tape to suffocate her daughter. Discrediting this claim, Anthony's defense attorneys were able to show the jury that DNA traces found on the duct tape could not be matched to their client (see photo on following page).[40]

RELEVANCE Evidence will not be admitted in court unless it is relevant to the case being considered. **Relevant evidence** is evidence that tends to prove or disprove a fact in question. Forensic proof that the bullets found in a victim's body were fired from a gun discovered in the suspect's pocket at the time of arrest, for example, is certainly relevant. The suspect's prior

record, showing a conviction for armed robbery ten years earlier, is, as we shall soon see, irrelevant to the case at hand and in most instances will be ruled inadmissible by the judge.

PREJUDICIAL EVIDENCE Evidence may be excluded if it would tend to distract the jury from the main issues of the case, mislead the jury, or cause jurors to decide the issue on an emotional basis.

Real Evidence In most cases involving a violent crime, prosecutors try to offer as much physical evidence of the crime as possible, showing the jury touching photographs of the victim before the crime and graphic photos of the victim after the crime, bloody pieces of clothing, and other evocative items. Defense attorneys usually try to exclude these items on the ground that they unfairly prejudice the jury against the defendant.

Judges generally will permit such evidence so long as it is not blatantly prejudicial. Several years ago, for example, Edward B. Fleury faced manslaughter charges after an eight-year-old boy named Christopher Bizilj accidentally shot and killed himself at a gun show sponsored by Fleury. During the trial, Judge Peter A. Velis of Hampden Superior Court in Springfield, Massachusetts, allowed jurors to see a video of the incident, in which a bullet from a 9mm Micro UZI pierces Bizilj's head. Velis, however, turned off the audio track so that jurors would not hear the boy's screams. "The greatest risk in this case is invoking any sympathy" for young Christopher, the judge explained.[41]

Evil Character Defense attorneys are likely to have some success precluding prosecutors from using prior purported criminal activities or actual convictions to show that the defendant has criminal propensities or an "evil character."[42] This concept is codified in the Federal Rules of Evidence, which state that evidence of "other crimes, wrongs, or acts is not admissible to prove the character of a person in order to show action in conformity therewith." Such evidence is allowed only when it does not apply to character construction and focuses instead on "motive, opportunity, intent, preparation, plan, knowledge, identity, or absence of mistake or accident."[43]

Although this legal concept has come under a great deal of criticism, it is consistent with the presumption-of-innocence standards discussed earlier. Arguably, if a prosecutor is allowed to establish that the defendant has shown antisocial or even violent traits in the past, this will prejudice the jury against the defendant in the present trial. Even if the judge instructs jurors that this prior evidence is irrelevant, human nature dictates that it will probably have a "warping influence" on the jurors' perception of the defendant.[44] Therefore, whenever possible, defense attorneys will keep such evidence from the jury.

The Prosecution's Case

Because the burden of proof is on the state, the prosecution is generally considered to have a more difficult task than the defense. The prosecutor attempts to establish guilt beyond a reasonable doubt by presenting the *corpus delicti* ("body of the offense" in

◼ Jennifer Welch, a crime scene investigator with the Orange County (Florida) Sheriff's Office, holds up duct tape found on Caylee Anthony's body. How did Casey Anthony's defense attorneys use this duct tape to create reasonable doubt that their client bound and killed her daughter?
Joe Burbank/MCT/Landov

Latin) of the crime to the jury. The *corpus delicti* is simply a legal term that refers to the substantial facts that show a crime has been committed. By establishing such facts through the presentation of relevant and nonprejudicial evidence, the prosecutor hopes to convince the jury of the defendant's guilt.

DIRECT EXAMINATION OF WITNESSES Witnesses are crucial to establishing the prosecutor's case against the defendant. The prosecutor will call witnesses to the stand and ask them questions pertaining to the sequence of events that the trial is addressing. This form of questioning is known as **direct examination.** During direct examination, the prosecutor will usually not be allowed to ask *leading questions*—questions that might suggest to the witness a particular desired response.

A leading question might be something like "So, Mrs. Williams, you noticed the defendant threatening the victim with a broken beer bottle?" If Mrs. Williams answers "yes" to this question, she has, in effect, been "led" to the conclusion that the defendant was, in fact, threatening with a broken beer bottle. The fundamental purpose behind testimony is to establish what actually happened, not what the trial attorneys would like the jury to believe happened. (A properly worded query would be, "Mrs. Williams, please describe the defendant's manner toward the victim during the incident.")

COMPETENCE AND RELIABILITY OF WITNESSES The rules of evidence include certain restrictions and qualifications pertaining to witnesses. Witnesses must have sufficient mental competence to understand the significance of testifying under oath. They must also be reliable in the sense that they are able to give a clear and reliable description of the events in question. If not, the prosecutor or defense attorney will make sure that the jury is aware of these shortcomings through *cross-examination.*

Cross-Examination

After the prosecutor has directly examined her or his witnesses, the defense attorney is given the chance to question the same witnesses. The Sixth Amendment states, "In all criminal prosecutions, the accused shall enjoy the right . . . to be confronted with witnesses against him." This **confrontation clause** gives the accused, through his or her attorneys, the right to cross-examine witnesses. **Cross-examination** refers to the questioning of an opposing witness during trial, and both sides of a case are allowed to do so.

QUESTIONING WITNESSES Cross-examination allows the attorneys to test the truthfulness of opposing witnesses and usually entails efforts to create doubt in the jurors' minds that the witness is reliable (see Figure 10.4 on the following page). After the defense has cross-examined a prosecution witness, the prosecutor may want to reestablish any reliability that might have been lost. The prosecutor can do so by again questioning the witness, a process known as *redirect examination.* Following the redirect examination, the defense attorney will be given the opportunity to ask further questions of prosecution witnesses, or *recross-examination.* Thus, each side has two opportunities to question

■ Cheri Young is subjected to direct examination during the campaign finance fraud trial of former North Carolina senator John Edwards, her husband's former employer. How do prosecutors use witnesses to establish the *corpus delicti* of an alleged crime?
AP Photo/Sara D. Davis, File

Direct Examination The examination of a witness by the attorney who calls the witness to the stand to testify.

Confrontation Clause The part of the Sixth Amendment that guarantees all defendants the right to confront witnesses testifying against them during the criminal trial.

Cross-Examination The questioning of an opposing witness during trial.

FIGURE 10.4 The Cross-Examination

The following is a transcript of a cross-examination of a government witness during a drug trial. Note that the defense attorney is not trying to establish any facts concerning the alleged crime. Instead, she is trying to create a negative picture of the witness in the minds of the jurors.

Defense: "You have thirteen children?"

Witness: "Unh huh" (affirmative)

Defense: "Made by thirteen different women?"

Witness: "Unh huh"

Defense: "Now and you are twenty-four years old?"

Witness: "Yes, m'am."

Defense: "So, out of the twenty-four years that you have been living, twenty years has been on the street, and almost four have been in prison?"

Witness: "Yes, you can say so."

Defense: "And out of the last two years that you have been on the street you had thirteen children?"

Witness: "Yes."

Rich Legg/iStockphoto

Source: The United States District Court for the Northern District of Georgia Atlanta Division, Transcript of Proceedings Before the Honorable Clarence Cooper, United States District Judge and a Jury, October 8, 1996. Docket Number: 1:95-CR-373-CC

a witness. The attorneys need not do so, but only after each side has been offered the opportunity will the trial move on to the next witness or the next stage.

HEARSAY Cross-examination is also linked to problems presented by *hearsay* evidence. **Hearsay** can be defined as any testimony given about a statement made by someone else. Literally, it is what someone heard someone else say. For the most part, hearsay is not admissible as evidence. When a witness offers hearsay, the person making the original remarks is not in court and therefore cannot be cross-examined. If such testimony were allowed, the defendant's Sixth Amendment right to confront witnesses against him or her would be violated.

The Illinois Exception As you might remember from the case that opened this chapter, both Stacy Peterson's pastor and her divorce lawyer were permitted to relate conversations they had with Stacy to the jury. Technically, this is hearsay, as Drew Peterson's lawyers did not have the opportunity to cross-examine Stacy regarding her statements. An Illinois statute, dubbed "Drew's Law," however, allows prosecutors to present hearsay evidence if they can prove by a "preponderance of the evidence"—rather than "beyond a reasonable doubt"—that the defendant took steps to make the witness unavailable to testify.[45] Prosecutors in the Peterson case were able to do so, essentially using a lower standard than is usually required in criminal trials to "prove" to the judge's satisfaction that Drew Peterson had caused Stacy's disappearance.

Interestingly, the fate of another alleged wife-murderer, Gabe Watson, detailed in the opening of Chapter 8, also hinged on hearsay evidence. In that case, Alabama prosecutors wanted the father of the alleged victim, Tina Watson, to testify that, shortly before her wedding, she told him that Gabe had asked her to increase her life insurance to $130,000. Gabe was the beneficiary of the policy, and, according to prosecutors, this provided him with a motive to kill Tina. The presiding judge ruled that this testimony was inadmissible hearsay, and Gabe never stood trial.

Hearsay An oral or written statement made by an out-of-court speaker that is later offered in court by a witness (not the speaker) concerning a matter before the court.

Other Exceptions There are a number of other exceptions to the hearsay rule, and as a result a good deal of hearsay evidence finds its way into criminal trials. For example, a hearsay statement is usually admissible if there seems to be little risk of a lie. Therefore, a statement made by someone who believes that his or her death is imminent—a "dying declaration" or a suicide note—is often allowed in court even though it is hearsay.[46] Similarly, the rules of most states allow hearsay when the statement contains an admission of wrongdoing *and* the speaker is not available to testify in court. The logic behind this exception is that a person generally does not make a statement against her or his own best interests unless it is true.[47]

Motion for a Directed Verdict A motion requesting that the court grant judgment in favor of the defense on the ground that the prosecution has not produced sufficient evidence to support the state's claim.

Motion for a Directed Verdict

After the prosecutor has finished presenting evidence against the defendant, the government will inform the court that it has rested the people's case. At this point, the defense may make a **motion for a directed verdict** (now also known as a *motion for judgment as a matter of law* in federal courts). Through this motion, the defense is basically saying that the prosecution has not offered enough evidence to prove that the accused is guilty beyond a reasonable doubt. If the judge grants this motion, which rarely occurs, then a judgment will be entered in favor of the defendant, and the trial is over.

The Defendant's Case

Assuming that the motion for a directed verdict is denied, the defense attorney may offer the defendant's case. Because the burden is on the state to prove the accused's guilt, the defense is not required to offer any case at all. It can simply "rest" without calling any witnesses or producing any real evidence and ask the jury to decide the merits of the case on what it has seen and heard from the prosecution.

PLACING THE DEFENDANT ON THE STAND If the defense does present a case, its first—and often most important—decision is whether the defendant will take the stand in her or his own defense. Because of the Fifth Amendment protection against self-incrimination, the defendant is not required to testify. Therefore, the defense attorney must make a judgment call. He or she may want to put the defendant on the stand if the defendant is likely to appear sympathetic to the jury or is well spoken and able to aid the defense's case. With a less sympathetic or less effective defendant, the defense attorney may decide that exposing the defendant before the jury presents too large a risk. Also, if the defendant testifies, she or he is open to cross-examination under oath from the prosecutor. In any case, remember that the prosecution cannot comment on a defendant's refusal to testify.[48]

CREATING A REASONABLE DOUBT Defense lawyers most commonly defend their clients by attempting to expose weaknesses in the prosecutor's case. Remember that if the defense attorney can create reasonable doubt concerning the client's guilt in the mind of just a single juror, the defendant has a good chance of gaining an acquittal or at least a *hung jury,* a circumstance explained later in the chapter.

Even if the prosecution can present seemingly strong evidence, a defense attorney may succeed by creating reasonable doubt. In an illustrative case, Jason Korey bragged to his friends that he had shot and killed Joseph Brucker in Pittsburgh, Pennsylvania, and a great deal of circumstantial evidence linked Korey to the killing. The police, however, could find no direct evidence: they could not link Korey to the murder weapon, nor could they match his footprints to those found at the crime scene. Michael Foglia, Korey's defense attorney, explained his client's bragging as an attempt to gain attention, not a true statement. Though this explanation may strike some as unlikely, in the absence of physical evidence it did create doubt in the jurors' minds, and Korey was acquitted.

(For a better idea of how this strategy works in court, see the feature *You Be the Defense Attorney—A Gang Murder* below.)

REASONABLE DOUBT AND SEXUAL ASSAULT Creating reasonable doubt is also very effective in cases that essentially rely on the word of the defendant against the word of the victim. In sexual-assault cases, for example, if the defense attorneys can create doubt about the victim's credibility—in other words, raise the possibility that he or she is lying—then they may prevail at trial. According to the Alcohol and Rape Study, carried out by researchers at Rutgers University and the University of New Hampshire, juries acquit about 90 percent of the time when the defendant says the sex was consensual and there is evidence that the alleged victim was drinking alcohol before the incident in question.[49] (The *CJ in Action* feature at the end of this chapter explores issues concerning evidence in sexual-assault cases in more detail.)

OTHER DEFENSE STRATEGIES The defense can choose among a number of strategies to generate reasonable doubt in the jurors' minds. It can present an *alibi defense,* by submitting evidence that the accused was not at or near the scene of the crime at the time the crime was committed. Another option is to attempt an *affirmative defense,* by presenting additional facts to the ones offered by the prosecution. Possible affirmative defenses, which we discussed in detail in Chapter 4, include the following:

1. Self-defense   2. Insanity   3. Duress   4. Entrapment

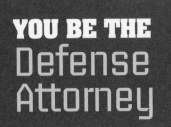

YOU BE THE
Defense
Attorney

Identify the primary method that defense attorneys use in most trials to weaken the prosecution's case against their client.

LEARNING OBJECTIVE 7

A GANG MURDER

THE SITUATION Your client is Daniel, a twenty-three-year-old member of a violent Los Angeles street gang. Daniel is charged with the first degree murder of Christopher, his best friend and fellow gang member. Christopher was killed because other gang members believed he had "snitched" about their criminal activity. According to prosecutors, Daniel lured Christopher to a garage, where other gang members hit him in the head with a shotgun and then stabbed him more than sixty times. During the trial, José, the prosecution's main witness, who admitted taking part in the stabbing while high on methamphetamine, testified that Daniel kicked Christopher's dead body. In her opening argument, the prosecutor told the jury that even though your client did not stab Christopher, he was just as guilty of murder as those who did.

THE LAW To find a defendant guilty, a jury must find *beyond a reasonable doubt* that he or she committed the crime. For Daniel to be guilty of first degree murder, the prosecution must prove that he acted with "malice aforethought" in luring Christopher to his death in the garage.

YOUR DECISION As a defense attorney, your job is to create reasonable doubt in the jurors' minds about Daniel's intent to lure Christopher to his death. Besides the facts presented above, other important details about this case include the following: (1) José, the prosecution's main witness, was allowed to plead guilty to a lesser charge of voluntary manslaughter in return for his testimony, and (2) José was dating Christopher's sister at the time of the murder. What argument will you make before the jury to create reasonable doubt?

[To see how a Los Angeles defense attorney argued in a case with similar facts, go to Example 10.1 in Appendix B.]

Somchai Rakin/Shutterstock.com

With an affirmative defense strategy, the defense attempts to prove that the defendant should be found not guilty because of certain circumstances surrounding the crime. An affirmative strategy can be difficult to carry out because it forces the defense to prove the reliability of its own evidence, not simply disprove the evidence offered by the prosecution.

The defense is often willing to admit that a certain criminal act took place, especially if the defendant has already confessed. In this case, the primary question of the trial becomes not whether the defendant is guilty, but what the defendant is guilty of. In these situations, the defense strategy focuses on obtaining the lightest possible penalty for the defendant. As we saw in the last chapter, this strategy is responsible for the high percentage of proceedings that end in plea bargains.

Rebuttal and Surrebuttal

After the defense closes its case, the prosecution is permitted to bring new evidence forward that was not used during its initial presentation to the jury. This is called the **rebuttal** stage of the trial. When the rebuttal stage is finished, the defense is given the opportunity to cross-examine the prosecution's new witnesses and introduce new witnesses of its own. This final act is part of the *surrebuttal*. After these stages have been completed, the defense may offer another motion for a directed verdict, asking the judge to find in the defendant's favor. If this motion is rejected, and it almost always is, the case is closed, and the opposing sides offer their closing arguments.

Closing Arguments

In their **closing arguments,** the attorneys summarize their presentations and argue one final time for their respective cases. In most states, the defense attorney goes first, and then the prosecutor. (In Colorado, Kentucky, and Missouri, the order is reversed.) An effective closing argument includes all of the major points that support the government's or the defense's case. It also emphasizes the shortcomings of the opposing party's case. Jurors will view a closing argument with some skepticism if it merely recites the central points of a party's claim or defense without also responding to the unfavorable facts or issues raised by the other side. Of course, neither attorney wants to focus too much on the other side's position, but the elements of the opposing position do need to be acknowledged and their flaws highlighted. (For an example of opposing closing arguments, see Figure 10.5 on the next page.)

One danger in the closing arguments is that an attorney will become too emotional and make remarks that are later deemed by appellate courts to be prejudicial. Furthermore, lawyers are not permitted to introduce any additional facts during a closing statement. If allowed to do so, lawyers would be able to "sneak in" new evidence without giving the opposing party a chance to challenge that evidence.[50] Once both attorneys have completed their remarks, the case is submitted to the jury, and the attorneys' role in the trial is, for the moment, complete.

SELF ASSESSMENT

Fill in the blanks and check your answers on page 343.

Evidence is any object or spoken _____ that can be used in a criminal trial to prove or disprove a _____ related to the crime. Evidence will not be admitted into the trial unless it is _____ and does not unfairly _____ the jury against the defendant by appealing to emotion rather than fact. The prosecution will usually try to build its case through _____ examination of its witnesses, which the defense will counter with a _____ -examination of its own. The defense's main goal is to create _____ _____ concerning the defendant's guilt in the minds of as many jurors as possible.

Rebuttal Evidence given to counteract or disprove evidence presented by the opposing party.

Closing Arguments Arguments made by each side's attorney after the cases for the plaintiff and defendant have been presented.

FIGURE 10.5 The Closing Argument

Defense attorneys for Keith Kidwell, charged with murdering convenience store worker Crayton Nelms in Bull City, North Carolina, argued that the case against their client was "flawed to the core." In her closing argument, district attorney Tracey Cline focused on one particular piece of evidence to contradict this assertion:

> Inside that [store] that morning, there were footprints, shoe impressions. All the ones that were in blood—and I'm not talking about what the kids put on their face at Halloween. Real blood. Blood that had once run warm inside a body. But all of the shoe prints in blood can be traced to Mr. Kidwell's shoes. Outside sole design, same physical size, general wear, similar features. Scientific words. You, each of you, had in your hands the picture of that bloody shoe print on Mr. Nelms' back and matched it up—I said matched—with [Kidwell's] shoe. Coincidence?

The jury found Kidwell guilty of first degree murder, and he was sentenced to life in prison without the possibility of parole.

Source: For a complete transcript of Cline's closing argument, go to **media2.newsobserver.com/smedia/2011/09/05/09/47/qSaKF. So.156.pdf**.

THE FINAL STEPS OF THE TRIAL AND POSTCONVICTION PROCEDURES

After closing arguments, the outcome of the trial is in the hands of the jury. In this section, we examine the efforts to give jurors the means necessary to make informed decisions about the guilt or innocence of the accused. We also look at the posttrial motions that can occur when the defense feels that the jurors, prosecution, or trial judge made errors that necessitate remedial legal action.

Jury Instructions

Before the jurors begin their deliberations, the judge gives the jury a **charge,** summing up the case and instructing the jurors on the rules of law that apply to the issues in the case. These charges, also called jury instructions, are usually prepared during a special *charging conference* involving the judge and the trial attorneys. In this conference, the attorneys suggest the instructions they would like to see be sent to the jurors, but the judge makes the final decision as to the charges submitted. If the defense attorney disagrees with the charges sent to the jury, he or she can enter an objection, thereby setting the stage for a possible appeal.

THE JUDGE'S ROLE The judge usually begins by explaining basic legal principles, such as the need to find the defendant guilty beyond a reasonable doubt. Then the jury instructions narrow to the specifics of the case at hand, and the judge explains to the jurors what facts the prosecution must have proved to obtain a conviction. If the defense strategy centers on an affirmative defense such as insanity or entrapment, the judge will discuss the relevant legal principles that the defense must have proved to obtain an acquittal.

The final segment of the charges discusses possible verdicts. These always include "guilty" and "not guilty," but some cases also allow for the jury to find "guilt by reason of

Charge The judge's instructions to the jury following the attorneys' closing arguments.

insanity" or "guilty but mentally ill." Juries are often charged with determining the seriousness of the crime as well, such as deciding whether a homicide is murder in the first degree, murder in the second degree, or manslaughter.

UNDERSTANDING THE INSTRUCTIONS A serious problem with jury instructions is that jurors often do not seem to understand them.[51] This situation is hardly surprising, as most average Americans do not have the education or legal background to disentangle the somewhat unfathomable jargon of the law. One study came to the unfortunate conclusion that juries that received no instructions whatsoever were basically as well equipped—or poorly equipped, as the case may be—as juries that did receive instructions.[52]

One solution is to simplify the language of the jury instructions. In 2005, California became the first state to move in this direction when state officials approved 2,048 pages of new "plain language" criminal jury instructions. So, for example, a juror in California will no longer read, "The law does not undertake to measure in units of time the length of the period during which the thought must be pondered before it can ripen into an intent to kill which is truly deliberate and premeditated." Instead, he or she will read, "The length of time the person spends considering whether to kill does not alone determine whether the killing is deliberate and premeditated."[53] Following California's lead, a number of states have taken similar steps to give jurors a better chance of properly following the judge's instructions.

Jury Deliberation

After receiving the charge, the jury begins its deliberations. Jury deliberation is a somewhat mysterious process, as it takes place in complete seclusion. Most of what is known about how a jury deliberates comes from mock trials or interviews with jurors after the verdict has been reached. A general picture of the deliberation process constructed from this research shows that the romantic notion of jurors with high-minded ideals of justice making eloquent speeches is, for the most part, not the reality. In approximately three out of every ten cases, the initial vote by the jury led to a unanimous decision. In 90 percent of the remaining cases, the majority eventually dictated the decision.[54]

One of the most important instructions that a judge normally gives the jurors is that they should seek no outside information during deliberation. The idea is that jurors should base their verdict *only* on the evidence that the judge has deemed admissible. In extreme cases, the judge will order that the jury be *sequestered,* or isolated from the public, during the trial and deliberation stages of the proceedings. Sequestration is used when deliberations are expected to be lengthy, or the trial is attracting a high amount of interest and the judge wants to keep the jury from being unduly influenced. Juries are usually sequestered in hotels and kept under the watch and guard of officers of the court.

The importance of *total* sequestration is reflected in a recent Colorado Supreme Court decision to overturn the death penalty of a man who was sentenced after the jurors consulted a Bible during deliberations. The court held that a Bible constituted an improper outside influence and a reliance on a "higher authority."[55]

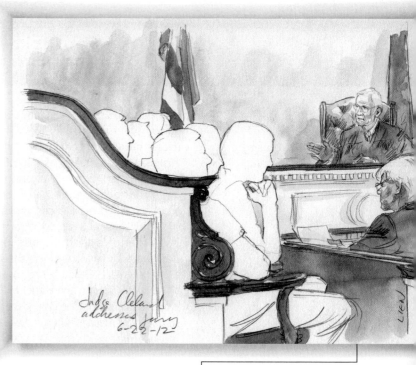

■ During the 2012 child sex abuse trial of former Penn State assistant football coach Jerry Sandusky in Bellefonte, Pennsylvania, Judge John Cleland told the jury, "It is not necessarily a crime for an adult to touch a child." The judge also said, "If [Sandusky] did not act out of sexual desire then he did not commit a crime even if he did act with poor judgment." Why do jurors need to hear these kinds of basic legal principles before they begin deliberating? Stringer/Reuters /Landov

Champion Studio/Shutterstock.com

One former juror, fresh from trial, complained that the members of the courtroom work group had not provided the jury with enough information to render a fair verdict. "We felt deeply frustrated at our inability to fill those gaps in our knowledge," he added. Until recently, frustrated jury members have lacked the means to carry out their own investigations in court. Today, however, jurors with smartphones and tablet computers can easily access news stories and online research tools. With these wireless devices, they can look up legal terms, blog and tweet about their experiences, and sometimes even try to contact other participants in the trial through "friend" requests on social media Web sites.

This access can cause serious problems for judges, whose responsibility it is to ensure that no outside information taints the jury's decision. During deliberations at the end of one recent trial in Florida concerning illegal Internet drug sales, the judge found that nine of the twelve jurors had conducted Google research about the case. One jury member even discovered that the defendant had previously prescribed drugs later used in a double suicide—information that the defense had successfully argued should be kept out of court. The judge had no choice but to declare a *mistrial,* requiring that the proceedings start again with a different jury.

Thinking about Wireless Devices in the Courtroom
The Sixth Amendment guarantees the accused the right to trial by an "impartial jury." How does the use of wireless devices in the courtroom threaten this right?

The Verdict

Once it has reached a decision, the jury issues a **verdict.** The most common verdicts are guilty and not guilty, though, as we have seen, juries may signify different degrees of guilt if instructed to do so. Following the announcement of a guilty or not guilty verdict, the jurors are discharged, and the jury trial proceedings are finished.

When a jury in a criminal trial is unable to agree on a unanimous verdict—or a majority in certain states—it returns with no decision. This is known as a **hung jury.** Following a hung jury, the judge will declare a mistrial, and the case will be tried again in front of a different jury if the prosecution decides to pursue the matter a second time. A judge can do little to reverse a hung jury, considering that "no decision" is just as legitimate a verdict as guilty or not guilty. In some states, if there are only a few dissenters to the majority view, a judge can send the jury back to the jury room under a set of rules set forth more than a century ago by the Supreme Court in *Allen v. United States* (1896).[56] The **Allen Charge,** as this instruction is called, asks the jurors in the minority to reconsider the majority opinion. Many jurisdictions do not allow *Allen* Charges on the ground that they improperly coerce jurors with the minority opinion to change their minds.[57]

For all of the attention they receive, hung juries are relatively rare. Juries are unable to come to a decision in only about 6 percent of all cases.[58] Furthermore, juries may be more lenient (or easy to "trick") than is generally perceived. One study found that juries were six times more likely than judges (in bench trials) to acquit a person who turns out to be guilty.[59] This statistic raises the question of *jury nullification,* which occurs when jurors "nullify" by using their own judgment to reach a verdict rather than following judicial instructions or the law.

Verdict A formal decision made by the jury.

Hung Jury A jury whose members are so irreconcilably divided in their opinions that they cannot reach a verdict.

Allen Charge An instruction by a judge to a deadlocked jury with only a few dissenters that asks the jurors in the minority to reconsider the majority opinion.

Although there is no way to measure the amount of jury nullification in American courts, it is believed to occur most often in cases involving controversial issues such as race, the death penalty, or drug offenses. Several years ago, for example, a drug case in Missoula, Montana, never made it to trial because prosecutors could not find enough jurors willing to convict someone of possessing one-sixteenth of an ounce of marijuana.[60]

Appeals

Even if a defendant is found guilty, the trial process is not necessarily over. In our criminal justice system, a person convicted of a crime has a right to appeal. An **appeal** is the process of seeking a higher court's review of a lower court's decision for the purpose of correcting or changing the lower court's judgment. A defendant who loses a case in a trial court cannot automatically appeal the conviction. The defendant normally must first be able to show that the trial court acted improperly on a question of law. Common reasons for appeals include the introduction of tainted evidence by the prosecution or faulty jury instructions delivered by the trial judge. In federal courts, about 18 percent of criminal convictions are appealed.[61]

DOUBLE JEOPARDY The appeals process is available only to the defense. If a jury finds the accused not guilty, the prosecution cannot appeal to have the decision reversed. To do so would infringe on the defendant's Fifth Amendment rights against multiple trials for the same offense. This guarantee against being tried a second time for the same crime is known as protection from **double jeopardy.** The prohibition against double jeopardy means that once a criminal defendant is found not guilty of a particular crime, the government may not reindict the person and retry him or her for the same crime. (Some nations allow for such retrials, as explained in the feature *Comparative Criminal Justice—Double Trouble* on the next page.)

The basic idea behind the double jeopardy clause, in the words of Supreme Court Justice Hugo Black, is that the state should not be allowed to

> make repeated attempts to convict an individual for an alleged offense, thereby subjecting him to embarrassment, expense, and ordeal and compelling him to live in a continuing state of anxiety and insecurity, as well as enhancing the possibility that though innocent he may be found guilty.[62]

There are several nuances to this rule, however. First, one state's prosecution will not prevent a different state or the federal government from prosecuting the same crime. Second, acquitted defendants can be sued in *civil* court for circumstances arising from the alleged wrongdoing on the theory that they are not being tried for the same *crime* twice. Third, a hung jury is *not* an acquittal for purposes of double jeopardy. So, if a jury is deadlocked, the government is free to seek a new trial.

THE APPEAL PROCESS There are two basic reasons for the appeal process. The first is to correct an error made during the initial trial. The second is to review policy. Because of this second function, the appellate courts are an important part of the flexible nature of the criminal justice system. When existing law has ceased to be effective or no longer reflects the values of society, an appellate court can effectively change the law through its decisions and the precedents that it sets.[63] A classic example was the *Miranda v. Arizona* decision (see Chapter 7), which, although it failed to change the fate of the defendant (he was found guilty on retrial), had a far-reaching impact on custodial interrogation of suspects.

It is also important to understand that once the appeal process begins, the defendant is no longer presumed innocent. The burden of proof has shifted, and the defendant is obligated to prove that her or his conviction should be overturned. The method of

LEARNING **8** OBJECTIVE Delineate circumstances in which a criminal defendant may be tried a second time for the same act.

DOUBLE TROUBLE

American college student Amanda Knox's long Italian nightmare began in Perugia on November 6, 2007. That day, she was arrested, along with her boyfriend, for killing her British roommate Meredith Kercher. In 2009, Knox (pictured at right) was convicted of murder, on the theory that Kercher's death was the result of a drug-fed orgy gone wrong. In 2011, an Italian appellate court overturned this conviction. The court based its ruling on shoddy investigative techniques by Italian law enforcement, which misread DNA evidence at the crime scene that pointed to a drug dealer named Rudy Guede as the obvious wrongdoer. After serving four years of a twenty-six-year prison sentence, Knox was freed and returned home to continue her education at the University of Washington in Seattle.

In March 2013, however, Italy's Court of Cassation reversed Knox's 2011 acquittal and ordered that her case be reviewed. This created the possibility that she would face a new trial and be convicted, again, for the same crime. In Italy, prosecutors routinely appeal acquittals. In the United States, because of constitutional protections against double jeopardy, defendants almost never face a second trial for the same crime. Knox called the Italian court's decision "painful," and it is unlikely that she will return to Italy to participate in the retrial.

AP Photo/ABC, Ida Mae Astute

FOR CRITICAL ANALYSIS

If Amanda Knox is found guilty in the second trial, the Italian government would probably ask the United States for her extradition (see Chapter 8). Should the U.S. government send her back to Italy under these circumstances? Why or why not?

LEARNING OBJECTIVE 9

List the five basic steps of an appeal.

filing an appeal differs slightly among the fifty states and the federal government, but the five basic steps are similar enough for summarization in Figure 10.6 on the facing page. For the most part, defendants are not required to exercise their right to appeal. The one exception involves the death sentence. Given the seriousness of capital punishment, the defendant is required to appeal the case, regardless of his or her wishes.

finality and Wrongful Convictions

Mandatory death sentence appeals lead to long stints on death row. According to the U.S. Department of Justice, prisoners sentenced to death spend, on average, almost fifteen years awaiting their execution.[64] Such a lengthy appeals process seems contrary to the concept of **finality,** which exists when the outcome of a criminal case can no longer be challenged by anyone. The benefits of finality are evident—once a case is over, all of the participants can redirect their energy to other activities. Furthermore, cases that drag on for years or even decades can weaken the public's confidence in the criminal justice system.

Several aspects of the criminal justice system discussed in this chapter directly promote finality. Statutes of limitations ensure that, after a reasonable amount of time, the government cannot prosecute most crimes. The protection against double jeopardy also protects suspects from the "fear and anxiety" of a second trial.

At the same time, however, finality also means that there is a point at which a convicted defendant will no longer be able to challenge the verdict, even though he or she may be innocent. For most of American history, finality had the upper hand over

Finality The end of a criminal case, meaning that the outcome of the case is no longer susceptible to challenge by prosecutors or the defendant.

innocence as far as postconviction procedures were concerned. Only during the past fifty years have appeals processes provided significant relief for those who wish to revisit aspects of the criminal trial after a final verdict has been delivered. The most serious threat to the primacy of finality, however, is the same DNA fingerprinting that has been a boon to law enforcement, as we saw in Chapter 6. As these techniques have become more effective, they have brought the problem of **wrongful convictions,** which occur when an innocent person is found guilty, into the national spotlight.

DNA EXONERATION DNA exonerates potential wrongdoers the same way it identifies them: by matching genetic material found at a crime scene to that of a suspect. (Or, conversely, by showing that the genetic material does not match the suspect's.) In 1998, for example, Johnny Williams was convicted of sexually assaulting a nine-year-old girl in Oakland, California. Despite the fact that he did not fit the girl's original description of her attacker, Williams was placed in a lineup and identified by the young victim. He told police more than forty times that he was innocent, but eventually confessed after being told that his DNA had been found on the girl's clothing. In 2013, new tests showed that the DNA traces on the clothing did not come from Williams, and his conviction was overturned.

According to the Innocence Project, a New York–based legal group, as of April 2013, 305 convicts have been exonerated by DNA evidence in the United States.[65] Given that state courts convict about 1.1 million adults each year,[66] this number may not seem very significant. People convicted of crimes do not have an automatic right to DNA checks of the evidence in their cases, however.[67] In most instances, the trial judge must approve the request, and if it is rejected, the convict must bring a lawsuit to force the issue.[68] Consequently, the DNA exonerations that have already taken place may represent a "random audit of convictions," meaning that the incidence of wrongful convictions may be a

■ On January 29, 2013, Doug Prade hugs a supporter in London, Ohio, after DNA evidence exonerated him of his wife's murder. Should prosecutors be disciplined for mistakenly bringing charges against innocent defendants such as Prade, who spent fifteen years in prison? Why or why not?
Phil Masturzo/*Akron Beacon Journal*/MCT/Newscom

Wrongful Conviction The conviction, either by verdict or by guilty plea, of a person who is factually innocent of the charges.

FIGURE 10.6 **The Steps of an Appeal**

1. The defendant, or *appellant,* files a **notice of appeal**—a short written statement outlining the basis of the appeal.

2. The appellant transfers the trial court record to the appellate court. This record contains items such as evidence and a transcript of the testimony.

3. Both parties file **briefs.** A brief is a written document that presents the party's legal arguments.

4. Attorneys from both sides present **oral arguments** before the appellate court.

5. Having heard from both sides, the judges of the appellate court retire to deliberate the case and make their decision. As described in Chapter 8, this decision is issued as a **written opinion.** Appellate courts generally do one of the following:

   • **Uphold** the decision of the lower court.

   • **Modify** the lower court's decision by changing only a part of it.

   • **Reverse** the decision of the lower court.

   • **Reverse and remand** the case, meaning that the matter is sent back to the lower court for further proceedings.

FIGURE 10.7 Wrongful Convictions and Unreliable Evidence

Johnny Williams, mentioned on the previous page, spent fourteen years in prison for attempted rape after being misidentified by the victim and making a false confession. Eyewitness misidentification and false confessions are two of the four most common reasons found for wrongful convictions later overturned by DNA evidence.

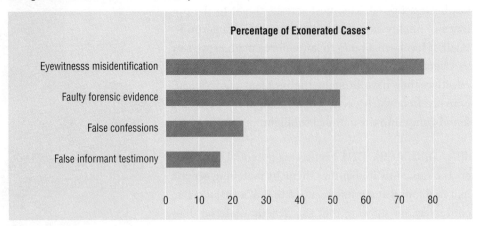

Percentage of Exonerated Cases*

Eyewitnesss misidentification
Faulty forensic evidence
False confessions
False informant testimony

0 10 20 30 40 50 60 70 80

* The total exceeds 100 percent because wrongful convictions can have more than one cause.
Source: The Innocence Project.

larger problem than the statistics indicate.[69] (Figure 10.7 above shows the most common causes of wrongful convictions.)

HABEAS CORPUS Even after the appeals process is exhausted, a convict many have access to one final procedure, known as ***habeas corpus*** (Latin for "you have the body"). *Habeas corpus* is a judicial order that commands a corrections official to bring a prisoner before a federal court so that the court can hear the convict's claim that he or she is being held illegally. A writ of *habeas corpus* differs from an appeal in that it can be filed only by someone who is imprisoned. In recent years, defense attorneys have successfully used the *habeas corpus* procedure for a number of their death row clients who have new DNA evidence proving their innocence.[70]

According to federal law, *habeas corpus* petitions must be filed no later than a year after the date of conviction. This restriction has proved problematic for inmates and their lawyers who may come across evidence of innocence after the deadline has passed. In 2012, a U.S. appeals court ruled that Floyd Perkins, a Michigan man serving a life sentence for murder, should be allowed to file a *habeas corpus* petition to prove his innocence despite missing the deadline by more than five years.[71]

Government lawyers appealed this decision, and the issue will ultimately be decided by the Supreme Court. At least one member of that body seems to disagree with extending the limits of finality in this manner. "Like other human institutions, courts and juries are not perfect," said Justice Antonin Scalia in an earlier case. "One cannot have a system of criminal punishment without accepting the possibility that someone will be punished mistakenly."[72]

SELF ASSESSMENT

Fill in the blanks and check your answers on page 343.

Once both the prosecution and the defense have completed their closing arguments, the judge will give the jury a _____ summing up the case and providing instructions on how to proceed. After the jury has _____ and reached a decision, it will announce a _____ of guilty or not guilty. If the jury cannot do so, a _____ jury occurs, and the judge will call a mistrial. If a defendant is convicted, he or she has the option of _____ this outcome based on a showing that the trial court acted improperly on a question of _____, not fact, during the proceedings.

Ankomando/Shutterstock.com

SOCIAL MEDIA & CJ

The Innocence Project strives to prevent wrongful convictions and reform the criminal justice system. To learn more about the organization, go to its Web site and click on the Facebook icon.

Habeas Corpus An order that requires corrections officials to bring an inmate before a court or a judge and explain why he or she is being held in prison.

CJ IN ACTION

RAPE SHIELD LAWS

Historically, the courtroom has been a hostile environment for victims of sexual assault. Because of a pervasive attitude labeled the "chastity requirement" by Professor Michelle Anderson of the City University of New York School of Law, rape victims who were perceived to be sexually virtuous were much more likely to be believed by jurors than those who had been sexually active.[73] If a woman had consented to sex before, so the line of thought went, she was more likely to do so again. Consequently, defense attorneys invariably and successfully focused on the accuser's sexual past, convincing juries that consent had been given in the present instance by establishing a pattern of consent in past ones. As we close this chapter, we will examine much-debated legislative efforts to make the courtroom "safe" for rape victims.

"UNCHASTITY" EVIDENCE

Rape shield laws keep specific evidence, including evidence about the victim's reputation and previous sexual conduct, out of the courtroom, except under certain circumstances.[74] Today, every state except Arizona has a rape shield law. (In Arizona, well-established case law, rather than a statute, declares evidence of the accuser's "unchastity" inadmissible.)[75] In 1978, Congress also imposed a rape shield law in federal courts.[76]

Rape shield laws do contain certain exceptions that allow the defense to use evidence of the accuser's prior sexual conduct to undermine the credibility of his or her testimony. For example, Federal Rule 412 states that evidence of "other sexual behavior" or the "sexual disposition" of a rape complainant is inadmissible *unless* it is offered *either* (1) to prove that a person other than the accused was the source of semen, injury, or other physical evidence, *or* (2) to prove consent *and* involves previous sexual behavior by the alleged victim with the defendant. In addition, the defense must show that the exclusion of the evidence would violate the constitutional rights of the defendant.[77]

THE CASE FOR RAPE SHIELD LAWS

- Without these laws, defense attorneys may subject victims of sexual assault to embarrassing and degrading cross-examination concerning their personal lives.

- These laws ensure that defendants are convicted or acquitted based on the relevant evidence, not the prejudices of jurors more focused on the sexual history of the accuser than on the facts of the case.

- These laws encourage victims to report incidents of sexual assault by protecting their privacy.

THE CASE AGAINST RAPE SHIELD LAWS

- The confrontation clause of the Sixth Amendment gives all defendants the right to question their accusers. By limiting this right, rape shield laws leave defendants in sexual-assault cases at the mercy of juries that do not know all the facts.

- In many instances, the victim's prior sexual history is relevant to the issue of whether she or he consented to the incident in question. These facts should not be hidden from the jury simply because they may cause an emotional reaction or deal with sexual issues.

- The many exceptions to rape shield laws, mentioned earlier, have effectively rendered them meaningless. According to the federal government, only 49 percent of those who have been sexually assaulted report the crime to the police.[78]

YOUR OPINION—WRITING ASSIGNMENT

A woman accuses two men of raping her in the back seat of a car. Both defendants claim that the sexual activity was consensual. At their trial, they want to present the following evidence from that night: (1) a fourth person had witnessed the accuser flirting aggressively with numerous men at a local bar; (2) the accuser had openly tried to seduce the older brother of one of the defendants; and (3) another witness had seen the accuser sitting on a soda crate in front of the defendants, one of whom was zipping up his pants.

Given the goals of rape shield laws and their exceptions discussed in this feature, which evidence, if any, concerning the above incident should be admitted before the jury? In cases such as this one, do you feel that rape shield laws properly balance the rights of the accuser and the rights of the accused? Before responding, you can review our discussions in this chapter concerning:

- Relevant and prejudicial evidence (page 328).

- The prosecutor's case (pages 328–329).

- The defendant's case (pages 331–333).

Your answer should include at least three full paragraphs.

CHAPTER SUMMARY

For more information on these concepts, look back to the Learning Objective icons throughout the chapter.

 Identify the basic protections enjoyed by criminal defendants in the United States. According to the Sixth Amendment, a criminal defendant has the right to a speedy and public trial by an impartial jury in the physical location where the crime was committed. Additionally, a person accused of a crime must be informed of the nature of the crime and be confronted with the witnesses against him or her. Further, the accused must be able to summon witnesses in her or his favor and have the assistance of counsel.

 Explain what "taking the Fifth" really means. The Fifth Amendment states that no person "shall be compelled in any criminal case to be a witness against himself." Thus, defendants do not have to testify if their testimony would implicate them in the crime. Witnesses may refuse to testify on this same ground. (Witnesses, though, are often granted immunity and thereafter can no longer take the Fifth.) In the United States, silence on the part of a defendant cannot be used by the jury in forming its opinion about guilt or innocence.

 List the requirements normally imposed on potential jurors. They must be (a) citizens of the United States; (b) over eighteen years of age; (c) free of felony convictions; (d) healthy enough to function on a jury; (e) sufficiently intelligent to understand the issues at trial; and (f) able to read, write, and comprehend the English language.

 Contrast challenges for cause and peremptory challenges during *voir dire*. A challenge for cause occurs when an attorney provides the court with a legally justifiable reason why a potential juror should be excluded—for example, the juror does not understand English. In contrast, peremptory challenges do not require any justification by the attorney and are usually limited to a small number. They cannot, however, be based, even implicitly, on race or gender.

 List the standard steps in a criminal jury trial. (a) Opening statements by the prosecutor and the defense attorney; (b) presentation of evidence, usually in the form of questioning by the prosecutor, known as direct examination; (c) cross-examination by the defense attorney of the same witnesses; (d) at the end of the prosecutor's presentation of evidence, motion

for a directed verdict by the defense (also called a motion for judgment as a matter of law in the federal courts), which is normally denied by the judge; (e) presentation of the defendant's case, which may include putting the defendant on the stand and direct examination of the defense's witnesses; (f) cross-examination by the prosecutor; (g) after the defense closes its case, rebuttal by the prosecution, which may involve new evidence that was not used initially by the prosecution; (h) cross-examination of the prosecution's new witnesses by the defense and introduction of new witnesses of its own, called the surrebuttal; (i) closing arguments by both the defense and the prosecution; (j) the charging of the jury by the judge, during which the judge sums up the case and instructs the jurors on the rules of law that apply; (k) jury deliberations; and (l) presentation of the verdict.

 Explain the difference between testimony and real evidence, between lay witnesses and expert witnesses, and between direct and circumstantial evidence. Testimony consists of statements by competent witnesses, whereas real evidence includes physical items that affect the case. A lay witness is an "average person," whereas an expert witness speaks with the authority of one who has professional training, advanced knowledge, or substantial experience in a specialized area. Direct evidence is evidence presented by witnesses as opposed to circumstantial evidence, which can create an inference that a fact exists, but does not directly establish the fact.

 Identify the primary method that defense attorneys use in most trials to weaken the prosecution's case against their client. To find a defendant guilty, a jury must believe beyond a reasonable doubt that he or she committed the crime. Therefore, defense attorneys will often present arguments and evidence designed to raise a reasonable doubt of guilt in the jurors' minds.

 Delineate circumstances in which a criminal defendant may be tried a second time for the same act. A defendant who is acquitted in a criminal trial may be sued in a civil case for essentially the same act. When an act is a crime under both state and federal law, a defendant who is acquitted in state court may be tried in federal court for the same act, and vice versa.

 List the five basic steps of an appeal. (a) The filing of a notice of appeal; (b) the transfer of the trial court record to the appellate court; (c) the filing of briefs; (d) the presentation of oral arguments; and (e) the issuance of a written opinion by the appellate judges, upholding the decision of the lower court, modifying part of the decision, reversing the decision, or reversing and remanding the case to the trial court.

QUESTIONS FOR **CRITICAL ANALYSIS**

1. Why is it important for the judge to tell jurors that a defendant's decision to remain silent during the trial cannot be taken as a sign of guilt?

2. How might the "CSI effect" have a positive impact on criminal trials from the standpoint of both prosecutor preparation and juror interest?

3. Police find a critically wounded man lying in the parking lot of a gas station. When they ask him what happened, he indicates that Mr. X shot him. Then, the man dies. Should the dead man's identification of Mr. X be allowed in court? Or is it inadmissible hearsay? Explain your answer. (To see how the United States Supreme Court ruled in a similar case, go to **www.scotusblog.com/case-files/cases/michigan-v-bryant**.)

4. Texas has a law called the Timothy Cole Compensation Act, under which people who are wrongfully convicted of crimes may collect $80,000 from the state for each year of unwarranted imprisonment. Do you think this is fair? Why or why not? What are the goals of this kind of legislation?

5. Why is the appeals process so important to the American criminal justice system? What would be some of the consequences if criminal defendants did not have the ability to appeal questionable convictions?

KEY **TERMS**

acquittal   317
Allen Charge   336
appeal   337
bench trial   316
challenge for cause   322
charge   334
circumstantial evidence   327
closing arguments   333
confrontation clause   329
cross-examination   329
direct evidence   327
direct examination   329

double jeopardy   337
evidence   325
expert witness   326
finality   338
habeas corpus   340
hearsay   330
hung jury   336
jury trial   316
lay witness   325
master jury list   320
motion for a directed verdict   331
opening statements   324

peremptory challenges   322
real evidence   325
rebuttal   333
relevant evidence   328
statute of limitations   316
testimony   325
venire   320
verdict   336
voir dire   321
wrongful conviction   339

SELF ASSESSMENT **ANSWER KEY**

Page 318: **i.** jury; **ii.** bench; **iii.** judge; **iv.** self-incrimination; **v.** innocent; **vi.** guilty; **vii.** state/prosecutor; **viii.** reasonable doubt

Page 324: **i.** *venire;* **ii.** *voir dire;* **iii.** cause; **iv.** peremptory; **v.** race; **vi.** gender

Page 333: **i.** testimony; **ii.** fact; **iii.** relevant; **iv.** prejudice; **v.** direct; **vi.** cross; **vii.** reasonable doubt

Page 340: **i.** charge; **ii.** deliberated; **iii.** verdict; **iv.** hung; **v.** appealing; **vi.** law

NOTES

1. Lawrence M. Friedman and Robert V. Percival, *The Roots of Justice* (Chapel Hill, NC: University of North Carolina Press, 1981).

2. Alexandra Natapoff, "Misdemeanors," *Southern California Law Review* 85 (2012), 105.

3. 407 U.S. 514 (1972).

4. 725 Illinois Compiled Statutes Section 5/103-5 (1992).

5. Bureau of Justice Statistics, *Felony Defendants in Large Urban Counties, 2006* (Washington, D.C.: U.S. Department of Justice, May 2010), Table 10, page 10.

6. 18 U.S.C. Section 3161.

7. 391 U.S. 145 (1968).

8. *Blanton v. Las Vegas*, 489 U.S. 538 (1989).

9. *Williams v. Florida*, 399 U.S. 102 (1970).

10. 435 U.S. 223 (1978).

11. *Apodaca v. Oregon*, 406 U.S. 404 (1972); and *Lee v. Louisiana*, No. 07-1523 (2008).

12. 332 U.S. 46 (1947).

13. Barton L. Ingraham, "The Right of Silence, the Presumption of Innocence, the Burden of Proof, and a Modest Proposal," *Journal of Criminal Law and Criminology* 85 (1994), 559–595.

14. 397 U.S. 358 (1970).

15. James P. Levine, "The Impact of Local Political Cultures on Jury Verdicts," *Criminal Justice Journal* 14 (1992), 163–164.

16. John W. Clark III, "The Utility of Jury Consultants in the Twenty-First Century," *Criminal Law Bulletin* (Spring 2006), 3.

17. Quoted in Colin Moynihan, "Wanted in Officer's Trial: Difficult-to-Shock Jurors," *New York Times* (February 9, 2013), A15.

18. *Lockhart v. McCree*, 476 U.S. 162 (1986).

19. *Witherspoon v. Illinois*, 391 U.S. 510 (1968).

20. John Kaplan and Jon R. Waltz, *The Trial of Jack Ruby* (New York: Macmillan, 1965), 91–94.

21. 380 U.S. 224 (1965).

22. 476 U.S. 79 (1986).

23. Eric L. Muller, "Solving the *Batson* Paradox: Harmless Error, Jury Representation, and the Sixth Amendment," *Yale Law Journal* 106 (October 1996), 93.

24. 499 U.S. 400 (1991).

25. 502 U.S. 1056 (1992).

26. *Snyder v. Louisiana*, 552 U.S. 472 (2008).

27. *Illegal Racial Discrimination in Jury Selection: A Continuing Legacy* (Montgomery, AL: Equal Justice Initiative, August 2010).

28. Catherine M. Grosso and Barbara O'Brien, "A Stubborn Legacy: The Overwhelming Importance of Race in Jury Selection in 173 Post-*Batson* North Carolina Capital Trials," *Iowa Law Review* 97 (2012), 1531.

29. Quoted in Shaila Dewan, "Study Finds Blacks Blocked from Southern Juries," *New York Times* (June 2, 2010), 14.

30. 511 U.S. 127 (1994).

31. Harry Kalven and Hans Zeisel, *The American Jury* (Boston: Little, Brown, 1966), 163–167.

32. Nancy Pennington and Reid Hastie, "The Story Model for Juror Decision Making," in *Inside the Juror: The Psychology of Juror Decision Making* (Cambridge, MA: Harvard University Press, 1983), 192, 194–195.

33. Federal Rule of Evidence 703.

34. Richard A. Epstein, "Judicial Control over Expert Testimony: Of Deference and Education," *Northwestern University Law Review* 87 (1993), 1156.

35. L. Timothy Perrin, "Expert Witnesses under Rules 703 and 803(4) of the Federal Rules of Evidence: Separating the Wheat from the Chaff," *Indiana Law Journal* 72 (Fall 1997), 939.

36. *Daubert v. Merrell Dow Pharmaceuticals*, 509 U.S. 579 (1993).

37. Committee on Identifying the Needs of the Forensic Science Community, *Strengthening Forensic Science in the United States: A Path Forward* (Washington, D.C.: National Academies Press, 2009), 269–278; Bradford T. Ulery, et al., "Accuracy and Reliability of Forensic Latent Fingerprint Decisions, *Proceedings of the National Academy of Sciences Early Edition* (April 5, 2011), 1–6; and Jason M. Tanger, Matthew B. Thompson, and Duncan J. McCarthy, "Identifying Fingerprint Expertise," *Psychological Science* (August 16, 2011), 995–997.

38. Lyn Haber and Ralph Norman Haber, "Scientific Validation of Fingerprint Evidence under *Daubert*," *Law, Probability, and Risk* 7 (2008), 87–109.

39. Donald E. Shelton, "Juror Expectations for Scientific Evidence in Criminal Cases: Perceptions and Reality about the 'CSI Effect' Myth," *Thomas M. Cooley Law Review* 27 (2010), at **lawreview.tmc.cooley.edu /Resources/Documents/1_27-1%20Shelton%20Article.pdf**.

40. Kyle Hightower, "Defense Focuses on DNA in Anthony Trial," *Associated Press* (June 16, 2011).

41. Quoted in Katie Zezima, "Judge Will Allow Jurors to See Video of 8-Year-Old Being Killed by Uzi at Gun Show," *New York Times* (December 8, 2010), A15.

42. Thomas J. Reed, "Trial by Propensity: Admission of Other Criminal Acts Evidenced in Federal Criminal Trials," *University of Cincinnati Law Review* 50 (1981), 713.

43. *Ibid.*

44. *People v. Zackowitz*, 254 N.Y. 192 (1930).

45. 725 I.L.C.S. 5/115-10.6 (West 2008).

46. Federal Rules of Procedure, Rule 804(b)(2).

47. Arthur Best, *Evidence: Examples and Explanations*, 4th ed. (New York: Aspen Law & Business, 2001), 89–90.

48. *Griffin v. California*, 380 U.S. 609 (1965).

49. Douglas D. Koski, "Alcohol and Rape Study," *Criminal Law Bulletin* 38 (2002), 21–159.

50. *United States v. Wright*, 625 F.3d 583, 611 (9th Cir. 2010).

51. Firoz Dattu, "Illustrated Jury Instructions," *Judicature* 82 (September /October 1998), 79.

52. Walter J. Steele, Jr., and Elizabeth Thornburg, "Jury Instructions: A Persistent Failure to Communicate," *Judicature* 74 (1991), 249–254.

53. Judicial Council of California, *Criminal Jury Instructions* (Eagan, MN: Thomson/West, 2005), no. 521.

54. David W. Broeder, "The University of Chicago Jury Project," *Nebraska Law Review* 38 (1959), 744–760.

55. *People v. Haran*, 109 P.3d 616 (Colo. 2005).

56. 164 U.S. 492 (1896).

57. *United States v. Fioravanti*, 412 F.2d 407 (3d Cir. 1969).

58. William S. Neilson and Harold Winter, "The Elimination of Hung Juries: Retrials and Nonunanimous Verdicts," *International Review of Law and Economics* (March 2005), 2.

59. Joseph L. Gastwirth and Michael D. Sinclair, "Diagnostic Test Methodology in the Design and Analysis of Judge-Jury Agreement Studies," *Jurimetrics Journal* 39 (Fall 1998), 59.

60. Gwen Florio, "Missoula District Court: Jury Pool in Marijuana Case Stages Mutiny," *The Missoulian* (December 19, 2010), at **missoulian.com/news /local/article_464bdc0a-0b36-11e0-a594-001cc4c03286.html**.

61. Bureau of Justice Statistics, *Federal Justice Statistics, 2009* (Washington, D.C.: U.S. Department of Justice, December 2011), 13, 18.

62. *Green v. United States,* 355 U.S. 184 (1957).

63. David W. Neubauer, *America's Courts and the Criminal Justice System,* 5th ed. (Belmont, CA: Wadsworth Publishing Co. 1996), 254.

64. Bureau of Justice Statistics, *Capital Punishment, 2010—Statistical Tables* (Washington, D.C.: U.S. Department of Justice, December 2011), Table 8, page 12.

65. The Innocence Project, "Innocence Project Case Files," at **www.innocenceproject.org/know**.

66. Bureau of Justice Statistics, *Felony Sentences in State Courts, 2006—Statistical Tables* (Washington, D.C.: U.S. Department of Justice, December 2009), 1.

67. *District Attorney's Office v. Osborne,* 557 U.S. 52 (2009).

68. Ethan Bronner, "Lawyers, Saying DNA Cleared Inmate, Pursue Access to Data," *New York Times* (January 4, 2013), A1.

69. Richard A. Rosen, "Innocence and Death," *North Carolina Law Review* (December 2003), 69–70.

70. William J. Morgan, Jr., "Justice in Foresight: Past Problems with Eyewitness Identification and Exoneration by DNA Technology," *Southern Regional Black Law Students Association Law Journal* (Spring 2009), 87.

71. *Perkins v. McQuiggin,* 670 F.3d 665 (2012).

72. *Kansas v. Marsh,* 548 U.S. 163, 199 (2006) (Scalia, J., concurring).

73. Michelle J. Anderson, "From Chastity Requirement to Sexuality License: Sexual Consent and a New Rape Shield Law," *George Washington Law Review* (February 2002), 51.

74. Michigan Compiled Laws Annotated Section 750.520j (West 1991).

75. *State ex rel. Pope v. Superior Court,* 545 P.2d 946, 953 (Ariz. 1996).

76. Federal Rule of Evidence 412(a)(1)–(2).

77. Federal Rule of Evidence 412(b)(1)(A)–(C).

78. Bureau of Justice Statistics, *Criminal Victimization, 2011* (Washington, D.C.: U.S. Department of Justice, October 2012), Table 8, page 8.

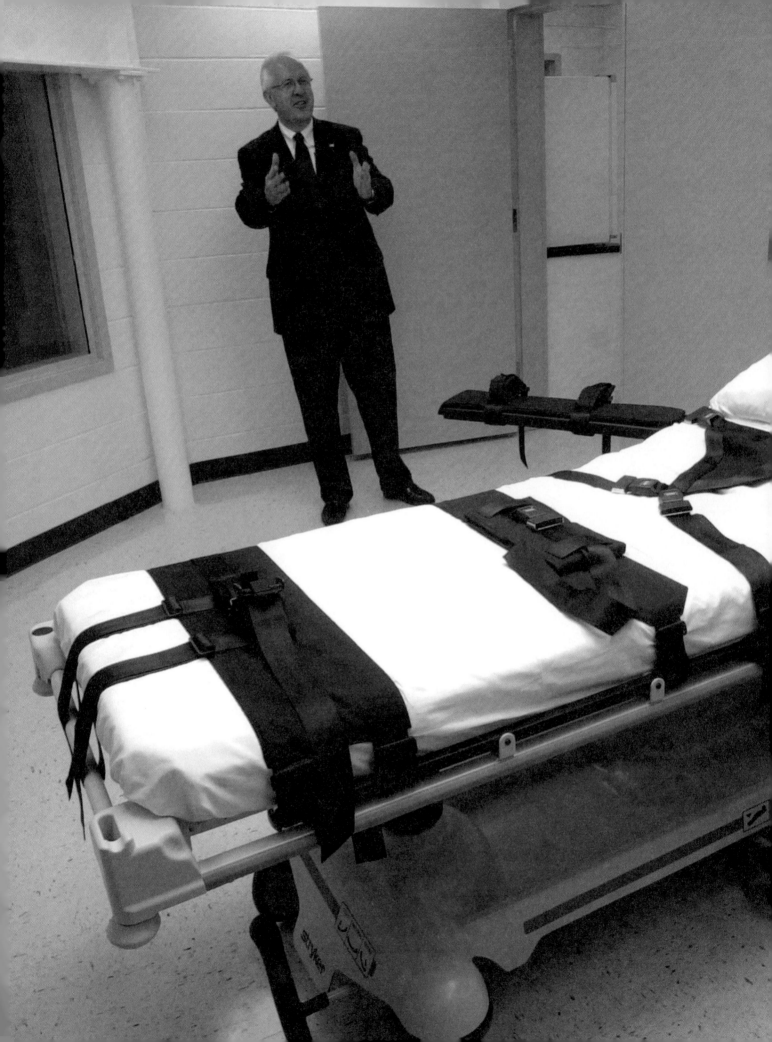

CHAPTER

11

Punishment and Sentencing

To target your study and review, look for these numbered Learning Objective icons throughout the chapter.

AP Photo/Dave Martin

ILLEGAL VIEWING

THREE WEEKS into their freshman year at Rutgers University in Piscataway, New Jersey, Dharun Ravi set up a hidden webcam to spy on roommate Tyler Clementi. Ravi then joined another Rutgers student in her room, where the pair briefly watched a live stream of Clementi embracing an older man. "I saw him making out with a dude. Yay," Ravi tweeted soon thereafter. Two days later, Ravi attempted to set up another viewing of his roommate's romantic activities. One day after that, Clementi took a train to nearby New York City and jumped to his death from the George Washington Bridge.

If Clementi had not committed suicide, Ravi's actions would have been, in the words of one observer, "a matter for the Rutgers resident advisers." Instead, the incident touched off a national debate on the evils of "gay bashing," and Ravi

AP Photo/Mel Evans

was arrested. In March 2012, a jury convicted him of invasion of privacy, tampering with evidence, and bias intimidation. Though these crimes generally carry light punishments, particularly for a first offender, Ravi faced a maximum of ten years in prison because of the bias intimidation charge. (For a review of the penalty enhancement aspects of hate crime laws, see Chapter 4.) Following the verdict, however, Judge Glenn Berman sentenced Ravi to spend thirty days in jail, complete three hundred hours of community service, receive counseling about "alternative lifestyles," and pay an $11,000 fine.

Many observers criticized the sentence as a "slap on the wrist." Ravi's punishment "doesn't feel harsh enough to deter other thoughtless young people from the same callous behavior," wrote columnist Lane Filler in *Newsday*. Judge Berman defended his decision by pointing out that, even though Ravi acted with "colossal insensitivity," nobody could have anticipated Clementi's suicide. "I can't find it in me to remand [Ravi] to state prison that houses people convicted of offenses such as murder, armed robbery, and rape," the judge said.

1. Did Judge Glenn Berman hand down an appropriate sentence in this case? Explain your answer.
2. Suzanne Goldberg, a law professor at Columbia University, compares Dharun Ravi's actions to those of a teenager who kills someone while driving and texting. "It shows the same disregard of human life and human dignity that stems in part from immaturity," she says. "The texters are not texting with the intent of causing someone's death, but if they cause injury or death, they are held accountable." What is your opinion of this comparison?
3. Do you think that a harsher punishment for Ravi would prevent other young people from acting with insensitivity toward homosexuals or other members of minority groups? Why or why not?

Dharun Ravi exits Middlesex County Jail in North Brunswick, New Jersey, after serving a short jail term for crimes related to spying on his college roommate with a webcam.

Gray wall studio/Shutterstock.com

THE PURPOSE OF SENTENCING

Professor Herbert Packer has said that punishing criminals serves two ultimate purposes: the "deserved infliction of suffering on evil doers" and "the prevention of crime."[1] Even this straightforward assessment raises several questions. How does one determine the sort of punishment that is "deserved"? How can we be sure that certain penalties "prevent" crime? Should criminals be punished solely for the good of society, or should their well-being also be taken into consideration? Should Judge Glenn Berman have sent a stronger "message" with a ten-year prison sentence in the Dharun Ravi case, or would such a punishment have unfairly made Ravi a "scapegoat" for a bigoted culture?[2]

Sentencing laws indicate how any given group of people has answered these questions, but do not tell us why they were answered in that manner. To understand why, we must first consider the four basic philosophical reasons for sentencing—retribution, deterrence, incapacitation, and rehabilitation. (For an introduction to these concepts, see Figure 11.1 below.)

Retribution

The oldest and most common justification for punishing someone is that he or she "deserved it"—as the Old Testament states, "an eye for an eye and a tooth for a tooth." Under a system of justice that favors **retribution,** a wrongdoer who has freely chosen to violate society's rules must be punished for the infraction. Retribution relies on the principle of **just deserts,** which holds that the severity of the punishment must be in proportion to the severity of the crime. Retributive justice is not the same as *revenge.* Whereas revenge implies that the wrongdoer is punished only with the aim of satisfying a victim or victims, retribution is more concerned with the needs of society as a whole.

The *principle of willful wrongdoing* is central to the idea of retribution. According to this principle, society is morally justified in punishing someone only if that person was aware that he or she committed a crime. Therefore, animals, children, and the mentally incapacitated are not responsible for their criminal actions, even though they may be a threat to the community.[3] Furthermore, the principles of retribution reject any wide-reaching social benefit as a goal of punishment. The philosopher Immanuel Kant (1724–1804), an early proponent of retribution in criminal justice, believed that punishment by a court

LEARNING OBJECTIVE **1** List and contrast the four basic philosophical reasons for sentencing criminals.

FIGURE 11.1 Sentencing Philosophies

In March 2013, Judge Vic VanderSchoor sentenced Dennis Huston to sixteen years in prison for embezzling nearly $3 million from government agencies in Franklin County, Washington. Although Huston's defense attorney asked for a lighter punishment because of his client's age (sixty-six years), the judge's sentence was in keeping with the four main philosophies of sentencing.

Retribution	Punishment is society's means of expressing condemnation of illegal acts such as embezzlement. In this case, Huston "violated the trust of each and every citizen of the county," said the judge.
Deterrence	Harsh sentences for embezzlement may convince others not to engage in that behavior. Prosecutors said that Huston's example would prevent other government employees "from going down that same road."
Incapacitation	While he is in prison, Huston will be unable to commit more crimes.
Rehabilitation	Huston reportedly used the stolen money to fuel his cocaine and gambling habits. While in prison, he can participate in treatment programs to address these problems.

Source: Kristen M. Kraemer, "Huston Sentenced to 16 Years in Franklin County Embezzlement Scandal," *Tri-City Herald* (Kennewick, WA) (March 27, 2013), at **www.tri-cityherald.com/2013/03/27/2331438/huston-sentenced-to-16-years.html**.

can never be inflicted merely as a means to promote some other good for the criminal himself or for civil society. It must always be inflicted upon him only because he has committed a crime. For a man can never be treated merely as a means to the purposes of another.[4]

In other words, punishment is an end in itself and cannot be justified by any future good that may result from a criminal's suffering.

One problem with retributive ideas of justice lies in proportionality. Whether or not one agrees with the death penalty, the principle behind it is easy to fathom: the punishment (death) often fits the crime (murder). But what about the theft of an automobile? How does one fairly determine the amount of time the thief must spend in prison for that crime? Should the type of car or the wealth of the car owner matter? Theories of retribution often have a difficult time providing answers to such questions.[5]

Deterrence

The concept of **deterrence** (as well as incapacitation and rehabilitation) takes a different approach than does retribution. That is, rather than seeking only to punish the wrongdoer, the goal of sentencing should be to prevent future crimes. By "setting an example," society is sending a message to potential criminals that certain actions will not be tolerated. Jeremy Bentham, a nineteenth-century British reformer who first articulated the principles of deterrence, felt that retribution was counterproductive because it does not serve the community. He believed that a person should be punished only when doing so is in society's best interests and that the severity of the punishment should be based on its deterrent value, not on the severity of the crime.[6]

GENERAL AND SPECIFIC DETERRENCE Deterrence can take two forms: general and specific. The basic idea of *general deterrence* is that by punishing one person, others will be discouraged from committing a similar crime. *Specific deterrence* assumes that an individual, after being punished once for a certain act, will be less likely to repeat that act because she or he does not want to be punished again.[7] Those who favored a more severe punishment for Dharun Ravi, whose offenses were covered in the opening of this chapter, often expressed themselves using principles of general deterrence. "You're making an example of Ravi in order to send a message to other people who might be bullying [and] to schools and parents and prosecutors who have not considered this a crime before," explained Marc Poirer of the Seton Hall University School of Law.[8]

Both forms of deterrence have proved problematic in practice. General deterrence assumes that a person commits a crime only after a rational decision-making process, in which he or she implicitly weighs the benefits of the crime against the possible costs of the punishment. This is not necessarily the case, especially for young offenders who tend to value the immediate rewards of crime over the possible future consequences. The argument for specific deterrence is somewhat weakened by the fact that a relatively small number of habitual offenders are responsible for the majority of certain criminal acts.

LOW PROBABILITY OF PUNISHMENT Another criticism of deterrence is that for most crimes, wrongdoers are unlikely to be caught, sentenced, and imprisoned. According to the National Crime Victimization Survey, only 49 percent of all violent crimes and 37 percent of all property crimes are even reported to the police.[9] Of those reported, only 48 percent of violent crimes and 19 percent of property crimes result in an arrest.[10] Then, as we saw in Chapter 9, case attrition further whittles down the number of arrestees who face trial and the possibility of imprisonment.

Thus, in general, potential criminals have less to fear from the criminal justice system than one might expect. Professors Paul H. Robinson of the University of Pennsylvania Law School and John M. Darley of Princeton University note that this low probability of punishment could be offset by making the punishment so severe that even the slightest chance of apprehension could act as a deterrent—for example, an eighty-five-year prison term for shoplifting or the loss of a hand for burglary.[11] Or punishments could be "advertised" to have a greater deterrent impact. In Iran, criminals are sometimes hanged in public.[12] Our society is, however, unwilling to accept these possibilities.

Incapacitation

"Wicked people exist," said James Q. Wilson. "Nothing avails except to set them apart from innocent people."[13] Wilson's blunt statement summarizes the justification for **incapacitation** as a form of punishment. As a purely practical matter, incarcerating criminals guarantees that they will not be a danger to society, at least for the length of their prison terms. At some level, the death penalty can also be justified in terms of incapacitation, as it prevents the offender from committing any future crimes.

In a Santa Ana, California, courtroom, Andrew Gallo reacts to his sentence of fifty-one years in prison for killing three people in a drunk driving automobile accident. How do theories of deterrence and incapacitation justify Gallo's punishment?
AP Photo/Mark Rightmire, Pool

THE IMPACT OF INCAPACITATION Several studies do support incapacitation's efficacy as a crime-fighting tool. Criminologist Isaac Ehrlich of the University at Buffalo estimated that a 1 percent increase in sentence length will produce a 1 percent decrease in the crime rate.[14] More recently, Avinash Singh Bhati of the Urban Institute in Washington, D.C., found that higher levels of incarceration lead to fewer violent crimes but have little impact on property crime rates.[15]

Incapacitation as a theory of punishment does suffer from several weaknesses. Unlike retribution, it offers no proportionality with regard to a particular crime. Giving a burglar a life sentence would certainly ensure that she or he would not commit another burglary. Does that justify such a severe penalty? Furthermore, incarceration protects society only until the criminal is freed. Many studies have shown that, on release, offenders may actually be more likely to commit crimes than before they were imprisoned.[16] In that case, incapacitation may increase likelihood of crime, rather than diminish it.

SELECTIVE AND COLLECTIVE INCAPACITATION Some observers believe that strategies of *selective incapacitation* should be favored over strategies of *collective incapacitation* for the best results. With collective incapacitation, all offenders who have committed a similar crime are imprisoned for the same time period. Selective incapacitation, in contrast, provides longer sentences for individuals, such as career criminals, who are judged more likely to commit further crimes if and when they are released. The problem with selective incapacitation, however, lies in the difficulty of predicting just who is at the greatest risk

Incapacitation A strategy for preventing crime by detaining wrongdoers in prison, thereby separating them from the community and reducing criminal opportunities.

to commit future crimes. Studies have shown that even the most effective methods of trying to predict future criminality are correct less than half of the time.[17]

Rehabilitation

For many, **rehabilitation** is the most "humane" goal of punishment. This line of thinking reflects the view that crime is a "social phenomenon" caused not by the inherent criminality of a person, but by factors in that person's surroundings. By removing wrongdoers from their environment and intervening to change their values and personalities, the rehabilitative model suggests, criminals can be "treated" and possibly even "cured" of their proclivities toward crime. Although studies of the effectiveness of rehabilitation are too varied to be easily summarized, it does appear that, in most instances, criminals who receive treatment are less likely to reoffend than those who do not.[18]

For the better part of the past three decades, the American criminal justice system has been characterized by a notable rejection of many of the precepts of rehabilitation in favor of retributive, deterrent, and incapacitating sentencing strategies that "get tough on crime." Recently, however, more jurisdictions are turning to rehabilitation as a cost-effective (and, possibly, crime-reducing) alternative to punishment, a topic that we will explore more fully in the next chapter. Furthermore, the American public may be more accepting of rehabilitative principles than many elected officials think. A survey by Zogby International, sponsored by the National Council on Crime and Delinquency, found that 87 percent of respondents favored rehabilitative services for nonviolent offenders, both before and after they leave prison.[19] (See the feature *Comparative Criminal Justice—The Norwegian Way* on the facing page to learn about a country where a national commitment to rehabilitation shapes sentencing practices.)

Restorative Justice

It would be a mistake to view the four philosophies we have just discussed as being mutually exclusive. For the most part, a society's overall sentencing direction is influenced by all four theories, with political and social factors determining which one is predominant at any one time. Political and social factors can also support new approaches to punishment. The influence of victims, for example, has contributed to the small but growing *restorative justice* movement in this country.

LISTENING TO THE VICTIM Despite the emergence of victim impact statements, which we will discuss later in the chapter, victims have historically been restricted from participating in the punishment process. Such restrictions are supported by the general assumption that victims are focused on vengeance rather than justice. According to criminologists Heather Strang of Australia's Center for Restorative Justice and Lawrence W. Sherman of the University of Pennsylvania, however, this is not always the case. After the initial shock of the crime has worn off, Strang and Sherman have found, victims are more interested in three things that have little to do with revenge: (1) an opportunity to participate in the process, (2) financial reparations, and (3) an apology.[20]

Restorative justice strategies focus on these concerns by attempting to repair the damage that a crime does to the victim, the victim's family, and society as a whole. This outlook relies on the efforts of the offender to "undo" the harm caused by the criminal act through an apology and **restitution,** or monetary compensation for losses suffered by the victim(s). Theoretically, the community also participates in the process by providing treatment programs and financial support that allow both offender and victim to reestablish themselves as productive members of society.[21]

THE NORWEGIAN WAY

In July 2011, thirty-three-year-old Anders Behring Breivik fatally shot sixty-nine people on Utoya Island off the coast of Norway. He also claimed responsibility for a bomb attack that killed another eight people in the capital city of Oslo. After a seven-month investigation, Norwegian prosecutors charged Breivik with committing a terrorist act. In the United States, Breivik would almost certainly have faced the death penalty for his multiple, violent offenses.

In Norway, however, a terror charge carries a maximum sentence of twenty-one years in prison. Indeed, the maximum sentence for most crimes in Norway, including premeditated murder, is twenty-one years. Like all European countries, Norway has no death penalty, and it has also abolished the life sentence as a possible form of punishment. This reflects the Norwegian criminal justice system's focus on rehabilitation rather than retribution or incapacitation. The goal in Norway is to return offenders to—rather than separate them from—society.

EXTENDED STAY

In August 2012, a panel of five judges found that Breivik is sane and sentenced him to "preventive detention." This means that, in 2033, Breivik's prison stay will be extended if he is found to pose a continuing threat to society—a likely outcome, given the brutality of his crimes. Still, the incident seems to have shaken the country's confidence in its system of punishment, which sees few offenders spending more than fourteen years behind bars. In a poll conducted six days after Breivik's attacks, 65 percent of Norwegians said that the penalties for serious crimes in their country were "too low."

FOR CRITICAL ANALYSIS

Norway's murder rate is minuscule—about 0.7 murders per 100,000 people. By comparison, the murder rate in the United States is 4.8 per 100,000. In general, violent crime is much more common in the United States than in Norway. How do you think these differences shape the two nations' divergent sentencing philosophies?

Convicted mass murderer Anders Behring Breivik makes a political statement during an appearance in an Oslo courtroom.
AP Photo/Frank Augstein, File

COMPENSATING THE VICTIM Programs based on the principles of restorative justice face several obstacles. Primarily, many criminal justice professionals regard these principles as too vague and "touchy-feely" to be useful.[22] Furthermore, federal and state sentencing laws do not address issues such as communication between victims and offenders. So supporters have to rely on sympathetic judges, prosecutors, and defense attorneys to implement restorative justice theories in court. Finally, many courts are unable or unwilling to enforce restitution orders. In recent years, courts in states such as Arizona ($831 million), Iowa ($533 million), and Pennsylvania ($638 million) have allowed massive amounts of uncollected restitution orders to build up.[23]

On a federal level, the Victims of Crime Act of 1984 established the Crime Victims Fund to provide financial aid for crime victims.[24] This program—financed by fines and penalties assessed on convicted federal offenders—distributes grants to state governments, which in turn pass the funds on to victims. In 2011, through the Crime Victims Fund, states paid nearly 150,000 claims to victims, totaling more than $430 million.[25]

Indeterminate Sentencing
An indeterminate term of incarceration in which a judge determines the minimum and maximum terms of imprisonment.

Determinate Sentencing A period of incarceration that is fixed by a sentencing authority and cannot be reduced by judges or other corrections officials.

VICTIM-OFFENDER DIALOGUE One increasingly popular offshoot of the restorative justice movement is *victim-offender dialogue (VOD).* This practice centers on face-to-face meetings between victims and offenders in a secure setting at the offender's prison. VOD allows the victims to speak directly to offenders about the criminal incident and how it has affected their lives. It also gives the offender a chance to apologize directly to the victim. Today, more than half of state corrections departments support VOD programs within their prisons.[26]

SELF ASSESSMENT

Fill in the blanks and check your answers on page 383.

The saying "an eye for an eye and a tooth for a tooth" reflects the concept of _____ as a justification for punishment. The goal of _____ is to prevent future crimes by "setting an example," while _____ purports to prevent crime by keeping offenders behind bars. Models of _____ suggest that criminals can be "treated" and possibly even "cured."

THE STRUCTURE OF SENTENCING

Philosophy not only is integral to explaining *why* we punish criminals, but also influences *how* we do so. The history of criminal sentencing in the United States has been characterized by shifts in institutional power among the three branches of the government. When public opinion moves toward more severe strategies of retribution, deterrence, and incapacitation, *legislatures* have responded by asserting their power over determining sentencing guidelines. In contrast, periods of rehabilitative justice are marked by a transfer of this power to the *administrative* and *judicial* branches.

Legislative Sentencing Authority

Because legislatures are responsible for making laws, these bodies are also initially responsible for passing the criminal codes that determine the length of sentences.

INDETERMINATE SENTENCING Penal codes with **indeterminate sentencing** policies set a minimum and maximum amount of time that a person must spend in prison. For example, the indeterminate sentence for aggravated assault could be three to nine years, or six to twelve years, or twenty years to life. Within these parameters, a judge can prescribe a particular term, after which an administrative body known as the *parole board* decides at what point the offender is to be released. A prisoner is aware that he or she is eligible for *parole* as soon as the minimum time has been served and that good behavior can further shorten the sentence.

Contrast indeterminate with determinate sentencing.

LEARNING
2
OBJECTIVE

DETERMINATE SENTENCING Disillusionment with the somewhat vague nature of indeterminate sentencing often leads politicians to support **determinate sentencing,** or fixed sentencing. As the name implies, in determinate sentencing an offender serves exactly the amount of time to which she or he is sentenced (minus "good time," described below). For example, if the legislature deems that the punishment for a first-time armed robber is ten years, then the judge has no choice but to impose a sentence of ten years, and the criminal will serve ten years minus good time before being freed.

"GOOD TIME" AND TRUTH IN SENTENCING Often, the amount of time prescribed by a judge bears little relation to the amount of time the offender actually spends behind bars. In states with indeterminate sentencing, parole boards have broad powers to release prisoners once they have served the minimum portion of their sentence. Furthermore, all but four states offer prisoners the opportunity to reduce their sentences by doing "**good time**"—or behaving well—as determined by prison administrators. (See Figure 11.2 below for an idea of the effects of good-time regulations and other early-release programs on state prison sentences.)

LEARNING OBJECTIVE 3 Explain why there is a difference between the sentence imposed by a judge and the actual sentence served by the prisoner.

Sentence-reduction programs promote discipline within a correctional institution and reduce overcrowding, so many prison officials welcome them. The public, however, may react negatively to news that a violent criminal has served a shorter term than ordered by a judge and pressure elected officials to "do something." In Illinois, for example, some inmates were serving less than half their sentences by receiving a one-day reduction in their term for each day of "good time." Under pressure from victims' groups, the state legislature passed a **truth-in-sentencing law** in 1995 that requires murderers and others convicted of serious crimes to complete at least 85 percent of their sentences with no time off for good behavior.[27]

As their name suggests, the primary goal of these laws is to provide the public with more accurate information about the actual amount of time an offender will spend behind bars. The laws also keep convicts incapacitated for longer periods of time. Fifteen years after Illinois passed its truth-in-sentencing law, those murderers subject to the legislation were spending an average of seventeen years more in prison than those not subject to the legislation. For sex offenders in the state, the difference was 3.5 years.[28] Today, forty states have instituted some form of truth-in-sentencing laws, though the future of such statutes is in doubt due to the pressure of overflowing prisons.

Administrative Sentencing Authority

Parole is a condition of early release in which a prisoner is released from a correctional facility but is not freed from the legal custody and supervision of the state. Generally, after an inmate has been released on parole, he or she is supervised by a parole officer for a specified amount of time. The decision of whether to parole an inmate lies with the parole board. Parole is a crucial aspect of the criminal justice system and will be discussed in detail in Chapter 12.

For now, it is important to understand the role rehabilitation theories play in *administrative sentencing authority.* The formation in 1910 of the U.S. Parole Commission

"Good Time" A reduction in time served by prisoners based on good behavior, conformity to rules, and other positive behavior.

Truth-in-Sentencing Laws Legislative attempts to ensure that convicts will serve approximately the terms to which they were initially sentenced.

FIGURE 11.2 Average Sentence Length and Estimated Time to Be Served in State Prison

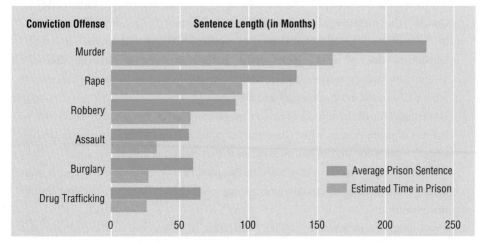

Source: Bureau of Justice Statistics, *National Corrections Reporting Program: Sentence Length of State Prisoners, by Offense, Admission Type, Sex, and Race* (January 20, 2011), "Table 9: First Releases from State Prison, 2008," at **bjs.ojp.usdoj.gov/index.cfm?ty=pbdetail&iid=2056**.

and similar commissions in the fifty states implied that the judge, though a legal expert, was not trained to determine when an inmate had been rehabilitated. Therefore, the sentencing power should be given to experts in human behavior, who were qualified to determine whether a convict was fit to return to society.[29]

Judicial Sentencing Authority

During the pretrial procedures and the trial itself, the judge's role is somewhat passive and reactive. She or he is primarily a "procedural watchdog," ensuring that the rights of the defendant are not infringed while the prosecutor and defense attorney dictate the course of action. At a traditional sentencing hearing, however, the judge is no longer an arbiter between the parties. She or he is now called on to exercise the ultimate authority of the state in determining the defendant's fate.

From the 1930s to the 1970s, when theories of rehabilitation held sway over the criminal justice system, indeterminate sentencing practices were guided by the theory of "individualized justice." Just as a physician gives specific treatment to individual patients depending on their particular health needs, the hypothesis goes, a judge needs to consider the specific circumstances of each individual offender in choosing the best form of punishment. Taking the analogy one step further, just as the diagnosis of a qualified physician should not be questioned, a qualified judge should have absolute discretion in making the sentencing decision. *Judicial discretion* rests on the assumption that a judge should be given ample leeway in determining punishments that fit both the crime and the criminal.[30] As we shall see later in the chapter, the growth of determinate sentencing has severely restricted judicial discretion in many jurisdictions.

JUDICIAL DISPOSITIONS Within whatever legislative restrictions apply, the sentencing judge has a number of options when it comes to choosing the proper form of punishment. These sentences, or *dispositions,* include:

1. *Capital punishment.* Reserved normally for those who commit first degree murder—that is, a premeditated killing—capital punishment is a sentencing option in thirty-two states. It is also an option in federal court, where a defendant can be put to death for murder, as well as for trafficking in a large amount of illegal drugs, *espionage* (spying), and *treason* (betraying the United States).

2. *Imprisonment.* Whether for the purpose of retribution, deterrence, incapacitation, or rehabilitation, a common form of punishment in American history has been imprisonment. In fact, it is used so commonly today that judges—and legislators—are having to take factors such as prison overcrowding into consideration when making sentencing decisions. The issues surrounding imprisonment will be discussed in Chapters 13 and 14.

3. *Probation.* One of the effects of prison overcrowding has been a sharp rise in the use of probation, in which an offender is permitted to live in the community under supervision and is not incarcerated. (Probation is covered in Chapter 12.) *Alternative sanctions* (also discussed in Chapter 12) combine probation with other dispositions such as electronic monitoring, house arrest, boot camps, and shock incarceration.

4. *Fines.* Fines can be levied by judges in addition to incarceration and probation or independently of other forms of punishment. When a fine is the only punishment, it usually reflects the judge's belief that the offender is not a threat to the commu-

nity and does not need to be imprisoned or supervised. In some instances, mostly involving drug offenders, a judge can order the seizure of an offender's property, such as his or her home.

OTHER FORMS OF PUNISHMENT Whereas fines are payable to the government, restitution and community service are seen as reparations to the injured party or to the community. As noted earlier, restitution is a direct payment to the victim or victims of a crime. Community service consists of "good works"—such as cleaning up highway litter or tutoring disadvantaged youths—that benefit the entire community. Along with restitution, *apologies* play an important role in restorative justice, discussed previously in this chapter. An apology is seen as an effort by the offender to recognize the wrongness of her or his conduct and acknowledge the impact that it has had on the victim and the community.

In some jurisdictions, judges have a great deal of discretionary power and can impose sentences that do not fall into any of these categories. This "creative sentencing," as it is sometimes called, has produced some interesting results. A judge in Painesville, Ohio, ordered a man who had stolen from a Salvation Army kettle to pass twenty-four hours as a homeless person. In Broward County, Florida, a man who shoved his wife was sentenced to "take her to Red Lobster," go bowling with her, and then undergo marriage counseling.[31] A Covington, Kentucky, teenager charged with disorderly conduct for falsely yelling "bingo" in a bingo hall was banned from saying that particular word for six months. Though these types of punishments are often ridiculed, many judges see them as a viable alternative to incarceration for less dangerous offenders.

The Sentencing Process

The decision of how to punish a wrongdoer is the end result of what Yale Law School professor Kate Stith and federal appeals court judge José A. Cabranes call the "sentencing ritual."[32] The two main participants in this ritual are the judge and the defendant, but prosecutors, defense attorneys, and probation officers also play a role in the proceedings. Individualized justice requires that the judge consider all the relevant circumstances in making sentencing decisions. Therefore, judicial discretion is often tantamount to *informed* discretion—without the aid of the other members of the courtroom work group, the judge would not have sufficient information to make the proper sentencing choice.

THE PRESENTENCE INVESTIGATIVE REPORT For judges operating under various states' indeterminate sentencing guidelines, information in the **presentence investigative report** is a valuable component of the sentencing ritual. Compiled by a probation officer, the report describes the crime in question, notes the suffering of any victims, and lists the defendant's prior offenses (as well as any alleged but uncharged criminal activity). The report also contains a range of personal data such as family background, work history, education, and community activities—information that is not admissible as evidence during trial. In putting together the presentence investigative report, the probation officer is

LEARNING OBJECTIVE 4 State who has input into the sentencing decision and list the factors that determine a sentence.

Presentence Investigative Report An investigative report on an offender's background that assists a judge in determining the proper sentence.

After Jason Householder, left, and John Stockum were convicted of criminal damaging for throwing beer bottles at a car, municipal court judge David Hostetler of Coshocton, Ohio, gave them a choice: jail time or a walk down Main Street in women's clothing. As you can see, they chose the dresses. What reasons might a judge have for handing down this sort of "creative" sentence?
AP Photo/Dante Smith/*Coshocton Tribune*

supposed to gain a "feel" for the defendant and communicate these impressions of the offender to the judge.

The report also includes a sentencing recommendation. This aspect has been criticized as giving probation officers too much power in the sentencing process, because less diligent judges would simply rely on the recommendation in determining punishment.[33] For the most part, however, judges do not act as if they were bound by the presentence investigative report. In the case that opened this chapter, for example, Judge Glenn Berman largely disregarded a report recommending that Dharun Ravi not receive any jail time or fine as punishment for his crimes.[34]

THE PROSECUTOR AND DEFENSE ATTORNEY To a certain extent, the adversary process does not end when the guilt of the defendant has been established. Both the prosecutor and the defense attorney are interviewed in the process of preparing the presentence investigative report, and both will try to present a version of the facts consistent with their own sentencing goals. The defense attorney in particular has a duty to make sure that the information contained in the report is accurate and not prejudicial toward his or her client. Depending on the norms of any particular courtroom work group, prosecutors and defense attorneys may petition the judge directly for certain sentences.

Because of the mechanics of plea bargaining, explained in Chapter 9, prosecutors have the ability to influence sentencing in ways that trouble many observers. For example, prosecutors can trade a promise of reduced prison time—through a plea bargain—for intelligence regarding ongoing criminal investigations. This practice, known derogatively as "snitching" on the part of an informant, is widespread. From 2008 to 2012, nearly 50,000 federal convicts, or about one in eight, were able to lessen their prison terms by providing information to federal law enforcement agents.[35] Many of these informants were able to reduce their sentences by as much as 50 percent.[36] Consequently, low-level criminals who do not have any information to trade often wind up with harsher sentences than their well-informed bosses.

SENTENCING AND THE JURY Juries also play an important role in the sentencing process. As we will see later in the chapter, it is the jury, and not the judge, who generally decides whether a convict eligible for the death penalty will in fact be executed. Additionally, six states—Arkansas, Kentucky, Missouri, Oklahoma, Texas, and Virginia—allow juries, rather than judges, to make the sentencing decision even when the death penalty is not an option. In these states, the judge gives the jury instructions on the range of penalties available, and then the jury makes the final decision.[37]

Juries have traditionally been assigned a relatively small role in felony sentencing, largely out of concern that jurors' lack of experience and legal expertise leaves them unprepared for the task. When sentencing by juries is allowed, the practice is popular with prosecutors because jurors are more likely than judges to give harsh sentences, particularly for drug crimes, sexual assault, and theft.[38]

Factors of Sentencing

The sentencing ritual strongly lends itself to the concept of individualized justice. With inputs—sometimes conflicting—from the prosecutor, attorney, and probation officer, the judge can be reasonably sure of getting the "full picture" of the crime and the criminal. In making the final decision, however, most judges consider two factors above all others: the seriousness of the crime and any mitigating or aggravating circumstances.

THE SERIOUSNESS OF THE CRIME As would be expected, the seriousness of the crime is the primary factor in a judge's sentencing decision. The more serious the crime, the harsher the punishment, for society demands no less. Each judge has his or her own methods of determining the seriousness of the offense. Many judges simply consider the "conviction offense," basing their sentence on the crime for which the defendant was convicted.

Other judges—some mandated by statute—focus instead on the "**real offense**" in determining the punishment. The "real offense" is based on the actual behavior of the defendant, regardless of the official conviction. For example, through a plea bargain, a defendant may plead guilty to simple assault when in fact he hit his victim in the face with a baseball bat. A judge, after reading the presentence investigative report, could decide to sentence the defendant as if he had committed aggravated assault, which is the "real" offense. Though many prosecutors and defense attorneys are opposed to "real offense" procedures, which can render a plea bargain meaningless, there is a growing belief in criminal justice circles that they bring a measure of fairness to the sentencing decision.[39]

MITIGATING AND AGGRAVATING CIRCUMSTANCES When deciding the severity of punishment, judges and juries are often required to evaluate the *mitigating* and *aggravating* *circumstances* surrounding the case. **Mitigating circumstances** are those circumstances, such as the fact that the defendant was coerced into committing the crime, that allow a lighter sentence to be handed down. In contrast, **aggravating circumstances,** such as a prior record, blatant disregard for the safety of others, or the use of a weapon, can

"Real Offense" The actual offense committed, as opposed to the charge levied by a prosecutor as the result of a plea bargain.

Mitigating Circumstances Any circumstances accompanying the commission of a crime that may justify a lighter sentence.

Aggravating Circumstances Any circumstances accompanying the commission of a crime that may justify a harsher sentence.

lead a judge or jury to inflict a harsher penalty than might otherwise be warranted (see Figure 11.3 below).

Aggravating circumstances play an important role in a prosecutor's decision to charge a suspect with capital murder. The criminal code of every state that employs the death penalty contains a list of aggravating circumstances that make an offender eligible for execution. Most of these codes require that the murder take place during the commission of felony, or create a grave risk of death for multiple victims, or interfere with the duties of law enforcement. (For a comprehensive rundown, go to **www.deathpenaltyinfo.org/aggravating-factors-capital-punishment-state**.) As you will see later in the chapter, mitigating factors such as mental illness and youth can spare an otherwise death-eligible offender from capital punishment.

JUDICIAL PHILOSOPHY Most states and the federal government spell out mitigating and aggravating circumstances in statutes, but there is room for judicial discretion in applying the law to particular cases. Judges are not uniform, or even consistent, in their opinions of which circumstances are mitigating or aggravating. One judge may believe that a fourteen-year-old is not fully responsible for his or her actions, while another may believe that teenagers should be treated as adults by criminal courts. A recent study in the journal *Science* found that, faced with a hypothetical situation in which a defendant suffered from brain damage, judges reduced the length of the sentence by about 7 percent.[40]

Often, a judge's personal philosophy will place her or him at odds with prosecutors. In November 2012, for example, three men from the West African country of Mali pleaded guilty in a New York City federal court to trafficking cocaine to raise money for international terrorist organizations. Federal prosecutors requested the maximum punishment of fifteen years in prison for each defendant. Instead, Judge Barbara S. Jones imposed far lesser sentences—about five years each for two of the men, and forty-six months for a third. Judge Jones based these decisions on her belief that the defendants, who had spent

FIGURE 11.3 **Aggravating and Mitigating Circumstances**

Aggravating Circumstances	Mitigating Circumstances
• An offense involved multiple participants, and the offender was the leader of the group.	• An offender acted under strong provocation, or other circumstances in the relationship between the offender and the victim make the offender's behavior less serious and therefore less deserving of punishment.
• A victim was particularly vulnerable.	
• A victim was treated with particular cruelty for which an offender should be held responsible.	• An offender played a minor or passive role in the offense or participated under circumstances of coercion or duress.
• The offense involved injury or threatened violence to others and was committed to gratify an offender's desire for pleasure or excitement.	• An offender, because of youth or physical impairment, lacked substantial capacity for judgment when the offense was committed.
• The degree of bodily harm caused, attempted, threatened, or foreseen by an offender was substantially greater than average for the given offense.	
• The degree of economic harm caused, attempted, threatened, or foreseen by an offender was substantially greater than average for the given offense.	
• The amount of contraband materials possessed by the offender or under the offender's control was substantially greater than average for the given offense.	

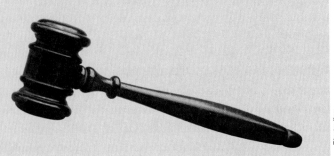

Photodisc

Source: American Bar Association.

most of their lives living in dire poverty, were motivated by financial need rather than anti-American, terrorist ideology.[41]

SELF ASSESSMENT

Fill in the blanks and check your answers on page 383.

_____ sentences set a minimum and a maximum amount of time a convict must spend in prison, whereas _____ sentences reflect the exact length of incapacitation, minus reductions for _____ _____ , or behaving well. Judges often rely on information contained in the _____ _____ report when making sentencing decisions. The primary factor in the sentencing process is the _____ of the crime for which the defendant was convicted. _____ circumstances allow a lighter sentence to be handed down, while _____ circumstances can lead to the imposition of a harsher penalty.

INCONSISTENCIES IN SENTENCING

For some, the natural differences in judicial philosophies, when combined with a lack of institutional control, raise important questions. Why should a bank robber in South Carolina and a bank robber in Michigan receive different sentences? Even federal indeterminate sentencing guidelines seem overly vague: a bank robber can receive a prison term from one day to twenty years, depending almost entirely on the judge.[42] Furthermore, if judges have freedom to use their discretion, do they not also have the freedom to misuse it?

Purported improper judicial discretion is often the first reason given for two phenomena that plague the criminal justice system: *sentencing disparity* and *sentencing discrimination*. Though the two terms are often used interchangeably, they describe different statistical occurrences—the causes of which are open to debate.

LEARNING **5** OBJECTIVE Explain some of the reasons why sentencing reform has occurred.

Sentencing Disparity

Justice would seem to demand that those who commit similar crimes should receive similar punishments. **Sentencing disparity** occurs when this expectation is not met in one of three ways:

1. Criminals receive similar sentences for different crimes of unequal seriousness.
2. Criminals receive different sentences for similar crimes.
3. Mitigating or aggravating circumstances have a disproportionate effect on sentences.

Most of the blame for sentencing disparities is placed at the feet of the judicial profession. Even with the restrictive presence of the sentencing reforms we will discuss shortly, judges have a great deal of influence over the sentencing decision, whether they are making that decision themselves or instructing the jury on how to do so. Like other members of the criminal justice system, judges are individuals, and their discretionary sentencing decisions reflect that individuality. Besides judicial discretion, several other causes have been offered as explanations for sentencing disparity, including differences between geographic jurisdictions and between federal and state courts.

GEOGRAPHIC DISPARITIES For offenders, the amount of time spent in prison often depends as much on where the crime was committed as on the crime itself. A comparison of the sentences for drug trafficking reveals that someone convicted of the crime in the Northern District of California faces an average of 78 months in prison, whereas a similar offender in northern Iowa can expect an average of 127 months.[43] The average

Sentencing Discrimination
A situation in which the length of a sentence appears to be influenced by a defendant's race, gender, economic status, or other factor not directly related to the crime he or she committed.

sentences imposed in the Fourth Circuit, which includes North Carolina, South Carolina, Virginia, and West Virginia, are consistently harsher than those in the Ninth Circuit, comprising most of the western states: 76 months longer for convictions related to kidnapping and 50 months longer for all offenses.[44] Such disparities can be attributed to a number of different factors, including local attitudes toward crime and available financial resources to cover the expenses of incarceration.

FEDERAL VERSUS STATE COURT DISPARITIES Because of different sentencing guidelines the punishment for the same crime in federal and state courts can also be dramatically different. In North Carolina, for example, a defendant convicted of distributing child pornography will rarely face a prison sentence of more than two years. If it is a first offense, he or she will most likely be placed on probation. Federal courts, however, have a mandatory five-year minimum prison term for any child pornography distribution conviction, with punishments often reaching twenty years because of aggravating circumstances.[45] Figure 11.4 below shows the sentencing disparities for certain crimes in the two systems.

Sentencing Discrimination

Sentencing discrimination occurs when disparities can be attributed to extralegal variables such as the defendant's gender, race, or economic standing.

RACE AND SENTENCING At first glance, racial discrimination would seem to be rampant in sentencing practices. Research by Cassia Spohn of Arizona State University and David Holleran of the College of New Jersey suggests that minorities pay a "punishment penalty" when it comes to sentencing.[46] In Chicago, Spohn and Holleran found that convicted African Americans were 12.1 percent more likely and convicted Hispanics were 15.3 percent more likely to go to prison than convicted whites. Another report released several years ago by the Illinois Disproportionate Justice Impact Study Commission found that African Americans were nearly five times more likely to be sentenced to

FIGURE 11.4 Average Maximum Sentences for Selected Crimes in State and Federal Courts

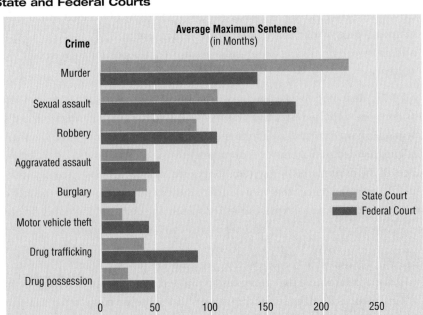

Source: Bureau of Justice Statistics, *Felony Sentences in State Courts, 2006—Statistical Tables* (Washington, D.C.: U.S. Department of Justice, December 2009), Table 1.6, page 9.

prison than whites for low-level drug crimes in that state.[47] Nationwide, about 38 percent of all inmates in state and federal prisons are African American,[48] even though members of that minority group make up only about 13 percent of the country's population and represent 28 percent of those arrested.[49]

Interestingly, Spohn and Holleran found that the rate of imprisonment rose significantly for minorities who were young and unemployed. This led them to conclude that the disparities between races were not the result of "conscious" discrimination on the part of the sentencing judges. Rather, faced with limited time to make decisions and limited information about the offenders, the judges would resort to stereotypes, considering not just race, but age and unemployment as well.[50] Another study, published in 2006, found that older judges and judges who were members of minority groups in Pennsylvania were less likely to send offenders to prison, regardless of their race.[51] Such research findings support the argument in favor of diversity among judges, discussed in Chapter 8.

Antwain Black, shown here celebrating with his mother, was one of thousands of inmates given an early release after federal crack cocaine sentencing laws were deemed discriminatory against African Americans. How does the appearance of discrimination—whether intended or not—harm the legitimacy of the criminal justice system? AP Photo/Seth Perlman

Comparing Sentences In addition, Spohn and Holleran found that none of the offender characteristics (race, age, employment) had an effect on the *length* of the prison sentence.[52] Not all the data support this premise, however. Several years ago, researchers from the University of Nevada at Reno found that African Americans received "significantly higher" minimum and maximum sentences than white defendants for felony convictions and drunk driving in that state.[53] National statistics on the matter are somewhat conflicting. According to the Bureau of Justice Statistics, African Americans' prison sentences are nine months longer, on average, for all violent crimes. Yet, for individual crimes such as weapons offenses and drug trafficking, whites, on average, receive marginally longer sentences.[54]

Crack Cocaine Sentencing Few sentencing policies have aroused as many charges of discrimination as those involving crack cocaine. Powder cocaine and crack, a crystallized form of the drug that is smoked rather than inhaled, are chemically identical. Under federal legislation passed in 1986, however, sentences for crimes involving crack were, in some instances, one hundred times more severe than for crimes involving powder cocaine.[55] The law was designed to combat the violence associated with the crack trade in American cities. Instead, say critics, it wound up harming those very areas, particularly African American communities. About 80 percent of federal crack defendants are African American.[56]

The U.S. Congress addressed this issue in 2010 by passing the Fair Sentencing Act, which reduces the legal disparity between the two forms of cocaine to eighteen to one for sentencing purposes.[57] A year later, the U.S. Sentencing Commission voted to apply the guidelines to those federal inmates already serving time for crack-related convictions.

This led to the immediate release of nearly 2,000 federal inmates, and, overall, lessened the sentences of about 6,600 such inmates by an average of twenty-nine months.[58] A number of states have taken similar steps to limit sentencing disparities between crack and powder cocaine offenses.[59]

WOMEN AND SENTENCING Few would argue that race or ethnicity should be a factor in sentencing decisions—the system should be "color-blind." Does the same principle apply to women? In other words, should the system be "gender-blind" as well—at least on a policy level? Congress answered that question in the Sentencing Reform Act of 1984, which emphasized the ideal of gender-neutral sentencing.[60]

Gender Differences In practice, however, this has not occurred. Women who are convicted of crimes are less likely to go to prison than men, and those who are incarcerated tend to serve shorter sentences. According to government data, on average, a woman receives a sentence that is twenty-nine months shorter than that of a man for a violent crime and nine months shorter for a property crime.[61] When adjusting for comparable arrest offenses, criminal histories, and other presentencing factors, Sonja B. Starr of the University of Michigan Law School found that male convicts receive sentences that are 60 percent more severe than those for women.[62] One study attributes these differences to the elements of female criminality: in property crimes, women are usually accessories, and in violent crimes, women are usually reacting to physical abuse. In both situations, the mitigating circumstances lead to lesser punishment.[63]

The Chivalry Effect Other evidence also suggests that a *chivalry effect,* or the idea that women should be treated more leniently than men, plays a large role in sentencing decisions. Several self-reported studies have shown that judges may treat female defendants more "gently" than males and that with women, judges are influenced by mitigating factors such as marital status and family background that they would ignore with men.[64]

In certain situations, however, a woman's gender can work against her. In October 2012, Texas prosecutors asked that Elizabeth Escalona receive forty-five years in prison for gluing her two-year-old daughter's hands to the wall and repeatedly beating the child. Instead, district judge Larry Mitchell sentenced Escalona to ninety-nine years in prison, more than double the prosecution's request. According to Keith Crew, a professor of sociology and criminology at the University of Northern Iowa, defendants who are seen as bad mothers often "get the hammer" from judges and juries.[65]

SELF ASSESSMENT

Fill in the blanks and check your answers on page 383.

Sentencing _____ occurs when similar crimes are punished with dissimilar sentences, while sentencing _____ is the result of judicial consideration of extralegal variables such as the defendant's race or gender.

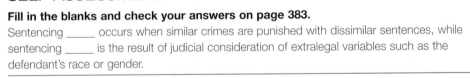

SENTENCING REFORM

Judicial discretion, then, appears to be a double-edged sword. Although it allows judges to impose a wide variety of sentences to fit specific criminal situations, it appears to fail to rein in a judge's subjective biases, which can lead to disparity and perhaps discrimination. Critics of judicial discretion believe that its costs (the lack of equality) outweigh its benefits (providing individualized justice). As Columbia law professor John C. Coffee noted:

If we wish the sentencing judge to treat "like cases alike," a more inappropriate technique for the presentation could hardly be found than one that stresses a novelistic portrayal of each offender and thereby overloads the decisionmaker in a welter of detail.[66]

In other words, Professor Coffee feels that judges are given too much information in the sentencing process, making it impossible for them to be consistent in their decisions. It follows that limiting judicial discretion would not only simplify the process but lessen the opportunity for disparity or discrimination. This attitude has spread through state and federal legislatures, causing extensive changes in sentencing procedures within the American criminal justice system.

Sentencing Guidelines

In an effort to eliminate the inequities of disparity by removing judicial bias from the sentencing process, many states and the federal government have turned to **sentencing guidelines,** which require judges to dispense legislatively determined sentences based on factors such as the seriousness of the crime and the offender's prior record.

STATE SENTENCING GUIDELINES In 1978, Minnesota became the first state to create a Sentencing Guidelines Commission with a mandate to construct and monitor the use of a determinate sentencing structure. The Minnesota Commission left no doubt as to the philosophical justification for the new sentencing statutes, stating unconditionally that retribution was its primary goal.[67] Today, about twenty states employ some form of sentencing guidelines with similar goals.

In general, these guidelines remove discretionary power from state judges by turning sentencing into a mathematical exercise. Members of the courtroom work group are guided by a *grid*, which helps them determine the proper sentence. Figure 11.5 on the following page shows the grid established by the Massachusetts sentencing commission. As in the grids used by most states, one axis ranks the type of crime, while the other refers to the offender's criminal history. In the grid for Massachusetts, the pink boxes indicate the "incarceration zone." A prison sentence is required for crimes in this zone. The yellow boxes delineate a "discretionary zone," in which the judge can decide between incarceration or intermediate sanctions, which you will learn about in the next chapter. The green boxes indicate the "intermediate sanction zone," in which only intermediate sanctions are to be levied.

Certain crimes are "staircased" in the Massachusetts grid, meaning that the same crime can result in different punishments based on other factors.[68] For example, assault and battery with a dangerous weapon (A&B DW) resulting in no injury or a minor injury is at offense seriousness level 3. When the crime results in a moderate but not life-threatening injury, it is at offense seriousness level 4. But when the injury is life threatening, the crime is at offense seriousness level 6—squarely in the "incarceration zone" regardless of the defendant's criminal history.

FEDERAL SENTENCING GUIDELINES In 1984, Congress passed the Sentencing Reform Act (SRA),[69] paving the way for federal sentencing guidelines that went into effect three years later. Similar in many respects to the state guidelines, the SRA also eliminated parole for federal prisoners and severely limited early release from prison due to good behavior.[70] The impact of the SRA and the state guidelines has been dramatic. Sentences have become harsher—by the mid-2000s, the average federal prison sentence was fifty months, more than twice as long as in 1984.[71]

Furthermore, much of the discretion in sentencing has shifted from the judge to the prosecutor. Because the prosecutor chooses the criminal charge, she or he can, in effect,

FIGURE 11.5 Massachusetts's Sentencing Guidelines

Sentencing Guidelines Grid

Level	Illustrative Offenses	Sentence Range				
9	Murder	Life	Life	Life	Life	Life
8	Manslaughter (Voluntary) Rape of a Child with Force Aggravated Rape Armed Burglary	96–144 Months	108–162 Months	120–180 Months	144–216 Months	204–306 Months
7	Armed Robbery Rape Mayhem	60–90 Months	68–102 Months	84–126 Months	108–162 Months	160–240 Months
6	Manslaughter (Involuntary) Armed Robbery (No Gun) A&B DW* (Significant Injury)	40–60 Months	45–67 Months	50–75 Months	60–90 Months	80–120 Months
5	Unarmed Robbery Unarmed Burglary Stalking in Violation of Order Larceny ($50,000 and over)	12–36 Months IS-IV IS-III IS-II	24–36 Months IS-IV IS-III IS-II	36–54 Months	48–72 Months	60–90 Months
4	Larceny (from a Person) A&B DW (Moderate Injury)* B&E** (Dwelling) Larceny ($10,000 to $50,000)	0–24 Months IS-IV IS-III IS-II	3–30 Months IS-IV IS-III IS-II	6–30 Months IS-IV IS-III IS-II	20–30 Months	24–36 Months
3	A&B DW (Minor or No Injury) B&E (Not Dwelling) Larceny ($250 to $10,000)	0–12 Months IS-IV IS-III IS-II IS-I	0–15 Months IS-IV IS-III IS-II IS-I	0–18 Months IS-IV IS-III IS-II IS-I	0–24 Months IS-IV IS-III IS-II	6–24 Months IS-IV IS-III IS-II
2	Assault Larceny (under $250)	IS-III IS-II IS-I	0–6 Months IS-III IS-II IS-I	0–6 Months IS-III IS-II IS-I	0–9 Months IS-IV IS-III IS-II IS-I	0–12 Months IS-IV IS-III IS-II IS-I
1	Driving after Suspended License Disorderly Conduct Vandalism	IS-II IS-I	IS-III IS-II IS-I	IS-III IS-II IS-I	0–3 Months IS-IV IS-III IS-II IS-I	0–6 Months IS-IV IS-III IS-II IS-I
	Criminal History Scale	**A** No/Minor Record	**B** Moderate Record	**C** Serious Record	**D** Violent/Repetitive	**E** Serious Violent

*A&B DW = Assault and Battery, Dangerous Weapon
**B&E = Breaking and Entering

The numbers in each cell represent the range from which the judge selects the maximum sentence (Not More Than). The minimum sentence (Not Less Than) is two-thirds of the maximum sentence and constitutes the initial parole eligibility date.

Sentencing Zones

- ☐ Incarceration Zone
- ☐ Discretionary Zone (incarceration/intermediate sanction)
- ☐ Intermediate Sanction Zone

Intermediate Sanction Levels

IS-IV	24-Hour Restriction
IS-III	Daily Accountability
IS-II	Standard Supervision
IS-I	Financial Accountability

present the judge with the range of sentences. Defendants and their defense attorneys realize this and are more likely to agree to a plea bargain, which is, after all, a "deal" with the prosecutor.[72]

JUDICIAL DEPARTURES Even in their haste to limit a judge's power, legislators realized that sentencing guidelines could not be expected to cover every possible criminal situation. Therefore, both state and federal sentencing guidelines allow an "escape hatch" of limited judicial discretion known as a **departure.** Judges in Massachusetts can "depart"

Departure A stipulation in many federal and state sentencing guidelines that allows a judge to adjust his or her sentencing decision based on the special circumstances of a particular case.

from the grid on the facing page if a case involves mitigating or aggravating circumstances.[73] In the case of Dharun Ravi that opened this chapter, Judge Glenn Berman made a significant departure from New Jersey guidelines that call for five-to-ten-year prison sentences for hate crimes.

Much to the disappointment of supporters of sentencing reform, a series of Supreme Court decisions handed down midway though the first decade of the 2000s held that federal sentencing guidelines were advisory only.[74] Since then, federal judges have taken advantage of their newfound freedom to depart from these guidelines. A 2012 study by the Transactional Records Access Clearinghouse found widespread sentencing disparities in federal courts, particularly in drug, weapons, and white-collar cases.[75] Furthermore, the U.S. Sentencing Commission reports that racial disparity in federal courts is again on the rise, with African American male defendants receiving sentences of about 20 percent greater lengths than white males who have been convicted of similar offenses.[76]

Mandatory Sentencing Guidelines

In an attempt to close even the limited loophole of judicial discretion offered by departures, politicians (often urged on by their constituents) have passed sentencing laws even more contrary to the idea of individualized justice. These **mandatory** (minimum) **sentencing guidelines** further limit a judge's power to deviate from determinate sentencing laws by setting firm standards for certain crimes. Forty-six states have mandatory sentencing laws for crimes such as selling illegal drugs, driving under the influence of alcohol, and committing any crime with a dangerous weapon. In Alabama, for example, any person caught selling illegal drugs must spend at least two years in prison, with five years added to the sentence if the sale takes place within three miles of a school or housing project.[77] Similarly, Congress has set mandatory minimum sentences for more than one hundred crimes, mostly drug offenses.

As might be expected, such laws are often unpopular with judges. After being forced to send a defendant to prison for fifty-five years for selling marijuana and illegally possessing a handgun, U.S. district judge Paul Cassell called the sentence "unjust, cruel, and irrational."[78] Furthermore, mandatory minimum sentences perpetuate many of the inconsistencies previously detailed concerning race, ethnicity, and gender. Nearly 70 percent of all convicts subject to mandatory minimum sentences are African American or Hispanic, and 90 percent of such convicts are men.[79]

"THREE-STRIKES" LEGISLATION **Habitual offender laws** are a common form of mandatory sentencing. Also known as "three-strikes-and-you're-out" laws, these statutes require that any person convicted of a third felony must serve a lengthy prison sentence. In many cases, the crime does not have to be of a violent or dangerous nature. Under Washington's habitual offender law, for example, a "persistent offender" is automatically sentenced to life even if the third felony offense happens to be "vehicular assault" (an automobile accident that causes injury), unarmed robbery, or attempted arson, among other lesser felonies.[80] Today, twenty-six states and the federal government employ "three-strikes" statutes, with varying degrees of severity.

"THREE STRIKES" IN COURT The United States Supreme Court paved the way for these three-strikes laws when it ruled in *Rummel v. Estelle* (1980)[81] that Texas's habitual offender statute did not constitute "cruel and unusual punishment" under the Eighth Amendment. Basically, the Court gave each state the freedom to legislate such laws in the

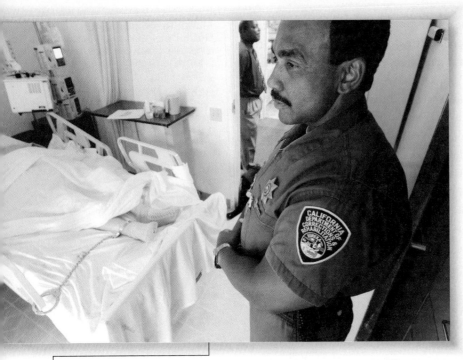

To reduce overcrowding in state prisons, California corrections officials are considering early release for seriously ill inmates such as the one shown here. How will the recent California ballot initiative changing the state's "three-strikes" law potentially alleviate prison overcrowding?
AP Photo/Noah Berger

manner that it deems proper. Twenty-three years later, in *Lockyer v. Andrade* (2003),[82] the Court upheld California's "three-strikes" law. The California statute allows prosecutors to seek penalties up to life imprisonment without parole on conviction of any third felony, including for nonviolent crimes. Leandro Andrade received fifty years in prison for stealing $153 worth of videotapes, his fourth felony conviction. A federal appeals court overturned the sentence, agreeing with Andrade's attorneys that it met the definition of cruel and unusual punishment.[83]

In a bitterly divided 5–4 decision, the Supreme Court reversed. Justice Sandra Day O'Connor, writing for the majority, stated that the sentence was not so "objectively" unreasonable that it violated the Constitution.[84] In his dissent, Justice David H. Souter countered that "[i]f Andrade's sentence is not grossly disproportionate, the principle has no meaning."[85] Basically, the justices who upheld the law said that if the California legislature—and by extension the California voters—felt that the law was reasonable, then the judicial branch was in no position to disagree.

Given the Court's *Andrade* decision, it was somewhat ironic when, in 2012, California voters decided that the state's three-strikes law was indeed unreasonable. That year, by a two-thirds vote, Californians passed a ballot initiative revising the law. Now, a life sentence will be imposed only when the third felony conviction is for a serious or violent crime.[86] Furthermore, the measure authorizes judges to resentence those inmates who are serving life prison terms in California prisons because of a nonviolent "third strike." An estimated 3,000 state inmates—including Leandro Andrade—became eligible for reduced sentences under the revised law.[87] In Chapter 13, we will see that numerous states are similarly rethinking mandatory minimum sentencing in an effort to reduce their large and costly prison populations.

Victim Impact Evidence

The final piece of the sentencing puzzle involves victims and victims' families. As was mentioned in the previous chapter, crime victims traditionally were banished to the peripheries of the criminal justice system. This situation has changed dramatically with the emergence of the victims' rights movement over the past few decades. Victims are now given the opportunity to testify—in person or through written testimony—during sentencing hearings about the suffering they experienced as the result of the crime. These **victim impact statements (VISs)** have proved extremely controversial, however, and even the Supreme Court has had a difficult time determining whether they cause more harm than good.

Victim Impact Statement (VIS) A statement to the sentencing body (judge, jury, or parole board) in which the victim is given the opportunity to describe how the crime has affected her or him.

BALANCING THE PROCESS The Crime Victims' Rights Act provides victims the right to be reasonably heard during the sentencing process,[88] and many state victims' rights laws contain similar provisions.[89] In general, these laws allow a victim (or victims) to tell his or her "side of the story" to the sentencing body, be it a judge, jury, or parole officer. In non-murder cases, the victim can personally describe the physical, financial, and emotional impact of the crime. When the charge is murder or manslaughter, relatives or friends can give personal details about the victim and describe the effects of her or his death. In almost all instances, the goal of the VIS is to increase the harshness of the sentence.

LEARNING
6
OBJECTIVE
Identify the arguments for and against the use of victim impact statements during sentencing hearings.

Most of the debate surrounding VISs centers on their use in the sentencing phases of death penalty cases. Supporters point out that the defendant has always been allowed to present character evidence in the hopes of dissuading a judge or jury from capital punishment. According to some, a VIS balances the equation by giving survivors a voice in the process. Presenting a VIS is also said to have psychological benefits for victims, who are no longer forced to sit in silence as decisions that affect their lives are made by others.[90] Finally, on a purely practical level, a VIS may help judges and juries make informed sentencing decisions by providing them with an understanding of all of the consequences of the crime. (For an example of a victim impact statement from a recent death penalty case, see Figure 11.6 below.)

THE RISKS OF VICTIM EVIDENCE Opponents of the use of VISs claim that they interject dangerously prejudicial evidence into the sentencing process, which should be governed by reason, not emotion. The inflammatory nature of VISs, they say, may distract judges and juries from the facts of the case, which should be the only basis for a sentence.[91] Furthermore, critics contend that a VIS introduces the idea of "social value" into the courtroom. In other words, judges and juries may feel compelled to base the punishment on the "social value" of the victim (his or her standing in the community, role as a family member, and the like) rather than the circumstances of the crime.

FIGURE 11.6 Victim Impact Statement (VIS)

In 2010, a Connecticut jury convicted Steven Hayes on sixteen counts of kidnapping, rape, and murder resulting from the deaths of Jennifer Hawke-Petit and her two daughters, seventeen-year-old Hayley and eleven-year-old Michaela. During the sentencing phase of the trial, Cynthia Hawke-Renn, Jennifer's sister, gave a VIS via videotape. A portion of the transcript is reprinted here. The jury eventually decided that Hayes deserved the death penalty for his crimes.

My sister gave me my middle name of Joy. I have always been a joyful person with a bubbly, happy-go-lucky attitude and you have taken that from me. I used to have trust and faith in humanity and you have taken that as well. I used to feel safe in my bed at night as did my children and you have destroyed that also. The very saddest thing in the world to me is that if you had just asked any of them for what you wanted you would have gotten all of it and more. . . . You did not have to murder or rape any of them. . . . We are to resist evil and I have to say I see you only as pure evil.

Along with her two daughters, Jennifer Hawke-Petit was tortured and murdered by Steven Hayes and an accomplice.
ZUMA Press/Newscom

Source: "Cynthia Hawke-Renn Delivers Statement at Hayes Sentencing," *Eyewitness News 3* (December 2, 2010), at **www.wfsb.com/news/25995640/detail.html**.

Capital Punishment The use of the death penalty to punish wrongdoers for certain crimes.

In 1991, the United States Supreme Court gave its approval to the use of VISs, allowing judges to decide whether the statements are admissible on a case-by-case basis just as they do with any other type of evidence.[92] Several years after this decision, Bryan Myers of the University of North Carolina at Wilmington and Jack Arbuthnot of Ohio University decided to test the prejudicial impact of the testimony in question. They ran simulated court proceedings with two groups of mock jurors: one group heard a "family member" give a VIS, while the other group did not. Of those mock jurors who ultimately voted for the death penalty, 67 percent had heard the VIS. In contrast, only 30 percent of those who did not hear it voted to execute the defendant.[93]

SELF ASSESSMENT

Fill in the blanks and check your answers on page 383.

With the aim of limiting judicial discretion, many states and the federal government have enacted sentencing _____. These laws have greatly _____ the length of prison sentences in the United States. The trend toward longer prison terms has also been influenced by _____ - _____ laws, a form of mandatory sentencing that requires increased punishment for a person convicted of multiple felonies. According to the United States Supreme Court, _____ _____ statements may be presented at sentencing hearings so long as they are not overly prejudicial.

CAPITAL PUNISHMENT— THE ULTIMATE SENTENCE

"You do not know how hard it is to let a human being die," Abraham Lincoln (1809–1865) once said, "when you feel that a stroke of your pen will save him." Despite these misgivings, during his four years in office Lincoln approved the execution of 267 soldiers, including those who had slept at their posts.[94] Our sixteenth president's ambivalence toward **capital punishment** is reflected in America's continuing struggle to reconcile the penalty of death with the morals and values of society. Capital punishment has played a role in sentencing since the earliest days of the Republic and—having survived a brief period of abolition between 1972 and 1976—continues to enjoy public support.

Still, few topics in the criminal justice system inspire such heated debate. Death penalty opponents such as legal expert Stephen Bright wonder whether "there comes a time when a society gets beyond some of the more primitive forms of punishment."[95] They point out that only twenty-three countries still employ the death penalty and that the United States is the sole Western democracy that continues the practice. Critics also claim that a process whose subjects are chosen by "luck and money and race" cannot serve the interests of justice.[96] Proponents believe that the death penalty serves as the ultimate deterrent for violent criminal behavior and that the criminals who are put to death are the "worst of the worst" and deserve their fate.

Today, about 3,100 convicts are living on "death row" in American prisons, meaning they have been sentenced to death and are awaiting execution. In the 1940s, as many as two hundred people were put to death in the United States in one year. As Figure 11.7 on the facing page shows, the most recent high-water mark was ninety-eight in 1999. Despite declines since then, states and the federal government are still regularly executing convicts. Consequently, the questions that surround the death penalty—Is it fair? Is it humane? Does it deter crime?—will continue to mobilize both its supporters and its detractors.

FIGURE 11.7 Executions in the United States, 1976 to 2012

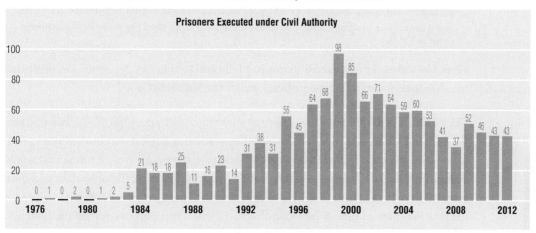

Source: Death Penalty Information Center.

Methods of Execution

In its early years, when the United States adopted the practice of capital punishment from England, it also adopted English methods, which included drawing and quartering and boiling the convict alive. By the nineteenth century, these techniques had been deemed "barbaric" and were replaced by hanging. Indeed, the history of capital punishment in America is marked by attempts to make the act more humane. The 1890s saw the introduction of electrocution as a less painful method of execution than hanging, and in 1890 in Auburn Prison, New York, William Kemmler became the first American to die in an electric chair.

The "chair" remained the primary form of execution until 1977, when Oklahoma became the first state to adopt lethal injection. Today, this method dominates executions in all thirty-two states that employ the death penalty. Sixteen states authorize at least two different methods of execution, meaning that electrocution (nine states), lethal gas (three states), hanging (three states), and the firing squad (two states) are still used on rare occasions.[97]

Many states employ a three-drug process to carry out lethal injections. First, the sedative sodium thiopental is administered to deaden pain. Then pancuronium bromide, a paralytic, immobilizes the prisoner. Finally, a dose of potassium chloride stops the heart. Members of the law enforcement and medical communities have long claimed that, if performed correctly, this procedure kills the individual quickly and painlessly. Others, however, contend that the second drug—the paralytic—masks any outward signs of distress and thus keeps observers from knowing whether the inmate suffers extreme pain before death.[98]

The Death Penalty and the Supreme Court

In 1890, William Kemmler challenged his sentence to die in New York's new electric chair (for murdering his mistress) on the grounds that electrocution infringed on his Eighth Amendment rights against cruel and unusual punishment.[99] Kemmler's challenge is historically significant in that it did not implicate the death penalty itself as being cruel and unusual, but only the method by which it was carried out. Many constitutional scholars believe that the framers never questioned the necessity of capital punishment, as long as due process is followed in determining the guilt of the suspect.[100] Accordingly, the Supreme Court rejected Kemmler's challenge, stating:

The Virginia Department of Corrections' electric chair is used only at the request of the inmate facing the death sentence. Why has lethal injection replaced the use of the "chair" in most American executions?
AP Photo/Virginia Department of Corrections

> Punishments are cruel when they involve torture or a lingering death; but the punishment of death is not cruel, within the meaning of that word as used in the Constitution. It implies there something inhuman and barbarous, something more than the mere extinguishment of life.[101]

Thus, the Court set a standard that it has followed to this day. No *method* of execution has ever been found to be unconstitutional by the Supreme Court.

SOCIAL MEDIA & CJ

Staffers at the **Death Penalty Information Center (DPIC)** regularly tweet about issues concerning capital punishment in the United States. To access this Twitter feed, go to the DPIC's Web page.

Ankomando/Shutterstock.com

THE *WEEMS* STANDARD For nearly eight decades following its decision in the *Kemmler* case, the Supreme Court was silent on the question of whether capital punishment was constitutional. In *Weems v. United States* (1910),[102] however, the Court made a ruling that would significantly affect the debate on the death penalty. In this case, the defendant had been sentenced to fifteen years of hard labor, a heavy fine, and a number of other penalties for the relatively minor crime of falsifying official records. The Court overturned the sentence, ruling that the penalty was too harsh considering the nature of the offense. Ultimately, in the *Weems* decision, the Court set three important precedents concerning sentencing:

1. Cruel and unusual punishment is defined by the changing norms and standards of society and therefore is not based on historical interpretations.
2. Courts may decide whether a punishment is unnecessarily cruel with regard to physical pain.
3. Courts may decide whether a punishment is unnecessarily cruel with regard to psychological pain.[103]

THE *BAZE* ENDORSEMENT In 2007, two convicted murderers in Kentucky asked the United States Supreme Court to invalidate the state's lethal injection procedure (see previous page) because of the possibility that it inflicted undetectable suffering. Nearly all of the scheduled executions in the United States were placed on hold while the Court deliberated this issue. In 2008, the Court ruled in *Baze v. Rees* that the mere possibility of pain "does not establish the sort of 'objectively intolerable risk of harm' that qualifies as cruel and unusual" punishment.[104]

Although executions resumed shortly after the *Baze* decision, a number of states changed the ingredients of the drug "cocktails" involved. Today, thirteen states have replaced sodium thiopental in their three-step processes with a similar sedative called pentobarbital, commonly used in this country to euthanize animals. In addition, seven states now use a single, very strong dose of pentobarbital to carry out the death penalty.[105]

Reforming the Death Penalty

In the 1960s, the Supreme Court became increasingly concerned about what it saw as serious flaws in the way the states administered capital punishment. Finally, in 1967, the Court put a moratorium on executions until it could "clean up" the process. The chance to do so came with the *Furman v. Georgia* case, decided in 1972.[106]

Identify the two stages that make up the bifurcated process of death penalty sentencing.

LEARNING
7
OBJECTIVE

THE BIFURCATED PROCESS In its *Furman* decision, by a 5–4 margin, the Supreme Court essentially held that the death penalty, as administered by the states, violated the Eighth Amendment. Justice Potter Stewart was particularly eloquent in his concurring opinion, stating that the sentence of death was so arbitrary as to be comparable to "being struck by lightning."[107] Although the *Furman* ruling invalidated the death penalty for more than six hundred offenders on death row at the time, it also provided the states with a window to make the process less arbitrary, therefore bringing their death penalty statutes up to constitutional standards.

The result was a two-stage, or *bifurcated*, procedure for capital cases. In the first stage, a jury determines the guilt or innocence of the defendant for a crime that has, by state statute, been determined to be punishable by death. If the defendant is found guilty, the jury reconvenes in the second stage and considers all aggravating and mitigating factors to decide whether the death sentence is in fact warranted. (See *Mastering Concepts—The Bifurcated Death Penalty Process* alongside.) Therefore, even if a jury finds the defendant guilty of a crime, such as first degree murder, that *may be* punishable by death, in the second stage it can decide that the circumstances surrounding the crime justify only a punishment of life in prison.

COURT APPROVAL The Supreme Court ruled in favor of Georgia's new bifurcated process in 1976, stating that the process removed the ability of a court to "wantonly and freakishly impose the death penalty."[108] The Court upheld similar procedures in Texas and Florida, establishing a model for all states to follow that would assure them protection from lawsuits based on Eighth Amendment grounds. On January 17, 1977, Gary Gilmore became the first American executed (by Utah) under the new laws, and today thirty-two states and the federal government have capital punishment laws based on the bifurcated process. (Note that state governments are responsible for almost all executions in this country. The federal government has carried out only three death sentences since 1963.)

THE JURY'S ROLE The Supreme Court reaffirmed the important role of the jury in death penalties in *Ring v. Arizona* (2002).[109] The case involved Arizona's bifurcated process: after the jury determined a defendant's guilt or innocence, it would be dismissed, and the judge alone would decide whether execution was warranted. The Court found that this procedure violated the defendant's Sixth Amendment right to a jury trial, ruling that juries must be involved in *both* stages of the bifurcated process. The decision invalidated death penalty laws in Arizona, Colorado, Idaho, Montana, and Nebraska, forcing legislatures in those states to hastily revamp their procedures. (To learn how a jury makes this difficult decision, see the feature *You Be the Juror—Life or Death?* on the following page.)

Some states still allow for a measure of judicial discretion in capital punishment decisions. In Alabama, Delaware, and Florida, the jury only recommends a sentence of death or life in prison. If the judge feels that the sentence is unreasonable, he or she can override the jury. In 2012, for example, an Alabama jury voted 9–3 that Gregory Henderson should serve a sentence of life in prison for running over and killing a law enforcement agent during a traffic stop. Nonetheless, Lee County circuit judge Jacob Walker, noting that the defendant showed no remorse for his intentional crime, overruled the jury's recommendation and sentenced Henderson to death.

MASTERING CONCEPTS
THE BIFURCATED DEATH PENALTY PROCESS

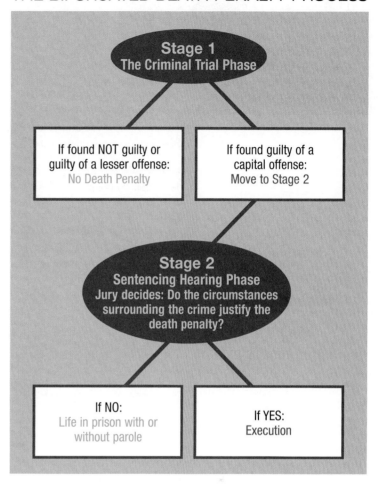

Stage 1
The Criminal Trial Phase

If found NOT guilty or guilty of a lesser offense:
No Death Penalty

If found guilty of a capital offense:
Move to Stage 2

Stage 2
Sentencing Hearing Phase
Jury decides: Do the circumstances surrounding the crime justify the death penalty?

If NO:
Life in prison with or without parole

If YES:
Execution

YOU BE THE Juror

LIFE OR DEATH?

THE SITUATION You are a member of the jury that found Robinson guilty of paying another man to kill his fourteen-year-old girlfriend Chelsea, who was pregnant with Robinson's child. During the trial, you heard evidence that Robinson wanted Chelsea dead so that she could not testify against him in a statutory rape trial. In your state, murder-for-hire is a capital offense, so now you and your fellow jury members must decide whether Robinson deserves the death penalty or, alternatively, life in prison for his crimes.

THE LAW Jurors must weigh aggravating factors against mitigating factors during the death penalty phase of criminal trials. If you believe that the aggravating factors surrounding Robinson's crime outweigh the mitigating factors, you must vote for him to be executed.

YOUR DECISION After presenting testimony from family and friends that Robinson experienced a difficult childhood without parental guidance, the defense attorney asks if there isn't "something in your heart that tells you that death isn't the appropriate punishment?" Indeed, according to state law, "mercy" can be a mitigating factor in this case. The prosecutor counters by saying, "Mercy? You can grant him the same mercy he granted Chelsea." The prosecutor also argues that the heinous nature of the crime is a strong aggravating factor, adding, "If this murder is not worthy of the death penalty, then what is?" After hearing these arguments, do you think that Robinson should receive the death penalty or a life prison sentence? Why?

[To see whether a Kansas jury chose the death sentence in similar circumstances, go to Example 11.1 in Appendix B.]

Somchai Rakin/Shutterstock.com

MITIGATING CIRCUMSTANCES Several mitigating circumstances will prevent a defendant found guilty of first degree murder from receiving the death penalty.

Insanity In 1986, the United States Supreme Court held that the Constitution prohibits the execution of a person who is insane. The Court failed to provide a test for insanity other than Justice Lewis F. Powell's statement that the Eighth Amendment "forbids the execution only of those who are unaware of the punishment they are about to suffer and why they are to suffer it." [110] Consequently, each state must come up with its own definition of "insanity" for death penalty purposes. A state may also force convicts on death row to take medication that will make them sane enough to be aware of the punishment they are about to suffer and why they are about to suffer it. [111]

Mental Handicap The Supreme Court's change of mind on the question of whether a mentally handicapped convict may be put to death underscores the continuing importance of the *Weems* test. In 1989, the Court rejected the argument that execution of a mentally handicapped person was "cruel and unusual" under the Eighth Amendment. [112] At the time, only two states barred execution of the mentally handicapped. Thirteen years later, eighteen states had such laws, and the Court decided that this increased number reflected "changing norms and standards of society." In *Atkins v. Virginia* (2002), [113] the Court used the *Weems* test as the main rationale for barring the execution of the mentally handicapped.

The *Atkins* ruling did not end controversy in this area, however, as it allowed state courts to make their own determinations concerning which inmates qualified as "mentally impaired" for death penalty purposes. In 2012, for example, Texas executed Marvin Wilson even though some tests showed that his IQ was below 70, a level accepted by many experts as the cutoff point for mental retardation. Although Wilson's lawyers spent years challenging their client's fate, numerous appellate courts, including the Supreme Court, upheld the right of Texas to execute Wilson, who had killed a police drug informant.[114]

Age Following the *Atkins* case, many observers, including four Supreme Court justices, hoped that the same reasoning would be applied to the question of whether convicts who committed the relevant crime when they were juveniles may be executed. These hopes were realized in 2005 when the Court issued its *Roper v. Simmons* decision, which effectively ended the execution of those who committed crimes as juveniles.[115] As in the *Atkins* case, the Court relied on the "evolving standards of decency" test, noting that a majority of the states, as well as every other civilized nation, prohibited the execution of offenders who committed their crimes before the age of eighteen. (See the feature *Landmark Cases—Roper v. Simmons* on the next page.) The *Roper* ruling required that seventy-two convicted murderers in twelve states be resentenced and took the death penalty "off the table" for dozens of pending cases in which prosecutors were seeking capital punishment for juvenile criminal acts.

Lawyers for convicted murderer Mark Anthony Soliz, shown here in a Cleburne, Texas, courtroom, are appealing their client's death sentence because he suffers from fetal alcohol syndrome. Do you believe that executing a person with this condition, which presumably impairs the functioning of the brain, should be prohibited by the U.S. Supreme Court? Why or why not?
Joyce Marshall/*Fort Worth Star-Telegram*/MCT via Getty Image

Debating the Sentence of Death

Of the topics covered in this textbook, few inspire such passionate argument as the death penalty. Many advocates believe that execution is "just deserts" for those who commit heinous crimes. In the words of Ernest van den Haag, death is the "only fitting retribution for murder that I can think of."[116] Opponents worry that retribution is simply another word for vengeance and that "the use of the death penalty by the state will increase the acceptance of revenge in our society and will give official sanction to a climate of violence."[117] As the debate over capital punishment continues, it tends to focus on several key issues: deterrence, fallibility, arbitrariness, and discrimination.

DETERRENCE Those advocates of the death penalty who wish to show that the practice benefits society often turn to the idea of deterrence. In other words, they believe that by executing convicted criminals, the criminal justice system discourages potential criminals from committing similar violent acts. (When people speak of "deterrence" with regard to the death penalty, they are usually referring to general deterrence rather than specific deterrence.) Deterrence was the primary justification for the frequent public executions carried out in this country before the 1830s and for the brutality of those events.

For Deterrence In 1975, Isaac Ehrlich, an economist then at the University of Chicago, estimated that if all those eligible for the death penalty had been executed, each

Roper v. Simmons

Explain why the U.S. Supreme Court abolished the death penalty for juvenile offenders.

When he was seventeen years old, Christopher Simmons abducted Shirley Cook, used duct tape to cover her eyes and mouth and bind her hands, and threw her to her death in a river. Although he bragged to his friends that he would "get away with it" because he was a minor, he was found guilty of murder and sentenced to death by a Missouri court. After the United States Supreme Court held, in 2002, that "evolving standards of decency" rendered the execution of mentally retarded persons unconstitutional, Simmons appealed his own sentence. His case gave the Court a chance to apply the "evolving standards of decency" test to death sentences involving offenders who were juveniles at the time they committed the underlying capital crime.

Roper v. Simmons
United States Supreme Court
543 U.S. 551 (2005)

IN THE WORDS OF THE COURT . . .
JUSTICE KENNEDY, MAJORITY OPINION

* * * *

The evidence of national consensus against the death penalty for juveniles is similar, and in some respects parallel, to the evidence *Atkins* held sufficient to demonstrate a national consensus against the death penalty for the mentally retarded.

* * * *

Three general differences between juveniles under 18 and adults demonstrate that juvenile offenders cannot with reliability be classified among the worst offenders. First, as any parent knows and as the scientific and sociological studies * * * tend to confirm, "[a] lack of maturity and an underdeveloped sense of responsibility are found in youth more often than in adults and are more understandable among the young. These qualities often result in impetuous and ill-considered actions and decisions." * * * In recognition of the comparative immaturity and irresponsibility of juveniles, almost every State prohibits those under 18 years of age from voting, serving on juries, or marrying without parental consent.

The second area of difference is that juveniles are more vulnerable or susceptible to negative influences and outside pressures, including peer pressure. * * * The third broad difference is that the character of a juvenile is not as well formed as that of an adult. The personality traits of juveniles are more transitory, less fixed.

These differences render suspect any conclusion that a juvenile falls among the worst offenders. * * * Retribution is not proportional if the law's most severe penalty is imposed on one whose culpability or blameworthiness is diminished, to a substantial degree, by reason of youth and immaturity.

DECISION
The Court found that, applying the Eighth Amendment in light of "evolving standards of decency," the execution of offenders who were under the age of eighteen when their crimes were committed was cruel and unusual punishment and therefore unconstitutional.

FOR CRITICAL ANALYSIS
In his majority opinion, Justice Kennedy noted that a number of countries, including China, Iran, and Pakistan, had recently ended the practice of executing juveniles, leaving the United States "alone in a world that has turned its face against the practice." What impact, if any, should international customs have on American criminal law?

Kentoh/Shutterstock.com

additional execution that would have taken place between 1933 and 1967 could have saved the lives of as many as eight murder victims.[118] Ehrlich's data were subjected to heavy criticism, but researchers, relying on statistical comparisons of death sentences, executions, and homicide rates in particular geographic areas, continue to find statistical proof of the deterrent effect of capital punishment. Several reports released in the first decade of the 2000s claim that each convict executed deters between three and eighteen future homicides.[119] More recent research suggests that if the death penalty does have a deterrent effect, it is small and relatively short-lived, influencing behavior only for about a month after an execution takes place.[120]

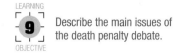

LEARNING **9** OBJECTIVE Describe the main issues of the death penalty debate.

Against Deterrence The main problem with studies that support the death penalty, say its critics, is that there are too few executions carried out in the United States each year to adequately determine their impact.[121] Furthermore, each study that "proves" the deterrent effect of the death penalty seems be matched by one that "disproves" the same premise.[122] In 2004, for example, criminal justice professors Lisa Stolzenberg and Stewart J. D'Alessio of Florida International University found no evidence that the number of executions had any effect on the incidence of murder in the Houston, Texas, area over a five-year period.[123]

In the end, the deterrence debate follows a familiar pattern. Opponents of the death penalty claim that murderers rarely consider the consequences of their act, and therefore it makes no difference whether capital punishment exists or not. Proponents counter that this proves the death penalty's deterrent value, because if the murderers *had* considered the possibility of execution, they would not have committed their crimes. (For a discussion of the moral component to this argument, see the feature *CJ in Action* at the end of the chapter.)

FALLIBILITY In a sense, capital punishment acts as the ultimate deterrent by rendering those executed incapable of committing further crimes. Incapacitation as a justification for the death penalty, though, rests on two questionable assumptions: (1) every convicted murderer is likely to recidivate, and (2) the criminal justice system is *infallible*. In other words, the system never convicts someone who is actually not guilty.

Wrongful Deaths? Although several executions from the 1980s and 1990s are coming under increased scrutiny,[124] no court has ever found that an innocent person has been executed in the United States. According to the Death Penalty Information Center, however, between 1973, when the Supreme Court had temporarily suspended capital punishment, and March 2013, 142 American men and women who had been convicted of capital crimes and sentenced to death—though not executed—were later found to be innocent. Over that same time period, 1,325 executions took place, meaning that for every nine convicts put to death during that period, about one death row inmate has been found innocent.[125]

Defense Issues The single factor that contributes the most to the criminal justice system's fallibility in this area is widely believed to be unsatisfactory legal representation. Many states and counties cannot or will not allocate adequate funds for death penalty cases, meaning that indigent capital defendants are often provided with a less-than-vigorous defense.

The case of convicted murderer Ronald Rompilla highlights the consequences of poor counsel in a capital case. During the sentencing phase of his trial, Rompilla's lawyers made two serious errors. First, they failed to challenge the prosecution's characterization of Rompilla's previous conviction for rape and assault. In fact, they never even looked at the file of that case. Second, they failed to provide the Pennsylvania jury with mitigating factors that would argue against a death sentence, such as their client's troubled childhood, severe alcoholism, and other mental illnesses. Not surprisingly, the jury ordered Rompilla's execution, a sentence that was eventually overturned by the United States Supreme Court due to ineffective counsel.[126]

ARBITRARINESS As noted earlier, one of the reasons it is so difficult to determine the deterrent effect of the death penalty is that it is rarely meted out. Despite the bifurcated process required by the Supreme Court's *Furman* ruling (discussed earlier in the chapter), a significant amount of arbitrariness appears to remain in the system. Only 2 percent of all defendants convicted of murder are sentenced to death, and, as we have seen, relatively few of those on death row are ever executed.[127]

The chances of a defendant in a capital trial being sentenced to death seem to depend heavily on, as we have just seen, the quality of the defense counsel and the jurisdiction where the crime was committed. As Figure 11.8 below shows, a convict's likelihood of being executed is strongly influenced by geography. Five states (Florida, Missouri, Oklahoma, Texas, and Virginia) account for more than two-thirds of all executions, while eighteen states and the District of Columbia do not provide for capital punishment within their borders. Thus, a person on trial for first degree murder in Idaho has a much better chance of avoiding execution than someone who has committed the same crime in Texas.

Discriminatory Effect and the Death Penalty

Whether or not capital punishment is imposed arbitrarily, some observers claim that it is not done without bias. A disproportionate number of those executed since 1976—just over one-third—have been African American, and today 42 percent of all inmates on death row are black.[128] Another set of statistics also continues to be problematic: in 257 cases involving interracial murders in which the defendant was executed between 1976 and March 2013, the defendant was African American and the victim was white. Over that same time period, only 19 cases involved a white defendant and a black victim.[129] In fact, although slightly less than half of murder victims are white, three out of every four executions involve white victims.[130]

FIGURE 11.8 Executions by State, 1976–2012

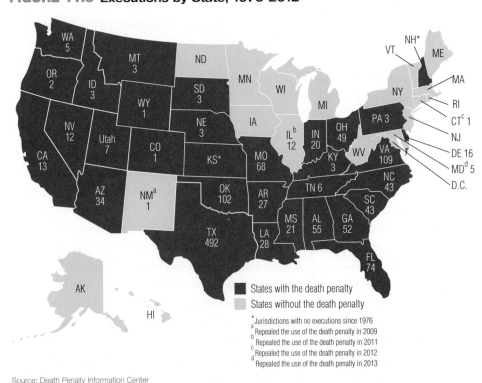

States with the death penalty
States without the death penalty

* Jurisdictions with no executions since 1976
a Repealed the use of the death penalty in 2009
b Repealed the use of the death penalty in 2011
c Repealed the use of the death penalty in 2012
d Repealed the use of the death penalty in 2013

Source: Death Penalty Information Center

THE *McCLESKEY* DECISION In *McCleskey v. Kemp* (1987),[131] the defense attorney for an African American sentenced to death for killing a white police officer used similar statistics to challenge Georgia's death penalty law. A study of two thousand Georgia murder cases showed that although African Americans were the victims of six out of every ten murders in the state, more than 80 percent of the cases in which death was imposed involved murders of whites.[132] In a 5–4 decision, the United States Supreme Court rejected the defense's claims, ruling that statistical evidence did not prove discriminatory intent on the part of Georgia's lawmakers.

One of the reasons the study was unpersuasive in the *McClesky* case is that statistics, as we noted in Chapter 3, are often imperfect tools to measure trends. Even though the studies mentioned above show that race has an effect on the probability of receiving the death penalty, to prove discrimination from a legal standpoint, race must be the *only* determinant. Thus, a study must show that race, and not other factors such as the severity of the crime, the criminal history of the defendant, and the quality of the defense attorney, was the determining factor.[133] Research by William M. Holmes of the Criminal Justice Center at the University of Massachusetts in Boston, for example, found that race did not account for wrongful convictions in capital cases. A much more important factor, according to Holmes, was education level, which correlates strongly with income.[134]

RACE AND THE DEATH PENALTY IN NORTH CAROLINA Despite the Supreme Court's *McCleskey* ruling, several years ago the North Carolina legislature passed the Racial Justice Act. This law allows death row inmates to challenge their sentences on the ground that their race played a significant role in the proceedings.[135] In April 2012, Marcus Robinson became the first death row inmate to take advantage of the new law by claiming that state prosecutors consistently discriminate against blacks in selecting juries for capital cases such as his. A state judge changed Robinson's sentence to life in prison without parole (see photo alongside.)

In 2013, after nearly all of the state's death row inmates filed claims requesting that their sentences be similarly reduced, North Carolina lawmakers repealed the legislation. "A white supremacist who murdered an African American could argue he was a victim of racism if blacks were on the jury," noted one legislator.[136]

The Immediate Future of the Death Penalty

As noted earlier in the chapter, the number of executions carried out each year in the United States has decreased dramatically since 1999. Other statistics also indicate a decline in death penalty activity. In 2012, only 77 people were sentenced to death, compared with 277 in 1999.[137] According to James S. Liebman, a law professor at Columbia University, prosecutors in 60 percent of the nation's counties no longer seek the death penalty, even with defendants who have been convicted of capital crimes.[138]

REASONS FOR THE DECLINE IN EXECUTIONS We have already addressed some of the reasons for the diminishing presence of executions in the criminal justice system. With its

Do you think that defendants such as Marcus Robinson, left, should be given the chance to show that race played an unfair role in their death sentences? What are the potential benefits and drawbacks of state legislation that allows for this type of appeal?
AP Photo/*The Fayetteville Observer,* Andrew Craft

decisions in the *Atkins* (2002) and *Roper* (2005) cases, the United States Supreme Court removed the possibility that hundreds of mentally handicapped and juvenile offenders could be sentenced to death. Furthermore, nearly all of the states that allow for the death penalty now permit juries to impose a sentence of life in prison without parole as an alternative to death. In Texas, the number of death sentences imposed each year dropped by about 50 percent after jurors were given the life-without-parole option, a trend that has been mirrored throughout the United States.[139]

Financial considerations are also starting to color the capital punishment picture. Because of the costs of intensive investigations, extensive *voir dire* (see Chapter 10), and lengthy appellate reviews, pursuing the death penalty can be very expensive. A study by the Urban Institute found that the average death penalty trial costs a state $2 million more than a murder trial in which capital punishment is not sought.[140] Stan Garnett, the district attorney in Boulder County, Colorado, points out that a single death penalty case costs state taxpayers $18 million, while the entire annual budget for his office is $4.6 million.[141] As state budgets come under increased pressure from declining revenues, officials are looking at capital punishment as an area of potential savings.

PUBLIC OPINION AND THE DEATH PENALTY In March 2013, after the Maryland legislature voted to ban the death penalty, state lieutenant governor Anthony Brown said, "Today is a victory for those who believe that fairness and truth and justice, and not retribution or bias, are fundamental to our core beliefs as Marylanders."[142] Maryland became the sixth state in six years to end capital punishment, along with Connecticut, Illinois, New Jersey, New Mexico, and New York.

Does this mean society's "standards of decency" are changing to the point that the death sentence is in danger of being completely abolished in the United States? Probably not. The Supreme Court has shown no interest in holding that the death penalty itself is unconstitutional. In addition to its *Baze* decision (discussed earlier in this section), in 2007 the Court made it easier for prosecutors to seek the death penalty by allowing them to remove potential jurors who express reservations about the practice.[143]

Although public support for the death penalty has been steadily dropping since the mid-1990s, one poll taken in 2013 showed that 63 percent of Americans still favor the practice.[144] (That percentage does, however, drop to about 50 percent when the choice is between execution and a sentence of life in prison without parole.)[145] Another poll found that 58 percent of the respondents favored an official moratorium on executions nationwide to consider the problem of wrongful death sentences.[146] In the 2000s, then, many Americans seem more interested in making the sentence of death fairer than in doing away with it altogether.

SELF ASSESSMENT

Fill in the blanks and check your answers on page 383.

By a large margin, _____ _____ is the most widespread method of execution in the United States today. According to the United States Supreme Court's *Weems* decision, "cruel and unusual punishment" under the Eighth Amendment is determined by the changing _____ _____ _____ of society. Following these guidelines, in 2002 the Court barred the execution of the _____ _____, and in 2005 it prohibited the execution of persons who were _____ at the time of their crime.

CJ IN ACTION

THE MORALITY OF THE DEATH PENALTY

William Petit was disappointed when his home state of Connecticut abolished the death penalty in 2012. The lone survivor of a home invasion that resulted in the brutal killings of his wife and two daughters, Petit said, "We believe in the death penalty because we believe it is really the only true, just punishment for certain heinous and depraved murders." He added that those who oppose capital punishment often lose sight of victims, "the people who died and can't be here to speak for themselves."[147] Like many Americans, Petit does not see the death penalty in terms of the Eighth Amendment, "changing norms and standards," or the bifurcated sentencing process. Rather, he sees it as a matter of right and wrong, a viewpoint we will examine in this *CJ in Action* feature.

THE "LIFE-LIFE TRADE-OFF"

In academic circles, discussion about the morality of the death penalty has generally focused on two concepts. Those who take a *utilitarian* approach believe that the "cost" of each execution is acceptable because of the "benefit" to society, usually expressed in terms of deterrence of future crimes. Those who favor the *deontological* approach reject this cost-benefit analysis on the grounds that an individual's right to life should never be sacrificed, not even for the greater good.

Robert Blecker, a professor at New York Law School, sees such arguments as too esoteric to explain our country's somewhat unique relationship with the death penalty. Blecker believes that, for many Americans, capital punishment is an expression of hatred toward the offender and the "wrongness" of his or her crime.[148] Viewed in this light, the death penalty, still popular in the United States, can be seen as an expression of society's collective moral judgment on those who commit murder.

THE CASE FOR
EXECUTION AS A MORAL ACT

- If the death penalty can prevent even a single future murder, then it is morally justifiable and perhaps even required by the government.

- Some crimes are so horrible that executing the person responsible is the only fitting response.

- The victim's family members often say that a murderer's execution brings them a sense of "closure" by allowing them to come to terms with their grief.

THE CASE AGAINST
EXECUTION AS A MORAL ACT

- The death penalty is an inherently cruel and barbaric act, and it is improper for the government of a civilized nation to kill its own citizens.

- Just as we would not permit a physician to remove the organs of a living person to save the lives of others who need organ transplants, we should not execute a criminal based on the principle that the act would save the lives of others.[149]

- Problems of arbitrariness, discrimination, and wrongful convictions rob the death penalty of any moral justification, leaving it nothing more than the pointless infliction of violence by the state.

YOUR OPINION—WRITING ASSIGNMENT

Patrick O. Kennedy spent five years on Louisiana's death row for raping his eight-year-old stepdaughter so violently that she required emergency surgery. Louisiana was one of six states that allowed the death penalty for certain sex crimes, mostly involving minors. In 2008, the United States Supreme Court found these laws to be unconstitutional, labeling as "cruel and unusual" any punishment that is not proportionate to the crime.[150] Kennedy's sentence was reduced to life in prison without parole.

How do the arguments concerning the morality of the death penalty apply when the punishment extends to other crimes besides murder? In general, do you think an argument can be made that people who rape children should be executed? Before responding, you can review our discussions in this chapter concerning:

- The purposes of sentencing, particularly retribution, deterrence, and incapacitation (pages 349–352).

- The debate over the death penalty, particularly the discussions of fallibility and arbitrariness (pages 377–378).

- Possible discrimination and the death penalty (pages 378–379).

Your answer should include at least three full paragraphs.

CHAPTER SUMMARY

For more information on these concepts, look back to the Learning Objective icons throughout the chapter.

 List and contrast the four basic philosophical reasons for sentencing criminals. (a) Retribution, (b) deterrence, (c) incapacitation, and (d) rehabilitation. Under the principle of retributive justice, the severity of the punishment is in proportion to the severity of the crime. Punishment is an end in itself. In contrast, the deterrence approach seeks to prevent future crimes by setting an example. Such punishment is based on its deterrent value and not necessarily on the severity of the crime. The incapacitation theory of punishment simply argues that a criminal in prison cannot inflict further harm on society. In contrast, the rehabilitation theory asserts that criminals can be rehabilitated in the appropriate prison environment.

 Contrast indeterminate with determinate sentencing. Indeterminate sentencing follows from legislative penal codes that set minimum and maximum amounts of incarceration time. Determinate sentencing carries a fixed amount of time, although this may be reduced for "good time."

 Explain why there is a difference between the sentence imposed by a judge and the actual sentence served by the prisoner. Although judges may decide on indeterminate sentencing, thereafter it is parole boards that decide when prisoners will be released after the minimum sentence is served.

 State who has input into the sentencing decision and list the factors that determine a sentence. The prosecutor, defense attorney, probation officer, and judge provide inputs. The factors considered in sentencing are (a) the seriousness of the crime, (b) mitigating circumstances, (c) aggravating circumstances, and (d) judicial philosophy.

 Explain some of the reasons why sentencing reform has occurred. One reason is sentencing disparity, which is indicative of a situation in which those convicted of similar crimes receive dissimilar sentences (often due to a particular judge's sentencing philosophy). Sentencing discrimination has also occurred on the basis of defendants' gender, race, or economic standing. An additional reason for sentencing reform has been a general desire to "get tough on crime."

 Identify the arguments for and against the use of victim impact statements during sentencing hearings. Proponents of victim impact statements believe that they allow victims to provide character evidence in the same manner as defendants have always been allowed to do and that they give victims a therapeutic "voice" in the sentencing process. Opponents argue that the statements bring unacceptable levels of emotion into the courtroom and encourage judges and juries to make sentencing decisions based on the "social value" of the victim rather than the facts of the case.

 Identify the two stages that make up the bifurcated process of death penalty sentencing. The first stage of the bifurcated process requires a jury to find the defendant guilty or not guilty of a crime that is punishable by execution. If the defendant is found guilty, then, in the second stage, the jury reconvenes to decide whether the death sentence is warranted.

 Explain why the U.S. Supreme Court abolished the death penalty for juvenile offenders. In its *Roper v. Simmons* decision, the Supreme Court ruled that national "evolving standards of decency" no longer justified the execution of juvenile offenders. Such offenders are understood to be less blameworthy than adults because of various issues relating to immaturity and irresponsibility.

 Describe the main issues of the death penalty debate. Many of those who favor capital punishment believe that it is "just deserts" for the most violent of criminals. Those who oppose it see the act as little more than revenge. There is also disagreement over whether the death penalty acts as a deterrent. The relatively high number of death row inmates who have been found innocent has raised questions about the fallibility of the process, while certain statistics seem to show that execution is rather arbitrary. Finally, many observers contend that capital punishment is administered unfairly with regard to members of minority groups.

QUESTIONS FOR CRITICAL ANALYSIS

1. Suppose that the U.S. Congress passed a new law that punished shoplifting with a mandatory eighty-five-year prison term. What would be the impact of the new law on shoplifting nationwide? Would such a harsh law be justified by its deterrent effect? What about imposing a similarly extreme punishment on a more serious crime— a mandatory sentence of life in prison for, say, drunk driving? Would such a law be in society's best interest? Why or why not?

2. Why are truth-in-sentencing laws generally popular among victims' rights advocates? Why might these laws not be so popular with prison administrators or government officials charged with balancing a state budget?

3. Harold is convicted of unarmed burglary after a trial in Boston, Massachusetts. He has no prior convictions. According to the grid on page 366, what punishment do the state guidelines require? What would his punishment be if he had a previous conviction for armed robbery, which means that he has a "serious" criminal record?

4. In Alabama, Delaware, and Florida, judges can override sentencing decisions made by juries. What are the arguments for and against giving judges this power?

5. Some observers believe that, by abolishing the death penalty, state officials in states such as Connecticut and Maryland have taken away an important bargaining chip for prosecutors to use during plea bargaining. Why might this be the case?

KEY TERMS

aggravating circumstances   359
capital punishment   370
departure   366
determinate sentencing   354
deterrence   350
"good time"   355
habitual offender laws   367
incapacitation   351

indeterminate sentencing   354
just deserts   349
mandatory sentencing
   guidelines   367
mitigating circumstances   359
presentence investigative report   357
"real offense"   359
rehabilitation   352

restitution   352
restorative justice   352
retribution   349
sentencing discrimination   362
sentencing disparity   361
sentencing guidelines   365
truth-in-sentencing laws   355
victim impact statement (VIS)   368

SELF ASSESSMENT ANSWER KEY

Page 354: i. retribution; **ii.** deterrence; **iii.** incapacitation; **iv.** rehabilitation

Page 361: i. Indeterminate; **ii.** determinate; **iii.** good time; **iv.** presentence investigative; **v.** seriousness; **vi.** Mitigating; **vii.** aggravating

Page 364: i. disparity; **ii.** discrimination

Page 370: i. guidelines; **ii.** increased; **iii.** three-strikes/ habitual offender; **iv.** victim impact

Page 380: i. lethal injection; **ii.** norms and standards; **iii.** mentally handicapped; **iv.** juveniles/minors

NOTES

1. Herbert L. Packer, "Justification for Criminal Punishment," in *The Limits of Criminal Sanction* (Palo Alto, CA: Stanford University Press, 1968), 36–37.

2. Jay Michaelson, "Can Suicide Be a Hate Crime?" *Newsweek* (March 19, 2012), 17.

3. Jami L. Anderson, "Reciprocity as a Justification for Retributivism," *Criminal Justice Ethics* (Winter/Spring 1997), 13–14.

4. Immanuel Kant, *Metaphysical First Principles of the Doctrine of Right*, trans. Mary Gregor (Cambridge, UK: Cambridge University Press, 1991), 331.

5. Harold Pepinsky and Paul Jesilow, *Myths That Cause Crime* (Cabin John, MD: Seven Locks Press, 1984).

6. Jeremy Bentham, *An Introduction to the Principles of Morals and Legislation 1789* (New York: Hafner Publishing Corp., 1961).

7. Brian Forst, "Prosecution and Sentencing," in *Crime*, ed. James Q. Wilson and Joan Petersilia (San Francisco: ICS Press, 1995), 376.

8. Quoted in Kate Zernike, "In Rutgers Spying Case, Voices for Gay Rights Urge Leniency," *New York Times* (May 21, 2012), A1.

9. Bureau of Justice Statistics, *Criminal Victimization, 2011* (Washington, D.C.: U.S. Department of Justice, October 2012), Table 8, page 8.

10. Federal Bureau of Investigation, *Crime in the United States, 2011* (Washington, D.C.: U.S. Department of Justice, 2012), at **www.fbi.gov /about-us/cjis/ucr/crime-in-the-u.s/2011/crime-in-the-u.s.-2011 /tables/table_25**.

11. Paul H. Robinson and John M. Darley, "The Utility of Desert," *Northwestern University Law Review* 91 (Winter 1997), 453.

12. Thomas Erdbrink, "Iran Resorts to Hangings in Public to Cut Crime," *New York Times* (January 21, 2013), A4.

13. James Q. Wilson, *Thinking about Crime* (New York: Basic Books, 1975), 235.

14. Isaac Ehrlich, "Participation in Illegitimate Activities: A Theoretical and Empirical Investigation," *Journal of Political Economy* 81 (May/June 1973), 521–564.

15. Avinash Singh Bhati, *An Information Theoretic Method for Estimating the Number of Crimes Averted by Incapacitation* (Washington, D.C.: Urban Institute, July 2007), 18–33.

16. Todd Clear, *Harm in Punishment* (Boston: Northeastern University Press, 1980).

17. Jan Chaiken, Marcia Chaiken, and William Rhodes, "Predicting Violent Behavior and Classifying Violent Offenders," in *Understanding and Preventing Violence*, ed. Albert J. Reiss, Jr., and Jeffrey A. Roth (Washington, D.C.: National Academy Press, 1994).

18. Patricia M. Clark, "An Evidence-Based Intervention for Offenders," *Corrections Today* (February/March 2011), 62–64.

19. Barry Krisberg and Susan Marchionna, *Attitudes of U.S. Voters toward Prisoner Rehabilitation and Reentry Policies* (Oakland, CA: National Council on Crime and Delinquency, April 2006), 1.

20. Heather Strang and Lawrence W. Sherman, "Repairing the Harm: Victims and Restorative Justice," *Utah Law Review* (2003), 15, 18, 20–25.

21. Todd R. Clear, George F. Cole, and Michael D. Reisig, *American Corrections*, 7th ed. (Belmont, CA: Thomson Wadsworth, 2006), 68–69.

22. Leena Kurki, "Restorative and Community Justice in the United States," in *Crime and Justice: A Review of Research*, vol. 27, ed. Michael Tonry (Chicago: University of Chicago Press, 2000), 253–303.

23. *Making Restitution Real* (Washington, D.C.: National Center for Victims of Crime, 2011), 3.

24. 42 U.S.C. Section 10601 (2006).

25. Office for Victims of Crime, "2011 Victims of Crime Act Performance Report," at **www.ojp.usdoj.gov/ovc/grants/vocanpr_vc11.html**.

26. Josh Allen, "Jon Wilson Helps Crime Victims Talk with Their Offenders," *The Christian Science Monitor Weekly* (April 9, 2012), 45.

27. Gregory W. O'Reilly, "Truth-in-Sentencing: Illinois Adds Yet Another Layer of 'Reform' to Its Complicated Code of Corrections," *Loyola University of Chicago Law Journal* (Summer 1996), 986, 999–1000.

28. David E. Olson, et al., *Final Report: The Impact of Illinois' Truth-in-Sentencing Law on Sentence Lengths, Time to Serve and Disciplinary Incidents of Convicted Murderers and Sex Offenders* (Chicago: Illinois Criminal Justice Information Authority, June 2009), 4–5.

29. Marvin Zalman, "The Rise and Fall of the Indeterminate Sentence," *Wayne Law Review* 24 (1977), 45, 52.

30. Paul W. Keve, *Crime Control and Justice in America: Searching for Facts and Answers* (Chicago: American Library Association, 1995), 77.

31. Danielle A. Alvarez, "Flowers, Dinner, Bowling—and Counseling—Ordered by Broward Judge in Domestic Case," *Sunsentinel.com* (February 7, 2012), at **articles.sun-sentinel.com/2012-02-07/news /fl-flowers-food-bowling-20120207_1_red-lobster-broward -judge-judge-johnjay-hurley**.

32. Kate Stith and José A. Cabranes, "Judging under the Federal Sentencing Guidelines," *Northwestern University Law Review* 91 (Summer 1997), 1247.

33. Mark M. Lanier and Claud H. Miller III, "Attitudes and Practices of Federal Probation Officers towards Pre-Plea/Trial Investigative Report Policy," *Crime & Delinquency* 41 (July 1995), 365–366.

34. Kate Zernike, "Judge Defends Penalty in Rutgers Spying Case, Saying It Fits Crime," *New York Times* (May 31, 2012), A22.

35. Brad Heath, "How Snitches Buy Their Freedom," *USA Today* (December 14–16, 2012), 1A.

36. *Ibid.,* 5A.

37. Nancy J. King and Rosevelt L. Noble, "Felony Jury Sentencing in Practice: A Three-State Study," *Vanderbilt Law Review* (2004), 1986.

38. Jena Iontcheva, "Jury Sentencing as Democratic Practice," *Virginia Law Review* (April 2003), 325.

39. Julie R. O'Sullivan, "In Defense of the U.S. Sentencing Guidelines Modified Real-Offense System," *Northwestern University Law Review* 91 (1997), 1342.

40. Lisa G. Aspinwall, Teneille R. Brown, and James Tabery, "The Double-Edged Sword: Does Biomechanism Increase or Decrease Judges' Sentencing of Psychopaths?" *Science* (August 2012), 846–849.

41. Benjamin Weiser, "Citing Terror Defendants' Motivation, Judge Shows Sentencing Leniency," *New York Times* (November 23, 2012), A27.

42. 18 U.S.C. Section 2113(a) (1994).

43. United States Sentencing Commission, "Statistical Information Packet, Fiscal Year 2011, Northern District of California," Table 7, at **www .ussc.gov/Data_and_Statistics/Federal_Sentencing_Statistics /State_District_Circuit/can11.pdf**; and "Statistical Information Packet, Fiscal Year 2011, Northern District of Iowa," Table 7, at **www .ussc.gov/Data_and_Statistics/Federal_Sentencing_Statistics /State_District_Circuit/2011/ian11.pdf**.

44. United States Sentencing Commission, "Statistical Information Packet, Fiscal Year 2011, Fourth Circuit," Table 7, at **www.ussc .gov/Data_and_Statistics/Federal_Sentencing_Statistics/State _District_Circuit/2011/4c11.pdf**; and "Statistical Information Packet, Fiscal Year 2011, Ninth Circuit," Table 7, at **www.ussc.gov /Data_and_Statistics/Federal_Sentencing_Statistics/State _District_Circuit/2011/9c11.pdf**.

45. Keith Williams, "Practical Child Porn Defense: Fighting the Pitchfork Mentality," *Aspatore* (July 2012), 3911.

46. Cassia Spohn and David Holleran, "The Imprisonment Penalty Paid by Young, Unemployed Black and Hispanic Male Offenders," *Criminology* 35 (2000), 281.

47. Illinois Disproportionate Justice Impact Study Commission, "Key Findings and Recommendations" (2011), at **www.senatedem.ilga .gov/phocadownload/PDF/Attachments/2011/djisfactsheet.pdf**.

48. Bureau of Justice Statistics, *Prisoners in 2011* (Washington, D.C.: U.S. Department of Justice, December 2012), Table 7, page 7.

49. Federal Bureau of Investigation, *Crime in the United States, 2011*, at **www.fbi.gov/aboutus/cjis/ucr/crime-in-the-u.s/2011/crime -in-the-u.s.-2011/tables/table-43**.

50. Spohn and Holleran, 301.

51. Brian Johnson, "The Multilevel Context of Criminal Sentencing: Integrating Judge- and County-Level Influences," *Criminology* (May 2006), 259–298.

52. Spohn and Holleran, 291.

53. Jeff German and Cy Ran, "Sentencing Study Finds Disparities You'd Expect," *Las Vegas Sun* (August 13, 2008), 1.

54. Bureau of Justice Statistics, *State Court Sentencing of Convicted Felons, 2006—Statistical Tables* (Washington, D.C.: U.S. Department of Justice, December 2009), Table 3.6, page 21.

55. Anti-Drug Abuse Act of 1986, Pub. L. No. 99-570, 100 Stat. 3207 (1986).

56. Solomon Moore, "Justice Department Seeks Equity in Sentences for Cocaine," *New York Times* (April 30, 2009), A17.

57. Pub. L. No. 111-220, Section 2, 124 Stat. 2372.

58. United States Sentencing Commission, "Preliminary Crack Retroactivity Data Report: Fair Sentencing Act" (December 2012), at **www.ussc.gov/Research_and_Statistics/Federal_Sentencing _Statistics/FSA_Amendment/2012-12_USSC_Crack_Retroactivity _Report_PostFSA.pdf**.

59. Nicole D. Porter and Valerie Wright, *Cracked Justice* (Washington, D.C.: The Sentencing Project, March 2011).

60. 28 U.S.C. Section 991 (1994).

61. Bureau of Justice Statistics, *Felony Sentences in State Courts, 2006—Statistical Tables* (Washington, D.C.: U.S. Department of Justice, December 2009), Table 3.5, page 20.

62. Sonja B. Starr, "Estimating Gender Disparities in Federal Criminal Cases," *University of Michigan Law and Economics Research Paper* (August 29, 2012), at **papers.ssrn.com/sol3/papers.cfm?abstract_id=2144002**.

63. Clarice Feinman, *Women in the Criminal Justice System,* 3d ed. (Westport, CT: Praeger, 1994), 35.

64. Darrell Steffensmeier, John Kramer, and Cathy Streifel, "Gender and Imprisonment Decisions," *Criminology* 31 (1993), 411.

65. Quoted in Kareem Fahim and Karen Zraick, "Seeing Failure of Mother as Factor in Sentencing," *New York Times* (November 17, 2008), A24.

66. John C. Coffee, "Repressed Issues of Sentencing," *Georgetown Law Journal* 66 (1978), 987.

67. J. S. Bainbridge, Jr., "The Return of Retribution," *ABA Journal* (May 1985), 63.

68. The Massachusetts Court System, "Introduction: Sentencing Guidelines," at **www.mass.gov/courts/formsandguidelines/sentencing/step1.html#step1**.

69. Pub. L. No. 98-473, 98 Stat. 1987, codified as amended at 18 U.S.C. Sections 3551–3742 and 28 U.S.C. Sections 991–998 (1988).

70. Julia L. Black, "The Constitutionality of Federal Sentences Imposed under the Sentencing Reform Act of 1984 after *Mistretta v. United States,*" *Iowa Law Review* 75 (March 1990), 767.

71. *Fifteen Years of Guidelines Sentencing: An Assessment of How Well the Federal Criminal Justice System Is Achieving the Goals of Sentencing Reform* (Washington, D.C.: U.S. Sentencing Commission, November 2004), 46.

72. Clear, Cole, and Reisig, 86.

73. Neal B. Kauder and Brian J. Ostrom, *State Sentencing Guidelines: Profiles and Continuum* (Williamsburg, VA: National Center for State Courts, 2008), 15.

74. *Blakely v. Washington,* 542 U.S. 296 (2004); *United States v. Booker,* 543 U.S. 220 (2005); and *Gall v. United States,* 552 U.S. 38 (2007).

75. Transactional Records Access Clearinghouse, "Wide Variations Seen in Federal Sentencing" (March 5, 2012), at **trac.syr.edu/whatsnew/email.120305.html**.

76. *Demographic Differences in Federal Sentencing Practices: An Update of the Booker Report's Multivariate Regression Analysis* (Washington, D.C.: U.S. Sentencing Commission, March 2010), C-3.

77. Alabama Code 1975 Section 20-2-79.

78. Quoted in Melinda Rogers, "Reluctant Utah Judge Orders Man to 57 Years in Prison for Gang Robberies," *Salt Lake Tribune* (December 15, 2011), at **www.sltrib.com/sltrib/mobile/53124012-90/maumauprison-angelos-court.html.csp**.

79. United States Sentencing Commission, *Report to Congress: Mandatory Minimum Penalties in the Federal Criminal Justice System* (Washington, D.C.: United States Sentencing Commission, October 2011), xxviii.

80. Washington Revised Code Annotated Section 9.94A.030.

81. 445 U.S. 263 (1980).

82. 538 U.S. 63 (2003).

83. *Lockyer v. Andrade,* 270 F.3d 743 (9th Cir. 2001).

84. *Lockyer v. Andrade,* 538 U.S. 63, 76 (2003).

85. *Ibid.,* 83.

86. Marisa Lagos and Ellen Huet, " 'Three Strikes' Law Changes Approved by Wide Margin," *San Francisco Chronicle* (November 7, 2012), A14.

87. Nicole D. Porter, *The State of Sentencing 2012* (Washington, D.C.: The Sentencing Project, January 2013), 4.

88. Justice for All Act of 2004, Pub. L. No. 108-405, 118 Stat. 2260.

89. Paul G. Cassell, "In Defense of Victim Impact Statements," *Ohio State Journal of Criminal Law* (Spring 2009), 614.

90. Edna Erez, "Victim Voice, Impact Statements, and Sentencing: Integrating Restorative Justice and Therapeutic Jurisprudence Principles in Adversarial Proceedings," *Criminal Law Bulletin* (September/October 2004), 495.

91. Bryan Myers and Edith Greene, "Prejudicial Nature of Impact Statements," *Psychology, Public Policy, and Law* (December 2004), 493.

92. *Payne v. Tennessee,* 501 U.S. 808 (1991).

93. Bryan Myers and Jack Arbuthnot, "The Effects of Victim Impact Evidence on the Verdicts and Sentencing Judgments of Mock Jurors," *Journal of Offender Rehabilitation* (1999), 95–112.

94. Walter Berns, "Abraham Lincoln (Book Review)," *Commentary* (January 1, 1996), 70.

95. Comments made at the Georgetown Law Center, "The Modern View of Capital Punishment," *American Criminal Law Review* 34 (Summer 1997), 1353.

96. David Bruck, quoted in Bill Rankin, "Fairness of the Death Penalty Is Still on Trial," *Atlanta Constitution-Journal* (July 29, 1997), A13.

97. Bureau of Justice Statistics, *Capital Punishment, 2010* (Washington, D.C.: U.S. Department of Justice, December 2011), 2.

98. *Baze v. Rees,* 217 S.W.3d 207 (Ky. 2006).

99. Larry C. Berkson, *The Concept of Cruel and Unusual Punishment* (Lexington, MA: Lexington Books, 1975), 43.

100. John P. Cunningham, "Death in the Federal Courts: Expectations and Realities of the Federal Death Penalty Act of 1994," *University of Richmond Law Review* 32 (May 1998), 939.

101. *In re Kemmler,* 136 U.S. 447 (1890).

102. 217 U.S. 349 (1910).

103. Pamela S. Nagy, "Hang by the Neck until Dead: The Resurgence of Cruel and Unusual Punishment in the 1990s," *Pacific Law Journal* 26 (October 1994), 85.

104. 553 U.S. 35 (2008).

105. Death Penalty Information Center, "State by State Lethal Injection," at **www.deathpenaltyinfo.org/state-lethal-injection**.

106. 408 U.S. 238 (1972).

107. 408 U.S. 309 (1972) (Stewart, concurring).

108. *Gregg v. Georgia,* 428 U.S. 153 (1976).

109. 536 U.S. 584 (2002).

110. *Ford v. Wainwright,* 477 U.S. 399, 422 (1986).

111. Vidisha Barua, "'Synthetic Sanity': A Way Around the Eighth Amendment?" *Criminal Law Bulletin* (July/August 2008), 561–572.

112. *Penry v. Lynaugh,* 492 U.S. 302 (1989).

113. 536 U.S. 304 (2002).

114. Michael Graczyk, "Marvin Wilson Set to Be Executed after U.S. Supreme Court Denies Request to Stay," *Associated Press* (August 7, 2012).

115. 543 U.S. 551 (2005).

116. Ernest van den Haag, "The Ultimate Punishment: A Defense," *Harvard Law Review* 99 (1986), 1669.

117. *The Death Penalty: The Religious Community Calls for Abolition* (pamphlet published by the National Coalition to Abolish the Death Penalty and the National Interreligious Task Force on Criminal Justice, 1988), 48.

118. Isaac Ehrlich, "The Deterrent Effect of Capital Punishment: A Question of Life and Death," *American Economic Review* 65 (June 1975), 397–417.

119. Hashem Dezhbakhsh, Paul H. Rubin, and Joanna M. Shepherd, "Does Capital Punishment Have a Deterrent Effect? New Evidence from Postmoratorium Panel Data," *American Law and Economics Review* 5 (2003), 344–376; H. Naci Mocan and R. Kaj Gittings, "Getting Off Death Row: Commuted Sentences and the Deterrent Effect of Capital Punishment," *Journal of Law and Economics* 46 (2003), 453–478; Joanna M. Shepherd, "Deterrence versus Brutalization: Capital Punishment's Differing Impact among States," *Michigan Law Review* 104 (2005),

203–255; and Paul R. Zimmerman, "State Executions, Deterrence, and the Incidence of Murder," *Journal of Applied Economics* 7 (2005), 163–193.

120. Kenneth C. Land, Raymond H. C. Teske, Jr., and Hui Zheng, "Overview of: 'The Differential Short-Term Impacts of Executions on Felony and Non-Felony Homicides," *Criminology & Public Policy* (August 2012), 539–563.

121. Richard Berk, "Can't Tell: Comments on 'Does the Death Penalty Save Lives?'" *Criminology and Public Policy* (November 2009), 845–851.

122. John J. Donohue and Justin Wolfers, "Uses and Abuses of Empirical Evidence in the Death Penalty Debate," *Stanford Law Review* 58 (2005), 791–845.

123. Lisa Stolzenberg and Stewart J. D'Alessio, "Capital Punishment, Execution Publicity, and Murder in Houston, Texas," *Journal of Criminal Law and Criminology* (Winter 2004), 351–379.

124. Roger C. Barnes, "Death Penalty Undermines Justice," *San Antonio Express-News* (July 12, 202), 6B.

125. Death Penalty Information Center, "Innocence and the Death Penalty," at **www.deathpenaltyinfo.org/innocence-and-death-penalty**.

126. *Rompilla v. Beard*, 545 U.S. 375 (2005).

127. Adam Liptak, "Geography and the Machinery of Death," *New York Times* (February 5, 2007), A10.

128. Deborah Fins, *Death Row U.S.A.* (New York: NAACP Legal Defense and Educational Fund, Spring 2012), 1.

129. Death Penalty Information Center, "National Statistics on the Death Penalty and Race," at **www.deathpenaltyinfo.org/race-death-row-inmates-executed-1976#defend**.

130. *Ibid.*

131. 481 U.S. 279 (1987).

132. David C. Baldus, George Woodworth, and Charles A. Pulaski, *Equal Justice and the Death Penalty: A Legal and Empirical Analysis* (Boston: Northeastern University Press, 1990), 140–197, 306.

133. Laura Argys and Naci Mocan, *Who Shall Live and Who Shall Die? An Analysis of Prisoners on Death Row in the United States* (Cambridge, MA: National Bureau of Economic Research, February 2003), 22.

134. William M. Holmes, "Who Are the Wrongly Convicted on Death Row?" in *Wrongly Convicted: When Justice Fails*, ed. Saundra Westervelt and John Humphrey (Piscataway, NJ: Rutgers University Press, 2001).

135. North Carolina General Statute Section 15A-2010 (2009).

136. Quoted in Kim Severson, "North Carolina Repeals Law Allowing Racial Bias Claim in Death Penalty Challenges," *New York Times* (June 6, 2013), A13.

137. *The Death Penalty in 2012: Year End Report* (Washington, D.C.: Death Penalty Information Center, December 2012), 1.

138. Quoted in Ethan Bronner, "Use of Death Sentences Continues to Fall in U.S.," *New York Times* (December 21, 2012), A24.

139. David McCord, "What's Messing with Texas Death Sentences?" *Texas Tech Law Review* (Winter 2011), 601–608.

140. Cited in "Saving Lives and Money," *The Economist* (March 14, 2009), 32.

141. Quoted in Bronner.

142. Quoted in Mark Morgenstein, "Maryland Legislature Votes to End Death Penalty," *CNN Justice* (March 15, 2013), at **www.cnn.com/2013/03/15/justice/maryland-death-penalty-ban**.

143. *Uttecht v. Brown*, 551 U.S. 1 (2007).

144. Gallup, "U.S. Death Penalty Support Stable at 63%" (January 9, 2013), at **www.gallup.com/poll/159770/death-penalty-support-stable.aspx**.

145. Gallup, "In U.S. 64% Support Death Penalty in Cases of Murder" (November 8, 2010), at **www.gallup.com/poll/144284/support-death-penalty-cases-murder.aspx**.

146. Richard C. Dieter, *A Crisis of Confidence: Americans' Doubts about the Death Penalty* (Washington, D.C.: Death Penalty Information Center, June 2007), 5, 9.

147. Quoted in Shannon Young, "Connecticut Senate Votes for Death Penalty Abolishment," *Associated Press* (April 6, 2012).

148. Quoted in Andrea Weigl, "Father Wants Killer to Die," *Raleigh (NC) News & Observer* (April 23, 2007), A1.

149. Claire Finkelstein, "A Contractarian Argument against the Death Penalty," *New York University Law Review* (October 2006), 1283.

150. *Kennedy v. Louisiana*, 554 U.S. 407 (2008).

12

Probation, Parole, and Intermediate Sanctions

To target your study and review, look for these numbered Learning Objective icons throughout the chapter.

AP Photo/*Rapid City Journal*, Benjamin Brayfield

LACKING COMMON SENSE

IN OKLAHOMA, second degree manslaughter occurs when a person commits a homicide because of "culpable negligence," or the failure to use ordinary care and caution. Eighteen-year-old Krysta Dawson certainly met that standard several years ago by putting her nine-month-old son James in a bathtub and leaving the room. When she returned, James was unresponsive, and the infant died in a hospital the next day. After initially investigating the drowning as an accident, Tulsa police eventually decided that Dawson's actions were criminal, and prosecutors charged her with second degree manslaughter. "A nine-month-old should never be left in that type of situation," said a local authority. "I think that is just common sense."

Dawson pleaded no contest to the charge, leaving her punishment in the hands of District Judge Clancy Smith. Given that Dawson's negligence directly led to the death of a child, one might have expected Smith to be severe. Judges, however, tend toward leniency in such cases. In 2009, a Morgan County, Colorado, judge sentenced Amanda Holbert to four years of probation for allowing her nine-month-old son to drown in a bathtub while she spoke on the telephone. The next year in Tampa, Florida, Katrina Brooks received five years' probation for similarly neglecting her infant son while on the phone, leading to his drowning death in a bathtub.

It seems that judges often consider the women in these situations as "loving and caring" mothers who made "a mistake," rather than violent criminals. So, it should have come as no surprise that Judge Smith sentenced Dawson to probation for James's death. As one of the conditions of staying out of prison, Dawson was required to inform local officials if she changed her address. Consequently, when Dawson subsequently moved to Arkansas without notifying the local district attorney's office, she broke the terms of her probation. As a result, in 2013 Dawson was rearrested and, this time, sentenced to spend four years behind bars.

1. Arguing that mothers in such cases deserve tough punishments including prison time, one prosecutor said, "These are clearly unnecessary deaths that are clearly preventable." In your opinion, how forgiving should the criminal justice system be with a mother whose negligence leads to an accidental homicide?
2. In general, what might be some of the arguments for allowing any nonviolent offender to serve her or his sentence in the community, under supervision, rather than in prison or jail?
3. Do you agree that Krysta Dawson should have been sent to prison for moving to Arkansas without notifying local officials and therefore breaking the terms of her probation agreement? Why might a court deal more harshly with this infraction than with Dawson's initial crime?

AP Photo/Madison County Sheriff's Department

Parents such as Thomas and Emilie Pinski of Edwardsville, Illinois, who accidentally allow their children to drown are often sentenced to probation by judges.

Gray wall studio/Shutterstock.com

THE JUSTIFICATION FOR COMMUNITY CORRECTIONS

LEARNING OBJECTIVE **1** Explain the justifications for community-based corrections programs.

Judges who decide not to send criminally negligent mothers such as Krysta Dawson, Amanda Holbert, and Katrina Brooks to prison or jail are hardly breaking new ground. Today, nearly 4 million offenders are serving their sentences in the community on *probation* rather than behind bars. In addition, approximately 850,000 convicts in the United States have been *paroled*, meaning that they are finishing their prison sentences "on the outside" under the supervision of correctional officers.[1]

America, says University of Minnesota law professor Michael Tonry, is preoccupied with the "absolute severity of punishment" and the "widespread view that only imprisonment counts."[2] Consequently, **community corrections** such as probation and parole are often considered a less severe, and therefore a less worthy, alternative to imprisonment. In reality, community corrections are crucially important. One in fifty adults in this country is living under community supervision,[3] and few criminal justice matters are more pressing than the need to successfully reintegrate these offenders into society.

Reintegration

A very small percentage of all convicted offenders have committed crimes that warrant life imprisonment or capital punishment. Most, at some point, will return to the community. Consequently, according to one group of experts, the task of the corrections system

> includes building or rebuilding solid ties between the offender and the community, integrating or reintegrating the offender into community life—restoring family ties, obtaining employment and an education, securing in the larger sense a place for the offender in the routine functioning of society.[4]

Considering that some studies have shown higher recidivism rates for offenders who are subjected to prison culture, a frequent justification of community-based corrections is that they help to reintegrate the offender into society.

Reintegration has a strong theoretical basis in rehabilitative theories of punishment. An offender is generally considered to be "rehabilitated" when he or she no longer represents a threat to other members of the community and therefore is believed to be fit to live in that community. In the context of this chapter and the two that follow, it will also be helpful to see reintegration as a process through which criminal justice officials such as probation and parole officers provide the offender with incentives to follow the rules of society. These incentives can be positive, such as enrolling the offender in a drug treatment program. They can also be negative—in particular, the threat of return to prison or jail for failure to comply. In all instances, criminal justice professionals must carefully balance the needs of the individual offender against the rights of law-abiding members of the community.

Diversion

Another justification for community-based corrections, based on practical considerations, is **diversion.** As you are already aware, many criminal offenses fall into the category of "petty," and it is well-nigh impossible, as well as unnecessary, to imprison every offender for every offense. Community-based corrections are an important means of diverting criminals to alternative modes of punishment so that scarce incarceration resources are consumed by only the most dangerous criminals. In his "strainer" analogy, corrections expert Paul H. Hahn likens this process to the workings of a kitchen strainer.

Community Corrections The correctional supervision of offenders in the community as an alternative to sending them to prison or jail.

Reintegration A goal of corrections that focuses on preparing the offender for a return to the community unmarred by further criminal behavior.

Diversion In the context of corrections, a strategy to divert those offenders who qualify away from prison and jail and toward community-based and intermediate sanctions.

In Dallas, street prostitutes such as the two shown here are often treated as crime victims and offered access to treatment and rehabilitation programs. How might society benefit if such offenders are kept out of jail or prison through these kinds of diversion programs? AP Photo/LM Otero, File

With each "shake" of the corrections "strainer," the less serious offenders are diverted from incarceration. At the end, only the most serious convicts remain in prison.[5] (The concept of diversion is closely linked to that of selective incapacitation, mentioned in Chapter 11.)

The diversionary role of community-based punishments has become more pronounced as prisons and jails have filled up over the past three decades. In fact, probationers and parolees now account for about 70 percent of all adults in the American corrections systems.[6] (To learn about another form of diversion, which focuses on the mental health system rather than the criminal justice system, see the *CJ in Action* feature at the end of this chapter.)

The "Low-Cost Alternative"

Not all of the recent expansion of community corrections can be attributed to acceptance of its theoretical underpinnings. Many politicians and criminal justice officials who do not look favorably on ideas such as reintegration and diversion have embraced programs to keep nonviolent offenders out of prison. The reason is simple: economics. The cost of constructing and maintaining prisons and jails, as well as housing and caring for inmates, has placed a great deal of pressure on corrections budgets across the country. Indeed, to cut prison operating costs, states are taking such steps as installing windmills and solar panels to save energy and using medical schools to provide less costly health care.[7]

Community corrections offer an enticing financial alternative to imprisonment. Data compiled by the Center for Economic and Policy Research suggest that for each nonviolent offender shifted from incarceration to community supervision, the federal government saves about $22,700, and state governments save about $23,200.[8] Not surprisingly, many jurisdictions are adopting policies that favor keeping offenders out of prison or jail cells. By diverting significant numbers of nonviolent criminals from state prisons to probation and parole, for example, New Hampshire estimates that it will save about $190 million, including new prison construction and operating costs, by 2021.[9] Officials can also require community-based criminals to finance their own supervision. In Oklahoma, probationers pay a $40 monthly fee to cover part of the costs of community corrections.[10]

SELF ASSESSMENT

Fill in the blanks and check your answers on page 417.

The three basic justifications for community corrections are (1) _____, which focuses on building or rebuilding the offender's ties with the community; (2) _____, a strategy that attempts to allocate scarce jail and prison space to only the most dangerous criminals; and (3) _____ considerations, as community corrections are generally _____ expensive than incarceration.

PROBATION: DOING TIME IN THE COMMUNITY

Probation A criminal sanction in which a convict is allowed to remain in the community rather than be imprisoned.

As Figure 12.1 on the facing page shows, **probation** is the most common form of punishment in the United States. Although it is administered differently in various jurisdictions, probation can be generally defined as the legal status of an offender who, after being convicted of a crime, has been directed by the sentencing court to remain in the community under the supervision of a probation service for a designated period of time and subject to certain conditions imposed by the court or by law.[11]

The theory behind probation is that certain offenders, having been found guilty of a crime, can be treated more economically and humanely by putting them under controls while still allowing them to live in the community. One of the advantages of probation has been that it provides for the rehabilitation of the offender while saving society the costs of incarceration. Despite probation's widespread use, certain participants in the criminal justice system question its ability to reach its rehabilitative goals. Critics point to the immense number of probationers and the fact that many of them are violent felons as evidence that the system is "out of control." Supporters contend that nothing is wrong with probation in principle, but admit that its execution must be adjusted to meet the goals of modern corrections.[12]

Sentencing and Probation

Probation is basically an arrangement between sentencing authorities and the offender. In traditional probation, the offender agrees to comply with certain terms for a specified amount of time in return for serving the sentence in the community. One of the primary benefits for the offender, besides not getting sent to a correctional facility, is that the length of the probationary period is usually considerably shorter than the length of a prison term (see Figure 12.2 on the next page).

The traditional form of probation is not the only arrangement that can be made. A judge can hand down a **suspended sentence,** under which a defendant who has been convicted and sentenced to be incarcerated is not required to serve the sentence. Instead, the judge puts the offender on notice, keeping open the option of reinstating the original sentence and sending the offender to prison or jail if he or she reoffends. In practice, suspended sentences are quite similar to probation.

ALTERNATIVE SENTENCING ARRANGEMENTS Judges can also combine probation with incarceration. Such sentencing arrangements include:

- *Split sentences.* In **split sentence probation,** also known as *shock probation,* the offender is sentenced to a specific amount of time in prison or jail, to be followed by a period of probation.
- *Shock incarceration.* In this arrangement, an offender is sentenced to prison or jail with the understanding that after a period of time, she or he may petition the court to be released on probation. Shock incarceration is discussed more fully later in the chapter.
- *Intermittent incarceration.* With intermittent incarceration, the offender spends a certain amount of time each week, usually during the weekend, in a jail, workhouse, or other government institution.

Split sentences are popular with judges, as they combine the "treatment" aspects of probation with the "punishment" aspects of incarceration. According to the U.S. Department of Justice, about a fifth of all probationers are also sentenced to some form of incarceration.[13]

CHOOSING PROBATION Generally, research has shown that offenders are most likely to be denied probation if they:

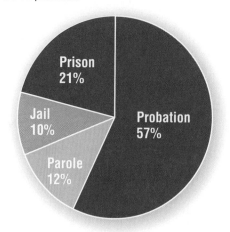

FIGURE 12.1 Probation in American Corrections

As you can see, the majority of convicts under the control of the American corrections system are on probation.

Source: Bureau of Justice Statistics, *Correctional Populations in the United States, 2011* (Washington, D.C.: U.S. Department of Justice, November 2012), Table 2, page 3.

LEARNING **2** OBJECTIVE Explain several alternative sentencing arrangements that combine probation with incarceration.

Suspended Sentence A judicially imposed condition in which an offender is sentenced after being convicted of a crime, but is not required to begin serving the sentence immediately.

Split Sentence Probation A sentence that consists of incarceration in a prison or jail, followed by a probationary period in the community.

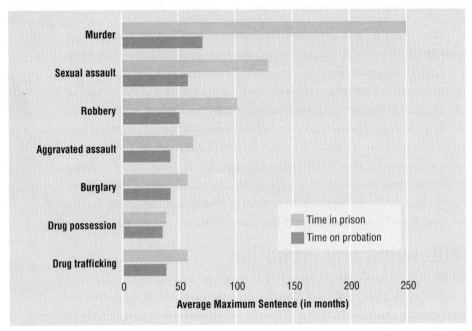

FIGURE 12.2 Average Length of Sentence: Prison versus Probation

As you can see, the average probation sentence is much shorter than the average prison sentence for most crimes.

Legend:
- Time in prison
- Time on probation

X-axis: Average Maximum Sentence (in months) — 0, 50, 100, 150, 200, 250

Categories: Murder, Sexual assault, Robbery, Aggravated assault, Burglary, Drug possession, Drug trafficking

Source: Bureau of Justice Statistics, *Felony Sentences in State Courts, 2006—Statistical Tables* (Washington, D.C.: U.S. Department of Justice, December 2009), Table 1.3.

LEARNING OBJECTIVE **3** Specify the conditions under which an offender is most likely to be denied probation.

- Are convicted on multiple charges.
- Were on probation or parole at the time of the arrest.
- Have two or more prior convictions.
- Are addicted to narcotics.
- Seriously injured the victim of the crime.
- Used a weapon during the commission of the crime.[14]

As might be expected, the chances of a felon being sentenced to probation are highly dependent on the seriousness of his or her crime. Only 18 percent of probationers in the United States have committed a violent crime, including domestic violence and sex offenses. The majority of probationers have been convicted of property crimes, drug offenses, or public order crimes such as drunk driving.[15]

As with the child-drowning cases discussed in the opening to this chapter, probation also allows judges to recognize that some offenders are less blameworthy than others. In 2013, for example, a judge in Arizona found himself with the difficult task of punishing eighty-six-year-old George Sanders for fatally shooting Virginia, his eighty-one-year-old wife. Virginia, who was suffering from a painful health condition, had begged George to end her life. In handing down his sentence of two years' probation, Judge John Ditsworth said that his decision tempered "justice with mercy."[16]

PROBATION DEMOGRAPHICS As in other areas of the criminal justice system, African Americans make up a higher percentage of the national probation population (31 percent) than the general population (13 percent). Fifty-four percent of probationers are white, and 13 percent are Hispanic.[17] The percentage of female probationers is significantly higher than female prison inmates (25 percent to 7 percent),[18] which is in keeping with the gender sentencing trends we discussed in the previous chapter. More detailed surveys of probationers reveal that they tend to be between the ages of twenty-one and thirty-nine, single, high school graduates, and have annual incomes of less than $20,000.[19]

Conditions of Probation

A judge may decide to impose certain conditions as part of a probation sentence. These conditions represent a "contract" between the judge and the offender, in which the latter agrees that if she or he does not follow certain rules, probation may be revoked (see Figure 12.3 below). The probation officer usually recommends the conditions of probation, but judges also have the power to set any terms they believe to be necessary. For example, as part of her five-year probationary sentence for drunk driving, actress Lindsay Lohan was required to complete 480 hours of community service and attend psychological counseling sessions four times a month.

PRINCIPLES OF PROBATION A judge's personal philosophy is often reflected in the probation conditions that she or he creates for probationers. In *In re Quirk* (1997),[20] for example, the Louisiana Supreme Court upheld the ability of a trial judge to impose church attendance as a condition of probation. Though judges have a great deal of discretion in setting the conditions of probation, they do operate under several guiding principles. First, the conditions must be related to the dual purposes of probation, which most federal and state courts define as (1) the rehabilitation of the probationer and (2) the protection of the community. Second, the conditions must not violate the U.S. Constitution, as probationers are generally entitled to the same constitutional rights as other prisoners.[21]

Of course, probationers do give up certain constitutional rights when they consent to the terms of probation. Most probationers, for example, agree to spot checks of their homes for contraband such as drugs or weapons, and they therefore have a diminished expectation of privacy.

In *United States v. Knights* (2001),[22] the United States Supreme Court upheld the actions of deputy sheriffs in Napa County, California, who searched a probationer's home without a warrant or probable cause. The unanimous decision was based on the premise that because those on probation are more likely to commit crimes, law enforcement agents "may therefore justifiably focus on probationers in a way that [they do] not on the ordinary citizen."[23]

FIGURE 12.3 Conditions of Probation

UNITED STATES DISTRICT COURT
FOR THE
DISTRICT OF COLUMBIA

To: _____ No. 84-417

Address: 1440 N St., N.W., #10, Wash., D.C.

In accordance with authority conferred by the United States Probation Law, you have been placed on probation this date, January 25, 2014 for a period of one year by the Hon. Thomas F. Hogan United States District Judge, sitting in and for this District Court at Washington, D.C.

CONDITIONS OF PROBATION

It is the order of the Court that you shall comply with the following conditions of probation:

(1)-You shall refrain from violation of any law (federal, state, and local). You shall get in touch immediately with your probation officer if arrested or questioned by a law enforcement officer.

(2)-You shall associate only with law-abiding persons and maintain reasonable hours.

(3)-You shall work regularly at a lawful occupation and support your legal dependents, if any, to the best of your ability. When out of work you shall notify your probation officer at once. You shall consult him prior to job changes.

(4)-You shall not leave the judicial district without permission of the probation officer.

(5)-You shall notify your probation officer immediately of any change in your place of residence.

(6)-You shall follow the probation officer's instructions.

(7)-You shall report to the probation officer as directed.

(8)-You shall not possess a firearm (handgun or rifle) for any reason.

The special conditions ordered by the Court are as follows:
    Imposition of sentence suspended, one year probation, Fine of $75 on each count.

I understand that the Court may change the conditions of probation, reduce or extend the period of probation, and at any time during the probation period or within the maximum probation period of 5 years permitted by law, may issue a warrant and revoke probation for a violation occurring during the probation period.

I have read or had read to me the above conditions of probation. I fully understand them and I will abide by them.

_____ Date _____
Probationer

You will report as follows: _____ as directed by your Probation Officer

_____ Date _____
U.S. Probation Officer

TYPES OF CONDITIONS Obviously, probationers who break the law are very likely to have their probation revoked. Other, less serious infractions may also result in revocation, as we saw with Krysta Dawson at the beginning of this chapter. The conditions placed on a probationer fall into three general categories:

- *Standard conditions,* which are imposed on all probationers. These include reporting regularly to the probation officer, notifying the agency of any change of address, not leaving the jurisdiction without permission, and remaining employed.
- *Punitive conditions,* which usually reflect the seriousness of the offense and are intended to increase the punishment of the offender. Such conditions include fines, community service, restitution, drug testing, and home confinement (discussed later).
- *Treatment conditions,* which are imposed to reverse patterns of self-destructive behavior. Such treatment generally includes counseling for drug and alcohol abuse, anger management, and mental health issues.

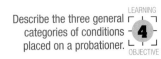

Describe the three general categories of conditions placed on a probationer. **LEARNING 4 OBJECTIVE**

Some observers feel that judges have too much discretion in imposing overly restrictive conditions that no person, much less one who has exhibited antisocial tendencies, could meet. Citing prohibitions on drinking liquor, gambling, and associating with "undesirables," as well as requirements such as meeting early curfews, the late University of Delaware professor Carl B. Klockars claimed that if probation rules were taken seriously, "very few probationers would complete their terms without violation."[24]

As more than six out of ten federal probationers do complete their terms successfully, Klockars's statement suggests that either probation officers are unable to determine that violations are taking place, or many of them are exercising a great deal of discretion in reporting minor probation violations. Perhaps the officers realize that violating probationers for every single "slip-up" is unrealistic and would add to the already significant problem of jail and prison overcrowding.

SOCIAL MEDIA **&CJ**

The world of the probation officer is illuminated through tweets provided by **Probation Officers@ ProbationNews.** You can become a follower by signing on to your Twitter account and searching for "probation officers."

Ankomando/Shutterstock.com

The Supervisory Role of the Probation Officer

The probation officer has two basic roles. The first is investigative and consists of conducting the presentence investigation (PSI), which was discussed in Chapter 11. The second is supervisory and begins as soon as the offender has been sentenced to probation. In smaller probation agencies, individual officers perform both tasks. In larger jurisdictions, the trend has been toward separating the responsibilities, with *investigating officers* handling the PSI and *line officers* concentrating on supervision.

Supervisory policies vary and are often a reflection of whether the authority to administer probation services is *decentralized* (under local, judicial control) or *centralized* (under state, administrative control). In any circumstance, however, certain basic principles of supervision apply. Starting with a preliminary interview, the probation officer establishes a relationship with the offender. This relationship is based on the mutual goal of both parties: the successful completion of the probationary period. Just because the line officer and the offender have the same goal, however, does not necessarily mean that cooperation will be a feature of probation.

THE USE OF AUTHORITY The ideal probation officer–offender relationship is based on trust. In reality, this trust often does not exist. Any incentive an offender might have to be completely truthful with a line officer is marred by one simple fact: self-reported wrongdoing can be used to revoke probation. Even probation officers whose primary mission is to rehabilitate are under institutional pressure to punish their clients for violating conditions of probation. One officer deals with this situation by telling his clients

> that I'm here to help them, to get them a job, and whatever else I can do. But I tell them too that I have a family to support and that if they get too far off track, I can't afford to put my job on the line for them. I'm going to have to violate them.[25]

In the absence of trust, most probation officers rely on their **authority** to guide an offender successfully through the sentence. An officer's authority, or ability to influence a person's actions without resorting to force, is based partially on her or his power to revoke probation. It also reflects her or his ability to impose a number of lesser sanctions. For example, if a probationer fails to attend a required alcohol treatment program, the officer can send him or her to a "lockup," or detention center, overnight. To be successful, a probation officer must establish this authority early in the relationship because it is the primary tool for persuading the probationer to behave in an acceptable manner.[26]

■ A Washington, D.C., probation officer makes phone curfew checks while her partner watches. Why is trust so often difficult to achieve between probation officers and offenders?
Mark Gail/*The Washington Post/*Getty Images

THE CASELOAD DILEMMA Even the most balanced, "firm but fair" approach to probation can be defeated by the problem of excessive *caseloads*. A **caseload** is the number of clients a probation officer is responsible for at any one time. Heavy probation caseloads seem inevitable: unlike a prison cell, a probation officer can always take "just one more" client. Furthermore, the ideal caseload size is very difficult to determine because different offenders require different levels of supervision.[27]

The consequences of disproportionate probation officer–probationer ratios are self-evident, however. When burdened with large caseloads, probation officers find it practically impossible to rigorously enforce the conditions imposed on their clients. Lack of surveillance leads to lack of control, which can undermine the very basis of a probationary system. In Sacramento County, California, where probation officers have caseloads of more than 120 each and more than 90 percent of all probationers are unsupervised, these offenders are responsible for 30 percent of the county's total arrests.[28]

Revocation of Probation

The probation period can end in one of two ways. Either the probationer successfully fulfills the conditions of the sentence, or the probationer misbehaves and probation is revoked, resulting in a prison or jail term. The decision of whether to revoke after a **technical violation**—such as failing to report a change of address or testing positive for drug use—is often a judgment call by the probation officer and therefore the focus of controversy. (See the feature *You Be the Probation Officer—A Judgment Call* on the following page to learn more about the issues surrounding revocation.)

As we have seen, probationers do not always enjoy the same protections under the U.S. Constitution as other members of society. The United States Supreme Court has not stripped these offenders of all rights, however. In *Mempa v. Rhay* (1967),[29] the Court

Authority The power designated to an agent of the law over a person who has broken the law.

Caseload The number of individual probationers or parolees under the supervision of a probation or parole officer.

Technical Violation An action taken by a probationer or parolee that, although not criminal, breaks the terms of probation or parole as designated by the court.

A JUDGMENT CALL

THE FACTS Your client, Alain, was convicted of selling drugs and given a split sentence—three years in prison and three years on probation. You meet Alain for the first time two days after his release, and you are immediately concerned about his mental health. His mother confirms your worries, telling you that Alain needs help. You refer him to a psychiatric hospital, but the officials there determine that he "does not require mental health treatment at this time." Several weeks later, Alain's mother tells you that he is staying out late at night and "hanging out with the wrong crowd," both violations of his probation agreement. After he tests positive for marijuana, you warn Alain that, after one more violation, you will revoke his probation and send him back to prison. He tells you that he is "feeling agitated" and "having intermittent rage." You refer him to a substance abuse and mental health treatment facility, where he tests positive for marijuana once again.

THE LAW For any number of reasons, but particularly for the failed drug tests, you can start revocation proceedings against Alain. These proceedings will almost certainly conclude with his return to prison.

YOUR DECISION On the one hand, Alain has violated the terms of his probation agreement numerous times. On the other hand, he has been convicted of only one crime—a drug violation—and you have no evidence that he is behaving violently or poses a danger to himself or others. Furthermore, Alain has strong family support and is willing to enter treatment for his substance abuse problems. Do Alain's technical violations cause you to begin the revocation process? Why or why not?

[To see how a Fairfield County, Connecticut, probation officer dealt with a similar situation, go to Example 12.1 in Appendix B.]

Somchai Rakin/Shutterstock.com

ruled that probationers were entitled to an attorney during the revocation process. Then, in *Morrissey v. Brewer* (1972) and *Gagnon v. Scarpelli* (1973),[30] the Court established a three-stage procedure by which the "limited" due process rights of probationers must be protected in potential revocation situations:

- *Preliminary hearing.* In this appearance before a "disinterested person" (often a judge), the facts of the violation or arrest are presented, and it is determined whether probable cause for revoking probation exists. This hearing can be waived by the probationer.
- *Revocation hearing.* During this hearing, the probation agency presents evidence to support its claim of violation, and the probationer can attempt to refute this evidence. The probationer has the right to know the charges being brought against him or her. Furthermore, probationers can testify on their own behalf and present witnesses in their favor, as well as confront and cross-examine adverse witnesses. A "neutral and detached" body must hear the evidence and rule on the validity of the proposed revocation.
- *Revocation sentencing.* If the presiding body rules against the probationer, then the judge must decide whether to impose incarceration and for what length of time. In a revocation hearing dealing with technical violations, the judge will often reimpose probation with stricter terms or intermediate sanctions.

In effect, this is a "bare-bones" approach to due process. Most of the rules of evidence that govern regular trials do not apply to revocation hearings. Probation officers are not, for example, required to read offenders their *Miranda* rights before questioning them about crimes they may have committed during probation. In *Minnesota v. Murphy* (1984),[31] the Supreme Court ruled that a meeting between probation officer and client does not equal custody and, therefore, the Fifth Amendment protection against self-incrimination does not apply, either.

Does Probation Work?

On March 28, 2013, Las Cruces, New Mexico, police arrested Cornelius Renteria for murdering his ex-girlfriend in her home. At the time of the murder, Renteria was on probation for kidnapping, child abuse, and aggravated assault charges. Indeed, probationers are responsible for a significant amount of crime. Each year, about 375,000 probationers return to prison or jail, many because of criminal behavior.[32] Such statistics raise a critical question—is probation worthwhile?

To measure the effectiveness of probation, one must first establish its purpose. Generally, as we saw earlier, the goal of probation is to reintegrate and divert as many offenders as possible while at the same time protecting the public. Specifically, probation and other community corrections programs are evaluated by their success in preventing *recidivism*—the eventual rearrest of the probationer.[33] Given that most probationers are first-time, nonviolent offenders, the system is not designed to prevent relatively rare outbursts of violence, such as the murder committed by Cornelius Renteria.

RISK FACTORS FOR RECIDIVISM About a quarter of all federal probationers are rearrested within five years of being placed under community supervision. There are several risk factors that make a probationer more likely to recidivate, including a criminal history, substance abuse problems, and unemployment.[34] Consequently, probation departments have attempted to focus attention on those probationers with the most risk factors.[35]

In addition, as far as reducing recidivism is concerned, the most effective probation strategy appears to be a mix of supervision (behavior monitoring) and treatment (behavior change). Researchers have labeled this a "hybrid" approach to probation, and numerous studies attest to the benefits of mixing "tough love" and treatment such as drug counseling and continuing education instead of focusing on one or the other.[36] Also, as noted earlier, caseloads matter. A recent study of probation practices in Iowa and Oklahoma found that the lower the caseload for each individual probation officer, the lower the rates of probationers being arrested for new crimes.[37]

NEW MODELS OF PROBATION In their efforts to cut the costs and caseloads associated with corrections, a number of jurisdictions are experimenting with new models of probation. Since 2004, for example, Hawaii's Office of the Attorney General has operated Hawaii's Opportunity Probation with Enforcement (HOPE) program under the "swift and certain" principle. The rules of HOPE are simple. Each substance abuse probationer must call the courthouse every day to learn if she or he is required to come in for urine tests for drugs, or *urinalysis*. If drugs are found in the probationer's system during one of these frequent tests, a short jail term—one to two weeks—is automatically served.[38] HOPE has resulted in large reductions in positive drug tests by probationers, and its 1,500 participants are significantly less likely to be rearrested than those not in the program.[39]

In 2000, with the approval of a ballot initiative, California embarked on an even more ambitious undertaking. The Substance Abuse and Crime Prevention Act changed

Courtesy Peggy McCarthy

PEGGY McCARTHY

LEAD PROBATION OFFICER

The best thing about my job is that every day is different. I may be in court first thing in the morning, and then in my office meeting with defendants or developing case plans. In the afternoon, I may be at the jail taking statements for court reports or out in the field seeing my defendants. If I work a late shift, I may be visiting counseling agencies or talking to collateral sources or doing surveillance. I may be organizing a search on a defendant's home or making an arrest. I may be working with the police to solve crimes or locate absconders. Or I may simply be completing administrative duties like filing or returning phone calls to defendants and/or their family members. Anything can happen at any time, and I have to be ready to respond. If a probation officer gets bored, something is wrong.

I take a great deal of pride in assisting defendants with the difficult task of making positive change in their lives. The rewards may be few and far between, but when a defendant with a history of substance abuse stays clean and sober for a year, when a gang-affiliated defendant secures a job and no longer associates with negative peers, or when a defendant who admittedly never liked school obtains a GED or diploma, that is when I realize that what I'm doing day in and day out is 100 percent worthwhile.

SOCIAL MEDIA CAREER TIP Manage your online reputation—or someone else will do it for you. Monitor your profile using tools such as iSearch, Pipl, and ZabaSearch. Check BoardTracker, BoardReader, and Omgili for information on what people are saying about you on message boards.

the state penal code to mandate probation for any first- or second-time drug offender arrested for a crime involving personal use.[40] As a condition of probation, the offender must complete a yearlong drug treatment program followed by six months of aftercare. A study by researchers at the University of California at Los Angeles found that, in the five years following the law's passage, the number of drug possession–related prison admissions in California decreased by 30 percent. During that same period, the state saved nearly $3,000 for each probationer in treatment rather than behind bars.[41]

SELF ASSESSMENT

Fill in the blanks and check your answers on page 417.

Offenders sentenced to probation serve their sentence in the _____ under the supervision of a _____ _____. If a probationer commits a _____ _____ by failing to follow the _____ of his or her probation, it may be revoked. If revocation occurs, the offender will be sent to _____. To a large extent, the effectiveness of probation programs is measured by _____, or the rate at which offenders are rearrested. In many instances, this effectiveness is compromised by the heavy _____ carried by probation officers.

THE PAROLE PICTURE

At any given time, about 850,000 Americans are living in the community on **parole,** or the *conditional* release of a prisoner after a portion of his or her sentence has been served behind bars. Parole allows the corrections system to continue to supervise an offender who is no longer incarcerated. As long as parolees follow the conditions of their parole,

Parole The conditional release of an inmate before his or her sentence has expired.

they are allowed to finish their terms outside the prison. If parolees break the terms of their early release, however, they face the risk of being returned to a penal institution.

Parole is based on three concepts:[42]

1. *Grace.* The prisoner has no right to be given an early release, but the government has granted her or him that privilege.
2. *Contract of consent.* The government and the parolee enter into an arrangement whereby the latter agrees to abide by certain conditions in return for continued freedom.
3. *Custody.* Technically, though no longer incarcerated, the parolee is still the responsibility of the state. Parole is an extension of corrections.

Because of good-time credits and parole, most prisoners do not serve their entire sentence in prison. In fact, the average felon serves only about half of the term handed down by the court.

Comparing Probation and Parole

Both probation and parole operate under the basic assumption that the offender serves her or his time in the community rather than in a prison or jail. The main differences between the two concepts—which sound confusingly similar—involve their circumstances. Probation is a sentence handed down by a judge following conviction and usually does not include incarceration. Parole is a conditional release from prison and occurs after an offender has already served some time in a correctional facility. (See *Mastering Concepts—Probation versus Parole* below for clarification.)

LEARNING OBJECTIVE **5** Identify the main differences between probation and parole.

MASTERING CONCEPTS
PROBATION VERSUS PAROLE

Probation and parole have many aspects in common. In fact, probation and parole are so similar that many jurisdictions combine them into a single agency. There are, however, some important distinctions between the two systems, as noted below.

	PROBATION	PAROLE
Basic Definition	An **alternative to imprisonment** in which a person who has been convicted of a crime is allowed to serve his or her sentence in the community subject to certain conditions and supervision by a probation officer.	An **early release** from a correctional facility, in which the convicted offender is given the chance to spend the remainder of her or his sentence under supervision in the community.
Timing	The offender is sentenced to a probationary term in place of a prison or jail term. If the offender breaks the conditions of probation, he or she is sent to prison or jail. Therefore, **probation generally occurs *before* imprisonment.**	Parole is a form of early release. Therefore, **parole occurs *after* an offender has spent time behind bars.**
Authority	**Probation is under the domain of the judiciary.** A judge decides whether to sentence a convict to probation, and a judge determines whether a probation violation warrants revocation and incarceration.	**Parole often falls under the domain of the parole board.** This administrative body determines whether the prisoner qualifies for early release and the conditions under which the parole must be served.
Characteristics of Offenders	As a number of studies have shown, probationers are normally less involved in the criminal lifestyle. Most of them are **first-time offenders who have committed nonviolent crimes.**	Many parolees have **spent months or even years in prison** and, besides abiding by conditions of parole, must make the difficult transition to "life on the outside."

FIGURE 12.4 Standard Conditions of Parole

The parolee must do the following:

- Stay within a certain area.
- Obtain permission before changing residence or employment.
- Obtain and maintain employment.
- Maintain acceptable, nonthreatening behavior.
- Not possess firearms or weapons.
- Report any arrest within twenty-four hours.
- Not use illegal drugs or alcohol or enter drinking establishments.
- Not break any state or local laws.
- Allow contacts by parole officers at home or employment without obstruction.
- Submit to search of person, residence, or motor vehicle at any time by parole officers.

CONDITIONS OF PAROLE In many ways, parole supervision is similar to probation supervision. Like probationers, offenders who are granted parole are placed under the supervision of community corrections officers and required to follow certain conditions. Certain parole conditions mirror probation conditions. All parolees, for example, must comply with the law, and they are generally responsible for reporting to their parole officer at certain intervals.

The frequency of these visits, along with the other terms of parole, is spelled out in the **parole contract,** which sets out the agreement between the state and the paroled offender. Under the terms of the contract, the state agrees to conditionally release the inmate, and the future parolee agrees that her or his conditional release will last only as long as she or he abides by the contract. (See Figure 12.4 on the left for a list of standard parole conditions.)

PAROLE REVOCATION A large number—about half—of parolees return to prison before the end of their parole period, most because they were convicted of a new offense or had their parole revoked.[43] **Parole revocation** is similar in many aspects to probation revocation. If the parolee commits a new crime, then a return to prison is very likely. If, however, the individual commits a technical violation by breaking a condition of parole, then parole authorities have discretion as to whether revocation proceedings should be initiated. A number of states, including Michigan, Missouri, and New York, have taken steps to avoid reincarcerating parolees for technical violations as part of their continuing efforts to reduce prison populations.[44]

When authorities do attempt to revoke parole for a technical violation, they must provide the parolee with a revocation hearing.[45] Although this hearing does not provide the same due process protections as a criminal trial, the parolee does have the right to be notified of the charges, to present witnesses, to speak in his or her defense, and to question any hostile witnesses (so long as such questioning would not place them in danger). In the first stage of the hearing, the parole authorities determine whether there is probable cause that a violation occurred. Then, they decide whether to return the parolee to prison.

PROBATION AND PAROLE OFFICERS Unlike police officers or sheriffs' deputies, probation and parole officers generally do not wear uniforms. Instead, they have badges that identify their position and agency. The duties of probation officers and parole officers are so similar that many small jurisdictions combine the two posts into a single position.

Given the supervisory nature of their professions, probation and parole officers are ultimately responsible for protecting the community by keeping their clients from committing crimes. There is also an element of social work in their duties, and these officers must constantly balance the needs of the community with the needs of the offender.[46] Parole officers in particular are expected to help the parolee readjust to life outside the correctional institution by helping her or him find a place to live and a job, and seeing that she or he receives any treatment that may be necessary.

Parole Contract An agreement between the state and the offender that establishes the conditions of parole.

Parole Revocation When a parolee breaks the conditions of parole, the process of withdrawing parole and returning the person to prison.

Discretionary Release

As you may recall from Chapter 11, corrections systems are classified by sentencing procedure—indeterminate or determinate. Indeterminate sentencing occurs when the legislature sets a range of punishments for particular crimes, and the judge and the parole board exercise discretion in determining the actual length of the prison term. For that reason, states with indeterminate sentencing are said to have systems of **discretionary release.**

ELIGIBILITY FOR PAROLE Under indeterminate sentencing, parole is not a right but a privilege. This is a crucial point, as it establishes the terms of the relationship between the inmate and the corrections authorities during the parole process. In *Greenholtz v. Inmates of the Nebraska Penal and Correctional Complex* (1979),[47] the Supreme Court ruled that inmates do not have a constitutionally protected right to expect parole, thereby giving states the freedom to set their own standards for determining parole eligibility. In most states that have retained indeterminate sentencing, a prisoner is eligible to be considered for parole release after serving a legislatively determined percentage of the minimum sentence—usually one-half or two-thirds—less any good time or other credits.

Not all convicts are eligible for parole. As we saw in Chapter 11, offenders who have committed the most serious crimes often receive life sentences without the possibility of early release. In general, life without parole is reserved for those who have committed first degree murder or are defined by statute as habitual offenders. Today, about one-third of convicts serving life sentences have no possibility of parole.[48]

PAROLE PROCEDURES A convict does not apply for parole. Rather, different jurisdictions have different procedures for determining discretionary release dates. In many states, the offender is eligible for discretionary release at the end of his or her minimum sentence minus good-time credits (see Chapter 11). For instance, in 2012, Michael Claudy was sentenced to five to ten years in prison for harassing female students at Shippensburg University in Pennsylvania. This means that he will become eligible for parole after serving five years, less good time. In other states, parole eligibility is measured at either one-third or one-half of the maximum sentence, or it is a matter of discretion for the parole authorities.

In most, but not all, states, the responsibility for making the parole decision falls to the **parole board,** whose members are generally appointed by the governor. According to the American Correctional Association, the parole board has four basic roles:

1. To decide which offenders should be placed on parole.
2. To determine the conditions of parole and aid in the continuing supervision of the parolee.
3. To discharge the offender when the conditions of parole have been met.
4. If a violation occurs, to determine whether parole privileges should be revoked.[49]

Most parole boards are small, made up of three to seven members. In many jurisdictions, board members' terms are limited to between four and six years. The requirements for board members vary. Nearly half the states have no prerequisites, while others require a bachelor's degree or some expertise in the field of criminal justice.

THE PAROLE DECISION Parole boards use a number of criteria to determine whether a convict should be given discretionary release. These criteria include the nature of the underlying offense, any prior criminal record, the inmate's behavior behind bars, and the attitude of the victim or the victim's family. In a system that uses discretionary parole, the actual release decision is made at a **parole grant hearing.** During this hearing, the entire board or a subcommittee reviews relevant information on the convict. Sometimes, but not always, the offender is interviewed.

Because the board members have only limited knowledge of each offender, key players in the case are often notified in advance of the parole hearing and asked to provide

LEARNING
6
OBJECTIVE

List the four basic roles of the parole board.

Discretionary Release The release of an inmate into a community supervision program at the discretion of the parole board within limits set by state or federal law.

Parole Board A body of appointed civilians that decides whether a convict should be granted conditional release before the end of his or her sentence.

Parole Grant Hearing A hearing in which the entire parole board or a subcommittee reviews information, meets the offender, and hears testimony from relevant witnesses to determine whether to grant parole.

Two parole board members consider the fate of inmate Michael Skakel during a recent parole grant hearing at the McDougall-Walker Correctional Institution in Suffield, Connecticut. In 1975, Skakel, then fifteen years old, beat another teenager to death with a golf club. Should inmates be allowed to speak at their parole grant hearings? Why or why not? Pool photo Jessica Hill/*Hartford Courant/ MCT* via Getty Images

comments and recommendations. These participants include the sentencing judge, the attorneys at the trial, the victims, and any law enforcement officers who may be involved. After these preparations, the typical parole hearing itself is very short—usually lasting just a few minutes.

As parole has become a more important tool for reducing prison populations, corrections authorities are making greater efforts to ensure that the process does not endanger the community. Each of Michigan's approximately 43,000 state prisoners, for example, is subjected to an annual evaluation to determine his or her "risk potential." As this numerical score improves, so do the inmate's chances for parole. State corrections officials are highly motivated to identify potential parolees: parole supervision costs about $2,130 a year, compared with about $34,000 a year for an offender in state prison.[50]

PAROLE DENIAL If parole is denied, the entire process is replayed at the next "action date," which depends on the nature of the offender's crimes and all relevant laws. In 2012, for example, Mark David Chapman was denied parole for the seventh time. About three decades earlier, Chapman had been convicted of murder for fatally shooting musician John Lennon in New York City and sentenced to twenty years to life in prison. Although Chapman had not had an infraction behind bars since 1994, the three parole board members told him that his release would "tend to trivialize the tragic loss of life which you caused as a result of this heinous, unprovoked, violent, cold and calculated crime."[51] (See the feature *You Be the Parole Board Member—Cause for Compassion?* on the facing page to learn more about the process of discretionary release.)

Parole Guidelines

Nearly twenty states have moved away from discretionary release systems to procedures that provide for **mandatory release.** Under mandatory release, offenders leave prison only when their prison terms have expired, minus adjustments for good time. No parole board is involved in this type of release, which is designed to eliminate discretion from the process.

Instead, in mandatory release, corrections officials rely on **parole guidelines** to determine the early release date. Similar to sentencing guidelines (see Chapter 11), parole guidelines determine a potential parolee's risk of recidivism using a mathematical equation. Under this system, inmates and corrections authorities know the *presumptive parole date* soon after the inmate enters prison. So long as the offender does not experience any disciplinary or other problems while incarcerated, he or she can be fairly sure of the time of release.[52]

Note that a number of states and the federal government claim to have officially "abolished" parole through truth-in-sentencing laws. (As described in Chapter 11, this form of legislation requires certain statutorily determined offenders to serve at least 85 percent of their prison terms.) For the most part, however, these laws simply emphasize prison terms that are "truthful," not necessarily "longer." Mechanisms for parole, by

Mandatory Release Release from prison that occurs when an offender has served the full length of his or her sentence, minus any adjustments for good time.

Parole Guidelines Standards that are used in the parole process to measure the risk that a potential parolee will recidivate.

CAUSE FOR COMPASSION?

LEARNING OBJECTIVE 7 Explain which factors influence the decision to grant parole.

THE SITUATION Thirty-seven years ago, Susan was convicted of first degree murder and sentenced to life in prison for taking part in a grisly killing spree in Los Angeles. Over the course of two days, Susan and her accomplices killed seven people. Susan stabbed one of the victims—a pregnant woman—sixteen times and wrote the word "PIG" on a door using another victim's blood. During her trial, Susan testified that "I was stoned, man, stoned on acid," at the time of her crimes. Now sixty-one years old, Susan is before your parole board, requesting release from prison. For most of her time behind bars, she has been a model prisoner, and she has apologized numerous times for her wrongdoing. Furthermore, her left leg has been amputated, the left side of her body is paralyzed, and she has been diagnosed with terminal brain cancer.

THE LAW You have a great deal of discretion in determining whether a prisoner should be paroled. Some of the factors you should consider are the threat the prisoner would pose to the community if released, the nature of the offense, and the level of remorse. In addition, California allows for "compassionate release" when an inmate is "terminally ill."

YOUR DECISION Susan obviously poses no threat to the community and is a viable candidate for compassionate release. Should she be set free on parole? Or are some crimes so horrific that the convict should never be given parole, no matter what the circumstances? Explain your vote.

[To see how a California parole board voted in a similar situation, go to Example 12.2 in Appendix B.]

---

whatever name, are crucial to the criminal justice system for several reasons. First, they provide inmates with an incentive to behave properly in the hope of an early release. Second, they reduce the costs related to incarceration by keeping down the inmate population, a critical concern for prison administrators.[53]

Victims' Rights and Parole

Mark David Chapman's chances of being granted parole, described earlier in this section, are hurt by the continuing wishes of Yoko Ono, John Lennon's widow, that he remain in prison. Victims' opinions are not, however, usually a deciding factor in the parole process. For example, more than forty years ago, Sirhan Sirhan shot and wounded William Weisel during an attack that took the life of U.S. Senator Robert F. Kennedy. In 2011, Weisel (see photo alongside) told a parole board at the Pleasant Valley State Prison in Coalinga, California, that he did not oppose Sirhan being granted parole. Regardless of Weisel's forgiveness, the parole board rejected Sirhan's appeal for release.[54]

The federal Crime Victims' Rights Act provides victims with the right to be reasonably notified of any parole proceedings and the right to attend and be reasonably

■ What are the arguments for and against allowing victims such as William Weisel to participate in the parole process?
AP Photo/Ben Margot

heard at such proceedings.[55] A number of states offer similar assurances of victim participation in the parole process. Even though such involvement is not decisive, victim statements can help parole boards fully appreciate the nature of the crime and the risk that the offender poses to the community if given conditional release.[56]

SELF ASSESSMENT

Fill in the blanks and check your answers on page 417.

Parole refers to the _____ release of an inmate from prison before the end of his or her _____. Once an inmate has been released from prison, the terms of his or her release are spelled out in a parole _____, and a _____ violation of these terms or, especially, the commission of a new crime will almost certainly result in a return to prison. In jurisdictions that have systems of discretionary release, a _____ _____ makes the parole decision. In contrast, with a _____ release, the inmate will not leave prison until her or his sentence has expired, minus good-time credits.

INTERMEDIATE SANCTIONS

Many observers feel that the most widely used sentencing options—imprisonment and probation—fail to reflect the immense diversity of crimes and criminals. **Intermediate sanctions** provide a number of additional sentencing options for those wrongdoers who require stricter supervision than that supplied by probation, but for whom imprisonment would be unduly harsh and counterproductive.[57] The intermediate sanctions discussed in this section are designed to match the specific punishment and treatment of an individual offender with a corrections program that reflects that offender's situation.

Dozens of different variations of intermediate sanctions are handed down each year. To cover the spectrum succinctly, two general categories of such sanctions will be discussed in this section: those administered primarily by the courts and those administered primarily by corrections departments, including day reporting centers, intensive supervision probation, shock incarceration, and home confinement. Remember that none of these sanctions are exclusive. They are often combined with imprisonment and probation and parole, and with each other.

Judicially Administered Sanctions

The lack of sentencing options is most frustrating for the person who, in the majority of cases, does the sentencing—the judge. Consequently, when judges are given the discretion to "color" a punishment with intermediate sanctions, they will often do so. In addition to imprisonment and probation, a judge has five sentencing options:

1. Fines.
2. Community service.
3. Restitution.
4. Pretrial diversion programs.
5. Forfeiture.

Fines, community service, and restitution were discussed in Chapter 11. In the context of intermediate sanctions, it is important to remember that these punishments are generally combined with incarceration or probation. For that reason, some critics feel the retributive or deterrent impact of such punishments is severely limited. Many European countries, in contrast, rely heavily on fines as the sole sanctions for a variety of crimes. (See the feature *Comparative Criminal Justice—Swedish Day-Fines* on the facing page.)

Intermediate Sanctions
Sanctions that are more restrictive than probation and less restrictive than imprisonment.

SWEDISH DAY-FINES

Few ideals are cherished as highly in our criminal justice system as equality. Most Americans take it for granted that individuals guilty of identical crimes should face identical punishments. From an economic perspective, however, this emphasis on equality renders our system decidedly unequal. Take two citizens, one a millionaire investment banker and the other a checkout clerk earning the minimum wage. Driving home from work one afternoon, each is caught by a traffic officer doing 80 miles per hour in a 55-mile-per-hour zone. The fine for this offense is $150. This amount, though equal for both, has different consequences: it represents mere pocket change for the investment banker, but a significant chunk out of the checkout clerk's weekly paycheck.

Restricted by a "tariff system" that sets specific amounts for specific crimes, regardless of the financial situation of the convict, American judges often refrain from using fines as a primary sanction. They either assume that poor offenders cannot pay the fine or worry that a fine will allow wealthier offenders to "buy" their way out of a punishment.

PAYING FOR CRIME

In searching for a way to make fines more effective sanctions, many reformers have seized on the concept of the "day-fine," as practiced in Sweden and several other European countries. In this system, which was established in the 1920s and 1930s, the fine amount is linked to the monetary value of the offender's daily income. Depending on the seriousness of the crime, a Swedish offender will be sentenced to 1 to 120 day-fines or, as combined punishment for multiple crimes, up to 200 day-fines.

For each day-fine unit assessed, the offender is required to pay one-thousandth of her or his annual gross income (minus a deduction for basic living expenses, as determined by the Prosecutor General's Office) to the court. Consequently, the day-fine system not only reflects the degree of the crime, but ensures that the economic burden will be equal for those with different incomes.

Swedish police and prosecutors can levy day-fines without court involvement. As a result, plea bargaining is nonexistent, and more than 80 percent of all offenders are sentenced to intermediate sanctions without a trial. The remaining cases receive full trials, with an acquittal rate of only 6 percent, compared with 32 percent in the United States.

FOR CRITICAL ANALYSIS

Do you think a "day-fine" system would be feasible in the United States? Why might it be difficult to implement in this country?

PRETRIAL DIVERSION PROGRAMS Not every criminal violation requires the courtroom process. Consequently, some judges have the discretion to order an offender into a **pretrial diversion program** during the preliminary hearing. (Prosecutors can also offer an offender the opportunity to join such a program in return for reducing or dropping the initial charges.) These programs represent an "interruption" of the criminal proceedings and are generally reserved for young or first-time offenders who have been arrested on charges of illegal drug use, child or spousal abuse, or sexual misconduct. Pretrial diversion programs usually include extensive counseling, often in a treatment center. If the offender successfully follows the conditions of the program, the criminal charges are dropped.

Several years ago, for example, New York Federal District Judge John Gleeson started offering certain drug-addicted defendants a deal: get clean, and you will not go to prison. The program's first graduate, Emily Leitch, had been arrested at New York City's Kennedy International Airport with about thirty pounds of cocaine in her luggage. For a year, Leitch was subjected to drug tests, took parenting courses, earned her high school equivalency diploma, and got a commercial bus driver's license. In February 2013, a prosecutor agreed to dismiss the drug trafficking charges against Leitch if she did not use drugs or get arrested for eighteen months. "I want to thank the federal government for giving me a chance," Leitch said following the proceedings.[58]

> **Pretrial Diversion Program**
> An alternative to trial offered by a judge or prosecutor, in which the offender agrees to participate in a specified counseling or treatment program in return for withdrawal of the charges.

In Pinellas County, Florida, Judge Dee Anna Farnell congratulates graduates of her drug court program. How does society benefit when an offender successfully completes a drug court program rather than being sent to prison or jail?
Scott Keeler/*Tampa Bay Times*/ ZUMAPRESS.com

PROBLEM-SOLVING COURTS Many judges have found opportunities to divert low-level offenders by presiding over problem-solving courts. In these comparatively informal courtrooms, judges attempt to address problems such as drug addiction, mental illness, and homelessness that often lead to the eventual rearrest of the offender.[59]

Drug Courts About three thousand problem-solving courts are operating in the United States. Although these specialized courts cover a wide variety of subjects, from domestic violence to juvenile crime to mental illness, the most common problem-solving courts are drug courts.

Although the specific procedures of drug courts vary widely, most follow a general pattern. Either after arrest or on conviction, the offender is given the option of entering a drug court program or continuing through the standard courtroom process. Those who choose the former come under the supervision of a judge who will oversee a mixture of treatment and sanctions designed to cure their addiction. When offenders successfully complete the program, the drug court rewards them by dropping all charges against them. Drug courts operate on the assumption that when a criminal addict's drug use is reduced, his or her drug-fueled criminal activity will also decline.

Growing Influence Research shows that drug courts reduce the probability of continued drug abuse and, consequently, lead to a significant reduction in recidivism rates of participants when compared with nonparticipants.[60] *Community courts,* which focus on quality-of-life offenses such as petty theft and prostitution, also have numerous benefits. A community court in New York City not only reduces participant recidivism rates, but also saves the municipal government about $1.4 million annually by keeping low-level offenders out of city jails.[61] As a result of this kind of success, problem-solving principles are moving beyond specialty courts into mainstream criminal courts, allowing judges to insert principles of restorative justice, which we discussed in Chapter 11, into their diversion efforts.

For example, more judges are taking advantage of *community dispute resolution centers* to move certain misdemeanors and minor criminal matters out of the court system completely. At these centers, specialists help the parties involved in a dispute—such as one involving vandalism or noise complaints—by *mediating,* or negotiating, a satisfactory outcome for both sides. In 2011, New York judges, prosecutors, and police officers referred more than 3,100 criminal cases to community dispute resolution centers, thus diverting the participants from the formal court system.[62]

FORFEITURE In 1970, Congress passed the Racketeer Influenced and Corrupt Organizations Act (RICO) in an attempt to prevent the use of legitimate business enterprises as shields for organized crime.[63] As amended, RICO and other statutes give judges the ability to implement forfeiture proceedings in certain criminal cases. **Forfeiture** is a process by which the government seizes property gained from or used in criminal activ-

Forfeiture The process by which the government seizes private property attached to criminal activity.

ity. For example, if a person is convicted for smuggling cocaine into the United States from South America, a judge can order the seizure of not only the narcotics, but also the speedboat the offender used to deliver the drugs to a pickup point off the coast of South Florida. In *Bennis v. Michigan* (1996),[64] the Supreme Court ruled that a person's home or car could be forfeited even though the owner was unaware that the property was connected to illegal activity.

Once property is forfeited, the government has several options. It can sell the property, with the proceeds going to the state and/or federal law enforcement agencies involved in the seizure. Alternatively, the government agency can use the property directly in further crime-fighting efforts or award it to a third party, such as an informant. Forfeiture can be financially rewarding—the U.S. Marshals Service manages nearly $4 billion worth of contraband and property impounded from criminals and criminal suspects. Each year, the agency shares about $580 million of these funds with state and local law enforcement agencies, with an additional $345 million going to crime victims.[65]

Day Reporting Centers

First used in Great Britain, **day reporting centers (DRCs)** are mainly tools to reduce jail and prison overcrowding. Although the offenders are allowed to live in the community rather than jail or prison, they must spend all or part of each day at a reporting center. In general, being sentenced to a DRC is an extreme form of supervision. With offenders under a single roof, they are much more easily monitored and controlled.

DRCs are instruments of rehabilitation as well. They often feature treatment programs for drug and alcohol abusers and provide counseling for a number of psychological problems, such as depression and anger management. Many of those found guilty in the Roanoke (Virginia) Drug Court, for example, are ordered to participate in a yearlong day reporting program. At the center, offenders meet with probation officers, submit to urine tests, and attend counseling and education programs, such as parenting and life-skills classes. After the year has passed, if the offender has completed the program to the satisfaction of the judge and has found employment, the charges will be dropped.[66]

Intensive Supervision Probation

Over the past several decades, a number of jurisdictions have turned to **intensive supervision probation (ISP)** to solve the problems associated with burdensome caseloads we discussed earlier in the chapter. ISP offers a more restrictive alternative to regular probation, with higher levels of face-to-face contact between offenders and officers and frequent modes of control such as urine tests for drugs. In New Jersey, for example, ISP officers have caseloads of only 20 offenders (compared with 115 for other probation officers in the state) and are provided with additional resources to help them keep tabs on their charges.[67] Different jurisdictions have different methods of determining who is eligible for ISP, but a majority of states limit ISP to offenders who do not have prior probation violations.

The main goal of ISP is to provide prisonlike control of offenders while keeping them out of prison. Critics of ISP believe that it "causes" high failure rates, as more supervision increases the chances that an offender will be caught breaking conditions of probation.[68] A recent comparison of ISP with DRCs, however, found the intensive supervision of ISP to be more effective. In the six months following termination of the program, DRC participants were more likely to be convicted for a new offense and to test positive for drugs than their ISP counterparts. The study suggests that when combined with services such as outpatient drug treatment and educational training, ISP can be effective in producing low rates of recidivism.[69]

Day Reporting Center (DRC) A community-based corrections center to which offenders report on a daily basis for treatment, education, and rehabilitation.

Intensive Supervision Probation (ISP) A punishment-oriented form of probation in which the offender is placed under stricter and more frequent surveillance and control than in conventional probation.

LEARNING OBJECTIVE **8** Contrast day reporting centers with intensive supervision probation.

Shock Incarceration

As the name suggests, **shock incarceration** is designed to "shock" criminals into compliance with the law. Following conviction, the offender is first sentenced to a prison or jail term. Then, usually within ninety days, he or she is released and resentenced to probation. The theory behind shock incarceration is that by getting a taste of the brutalities of the daily prison grind, the offender will be shocked into a crime-free existence.

■ Inmates engage in morning calisthenics at the Impact Incarceration Program in Illinois. In theory, why would boot camps like this one benefit first-time nonviolent offenders more than a jail or prison sentence?
Journal Courier/The Image Works Image

THE VALUE OF SHOCK In the past, shock incarceration was targeted primarily toward youthful, first-time offenders, who were thought to be more likely to be "scared straight" by a short stint behind bars. Recent data show, however, that 20 percent of all adults sentenced to probation spend some time in jail or prison before being released into the community.[70] Critics of shock incarceration are dismayed by this trend. They argue that the practice needlessly disrupts the lives of low-level offenders who would not otherwise be eligible for incarceration and exposes them to the mental and physical hardships of prison life (which we will discuss in Chapter 14).[71] Furthermore, there is little evidence that shock probationers fare any better than regular probationers when it comes to recidivism rates.[72]

BOOT CAMPS The *boot camp* is a variation on traditional shock incarceration. Instead of spending the "shock" period of incarceration in prison or jail, offenders are sent to a boot camp. Modeled on military basic training, these camps are generally located within prisons and jails, though some can be found in the community. The programs emphasize strict discipline, manual labor, and physical training. They are designed to instill self-responsibility and self-respect in participants, thereby lessening the chances that they will return to a life of crime. More recently, boot camps have also emphasized rehabilitation, incorporating such components as drug and alcohol treatment programs, anger-management courses, and vocational training.[73]

The first boot camp opened in Georgia in 1983. At the peak of their popularity in the mid-1990s, about 120 local, state, and federal boot camps housed more than seven thousand inmates. Around that time, however, studies began to show that the camps were not meeting their goals of improving rearrest rates while reducing prison populations and corrections budgets.[74] By 2000, nearly one-third of the boot camps had closed, and in 2005 the Federal Bureau of Prisons announced plans to discontinue its boot camp program.

Because of their rehabilitative and disciplinarian features, boot camps remain popular in the juvenile corrections system, and there is some evidence that they can be effective. Pennsylvania's Motivational Boot Camp Program, for instance, averages approximately four hundred admissions a year. The program reduces the amount of time

Shock Incarceration A short period of incarceration that is designed to deter further criminal activity by "shocking" the offender with the hardships of imprisonment.

participants spend in the state's corrections system by about sixteen months, saving taxpayers just over $38,000 per offender. Pennsylvania authorities make no claims, however, that the boot camp reduces recidivism rates.[75]

Home Confinement and Electronic Monitoring

Various forms of **home confinement**—in which offenders serve their sentences not in a government institution but at home—have existed for centuries. It has often served, and continues to do so, as a method of political control, used by totalitarian regimes to isolate and silence dissidents. For purposes of general law enforcement, home confinement was impractical until relatively recently. After all, one could not expect offenders to keep their promises to stay at home, and the personnel costs of guarding them were prohibitive. In the 1980s, however, with the advent of **electronic monitoring,** or using technology to guard the prisoner, home confinement became more viable. Today, all fifty states and the federal government have home monitoring programs with about 130,000 offenders, including probationers and parolees, participating at any one time.[76]

THE LEVELS OF HOME MONITORING Home monitoring has three general levels of restriction:

1. *Curfew,* which requires offenders to be in their homes at specific hours each day, usually at night.
2. *Home detention,* which requires that offenders remain home at all times, with exceptions being made for education, employment, counseling, or other specified activities such as the purchase of food or, in some instances, attendance at religious ceremonies.
3. *Home incarceration,* which requires the offender to remain home at all times, save for medical emergencies.

LEARNING **9** OBJECTIVE List the three levels of home monitoring.

Under ideal circumstances, home confinement serves many of the goals of intermediate sanctions. It protects the community. It saves public funds and space in correctional facilities by keeping convicts out of institutional incarceration. It meets public expectations of punishment for criminals. Uniquely, home confinement also recognizes that convicts, despite their crimes, play important roles in the community, and allows them to continue in those roles. An offender, for example, may be given permission to leave confinement to care for elderly parents.

Home confinement is also lauded for giving sentencing officials the freedom to match the punishment with the needs of the offender. In Missouri, for instance, the conditions of detention for a musician required him to remain at home during the day, but allowed him to continue his career at night. In addition, he was obliged to make antidrug statements before each performance, to be verified by the manager at the club where he appeared.

TYPES OF ELECTRONIC MONITORING According to some reports, the inspiration for electronic monitoring was a *Spider-Man* comic book in which the hero was trailed by the use of an electronic device on his arm. In 1979, a New Mexico judge named

■ Offenders who are confined to their homes are often monitored by electronic devices like this one, which fits around the ankle. What are some of the benefits of electronic monitoring as an intermediate sanction?
Damon Higgins/ZUMA Press/Newscom

Jack Love, having read the comic, convinced an executive at Honeywell, Inc., to begin developing similar technology to supervise convicts.[77]

Two major types of electronic monitoring have grown out of Love's initial concept. The first is a "programmed contact" program, in which the offender is contacted periodically by telephone or beeper to verify his or her whereabouts. Verification is obtained via a computer that uses voice or visual identification techniques or by requiring the offender to enter a code in an electronic box when called. The second is a "continuously signaling" device, worn around the convict's wrist, ankle, or neck. A transmitter in the device sends out a continuous signal to a "receiver-dialer" device located in the offender's dwelling. If the receiver device does not detect a signal from the transmitter, it informs a central computer, and the police are notified.[78]

TECHNOLOGICAL ADVANCES IN ELECTRONIC MONITORING As electronic monitoring technology has evolved, the ability of community corrections officials to target specific forms of risky behavior has greatly increased. A Michigan court, for example, has begun placing black boxes in the automobiles of repeat traffic law violators. Not only do these boxes record information about the offenders' driving habits for review by probation officers, but they also emit a loud beep when the car goes too fast or stops too quickly. Another device—an ankle bracelet—is able to test a person's sweat for alcohol levels and transmit the results over the Internet.

CJ& TECHNOLOGY   GLOBAL POSITIONING SYSTEM (GPS)

AP Photo/Jeff T. Green

After probationer Henry L. Murray committed a series of robberies in the Gainesville, Florida, area, he fled north into Georgia. Murray may have felt he was beyond the reach of the law, but Georgia authorities soon found him, thanks in large part to the global positioning system (GPS) device strapped to his ankle. GPS technology is a form of tracking technology that relies on twenty-four military satellites orbiting thousands of miles above the earth. The satellites transmit signals to each other and to a receiver on the ground, allowing a monitoring station to determine the location of a receiving device to within a few feet. GPS provides a much more precise level of supervision than regular electronic monitoring. A probationer like Murray wears a transmitter, similar to a traditional electronic monitor, around his or her ankle or wrist. This transmitter communicates with a portable tracking device (PTD), a small box that uses the military satellites to determine the probationer's movements.

GPS technology can be used either "actively" to constantly monitor the subject's whereabouts, or "passively" to ensure that the offender remains within the confines of a limited area determined by a judge or probation officer. Inclusion and exclusion zones are also important to GPS supervision. Inclusion zones are areas such as a home or workplace where the offender is expected to be at certain times. Exclusion zones are areas such as parks, playgrounds, and schools where the offender is not permitted to go. GPS-linked computers can alert officials immediately when an exclusion zone has been breached and create a computerized record of the probationer's movements for review at a later time. Despite the benefits of this technology, it is rarely implemented. According to the Bureau of Justice Statistics, only about eight thousand probationers are currently being tracked by GPS.

Thinking about GPS

How might GPS monitoring be used to improve and overhaul the American bail system, covered in Chapter 9?

EFFECTIVENESS OF HOME CONFINEMENT Because most participants in home confinement programs are low-risk offenders, their recidivism rates are quite low. Indeed, these programs appear to be no more or less effective than those that rely on human supervision, with most of their upside coming from the benefits mentioned earlier, such as cost savings and offender freedom.[79] One concern about home confinement is that offenders are often required to defray program costs, which can be as high as $100 per week. Consequently, those who cannot afford to pay for electronic monitoring may not be eligible. Furthermore, families of offenders confined to the home can experience high levels of stress and a loss of privacy.[80] In general, however, those who successfully complete a home confinement term seem to benefit in areas such as obtaining and holding employment.[81]

Widen the Net The criticism that intermediate sanctions designed to divert offenders from prison actually increase the number of citizens who are under the control and surveillance of the American corrections system.

Widening the Net

As mentioned above, most of the convicts chosen for intermediate sanctions are low-risk offenders. From the point of view of the corrections official doing the choosing, this makes sense. Such offenders are less likely to commit crimes and attract negative publicity. This selection strategy, however, appears to invalidate one of the primary reasons intermediate sanctions exist: to reduce prison and jail populations. If most of the offenders in intermediate sanctions programs would otherwise have received probation, then the effect on these populations is nullified. Indeed, studies have shown this to be the case.[82]

At the same time, intermediate sanctions broaden the reach of the corrections system. In other words, they increase rather than decrease the amount of control the state exerts over the individual. Suppose a person is arrested for a misdemeanor such as shoplifting and, under normal circumstances, would receive probation. With access to intermediate sanctions, the judge may add a period of home confinement to the sentence. Critics contend that such practices **widen the net** of the corrections system by augmenting the number of citizens who are under the control and surveillance of the state and also *strengthen the net* by increasing the government's power to intervene in the lives of its citizens.[83] Technological advances—such as the black boxes in automobiles, sweat-testing ankle bracelets, and GPS devices mentioned in this chapter—will only accelerate the trend.

SELF ASSESSMENT

Fill in the blanks and check your answers on page 417.

Judicially administered sanctions include fines, restitution, and _____, a process in which the government seizes property connected to illegal activity. Offenders may also be sentenced to spend part of their time at _____ _____ _____, where they receive treatment and are more easily _____ by corrections officials. _____ _____, or militaristic programs designed to instill self-responsibility, are a form of _____ incarceration. Home confinement, another intermediate sanction, has become more effective in recent years thanks to technology known as _____ _____.

THE PARADOX OF COMMUNITY CORRECTIONS

Despite their many benefits, including cost savings, treatment options, and the ability to divert hundreds of thousands of nonviolent wrongdoers from prisons and jails, community-based corrections programs suffer from a basic paradox: the more effectively

How do policies that favor increased surveillance of clients by probation officers contribute to the paradox of community corrections?
Los Angeles County Probation Department

offenders are controlled, the more likely they are to be caught violating the terms of their conditional release. As you may have noticed, the community supervision programs discussed in this chapter are evaluated according to rates of recidivism and revocation, with low levels of each reflecting a successful program. Increased control and surveillance, however, will necessarily raise the level of violations, thus increasing the probability that any single violation will be discovered. Therefore, as factors such as the number of conditions placed on probationers and the technological proficiency of electronic monitoring devices increase, so, too, will the number of offenders who fail to meet the conditions of their community-based punishment.

One observer calls this the "quicksand" effect of increased surveillance. Instead of helping offenders leave the corrections system, increased surveillance pulls them more deeply into it.[84] The quicksand effect can be quite strong, according to researchers Barbara Sims of Penn State University–Harrisburg and Mark Jones of East Carolina University. In a study of North Carolina corrections data, Sims and Jones found that 26 percent of the probationers whose probation terms were revoked had been guilty of violations such as failing a single drug test. The researchers believe this strategy is overly punitive, given the difficulties of breaking an addiction.[85]

CJ IN ACTION

INVOLUNTARY COMMITMENT OF THE MENTALLY ILL

Most people who suffer from mental illness are not criminals, and most criminals are not mentally ill. As we saw in Chapter 2, however, there appears to be a correlation between mental illness and violent behavior. So, under certain circumstances that we will explore in this *CJ in Action* feature, mental health professionals have the same powers as criminal justice professionals—they can restrict the freedom of potentially dangerous individuals for the good of society. As in the criminal justice system, however, this power is fraught with controversy and fears of making the wrong decision.

THE NEED FOR TREATMENT

Cousins Jesse Ramirez, seven, and Edwin Pellecier, ten, were playing in a Phoenix park when, for no apparent reason, Joe Gallegos killed them with a baseball bat. As it became clear that Gallegos suffered from schizophrenia and other mental ailments, many community members wondered why he was on the streets. Arizona, like every other state, has an *involuntary civil commitment* law, under which mentally ill individuals can be held in custody and committed to a psychiatric hospital against their wishes. Involuntary commitment, like imprisonment for criminals, raises due process concerns because it involves a significant deprivation of liberty.[86] Therefore, states must devise procedures that protect the rights of mentally ill individuals during this process.

Arizona actually has a fairly flexible involuntary commitment law. Anyone with knowledge of a person's unstable behavior—such as a parent, teacher, or friend—can petition for a court-ordered mental health evaluation. Then, if the court finds a "need for treatment," the person can be involuntarily committed.[87] Indeed, prior to committing double murder, Joe Gallegos was involuntarily committed twice by family members. Both times, he was released when medical authorities decided that he did not pose a threat to himself or others. When discussing issues of mental health and crime, one question inevitably arises: Should we make it easier to involuntarily commit mentally ill individuals, for their safety and our own?

THE CASE FOR LENIENT INVOLUNTARY COMMITMENT STANDARDS

- More lenient standards would allow for the care and rehabilitation of individuals who need treatment and are not receiving it.

- Such standards would protect society from the dangers posed by the untreated mentally ill.

- Treatment before arrest would also prevent many criminal acts from taking place and spare society the costs of incarceration.[88]

THE CASE AGAINST LENIENT INVOLUNTARY COMMITMENT STANDARDS

- Such standards infringe on the rights of the mentally ill. As the United States Supreme Court has stated, "the mere presence of mental illness does not disqualify a person from preferring his home to the comforts of an institution."[89]

- Only a small percentage of people with mental illnesses behave violently, and it is very difficult to predict whether a person will present a future danger. More lenient commitment standards would strip many harmless people of their freedoms unnecessarily.[90]

- States do not have the funds or the capacity to treat a large influx of new psychiatric patients.

WRITING ASSIGNMENT—YOUR OPINION

As you have seen throughout this textbook, substance abuse has a strong connection to criminality. For that reason, the American corrections system routinely mandates substance abuse treatment for those under community supervision or behind bars. But what if alcohol or drug problems could be addressed before the first arrest? Research shows that early treatment improves an addict's ability to stay off drugs and alcohol, and therefore lessens the chances of future wrongdoing.[91]

Would you support a law, similar to Arizona's involuntary commitment law, that would allow concerned parties—family members, co-workers, or friends—to petition a court for involuntary substance abuse treatment? In other words, the law would permit one adult to force another adult, with judicial approval, to get treatment for drug or alcohol abuse. How could such a law be written to balance individual rights and society's need for protection? Would it successfully divert potential offenders from the criminal justice system? Before responding, you can review our discussions in this chapter concerning:

- Diversion (pages 391–392)

- Drug courts (page 408)

- Widening the net (page 413)

Your answer should include at least three full paragraphs.

CHAPTER SUMMARY

For more information on these concepts, look back to the Learning Objective icons throughout the chapter.

 Explain the justifications for community-based corrections programs. One justification involves reintegration of the offender into society. Reintegration restores family ties, encourages employment and education, and secures a place for the offender in the routine functioning of society. Other justifications involve diversion and cost savings. By diverting criminals to alternative modes of punishment, further overcrowding of jail and prison facilities can be avoided, as can the costs of incarcerating the offenders.

 Explain several alternative sentencing arrangements that combine probation with incarceration. With a suspended sentence, a convicted offender is not required to serve the sentence, but the judge has the option of reinstating the sentence if the person reoffends. In addition, there are three other general types of sentencing arrangements: (a) split sentence probation, in which the judge specifies a certain time in jail or prison followed by a certain time on probation; (b) shock incarceration, in which a judge sentences an offender to be incarcerated, but allows that person to petition the court to be released on probation; and (c) intermittent incarceration, in which an offender spends a certain amount of time each week in jail or in a halfway house or another government institution.

 Specify the conditions under which an offender is most likely to be denied probation. The offender (a) has been convicted of multiple charges, (b) was on probation or parole when arrested, (c) has two or more prior convictions, (d) is addicted to narcotics, (e) seriously injured the victim of the crime, or (f) used a weapon while committing the crime.

 Describe the three general categories of conditions placed on a probationer. (a) Standard conditions, such as requiring that the probationer notify the agency of a change of address, not leave the jurisdiction without permission, and remain employed; (b) punitive conditions, such as restitution, community service, and home confinement; and (c) treatment conditions, such as required drug or alcohol treatment.

 Identify the main differences between probation and parole. Probation is a sentence handed down by a judge that generally acts as an alternative to incarceration. Parole is a form of early release from prison determined by a parole authority, often a parole board. Probationers are usually first-time offenders who have committed nonviolent crimes, while parolees have often spent significant time in prison.

 List the four basic roles of the parole board. Parole boards (a) decide which inmates should be granted parole, (b) determine the conditions of parole, (c) resolve when an offender has satisfied his or her parole requirements, and (d) determine whether parole privileges should be revoked if a violation has occurred.

 Explain which factors influence the decision to grant parole. In deciding whether to grant parole, parole board members primarily consider the severity of the underlying crime and the threat the offender will pose to the community if released. Other factors include the offender's level of remorse and his or her behavior while incarcerated.

 Contrast day reporting centers with intensive supervision probation. In a day reporting center, the offender is allowed to remain in the community, but must spend all or part of each day at the reporting center. While at the center, offenders meet with probation officers, submit to drug tests, and attend counseling and education programs. With intensive supervision probation (ISP), more restrictions are imposed, and there is more face-to-face contact between offenders and probation officers. ISP may also include electronic surveillance.

 List the three levels of home monitoring. (a) Curfew, which requires that the offender be at home during specified hours; (b) home detention, which requires that the offender be at home except for education, employment, and counseling; and (c) home incarceration, which requires that the offender be at home at all times except for medical emergencies.

QUESTIONS FOR CRITICAL ANALYSIS

1. Why might probationers or parolees want to limit their social media activity? Give an example of a circumstance in which a Facebook posting could cause probation or parole to be revoked.

2. Review our discussion of Hawaii's Opportunity Probation with Enforcement (HOPE). What might explain why second violations of the urine tests are rare?

3. In many jurisdictions, parolees can be stopped and searched by parole or police officers at any time, even if there is no probable cause that the parolee has committed a crime. How can these types of stops and searches be justified?

4. How might technology such as GPS-enhanced electronic monitoring ease the caseload burden of probation officers?

5. In your own words, explain what the phrase "widening the net" means. What might be some of the unintended consequences of increasing the number of offenders who are supervised by corrections officers in the community?

KEY TERMS

authority 397
caseload 397
community corrections 391
day reporting center (DRC) 409
discretionary release 403
diversion 391
electronic monitoring 411
forfeiture 408
home confinement 411

intensive supervision probation (ISP) 409
intermediate sanctions 406
mandatory release 404
parole 400
parole board 403
parole contract 402
parole grant hearing 403
parole guidelines 404

parole revocation 402
pretrial diversion program 407
probation 392
reintegration 391
shock incarceration 410
split sentence probation 393
suspended sentence 393
technical violation 397
widen the net 413

SELF ASSESSMENT ANSWER KEY

Page 392: **i.** reintegration; **ii.** diversion; **iii.** cost; **iv.** less

Page 400: **i.** community; **ii.** probation officer; **iii.** technical violation; **iv.** conditions; **v.** prison or jail; **vi.** recidivism; **vii.** caseloads

Page 406: **i.** conditional; **ii.** sentence; **iii.** contract; **iv.** technical; **v.** parole board; **vi.** mandatory

Page 413: **i.** forfeiture; **ii.** day reporting centers; **iii.** supervised; **iv.** Boot camps; **v.** shock; **vi.** electronic monitoring

NOTES

1. Bureau of Justice Statistics, *Probation and Parole in the United States, 2011* (Washington, D.C.: U.S. Department of Justice, November 2012), 1–2.

2. Michael Tonry, *Sentencing Matters* (New York: Oxford Press, 1996), 28.

3. *Probation and Parole in the United States, 2011,* 2.

4. Corrections Task Force of the President's Commission on Law Enforcement and Administration of Justice (1967).

5. Paul H. Hahn, *Emerging Criminal Justice: Three Pillars for a Proactive Justice System* (Thousand Oaks, CA: Sage Publications, 1998), 106–108.

6. Bureau of Justice Statistics, *Correctional Populations in the United States, 2011* (Washington, D.C.: U.S. Department of Justice, November 2012), Table 2, page 3.

7. "Cutting Costs: How States Are Addressing Corrections Budget Shortfalls," *Corrections Directions* (December 2008), 6.

8. John Schmitt, Kris Warner, and Sarika Gupta, *The High Budgetary Cost of Incarceration* (Washington, D.C.: Center for Economic and Policy Research, June 2010), Table 4, page 11.

9. Donna Lyons, "States Are Reshaping Policies to Save Money and Maintain Public Safety with 'Justice Reinvestment' Reforms," *State Legislature Magazine* (January 2013), at **www.ncsl.org/issues -research/justice/high-yield-corrections.aspx.**

10. Nathan Koppel, "Probation Pays Bills for Prosecutors," *Wall Street Journal* (February 12, 2012), A2.

11. Paul W. Keve, *Crime Control and Justice in America* (Chicago: American Library Association, 1995), 183.

12. Gerald Bayens and John Ortiz Smykla, *Probation, Parole, & Community-Based Corrections* (New York: McGraw-Hill, 2013), 186–217.

13. Bureau of Justice Statistics, *Probation and Parole in the United States, 2010* (Washington, D.C.: U.S. Department of Justice, December 2011), Appendix table 3, page 31.

14. Joan Petersilia and Susan Turner, *Prison versus Probation in California: Implications for Crime and Offender Recidivism* (Santa Monica, CA: RAND Corporation, 1986).

15. *Probation and Parole in the United States, 2011,* Appendix table 3, page 17.

16. Brian Skoloff, "George Sanders Gets Probation in Mercy Killing," *Associated Press* (March 29, 2013).

17. *Probation and Parole in the United States, 2011,* Appendix table 3, page 17.

18. *Ibid.;* and Bureau of Justice Statistics, *Prisoners in 2011* (Washington, D.C.: U.S. Department of Justice, December 2012), Table 1, page 2.

19. Sharyn Adams, Lindsay Bostwick, and Rebecca Campbell, *Examining Illinois Probationer Characteristics and Outcomes* (Chicago: Illinois Criminal Justice Information Authority, September 2011), Table 1, pages 16–17.

20. 705 So.2d 172 (La. 1997).

21. Neil P. Cohen and James J. Gobert, *The Law of Probation and Parole* (Colorado Springs, CO: Shepard's/McGraw-Hill, 1983), Section 5.01, 183–184; Section 5.03, 191–192.

22. 534 U.S. 112 (2001).

23. *Ibid.,* 113.

24. Carl B. Klockars, Jr., "A Theory of Probation Supervision," *Journal of Criminal Law, Criminology, and Police Science* 63 (1972), 550–557.

25. *Ibid.,* 551.

26. Hahn, 116–118.

27. Matthew T. DeMichele, *Probation and Parole's Growing Caseloads and Workload Allocation: Strategies for Managerial Decision Making* (Lexington, KY: American Probation and Parole Association, May 2007).

28. Brad Branna, "Sacramento County Probation Officers Have Highest Caseload in State," *Sacramento Bee* (April 10, 2013), at **www.sacbee .com/2013/04/10/5329755/sacramento-county-probation -officers.html**.

29. 389 U.S. 128 (1967).

30. *Morrissey v. Brewer,* 408 U.S. 471 (1972); and *Gagnon v. Scarpelli,* 411 U.S. 778 (1973).

31. 465 U.S. 420 (1984).

32. *Probation and Parole in the United States, 2011,* table 4, page 6.

33. Jennifer L. Skeem and Sarah Manchak, "Back to the Future: From Klockars' Model of Effective Supervision to Evidence-Based Practice in Probation," *Journal of Offender Rehabilitation* 47 (2008), 231.

34. William Rhodes, et al., *Recidivism of Offenders on Federal Community Supervision* (Cambridge, MA: Abt Associates, December 2012), 8, 12–13.

35. Elizabeth K. Drake, Steve Aos, and Robert Barnoski, *Washington's Offender Accountability Act: Final Report on Recidivism Outcomes* (Olympia, WA: Washington State Institute for Public Policy, January 2010).

36. Skeem and Manchak, 226–229.

37. Sarah K. Jalbert, et al., *A Multi-Site Evaluation of Reduced Probation Caseload Size in an Evidence-Based Setting* (Cambridge, MA: Abt Associates, March 2011), 8–10.

38. Graeme Wood, "Prison without Walls," *The Atlantic* (September 2010), 92–93.

39. Angela Hawken and Mark Kleiman, *Managing Drug Involved Probationers and Swift and Certain Sanctions: Evaluating Hawaii's HOPE* (Washington, D.C.: U.S. Department of Justice, December 2009), 4.

40. California Penal Code Sections 1210, 1210.1 (West Supp. 2004); and California Health and Safety Code Sections 11999.4–11999.13 (West Supp. 2004).

41. Douglas Longshore, Angela Hawken, Darren Urada, and M. Douglas Anglin, *Evaluation of the Substance Abuse and Crime Prevention Act: SACPA Cost-Analysis Report (First and Second Years)* (Los Angeles: UCLA Integrated Substance Abuse Programs, 2006), 5.

42. Todd R. Clear, George F. Cole, and Michael D. Reisig, *American Corrections,* 9th ed. (Belmont, CA: Wadsworth Cengage Learning, 2011), 408.

43. *Probation and Parole in the United States, 2011,* table 6, page 8.

44. Joseph Walker, "Rules May Help Parolees Avoid Jail for Small Errors," *New York Times* (January 5, 2012), at **cityroom.blogs.nytimes .com/2012/01/05/rating-a-parolees-risk-before-a-return-to-prison**.

45. *Morrissey v. Brewer,* 408 U.S. 471 (1972).

46. Todd R. Clear and Edward Latessa, "Probation Officer Roles in Intensive Supervision: Surveillance versus Treatment," *Justice Quarterly* 10 (1993), 441–462.

47. 442 U.S. 1 (1979).

48. Marie Gottschalk, "Days without End: Life Sentences and Penal Reform," *Prison Legal News* (April 11, 2013), at **www.prisonlegalnews .org/24102_displayArticle.aspx**.

49. William Parker, *Parole: Origins, Development, Current Practices, and Statutes* (College Park, MD: American Correctional Association, 1972), 26.

50. "Michigan Lets Prisoners Go—and Saves a Bundle," *Bloomberg Businessweek* (December 11, 2011), 16.

51. Quoted in Michael Virtanen, "Chapman Denied Parole a Seventh Time," *Associated Press* (August 24, 2012).

52. Clear, Cole, and Reisig, 420–421.

53. Mark P. Rankin, Mark H. Allenbaugh, and Carlton Fields, "Parole's Essential Role in Bailing Out Our Nation's Criminal Justice Systems," *Champion* (January 2009), 47–48.

54. Quoted in Deanna Durante and Karen Araiza, "Wife's Family Protests Killer Husband's Release," *NBC10 Philadelphia* (January 17, 2013), at **www.nbcphiladelphia.com/news/local/Robb-Victim-Family -Upset-Murderer-Paroled-187229111.html**.

55. 18 U.S.C. Section 3771(a)(4) (2006).

56. Frances P. Bernat, et al., "Victim Impact Laws and the Parole Process in the United States: Balancing Victim and Inmate Rights and Interests," *International Review of Victimology* 3 (1994), 134.

57. Norval Morris and Michael Tonry, *Between Prison and Probation: Intermediate Punishments in a Rational Sentencing System* (Oxford: Oxford University Press, 1990).

58. Quoted in Mosi Secret, "Outside Box, Federal Judges Offer Addicts a Free Path," *New York Times* (March 2, 2013), A1.

59. West Huddleston and Douglas B. Marlowe, *Painting the Current Picture: A National Report on Drug Courts and Other Problem-Solving Programs in the United States* (Alexandria, VA: National Drug Court Institute, July 2011).

60. Shelli B. Rossman, et al., *The Multi-Site Adult Drug Court Evaluation: Executive Summary* (Washington, D.C.: Urban Institute, November 2011), 5.

61. Kelli Henry and Dana Kralstein, *Community Courts: The Research Literature* (New York: Center for Court Innovation, 2011), 8, 12.

62. *Community Dispute Resolution Centers Program: Annual Report 2010– 2011* (New York: New York State Unified Court System, February 2012), 14.

63. 18 U.S.C. Sections 1961–1968.

64. 516 U.S. 442 (1996).

65. David Ashenfelter, "Police Gain Millions from Forfeited Assets," *Detroit Free Press* (February 27, 2012), A3.

66. Model State Drug Court Legislation Committee, *Model State Drug Court Legislation: Model Drug Offender Accountability and Treatment Act* (Alexandria, VA: National Drug Court Institute, May 2004), 42.

67. New Jersey Courts, "ISP Fact Sheet," at **www.judiciary.state.nj.us /probsup/11556_overviewfactsheet.pdf**.

68. Joan Petersilia and Susan Turner, "Intensive Probation and Parole," *Crime and Justice* 17 (1993), 281–335.

69. Douglas J. Boyle, et al., *Outcomes of a Randomized Trial of an Intensive Community Corrections Program—Day Reporting Center— for Parolees, Final Report for the National Institute of Justice* (October 2011), 3–4.

70. *Probation and Parole in the United States, 2010,* Appendix table 3, page 31.

71. Clear, Cole, and Reisig, 125.

72. Paul Stageberg and Bonnie Wilson, *Recidivism Among Iowa Probationers* (Des Moines, IA: The Iowa Division of Criminal and Juvenile Justice

Planning, July 2005); and Paul Koniceck, *Five Year Recidivism Follow-Up Offender Releases* (Columbus, OH: Ohio Department of Rehabilitation and Correction, August 1996).

73. Dale Parent, *Correctional Boot Camps: Lessons from a Decade of Research* (Washington, D.C.: U.S. Department of Justice, June 2003), 6.

74. *Ibid.,* 8, 11–12.

75. Cynthia A. Kempinen, "Pennsylvania's Motivational Boot Camp Program: What Have We Learned over the Last Seventeen Years?" *Pennsylvania Commission on Sentencing Research Bulletin* (March 2011), 1.

76. Robert S. Gable, "Left to Their Own Devices: Should Manufacturers of Offender Monitoring Equipment Be Liable for Design Defect?" *University of Illinois Journal of Law, Technology, and Policy* (Fall 2009), 334.

77. Josh Kurtz, "New Growth in a Captive Market," *New York Times* (December 31, 1989), 12.

78. Edna Erez, Peter R. Ibarra, and Norman A. Lurie, "Electronic Monitoring of Domestic Violence Cases—A Study of Two Bilateral Programs," *Federal Probation* (June 2004), 15–20.

79. Office of Justice Programs, *Home Confinement/Electronic Monitoring Literature Review* (Washington, D.C.: U.S. Department of Justice, 2009).

80. William Bales, et al., *A Quantitative and Qualitative Assessment of Electronic Monitoring* (Tallahassee, FL: Florida State University Center for Criminology and Public Policy Research, January 2010), 89–92.

81. Terry Baumer and Robert Mendelsohn, *The Electronic Monitoring of Nonviolent Convicted Felons* (Washington, D.C.: National Institute of Justice, 1992).

82. Michael Tonry and Mary Lynch, "Intermediate Sanctions," in *Crime and Justice,* vol. 20, ed. Michael Tonry (Chicago: University of Chicago Press, 1996), 99.

83. Dennis Palumbo, Mary Clifford, and Zoann K. Snyder-Joy, "From Net Widening to Intermediate Sanctions: The Transformation of Alternatives to Incarceration from Benevolence to Malevolence," in *Smart Sentencing: The Emergence of Intermediate Sanctions,* ed. James M. Byrne, Arthur Lurigio, and Joan Petersilia (Newbury Park, CA: Sage, 1992), 231.

84. Keve, 207.

85. Barbara Sims and Mark Jones, "Predicting Success or Failure on Probation: Factors Associated with Felony Probation Outcomes," *Crime and Delinquency* (July 1997), 314–327.

86. *Addington v. Texas,* 441 U.S. 418, 425 (1979).

87. Arizona Revised Statute Section 36-3701 (Supp. 2000).

88. Andrew P. Wilper, et al., "The Health and Health Care of U.S. Prisoners: Results of a National Survey," *American Journal of Public Health* (April 2009), 673–679.

89. *O'Connor v. Donaldson,* 422 U.S. 563, 575 (1975).

90. Jacob Sullum, "The Slippery Slope of Locking Up Loons," *Chicago Sun-Times* (January 19, 2011), 27.

91. David Farabee, et al., "The Effectiveness of Coerced Treatment for Drug-Abusing Offenders," *Federal Probation* 2 (1998), 3–7.

CHAPTER

13

Prisons and Jails

AP Photo/Rich Pedroncelli

To target your study and review, look for these numbered Learning Objective icons throughout the chapter.

COST CUTTING IN CORRECTIONS

THE FLORIDA Department of Corrections was facing two major problems. First, it was under orders from the governor to reduce its annual $2.4 billion budget. Second, thanks to dropping crime rates, it had too many prison beds (116,000) for too few prisoners (101,000). Given that, in the words of one state legislator, no "tooth fairy" was likely to come to the rescue with extra funds, Florida corrections officials decided to take a step that would have been unthinkable even five years earlier. In 2012, hoping to alleviate both of its problems, the state announced the closing of seven prisons with the goal of saving $76 million.

Florida has not been alone in taking such drastic steps to reduce corrections costs. Also in 2012, Illinois decided to end operations at two of its prisons, and since 2009 Michigan and New York have shut down eight and seven prisons, respectively. Numerous states have also taken steps to steer nonviolent offenders to community corrections, thereby reserving expensive prison space for riskier criminals. These policy choices reflect a small but significant trend in American corrections: fewer inmates. In 2010, the total U.S. prison population declined for the first time in nearly four decades. Then, in 2011 and 2012, the number of inmates decreased again.

To be sure, the decreases were slight—totaling about 1 percent—and do little to threaten our nation's title as "the globe's leading incarcerator." About 2.3 million Americans are in prison and jail. The United States locks up six times as many of its citizens as Canada does, and seven times as many as most European democracies. Still, the fact that state politicians are willing to accept policies that reduce the number of inmates represents a sea change in the country's corrections strategies. Texas, for example, recently lowered its prison population by more than one thousand by directing eligible inmates into rehabilitation programs that improved their prospects of an early release. According to Jerry Madden, a state representative from Plano, this does not mean that Texans have stopped being "tough on crime." Rather, it shows that "We [are] being smart."

1. Closing a prison does have negative consequences. It can put prison employees out of work, hurting the local economy. It also requires that inmates be transferred to other prisons, which often forces their families to drive greater distances for visits. Are these negatives acceptable in light of the cost savings associated with prison closings? Why or why not?

2. By most measures, the United States imprisons more of its citizens any other country in the world. Economic considerations aside, what is your opinion of our dramatically high incarceration rates?

3. In their continuing efforts to cut corrections costs, some Florida officials want private health-care companies to provide medical treatment to state inmates. For the most part, the government is responsible for prison-related services in this country. Do you think that private companies should be allowed to provide such services? Explain your answer.

AP Photo/Rich Pedroncelli, File

About 2.3 million inmates are incarcerated in the United States, including this group exercising in the main yard at the Pelican Bay State Prison near Crescent City, California.

Gray wall studio/Shutterstock.com

A SHORT HISTORY OF AMERICAN PRISONS

Penitentiary An early form of correctional facility that emphasized separating inmates from society and from each other.

Today's high rates of imprisonment—often referred to as evidence of "mass incarceration" in the United States—are the result of many criminal justice strategies that we have discussed in this textbook. These include truth-in-sentencing guidelines, relatively long sentences for gun and drug crimes, "three-strikes" habitual offender laws, and judicial freedom to incarcerate convicts for relatively minor criminal behavior. At the base of all these policies is a philosophy that sees prisons primarily as instruments of punishment. The loss of freedom imposed on inmates is the penalty for the crimes they have committed. Punishment has not, however, always been the main reason for incarceration in this country.

English Roots

The prisons of eighteenth-century England, known as "bridewells" after London's Bridewell Palace, had little to do with punishment. These facilities were mainly used to hold debtors or those awaiting trial, execution, or banishment from the community. (In many ways, as will be made clear, these facilities resembled the modern jail.) English courts generally imposed one of two sanctions on convicted felons: they turned them loose, or they executed them.[1] To be sure, most felons were released, pardoned either by the court or the clergy after receiving a whipping or a branding.

The correctional system in the American colonies differed very little from that of their motherland. If anything, colonial administrators were more likely to use corporal punishment than their English counterparts, and the death penalty was not uncommon in early America. The one dissenter was William Penn, who adopted the "Great Law" in Pennsylvania in 1682. Based on Quaker ideals of humanity and rehabilitation, this criminal code forbade the use of torture and mutilation as forms of punishment. Instead, felons were ordered to pay restitution of property or goods to their victims. If the offenders did not have sufficient property to make restitution, they were placed in a prison, which was primarily a "workhouse."[2] The death penalty was still allowed under the "Great Law," but only in cases of premeditated murder. Penn proved to be an exception, however, and the path to reform was much slower in the colonies than in England.

Walnut Street Prison: The First Penitentiary

On William Penn's death in 1718, the "Great Law" was rescinded in favor of a harsher criminal code, similar to those of the other colonies. At the time of the American Revolution, however, the Quakers were instrumental in the first broad swing of the incarceration pendulum from punishment to rehabilitation. In 1776, Pennsylvania passed legislation ordering that offenders be reformed through treatment and discipline rather than simply beaten or executed.[3] Several states, including Massachusetts and New York, quickly followed Pennsylvania's example.

Pennsylvania continued its reformist ways by opening the country's first **penitentiary** in a wing of Philadelphia's Walnut Street Jail in 1790. The penitentiary operated on the assumption that silence and labor provided the best hope of rehabilitating the criminal spirit. Remaining silent would force the prisoners to think about their crimes, and eventually the weight of conscience would lead to repentance. At the same time, enforced labor would attack the problem of idleness—regarded as the main cause of crime by penologists of the time.[4] Consequently, inmates at Walnut Street were isolated from one another in solitary rooms and kept busy with constant menial chores.

Contrast the Pennsylvania and the New York penitentiary theories of the 1800s. LEARNING OBJECTIVE **1**

Eventually, the penitentiary at Walnut Street succumbed to the same problems that continue to plague institutions of confinement: overcrowding and excessive costs. As an influx of inmates forced more than one person to be housed in a room, maintaining silence became nearly impossible. By the early 1800s, officials could not find work for all of the convicts, so many were left idle.

The Great Penitentiary Rivalry: Pennsylvania versus New York

The apparent lack of success at Walnut Street did little to dampen enthusiasm for the penitentiary concept. Throughout the first half of the nineteenth century, a number of states reacted to prison overcrowding by constructing new penitentiaries. Each state tended to have its own peculiar twist on the roles of silence and labor, and two such systems—those of Pennsylvania and New York—emerged to shape the debate over the most effective way to run a prison.

THE PENNSYLVANIA SYSTEM After the failure of Walnut Street, Pennsylvania constructed two new prisons: the Western Penitentiary near Pittsburgh (opened in 1826) and the Eastern Penitentiary in Cherry Hill, near Philadelphia (1829). The Pennsylvania system took the concept of silence as a virtue to new extremes. Based on the idea of **separate confinement,** these penitentiaries were constructed with back-to-back cells facing outward from the center. (See Figure 13.1 below for the layout of the original Eastern Penitentiary.) To protect each inmate from the corrupting influence of the others, prisoners worked, slept, and ate alone in their cells. Their only contact with other human beings came in the form of religious instruction from a visiting clergyman or prison official.[5]

THE NEW YORK SYSTEM If Pennsylvania's prisons were designed to transform wrong-doers into honest citizens, those in New York focused on obedience. When New York's Newgate Prison (built in 1791) became overcrowded, the state authorized the construction of Auburn Prison, which opened in 1816. Auburn initially operated under many of the same assumptions that guided the penitentiary at Walnut Street. Solitary confinement, however, seemed to lead to an inordinate amount of sickness, insanity, and even suicide among inmates, and it was abandoned in 1822. Nine years later, Elam Lynds became warden at Auburn and instilled the **congregate system,** also known as the Auburn system. Like Pennsylvania's separate confinement system, the congregate system was based on silence and labor. At Auburn, however, inmates worked and ate together, with silence enforced by prison guards.[6]

If either state can be said to have "won" the debate, it was New York. The Auburn system proved more popular, and a majority of the new prisons built during the first half of the nineteenth century followed New York's lead, though mainly for economic reasons rather than philosophical ones. New York's penitentiaries were cheaper to build because they did not require so much space. Furthermore, inmates in New York were employed in workshops, whereas those in Pennsylvania toiled alone in their cells. Consequently, the Auburn system was better positioned to exploit prison labor in the early years of widespread factory production.

FIGURE 13.1 The Eastern Penitentiary

As you can see, the Eastern Penitentiary was designed in the form of a "wagon wheel," known today as the radial style. The back-to-back cells in each "spoke" of the wheel faced outward from the center to limit contact between inmates. What was the primary goal of this design?

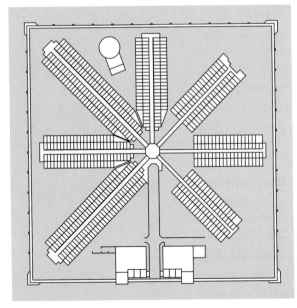

The Reformers and the Progressives

The Auburn system did not go unchallenged. In the 1870s, a group of reformers argued that fixed sentences, imposed silence, and isolation did nothing to improve prisoners. These critics proposed that penal institutions should offer the promise of early release as a prime tool for rehabilitation. Echoing the views of the Quakers a century earlier, the reformers presented an ideology that would heavily influence American corrections for the next century.

This "new penology" was put into practice at New York's Elmira Reformatory in 1876 (see the photo alongside). At Elmira, good behavior was rewarded by early release, and misbehavior was punished with extended time under a three-grade system of classification. On entering the institution, the offender was assigned a grade of 2. If the inmate followed the rules and completed work and school assignments, after six months he was moved up to grade 1, the necessary grade for release. If, however, the inmate broke institutional rules, he was lowered to grade 3. A grade 3 inmate needed to behave properly for three months before he could return to grade 2 and begin to work back toward grade 1 and eventual release.[7]

Although other penal institutions did not adopt the Elmira model, its theories came into prominence in the first two decades of the twentieth century thanks to the Progressive movement in criminal justice. The Progressives—linked to the positivist school of criminology discussed in Chapter 2—believed that criminal behavior was caused by social, economic, and biological factors and, therefore, a corrections system should have a goal of treatment, not punishment. Consequently, they trumpeted a **medical model** for prisons, which held that institutions should offer a variety of programs and therapies to cure inmates of their "ills," whatever the root causes. The Progressives were largely responsible for the spread of indeterminate sentences (Chapter 11), probation (Chapter 12), intermediate sanctions (Chapter 12), and parole (Chapter 12) in the first half of the twentieth century.

The Reassertion of Punishment

Even though the Progressives had a great influence on the corrections system as a whole, their theories had little impact on the prisons themselves. Many of these facilities had been constructed in the nineteenth century and were impervious to change. More important, prison administrators usually did not agree with the Progressives and their followers, so the day-to-day lives of most inmates varied little from the congregate system of Auburn Prison.

Academic attitudes began to shift toward the prison administrators in the mid-1960s. Then, in 1974, the publication of Robert Martinson's famous "What Works?" essay provided opponents of the medical model with statistical evidence that rehabilitation efforts did nothing to lower recidivism rates.[8] This is not to say that Martinson's findings went unchallenged. A number of critics argued that rehabilitative programs could be successful.[9] In fact, Martinson himself retracted most of his claims in a little-noticed

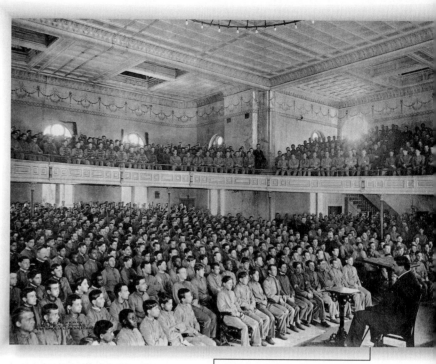

Inmates of the Elmira Reformatory in New York attend a presentation at the prison auditorium. To what extent do you believe that treatment should be a part of the incarceration of criminals?
Corbis

Medical Model A model of corrections in which the psychological and biological roots of an inmate's criminal behavior are identified and treated.

article published five years after his initial report.[10] Attempts by Martinson and others to "set the record straight" went largely unnoticed, however, as crime rose sharply in the early 1970s. This trend led many criminologists and politicians to champion "get tough" measures to deal with criminals they now considered "incurable." By the end of the 1980s, the legislative, judicial, and administrative strategies that we have discussed throughout this text had positioned the United States for an explosion in inmate populations and prison construction unparalleled in the nation's history.

The Role of Prisons in Modern Society

For reasons that we will explain later in the chapter, the number of federal and state prisoners quadrupled between 1980 and 2010.[11] This increase reflects the varied demands placed on the modern American penal institution. As University of Connecticut sociologist Charles Logan once noted, Americans expect prisons to "correct the incorrigible, rehabilitate the wretched . . . restrain the dangerous, and punish the wicked."[12] Basically, prisons exist to make society a safer place. Whether this is to be achieved through retribution, deterrence, incapacitation, or rehabilitation—the four justifications of corrections introduced in Chapter 11—depends on the operating philosophy of the individual penal institution.

Three general models of prisons have emerged to describe the different schools of thought behind prison organization:

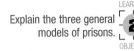

Explain the three general models of prisons. **LEARNING 2 OBJECTIVE**

- The *custodial model* is based on the assumption that prisoners are incarcerated for reasons of incapacitation, deterrence, and retribution. All decisions within the prison—such as what form of recreation to provide the inmates—are made with an eye toward security and discipline, and the daily routine of the inmates is highly controlled. The custodial model has dominated the most restrictive prisons in the United States since the 1930s.
- The *rehabilitation model* stresses the ideals of individualized treatment that we discussed in Chapter 11. Security concerns are often secondary to the well-being of the individual inmate, and a number of treatment programs are offered to aid prisoners in changing their criminal and antisocial behavior. The rehabilitation model came into prominence during the 1950s and enjoyed widespread popularity until it began to lose general acceptance in the 1970s and 1980s.
- In the *reintegration model,* the correctional institution serves as a training ground for the inmate to prepare for existence in the community. Prisons that have adopted this model give the prisoners more responsibility during incarceration and offer halfway houses and work programs (both discussed in Chapter 14) to help them reintegrate into society. This model is becoming more influential, as corrections officials react to problems such as prison overcrowding.[13]

Competing views of the prison's role in society are at odds with these three "ideal" perspectives. Professor Alfred Blumstein argues that prisons create new criminals, especially with regard to nonviolent drug offenders. Not only do these nonviolent felons become socialized to the criminal lifestyle while in prison, but the stigma of incarceration makes it more difficult for them to obtain employment on release. Their only means of sustenance "on the outside" is to apply the criminal methods they learned in prison.[14] A study by criminal justice professors Cassia Spohn of Arizona State University and David Holleran of the College of New Jersey found that convicted drug offenders who were sentenced to prison were 2.2 times more likely to be incarcerated for a new offense than those sentenced to probation.[15]

PRISON ORGANIZATION AND MANAGEMENT

The United States has a dual prison system that parallels its dual court system, which we discussed in Chapter 8. The Federal Bureau of Prisons (BOP) currently operates about one hundred confinement facilities, ranging from prisons to immigration detention centers to community corrections institutions.[16] In the federal corrections system, a national director, appointed by the president, oversees six regional directors and a staff of over 35,000 employees. All fifty states also operate state prisons, which number over 1,700 and make up more than 90 percent of the country's correctional facilities.[17] Governors are responsible for the organization and operation of state corrections systems, which vary widely based on each state's geography, *demographics* (population characteristics), and political culture.

Generally, those offenders sentenced in federal court for breaking federal law serve their time in federal prisons, and those offenders sentenced in state court for breaking state law serve their time in state prisons. As you can see in Figure 13.2 below, federal prisons hold relatively few violent felons, because relatively few federal laws involve violent crime. At the same time, federal prisons are much more likely to hold public order offenders, a group that includes violators of federal immigration law.

FIGURE 13.2 Types of Offenses of Federal and State Prison Inmates

As the comparison below shows, state prisoners are most likely to have been convicted of violent crimes, while federal prisoners are most likely to have been conficted of drug and public order offenses.

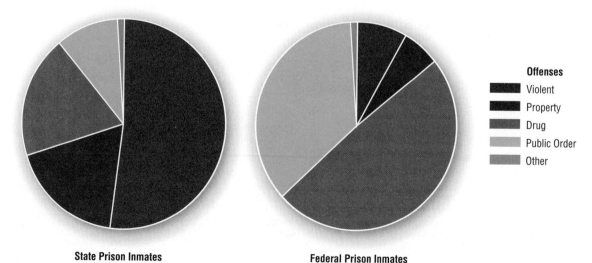

State Prison Inmates   **Federal Prison Inmates**

Offenses
- Violent
- Property
- Drug
- Public Order
- Other

Source: Bureau of Justice Statistics, *Prisoners in 2011* (Washington, D.C.: U.S. Department of Justice, December 2012), Appendix table 8, page 27; and Appendix table 12, page 29.

Warden The prison official who is ultimately responsible for the organization and performance of a correctional facility.

Prison Administration

Whether the federal government or a state government operates a prison, its administrators have the same general goals, summarized by Charles Logan as follows:

> The mission of a prison is to keep prisoners—to keep them in, keep them safe, keep them in line, keep them healthy, and keep them busy—and to do it with fairness, without undue suffering and as efficiently as possible.[18]

Considering the environment of a prison—an enclosed world inhabited by people who are generally violent and angry and would rather be anywhere else—Logan's mission statement is somewhat unrealistic. A prison staff must supervise the daily routines of hundreds or thousands of inmates, a duty that includes providing them with meals, education, vocational programs, and different forms of leisure. The smooth operation of this supervision is made more difficult—if not, at times, impossible—by budgetary restrictions, overcrowding, and continual inmate turnover.

FORMAL PRISON MANAGEMENT In some respects, the management structure of a prison is similar to that of a police department, as discussed in Chapter 6. Both systems rely on a hierarchical (top-down) *chain of command* to increase personal responsibility. Both assign different employees to specific tasks, though prison managers have much more direct control over their subordinates than do police managers. The main difference is that police departments have a *continuity of purpose* that is sometimes lacking in prison organizations. All members of a police force are, at least theoretically, working to reduce crime and apprehend criminals. In a prison, this continuity is less evident. An employee in the prison laundry service and one who works in the visiting center have little in common. In some instances, employees may even have cross-purposes: a prison guard may want to punish an inmate, while a counselor in the treatment center may want to rehabilitate her or him.

Consequently, a strong hierarchy is crucial for any prison management team that hopes to meet Charles Logan's expectations. As Figure 13.3 below shows, the **warden** (also known as a superintendent) is ultimately responsible for the operation of a prison. He or she oversees deputy wardens, who in turn manage the various organizational lines of the institution. The custodial employees, who deal directly with the inmates and make

Describe the formal prison management system, and indicate the three most important aspects of prison governance. **LEARNING OBJECTIVE 3**

FIGURE 13.3 Organizational Chart for a Typical Correctional Facility

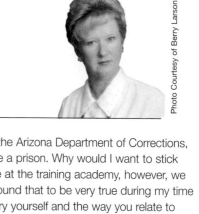

Photo Courtesy of Berry Larson

BERRY LARSON
PRISON WARDEN

Before I began my career as a correctional officer for the Arizona Department of Corrections, I had several people question my desire to work inside a prison. Why would I want to stick myself somewhere so unpleasant and stressful? While at the training academy, however, we were taught that "approach determines response." I found that to be very true during my time as a correctional officer. It is all about the way you carry yourself and the way you relate to the inmates. An inmate can tell if you are trying to be someone you are not. They can also tell if you are afraid. I never had to use physical force once in all the time I was a correctional officer—officer presence and nonverbal/verbal communication is usually sufficient to handle any situation, as long as you keep control of your emotions.

As warden of the Arizona State Prison Complex–Lewis, my duties include touring the units; attending special events such as inmate graduations for GED and vocational programs; managing emergency situations such as power outages, fights and assaults, and staff injuries; and eradicating all criminal activity from the facility. Many, if not most, of our inmates came to us in pretty bad shape—little or no education, a substance abuse history, or mental health or behavioral issues. These young men have spent their lives watching television and playing video games and simply do not have the skills to be successful in life. We try to remedy the situation by providing them with educational and vocational programs and "life-skills" classes that promote civil and productive behavior.

SOCIAL MEDIA CAREER TIP Regularly reevaluate your social media tools and the methods you use to keep up to date in your fields of interest. If you are still using the same tools as a year ago, you probably aren't keeping up with the latest developments in Internet technology.

---

up more than half of a prison's staff, operate under a militaristic hierarchy, with a line of command passing from the deputy warden to the captain to the correctional officer.

GOVERNING PRISONS The implications of prison mismanagement can be severe. While studying a series of prison riots, sociologists Bert Useem and Peter Kimball found that breakdown in managerial control commonly preceded such acts of mass violence.[19] During the 1970s, for example, conditions at the State Penitentiary in New Mexico deteriorated significantly. Inmates were increasingly the targets of random and harsh treatment at the hands of the prison staff, while at the same time a reduction in structured activities left prison life "painfully boring."[20] The result, in 1980, was one of the most violent prison riots in the nation's history.

What sort of prison management is most suited to avoid such situations? Although there is no single "best" form of prison management, political scientist John DiIulio believes that, in general, the sound governance of correctional facilities is a matter of order, amenities, and services:

- *Order* can be defined as the absence of misconduct such as murder, assault, and rape. Many observers, including DiIulio, believe that, having incarcerated a person, the state has a responsibility to protect that person from disorder in the correctional institution.

Classification The process through which prison officials determine which correctional facility is best suited to the individual offender.

Maximum-Security Prison A correctional institution designed and organized to control and discipline dangerous felons, as well as prevent escape.

- *Amenities* are those comforts that make life "livable," such as clean living conditions, acceptable food, and entertainment. One theory of incarceration holds that inmates should not enjoy a quality of life comparable to life outside prison. Without the basic amenities, however, prison life becomes unbearable, and inmates are more likely to lapse into disorder.
- *Services* include programs designed to improve an inmate's prospects on release, such as vocational training, remedial education, and drug treatment. Again, many feel that a person convicted of a crime does not deserve to participate in these kinds of programs, but they have two clear benefits. First, they keep the inmate occupied and focused during her or his sentence. Second, they reduce the chances that the inmate will go back to a life of crime after she or he returns to the community.[21]

According to DiIulio, in the absence of order, amenities, and services, inmates will come to see their imprisonment as not only unpleasant but unfair, and they will become much more difficult to control.[22] Furthermore, weak governance encourages inmates to come up with their own methods of regulating their lives. As we shall see in the next chapter, the result is usually high levels of violence and the expansion of prison gangs and other unsanctioned forms of authority.

Types of Prisons

One of the most important aspects of prison administration occurs soon after a defendant has been convicted of a crime. In this **classification** process, administrators determine what sort of correctional facility provides the best "fit" for each individual convict. In general, prison administrators rely on three criteria for classification purposes:

1. The seriousness of the crime committed.
2. The risk of future criminal or violent conduct.
3. The need for treatment and rehabilitation programs.[23]

In the federal prison system, this need to classify—and separate—different kinds of offenders has led to six different levels of correctional facilities. Inmates in level 1 facilities are usually nonviolent and require the least amount of security, while inmates in level 6 facilities are the most dangerous and require the harshest security measures. (Many states also use the six-level system, an example of which can be seen in Figure 13.4 on the facing page.) To simplify matters, most observers refer to correctional facilities as being one of three levels—minimum, medium, or maximum. A fourth level—the supermaximum-security prison, known as the "supermax"—is relatively rare and extremely controversial due to its hyperharsh methods of punishing and controlling the most dangerous prisoners.

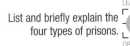

List and briefly explain the four types of prisons.

LEARNING
4
OBJECTIVE

MAXIMUM-SECURITY PRISONS In a certain sense, the classification of prisoners today owes a debt to the three-grade system developed at the Elmira Reformatory, discussed earlier in the chapter. Once wrongdoers enter a corrections facility, they are constantly graded on behavior. Those who serve "good time," as we have seen, are often rewarded with early release. Those who compile extensive misconduct records are usually housed, along with violent and repeat offenders, in **maximum-security prisons.** The names of these institutions—Folsom, San Quentin, Sing Sing, Attica—conjure up foreboding images of concrete and steel jungles, with good reason.

Maximum-security prisons are designed with full attention to security and surveillance. In these institutions, inmates' lives are programmed in a militaristic fashion

FIGURE 13.4 Security Levels of Correctional Facilities in Virginia

The security levels of correctional facilities in Virginia are graded from level 1 to level 6. As you can see, level 1 facilities are for those inmates who pose the least amount of risk to fellow inmates, staff members, and themselves. Level 6 facilities are for those who are considered the most dangerous by the Virginia Department of Corrections.

LEVEL 1 - LOW
No first or second degree murder, robbery, sex-related crime, kidnapping/abduction, felonious assault (current or prior), flight/escape history, carjacking, or malicious wounding. No disruptive behavior.

LEVEL 1 - HIGH
No first or second degree murder, robbery, sex-related crime, kidnapping/abduction, felonious assault (current or prior), flight/escape history. No disruptive behavior for at least past 24 months.

LEVEL 2
For initial assignment only. No escape history for past 5 years. No disruptive behavior for at least past 24 months prior to transfer to any less secure facility.

LEVEL 3
Single, multiple, and life+ sentences.* Must have served 20 consecutive years on sentence. No disruptive behavior for at least past 24 months prior to transfer to any less secure facility.

LEVEL 4
Single, multiple, and life+ sentences. No disruptive behavior for at least past 24 months prior to transfer to any less secure facility.

LEVEL 5
Same as level 4 except with fewer opportunities to participate in programs and jobs, fewer visitation and phone access privileges, and less freedom of movement within the facility. No disruptive behavior for at least past 24 months prior to transfer to any less secure facility.

LEVEL 6
Single, multiple, and life+ sentences. Profile of inmates: disruptive, assaultive, severe behavior problems, predatory-type behavior, escape risk. No disruptive behavior for at least past 24 months prior to transfer to any less secure facility.

* "Life +" means a life sentence plus extra years in case of an early release.

Source: Virginia Department of Corrections.

to keep them from escaping or from harming themselves or the prison staff. About a quarter of the prisons in the United States are classified as maximum security, and these institutions house about a third of the country's prisoners.

The Design Maximum-security prisons tend to be large—holding more than a thousand inmates—and they have similar features. The entire operation is usually surrounded by concrete walls that stand twenty to thirty feet high and have also been sunk deep into the ground to deter tunnel escapes. Fences reinforced with razor-ribbon barbed wire that can be electrically charged may supplement these barriers. The prison walls are studded with watchtowers, from which guards armed with shotguns and rifles survey the movement of prisoners below. The designs of these facilities, though similar, are not uniform. Though correctional facilities built using the radial design pioneered by the Eastern Penitentiary still exist, several other designs have become prominent in more recently constructed institutions. For an overview of these designs, including the radial design, see Figure 13.5 on page 433.

Inmates live in cells, most of them with similar dimensions to those found in the Topeka Correctional Facility, a maximum-security prison in Topeka, Kansas: eight feet by fourteen feet with cinder block walls.[24] The space contains bunks, a toilet, a sink, and possibly a cabinet or closet. Cells are located in rows of *cell blocks*, each of which forms its own security unit, set off by a series of gates and bars. A maximum-security institution is essentially a collection of numerous cell blocks, each constituting its own prison within a prison.

Most prisons, regardless of their design, have cell blocks that open into sprawling prison yards, where the inmates commingle daily. The "prison of the future," however, rejects this layout. Instead, it relies on a podular design, as evident at the Two Rivers Correctional Institution in Umatilla, Oregon. At Two Rivers, which opened in 2007, fourteen housing pods contain ninety-six inmates each. Each unit has its own yard, so inmates rarely, if ever, interact with members of other pods. This design gives administrators the flexibility to, for example, place violent criminals in pod A and white-collar criminals in pod B without worrying about mixing the two different security levels.[25]

Security Measures Within maximum-security prisons, inmates' lives are dominated by security measures. Whenever they move from one area of the prison to another, they do so in groups and under the watchful eye of armed correctional officers. Television surveillance cameras may be used to monitor their every move, even when sleeping, showering, or using the toilet. They are subject to frequent pat-downs or strip searches at the guards' discretion. Constant "head counts" ensure that every inmate is where he or she should be. Tower guards—many of whom have orders to shoot to kill in the case of a disturbance or escape attempt—constantly look down on the inmates as they move around outdoor areas of the facility.

CJ & TECHNOLOGY — TRACKING INMATES

Black Creek/TSI PRISM

Technology has added significantly to the overall safety of maximum-security prisons. Walk-through metal detectors and X-ray body scanners, for example, can detect weapons or other contraband hidden on the body of an inmate. The most promising new technology in this field, however, relies on radio frequency identification (RFID). About the size of two grains of rice, an RFID tag consists of a glass capsule that contains a computer chip, a tiny copper antenna, and an electrical device known as a "capacitor" that transmits the data in the chip to an outside scanner. In the prison context, RFID works as a high-tech head count: inmates wear bracelets tagged with the microchips while correctional officers wear small RFID devices resembling pagers.

Guided by a series of radio transmitters and receivers, the system is able to pinpoint the location of inmates and guards within twenty feet. Every two seconds, radio signals "search out" the location of each inmate and guard, and relay this information to a central computer. On a grid of the prison, an inmate shows up as a yellow dot and a correctional officer as a blue dot. Many RFID systems also store all movements in a database for future reference. "[RFID] completely revolutionizes a prison because you know where everyone is—not approximately but exactly where they are," remarked an official at the National Institute of Justice.

Thinking about RFID Tracking
Review the discussion of crime mapping and "hot spots" in Chapter 6. Drawing on your knowledge of crime-mapping technology, discuss how RFID technology can reduce violence and other misconduct such as drug sales in prisons.

SUPERMAX PRISONS About thirty states and the Federal Bureau of Prisons (BOP) operate **supermax** (short for supermaximum security) **prisons,** which are supposedly reserved for the "worst of the worst" of America's corrections population. Many of the inmates in these facilities are deemed high risks to commit murder behind bars—about a quarter of the occupants of the BOP's U.S. Penitentiary Administrative Maximum (ADX) in Florence, Colorado, have killed other prisoners or assaulted correctional officers elsewhere.

Supermax prisons are also used as punishment for offenders who commit serious disciplinary infractions in maximum-security prisons, or for those inmates who become involved

Supermax Prison A correctional facility reserved for those inmates who have extensive records of misconduct.

FIGURE 13.5 Prison Designs

The Radial Design

The wagon wheel form of the radial design was created with the dual goals of separation and control. Inmates are separated from one another in their cells on the "spokes" of the wheel, and prison officials can control the activities of the inmates from the control center in the "hub" of the wheel.

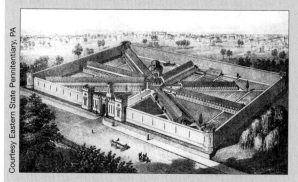

Courtesy Eastern State Penitentiary, PA

The Telephone-Pole Design

The main feature of this design is a long central corridor that serves as a means for transporting inmates from one part of the facility to another. Branching off from this main corridor are the functional areas of the facility: housing, food services, workshops, a treatment programs room, and other services.

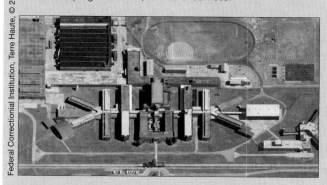

Federal Correctional Institution, Terre Haute, © 2013 Google Maps

Source: Text adapted from Todd R. Clear, George F. Cole, and Michael D. Reisig, *American Corrections*, 9th ed. (Belmont, CA: Cengage Learning, 2010), 267–268.

The Courtyard Style

In the courtyard-style prison, a courtyard replaces the transportation function of the "pole" in the telephone-pole prison. The prison buildings form a square around the courtyard, and to get from one part of the facility to another, the inmates go across the courtyard.

St. Cloud Minnesota State Prison, © 2013 Google Maps

The Campus Style

Some of the newer minimum-security prisons have adopted the campus style, which had previously been used in correctional facilities for women and juveniles. As on a college campus, housing units are scattered among functional units such as the dining room, recreation area, and treatment centers.

Acacia Prison, Western Australia Department of Corrective Services

with prison gangs.[26] In addition, a growing number of supermax occupants are either high-profile individuals who would be at constant risk of attack in a general prison population or convicted terrorists such as Faisal Shahzad, who attempted to detonate a bomb in New York City's Times Square in 2010; Ted "the Unabomber" Kaczynski; and Terry Nichols, who was involved in the bombing of a federal office building in Oklahoma City in 1995.

A Controlled Environment The main purpose of a supermax prison is to strictly control the inmates' movement, thereby limiting (or eliminating) situations that could lead to breakdowns in discipline. The conditions at California's Security Housing Unit (SHU) at Pelican Bay State Prison are representative of most supermax institutions. Prisoners are confined to their one-person cells for twenty-three hours each day under video camera surveillance. They receive meals through a slot in the door. The cells measure eight by ten feet in size and are windowless. Fluorescent lights are continuously on, day and night, making it difficult for inmates to enjoy any type of privacy or sleep.[27]

For the most part, supermax prisons operate in a state of perpetual **lockdown,** in which all inmates are confined to their cells and social activities such as meals, recreational sports, and treatment programs are nonexistent. For the sixty minutes of each day that SHU inmates are allowed out of their cells (compared with twelve to sixteen hours in regular maximum-security prisons), they may either shower or exercise in an enclosed, concrete "yard" covered by plastic mesh. Prisoners are strip-searched before and after leaving their cells, and are placed in waist restraints and handcuffs on their way to and from the "yard" and showers.[28]

Supermax Syndrome Many prison officials support the proliferation of supermax prisons because they provide increased security for the most dangerous inmates. These proponents believe that the harsh reputation of the facilities will deter convicts from misbehaving for fear of transfer to a supermax. Nevertheless, the supermax has aroused a number of criticisms. Amnesty International and other human rights groups assert that the facilities violate standards for proper treatment of prisoners. At Wisconsin's Supermax Correctional Facility, for example, the cells have no air-conditioning or windows, and average temperatures during the summer top 100 degrees.[29]

Furthermore, while studying prisoners at California's Pelican Bay facility, a Harvard University psychiatrist found that 80 percent suffered from what he called "SHU [security housing unit] syndrome," a condition brought on by long periods of isolation.[30] Further research on SHU syndrome shows that supermax inmates manifest a number of psychological problems, including massive anxiety, hallucinations, and acute confusion.[31] We will take a closer look at the merits and drawbacks of solitary confinement, a method of inmate punishment that extends well beyond supermax prisons, in the *CJ in Action* feature that ends this chapter.

MEDIUM- AND MINIMUM-SECURITY PRISONS Medium-security prisons hold about 45 percent of the prison population and minimum-security prisons 20 percent. Inmates at **medium-security prisons** have for the most part committed less serious crimes than those housed in maximum-security prisons and are not considered high risks for escaping or causing harm. Consequently, medium-security institutions are not designed for control to the same extent as maximum-security prisons and have a more relaxed atmosphere. These facilities also offer more educational and treatment programs and allow for more contact between inmates. Medium-security prisons are rarely walled, relying instead on high fences. Prisoners have more freedom of movement within the structures, and the levels of surveillance are much lower. Living quarters are less restrictive as well—many of the newer medium-security prisons provide dormitory housing.

A **minimum-security prison** seems at first glance to be more like a college campus than an incarceration facility. Most of the inmates at these institutions are first-time offenders who are nonviolent and well behaved. A high percentage are white-collar criminals. Indeed, inmates are often transferred to minimum-security prisons as a

■ What security measures can you identify from this photo of a cell block at Arizona State Prison in Florence?
AP Photo/Matt York

reward for good behavior in other facilities. Therefore, security measures are lax compared with even medium-security prisons. Unlike medium-security institutions, minimum-security prisons do not have armed guards. Prisoners are provided with amenities such as television sets and computers in their rooms. They also enjoy freedom of movement, and are allowed off prison grounds for educational or employment purposes to a much greater extent than those held in more restrictive facilities.

Some critics have likened minimum-security prisons to "country clubs," but in the corrections system, everything is relative. A minimum-security prison may seem like a vacation spot when compared with the horrors of Sing Sing, but it still represents a restriction of personal freedom and separates the inmate from the outside world. (The feature *Comparative Criminal Justice—Prison Lite* below provides a look at Norway's approach to incarceration, in which even the worst offenders are afforded the minimum-security experience.)

SELF ASSESSMENT

Fill in the blanks and check your answers on page 450.

The management of a prison is hierarchical, with the _____ (also known as a superintendent) at the top of the power structure. _____ is a crucial component of prison management, as it determines the security requirements needed to safely incarcerate each individual offender. Those offenders who have been convicted of violent crimes and repeat offenders are most likely to be sent to _____-security prisons. If a prisoner assaults another inmate or a correctional officer, prison officials may decide to transfer him or her to a _____ prison.

saicle

COMPARATIVE
CRIMINAL JUSTICE

PRISON LIFE

While Norwegian mass killer Anders Breivik, whose murder of seventy-seven people was detailed in this feature in Chapter 11, was being held in prison for trial, he had plenty to keep him busy. Breivik enjoyed access to a television and a computer, three cells for extra space, and regular visits from prison staff. "He's a human being. He has human rights," said a facility spokeswoman. "This is about creating a humane prison regime."

In Norway, incarceration is based on the premise that loss of liberty is punishment enough for offenders. Consequently, the prisons themselves are made as pleasant as possible. For example, Halden Fengsel prison, which houses murderers and rapists, provides amenities such as a recording studio, a "kitchen laboratory" for cooking classes, and a two-bedroom house where inmates can house their families for overnight visits. An inmate at the Skien maximum-security island prison compares his incarceration to "living in a village." He adds, "Everybody has to work. But we have free time so we can do some fishing, or in summer we can swim off the beach. We know we are prisoners but here we feel like people."

Norway's methods have, it appears, created certain expectations among its inmates. After spending several months in prison following his 2012 conviction, Anders Breivik wrote a letter to authorities protesting the conditions of his imprisonment. Among the complaints: not enough butter for his bread, cold coffee, and no skin moisturizer.

FOR CRITICAL ANALYSIS

In the United States, life behind bars has long been predicated on the *principle of least eligibility,* which holds that the least advantaged members of society outside prison should lead a better existence than any prison or jail inmate. Do you favor the American or the Norwegian approach to prison conditions? Why?

INMATE POPULATION TRENDS

As Figure 13.6 below shows, the number of Americans in prison or jail has increased dramatically in the past three decades. This growth can be attributed to a number of factors, starting with the enhancement and stricter enforcement of the nation's illegal drug laws.

Factors in Prison Population Growth

There are more people in prison and jail for drug offenses today than there were for *all* offenses in the early 1970s.[32] In 1980, about 19,000 drug offenders were incarcerated in state prisons and 4,800 drug offenders were in federal prisons. Thirty-one years later, state prisons held about 258,000 inmates who had been arrested for drug offenses, and the number of drug offenders in federal prisons had risen to almost 95,000 (representing about half of all inmates in federal facilities).[33]

INCREASED PROBABILITY OF INCARCERATION The growth of America's inmate population also reflects the reality that the chance of someone who is arrested going to prison today is much greater than it was thirty years ago. Most of this growth took place in the 1980s, when the likelihood of incarceration in a state prison after arrest increased fivefold for drug offenses, threefold for weapons offenses, and twofold for crimes such as sexual assault, burglary, auto theft, and larceny.[34] For federal crimes, the proportion of convicted defendants being sent to prison rose from 54 percent in 1988 to 86 percent in 2011.[35]

INMATES SERVING MORE TIME In Chapter 11, we discussed a number of "get tough" sentencing laws passed in reaction to the crime wave of the 1970s and 1980s. These measures, including sentencing guidelines, mandatory minimum sentences, and truth-in-sentencing laws, have significantly increased the length of prison terms in the United States.[36] In California, for example, by 2011 a quarter of the inmate population had been sentenced under the state's "three-strikes" law, and the terms for these inmates were nine years longer because of that legislation.[37]

List the factors that have LEARNING caused the prison population to grow dramatically in the last several decades. OBJECTIVE **5**

FIGURE 13.6 The Inmate Population of the United States

The total number of inmates in the United States has risen from 744,208 in 1985 to about 2.3 million in 2012.

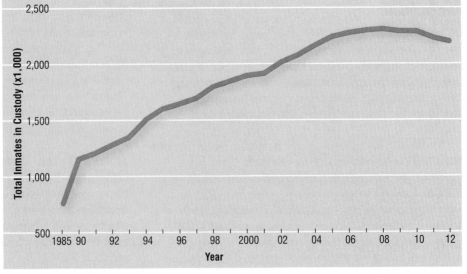

Source: U.S. Department of Justice.

Overall, inmates released from state prison in 2009 spent an average of nine months—about 36 percent—longer behind bars than those inmates released in 1990.[38] On the federal level, in the fifteen years after the passage of the Sentencing Reform Act of 1984, the average time served in federal prison increased more than 50 percent.[39] Furthermore, about 140,000 state prisoners and 4,000 federal prisoners are serving life prison terms with no chance of release, up from about 34,000 and 400, respectively, in the mid-1980s.[40]

FEDERAL PRISON GROWTH Even though, as noted at the beginning of this chapter, the overall prison population of the United States recently has started to decrease, this is not the case for federal prison populations. In 2011, the number of federal prisoners

■ A female inmate at the Ohio Reformatory for Women in Marysville, Ohio, works on a state flag in the prison workshop. How have female prison inmate population trends been inconsistent with overall prison inmate population trends in recent years?
Ty Wright/Bloomberg via Getty Images

increased by 3.4 percent.[41] Indeed, between 2000 and 2011, the federal prison population grew 58 percent, from about 125,000 to just over 197,000.[42]

Besides the increase in federal drug offenders already mentioned, this growth can be attributed to increased federal law enforcement attention to weapons crimes and immigration law violations. Between 1998 and 2010, the number of weapons offenders in federal prison almost tripled.[43] During that same time period, the number of immigration offenders saw similar increases, as the result of which a third of all federal inmates are now Hispanic.[44] Furthermore, in 2013, approximately 14,200 women were behind bars in federal prison, about double their numbers in 1995.[45] Women still account for only 7 percent of all inmates in the United States, but their rates of imprisonment have been growing more rapidly than those of men for the last decade.[46]

The Costs of Incarceration

The escalation in the U.S. prison population has been accompanied by increased costs. Today, the states together spend nearly $40 billion a year to operate their corrections systems—up from $12 billion in 1987. Twelve states allocate in excess of $1 billion a year for corrections-related services, often spending more on prisons than on education or health care.[47] Several years ago, California had a $20 billion budget deficit and was spending $10 billion a year on its prisons.[48] Arizona, which faces a similar problem, has decided to charge $25 for family and friend visits to inmates in its prison system as a fund-raising measure.[49]

Decarceration

For most states looking to cut correction costs, the focus has been on *decarceration,* or the reduction of inmate populations. As recently as 2007, one expert lamented the unwillingness of corrections authorities to decarcerate, calling the strategy "practically virgin territory."[50] This is no longer the case, as the high cost of imprisonment has caused policymakers to consider a number of different methods to reduce the number of people in prison. In general, decarceration relies on three strategies:

Private Prisons Correctional facilities operated by private corporations instead of the government and, therefore, reliant on profits for survival.

1. Decreasing the probability that nonviolent offenders will be sentenced to prison.
2. Increasing the rate of release of nonviolent offenders from prison.
3. Decreasing the rate of imprisonment for probation and parole violators.[51]

Many states have adopted one or more of these approaches. Texas, as noted at the beginning of the chapter, now diverts a large number of nonviolent offenders to drug treatment in the community. Corrections officials in Michigan, Missouri, and New York are making a concerted effort to avoid reincarcerating parolees for technical violations.[52]

In response to a U.S. Supreme Court ruling that we will discuss in the next chapter, California has implemented a "realignment" strategy to reduce rates of imprisonment for low-level criminals. As a result, from 2011 to 2012, the number of offenders admitted to California prisons dropped by nearly 19 percent, and the state's prison population fell from 164,200 to 135,800.[53] Nationwide in 2011, state prison releases exceeded prison admissions by nearly 20,000.[54] (To better understand the possible consequences of decarceration on crime rates, see the feature *Myth versus Reality—Does Putting Criminals in Prison Reduce Crime?* on the facing page.)

SELF ASSESSMENT

Fill in the blanks and check your answers on page 450.

Of all the factors in the growth of the prison population in the last several decades, stricter enforcement of the nation's _____ laws has had the greatest impact. Other factors contributing to this growth include (1) increased probability of _____ , (2) increased _____ of time served in prison, and (3) the growth of the _____ prison system. Many states are adopting strategies of _____ designed to reduce their inmate populations and the costs associated with their corrections systems.

THE EMERGENCE OF PRIVATE PRISONS

As the prison population soared at the end of the twentieth century, state corrections officials faced a serious problem: too many inmates, not enough prisons. "States couldn't build space fast enough," explains corrections expert Martin Horn. "And so they had to turn to the private sector."[55] With corrections exhibiting all appearance of "a recession-proof industry," American businesses eagerly entered the market.

Today, **private prisons,** or prisons run by private firms to make a profit, are an important part of the criminal justice system. About two dozen private companies operate more than two hundred facilities across the United States. The two largest corrections firms, Corrections Corporation of America (CCA) and the GEO Group, Inc., manage about 130 correctional facilities and generate about $3.3 billion in annual revenue combined.[56] By 2011, private penal institutions housed over 130,000 inmates, representing 8.2 percent of all prisoners in the state and federal corrections systems.[57]

Why Privatize?

It would be a mistake to automatically assume that private prisons are less expensive to run than public ones. Nevertheless, the incentive to privatize is primarily financial.

COST EFFICIENCY In the 1980s and 1990s, a number of states and cities reduced operating costs by transferring government-run services such as garbage collection and road maintenance to the private sector. Similarly, private prisons can often be run more cheaply and efficiently than public ones for the following reasons:

List the reasons why LEARNING private prisons can often be run more cheaply than public ones. OBJECTIVE **6**

MYTH vs REALITY

Does Putting Criminals in Prison Reduce Crime?

Since the early 1990s, violent crime rates in the United States have been stable or declining. Yet, during the same period, as Figure 13.6 earlier in the chapter shows, the number of imprisoned Americans has climbed precipitously. The correlation between these two trends is the subject of much discussion among crime experts.

THE MYTH Crime falls when the prison population rises. This can be attributed to the effects of deterrence and incapacitation, theories of punishment we discussed in Chapter 11. First, the threat of prison deters would-be criminals from committing crimes. Second, a prison inmate is incapable of committing crimes against the public because he or she has been separated from the community.

THE REALITY Numerous statistical examples discredit a direct, sustained link between decreased crime rates and increased prison populations. Canada, for example, experienced a decline in crime rates similar to the United States in the 1990s without any increase in national incarceration levels. Furthermore, by one measurement, New York City has seen crime decrease by a remarkable 80 percent since the early 1990s. Yet, during the 2000s, the city has been locking up fewer people than it was at the height of its late-1980s crime wave.

According to one theory, massive incarceration accounted for about a quarter of the crime drop of the 1990s, as many of the most violent offenders were removed from society and remain behind bars. Since then, however, a large percentage of new prison admissions have been drug law offenders and probation/parole violators. The data tell us that removing these sorts of criminals from the community has a relatively limited effect on violent and property crime rates. In fact, their absence from their homes may even contribute to criminal activity. As we discussed in Chapter 2, many criminologists believe that widespread family disruption greatly increases the incidence of crime in a community.

Additionally, some experts believe that prisons are "schools of crime" that "teach" low-level offenders to be habitual criminals. If this is true, many inmates are more likely to commit crimes after their release from prison than they would have been if they had never been incarcerated in the first place.

FOR CRITICAL ANALYSIS

How might the new trend of decarceration give criminologists a chance to test theories regarding the correlation between incarceration levels and crime rates?

- *Labor costs.* The wages of public employees account for nearly two-thirds of a prison's operating expenses. Although private corrections firms pay base salaries comparable to those enjoyed by public prison employees, their nonunionized staffs receive lower levels of overtime pay, workers' compensation claims, sick leave, and health-care insurance.

- *Competitive bidding.* Because of the profit motive, private corrections firms have an incentive to buy goods and services at the lowest possible price.

- *Less red tape.* Private corrections firms are not part of the government bureaucracy and therefore do not have to contend with the massive amount of paperwork that can clog government organizations.[58]

In 2005, the National Institute of Justice released the results of a five-year study comparing low-security public and private prisons in California. The government agency found that private facilities cost taxpayers between 6 and 10 percent less than public ones.[59] More recent research conducted at Vanderbilt University found that states saved about $15 million annually when they supplemented their corrections systems with privately managed institutions.[60]

OVERCROWDING AND OUTSOURCING Private prisons are becoming increasingly attractive to state governments faced with the competing pressures of tight budgets and overcrowded corrections facilities. Lacking the funds to alleviate overcrowding by building

■ The Saguaro Correctional Facility in Eloy, Arizona—privately operated by the Corrections Corporation of America—has been criticized for only accepting inmates who are in relatively good health. If true, why would this strategy make financial sense for private prisons?
Monica Almeida/*New York Times*/Redux Pictures

more prisons, state officials are turning to the private institutions for help. Often, the private prison is out of state, which leads to the "outsourcing" of inmates. Hawaii, for example, sends about one-third of its 6,000 inmates to private prisons in Arizona.[61] California has alleviated its chronic overcrowding problems by sending more than 10,000 inmates to private institutions in Arizona, Colorado, Michigan, Minnesota, Missouri, Montana, and Oklahoma.[62]

The Argument against Private Prisons

The assertion that private prisons offer economic benefits is not universally accepted. A number of studies have found that private prisons are no more cost-effective than public ones.[63] Furthermore, opponents of private prisons worry that, despite the assurances of corporate executives, private corrections companies will "cut corners" to save costs, denying inmates important security guarantees in the process.

SAFETY CONCERNS Criticism of private prisons is somewhat supported by the anecdotal evidence. Certainly, these institutions have been the setting for a number of violent incidents over the past several years. In 2010, Hanni Elabed was severely beaten by another inmate at the Idaho Correctional Center (ICC), operated by CCA. Eight minutes passed before guards finally intervened to save Elabed, who was left permanently brain damaged. As part of the resulting lawsuit, a former employee said, "It is clear to me that ICC was more interested in making a profit than reducing prisoner violence."[64] In 2012, another CCA facility experienced a riot that ended with the death of a correctional officer and twenty other injuries. During this disturbance at the Adams County Correctional Center in Natchez, Mississippi, three hundred inmates used broomsticks and other homemade weapons to control the facility for nearly eight hours.[65]

Apart from anecdotal evidence, various studies have also uncovered disturbing patterns of misbehavior at private prisons. For example, in the year after CCA took over operations of Ohio's Lake Erie Correctional Institution from the state corrections department, the number of assaults against correctional officers and inmates increased by over 40 percent.[66] In addition, research conducted by Curtis R. Blakely of the University of South Alabama and Vic W. Bumphus of the University of Tennessee at Chattanooga found that a prisoner in a private correctional facility was twice as likely to be assaulted by a fellow inmate as a prisoner in a public one.[67]

PHILOSOPHICAL CONCERNS Other critics see private prisons as inherently unjust, even if they do save tax dollars or provide enhanced services. These observers believe that corrections is not simply another industry, like garbage collection or road maintenance, and that only the government has the authority to punish wrongdoers. In the words of John DiIulio:

> It is precisely because corrections involves the deprivation of liberty, precisely because it involves the legally sanctioned exercise of coercion by some citizens over others, that it must remain wholly within public hands.[68]

Furthermore, some observers note, if a private corrections firm receives a fee from the state for each inmate housed in its facility, does that not give management an incentive to increase the amount of time each prisoner serves? Though government parole boards make the final decision on an inmate's release from private prisons, the company could manipulate misconduct and good behavior reports to maximize time served and, by extension, higher profits.[69] "You can put a dollar figure on each inmate that is held at a private prison," says Alex Friedmann of *Prison Legal News*. "They are treated as commodities. And that's very dangerous and troubling when a company sees the people it incarcerates as nothing more than a money stream."[70]

The Future of Privatization in the Corrections Industry

In February 2012, Florida's Senate narrowly defeated a bill that would have privatized the state's entire corrections system.[71] The vote seemed to bode ill for what was once considered a recession-proof industry. Indeed, with more states reducing their prison populations, there are signs that the growth of private prisons has stagnated. Between 2010 and 2011, the number of state inmates in private prisons dropped by about 2,000.[72] In an effort to find new avenues of business, CCA recently sent a letter to forty-eight states in which the company offered to purchase unwanted public prisons. So far, only one state has taken this step: Ohio sold the aforementioned Lake Erie Correctional Institution to CCA for nearly $73 million.

Still, most experts see continued profitability for private prisons, for two reasons. First, shrinking budgets may force states to look for less costly alternatives to housing inmates in public prisons. Second, as the number of federal prisoners increases, the Federal Bureau of Prisons has turned to private prisons to expand its capacity. Between 2000 and 2011, the number of federal inmates in private prisons more than doubled, from about 15,500 to about 38,500.[73] The current emphasis on imprisoning violators of immigration law seems likely to ensure that this trend will continue.

SELF ASSESSMENT

Fill in the blanks and check your answers on page 450.

The incentive for using private prisons is primarily _____. Prison officials also feel pressure to send inmates to private prisons to alleviate _____ of public correctional facilities. Critics of private prisons claim that as a result of their cost-cutting measures, inmates are denied important _____ guarantees and thus may be put in physical danger. The industry's future seems assured, however, because of increased demand for prison beds for immigration law violators on the part of the _____ government.

JAILS

Although prisons and prison issues dominate the public discourse on corrections, there is an argument to be made that jails are the dominant penal institutions in the United States. In general, a prison is a facility designed to house people convicted of felonies for lengthy periods of time, while a **jail** is authorized to hold pretrial detainees and offenders who have committed misdemeanors. On any given day, about 744,000 inmates are in jail in this country, and jails admit almost 12 million persons over the course of an entire year.[74] Nevertheless, jail funding is often the lowest priority for the tight budgets of local governments, leading to severe overcrowding and other dismal conditions.

Many observers see this negligence as having far-reaching consequences for criminal justice. Jail is often the first contact that citizens have with the corrections system. It is at this point that treatment and counseling have the best chance to deter future

LEARNING OBJECTIVE **7** Summarize the distinction between jails and prisons, and indicate the importance of jails in the American corrections system.

Jail A facility, usually operated by the county government, used to hold persons awaiting trial or those who have been found guilty of misdemeanors.

criminal behavior.[75] By failing to take advantage of this opportunity, says Professor Franklin Zimring of the University of California at Berkeley School of Law, corrections officials have created a situation in which "today's jail folk are tomorrow's prisoners."[76] (To better understand the role that these two correctional institutions play in the criminal justice system, see *Mastering Concepts—The Main Differences between Prisons and Jails* below.)

The Jail Population

Like their counterparts in state prisons, jail inmates are overwhelmingly young male adults. About 45 percent of jail inmates are white, 38 percent are African American, and 15 percent are Hispanic.[77] The main difference between state prison and jail inmates involves their criminal activity. As Figure 13.7 on the facing page shows, jail inmates are more likely to have been convicted of nonviolent crimes than their counterparts in state prison.

PRETRIAL DETAINEES A significant number of those detained in jails technically are not prisoners. They are **pretrial detainees** who have been arrested by the police and, for a variety of reasons that we discussed in Chapter 9, are unable to post bail. Pretrial detainees are, in many ways, walking legal contradictions. According to the U.S. Constitution, they are innocent until proved guilty. At the same time, by being incarcerated while awaiting trial, they are denied a number of personal freedoms and are subjected to the poor conditions of many jails. In *Bell v. Wolfish* (1979), the Supreme Court rejected the notion that this situation is inherently unfair by refusing to give pretrial detainees greater legal protections than sentenced jail inmates have.[78] In essence, the Court recognized that treating pretrial detainees differently from convicted jail inmates would place too much of a burden on corrections officials and was therefore impractical.[79] (To learn about another area where the courts have deferred to jail authorities, see the feature *A Question of Ethics—The Strip Search* on page 444.)

SENTENCED JAIL INMATES According to the U.S. Department of Justice, about 40 percent of those in jail have been convicted of their current charges.[80] In other words, they have been found guilty of a crime, usually a misdemeanor, and sentenced to time in jail. The typical jail term lasts between thirty and ninety days, and rarely does a prisoner spend

MASTERING CONCEPTS
THE MAIN DIFFERENCES BETWEEN PRISONS AND JAILS

	PRISONS	JAILS
1.	. . . are operated by the federal and state governments.	. . . are operated by county and city governments.
2.	. . . hold inmates who may have lived quite far away before being arrested.	. . . hold mostly inmates from the local community.
3.	. . . house only those who have been convicted of a crime.	. . . house those who are awaiting trial or have recently been arrested, in addition to convicts.
4.	. . . generally hold inmates who have been found guilty of serious crimes and received sentences of longer than one year.	. . . generally hold inmates who have been found guilty of minor crimes and are serving sentences of less than a year.
5.	. . . often offer a wide variety of rehabilitation and educational programs for long-term prisoners.	. . . due to smaller budgets, tend to focus only on the necessities of safety, food, and clothing.

FIGURE 13.7 Types of Offenses of Prison and Jail Inmates

As the comparison below shows, jail inmates are more likely than state prisoners to have been convicted of nonviolent crimes. This underscores the main function of jails: to house less serious offenders for a relatively short period of time.

State Prison Inmates   Jail Inmates

Offenses
- Violent
- Property
- Drug
- Public order
- Other

Source: Bureau of Justice Statistics, *Prisoners in 2011* (Washington, D.C.: U.S. Department of Justice, December 2011), Appendix table 8, page 27; and Bureau of Justice Statistics, *Profile of Jail Inmates, 2002* (Washington, D.C.: U.S. Department of Justice, July 2004), 1.

more than one year in jail for any single crime. Often, a judge will credit the length of time the convict has spent in detention waiting for trial—known as **time served**—toward his or her sentence. This practice acknowledges two realities of jails:

1. Terms are generally too short to allow the prisoner to gain any benefit (that is, rehabilitation) from the jail's often limited or nonexistent treatment facilities. Therefore, the jail term can serve no purpose except to punish the wrongdoer. (Judges who believe jail time can serve purposes of deterrence and incapacitation may not agree with this line of reasoning.)
2. Jails are chronically overcrowded, and judges need to clear space for new offenders.

> **Time Served** The period of time a person denied bail (or unable to pay it) has spent in jail prior to his or her trial.

OTHER JAIL INMATES Pretrial detainees and those convicted of misdemeanors make up the majority of the jail population. Jail inmates also include probation and parole violators, the mentally ill, juveniles awaiting transfer to juvenile authorities, and immigration law violators being held for the federal government. Increasingly, jails are also called on to handle the overflow from state prisons. To comply with a United States Supreme Court order to reduce its prison population, California corrections officials plan to divert an estimated 75,000 inmates from its prisons to its jails by 2015.[81]

THE SOCIOLOGY OF JAIL According to sociologist John Irwin, the unofficial purpose of a jail is to manage society's "rabble," so called because

> [they] are not well integrated into conventional society, they are not members of conventional social organizations, they have few ties to conventional social networks, and they are carriers of unconventional values and beliefs.[82]

In Irwin's opinion, rabble who act violently are arrested and sent to prison. The jail is reserved for merely offensive rabble, whose primary threat to society lies in their failure to conform to its behavioral norms. Approximately six out of ten jail inmates, for example, suffer from some form of mental illness.[83] This concept of rabble has been used by some critics of American corrections to explain the disproportionate number of poor and minority groups who may be found in the nation's jails at any time.

A QUESTION OF ETHICS

The Strip Search

Explain why the U.S. Supreme Court upheld the practice of strip searching all jail inmates, including those how have not been charged with a crime.

THE SITUATION During a stop, New Jersey police officers determined that Albert Florence had an outstanding warrant for an unpaid fine related to a previous traffic infraction. Even though this is not a criminal offense, the officers arrested Florence and took him to the Burlington County Jail. At the jail, correctional officers subjected him to a strip search, a highly invasive procedure that includes a shower and a search of the suspect's genitals and rectum.

THE ETHICAL DILEMMA Jail officials routinely strip search new entrants to (1) detect lice and other contagious medical conditions, (2) look for evidence of gang membership such as tattoos, and (3) prevent smuggling of drugs or weapons. As with Florence, however, the subject of the strip search often has not been charged with committing a crime. In such cases, say some observers, strip searches represent "a serious affront to human dignity and to individual privacy" and should be used only when there is reasonable suspicion that the inmate is carrying contraband.

WHAT IS THE SOLUTION? The U.S. Supreme Court has ruled that jail authorities may, using their discretion, conduct strip searches whenever they see fit, even if the inmate is not suspected of committing a crime and there is no evidence that he or she is carrying contraband. Justice Anthony Kennedy pointed out that "people detained for minor offenses can turn out to be the most devious and dangerous criminals." Do you agree that noncriminals such as Florence, detained for traffic violations and not suspected of any other wrongdoing, should be subjected to strip searches in jails? Why or why not?

Manfredxy/Shutterstock.com

Jail Administration

Of the nearly 3,370 jails in the United States, more than 2,700 are operated on a county level by an elected sheriff. Most of the remainder are under the control of municipalities, although six state governments (Alaska, Connecticut, Delaware, Hawaii, Rhode Island, and Vermont) manage jails. The capacity of jails varies widely. The Los Angeles County Men's Central Jail holds nearly 7,000 people, but jails that large are the exception rather than the rule. Forty percent of all jails in this country house fewer than 50 inmates.[84]

SOCIAL MEDIA & CJ

The **Los Angeles County Sheriff's Department** operates the largest jail in the United States. The law enforcement agency's Web site provides a link to its Facebook page, which has information about the jail and other aspects of criminal justice in Los Angeles.

Ankomando/Shutterstock.com

THE "BURDEN" OF JAIL ADMINISTRATION Given that the public's opinion of jails ranges from negative to indifferent, some sheriffs neglect their jail management duties. Instead, they focus on high-visibility issues such as putting more law enforcement officers on the streets and improving security in schools. In fact, a jail usually receives publicity only after an escape or an incident in which inmates are abused by jailers. Nonetheless, with their more complex and diverse populations, jails are often more difficult to manage than prisons. Jails hold people who have never been incarcerated before, people under the influence of drugs or alcohol at the time of their arrival, the mentally ill, and people who exhibit a range of violent behavior—from nonexistent to extreme—that only adds to the unpredictable atmosphere.[85]

Despite some sheriffs' general apathy toward jails, few would be willing to give up their management duties. As troublesome as they may be, jails can be useful in other ways. The sheriff appoints a jail administrator, or deputy sheriff, to oversee the day-to-day operations of the facility. The sheriff also has the power to hire other staff members, such as deputy jailers. The sheriff may award these jobs to people who helped her or him get elected, and, in return, jail staffers can prove helpful to the sheriff in future elections. Furthermore, jails pay. For example, the federal government reimburses the Rappahannock Regional Jail in Stafford, Virginia, $60 a day to house immigration violators awaiting the resolution of their cases.[86]

THE CHALLENGES OF OVERCROWDING In many ways, the sheriff is placed in an untenable position when it comes to jail overcrowding. He or she has little control over the number of people who are sent to jail—that power resides with prosecutors and judges. Nevertheless, the jail is expected to find space to hold all comers, regardless of its capacity. A sheriff from Kane County, Utah, describes the situation:

> We have people who should get sixty or ninety days, and they just do a weekend and we kick them out. Unless we get a real habitual abuser, we have no choice but to set them free. Most of the time we're pretty sure they will be back in a couple of days with a new offense.[87]

Living Conditions Chronic overcrowding makes the jail experience a miserable one for most inmates. Cells intended to hold one or two people are packed with up to six. Often, inmates are forced to sleep in hallways. In such stressful situations, tempers flare, leading to violent, aggressive behavior. The close proximity and unsanitary living conditions also lead to numerous health problems. In the words of one observer, jail inmates

> share tight space day and night, struggle with human density never before experienced (unless earlier in jail), and search hopelessly for even a moment of solitude. . . . [The congested conditions offer] inmates next to nothing except a stifling idleness that is almost sure to make them worse for the experience. If hard time in prison or jail is time without meaning, there might be no equal to long periods of time in the seriously overcrowded living areas of jails; for above all else (and clearly in comparison to time in prison), jail time is dead time.[88]

Such conditions also raise basic questions of justice: as we noted earlier, many of the inmates in jail have not yet been tried and must be presumed innocent.

A New Trend? Fortunately, at least for some jail managers, the situation seems to be improving. Between June 2010 and June 2011, the nation's jail inmate population dropped for the third consecutive year, the first such decline since the early 1980s.[89] To a large extent, this decrease was caused by reductions in jail populations in larger counties: two-thirds of jail jurisdictions with a thousand or more inmates reported a decline. Spurred by the same factors that have led to a reduction in state prison inmates, discussed earlier in this chapter, in 2011 U.S. jails averaged only 84 percent capacity, the lowest rate in a decade.[90] Also, jails have continued to add new beds—nearly 10,500 in 2010–2011—which has helped relieve overcrowding, if not pressures on local and state budgets.[91]

■ Sheriff Joe Chapman, right talks to an inmate at the Walton County Jail in Monroe, Georgia. Some corrections experts believe that jails are more difficult to manage than prisons. Why do you agree or disagree with this assertion?
Matt McClain/*The Washington Post* via Getty Images

New-Generation Jails

For most of the nation's history, the architecture of a jail was secondary to its purpose of keeping inmates safely locked away. Consequently, most jails in the United States continue to resemble those from the days of the Walnut Street Jail in Philadelphia. In this *traditional*, or *linear design*, jail cells are located along a corridor. To supervise the inmates while they are in their cells, custodial officers must walk up and down the corridor, so the number of prisoners they can see at any one time is severely limited. With this limited supervision, inmates can more easily break institutional rules.

PODULAR DESIGN In the 1970s, planners at the Bureau of Federal Prisons decided to upgrade the traditional jail design with the goal of improving conditions for both the staff and the inmates. The result was the **new-generation jail,** which differs significantly from its predecessors.[92] The layout of the new facilities makes it easier for the staff to monitor cell-confined inmates. The basic structure of the new-generation jail is based on a podular design. Each "pod" contains "living units" for individual prisoners. These units, instead of lining up along a straight corridor, are often situated in a triangle so that a staff member in the center of the triangle has visual access to nearly all the cells.

Daily activities such as eating and showering take place in the pod, which also has an outdoor exercise area. Treatment facilities are also located in the pod, allowing greater access for the inmates. During the day, inmates stay out in the open and are allowed back in their cells only when given permission. The officer locks the door to the cells from his or her control terminal.

DIRECT SUPERVISION APPROACH The podular design also enables a new-generation jail to be managed using a **direct supervision approach.**[93] One or more jail officers are stationed in the living area of the pod and are therefore in constant interaction with all prisoners in that particular pod. Some new-generation jails even provide a desk in the center of the living area, which sends a very different message to the prisoners than the traditional control booth (see photo alongside). Theoretically, jail officials who have constant contact with inmates will be able to stem misconduct quickly and efficiently and will also be able to recognize "danger signs" from individual inmates and stop outbursts before they occur. (As noted earlier in the chapter, corrections officials are using aspects of podular design when building new prisons, for many of the same reasons that the trend has been popular in jails.)

SELF ASSESSMENT

Fill in the blanks and check your answers on page 450.

A significant number of the people in jail are not prisoners, but rather _____ _____ who are unable to post bail and await trial. About 40 percent have been _____ of their current charges, meaning that the jail sentence is punishment for a crime—usually a _____ and not a felony. Most jails are operated on a local level by the county _____.

■ How does the layout of this direct supervision jail differ from that of the maximum-security prison pictured on page 434? What do these differences tell you about the security precautions needed for jail inmates as opposed to prison inmates?
Photo courtesy Bergen County Sheriff's Office, Bergen, NJ

THE CONSEQUENCES OF OUR HIGH RATES OF INCARCERATION

■ A mother and child wait outside the Donald W. W. Wyatt Detention Facility in Central Falls, Rhode Island. What are the possible consequences of having a parent behind bars for the affected children and for American society as a whole? Suzanne DeChillo/*New York Times*/Redux

For many observers, especially those who support the crime control theory of criminal justice, America's high rate of incarceration has contributed significantly to the drop in the country's crime rates.[94] At the heart of this belief is the fact, which we discussed in Chapter 2, that most crimes are committed by a relatively small group of repeat offenders. Several studies have tried to corroborate this viewpoint, with varying results—estimates of the number of crimes committed each year by habitual offenders range from 3 to 187.[95] If one accepts the higher estimate, each year a repeat offender spends in prison prevents a significant number of criminal acts.

Criminologists, however, note the negative consequences of America's immense prison and jail population. For one, incarceration can have severe social consequences for communities and the families that make up those communities. About 2.7 million minors in this country—one in twenty-eight—have a parent in prison.[96] These children are at an increased risk of suffering from poverty, depression, and academic problems, as well as higher levels of juvenile delinquency and eventual incarceration themselves.[97] Studies also link high imprisonment rates to increased incidence of sexually transmitted diseases and teenage pregnancy, as the separation caused by incarceration wreaks havoc on interpersonal relationships.[98]

LEARNING OBJECTIVE **9** Indicate some of the consequences of our high rates of incarceration.

In addition, incarceration denies one of the basic rights of American democracy—the right to vote—to about 5.9 million Americans with criminal records.[99] A number of states and the federal government *disenfranchise,* or take away the ability to vote, from those convicted of felonies. This has a disproportionate impact on minority groups, weakening their voice in the democratic debate. Today, African American males are incarcerated at a rate more than six times that of white males and almost three times that of Hispanic males.[100] With more black men behind bars than enrolled in the nation's colleges and universities, Marc Mauer of the Sentencing Project believes that the "ripple effect on their communities and on the next generation of kids, growing up with their fathers in prison, will certainly be with us for at least a generation."[101]

Whether our incarceration situation is "good" or "bad" depends to a large extent on one's personal philosophy. In the end, it is difficult to do a definitive cost-benefit analysis for each person incarcerated, weighing the benefits of preventing crimes that might (or might not) have been committed by an inmate against the costs to the convict's family and society. One thing that can be stated with some certainty is that, even with the growing interest in diversion and rehabilitation described in the previous chapter, the American prison system will remain one of the largest in the world for the foreseeable future.

SOLITARY CONFINEMENT: SENSELESS SUFFERING?

California corrections officials were convinced that Ernesto Lira, who had been imprisoned for possession of three grams of methamphetamine, was a gang member. As a result, they put him in a windowless eight-by-twelve foot cell. For eight years, twenty-three hours a day, his only companions were a family of spiders that he watched, "season by season, year by year." After Lira was released from prison, he put blankets over his bedroom windows to block out any light. He also suffered from depression and avoided crowds. "He's not the same person at all," said his sister. "Whatever happened, the experience he had in there changed him."[102] In this *CJ in Action* feature, we will examine the widespread practice of solitary confinement, condemned by critics as inhumane but heralded by supporters as an invaluable tool of prison management.

ENFORCED ISOLATION

Although conditions of solitary confinement vary, in general the term refers to the confinement of an inmate alone in a small cell for most or all of the day with minimal environmental stimulation and social interaction. Most solitary confinement cells measure approximately ten feet by six feet. Furnished with only a sink, toilet, and concrete bed, they have no windows or barred doors that would let in natural light.

As a rule, inmates are not sentenced to solitary confinement by a judge, and the assignment has no connection to the severity of the original offense. Rather, these isolation cells are reserved for prisoners who commit disciplinary violations once in prison or are deemed a security risk to themselves or others. According to estimates, at least 25,000 inmates—and probably significantly more—are in solitary confinement in American prisons at any given time.[103]

THE CASE FOR SOLITARY CONFINEMENT

- Prison officials see the threat of solitary confinement as a vital tool in maintaining order and discipline. Because human contact is one of the few privileges that inmates enjoy, they have a strong incentive to conform to the rules of the institution rather than risk losing that privilege.

- Solitary confinement protects prison staff and inmates alike by removing violent convicts from the general inmate population.

- Solitary confinement can be a form of rehabilitation, as it separates the inmate from negative influences.

THE CASE AGAINST SOLITARY CONFINEMENT

- Solitary confinement causes severe damage to the mental health of prisoners. Researchers have identified a number of resulting symptoms, including intense anxiety, hallucinations, violent fantasies, and reduced impulse control.[104]

- The majority of inmates who suffer the psychological harm of solitary confinement will eventually be returned to society, which will have to bear the burden of their mental illness.[105]

- Because prison officials have unfettered discretion in deciding who gets sent to solitary confinement and for how long, the practice is rife with abuse.

YOUR OPINION—WRITING ASSIGNMENT

To many observers, the drawbacks of solitary confinement lie in its practice, not its principles. Although it may be useful in controlling inmate populations, solitary confinement procedures suffer from failure to properly monitor the medical and psychological state of those in "the Hole," confinement for trivial offenses like "talking back" to corrections officials, and unacceptably long periods of isolation. The courts have shown no inclination to rein in these abuses, as judges tend to be extremely deferential to the decisions and policies of prison officials.

Today, no federal laws control the use of solitary confinement. Only one state, Washington, places a limit—twenty days—on the length of time an inmate may be kept in isolation.[106] If you were to draft a law regulating the use of solitary confinement, what elements would your law contain? Would you, like the courts, give prison officials a "free hand," or would you restrict their discretion? Would you allow prisoners to challenge their solitary confinement in court? Before responding, you can review our discussions in this chapter concerning:

- The three general models of prison organization (page 426).

- Maximum-security and supermax prisons (pages 430–434).

- Prison administration (pages 428–430).

Your answer should include at least three full paragraphs.

CHAPTER SUMMARY

For more information on these concepts, look back to the Learning Objective icons throughout the chapter.

 Contrast the Pennsylvania and the New York penitentiary theories of the 1800s. Basically, the Pennsylvania system imposed total silence on its prisoners. Based on the concept of separate confinement, penitentiaries were constructed with back-to-back cells facing both outward and inward. Prisoners worked, slept, and ate alone in their cells. In contrast, New York used the congregate system: silence was imposed, but inmates worked and ate together.

 Explain the three general models of prisons. (a) The custodial model assumes the prisoner is incarcerated for reasons of incapacitation, deterrence, and retribution. (b) The rehabilitation model puts security concerns second and the well-being of the individual inmate first. As a consequence, treatment programs are offered to prisoners. (c) The reintegration model sees the correctional institution as a training ground for preparing convicts to reenter society.

 Describe the formal prison management system, and indicate the three most important aspects of prison governance. A formal system is militaristic with a hierarchical (top-down) chain of command; the warden (or superintendent) is on top, then deputy wardens, and last, custodial employees. Sound governance of a correctional facility requires officials to provide inmates with a sense of order, amenities such as clean living conditions and acceptable food, and services such as vocational training and remedial education programs.

 List and briefly explain the four types of prisons. (a) Maximum-security prisons, which are designed mainly with security and surveillance in mind. Such prisons are usually large and consist of cell blocks, each of which is set off by a series of gates and bars. (b) Medium-security prisons, which offer considerably more educational and treatment programs and allow more contact between inmates. Such prisons are usually surrounded by high fences rather than by walls. (c) Minimum-security prisons, which permit prisoners to have television sets and computers and often allow them to leave the grounds for educational and employment purposes. (d) Supermaximum-security (supermax) prisons, in which prisoners are confined to one-person cells for up to twenty-three hours per day under constant video camera surveillance.

 List the factors that have caused the prison population to grow dramatically in the last several decades. (a) The enhancement and stricter enforcement of the nation's drug laws; (b) increased probability of incarceration; (c) inmates serving more time for each crime; (d) federal prison growth; and (e) rising incarceration rates for women.

 List the reasons why private prisons can often be run more cheaply than public ones. (a) Labor costs are lower because private prison employees are nonunionized and receive lower levels of overtime pay, sick leave, and health care. (b) Competitive bidding requires the operators of private prisons to buy goods and services at the lowest possible prices. (c) There is less red tape in a private prison facility.

 Summarize the distinction between jails and prisons, and indicate the importance of jails in the American corrections system. Generally, a prison is for those convicted of felonies who will serve lengthy periods of incarceration, whereas a jail is for those who have been convicted of misdemeanors and will serve less than a year of incarceration. Jails also hold individuals awaiting trial, juveniles awaiting transfer to juvenile authorities, probation and parole violators, and the mentally ill. In any given year, approximately 12 million people are admitted to jails, and therefore jails often provide the best chance for treatment or counseling that may deter future criminal behavior by these low-level offenders.

 Explain why the U.S. Supreme Court upheld the practice of strip searching all jail inmates, including those who have not been charged with a crime. In general, American courts are reluctant to require jail authorities to have different policies for different classes of jail inmates. When it comes to strip searches, the Supreme Court ruled that jail authorities may, at their discretion, strip search any inmate for reasons relating to jail hygiene and security.

 Indicate some of the consequences of our high rates of incarceration. Some people believe that the reduction in the country's crime rate is a direct result of increased incarceration rates. Others believe that high incarceration rates are having increasingly negative social consequences, such as financial hardships, reduced supervision and discipline of children, and a general deterioration of the family structure when one parent is in prison.

QUESTIONS FOR **CRITICAL ANALYSIS**

1. According to the American Civil Liberties Union, states could save $16 billion a year by releasing low-risk prisoners who are age fifty and older. This estimate is based on the fact that risk of recidivism decreases with age. What are the arguments for and against using age as a primary reason for early release from prison?

2. Supermax prisons operate in a state of perpetual lockdown. Why might a warden institute a lockdown in a maximum-security prison?

3. Do you agree with the argument that private prisons are inherently injust, no matter what costs they may save taxpayers? Why or why not?

4. Why have pretrial detainees been called "walking legal contradictions"? What are the practical reasons why pretrial detainees will continue to be housed in jails prior to trial, regardless of whether their incarceration presents any constitutional irregularities?

5. What are the arguments for and against taking away the ability to vote from those Americans convicted of committing a felony? What is your opinion of this form of disenfranchisement?

KEY **TERMS**

classification   430
congregate system   424
direct supervision approach   446
jail   441
lockdown   434
maximum-security prison   430

medical model   425
medium-security prison   434
minimum-security prison   434
new-generation jails   446
penitentiary   423
pretrial detainees   442

private prisons   438
separate confinement   424
supermax prison   432
time served   443
warden   428

SELF ASSESSMENT **ANSWER KEY**

Page 427: i. separate; **ii.** congregate; **iii.** silence; **iv.** cheaper; **v.** labor; **vi.** medical

Page 435: i. warden; **ii.** Classification; **iii.** maximum; **iv.** supermax

Page 438: i. drug; **ii.** incarceration/imprisonment; **iii.** length; **iv.** federal; **v.** decarceration

Page 441: i. financial; **ii.** overcrowding; **iii.** security/safety; **iv.** federal

Page 446: i. pretrial detainees; **ii.** convicted; **iii.** misdemeanor; **iv.** sheriff

NOTES

1. James M. Beattie, *Crime and the Courts in England, 1660–1800* (Princeton, NJ: Princeton University Press, 1986), 506–507.

2. Samuel Walker, *Popular Justice* (New York: Oxford University Press, 1980), 11.

3. Michael Meranze, *Laboratories of Virtue: Punishment, Revolution, and Authority in Philadelphia, 1760–1835* (Chapel Hill, NC: University of North Carolina Press, 1996), 55.

4. Negley K. Teeters, *The Cradle of the Penitentiary: The Walnut Street Jail at Philadelphia, 1773–1835* (Philadelphia: Pennsylvania Prison Society, 1955), 30.

5. Negley K. Teeters and John D. Shearer, *The Prison at Philadelphia's Cherry Hill* (New York: Columbia University Press, 1957), 142–143.

6. Henry Calvin Mohler, "Convict Labor Policies," *Journal of the American Institute of Criminal Law and Criminology* 15 (1925), 556–557.

7. Zebulon Brockway, *Fifty Years of Prison Service* (Montclair, NJ: Patterson Smith, 1969), 400–401.

8. Robert Martinson, "What Works? Questions and Answers about Prison Reform," *Public Interest* 35 (Spring 1974), 22.

9. See Ted Palmer, "Martinson Revisited," *Journal of Research on Crime and Delinquency* (1975), 133; and Paul Gendreau and Bob Ross, "Effective Correctional Treatment: Bibliotherapy for Cynics," *Crime & Delinquency* 25 (1979), 499.

10. Robert Martinson, "New Findings, New Views: A Note of Caution Regarding Sentencing Reform," *Hofstra Law Review* 7 (1979), 243.

11. Byron Eugene Price and John Charles Morris, eds., *Prison Privatization: The Many Facets of a Controversial Industry, Volume 1* (Santa Barbara: Praeger, 2012), 58.

12. Charles H. Logan, *Criminal Justice Performance Measures in Prisons* (Washington, D.C.: U.S. Department of Justice, 1993), 5.

13. Todd R. Clear and George F. Cole, *American Corrections,* 4th ed. (Belmont, CA: Wadsworth Publishing Co., 1997), 245–246.

14. Alfred Blumstein, "Prisons," in *Crime,* ed. James Q. Wilson and Joan Petersilia (San Francisco: ICS Press, 1995), 392.

15. Cassia Spohn and David Holleran, "The Effect of Imprisonment on Recidivism Rates of Felony Offenders: A Focus on Drug Offenders," *Criminology* (May 1, 2002), 329–357.

16. Bureau of Justice Statistics, *Census of State and Federal Correctional Facilities, 2005* (Washington, D.C.: U.S. Department of Justice, October 2008), 2.

17. *Ibid.*

18. Charles H. Logan, "Well Kept: Comparing Quality of Confinement in a Public and Private Prison," *Journal of Criminal Law and Criminology* 83 (1992), 580.

19. Bert Useem and Peter Kimball, *Stages of Siege: U.S. Prison Riots, 1971–1986* (New York: Oxford University Press, 1989).

20. Bert Useem, "Disorganization and the New Mexico Prison Riot of 1980," *American Sociology Review* 50 (1985), 685.

21. John J. DiIulio, *Governing Prisons* (New York: Free Press, 1987), 12.

22. *Ibid.*

23. Todd R. Clear, George F. Cole, and Michael D. Reisig, *American Corrections,* 9th ed. (Belmont, CA: Wadsworth Cengage Learning, 2010), 162.

24. Heather Stokes, "The Design to Aging Foundations" (November 13, 2012), at **prezi.com/l3mrp0gvomor/the-design-to-aging-foundations**.

25. Douglas Page, "The Prison of the Future," *Law Enforcement Technology* (January 2012), 11–13.

26. *Madrid v. Gomez,* 889 F.Supp. 1146 (N.D. Cal. 1995).

27. Keramet Reiter, *Parole, Snitch, or Die: California's Supermax Prisons and Prisoners, 1987–2007* (Berkeley, CA: University of California Institute for the Study of Social Change, 2010), 1.

28. "Facts about Pelican Bay's SHU," *California Prisoner* (December 1991).

29. *Jones-El et al. v. Berge and Lichter,* 164 F.Supp.2d 1096 (2001).

30. Robert Perkinson, "Shackled Justice: Florence Federal Penitentiary and the New Politics of Punishment," *Social Justice* (Fall 1994), 117–123.

31. Terry Kuppers, *Prison Madness: The Mental Health Crisis behind Bars and What We Must Do about It* (San Francisco: Jossey-Bass, 1999), 56–64.

32. Steven D. Levitt, "Understanding Why Crime Fell in the 1990s: Four Factors That Explain the Decline and Six That Do Not," *Journal of Economic Perspectives* (Winter 2004), 177.

33. Bureau of Justice Statistics, *Prisoners in 2011* (Washington, D.C.: U.S. Department of Justice, December 2012), Appendix table 7, page 26, and appendix table 12, page 29.

34. Allen J. Beck, "Growth, Change, and Stability in the U.S. Prison Population, 1980–1995," *Corrections Management Quarterly* (Spring 1997), 9–10.

35. U.S. District Courts, "Criminal Defendants Sentenced after Conviction, by Offense, during the 12-Month Period Ending September 30, 2011" at **www.uscourts.gov/uscourts/Statistics/JudicialBusiness/2011/appendices/D05Sep11.pdf**.

36. Joan Petersilia, "Beyond the Prison Bubble," *Wilson Quarterly* (Winter 2011), 27.

37. California State Auditor, *Inmates Sentenced under the Three Strikes Law and a Small Number of Inmates Receiving Specialty Care Represent Significant Costs* (Sacramento, CA: Bureau of State Audits, May 2011), 1.

38. *Time Served: The High Cost, Low Return of Longer Prison Terms* (Washington, D.C.: The Pew Center on the States, June 2012), 2.

39. *Fifteen Years of Guidelines Sentencing: An Assessment of How Well the Federal Criminal Justice System Is Achieving the Goals of Sentencing Reform* (Washington, D.C.: U.S. Sentencing Commission, November 2004), 46.

40. *Old Behind Bars: The Aging Prison Population of the United States* (New York: Human Rights Watch, January 2012), 33–34.

41. *Prisoners in 2011,* 1.

42. *Ibid.,* Table 5, page 6.

43. Kamala Mallik-Kane, Barbara Parthasarathy, and William Adams, *Examining Growth in the Federal Prison Population, 1998 to 2010* (Washington, D.C.: Urban Institute, September 2012), 4.

44. Mark Motivans, *Immigration Offenders in the Federal Justice System, 2010* (Washington, D.C.: U.S. Department of Justice, July 2012), 1; and Federal Bureau of Prisons, "Quick Facts about the Bureau of Prisons" (March 30, 2013), at **www.bop.gov/news/quick.jsp**.

45. "Quick Facts about the Bureau of Prisons"; and Bureau of Justice Statistics, *Prison and Jail Inmates, 1995* (Washington, D.C.: U.S. Department of Justice, August 1996), Table 6, page 6.

46. *Prisoners in 2011,* Table 1, page 2.

47. Christian Henrichson and Ruth Delaney, *The Price of Prisons: What Incarceration Costs Taxpayers* (New York: Center for Sentencing and Corrections, January 2012), 6, 8.

48. Rosemary Gartner, Anthony N. Doob, and Franklin E. Zimring, "The Past as Prologue? Decarceration in California Then and Now," *Criminology & Public Policy* (May 2011), 292.

49. Erica Goode, "Inmate Visits Now Carry Added Cost in Arizona," *New York Times* (September 5, 2011), A10.

50. James B. Jacobs, "Finding Alternatives to the Carceral State," *Social Research* (Summer 2007), 695.

51. Gartner, Doob, and Zimring, 294–296.

52. Joseph Walker, "Rules May Help Parolees Avoid Jail for Small Errors," *New York Times* (January 5, 2012), at **cityroom.blogs.nytimes.com/2012/01/05/rating-a-parolees-risk-before-a-return-to-prison**.

53. *Prisoners in 2011,* Table 3, page 5; and Mike Males, *Update: Eight Months in Realignment: Dramatic Reductions in California's Prisoners* (San Francisco, CA: Center on Juvenile & Criminal Justice, June 2012), 4.

54. *Prisoners in 2011,* 1.

55. Quoted in Scott Cohn, "Private Prison Industry Grows Despite Critics," *cnbc.com* (October 18, 2011), at **www.nbcnews.com/id/44936562/ns/business-cnbc_tv/t/private-prison-industry-grows-despite-critics/#.UW6vC7_zdzU**.

56. Suevon Lee, "By the Numbers: The U.S.'s Growing For-Profit Detention Industry," *ProPublica* (June 20, 2012), at **www.propublica.org/article/by-the-numbers-the-u.s.s-growing-for-profit-detention-industry**.

57. *Prisoners in 2011,* Appendix table 15, page 32.

58. "A Tale of Two Systems: Cost, Quality, and Accountability in Private Prisons," *Harvard Law Review* (May 2002), 1872.

59. Douglas C. McDonald and Kenneth Carlson, *Contracting for Imprisonment in the Federal Prison System: Cost and Performance of the Privately Operated Taft Correctional Institution* (Cambridge, MA: Abt Associates, Inc., October 2005), vii.

60. Vanderbilt University Law School, "New Study Shows Benefits of Having Privately and Publicly Managed Prisons in the Same State" (November 25, 2008), at **law.vanderbilt.edu/article-search/article-detail/index.aspx?nid=213**.

61. Nelson Daranciang, "Isle Inmates Brought Home," *Honolulu Star-Advertiser* (January 28, 2011), A3.

62. John Tunison, "Baldwin Prisoners Will Be Classified Medium Security," *Grand Rapids (MI) Press* (December 11, 2010), A4.

63. "Behind the Bars: Experts Question Benefits of Private Prisons," *Kentucky Courier Journal* (July 5, 2010), at **www.courier-journal.com/article/20100705/NEWS01/7050312/Behind-Bars-Experts-question-benefitsprivate-prisons**.

64. Quoted in Cohn.

65. Robbie Brown, "Mississippi Prison on Lockdown after Guard Dies," *New York Times* (May 23, 2012), A12.

66. Gregory Geisler, *CIIC: Lake Erie Correctional Institution* (Columbus, OH: Correctional Institution Inspection Committee, January 2013), 16.

67. Curtis R. Blakely and Vic W. Bumphus, "Private and Public Sector Prisons," *Federal Probation* (June 2004), 27.

68. John DiIulio, "Prisons, Profits, and the Public Good: The Privatization of Corrections," in *Criminal Justice Center Bulletin* (Huntsville, TX: Sam Houston State University, 1986).

69. Richard L. Lippke, "Thinking about Private Prisons," *Criminal Justice Ethics* (Winter/Spring 1997), 32.

70. Quoted in Cohn.

71. Steve Bousquet, "Nine Defectors Sink Private Prison Plan," *Tampa Bay Times* (February 15, 2012), 1A.

72. *Prisoners in 2011*, Appendix table 15, page 32.

73. *Ibid.*

74. Bureau of Justice Statistics, *Jail Inmates at Midyear 2012—Statistical Tables* (Washington, D.C.: U.S. Department of Justice, May 2013), 1, 4.

75. Arthur Wallenstein, "Jail Crowding: Bringing the Issue to the Corrections Center Stage," *Corrections Today* (December 1996), 76–81.

76. Quoted in Fox Butterfield, "'Defying Gravity,' Inmate Population Climbs," *New York Times* (January 19, 1998), A10.

77. *Jail Inmates at Midyear 2011—Statistical Tables*, Table 6, page 6.

78. 441 U.S. 520 (1979).

79. *Ibid.*, at 546.

80. *Jail Inmates at Midyear 2011—Statistical Tables*, Table 12, page 10.

81. Vauhini Vara and Bobby White, "County Jails Prepare for Extra Guests," *Wall Street Journal* (August 10, 2011), A4.

82. John Irwin, *The Jail: Managing the Underclass in American Society* (Berkeley, CA: University of California Press, 1985), 2.

83. Bureau of Justice Statistics, *Mental Health Problems of Prison and Jail Inmates* (Washington, D.C.: U.S. Department of Justice, September 2006), 1.

84. Bureau of Justice Statistics, *Census of Jail Facilities, 2006* (Washington, D.C.: U.S. Department of Justice, December 2011), 14.

85. Philip L. Reichel, *Corrections: Philosophies, Practices, and Procedures,* 2d ed. (Boston: Allyn & Bacon, 2001), 283.

86. Cathy Dyson, "Loss of Federal Inmates Shackles Regional Jail," *The Free Lance-Star (Fredericksburg, VA)* (March 9, 2013), at **news. fredericksburg.com/newsdesk/2013/03/09/loss-of-federal -inmates-shackles-regional-jail/#**.

87. Quoted in Greg Burton, "Jail Builders Race to Keep Up with Demand," *Salt Lake City Tribune* (May 8, 1998), N31.

88. Robert G. Lawson, "Turning Jails into Prisons—Collateral Damage from Kentucky's 'War on Crime,'" *Kentucky Law Journal* (2006–2007), 1.

89. *Jail Inmates at Midyear 2011—Statistical Tables*, 1.

90. *Ibid.*, 2.

91. *Ibid.*

92. R. L. Miller, "New Generation Justice Facilities: The Case for Direct Supervision," *Architectural Technology* 12 (1985), 6–7.

93. David Bogard, Virginia A. Hutchinson, and Vicci Persons, *Direct Supervision Jails: The Role of the Administrator* (Washington, D.C.: National Institute of Corrections, February 2010), 1–2.

94. Dan Seligman, "Lock 'Em Up," *Forbes* (May 23, 2005), 216–217.

95. Franklin E. Zimring and Gordon Hawkins, *Incapacitation: Penal Confinement and the Restraint of Crime* (New York: Oxford University Press, 1995), 38, 40, 145.

96. Bruce Western and Becky Pettit, *Collateral Costs: Incarceration's Effect on Economic Mobility* (Washington, D.C.: The Pew Charitable Trusts, 2010), 4.

97. John Tierney, "Prison and the Poverty Trap," *New York Times* (February 19, 2013), D1.

98. *Ibid.*

99. Christopher Uggen, Sarah Shannon, and Jeff Manza, *State-Level Estimates of Felon Disenfranchisement in the United States, 2010* (Washington, D.C.: The Sentencing Project, July 2012), 1.

100. Bureau of Justice Statistics, *Prisoners in 2010* (Washington, D.C.: U.S. Department of Justice, December 2011), Appendix table 14, page 27.

101. Quoted in Fox Butterfield, "Study Finds 2.6% Increase in U.S. Prison Population," *New York Times* (July 28, 2003), A8.

102. Quoted in Erica Good, "Fighting a Drawn-Out Battle against Solitary Confinement," *New York Times* (March 31, 2012), A1.

103. Erica Goode, "Prisons Rethink Isolation, Saving Money, Lives, and Sanity," *New York Times* (March 11, 2012), A1.

104. Bruce Arrigo and Jennifer Leslie Bullock, "The Psychological Effects of Solitary Confinement on Prisoners in Supermax Units," *International Journal of Offender Therapy and Comparative Criminology* (December 2008), 622–640.

105. Matthew Lowen and Caroline Isaacs, *Lifetime Lockdown: How Isolation Conditions Impact Prisoner Reentry* (Tucson, AZ: American Friends Service Committee, August 2012).

106. Washington Revised Code Section 10.64.060 (2005).

CHAPTER

14

Behind Bars: The Life of an Inmate

CHAPTER OUTLINE		CORRESPONDING LEARNING OBJECTIVES
Prison Culture		Explain the concept of prison as a total institution.
		Describe a risk run by corrections officials who fail to provide adequate medical care to the inmates under their control.
Prison Violence		Indicate some of the reasons for violent behavior in prisons.
Correctional Officers and Discipline		List and briefly explain the six general job categories among correctional officers.
		Describe the hands-off doctrine of prisoner law and indicate two standards used to determine if prisoners' rights have been violated.
Inside a Women's Prison		Explain the aspects of imprisonment that prove challenging for incarcerated mothers and their children.
Return to Society		Contrast parole, expiration release, pardon, and furlough.
		Explain the goal of prisoner reentry programs.
		Indicate typical conditions for release for a paroled child molester.

To target your study and review, look for these numbered Learning Objective icons throughout the chapter.

Noah Berger/Bloomberg via Getty Images

BUSINESS AS USUAL

ON JUNE 5, 2012, inmates at the Lee Correctional Institution in Bishopville, South Carolina, ambushed a correctional officer who was escorting a nurse during her evening rounds. The nurse narrowly escaped, and the correctional officer was held hostage for more than six hours before being rescued, relatively unharmed, by local law enforcement. Although state officials promised to review the incident, about three months later inmates wielding homemade knives seized another correctional officer at the same prison. The officer suffered stab wounds and was locked in a broom closet.

"It's part of the business," said South Carolina Corrections Department spokesman Clark Newsom of the two kidnappings. "We're dealing with very dangerous criminals here." Some observers felt, however, that poor management decisions had increased the danger levels at the maximum-security prison. One prison official warned that such outbursts were a natural consequence of inmates being treated like "wild animals." During the first incident, prisoners demanded improvements in their living conditions, including better medical care, access to reading material, and hot meals. Both kidnappings took place during "off hours," when one correctional officer was responsible for guarding as many as 250 inmates.

In 2013, South Carolina Governor Nikki Haley proposed spending an additional $18 million on state prisons. Part of the funds would go toward hiring more security personnel and buying new ovens for woefully ill-equipped prison kitchens. The proposal was, however, resisted by legislators who felt the resources should go to other, worthier areas of need. This attitude is in keeping with the "no frills" movement in American corrections, which has succeeded in removing most amenities from inmates' lives. Many state prisons ban weightlifting, televisions, radios, adult magazines, and conjugal visits. All states and the federal government have limited smoking in their correctional facilities, and some institutions spend less than $2 a day per inmate on meals. Consequently, life in today's penal institutions has been described as "grindingly dull routine interrupted by occasional flashes of violence and brutality."

Gray wall studio/Shutterstock.com

AP Photo/The State, Jason Clark, File

1. What is your opinion of the "no frills" movement in American corrections? Should an inmate's life be nothing more than "dull routine"? Explain your answer.
2. In the last chapter, you learned that prison officials often keep violent offenders in lockdown, restricting them to their cells for most of the day. Correctional officers at the Lee Correctional Institution favor lockdown as a security measure, particularly given the facility's low staffing levels. In contrast, an inmate compares the experience to being a "dog in a cage." He suggests that giving prisoners more freedom would relieve "a lot of stress" and avoid situations such as the two kidnappings described above. Which viewpoint do you favor? Why?
3. In both incidents, inmates using cell phones alerted prison administrators that a correctional officer had been captured. This is somewhat ironic, as inmates are banned from having cell phones and smartphones. Why is such a ban necessary for prison security?

Inmates at the Lee Correctional Institution in Bishopville, South Carolina, seized members of the prison staff on two separate occasions in 2012.

PRISON CULTURE

In this chapter, we will look at the life of the imprisoned convict, starting with the realities of an existence behind bars and finishing with the challenges of returning to free society. Along the way, we will discuss violence in prison, correctional officers, women's prisons, different types of release, and several other issues that are at the forefront of American corrections today. To start, we must understand the forces that shape prison culture and how those forces affect the overall operation of the correctional facility.

Any institution, whether a school, a bank, or a police department, has an organizational culture—a set of values that help the people in the organization understand what actions are acceptable and what actions are unacceptable. According to a theory put forth by the influential sociologist Erving Goffman, prison cultures are unique because prisons are **total institutions** that encompass every aspect of an inmate's life. Unlike a student or a bank teller, a prisoner cannot leave the institution or have any meaningful interaction with outside communities. Others arrange every aspect of daily life, and all prisoners are required to follow this schedule in the same manner.[1]

Inmates develop their own argot, or language (see Figure 14.1 below). They create their own economy, which, in the absence of currency, is based on the barter of valued items such as food, contraband, and sexual favors. They establish methods of determining power, many of which, as we shall see, involve violence. Isolated and heavily regulated, prisoners create a social existence that is, out of both necessity and design, separate from the outside world.

Adapting to Prison Society

On arriving at prison, each convict attends an orientation session and receives a "Resident's Handbook." The handbook provides information such as meal and official count times, disciplinary regulations, and visitation guidelines. The norms and values of the prison society, however, cannot be communicated by the staff or learned from a handbook. As first described by Donald Clemmer in his classic 1940 work, *The Prison Community*, the process of **prisonization**—or adaptation to the prison culture—advances as the inmate gradually understands what constitutes acceptable behavior in the institution, as defined not by the prison officials but by other inmates.[2]

In studying prisonization, criminologists have focused on two areas: how prisoners change their behavior to adapt to life behind bars, and how life behind bars has changed because of inmate behavior. Sociologist John Irwin has identified several patterns of inmate behavior, each one driven by the inmate's personality and values:

Total Institution An institution, such as a prison, that provides all of the necessities for existence to those who live within its boundaries.

Prisonization The socialization process through which a new inmate learns the accepted norms and values of the prison culture.

LEARNING
OBJECTIVE 1 Explain the concept of prison as a total institution.

FIGURE 14.1 Prison Slang

Ace Another word for "dollar."

Bang A fight to the death, or shoot to kill.

Base head A cocaine addict.

B.G. "Baby gangster," or someone who has never shot another person.

Booty bandit An incarcerated sexual predator who preys on weaker inmates, called "punks."

Bug A correctional staff member, such as a psychiatrist, who is deemed untrustworthy or unreliable.

Bumpin' titties Fighting.

Catch cold To get killed.

Chiva Heroin.

Dancing on the blacktop Getting stabbed.

Diddler Child molester or pedophile.

Green light Prison gang term for a contract killing.

Hacks Correctional officers.

Jug-up Mealtime.

Lugger An inmate who smuggles in and possesses illegal substances.

Punk An inmate subject to rape, usually more submissive than most inmates.

Ride with To perform favors, including sexual favors, for a convict in return for protection or prison-store goods.

Shank Knife.

Tits-up An inmate who has died.

Topped Committed suicide.

Source: **www.insideprison.com/glossary.asp**.

1. Professional criminals adapt to prison by "doing time." In other words, they follow the rules and generally do whatever is necessary to speed up their release and return to freedom.

2. Some convicts, mostly state-raised youths or those frequently incarcerated in juvenile detention centers, are more comfortable inside prison than outside. These inmates serve time by "jailing," or establishing themselves in the power structure of prison culture.

3. Other inmates take advantage of prison resources such as libraries or drug treatment programs by "gleaning," or working to improve themselves to prepare for a return to society.

4. Finally, "disorganized" criminals exist on the fringes of prison society. These inmates may have mental impairments or low levels of intelligence and find it impossible to adapt to prison culture on any level.[3]

The process of categorizing prisoners has a theoretical basis, but it serves a practical purpose as well, allowing administrators to reasonably predict how different inmates will act in certain situations. An inmate who is "doing time" generally does not present the same security risk as one who is "jailing."

Who Is in Prison?

The culture of any prison is heavily influenced by its inmates. Their values, beliefs, and experiences will be reflected in the social order that exists behind bars. As we noted in the last chapter, the past three decades have seen incarceration rates of women and minority groups rise sharply. Furthermore, the arrest patterns of inmates have changed over that time period. A prisoner today is much more likely to have been incarcerated on a drug charge or immigration violation than was the case in the 1980s. Today's inmate is also more likely to behave violently behind bars—a situation that will be addressed shortly.

AN AGING INMATE POPULATION In recent years, the most significant demographic change in the prison population involves age. Though the majority of inmates are still under thirty-four years old, as you can see in Figure 14.2 on the left, the number of state and federal prisoners over the age of forty has increased dramatically since the mid-1990s. Several factors have contributed to this upsurge, including longer prison terms, mandatory prison terms, recidivism, and higher levels of crimes—particularly violent crimes—committed by older offenders.[4]

AN AILING INMATE POPULATION Overall, about 40 percent of state and federal prisoners suffer from at least one form of illness other than a cold, the most common ailments being arthritis, hypertension, tuberculosis, and asthma.[5] In some areas, the news concerning inmate health is positive. For example, AIDS-related deaths in prisons declined 76 percent between 2001 and 2010.[6] Given the frailties of older

FIGURE 14.2 The Aging Prison Population

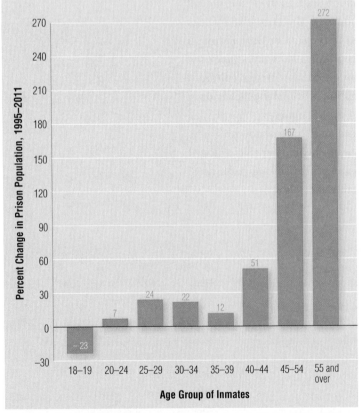

Sources: Bureau of Justice Statistics, *Prisoners in 2003* (Washington, D.C.: U.S. Department of Justice, November 2004), Table 10, page 8; Bureau of Justice Statistics, *Prisoners in 2011* (Washington, D.C.: U.S. Department of Justice, December 2012), Table 7, page 7.

inmates, however, prisons and jails are now holding more people with medical issues than in the past. Poor health is the cause of nine of ten inmate deaths in state prisons, with heart disease and cancer accounting for nearly half of these fatalities.[7] Not surprisingly, the mortality rates of inmates fifty-five and older from heart disease and cancer are five times higher than for any other age group.[8]

Corrections budgets are straining under the financial pressures caused by the health-care needs of aging inmates. According to the American Civil Liberties Union, an elderly inmate is two times more expensive to house than a younger inmate.[9] In Georgia, prisoners sixty-five years or older have average annual medical expenses of about $8,500, compared with an average annual medical expense of $961 for those inmates under sixty-five.[10] Given the burden of inmate medical costs, state corrections officials may be tempted to cut such services whenever possible. As the feature *Landmark Cases— Brown v. Plata* on the next page shows, however, prisoners have a constitutional right to adequate health care.

MENTAL ILLNESS BEHIND BARS Another factor in rising correctional health-care costs is the high incidence of mental illness in American prisons and jails. During the 1950s and 1960s, nearly 600,000 mental patients lived in public hospitals, often against their will. A series of scandals spotlighting the poor medical services and horrendous living conditions in these institutions led to their closure and the elimination of much of the nation's state-run mental health infrastructure.[11] Many mentally ill people now receive no supervision whatsoever, and some inevitably commit deviant or criminal acts.

As a result, in the words of criminal justice experts Katherine Stuart van Wormer and Clemens Bartollas, jails and prison have become "the dumping grounds for people whose bizarre behavior lands them behind bars."[12] Nationwide, 60 percent of jail inmates and 56 percent of state prisoners suffer from some form of mental illness.[13] As with aging and ailing prisoners, correctional facilities are required by law to provide treatment to mentally ill inmates, thus driving the costs associated with their confinement well above the average.[14] For reasons that should become clear over the course of this chapter, correctional facilities are not designed to foster mental well-being, and indeed inmates with mental illnesses often find that their problems are exacerbated by the prison environment.[15]

Rehabilitation and Prison Programs

In Chapter 11, we saw that rehabilitation is one of the basic theoretical justifications for punishment. **Prison programs,** which include any organized activities designed to foster rehabilitation, benefit inmates in several ways. On a basic level, these programs get prisoners out of their cells and alleviate the boredom that marks prison and jail life. The programs also help inmates improve their health and skills, giving them a better chance of reintegration into society after release. Consequently, nearly every federal and state prison in the United States offers some form of rehabilitation.[16]

Prison programs are limited, however. Many inmates suffering from mental illness would benefit from medication and twenty-four-hour psychiatric care. Yet these services are quite rare behind bars, mostly due to their high costs.[17] In addition, as many state prison systems face budget restraints, rehabilitation programs are increasingly subject to a *cost-benefit* analysis. In other words, for each dollar spent on a program, how many dollars are saved? These savings can be difficult to calculate, but researchers have become skilled at

Prison Programs Organized activities for inmates that are designed to improve their physical and mental health, provide them with vocational skills, or simply keep them busy while incarcerated.

■ Why is it beneficial for prisoners such as these two Colorado inmates, seen working on mannequin heads during a cosmetology class, to receive job training while still incarcerated? AP Photo/*The Daily Record,* Jeff Shane

LANDMARK CASES:
Brown v. Plata

Describe a risk run by corrections officials who fail to provide adequate medical care to the inmates under their control.

LEARNING 2 OBJECTIVE

California's thirty-three prisons are designed to hold 80,000 inmates. For most of the first decade of the 2000s, these facilities housed around 160,000 inmates. "It's an unacceptable working environment for everyone," said a former state corrections official. "It leads to greater violence, more staff overtime, and a total inability to deal with health care and mental illness issues." In 2009, a federal court agreed, ordering the state to reduce its prison population by 30,000 in two years. California officials appealed, giving the U.S. Supreme Court a chance to rule on the importance of medical care for inmates in this country.

Brown v. Plata
United States Supreme Court
131 S.Ct. 1910 (2011)

IN THE WORDS OF THE COURT . . .
JUSTICE KENNEDY, MAJORITY OPINION

* * * *

For years the medical and mental health care provided by California's prisons has fallen short of minimum constitutional requirements and has failed to meet prisoners' basic health needs. Needless suffering and death have been the well documented result.

* * * *

Prisoners are crammed into spaces neither designed nor intended to house inmates. As many as 200 prisoners may live in a gymnasium, monitored by as few as two or three correctional officers. * * * The consequences of overcrowding include "increased, substantial risk for transmission of infectious illness" and a suicide rate "approaching an average of one per week." * * * A correctional officer testified that, in one prison, up to 50 sick inmates may be held together in a 12- by 20-foot cage for up to five hours awaiting treatment. The number of staff is inadequate, and prisoners face significant delays in access to care. A prisoner with severe abdominal pain died after a 5-week delay in referral to a specialist; a prisoner with "constant and extreme" chest pain died after an 8-hour delay in evaluation by a doctor; and a prisoner died of testicular cancer after a "failure of MDs to work up for cancer in a young man with 17 months of testicular pain."

* * * *

A prison that deprives prisoners of basic sustenance, including adequate medical care, is incompatible with the concept of human dignity and has no place in civilized society.

DECISION
The Court found that severe overcrowding in California state prisons denied inmates satisfactory levels of mental and physical health care and therefore amounted to unconstitutional cruel and unusual punishment. It ordered the state to reduce the prison population to 137.5 percent of capacity—about 110,00 inmates—by June 2013. (As of May 2013, California's prison population stood at nearly 120,000.)

FOR CRITICAL ANALYSIS
In his dissent, Justice Alito wrote, "I fear that today's decision will lead to a grim roster of victims." What might be some of the reasons behind this fear? What steps could California corrections officials take to alleviate Alito's worries?

Kentoh/Shutterstock.com

measuring reductions in future criminal behavior—and the costs such behavior would have imposed on society—to determine the usefulness of prison programs.

SUBSTANCE ABUSE TREATMENT As we have seen throughout this textbook, there is a strong link between crime and abuse of drugs and alcohol. According to the National Center on Addiction and Substance Abuse (CASA) at New York's Columbia University, 1.5 million prison and jail inmates in the United States meet the medical criteria for substance abuse or addiction. Also according to CASA, only 11 percent of these inmates have received any type of professional treatment behind bars.[18] The most effective substance abuse programs for prisoners require trained staff, lengthy periods of therapy, expensive medication, and community aftercare, but such programs carry a price tag of nearly $10,000 per inmate. If every eligible prisoner in the United States received such treatment, the cost would be $12.6 billion. Researchers at CASA contend, however, that "the nation would break even in a year" if just one in ten of these inmates remained substance and crime free and employed for one year after release from prison.[19]

VOCATIONAL AND EDUCATIONAL PROGRAMS Even if an ex-convict does stay substance free, he or she will have a difficult time finding a steady paycheck. Employers are only about half as likely to hire job applicants with criminal records as they are those with "clean sheets."[20] To overcome this handicap, more than half of all American prisons offer *vocational* training, or prison programs that provide inmates with skills necessary to find a job. The California Institute for Men at Chino, for example, gives certain convicts the chance to complete a program in commercial diving. Nine out of ten prisons also attempt to educate their inmates, offering literacy training, GED (general equivalency degree) programs, and other types of instruction.[21]

Some evidence suggests that such efforts can have a positive effect on rates of reoffending. The Arkansas Department of Corrections figures that GED programs in its jails have cut the state's recidivism rate by 8 percent.[22] Only about 6 percent of the commercial divers from Chino return to prison within three years, compared with California's 70 percent overall recidivism rate.[23] Proponents of such efforts also point to their potential financial benefits. Researchers at the Washington State Institute for Public Policy estimate that every $1,182 spent for inmate vocational training saves $6,806 in future criminal justice costs and that every $962 spent on inmate education saves $5,306 in future criminal justice costs.[24]

At one time, the federal government provided grants that helped eligible inmates earn college degrees while in prison. This Pell Grant program was discontinued as part of the "no frills" movement mentioned in the opening of the chapter, after critics successfully argued that any available educational funds should go to non-prisoners.[25] Today, fewer than 3,000 inmates earn their associate's or bachelor's degree behind bars each year. Not only do most correctional facilities lack the financial resources to provide such postsecondary degrees, but they also lack facilities, technology (for online classes), and qualified instructors.[26]

SELF ASSESSMENT

Fill in the blanks and check your answers on page 485.

Prison culture is different from the cultures of schools or workplaces because prison is a _____ _____ that dominates every aspect of the inmate's life. Inmates create their own _____, or language, and develop their own _____ based on bartering food, contraband, and sexual favors. In recent decades, the prison culture has been affected by the increased average _____ of inmates, which has led to skyrocketing _____-_____ costs for federal and state corrections systems. Prison programs such as substance abuse treatment and _____ training, which helps improve inmates' job skills, are often justified by _____-benefit analyses.

PRISON VIOLENCE

Prisons and jails are dangerous places to live. Prison culture is predicated on violence—one observer calls the modern institution an "unstable and violent jungle."[27] Prison guards use the threat of violence (and, at times, its reality) to control the inmate population. Sometimes, the inmates strike back. Each year, federal correctional officers are subjected to about eighty assaults and 1,500 less serious attacks such as shoving and pushing.[28]

Deprivation Model A theory that inmate aggression is the result of the frustration inmates feel at being deprived of freedom, consumer goods, sex, and other staples of life outside the institution.

Relative Deprivation The theory that inmate aggression is caused when freedoms and services that the inmate has come to accept as normal are decreased or eliminated.

Indicate some of the reasons for violent behavior in prisons.

LEARNING
3
OBJECTIVE

Among the prisoners, violence is used to establish power and dominance. On occasion, this violence leads to death. About fifty-five inmates in state prisons and twenty inmates in local jails are murdered by fellow inmates each year.[29] (Note, though, that this homicide rate is lower than the national average.) With nothing but time on their hands, prisoners have been known to fashion deadly weapons out of everyday items such as toothbrushes and mop handles. To carry out their attack on a correctional officer at South Carolina's Lee Correctional Institution, discussed in the chapter opening, inmates fashioned knives out of sawed-off parts of fiberglass shower stalls.

Violence in Prison Culture

Until the 1970s, prison culture emphasized "noninterference" and did not support inmate-on-inmate violence. Prison "elders" would themselves punish any of their peers who showed a proclivity toward assaulting fellow inmates. Today, in contrast, violence is used to establish the prisoner hierarchy by separating the powerful from the weak. Humboldt State University's Lee H. Bowker has identified several other reasons for violent behavior:

- It provides a deterrent against being victimized, as a reputation for violence may eliminate an inmate as a target of assault.
- It enhances self-image in an environment that does not respect other attributes, such as intelligence.
- In the case of rape, it gives sexual relief.
- It serves as a means of acquiring material goods through extortion or outright robbery.[30]

The **deprivation model** can be used to explain the high level of prison violence. According to this model, the stressful and oppressive conditions of prison life lead to aggressive behavior on the part of inmates. Prison researcher Stephen C. Light found that when conditions such as overcrowding worsen, inmate misconduct often increases.[31] In these circumstances, the violent behavior may not have any express purpose—it may just be a means of relieving tension.

■ A correctional official displays a set of homemade knives, also known as *shivs,* made by inmates at Attica Correctional Facility in Attica, New York. What are some of the reasons that violence flourishes behind bars?
AP Photo/David Duprey

Riots

The deprivation model is helpful, though less convincing, in searching for the roots of collective violence. As far back as the 1930s, sociologist Frank Tannenbaum noted that harsh prison conditions can cause tension to build among inmates until it eventually explodes in the form of mass violence.[32] Living conditions among prisons are fairly constant, however, so how can the seemingly spontaneous outbreak of prison riots be explained?

Researchers have addressed the seeming randomness of prison violence by turning to the concept of **relative deprivation.** These theories focus on the gap between what is expected in a certain situation and what is achieved. Criminologist Peter C. Kratcoski has argued that because prisoners enjoy such meager privileges to begin with, any further deprivation can spark disorder.[33] A number of prison experts have noted that collective violence occurs in response to heightened measures of security at corrections facilities.[34] Thus, the violence is primarily a reaction to additional reductions in freedom for inmates, who enjoy very little freedom to begin with.

Riots, which have been defined as situations in which a number of prisoners are beyond institutional control for a significant amount of time, are relatively rare. These incidents are marked by extreme levels of inmate-on-inmate violence and can often be attributed, at least in part, to poor living conditions and inadequate prison administration. For example, a recent riot at the Adams County Correctional Center in Natchez, Mississippi, that left one correctional officer dead and twenty others injured was sparked by inmate protests over poor food and lack of medical care. Afterwards, a prisoner said, "The guard that died yesterday was a sad tragedy, but the situation is simple: if you treat a human as an animal for over two years, the response will be as an animal."[35]

Issues of Race and Ethnicity

On the morning of March 3, 2013, a huge brawl broke out at the Arizona State Prison Complex in Tucson, with three hundred white and Hispanic inmates battling one hundred African American inmates. Race plays a major role in prison life, and prison violence is often an outlet for racial tension. As prison populations have changed over the past three decades, with African Americans and Hispanics becoming the majority in many penal institutions, issues of race and ethnicity have become increasingly important to prison administrators and researchers.

SEPARATE WORLDS As early as the 1950s, researchers were noticing different group structures in inmate life. At that time, for example, prisoners at California's Soledad Prison informally segregated themselves according to geography as well as race: Tejanos (Mexicans raised in Texas), Chicanos, blacks from California, blacks from the South and Southwest, and the majority whites all formed separate social worlds.[36]

Leo Carroll, professor of sociology at the University of Rhode Island, has written extensively about how today's prisoners are divided into hostile groups, with race determining nearly every aspect of an inmate's life, including friends, job assignments, and cell location.[37] Carroll's research has also shown how minority groups in prison have seized on race to help form their prison identities.[38]

PRISON SEGREGATION More than four decades ago, the United States Supreme Court put an end to the widespread practice of **prison segregation,** under which correctional officials would place inmates in cells or blocks with those of a similar race or ethnicity.[39] According to the Supreme Court, prison segregation was unconstitutional because government officials were discriminating against individuals based on their skin color. Years after this ruling, however, the California Department of Corrections began implementing an unwritten policy of putting all new and transferred male inmates in cells with inmates of the same race or ethnicity for the first sixty days of incarceration. The goal of this policy was to determine if an inmate was a member of a race-based gang before allowing him to live in integrated quarters.

In 2005, the Supreme Court struck down California's version of prison segregation.[40] The Court did, however, leave prison officials with an "out." They can still segregate prisoners in an "emergency situation."[41] Thus, a year after the decision, when more than two thousand African American and Hispanic inmates at the Pitchless Detention Center in Castaic, California, battled each other for several hours, temporary segregation of the

Prison Segregation The practice of separating inmates based on a certain characteristic, such as age, gender, type of crime committed, or race.

Prison Gang A group of inmates who band together within the corrections system to engage in social and criminal activities.

Security Threat Group (STG) A group of three or more inmates who engage in activity that poses a threat to the safety of other inmates or the prison staff.

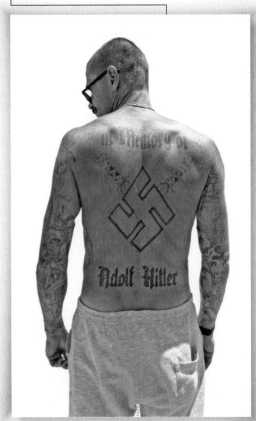

A member of the Aryan Brotherhood in California's Calipatria State Prison. This particular prison gang espouses white supremacy, but for the most part its leadership focuses on illegal activities such as extortion and drug trafficking. Why might an inmate join a prison gang?
Mark Allen Johnson/ZUMA

two groups was deemed justified under the circumstances. Even so, segregation proved to be only a short-term remedy. A week later Hispanic inmates threw bunk beds and other items at their African American counterparts in a dayroom in the nearby Los Angeles Men's Central Jail, sparking a disturbance that resulted in the death of a black inmate. As one observer pointed out, racial segregation "will never solve the underlying problems in L.A. County's jails."[42]

Prison Gangs and Security Threat Groups (STGs)

In many instances, racial and ethnic identification is the primary focus of the **prison gang**—a clique of inmates who join together in an organizational structure. Gang affiliation is often the cause of inmate-on-inmate violence. For decades, the California prison system has been plagued by feuds involving various gangs such as the Mexican Mafia, composed of U.S.-born inmates of Mexican descent, and their enemies, a spin-off organization called La Nuestra Familia.

In part, the prison gang is a natural result of life in the modern prison. As one expert says of these gangs:

> Their members have done in prison what many people do elsewhere when they feel personally powerless, threatened, and vulnerable. They align themselves with others, organize to fight back, and enhance their own status and control through their connection to a more powerful group.[43]

In addition to their important role in the social structure of correctional facilities, prison gangs participate in a wide range of illegal economic activities within these institutions, including prostitution, drug selling, gambling, and loan sharking. A study released in 2011 by Alan J. Drury and Matt DeLisi of Iowa State University found that gang members were more likely to be involved in prison misconduct than those inmates who had been convicted of murder.[44]

THE PREVALENCE OF PRISON GANGS Recent research places the rate of gang membership at 11.7 percent in federal prisons, 13.4 percent in state prisons, and 15.6 percent in jails.[45] When the National Gang Crime Research Center surveyed prison administrators, however, almost 95 percent said that gang recruitment took place at their institutions, so the overall prevalence of gangs is probably much higher.[46] Los Angeles correctional officials believe that eight out of every ten inmates in their city jails are gang affiliated.

In many instances, prison gangs are extensions of street gangs. Indeed, investigators believe leaders of the Mexican Mafia put out a contract for (green lighted) the violence in the Los Angeles jails discussed earlier in retaliation for an attack that took place on the city streets. Though the stereotypical gang is composed of African Americans or Hispanics, the majority of large prisons also have white, or "Aryan," gangs. One of the largest federal capital prosecutions in U.S. history, involving thirty-two counts of murder, focused on a major prison gang known as the Aryan Brotherhood. (See Figure 14.3 on the facing page.)

COMBATING PRISON GANGS In their efforts to combat the influence of prison gangs, over the past decade correctional officials have increasingly turned to the **security threat group (STG)** model. Generally speaking, an STG is an identifiable group of three or more individuals who pose a threat to the safety of other inmates or members of the corrections community.

FIGURE 14.3 The Top Prison Gangs in the United States

Certain prison gangs, such as the Crips and the Bloods, are offshoots of street gangs and gained influence behind bars because so many of their members have been incarcerated. Others, such as the Aryan Brotherhood and the Mexican Mafia, formed in prison and expanded to the streets. Listed here are seven of the most dangerous gangs operating in the American prison system today.

Aryan Brotherhood

White

Origins: Prison gang, formed in San Quentin State Prison in 1967, as white protection against blacks.

Allies: Mexican Mafia

Rivals: Black Guerrilla Family

Signs/Symbols: Swastika, SS Lightning bolts, numbers "666" (Satan, evil) and "88" (to signify the eighth letter of the alphabet, or HH), HH for "Heil Hitler," letters "AB," shamrock (a symbol of their original Irish membership), Nordic dagger on shield with lightning bolts.

Black Guerrilla Family

African American

Origins: Prison gang, founded by incarcerated Black Panthers in San Quentin State Prison in the mid-1960s.

Allies: La Nuestra Familia

Rivals: Aryan Brotherhood

Signs/Symbols: Crossed sabers, machetes, rifles, shotguns with the letters "B G F." A black dragon squeezing the life out of a prison guard by a prison tower.

Bloods

African American

Origins: Street gang, formed in Los Angeles in the 1960s, as a defense against the Crips.

Allies: People Nation (Chicago gang), La Nuestra Familia

Rivals: Crips, Aryan Brotherhood

Signs/Symbols: The color red, red bandannas or rags, the word "Piru" (the original Blood gang), crossed-out "c" in words as disrespect for Crips, other anti-Crip graffiti, hand signal spells "blood."

Crips

African American

Origins: Street gang, formed in the Central Avenue area of Los Angeles in the late 1960s.

Allies: Black Guerrilla Family, La Nuestra Familia

Rivals: Bloods, Aryan Brotherhood, Vice Lords

Signs/Symbols: The color blue, blue bandannas and rags, use the letter "c" in place of "b" in writing as disrespect for Bloods, calling each other "Cuzz," calling themselves "Blood Killas" (BK), wearing British Knight (BK) tennis shoes.

Mexican Mafia (EMC)

Mexican American/Hispanic

Origins: Prison gang, formed in Los Angeles in the Deuel Vocational Institution in the late 1950s. Foot soldiers and related Southern California street gangs are called Sureños.

Allies: Aryan Brotherhood

Rivals: Black Guerrilla Family, La Nuestra Familia

Signs/Symbols: The national symbol of Mexico, an eagle and a snake, on a flaming circle, lying on crossed knives. The color blue, the number 13.

Mara Salvatrucha 13 (MS-13)

Hispanic

Origins: Largest street gang in North America, originated in El Salvador and formed in Los Angeles in the 1980s.

Allies: Mexican Mafia

Rivals: MS-18 (LA gang)

Yuri Cortez/AFP/Getty Images

Signs/Symbols: Most Mara Salvatrucha members are covered in tattoos, even on their faces. Common markings include "MS," "13," "Salvadorian Pride," "Devil Horns."

La Nuestra Familia

Mexican American/Hispanic

Origins: Prison gang, formed in Soledad Prison in the late 1960s, as a reaction to the Mexican Mafia. Based in Northern California, foot soldiers outside of prison are called Norteños.

Allies: Black Guerrilla Family, Bloods, Crips

Rivals: Mexican Mafia, Mara Salvatrucha

Signs/Symbols: Large tattoos, often on the entire back. The initials NF, LNF, ENE, and F. The number 14 for "N," the fourteenth letter in the alphabet, stands for Norte or Norteño. The color red, Nebraska cornhuskers' caps with the letter N. A sombrero with a dagger is a common NF symbol.

Sources: "Gangs or Us," at **www.gangsorus.com/index.html**; and "Prison Gang Profiles," at **www.insideprison.com/prison_gang_profiles.asp**.

About two-thirds of all prisons have a correctional officer who acts as an STG coordinator.[47] This official is responsible for determining groups of individuals (not necessarily members of a prison gang) that qualify as STGs and taking appropriate measures.

In many instances, these measures are punitive. Prison officials, for example, have reduced overall levels of violence significantly by putting gang members in solitary confinement, away from the general prison population. Other punitive measures include restrictions on privileges such as family visits and prison program participation, as well as delays of parole eligibility.[48] Treatment philosophies also have a place in these strategies. New York prison administrators have increased group therapy and anger-management classes for STGs, a decision they credit for low murder rates in their state prisons.[49]

Prison Rape

In contrast to riots, the problem of sexual assault in prisons receives very little attention from media sources. This can be partly attributed to the ambiguity of the subject. The occurrence of rape in prisons and jails is undisputed, but determining exactly how widespread the problem is has proved complicated. Prison officials, aware that any sexual contact is prohibited in most penal institutions, are often unwilling to provide realistic figures for fear of negative publicity. Even when they are willing, they may be unable to do so. Most inmates are ashamed of being rape victims and refuse to report sexual assaults. Consequently, it has been difficult to come up with consistent statistics for sexual assault in prison. To remedy this situation, in 2003 Congress passed the Prison Rape Elimination Act, which mandates that prison officials collect data on the extent of the problem in their facilities.[50] According to a recent survey conducted because of this legislation, about one in ten former state prisoners reports having been sexually victimized by other inmates or prison staff while incarcerated.[51]

Prison rape, like all rape, is considered primarily an act of violence rather than sex. Inmates subject to rape ("punks") are near the bottom of the prison power structure and, in some instances, may accept rape by one particularly powerful inmate in return for protection from others.[52] Abused inmates often suffer from rape trauma syndrome and a host of other psychological ailments, including suicidal tendencies. Many prisons do not offer sufficient medical treatment for rape victims, nor does the prison staff take the necessary measures to protect obvious targets of rape—young, slightly built, nonviolent offenders. Furthermore, correctional officials are rarely held responsible for inmate-on-inmate violence.

SELF ASSESSMENT

Fill in the blanks and check your answers on page 485.

Some researchers rely on the _____ model, which focuses on the stressful and oppressive conditions of incarceration, to explain general prison violence. The concept of _____ _____, based on the gap between an inmate's expectations and reality, is used to explain the conditions that lead to prison riots. The strategy of prison _____, in which officials assign inmates of different races to separate living areas, has been used at times to control violence started by prison _____, or criminal organizations that operate behind bars.

CORRECTIONAL OFFICERS AND DISCIPLINE

Ideally, the presence of correctional officers—the standard term used to describe prison guards—has the effect of lessening violence in American correctional institutions. Practically speaking, this is indeed the case. Without correctional officers, the prison would be a place of anarchy. But in the highly regulated, oppressive environment of the prison, correctional officers must use the threat of violence, if not actual violence, to instill discipline and keep order. Thus, the relationship between prison staff and inmates is marked by mutual distrust. Consider the two following statements, the first made by a correctional officer and the second by a prisoner:

[My job is to] protect, feed, and try to educate scum who raped and brutalized women and children . . . who, if I turn my back, will go into their cell, wrap a blanket around their cellmate's legs, and threaten to beat or rape him if he doesn't give sex, carry contraband, or fork over radios, money, or other goods willingly. And they'll stick a shank in me tomorrow if they think they can get away with it.[53]

The pigs in the state and federal prisons . . . treat me so violently, I cannot possibly imagine a time I could ever have anything but the deepest, aching, searing hatred for them. I can't begin to tell you what they do to me. If I were weaker by a hair, they would destroy me.[54]

It may be difficult for an outsider to understand the emotions that fuel such sentiments. French philosopher Michel Foucault points out that discipline, both in prison and in the general community, is a means of social organization as well as punishment.[55] Discipline is imposed when a person behaves in a manner that is contrary to the values of the dominant social group. Correctional officers and inmates have different concepts of the ideal structure of prison society, and, as the two quotations just cited demonstrate, this conflict generates intense feelings of fear and hatred, which often lead to violence.

In high-security prisons, correctional officers such as these two at the supermax prison in Tamms, Illinois, monitor even the most mundane of inmate activities, including working, exercising, eating, and showering. How might this constant surveillance contribute to tension between correctional officers and prisoners?
John Smierciak/MCT/Landov

Prison Employment

At the time of the violence at the Lee Correctional Institution described at the beginning of this chapter, the facility had fifty-four job openings for correctional officers. Given the low starting salary for the post—about $25,000—and dangerous working conditions, it is not surprising that the prison was having a difficult time with recruiting. In general, however, there are numerous benefits to a career as a correctional officer. Because the position is a civil service (government) job, it offers steady benefits and employment security. In some states, such as California and New York, salaries can reach $70,000. Furthermore, because of a professionalism movement in hiring, the standards of correctional officers have risen dramatically in the past few decades.[56]

BECOMING A CORRECTIONAL OFFICER Most prospective correctional officers are required to pass the civil service exam in their state of employment. Furthermore, as with police cadets (see Chapter 5), correctional officers usually go through a military-style training program prior to deployment in a prison. This program incorporates classwork and physical training, including instruction in areas such as self-defense, inmate control, and protection against communicable disease. Like police cadets, correctional officer trainees also go through a period of supervision with an experienced co-worker, in which they learn not only the job's specific techniques and procedures, but also about the prison environment and subculture.[57]

RANK AND DUTIES The custodial staff at most prisons is organized according to four general ranks—captain, lieutenant, sergeant, and officer. In keeping with the militaristic model, captains are primarily administrators who deal directly with the warden on custodial issues. Lieutenants are the disciplinarians of the prison, responsible for policing and transporting the inmates. Sergeants oversee platoons of officers in specific parts of the prison, such as various cell blocks or work spaces.

Lucien X. Lombardo, professor of sociology and criminal justice at Old Dominion University, has identified six general job categories among correctional officers:[58]

LEARNING

List and briefly explain the six general job categories among correctional officers.

4

OBJECTIVE

1. *Block officers.* These employees supervise cell blocks containing as many as four hundred inmates, as well as the correctional officers on block guard duty. In general, the block officer is responsible for the well-being of the inmates. He or she tries to ensure that the inmates do not harm themselves or other prisoners and also acts as something of a camp counselor, dispensing advice and seeing that inmates understand and follow the rules of the facility.

2. *Work detail supervisors.* In many penal institutions, the inmates work in the cafeteria, the prison store, the laundry, and other areas. Work detail supervisors oversee small groups of inmates as they perform their tasks.

3. *Industrial shop and school officers.* These officers perform maintenance and security functions in workshop and educational programs. Their primary responsibility is to make sure that inmates are on time for these programs and do not cause any disturbances during the sessions.

4. *Yard officers.* Officers who work the prison yard usually have the least seniority, befitting the assignment's reputation as dangerous and stressful. These officers must be constantly on alert for breaches in prison discipline or regulations in the relatively unstructured environment of the prison yard.

5. *Tower guards.* These officers spend their entire shifts, which usually last eight hours, in isolated, silent posts high above the grounds of the facility. Although their only means of communication are walkie-talkies or cellular devices, the safety benefits of the position can outweigh the loneliness that comes with the job.

6. *Administrative building assignments.* Officers who hold these positions provide security at prison gates, oversee visitation procedures, act as liaisons for civilians, and handle administrative tasks such as processing the paperwork when an inmate is transferred from another institution.

Discipline

As Erving Goffman noted in his essay on the "total institution," in the general society adults are rarely placed in a position where they are "punished" as a child would be.[59] Therefore, the strict disciplinary measures imposed on prisoners come as something of a shock and can provoke strong defensive reactions. Correctional officers who must deal with these responses often find that disciplining inmates is the most difficult and stressful aspect of their job.

SANCTIONING PRISONERS As mentioned earlier, one of the first things that an inmate receives on entering a correctional facility is a manual that details the rules of the prison or jail, along with the punishment that will result from rule violations. These handbooks can be quite lengthy—running one hundred pages in some instances—and specific. Not only will a prison manual prohibit obvious misconduct such as violent or sexual activity, gambling, and possession of drugs or currency, but it also addresses matters of daily life such as personal hygiene, dress codes, and conduct during meals.

Correctional officers enforce the prison rules in much the same way that a highway patrol officer enforces traffic regulations. For a minor violation, the inmate may be "let off easy" with a verbal warning. More serious infractions will result in a "ticket," or a report forwarded to the institution's disciplinary committee.[60] The disciplinary committee generally includes several correctional officers and, in some instances, outside citizens or even inmates. Although, as we shall see, the United States Supreme Court has ruled that an inmate must be given a "fair hearing" before being disciplined,[61]

Inmates at the Deuel Vocational Institution in Tracy, California, walk a lap in the facility's recreation yard. What challenges does this environment pose for correctional officers who must impose discipline in such a setting?
Noah Berger/Bloomberg via Getty Images

in reality he or she has very little ability to challenge the committee's decision. Depending on the seriousness of the violation, sanctions can range from a loss of privileges such as visits from family members to the unpleasantness of solitary confinement, discussed in the previous chapter.

USE OF FORCE Most correctional officers prefer to rely on the "you scratch my back and I'll scratch yours" model for controlling inmates. In other words, as long as the prisoner makes a reasonable effort to conform to institutional rules, the correctional officer will refrain from taking disciplinary steps. Of course, the staff-inmate relationship is not always marked by cooperation, and correctional officers often find themselves in situations where they must use force.

Legitimate Security Interests Generally, courts have been unwilling to put too many restrictions on the use of force by correctional officers. As we saw with police officers in Chapter 6, correctional officers are given great leeway to use their experience to determine when force is warranted. In *Whitley v. Albers* (1986),[62] the Supreme Court held that the use of force by prison officials violates an inmate's Eighth Amendment protections only if the force amounts to "the unnecessary and wanton infliction of pain." Excessive force can be considered "necessary" if the legitimate security interests of the penal institution are at stake. Consequently, an appeals court ruled that when officers at a Maryland prison formed an "extraction team" to remove the leader of a riot from his cell, beating him in the process, the use of force was justified given the situation.[63]

In general, courts have found that the "legitimate security interests" of a prison or jail justify the use of force when the correctional officer is[64]

1. Acting in self-defense.
2. Acting to defend the safety of a third person, such as a member of the prison staff or another inmate.
3. Upholding the rules of the institution.
4. Preventing a crime such as assault, destruction of property, or theft.
5. Preventing an escape effort.

In addition, most prisons and jails have written policies that spell out the situations in which their employees may use force against inmates.

The "Malicious and Sadistic" Standard The judicial system has not, however, given correctional officers total freedom of discretion to apply force. In *Hudson v. McMillan* (1992),[65] the Supreme Court ruled that minor injuries suffered by a convict at the hands of a correctional officer following an argument did violate the inmate's rights, because there was no security concern at the time of the incident. In other words, the issue is not *how much* force was used, but whether the officer used the force as part of a good faith effort to restore discipline or acted "maliciously and sadistically" to cause harm. This "malicious and sadistic" standard has been difficult for aggrieved prisoners to meet: in the ten years following the *Hudson* decision, only about 20 percent of excessive force lawsuits against correctional officials were successful.[66]

About a quarter of the security staff at Sing Sing Correctional Facility in Ossining, New York—shown here—are women. What are some of the challenges that face female correctional officers who work in a men's maximum-security prison?
Susan Farley/*New York Times*/Redux Pictures

Female Correctional Officers

Security concerns were the main reason that, for many years, prison administrators refused to hire women as correctional officers in men's prisons. The consensus was that women were not physically strong enough to subdue violent male inmates and that their mere presence in the predominantly masculine prison world would cause disciplinary breakdowns.[67] As a result, in the 1970s a number of women brought lawsuits against state corrections systems, claiming that they were being discriminated against on the basis of their gender. For the most part, these legal actions were successful in opening the doors to men's prisons for female correctional officers (and vice versa).[68] Today, more than 150,000 women work in correctional facilities, many of them in constant close contact with male inmates.[69]

As it turns out, female correctional officers have proved just as effective as their male counterparts in maintaining discipline in men's prisons.[70] Furthermore, evidence shows that women prison staff can have a calming influence on male inmates, thus lowering levels of prison violence.[71] The primary problem caused by women working in male prisons, it seems, involves sexual misconduct. According to the federal government, nearly 60 percent of prison staff members who engage in sexual misconduct are female, suggesting a disturbing amount of consensual sex with inmates.[72] As we will see in the next section, similar issues exist between male correctional officers and female inmates, though in those cases the sexual contact is much more likely to be coerced.

Protecting Prisoners' Rights

Describe the hands-off doctrine of prisoner law and indicate two standards used to determine if prisoners' rights have been violated.

LEARNING
5
OBJECTIVE

The general attitude of the law toward inmates is summed up by the Thirteenth Amendment to the U.S. Constitution:

> Neither slavery nor involuntary servitude, except as a punishment for crime whereof the party shall have been duly convicted, shall exist within the United States.

"Hands-Off" Doctrine The unwritten judicial policy that favors noninterference by the courts in the administration of prisons and jails.

In other words, inmates do not have the same guaranteed rights as other Americans. For most of the nation's history, courts have followed the spirit of this amendment by applying the **"hands-off"** doctrine of prisoner law. This (unwritten) doctrine assumes that the care of inmates should be left to prison officials and that it is not the place of judges to intervene in penal administrative matters.

At the same time, the United States Supreme Court has stated that "[t]here is no iron curtain between the Constitution and the prisons of this country."[73] Consequently, like so many other areas of the criminal justice system, the treatment of prisoners is based on a balancing act—here, between the rights of prisoners and the security needs of the correctional institutions. Of course, as just noted, inmates do not have the same civil rights as do other members of society. In 1984, for example, the Supreme Court ruled that arbitrary searches of prison cells are allowed under the Fourth Amendment because inmates have no reasonable expectation of privacy[74] (see Chapter 7 for a review of this expectation).

THE "DELIBERATE INDIFFERENCE" STANDARD As for those constitutional rights that inmates do retain, in 1976 the Supreme Court established the **"deliberate indifference"** standard. In the case in question, *Estelle v. Gamble,*[75] an inmate had claimed to be the victim of medical malpractice. In his majority opinion, Justice Thurgood Marshall wrote that prison officials violated a convict's Eighth Amendment rights if they "deliberately" failed to provide him or her with necessary medical care. At the time, the decision was hailed as a victory for prisoners' rights, and it continues to ensure that a certain level of health care is provided. Defining "deliberate" has proved difficult, however. Does it mean that prison officials "should have known" that an inmate was placed in harm's way, or does it mean that officials purposefully placed the inmate in that position?

The Supreme Court seems to have taken the latter position. In *Wilson v. Seiter* (1991),[76] for example, inmate Pearly L. Wilson filed a lawsuit alleging that certain conditions of his confinement—including overcrowding; excessive noise; inadequate heating, cooling, and ventilation; and unsanitary bathroom and dining facilities—were cruel and unusual. The Court ruled against Wilson, stating that he had failed to prove that these conditions, even if they existed, were the result of "deliberate indifference" on the part of prison officials.

"IDENTIFIABLE HUMAN NEEDS" In its *Wilson* decision, the Supreme Court created the **"identifiable human needs"** standard for determining Eighth Amendment violations. The Court asserted that a prisoner must show that the institution has denied her or him a basic need such as food, warmth, or exercise.[77] The Court mentioned only these three needs, however, forcing the lower courts to determine for themselves what other needs, if any, fall into this category.

For example, a number of inmate lawsuits have been filed in response to the use of *nutraloaf*—an unpleasant concoction of nondairy cheese, powdered milk, tomato paste, and dehydrated potato flakes—as prison food (see photo alongside). These lawsuits make the argument that nutraloaf is so distasteful as to be cruel and unusual punishment. One plaintiff in Milwaukee, Wisconsin, claimed that he became so violently ill after eating nutraloaf that his body weight fell 8 percent due to excessive vomiting. In general, these lawsuits have failed, as courts have been reluctant to create a constitutional right to "decent prison food."[78]

Because of the Supreme Court's *Estelle* decision described above, prisoners do have a well-established right to "adequate" medical care. "Adequate" has been interpreted to mean a level of care comparable to what the inmate would receive if he or she were not behind bars.[79] This concept has not always proved popular with the general public. In 2012, a federal judge in Boston

"Deliberate Indifference" The standard for establishing a violation of an inmate's Eighth Amendment rights, requiring that prison officials were aware of harmful conditions in a correctional institution *and* failed to take steps to remedy those conditions.

"Identifiable Human Needs" The basic human necessities that correctional facilities are required by the Constitution to provide to inmates.

■ Many prisons punish misbehaving inmates by feeding them nutraloaf. Do you have any concerns about this form of punishment? Explain your answer.
AP Photo/Andy Duback

commanded Massachusetts to cover the costs of gender reassignment surgery for a male inmate who had murdered his wife twelve years earlier. After numerous complaints from taxpayers, the judge rescinded his order. Furthermore, as noted earlier in the chapter, several years ago the Supreme Court asserted, controversially, that the overcrowding of California's state prisons was so severe that it denied inmates satisfactory levels of health care.[80]

THE FIRST AMENDMENT IN PRISON The First Amendment reads, in part, that the federal government "shall make no law respecting an establishment of religion, or prohibiting the free exercise thereof; or abridging the freedom of speech." In the 1970s, the prisoners' rights movement forced open the "iron curtain" to allow the First Amendment behind bars. In 1974, for example, the Supreme Court held that prison officials can censor inmate mail only if doing so is necessary to maintain prison security.[81] The decade also saw court decisions protecting inmates' access to group worship, instruction by clergy, special dietary requirements, religious publications, and other aspects of both mainstream and nonmainstream religions.[82]

Judges will limit some of these protections when an obvious security interest is at stake. In 2010, for example, a Pennsylvania prison was allowed to continue banning religious headscarves because of legitimate concerns that the scarves could be used to conceal drugs or strangle someone.[83] In general, however, the judicial system's commitment to freedom of speech and religion behind bars remains strong. (This commitment may have a particularly dangerous side effect, as you can see in the feature *Countering Domestic Terrorism—Prislam* on the facing page.)

SELF ASSESSMENT

Fill in the blanks and check your answers on page 485.

Correctional officers known as _____ _____ are responsible for the daily well-being of the inmates in their cells. Perhaps the most stressful and important aspect of a correctional officer's job is enforcing _____ among the inmates. To do so, the officers may use force when a _____ security interest is being served. Courts will not, however, accept any force that is "_____ and sadistic." To prove that prison officials violated the _____ Amendment's prohibitions against cruel and unusual punishment, the inmate must first show that the officials acted with "_____ indifference" in taking or not taking an action.

INSIDE A WOMEN'S PRISON

When the first women's prison in the United States opened in 1839 on the grounds of New York's Sing Sing institution, the focus was on rehabilitation. Prisoners were prepared for a return to society with classes on reading, knitting, and sewing. Early women's reformatories had few locks or bars, and several included nurseries for the inmates' young children. Today, the situation is dramatically different. "Women's institutions are literally men's institutions, only we pull out the urinals," remarks Meda Chesney-Lind, a criminologist at the University of Hawaii.[84] Given the different circumstances surrounding male and female incarceration, this uniformity can have serious consequences for the women imprisoned in this country.

Characteristics of Female Inmates

Male inmates outnumber female inmates by approximately nine to one, and there are only about a hundred women's correctional facilities in the United States. Consequently, most research concerning the American corrections system focuses on male inmates

PRISLAM

Islam is the fastest-growing religion in the American prison system. According to one U.S. Justice Department study, about 30,000 to 40,000 federal prisoners convert to Islam each year. For the vast majority of inmates who choose "Prislam," as correctional officials have come to call the practice, the conversion is not political. Rather, the religion acts as a stabilizing force in their lives, helping them break the destructive patterns that caused them to be incarcerated in the first place.

From time to time, however, Prislam finds itself tainted by the specter of radical Islamic terrorism. In May 2009, for example, four Muslim men were accused of planning to bomb synagogues and shoot down military aircraft with Stinger missiles in the New York City area. Two of the plotters—Laguerre Payen and Onta Williams—are believed to have converted while in prison. Over a decade ago, the Islamic terrorist group Jam'yyat Al-Islam Al Saheeh (JIS), which was formed in Sacramento's Folsom Prison, launched a conspiracy to "kill infidels" in Southern California. Both Richard Reid, the "shoe bomber" who attempted to blow up an international flight in 2001, and José Padilla, convicted in 2007 of aiding terrorists, were prison converts to Islam.

"PEOPLE SHOULD BE WORRIED" Many American Muslims discount the connection between Islamic inmates and terrorist activity. If a radical prisoner with terrorist tendencies is "an unreformed sociopath who happens to be a Muslim, [then] Islam is not to be blamed for his condition," says Iman Talib Abdur-Rashid, a chaplain in the New York City prison system.

Still, the Federal Bureau of Prisons is taking steps to prevent the radicalization of federal inmates, including monitoring religious meetings and screening written religious materials. The worry is that the degradations and frustrations of prison life will drive unstable prisoners toward terrorism. "People should be worried about us. People in prison feel there is no way out," says Jehmahl, a murderer who converted to Islam while behind bars and subsequently joined JIS. "This is not so much about Islam. I'm radical. Radical means that you're holding no foundation. That's what the suicide bombers do. There's nothing but God left so let's go find a bomb."

FOR CRITICAL ANALYSIS American John Walker Lindh is serving a twenty-year prison sentence at a maximum-security prison in Indiana for giving aid to terrorist forces overseas. In 2013, Lindh filed a complaint claiming that prison authorities were improperly prohibiting him and other Muslim inmates from praying together in a group five times day, as required by their faith. Should corrections officials be able to ban this type of group prayer? Why or why not?

and men's prisons. Enough data exist, however, to provide a useful portrait of women behind bars. Female inmates are typically low income and undereducated, and have a history of unemployment. Female offenders are much less likely than male offenders to have committed a violent offense. Most are incarcerated for a nonviolent drug or property crime.[85] As Figure 14.4 on the next page shows, the demographics of female prisoners are similar to those of their male counterparts. That is, the majority of female inmates are under the age of forty, and the population is disproportionately African American.

A HISTORY OF ABUSE The single factor that most distinguishes female prisoners from their male counterparts is a history of physical or sexual abuse. A self-reported study conducted by the federal government indicates that 55 percent of female jail inmates have been abused at some point in their lives, compared with only 13 percent of male jail inmates.[86] Fifty-seven percent of women in state prisons and 40 percent of women in federal prisons report some form of past abuse—both figures are significantly higher than those for male prisoners.[87] Health experts believe that these levels of abuse are related to the significant amount of drug and/or alcohol addiction that plagues the female prison population, as well as to the mental illness problems that such addictions can cause or exacerbate.[88]

OTHER HEALTH PROBLEMS In fact, about 25 percent of women in state prisons have been diagnosed with mental disorders such as post–traumatic stress disorder (PTSD),

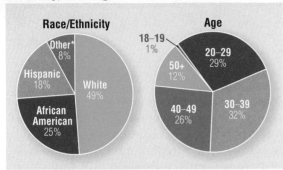
Explain the aspects of imprisonment that prove challenging for incarcerated mothers and their children. **LEARNING OBJECTIVE 6**

SOCIAL MEDIA & CJ

To learn more about corrections in this country, go to Twitter and locate "correctionsone." You'll see tweets gathered by the staff at **CorrectionsOne.com**, an online resource for news relating to American prisons and jails.

Ankomando/Shutterstock.com

depression, and substance abuse. PTSD, in particular, is found in women who have experienced sexual or physical abuse.[89] Furthermore, more women than men enter prisons and jails with health problems due to higher instances of poverty, inadequate health care, and substance abuse.[90] Not only do women prisoners have high rates of breast and cervical cancer, but they are also 50 percent more likely than men to be HIV positive and are at significantly greater risk for lung cancer.[91] The health risks and medical needs are even higher for the 5 percent of the female prison population who enter the correctional facility while pregnant. One study estimates that 20 to 35 percent of women inmates visit the infirmary each day, compared with 7 to 10 percent of male inmates.[92]

The Motherhood Problem

Drug and alcohol use within a women's prison can be a function of the anger and depression many inmates experience due to being separated from their children. An estimated seven out of every ten female prisoners have at least one minor child. About 1.7 million American children have a mother who is under correctional supervision.[93] Given the scarcity of women's correctional facilities, inmates are often housed at great distances from their children. One study found that almost two-thirds of women in federal prison are more than five hundred miles from their homes.[94]

Further research indicates that an inmate who serves her sentence more than fifty miles from her residence is much less likely to receive phone calls or personal visits from family members. For most inmates and their families, the costs of "staying in touch" are too high.[95] This kind of separation can have serious consequences for the children of inmates. When a father goes to prison, his children are likely to live with their mother. When a mother is incarcerated, however, her children are likely to live with other relatives or, in about 11 percent of the cases, be sent to foster care.[96] Only six states—California, Indiana, Nebraska, New York, Ohio, and Washington—provide facilities where inmates and their infant children can live together, and even in these facilities nursery privileges generally end once the child is eighteen months old.

The Culture of Women's Prisons

After spending five years visiting female inmates in the Massachusetts Correctional Institution (MCI) at Framingham, journalist Cristina Rathbone observed that the medium-security facility seemed "more like a high school than a prison."[97] The prisoners were older and tougher than high school girls, but they still divided into cliques, with the "lifers" at the top of the hierarchy and "untouchables" such as child abusers at the bottom. Unlike in men's prisons, where the underground economy revolves around drugs and weapons, at MCI-Framingham the most treasured contraband items are clothing, food, and makeup.[98]

THE PSEUDO-FAMILY Although both men's and women's prisons are organized with the same goals of control and discipline, the cultures within the two institutions are generally very different. As we have seen, male prison society operates primarily on the basis of power. Deprived of the benefits of freedom, male prisoners tend to create a violent environment that bears little relation to life on the outside.[99] In contrast, researchers have found that women prisoners prefer to re-create their outside identities by forming social networks that resemble, as noted earlier, high school cliques or, more commonly, the traditional family structure.[100] In these pseudo-families, inmates often play specific roles, with the more experienced convicts acting as "mothers" to younger, inexperienced "daughters." As one observer noted, the younger women rely on their "moms" for emotional support, companionship, loans, and even discipline.[101]

Such a family unit may have a "married" couple at its head, sometimes with a lesbian assuming the role of the father figure. Indeed, homosexuality in women's prisons often manifests itself through the formation of another traditional family model: the monogamous couple.[102] For the most part, sex between inmates plays a different role in women's prisons than in men's prisons. In the latter, rape is an act of aggression and power rather than sex, and "true" homosexuals are relegated to the lowest rungs of the social hierarchy. By contrast, women inmates who engage in sexual activity are not automatically labeled homosexual, and lesbians are not hampered in their social-climbing efforts.[103]

■ Female inmates at the Women's Eastern Reception, Diagnostic and Correctional Center in Vandalia, Missouri, visit with their daughters and granddaughters. Why is it difficult for many mothers behind bars to see their children?
AP Photo/Whitney Curtis

SEXUAL VIOLENCE AND PRISON STAFF Compared with men's prisons, women's prisons have extremely low levels of race-based, gang-related physical aggression.[104] Furthermore, though rates of sexual victimization can be high, most such episodes involve abusive sexual contacts such as unwanted touching rather than sexual assault or rape.[105] One form of serious prison violence that does plague women prisoners, however, is sexual misconduct by prison staff. Although no large-scale study on sexual abuse of female inmates by male correctional officers exists, a number of state-level studies suggest that it is widespread.[106] A complaint recently filed with the U.S. Department of Justice claimed that sexual misconduct by male correctional staff toward inmates at Alabama's Tutwiler Prison for Women is "commonplace" and consistently goes unpunished.[107]

Given that in many corrections systems, more than half of all staff members in women's prisons are men, such problems seem inevitable.[108] To start with, security procedures such as the pat-down and, in more extreme cases, the strip search become problematic when a female inmate and a male correctional officer are involved. The conditions in most prisons—including lack of privacy, inadequate grievance procedures, and harsh treatment of whistleblowers—only add to the potential for abuse of power in this area. Dr. Kerry Kupers, who has studied the effects of prison sexual assault, believes that it contributes to the PTSD, depression, anxiety, and other mental illnesses suffered by so many women prisoners.[109]

SELF ASSESSMENT

Fill in the blanks and check your answers on page 485.

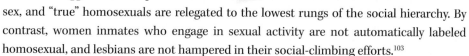

The majority of female inmates have been arrested for nonviolent _____ or property crimes. On admission to a correctional facility, women report much higher levels of physical and sexual _____ than their male counterparts, and female inmates often suffer from depression because they are separated from their _____. While levels of physical violence are relatively low in women's prisons, female inmates do face a greater threat of sexual assault from _____ _____ than male inmates do.

RETURN TO SOCIETY

With only a few weeks left to serve on his prison sentence for drug charges, John Cadogan was worried. As he explained in a group therapy session at the men's state prison in Chino, California, his meth-addicted ex-girlfriend wanted to see him "on the outside." Cadogan feared that she was going to tempt him to restart his own drug use. The other inmates agreed that the situation was fraught with difficulty. "It's like playing Russian roulette with a loaded gun," said one.[110]

Each year, about 700,000 inmates are released from American prisons. Many, such as Cadogan, face numerous challenges in their efforts to avoid relapse and reincarceration. More so than in the past, however, ex-convicts are not facing these challenges alone. Given the benefits to society of reducing recidivism, corrections officials and community leaders are making unprecedented efforts to help newly released prisoners establish crime-free lives.

Types of Prison Release

Contrast parole, expiration release, pardon, and furlough.

LEARNING 7 OBJECTIVE

The vast majority of all inmates leaving prison—about 80 percent—do so through one of the parole mechanisms discussed in Chapter 12. Of the remaining 20 percent, most are given an **expiration release**.[111] Also known as "maxing out," expiration release occurs when an inmate has served the maximum amount of time on the initial sentence, minus reductions for good-time credits, and is not subjected to community supervision. Another, quite rare unconditional release is a **pardon**, a form of executive clemency. The president (on the federal level) and the governor (on the state level) can grant a pardon, or forgive a convict's criminal punishment. Most states have a board of pardons—affiliated with the parole board—that makes recommendations to the governor in cases in which it believes a pardon is warranted. Most pardons involve obvious miscarriages of justice, though sometimes a governor will pardon an individual to remove the stain of conviction from her or his criminal record.

Certain temporary releases also exist. Some inmates, who qualify by exhibiting good behavior and generally proving that they do not represent a risk to society, are allowed to leave the prison on **furlough** for a certain amount of time, usually between a day and a week. At times, a furlough is granted because of a family emergency, such as a funeral. Furloughs can be particularly helpful for an inmate who is nearing release and can use them to ease the readjustment period. Finally, *probation release* occurs following a short period of incarceration at the back end of shock probation, which we discussed in Chapter 12. Generally, however, as you have seen, probationers experience community supervision in place of a prison term.

The Challenges of Reentry

Expiration Release The release of an inmate from prison at the end of his or her sentence without any further correctional supervision.

Pardon An act of executive clemency that overturns a conviction and erases mention of the crime from the person's criminal record.

Furlough Temporary release from a prison for purposes of vocational or educational training, to ease the shock of release, or for personal reasons.

Prisoner Reentry A corrections strategy designed to prepare inmates for a successful return to the community and to reduce their criminal activity after release.

What steps can corrections officials take to lessen the possibility that ex-convicts will reoffend following their release? Efforts to answer that question have focused on programs that help inmates make the transition from prison to the outside. In past years, these programs would have come under the general heading of "rehabilitation," but today corrections officials and criminologists refer to them as part of the strategy of **prisoner reentry**. The concept of reentry has come to mean many things to many people. For our purposes, keep in mind the words of Joan Petersilia of the University of California at Irvine, who defines *reentry* as encompassing "all activities and programming conducted to prepare ex-convicts to return safely to the community and to live as law abiding citizens."[112] In other words, whereas rehab is focused on the individual offender, *reentry* encompasses the released convict's relationship with society.

Barriers to Reentry

Perhaps the largest obstacle to successful prisoner reentry is the simple truth that life behind bars is very different from life on the outside. As one inmate explains, the "rules" of prison survival are hardly compatible with good citizenship:

> An unexpected smile could mean trouble. A man in uniform was not a friend. Being kind was a weakness. Viciousness and recklessness were to be respected and admired.[113]

The prison environment also insulates inmates. They are not required to make the day-to-day decisions that characterize a normal existence beyond prison bars. Depending on the length of incarceration, a released inmate must adjust to an array of economic, technological, and social changes that took place while she or he was behind bars. Common acts such as using an ATM or a smartphone may be completely alien to someone who has just completed a long prison term.

CHALLENGES OF RELEASE Other obstacles hamper reentry efforts. Housing can be difficult to secure, as many private property owners refuse to rent to someone with a criminal record, and federal and state laws restrict public housing options for ex-convicts. A criminal past also limits the ability to find employment, as does the lack of job skills of someone who has spent a significant portion of his or her life in prison. Felix Mata, who works with ex-convicts in Baltimore, Maryland, estimates that the average male prisoner returning to that city has only $50 in his pocket and owes $8,000 in child support. Furthermore, these men generally have no means of transportation, no place to live, and no ability to gain employment. At best, most ex-prisoners can expect to earn no more than $8,500 annually the first few years after being released.[114]

These economic barriers can be complicated by the physical and mental condition of the freed convict. We have already discussed the high incidence of substance abuse among prisoners and the health-care needs of aging inmates. In addition, one study concluded that as many as one in five Americans leaving jail or prison is seriously mentally ill.[115] (See Figure 14.5 below for a list of the hardships commonly faced by former inmates in their first year out of prison.)

FIGURE 14.5 Prisoner Reentry Issues

Researchers from the Urban Institute in Washington, D.C., asked nearly three hundred former prisoners (all male) in the Cleveland, Ohio, area about the most pressing issues they faced in their first year after release. The answers provide a useful snapshot of the many challenges of reentry.

1. *Housing.* Nearly two-thirds of the men were living with family members, and about half considered their housing situation "temporary." Many were concerned about their living environment: half said that drug dealing was a major problem in their neighborhoods, and almost 25 percent were living with drug and alcohol abusers.

2. *Employment.* After one year, only about one-third of the former inmates had a full-time job, and another 11 percent were working part-time.

3. *Family and friends.* One in four of the men identified family support as the most important thing keeping them from returning to criminality. Another 16 percent said that avoiding certain people and situations was the most crucial factor in their continued good behavior.

4. *Programs and services.* About two-thirds of the former inmates had taken part in programs and services such as drug treatment and continuing education.

5. *Health.* More than half of the men reported suffering from a chronic health condition, and 29 percent showed symptoms of depression.

6. *Substance use.* About half of the men admitted to weekly drug use or alcohol intoxication. Men who had strong family ties and those who were required to maintain telephone contact with their parole officer were less likely to engage in frequent substance use.

7. *Parole violation and recidivism.* More than half of the former inmates reported that they had violated the conditions of their parole, usually by drug use or having contact with other parolees. Fifteen percent of the men returned to prison in the year after release. Four out of five of the returns were the result of a new crime.

Source: Christy A. Visher and Shannon M. E. Courtney, *One Year Out: Experience of Prisoners Returning to Cleveland* (Washington, D.C.: Urban Institute, April 2007), 2.

THE THREAT OF RELAPSE All of these problems conspire to make successful reentry difficult to achieve. Perhaps it is not surprising that research conducted by the Pew Center on the States found that 43 percent of ex-prisoners are back in prison or jail within three years of their release dates.[116] These figures highlight the problem of recidivism among those released from incarceration.

Even given the barriers to reentry we have discussed, these rates of recidivism seem improbably high. Regardless of their ability to find a job or housing, many ex-convicts are fated to run afoul of the criminal justice system. Psychologists Edward Zamble and Vernon Quinsey explain the phenomenon as a *relapse process*.[117] Take the hypothetical example of an ex-convict who gets in a minor automobile accident while driving from his home to his job one morning. The person in the other car gets out and starts yelling at the ex-convict, who "relapses" and reacts just as he would have in prison—by punching the other person in the face. The ex-convict is then convicted of assault and battery and given a harsh prison sentence because of his criminal record.

Promoting Desistance

One ex-inmate compared the experience of being released to entering a "dark room, knowing that there are steps in front of you and waiting to fall."[118] The goal of reentry is to act as a flashlight for convicts by promoting **desistance,** a general term used to describe the continued abstinence from offending and the reintroduction of offenders into society. Certainly, the most important factor in the process is the individual convict. She or he has to *want* to desist and take steps to do so. In most cases, however, ex-inmates are going to need help—help getting an education, help finding and keeping a job, and help freeing themselves from harmful addictions to drugs and alcohol. Corrections officials are in a good position to offer this assistance, and their efforts in doing so form the backbone of the reentry movement.

Preparation for reentry starts behind bars. In addition to the rehabilitation-oriented prison programs discussed earlier in the chapter, most correctional facilities offer "life skills" classes to inmates. This counseling covers topics such as finding and keeping a job, locating a residence, understanding family responsibilities, and budgeting. After release, however, former inmates often find it difficult to continue with educational programs and counseling as they struggle to readjust to life outside prison. Consequently, parole supervising agencies operate a number of programs to facilitate offenders' desistance efforts while, at the same time, protecting the community to the greatest extent possible.

Explain the goal of prisoner reentry programs.

LEARNING

8

OBJECTIVE

WORK RELEASE AND HALFWAY HOUSES As is made clear in Figure 14.5 on the previous page, work and lodging are crucial components of desistance. Corrections officials have several options in helping certain parolees—usually low-risk offenders—find employment and a place to live during the supervision period. Nearly a third of correctional facilities offer **work release programs,** in which prisoners nearing the end of their sentences are given permission to work at paid employment in the community.[119]

Inmates on work release must either return to the correctional facility in the evening or live in community residential facilities known as **halfway houses.** These facilities, also available to other parolees and those who have finished their sentences, are often remodeled hotels or private homes. They provide a less institutionalized living environment than a prison or jail for a small number of offenders (usually between ten and twenty-five). Halfway houses can be tailored to the needs of the former inmate. Many

Desistance The process through which criminal activity decreases and reintegration into society increases over a period of time.

Work Release Program Temporary release of convicts from prison for purposes of employment. The offenders may spend their days on the job, but must return to the correctional facility at night and during the weekend.

Halfway House A community-based form of early release that places inmates in residential centers and allows them to reintegrate with society.

Photo Courtesy of Julie Howe

JULIE HOWE

HALFWAY HOUSE PROGRAM MANAGER

Early on in my career, I felt a bit intimidated by the clients simply because of my discomfort, not by their behavior. I started out very stern and learned later that it was better to start strong and to lighten up later rather than the reverse. The clients respect you more and know to take you seriously. My first client as a case manager was a real eye-opener. He was in his fifties, and I was in my early twenties. Earning his trust was quite a challenge. In the end he learned to respect me, and I learned different techniques when working with offenders.

My favorite part of my job is that I know that I have an impact on people's lives. If I can assist someone to become sober, responsible, employed, and self-sufficient, I am also having an impact on the community and those whom my clients' lives touch. I never get tired of hearing clients say thanks and knowing their lives are forever changed when they realize their potential and value. I also love that I have the opportunity to influence the behavior of others and shape their future. What an awesome responsibility!

SOCIAL MEDIA CAREER TIP Don't misrepresent facts or tell lies of omission online. Doing so in front of millions of online viewers virtually ensures you will be caught, and such untruths can fatally damage career possibilities.

communities, for example, offer substance-free transitional housing for those whose past criminal behavior was linked to drug or alcohol abuse.

WHAT WORKS IN REENTRY Substance abuse treatment can have a significant impact on desistance. Federal prisoners who receive such treatment in the community as a follow-up to prison programs are 16 percent less likely to return to prison and 15 percent less likely to resume drug use than those who do not.[120] Employment aid is also essential. Several years ago, the mayor of Newark, New Jersey, created an Office of Reentry to help ex-inmates find jobs. Of those who are successful, only 10 percent are likely to reoffend.[121]

The incentive to reduce recidivism—thereby holding down inmate populations—has spurred a number of states to implement far-reaching desistance programs. The Michigan Prison Reentry Initiative, for example, establishes an individualized "transition plan" for all released inmates. This plan, which includes not only substance abuse treatment and employment aid but transportation, housing, and life skills counseling, is credited with reducing Michigan's recidivism rate among parolees by 18 percent.[122]

The Special Case of Sex Offenders

Despite the beneficial impact of reentry efforts, one group of wrongdoers has consistently been denied access to such programs: those convicted of sex crimes. The eventual return of these offenders to society causes such high levels of community anxiety that the criminal justice system has not yet figured out what to do with them.

FEAR OF SEX OFFENDERS According to one poll, 66 percent of Americans are "very concerned" about child molesters, compared with 52 percent who expressed such concern about violent criminals and 36 percent about terrorists.[123] To a large degree, this attitude reflects the widespread belief that convicted sex offenders cannot be "cured" of their criminality and therefore are destined to continue committing sex offenses after their release from prison.[124]

It is true that the medical health profession has had little success in treating the "urges" that lead to sexually deviant or criminal behavior.[125] This has not, however, translated into rampant recidivism among sex offenders when compared to other types of criminals. According to the U.S. Department of Justice, the rearrest rates of rapists (46 percent) and those convicted of other forms of sexual assault (41 percent) are among the lowest for all offenders.[126] Furthermore, after analyzing eighty-two recidivism studies, Canadian researchers R. Karl Hanson and Kelly Morton-Bourgon found that only 14 percent of sex offenders were apprehended for another sex crime after release from prison or jail. On average, such offenders were significantly more likely to be rearrested for nonsexual criminal activity, if they were rearrested at all.[127]

CONDITIONS OF RELEASE Whatever their recidivism rates, sex offenders are subject to extensive community supervision after being released from prison. Generally, they are supervised by parole officers and live under the same threat of revocation as other parolees. Specifically, many sex offenders—particularly child molesters—have the following special conditions of release:

LEARNING

Indicate typical conditions for release for a paroled child molester.

9

OBJECTIVE

- No contact with children under the age of eighteen.
- Psychiatric treatment.
- Must stay a certain distance from schools or parks where children are present.
- Cannot own toys that may be used to lure children.
- Cannot have a job or participate in any activity that involves children.

Recently, states have taken steps to further restrict access of sex offenders to minors over the Internet. In 2012, a federal judge upheld an Indiana law that bans sex offenders from accessing Facebook and other social networking sites used by children. That same year, in New York, providers of online video games such as Xbox Live and PlayStation agreed to close the accounts of more than 3,500 sex offenders. As you will see in the *CJ in Action* feature at the end of this chapter, more than half of the states and hundreds of municipalities have passed *residency restrictions* for convicted sex offenders. These laws ban sex offenders from living within a certain distance of places where children naturally congregate.

SEX OFFENDER NOTIFICATION LAWS Perhaps the most dramatic step taken by criminal justice authorities to protect the public from sex crimes involves *sex offender registries,* or databases that contain sex offenders' names, addresses, photographs, and other information. The movement to register sex offenders started about two decades ago, after seven-year-old Megan Kanka of Hamilton Township, New Jersey, was raped and murdered by a twice-convicted pedophile (an adult sexually attracted to children) who had moved into her neighborhood after being released from prison on parole. The next year, in response to public outrage, the state passed a series of laws known collectively as the New Jersey Sexual Offender Registration Act, or "Megan's Law."[128] Today, all fifty states and the federal government have their own version of Megan's Law, or a **sex offender notification law,** which requires local law authorities to alert the public when a sex offender has been released into the community.

Sex Offender Notification Law Legislation that requires law enforcement authorities to notify people when convicted sex offenders are released into their neighborhood or community.

Active and Passive Notification No two sex offender notification laws have exactly the same provisions, but all are designed with the goal of allowing the public to learn the identities of convicted sex offenders living in their midst. In general, the laws demand that a paroled sex offender notify local law enforcement authorities on taking up residence in a state. In Georgia, for example, paroled sex offenders are required to present themselves to both the local sheriff and the superintendent of the public school district where they plan to live.[129] This registration process must be renewed every time the parolee changes address.

The authorities, in turn, notify the community of the sex offender's presence through the use of one of two models. Under the "active" model, the authorities directly notify the community or community representatives. Traditionally, this notification has taken the form of bulletins or posters, distributed and posted within a certain distance from the offender's home. Now, however, a number of states use e-mail alerts to fulfill notification obligations. In the "passive" model, information on sex offenders is made open and available for public scrutiny.

Effectiveness of Sex Offender Registries In 2006, Congress passed the Adam Walsh Child Protection and Safety Act, which established a national registry of sex offenders.[130] In addition, all fifty states operate sex offender registries with data on registered sex offenders in their jurisdictions. (For an idea of how this process works, you can visit the Federal Bureau of Investigation's Sex Offender Registry Web site.) The total number of registered sex offenders in the United States is about 740,000. These registries are quite popular with the public and even appear to affect property values. Homes in the proximity of a registered sex offender lose about $5,500 in value.[131]

Do sex offender registries actually protect the public? Perhaps not. According to Amanda Agan of the University of Chicago, rates of sex offenses have not declined in response to sex offender registries. Agan's research also shows that areas with elevated concentrations of registered sex offenders do not experience elevated levels of sex crimes.[132] One reason for this may be the fact, mentioned earlier, that sex offenders do not have particularly high rates of sex crime recidivism. Furthermore, almost nine of ten sex crimes are committed by people who have no history of such offenses and thus are not registered.[133] Finally, sex offender laws are so broad that many of those registered have been convicted of crimes such as indecent exposure or public urination that do not involve a sexual act or sexual contact.[134]

CJ & TECHNOLOGY — CRIME REGISTRIES

Those offenders who have been convicted of motor vehicle theft are rearrested at a rate of nearly 80 percent. Given that this number is nearly twice the recidivism rate for sex offenders, one commentator wonders whether there should be "registry lists that warn the public where they ought to avoid parking or which neighborhoods contain car thieves."

Although no car thief notification laws are on the horizon, local politicians are experimenting with registries for other types of criminals. Suffolk County, New York, has an online registry of animal abusers. Since 2012, convicted murderers released in Illinois have had to register with state authorities, much like sex offenders. Maine and Texas are considering placing registries for drunk drivers on the Internet. "You'd be hard pressed to find a more politically popular movement in recent years," says Wayne Logan, a professor at Florida State University.

State of California Department of Justice/ Megan's Law Homepage

Thinking about Crime Registries

One critic has called all crime registries instruments for "public shaming" with few other tangible benefits. Do you agree? Why or why not?

CIVIL CONFINEMENT To many, any type of freedom, even if encumbered by notification requirements, is too much freedom for a sex offender. "The issue is, what can you do short of putting them all in prison for the rest of their lives?" complained one policymaker.[135] In fact, many jurisdictions have devised a method to keep sex offenders off the streets for, if not their entire lives, then close to it.

A number of states have passed **civil confinement** laws that allow corrections officials to keep sex offenders locked up in noncorrectional facilities such as psychiatric hospitals after the conclusion of their prison terms. Under these laws, which we first encountered in Chapter 12 in connection with the mentally ill, corrections officials can keep sexual criminals confined indefinitely, as long as they are deemed a danger to society. Given the recidivism rates of sex offenders, civil confinement laws essentially give the state the power to detain this class of criminal indefinitely—a power upheld by the United States Supreme Court in 2010.[136]

SELF ASSESSMENT

Fill in the blanks and check your answers on page 485.

Ex-convicts often struggle to succeed after being released from prison because their limited skills make it difficult to find _____. The resulting financial troubles hamper the offender's ability to secure _____, which makes it more likely that he or she will recidivate. One way in which the corrections system tries to reverse this process is by offering _____ programs that include job training and work release opportunities. Corrections officials also promote _____, or the process by which a former inmate stops committing crimes, by allowing certain low-risk offenders to live in _____ houses, where they can receive specialized treatment. Sex offender _____ laws, also known as Megan's laws, mandate that law enforcement officials must alert the public when a sex offender has moved into the community.

Residents of Phelan, California, protest the opening of a proposed group home for sex offenders in their neighborhood. What are some of the reasons that community members fear the nearby presence of freed sex offenders? Are these fears justified? Why or why not?
AP Photo/Francis Specker

CJ IN ACTION

A SECOND LOOK AT RESIDENCY LAWS

In 2006, residents of Southampton, New York, noticed that convicted sex offenders were crowding into cheap hotel rooms. To end this practice, local authorities came up with a "temporary solution" by providing two large trailers to house about forty of these ex-convicts. In 2013, with nowhere else to go, the sex offenders were still in the trailers. "A murderer can live wherever he wants," complains Troy Wallace, who spent six months in prison for sexual abusing a fifteen-year-old. "I have to live in a trailer."[137] Wallace and the other sex offenders were having difficulty finding housing as a result of the city's residency law, an increasingly common and popular method for protecting children that, as we will discuss in this *CJ in Action* feature, may have unexpected consequences.

ZONING RESTRICTIONS FOR SEX OFFENDERS

More than half of the states and hundreds of municipalities have passed residency restrictions for convicted sex offenders. These laws ban sex offenders from living within a certain distance from places where children naturally congregate. In New Jersey, for example, "high-risk" offenders cannot take up residence within 3,000 feet of any school, park or campground, church, theater, bowling alley, library, or convenience store.[138] (For medium- and low-risk offenders, the distances are 2,500 feet and 1,000 feet, respectively.) The overlapping "off-limits zones" created by residency requirements can dramatically limit where a sex offender can find affordable housing, as was the case with Troy Wallace and the other sex offenders living in the Southampton trailers.

THE CASE FOR SEX OFFENDER RESIDENCY RESTRICTIONS

- Forbidding sex offenders from residing near schools and other areas that attract large groups of children decreases their access to these children, thus reducing the risk that they will reoffend. Research conducted by Jeffrey Walker of the University of Arkansas found that child molesters are nearly twice as likely to live near schools as offenders convicted of sexually assaulting adults.[139]

- The residency requirements are reassuring to parents and are generally very popular with the public.

- The right of convicted sex offenders to choose where they live is less important than the protection of law-abiding citizens.

THE CASE AGAINST SEX OFFENDER RESIDENCY RESTRICTIONS

- The laws push sex offenders into less populated areas or homelessness, which makes it much more difficult for law enforcement and corrections agents to keep tabs on them. "Probation and parole supervisors cannot effectively monitor offenders who are living under bridges, in parking lots, in tents at parks or interstate truck stops," says Elizabeth Barnhill of the Iowa Coalition against Sexual Assault.[140]

- The laws are inadequate. Studies have shown that strangers commit only about 10 percent of all sexual offenses against children. The perpetrators of such crimes are much more likely to be family members, friends, or other acquaintances.[141]

- The laws create a false sense of security. If a sex offender wants to get to a child, a residency requirement cannot stop him or her from simply getting in a car or walking to find a victim.

YOUR OPINION—WRITING ASSIGNMENT

Many residence requirements prohibit convicted sex offenders from living within a certain distance of a public park. To force these offenders out of their neighborhoods, many communities are building small "pocket" parks, some of them so tiny as to barely have enough room for a swing set. What is your opinion of this strategy? How do you feel about residency laws in general? Do these regulations constitute extra punishment for convicts who have already, at least in theory, paid their debt for their crimes?

As an alternative, should certain sex offenders be sentenced to life in prison without parole, sparing the criminal justice system the need to create awkward laws like residency requirements and civil confinement? Before responding, you can review our discussions in this chapter concerning:

- Barriers to reentry (pages 477–478).

- Fear of sex offenders (pages 479–480).

- Civil confinement (page 481).

Your answer should include at least three full paragraphs.

CHAPTER SUMMARY

For more information on these concepts, look back to the Learning Objective icons throughout the chapter.

 Explain the concept of prison as a total institution. Though many people spend time in partial institutions—schools, companies where they work, and religious organizations—only in prison is every aspect of an inmate's life controlled, and that is why prisons are called total institutions. Every detail for every prisoner is fully prescribed and managed.

 Describe a risk run by corrections officials who fail to provide adequate medical care to the inmates under their control. In the first decade of the 2000s, medical care for inmates in California's prison system was severely compromised by extreme overcrowding. As a result, the U.S. Supreme Court ordered state corrections officials to release 30,000 inmates so that standards of health care in the prison could be more compatible "with the concept of human dignity."

 Indicate some of the reasons for violent behavior in prisons. (a) To separate the powerful from the weak and establish a prisoner hierarchy; (b) to minimize one's own probability of being a target of assault; (c) to enhance one's self-image; (d) to obtain sexual relief; and (e) to obtain material goods through extortion or robbery.

 List and briefly explain the six general job categories among correctional officers. (a) Block officers, who supervise cell blocks or are on block guard duty; (b) work detail supervisors, who oversee the cafeteria, prison store, and laundry, for example; (c) industrial shop and school officers, who generally oversee workshop and educational programs; (d) yard officers, who patrol the prison yard when prisoners are allowed there; (e) tower guards, who work in isolation; and (f) those who hold administrative building assignments, such as prison gate guards and overseers of visitation procedures.

 Describe the hands-off doctrine of prisoner law and indicate two standards used to determine if prisoners' rights have been violated. The hands-off doctrine assumes that the care of prisoners should be left to prison officials and that it is not the place of judges to intervene. Nonetheless, the Supreme Court has created two standards to be used by the courts in determining whether a prisoner's Eighth Amendment protections against cruel and unusual punishment have been violated. Under the "deliberate indifference" standard, prisoners must show that prison officials were aware of harmful conditions at the facility but failed to remedy them. Under the "identifiable human needs" standard, prisoners must show that they were denied a basic need such as food, warmth, or exercise.

 Explain the aspects of imprisonment that prove challenging for incarcerated mothers and their children. Besides the anxiety that results from any separation of parent and child, incarcerated mothers often find it difficult to stay in contact with their children due to long distances between the prison and home. Furthermore, when a mother is imprisoned, her children are more likely not only to be separated from their father, but also to wind up in foster care.

 Contrast parole, expiration release, pardon, and furlough. Parole is an early release program for those incarcerated. Expiration release occurs when the inmate has served the maximum time for her or his initial sentence minus good-time credits. A pardon can be given only by the president or one of the fifty governors. Furlough is a temporary release while in jail or prison.

 Explain the goal of prisoner reentry programs. Based on the ideals of promoting desistance, these programs have two main objectives: (a) to prepare a prisoner for a successful return to the community, and (b) to protect the community by reducing the chances that the ex-convict will continue her or his criminal activity after release from prison.

 Indicate typical conditions for release for a paroled child molester. (a) Have no contact with children under the age of sixteen; (b) continue psychiatric treatment; (c) keep away from schools or parks where children are present; (d) cannot own toys that may be used to lure children; and (e) cannot have a job or participate in any activity that involves children.

QUESTIONS FOR **CRITICAL ANALYSIS**

1. Prisoner X is serving fourteen years in prison for robbery. He has fallen ill, and only a $1 million heart transplant will save his life. Are corrections officials *required* to pay for the heart transplant? Should they be required to do so? Explain your answers.

2. In the last chapter, you learned about the principle of least eligibility, which holds that inmates should not receive any benefits that are unavailable to the least advantaged members of outside society. Do you agree with the principle of least eligibility? If so, do you believe that prison programs such as substance abuse treatment and vocational training should be discontinued? Why or why not? If you disagree with the principle, how can you justify such programs beyond their benefits for individual inmates? Explain your answers.

3. Several years ago, sheriff's deputies ordered one hundred inmates at a Los Angeles County jail to strip naked, removed the mattresses from their cells, and left them with nothing to cover themselves but blankets for twenty-four hours. Are these steps—taken to quell racially motivated violence—morally acceptable? Are they legal?

4. How does the process of prisonization differ between male and female inmates?

5. What is the main justification for legislation that prohibits convicted sex offenders from accessing Facebook and online video games? What is your opinion of such legislation?

KEY **TERMS**

civil confinement   482
"deliberate indifference"   471
deprivation model   462
desistance   478
expiration release   476
furlough   476
halfway house   478

"hands-off" doctrine   470
"identifiable human needs"   471
pardon   476
prison gang   464
prison programs   459
prison segregation   463
prisoner reentry   476

prisonization   457
relative deprivation   462
security threat group (STG)   464
sex offender notification law   480
total institution   457
work release program   478

SELF ASSESSMENT **ANSWER KEY**

Page 461: i. total institution; **ii.** argot; **iii.** economies; **iv.** age; **v.** health-care; **vi.** vocational; **vii.** cost

Page 466: i. deprivation; **ii.** relative deprivation; **iii.** segregation; **iv.** gangs

Page 472: i. block officers; **ii.** discipline; **iii.** legitimate; **iv.** malicious; **v.** Eighth; **vi.** deliberate

Page 475: i. drug; **ii.** abuse; **iii.** children; **iv.** correctional officers

Page 482: i. employment; **ii.** housing; **iii.** reentry; **iv.** desistance; **v.** halfway; **vi.** notification

NOTES

1. Erving Goffman, "On the Characteristics of Total Institutions," in *Asylums: Essays on the Social Situation of Mental Patients and Other Inmates* (New York: Doubleday, 1961), 6.

2. Donald Clemmer, *The Prison Community* (Boston: Christopher, 1940).

3. John Irwin, *Prisons in Turmoil* (Boston: Little, Brown, 1980), 67.

4. *Old Behind Bars: The Aging Prison Population in the United States* (Human Rights Watch, 2012), 24–42.

5. Bureau of Justice Statistics, "Medical Problems of Prisoners," April 2008, "Highlights" and Table 2, at **www.ojp.usdoj.gov/bjs/pub/pdf/mpp.pdf**.

6. Bureau of Justice Statistics, *Mortality in Local Jails and State Prisons, 2000–2010—Statistical Tables* (Washington, D.C.: U.S. Department of Justice, December 2012), 3.

7. *Ibid.,* Table 13, page 14.

8. *Ibid.,* 3.

9. *At America's Expense: The Mass Incarceration of the Elderly* (New York: American Civil Liberties Union, June 2012), vii.

10. *Old Behind Bars: The Aging Prison Population in the United States,* 76.

11. Michael Vitiello, "Addressing the Special Problems of Mentally Ill Prisoners: A Small Piece of the Solution to Our Nation's Prison Crisis," *Denver University Law Review* (Fall 2010), 57–62.

12. Katherine Stuart van Wormer and Clemens Bartollas, *Women and the Criminal Justice System,* 3d ed. (Upper Saddle River, NJ: Pearson Education, 2011), 143.

13. Bureau of Justice Statistics, *Mental Health Problems of Prison and Jail Inmates* (Washington, D.C.: U.S. Department of Justice, September 2006), 1.

14. Fred Osher, et al., *Adults with Behavioral Health Needs Under Correctional Supervision: A Shared Framework for Reducing Recidivism and Promoting Recovery* (New York: Council of State Governments Justice Center, 2012), 8.

15. William Kanapaux, "Guilty of Mental Illness," *Psychiatric Times* (January 1, 2004), at **www.psychiatrictimes.com/forensic-psych /content/article/10168/47631**.

16. Bureau of Justice Statistics, *Census of State and Federal Correctional Facilities, 2005* (Washington, D.C.: U.S. Department of Justice, October 2008), 6.

17. Todd R. Clear, George F. Cole, and Michael D. Reisig, *American Corrections*, 9th ed (Belmont, CA: Wadsworth Cengage Learning, 2011), 381.

18. *Behind Bars II: Substance Abuse and America's Prison Population* (New York: The National Center on Addiction and Substance Abuse at Columbia University, February 2010), 4.

19. Ibid., 83–84.

20. Devah Pager and Bruce Western, *Investigating Prisoner Reentry: The Impact of Conviction Status on the Employment Prospects of Young Men* (Washington, D.C.: National Institute of Justice, October 2009), 6.

21. *Census of State and Federal Correctional Facilities, 2005*, 6.

22. Ron Barnett, "Incarcerated Getting Educated," *USA Today* (September 26, 2008), 2A.

23. Kevin Johnson, "Prison Diving Program Anchors Former Inmates," *USA Today* (July 14, 2008), 4A.

24. Steve Aos, Marna Miller, and Elizabeth Drake, *Evidence-Based Public Policy Options to Reduce Future Prison Construction, Criminal Justice Costs, and Crime Rates* (Olympia, WA: Washington State Institute for Public Policy, 2006), Exhibit 4, page 9.

25. Wendy Erisman and Jeanne B. Contardo, *Learning to Reduce Recidivism: A 50-State Analysis of Postsecondary Correctional Education Policy* (Washington, D.C.: Institute for Higher Education Policy, 2005), 1.

26. Laura E. Gorgol and Brian A. Sponsler, *Unlocking Potential: Results of a National Survey of Postsecondary Education in State Prisons* (Washington, D.C.: Institute for Higher Education Policy, May 2011), 10–15.

27. Robert Johnson, *Hard Time: Understanding and Reforming the Prison*, 2d ed. (Belmont, CA: Wadsworth, 1996), 133.

28. Federal Bureau of Prisons report, cited in Kevin Johnson, "Report Points to Prison Security Failures," *USA Today* (June 8, 2009), 3A.

29. *Mortality in Local Jails and State Prisons, 2000–2010—Statistical Tables*, Table 1, page 5; and Table 12, page 13.

30. Lee H. Bowker, *Prison Victimization* (New York: Elsevier, 1981), 31–33.

31. Stephen C. Light, "The Severity of Assaults on Prison Officers: A Contextual Analysis," *Social Science Quarterly* 71 (1990), 267–284.

32. Frank Tannenbaum, *Crime and Community* (Boston: Ginn & Co., 1938).

33. Randy Martin and Sherwood Zimmerman, "A Typology of the Causes of Prison Riots and an Analytical Extension to the 1986 Virginia Riot," *Justice Quarterly* 7 (1990), 711–737.

34. Bert Useem, "Disorganization and the New Mexico Prison Riot of 1980," *American Sociological Review* 50 (1985), 677–688.

35. Quoted in R. L. Nave, "Private Prisons, Public Problems," *Jackson (MS) Free Press* (June 6, 2012), at **www.jacksonfreepress.com/news/2012/ jun/06/private-prisons-public-problems**.

36. Irwin, 47.

37. Leo Carroll, "Race, Ethnicity, and the Social Order of the Prison," in *The Pains of Imprisonment*, ed. R. Johnson and H. Toch (Beverly Hills, CA: Sage, 1982).

38. Leo Carroll, *Hacks, Blacks, and Cons: Race Relations in a Maximum-Security Prison* (Lexington, MA: Lexington Books, 1988), 78.

39. *Lee v. Washington*, 390 U.S. 333 (1968).

40. *Johnson v. California*, 543 U.S. 499 (2005).

41. Ibid., at 508.

42. Jody Kent, "Race Walls Won't End Jail Riots," *Los Angeles Times* (February 12, 2006), M3.

43. Craig Haney, "Psychology and the Limits of Prison Pain," *Psychology, Public Policy, and Law* (December 1977), 499.

44. Alan J. Drury and Matt DeLisi, "Gangkill: An Exploratory Empirical Assessment of Gang Membership, Homicide Offending, and Prison Misconduct," *Crime & Delinquency* (January 2011), 130–146.

45. *A Study of Gangs and Security Threat Groups in America's Adult Prisons and Jails* (Indianapolis: National Major Gang Task Force, 2002).

46. George W. Knox, *The Problem of Gangs and Security Threat Groups (STGs) in American Prisons Today: Recent Research Findings from the 2004 Prison Gang Survey*, available at **www.ngcrc.com/corr2006.html**.

47. Ibid.

48. John Winterdyk and Rick Ruddell, "Managing Prison Gangs: Results from a Survey of U.S. Prison Systems," *Journal of Criminal Justice* 38 (2010), 733–734.

49. Alan Gomez, "States Make Prisons Far Less Deadly," *USA Today* (August 22, 2008), 3A.

50. 42 U.S.C. Sections 15601–15609 (2006).

51. Bureau of Justice Statistics, *Sexual Victimization Reported by Former State Prisoners, 2008* (Washington, D.C.: U.S. Department of Justice, May 2012), 5.

52. James E. Robertson, "The Prison Rape Elimination Act of 2003: A Primer," *Criminal Law Bulletin* (May/June 2004), 270–273.

53. Quoted in John J. DiIulio, Jr., *No Escape: The Future of American Corrections* (New York: Basic Books, 1991), 268.

54. Jack Henry Abbott, *In the Belly of the Beast* (New York: Vintage Books, 1991), 54.

55. Michel Foucault, *Discipline and Punish: The Birth of the Prison* (New York: Pantheon Books, 1977), 128.

56. Clear, Cole, and Reisig, 333.

57. Ibid., 335.

58. Lucien X. Lombardo, *Guards Imprisoned: Correctional Officers at Work* (Cincinnati, OH: Anderson Publishing Co., 1989), 51–71.

59. Goffman, 7.

60. Clear, Cole, and Reisig, 333.

61. *Wolff v. McDonnell*, 418 U.S. 539 (1974).

62. 475 U.S. 312 (1986).

63. *Stanley v. Hejirika*, 134 F.3d 629 (4th Cir. 1998).

64. Christopher R. Smith, *Law and Contemporary Corrections* (Belmont, CA: Wadsworth, 1999), Chapter 6.

65. 503 U.S. 1 (1992).

66. Darrell L. Ross, "Assessing *Hudson v. McMillan* Ten Years Later," *Criminal Law Bulletin* (September/October 2004), 508.

67. Van Wormer and Bartollas, 387.

68. Cristina Rathbone, *A World Apart: Women, Prison, and a Life behind Bars* (New York: Random House, 2006), 46.

69. Carl Nink et al., *Women Professionals in Corrections: A Growing Asset* (Centerville, UT: MTC Institute, August 2008), 1.

70. Denise L. Jenne and Robert C. Kersting, "Aggression and Women Correctional Officers in Male Prisons," *Prison Journal* (1996), 442–460.

71. Nink et al., 8–9.

72. Matt Gouras, "Female Prison Guards Often behind Sex Misconduct," *Associated Press* (March 14, 2010).

73. *Wolff v. McDonnell*, 539.

74. *Hudson v. Palmer*, 468 U.S. 517 (1984).

75. 429 U.S. 97 (1976).

76. 501 U.S. 294 (1991).

77. *Wilson v. Seiter*, 501 U.S. 294, 304 (1991).

78. Adam Cohen, "Can Food Be Cruel and Unusual Punishment?" *Time* (August 2, 2012), at **ideas.time.com/2012/04/02/can-food -be-cruel-and-unusual-punishment**.

79. *Woodall v. Foti*, 648 F.2d, 268, 272 (5th Cir. 1981).

80. *Brown v. Plata*, 563 U.S. ____ (2011).

81. *Procunier v. Martinez,* 416 U.S. 396 (1974).

82. *Cruz v. Beto,* 405 U.S. 319 (1972); *Gittlemacker v. Prasse,* 428 F.2d 1 (3d Cir. 1970); and *Kahane v. Carlson,* 527 F.2d 492 (2d Cir. 1975).

83. Maryclaire Dale, "Court Says Pa. Prison Can Ban Muslim Scarf," *Associated Press* (August 2, 2010).

84. Quoted in Alexandra Marks, "Martha Checks in Today," *Seattle Times* (October 8, 2004), A8.

85. Bureau of Justice Statistics, *Sourcebook of Criminal Justice,* 3d ed. (Washington, D.C.: U.S. Department of Justice, 2003), Table 6.56, page 519; and Bureau of Justice Statistics, *Prisoners in 2011* (Washington, D.C.: U.S. Department of Justice, December 2012), Table 9, page 9.

86. Bureau of Justice Statistics, *Profile of Jail Inmates, 2002* (Washington, D.C.: U.S. Department of Justice, July 2004), 10.

87. Bureau of Justice Statistics, *Prior Abuse Reported by Inmates and Probationers* (Washington, D.C.: U.S. Department of Justice, April 1999), 2.

88. *Caught in the Net: The Impact of Drug Policies on Women and Families* (Washington, D.C.: American Civil Liberties Union, 2004), 18–19.

89. Allen J. Beck and Laura M. Maruschak, *Mental Health Treatment in State Prisons, 2000* (Washington, D.C.: U.S. Department of Justice, July 2001), 1.

90. Barbara Bloom, Barbara Owen, and Stephanie Covington, *Gender Responsive Strategies: Research, Practice, and Guiding Principles for Women Offenders* (Washington, D.C.: National Institute of Corrections, 2003), 6.

91. *Ibid.,* 7.

92. *Ibid.,* 6.

93. Sarah Schirmer, Ashley Nellis, and Marc Mauer, *Incarcerated Parents and Their Children: Trends 1991–2007* (Washington, D.C.: The Sentencing Project, February 2009), 2.

94. Kelly Bedard and Eric Helland, "Location of Women's Prisons and the Deterrent Effect of 'Harder' Time," *International Review of Law and Economics* (June 2004), 152.

95. *Ibid.*

96. Schirmer, Nellis, and Mauer, 5.

97. Rathbone, 4.

98. *Ibid.,* 158.

99. Van Wormer and Bartollas, 137–138.

100. Barbara Bloom and Meda Chesney-Lind, "Women in Prison," in Roslyn Muraskin, ed., *It's a Crime: Women and Justice,* 4th ed. (Upper Saddle River, NJ: Prentice Hall, 2007), 542–563.

101. Piper Kerman, *Orange Is the New Black: My Year in a Women's Prison* (New York: Spiegal and Grau, 2011), 131.

102. Esther Heffernan, *Making It in Prison: The Square, the Cool, and the Life* (New York: Wiley, 1972), 91.

103. Leanne F. Alarid, "Female Inmate Subcultures," in *Corrections Contexts: Contemporary and Classical Readings,* ed. James W. Marquart and Jonathan R. Sorenson (Los Angeles: Roxbury Publishing Co., 1997), 136–137.

104. Barbara Owen et al., *Gendered Violence and Safety: A Contextual Approach to Improving Security in Women's Facilities,* December 2008, 12–14, at **www.ncjrs.gov/pdffiles1/nij/grants/225340.pdf**.

105. Nancy Wolff, Cynthia Blitz, Jing Shi, Jane Siegel, and Ronet Bachman, "Physical Violence inside Prisons: Rates of Victimization," *Criminal Justice and Behavior* 34 (2007), 588–604.

106. Van Wormer and Bartollas, 146–148.

107. Equal Justice Initiative, "Investigation into Sexual Violence at Tutwiler Prison for Women" (May 2012), at **www.eji.org/files/EJI%20Findings _from_Tutwiler_Investigation.pdf**.

108. Jocelyn M. Pollock, *Women, Prison and Crime* (Belmont, CA: Wadsworth, 2002), 52.

109. Cited in Bloom, Owen, and Covington, 26.

110. Quoted in Sean J. Miller, "When Prison Doors Swing Open," *Christian Science Monitor Weekly* (May 21, 2012), 29.

111. Bureau of Justice Statistics, "Reentry Trends in the United States," at **www.bjs.gov/content/reentry/reentry.cfm**.

112. Joan Petersilia, *When Prisoners Come Home: Parole and Prisoner Reentry* (New York: Oxford University Press, 2003), 39.

113. Victor Hassine, *Life without Parole: Living in Prison Today,* ed. Thomas J. Bernard and Richard McCleary (Los Angeles: Roxbury Publishing Co., 1996), 12.

114. Christy A. Visher, Sara A. Debus-Sherrill, and Jennifer Yahner, "Employment after Prison: A Longitudinal Study of Former Prisoners," *Justice Quarterly* 28 (2011), 713.

115. *Ill Equipped: U.S. Prisons and Offenders with Mental Illness* (New York: Human Rights Watch, 2003).

116. Pew Center on the States, *State of Recidivism: The Revolving Door of America's Prisons* (Washington, D.C.: The Pew Charitable Trusts, April 2011), 2.

117. Edward Zamble and Vernon Quinsey, *The Criminal Recidivism Process* (Cambridge, England: Cambridge University Press, 1997).

118. Quoted in Kevin Johnson, "After Years of Solitary, Freedom Is Hard to Grasp," *USA Today* (June 9, 2005), 2A.

119. *Census of State and Federal Correctional Facilities, 2005,* Table 6, page 5.

120. Alan Ellis and Todd Bussert, "Looking at the BOP's Amended RDAP Rules," *Criminal Justice* (Fall 2011), 37.

121. "They All Come Home," *The Economist* (April 23, 2011), 34.

122. Justice Center, *States Report Reductions in Recidivism* (Lexington, KY: The Council of State Governments, September 2012), 3.

123. "The Greatest Fear," *The Economist* (August 26, 2006), 25.

124. James F. Quin, Craig J. Forsyth, and Carla Mullen-Quinn, "Societal Reaction to Sex Offenders: A Review of the Origins and Results of the Myths Surrounding Their Crimes and Treatment Amenability," *Deviant Behavior* 25 (2004), 215–232.

125. Belinda Brooks Gordon and Charlotte Bilby, "Psychological Interventions for Treatment of Adult Sex Offenders," *British Medical Journal* (July 2006), 5–6.

126. Bureau of Justice Statistics, *Recidivism of Prisoners Released in 1994* (Washington, D.C.: U.S. Department of Justice, June 2002), Table 9, page 8.

127. R. Karl Hanson and Kelly Morton-Bourgon, "The Characteristics of Persistent Sexual Offenders: A Meta-Analysis of Recidivism Studies, *Journal of Consulting and Clinical Psychology* 73 (2005), 1154–1163.

128. New Jersey Revised Statute Section 2C:7-8(c) (1995).

129. Georgia Code Annotated Section 42-9-44.1(b)(1).

130. Public Law Number 109-248, Section 116, 120 Statute 595 (2006).

131. Leigh Linden and Jonah Rockoff, "Estimates of the Impact of Crime Risk on Property Values from Megan's Laws," *American Economic Review* 98 (2008), 1103–1127.

132. Amanda Y. Agan, "Sex Offender Registries: Fear without Function?" *Journal of Law and Economics* (February 2011), 207–239.

133. Jamie Fellner, ed., *No Easy Answers: Sex Offenders Laws in the U.S.* (New York: Human Rights Watch, 2007), 25.

134. Agan.

135. Abby Goodnough, "After Two Cases in Florida, Crackdown on Molesters," *Law Enforcement News* (May 2004), 12.

136. *United States v. Comstock,* 560 U.S. ____ (2010).

137. Quoted in Michael Schwirtz, "In 2 Trailers, the Neighbors Nobody Wants," *New York Times* (February 5, 2013), A1.

138. New Jersey Statutes Annotated Section 2C: 7-3.

139. Wendy Kock, "Sex-Offender Residency Laws Get a Second Look," *USA Today* (February 26, 2007), 1A.

140. Quoted in Jenifer Warren, "Sex Crime Residency Laws Exile Offenders," *Los Angeles Times* (October 30, 2006), 1.

141. Bureau of Justice Statistics, *Recidivism of Sex Offenders Released from Prison in 1994* (Washington, D.C.: U.S. Department of Justice, November 2003), 36; and Luis Rosell, "Sex Offenders: Pariahs of the 21st Century?" *William Mitchell Law Review* (2005), 419.

CHAPTER

15

The Juvenile Justice System

Carline Jean/Sun Sentinel/MCT via Getty Images

CHAPTER OUTLINE	CORRESPONDING LEARNING OBJECTIVES	
The Evolution of American Juvenile Justice		Describe the child-saving movement and its relationship to the doctrine of *parens patriae*.
		List the four major differences between juvenile courts and adult courts.
		Identify and briefly describe the single most important U.S. Supreme Court case with respect to juvenile justice.
Determining Delinquency Today		Describe the reasoning behind recent U.S. Supreme Court decisions that have lessened the harshness of sentencing outcomes for violent juvenile offenders.
Trends in Juvenile Delinquency		Explain how law enforcement's emphasis on domestic violence has influenced female juvenile arrest patterns.
Factors in Juvenile Delinquency		Describe the one variable that always correlates highly with juvenile crime rates.
		Indicate some of the reasons why youths join gangs.
First Contact: The Police and Pretrial Procedures		List the factors that normally determine what police do with juvenile offenders.
		Describe the four primary stages of pretrial juvenile justice procedure.
Trying and Punishing Juveniles		Explain the distinction between an adjudicatory hearing and a disposition hearing.

To target your study and review, look for these numbered Learning Objective icons throughout the chapter.

BLOODY SUNDAY

LIKE MANY teenagers, fifteen-year-old Nehemiah Griego of Albuquerque, New Mexico, was frustrated with his mother. The way that Nehemiah dealt with this frustration was, however, anything but commonplace. Around 1 A.M. on January 19, 2013, Nehemiah sneaked into his parents' upstairs bedroom and, using a family rifle, fatally shot his sleeping mother, Sara. Next, he used the weapon to kill his nine-year-old brother and two sisters, aged five and two. Nehemiah then waited five hours in a downstairs bathroom for his father to return home from work. When Greg Griego walked in the front door, his son shot him as well, resulting in the fifth and final death of that Sunday morning.

According to Bernalillo County law enforcement authorities, Nehemiah had been planning the killings for at least a week, spending much of that time playing violent video games. The teenager had also planned to murder his girlfriend's family and then start shooting random strangers at a local Wal-Mart, with the expectation that he would not survive the expected gunfire exchange with police. Instead, Nehemiah texted a photo of his dead mother to his girlfriend and spent most of the rest of the day with her before being arrested.

Because of the level of premeditation and the horrific nature of the murders, prosecutors decided to charge Nehemiah as an adult rather than a juvenile. If convicted of all the charges against him, including five counts of murder, he faced more than two hundred years in prison. Nehemiah's remaining family members disagreed with this strategy. His uncle, Eric Griego, told reporters that Nehemiah should be given "the fairest chance to turn his life around." Griego also said that his nephew should "not be cast away to an adult prison system where he can never have an opportunity for redemption."

1. Do you agree with Eric Griego that his nephew should be given a chance "to turn his life around"? Or does the shocking nature of these crimes require that the teenager spend the rest of his life in prison? Explain your answer.

2. About six months before the events in Albuquerque, the U.S. Supreme Court invalidated state laws that require life-without-parole prison terms for juveniles who commit murder. In her majority opinion, Justice Elena Kagan wrote that such sentences do not take into account juvenile traits such as "immaturity, impetuosity, and failure to appreciate risks and consequences." Do you agree with the Court that juveniles are not as blameworthy as adults and should not automatically be sentenced to die in prison? Why or why not?

3. If you were Nehemiah Griego's defense attorney, how would you argue that your client does not deserve to spend the rest of his life in prison without the chance for parole? What aspects of Nehemiah's behavior would you focus on?

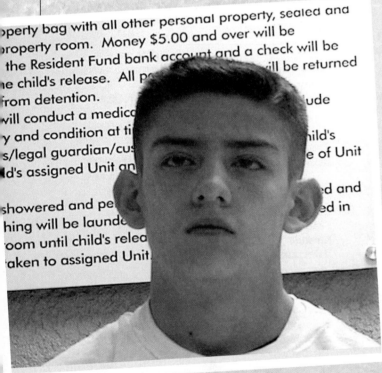

AP/Handout photo from Bernalillo County Sheriff's Department

In January 2013, fifteen-year-old Nehemiah Griego of Albuquerque, New Mexico, was arrested for killing five family members.

THE EVOLUTION OF AMERICAN JUVENILE JUSTICE

A difficult question—asked every time a younger offender such as Nehemiah Griego commits a heinous act of violence—lies at the heart of the juvenile justice debate: Should such acts by youths be given the same weight as those committed by adults, or should they be seen as "mistakes" that can be corrected by care and counseling? From its earliest days, the American juvenile justice system has operated as an uneasy compromise between "rehabilitation and punishment, treatment and custody."[1]

At the beginning of the 1800s, juvenile offenders were treated the same as adult offenders—they were judged by the same courts and sentenced to the same severe penalties. This situation began to change soon after, as urbanization and industrialization created an immigrant underclass that was, at least in the eyes of many reformers, predisposed to deviant activity. Certain members of the Progressive movement, known as the child savers, began to take steps to "save" children from these circumstances, introducing the idea of rehabilitating delinquents in the process.

The Child-Saving Movement

In general, the child savers favored the doctrine of *parens patriae,* which holds that the state has not only a right but also a duty to care for children who are neglected, delinquent, or in some other way disadvantaged. Juvenile offenders, the child savers believed, required treatment, not punishment, and they were horrified at the thought of placing children in prisons with hardened adult criminals. In 1967, then Supreme Court justice Abe Fortas said of the child savers:

LEARNING
1
OBJECTIVE

Describe the child-saving movement and its relationship to the doctrine of *parens patriae*.

> They believed that society's role was not to ascertain whether the child was "guilty" or "innocent," but "What is he, how has he become what he is, and what had best be done in his interest and in the interest of the state to save him from a downward career." The child—essentially good, as they saw it—was made "to feel that he is the object of [the government's] care and solicitude," not that he was under arrest or on trial.[2]

Child-saving organizations convinced local legislatures to pass laws that allowed them to take control of children who exhibited criminal tendencies or had been neglected by their parents. To separate these children from the environment in which they were raised, the organizations created a number of institutions, the best known of which was New York's House of Refuge. Opening in 1825, the House of Refuge implemented many of the same reformist measures popular in the penitentiaries of the time, meaning that its charges were subjected to the healthful influences of hard study and labor. Although the House of Refuge was criticized for its harsh discipline (which caused many boys to run away), similar institutions sprang up throughout the Northeast during the middle of the 1800s.

The Illinois Juvenile Court

The efforts of the child savers culminated with the passage of the Illinois Juvenile Court Act in 1899. The Illinois legislature created the first court specifically for juveniles, guided by the principles of *parens patriae* and based on the belief that children are not fully responsible for criminal conduct and are capable of being rehabilitated.[3]

The Illinois Juvenile Court and those in other states that followed in its path were (and, in many cases, remain) drastically different from adult courts:

LEARNING
2
OBJECTIVE

List the four major differences between juvenile courts and adult courts.

- *No juries.* The matter was decided by judges who wore regular clothes instead of black robes and sat at a table with the other participants rather than behind a

Status Offender A juvenile who has engaged in behavior deemed unacceptable for those under a certain statutorily determined age.

Juvenile Delinquency Behavior that is illegal under federal or state law that has been committed by a person who is under an age limit specified by statute.

bench. Because the primary focus of the court was on the child and not the crime, the judge had wide discretion in disposing of each case.

- *Different terminology.* To reduce the stigma of criminal proceedings, "petitions" were issued instead of "warrants." The children were not "defendants," but "respondents," and they were not "found guilty" but "adjudicated delinquent."

- *No adversarial relationship.* Instead of trying to determine guilt or innocence, the parties involved in the juvenile court worked together in the best interests of the child, with the emphasis on rehabilitation rather than punishment.

- *Confidentiality.* To avoid "saddling" the child with a criminal past, juvenile court hearings and records were kept sealed, and the proceedings were closed to the public.

By 1945, every state had a juvenile court system modeled after the first Illinois court. For the most part, these courts were able to operate without interference until the 1960s and the onset of the juvenile rights movement.

Juvenile Delinquency

After the first juvenile court was established in Illinois, the Chicago Bar Association described its purpose as, in part, to "exercise the same tender solicitude and care over its neglected wards that a wise and loving parent would exercise with reference to his [or her] own children under similar circumstances."[4] In other words, the state was given the responsibility of caring for those minors whose behavior seemed to show that they could not be controlled by their parents. As a result, many **status offenders** found themselves in the early houses of refuge and continue to be placed in state-run facilities today. A status offense is an act that, if committed by a juvenile, is considered illegal and grounds for possible state custody. The same act, if committed by an adult, does not warrant law enforcement action. (See Figure 15.1 below for a list of the most common status offenses.)

In contrast, **juvenile delinquency** refers to conduct that would also be criminal if committed by an adult. According to federal law and the laws of most states, a juvenile delinquent is someone who has not yet reached his or her eighteenth birthday—the age of adult criminal responsibility—at the time of the offense in question. In two states (New York and North Carolina), persons aged sixteen are considered adults, and eleven other states confer adulthood on seventeen-year-olds for purposes of criminal law.

Under certain circumstances, discussed later in this chapter, children under these ages can be tried in adult courts and incarcerated in adult prisons and jails. Remember that Nehemiah Griego was fifteen years old when he was charged as an adult for the murders of five family members, described in the opening of the chapter. By contrast, in 2013, high school football players Trent Mays, aged seventeen, and Ma'lik Richmond, aged sixteen, were found to be *delinquent beyond a reasonable doubt* of sexually assaulting an intoxicated sixteen-year-old girl in Steubenville, Ohio (see photo on the next page). Because they were adjudicated as juveniles, Mays and Richmond cannot be incarcerated past their twenty-first birthdays. Griego, charged as an adult, faced the possibility of spending at least two hundred years behind bars.

FIGURE 15.1 Status Offenses

1. Smoking cigarettes	5. Running away from home
2. Drinking alcohol	6. Violating curfew
3. Being truant (skipping school)	7. Participating in sexual activity
4. Disobeying teachers	8. Using profane language

Constitutional Protections and the Juvenile Court

Though the ideal of the juvenile court seemed to offer the "best of both worlds" for juvenile offenders, in reality the lack of procedural protections led to many children being arbitrarily punished not only for crimes, but for status offenses as well. Juvenile judges were treating all violators similarly, which led to many status offenders being incarcerated in the same institutions as violent delinquents. In response to a wave of lawsuits demanding due process rights for juveniles, the United States Supreme Court issued several rulings in the 1960s and 1970s that significantly changed the juvenile justice system.

■ Depending on the state, juvenile offenders found to be delinquent such as Trent Mays, left, and Ma'lik Richmond usually will not be incarcerated past their twenty-first birthdays. Is this a just punishment? Why or why not?
AP Photo/Keith Srakocic, Pool

KENT V. UNITED STATES The first decision to extend due process rights to children in juvenile courts was *Kent v. United States* (1966).[5] The case concerned sixteen-year-old Morris Kent, who had been arrested for breaking into a woman's house, stealing her purse, and raping her. Because Kent was on juvenile probation, the state sought to transfer his trial for the crime to an adult court (a process to be discussed later in the chapter).

Without giving any reasons for his decision, the juvenile judge consented to this judicial waiver, and Kent was sentenced in the adult court to a thirty- to ninety-year prison term. The Supreme Court overturned the sentence, ruling that juveniles have a right to counsel and a hearing in any instance in which the juvenile judge is considering sending the case to an adult court. The Court stated that, in jurisdiction waiver cases, a child receives "the worst of both worlds," getting neither the "protections accorded to adults" nor the "solicitous care and regenerative treatment" offered in the juvenile system.[6]

IN RE GAULT The *Kent* decision provided the groundwork for *In re Gault* one year later. Considered by many the single most important case concerning juvenile justice, *In re Gault* involved a fifteen-year-old boy who was arrested for allegedly making a lewd phone call while on probation.[7] In its decision, the Supreme Court held that juveniles facing a loss of liberty were entitled to many of the same basic procedural safeguards granted to adult offenders in this country. (See the feature *Landmark Cases: In re Gault* on the next page.)

OTHER IMPORTANT COURT DECISIONS Over the next ten years, the Supreme Court handed down three more important rulings on juvenile court procedure. The ruling in *In re Winship* (1970)[8] required the government to prove "beyond a reasonable doubt" that a juvenile had committed an act of delinquency, raising the burden of proof from a "preponderance of the evidence." In *Breed v. Jones* (1975),[9] the Court held that the Fifth Amendment's double jeopardy clause prevented a juvenile from being tried in an adult court for a crime that had already been adjudicated in juvenile court. In contrast, the decision in *McKeiver v. Pennsylvania* (1971)[10] represented an instance in which the Court did not move the juvenile court further toward the adult model. In that case, the Court ruled that the Constitution did not give juveniles the right to a jury trial.

In re Gault

Identify and briefly describe the single most important U.S. Supreme Court case with respect to juvenile justice. **3** LEARNING OBJECTIVE

In 1964, fifteen-year-old Gerald Gault and a friend were arrested for making lewd telephone calls to a neighbor in Gila County, Arizona. Gault, who was on probation, was placed under custody with no notice given to his parents. The juvenile court in his district held a series of informal hearings to determine Gault's punishment. During these hearings, no records were kept, Gault was not afforded the right to counsel, and the complaining witness was never made available for questioning. At the close of the hearing, the judge sentenced Gault to remain in Arizona's State Industrial School until the age of twenty-one. Gault's lawyers challenged this punishment, arguing that the proceedings had denied their client his due process rights. Eventually, the matter reached the United States Supreme Court.

In re Gault
United States Supreme Court
387 U.S. 1 (1967)

IN THE WORDS OF THE COURT . . .
JUSTICE FORTAS, MAJORITY OPINION

* * * *

From the inception of the juvenile court system, wide differences have been tolerated—indeed insisted upon—between the procedural rights accorded to adults and those of juveniles. In practically all jurisdictions, there are rights granted to adults which are withheld from juveniles.

* * * *

The absence of substantive standards has not necessarily meant that children receive careful, compassionate, individualized treatment. The absence of procedural rules based upon constitutional principle has not always produced fair, efficient, and effective procedures.

Departures from established principles of due process have frequently resulted not in enlightened procedure, but in arbitrariness.

* * * *

Ultimately, however, we confront the reality of that portion of the Juvenile Court process with which we deal in this case. A boy is charged with misconduct. The boy is committed to an institution where he may be restrained of liberty for years.* * * His world becomes "a building with whitewashed walls, regimented routine and institutional hours. . . ." Instead of mother and father and sisters and brothers and friends and classmates, his world is peopled by guards, custodians, state employees, and "delinquents" confined with him for anything from waywardness to rape and homicide. In view of this, it would be extraordinary if our Constitution did not require the procedural regularity and the exercise of care implied in the phrase "due process." Under our Constitution, the condition of being a boy does not justify a kangaroo court.

* * * *

DECISION
The Court held that juveniles were entitled to the basic procedural safeguards afforded by the U.S. Constitution, including the right to advance notice of charges, the right to counsel, the right to confront and cross-examine witnesses, and the privilege against self-incrimination. The decision marked a turning point in juvenile justice in this country: no longer would informality and paternalism be the guiding principles of juvenile courts. Instead, due process would dictate the adjudication process, much as in an adult court.

FOR CRITICAL ANALYSIS
What might be some of the negative consequences of the *In re Gault* decision for juveniles charged with committing delinquent acts? Can you think of any reasons why juveniles should not receive the same due process protections as adult offenders?

Kentoh/Shutterstock.com

SELF ASSESSMENT
Fill in the blanks and check your answers on page 520.
At its inception, the American juvenile justice system was guided by the principles of _____ _____, which holds that the state has a responsibility to look after children when their parents cannot do so. In general, juveniles are involved in two types of wrongdoing: (1) acts that would not be crimes if committed by adults, or _____ _____, and (2) acts that would be crimes if committed by an adult, or juvenile _____.

DETERMINING DELINQUENCY TODAY

In the eyes of many observers, the net effect of the Supreme Court decisions during the 1966–1975 period was to move juvenile justice away from the ideals of the child savers. As a result of these decisions, many young offenders would find themselves in a formalized system that is often indistinguishable from its adult counterpart. But, though the Court has recognized that minors charged with crimes possess certain constitutional rights, it has failed to dictate at what age these rights should be granted. Consequently, the legal status of children in the United States varies depending on where they live, with each state making its own policy decisions on the crucial questions of age and competency.

The Age Question

One day several years ago, a twelve-year-old boy was playing with toy trucks and planes in the backyard of his family's Burlington, Colorado, home. Minutes later, he fatally shot his parents, Charles and Marilyn Long, with a .357 Magnum revolver.

In Chapter 4, we saw that early American criminal law recognized infancy as a defense against criminal charges. At that time, on attaining fourteen years of age, a youth was considered an adult and treated accordingly by the criminal justice system. Today, as Figure 15.2 below shows, the majority of states, including Colorado (as well as the District of Columbia), allow for the prosecution of juveniles under the age of thirteen as adults. Thus, Colorado officials had the option of prosecuting the Longs' son for murder as an adult, despite his tender years. Instead, despite the wishes of some Long family members, district attorney Robert E. Watson decided to keep the boy in the state's juvenile justice system. "If you're looking for an adult explanation for why this kid went from playing in dirt to commit murder you'll never get one," said Watson. "This lies in the mind of a very immature twelve-year-old."[11]

As noted earlier, when juveniles who remain in juvenile court are found guilty, they receive "limited" sentences. Under these circumstances, they cannot remain incarcerated in juvenile detention centers past their eighteenth or twenty-first birthday. Consequently, a Colorado juvenile judge eventually sentenced the boy who shot and killed his parents to seven years in juvenile detention.

The Culpability Question

Many researchers believe that by the age of fourteen, an adolescent has the same ability as an adult to make a competent decision. Nevertheless, according to some observers, a juvenile's ability to theoretically understand the difference between "right"

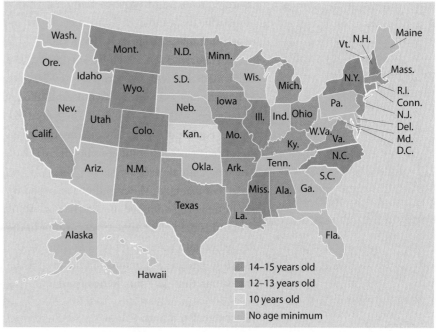

FIGURE 15.2 The Minimum Age at Which a Juvenile Can Be Tried as an Adult

- 14–15 years old
- 12–13 years old
- 10 years old
- No age minimum

Source: National Center for Juvenile Justice.

and "wrong" does not mean that she or he should be held to the same standards of competency as an adult.

JUVENILE BEHAVIOR A study released in 2003 by the Research Network on Adolescent Development and Juvenile Justice found that 33 percent of juvenile defendants in criminal courts had the same low level of understanding of legal matters as mentally ill adults who had been found incompetent to stand trial.[12] Legal psychologist Richard E. Redding believes that

> adolescents' lack of life experience may limit their real-world decision-making ability. Whether we call it wisdom, judgment, or common sense, adolescents may not have nearly enough.[13]

Juveniles are generally more impulsive, more likely to engage in risky behavior, and less likely to calculate the long-term consequences of any particular action. Furthermore, adolescents are far more likely to respond to peer pressure than are adults. The desire for acceptance and approval may drive them to commit crimes: juveniles are arrested as part of a group at much higher rates than adults.[14] Furthermore, juveniles are less likely than adults to display remorse immediately following a violent act. As a result, they are often penalized by the courts for showing "less grief than the system demands."[15]

DIMINISHED GUILT The "diminished culpability" of juveniles was one of the reasons given by the United States Supreme Court in its landmark decision in *Roper v. Simmons* (2005).[16] As we saw in Chapter 11, that case forbade the execution of offenders who were under the age of eighteen when they committed their crimes. In his majority opinion, Justice Anthony Kennedy wrote that because minors cannot fully comprehend the consequences of their actions, the two main justifications for the death penalty—retribution and deterrence—do not "work" with juvenile wrongdoers.[17]

Life Imprisonment Issues The Supreme Court applied the same reasoning in two later cases that have dramatically affected the sentencing of violent juvenile offenders. First, in *Graham v. Florida* (2010),[18] the Court held that juveniles who commit crimes that do not involve murder may not be sentenced to life in prison without the possibility of parole. According to Justice Kennedy, who wrote the majority opinion, state officials must give these inmates "some meaningful opportunity to obtain release based on demonstrated maturity and rehabilitation."[19]

Then, with *Miller v. Alabama* (2012),[20] the Court banned laws in twenty-eight states that made life-without-parole sentences *mandatory* for juveniles convicted of murder. The case focused on the fate of Evan Miller, who was fourteen years old when he killed a neighbor with a baseball bat. The ruling did not signify that juvenile offenders such as Miller could not, under any circumstances, be sentenced to life without parole. Rather, the Court stated that judges must have the discretion to weigh the mitigating factors in each individual case.

For example, Miller had been abused by his stepfather and neglected by his alcoholic and drug-addicted mother, had spent most of his life in foster care, and had tried to commit suicide four times.[21] According to the Court, this type of personal history must be taken into account when determining the proper sentence for a juvenile murderer. Such mitigating factors may indicate that the offender has the potential to be rehabilitated and therefore should be afforded the possibility of parole.

Resentencing Issues Following the Supreme Court's *Miller* decision, the future of more than 2,000 inmates currently serving life-without-parole sentences in the United States

Describe the reasoning behind recent U.S. Supreme Court decisions that have lessened the harshness of sentencing outcomes for violent juvenile offenders.

LEARNING
4
OBJECTIVE

for crimes committed as juveniles is uncertain. Depending on the state in which they are imprisoned, many of these offenders will probably receive resentencing hearings. These hearings will give courts the ability to hear evidence of mitigating factors and, if appropriate, reduce punishments. This process could take years to complete, however, and many judges will be hesitant to provide parole opportunities to offenders who have committed horrific crimes.

In other instances, states have taken administrative or legislative steps to address the issue. A week after the *Miller* ruling, for example, Iowa Governor Terry Branstad commuted the sentences of all inmates serving mandatory life terms in state prisons for murders committed as juveniles. He then immediately resentenced these inmates to life in prison with the possibility of parole after sixty years—touching off several lawsuits claiming that the governor had violated the "spirit" of the *Miller* decision.[22]

SELF ASSESSMENT

Fill in the blanks and check your answers on page 520.

The age at which a child can be held criminally responsible for his or her actions differs from _____ to _____. Many experts believe that minors should not be held to the same level of competency as adults, partially because they are more _____ and more likely to respond to _____ pressure. This "diminished culpability" was one of the reasons the United States Supreme Court gave in 2005 for prohibiting the _____ _____ for offenders who were under the age of eighteen when they committed their crimes.

In 2013, juvenile offender T. J. Lane was sentenced to life in prison without the possibility of parole for killing three students during a shooting spree at Chardon High School in Chardon, Ohio. According to the U.S. Supreme Court's *Miller* decision, under what circumstances can juveniles receive life-without-parole sentences? Do you agree with the Court's ruling?
AP Photo/Mark Duncan

TRENDS IN JUVENILE DELINQUENCY

When asked, juveniles will admit to a wide range of illegal or dangerous behavior, including carrying weapons, getting involved in physical fights, driving after drinking alcohol, and stealing or deliberately damaging school property.[23] Has the juvenile justice system been effective in controlling and preventing this kind of misbehavior, as well as more serious acts?

To answer this question, many observers turn to the Federal Bureau of Investigation's Uniform Crime Report (UCR), initially covered in Chapter 3. Because the UCR breaks down arrest statistics by age of the arrestee, it has been considered the primary source of information on the presence of juveniles in America's justice system. This does not mean, however, that the UCR is completely reliable when it comes to measuring juvenile delinquency. The process measures only those juveniles who were caught and therefore does not accurately reflect all delinquent acts in any given year. Furthermore, it measures the number of arrests but not the number of arrestees, meaning that—due to repeat offenders—the number of juveniles actually in the system could be below the number of juvenile arrests.

Delinquency by the Numbers

With these cautions in mind, UCR findings are quite clear as to the extent of juvenile delinquency in the United States today. In 2011, juveniles accounted for 12.7 percent of violent crime arrests and 11.8 percent of criminal activity arrests in general.[24] According to the 2011 UCR, juveniles were responsible for

- 8 percent of all murder arrests.
- 19 percent of all aggravated assault arrests.
- 14 percent of all forcible rapes.

- 18 percent of all weapons arrests.
- 22 percent of all robbery arrests.
- 20 percent of all Part I property crimes.
- 19 percent of all drug offenses.

The Rise and Fall of Juvenile Crime

As Figure 15.3 below shows, juvenile arrest rates for violent crimes have fluctuated dramatically over the past three decades. In the 2000s, with a few exceptions, juvenile crime in the United States has decreased at a rate similar to that of adult crime, as discussed earlier in this textbook. From 1997 to 2009, juvenile court delinquency caseloads declined by 20 percent.[25] Not surprisingly, the drop in juvenile arrests and court appearances has led to fewer juveniles behind bars. The national population of juvenile inmates decreased 12 percent between 2006 and 2008, allowing officials in some states, including California, Ohio, and Texas, to close juvenile detention facilities.[26]

A number of theories have been put forth to explain this downturn in juvenile offending. Some observers point to the increase in police action against "quality-of-life" crimes such as loitering, which they believe stops juveniles before they have a chance to commit more serious crimes. Similarly, about 80 percent of American municipalities enforce juvenile curfews, which restrict the movement of minors during certain hours, usually after dark.[27] In 2011, law enforcement made nearly 60,000 arrests for curfew and loitering law violations.[28] Furthermore, hundreds of local programs designed to educate children about the dangers of drugs and crime operate across the country. Though the results of such community-based efforts are difficult, if not impossible, to measure—it cannot be assumed that children would have become delinquent if they had not participated—these programs are generally considered a crucial element of keeping youth crime under control.[29]

FIGURE 15.3 Arrest Rates of Juveniles

After rising dramatically in the mid-1990s, juvenile arrest rates for violent crimes have—with a few exceptions—continued to drop steadily in the 2000s.

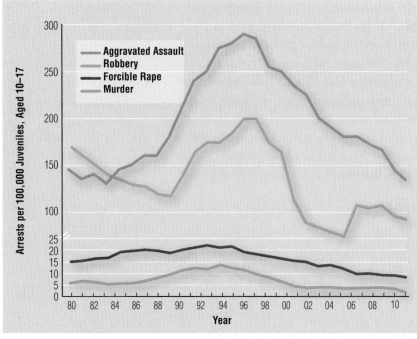

Source: Office of Juvenile Justice and Delinquency Prevention, *Statistical Briefing Book*, at **www.ojjdp.ncjrs.org/ojstatbb/ crime/JAR.asp**.

Girls in the Juvenile Justice System

Although overall rates of juvenile offending have been dropping, arrest rates for girls are declining more slowly than those for boys. Between 1997 and 2009, the number of cases involving males in delinquency courts declined 24 percent, while the female caseload in such courts declined by only 1 percent.[30] Self-reported studies show, however, that there has been little change in girls' violent behavior over the past few decades.[31] Why, then, is the presence of girls in the juvenile and criminal justice system increasing relative to their male counterparts?

A GROWING PRESENCE Although girls have for the most part been treated more harshly than boys for status offenses,[32] a "chivalry effect" (see Chapter 11) has traditionally existed in other areas of the juvenile justice system. In the past, police were likely to arrest offending boys while allowing girls to go home to the care of their families for similar behavior. This is no longer the case. According to the Office of Juvenile Justice and Delinquency Prevention, juvenile courts handled twice as many cases involving girls in 2009 as they did in 1985.[33] A particular problem area for girls appears to be the crime of assault. In 2011, females accounted for 24 percent of all juvenile arrests for aggravated assault and 36 percent of those arrests for simple assault, higher percentages than for other violent crimes.[34]

 A police officer interviews two teenage girls who were involved in a fight in Tucson, Arizona. What are some of the reasons that the arrest rate for female juveniles has increased over the past few decades?
Photo by Scott Olson/Getty Images

FAMILY-BASED DELINQUENCY Criminologists disagree on whether rising arrest rates for female juveniles reflect a change in behavior or a change in law enforcement practices. A significant amount of data supports the latter proposal, especially research showing that police are much more likely to make arrests in situations involving domestic violence than they were even a decade ago. Experts have found that girls are four times more apt to fight with parents or siblings than are boys, who usually engage in violent encounters with strangers. Consequently, a large percentage of female juvenile arrests for assault arise out of family disputes—arrests that until relatively recently would not have been made.[35]

Evidence also shows that law enforcement agents continue to treat girls more harshly for some status offenses. More girls than boys are arrested for the status offense of running away from home,[36] for example, even though studies show that male and female juveniles run away from home with equal frequency.[37] Criminologists who focus on issues of gender hypothesize that such behavior is considered normal for boys, but is seen as deviant for girls and therefore more deserving of punishment.[38]

LEARNING 5 OBJECTIVE Explain how law enforcement's emphasis on domestic violence has influenced female juvenile arrest patterns.

School Violence and Bullying

One Thursday morning in January 2013, sixteen-year-old Bryan Oliver walked into a science class at Taft Union High School in Kern County, California, with a shotgun. Oliver opened fire, wounding one student, and was later charged with premeditated attempted murder. The incident was every student's (and teacher's and parent's) worst nightmare. Like other episodes of school violence, it received heavy media coverage, fanning fears that our schools are unsafe.

SAFE SCHOOLS Research does show that juvenile victimization and delinquency rates increase during the school day, and the most common juvenile crimes, such as simple assaults, are most likely to take place on school grounds.[39] In spite of well-publicized mass shootings such as the one that took place at Sandy Hook Elementary School in Newtown, Connecticut, in December 2012, however, violent crime is not commonplace in American schools. In fact, school-age youths are more than fifty times more likely to be murdered away from school than on a campus.[40] Furthermore, between 1995 and 2011, victimization rates of students for nonfatal crimes at school declined significantly, meaning that, in general, schools are safer today than they were in the recent past.[41]

For the most part, these statistics mirror the downward trend of all criminal activity in the United States since the mid-1990s. In addition, since the fatal shootings of fourteen students and a teacher at Columbine High School near Littleton, Colorado, in 1999, many schools have improved security measures. From 1999 to 2011, the percentage of American schools using security cameras to monitor their campuses increased from 19 to 61 percent. Today, 92 percent of public schools control access to school buildings by locking or monitoring their doors.[42] Furthermore, many districts rely on law enforcement officers to patrol school grounds, a controversial practice that we will cover in the *CJ in Action* feature at the end of the chapter.

The Columbine shootings also led many schools to adopt "zero tolerance" policies when it comes to student behavior. These policies require strict punitive measures, such as suspension, expulsion, or referral to the police, for *any* breach of the school's disciplinary code. On January 2, 2013, for instance, a first-grader at Roscoe Nix Elementary School in Silver Spring, Maryland, was suspended for pointing his fingers in the shape of a gun. Finally, the increasing number of high-profile shootings on school grounds has spurred students themselves to take preventive action. Such was the case in December 2012 when students at Laurel High School in Laurel, Maryland, warned authorities about a classmate's increasingly disturbing behavior. School security searched the young man's locker, finding graphs, charts, and diagrams suggesting a future attack.

BULLIED STUDENTS According to Kern County law enforcement officials, Bryan Oliver, mentioned at the beginning of this section, did not choose his targets in the science class at random. Oliver was specifically trying to harm two students who had *bullied* him for his social awkwardness and bookishness. Broadly defined as repeated, aggressive behavior with physical (hitting, punching, and spitting) and verbal (teasing, name calling, and spreading false rumors) components, **bullying** has traditionally been seen more as an inevitable rite of passage than as deviant behavior. In recent years, however, society has become more aware of the negative consequences of bullying, underscored by a number of high-profile "bullycides." In April 2012, for example, fourteen-year-old Kenneth Weishuhn hanged himself in the garage of his home in Primghar, Iowa, after being subjected to anti-gay slurs at South O'Brien High School. Weishuhn was at least the fifth American teenage boy to commit suicide after being bullied about his sexuality since 2009.

According to data gathered by the federal government, 28 percent of students aged twelve to eighteen have been victims of bullying.[43] In particular, gay students are targeted—nine out of ten report being bullied each year.[44] As a response to this problem, every state but Montana has passed anti-bullying legislation. These laws focus mostly on "soft" measures, such as training school personnel how to recognize and respond to bullying.[45] As yet, state legislatures have been reluctant to take "harder" measures such as specifically defining bullying as a crime. For instance, no criminal charges were filed against the students who repeatedly harassed Kenneth Weishuhn before his death.

Such harder measures may ultimately come in response to civil lawsuits filed by parents of bullied children across the country. In March 2010, for example, thirteen-year-old Jon Carmichael of Cleburne, Texas, hanged himself after multiple acts of torment by fellow students, including being thrown into a trash can and having his head flushed in a toilet. On the anniversary of their son's death in 2011, Carmichael's parents sued the Joshua Independent School District for $20 million, claiming that staff and students were aware of the bullying on school grounds and did nothing to prevent it.[46]

Although it is not clear whether bullying in general is more prevalent now than in the past, one form of bullying is definitely on the rise. As the Internet, texting, and social networking sites such as Facebook have become integral parts of youth culture, so, it seems, has cyberbullying. Studies have shown that between one-fifth and one-third of American teenagers are targets of cyberbullying, which occurs when a person uses computers, smartphones, or other electronic devices to inflict willful and repeated emotional harm.

Cyberbullying returned to the national spotlight in September 2012 when fifteen-year-old Audrie Pott of Saratoga, California, committed suicide after photos of a sexual assault in which she was the victim were disseminated via smartphone. Pott was the fourth young woman in the United States and Canada since 2009 to take her life as a result of this sort of humiliation. To many, cyberbullying can be even more devastating than "old school" bullying. Not only does the anonymity of cyberspace seem to embolden perpetrators, causing them to be more vicious than they might be in person, but, as one expert points out, when bullying occurs online, "you can't get away from it."

Cheryl E. Davis/Shutterstock

Thinking about Cyberbullying

How should the criminal justice system respond to cyberbullying, if at all?

SELF ASSESSMENT

Fill in the blanks and check your answers on page 520.

The crime rate for juveniles has generally been _____ for more than a decade. Despite this trend, more _____ are getting involved with the juvenile justice system today than at any time in recent history. _____ violence is another area in which crime rates have dropped since the 1990s, thanks, in part, to greater security measures such as surveillance cameras and locked building doors. _____, in both its traditional and electronic forms, remains a problem, however, and is increasingly being addressed by school administrators and state legislators.

FACTORS IN JUVENILE DELINQUENCY

As we discussed in Chapter 2, an influential study conducted by Professor Marvin Wolfgang and several colleagues in the early 1970s introduced the "chronic 6 percent" to criminology. The researchers found that out of one hundred boys, six will become chronic offenders, meaning that they are arrested five or more times before their eighteenth birthdays. Furthermore, Wolfgang and his colleagues determined that these chronic offenders are responsible for half of all crimes and two-thirds of all violent crimes within any given cohort (a group of persons who have similar characteristics).[47] Does this "6 percent rule" mean that no matter what steps society takes, six out of every hundred juveniles are "bad seeds" and will act delinquently? Or does it point to a situation in which a small percentage of children may be more likely to commit crimes under certain circumstances?

Most criminologists favor the second interpretation. In this section, we will examine the four factors that have traditionally been used to explain juvenile criminal behavior and violent crime rates: age, substance abuse, family problems, and gangs. Keep in mind, however, that the factors influencing delinquency are not limited to these topics

Aging Out A term used to explain the fact that criminal activity declines with age.

Age of Onset The age at which a juvenile first exhibits delinquent behavior.

(see Figure 15.4 below). Researchers are constantly interpreting and reinterpreting statistical evidence to provide fresh perspectives on this very important issue.

For example, Dutch criminologists have proposed the Music Marker Theory to explain correlations between listening to certain types of music and juvenile delinquency. This theory holds that twelve-year-olds who prefer music that is associated with rebellion (heavy metal, gothic, punk, hip-hop) are more likely to exhibit delinquent behavior when they are older than adolescents who prefer conventional music such as pop or "highbrow" music such as classical or jazz. These criminologists believe that, at such a young age, most children have few opportunities to break society's rules. Children can decide what music they prefer, however, and this choice may be an early sign of rebellious or antisocial tendencies.[48]

The Age-Crime Relationship

Crime statistics are fairly conclusive on one point: the older a person is, the less likely he or she will exhibit criminal behavior. Self-reported studies confirm that most people are involved in some form of criminal behavior—however "harmless"—during their early years. In fact, Terrie Moffitt of Duke University has said that "it is statistically aberrant to refrain from crime during adolescence."[49] So, why do the vast majority of us not become chronic offenders?

According to many criminologists, particularly Travis Hirschi and Michael Gottfredson, any group of at-risk persons—regardless of gender, race, intelligence, or class—will commit fewer crimes as they grow older.[50] This process is known as **aging out** (or, sometimes, *desistance,* a term we first encountered in the previous chapter). Professor Robert J. Sampson and his colleague John H. Laub believe that this phenomenon is explained by certain events, such as marriage, employment, and military service, which force delinquents to "grow up" and forgo criminal acts.[51]

Another view sees the **age of onset,** or the age at which the youth begins delinquent behavior, as a consistent predictor of future criminal behavior. One study compared recidivism rates between juveniles first judged to be delinquent before the age of fifteen and those first adjudicated delinquent after the age of fifteen. Of the seventy-one subjects who made up the first group, 32 percent became chronic offenders. Of the sixty-five who made up the second group, none became chronic offenders.[52] Furthermore, according to the Office of Juvenile Justice and Delinquency Prevention, the earlier a youth enters the juvenile justice system, the more likely he or she will become a violent offender.[53] This research suggests that juvenile justice resources should be concentrated on the youngest offenders, with the goal of preventing crime and reducing the long-term risks for society.

Describe the one variable that always correlates highly with juvenile crime rates. — LEARNING OBJECTIVE 6

FIGURE 15.4 Risk Factors for Juvenile Delinquency

The characteristics listed here are generally accepted as "risk factors" for juvenile delinquency. In other words if one or more of these factors are present in a juvenile's life, he or she has a greater chance of exhibiting delinquent behavior— though such behavior is by no means a certainty.

Family	• Single parent/lack of parental role model • Parental or sibling drug/alcohol abuse • Extreme economic deprivation • Family members in a gang or in prison
School	• Academic frustration/failure • Learning disability • Negative labeling by teachers • Disciplinary problems
Community	• Social disorganization (refer to Chapter 2) • Presence of gangs and obvious drug use in the community • Availability of firearms • High crime/constant feeling of danger • Lack of social and economic opportunities
Peers	• Delinquent friends • Friends who use drugs or who are members of gangs • Lack of "positive" peer pressure
Individual	• Tendency toward aggressive behavior • Inability to concentrate or focus/easily bored/hyperactive • Alcohol or drug use • Fatalistic/pessimistic viewpoint

Substance Abuse

As we have seen throughout this textbook, substance abuse plays a strong role in criminal behavior for adults. The same can certainly be said for juveniles. According to the University of

Michigan's Institute for Social Research, 27 percent of American tenth-graders and 40 percent of American twelfth-graders are regular alcohol drinkers, increasing their risks for violent behavior, delinquency, academic problems, and unsafe sexual behavior.[54] Regular marijuana use among high school seniors reached a thirty-year high in 2011, and more juveniles are abusing synthetic drugs (described in Chapter 2) than ever before.[55] (See Figure 15.5 on the right for an overview of juvenile drug use in the United States.)

A STRONG CORRELATION As with adults, substance abuse among juveniles seems to play a major role in offending. Drug use is associated with a wide range of antisocial and illegal behaviors by juveniles, from school suspensions to large-scale theft.[56] Nearly all young offenders (94 percent) entering juvenile detention self-report drug use at some point in their lives, and 85 percent have used drugs in the previous six months.[57] According to the Arrestee Drug Abuse Monitoring Program, nearly 60 percent of male juvenile detainees and 46 percent of female juvenile detainees test positive for drug use at the time of their offense.[58] Drug use is a particularly strong risk factor for girls: 75 percent of young women incarcerated in juvenile facilities report regular drug and alcohol use—starting at the age of fourteen—and one study found that 87 percent of female teenage offenders need substance abuse treatment.[59]

STRONG CAUSATION? The correlation between substance abuse and offending for juveniles seems obvious. Does this mean that substance abuse *causes* juvenile offending? Researchers make the point that most youths who become involved in antisocial behavior do so before their first experience with alcohol or drugs. Therefore, it would appear that substance abuse is a form of delinquent behavior rather than its cause.[60] Still, a recent study of adolescent offenders did find that substance abuse treatment reduces criminal behavior in the short term, suggesting that, at the least, the use of illegal drugs is an integral component of the juvenile delinquent lifestyle.[61]

Child Abuse and Neglect

Abuse by parents also plays a substantial role in juvenile delinquency. **Child abuse** can be broadly defined as the infliction of physical or emotional damage on a child. Similar though not the same, **child neglect** refers to deprivations—of love, shelter, food, and proper care—children undergo by their parents. According to the National Survey of Children's Exposure to Violence, one in ten children in the United States experience mistreatment at the hands of a close family member.[62]

Children in homes characterized by violence or neglect suffer from a variety of physical, emotional, and mental health problems at a much greater rate than their peers.[63] This, in turn, increases their chances of engaging in delinquent behavior. One survey of violent juveniles showed that 75 percent had been subjected to severe abuse by a family member and 80 percent had witnessed violence in their homes.[64] Nearly half of all juveniles—and 80 percent of girls—sentenced to life in prison suffered high rates of abuse.[65]

FIGURE 15.5 Drug Use among Juveniles

Among Americans aged twelve to seventeen, the percentage who admit to using illegal drugs in the past month dropped each year from 2002 to 2008 before rising in 2009 and holding steady in the two years that followed.

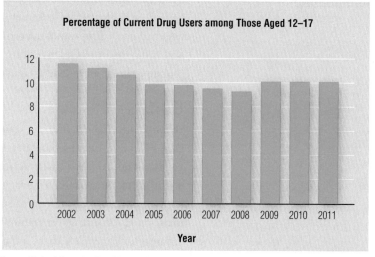

Percentage of Current Drug Users among Those Aged 12–17

Source: National Survey on Drug Use and Health, 2003–2012.

Child Abuse Mistreatment of children by causing physical, emotional, or sexual damage without any plausible explanation, such as an accident.

Child Neglect A form of child abuse in which the child is denied certain necessities such as shelter, food, care, and love.

Cathy Spatz Widom, currently a professor of psychology at John Jay College of Criminal Justice, compared the arrest records of two groups of subjects—one made up of 908 cases of substantiated parental abuse and neglect and the other made up of 667 children who had not been abused or neglected. Widom found that those who had been abused or neglected were 53 percent more likely to be arrested as juveniles than those who had not.[66] Simply put, according to researchers Janet Currie of Columbia University and Erdal Tekin of Georgia State University, "child maltreatment roughly doubles the probability that an individual engages in many types of crime."[67]

Gangs

When youths cannot find the stability and support they require in the family structure, they will often turn to their peers. This is just one explanation for why juveniles join **youth gangs.** Although jurisdictions may have varying definitions, for general purposes a youth gang is viewed as a group of three or more persons who (1) self-identify as an entity separate from the community by special clothing, vocabulary, hand signals, and names and (2) engage in criminal activity. According to an exhaustive survey of law enforcement agencies, there are probably around 33,000 gangs with approximately 1.4 million members in the United States.[68]

Juveniles who have experienced the risk factors discussed in this section are more likely to join a gang, and once they have done so, they are more likely to engage in delinquent and violent behavior than nongang members.[69] Statistics show high levels of gang involvement in most violent criminal activities in the United States.[70] One-half of all murders in Chicago and one-third of all murders in Los Angeles are gang related.[71] Furthermore, a study of criminal behavior among juveniles in Seattle found that gang members were considerably more likely to commit crimes than at-risk youths who shared many characteristics with gang members but were not affiliated with any gang (see Figure 15.6 below).

WHO JOINS GANGS? The average gang member is seventeen to eighteen years old, though members tend to be older in cities with long traditions of gang activity such as Chicago

FIGURE 15.6 Comparison of Gang and Nongang Delinquent Behavior

Taking self-reported surveys of subjects aged thirteen to eighteen in the Seattle area, researchers for the Office of Juvenile Justice and Delinquency Prevention found that gang members were much more likely to exhibit delinquent behavior than nongang members.

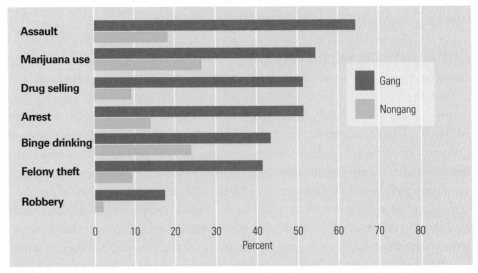

Source: Karl G. Hill, Christina Lui, and J. David Hawkins, *Early Precursors of Gang Membership: A Study of Seattle Youth* (Washington, D.C.: Office of Juvenile Justice and Delinquency Prevention, December 2001), Figure 1, page 2.

and Los Angeles. Although it is difficult to determine with any certainty the makeup of gangs as a whole, one recent survey found that 49 percent of all gang members in the United States are Hispanic, 35 percent are African American, and 9 percent are white, with the remaining 7 percent belonging to other racial or ethnic backgrounds.[72]

Though gangs tend to have racial or ethnic characteristics—that is, one group predominates in each gang—many researchers do not believe that race or ethnicity is the dominant factor in gang membership. Instead, gang members seem to come from lower-class or working-class communities, mostly in urban areas but with an increasing number from the suburbs and rural counties. In addition, researchers are finding that adolescents who will eventually join a gang display significantly higher levels of delinquent behavior than those who will never become involved in gang activity.[73]

A very small percentage of youth gang members are female. In many instances, girls associate themselves with gangs, even though they are not considered members. Generally, girls assume subordinate gender roles in youth gangs, providing emotional, physical, and sexual services for the dominant males.[74] Still, almost half of all youth gangs report having female members, and, as in other areas of juvenile crime and delinquency, involvement of girls in gangs is increasing.[75]

■ In Los Angeles, a gang member signifies his allegiance to the "Street Villains" through a series of elaborate tattoos. What role does identity play in a juvenile's decision to join a gang?
Kevork Djansezian/Getty Images

WHY DO YOUTHS JOIN GANGS? Gang membership often appears to be linked with status in the community. This tends to be true of both males and females. Many teenagers, feeling alienated from their families and communities, join gangs for the social relationships and the sense of identity a gang can provide.

LEARNING
7
OBJECTIVE

Indicate some of the reasons why youths join gangs.

A number of youths, especially those who live in high-crime neighborhoods, see gang membership as a necessity—joining a gang is a form of protection against violence from other gangs. For example, Mara Salvatrucha (MS-13) was formed by the children of immigrants who fled the civil war of El Salvador for Los Angeles in the 1980s. Finding themselves easy prey for the established local gangs, these young Salvadorans started MS-13 as a protective measure.

Excitement is another attraction of the gang life, as is the economic incentive of enjoying the profits from illegal gang activities such as dealing drugs or robbery. Finally, some teenagers are forced to join gangs by the threat of violence from gang members.

Guns

The Seattle survey represented in Figure 15.6 also found that gang members were much more likely to own firearms or have friends who did than nongang members.[76] Indeed, recent research shows that urban minority youths who are gang members and have engaged in violent behavior are six times more likely to own a gun than those urban minority youths who avoid such activities.[77] Gang members are also much more likely to believe that they need a gun for protection and to be involved in gun-related crimes.[78]

The harmful link between juveniles and guns is hardly limited to gang members, however. Indeed, one explanation for the increase in youth violence in the late 1980s and early 1990s points to the unprecedented access minors had to illegal weapons during that time. According to Carnegie Mellon University's Alfred Blumstein:

> [Y]outh have always fought with each other. But when it's a battle with fists, the dynamics run much more slowly. With a gun, it evolves very rapidly, too fast for a third party to intervene. That also raises the stakes and encourages others to arm themselves, thereby triggering a preemptive strike: "I better get him before he gets me."[79]

The role that guns play in exacerbating school violence is particularly troubling. From January 1, 2013, to February 1, 2013, there were almost fifty incidents in the United States in which guns were found on students at school or in their lockers.[80] According to the Centers for Disease Control, 8.6 percent of male students and 1.4 percent of female students will carry a gun at least once during any given year.[81]

SELF ASSESSMENT

Fill in the blanks and check your answers on page 520.

Criminologists have identified a number of _____ factors that increase the probability of juvenile misbehavior. One is youth. Studies of a process called _____ _____ show that children commit fewer offenses as they grow older. According to two researchers, _____ _____ at the hands of parents or guardians doubles the chances of delinquency. Youth who become involved in _____ are also more likely to engage in criminal activity than those who do not.

FIRST CONTACT: THE POLICE AND PRETRIAL PROCEDURES

As part of the Juvenile Robbery Intervention Program, New York City detectives spend hours monitoring the Facebook pages and Twitter accounts of teenagers at risk for gang involvement and violent crime. Most commonly, however, contact between juvenile offenders and law enforcement takes place on the streets, initiated by a police officer on patrol who either apprehends the juvenile while he or she is committing a crime or answers a call for service. (See Figure 15.7 on the facing page for an overview of the juvenile justice process.) The youth is then passed on to an officer of the juvenile court, who must decide how to handle the case.

Police Discretion and Juvenile Crime

Police arrest about 1.1 million youths under the age of eighteen each year. In most states, police officers must have probable cause to believe that the minor has committed an offense, just as they would if the suspect was an adult. Police power with regard to juveniles is greater than with adults, however, because police can take youths into custody for status offenses, such as possession of alcohol or truancy. In these cases, the officer is acting *in loco parentis,* or in the place of the parent. The officer's role is not necessarily to punish the youths, but to protect them from harmful behavior.

LOW-VISIBILITY DECISION MAKING Police officers also have a great deal of discretion in deciding what to do with juveniles who have committed crimes or status offenses. Juvenile justice expert Joseph Goldstein labels this discretionary power **low-visibility decision making** because it relies on factors that the public is not generally in a position to understand or criticize. When a grave offense has taken place, a police officer may decide to formally arrest the juvenile, send him or her to juvenile court, or place the youth under the care of a social-service organization. In less serious situations, the

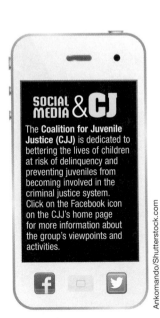

FIGURE 15.7 The Juvenile Justice Process

This diagram shows the possible tracks that a young person may take after her or his first contact with the juvenile justice system (usually a police officer).

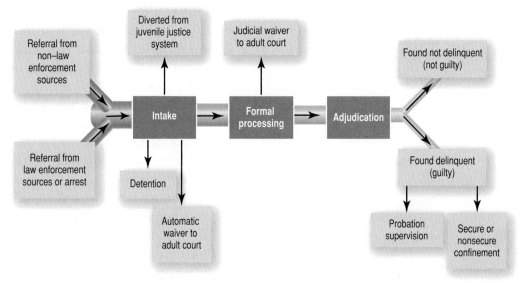

Source: Office of Juvenile Justice and Delinquency Prevention.

officer may simply issue a warning or take the offender to the police station and release the child into the custody of her or his parents.

In making these discretionary decisions, police generally consider the following factors:

LEARNING **8** OBJECTIVE List the factors that normally determine what police do with juvenile offenders.

- The nature of the child's offense.
- The offender's past history of involvement with the juvenile justice system.
- The setting in which the offense took place.
- The ability and willingness of the child's parents to take disciplinary action.
- The attitude of the offender.
- The offender's race and gender.

Law enforcement officers notify the juvenile court system that a particular young person requires its attention through a process known as a **referral.** Anyone with a valid reason, including parents, relatives, welfare agencies, and school officials, can refer a juvenile to the juvenile court. The vast majority of cases in juvenile courts, however, are referred by the police.[82]

ARRESTS AND MINORITY YOUTHS
As in other areas of the criminal justice system, members of minority groups are disproportionately represented in juvenile arrests. The violent crime arrest rate for African American juveniles is about four times that for white juveniles, and the property arrest crime rate for black juveniles is double that of whites. Furthermore, African American juveniles are referred to juvenile court twice as often as their white peers.[83]

A great deal of research, much of it contradictory, has been done to determine whether these statistics reflect inherent racism in the juvenile justice system or whether social factors are to blame.[84] One large-scale study, performed by federal government crime researchers Carl E. Pope and Howard Snyder using the National Incident-Based Reporting System, found that nonwhite offenders were no more likely than white offenders to be arrested for the same delinquent behavior.[85]

Referral The notification process through which a law enforcement officer or other concerned citizen makes the juvenile court aware of a juvenile's unlawful or unruly conduct.

FIGURE 15.8 Juvenile Arrest Rates by Race

Using the FBI's Uniform Crime Report, statisticians can determine the rates of arrest for persons aged ten to seventeen in the United States. As you can see, the rate of arrests per 100,000 juveniles remains considerably higher for African Americans than for other racial groups.

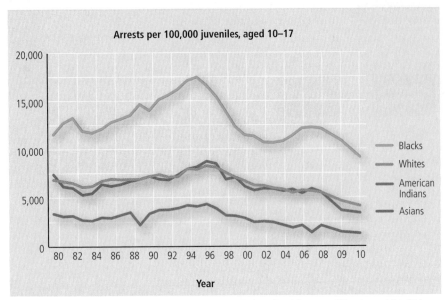

Arrests per 100,000 juveniles, aged 10–17

Legend:
- Blacks
- Whites
- American Indians
- Asians

Year

Source: Office of Juvenile Justice and Delinquency Prevention, "Juvenile Arrest Trends," at **www.ojjdp.ncjrs.org/ojstatbb/crime/JAR_Display.asp?ID=qa05260&text=yes**.

FAILING THE "ATTITUDE TEST" In general, though, as Figure 15.8 on the left shows, police officers do seem more likely to arrest members of minority groups. Although this may be partially attributed to the social factors discussed in Chapter 2, it also appears that minority youths often fail the "attitude test" during interactions with police officers. After the seriousness of the offense and past history, the most important factor in the decision of whether to arrest or release appears to be the offender's attitude. An offender who is polite and apologetic generally has a better chance of being released. If the juvenile is hostile or unresponsive, the police are more likely to place him or her in custody for even a minor offense.[86]

Furthermore, police officers who do not live in the same community with minority youths may misinterpret normal behavior as disrespectful or delinquent and act accordingly.[87] This "culture gap" is of crucial importance to police-juvenile relations and underscores the community-oriented policing goal of having law enforcement agents be more involved in the communities they patrol, as we discussed in Chapter 6.

Juveniles and *Miranda* Rights

The privacy and *Miranda* rights of juveniles are protected during contact with law enforcement officers, though not to the same extent as for adults. In most jurisdictions, the Fourth Amendment ban against unreasonable searches and seizures and Fifth Amendment safeguards against custodial self-incrimination apply to juveniles. In other words, juvenile court judges cannot use illegally seized evidence in juvenile hearings, and police must read youths their *Miranda* rights after arrest.

In *Fare v. Michael C.* (1979),[88] the Supreme Court clarified law enforcement officials' responsibilities with regard to *Miranda* warnings and juveniles. The case involved a boy who had been arrested on suspicion of murder. After being read his rights, the youth asked to speak to his probation officer. The request was denied. The boy eventually confessed to the crime. The Court ruled that juveniles may waive their right to protection against self-incrimination and that admissions made to the police in the absence of counsel are admissible.

More recently, in *J.D.B. v. North Carolina* (2011),[89] the Court was asked to review a case involving a thirteen-year-old student who was pulled from class by a uniformed police officer and questioned about items stolen from neighboring homes. The student eventually confessed to his involvement in the burglaries. His lawyers challenged the resulting conviction on the ground that their client was never read his *Miranda* rights. The Court ruled that age is not a *decisive* factor in determining whether a suspect believes himself or herself to be "in custody" for purposes of interrogation. (See Chapter 7 to review the

Miranda procedure.) It is a *relevant* factor, however, given that a reasonable juvenile may view the circumstances differently than would a reasonable adult.[90] As can be seen in the feature *A Question of Ethics—Interrogating Children* below, police may be taking a chance if they rely on the testimony of young suspects and witnesses.

Intake

As noted earlier, if, following arrest, a police officer feels the offender warrants the attention of the juvenile justice process, the officer will refer the youth to juvenile court. Once this step has been taken, a complaint is filed with a special division of the juvenile court, and the **intake** process begins. Intake may be followed by diversion to a community-based program, transfer to an adult court, or detention to await trial in juvenile court. Thus, intake, diversion, transfer, and detention are the four primary stages of pretrial juvenile justice procedure.

During intake, an official of the juvenile court—usually a probation officer, but sometimes a judge—must decide, in effect, what to do with the offender. The intake officer has several options during intake.

1. Simply dismiss the case, releasing the offender without taking any further action. This occurs in about one in five cases, usually because the judge cannot determine a sufficient reason to continue.[91]
2. Divert the offender to a social-services program, such as drug rehabilitation or anger management.
3. File a **petition** for a formal court hearing. The petition is the formal document outlining the charges against the juvenile.
4. Transfer the case to an adult court, where the offender will be tried as an adult.

Intake The process by which an official of the court must decide whether to file a petition, release the juvenile, or place the juvenile under some other form of supervision.

Petition The document filed with a juvenile court alleging that the juvenile is a delinquent or a status offender and requesting that the court either hear the case or transfer it to an adult court.

LEARNING
9
OBJECTIVE
Describe the four primary stages of pretrial juvenile justice procedure.

A QUESTION OF ETHICS — Interrogating Children

THE SITUATION The body of an eleven-year-old girl named Ryan Harris has been found in a lot behind an empty building. Evidence shows that Ryan was beaten and sexually assaulted before her death. Chicago police believe that a seven-year-old boy has knowledge of the circumstances surrounding the murder. Two detectives isolate the boy in an empty room at the police station and ask him if he knows what a lie is. "You should never lie," the boy answers.

Each of the detectives takes one of the boy's hands and asks him about Harris. The seven-year-old admits to throwing a brick at the girl and knocking her off her bicycle, and then dragging her body into the weeds with the help of an eight-year-old friend. After corroborating the story with this accomplice, the police detain the boys and classify the case of Ryan Harris as "Cleared/Closed by Arrest."

THE ETHICAL DILEMMA The law allows police to interrogate a juvenile of any age without a parent or guardian being present. In these situations, the police must only make a "reasonable attempt" to contact the parents, after which they can question the child. Indeed, as we saw in the text, the rules for interrogating juveniles are almost indistinguishable from those that apply to adults.

Police questioning of children does, however, raise ethical and practical questions. How can children as young as the ones involved in this case understand the concept or consequences of waiving their *Miranda* rights, as both boys did? Isn't any situation in which police officers are alone in a room with a child inherently coercive?

WHAT IS THE SOLUTION? How reliable do you consider the statements of juveniles, especially those as young as the boys in the Harris murder? Regardless of the law, how should police approach the interrogation of children who may not fully understand the concept of constitutional rights? (In this case, although the police did not break any rules, their strategy backfired. After a forensic examination found semen—which boys so young could not have produced—on the girl's torn underwear, the suspects were immediately released and the investigation reopened.)

Manfredxy/Shutterstock.com

Judicial Waiver The process in which the juvenile judge, based on the facts of the case at hand, decides that the alleged offender should be transferred to adult court.

Automatic Transfer The process by which a juvenile is transferred to adult court as a matter of state law.

With regard to status offenses, judges have sole discretion to decide whether to process the case or *divert* the youth to another juvenile service agency.

Pretrial Diversion

In the early 1970s, Congress passed the first Juvenile Justice and Delinquency Prevention (JJDP) Act, which ordered the development of methods "to divert juveniles from the traditional juvenile justice system."[92] Within a few years, hundreds of diversion programs had been put into effect. Today, diversion refers to the process of removing low-risk offenders from the formal juvenile justice system by placing them in community-based rehabilitation programs.

Diversion programs vary widely, but fall into three general categories:

1. *Probation.* In this program, the juvenile is returned to the community, but placed under the supervision of a juvenile probation officer. If the youth breaks the conditions of probation, he or she can be returned to the formal juvenile system.
2. *Treatment and aid.* Many juveniles have behavioral or medical conditions that contribute to their delinquent behavior, and many diversion programs offer remedial education, drug and alcohol treatment, and other forms of counseling to alleviate these problems.
3. *Restitution.* In these programs, the offender "repays" her or his victim, either directly or symbolically through community service.[93]

Proponents of diversion programs include many labeling theorists (see Chapter 2), who believe that contact with the formal juvenile justice system "labels" the youth a delinquent, which leads to further delinquent behavior. Increasingly, juvenile justice practitioners are relying on principles of restorative justice (see Chapter 11) to divert adolescents from formal institutions. For example, in Barron County, Wisconsin, delinquents have access to victim-offender conferences, underage drinking and anger-management workshops, and group intervention courses for chronic offenders.[94] Juvenile drug courts, modeled on the adult drug courts we discussed in Chapter 12, have also had some success in this area.[95]

Transfer to Adult Court

One side effect of diversionary programs is that the youths who remain in the juvenile courts are more likely to be seen as "hardened" and thus less amenable to rehabilitation. This, in turn, increases the likelihood that the offender will be transferred to an adult court, a process in which the juvenile court waives jurisdiction over the youth. As the American juvenile justice system has shifted away from ideals of treatment and toward punishment, transfer to adult court has been one of the most popular means of "getting tough" on delinquents.

METHODS OF TRANSFER There are three types of transfer laws, and most states use more than one of them depending on the jurisdiction and the seriousness of the offense. Juveniles are most commonly transferred to adult courts through **judicial waiver,** in which the juvenile judge is given the power to determine whether a young offender's case will be waived to adult court. The judge makes this decision based on the offender's age, the nature of the offense, and any criminal history. All but five states employ judicial waiver.

Twenty-nine states have taken the waiver responsibility out of judicial hands through **automatic transfer,** also known as *legislative waiver.* In these states, the legislatures have designated certain conditions—usually involving serious crimes such as murder and rape—under which a juvenile case is automatically "kicked up" to adult court.

In Rhode Island, for example, a juvenile aged sixteen or older with two prior felony adjudications will automatically be transferred on being accused of a third felony.[96]

Fifteen states also allow for **prosecutorial waiver,** in which prosecutors are allowed to choose whether to initiate proceedings in juvenile or criminal court when certain age and offense conditions are met. In twenty-five states, criminal court judges also have the freedom to send juveniles who were transferred to adult court back to juvenile court. Known as *reverse transfer* statutes, these laws are designed to provide judges with a measure of discretion even when automatic transfer takes place.

INCIDENCE OF TRANSFER Each year, about 8,000 delinquency cases are waived to adult criminal court—less than 0.5 percent of all cases that reach juvenile court.[97] As we saw earlier in the chapter, those juveniles who commit the most violent felonies are the most likely to be transferred. For example, when she was thirteen years old, Tyasia Jackson was arrested for killing her two-year-old step-sister Sasha Ray in Waldrop Trail, Georgia. Under state law, prosecutors have the discretion to charge thirteen-year-olds who have committed capital crimes either as juveniles as adults.[98] In this case, given that Jackson stabbed Ray seven times and then left her in the backyard of their family home, prosecutors decided that the defendant warranted transfer to adult court.

TRANSFER AND ADULT CORRECTIONS Proponents of transferring juveniles to the adult justice system contend that violent juvenile offenders pose a risk to nonviolent offenders in juvenile detention centers. Thus, their removal makes the juvenile justice system safer. Critics of the practice point out that, by the same token, adult prisons and jails can be very dangerous places for young offenders. Research shows that juveniles in jails have the highest suicide rates of all inmates and suffer disproportionate levels of physical and sexual abuse.[99]

Data also indicate that juveniles transferred to adult correctional facilities have higher recidivism rates than those who remain in the juvenile justice system.[100] Experts have several theories to explain this pattern, including the negative effect of labeling juveniles as "felons" (to review labeling theory, see Chapter 2) and the decreased opportunities for family support in adult correctional facilities.[101] Furthermore, evidence suggests that younger inmates will gain knowledge of the criminal lifestyle from older, more experienced prisoners. "You can learn a whole lot more bad things in here than good," said one juvenile inmate from his cell in an Arizona adult prison.[102]

Detention

Once the decision has been made that the offender will face adjudication in a juvenile court, the intake official must decide what to do with him or her until the start of the trial. Generally, the juvenile is released into the custody of parents or a guardian—most

Inmates at the Beaumont Juvenile Correctional Center in Beaumont, Virginia, take part in a Russian literature class. What are some of the arguments for keeping juvenile offenders separate from adult inmates? In your opinion, under what circumstances should juvenile offenders be sent to adult correctional facilities? Photo by Bonnie Jo Mount/*The Washington Post* via Getty Images

Prosecutorial Waiver A procedure used in situations where the prosecutor has discretion to decide whether a case will be heard by a juvenile court or an adult court.

jurisdictions favor this practice in lieu of setting money bail for youths. The intake officer may also place the offender in **detention,** or temporary custody in a secure facility, until the disposition process begins. Once a juvenile has been detained, most jurisdictions require that a **detention hearing** be held within twenty-four hours. During this hearing, the offender has several due process safeguards, including the right to counsel, the right against self-incrimination, and the right to cross-examine and confront witnesses.

In justifying its decision to detain, the court will usually address one of three issues:

1. Whether the child poses a danger to the community.
2. Whether the child will return for the adjudication process.
3. Whether detention will provide protection for the child.

The Supreme Court upheld the practice of preventive detention (see Chapter 9) for juveniles in *Schall v. Martin* (1984)[103] by ruling that youths can be detained if they are deemed a "risk" to the safety of the community or to their own welfare. Partly as a result, the number of detained juveniles increased by 29 percent between 1985 and 2009.[104]

SELF ASSESSMENT

Fill in the blanks and check your answers on page 520.

If the circumstances are serious enough, a police officer can formally _____ an offending juvenile. Otherwise, the officer can _____ the juvenile to the juvenile court system or place her or him in the care of a _____-service organization. During the _____ process, a judge or juvenile probation officer decides the immediate fate of the juvenile delinquent. One of the options is _____, in which low-risk offenders are placed in community rehabilitation programs. If the judge believes that the seriousness of the offense so warrants, he or she can transfer the juvenile into the adult court system through a process called judicial _____.

TRYING AND PUNISHING JUVENILES

In just over half of all referred cases, the juvenile is eventually subject to formal proceedings in juvenile court.[105] As noted earlier, changes in the juvenile justice system since *In re Gault* (1967) have led many to contend that juvenile courts have become indistinguishable, both theoretically and practically, from adult courts.[106] Just over half of the states, for example, permit juveniles to request a jury trial under certain circumstances. As the *Mastering Concepts* feature on the facing page explains, however, juvenile justice proceedings may still be distinguished from the adult system of criminal justice, and these differences are evident in the adjudication and disposition of the juvenile trial.

Adjudication

During the adjudication stage of the juvenile justice process, a hearing is held to determine whether the offender is delinquent or in need of some form of court supervision. Most state juvenile codes dictate a specific set of procedures that must be followed during the **adjudicatory hearing,** with the goal of providing the respondent with "the essentials of due process and fair treatment." Consequently, the respondent in an adjudicatory hearing has the right to notice of charges, counsel, and confrontation and cross-examination, and the privilege against self-incrimination. Furthermore, "proof beyond a reasonable doubt" must be established to find the child delinquent. When the child admits guilt—that is, admits to the charges of the initial petition—the judge must ensure that the admission was voluntary.

Explain the distinction between an adjudicatory hearing and a disposition hearing. **LEARNING OBJECTIVE 10**

MASTERING CONCEPTS
THE JUVENILE JUSTICE SYSTEM VERSUS THE CRIMINAL JUSTICE SYSTEM

AP Photo/Columbus Dispatch, James D. DeCamp

When the juvenile justice system was first established in the United States, its participants saw it as being separate from the adult criminal justice system. Indeed, the two systems remain separate in many ways. There are, however, a number of similarities between juvenile and adult justice. Here, we summarize both the similarities and the differences.

SIMILARITIES	DIFFERENCES		
		Juvenile System	**Adult System**
• The right to receive the *Miranda* warnings.	**Purpose**	Rehabilitation of the offender.	Punishment.
• Procedural protections when making an admission of guilt.	**Arrest**	Juveniles can be arrested for acts (status offenses) that are not criminal for adults.	Adults can be arrested only for acts made illegal by the relevant criminal code.
• Prosecutors and defense attorneys play equally important roles.	**Wrongdoing**	Considered a "delinquent act."	A crime.
	Proceedings	Informal; closed to public.	Formal and regimented; open to public.
• The right to be represented by counsel at the crucial stages of the trial process.	**Information**	Courts may NOT release information to the press.	Courts MUST release information to the press.
• Access to plea bargains.	**Parents**	Play significant role.	Play no role.
	Release	Into parent/guardian custody.	May post bail when appropriate.
• The right to a hearing and an appeal.	**Jury trial**	In some states, juveniles do NOT have this right.	All adults have this right.
• The standard of evidence is proof beyond a reasonable doubt.	**Searches**	Juveniles can be searched in school without probable cause.	No adult can be searched without probable cause.
• Offenders can be placed on probation by the judge.	**Records**	Juvenile's record is sealed at age of adult criminal responsibility.	Adult's criminal record is permanent.
• Offenders can be held before adjudication if the judge believes them to be a threat to the community.	**Sentencing**	Juveniles are placed in separate facilities from adults.	Adults are placed in county jails or state or federal prisons.
• Following trial, offenders can be sentenced to community supervision.	**Death penalty**	No death penalty.	Death penalty for certain serious crimes under certain circumstances.

At the close of the adjudicatory hearing, the judge is generally required to rule on the legal issues and evidence that have been presented. Based on this ruling, the judge determines whether the respondent is delinquent or in need of court supervision. Alternatively, the judge can dismiss the case based on a lack of evidence. It is important to remember that finding a child delinquent is *not* the same as convicting an adult of a crime. A delinquent does not face the same restrictions imposed on adult convicts in some states, such as limits on the right to vote and to run for political office (discussed in Chapter 13).

Disposition

Once a juvenile has been adjudicated delinquent, the judge must decide what steps will be taken toward treatment and/or punishment. Most states provide for a *bifurcated* process in which a separate **disposition hearing** follows the adjudicatory hearing. Depending on state law, the juvenile may be entitled to counsel at the disposition hearing.

Disposition Hearing Similar to the sentencing hearing for adults, a hearing in which the juvenile judge or officer decides the appropriate punishment for a youth found to be delinquent or a status offender.

Predisposition Report A report prepared during the disposition process that provides the judge with relevant background material to aid in the disposition decision.

Graduated Sanctions The practical theory in juvenile corrections that a delinquent or status offender should receive a punishment that matches in seriousness the severity of the wrongdoing.

SENTENCING JUVENILES In an adult trial, the sentencing phase is primarily concerned with the needs of the community to be protected from the convict. In contrast, a juvenile judge uses the disposition hearing to determine a sentence that will serve the needs of the child. For assistance in this crucial process, the judge will order the probation department to gather information on the juvenile and present it in the form of a **predisposition report.** The report usually contains information concerning the respondent's family background, the facts surrounding the delinquent act, and interviews with social workers, teachers, and other important figures in the child's life.

JUDICIAL DISCRETION In keeping with the rehabilitative tradition of the juvenile justice system, juvenile judges generally have a great deal of discretion in choosing one of several disposition possibilities. A judge can tend toward leniency, delivering only a stern reprimand or warning before releasing the juvenile into the custody of parents or other legal guardians. Otherwise, the choice is among incarceration in a juvenile correctional facility, probation, or community treatment. In most cases, the seriousness of the offense is the primary factor used in determining whether to incarcerate a juvenile, though history of delinquency, family situation, and the offender's attitude are all relevant.

Further indication of the treatment goals of juvenile courts can be found in the indeterminate sentencing practices that, until recently, dominated disposition. Under this system, correctional administrators were given the freedom to decide when a delinquent had been sufficiently rehabilitated and could be released. Today, nearly half of the states have enacted determinate or minimum mandatory sentencing laws that cover convicted juvenile offenders. Such statutes shift the focus of disposition from the treatment needs of the delinquent to society's desire to punish and incapacitate.

Juvenile Corrections

In general, juvenile corrections are based on the concept of **graduated sanctions**—that is, the severity of the punishment should fit the crime. Consequently, status and first-time offenders are diverted or placed on probation, repeat offenders find themselves in intensive community supervision or treatment programs, and serious and violent offenders are placed in correctional facilities.[107]

As society's expectations of the juvenile justice system have changed, so have the characteristics of its corrections programs. In some cities, for example, juvenile probation officers join police officers on the beat. Because the former are not bound by the same search and seizure restrictions as other law enforcement officials, this interdepartmental teamwork provides more opportunities to fight youth crime aggressively. Juvenile correctional facilities are also changing their operations to reflect public mandates that they should both reform and punish. Also, note that about 6,000 juveniles are in adult jails and another 25,000 are serving time in adult prisons.[108]

JUVENILE PROBATION The most common form of juvenile corrections is probation—33 percent of all delinquency cases disposed of by juvenile courts result in conditional diversion. The majority of all adjudicated delinquents (60 percent) will never receive a disposition more severe than being placed on probation.[109] These statistics reflect a general understanding among juvenile court judges and other officials that a child should normally be removed from her or his home only as a last resort.

The organization of juvenile probation is very similar to adult probation (see Chapter 12), and juvenile probationers are increasingly subjected to electronic monitoring and other supervisory tactics. The main difference between the two programs lies in the attitude toward the offender. Adult probation officers have an overriding responsibility to protect the community from the probationer, while juvenile probation officers are expected to take the role of a mentor or a concerned relative in looking after the needs of the child.

CONFINING JUVENILES About 70,000 American youths (down from approximately 107,000 in 1995) are incarcerated in public and private juvenile correctional facilities in the United States.[110] Most of these juveniles have committed crimes against people or property, but a significant number (about 15 percent) have been incarcerated for technical violations of their probation or parole agreements.[111] After deciding that a juvenile needs to be confined, the judge has two sentencing options: nonsecure juvenile institutions and secure juvenile institutions.

Juvenile inmates prepare to enter a dormitory at Texas's Marlin Orientation and Assessment Unit. What might be some of the reasons that juvenile correctional facilities often operate similarly to adult prisons and jails?
Michael Ainsworth/*Dallas Morning News*/Corbis

Nonsecure Confinement Some juvenile delinquents do not require high levels of control and can be placed in **residential treatment programs.** These programs, run by either probation departments or social-services departments, allow their subjects freedom of movement in the community. Generally, this freedom is predicated on the juveniles following certain rules, such as avoiding alcoholic beverages and returning to the facility for curfew. Residential treatment programs can be divided into four categories:

1. *Foster care programs,* in which the juveniles live with a couple who act as surrogate parents.
2. *Group homes,* which generally house between twelve and fifteen youths and provide treatment, counseling, and education services by a professional staff.
3. *Family group homes,* which combine aspects of foster care and group homes, meaning that a single family, rather than a group of professionals, looks after the needs of the young offenders.
4. *Rural programs,* which include wilderness camps, farms, and ranches where between thirty and fifty children are placed in an environment that provides recreational activities and treatment programs.

Secure Confinement Secure facilities are comparable to the adult prisons and jails we discussed in Chapters 13 and 14. These institutions go by a confusing array of names depending on the state in which they are located, but the two best known are boot camps and training schools. A **boot camp** is the juvenile variation of shock probation.

As we noted in Chapter 12, boot camps are modeled after military training for new recruits. Boot camp programs are based on the theory that by giving wayward youths a taste of the "hard life" of military-like training for short periods of time, usually no longer than 180 days, they will be "shocked" out of a life of crime. New York's Camp Monterey Shock Incarceration Facility is typical of the boot camp experience. Inmates are grouped in platoons and live in dormitories. They spend eight hours a day training, drilling, and

Residential Treatment Program A government-run facility for juveniles whose offenses are not deemed serious enough to warrant incarceration in a training school.

Boot Camp A variation on traditional shock incarceration in which juveniles (and some adults) are sent to secure confinement facilities modeled on military basic training camps instead of prison or jail.

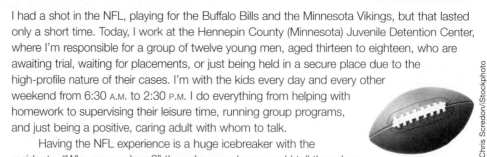

CAREERS IN CJ

CARL McCULLOUGH, SR.

RESIDENT YOUTH WORKER

Photo Courtesy of Carl McCullough, Sr.

Chris Scredon/iStockphoto

FASTFACTS

RESIDENT YOUTH WORKER, JOB DESCRIPTION:

- Provide safety, security, custodial care, discipline, and guidance. Play a critical role in the rehabilitation of youth and, as a result, have a potentially great impact on a youth's success during and after his or her incarceration.

WHAT KIND OF TRAINING IS REQUIRED?

- A bachelor's degree in human services, behavioral science, or a related field.
- Professional and respectful verbal communication skills.

ANNUAL SALARY RANGE?

- $16,840 – $44,940

I had a shot in the NFL, playing for the Buffalo Bills and the Minnesota Vikings, but that lasted only a short time. Today, I work at the Hennepin County (Minnesota) Juvenile Detention Center, where I'm responsible for a group of twelve young men, aged thirteen to eighteen, who are awaiting trial, waiting for placements, or just being held in a secure place due to the high-profile nature of their cases. I'm with the kids every day and every other weekend from 6:30 A.M. to 2:30 P.M. I do everything from helping with homework to supervising their leisure time, running group programs, and just being a positive, caring adult with whom to talk.

Having the NFL experience is a huge icebreaker with the residents. "Why are you here?" they always ask me, and I tell them I am here because I care about them, because I want to see a change, and because I'd like to help them believe that something better is possible. To do this job well, you have to be good at building relationships. It helps to know how to work with different cultures as well. Then you have to have patience; without it you won't last long. You know they are going to test you, to see what they can and can't get away with. You also have to be willing to learn a few things from them. You have to be a good listener.

SOCIAL MEDIA CAREER TIP Potential employers want information about you, but they do not want your life story. To capitalize on two primary benefits of social media, personalize your message and be concise.

doing hard labor, and also participate in programs such as basic adult education and job skills training.[112]

No juvenile correctional facility is called a "prison." This does not mean they lack a strong resemblance to prisons. The facilities that most closely mimic the atmosphere at an adult correctional facility are **training schools,** alternatively known as youth camps, youth development centers, industrial schools, and several other similar titles. Whatever the name, these institutions claim to differ from their adult countparts by offering a variety of programs to treat and rehabilitate the young offenders. In reality, training schools are plagued by many of the same problems as adult prisons and jails, including high levels of inmate-on-inmate violence, substance abuse, gang wars, and overcrowding.

AFTERCARE Juveniles leave correctional facilities through an early release program or because they have served the length of their sentences. Juvenile corrections officials recognize that many of these children, like adults, need assistance readjusting to the outside world. Consequently, released juveniles are often placed in **aftercare** programs. Based on the same philosophy that drives the prisoner reentry movement (discussed in the previous chapter), aftercare programs are designed to offer services for the juveniles, while at the same time supervising them to reduce the chances of recidivism. The ideal aftercare program includes community support groups, aid in finding and keeping employment, and continued monitoring to ensure that the juvenile is able to deal with the demands of freedom.

Training School A correctional institution for juveniles found to be delinquent or status offenders.

Aftercare The variety of therapeutic, educational, and counseling programs made available to juvenile delinquents (and some adults) after they have been released from a correctional facility.

Juvenile Justice and Recidivism

It is difficult to state the effectiveness of juvenile adjudication, corrections, and aftercare with much certainty. No nationwide recidivism rate for juveniles has been calculated. Indeed, such a figure would be somewhat meaningless, given that state juvenile justice systems vary dramatically, as do their definitions of reoffending.[113]

Overall, however, nearly 60 percent of juveniles who have been referred to juvenile court are "rereferred" before turning eighteen years old.[114] More troubling is the notion that many juvenile offenders are likely, if not destined, to become adult offenders. A recent report of Illinois's juvenile justice system criticized it as "a 'feeder system' to the adult criminal justice system and a cycle of crime, victimization, and incarceration."[115]

SELF ASSESSMENT

Fill in the blanks and check your answers on page 520.

A juvenile offender's delinquency is determined during the _____ hearing, which is similar in many ways to an adult trial. If the juvenile is found to be delinquent, her or his sentence is determined during the _____ hearing. The most common form of juvenile corrections is _____. If the judge decides that the juvenile needs more stringent supervision, he or she can sentence the offender to a _____ facility such as a residential treatment program. If the juvenile's offense has been particularly serious, she or he will most likely be sent to a secure confinement facility such as a _____ camp or a _____ school.

POLICE IN SCHOOLS

After the December 2012 shooting spree at an elementary school in Newtown, Connecticut, that left twenty first-graders and six staff dead, a single question echoed across the country: What do we do to protect our children? Both the White House and the National Rifle Association of America (NRA) gave a similar answer. President Barack Obama's administration sought $150 million to help educators hire up to 1,000 on-site police officers, while the NRA called for every school in the nation to be patrolled by armed guards. These widely debated suggestions raise another question, addressed in this *CJ in Action* feature: Do police in schools create more problems than they solve?

SECURITY OR DISCIPLINE?

In the 1970s, law enforcement officers were present in only about 1 percent of American schools. This percentage began to rise in the 1980s, when juvenile crime rates increased dramatically. Then, in 1999, two high school seniors killed twelve students and one teacher at Colorado's Columbine High School, leading to a wave of financing for school police. By 2010, about half of all public schools had assigned police officers, and about 17,000 School-Resource Officers (SROs) were patrolling school hallways.[116] SROs have the same powers as any other police officer, including the ability to issue criminal citations to students who break the law on school grounds.

In theory, armed SROs have the ability to respond quickly to emergency situations and disable shooters such as Newtown's Adam Lanza before the violence escalates. "The only thing that stops a bad guy with a gun," says NRA leader Wayne LaPierre, "is a good guy with a gun."[117] In practice, SROs spend much more time on disciplinary issues than security issues. For example, Texas SROs hand out approximately 300,000 "Class C" misdemeanor citations to students each year for offenses such as acting up in the classroom, getting in fights, or smoking cigarettes. "The problem," says an SRO from Phoenix, Arizona, "is the school at times says, 'Oh, we've got a cop. Let him [or her] take care of things.'"[118]

THE CASE FOR POLICE IN SCHOOLS

- Having armed, trained law enforcement personnel in schools increases the level of safety at the schools, just as it would anywhere else.

- A police presence acts as a deterrent against a school attack. In the words of one commentator, "Rampaging gunmen seek victims at places where they expect no immediate resistance."[119]

- SROs help teachers deal with increasingly dangerous students, who, according to an Austin, Texas, educator, "can be very threatening. The police get called because that way the teacher can go on with teaching instead of wasting half the class dealing with one child, and it sends a message to the other kids."[120]

THE CASE AGAINST POLICE IN SCHOOLS

- The United States does not have unlimited supplies of law enforcement agents. Putting police in schools means taking them away from other parts of the community.

- Many school districts cannot afford the expense. The School Superintendents Association estimates that placing an officer in every American school, as the NRA suggests, would cost more than $5 billion.[121]

- Police in schools lead to a "school-to-prisons pipeline" in which minor behavior problems are referred to criminal courts, saddling hundreds of thousands of students with criminal records. As a consequence, these children are more likely to drop out of school and have future interactions with the criminal justice system.[122]

YOUR OPINION—WRITING ASSIGNMENT

Financial considerations aside, law enforcement will continue to patrol the hallways of many of the nation's public schools. The challenge, then, is to stop "criminalizing our children for nonviolent offenses," as one Texas judge says.[123] Why do you think that an SRO would cite a student for, as has happened, spraying herself with perfume in class or pouring milk on another student? How should SRO discretion be limited to best meet the goal of protecting students without arresting too many of them in the process? Before responding, you can review our discussions in this chapter concerning:

- The culpability of juveniles (pages 495–497).

- School violence and bullying (pages 499–501).

- Police discretion and juvenile crime (pages 506–508).

Your answer should include at least three full paragraphs.

CHAPTER SUMMARY

For more information on these concepts, look back to the Learning Objective icons throughout the chapter.

Describe the child-saving movement and its relationship to the doctrine of *parens patriae*. Under the doctrine of *parens patriae*, the state has a right and a duty to care for neglected, delinquent, or disadvantaged children. The child-saving movement, based on the doctrine of *parens patriae*, started in the 1800s. Its followers believed that juvenile offenders require treatment rather than punishment.

List the four major differences between juvenile courts and adult courts. (a) No juries, (b) different terminology, (c) limited adversarial relationship, and (d) confidentiality.

Identify and briefly describe the single most important U.S. Supreme Court case with respect to juvenile justice. The case was *In re Gault*, decided by the Supreme Court in 1967. In this case a minor was arrested for allegedly making an obscene phone call. His parents were not notified and were not present during the juvenile court judge's decision-making process. In this case, the Supreme Court held that juveniles are entitled to many of the same due process rights granted to adult offenders, including notice of charges, the right to counsel, the privilege against self-incrimination, and the right to confront and cross-examine witnesses.

Describe the reasoning behind recent U.S. Supreme Court decisions that have lessened the harshness of sentencing outcomes for violent juvenile offenders. In banning capital punishment and limiting the availability of life sentences without parole for offenders who committed their crimes as juveniles, the Supreme Court has focused on the concept of "diminished capacity." This concept is based on the notion that violent juvenile offenders cannot fully comprehend the consequences of their actions and are more deserving of the opportunity for rehabilitation than adult violent offenders.

Explain how law enforcement's emphasis on domestic violence has influenced female juvenile arrest patterns. Girls are much more likely to fight with parents and siblings than are boys, whose physical confrontations tend to involve strangers. Because police officers have taken a more aggressive stand against domestic violence, they are more likely to arrest female juveniles involved in family disputes now than they were in the past.

Describe the one variable that always correlates highly with juvenile crime rates. The older a person is, the less likely he or she will exhibit criminal behavior. This process is known as aging out. Thus, persons in any at-risk group will commit fewer crimes as they get older.

Indicate some of the reasons why youths join gangs. Some alienated teenagers join gangs for the social relationships and the sense of identity that gangs can provide. Youths living in high-crime neighborhoods join gangs as a form of protection. The excitement of belonging to a gang is another reason to join.

List the factors that normally determine what police do with juvenile offenders. The arresting police officers consider (a) the nature of the offense, (b) the youthful offender's past criminal history, (c) the setting in which the offense took place, (d) whether the parents can take disciplinary action, (e) the attitude of the offender, and (f) the offender's race and gender.

Describe the four primary stages of pretrial juvenile justice procedure. (a) Intake, in which an official of the juvenile court engages in a screening process to determine what to do with the youthful offender; (b) pretrial diversion, which may consist of probation, treatment and aid, and/or restitution; (c) jurisdictional waiver to an adult court, in which case the youth leaves the juvenile justice system; and (d) some type of detention, in which the youth is held until the disposition process begins.

Explain the distinction between an adjudicatory hearing and a disposition hearing. An adjudicatory hearing is essentially a "trial." Defense attorneys may be present during the adjudicatory hearing in juvenile courts. In many states, once adjudication has occurred, there is a separate disposition hearing that is similar to the sentencing phase in an adult court. At this point, the court, often aided by a predisposition report, determines the sentence that serves the "needs" of the child.

QUESTIONS FOR CRITICAL ANALYSIS

1. What is the difference between a status offense and a crime? What punishments do you think should be imposed on juveniles who commit status offenses?

2. In many prisons, juveniles serving life sentences without the possibility of parole are not allowed to take educational or vocational training classes. What is the reasoning behind this policy? What is your opinion of this policy?

3. Do you think that bullying should be punishable as a felony along the same lines as assault? (For the definition of assault, go back to Chapter 1.) Why or why not?

4. Several years ago, eight Florida teenagers ranging in age from fourteen to eighteen beat a classmate so badly that she suffered a concussion. According to law enforcement officials, the teenagers recorded the assault so that they could post it on the Internet. If you were a prosecutor and could either waive these teenagers to adult court or refer them to the juvenile justice system, which option would you choose? What other information would you need to make your decision?

5. Forty-four states have enacted parental responsibility statutes, which make parents responsible for the offenses of their children. Seventeen of these states hold parents criminally liable for their children's actions, punishing the parents with fines, community service, and even incarceration. What is your opinion of these laws—particularly those with criminal sanctions for parents?

KEY TERMS

adjudicatory hearing   512
aftercare   516
age of onset   502
aging out   502
automatic transfer   510
boot camp   515
bullying   500
child abuse   503
child neglect   503

detention   512
detention hearing   512
disposition hearing   513
graduated sanctions   514
intake   509
judicial waiver   510
juvenile delinquency   492
low-visibility decision making   506
parens patriae   491

petition   509
predisposition report   514
prosecutorial waiver   511
referral   507
residential treatment
   program   515
status offender   492
training school   516
youth gang   504

SELF ASSESSMENT ANSWER KEY

Page 494: i. *parens patriae;* **ii.** status offenses; **iii.** delinquency

Page 497: i. state; **ii.** state; **iii.** impulsive; **iv.** peer; **v.** death penalty

Page 501: i. declining; **ii.** girls; **iii.** School; **iv.** Bullying

Page 506: i. risk; **ii.** aging out; **iii.** child abuse/child neglect; **iv.** gangs

Page 512: i. arrest; **ii.** refer; **iii.** social; **iv.** intake; **v.** diversion; **vi.** waiver

Page 517: i. adjudicatory; **ii.** disposition; **iii.** probation; **iv.** nonsecure; **v.** boot; **vi.** training

NOTES

1. Jennifer M. O'Connor and Lucinda K. Treat, "Getting Smart about Getting Tough: Juvenile Justice and the Possibility of Progressive Reform," *American Criminal Law Review* 33 (Summer 1996), 1299.

2. *In re Gault,* 387 U.S. 1, at 15 (1967).

3. Samuel Davis, *The Rights of Juveniles: The Juvenile Justice System,* 2d ed. (New York: C. Boardman Co., 1995), Section 1.2.

4. Quoted in Anthony Platt, *The Child Savers* (Chicago: University of Chicago Press, 1969), 119.

5. 383 U.S. 541 (1966).

6. *Ibid.*, 556.

7. 387 U.S. 1 (1967).

8. 397 U.S. 358 (1970).

9. 421 U.S. 519 (1975).

10. 403 U.S. 528 (1971).

11. Quoted in "Colo. Boy Pleads Guilty to Killing Parents," *Associated Press* (September 29, 2011).

12. Research Network on Adolescent Development and Juvenile Justice, *Youth on Trial: A Developmental Perspective on Juvenile Justice* (Chicago: John D. & Catherine T. MacArthur Foundation, 2003), 1.

13. Richard E. Redding, "Juveniles Transferred to Criminal Court: Legal Reform Proposals Based on Social Science Research," *Utah Law Review* (1997), 709.

14. Howard N. Snyder and Melissa Sickmund, *Juvenile Offenders and Victims: A National Report* (Washington, D.C.: U.S. Department of Justice, 1995), 47.

15. Martha Grace Duncan, "'So Young and So Untender': Remorseless Children and the Expectations of the Law," *Columbia Law Review* (October 2002), 1469.

16. 543 U.S. 551 (2005).

17. *Ibid.*, 567.

18. 130 S.Ct. 2011 (2010).

19. *Ibid.*, at 2030.

20. 132 S. Ct. 2455 (2012).

21. *Ibid.*, ar 2463.

22. Scott Michels, "A Reprieve for Juvenile Lifers?" *The Crime Report* (July 26, 2012), at **www.thecrimereport.org/news/articles/2012-07-a-reprieve-for-juvenile-lifers**.

23. *Surveillance Summaries: Youth Risk Behavior Surveillance—United States, 2011* (Washington, D.C.: Centers for Disease Control and Prevention, June 8, 2012).

24. Federal Bureau of Investigation, *Crime in the United States, 2011* (Washington, D.C.: U.S. Department of Justice, 2012), at **www.fbi.gov/about-us/cjis/ucr/crime-in-the-u.s/2011/crime-in-the-u.s.-2011/tables/table-38**.

25. Charles Puzzanchera, Benjamin Adams, and Sarah Hockenberry, *Juvenile Court Statistics 2009* (Washington, D.C.: National Center for Juvenile Justice, May 2012), 7.

26. Office of Juvenile Justice and Delinquency Prevention, *Juvenile Residential Facility Census, 2008: Selected Findings* (Washington, D.C.: U.S. Department of Justice, July 2011), 1; and Todd Richmond, "Fewer Young Criminals Push States to Close Prisons," *Associated Press* (June 7, 2010).

27. David McDowell, "Juvenile Curfew Laws and Their Influence on Crime," *Federal Probation* (December 2006), 58.

28. *Crime in the United States, 2011,* at **www.fbi.gov/about-us/cjis/ucr/crime-in-the-u.s/2011/crime-in-the-u.s.-2011/tables/table-38**.

29. Office of Juvenile Justice and Delinquency Prevention, "Community Prevention Grants Program," at **www.ojjdp.gov/cpg**.

30. Puzzanchera, Adams, and Hockenberry, 12.

31. Sara Goodkind et al., "Are Girls Really Becoming More Delinquent? Testing the Gender Convergence Hypothesis by Race and Ethnicity, 1976–2005," *Children and Youth Services Review* (August 2009), 885–889.

32. Kimberly Kempf-Leonard and Lisa Sample, "Disparity Based on Sex: Is Gender-Specific Treatment Warranted?" *Justice Quarterly* 17 (2000), 89–128.

33. Crystal Knoll and Melissa Sickmund, *Delinquency Cases in Juvenile Court, 2009* (Washington, D.C.: Office of Juvenile Justice and Delinquency Prevention, October 2012), 2.

34. *Crime in the United States, 2011,* at **www.fbi.gov/about-us/cjis/ucr/crime-in-the-u.s/2011/crime-in-the-u.s.-2011/tables/table-33**.

35. Margaret A. Zahn et al., "The Girls Study Group—Charting the Way to Delinquency Prevention for Girls," *Girls Study Group: Understanding and Responding to Girls' Delinquency* (Washington, D.C.: Office of Juvenile Justice and Delinquency Prevention, October 2008), 3.

36. Puzzanchera, Adams, and Hockenberry, 77.

37. Melissa Sickmund and Howard N. Snyder, *Juvenile Offenders and Victims: 1999 National Report* (Washington, D.C.: Office of Juvenile Justice and Delinquency Prevention, 1999), 58.

38. Meda Chesney-Lind, *The Female Offender: Girls, Women, and Crime* (Thousand Oaks, CA: Sage Publications, 1997).

39. Denise C. Gottfredson and David A. Soulé, "The Timing of Property Crime, Violent Crime, and Substance Abuse among Juveniles," *Journal of Research in Crime and Delinquency* (February 2005), 110–120.

40. National Center for Education Statistics and Bureau of Justice Statistics, *Indicators of School Crime and Safety: 2011* (Washington, D.C.: U.S. Department of Justice, February 2012), 6.

41. *Ibid.*, 10–15.

42. *Ibid.*, 82–83.

43. *Ibid.*, 44.

44. Jessica Bennett, "From Lockers to Lockup," *Newsweek* (October 11, 2010), 39.

45. Adam J. Speraw, "No Bullying Allowed: A Call for a National Anti-Bullying Statute to Promote a Safer Learning Environment in American Public Schools," *Valparaiso University Law Review* (Summer 2010), 1151–1198.

46. Natalie DiBlasio, "More Cases of Bullying Are Ending Up in Court," *USA Today* (September 12, 2011), 3A.

47. Marvin E. Wolfgang, *From Boy to Man, from Delinquency to Crime* (Chicago: University of Chicago Press, 1987).

48. Tom F.M. ter Bogt, Loes Keijsers, and Wim H.J. Meeus, "Early Adolescent Music Preferences and Minor Delinquency," *Pediatrics* (February 2013), 380–389.

49. Quoted in John H. Laub and Robert J. Sampson, "Understanding Desistance from Crime," in *Crime and Justice: A Review of Research* (Chicago: University of Chicago Press, 2001), 6.

50. Travis Hirschi and Michael Gottfredson, "Age and the Explanation of Crime," *American Journal of Sociology* 89 (1982), 552–584.

51. Robert J. Sampson and John H. Laub, "A Life-Course View on the Development of Crime," *Annals of the American Academy of Political and Social Science* (November 2005), 12.

52. David P. Farrington, "Offending from 10 to 25 Years of Age," in *Prospective Studies of Crime and Delinquency*, ed. Katherine Teilmann Van Dusen and Sarnoff A. Mednick (Boston: Kluwer-Nijhoff Publishers, 1983), 17.

53. Office of Juvenile Justice and Delinquency Prevention, *Juveniles in Court* (Washington, D.C.: U.S. Department of Justice, June 2003), 29.

54. Lloyd D. Johnston et al., *Monitoring the Future: National Results on Adolescent Drug Use—Overview of Key Findings, 2011* (Ann Arbor, MI: Institute for Social Research, February 2012), 36.

55. Anahad O'Connor, "Regular Marijuana Use by High School Students Hits New Peak, Report Finds," *New York Times* (December 15, 2011), A16.

56. Carl McCurley and Howard Snyder, *Co-occurrence of Substance Abuse Behaviors in Youth* (Washington, D.C.: Office of Juvenile Justice and Delinquency Prevention, 2008).

57. Gary McClelland, Linda Teplin, and Karen Abram, "Detection and Prevalence of Substance Abuse among Juvenile Detainees," *Juvenile Justice Bulletin* (Washington, D.C.: Office of Juvenile Justice and Delinquency Prevention, June 2004), 10.

58. Arrestee Drug Abuse Monitoring Program, *Preliminary Data on Drug Use and Related Matters among Adult Arrestees and Juvenile Detainees* (Washington, D.C.: National Institute of Justice, 2003).

59. National Mental Health Association, "Mental Health and Adolescent Girls in the Justice System," at **www.nmha.org/children/justjuv/girlsjj.cfm**.

60. Larry J. Siegel and Brandon C. Welsh, *Juvenile Delinquency: The Core*, 4th ed. (Belmont, CA: Wadsworth Cengage Learning, 2011), 268.

61. Edward P. Mulvey, *Highlights from Pathways to Desistance: A Longitudinal Study of Serious Adolescent Offenders* (Washington, D.C.: Office of Juvenile Justice and Delinquency Prevention, March 2011), 1–3.

62. Sherry Hamby et al., *Juvenile Justice Bulletin: Children's Exposure to Intimate Partner Violence and Other Family Violence* (Washington, D.C.: Office of Juvenile Justice and Delinquency Prevention, October 2011), 1.57.

63. Kimberly A. Tyler and Katherine A. Johnson, "A Longitudinal Study of the Effects of Early Abuse on Later Victimization among High-Risk Adolescents," *Violence and Victims* (June 2006), 287–291.

64. Grover Trask, "Defusing the Teenage Time Bombs," *Prosecutor* (March/April 1997), 29.

65. Ashley Nellis, *The Lives of Juvenile Lifers: Findings from a National Survey* (Washington, D.C.: The Sentencing Project, March 2012), 2.

66. Cathy Spatz Widom, *The Cycle of Violence* (Washington, D.C.: National Institute of Justice, October 1992).

67. Janet Currie and Erdal Tekin, *Does Child Abuse Cause Crime?* (Atlanta: Andrew Young School of Policy Studies, April 2006), 27–28.

68. *2011 National Gang Threat Assessment—Emerging Trends* (Washington, D.C.: National Gang Intelligence Center, 2012), 9.

69. Chris Melde and Finn-Aage Esbensen, "Gang Membership as a Turning Point in the Life Course," *Criminology* (August 2011), 513–546.

70. *2011 National Gang Threat Assessment—Emerging Trends*, 15–17.

71. James C. Howell et al., "U.S. Gang Problems Trends and Seriousness, 1996–2009," *National Gang Center Bulletin Number 6* (May 2011), 10.

72. "Race/Ethnicity of Gang Members," *National Youth Gang Survey Analysis* (Institute for Intergovernmental Research/National Youth Gang Center, 2009), at **www.iir.com/nygc/nygsa**.

73. Rachel A. Gordon, Benjamin B. Lahey, Eriko Kawai, Rolf Loeber, and Magda Stouthamer-Loeber, "Antisocial Behavior and Youth Gang Membership: Selection and Socialization," *Criminology* (February 2004), 55–89.

74. National Alliance of Gang Investigators Associates, *2005 National Gang Threat Assessment* (Washington, D.C.: Bureau of Justice Assistance, 2005), 10–11.

75. Angela Wolf and Livier Gutierrez, *It's About Time: Prevention and Intervention Services for Gang-Affiliated Girls* (National Council on Crime and Delinquency, March 2012), 1–2.

76. Karl G. Hill, Christina Lui, and J. David Hawkins, *Early Precursors of Gang Membership: A Study of Seattle Youth* (Washington, D.C.: Office of Juvenile Justice and Delinquency Prevention, December 2001).

77. Richard Spano and John M. Bollard, "Is the Nexus of Gang Membership, Exposure to Violence, and Violent Behavior a Key Determinant of First Time Gun Carrying for Urban Minority Youth?" *Justice Quarterly* 28 (2011), 838–862.

78. Beth Bjerregaard and Alan J. Lizotte, "Gun Ownership and Gang Membership," *Journal of Criminal Law and Criminology* 86 (1995), 49.

79. Quoted in Gracie Bond Staples, "Guns in School," *Fort Worth Star-Telegram* (June 3, 1998), 1.

80. M. Alex Johnson, "Pistol-Packing Pupils Becoming an Everyday Occurrence," *NBC News.com* (February 5, 2013), at **usnews.nbcnews.com/_news/2013/02/05/16841405-pistol-packing-pupils-becoming-an-everyday-occurrence?lite**.

81. Centers for Disease Control and Prevention, "Youth Risk Behavior Surveillance—United States, 2011," *Morbidity and Mortality Weekly Report* (June 8, 2012), 7.

82. Puzzanchera, Adams, and Hockenberry, 31.

83. Neelum Arya and Ian Augarten, *Critical Condition: African-American Youth in the Justice System* (Washington, D.C.: Campaign for Youth and Justice, 2008), 17–20.

84. Carl E. Pope and Howard N. Snyder, *Race as a Factor in Juvenile Arrests* (Washington, D.C.: Office of Juvenile Justice and Delinquency Prevention, April 2003), 1.

85. *Ibid.*, 4.

86. National Institute of Justice, *The Code of the Street and African-American Adolescent Violence* (Washington, D.C.: U.S. Department of Justice, February 2009), 7, 10, 14.

87. George S. Bridges and Sara Steen, "Racial Disparities in Official Assessments of Juvenile Offenders," *American Sociological Review* 63 (1998), 554.

88. 422 U.S. 23 (1979).

89. 131 S.Ct. 2394 (2011).

90. *Ibid.*, at 2403.

91. Knoll and Sickmund, 3.

92. 42 U.S.C. Sections 5601–5778 (1974).

93. S'Lee Arthur Hinshaw II, "Juvenile Diversion: An Alternative to Juvenile Court," *Journal of Dispute Resolution* (1993), 305.

94. Ted Gordon Lewis, "Barron County Restorative Justice Programs: A Partnership Model for Balancing Community and Government Resources for Juvenile Justice Services," *Journal of Juvenile Justice* (Fall 2011), 17–32.

95. Audrey Hickert et al., "Impact of Juvenile Drug Courts on Drug Use and Criminal Behavior," *Journal of Juvenile Justice* (Fall 2011), 60–77.

96. Rhode Island General Laws Section 14-1-7.1 (1994 and Supp. 1996).

97. Knoll and Sickmund, 3.

98. Code of Georgia, Section 15-11-39.

99. *Falling Through the Cracks: A New Look at Ohio Youth in the Adult Criminal Justice System* (Covington, KY: Children's Law Center, 2012), 2.

100. Richard E. Redding, *Juvenile Transfer Laws: An Effective Deterrent to Delinquency?* (Washington, D.C.: Office of Juvenile Justice and Delinquency Prevention, June 2010), 4.

101. Richard E. Redding, "Juvenile Transfer Laws: An Effective Deterrent to Delinquency?" *Juvenile Justice Bulletin* (Washington, D.C.: Office of Juvenile Justice and Delinquency Prevention, August 2008), 7.

102. Quoted in Judi Villa, "Adult Prisons Harden Teens," *Arizona Republic* (November 14, 2004), A27.

103. 467 U.S. 253 (1984).

104. Puzzanchera, Adams, and Hockenberry, 32.

105. Knoll and Sickmund, 3.

106. Barry C. Feld, "Criminalizing the American Juvenile Court," *Crime and Justice* 17 (1993), 227–254.

107. Eric R. Lotke, "Youth Homicide: Keeping Perspective on How Many Children Kill," *Valparaiso University Law Review* 31 (Spring 1997), 395.

108. Bureau of Justice Statistics, *Jail Inmates at Midyear 2011—Statistical Tables* (Washington, D.C.: U.S. Department of Justice, April 2012), 1; and Bureau of Justice Statistics, *Prisoners in 2009* (Washington, D.C.: U.S. Department of Justice, December 2010), Appendix table 13, page 27.

109. Knoll and Sickmund, 3.

110. *Reducing Youth Incarceration in the United States* (Baltimore, MD: The Annie E. Casey Foundation, February 2013), 1.

111. Howard N. Snyder and Melissa Sickmund, *Juvenile Offenders and Victims: 2006 National Report* (Washington, D.C.: National Center for Juvenile Justice, March 2006), 98.

112. Dean John Champion, *The Juvenile Justice System: Delinquency, Processing, and the Law*, 5th ed. (Upper Saddle River, NJ: Pearson Prentice Hall, 2007), 581–582.

113. Snyder and Sickmund, *Juvenile Offenders and Victims: 2006 National Report*, 234.

114. *Ibid.*, 235.

115. *Youth Reentry Improvement Report* (Springfield, IL: Illinois Juvenile Justice Commission, November 2011), 9.

116. Barbara Raymond, "Assigning Police Officers to Schools," Center for Problem-Oriented Policing, *Response Guide No. 10* (2010), at **www.popcenter.org/Responses/school_police/print**.

117. Quoted in Jason Hunsicker and Taylor Muller, "Making Schools Safer," *Daily Guide (Waynesville, MO)* (March 30, 2013), 1.

118. Quoted in Susan Ferriss, "Should Schools Have More Police— or Fewer? States Disagree," *Denver Post* (March 5, 2013) at **www.denverpost.com/politics/ci_22714286/should-schools-have-more-police-or-fewer-states**.

119. Stephen P. Halbrook, "Armed School Guards: Best Bet to Stop Future Newtowns," *San Antonio Express-News* (February 6, 2013), 4.

120. Quoted in Chris McGreal, "The U.S. Schools with Their Own Police," *The Guardian* (January 9, 2012), at **www.guardian.co.uk/world/2012/jan/09/texas-police-schools**.

121. Teresa Welsh, "Should the Federal Government Pay for Armed Guards in Public Schools?" *U.S. News & World Report* (April 3, 2013), at **www.usnews.com/opinion/articles/2013/04/03/should-the-federal-government-pay-for-armed-guards-in-public-schools**.

122. Catherin Y. Kim and I. India Geronimo, *Policing in Schools* (New York: American Civil Liberties Union, 2009), 8–13.

123. Quoted in Erik Eckholm, "With Police in Schools, More Children in Court," *New York Times* (April 12, 2013), A1.

CHAPTER

16

Today's Challenges:
The Terror Threat, Cyber Crime, and White-Collar Crime

CHAPTER OUTLINE	CORRESPONDING LEARNING OBJECTIVES	
The Terror Threat		Describe the concept of *jihad* as practiced by al Qaeda and its followers.
		Identify three important trends in international terrorism.
		Explain the primary difference between the U.S. government's treatment of enemy combatants and the treatment of terrorist suspects under the jurisdiction of the criminal justice system.
Cyber Crime		Distinguish cyber crime from "traditional" crime.
		Describe the three following forms of malware: (a) botnets, (b) worms, and (c) viruses.
		Explain how the Internet has contributed to piracy of intellectual property.
		Outline the three major reasons why the Internet is conducive to the dissemination of child pornography.
White-Collar Crime		Indicate some of the ways that white-collar crime is different from violent or property crime.
		Explain the concept of corporate violence.

To target your study and review, look for these numbered Learning Objective icons throughout the chapter.

Reuters/Jim Urquhart

DO-IT-YOURSELF TERROR

SAMIR KHAN'S advice for his fellow Islamic *jihadists* was simple and straightforward: think small. Khan, an American who moved to the Middle East to start the online magazine *Inspire,* thought that terrorist actions on the scale of the September 11, 2001, attacks against the United States were no longer feasible. Instead, he wrote, solo, under-the-radar operations have a better chance of success. "The effect is much greater, it always embarrasses the enemy, and these types of individual decision-making attacks are nearly impossible for [anti-terrorism efforts] to contain," Khan counseled.

Khan was killed by an American drone strike in Yemen in 2011, but his words echoed loudly on April 15, 2013. That day, Tamerlan Tsarnaev, 26, and his younger brother Dzhokhar, 19, apparently detonated two bombs near the finish line of the Boston Marathon, killing three and wounding more than 260. The Tsarnaevs allegedly fashioned the bombs by packing pressure cookers with nails, ball bearings, and black powder taken from fireworks. The devices were triggered by simple egg timers. Following his capture, Dzhokhar admitted that the pressure-cooker explosives were created using instructions found in *Inspire,* which frequently published Web articles with titles such as "Make a Bomb in the Kitchen of Your Mom."

Dzhokhar also told authorities that he and his brother, who was killed during a police chase, were motivated by religious fervor but had not received any help from international terrorist organizations. In 2012, Tamerlan did spend several months in Dagestan, a republic of Russia that is marked by violence committed by and against Islamic separatists. On his return, he made a YouTube playlist that indicated a growing interest in Islamic radicalism. Even so, the brothers—who had lived in the Boston area for about ten years—were fully assimilated in American culture and proved skillful at hiding their plans from close acquaintances. When surveillance images of the as-yet-unidentified bombers showed up on the Internet, one of Dzhokhar's friends noted his resemblance to the suspect. "LOL," Dzhokhar replied. "You better not text me."

1. Following the Boston Marathon bombings, Phillip Mudd, a former federal counterterrorism official, said, "I was surprised that this didn't happen sooner." Do you share Mudd's somewhat pessimistic outlook? What factors make attacks by homegrown terrorists such as the Tsarnaev brothers difficult to prevent?

2. Should the federal government make it a crime to publish bomb-making instructions online? Why or why not?

3. In a poll taken shortly after Dzhokhar Tsarnaev's capture, 70 percent of Americans indicated that, if convicted of carrying out the bombings, he should receive the death penalty. What punishment do you think best fits this act of terror?

AP Photo/FBI

Law enforcement used street-level surveillance cameras to identify Dzokhar Tsarnaev, left, and his brother Tamerlan, right, as the primary suspects in the Boston Marathon bombings.

Gray wall studio/Shutterstock.com

THE TERROR THREAT

Nonstate Actor An entity that plays a role in international affairs but does not represent any established state or nation.

It took law enforcement officials only three days to identify the Tsarnaev brothers using video footage following the pressure-cooker bombings at the Boston Marathon. During those three days, speculation as to the identity of those responsible for the attacks was rampant. Some pointed to international Islamic plotters, others to right-wing radicals, still others—correctly—to homegrown extremists. There was little doubt, however, that the bombings were, in the words of President Barack Obama, "an act of terror."[1]

In the first chapter of this textbook, we defined terrorism as the use of violence in furtherance of political or social objectives. Today, the dominant strain of terrorism mixes political goals with very strong religious affiliations. As the carnage of the Boston Marathon bombings underscores, modern terrorism is also characterized by extreme levels of violence. The January 24, 2011, suicide bombing at Russia's busiest airport in Moscow killed at least 35 people and injured 150 more. The three-day November 2008 raid on the financial district of Mumbai, India, left 173 dead and more than 300 wounded. And, of course, the September 11, 2001, attacks on New York and Washington, D.C., claimed nearly 3,000 lives. Indeed, the power of terrorism is a direct result of the fear caused by this violence—not only the fear that such atrocities will be repeated, but also that next time, they will be much worse.

The Global Context of Terrorism

Generally, terrorist acts are not the acts of nations or legally appointed governments. Rather, terror is the realm of **nonstate actors** such as Tamerlan and Dzhokhar Tsarnaev, free of control by or allegiance to any nation, who use violence to further their own goals. At the same time, as David A. Westbrook of the University at Buffalo (New York) points out, the large scale and financial resources of some modern terrorist organizations make them as powerful as many nations, if not more so.[2]

In addition, the high body counts associated with the worst terrorist acts seem better described in terms of war than of crime, which in most cases involves two people—the criminal and the victim. Thus, perhaps the most satisfying description of terrorism is as a "supercrime" that incorporates many of the characteristics of international warfare.[3] Indeed, it often seems that the United States is "at war" with al Qaeda, the organization responsible for the September 11, 2001, attacks against this country.

AL QAEDA VERSUS THE UNITED STATES On May 1, 2011, a team of U.S. Navy Seals in helicopters descended on a three-story house in Abbottabad, a town located about thirty miles northeast of Islamabad, the capital of Pakistan. Forty minutes later, they left with the body of Osama bin Laden, whom they had killed after a shootout with his bodyguards. "Justice has been done," said President Obama, echoing the sentiments of many Americans for whom the event marked a symbolic triumph in the struggle against international terrorism.[4]

■ Volunteers search a destroyed vehicle following a suicide bombing that killed nine people in Peshawar, Pakistan, on April 16, 2013. The attack targeted an election campaign rally and was evidently carried out by the Taliban, a group that opposes Pakistan's political process. Explain why such acts of violence are considered "terrorism."
A. Majeed/AFP/Getty Images

Describe the concept of *jihad* as practiced by al Qaeda and its followers.

LEARNING
1
OBJECTIVE

Osama bin Laden and al Qaeda Osama bin Laden's al Qaeda organization grew out of a network of volunteers who migrated to Afghanistan in the 1980s to rid that country of foreign occupiers. (Ironically, in light of later events, bin Laden and his comrades received significant American financial aid.) For bin Laden, these efforts took the form of *jihad*, a controversial term that also has been the subject of much confusion. Contrary to what many think, *jihad* does not mean "holy war." Rather, it refers to three kinds of struggle, or exertion, required of the Muslim faithful: (1) the struggle against the evil in oneself, (2) the struggle against the evil outside oneself, and (3) the struggle against nonbelievers.[5] Many Muslims believe that this struggle can be achieved without violence and denounce the form of *jihad* practiced by al Qaeda. Clearly, however, bin Laden and his followers rejected the notion that *jihad* can be accomplished through peaceable efforts.

In the 1990s, bin Laden began to turn his attention to the United States, and al Qaeda set its sights on American interests abroad. In 1998, for example, the organization bombed two U.S. embassies in Africa, killing 231 people. Two years later, al Qaeda agents launched a suicide attack on the U.S.S. *Cole,* a Navy destroyer docked in Aden, a port in the small Middle Eastern country of Yemen, during which seventeen U.S. sailors died.

About a year after the September 11, 2001, attacks, bin Laden wrote a letter to the American people outlining the reasons behind al Qaeda's opposition to the U.S. government. These included American support for Israel, which is widely seen as an enemy to Muslims, and U.S. exploitation of Islamic countries for their oil. Furthermore, bin Laden criticized the presence of U.S. military forces in the Middle East, "spreading your ideology and thereby polluting the hearts of our people."[6]

A Continuing Threat Two years before his death, Osama bin Laden boasted that his disciples would "continue *jihad* for another seven years, seven years after that, and even seven years more after."[7] A year after bin Laden's death, however, Matthew Olsen, the director of the National Counterterrorism Center, said that the "core al Qaeda," which operates out of Pakistan, "was at its weakest point in the last ten years."[8] More than half of the group's leaders had been killed by American military raids and drone strikes, and its members were focused more on survival than on planning large-scale terrorist operations.[9]

Weakened as it may be, al Qaeda is still a formidable organization. It now relies on a loose affiliation of franchises that operate in Iraq, Yemen, Somalia, Nigeria, and other nations—"more of a McDonald's . . . than a General Motors," in the words of one expert.[10] For example, an al Qaeda spinoff operating out of Algeria has been linked with the killings of four Americans in Benghazi, Libya, on September 11, 2012. In April 2013, Canadian authorities foiled an alleged plot to bomb a passenger train supported by al Qaeda elements in Iran. Overall, al Qaeda affiliates conducted more operations in the year after bin Laden's death than they did in the final year of his life.[11] (See Figure 16.1 on the facing page for a description of some of al Qaeda's "franchises.")

Self-Radicalization Despite heavy activity by al Qaeda splinter groups near their home bases in the Middle East, one U.S. official says that is it "really hard to imagine" one of them "gathering together the resources, the talent, and the money to mount another 9/11-type of attack."[12] As an alternative, al Qaeda propagandists such as Samir Khan, introduced in the opening to this chapter, use the Internet to try to recruit "lonely people who are looking for a cause."[13]

FIGURE 16.1 Al Qaeda's Global Partners

The Islamist groups described in this figure are loosely affiliated with the "original" al Qaeda. They have a number of different goals, showing the diversity of international terrorist groups that base themselves in the Middle East.

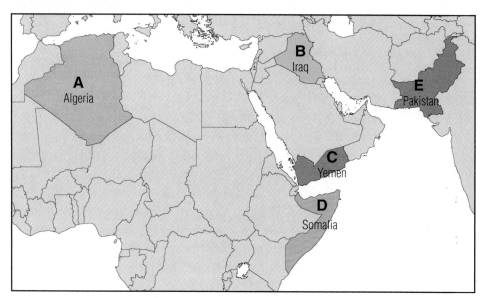

GROUP	GOALS	HIGH-PROFILE ACTIVITY
A. Al Qaeda in Islamic Maghreb (AQIM)	Remove Algeria's government, attack U.S.	In 2007, detonated car bombs outside the Algerian prime minister's office and several police stations—the blasts killed more than 30 and wounded more than 150.
B. Al Qaeda in Iraq (AQI)	Harass American military in Iraq; oust elected Iraqi government.	Destabilizes Iraqi society with numerous suicide bombing attacks on U.S. military personnel and local civilians.
C. Al Qaeda in the Arabian Peninsula (AQAP)	Establish safe haven for like-minded terrorists in Yemen.	Trained underwear suicide bomber, who attempted to destroy a Northwest Airlines flight to Detroit in 2009, shipped packages containing bombs to Jewish religious centers in Chicago in 2010.
D. Al Shabaab	Establish Islamic law in Somalia.	In 2010, set off bombs in two Ugandan bars that were screening soccer's World Cup tournament, killing at least 70 people.
E. Lashkar-e-Taiba	Establish Islamic rule in India; unite Muslims in region.	Launched three days of coordinated attacks in Mumbai, India, in 2008, killing 164 and wounding 308.

Such was certainly the case with Major Nidal Hasan, a U.S. Army psychiatrist who fatally shot thirteen people in Fort Hood, Texas, in 2009. Hasan was influenced by the online writings of Anwar al-Awlaki, a radical U.S.-born cleric affiliated with al Qaeda in the Arabian Peninsula. (Al-Awlaki was killed in the same drone strike that ended Khan's life.) In turn, Hasan is held up as a positive example in a video produced by the "core" al Qaeda in Pakistan called "You Are Only Responsible for Yourself." This video urges Muslims in the United States and Europe to stage terrorist attacks without orders from foreign operatives.[14]

"Self-radicalized" terrorists such as Nidal Hasan and the Tsarnaev brothers have the ability to operate under law enforcement's radar up until the moment they strike. This ability is often used as justification for preventive policing, described in Chapter 6, which relies on informants and undercover agents to stop homegrown terrorist plots before they develop. Such tactics can be effective on the international level as well. Several years ago, for example, a double agent posing as a suicide bomber managed to infiltrate al Qaeda in the Arabian Peninsula. When, in 2012, this agent was given a mission to destroy a U.S.-bound airplane with a bomb to be hidden in his clothing, he delivered the explosive device to American intelligence agents instead.[15]

TERRORISM TRENDS FOR THE FUTURE Smaller operations involving American-born terrorists influenced by international sources reflect several trends identified by homeland security expert Brian M. Jenkins. Each of these trends de-emphasizes the importance of any single, dominant organization such as al Qaeda:[16]

Identify three important trends in international terrorism.

LEARNING
2
OBJECTIVE

1. *Terrorists have developed more efficient methods of financing their operations* through avenues such as Internet fund-raising, drug trafficking, and money laundering schemes.

2. *Terrorists have developed more efficient organizations* based on the small-business model, in which individuals are responsible for different tasks including recruiting, planning, propaganda, and social services such as supporting the families of suicide bombers. These "employees" do not answer to a single leader but rather function as a network that is quick to adjust and difficult to infiltrate.

3. *Terrorists have exploited new communications technology to mount global campaigns,* relying on the Internet for immediate, direct communication among operatives and as a crucial recruiting tool. Furthermore, large numbers of "jihobbyists" are operating online, disseminating extremist writings and videos and using social media to spread the terrorist message in cyberspace.

As you may have noted, each of these trends favors the global terrorism movement. Indeed, Jenkins finds that today's *jihadists* are dangerous, resilient survivors who have achieved some strategic results and are determined to continue attacking their enemies. "Destroying their terrorist enterprise," he concludes, "will take years."[17]

Terrorists in Court

On the morning of September 12, 2001, al Qaeda spokesman Sulaiman Abu Ghaith stood by the side of his father-in-law, Osama bin Laden, and celebrated the previous day's attacks against the United States. Almost twelve years later, in February 2013, American agents arrested Abu Ghaith in the Middle Eastern country of Jordan. Abu Ghaith was immediately brought to a federal court in New York City, where he pleaded not guilty to charges of conspiring to kill Americans. A number of politicians disagreed with this strategy, arguing that Abu Ghaith should be treated as a military prisoner and, in the words of Kentucky Republican Senator Mitch McConnell, "interrogated without having to overcome the objections of his civilian lawyers."[18] The debate over "what to do" with suspected terrorists has divided American lawmakers for more than a decade and appears set to continue well into the future.

THE CRIMINAL JUSTICE MODEL Under the *criminal justice model* of homeland security, terrorism is treated like any other crime. That is, the law enforcement, court, and corrections systems work together to deter terrorist activity through the threat of arrest and punishment, as is the case with Sulaiman Abu Ghaith. Since the September 11, 2001, attacks, the criminal justice system has, as we have seen throughout this textbook, been very active in apprehending, prosecuting, and convicting terrorist suspects.

From 2001 to 2011, nearly 500 individuals were convicted in sixty different federal courts in thirty-seven states. About 220 of these defendants violated federal laws related directly to international terrorism such as the use of *weapons of mass destruction* and conspiracy to murder Americans in foreign countries.[19] (**Weapon of mass destruction** is an umbrella term used to cover deadly instruments that represent a significant threat to persons or property.) At the end of 2012, the Federal Bureau of Prisons was holding 362 people convicted in terrorism-related cases. Of these inmates, 269 were found guilty in connection with international terrorism.[20]

THE MILITARY MODEL From 2001 to 2009, the administration of President George W. Bush made it clear that, besides the criminal justice model, there was a parallel response to the terrorist threat: the *military model*. Although the scope of this textbook does not include U.S. military actions in Afghanistan, Iraq, and other global "hot spots," the militarization of the fight against terrorists did lead to several developments with repercussions for the criminal justice system.

Under President Bush, the U.S. Department of Defense was authorized to designate certain terrorist suspects detained during the course of military operations as **enemy combatants.** According to the policy at the time, this designation allowed a suspect to be "held indefinitely until the end of America's war on terrorism or until the military determines on a case-by-case basis that the particular detainee no longer poses a threat to the United States or its allies."[21] As a result, about eight hundred enemy combatants were transferred to the U.S. Naval Base at Guantánamo Bay, Cuba (GTMO).

At the time, American officials insisted that, because these al Qaeda and Afghanistan-based operatives had been captured during military operations, they could be held indefinitely without being charged with any wrongdoing.[22] The detainees were denied access to legal representation or family members and were subjected to harsh interrogation tactics such as simulated drowning, sleep and food deprivation, physical stress positions, and isolation.[23] As a result of the conditions at GTMO, the U.S. government has come under a great deal of international criticism, particularly from Arab and Muslim countries and from those non-Muslim nations, such as Australia and Great Britain, whose citizens have been held at the detention center.

Political Issues By 2013, only about 170 detainees remained at GTMO, with the rest having been released or repatriated to their home countries. The Obama administration has indicated a strong desire to close down the facility, and no new prisoners have been sent to GTMO since President Obama took office in 2009. Indeed, that year the president proposed moving all GTMO detainees to a supermax prison in Illinois. As a response, the U.S. Congress passed legislation that barred the transfer of any detained

■ In March 2013, Abdel Hameed Shehadeh, right, was convicted in federal court of lying to FBI agents about his intention to travel to Pakistan and join a terrorist organization. Do you think that such behavior is criminal? Why or why not? How is Shehadeh's conviction an example of the criminal justice model of homeland security?
AP Photo/Elizabeth Williams

Weapon of Mass Destruction A weapon that has the capacity to cause large number of casualties or significant property damage.

Enemy Combatant An individual who has supported foreign terrorist organizations such as al Qaeda that are engaged in hostilities against the military operations of the United States.

enemy combatants onto domestic soil.[24] (See the feature *You Be the President—The Enemy Within?* below to learn how this issue resurfaced following the capture of one of the Boston Marathon bombers.)

Security Issues Regardless of congressional opposition, the president does have the option of using an executive waiver to transfer GTMO detainees to the mainland United States. Despite his misgivings about "keeping individuals in no man's land in perpetuity,"[25] as of the summer of 2013 President Obama had not taken advantage of this waiver. The reason: many homeland security officials believe that these detainees still pose a threat. About one in seven released from GTMO has returned, or is suspected of having returned, to terrorist activities.[26] One former prisoner, Said Ali al-Shihri, became the deputy leader of al Qaeda operations in Yemen.[27]

In 2008, the United States Supreme Court ruled that GTMO detainees should have a "meaningful opportunity" to challenge their incarceration in court.[28] Four years later, however, even though the federal government had provided no such opportunity, the Court refused to revisit the issue.[29] Furthermore, at least fifty GTMO inmates are con-

THE ENEMY WITHIN?

Explain the primary difference between the U.S. government's treatment of enemy combatants and the treatment of terrorist suspects under the jurisdiction of the criminal justice system.

LEARNING **3** **OBJECTIVE**

Somchai Rakin/Shutterstock.com

THE FACTS As Dzhokhar Tsarnaev recovered from life-threatening injuries in a Boston hospital bed, a number of lawmakers insisted that he be treated as a war criminal rather than a common criminal. Certainly, the carnage that resulted from two pressure-cooker bombs detonated during the Boston Marathon by Dzhokhar and his brother Tamerlan resembled a battlefield more than a crime scene. Furthermore, if designated an enemy combatant, Dzokhar could be interrogated by federal agents without the protections afforded to criminal suspects in this country. "We're at war," said South Carolina Republican Senator Lindsey Graham. "The idea that the only way we can question [Dzhokhar] about national security matters is to go through his lawyer—that is absolutely crazy."

THE LAW According to federal statute, an enemy combatant must be a foreign national associated with al Qaeda in some capacity. Dzhokhar is a U.S. citizen, and although he and his brother seem to have been influenced by al Qaeda propaganda, there is no evidence that either had any direct contact with the terrorist organization. In 2004, however, the U.S. Supreme Court suggested that, in "narrow circumstances," there is "no bar to this nation's holding one of its own citizens as an enemy combatant."

YOUR DECISION Senator Graham of South Carolina does not suggest that Dzhokhar be transferred directly from his hospital bed to a military prison. Rather, Graham wants him to be interrogated for thirty days as an enemy combatant to determine whether he and his brother have more substantial ties to al Qaeda. As president, you have a great deal of discretion to determine when "narrow circumstances" exist. Should Dzhokhar be designated an enemy combatant for purposes of interrogation, or should he be arrested and provided the protections of the criminal justice system?

To see how the administration of President Barack Obama dealt with this situation, go to Example 16.1 in Appendix B.

sidered too dangerous for release. Federal officials will review their status periodically, but in theory they could be held indefinitely.[30] In the spring of 2013, frustration over the possibility of indefinite detention led to hunger strikes involving nearly one hundred GTMO detainees.

MILITARY JUSTICE Besides indefinite detention, the other possibility for those who remain incarcerated at GTMO involves **military tribunals,** which are carried out at the naval base. Such tribunals—also known as *military commissions*—offer more limited protections than those afforded to defendants in civilian courts, as described in Chapter 10. In a tribunal, the accused does not have the right to a trial by jury, as guaranteed by the Sixth Amendment. Instead, a panel of at least five military commissioners acts in place of the judge and jury and decides questions of both "fact and law."

Only two-thirds of the panel members need to agree for a conviction, in contrast to the unanimous jury required by criminal trials. Furthermore, evidence that would be inadmissible in criminal court, such as some forms of hearsay testimony (discussed in Chapter 10) and "fruit of the poisoned tree" from unreasonable searches and seizures (discussed in Chapter 7), is allowed before these tribunals.[31] (See Figure 16.2 below for an overview of the rules that govern military trials.)

Coerced Interrogation Perhaps the most high-profile detainee being held at GTMO is Khalid Sheikh Mohammed, the self-proclaimed "mastermind" behind the September 11, 2001, attacks. Initially, the Bush administration decided to try Mohammed and four of his colleagues using military tribunals. When President Obama took office, he announced that the proceedings would be moved to a federal court in New York City.

These plans were derailed, thanks to the outcome of the first trial of a GTMO detainee in civilian criminal court. The defendant in that case, a Tanzanian citizen named Ahmed Khalfan Ghailani, was an integral member of a 1998 al Qaeda plot that led to the bombing of two American embassies in East Africa. In 2011, a federal jury in New York convicted Ghailani of one count of conspiracy to destroy government

FIGURE 16.2 Military Trials for Terrorist Suspects

The guidelines for military tribunals can be found in the Military Commissions Act of 2009. Several basic questions concerning the procedures used in such tribunals are answered below.

Who is eligible to appear before a military tribunal?

Only "unprivileged enemy belligerents" can be tried by a military tribunal. A person is considered an "unprivileged enemy belligerent" if he or she

A. Has engaged in hostilities against the United States or one of its military allies;

B. Has purposefully and materially supported hostilities against the United States or one of its military allies; or

C. Was a member of al Qaeda at the time of the offense.

Who decides the suspect's guilt or innocence?

A suspect's fate will be decided by a tribunal of at least five military officers. The vote will be conducted in secret, and a two-thirds majority is necessary to find the suspect guilty.

What procedural protections will the suspect be granted during military tribunals?

The military tribunals provide the following procedural protections:

A. The right of the accused to present witnesses in his or her defense and cross-examine hostile witnesses.

B. Protection against self-incriminating statements (see Chapter 10).

C. A ban on statements obtained through cruel, inhuman, or degrading treatment.

D. The ability to offer the affirmative defense of mental disease or defect (see Chapter 4).

Source: Military Commissions Act of 2009, Public Law No. 111-84, Sections 1801–1807, 123 Stat. 2190 (2009).

Detainees in orange jumpsuits sit in a holding area at the U.S. Naval Base at Guantánamo Bay, Cuba. Do you think non-U.S. citizens who are in the custody of the U.S. military should be protected by our Constitution? Why or why not?
Reuters/U.S. Department of Defense/Petty Officer 1st class Shane T. McCoy/Handout

buildings and property, and Judge Lewis A. Kaplan sentenced him to life in federal prison. At the same time, however, Ghailani was acquitted of more than 280 counts of conspiracy and murder, partially because the judge disallowed damning evidence that had been improperly obtained through coerced interrogation. As you may recall from Chapter 7, such evidence is not admissible in criminal court.

By the federal government's own admission, its agents subjected 9/11 "mastermind" Mohammed to waterboarding more than 180 times during questioning.[32] Waterboarding is a technique that involves repeatedly pouring water down the throat of the subject to reproduce the feeling of drowning. If the fruits of coerced interrogation were not allowed in Ghailani's criminal trial, then a great deal of evidence would similarly be inadmissible with regard to Mohammed. Consequently, spurred by pressure from Congress, the Obama administration decided to adjudicate Mohammed and his associates in a military tribunal, where they face the death penalty in proceedings that commenced in May 2012.

The Future of GTMO By May 2013, only seven of the 779 prisoners housed at GTMO had been convicted by military tribunals.[33] To improve these odds, federal officials have decided, when possible, to offer plea bargains—particularly to "low-value" detainees who have not committed violence against Americans.[34] The pace of such efforts has been slow, however, and tribunals of "high-value" detainees such as Khalid Sheikh Mohammed are expected to take years to complete. As a result, it will take an act of formidable political will from the Obama administration to close down GTMO in the foreseeable future.

Border Security

In its final report on the events that led up to September 11, 2001, the 9/11 Commission had plenty of blame to spread around. Poor preparation for a terrorist attack, poor performances by the Federal Bureau of Investigation (FBI) and other domestic law enforcement agencies, and poor intelligence gathering by the Central Intelligence Agency (CIA) were all highlighted as causes for concern. The commission seemed particularly disturbed, however, at the ease with which proven and potential terrorists could enter the United States. "Protecting borders was not a national security issue before 9/11," the report remarked, with more than a hint of disbelief.[35] The protection of our national borders has certainly become an issue since the commission published its report, though questions remain as to whether homeland security has significantly improved as a result.

REGULATED POINTS OF ENTRY People and goods legally enter the United States through checkpoints at airports, seaports, and guarded land stations. At these regulated points of entry, government agents check documents such as passports and *visas* and inspect luggage and cargo to ensure compliance with immigration and trade laws. (A **visa** is a document issued by the U.S. State Department that indicates the conditions under

Visa Official authorization allowing a person to travel to and within the issuing country.

which a holder can enter and travel within the United States.) The task is immense. Close to 100 million foreign visitors arrive at America's more than one hundred international airports each year, with millions more passing through patrol stations along our borders with Mexico and Canada.

Illegal Presence The September 11 plot exposed, among other homeland security failures, a weakness in America's immigration system: an inability to track foreigners who fail to conform to the terms of their visas and are therefore illegally present in the United States. Five of the 9/11 hijackers had violated their visas—and were therefore eligible for removal from the country—before they carried out the attacks. To remedy this situation, the Department of Homeland Security created the United States Visitor and Immigrant Status Indicator Technology (US-VISIT) program. Under US-VISIT, which started in 2004, most foreigners entering the United States on visas are subject to fingerprinting and a facial scan using digital photography. Their names are also checked against criminal records and watch lists for suspected terrorists.

Although the program has been effective in recording the entry of foreigners, it has been less successful in following their movements once they are in the United States. Furthermore, without the cooperation of the visitor, US-VISIT is unable to confirm when, or if, she or he has left the country. As a result, about 200,000 non-U.S. citizens intentionally overstay their visas each year.[36] Amine El Khalifi, a Moroccan citizen who pleaded guilty in 2012 to an attempted suicide bombing of the U.S. Capitol Building in Washington, D.C., had overstayed his visa by twelve years at the time of his arrest.

Screening Challenges On April 13, 2013, customs officials at the Detroit Metro Airport in Romulus, Michigan, noticed that that a page had been removed from the passport of Saudi Arabian citizen Hussain Al Khawahir. As a result, they examined Al Khawahir's luggage and found a pressure cooker similar to the model used in the Boston Marathon bombings we have been discussing in this chapter.

One of the hallmarks of homeland security has been increased scrutiny of travelers at the nation's airports. The Department of Homeland Security's Transportation Security Administration (TSA) has overseen significant changes in the way airports screen passengers, luggage, and cargo. Border personnel, both at home and abroad, have been trained to scrutinize all foreigners entering the United States for "terrorist risk factors." The FBI's Terrorist Screening Center has also compiled a "no fly" list of individuals who are deemed to pose a risk of terrorist activity and therefore are not allowed to board flights leaving or entering the United States.

Screening Failure Sometimes port-of-entry strategies succeed, and sometimes they fail. For instance, the name of Tamerlan Tsarnaev, one of the suspects in the Boston Marathon bombing, was on a government "no fly" list at the time he left the United States for a six-month trip to predominantly Muslim regions of Russia in 2012. Because of spelling errors in Tsarnaev's name, his travel did not trigger any government reaction.[37]

In addition, two of the risk factors mentioned above are the purchase of a one-way plane ticket with cash and failure to check any luggage for a long flight. These behavior patterns may indicate a traveler who wishes to keep his or her identity hidden and has no plans for a return flight. On December 25, 2009, Umar Abdulmutallab followed this pattern exactly. Yet, he was allowed to board Northwest Flight 253 from Amsterdam to Detroit with a bomb hidden in this underwear. Abdulmutallab's suicide mission failed largely thanks to the bomb's failure to detonate.

Johan Swanepoel/
Shutterstock.com

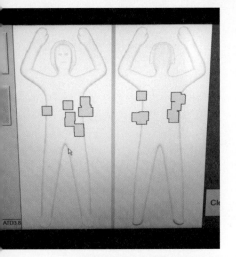

Photo by David L Ryan/*The Boston Globe*
via Getty Images

The "underwear bomb" carried by Umar Abdulmutallab onto the flight from Amsterdam to Detroit did not trigger the airport metal detector he passed through because it was not made of metal. Instead, it was fashioned out of plastic, the apparent creation of a bomb maker associated with al Qaeda in the Arabian Peninsula (AQAP) named Ibrahim al-Asiri. In response, the TSA has installed full-body scanners at nearly two hundred airports in the United States. These scanners, at least theoretically, are better able to detect nonmetallic explosives.

There are indications, however, that the body scanners have not dissuaded AQAP's efforts to get explosives onto American airliners. Two years after Abdulmutallab's failed attempt, federal agents uncovered a more sophisticated version of the original underwear bomb, thanks to the undercover agent mentioned previously who had infiltrated AQAP in Yemen. Furthermore, some U.S. intelligence agents believe that al-Asiri is working on a bomb that would be surgically implanted in the body of a suicidal subject. "The idea is to insert the device in the terrorist's love handle," said one government source. Though seemingly far-fetched, such reports raise the uncomfortable specter of explosive devices that the TSA is unable to detect.

Thinking about the "Body Bomb"

Recognizing the possibility that potential suicide bombers may be able to get dangerous devices on airplanes without being detected, the TSA has trained some security screeners in the art of the "chat down." These screeners should be able to spot passengers who are security risks by their facial expressions, body language, and speech patterns. What are some of the potential benefits and drawbacks of this form of airport security?

UNREGULATED BORDER ENTRY Every year hundreds of thousands of non-U.S. citizens, unable to legally obtain visas, enter the country illegally by crossing the large, unregulated stretches of our borders with Mexico and Canada. Securing these border areas has proved problematic, if not impossible, for the various homeland security agencies. As a result, the border areas provide a conduit for illegal drugs, firearms and other contraband, illegal immigrants, and, possibly, terrorists and weapons of mass destruction to be smuggled into the country.

A Logistical Nightmare The main problem for the U.S. Border Patrol and local law enforcement agents in trying to stem this flow is logistics. The U.S.-Canadian border extends for 3,957 miles (not counting Alaska), and the border with Mexico stretches for 1,954 miles. Much of the borderland consists of uninhabited plains and woodland to the north and desert and scrubland to the south. To compensate, the homeland security presence on the Mexican border has never been greater.

The Department of Homeland Security (DHS) has fenced off about 650 miles of the border, mostly near international bridges and urban areas. About 21,500 Border Patrol agents are deployed in this area, operating 16,875 vehicles, 269 aircraft, 300 boats, 300 camera towers, and a number of aerial drones.[38] Even so, the Government Accountability Office estimates that only 44 percent of the southwestern border is under "operational control."[39] Furthermore, several years ago DHS canceled a project to build a "virtual fence"—consisting of sensors, cameras, and other surveillance technology—along the border because of high costs and low efficiency.

CAREERS IN CJ

Photo Courtesy of Paul Morris

PAUL MORRIS

CUSTOMS AND BORDER PROTECTION AGENT

The most memorable day of my career was, without a doubt, September 11, 2001. That morning, as I watched the fall of the Twin Towers, I knew that things were going to be different. Personally, the attacks left me with a resolve to ensure, to the maximum extent possible, that nothing similar ever happens again. Professionally, that day marked a sea charge with respect to how the federal border agencies viewed border security. Ever since, our anti-terrorism mission has been elevated above our other responsibilities, such as controlling illegal immigration, protecting our agricultural interests, and stopping the flow of illegal narcotics into this country.

To be sure, as each of these tasks is crucially important, the extra burdens of anti-terrorism pose a significant challenge. With the volume of vehicles, cargo, and persons crossing our borders, there can be no guarantees that a potential terrorist or weapon of mass destruction cannot slip across the border. Nevertheless, with advanced identification technology, increased personnel, and a more efficient infrastructure, I am confident that the possibility of such a breach is low.

SOCIAL MEDIA CAREER TIP Consider setting up personal and career-oriented Facebook pages or Twitter accounts and keeping your posts on each separated. Remember, though, that just because material is on your "personal" page or account, it still may be seen by others outside your network.

www.dhs.gov

Terrorist Crossings Many national security officials worry that the porous nature of America's borders will prove too tempting for terrorist organizations to resist. These fears have led to increased homeland security measures along the U.S.-Canadian border, which had previously received much less attention than southern crossing routes. Still, smugglers have little problem getting marijuana, Ecstasy, and methamphetamine (heading south) and tax-free cigarettes, weapons, and cocaine (heading north) across the divide.[40] A 2011 government report, citing the threat of "known terrorist organizations" operating in Canada, determined that just thirty-two miles of the northern border have an acceptable level of security.[41] Despite these worries, as of late 2013 no high-level terrorist suspects are known to have taken an illegal land route into the United States.

Cyberattacks—The Future of Terrorism?

On the morning of August 15, 2012, employees of the Saudi Arabian oil company Saudi Aramco who turned on their computer screens at work were in for a surprise. Instead of accessing documents, spreadsheets, or e-mails, they saw an image of a burning American flag. Though it caused the oil company significant cost and inconvenience, this **cyberattack** was probably designed to make a political statement protesting the company's ties with the United States.[42] Such unlawful attempts to disrupt computer systems have the potential to do much greater damage, and are considered by many homeland security experts to be the next great challenge of international terrorism.

Cyberattack An attempt to damage or disrupt computer systems or electronic networks operated by computers.

This map shows the locations of 7,200 key industrial control systems identified by the Department of Homeland Security as potential targets of a terrorist attack. Why is it important that each of these control systems is directly linked to the Internet?
Courtesy U.S. Department of Homeland Security

INFRASTRUCTURE SECURITY In the context of homeland security, concern about cyberattacks focuses on the ability of outside parties to attack our infrastructure. As you may recall from Chapter 5, a nation's infrastructure includes large-scale operations that control supplies of energy, transportation, food, and public health. According to the Department of Homeland Security, America's infrastructure suffered two hundred cyberattacks in 2012, though none caused widespread disruption of services.[43]

In general, cyberattacks are carried out by the use of malicious computer programs known as *malware*—discussed later in the chapter—that damage computer systems. In particular, malware can be designed to create *denial-of-service*, a situation in which the targeted operation can no longer function.[44] In 2009, for example, malware known as Stuxnet effectively sabotaged the operation of Iran's nuclear facilities. The worst-case scenario involving cyberattacks would, in the words of one American homeland security official, make "9/11 look like a tea party."[45] Among the possible catastrophes: gas pipelines destroyed, national bank records wiped clean, 911 call centers jammed, air traffic control centers shut down, and hospitals rendered inoperable.

STATE ACTORS As much as international terrorist organizations such as al Qaeda might desire these types of results, cyberattacks remain beyond their abilities for the time being. Creating malware such as Stuxnet requires the work of numerous well-trained computer experts and costs upwards of $1 million.[46] In fact, most large-scale cyberattacks today involve nations rather than individuals. Stuxnet was probably created with the support of the governments of the United States and Israel. Iran, in turn, is believed to be behind the cyberattack on Saudi Aramco described above. In September 2012, Chinese operatives apparently gained access to the computer system of Telvent, a company that monitors half the oil and gas pipelines in North America.

Consequently, large-scale cyberattacks are treated as a military problem. Still, the possibility that nonstate actors will, at some point, have the technical ability to launch a widespread computer attack is a growing concern for anti-terrorism law enforcement agencies. Private companies, which may not have the funds or expertise to protect against cyberattacks, control about 90 percent of the infrastructure in the United States. Several years ago, a computer expert showed that it would be relatively easy to manipulate the equipment that chemically treats California's drinking water.[47] According to James Lewis of the Center for Strategic and International Studies, America suffers from a "misplaced sense of invulnerability" when it comes to cyberattacks, just as it did regarding international terrorism prior to September 11, 2001.[48]

SELF ASSESSMENT

Fill in the blanks and check your answers on page 556.

Terrorists are _____ actors, meaning that they are not affiliated with any established nation. Under the criminal justice model of homeland security, terrorist acts are treated like _____, and terrorists are prosecuted in _____ courts. Under the military model, suspected terrorists are designated _____ _____ and tried by military _____. In the future, international terrorist organizations may develop the technical expertise to launch _____ against the infrastructure of the United States.

CYBER CRIME

"No one expected the Internet to become a critical global infrastructure," an international security expert told lawmakers in Washington, D.C., several years ago. "The Internet is incredibly valuable, but it's easy to attack."[49]

The expert was speaking about cyberattacks, but he easily could have been describing many other areas where the World Wide Web and the criminal justice system intersect. In May 2013, for example, federal prosecutors brought charges against seven men who were part of a global crime ring that stole $45 million from automated teller machines (ATMs). The "ingenious" scheme started when its ringleaders used the Internet to break into the computer system of an Indian company that handles prepaid debit-card transactions for Visa and MasterCard. The cyber criminals then raised the withdrawal limits on numerous debit accounts, and provided operatives in twenty-seven countries with the account numbers and passwords. These accomplices then made about 4,500 fraudulent ATM transactions over the course of several hours. The seven Americans, working in New York City, stole about $2.8 million.[50]

"In the place of guns and masks, this cyber crime organization used laptops and the Internet," said one of the federal prosecutors involved in the case.[51] In fact, guns and masks are no longer the preferred tools of bank robbers. From 2001 to 2011, the rate of bank robberies in the United States dropped by half, a trend industry insiders explain by pointing to the rise in criminal operations such as the ATM scheme. "Clearly, as more and more transactions become electronic, more bank crimes become electronic," says Doug Johnson of the American Bankers Association.[52]

Computer Crime and the Internet

Nearly every business in today's economy, banks included, relies on computers to conduct its daily affairs and to provide consumers with easy access to its products and services. Furthermore, more than 500 million American household devices are now connected to the Internet, and the proliferation of handheld Internet devices has made it possible to be online at almost any time or place. In short, the Internet has become a place where large numbers of people interact socially and commercially. In any such environment, wrongdoing has an opportunity to flourish.

The U.S. Department of Justice broadly defines **computer crime** as "any violation of criminal law that involves a knowledge of computer technology for [its] perpetration, investigation, or prosecution."[53] More specifically, computer crimes can be divided into three categories, according to the computer's role in the particular criminal act:[54]

1. The computer is the *object* of a crime, such as when the computer itself or its software is stolen.
2. The computer is the *subject* of a crime, just as a house is the subject

"*You know, you can do this just as easily online.*"

of a burglary. This type of computer crime occurs, for example, when someone "breaks into" a computer to steal personal information such as a credit-card number.

3. The computer is the *instrument* of a crime, as when the plotters of the ATM scheme detailed above used a computer to manipulate the withdrawal limits on thousands of prepaid debit cards.

In this chapter, we will be using a broader term, **cyber crime,** to describe any criminal activity occurring via a computer in the virtual community of the Internet. It is very difficult, if not impossible, to determine how much cyber crime actually takes place. Often, people never know that they have been the victims of this type of criminal activity. Furthermore, businesses sometimes fail to report such crimes for fear of losing customer confidence. Nonetheless, in 2012, the Internet Crime Complaint Center (IC3), operated as a partnership between the FBI and the National White Collar Crime Center, received about 290,000 complaints representing just over $525 million in victim losses.[55] According to the Norton Cybercrime Report, nearly 70 percent of all adults who use the Internet have been victimized by cyber crime, with annual global losses exceeding $380 billion.[56]

Cyber Crimes against Persons and Property

Most cyber crimes are not "new" crimes. Rather, they are existing crimes in which the Internet is the instrument of wrongdoing. The challenge for law enforcement is to apply traditional laws, which were designed to protect persons from physical harm or to safeguard their physical property, to crimes committed in cyberspace. This challenge is made all the greater by two aspects of the Internet that may aid the perpetrators of cyber crimes—the anonymity it provides and the ease with which large amounts of information may be transferred quickly. Here, we look at several types of activity that constitute "updated" crimes against persons and property—online consumer fraud, cyber theft, and cyberstalking.

Distinguish cyber crime from "traditional" crime.

LEARNING

4

OBJECTIVE

CYBER CONSUMER FRAUD The expanding world of e-commerce has created many benefits for consumers. It has also led to some challenging problems, including fraud conducted via the Internet. In general, fraud is any misrepresentation knowingly made with the intention of deceiving another person. Furthermore, the victim must reasonably rely on the fraudulent information to her or his detriment. **Cyber fraud,** then, is fraud committed over the Internet. Scams that were once conducted solely by mail or phone can now be found online, and new technology has led to increasingly more creative ways to commit fraud. Online dating scams, for example, have increased dramatically in recent years, with fraudsters creating fake profiles to deceive unwitting romantic partners. According to the IC3, in 2012 online romance scam artists defrauded victims out of more than $55 million.[57] In one case, a fictitious American solider in Iraq convinced his online "sweetheart" that he had been kidnapped and needed $250,000 from her to buy his freedom.

As you can see in Figure 16.3 on the left, fraud accounts for the largest percentage of losses related to consumer cyber crime. Two widely reported forms of cyber crime are *advance fee fraud* and *online auction fraud*. In the simplest form of advance fee fraud, consumers order and pay for items such as automobiles or antiques that are never delivered. Online auction fraud is also fairly straightforward. A person lists an item for auction, on either a legitimate or a fake auction site, and then refuses to send the product after

FIGURE 16.3 The Costs of Cyber Crime

After polling adults in twenty-four countries, including the United States, researchers associated with the American security software company Symantec estimated that nearly 1.5 million computer users worldwide are victims of cyber crime each day. As the graph below shows, 85 percent of the financial costs associated with cyber crime are the result of fraud, theft, or computer repairs made necessary by the wrongdoing.

Other 15%

Theft 17%

Fraud 42%

Repairs 26%

Source: *2012 Norton Cybercrime Report* (Mountain View, CA: Symantec, 2012), 4, 6.

receiving payment. In 2012, for example, the FBI uncovered a scheme in which an Oregon couple took photos of items on store shelves, offered them for auction on the Internet, and collected more than $300,000 from unsuspecting bidders.

CYBER THEFT In cyberspace, thieves are not subject to the physical limitations of the "real" world. A thief can steal data stored in a networked computer with network access from anywhere on the globe. Only the speed of the connection and the thief's computer equipment limit the quantity of data that can be stolen.

Identity Theft This freedom from physical limitations has led to a marked increase in **identity theft,** which occurs when the wrongdoer steals a form of identification—such as a name, date of birth, or Social Security number—and uses the information to access the victim's financial resources. According to the federal government, about 7 percent of American households have at least one member who has been the victim of identity theft.[58]

More than half of identity theft involves the misappropriation of an existing credit-card account.[59] In the "real world," this is generally accomplished by stealing an actual credit card. Online, an identity thief can steal financial information by fooling Web sites into thinking that he or she is the actual account holder. For example, important personal information such as one's birthday, hometown, or employer that is available on social media sites such as Facebook can be used to convince a third party to reveal the victim's Social Security or bank account number.

The more personal information a cyber criminal obtains, the easier it is for him or her to find a victim's online user name. Once the online user name has been compromised, the easier it is to steal a victim's password, which is often the last line of defense to financial information. Numerous software programs aid identity thieves in illegally obtaining passwords. A technique called *keystroke logging,* for example, relies on software that embeds itself in a victim's computer and records every keystroke made on that computer. User names and passwords are then recorded and sold to the highest bidder. Internet users should also be wary of any links contained within e-mails sent from an unknown source, as these links can sometimes be used to illegally obtain personal information. (See Figure 16.4 below for some hints on how to protect your online passwords.)

Phishing A distinct form of identity theft known as **phishing** adds a different wrinkle to this particular form of cyber crime. In a phishing attack, the perpetrators "fish" for financial

Identity Theft The theft of personal information, such as a person's name, driver's license number, or Social Security number.

Phishing Sending an unsolicited e-mail that falsely claims to be from a legitimate organization in an attempt to acquire sensitive information from the recipient.

FIGURE 16.4 Protecting Online Passwords

Once an online password has been compromised, the information on the protected Web site is fair game for identity thieves. By following these simple rules, you can strengthen the protection provided by your online passwords.

1. **Don't** use existing words such as your pet's name or your hometown. Such words are easy for computer identity theft programs to decode.
2. **Do** use at least eight characters in your passwords, with a nonsensical combination of upper- and lower-case letters, numbers, and symbols. A weak password is "scout1312." A strong password is "4X$dQ%3Z9j."
3. **Don't** use the same username and password for different Web accounts. If you do, then each account is in danger if one account is compromised.
4. **Do** use a different password for each Web account. If necessary, write down the various passwords and keep the list in a safe place.
5. **Don't** use information that can be easily found online or guessed at in choosing the questions that Web sites use to verify your password. That is, don't select questions such as "What is your birthday?" or "What is your city of birth?" Instead, choose questions with obscure answers that you are certain to remember or can easily look up.
6. **Don't** log on to any Web site if you are connected to the Internet via a wireless network (Wi-Fi) that is not itself password protected.

Cyberstalking The crime of stalking, committed in cyberspace through the use of e-mail, text messages, or another form of electronic communication.

Several years ago, Patrick Macchione was convicted of cyberstalking a fellow University of Central Florida student. Do you agree that cyberstalking can cause just as much "reasonable fear" in a victim as physical stalking? Why or why not?
Photo Courtesy of Seminole County Sheriff's Office

data and passwords from consumers by posing as a legitimate business such as a bank or credit-card company. The "phisher" sends an e-mail asking the recipient to "update" or "confirm" vital information, often with the threat that an account or some other service will be discontinued if the information is not provided. Once the unsuspecting target enters the information, the phisher can use it to masquerade as the person or to drain his or her bank or credit account.

In 2012, thousands of unwitting users were fooled by e-mails allegedly sent by local utility companies offering federal aid—apparently authorized by President Barack Obama—in paying their electrical bills. Victims were required to provide their Social Security number to ensure that they qualified for the help. Over the past several years, dozens of companies, including Amazon.com, Zappos.com, and LinkedIn, have been forced to warn consumers that fraudulent e-mails asking for personal and financial information had been sent in the companies' names.

Phishing scams have also spread to other areas, such as text messaging and social-networking sites. Nearly 13 percent of all phishing, for example, takes place using Facebook alerts.[60] A new form of this fraud, called spear phishing, is much more difficult to detect because the messages seem to have come from co-workers, friends, or family workers. "It's a really nasty tactic because it's so personalized," explains security expert Bruce Schneier. "It's an e-mail from your mother saying she needs your Social Security number for the will she's doing."[61]

CYBER AGGRESSION AND THE NEW MEDIA The growing use of mobile devices such as smartphones and tablets has added another outlet for online criminal activity. About 10 percent of cyber crime now targets such devices.[62] In particular, widespread smartphone use seems to have exacerbated cyberbullying, which we discussed in the context of school crime in the previous chapter. According to a recent survey, American teenagers who consider themselves "heavy users" of their cell phones are much more likely to experience cyberbullying than those who consider themselves "normal users" of the devices.[63]

In 2009, the U.S. Department of Justice released a landmark study that shed light on the high incidence of stalking in the United States. Defined as a "credible threat" that puts a person in reasonable fear for her or his safety or the safety of the person's immediate family, stalking, according to the study, affects approximately 3.4 million Americans each year.[64] About one in four of these victims experiences a form of **cyberstalking,** in which the perpetrator uses e-mail, text messages, or some other form of electronic communication to carry out his or her harassment.[65] Nearly every state and the federal government have passed legislation to combat this criminal behavior. For instance, in January 2012, Patrick Macchione was sentenced to four years in state prison for cyberstalking fellow University of Central Florida student Kristen Pratt. Macchione sent death threats to Pratt using Twitter, posted lewd messages to her Facebook account, and directed nearly thirty threatening videos at her on YouTube (see photo alongside).

Cyber Crimes in the Business World

Just as cyberspace can be a dangerous place for consumers, it presents a number of hazards for businesses that wish to offer their services on the Internet. In the ATM "bank robbery" case described earlier in the section, the victims were not individual bank account holders but rather two banks—both located in the Middle East—that supplied funds for the debit cards involved. The same circumstances that enable companies to reach a large number of consumers also leave them vulnerable to cyber crime. For example, in 2012 federal law enforcement agents arrested Dutch citizen David Schrooten for infecting the online sales systems of several Seattle businesses with spyware programs. This spyware collected at least 44,000 credit-card numbers, subsequently sold by Schrooten to third parties for fraudulent use.

HACKERS David Schrooten is a particular type of cyber criminal known as a *hacker*. **Hackers** are people who use one computer to illegally access another. The danger posed by hackers has increased significantly because of **botnets,** or networks of computers that have been appropriated by hackers without the knowledge of their owners. A hacker will secretly install a program on thousands, if not millions, of personal computer "robots," or "bots," that allows him or her to forward transmissions to an even larger number of systems. The program attaches itself to the host computer when someone operating the computer opens a fraudulent e-mail.

LEARNING **5** OBJECTIVE Describe the three following forms of malware: (a) botnets, (b) worms, and (c) viruses.

Malware Programs that create botnets are one of the latest forms of *malware*, a term that refers to any program that is harmful to a computer or, by extension, a computer user. A **worm,** for example, is a software program that is capable of reproducing itself as it spreads from one computer to the next. A **virus,** another form of malware, is also able to reproduce itself, but must be attached to an "infested" host file to travel from one computer network to another. Worms and viruses can be programmed to perform a number of functions, such as prompting host computers to continually "crash" and reboot, or otherwise infect the system.

Malware is increasingly being used to target specific companies or organizations. In 2011, for example, hackers used malware to carry out a targeted attack on Sony's PlayStation network, thus gaining access to personal information and, possibly, the credit-card numbers of 77 million online gamers worldwide. Sony, a Japanese company, was forced to shut down the network for twenty-four days, costing the company $170 million. The Ponemon Institute, a private research organization, estimates that individual American businesses lose an average of $8.9 million a year because of malware and other cyber crime.[66]

The Spread of Spam Businesses and individuals alike are targets of **spam,** or unsolicited "junk e-mails" that flood virtual mailboxes with advertisements, solicitations, and other messages. Considered relatively harmless in the early days of the Internet, in 2012, an average of 87 billion spam messages were being sent each day. Nearly 2 billion of these spam messages contained some form of malware.[67] To rectify this situation, in 2003 Congress passed the Controlling the Assault of Non-Solicited Pornography and Marketing Act (CAN-SPAM), which requires all unsolicited e-mails to be labeled and to include opt-out provisions and the sender's physical address.[68]

Spam is also the preferred method of phishing, the identity theft scam described earlier. By sending millions or even billions of these fraudulent e-mails, phishers need only entice a few users to "take the bait" to ensure a successful and lucrative operation. Finally, "social" spam is becoming more common on social-networking sites such as Facebook. This form of hacking relies on fake messages, such as "hey, check out this free iPad," that appear to be from a friend rather than an unknown company. The message includes a link to download a coupon for the free product. In reality, however, by clicking on the link, the unsuspecting user has allowed malware to infect his or her computer.

PIRATING INTELLECTUAL PROPERTY ONLINE Most people think of wealth in terms of houses, land, cars, stocks, and bonds. Wealth, however, also includes **intellectual property,** which consists of the products that result from intellectual, creative processes.

Hacker A person who uses one computer to break into another.

Botnet A network of computers that have been appropriated without the knowledge of their owners and used to spread harmful programs via the Internet; short for *robot network*.

Worm A computer program that can automatically replicate itself and interfere with the normal use of a computer. A worm does not need to be attached to an existing file to move from one network to another.

Virus A computer program that can replicate itself and interfere with the normal use of a computer. A virus cannot exist as a separate entity and must attach itself to another program to move through a network.

Spam Bulk e-mails, particularly of commercial advertising, sent in large quantities without the consent of the recipient.

Intellectual Property Property resulting from intellectual, creative processes.

The government provides various forms of protection for intellectual property, such as copyrights and patents. These protections ensure that a person who writes a book or a song or creates a software program is financially rewarded if that product is sold in the marketplace.

Explain how the Internet has contributed to piracy of intellectual property.
LEARNING
6
OBJECTIVE

Intellectual property such as books, films, music, and software is vulnerable to "piracy"—the unauthorized copying and use of the property. In the past, copying intellectual products was time consuming, and the quality of the pirated copies was clearly inferior. In today's online world, however, things have changed. Simply clicking a mouse can now reproduce millions of unauthorized copies, and pirated duplicates of copyrighted works obtained via the Internet are often exactly the same as the original, or close to it.

The Business Software Alliance estimates that 42 percent of all business software is pirated, costing software makers more than $63.4 billion in 2012.[69] (In the *CJ in Action* feature at the end of this chapter, we will discuss the moral and legal components of illegally downloading intellectual property.)

Cyber Crimes against the Community

One of the greatest challenges cyberspace presents for law enforcement is how to enforce laws governing activities that are prohibited under certain circumstances but are not always illegal. Such laws generally reflect the will of the community, which recognizes behavior as acceptable under some circumstances and unacceptable under others. Thus, while it is legal in many areas to sell a pornographic video to a fifty-year-old, it is never legal to sell the same item to a fifteen-year-old. Similarly, placing a bet on a football game with a bookmaker in Las Vegas, Nevada, is legal, but doing the same thing with a bookmaker in Cleveland, Ohio, is not. Of course, in cyberspace it is often impossible to know whether the customer buying porn is age fifty or fifteen, or if the person placing the bet is in Las Vegas or Cleveland.

ONLINE PORNOGRAPHY The Internet has been a boon to the pornography industry. Twelve percent of all Web sites have pornographic content, and these sites generate $4.2 billion in revenue a year.[70] Though no general figures are available, the Internet has undoubtedly also been a boon to those who illegally produce and sell material depicting sexually explicit conduct involving a child—child pornography. As we have seen with other cyber crimes, the Internet is conducive to child pornography for a number of reasons:

Outline the three major reasons why the Internet is conducive to the dissemination of child pornography.
LEARNING
7
OBJECTIVE

- *Speed.* The Internet is the fastest means of sending visual material over long distances. Child pornographers can deliver their material faster and more securely online than through regular mail.
- *Security.* Any illegal material that passes through the hands of a mail carrier is inherently in danger of being discovered. This risk is significantly reduced with e-mail. Furthermore, Internet sites that offer child pornography can protect their customers with passwords, which keep random Web surfers (or law enforcement agents) from stumbling on the site of chat rooms.
- *Anonymity.* Obviously, anonymity is the most important protection offered by the Internet for sellers and buyers of child pornography, as it is for any person engaged in illegal behavior in cyberspace.[71]

Because of these three factors, courts and lawmakers have had a difficult time controlling the dissemination of illegal sexual content via the Internet. In 2008, however, the United States Supreme Court upheld a federal law known as the Protect Act. This legislation makes it a crime to exchange "any material or purported material" online that would cause "another to believe" it depicted a minor engaged in sex, whether "actual or simulated."[72] Essentially, this law gives prosecutors the power they need to arrest purveyors of virtual child pornography, which uses computer images—not real children—to depict sexual acts.

GAMBLING IN CYBERSPACE In general, gambling is illegal. All states have statutes that regulate gambling—defined as any scheme that involves the distribution of property by chance among persons who have risked something of value for the opportunity to receive the property. In some states, certain forms of gambling, such as casino gambling or horse racing, are legal. Many states also have legalized state-operated lotteries, as well as lotteries, such as Bingo, conducted for charitable purposes. A number of states also allow gambling on Native American reservations.

In 2013, Nevada became the first state to legalize online poker within its borders. What are some of the benefits and drawbacks of allowing states to take this step? Nathan Alliard/Getty Images

In the past, this mixed bag of gambling laws has presented a legal quandary: Can citizens in a state that does not allow gambling place bets to a Web site located in a state that does? After all, states have no constitutional authority over activities that take place in other states. Complicating the problem was the fact that many Internet gambling sites are located outside the United States in countries where Internet gambling is legal, and no state government has authority over activities that take place in other countries. In 2006, Congress, concerned about money laundering stemming from online gambling, the problem of addiction, and underage gambling, passed legislation that greatly strengthened efforts to reduce online gaming. The Unlawful Internet Gambling Enforcement Act of 2006 cuts off the money flow to Internet gambling sites by barring the use of electronic payments, such as credit-card transactions, at those sites.[73]

The environment for online gambling changed dramatically in 2011. That year, the U.S. Department of Justice released a memo essentially allowing states to operate gambling Web sites as long as the bets do not involve a "sporting event or contest."[74] In April 2013, this led to the United States' first legal online poker site, operating out of Nevada. Other states, including Delaware and New Jersey, are expected to follow suit. The challenge is that, according to federal law, these sites must be *intrastate*. In other words, someone using the Nevada poker Web site must be in the state of Nevada. Given the difficulty of determining an Internet user's physical location, states will undoubtedly struggle to keep their new online gambling Web sites within the parameters of the law.[75]

Fighting Cyber Crime

One Monday afternoon several years ago, $1.2 million disappeared from the bank account of Lifestyle Forums & Displays, a mannequin maker and importer based in Brooklyn, New York. Lloyd Keilson, the company's chief executive officer, notified both the FBI and the New York City Police Department, but neither was able to help. An FBI agent told Keilson that cyberthieves had used an unknown virus to carry out the theft and were therefore untraceable.[76]

"The dynamics of the Internet and cyberspace are so fast that we have a hard time staying ahead of the adversary," admits former U.S. Secret Service agent Robert D. Rodriguez.[77] As already noted in this chapter, the Internet provides an ideal environment for the "underground" of society. With hundreds of millions of users in every corner of the globe transferring unimaginable amounts of information almost instantaneously, the Internet has proved resistant to government regulation. In addition, although a number of countries have tried to "control" the Internet (see the feature *Comparative Criminal Justice—The Great Firewall of China* below), the U.S. government has generally adopted a hands-off attitude to better promote the free flow of ideas and encourage the growth of electronic commerce. Thus, in this country cyberspace is, for the most part, unregulated, making efforts to fight cyber crime all the more difficult.

CHALLENGES FOR LAW ENFORCEMENT In trying to describe the complexities of fighting cyber crime, Michael Vatis, former director of the FBI's National Infrastructure Protection Center, imagines a bank robbery during which the police arrive just as "the

COMPARATIVE
CRIMINAL JUSTICE

Saicle/Shutterstock.com

THE GREAT FIREWALL OF CHINA

The online anonymity enjoyed by many Americans on the Internet is increasingly hard to come by in China. In 2012, the Chinese government imposed new rules that require Internet users in that country to provide service providers with their real names. The regulations also require the service providers to report suspicious online activity, such as viewing pornography or the use of words such as *freedom* or *democracy,* to the authorities. Observers have little doubt that the changes are designed to restrict freedom of speech on the Internet. In the past, Chinese bloggers have been jailed for making politically sensitive comments or accusing local officials of wrongdoing.

In the United States, the issue of whether the government should regulate the Internet—and, if so, how much—is hotly debated. In China, the question was answered long before the Internet was even imagined. Since the 1950s, the Chinese Communist Party has exercised strict control over all forms of information, including newspapers, television, radio, movies, and books. Today, under the auspices of the Ministry of Information Industry, that control has been extended to the World Wide Web.

Under broad laws that prohibit, among other things, "destroying the order of society" and "making falsehoods or distorting the truth," Chinese censors have free rein to limit the flow of information through government-controlled Internet service providers. The "Great Firewall," as this system is sometimes called, routinely blocks more than a million Web sites. Many of the sites are pornographic, but the obstruction also extends to Facebook, Twitter, YouTube, and Evite. These steps anger many Chinese citizens, and a number of blogs in the country are dedicated to "tearing down the Great Firewall." One bookstore owner refused to install government-mandated monitoring software onto her establishment's Wi-Fi system, instead choosing to disconnect the service. She decried the "Orwellian surveillance system that forces my customers to disclose their identity to a government that wants to monitor how they use the Internet."

FOR CRITICAL ANALYSIS

How would China-style Internet censorship affect cyber crime in the United States? Under what circumstances, if any, would Americans accept such levels of Internet control by the government?

demand note and fingerprints are vanishing, the security camera is erasing its own images, and the image of the criminal is being erased from the mind of the teller."[78] The difficulty of gathering evidence is just one of the challenges that law enforcement officers face in dealing with cyber crime.

Cyber Forensics Police officers cannot put yellow tape around a computer screen or dust a Web site for fingerprints. The best, and often the only, way to fight computer crime is with technology that gives law enforcement agencies the ability to "track" hackers and other cyber criminals through the Internet. But, as Michael Vatis observed, these efforts are complicated by the fact that digital evidence can be altered or erased even as the cyber crime is being committed. In Chapter 6, we discussed forensics, or the application of science to find evidence of criminal activity. Within the past two decades, a branch of this science known as **cyber forensics** has evolved to gather evidence of cyber crimes.

The main goal of cyber forensics is to gather **digital evidence,** or information of value to a criminal investigation that is stored on, received by, or transmitted by an electronic device such as a computer. Sometimes, this evidence is not particularly difficult to find. In the Steubenville, Ohio, sexual assault case mentioned in Chapter 15, for example, the two young suspects recorded their crimes on cell phones and then posted the evidence on social media. A twelve-minute cell phone video even featured a witness mocking the unconscious victim as "dead" and "so raped."[79]

For more complex investigations, experts in cyber forensics can employ software that retraces a suspect's digital movements. Such software works by creating a digital duplicate of the targeted hard drive, enabling cyber sleuths to break access codes, determine passwords, and search files.[80] "Short of taking your hard drive and having it run over by a Mack truck," says one expert, "you can't be sure that anything is truly deleted from your computer."[81] The latest challenge to cyber investigators is posed by *cloud computing,* in which data are stored not in a physical location but in a virtual, shared computing platform that is linked simultaneously to a number of different computers. Therefore, law enforcement officers investigating wrongdoing in the "cloud" may not have full control of the "crime scene."[82] (The growing importance of cyber crime has led a number of universities to offer graduate certificates in cyber forensics. To learn about one, go to the Web site of the Marshall University Forensic Science Center.)

Jurisdictional Challenges Regardless of what type of cyber crime is being investigated, law enforcement agencies are often frustrated by problems of jurisdiction (explained more fully in Chapter 8). Jurisdiction is primarily based on physical geography—each country, state, and nation has jurisdiction, or authority, over crimes that occur within its boundaries. The Internet, however, destroys these traditional notions because geographic boundaries simply do not exist in cyberspace.

To see how this can affect law enforcement efforts, let's consider a hypothetical cyberstalking case. Phil, who lives in State A, has been sending e-mails containing graphic sexual threats to Stephanie, who lives in State B. Where has the crime taken place? Which police department has authority to arrest Phil, and which court system has authority to try him? To further complicate matters, what if State A has not yet added cyberstalking to its criminal code, while State B has? Does that mean that Phil has not committed a crime in his home state, but has committed one in Stephanie's?

The federal government has taken to answering this question by stating that Phil has committed a crime wherever it says he has. The Sixth Amendment to the U.S. Constitution states that federal criminal cases should be tried in the district in which

Cyber Forensics The application of computer technology to finding and utilizing evidence of cyber crimes.

Digital Evidence Information or data of value to a criminal investigation that is either stored or transmitted by electronic means.

A special agent with U.S. Immigration and Customs Enforcement (ICE) poses in front of the agency's Cyber Crimes Center in Fairfax, Virginia. Why are federal agencies such as ICE generally better positioned to fight cyber crime than local law enforcement agencies?
Richard Clement/Reuters/Landov

the offense was committed.[83] Because the Internet is "everywhere," the federal government has a great deal of leeway in choosing the venue in which an alleged cyber criminal will face trial. In the hacking case of David Schrooten discussed earlier in the chapter, for example, federal authorities claimed jurisdiction even though Schrooten was never physically in Seattle while harvesting credit-card numbers from local businesses. The victims and their computers were, however, in Seattle, thus providing a basis for jurisdiction. "You cannot hide in cyberspace," said U.S. Attorney Jenny Durkan after Schrooten's arrest. "We will find you."[84]

FEDERAL LAW ENFORCEMENT AND CYBER CRIME

Because of its freedom from jurisdictional restraints, the federal government has traditionally taken the lead in law enforcement efforts against cyber crime. This is not to say that little cyber crime prevention occurs on the local level. Most major metropolitan police departments have created special units to fight cyber crime. In general, however, only a handful of local police and sheriffs' departments have the resources to support a squad of cyber investigators. Among state law enforcement agencies, only California has a large cyber crime unit, with twenty investigators who focus on wrongdoing such as identity theft, Internet scams, online child pornography, and theft of intellectual property. Other state efforts in this area generally focus on a single cyber crime, particularly online child pornography.

As the primary crime-fighting unit of the federal government, the FBI has taken the lead in law enforcement efforts against cyber crime. The FBI has the primary responsibility for enforcing all federal criminal statutes involving computer crimes. In 1998, the Bureau added a Cyber Division dedicated to investigating computer-based crimes. The Cyber Division and its administrators coordinate the FBI's efforts in cyberspace, specifically its investigations into computer crimes and intellectual property theft. The division also has jurisdiction over the Innocent Images National Initiative (IINI), the agency's online child-pornography subdivision.

In addition, the FBI has developed several Cyber Action Teams (CATs), which combine the skills of some twenty-five law enforcement agents, cyber forensics investigators, and computer programming experts. Today, cyber crime is the FBI's third-highest priority (after counterterrorism and counterintelligence), and each of the Bureau's fifty-six field divisions has at least one agent who focuses solely on crimes committed on the Internet.

SELF ASSESSMENT

Fill in the blanks and check your answers on page 556.

Web thieves have opportunities to practice _____ theft because of the large amount of personal financial information that is stored on the Internet. A _____ is someone who gains illegal access to one computer using another computer. These wrongdoers sometimes use _____, or networks of hijacked computers, to carry out various improper online activities, including the illegal spread of junk e-mails known as _____. Because of jurisdictional issues, most law enforcement efforts to combat cyber crime are coordinated by the _____ government.

WHITE-COLLAR CRIME

A woman in Huntsville, Alabama, squanders $60,000 in student loans on house bills and "entertainment." The owners of the Glory Pharmacy in Hernando County, Florida, knowingly accept 1,400 fake prescriptions for the painkiller oxycodone. A New Jersey defense contractor sells the U.S. Army faulty helicopter parts. A former Massachusetts state treasurer is indicted for using lottery funds to finance an unsuccessful campaign to become governor.

These court cases represent a variety of criminal behavior with different motives, different methods, and different victims. Yet they all fall into the category of *white-collar crime,* an umbrella term for wrongdoing marked by deceit and scandal rather than violence. As we mentioned in Chapter 1, white-collar crime has a broad impact on the global economy, causing American businesses alone approximately $300 billion in losses each year.[85] Despite its global and national importance, however, white-collar crime has consistently challenged a criminal justice system that struggles to define the problem, much less effectively combat it.

What Is White-Collar Crime?

White-collar crime is not an official category of criminal behavior measured by the federal government in the Uniform Crime Report. Rather, it covers a broad range of illegal acts involving "lying, cheating, and stealing," according to the FBI's Web site on the subject.[86] To give a more technical definition, white-collar crimes are financial activities characterized by deceit and concealment that do not involve physical force or violence. Figure 16.5 below lists and describes some common types of white-collar crime.

LEARNING **8** OBJECTIVE Indicate some of the ways that white-collar crime is different from violent or property crime.

FIGURE 16.5 White-Collar Crimes

Embezzlement
Embezzlement is a form of employee fraud in which an individual uses his or her position within an organization to *embezzle,* or steal, the employer's funds, property, or other assets. Pilferage is a less serious form of employee fraud in which the individual steals items from the workplace.

Tax Evasion
Tax evasion occurs when taxpayers underreport (or do not report) their taxable income or otherwise purposely attempt to evade a tax liability.

Digital Vision CD

Credit-Card and Check Fraud
Credit-card fraud involves obtaining credit-card numbers through a variety of schemes (such as stealing them from the Internet) and using the numbers for personal gain. Check fraud includes writing checks that are not covered by bank funds, forging checks, and stealing traveler's checks.

Mail and Wire Fraud
This umbrella term covers all schemes that involve the use of mail, radio, television, the Internet, or a telephone to intentionally deceive in a business environment.

PhotoDisc/Getty Images

Securities Fraud
Securities fraud covers illegal activity in the stock market. Stockbrokers who steal funds from their clients are guilty of securities fraud, as are those who engage in *insider trading,* which involves buying or selling securities on the basis of information that has not been made available to the public.

Bribery
Also known as *influence peddling,* bribery occurs in the business world when somebody within a company or government sells influence, power, or information to a person outside the company or government who can benefit. A county official, for example, could give a construction company a lucrative county contract to build a new jail. In return, the construction company would give some of the proceeds, known as a *kickback,* to the official.

Consumer Fraud
This term covers a wide variety of activities designed to defraud consumers, from selling counterfeit art to offering "free" items, such as electronic devices or vacations, that include a number of hidden charges.

Insurance Fraud
Insurance fraud involves making false claims in order to collect insurance payments. Faking an injury in order to receive payments from a workers' compensation program, for example, is a form of insurance fraud.

Digital Vision CD

DIFFERENT TECHNIQUES To differentiate white-collar crime from "regular" crime, criminologists Michael L. Benson of the University of Cincinnati and Sally S. Simpson of the University of Maryland focus on technique. For example, in an ordinary burglary, a criminal uses physical means, such as picking a lock, to get somewhere he or she should not be—someone else's home—to do something that is clearly illegal. Furthermore, the victim is a specific identifiable individual—the homeowner. In contrast, white-collar criminals usually (1) have legal access to the place where the crime occurs; (2) are spatially separated from the victim, who is often unknown; and (3) behave in a manner that is, at least superficially, legitimate.[87]

Benson and Simpson also identify three main techniques used by white-collar criminals to carry out their crimes:[88]

■ Several years ago, Rita Crundwell was convicted of stealing more than $54 million from the city of Dixon, Illinois, for which she had been working as a financial officer. Why does Crundwell's wrongdoing fall into the category of white-collar crime?
AP Photo/Sauk Valley Media, Alex T. Paschal, File

1. *Deception.* White-collar crime almost always involves a party who deceives and a party who is deceived. The nation's federal Medicare system, which provides health insurance for those sixty-five years of age and older, is a frequent target of deceptive practices. For example, in 2013, the FBI arrested six Detroit-area in-home health-care providers who recruited dishonest Medicare beneficiaries to request costly and unnecessary nursing services. When the federal government reimbursed these health-care providers for the home care—which was never actually performed—the white-collar criminals kept the funds for themselves.

2. *Abuse of trust.* A white-collar criminal often operates in a position of trust and misuses that trust for personal benefit. In 2013, for example, the FBI arrested three men for stealing about $6.7 million from a victim by convincing him that they invested the funds in large blocks of Facebook, Inc., stock.

3. *Concealment and conspiracy.* To continue their illegal activities, white-collar criminals need to conceal those activities. In *odometer fraud,* for example, an automobile dealership "rolls back" the odometers of used cars so that a higher price can be charged for the vehicles. As soon as the fraud is discovered, the scheme can no longer succeed.

VICTIMS OF WHITE-COLLAR CRIME As the above examples show, sometimes the victim of a white-collar crime is obvious. A fraudulent stockbroker is stealing directly from his or her clients, and odometer fraud denies consumers the actual value of their purchased automobiles. But who was victimized in the fraudulent Medicare benefits scheme? In that instance, the "victims" were the U.S. taxpayers, who collectively had to cover the cost of the unwarranted benefits. Often, white-collar crime does not target individuals but rather large groups or even abstract concepts such as "society" or "the environment."

CORPORATE WHITE-COLLAR CRIME For legal purposes, a corporation can be treated as a person capable of forming the intent necessary to commit a crime. For instance, the Deepwater Horizon oil spill off the coast of Louisiana in April 2010 caused a great deal of obvious harm. Eleven workers were killed in the oil rig explosion that caused the spill, and the Louisiana coastline suffered immense ecological damage, threatening the livelihoods of thousands of seafood suppliers. In November 2012, BP, the corporation that operated Deepwater Horizon, pleaded guilty to fourteen different criminal charges relating to the incident. The company agreed to pay $4.5 billion in fines and submit to four years of government monitoring of its safety practices and ethics. (Three BP officers aboard the oil rig at the time of the accident were also individually charged with one count of manslaughter for each of the workers who died in the explosion.)

Regulating and Policing White-Collar Crime

In 2012, Genwal Resources, Inc., which operates the Crandall Canyon coal mine in central Utah, pleaded guilty to two misdemeanor charges of violating health and safety standards and paid a $500,000 fine. The charges stemmed from a collapse at the mine that ultimately killed six miners, two rescuers, and a government inspector. The deaths of nine people because of Genwal Resources' failure to enforce safety measures at its coal mine are an example of *corporate violence.* In contrast to assaults committed by individual people, **corporate violence** is a result of policies or actions undertaken by a corporation. In the United States, parallel regulatory and criminal systems have evolved to prevent corporate violence and other forms of white-collar crime.

LEARNING
9
OBJECTIVE

Explain the concept of corporate violence.

THE REGULATORY JUSTICE SYSTEM Although most white-collar crimes cause harm, these harms are not necessarily covered by criminal statutes. Indeed, more often they are covered by *administrative* laws, which we first encountered in Chapter 4. Such laws make up the backbone of the U.S. regulatory system, through which the government attempts to control the actions of individuals, corporations, and other institutions. The goal of **regulation** is not prevention or punishment as much as **compliance,** or the following of regulatory guidelines.[89] For example, as part of their efforts to clean up the massive oil spill of 2010, BP and government agencies used dispersants, which cause oil to disintegrate in water. Agents from the Environmental Protection Agency (EPA) monitored levels of these chemicals to ensure that further damage was not done to the Gulf of Mexico (see the photo alongside).[90]

The EPA—which regulates practices relating to air quality, water quality, and toxic waste—is one of the federal administrative agencies whose compliance oversight brings them into contact with white-collar crime. Another, the Occupational Safety and Health Administration (OSHA), enforces workplace health and safety standards. In addition, the Federal Trade Commission regulates business interactions, and the Securities and Exchange Commission (SEC) ensures that financial markets such as the New York Stock Exchange operate in a fair manner.

LAW ENFORCEMENT AND WHITE-COLLAR CRIME In general, when officials at a regulatory agency find that criminal prosecution is needed to punish a particular violation, they will refer the matter to the U.S. Department of Justice. Either through such referrals or at their own discretion, federal officials prosecute white-collar crime using the investigatory powers of several different federal law enforcement agencies. The FBI has become the lead agency when it comes to white-collar crime, particularly in response to the recent financial scandals, as we shall soon see. The U.S. Postal Inspection Service is also quite

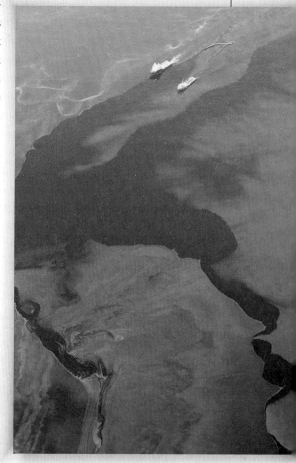

■ What role did the Environmental Protection Agency (EPA) play in monitoring efforts to clean up the oil slick from the Deepwater Horizon oil spill? Why is the EPA considered a regulatory agency and not a law enforcement agency?
Ted Jackson/*The Times-Picayune*/Landov

active in such investigations, as fraudulent activities often involve the U.S. mail. In addition, the Internal Revenue Service's Criminal Investigative Division has jurisdiction over a wide variety of white-collar crimes, including tax fraud, and operates perhaps the most effective white-collar crime lab in the country.[91]

Local and state agencies also investigate white-collar crimes, but because of the complexity and costs of such investigations, most are handled by the federal government. Federal prosecutors are also in a unique position to enforce the federal Racketeer Influenced and Corrupt Organizations Act (RICO), which we discussed briefly in Chapter 12. Originally designed to combat organized crime, RICO makes it illegal to receive income through a pattern of *racketeering*.[92] The definition of **racketeering** is so inclusive—basically covering any attempt to earn illegal income involving more than one person—that it can be used against a broad range of white-collar wrongdoing. Several years ago, for example, federal prosecutors used RICO to convict eleven tobacco companies for misleading the American public about the addictive qualities of cigarettes.

White-Collar Crime in the 2000s

The decade that ended in 2010 was marked by two periods of financial scandal. First, in 2001 and 2002, fraudulent accounting practices led to the demise of giant corporations such as Enron and Worldcom, costing investors tens of billions of dollars. Then, near the end of the decade, the collapse of the subprime mortgage market caused millions of Americans to lose their homes to foreclosure and led to the collapse of major financial institutions such as Lehman Brothers and Washington Mutual. In the latter period, headlines focused on widespread *mortgage fraud,* or dishonest practices relating to home loans, along with the misdeeds of Bernard Madoff. Before his 2008 arrest, Madoff managed to defraud thousands of investors out of approximately $65 billion.

As has often occurred in U.S. history, these scandals and the concurrent economic downturns led to greater regulation and criminalization of white-collar crime. In 1934, for example, in the wake of the Great Depression, Congress established the SEC to watch over the American economy.[93] Similarly, in 2002 Congress passed legislation which, among other things, enhanced the penalties for those convicted of white-collar crimes.[94] (See the feature *Myth versus Reality—Soft Time for White-Collar Crime* on the facing page.) In response to the "Great Recession" of 2008 and 2009, the FBI created the National Mortgage Fraud Team and began to crack down on a variety of white-collar crimes. Indeed, FBI agents are increasingly using aggressive tactics such as going undercover, planting wiretaps, and raiding offices—tactics previously reserved for drug dealers, mobsters, and terrorists—against white-collar criminals.[95]

SELF ASSESSMENT

Fill in the blanks and check your answers on page 556.

According to the FBI, white-collar crimes are economic activities characterized by _____ and concealment that do not involve _____. Administrative agencies such as the _____ Protection Agency make up the backbone of the U.S. regulatory system, which combats white-collar crime by requiring _____ with certain guidelines. A powerful tool for law enforcement in combating white-collar crimes, _____ can be used against groups or organizations that attempt to earn income illegally.

MYTH vs REALITY

Soft Time for White-Collar Crime

During the 1980s, the nation was rocked by a series of financial scandals including the "savings and loan crisis." As a result of this debacle, dozens of financial institutions failed, eventually costing American taxpayers more than $160 billion. To the outrage of many, the high-profile white-collar criminals from the era received relatively light prison sentences for their fraudulent behavior. Corrupt Louisiana financier Herman K. Beebe spent less than a year in prison. Michael Milken, "the junk bond king" who pleaded guilty to violating securities laws, was released after twenty-two months. Bank president Charles Keating, Jr., whose actions wiped out the savings of more than 20,000 customers, served four and a half years.

THE MYTH White-collar criminals, with their high-priced lawyers and friends in high places, receive light penalties. Even though their wrongdoing causes a great deal of suffering, they are not treated as harshly by the criminal justice system as petty thieves or low-level drug dealers.

THE REALITY The political response to the financial scandals of the early 2000s focused on increasing penalties for white-collar criminals. In November 2001, the U.S. Sentencing Commission increased its recommended punishments for businesspersons who commit fraud, particularly when the misdeeds involve losses in excess of $100 million. Then, in 2002, Congress passed the White Collar Crime Penalty Enhancement Act, which doubled the maximum sentences for some corporate frauds.

The results have been striking. In March 2010, a U.S. district judge sentenced Robert Thompson to 309 years in prison for targeting the elderly in a series of scams. That same year, Bernie Madoff, discussed in the text, received a 150-year prison term. In June 2012, Allen Stanford was sentenced to 110 years in prison for defrauding investors out of more than $7 billion over the course of two decades. Although judges still have great leeway to depart from the guidelines when sentencing white-collar criminals, public outrage at white-collar crime has apparently created an environment in which harsh punishments are the rule rather than the exception.

FOR CRITICAL ANALYSIS
What are some of the justifications for punishing white-collar criminals such as Robert Thompson and Bernie Madoff so harshly? Are there any reasons to be lenient with those whose crimes do not physically harm their victims?

HACKING FOR OPEN ACCESS

"We need to take information, wherever it is stored, make our copies, and share them with the world."[96] Such was the opinion of expert computer programmer Aaron Swartz, and, in 2011, he put his words into action. That year, Swartz was arrested in Boston on charges of hacking into the network of the Massachusetts Institute of Technology and illegally downloading nearly 5 million articles from JSTOR, an online database of academic journals. On January 11, 2013, apparently distraught over the possibility of a lengthy prison sentence, Swartz hanged himself. The twenty-six-year-old's suicide touched off a firestorm of debate over the availability of information on the Internet—the topic of this chapter's *CJ in Action* feature.

BREAKING THE LAW

Federal authorities had indicted Swartz on thirteen charges of violating the Computer Fraud and Abuse Act (CFAA). Broadly speaking, the CFAA is designed to punish those who illegally access a computer.[97] Federal agents estimated that Swartz had illegally downloaded about 18 million pages of protected data from the scientific journals on the JSTOR Web site. At eight cents a page, that worked out to a $1.5 million hacking job, meaning that, under federal sentencing guidelines, Swartz faced as much as thirty-five years in prison and a $1 million fine.

Swartz's supporters called the federal government's prosecution unfair, pointing out that his behavior—though illegal—was not carried out for personal gain. Swartz was a leader of the "Open Access" movement, a loose organization of Internet activists dedicated to making information such as JSTOR's often costly scientific journals available online at no charge. Others, though sympathetic to Swartz's plight, felt that he had clearly broken the law. "People who have data in computers want them to be confidential," said Michael Sussmann, a lawyer who specializes in Internet issues.[98]

THE CASE FOR HACKING
TO PROVIDE OPEN ACCESS

• According to Swartz, "Stealing is wrong. But downloading isn't stealing. If I shoplift an album from my local record store, no one else can buy it. But when I download a song, no one loses it and another person gets it. There's no ethical problem."[99]

• Tax dollars support much of the research in scholarly and scientific journals, and therefore the content of these journals should be provided to the public at no cost.

• Most people, particularly students, cannot afford to purchase this information, creating what Open Access advocate Carl Malamud calls a "members-only country club of knowledge."[100]

THE CASE AGAINST HACKING
TO PROVIDE OPEN ACCESS

• In the words of U.S. Attorney Carmen Ortiz, who prosecuted Swartz, "stealing is stealing, whether you use a computer command or a crowbar."[101]

• The principle of free information is misguided. Producing academic articles involves labor, and most of the people who provide such labor want to be paid. In many cases, these people cannot afford to work for free.

• Punishing those who hack computers for supposedly "noble" causes provides a deterrent to all hacking—much of which is carried out for illicit financial gain.

YOUR OPINION—WRITING ASSIGNMENT

Several years ago, the U.S. government requested the extradition of Richard O'Dwyer, a twenty-four-year-old who lived in northern England. According to federal prosecutors, O'Dwyer operated a Web site that helped users find pirated American movies and television shows. That is, although O'Dwyer's site did not contain any illegally downloaded content itself, it provided links to other sites that did. Through advertising, O'Dwyer made about $230,000 from his site, which was established through a British server.[102] Some observers criticized the U.S. government for seeking a ten-year prison term for O'Dwyer, pointing out that it is not usually against the law to establish what is essentially a search engine.

Does the United States have jurisdiction over O'Dwyer and his Web site? Do you think that he is committing a crime by providing an outlet for others to illegally download copyrighted material? How do you compare the activities of O'Dwyer to the Open Access movement championed by Aaron Swartz? Before responding, you can review our discussions in the chapter concerning:

• Pirating intellectual property online (pages 543–544).

• Cyber crime jurisdictional challenges (pages 547–548).

Your answer should include at least three full paragraphs.

CHAPTER SUMMARY

For more information on these concepts, look back to the Learning Objective icons throughout the chapter.

 Describe the concept of *jihad* as practiced by al Qaeda and its followers. *Jihad* is a term for the struggle against evil that the Muslim faith demands of its adherents. As practiced by al Qaeda and other religious extremist groups, the tenets of *jihad* require violent action against "evil" nonbelievers, a viewpoint that is rejected by the majority of Muslims.

 Identify three important trends in international terrorism. (a) Terrorists have developed more efficient methods of financing their operations. (b) Terrorists have developed more efficient organizations based on the small-business model. (c) Terrorists have exploited new communications technology to mount global campaigns.

 Explain the primary difference between the U.S. government's treatment of enemy combatants and the treatment of terrorist suspects under the jurisdiction of the criminal justice system. Enemy combatants are taken into the custody of the U.S. military and do not enjoy the same level of constitutional protection as do terrorist suspects charged with criminal behavior. For example, enemy combatants have been subjected to indefinite detention, and their cases are adjudicated by military tribunals, not civilian criminal courts.

 Distinguish cyber crime from "traditional" crime. Most cyber crimes are not "new" types of crimes. Rather, they are traditional crimes committed in cyberspace. Perpetrators of cyber crimes are often aided by certain aspects of the Internet, such as its ability to cloak the user's identity and its effectiveness as a conduit for transferring—or stealing—large amounts of information very quickly.

 Describe the three following forms of malware: (a) botnets, (b) worms, and (c) viruses. (a) A botnet is a network of computers that have been hijacked without the knowledge of their owners and used to spread harmful programs across the Internet. (b) A worm is a damaging software program that reproduces itself as it moves from computer to computer. (c) A virus is a damaging software program that must be attached to an "infested" host file to transfer from one computer to the next.

 Explain how the Internet has contributed to piracy of intellectual property. In the past, copying intellectual property such as films and music was time consuming, and the quality of the pirated copies was vastly inferior to that of the originals. On the Internet, however, millions of unauthorized copies of intellectual property can be reproduced at the click of a mouse, and the quality of these items is often the same as that of the original, or close to it.

 Outline the three major reasons why the Internet is conducive to the dissemination of child pornography. The Internet provides (a) a quick way to transmit child pornography from providers to consumers; (b) security such as untraceable e-mails and password-protected Web sites and chat rooms; and (c) anonymity for buyers and sellers of child pornography.

 Indicate some of the ways that white-collar crime is different from violent or property crime. A wrongdoer committing a standard crime usually uses physical means to get somewhere he or she legally should not be in order to do something clearly illegal. Also, the victims of violent and property crimes are usually easily identifiable. In contrast, a white-collar criminal usually has legal access to the crime scene where he or she is doing something seemingly legitimate. Furthermore, victims of white-collar crimes are often unknown or unidentifiable.

 Explain the concept of corporate violence. Corporate violence occurs when a corporation implements policies that ultimately cause harm to individuals or the environment.

QUESTIONS FOR CRITICAL ANALYSIS

1. Using your own words, what is the definition of *terrorism?*

2. According to Donna Marsh, whose pregnant daughter was killed on September 11, 2001, in New York City, it is "unconscionable" to hold terrorism suspects for nearly a decade without trial, and it "demeans the United States' justice system" to say these suspects cannot be tried in civilian courts. What is your opinion of these statements?

3. According to several studies, someone who is a victim of a cyber crime such as identity theft has a relatively high risk of being a victim of the same crime again. Why do you think this is the case?

4. Consider the following proposed state law: *It is unlawful for any person, with intent to terrify, intimidate, threaten, harass, annoy, or offend, to use ANY ELECTRONIC OR DIGITAL DEVICE and use any obscene, lewd, or profane language.* What is your opinion of this statute? What might be some of its unforeseen consequences?

5. Law enforcement agencies have extensively employed antiracketeering laws such as RICO in combating drug dealers and criminal gangs. (To review RICO, go to page 000.) Why would such legislation be useful in prosecuting these non-white-collar criminals?

KEY TERMS

botnet 543
compliance 551
computer crime 539
corporate violence 551
cyberattack 537
cyber crime 540
cyber forensics 547
cyber fraud 540

cyberstalking 542
digital evidence 547
enemy combatant 531
hacker 543
identity theft 541
intellectual property 543
military tribunal 533
nonstate actor 527

phishing 541
racketeering 552
regulation 551
spam 543
virus 543
visa 534
weapon of mass destruction 531
worm 543

SELF ASSESSMENT ANSWER KEY

Page 538: i. nonstate; **ii.** crimes; **iii.** criminal/civilian; **iv.** enemy combatants; **v.** tribunals/commissions; **vi.** cyberattacks

Page 548: i. identity; **ii.** hacker; **iii.** botnets; **iv.** spam; **v.** federal

Page 552: i. deceit; **ii.** violence/physical force; **iii.** Environmental; **iv.** compliance; **v.** RICO/antiracketeering laws

NOTES

1. Quoted in Kira Zalan, "Anatomy of an Investigation," *U.S. News Weekly* (April 19, 2013), 4.

2. David A. Westbrook, "Bin Laden's War," *Buffalo Law Review* (December 2006), 981–1012.

3. George P. Fletcher, "The Indefinable Concept of Terrorism," *Journal of International Criminal Justice* (November 2006), 894–911.

4. Quoted in Kimberly Dozier and David Espo, "U.S. Kills Osama bin Laden Decade after 9/11 Attacks," *Associated Press* (May 2, 2011).

5. Ahmed S. Hashim, "Al-Qaida: Origins, Goals, and Grand Strategy," in *The McGraw-Hill Homeland Security Handbook,* ed. David G. Kamien (New York: McGraw-Hill, 2006), 24.

6. Quoted in *ibid.,* 9.

7. Quoted in "The Growing, and Mysterious, Irrelevance of al Qaeda," *The Economist* (January 24, 2009), 64.

8. Quoted in Steve Coll, "Name Calling," *New Yorker* (March 4, 2013), 17.

9. Brian Michael Jenkins, *New Challenges to U.S. Counterterrorism Efforts: An Assessment of the Current Terrorist Threat* (Santa Monica, CA: RAND Corporation, July 2012), 2.

10. Quoted in Josh Meyer, "Small Groups Seen as Biggest Threat in U.S.," *Los Angeles Times* (August 16, 2007), 1.

11. "Al Qaida: No Longer a Real Threat?" *The Week* (May 11, 2012), 18.

12. Quoted in Siobhan Gorman, "Terror Risk Falls, U.S. Officials Say," *Wall Street Journal* (April 28–29, 2012), A4.

13. Quoted in Scott Shane, "A Homemade Style of Terror: Jihadists Push New Tactics," *New York Times* (May 6, 2013), A1.

14. *Ibid.*

15. Daniel Klaidman and Christopher Dickey, "The Body Bomb," *Newsweek* (May 21, 2012), 20.

16. Brian Michael Jenkins, "The New Age of Terrorism," in *The McGraw-Hill Homeland Security Handbook,* ed. David G. Kamien (New York: McGraw-Hill, 2006), 117–129.

17. *Ibid.,* 128.

18. Quoted in Marc Santora and William K. Rashbaum, "Bin Laden Relative Pleads Not Guilty in Terrorism Case," *New York Times* (March 9, 2013), A14.

19. "Nearly 500 Convicted on Terror-Related Charges since 9/11: Report," *Reuters* (July 12, 2012).

20. Scott Shane, "Beyond Guantánamo, a Web of Prisons for Terrorism Inmates," *New York Times* (December 11, 2011), A1.

21. *In re Guantánamo Detainee Cases,* 535 F.Supp.2d 443, 447 (D.D.C. 2005).

22. Richard M. Pious, *The War on Terrorism and the Rule of Law* (Los Angeles: Roxbury Publishing Co., 2006), 165–166.

23. Michael Greenberger, "You Ain't Seen Nothin' Yet: The Inevitable Post-Hamdan Conflict between the Supreme Court and the Political Branches," *Maryland Law Review* 66 (2007), 805, 807.

24. Public Law Number 111-383 (January 7, 2011).

25. Quoted in Charlie Savage, "Obama Renews Push to Close Cuba Prison," *New York Times* (May 1, 2013), A1.

26. "One in 7 Who Leave Guantanamo Involved in Terrorism," *Reuters* (May 26, 2009).

27. Brian Bennett, "Former Detainees Now Plot in Yemen," *Los Angeles Times* (November 2, 2010), A1.

28. *Boumediene v. Bush,* 553 U.S. 723 (2008).

29. Adam Liptak, "Justices Reject Detainees' Appeal, Leaving Cloud over Earlier Guantánamo Ruling," *New York Times* (June 12, 2012), A14.

30. Charlie Savage, "U.S. Prepares to Lift Ban on Guantanamo Cases," *New York Times* (January 20, 2011), A1.

31. Military Commission Act of 2009, Pub. L. No. 111-84, Sections 1801–1807, 123 Stat. 2190 (2009).

32. Richard A. Serrano, "9/11 Defense Team Calls Tribunal Unjust," *Los Angeles Times* (May 7, 2012), A8.

33. "The Oubliette," *The Economist* (May 4, 2013), 27.

34. Charlie Savage, "Delays Keep Former Qaeda Child Soldier at Guantánamo, Despite Plea Deal," *New York Times* (March 25, 2012), 18.

35. National Commission on Terrorist Attacks upon the United States, *The 9/11 Commission Report: Executive Summary* (Washington, D.C.: National Commission on Terrorist Attacks upon the United States, 2004), 14.

36. James C. McKinley, Jr., and Julia Preston, "U.S. Can't Trace Foreign Visitors on Expired Visas," *New York Times* (October 12, 2009), A1.

37. Eric Schmitt and Michael S. Schmidt, "2 U.S. Agencies Added Boston Bomb Suspect to Watch Lists," *New York Times* (April 25, 2013), A20.

38. "Securing the Border," *The Week* (March 22, 2013), 11.

39. Rebecca Gambler, *Goals and Measures Not Yet in Place to Inform Border Security Status and Resource Needs* (Washington, D.C.: United States Government Accountability Office, February 26, 2013), 16.

40. Chris Hawley, "Border Agents in North Fight Drug War on Ice," *Associated Press* (February 15, 2011).

41. *Border Security: Enhanced DHS Oversight and Assessment of Interagency Coordination Is Needed for Northern Border* (Washington, D.C.: U.S. Government Accountability Office, December 2010), 2, 10.

42. Nicole Perloth, "Cyberattack on Saudi Firm Disquiets U.S.," *New York Times* (October 24, 2012), A1.

43. Nicole Perloth, David E. Sanger, and Michael S. Schmidt, "As Hacking Against U.S. Rises, Experts Try to Pin Down Motive," *New York Times* (March 4, 2013), A1.

44. Gabriel K. Park, "Granting an Automatic Authorization for Military Response: Protecting National Criminal Infrastructure from Cyberattack," *Brooklyn Journal of International Law* 38 (2013), 801–802.

45. Quoted in "Hype and Fear," *The Economist* (December 8, 2012), 62.

46. Ben Flanagan, "Former CIA Chief Speaks Out on Iran Stuxnet Attack," *The National* (December 15, 2011), at **www.thenational .ae/thenationalconversation/industry-insights/technology /former-cia-chief-speaks-out-on-iran-stuxnet-attack**.

47. Ken Dilanian, "Beware the Coming Cyber Attack," *The Week* (April 8, 2011), 14.

48. James Lewis, "Examining the Cyber Threat to Critical Infrastructure and The American Economy," *Hearing before the Subcommittee on Cybersecurity, Infrastructure Protection, and Security Technologies* (Washington, D.C.: U.S. Government Printing Office, 2012), 41.

49. *Ibid.*

50. Colleen Long and Martha Mendoza, "Bank Heist Impressed Cyber Crime Experts," *Associated Press* (May 10, 2013).

51. Quoted in Marc Santora, "In Hours, Thieves Took $45 Million in A.T.M. Scheme," *New York Times* (May 10, 2013), A1.

52. Jack Nicas, "Crime That No Longer Pays," *Wall Street Journal* (February 5, 2013), A3.

53. National Institute of Justice, *Computer Crime: Criminal Justice Resource Manual* (Washington, D.C.: U.S. Department of Justice, 1989), 2.

54. *Ibid.*

55. Internet Crime Complaint Center, *IC3 2012 Internet Crime Report* (Glen Allen, VA: National White Collar Crime Center, 2013), 4.

56. Symantec, press release, "Norton Study Calculates Cost of Global Cybercrime" (September 7, 2011), at **ww.symantec.com/about /news/release/article.jsp?prid=20110907_02**.

57. Internet Crime Complaint Center, 16.

58. Bureau of Justice Statistics, *Identity Theft Reported by Households, 2005–2010* (Washington, D.C.: U.S. Department of Justice, November 2011), 1.

59. *Ibid.,* Table 4, page 5.

60. Benny Evangelista Alejandro Martinez-Cabrera, "Big Jump in Number of People on Twitter," *San Francisco Chronicle* (September 4, 2010), D2.

61. Quoted in Matt Richtel and Verne G. Kopytoff, "E-Mail Fraud Hides behind Friendly Face," *New York Times* (June 3, 2011), A1.

62. Ben Rooney, "Cybercrime Exacts a Daily Toll," *Wall Street Journal* (September 12, 2011), 29.

63. Openet, press release, "Openet-Sponsored Study Reveals 41 Percent of Teenagers Experience Cyber-bullying" (January 18, 2012), at **www .openet.com/company/news-events/pressreleases?id=482**.

64. Bureau of Justice Statistics, *Stalking Victimization in the United States* (Washington, D.C.: U.S. Department of Justice, January 2009), 1.

65. *Ibid.*

66. *2012 Cost of Cyber Crime Study: United States* (Traverse City, MI: Ponemon Institute, October 2012), 1.

67. Eduard Kovacs, "87 Billion Spam Emails Sent Out Each Day in Q3 of 2012, Commtouch Reports," *Softpedia* (October 25, 2012), at **news .softpedia.com/news/87-Billion-Spam-Emails-Sent-Out-Each -Day-in-Q3-of-2012-Commtouch-Reports-302232.shtml**.

68. 15 U.S.C. Sections 7701–7713 (2003).

69. *Shadow Market: 2011 BSA Global Software Piracy Study* (Washington, D.C.: Business Software Alliance, May 2012), 1.

70. "The Internet Porn 'Epidemic': By the Numbers," *The Week* (June 17, 2010), at **theweek.com/article/index/204156/theinternet-porn -epidemic-by-the-numbers**.

71. William R. Graham, Jr., "Uncovering and Eliminating Child Pornography Rings on the Internet," *Law Review of Michigan State University Detroit College of Law* (Summer 2000), 466.

72. *United States v. Williams,* 533 U.S. 285 (2008).

73. 31 U.S.C. Sections 5361 *et seq.* (2006).

74. Memorandum Opinion for the Assistant Attorney General, Criminal Division, "Whether Proposals by Illinois and New York to Use the Internet and Out-of-State Transaction Processors to Sell Lottery

Tickets to In-State Adults Violate the Wire Act" (September 20, 2011), at **www.justice.gov/olc/2011/state-lotteries-opinion.pdf**.

75. Cyrus Farivar, "State-by-State, America Keeps Betting on Online Poker and Gambling," *Arstechnica.com* (May 19, 2013), at **arstechnica .com/business/2013/05/state-by-state-america-keeps-betting -on-online-poker-and-gambling**.

76. Sarah E. Needleman, "Cybercriminals Sniff Out Vulnerable Firms," *Wall Street Journal* (July 5, 2012), B7.

77. Quoted in Santora.

78. Quoted in Richard Rapaport, "Cyberwars: The Feds Strike Back," *Forbes* (August 23, 1999), 126.

79. "Steubenville: A Very Modern Rape Case," *The Week* (March 29, 2013), 19.

80. Matthew Boyle, "The Latest Hit: CSI in Your Hard Drive," *Fortune* (November 14, 2005), 39.

81. Quoted in "Cybersleuths Find Growing Role in Fighting Crime," HPC Wire, at **www.hpcwire.com/hpc-bin/artread.pl?direction=Current &articlenumber=19864**.

82. George Grispos and William B. Glisson, "Calm Before the Storm: The Challenges of Cloud Computing in Digital Forensics," *International Journal of Digital Crime and Forensics* (2012), 28–48.

83. Laurie P. Cohen, "Internet's Ubiquity Multiplies Venues to Try Web Crimes," *Wall Street Journal* (February 12, 2007), B1.

84. Quoted in "David Benjamin Schrooten, aka 'Fortezza,' Dutch Hacker, Pleads Not Guilty to Mass U.S. Credit Card Theft," *Associated Press* (June 12, 2012).

85. Legal Information Institute, "White Collar Crime," at **www.law. cornell.edu/wex/white-collar_crime**.

86. The Federal Bureau of Investigation, "White-Collar Crime" at **www.fbi .gov/about-us/investigate/white_collar/whitecollarcrime**.

87. Michael L. Benson and Sally S. Simpson, *White-Collar Crime: An Opportunity Perspective* (New York: Routledge, 2009), 79–80.

88. *Ibid.,* 81–87.

89. *Ibid.,* 189.

90. Raffi Khatchadourain, "The Gulf War," *The New Yorker* (March 14, 2011), 51–53.

91. David O. Friedrichs, *Trusted Criminals: White Collar Crime in Contemporary Society,* 4th ed. (Belmont, CA: Wadsworth Cengage Learning, 2010), 278–283.

92. Lawrence Salinger, *Encyclopedia of White-Collar and Corporate Crime,* 2d ed. (Thousand Oaks, CA: Sage, 2004), 361.

93. 15 U.S.C. Sections 78a *et seq.*

94. White-Collar Crime Penalty Enhancement Act of 2002, 18 U.S.C. Sections 1341, 1343, 1349–1350.

95. Peter Lattman and William K. Rashbaum, "A Trader, an F.B.I. Witness, and Then a Suicide," *Reuters* (June 2, 2011).

96. Aaron Swartz, "The Guerilla Open Access Manifesto" (2008), at **archive .org/stream/GuerillaOpenAccessManifesto/Goamjuly2008 _djvu.txt**.

97. Counterfeit Access Device and Computer Fraud and Abuse Act of 1984, Public Law Number 98-473, 98 Statute 2190 (codified as amended at 18 U.S.C. Section 1030 (2006)).

98. Quoted in Peter Schworm and Shelley Murphy, "Critics Say U.S. Cyber Law Invites Harsh Prosecutions," *Boston Globe* (January 25, 2013), A1.

99. Quoted in Larissa MacFarquhar, "Requiem for a Dream," *The New Yorker* (March 11, 2013), 56.

100. Quoted in Jessica Guynn, "In Death, a Hero or Criminal?" *Baltimore Sun* (February 1, 2013), 16A.

101. Quoted in Schworm and Murphy.

102. Somni Sengupta, "U.S. Pursuing a Middleman in Web Piracy," *New York Times* (July 13, 2012), A1.

The Constitution of the United States

PREAMBLE

We the People of the United States, in Order to form a more perfect Union, establish Justice, insure domestic Tranquility, provide for the common defence, promote the general Welfare, and secure the Blessings of Liberty to ourselves and our Posterity, do ordain and establish this Constitution for the United States of America.

ARTICLE I

Section 1. All legislative Powers herein granted shall be vested in a Congress of the United States, which shall consist of a Senate and House of Representatives.

Section 2. The House of Representatives shall be composed of Members chosen every second Year by the People of the several States, and the Electors in each State shall have the Qualifications requisite for Electors of the most numerous Branch of the State Legislature.

No Person shall be a Representative who shall not have attained to the Age of twenty five Years, and been seven Years a Citizen of the United States, and who shall not, when elected, be an Inhabitant of that State in which he shall be chosen.

Representatives and direct Taxes shall be apportioned among the several States which may be included within this Union, according to their respective Numbers, which shall be determined by adding to the whole Number of free Persons, including those bound to Service for a Term of Years, and excluding Indians not taxed, three fifths of all other Persons. The actual Enumeration shall be made within three Years after the first Meeting of the Congress of the United States, and within every subsequent Term of ten Years, in such Manner as they shall by Law direct. The Number of Representatives shall not exceed one for every thirty Thousand, but each State shall have at Least one Representative; and until such enumeration shall be made, the State of New Hampshire shall be entitled to chuse three, Massachusetts eight, Rhode Island and Providence Plantations one, Connecticut five, New York six, New Jersey four, Pennsylvania eight, Delaware one, Maryland six, Virginia ten, North Carolina five, South Carolina five, and Georgia three.

When vacancies happen in the Representation from any State, the Executive Authority thereof shall issue Writs of Election to fill such Vacancies.

The House of Representatives shall chuse their Speaker and other Officers; and shall have the sole Power of Impeachment.

Section 3. The Senate of the United States shall be composed of two Senators from each State, chosen by the Legislature thereof, for six Years; and each Senator shall have one Vote.

Immediately after they shall be assembled in Consequence of the first Election, they shall be divided as equally as may be into three Classes. The Seats of the Senators of the first Class shall be vacated at the Expiration of the second Year, of the second Class at the Expiration of the fourth Year, and of the third Class at the Expiration of the sixth Year, so that one third may be chosen every second Year; and if Vacancies happen by Resignation, or otherwise, during the Recess of the Legislature of any State, the Executive thereof may make temporary Appointments until the next Meeting of the Legislature, which shall then fill such Vacancies.

No Person shall be a Senator who shall not have attained to the Age of thirty Years, and been nine Years a Citizen of the United States, and who shall not, when elected, be an Inhabitant of that State for which he shall be chosen.

The Vice President of the United States shall be President of the Senate, but shall have no Vote, unless they be equally divided.

The Senate shall chuse their other Officers, and also a President pro tempore, in the Absence of the Vice President, or when he shall exercise the Office of President of the United States.

The Senate shall have the sole Power to try all Impeachments. When sitting for that Purpose, they shall be on Oath or Affirmation. When the President of the United States is tried, the Chief Justice shall preside: And no Person shall be convicted without the Concurrence of two thirds of the Members present.

Judgment in Cases of Impeachment shall not extend further than to removal from Office, and disqualification to hold and enjoy any Office of honor, Trust, or Profit under the United States: but the Party convicted shall nevertheless be liable and subject to Indictment, Trial, Judgment, and Punishment, according to Law.

Section 4. The Times, Places and Manner of holding Elections for Senators and Representatives, shall be prescribed in each State by the Legislature thereof; but the Congress may at any time by Law make or alter such Regulations, except as to the Places of chusing Senators.

The Congress shall assemble at least once in every Year, and such Meeting shall be on the first Monday in December, unless they shall by Law appoint a different Day.

Section 5. Each House shall be the Judge of the Elections, Returns, and Qualifications of its own Members, and a Majority of each shall constitute a Quorum to do Business; but a smaller Number may adjourn from day to day, and may be authorized to compel the Attendance of absent Members, in such Manner, and under such Penalties as each House may provide.

Each House may determine the Rules of its Proceedings, punish its Members for disorderly Behavior, and, with the Concurrence of two thirds, expel a Member.

Each House shall keep a Journal of its Proceedings, and from time to time publish the same, excepting such Parts as may in their Judgment require Secrecy; and the Yeas and Nays of the Members of either House on any question shall, at the Desire of one fifth of those Present, be entered on the Journal.

Neither House, during the Session of Congress, shall, without the Consent of the other, adjourn for more than three days, nor to any other Place than that in which the two Houses shall be sitting.

Section 6. The Senators and Representatives shall receive a Compensation for their Services, to be ascertained by Law, and paid out of the Treasury of the United States. They shall in all Cases, except Treason, Felony and Breach of the Peace, be privileged from Arrest during their Attendance at the Session of their respective Houses, and in going to and returning from the same; and for any Speech or Debate in either House, they shall not be questioned in any other Place.

No Senator or Representative shall, during the Time for which he was elected, be appointed to any civil Office under the Authority of the United States, which shall have been created, or the Emoluments whereof shall have been increased during such time; and no Person holding any Office under the United States, shall be a Member of either House during his Continuance in Office.

Section 7. All Bills for raising Revenue shall originate in the House of Representatives; but the Senate may propose or concur with Amendments as on other Bills.

Every Bill which shall have passed the House of Representatives and the Senate, shall, before it become a Law, be presented to the President of the United States; If he approve he shall sign it, but if not he shall return it, with his Objections to the House in which it shall have originated, who shall enter the Objections at large on their Journal, and proceed to reconsider it. If after such Reconsideration two thirds of that House shall agree to pass the Bill, it shall be sent together with the Objections, to the other House, by which it shall likewise be reconsidered, and if approved by two thirds of that House, it shall become a Law. But in all such Cases the Votes of both Houses shall be determined by Yeas and Nays, and the Names of the Persons voting for and against the Bill shall be entered on the Journal of each House respectively. If any Bill shall not be returned by the President within ten Days (Sundays excepted) after it shall have been presented to him, the Same shall be a Law, in like Manner as if he had signed it, unless the Congress by their Adjournment prevent its Return in which Case it shall not be a Law.

Every Order, Resolution, or Vote, to which the Concurrence of the Senate and House of Representatives may be necessary (except on a question of Adjournment) shall be presented to the President of the United States; and before the Same shall take Effect, shall be approved by him, or being disapproved by him, shall be repassed by two thirds of the Senate and House of Representatives, according to the Rules and Limitations prescribed in the Case of a Bill.

Section 8. The Congress shall have Power To lay and collect Taxes, Duties, Imposts and Excises, to pay the Debts and provide for the common Defence and general Welfare of the United States; but all Duties, Imposts and Excises shall be uniform throughout the United States;

To borrow Money on the credit of the United States;

To regulate Commerce with foreign Nations, and among the several States, and with the Indian Tribes;

To establish an uniform Rule of Naturalization, and uniform Laws on the subject of Bankruptcies throughout the United States;

To coin Money, regulate the Value thereof, and of foreign Coin, and fix the Standard of Weights and Measures;

To provide for the Punishment of counterfeiting the Securities and current Coin of the United States;

To establish Post Offices and post Roads;

To promote the Progress of Science and useful Arts, by securing for limited Times to Authors and Inventors the exclusive Right to their respective Writings and Discoveries;

To constitute Tribunals inferior to the supreme Court;

To define and punish Piracies and Felonies committed on the high Seas, and Offenses against the Law of Nations;

To declare War, grant Letters of Marque and Reprisal, and make Rules concerning Captures on Land and Water;

To raise and support Armies, but no Appropriation of Money to that Use shall be for a longer Term than two Years;

To provide and maintain a Navy;

To make Rules for the Government and Regulation of the land and naval Forces;

To provide for calling forth the Militia to execute the Laws of the Union, suppress Insurrections and repel Invasions;

To provide for organizing, arming, and disciplining, the Militia, and for governing such Part of them as may be employed in the Service of the United States, reserving to the States respectively, the Appointment of the Officers, and the Authority of training the Militia according to the discipline prescribed by Congress;

To exercise exclusive Legislation in all Cases whatsoever, over such District (not exceeding ten Miles square) as may, by Cession of particular States, and the Acceptance of Congress, become the Seat of the Government of the United States, and to exercise like Authority over all Places purchased by the Consent of the Legislature of the State in which the Same shall be, for the Erection of Forts, Magazines, Arsenals, dock-Yards, and other needful Buildings;—And

To make all Laws which shall be necessary and proper for carrying into Execution the foregoing Powers, and all other Powers vested by this Constitution in the Government of the United States, or in any Department or Officer thereof.

Section 9. The Migration or Importation of such Persons as any of the States now existing shall think proper to admit, shall not be prohibited by the Congress prior to the Year one thousand eight hundred and eight, but a Tax or duty may be imposed on such Importation, not exceeding ten dollars for each Person.

The privilege of the Writ of Habeas Corpus shall not be suspended, unless when in Cases of Rebellion or Invasion the public Safety may require it.

No Bill of Attainder or ex post facto Law shall be passed.

No Capitation, or other direct, Tax shall be laid, unless in Proportion to the Census or Enumeration herein before directed to be taken.

No Tax or Duty shall be laid on Articles exported from any State.

No Preference shall be given by any Regulation of Commerce or Revenue to the Ports of one State over those of another: nor shall Vessels bound to, or from, one State be obliged to enter, clear, or pay Duties in another.

No Money shall be drawn from the Treasury, but in Consequence of Appropriations made by Law; and a regular Statement and Account of the Receipts and Expenditures of all public Money shall be published from time to time.

No Title of Nobility shall be granted by the United States: And no Person holding any Office of Profit or Trust under them, shall, without the Consent of the Congress, accept of any present, Emolument, Office, or Title, of any kind whatever, from any King, Prince, or foreign State.

Section 10. No State shall enter into any Treaty, Alliance, or Confederation; grant Letters of Marque and Reprisal; coin Money; emit Bills of Credit; make any Thing but gold and silver Coin a Tender in Payment of Debts; pass any Bill of Attainder, ex post facto Law, or Law impairing the Obligation of Contracts, or grant any Title of Nobility.

No State shall, without the Consent of the Congress, lay any Imposts or Duties on Imports or Exports, except what may be absolutely necessary for executing its inspection Laws: and the net Produce of all Duties and Imposts, laid by any State on Imports or Exports, shall be for the Use of the Treasury of the United States; and all such Laws shall be subject to the Revision and Controul of the Congress.

No State shall, without the Consent of Congress, lay any Duty of Tonnage, keep Troops, or Ships of War in time of Peace, enter into any Agreement or Compact with another State, or with a foreign Power, or engage in War, unless actually invaded, or in such imminent Danger as will not admit of delay.

ARTICLE II

Section 1. The executive Power shall be vested in a President of the United States of America. He shall hold his Office during the Term of four Years, and, together with the Vice President, chosen for the same Term, be elected, as follows:

Each State shall appoint, in such Manner as the Legislature thereof may direct, a Number of Electors, equal to the whole Number of Senators and Representatives to which the State may be entitled in the Congress; but no Senator or Representative, or Person holding an Office of Trust or Profit under the United States, shall be appointed an Elector.

The Electors shall meet in their respective States, and vote by Ballot for two Persons, of whom one at least shall not be an Inhabitant of the same State with themselves. And they shall make a List of all the Persons voted for, and of the Number of Votes for each; which List they shall sign and certify, and transmit sealed to the Seat of the Government of the United States, directed to the President of the Senate. The President of the Senate shall, in the Presence of the Senate and House of Representatives, open all the Certificates, and the Votes shall then be counted. The Person having the greatest Number of Votes shall be the President, if such Number be a Majority of the whole Number of Electors appointed; and if there be more than one who have such Majority, and have an equal Number of Votes, then the House of Representatives shall immediately chuse by Ballot one of them for President; and if no Person have a Majority, then from the five highest on the List the said House shall in like Manner chuse the President. But in chusing the President, the Votes shall be taken by States, the Representation from each State having one Vote; A quorum for this Purpose shall consist of a Member or Members from two thirds of the States, and a Majority of all the States shall be necessary to a Choice. In every Case, after the Choice of the President, the Person having the greater Number of Votes of the Electors shall be the Vice President. But if there should remain two or more who have equal Votes, the Senate shall chuse from them by Ballot the Vice President.

The Congress may determine the Time of chusing the Electors, and the Day on which they shall give their Votes; which Day shall be the same throughout the United States.

No person except a natural born Citizen, or a Citizen of the United States, at the time of the Adoption of this Constitution, shall be eligible to the Office of President; neither shall any Person be eligible to that Office who shall not have attained to the Age of thirty five Years, and been fourteen Years a Resident within the United States.

In Case of the Removal of the President from Office, or of his Death, Resignation or Inability to discharge the Powers and Duties of the said Office, the same shall devolve on the Vice President, and the Congress may by Law provide for the Case of Removal, Death, Resignation or Inability, both of the President and Vice President, declaring what Officer shall then act as President, and such Officer shall act accordingly, until the Disability be removed, or a President shall be elected.

The President shall, at stated Times, receive for his Services, a Compensation, which shall neither be increased nor diminished during the Period for which he shall have been elected, and he shall not receive within that Period any other Emolument from the United States, or any of them.

Before he enter on the Execution of his Office, he shall take the following Oath or Affirmation: "I do solemnly swear (or affirm) that I will faithfully execute the Office of President of the United States, and will to the best of my Ability, preserve, protect and defend the Constitution of the United States."

Section 2. The President shall be Commander in Chief of the Army and Navy of the United States, and of the Militia of the several States, when called into the actual Service of the United States; he may require the Opinion, in writing, of the principal Officer in each of the executive Departments, upon any Subject relating to the Duties of their respective Offices, and he shall have Power to grant Reprieves and Pardons for Offenses against the United States, except in Cases of Impeachment.

He shall have Power, by and with the Advice and Consent of the Senate to make Treaties, provided two thirds of the Senators present concur; and he shall nominate, and by and with the Advice and Consent of the Senate, shall appoint Ambassadors, other public Ministers and Consuls, Judges of the supreme Court, and all other Officers of the United States, whose Appointments are not herein otherwise provided for, and which shall be established by Law; but the Congress may by Law vest the Appointment of such inferior Officers, as they think proper, in the President alone, in the Courts of Law, or in the Heads of Departments.

The President shall have Power to fill up all Vacancies that may happen during the Recess of the Senate, by granting Commissions which shall expire at the End of their next Session.

Section 3. He shall from time to time give to the Congress Information of the State of the Union, and recommend to their Consideration such Measures as he shall judge necessary and expedient; he may, on extraordinary Occasions, convene both Houses, or either of them, and in Case of Disagreement between them, with Respect to the Time of Adjournment, he may adjourn them to such Time as he shall think proper; he shall receive Ambassadors and other public Ministers; he shall take Care that the Laws be faithfully executed, and shall Commission all the Officers of the United States.

Section 4. The President, Vice President and all civil Officers of the United States, shall be removed from Office on Impeachment for, and Conviction of, Treason, Bribery, or other high Crimes and Misdemeanors.

ARTICLE III

Section 1. The judicial Power of the United States, shall be vested in one supreme Court, and in such inferior Courts as the Congress may from time to time ordain and establish. The Judges, both of the supreme and inferior Courts, shall hold their Offices during good Behaviour, and shall, at stated Times, receive for their Services a Compensation, which shall not be diminished during their Continuance in Office.

Section 2. The judicial Power shall extend to all Cases, in Law and Equity, arising under this Constitution, the Laws of the United States, and Treaties made, or which shall be made, under their Authority;—to all Cases affecting Ambassadors, other public Ministers and Consuls;—to all Cases of admiralty and maritime Jurisdiction;—to Controversies to which the United States shall be a Party;—to Controversies between two or more States;—between a State and Citizens of another State;—between Citizens of different States;—between Citizens of the same State claiming Lands under Grants of different States, and between a State, or the Citizens thereof, and foreign States, Citizens or Subjects.

In all Cases affecting Ambassadors, other public Ministers and Consuls, and those in which a State shall be a Party, the supreme Court shall have original Jurisdiction. In all the other Cases before mentioned, the supreme Court shall have appellate Jurisdiction, both as to Law and Fact, with such Exceptions, and under such Regulations as the Congress shall make.

The Trial of all Crimes, except in Cases of Impeachment, shall be by Jury; and such Trial shall be held in the State where the said Crimes shall have been committed; but when not committed within any State, the Trial shall be at such Place or Places as the Congress may by Law have directed.

Section 3. Treason against the United States, shall consist only in levying War against them, or, in adhering to their Enemies, giving them Aid and Comfort. No Person shall be convicted of Treason unless on the Testimony of two Witnesses to the same overt Act, or on Confession in open Court.

The Congress shall have Power to declare the Punishment of Treason, but no Attainder of Treason shall work Corruption of Blood, or Forfeiture except during the Life of the Person attainted.

ARTICLE IV

Section 1. Full Faith and Credit shall be given in each State to the public Acts, Records, and judicial Proceedings of every other State. And the Congress may by general Laws prescribe the Manner in which such Acts, Records and Proceedings shall be proved, and the Effect thereof.

Section 2. The Citizens of each State shall be entitled to all Privileges and Immunities of Citizens in the several States.

A Person charged in any State with Treason, Felony, or other Crime, who shall flee from Justice, and be found in another State, shall on Demand of the executive Authority of the State from which he fled, be delivered up, to be removed to the State having Jurisdiction of the Crime.

No Person held to Service or Labour in one State, under the Laws thereof, escaping into another, shall, in Consequence of any Law or Regulation therein, be discharged from such Service or Labour, but shall be delivered up on Claim of the Party to whom such Service or Labour may be due.

Section 3. New States may be admitted by the Congress into this Union; but no new State shall be formed or erected within the Jurisdiction of any other State; nor any State be formed by the Junction of two or more States, or Parts of States, without the Consent of the Legislatures of the States concerned as well as of the Congress.

The Congress shall have Power to dispose of and make all needful Rules and Regulations respecting the Territory or other Property belonging to the United States; and nothing in this Constitution shall be so construed as to Prejudice any Claims of the United States, or of any particular State.

Section 4. The United States shall guarantee to every State in this Union a Republican Form of Government, and shall protect each of them against Invasion; and on Application of the Legislature, or of the Executive (when the Legislature cannot be convened) against domestic Violence.

ARTICLE V

The Congress, whenever two thirds of both Houses shall deem it necessary, shall propose Amendments to this Constitution, or, on the Application of the Legislatures of two thirds of the several States, shall call a Convention for proposing Amendments, which, in either Case, shall be valid to all Intents and Purposes, as part of this Constitution, when ratified by the Legislatures of three fourths of the several States, or by Conventions in three fourths thereof, as the one or the other Mode of Ratification may be proposed by the Congress; Provided that no Amendment which may be made prior to the Year One thousand eight hundred and eight shall in any Manner affect the first and fourth Clauses in the Ninth Section of the first Article; and that no State, without its Consent, shall be deprived of its equal Suffrage in the Senate.

ARTICLE VI

All Debts contracted and Engagements entered into, before the Adoption of this Constitution shall be as valid against the United States under this Constitution, as under the Confederation.

This Constitution, and the Laws of the United States which shall be made in Pursuance thereof; and all Treaties made, or which shall be made, under the Authority of the United States, shall be the supreme Law of the Land; and the Judges in every State shall be bound thereby, any Thing in the Constitution or Laws of any State to the Contrary notwithstanding.

The Senators and Representatives before mentioned, and the Members of the several State Legislatures, and all executive and judicial Officers, both of the United States and of the several States, shall be bound by Oath or Affirmation, to support this Constitution; but no religious Test shall ever be required as a Qualification to any Office or public Trust under the United States.

ARTICLE VII

The Ratification of the Conventions of nine States shall be sufficient for the Establishment of this Constitution between the States so ratifying the Same.

AMENDMENT I [1791]

Congress shall make no law respecting an establishment of religion, or prohibiting the free exercise thereof; or abridging the freedom of speech, or of the press; or the right of the people peaceably to assembly, and to petition the Government for a redress of grievances.

AMENDMENT II [1791]

A well regulated Militia, being necessary to the security of a free State, the right of the people to keep and bear Arms, shall not be infringed.

AMENDMENT III [1791]

No Soldier shall, in time of peace be quartered in any house, without the consent of the Owner, nor in time of war, but in a manner to be prescribed by law.

AMENDMENT IV [1791]

The right of the people to be secure in their persons, houses, papers, and effects, against unreasonable searches and seizures, shall not be violated, and no Warrants shall issue, but upon probable cause, supported by Oath or affirmation, and particularly describing the place to be searched, and the persons or things to be seized.

AMENDMENT V [1791]

No person shall be held to answer for a capital, or otherwise infamous crime, unless on a presentment or indictment of a Grand Jury, except in cases arising in the land or naval forces, or in the Militia, when in actual service in time of War or public danger; nor shall any person be subject for the same offence to be twice put in jeopardy of life or limb; nor shall be compelled in any criminal case to be a witness against himself, nor be deprived of life, liberty, or property, without due process of law; nor shall private property be taken for public use, without just compensation.

AMENDMENT VI [1791]

In all criminal prosecutions, the accused shall enjoy the right to a speedy and public trial, by an impartial jury of the State and district wherein the crime shall have been committed, which district shall have been previously ascertained by law, and to be informed of the nature and cause of the accusation; to be confronted with the witnesses against him;

to have compulsory process for obtaining witnesses in his favor, and to have the Assistance of Counsel for his defence.

AMENDMENT VII [1791]

In Suits at common law, where the value in controversy shall exceed twenty dollars, the right of trial by jury shall be preserved, and no fact tried by jury, shall be otherwise reexamined in any Court of the United States, than according to the rules of the common law.

AMENDMENT VIII [1791]

Excessive bail shall not be required, nor excessive fines imposed, nor cruel and unusual punishments inflicted.

AMENDMENT IX [1791]

The enumeration in the Constitution, of certain rights, shall not be construed to deny or disparage others retained by the people.

AMENDMENT X [1791]

The powers not delegated to the United States by the Constitution, nor prohibited by it to the States, are reserved to the States respectively, or to the people.

AMENDMENT XI [1798]

The Judicial power of the United States shall not be construed to extend to any suit in law or equity, commenced or prosecuted against one of the United States by Citizens of another State, or by Citizens or Subjects of any Foreign State.

AMENDMENT XII [1804]

The Electors shall meet in their respective states, and vote by ballot for President and Vice-President, one of whom, at least, shall not be an inhabitant of the same state with themselves; they shall name in their ballots the person voted for as President, and in distinct ballots the person voted for as Vice-President, and they shall make distinct lists of all persons voted for as President, and of all persons voted for as Vice-President, and of the number of votes for each, which lists they shall sign and certify, and transmit sealed to the seat of the government of the United States, directed to the President of the Senate;—The President of the Senate shall, in the presence of the Senate and House of Representatives, open all the certificates and the votes shall then be counted;—The person having the greatest number of votes for President, shall be the President, if such number be a majority of the whole number of Electors appointed; and if no person have such majority, then from the persons having the highest numbers not exceeding three on the list of those voted for as President, the House of Representatives shall choose immediately, by ballot, the President. But in choosing the President, the votes shall be taken by states, the representation from each state having one vote; a quorum for this purpose shall consist of a member or members from two-thirds of the states, and a majority of all states shall be necessary to a choice. And if the House of Representatives shall not choose a President whenever the right of choice

shall devolve upon them, before the fourth day of March next following, then the Vice-President shall act as President, as in the case of the death or other constitutional disability of the President.—The person having the greatest number of votes as Vice-President, shall be the Vice-President, if such number be a majority of the whole number of Electors appointed, and if no person have a majority, then from the two highest numbers on the list, the Senate shall choose the Vice-President; a quorum for the purpose shall consist of two-thirds of the whole number of Senators, and a majority of the whole number shall be necessary to a choice. But no person constitutionally ineligible to the office of President shall be eligible to that of Vice-President of the United States.

AMENDMENT XIII [1865]

Section 1. Neither slavery nor involuntary servitude, except as a punishment for crime whereof the party shall have been duly convicted, shall exist within the United States, or any place subject to their jurisdiction.

Section 2. Congress shall have power to enforce this article by appropriate legislation.

AMENDMENT XIV [1868]

Section 1. All persons born or naturalized in the United States, and subject to the jurisdiction thereof, are citizens of the United States and of the State wherein they reside. No State shall make or enforce any law which shall abridge the privileges or immunities of citizens of the United States; nor shall any State deprive any person of life, liberty, or property, without due process of law; nor deny to any person within its jurisdiction the equal protection of the laws.

Section 2. Representatives shall be apportioned among the several States according to their respective numbers, counting the whole number of persons in each State, excluding Indians not taxed. But when the right to vote at any election for the choice of electors for President and Vice President of the United States, Representatives in Congress, the Executive and Judicial officers of a State, or the members of the Legislature thereof, is denied to any of the male inhabitants of such State, being twenty-one years of age, and citizens of the United States, or in any way abridged, except for participation in rebellion, or other crime, the basis of representation therein shall be reduced in the proportion which the number of such male citizens shall bear to the whole number of male citizens twenty-one years of age in such State.

Section 3. No person shall be a Senator or Representative in Congress, or elector of President and Vice President, or hold any office, civil or military, under the United States, or under any State, who having previously taken an oath, as a member of Congress, or as an officer of the United States, or as a member of any State legislature, or as an executive or judicial officer of any State, to support the Constitution of the United States, shall have engaged in insurrection or rebellion against the same, or given aid or comfort to the enemies thereof. But Congress may by a vote of two-thirds of each House, remove such disability.

Section 4. The validity of the public debt of the United States, authorized by law, including debts incurred for payment of pensions and bounties for services in suppressing insurrection or rebellion, shall not be questioned. But neither the United States nor any State shall assume or pay any debt or obligation incurred in aid of insurrection or rebellion against the United States, or any claim for the loss or emancipation of any slave; but all such debts, obligations and claims shall be held illegal and void.

Section 5. The Congress shall have power to enforce, by appropriate legislation, the provisions of this article.

AMENDMENT XV [1870]

Section 1. The right of citizens of the United States to vote shall not be denied or abridged by the United States or by any State on account of race, color, or previous condition of servitude.

Section 2. The Congress shall have power to enforce this article by appropriate legislation.

AMENDMENT XVI [1913]

The Congress shall have power to lay and collect taxes on incomes, from whatever source derived, without apportionment among the several States, and without regard to any census or enumeration.

AMENDMENT XVII [1913]

Section 1. The Senate of the United States shall be composed of two Senators from each State, elected by the people thereof, for six years; and each Senator shall have one vote. The electors in each State shall have the qualifications requisite for electors of the most numerous branch of the State legislatures.

Section 2. When vacancies happen in the representation of any State in the Senate, the executive authority of such State shall issue writs of election to fill such vacancies: *Provided,* That the legislature of any State may empower the executive thereof to make temporary appointments until the people fill the vacancies by election as the legislature may direct.

Section 3. This amendment shall not be so construed as to affect the election or term of any Senator chosen before it becomes valid as part of the Constitution.

AMENDMENT XVIII [1919]

Section 1. After one year from the ratification of this article the manufacture, sale, or transportation of intoxicating liquors within, the importation thereof into, or the exportation thereof from the United States and all territory subject to the jurisdiction thereof for beverage purposes is hereby prohibited.

Section 2. The Congress and the several States shall have concurrent power to enforce this article by appropriate legislation.

Section 3. This article shall be inoperative unless it shall have been ratified as an amendment to the Constitution by the legislatures of the several States, as provided in the Constitution, within seven years from the date of the submission hereof to the States by the Congress.

AMENDMENT XIX [1920]

Section 1. The right of citizens of the United States to vote shall not be denied or abridged by the United States or by any State on account of sex.

Section 2. Congress shall have power to enforce this article by appropriate legislation.

AMENDMENT XX [1933]

Section 1. The terms of the President and Vice President shall end at noon on the 20th day of January, and the terms of Senators and Representatives at noon on the 3d day of January, of the years in which such terms would have ended if this article had not been ratified; and the terms of their successors shall then begin.

Section 2. The Congress shall assemble at least once in every year, and such meeting shall begin at noon on the 3d day of January, unless they shall by law appoint a different day.

Section 3. If, at the time fixed for the beginning of the term of the President, the President elect shall have died, the Vice President elect shall become President. If the President shall not have been chosen before the time fixed for the beginning of his term, or if the President elect shall have failed to qualify, then the Vice President elect shall act as President until a President shall have qualified; and the Congress may by law provide for the case wherein neither a President elect nor a Vice President elect shall have qualified, declaring who shall then act as President, or the manner in which one who is to act shall be selected, and such person shall act accordingly until a President or Vice President shall have qualified.

Section 4. The Congress may by law provide for the case of the death of any of the persons from whom the House of Representatives may choose a President whenever the right of choice shall have devolved upon them, and for the case of the death of any of the persons from whom the Senate may choose a Vice President whenever the right of choice shall have devolved upon them.

Section 5. Sections 1 and 2 shall take effect on the 15th day of October following the ratification of this article.

Section 6. This article shall be inoperative unless it shall have been ratified as an amendment to the Constitution by the legislatures of three-fourths of the several States within seven years from the date of its submission.

AMENDMENT XXI [1933]

Section 1. The eighteenth article of amendment to the Constitution of the United States is hereby repealed.

Section 2. The transportation or importation into any State, Territory, or possession of the United States for delivery or use therein of intoxicating liquors, in violation of the laws thereof, is hereby prohibited.

Section 3. This article shall be inoperative unless it shall have been ratified as an amendment to the Constitution by conventions in the several States, as provided in the Constitution, within seven years from the date of the submission hereof to the States by the Congress.

AMENDMENT XXII [1951]

Section 1. No person shall be elected to the office of the President more than twice, and no person who has held the office of President, or acted as President, for more than two years of a term to which some other person was elected President shall be elected to the office of President more than once. But this Article shall not apply to any person holding the office of President when this Article was proposed by the Congress, and shall not prevent any person who may be holding the office of President, or acting as President, during the term within which this Article becomes operative from holding the office of President or acting as President during the remainder of such term.

Section 2. This article shall be inoperative unless it shall have been ratified as an amendment to the Constitution by the legislatures of three-fourths of the several States within seven years from the date of its submission to the States by the Congress.

AMENDMENT XXIII [1961]

Section 1. The District constituting the seat of Government of the United States shall appoint in such manner as the Congress may direct:

A number of electors of President and Vice President equal to the whole number of Senators and Representatives in Congress to which the District would be entitled if it were a State, but in no event more than the least populous state; they shall be in addition to those appointed by the states, but they shall be considered, for the purposes of the election of President and Vice President, to be electors appointed by a state; and they shall meet in the District and perform such duties as provided by the twelfth article of amendment.

Section 2. The Congress shall have power to enforce this article by appropriate legislation.

AMENDMENT XXIV [1964]

Section 1. The right of citizens of the United States to vote in any primary or other election for President or Vice President, for electors for President or Vice President, or for Senator or Representative in Congress, shall not be denied or abridged by the United States, or any State by reason of failure to pay any poll tax or other tax.

Section 2. The Congress shall have power to enforce this article by appropriate legislation.

AMENDMENT XXV [1967]

Section 1. In case of the removal of the President from office or of his death or resignation, the Vice President shall become President.

Section 2. Whenever there is a vacancy in the office of the Vice President, the President shall nominate a Vice President who shall take office upon confirmation by a majority vote of both Houses of Congress.

Section 3. Whenever the President transmits to the President pro tempore of the Senate and the Speaker of the House of Representatives his written declaration that he is unable to discharge the powers and duties of his office, and until he transmits to them a written declaration to the contrary, such powers and duties shall be discharged by the Vice President as Acting President.

Section 4. Whenever the Vice President and a majority of either the principal officers of the executive departments or of such other body as Congress may by law provide, transmit to the President pro tempore of the Senate and the Speaker of the House of Representatives their written declaration that the President is unable to discharge the powers and duties of his office, the Vice President shall immediately assume the powers and duties of the office as Acting President.

Thereafter, when the President transmits to the President pro tempore of the Senate and the Speaker of the House of Representatives his written declaration that no inability exists, he shall resume the powers and duties of his office unless the Vice President and a majority of either the principal officers of the executive department or of such other body as Congress may by law provide, transmit within four days to the President pro tempore of the Senate and the Speaker of the House of Representatives their written declaration that the President is unable to discharge the powers and duties of his office. Thereupon Congress shall decide the issue, assembling within forty-eight hours for that purpose if not in session. If the Congress, within twenty-one days after receipt of the latter written declaration, or, if Congress is not in session, within twenty-one days after Congress is required to assemble, determines by two-thirds vote of both Houses that the President is unable to discharge the powers and duties of his office, the Vice President shall continue to discharge the same as Acting President; otherwise, the President shall resume the powers and duties of his office.

AMENDMENT XXVI [1971]

Section 1. The right of citizens of the United States, who are eighteen years of age or older, to vote shall not be denied or abridged by the United States or by any State on account of age.

Section 2. The Congress shall have power to enforce this article by appropriate legislation.

AMENDMENT XXVII [1992]

No law, varying the compensation for the services of the Senators and Representatives, shall take effect, until an election of Representatives shall have intervened.

Appendix B

You Be the _____: What Actually Happened

1.1 In general, state legislators reject the idea of banning distracted walking as unwarranted government interference. Over the past several years, distracted walking bills have failed in Arkansas, Illinois, and New York. Recently, the Utah Transit Authority did adopt a rule that subjects anyone who crosses the light rail tracks on the streets of Salt Lake City while distracted by an electronic device to a $50 fine. The state legislature refused, however, to implement the rule statewide. "Look, I get distracted all the time," said one Utah lawmaker who opposed the proposal. "Walking on sidewalks, in stores and malls, and maybe in a crosswalk sometimes I'm using my cellphone. But I try to stay connected to my environment. I never thought the government needed to cite me for using my cellphone in a reasonable manner."

4.1 The appellate court refused to throw out the charges. Although Emil was unconscious at the time his car struck the schoolgirls, he had made the initial decision to get behind the wheel despite the knowledge that he suffered from epileptic seizures. In other words, the *actus reus* in this crime was not Emil's driving into the girls, but his decision to drive in the first place. That decision was certainly voluntary and therefore satisfies the requirements of *actus reus*. Note that if Emil had never had an epileptic seizure before and had no idea that he suffered from that malady, the court's decision would probably have been different.

6.1 Deputy Timothy Scott ended the pursuit by applying his push bumper to the rear of Victor Harris's car. As a result, Harris lost control of his vehicle and spun off the side of the road. In the crash, Harris was badly injured, losing the ability to use his arms and legs. The question of whether Scott made the right decision eventually reached the United States Supreme Court. Ruling in the police officer's favor, the Court stated that Scott had acted reasonably under the circumstances, given the threat that Harris posed to others. The Court added that Harris intentionally placed himself in danger with his reckless actions and therefore could not blame Scott for injuries suffered in the resulting crash.

6.2 As these events actually played out, fifteen Cincinnati law enforcement officers had surrounded a suspect named Lorenzo Collins when he brandished the brick, and the two officers closest to Collins fatally shot him. The two officers were cleared of any wrongdoing, given that a reasonable officer in their position could have seen the brick as an instrument that could cause death or serious bodily harm. The court of public opinion, however, was against the police officers, who were accused by members of the community of needlessly killing a mentally unstable man who was carrying a brick, not a knife or a gun.

7.1 The United States Supreme Court upheld Michael's conviction, ruling that as long as police officers have probable cause to believe that a traffic violation has occurred, the "real" reason for making the stop is irrelevant. As Justice Antonin Scalia put it, "Subjective intentions play no role in ordinary, probable-cause, Fourth Amendment analysis." In practical terms, this ruling gives law enforcement agents the ability to confirm "hunches" about serious illegal behavior as long as the target of these hunches commits even the most minor traffic violation. Such violations could include failing to properly signal during a turn, or making a rolling stop at a stop sign, or driving five miles over the posted speed limit.

9.1 The North Carolina prosecutor in this case charged Judy Norman with first degree murder, reasoning that self-defense did not apply because Judy did not face any *imminent* danger from her husband, John. Despite his threats and the years of abuse, John was, at the time of his murder, asleep and thus incapable of harming her. A jury in the case, however, found Judy guilty of voluntary manslaughter only, and she was sentenced to six years in prison. This case gained national attention because the trial court refused to allow evidence of *battered woman syndrome (BWS)* to be presented to the jury. The term describes the psychological state a person descends into following a lengthy period of physical abuse. In a courtroom, an expert might argue that anyone suffering from this syndrome is in a constant, and reasonable, fear for her or his life. Some states do allow evidence of BWS to support the defendant's claim of self-defense in these sorts of cases, and it has been effective. A New York woman who shot her abusive husband as he slept, for example, was acquitted after a jury accepted her self-defense claims, bolstered by expert testimony on BWS.

10.1 In defending Daniel Aguilar against charges regarding Christopher Ash's murder, defense attorney Antonio Bestard's primary argument was that his client did not know that Ash was going to be killed in the garage. After all, they were best friends. Along the same lines, Bestard argued that Aguilar was forced to lure his friend to the garage by older gang members, who would have killed Aguilar had he refused. Bestard also attacked the credibility of the main witness, José Covarrubias, who not only was under the influence of drugs on the night of the murder and sleeping with the victim's sister, but also had received a lighter sentence of twenty-two years in return for testifying against fellow gang members. Bestard suggested that Covarrubias had an incentive to lie to law enforcement officials to get a lighter sentence. In the end, however, the jury found Aguilar guilty of first degree murder, and he was sentenced to life in prison without parole.

11.1 Before the sentencing phase of this trial began, Sedgwick County (Kansas) District Judge Ben Burgess allowed the prosecution to tell the jury that Elgin Robinson's murder-for-hire plot was "heinous, atrocious, and cruel." The defense had argued unsuccessfully that, as Robinson did not commit the murder himself, the crime's heinousness should not be an aggravating factor. Despite this ruling, after four hours of deliberation, the jury could not reach a unanimous verdict for the death penalty, with jurors voting 9–3 in favor of execution. By Kansas law, therefore, Robinson was sentenced to life in prison. Alabama and Florida are the only states that do not require a unanimous verdict for a jury to sentence a convict to be executed. Alabama requires ten votes, and Florida requires seven votes to impose the death penalty.

12.1 Alain LeConte's probation officer did not take any steps to revoke his probation. The issue became moot, however, when LeConte was arrested for killing a gas station attendant during an armed robbery in Norwalk, Connecticut. The crime took place between his first and second failed drug tests. LeConte's probation officer came under a great deal of criticism for failing to revoke his probation, but she received support from her supervisor. "We can only do so much," he said. "[LeConte's] probation officer went out of her way to assist this young man, but unfortunately it wasn't successful." The supervisor also pointed out that LeConte had no known history of violent behavior and had been a generally cooperative probationer when it came to getting treatment. This case underscores the difficult aspects of a probation officer's job. A misjudgment, even if it was based on a reasonable evaluation of the situation, can end in tragedy.

12.2 Susan Atkins was a disciple of cult leader Charles Manson and, in the summer of 1969, participated in one of the most sensationalized mass murders in American history. The woman Atkins stabbed sixteen times was Sharon Tate, an actress and the wife of film director Roman Polanski. On September 2, 2009, the California Board of Parole unanimously denied compassionate release for Atkins, marking the eighteenth time she had been refused parole. Three months later, Atkins died of brain cancer. Her case highlights the extent to which parole boards are often swayed by the nature of the crime above all other considerations.

16.1 On April 22, 2013, federal authorities charged Dzhokhar Tsarnaev with one count of using and conspiring to use a weapon of mass destruction resulting in death and one count of malicious destruction of property by means of an explosive device resulting in death. White House spokesman Jay Carney said that because Dzhokhar is a U.S. citizen, it would not have been appropriate to designate him an enemy combatant. In general, the Obama administration has indicated its preference for trying all terrorist suspects apprehended in the United States through the criminal justice system.

Appendix C

Table of Cases

Glossary

A

acquittal A declaration following a trial that the individual accused of the crime is innocent in the eyes of the law and thus is absolved from the charges.

actus reus (pronounced *ak*-tus *ray*-uhs). A guilty (prohibited) act.

adjudicatory hearing The process through which a juvenile court determines whether there is sufficient evidence to support the initial petition.

administrative law The body of law created by administrative agencies (in the form of rules, regulations, orders, and decisions) in order to carry out their duties and responsibilities.

adversary system A legal system in which the prosecution and defense are opponents, or adversaries, and present their cases in the light most favorable to themselves.

affidavit A written statement of facts, confirmed by the oath or affirmation of the party making it and made before a person having the authority to administer the oath or affirmation.

affirmative action A hiring or promotion policy favoring those groups, such as women, African Americans, or Hispanics, who have suffered from discrimination in the past or continue to suffer from discrimination.

aftercare The variety of therapeutic, educational, and counseling programs made available to juvenile delinquents (and some adults) after they have been released from a correctional facility.

age of onset The age at which a juvenile first exhibits delinquent behavior.

aggravating circumstances Any circumstances accompanying the commission of a crime that may justify a harsher sentence.

aging out A term used to explain the fact that criminal activity declines with age.

alibi A defense offered by a person accused of a crime showing that she or he was elsewhere at the time the crime took place.

***Allen* charge** An instruction by a judge to a deadlocked jury with only a few dissenters that asks the jurors in the minority to reconsider the majority opinion.

appeal The process of seeking a higher court's review of a lower court's decision for the purpose of correcting or changing this decision.

appellate courts Courts that review decisions made by lower courts, such as trial courts; also known as *courts of appeals.*

arraignment A court proceeding in which the suspect is formally charged with the criminal offense stated in the indictment.

arrest To take into custody a person suspected of criminal activity.

arrest warrant A written order, based on probable cause and issued by a judge or magistrate, commanding that the person named on the warrant be arrested by the police.

assault A threat or an attempt to do violence to another person that causes that person to fear immediate physical harm.

attempt The act of taking substantial steps toward committing a crime while having the ability and the intent to commit the crime, even if the crime never takes place.

attendant circumstances The facts surrounding a criminal event that must be proved to convict the defendant of the underlying crime.

attorney-client privilege A rule of evidence requiring that communications between a client and his or her attorney be kept confidential, unless the client consents to disclosure.

attorney general The chief law officer of a state; also, the chief law officer of the nation.

authority The power designated to an agent of the law over a person who has broken the law.

automatic transfer The process by which a juvenile is transferred to adult court as a matter of state law.

B

bail The dollar amount or conditions set by the court to ensure that an individual accused of a crime will appear for further criminal proceedings.

bail bond agent A businessperson who agrees, for a fee, to pay the bail amount if the accused fails to appear in court as ordered.

ballistics The study of firearms, including the firing of the weapon and the flight of the bullet.

ballot initiative A procedure in which the citizens of a state, by collecting enough signatures, can force a public vote on a proposed change to state law.

battery The act of physically contacting another person with the intent to do harm, even if the resulting injury is insubstantial.

bench trial A trial conducted without a jury, in which a judge makes the determination of the defendant's guilt or innocence.

beyond a reasonable doubt The degree of proof required to find the defendant in a criminal trial guilty of committing the crime. The defendant's guilt must be the only reasonable explanation for the criminal act before the court.

bill of rights The first ten amendments to the U.S. Constitution.

biology The science of living organisms, including their structure, function, growth, and origin.

biometrics Methods to identify a person based on his or her unique physical characteristics, such as fingerprints or facial configuration.

blue curtain A metaphorical term used to refer to the value placed on secrecy and the general mistrust of the outside world shared by many police officers.

body armor Protective covering that is worn under a police officer's clothing and designed to minimize injury from being hit by a fired bullet.

booking The process of entering a suspect's name, offense, and arrival time into the police log following her or his arrest.

boot camp A variation on traditional shock incarceration in which juveniles (and some adults) are sent to secure confinement facilities modeled on military basic training camps instead of prison or jail.

botnet A network of computers that have been appropriated without the knowledge of their owners and used to spread harmful programs via the Internet; short for *robot network*.

Boykin **form** A form that must be completed by a defendant who pleads guilty. The defendant states that she or he has done so voluntarily and with full comprehension of the consequences.

broken windows theory Wilson and Kelling's theory that a neighborhood in disrepair signals that criminal activity is tolerated in the area. By cracking down on quality-of-life crimes, police can reclaim the neighborhood and encourage law-abiding citizens to live and work there.

bullying Overt acts taken by students with the goal of intimidating, harassing, or humiliating other students.

bureaucracy A hierarchically structured administrative organization that carries out specific functions.

burglary The act of breaking into or entering a structure (such as a home or office) without permission for the purpose of committing a felony.

burnout A mental state that occurs when a person suffers from exhaustion and has difficulty functioning normally as a result of overwork and stress.

C

capital crime A criminal act that makes the offender eligible to receive the death penalty.

capital punishment The use of the death penalty to punish wrongdoers for certain crimes.

case attrition The process through which prosecutors, by deciding whether to prosecute each person arrested, effect an overall reduction in the number of persons prosecuted.

case law The rules of law announced in court decisions.

caseload The number of individual probationers or parolees under the supervision of a probation or parole officer.

causation The relationship in which a change in one measurement or behavior creates a recognizable change in another measurement or behavior.

challenge for cause A *voir dire* challenge for which an attorney states the reason why a prospective juror should not be included on the jury.

charge The judge's instructions to the jury following the attorneys' closing arguments.

child abuse Mistreatment of children by causing physical, emotional, or sexual damage without any plausible explanation, such as an accident.

child neglect A form of child abuse in which the child is denied certain necessities such as shelter, food, care, and love.

choice theory A school of criminology that holds that wrongdoers act as if they weigh the possible benefits of criminal or delinquent activity against the expected costs of being apprehended.

circumstantial evidence Indirect evidence that is offered to establish, by inference, the likelihood of a fact that is in question.

citizen oversight The process by which citizens review complaints brought against individual police officers or police departments.

civil confinement The practice of confining individuals against their will if they present a danger to the community.

civil law The branch of law dealing with the definition and enforcement of all private or public rights, as opposed to criminal matters.

civil liberties The basic rights and freedoms for American citizens guaranteed by the U.S. Constitution, particularly in the Bill of Rights.

classical criminology A school of criminology based on the belief that individuals have free will to engage in any behavior, including criminal behavior.

classification The process through which prison officials determine which correctional facility is best suited to the individual offender.

clearance rate A comparison of the number of crimes cleared by arrest and prosecution with the number of crimes reported during any given time period.

closing arguments Arguments made by each side's attorney after the cases for the plaintiff and defendant have been presented.

coercion The use of physical force or mental intimidation to compel a person to do something—such as confess to committing a crime—against her or his will.

cold case A criminal investigation that has not been solved after a certain amount of time.

cold hit The establishment of a connection between a suspect and a crime, often through the use of DNA evidence, in the absence of an ongoing criminal investigation.

common law The body of law developed from custom or judicial decisions in English and U.S. courts and not attributable to a legislature.

community corrections The correctional supervision of offenders in the community as an alternative to sending them to prison or jail.

community policing A policing philosophy that emphasizes community support for and cooperation with the police in preventing crime.

competency hearing A court proceeding to determine whether the defendant is mentally well enough to understand the charges filed against him or her and cooperate with a lawyer in presenting a defense.

compliance The state of operating in accordance with governmental standards.

computer crime Any wrongful act that is directed against computers and computer parts or that involves wrongful use or abuse of computers or software.

concurrent jurisdiction The situation that occurs when two or more courts have the authority to preside over the same criminal case.

concurring opinions Separate opinions prepared by judges who support the decision of the majority of the court but who want to make or clarify a particular point or to voice disapproval of the grounds on which the decision was made.

conducted energy device (CED) A less lethal weapon designed to disrupt a target's central nervous system by means of a charge of electrical energy.

confidential informant (CI) A human source for police who provides information concerning illegal activity in which he or she is involved.

conflict model A criminal justice model in which the content of criminal law is determined by the groups that hold economic, political, and social power in a community.

confrontation clause The part of the Sixth Amendment that guarantees all defendants the right to confront witnesses testifying against them during the criminal trial.

congregate system A nineteenth-century penitentiary system developed in New York in which inmates were kept in separate cells during the night but worked together in the daytime under a code of enforced silence.

consensus model A criminal justice model in which the majority of citizens in a society share the same values and beliefs. Criminal acts are acts that conflict with these values and beliefs and that are deemed harmful to society.

consent searches Searches by police that are made after the subject of the search has agreed to the action. In these situations, consent, if given of free will, validates a warrantless search.

conspiracy A plot by two or more people to carry out an illegal or harmful act.

constitutional law Law based on the U.S. Constitution and the constitutions of the various states.

coroner The medical examiner of a county, usually elected by popular vote.

corporate violence Physical harm to individuals or the environment that occurs as the result of corporate policies or decision making.

corpus delicti The body of circumstances that must exist for a criminal act to have occurred.

correlation The relationship between two measurements or behaviors that tend to move in the same direction.

courtroom work group The social organization consisting of the judge, prosecutor, defense attorney, and other court workers.

crime An act that violates criminal law and is punishable by criminal sanctions.

crime control model A criminal justice model that places primary emphasis on the right of society to be protected from crime and violent criminals.

crime mapping Technology that allows crime analysts to identify trends and patterns of criminal behavior within a given area.

criminal justice system The interlocking network of law enforcement agencies, courts, and corrections institutions designed to enforce criminal laws and protect society from criminal behavior.

criminology The scientific study of crime and the causes of criminal behavior.

cross-examination The questioning of an opposing witness during trial.

custodial interrogation The questioning of a suspect after that person has been taken into custody. In this situation, the suspect must be read his or her *Miranda* rights before interrogation can begin.

custody The forceful detention of a person, or the perception that a person is not free to leave the immediate vicinity.

cyberattack An attempt to damage or disrupt computer systems or electronic networks operated by computers.

cyber crime A crime that occurs online, in the virtual community of the Internet, as opposed to in the physical world.

cyber forensics The application of computer technology to finding and utilizing evidence of cyber crimes.

cyber fraud Any misrepresentation knowingly made over the Internet with the intention of deceiving another and on which a reasonable person would and does rely to his or her detriment.

cyberstalking The crime of stalking, committed in cyberspace through the use of e-mail, text messages, or another form of electronic communication.

D

day reporting center (DRC) A community-based corrections center to which offenders report on a daily basis for treatment, education, and rehabilitation.

deadly force Force applied by a police officer that is likely or intended to cause death.

defendant In a civil court, the person or institution against whom an action is brought. In a criminal court, the person or entity who has been formally accused of violating a criminal law.

defense attorney The lawyer representing the defendant.

delegation of authority The principles of command on which most police departments are based, in which personnel take orders from and are responsible to those in positions of power directly above them.

"deliberate indifference" The standard for establishing a violation of an inmate's Eighth Amendment rights, requiring that prison officials were aware of harmful conditions in a correctional institution *and* failed to take steps to remedy those conditions.

departure A stipulation in many federal and state sentencing guidelines that allows a judge to adjust his or her sentencing decision based on the special circumstances of a particular case.

deprivation model A theory that inmate aggression is the result of the frustration inmates feel at being deprived of freedom, consumer goods, sex, and other staples of life outside the institution.

desistance The process through which criminal activity decreases and reintegration into society increases over a period of time.

detective The primary police investigator of crimes.

detention The temporary custody of a juvenile in a secure facility after a petition has been filed and before the adjudicatory process begins.

detention hearing A hearing to determine whether a juvenile should be detained, or remain detained, while waiting for the adjudicatory process to begin.

determinate sentencing A period of incarceration that is fixed by a sentencing authority and cannot be reduced by judges or other corrections officials.

deterrence The strategy of preventing crime through the threat of punishment.

deviance Behavior that is considered to go against the norms established by society.

differential response A strategy for answering calls for service in which response time is adapted to the seriousness of the call.

digital evidence Information or data of value to a criminal investigation that is either stored or transmitted by electronic means.

directed patrol A patrol strategy that is designed to focus on a specific type of criminal activity at a specific time.

direct evidence Evidence that establishes the existence of a fact that is in question without relying on inference.

direct examination The examination of a witness by the attorney who calls the witness to the stand to testify.

direct supervision approach A process of prison and jail administration in which correctional officers are in continuous physical contact with inmates during the day.

discovery Formal investigation by each side prior to trial.

discretion The ability of individuals in the criminal justice system to make operational decisions based on personal judgment instead of formal rules or official information.

discretionary release The release of an inmate into a community supervision program at the discretion of the parole board within limits set by state or federal law.

discrimination The illegal use of characteristics such as gender or race by employers when making hiring or promotion decisions.

disposition hearing Similar to the sentencing hearing for adults, a hearing in which the juvenile judge or officer decides the appropriate punishment for a youth found to be delinquent or a status offender.

dissenting opinions Separate opinions in which judges disagree with the conclusion reached by the majority of the court and expand on their own views about the case.

diversion In the context of corrections, a strategy to divert those offenders who qualify away from prison and jail and toward community-based and intermediate sanctions.

DNA fingerprinting The identification of a person based on a sample of her or his DNA, the genetic material found in the cells of all living things.

docket The list of cases entered on a court's calendar and thus scheduled to be heard by the court.

domestic terrorism Acts of terrorism that take place on U.S. soil without direct foreign involvement.

double jeopardy To twice place at risk (jeopardize) a person's life or liberty. Constitutional law prohibits a second prosecution in the same court for the same criminal offense.

double marginality The double suspicion that minority law enforcement officers face from their white colleagues and from members of the minority community to which they belong.

drug Any substance that modifies biological, psychological, or social behavior. In particular, an illegal substance with those properties.

Drug Enforcement Administration (DEA) The federal agency responsible for enforcing the nation's laws and regulations regarding narcotics and other controlled substances.

dual court system The separate but interrelated court system of the United States, made up of the courts on the national level and the courts on the state level.

due process clause The provisions of the Fifth and Fourteenth Amendments to the Constitution that guarantee that no person shall be deprived of life, liberty, or property without due process of law.

due process model A criminal justice model that places primacy on the right of the individual to be protected from the power of the government.

duress Unlawful pressure brought to bear on a person, causing the person to perform an act that he or she would not otherwise perform.

duty The moral sense of a police officer that she or he should behave in a certain manner.

duty to retreat The requirement that a person claiming self-defense prove that she or he first took reasonable steps to avoid the conflict that resulted in the use of deadly force.

E

electronic monitoring A technique of probation supervision in which the offender's whereabouts are kept under surveillance by an electronic device.

electronic surveillance The use of electronic equipment by law enforcement agents to record private conversations or observe conduct that is meant to be private.

enemy combatant An individual who has supported foreign terrorist organizations such as al Qaeda that are engaged in hostilities against the military operations of the United States.

entrapment A defense in which the defendant claims that he or she was induced by a public official—usually an undercover agent or police officer—to commit a crime that he or she would otherwise not have committed.

ethics The moral principles that govern a person's perception of right and wrong.

evidence Anything that is used to prove the existence or nonexistence of a fact.

exclusionary rule A rule under which any evidence that is obtained in violation of the accused's rights, as well as any evidence derived from illegally obtained evidence, will not be admissible in criminal court.

exigent circumstances Situations that require extralegal or exceptional actions by the police.

expert witness A witness with professional training or substantial experience qualifying her or him to testify on a certain subject.

expiration release The release of an inmate from prison at the end of his or her sentence without any further correctional supervision.

extradition The process by which one jurisdiction surrenders a person accused or convicted of violating another jurisdiction's criminal law to the second jurisdiction.

F

Federal Bureau of Investigation (FBI) The branch of the Department of Justice responsible for investigating violations of federal law.

federalism A form of government in which a written constitution provides for a division of powers between a central government and several regional governments.

felony A serious crime, usually punishable by death or imprisonment for a year or longer.

felony-murder An unlawful homicide that occurs during the attempted commission of a felony.

field training The segment of a police recruit's training in which he or she is removed from the classroom and placed on the beat, under the supervision of a senior officer.

finality The end of a criminal case, meaning that the outcome of the case is no longer susceptible to challenge by prosecutors or the defendant.

forensics The application of science to establish facts and evidence during the investigation of crimes.

forfeiture The process by which the government seizes private property attached to criminal activity.

formal criminal justice process The model of the criminal justice process in which participants follow formal rules to create a smoothly functioning disposition of cases from arrest to punishment.

frisk A pat-down or minimal search by police to discover weapons.

fruit of the poisoned tree Evidence that is acquired through the use of illegally obtained evidence and is therefore inadmissible in court.

furlough Temporary release from a prison for purposes of vocational or educational training, to ease the shock of release, or for personal reasons.

G

genetics The study of how certain traits or qualities are transmitted from parents to their offspring.

"good faith" exception The legal principle that evidence obtained with the use of a technically invalid search warrant is admissible during trial if the police acted in good faith when they sought the warrant from a judge.

"good time" A reduction in time served by prisoners based on good behavior, conformity to rules, and other positive behavior.

graduated sanctions The practical theory in juvenile corrections that a delinquent or status offender should receive a punishment that matches in seriousness the severity of the wrongdoing.

grand jury The group of citizens called to decide whether probable cause exists to believe that a suspect committed the crime with which she or he has been charged.

gun control Efforts by a government to regulate or control the sale of guns.

H

habeas corpus An order that requires corrections officials to bring an inmate before a court or a judge and explain why he or she is being held in prison.

habitual offender laws Statutes that require lengthy prison sentences for those who are convicted of multiple felonies.

hacker A person who uses one computer to break into another.

halfway house A community-based form of early release that places inmates in residential centers and allows them to reintegrate with society.

"hands-off" doctrine The unwritten judicial policy that favors noninterference by the courts in the administration of prisons and jails.

hate crime law A statute that provides for greater sanctions against those who commit crimes motivated by bias against an individual or a group based on race, ethnicity, religion, gender, sexual orientation, disability, or age.

hearsay An oral or written statement made by an out-of-court speaker that is later offered in court by a witness (not the speaker) concerning a matter before the court.

home confinement A community-based sanction in which offenders serve their terms of incarceration in their homes.

homeland security A concerted national effort to prevent terrorist attacks within the United States and reduce the country's vulnerability to terrorism.

hormone A chemical substance, produced in tissue and conveyed in the bloodstream, that controls certain cellular and body functions such as growth and reproduction.

hot spots Concentrated areas of high criminal activity that draw a directed police response.

hung jury A jury whose members are so irreconcilably divided in their opinions that they cannot reach a verdict.

hypothesis A possible explanation for an observed occurrence that can be tested by further investigation.

I

"identifiable human needs" The basic human necessities that correctional facilities are required by the Constitution to provide to inmates.

identity theft The theft of personal information, such as a person's name, driver's license number, or Social Security number.

impeachment The formal process by which a public official is charged with misconduct that could lead to his or her removal from office.

incapacitation A strategy for preventing crime by detaining wrongdoers in prison, thereby separating them from the community and reducing criminal opportunities.

inchoate offenses Conduct deemed criminal without actual harm being done, provided that the harm that would have occurred is one the law tries to prevent.

incident-driven policing A reactive approach to policing that emphasizes a speedy response to calls for service.

indeterminate sentencing An indeterminate term of incarceration in which a judge determines the minimum and maximum terms of imprisonment.

indictment A charge or written accusation, issued by a grand jury, that probable cause exists to believe that a named person has committed a crime.

"inevitable discovery" exception The legal principle that illegally obtained evidence can be admissible in court if police using lawful means would have "inevitably" discovered it.

infancy A condition that, under early American law, excused young wrongdoers of criminal behavior because presumably they could not understand the consequences of their actions.

informal criminal justice process A model of the criminal justice system that recognizes the informal authority exercised by individuals at each step of the criminal justice process.

information The formal charge against the accused issued by the prosecutor after a preliminary hearing has found probable cause.

infraction In most jurisdictions, a noncriminal offense for which the penalty is a fine rather than incarceration.

infrastructure The services and facilities that support the day-to-day needs of modern life, such as electricity, food, transportation, and water.

initial appearance An accused's first appearance before a judge or magistrate following arrest.

insanity A defense for criminal liability that asserts a lack of criminal responsibility due to mental instability

intake The process by which an official of the court must decide whether to file a petition, release the juvenile, or place the juvenile under some other form of supervision.

intellectual property Property resulting from intellectual, creative processes.

intelligence-led policing An approach that measures the risk of criminal behavior associated with certain individuals or locations so as to predict when and where such criminal behavior is most likely to occur in the future.

intensive supervision probation (ISP) A punishment-oriented form of probation in which the offender is placed under stricter and more frequent surveillance and control than in conventional probation.

intermediate sanctions Sanctions that are more restrictive than probation and less restrictive than imprisonment.

internal affairs unit (IAU) A division within a police department that receives and investigates complaints of wrongdoing by police officers.

interrogation The direct questioning of a suspect to gather evidence of criminal activity and to try to gain a confession.

intoxication A defense for criminal liability in which the defendant claims that the taking of intoxicants rendered him or her unable to form the requisite intent to commit a criminal act.

involuntary manslaughter A homicide in which the offender had no intent to kill her or his victim.

irresistible-impulse test A test for the insanity defense under which a defendant who knew his or her action was wrong may still be found insane if he or she was unable, as a result of a mental deficiency, to control the urge to complete the act.

J

jail A facility, usually operated by the county government, used to hold persons awaiting trial or those who have been found guilty of misdemeanors.

judicial misconduct A general term describing behavior—such as accepting bribes or consorting with known felons—that diminishes public confidence in the judiciary.

judicial review The power of a court—particularly the United States Supreme Court—to review the actions of the executive and legislative branches and, if necessary, declare those actions unconstitutional.

judicial waiver The process in which the juvenile judge, based on the facts of the case at hand, decides that the alleged offender should be transferred to adult court.

jurisdiction The authority of a court to hear and decide cases within an area of the law or a geographic territory.

jury trial A trial before a judge and a jury.

just deserts A sanctioning philosophy based on the assertion that criminals deserve to be punished for breaking society's rules.

justice The quality of fairness that must exist in the processes designed to determine whether individuals are guilty of criminal wrongdoing.

juvenile delinquency Behavior that is illegal under federal or state law that has been committed by a person who is under an age limit specified by statute.

L

larceny The act of taking property from another person without the use of force with the intent of keeping that property.

lay witness A witness who can truthfully and accurately testify on a fact in question without having specialized training or knowledge.

liability In a civil court, legal responsibility for one's own or another's actions.

lockdown A disciplinary action taken by prison officials in which all inmates are ordered to their quarters and nonessential prison activities are suspended.

low-visibility decision making A term used to describe the discretionary power police have in determining what to do with misbehaving juveniles.

M

magistrate A public civil officer or official with limited judicial authority within a particular geographic area, such as the authority to issue an arrest warrant.

mala in se A descriptive term for acts that are inherently wrong, regardless of whether they are prohibited by law.

mala prohibita A descriptive term for acts that are made illegal by criminal statute and are not necessarily wrong in and of themselves.

mandatory arrest law Requires a police officer to detain a person for committing a certain type of crime as long as there is probable cause that he or she committed the crime.

mandatory release Release from prison that occurs when an offender has served the full length of his or her sentence, minus any adjustments for good time.

mandatory sentencing guidelines Statutorily determined punishments that must be applied to those who are convicted of specific crimes.

master jury list The list of citizens in a court's district from which a jury can be selected; compiled from voter-registration lists, driver's license lists, and other sources.

maximum-security prison A correctional institution designed and organized to control and discipline dangerous felons, as well as prevent escape.

medical model A model of corrections in which the psychological and biological roots of an inmate's criminal behavior are identified and treated.

medium-security prison A correctional institution that houses less dangerous inmates and therefore uses less restrictive measures to prevent violence and escapes.

mens rea (pronounced *mehns ray*-uh). Mental state, or intent. A wrongful mental state is usually as necessary as a wrongful act to establish criminal liability.

military tribunal A court that is operated by the military rather than the criminal justice system and is presided over by military officers rather than judges.

minimum-security prison A correctional institution designed to allow inmates, most of whom pose low security risks, a great deal of freedom of movement and contact with the outside world.

Miranda rights The constitutional rights of accused persons taken into custody by law enforcement officials, such as the right to remain silent and the right to counsel.

misdemeanor A criminal offense that is not a felony; usually punishable by a fine and/or a jail term of less than one year.

Missouri plan A method of selecting judges that combines appointment and election.

mitigating circumstances Any circumstances accompanying the commission of a crime that may justify a lighter sentence.

M'Naghten rule A common law test of criminal responsibility, derived from *M'Naghten's* Case in 1843, that relies on the defendant's inability to distinguish right from wrong.

Model Penal Code A statutory text created by the American Law Institute that sets forth general principles of criminal responsibility and defines specific offenses.

morals Principles of right and wrong behavior, as practiced by individuals or by society.

motion for a directed verdict A motion requesting that the court grant judgment in favor of the defense on the ground that the prosecution has not produced sufficient evidence to support the state's claim.

murder The unlawful killing of one human being by another.

N

necessity A defense against criminal liability in which the defendant asserts that circumstances required her or him to commit an illegal act.

negligence A failure to exercise the standard of care that a reasonable person would exercise in similar circumstances.

neurotransmitter A chemical that transmits nerve impulses between nerve cells and from nerve cells to the brain.

new-generation jail A type of jail that is distinguished architecturally from its predecessors by a design that encourages interaction between inmates and jailers and that offers greater opportunities for treatment.

night watch system An early form of American law enforcement in which volunteers patrolled their community from dusk to dawn to keep the peace.

noble cause corruption Knowing misconduct by a police officer with the goal of attaining what the officer believes is a "just" result.

nolo contendere Latin for "I will not contest it." A criminal defendant's plea, in which he or she chooses not to challenge, or contest, the charges brought by the government.

nonpartisan elections Elections in which candidates are presented on the ballot without any party affiliation.

nonstate actor An entity that plays a role in international affairs but does not represent any established state or nation.

O

opening statements The attorneys' statements to the jury at the beginning of the trial.

opinions Written statements by the judges expressing the reasons for the court's decision in a case.

oral arguments The verbal arguments presented in person by attorneys to an appellate court. Each attorney presents reasons why the court should rule in his or her client's favor.

organized crime Illegal acts carried out by illegal organizations engaged in the market for illegal goods or services, such as illicit drugs or firearms.

P

pardon An act of executive clemency that overturns a conviction and erases mention of the crime from the person's criminal record.

parens patriae A doctrine that holds that the state has a responsibility to look after the well-being of children and to assume the role of parent if necessary.

parole The conditional release of an inmate before his or her sentence has expired.

parole board A body of appointed civilians that decides whether a convict should be granted conditional release before the end of his or her sentence.

parole contract An agreement between the state and the offender that establishes the conditions of parole.

parole grant hearing A hearing in which the entire parole board or a subcommittee reviews information, meets the offender, and hears testimony from relevant witnesses to determine whether to grant parole.

parole guidelines Standards that are used in the parole process to measure the risk that a potential parolee will recidivate.

parole revocation When a parolee breaks the conditions of parole, the process of withdrawing parole and returning the person to prison.

partisan elections Elections in which candidates are affiliated with and receive support from political parties.

patronage system A form of corruption in which the political party in power hires and promotes police officers, receiving job-related "favors" in return.

penitentiary An early form of correctional facility that emphasized separating inmates from society and from each other.

peremptory challenges Voir dire challenges to exclude potential jurors from serving on the jury without any supporting reason or cause.

petition The document filed with a juvenile court alleging that the juvenile is a delinquent or a status offender and requesting that the court either hear the case or transfer it to an adult court.

phishing Sending an unsolicited e-mail that falsely claims to be from a legitimate organization in an attempt to acquire sensitive information from the recipient.

plaintiff The person or institution that initiates a lawsuit in civil court proceedings by filing a complaint.

plain view doctrine The legal principle that objects in plain view of a law enforcement agent who has the right to be in a position to have that view may be seized without a warrant and introduced as evidence.

plea bargaining The process by which the accused and the prosecutor work out a mutually satisfactory conclusion to the case, subject to court approval.

police corruption The abuse of authority by a law enforcement officer for personal gain.

police subculture The values and perceptions that are shared by members of a police department and, to a certain extent, by all law enforcement agents.

policy A set of guiding principles designed to influence the behavior and decision making of police officers.

positivism A school of the social sciences that sees criminal and delinquent behavior as the result of biological, psychological, and social forces.

precedent A court decision that furnishes an example of authority for deciding subsequent cases involving similar facts.

predisposition report A report prepared during the disposition process that provides the judge with relevant background material to aid in the disposition decision.

preliminary hearing An initial hearing in which a magistrate decides if there is probable cause to believe that the defendant committed the crime with which he or she is charged.

preponderance of the evidence The degree of proof required to decide in favor of one side or the other in a civil case. In general, this requirement is met when a plaintiff proves that a fact more likely than not is true.

presentence investigative report An investigative report on an offender's background that assists a judge in determining the proper sentence.

pretrial detainees Individuals who cannot post bail after arrest and are therefore forced to spend the time prior to their trial incarcerated in jail.

pretrial diversion program An alternative to trial offered by a judge or prosecutor, in which the offender agrees to participate in a specified counseling or treatment program in return for withdrawal of the charges.

preventive detention The retention of an accused person in custody due to fears that she or he will commit a crime if released before trial.

prisoner reentry A corrections strategy designed to prepare inmates for a successful return to the community and to reduce their criminal activity after release.

prison gang A group of inmates who band together within the corrections system to engage in social and criminal activities.

prison programs Organized activities for inmates that are designed to improve their physical and mental health, provide them with vocational skills, or simply keep them busy while incarcerated.

prison segregation The practice of separating inmates based on a certain characteristic, such as age, gender, type of crime committed, or race.

prisonization The socialization process through which a new inmate learns the accepted norms and values of the prison culture.

private prisons Correctional facilities operated by private corporations instead of the government and, therefore, reliant on profits for survival.

private security The practice of private corporations or individuals offering services traditionally performed by police officers.

proactive arrests Arrests that occur because of concerted efforts by law enforcement agencies to respond to a particular type of criminal or criminal behavior.

probable cause Reasonable grounds to believe the existence of facts warranting certain actions, such as the search or arrest of a person.

probation A criminal sanction in which a convict is allowed to remain in the community rather than be imprisoned.

probationary period A period of time at the beginning of a police officer's career during which she or he may be fired without cause.

problem-oriented policing A policing philosophy that requires police to identify potential criminal activity and develop strategies to prevent or respond to that activity.

problem-solving courts Lower courts that have jurisdiction over one specific area of criminal activity, such as illegal drugs or domestic violence.

procedural criminal law Rules that define the manner in which the rights and duties of individuals may be enforced.

procedural due process A provision in the Constitution that states that the law must be carried out in a fair and orderly manner.

professionalism Adherence to a set of values that show a police officer to be of the highest moral character.

professional model A style of policing advocated by August Vollmer and O. W. Wilson that emphasizes centralized police organizations, increased use of technology, and a limitation of police discretion through regulations and guidelines.

property bond An alternative to posting bail in cash, in which the defendant gains pretrial release by providing the court with property valued at the bail amount as assurance that he or she will return for trial.

prosecutorial waiver A procedure used in situations where the prosecutor has discretion to decide whether a case will be heard by a juvenile court or an adult court.

psychoactive drugs Chemicals that affect the brain, causing changes in emotions, perceptions, and behavior.

psychoanalytic theory Sigmund Freud's theory that attributes our thoughts and actions to unconscious motives.

psychology The scientific study of mental processes and behavior.

public defenders Court-appointed attorneys who are paid by the state to represent defendants who are unable to hire private counsel.

public order crime Behavior that has been labeled criminal because it is contrary to shared social values, customs, and norms.

public prosecutors Individuals, acting as trial lawyers, who initiate and conduct cases in the government's name and on behalf of the people.

R

racial profiling The practice of targeting people for police action based solely on their race, ethnicity, or national origin.

racketeering The criminal action of being involved in an organized effort to engage in illegal business transactions.

random patrol A patrol strategy that relies on police officers monitoring a certain area with the goal of detecting crimes in progress or preventing crime due to their presence. Also known as *general* or *preventive patrol.*

reactive arrests Arrests that come about as part of the ordinary routine of police patrol and responses to calls for service.

real evidence Evidence that is brought into court and seen by the jury, as opposed to evidence that is described for a jury.

"real offense" The actual offense committed, as opposed to the charge levied by a prosecutor as the result of a plea bargain.

reasonable force The degree of force that is appropriate to protect the police officer or other citizens and is not excessive.

rebuttal Evidence given to counteract or disprove evidence presented by the opposing party.

recidivism The act of committing a new crime after a person has already been punished for a previous crime by being convicted and sent to jail or prison.

recklessness The state of being aware that a risk does or will exist and nevertheless acting in a way that consciously disregards this risk.

recruitment The process by which law enforcement agencies develop a pool of qualified applicants from which to select new members.

referral The notification process through which a law enforcement officer or other concerned citizen makes the juvenile court aware of a juvenile's unlawful or unruly conduct.

regulation Governmental control of society through rules and laws that is generally carried out by administrative agencies.

rehabilitation The philosophy that society is best served when wrongdoers are provided the resources needed to eliminate criminality from their behavioral pattern.

reintegration A goal of corrections that focuses on preparing the offender for a return to the community unmarred by further criminal behavior.

relative deprivation The theory that inmate aggression is caused when freedoms and services that the inmate has come to accept as normal are decreased or eliminated.

release on recognizance (ROR) A judge's order that releases an accused from jail with the understanding that he or she will return of his or her own will for further proceedings.

relevant evidence Evidence tending to make a fact in question more or less probable than it would be without the evidence. Only relevant evidence is admissible in court.

residential treatment program A government-run facility for juveniles whose offenses are not deemed serious enough to warrant incarceration in a training school.

response time The rapidity with which calls for service are answered.

restitution Monetary compensation for damages done to the victim by the offender's criminal act.

restorative justice An approach to punishment designed to repair the harm done to the victim and the community by the offender's criminal act.

retribution The philosophy that those who commit criminal acts should be punished based on the severity of the crime and that no other factors need be considered.

robbery The act of taking property from another person through force, threat of force, or intimidation.

rule of four A rule of the United States Supreme Court that the Court will not issue a writ of *certiorari* unless at least four justices approve of the decision to hear the case.

rule of law The principle that the rules of a legal system apply equally to all persons, institutions, and entities—public or private—that make up a society.

S

search The process by which police examine a person or property to find evidence that will be used to prove guilt in a criminal trial.

search warrant A written order, based on probable cause and issued by a judge or magistrate, commanding that police officers or criminal investigators search a specific person, place, or property to obtain evidence.

searches and seizures The legal term, as found in the Fourth Amendment to the U.S. Constitution, that generally refers to the searching for and the confiscating of evidence by law enforcement agents.

searches incidental to arrests Searches for weapons and evidence that are conducted on persons who have just been arrested.

security threat group (STG) A group of three or more inmates who engage in activity that poses a threat to the safety of other inmates or the prison staff.

seizure The forcible taking of a person or property in response to a violation of the law.

self-defense The legally recognized privilege to protect one's self or property from injury by another.

sentencing discrimination A situation in which the length of a sentence appears to be influenced by a defendant's race, gender, economic status, or other factor not directly related to the crime he or she committed.

sentencing disparity A situation in which those convicted of similar crimes do not receive similar sentences.

sentencing guidelines Legislatively determined guidelines that judges are required to follow when sentencing those convicted of specific crimes.

separate confinement A nineteenth-century penitentiary system developed in Pennsylvania in which inmates were kept separate from each other at all times, with daily activities taking place in individual cells.

sex offender notification law Legislation that requires law enforcement authorities to notify people when convicted sex offenders are released into their neighborhood or community.

sexual assault Forced or coerced sexual intercourse (or other sexual acts).

sexual harassment A repeated pattern of unwelcome sexual advances and/or obscene remarks in the workplace. Under certain circumstances, sexual harassment is illegal and can be the basis for a civil lawsuit.

sheriff The primary law enforcement officer in a county, usually elected to the post by a popular vote.

shock incarceration A short period of incarceration that is designed to deter further criminal activity by "shocking" the offender with the hardships of imprisonment.

social disorganization theory The theory that deviant behavior is more likely in communities where social institutions such as the family, schools, and the criminal justice system fail to exert control over the population.

socialization The process through which a police officer is taught the values and expected behavior of the police subculture.

sociology The study of the development and functioning of groups of people who live together within a society.

spam Bulk e-mails, particularly of commercial advertising, sent in large quantities without the consent of the recipient.

split sentence probation A sentence that consists of incarceration in a prison or jail, followed by a probationary period in the community.

stare decisis (pronounced *ster*-ay dih-*si-ses*). A legal doctrine under which judges are obligated to follow the precedents established under prior decisions.

status offender A juvenile who has engaged in behavior deemed unacceptable for those under a certain statutorily determined age.

statute of limitations A law limiting the amount of time prosecutors have to bring criminal charges against a suspect after the crime has occurred.

statutory law The body of law enacted by legislative bodies.

statutory rape A strict liability crime in which an adult engages in a sexual act with a minor.

stop A brief detention of a person by law enforcement agents for questioning.

street gang A group of people, usually three or more, who share a common identity and engage in illegal activities.

stressors The aspects of police work and life that lead to feelings of stress.

strict liability crimes Certain crimes, such as traffic violations, in which the defendant is guilty regardless of her or his state of mind at the time of the act.

substantial-capacity test (ALI/MPC test) A test for the insanity defense that states that a person is not responsible for criminal behavior when he or she "lacks substantial capacity" to understand that the behavior is wrong or to know how to behave properly.

substantive criminal law Law that defines the rights and duties of individuals with respect to one another.

substantive due process The constitutional requirement that laws used in accusing and convicting persons of crimes must be fair.

supermax prison A correctional facility reserved for those inmates who have extensive records of misconduct.

supremacy clause A clause in the U.S. Constitution establishing that federal law is the "supreme law of the land" and shall prevail when in conflict with state constitutions or statutes.

suspended sentence A judicially imposed condition in which an offender is sentenced after being convicted of a crime, but is not required to begin serving the sentence immediately.

system A set of interacting parts that, when functioning properly, achieve a desired result.

T

technical violation An action taken by a probationer or parolee that, although not criminal, breaks the terms of probation or parole as designated by the court.

terrorism The use or threat of violence to achieve political objectives.

testimony Verbal evidence given by witnesses under oath.

testosterone The hormone primarily responsible for the production of sperm and the development of male secondary sex characteristics such as the growth of facial and pubic hair and the change of voice pitch.

theory An explanation of a happening or circumstance that is based on observation, experimentation, and reasoning.

time served The period of time a person denied bail (or unable to pay it) has spent in jail prior to his or her trial.

total institution An institution, such as a prison, that provides all of the necessities for existence to those who live within its boundaries.

trace evidence Evidence such as a fingerprint, blood, or hair found in small amounts at a crime scene.

training school A correctional institution for juveniles found to be delinquent or status offenders.

trial courts Courts in which most cases usually begin and in which questions of fact are examined.

truth-in-sentencing laws Legislative attempts to ensure that convicts will serve approximately the terms to which they were initially sentenced.

U

U.S. Customs and Border Protection (CBP) The federal agency responsible for protecting U.S. borders and facilitating legal trade and travel across those borders.

U.S. Immigration and Customs Enforcement (ICE) The federal agency that enforces the nation's immigration and customs laws.

U.S. Secret Service A federal law enforcement organization with the primary responsibility of protecting the president, the president's family, the vice president, and other important political figures.

V

venire The group of citizens from which the jury is selected.

verdict A formal decision made by the jury.

victim Any person who suffers physical, emotional, or financial harm as the result of a criminal act.

victim impact statement (VIS) A statement to the sentencing body (judge, jury, or parole board) in which the victim is given the opportunity to describe how the crime has affected her or him.

virus A computer program that can replicate itself and interfere with the normal use of a computer. A virus cannot exist as a separate entity and must attach itself to another program to move through a network.

visa Official authorization allowing a person to travel to and within the issuing country.

voir dire The preliminary questions that the trial attorneys ask prospective jurors to determine whether they are biased or have any connection with the defendant or a witness.

voluntary manslaughter A homicide in which the intent to kill was present in the mind of the offender, but malice was lacking.

W

warden The prison official who is ultimately responsible for the organization and performance of a correctional facility.

warrantless arrest An arrest made without first seeking a warrant for the action.

weapon of mass destruction A weapon that has the capacity to cause large number of casualties or significant property damage.

white-collar crime Nonviolent crimes committed by business entities or individuals to gain a personal or business advantage.

widen the net The criticism that intermediate sanctions designed to divert offenders from prison actually increase the number of citizens who are under the control and surveillance of the American corrections system.

work release program Temporary release of convicts from prison for purposes of employment. The offenders may spend their days on the job, but must return to the correctional facility at night and during the weekend.

worm A computer program that can automatically replicate itself and interfere with the normal use of a computer. A worm does not need to be attached to an existing file to move from one network to another.

writ of *certiorari* A request from a higher court asking a lower court for the record of a case. In essence, the request signals the higher court's willingness to review the case.

wrongful conviction The conviction, either by verdict or by guilty plea, of a person who is factually innocent of the charges.

Y

youth gang A self-formed group of youths with several identifiable characteristics, including a gang name and other recognizable symbols, a geographic territory, and participation in illegal activities.

Name Index

Subject Index

exigent circumstances, 232–233
 intent and, 232
 knock and announce rule, 233
 mandatory arrest policies, 171
 minority youths and, 507–508
 proactive, 187
 reactive, 186–187
 seizure or detention, 232
 understanding of, 232
 with a warrant, 232–233
 without a warrant, 233–234
Arrest warrant, 232–233
Arson, 8, 75
Aryan Brotherhood, 464, 465
Asian Americans
 crime and, 87
 as judges, 269–270
 as law enforcement officers, 145–146, 148–149
Assault
 defined, 7
 gangs and, 504
Assembly-line justice, 273
Assistant prosecutors, 282
Association, probable cause based on, 214
Association of Certified Fraud Examiners, 9
Attempt, 107
Attendant circumstances, 112–113
Attention deficit hyperactivity disorder (ADHD), 41
Attitude test, 508
Attorney-client privilege
 defense attorneys, 289
 defined, 289
 exceptions to, 289
Attorney general, 281–282
Attorneys. *See* Defense attorneys; Prosecutors
Auburn Prison, 424
Auburn system, 424
Aurora, Colorado shooting, 36
Authority
 delegation of, 173
 as element of arrest, 232
 of probation officer, 396–397
 use of force and, 193–196
Automatic License Plate Recognition (ALPR), 138, 226
Automatic transfer, 510

Automobiles
 Automatic License Plate Recognition (ALPR) technology, 226
 containers within vehicle, 223–224
 high-tech cop cars, 138
 officers killed in automobile accidents, 192
 patrol cars and reform era, 138
 pretextual stops, 223
 protective searches, 223
 searches of, 222–224
 warrantless searches of, 222–223

B

Bail
 average amounts, 293
 bail setting, 291–293
 defined, 291
 guidelines, 291–293
 overcrowded jails and, 293
 posting, 294
 purpose of, 291
 reasonable, 291
 risk and, 293
 ten percent cash bail, 294–295
 uncertainty and, 293
Bail bond agent, 294–295
Bailiff, 271
Bail Reform Act, 295
Bail tariffs, 291–292
Ballistics, 182–183
Ballot initiatives, 102
Baltimore City Police Department, 198–199
Baltimore Police Department, 137
Bath salts, 57
Battery, 7, 126
Beats, 173
Bench trial, 316
Benghazi attack, 528
Berkeley Police Department, 138
Beyond a reasonable doubt, 70
Bifurcated death penalty process, 372–373
Bigamy, 71, 104–105
Bill of attainder, 122
Bill of Rights. *See also* individual amendments
 defined, 122
 procedural safeguards and, 121–123

bin Laden, Osama
 al Qaeda and, 527–528
 death of, 527
 jihad, 528
 terrorism against U.S., 527–530
Biological theories of crime, 40–43
Biology, 40
Biometrics, 20–21
Black Guerrilla Family, 465
Block officers, 468
Bloods, 465
Blue curtain, 191
Body armor, 192
Body bomb, 536
Body-mounted video cameras, 200
Booking, 292
 Fifth Amendment and, 241
Boot camps, 410–411, 515–516
Border Patrol, 153–154
 securing Mexican and Canadian borders, 536
 totality of circumstances test, 228
 virtual fence, 536
Border security, 534–537
 airport screening and TSA, 535
 no fly list, 535
 regulated points of entry, 534–535
 screening challenges, 535
 securing Mexican and Canadian borders, 536–537
 unregulated points of entry, 536–537
 US-VISIT program, 535
Boston Marathon bombing, 24, 526–527, 535
Boston Police Department, 137
Botnets, 543
Boykin form, 305
Brain, crime and, 41–42
Bribery, 198, 549
 during political era of policing, 137
Bridewell Place, 423
Broken windows effect, 51, 59
Broward County (Florida) Sheriff's Department, 200
Brownsville Police Department, 168, 190
Bullycides, 500
Bullying
 anti-bullying legislation, 500

cyberbullying, 501, 542
  defined, 500
Burden of proof, 69–70
Bureaucracy, 172
  courts as, 252
Bureau of Alcohol, Tobacco,
    Firearms and Explosives
    (ATF), responsibilities of, 158
Burglary, 105
  average length of sentence, 394
  defined, 8, 75
  degree of, 108
  sentencing disparity, 361
Burnout, 193
Bush, George W., military model
    for terrorist threat, 531
Business Software Alliance, 544

C

Caffeine, 72
Calls for service, 174–175
  cold calls for, 184, 185
  hot calls for, 184, 185
  response time and efficiency,
    183–184
Campus style, 433
Cannabinoids, synthetic, 57
Capital crime, 27
Capitalism, vs. Marxism, 47–48
Capital offenses, 70
Capital punishment. *See also*
    Death penalty
  defined, 370
  as form of punishment, 356
Case citations, 33
Case law, 102–103
Caseload, probation officers, 397
Cases
  case attrition, 298–300
  priorities, 300
Castle Rock Police Department,
    171–172
Causation
  as element of crime, 112
  theory of criminology, 37
Cayce Police Department, 170
Cell block, 431
Center for Economic and Policy
    Research, 392
Centers for Disease Control, 68
Chain of command, police
    departments and, 173
Challenges for cause, 322
Champaign (Illinois) Police
    Department, 161

Charge to jury, 334
Charging conference, 334
Chastity requirement, 341
Chemical weapons
    investigations, 226
Chicago
  anti-loitering ordinance and
    gangs, 5
  homicide rate and, 4, 21, 44
Chicago Police Department, 137
Chicago school, 44
Child abuse, 503–504
Child neglect, 503–504
Children. *See also* Juveniles
  abuse of, 503–504
  infancy defense, 114
  life course theories of crime
    and childhood, 52–53
  neglect of, 503–504
  online child pornography, 9
  parens patriae, 491
Child savers, 491
China, Internet firewall, 546
Chivalry effect, 498–499
Choice theory, 38–40
  death penalty and, 40
  public policy and, 40
Chronic 6 percent, 59, 501
Chronic offender, 58–59
Cincinnati Police Department,
    137
Circuit judges, 99
Circumstantial evidence, 327
Citizen oversight, 199–200
City attorney, 281
Civil confinement, 482
Civil law
  burden of proof, 69–70
  compared to criminal law, 69,
    70
  defined, 69
  preponderance of evidence, 70
  responsibility and, 69
Civil liberties
  defined, 23
  homeland security and, 23–24
Civil Rights Act, 146
Civil suits, double jeopardy, 337
Class, crime and, 85–87
Classical criminology, 38–39
Classification, of prisoners, 430
Clean Water Act, 102
Clearance rates
  cold cases and, 179
  declining, 179

Clerk of the court, 271
Closed-circuit television (CCTV)
    cameras, 225–226
Closing arguments, 333
Cloud computing, 547
Coast Guard, 153, 155
Cocaine, 72, 73
  crack, 84
  crime trends and, 84
Cockfighting, 105
Code of Hammurabi, 99
Code of Israelites, 99
Code of Justinian, 99
CODIS, 182
Coercion
  confession and, 234
  inherent, 235
Cold cases
  databases and cold hit,
    181–182
  defined, 179
Cold hit, 181–182
Cole, U.S.S., bombing of, 528
Collective incapacitation,
    351–352
Columbine school shooting, 500,
    518
Commission on Law
    Observance and
    Enforcement, 137
Common law, 99–100
  defined, 99
  English, 99–100
Community-based corrections,
    15
Community corrections,
    391–415
  cost of, 392
  diversion, 391–392
  intermediate sanctions,
    406–413
  justification for, 391–392
  low-cost alternative, 392
  number of people in, 391
  paradox of, 413–414
  probation, 392–400
  reintegration, 391
Community courts, 408
Community dispute resolution
    centers, 408
Community policing, 134
  criticism of, 189
  defined, 188
  historical perspective on, 139
  as quiet revolution, 188

as form of punishment, 356–357
Fingerprint readers, 20
Fingerprints
    challenging evidence of, 327
    DNA fingerprinting, 180–181
    human fingerprinting, 180
Firearms. *See* Guns
Fire marshal, 13
First Amendment
    counterterrorism efforts, 24
    "crush" videos, 262
    hate crime law and, 126
    prisoners' rights and, 472
Fish, game and watercraft
        wardens, 13, 153
Flag burning, 101
Flash-robs, 28
Fleeing felon rule, 195
Folsom Prison, 430
Food and Drug Administration
        (FDA), 102
Force
    amount of, in self-defense, 119
    authority and, 193–196
    deadly, 119, 194
    incidence of use of, 194
    less lethal weapons, 196
    nondeadly, 119, 194
    by prison officials, 469–470
    reasonable, 194, 195
    Supreme Court decisions on,
        194–195
    tasers and, 196
    use of force matrix, 194
Force multiplier, electronic
        surveillance as, 225
Foreign Intelligence
        Surveillance Act (FISA),
        226–227
Forensics, 179–182
    ballistics, 179–180
    crime scene, 179–180
    cyber crimes and, 547
    DNA fingerprinting, 180–181
    human fingerprinting, 180
    trace evidence, 179
Forensic scientist, 180
Forfeiture, 408–409
Formal criminal justice process,
        15
Foster care programs, 515
Four Loko, 7
Fourteenth Amendment, 122
Fourth Amendment, 122,
        213–216

arbitrary searches in prison
        cells, 471
automobile searches, 222, 223
counterterrorism efforts and,
        24
exclusionary rule, 215–216
garbage and, 217
good faith exception, 216
inevitable discovery exception,
        216
juveniles and, 508
Patriot Act and, 226–227
probable cause, 213–215
reasonableness, 213
search warrants, 219
France, training for judges, 269
Fraud
    cyber, 540–541
    types of, 549
    white-collar crime and, 549
Frisk
    defined, 229
    reasonable suspicion, 229, 230
Fruit of the poisoned tree, 215,
        239
Furlough, 476

G

Gambling, 8, 9
    online, 9, 545
Gang investigator, 8
Gangs
    Chicago and anti-loitering
        ordinance, 5
    defined, 504
    girls in, 505
    guns and, 22, 505
    historical perspective on, 504
    membership in, 21
    prison, 464–466
    as risk factor for juvenile
        delinquency, 504–505
    street, 21
    violence and, 4
Gangster Disciples, 21
Garbage, privacy and, 216–217
Gashte Ershad, 134
GED programs, 461
Gender
    jury selection, 324
    juvenile delinquency and,
        498–499
    sentencing discrimination, 364
    social conflict theory and, 48
General deterrence, 350

General (unlimited) jurisdiction,
        255, 259
General strain theory, 46
General Theory of Crime, A
        (Gottfredson & Hirschi), 52
Genetics
    crime and, 40–41
    defined, 40
    MAOA gene, 40–41
Genetic witness, 182
Genwal Resources, Inc., 551
GEO Group, Inc., 438
Good faith exception, 216
Good time, 354–355
GPS
    electronic monitoring and, 412
    privacy and electronically
        following automobiles,
        217–218, 226
Graduated sanction, 514
Grand jury, 292, 296–297
    requirements of, by states,
        297
    as rubber stamp, 296–297
    as shield and sword, 296
Great Law, 423
Gross misdemeanor, 71
Group A offenses, 77
Group homes, 515
Guantánamo Bay, Cuba
        (GTMO), 531–534
    coerced interrogation,
        533–534
    future of, 534
    military tribunal, 533
    transferring prisoners to U.S.,
        531–533
Guilt
    factual, 283
    legal, 283
Guilty
    beyond a reasonable doubt,
        318
    criminal law and, 69
    defense attorneys defending,
        285, 289
    plea bargaining, 302–306
    pleading, 302–306
Guilty but mentally ill statutes,
        116
Guilty plea, 292, 302–306
    misdemeanor cases at initial
        appearance, 291
Gun control
    after Newtown, 103

concealed weapon laws, 105
defined, 22
vs. gun rights, 29
mental illness and, 90
Gun Control Act, 158
Gun courts, 259
Guns
AFT responsibilities and,
158
crime and, 22
deaths from, 22, 29
gangs and, 22, 505
increase prison population
and weapon crimes, 437
juvenile delinquency and,
505–506
juveniles' access to, 506
ownership rate, 22
violence and, 4

H

Habeas corpus
petition, 340
writ of, 121–122
Habitual Criminal Sterilization
Act, 124
Habitual offender laws, 367
Hackers, 543
Hacking/cracking, 9, 554
Halfway house program
manager, 479
Halfway houses, 15, 478–479
Hallcrest Report II, 160
Hand geometry scanners, 20
Hands-off doctrine, 470–471
Hate crime laws, 112–113, 126
Hate crimes, 77
Hawaii's Opportunity Probation
with Enforcement (HOPE),
399
Hazing, 280
Health-care fraud, FBI sweep
targeting, 14
Hearsay, 330–331
Heroin, addiction and, 72
High-speed pursuits
deaths from, 170
discretion and, 170–171
Highway patrol, 13
number of agencies, 152
purpose of, 152
vs. state police, 152
Hijab, 134
Hillsborough (New Jersey) Police
Department, 28

Hispanics
biases in policing and, 197–198
crime and, 87
death penalty and, 379
as fastest-growing minority
group in prisons, 87
gang membership, 505
incarceration rate of, 27
increasing prison population
and immigration offenses,
437
as judges, 269–270
juvenile arrests and, 507–508
as law enforcement officers,
145–146, 148–149
prison violence and, 463–464
on probation, 394
racial profiling and S.B. 1070,
230–231
racial threat theory, 48
risk of victimization, 82
sentencing discrimination
and, 362
stops and, 229–230
Home confinement, 411–413
defined, 411
effectiveness of, 413
levels of, 411
Home detention, 411
Home incarceration, 411
Homeland security, 527–538
al Qaeda vs. United States,
527–530
border security, 534–537
civil liberties and, 23–24
crime control model and, 19
criminal justice model of,
530–531
cyberattacks, 537–538
defined, 23
domestic terrorism, 24
global context of terrorism,
527–530
infrastructure security, 538
military model, 531–534
Patriot Act and, 23
preventive policing and
domestic terrorism, 528–
539
terrorist in court, 530–534
Homeland Security, Department
of (DHS)
creation of, 13, 153
Customs and Border
Protection (CBP), 153–154

Immigration and Customs
Enforcement (ICE),
154–155
Secret Service, 155
Homicide. *See also* Murder
mens rea, 108–109
race and, 85
by relative or acquaintance, 75
Honesty, ethical dilemmas of,
202
Honor killings, 71
Horizontal overcharging, 305
Hormones
aggression and, 41
postpartum psychosis, 41
Hot-spot policing, 20
Hot spots, 59, 84, 186
Hot-spot technology, 140
House of Refuge, 491
Hung jury, 317, 331, 336
double jeopardy and, 337
Hydrocodone, 56
Hypothesis, defined, 37

I

Id, 43
Identifiable human needs,
471–472
Identification process, 240–241
lineups, 240
nontestimonial evidence, 241
photo arrays, 240
showups, 240
Identity theft, 9, 541
Illicit drugs, 72–73
Illinois Juvenile Court Act,
491–492
Immigration
increase in prison population
and violations of, 437
racial profiling and, 230–231
Immigration and Customs
Enforcement (ICE)
under Homeland Security
Department, 153, 154
responsibilities of, 154
Secure Communities initiative,
155
Impeachment, of federal judges,
268
Imprisonment, as form of
punishment, 356
Incapacitation
collective, 351–352
death penalty, 377

National Survey on Drug Use and Health (NSDUH), 22, 56, 503
National White Collar Crime Center, 540
Native Americans
  crime and, 87
  jurisdiction on Indian reservations, 256
NC4 Safecop software, 138
Necessity, as defense under criminal law, 120
Negative emotionality, 47
Negligence, criminal, 108
Neurophysiology, 41
Neurotransmitters, 41
Newgate Prison, 424
New-generation jails, 446
New Orleans Police Department (NOPD), 137, 199
Newtown shooting, 22, 29, 90, 158
New York Police Department (NYPD)
  corruption and, 198
  crime-mapping system, 186
  diversity of officers, 148
  establishment of, 137
  homeland security and, 141
  internal affairs unit, 199
  size of department, 150
  stops, 230
New York Stock Exchange, 551
New York system, 424
Next Generation 911, 184
Nicotine, 72
Night watch system, 136
Noble cause corruption, 201
No-drop policies, 91
Nolle prosequi, 299
Nolo contendere plea, 302
Nondeadly force, 119, 194
Nonpartisan elections, 266
Nonstate actors, 527
Nontestimonial evidence, 241
Nonviolent offenders, reducing rates of imprisonment of, 437–438
Norepinephrine, 41
Norton Cybercrime Report, 540
Norway, prison system, 435
Norwegian criminal justice system, 353
Not guilty plea, 306

Notification laws, sex offenders, 480–481

O

Obama, Barack
  closing GTMO, 531
  on death of bin Laden, 527
  on predator drones, 123
Observation, probable cause based on, 214
Occupational Safety and Health Administration (OSHA), 102, 551
Occupy Cleveland movement, 178
OC pepper spray, 196
Odometer fraud, 550
Officer Down Memorial Page, 191
Officer-initiated activities, 175
Officers. See Law enforcement officers
Oklahoma bombing, 103
Omission, act of, 107
Omnibus Crime Control and Safe Streets Act, 139
Online auction fraud, 540–541
Online crimes. See also Cyber crimes
  child pornography, 9
  gambling, 9
Online dating scams, 540
Open access movement, 554
Opening statement, 324–325
Operation Heat Wave, 188
Operations, 173
Opinions, 256
Oral arguments, 263
Organized crime, 9
Original jurisdiction, 255
Overcharging, 305
Oxycodone, 56

P

Pardon, 476
Parens patriae, 491
Parole
  administrative sentencing authority and, 355–356
  authority, 401
  characteristics of offenders, 401
  compared to probation, 401–402
  concepts based on, 401

conditions of, 402
decarceration and, 438, 439
defined, 15, 400, 401
denial of, 404
discretionary release, 402–404
eligibility for, 354, 403
federal sentencing guidelines and, 365–366
guidelines for, 404–405
halfway houses, 478–479
life without, 403
mandatory release, 404–405
parole contract, 402
parole grant hearing, 403–404
parole officer and, 402
preparation for reentry behind bars, 478
promoting desistance, 478–479
rehabilitation and, 355
revocation of, 402
technical violation, 402
timing of, 401
truth in sentencing and, 404
victims' rights and, 405–406
work release programs, 478
Parole board, 354
  defined, 403
  good time and, 354–355
  historical perspective on, 355–356
  indeterminate sentencing and, 354
  parole hearing, 403–404
  roles of, 403
Parole Commission, U.S., 355–356
Parole contract, 402
Parole officers
  presentence investigation report, 396
  role of, 402
Parole revocation, 402
Particularity requirement of search warrants, 219
Part I offenses, 75
Part II offenses, 75–76
Partisan elections, 266
Patriot Act
  crime control model and, 23
  key provisions of, 23
  passage of, 23
  surveillance and, 226–227
Patrol, 174–176
  activities of, 175

Property crime
  defined, 8
  by juveniles, 498
Prosecuting attorney, 281
Prosecutorial waiver, 511
Prosecutors, 281–284
  assembly-line justice and, 273
  assistant prosecutors, 282
  attorney general and, 281–282
  burden of proving guilt, 318
  case attrition, 298–300
  case priorities, 300
  charging and, 301
  charging conference, 334
  closing arguments of, 333
  as crime fighter, 283
  direct examination of
    witnesses, 329
  discretion and, 17, 281–282,
    297–301
  double jeopardy, 337
  duties of, 281
  as elected official, 282–283
  establishing probable cause
    pretrial, 295–297
  evidence and, 325
  federal sentencing guidelines
    and, 365–366
  grand jury and, 296–297
  hearsay, 330–331
  information issued by, 296
  jury selection, 321–324
  no-drop policies for domestic
    violence cases, 91
  office of, 281–282
  opening statements, 324–325
  organization of, 282
  overcharging, 305
  plea bargaining, 303, 358–359
  police-prosecutor conflict, 283
  power of, 281
  preliminary hearing, 295–296
  rebuttal, 333
  redirect examination, 329–330
  screening process, 297–301
  in sentencing process, 358–359
  strict standard of proof, 318
  use of social media, 28
  victims and, 283–284
Prostitution, 8, 9, 72
Protect Act, 544–545
Psychoactive drugs, 22
Psychoanalytic theory, 42
Psychological theories of crime,
  40–43

Psychology
  crime and, 42–43
  defined, 40
Public defenders
  attorney-client relationship,
    288
  caseload of, 287
  defense counsel programs, 286
  defined, 286
  effectiveness of, 286–287
  eligibility issues, 286
  role of, 286
  Strickland standard, 288
Public order crime, 8
Public policy
  choice theory and, 40
  life course theories and, 53
  social conflict theory and, 49
  social process theory and,
    51–52
  social structure theory and, 47
  trait theory and, 43
Public prosecutors, 281–284
Pulling levers, 190
Punishment
  cruel and unusual
    punishment, 371–372
  death penalty, 370–381
  forms of, 356–357
  goals of, 39
  intermediate sanctions,
    406–413
  probation as, 392

Q

Questions of fact, 255
Questions of law, 256

R

Race
  bias in policing, 196–198
  consequences of high
    incarceration rate and, 447
  crime trends and, 85–87
  death penalty and, 378–388
  drug crime and, 86
  homicide and, 85
  incarceration and, 27
  jury selection and, 322–324
  prison violence and, 463–464
  racial threat theory, 48
  and reasonable suspicion,
    229–231
  risk of victimization and, 82
  sentencing and, 362–364

  social conflict theory and, 48
  stereotyping and drug crime,
    86
Racial Justice Act, 379
Racial profiling
  Constitution and, 242
  defined, 230
  immigration and, 230–231
  S.B. 1070 and, 230–231
Racial threat theory, 48
Racketeer Influenced and
    Corrupt Organizations Act
    (RICO), 408, 552
Racketeering, 552
Radial design, 433
Radio frequency identification
    (RFID) tags, 432
Random patrol, 184–185
Rape, 7
  chastity requirement, 341
  as common crime against
    women, 88
  crime statistics and, 76
  defined, 68–69, 75, 76, 78
  by juveniles, 497
  prisons and, 466
  rape shield laws, 341
  rate of in UCR compared to
    NCVS, 78
  statutory rape, 110
  use of force and, 68
  in women's prisons, 475
Rape, Abuse, and Incest
    National Network, 69
Rape shield laws, 341
Rational choice theory, 39
Reactive arrests, 186–187
Real evidence, 325, 328
Real offense, 359
Reasonable bail, 291
Reasonable doubt, 318
  creating, in defendant's case,
    332
  juveniles and, 493
  sexual-assault cases and, 332
Reasonable force, 194, 195
Reasonable suspicion
  frisk, 229, 230
  race and, 229–231
  Terry case and, 228
  totality of the circumstances,
    228
Rebuttal, 333
Recidivism, 27
  juveniles and, 517

Sexual harassment, of female police officers, 147
Shakedowns, 198
Sheriffs
county law enforcement and, 13
defined, 150
jail administration by, 444–445
vs. local police departments, 151
number of departments, 151
political aspect of, 150–151
size and responsibility of departments, 151
Shifts, 173
Shock incarceration, 393
boot camp, 410–411
defined, 410
value of, 410
Shock probation, 393, 515
Showups, 240
SHU (security housing unit) syndrome, 434
Sing Sing, 430
Sixth Amendment, 122
counterterrorism efforts and, 24
cross-examination and, 329
death penalty, 373
defense attorneys and, 284, 285, 286, 287
impartial jury, 316
interrogation, 235
jurisdiction and cyber crime, 547–548
pretrial detention and, 291
showups and photo arrays, 241
speedy trial and, 315–316
trial by jury, 319
Sixth sense, 169
Social conflict theories, 47–49
Social disorganization theory, 44–45
disorganized zones, 44–45
drug use and, 54
stages of, 45
value of role models, 45
Socialization, 190–191
Social media
background check using, 144
flash-robs, 28
impact on criminal justice system, 27–28
police department's use of, 132, 142

Social process theories, 49–52
control theory, 51
labeling theory, 51
learning theory, 49–50
public policy and, 51–52
Social psychology, 43
Social reality of crime, 47–48
Sociological theories of crime, 44–47
Solitary confinement, 447
Span of control, 173
Special prosecution, 282
Specialty courts, 259
Specific deterrence, 350
Spectator demonstrations, 319
Speech, freedom of
counterterrorism efforts, 24
"crush" videos, 262
Speedy trial, 315–316
Speedy Trial Act, 315, 316
Split sentence probation, 393
Spoils system, 137
Stalking
as common crime against women, 88
cyberstalking, 542
Stand your ground law, 119–120
StarChase launcher, 138
Stare decisis, 102–103
State attorney, 281
State court system
court of appeal, 259–260
courts of limited jurisdiction, 257–2259
in dual court system, 256–257
excessive caseload and, 273
jurisdiction and, 253–254
magistrate courts, 258–259
organization of, 257–258
selection of judges, 266–268
sentencing disparity, 362
specialty courts, 259
state prisons for, 427
trial courts of general jurisdiction, 259
State government
federalism and, 12
police power and, 12
State law enforcement, 13
State police, 13
vs. highway patrol, 152
number of departments, 152
purpose of, 152
State statues, as source of criminal law, 101

Station, 173
Status offenders, 492
low-visibility decision making and, 506–507
treatment of girls, 499
Statute of limitations, 316
Statutes, as source of criminal law, 100–102
Statutory law, 100–102
Statutory rape, 110
Step Up to Law Enforcement program, 146
Stimulants, 72
Stop and frisk, 227–231
Stop-and-identify laws, 229
Stops, 228–231
compared to arrest, 231
defined, 229
length of time and, 229
pretextual, 223
reasonable suspicion, 228
Terry case and, 228
totality of the circumstances, 228
Strain theory, 46–47
Street gangs, 21
Stress, on-the-job pressures and, 192–193
Stressors, 193
Strict liability crimes, 109–110
Strip search, 445
Stuxnet, 538
Subculture. *See* Police subculture
Subculture theory, 47
Subject-matter jurisdiction, 255
Substance abuse
juvenile delinquency and, 502–503
treatment for, in prisons, 460–461
Substance Abuse and Crime Prevention Act, 399–400
Substantial-capacity test (ALI/MPC) test, 115
Substantive criminal law, 100, 121
Substantive due process, 124
Suicide
physician-assisted, 6, 12
of police officers, 193
Supercrime, 527
Superego, 43
Supermax prison, 432–434
Supremacy clause, 101

tracking inmates in prison, 432
wireless devices in courtroom, 335
Telephone-pole design, 433
Television, violence on, and crime, 50
Temporary release, 476
Ten percent cash bail, 294–295
Tenth Amendment, 100
Terrorism, 527–538. *See also specific events of terrorism*
al Qaeda vs. United States, 527–530
border security, 534–537
Boston Marathon bombing, 526–527
civil liberties and counterterrorism, 23–24
counterterrorism strategies
intelligence-led policing, 141–142
local police department and anti-terrorism efforts, 141–142
Suspicious Activity Report (SAR), 141
in court, 530–534
criminal justice model, 530–531
enemy combatants, 531
Guantánamo Bay, Cuba (GTMO), 531–534
military model, 531–533
military tribunals, 533–534
number of convicted terrorists, 531
crime control model and, 23
cyberattacks as future of, 537–538
defined, 23, 25, 527
domestic, 24
entrapment issues, 178–179
future trends, 539
global context of, 527–530
homeland security and, 23–24
jihad and, 528
material support for, and AEDPA, 103–104
Oslo, Norway, bomb attack, 353
Patriot Act and, 23
police academy training in, 145
preventive policing and domestic terrorism, 177–178, 528–539

Prislam and, 473
self-radicalization, 528–539
as supercrime, 527
as warfare, 527
Terrorism investigations, 226
Testimony
defined, 325
as evidence, 325–327
Testosterone, aggression and, 41
Texting-while-driving laws, 12, 17, 18
Theft
cyber, 541–542
defined, 75
gangs and, 504
identity, 541
as misdemeanor or felony, 112
motor vehicle, 8
as property crime, 8
Theory. *See* Crime theories
Thermal imagers, 224–225
Thirteenth Amendment, prisoners' rights, 470
Three-strike laws, 102, 367–368
Thrill offenders, 39
Time served, 443
Tokenism, 147
Topeka Correctional Facility, 431
Tort, 69
Total institution, 457
Totality of the circumstances, 228
Touch DNA, 182
Tours, 173
Tower guards, 468
Trace evidence, 179
Traditional jail design, 446
Traffic laws, 105
Training schools, 516
Trait theory, 40, 43
Transactional Records Access Clearinghouse, 367
Transportation Security Administration (TSA), 156
airport screening and, 535
Treasury Department, 159
Trial court administrator, 323
Trial courts
defined, 255
jurisdiction and, 255
Trial judges
administrative role of, 265
roles and responsibilities of, 264–265
before trial, 264–265

during trial, 265
Trials
bench, 316
change of venue, 318
elements of
appeals, 337–338
closing arguments, 333
cross-examination, 329–331
defendant's case, 331–333
jury deliberation, 335
jury instructions, 334–335
motion for a directed verdict, 331
opening statements, 324–325
overview of steps in, 325
prosecution's case, 328–329
rebuttal and surrebuttal, 333
role of evidence, 325–328
verdict, 336–337
jury selection, 318–324
pleading guilty, 302–306
pretrial procedures
establishing probable cause, 295–297
grand jury, 296–297
pleading guilty, 302–306
preliminary hearing, 295–296
pretrial detention, 291–295
prosecutorial screening process, 297–301
special features of criminal trials, 315–318
presumption of innocence, 317–318
privilege against self-incrimination, 317
role of jury, 316–317
speedy trial, 315–316
strict standard of proof, 318
spectator demonstrations, 319
speedy, 315–316
statute of limitations, 316
steps leading to, 292
Truth-in-sentencing laws, 355
increased length of prison terms, 436
mandatory release and, 404
Tucson Police Department, budget and response times, 183
Tulsa Police Department, 14
"Tweets-by-beat" initiative, 132
Twin studies, 40
Twitter, 28, 132, 142, 144

Two Rivers Correctional
   Institution, 431–432

U

UCR. *See* Uniform Crime Report
   (UCR)
Unconscious, 42
Undercover officers, 177
Underwear bomber, 535, 536
Uniform Code of Military
   Justice, 255
Uniform Crime Report (UCR),
   74–76, 133
   compared to NCVS, 78
   compared to NIBRS, 77
   defined, 74
   discretionary distortions in, 76
   information based on, 74
   juvenile delinquency and,
      497–498
   Part I offenses, 75
   Part II offenses, 75–76
   underreporting crime, 76
United States Reports, 33
United States Visitor and
   Immigrant Status Indicator
   Technology (US-VISIT)
   program, 535
Universal jurisdiction, 255
Unlawful Internet Gambling
   Enforcement Act, 545
USA Patriot Act. *See* Patriot Act
U.S. attorney, 281
Use of force. *See* Force
Use of force matrix, 194
U.S. Marshals Service
   creation of, 158
   responsibilities of, 158

V

Vehicles, searches of, 222–224
Venire, 320–321
Vera Institute, 293
Verdict, 336–337
   motion for a directed verdict,
      331
Vertical overcharging, 305
Victim advocates, 81, 88
Victim impact statement,
   368–370
Victimization
   mental illness as risk factor
      for, 90
   repeat, 82
   risks of, 81–83

Victimless crimes, 8
Victim-offender dialogue (VOD),
   354
Victims of crime, 79–83
   chastity requirement, 341
   civil lawsuits brought by, 337
   compensating, 353
   creating reasonable doubt
      about credibility, 332
   impact evidence and
      sentencing, 368–370
   listening to, 352
   parole and rights of, 405–406
   plea bargaining and, 303–304
   prosecutors and, 283–284
   repeat victimization, 82
   restorative justice, 352–354
   rights of
      advocating for victims, 24–25
      defined, 25
      emergence of, 24–26
      enforceability of, 80
      informed, present and heard
         rights, 80
      legal rights of, 80
      legislative efforts, 25–26
      prosecutors and, 284
      restitution, 80
   risks of victimization, 81–83
   routine activities theory, 82
   services for, 81
   surveys of, 77–79
   uncooperative, 300
   unreliable, 300
   vengeance and, 81
   victim-offender dialogue
      (VOD), 354
   of white-collar crime, 550
   women as, 88–89
Victims of Crime Act, 353
Victims' Rights Amendment,
   122–123
Victim surveys, 77–79
Video games, violence in, and
   crime, 50
Video surveillance, 225–226
Violence
   corporate violence, 551
   in prisons, 462–463
   in schools, 499–500
   on television and crime, 50
Violent crimes
   categories of, 7
   defined, 7
   juveniles, 497–498

Virus, 543
Visa, 534–535
Vocational training, for
   prisoners, 461
Voir dire, 321–322
Voluntary manslaughter, 109

W

Waiver
   automatic, 510
   judicial, 510
   legislative, 510
   prosecutorial, 511
Walnut Street Jail, 423–424
Warden, 428–429
War on drugs, 86
War on terrorism, material
   witness law, 125
Warrant, 212
Warrantless arrest, 233–234
Warrants
   arrests with, 232–233
   arrests without, 233–234
   exigent circumstances, 212
Warrior gene, 40–41
Washington, D.C. Police
   Department, 150
   diversity of officers, 148
Washington Mutual, 552
Washington State Highway
   Patrol, 152
Waterboarding, 534
Weapons crimes, increase in
   prison population, 437
Weapons of mass destruction,
   531
Wedding cake model of criminal
   justice, 315
Western Penitentiary, 424
White-collar crime, 549–553
   in the 2000s, 552
   characteristics of, 549
   corporate violence, 551
   by corporations, 550–551
   cost of, to businesses
      worldwide, 9
   defined, 9, 549
   examples of, 549
   law enforcement and, 551–552
   regulating, 551
   soft on, 553
   techniques used in, 550
   victims of, 550
White Collar Crime Penalty
   Enhancement Act, 553

SUBJECT INDEX I-27